CONNECT TO Explore

 Connect History guides students through the process of analyzing the documents, works of art, and maps in **WEST** to teach them how historians uncover meaning by investigating different types of primary sources.

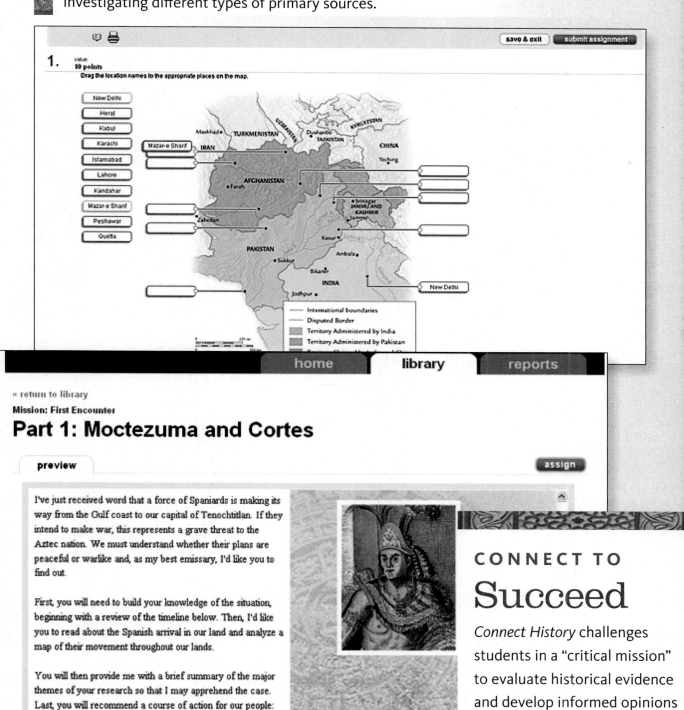

CONNECT TO Succeed

Connect History challenges students in a "critical mission" to evaluate historical evidence and develop informed opinions on historical issues and decisions that shaped Western civilization and still impact us today.

WEST

EXPERIENCE WESTERN CIVILIZATION

DENNIS SHERMAN
John Jay College
City University of New York

JOYCE SALISBURY
University of Wisconsin–Green Bay

McGraw Hill

Connect
Learn
Succeed™

Published by McGraw-Hill, an imprint of The McGraw-Hill Companies, Inc., 1221 Avenue of the Americas, New York, NY 10020. Copyright © 2012. All rights reserved. No part of this publication may be reproduced or distributed in any form or by any means, or stored in a database or retrieval system, without the prior written consent of The McGraw-Hill Companies, Inc., including, but not limited to, in any network or other electronic storage or transmission, or broadcast for distance learning.

This book is printed on acid-free paper.

Printed in the United States of America

1 2 3 4 5 6 7 8 9 0 QDB/QDB 1 0 9 8 7 6 5 4 3 2 1

ISBN: 978-0-07-340700-5
MHID: 0-07-340700-3

Sponsoring Editor: *Matthew Busbridge*
Marketing Manager: *Stacy Best Ruel*
Developmental Editor: *Laura Wilk*
Editorial Coordinators: *Jaclyn Mautone, Maureen West*
Production Editor: *Carey Eisner*
Manuscript Editor: *Margaret Moore*
Design Manager: *Cassandra Chu*
Text Designer: *Maureen McCutcheon*
Cover Designer: *Linda Beaupre*
Art Editor: *Robin Mouat*
Illustrator: *Patti Isaacs*
Photo Research Coordinator: *Alexandra Ambrose*
Photo Researcher: *Judy Mason*
Buyer: *Sherry Kane*
Media Project Managers: *Andrea Helmbolt, Mathew Sletten, Jennifer Barrick*
Digital Product Manager: *Jay Gubernick*
Composition: *10.5/12 Adobe Garamond Pro Regular by Lachina Publishing Services*
Printing: *45# New Era Thin, Quad Graphics Dubuque*

Vice President Editorial: *Michael Ryan*
Publisher: *Chris Freitag*
Editorial Director: *William R. Glass*
Managing Development Editor: *Nancy Crochiere*

Cover: W: Visual Language; E: Jason Brindel Commercial/Alamy; S: Detail: Procession of the Eucharist in the Piazza San Marco, Venice, Italy, 1496 by Gentile Bellini (1429–1507)/Accademia, Venice, Italy/Erich Lessing/Art Resource, NY; T: Balean/TopFoto/The Image Works

Credits: The credits section for this book begins on page C-1 and is considered an extension of the copyright page.

Library of Congress Cataloging-in-Publication Data
Sherman, Dennis.
  West : experience western civilization / Dennis Sherman, Joyce
Salisbury.
    p. cm.
  Includes index.
  ISBN-13: 978-0-07-340700-5 (softcover : acid-free paper)
  ISBN-10: 0-07-340700-3 (softcover : acid-free paper)
1. Civilization, Western—History—Sources. 2. Civilization,
Western—History—Textbooks. I. Salisbury, Joyce E. II. Title.
  CB245.S464 2011
  909'.09821—dc23

                              2011035722

The Internet addresses listed in the text were accurate at the time of publication. The inclusion of a website does not indicate an endorsement by the authors or McGraw-Hill, and McGraw-Hill does not guarantee the accuracy of the information presented at these sites.

www.mhhe.com

About the Authors

DENNIS SHERMAN

Dennis Sherman is Professor of History at John Jay College, the City University of New York. He received his B.A. (1962) and J.D. (1965) degrees from the University of California at Berkeley and his Ph.D. (1970) from the University of Michigan. He was Visiting Professor at the University of Paris (1978–1979, 1985). He received the Ford Foundation Prize Fellowship (1968–1969, 1969–1970), a fellowship from the Council for Research on Economic History (1971–1972), and fellowships from the National Endowment for the Humanities (1973–1976). His publications include *A Short History of Western Civilization*, Eighth Edition (coauthor), *Western Civilization: Sources, Images, and Interpretations*, Eighth Edition, *World History: Sources, Images, and Interpretations*, Fourth Edition, a series of introductions in the Garland Library of War and Peace, several articles and reviews on nineteenth-century French economic and social history in American and European journals, and several short stories and poems in literary reviews. He is the recipient of John Jay College's "Outstanding Teacher of the Year" award.

JOYCE SALISBURY

Joyce Salisbury is Professor Emerita of History at the University of Wisconsin–Green Bay, where she taught history to undergraduates for more than twenty years. She received a Ph.D. in medieval history from Rutgers University in New Jersey. She is a respected historian who has published many articles and has written or edited more than ten books, including the critically acclaimed *Perpetua's Passion: Death and Memory of a Young Roman Woman, The Blood of Martyrs: Unintended Consequences of Ancient Violence, The Encyclopedia of Women in the Ancient World,* and *The Greenwood Encyclopedia of Daily Life,* which won many awards for its creative organization and timely presentation of the material. In 2010, Salisbury published a second edition of her classic work on the history of attitudes toward animals: *The Beast Within: Humans and Animals in the Middle Ages.* Salisbury is an award-winning teacher who was named "Professor of the Year for Wisconsin in 1991" by CASE (Council for Advancement and Support of Education), a prestigious national organization. Since retiring from the University of Wisconsin–Green Bay, Salisbury has taught twice on Semester at Sea, a program sponsored by the University of Virginia that teaches students as they circumnavigate the world. Salisbury brought a global perspective to the history of Western civilization while teaching abroad, and this edition of the book has benefited from her interaction with students as they make sense of our twenty-first-century global civilization.

Brief Contents

Contents

THE ROOTS OF WESTERN CIVILIZATION 1

The Ancient Middle East to the Sixth Century B.C.E.

THE CONTEST FOR EXCELLENCE

2

Greece, 2000–338 B.C.E.

THE POLEIS BECOME COSMOPOLITAN

3

The Hellenistic World, 336–150 B.C.E.

PRIDE IN FAMILY AND CITY

4

Rome from Its Origins Through the Republic, 753–44 B.C.E.

TERRITORIAL AND CHRISTIAN EMPIRES

5

The Roman Empire, 31 B.C.E.–410 C.E.

A WORLD DIVIDED

6

Western Kingdoms, Byzantium, and the Islamic World, ca. 376–1000

THE STRUGGLE TO BRING ORDER

7

The Early Middle Ages, ca. 750–1000

ORDER RESTORED   8

The High Middle Ages, 1000–1300

"ALONE BEFORE GOD"

11

Religious Reform and Warfare, 1500–1648

FAITH, FORTUNE, AND FAME

12

European Expansion, 1450–1700

THE STRUGGLE FOR SURVIVAL AND SOVEREIGNTY

13

Europe's Social and Political Order, 1600–1715

A NEW WORLD OF REASON AND REFORM

14

The Scientific Revolution and the Enlightenment, 1600–1800

COMPETING FOR POWER AND WEALTH 15
The Old Regime, 1715–1789

OVERTURNING THE POLITICAL AND SOCIAL ORDER 16
The French Revolution and Napoleon, 1789–1815

FACTORIES, CITIES, AND FAMILIES IN THE INDUSTRIAL AGE

17

The Industrial Revolution, 1780–1850

MODERN LIFE AND THE CULTURE OF PROGRESS

21

Western Society, 1850–1914

MASS POLITICS AND IMPERIAL DOMINATION

20

Democracy and the New Imperialism, 1870–1914

DESCENDING INTO THE TWENTIETH CENTURY

22

World War and Revolution, 1914–1920

DARKENING DECADES

23

Recovery, Dictators, and Depression, 1920–1939

INTO THE FIRE AGAIN

24

World War II, 1939–1945

SUPERPOWER STRUGGLES AND GLOBAL TRANSFORMATIONS

25

The Cold War, 1945–1980s

INTO THE TWENTY-FIRST CENTURY **26**

The Present in Perspective

List of Primary Source Documents

EXPLORING THE PAST

List of Features

Experience Success in *History*

Connect to the Experience of History

History is more than words. **WEST** immerses students in Western civilization across time. The historical narrative comes to life with dynamic interactive primary sources, riveting images, and digitally enhanced maps that engage students' senses to give them a better appreciation for the people, places, and events that make up history.

Connect the Past to the Present

History is about making connections. **WEST**'s framework guides students through history, assessing their understanding as they progress, and inviting them to apply what they've learned to develop informed opinions on historical issues and debates. **WEST** presents students with practice and support understanding the cause-and-effect relationships between events over time and continents.

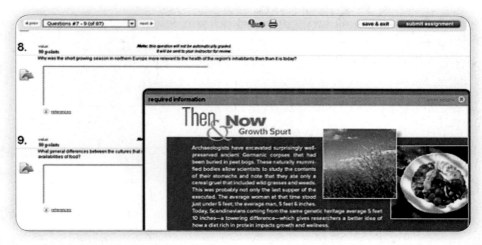

Connect to Success in History

History is an active process. **WEST** is an active program. **WEST** challenges students to investigate primary sources, scrutinize historical images, and explore maps to acquire and build the analytical skills necessary to identify how the past influenced the present and, ultimately, grasp how our actions today will shape our future tomorrow.

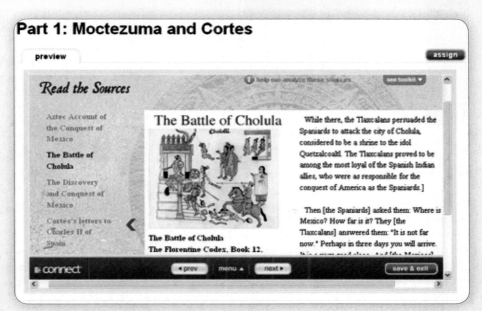

WEST Features

Then & Now

Then & Now
Pyrotechnics in the Theater

Shakespeare used music and fireworks to excite audiences who attended his popular plays. In 1613, theatrical cannons filled with gunpowder and fireworks misfired, catching the thatched roof and wooden beams on fire, burning the theater down. Today, despite fire safety rules to prevent similar fire hazards, performers still find pyrotechnics the most dramatic way to get their audiences' attention. But just like in Shakespeare's time, injuries are unavoidable. In recent years, performers like Michael Jackson, Metallica, and Mötley Crüe have all suffered injuries when fireworks on stage went awry.

Vibrant photos illustrate connections between the past and present. By establishing a visual point of reference, students see the evolution of material goods, as well as ideas, over time.

Exploring the Past

Garibaldi Appeals to Italians for Support

The campaign that resulted in the unification of Italy required not just idealism but also a realistic outlook and daring action. With his political manipulations, Cavour provided the realism. With his invasion of Sicily in 1860, Giuseppe Garibaldi provided the daring action.

The brave man finds an arm everywhere. Listen not to the voice of cowards, but arm, and let us fight for our brethren, who will fight for us tomorrow.

A band of those who fought with me the country's battles marches with me to the fight. Good and generous, they will fight for their country to the last drop of their blood, nor ask for other reward than a

Exploring the Past

Two primary sources in each chapter help students explore how historians uncover details about the people, places, and events that comprise the historical narrative. Accompanying critical thinking questions can be assigned in Connect.

Art Investigation

Wolf Vostell, *Miss America*
1968

Each chapter features critical works of art and provides guided analyses to assist students in thinking about the role of art in Western civilization. Accompanying critical thinking questions in Connect can be assigned to assess students' comprehension and invite them to think about each piece in the larger context of the chapter.

Past Lives

Biographical profiles reveal the power of individuals to influence history. Accompanying critical thinking questions encourage students to consider the significance of the individual's actions to larger developments in Western civilization.

Past Lives

Käthe Kollwitz (1867–1945)

By the eve of World War I, Käthe Kollwitz's prints, drawings, and posters had made her one of Germany's leading artists. "[M]y art has purpose," she said. "I want to be effective in this time when people are so helpless and in need of aid."

In early August 1914, just after World War I broke out, the Kollwitz family heard German

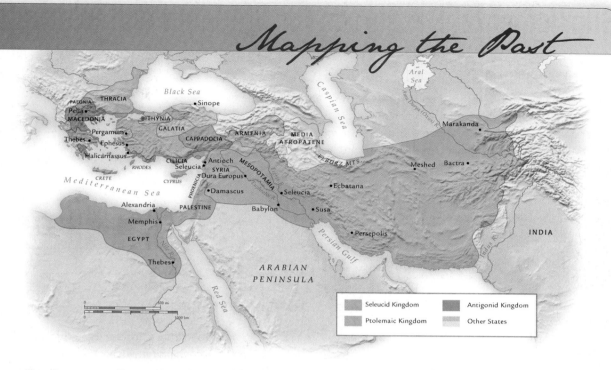

Mapping the Past

The Successor States After the Death of Alexander, ca. 240 B.C.E. **This map shows the breakup of Alexander's empire into three states and illustrates the relative sizes of the successor kingdoms. Based on your analysis of previous maps, as well as the information in the text, what were the historical and geographic reasons for the differing sizes of the successor kingdoms?**

Mapping the Past

Key maps in each chapter are highlighted to help students build geography skills and consider the significance of geography in history. Accompanying critical thinking questions provide a framework for their investigations.

connect to today

Value Systems

Key values of the Renaissance included individualism over community, realism over faith, and activism over obedience. In what ways do you think contemporary society and culture still exhibit the values of the Renaissance?

Connect to Today

Crucial events in history are highlighted in each chapter, inviting students to apply the lessons of the past to the present day.

OPINION

What do you think was the most important result of Cold War tension on international affairs in the Western and non-Western worlds?

Opinion

Critical thinking questions presented at decisive points in each chapter challenge students to develop informed opinions on the larger historical issues in the chapter reading.

Supplemental Resources for Students and Instructors

Online Learning Center

The Online Learning Center, at **www.mhhe.com/west**, contains several instructor tools, including a link to the faculty guide on Primary Source Investigator (**www.mhhe.com/psi**), PowerPoint presentations for each chapter, and the computerized test bank. The instructor side of the OLC is password protected to prevent tampering. Please contact your local McGraw-Hill representative for details.

Videos

Created and narrated by Joyce Salisbury, this three-video collection illuminates the author's lectures on the Middle Ages with the sculpture and fine art of the times. Available to adopters through your local McGraw-Hill representative, this unique series contains a video on each of the following topics: medieval women, medieval Judaism, and medieval life. A wide range of videos on classic and contemporary topics in history is available through the Films for the Humanities and Sciences collection. Instructors can illustrate classroom discussions and enhance lectures by selecting from a series of videos that are correlated to complement **WEST**. Contact your local McGraw-Hill sales representatives for further information.

Primary Source Investigator

McGraw-Hill's Primary Source Investigator (PSI), available online at **www.mhhe.com/psi**, is designed to support and enrich the text discussion in **WEST**, 1e. PSI gives instructors and students access to more than 650 primary and secondary sources, including documents, images, maps, and videos. Students can use these resources to formulate and defend their arguments, as well as further their understanding of the topics discussed in each chapter. All assets are also indexed alphabetically as well as by type, subject, place, and time period, allowing students and instructors to locate them quickly and easily.

Acknowledgments

BOARD OF ADVISORS

Stephen Andrews, *Central New Mexico Community College*
Cassandra Cookson, *Lee College*
Martin Ederer, *Buffalo State College*
Christopher Gehrz, *Bethel University*
Wendy Gunderson, *Collin County Community College*
Stephen Lopez, *San Jacinto College*
David Meskill, *Dowling College*
David Mock, *Tallahassee Community College*
Jessica Patton, *Tarrant County College*
Michael Prahl, *Hawkeye Community College*
Manfred Silva, *El Paso Community College Northwest*
Armando Villarreal, *Tarrant County College*
Roger Ward, *Collin County Community College*

REVIEWERS

Stephen J. Andrews, *Central New Mexico Community College*
Douglas C. Baxter, *Ohio University*
Mark Clark, *University of Virginia's College at Wise*
Ron Dufour, *Rhode Island College*
Ana Fodor, *Danville Community College*
Philip Hnatkovich, *Penn State University*
Adam Howard, *Northern Virginia Community College*
Matthew E. Keith, *The Ohio State University*
William Lipkin, *Seton Hall University*
Michael Mackey, *Community College of Denver*
Anthony Makowski, *Delaware County Community College*
Jeannine Olson, *Rhode Island College*
Mark Roehrs, *Lincoln Land Community College*
Leslie Schuster, *Rhode Island College*
Rebecca Woodham, *Wallace Community College*

SYMPOSIUM ATTENDEES

Donna Allen, *Glendale Community College*
Patrick Brennan, *Gulf Coast Community College*
Tamara Chaplin, *University of Illinois at Urbana-Champaign*
Charles Connell, *Northern Arizona University*
Derrick Griffey, *Gadsden State Community College*
Lloyd Johnson, *Campbell University*
Sarah Jurenka, *Bishop State Community College*
Bill Kamil, *Sinclair Community College*
Lynn Lubamersky, *Boise State University*
Michael J. Mullin, *Augustana College*
Troy Paddock, *Southern Connecticut State University*
Valor Pickett, *Northwest Arkansas Community College*
Sean Pollock, *Wright State University*
Michael Prahl, *Hawkeye Community College*
Matthew Ruane, *Florida Institute of Technology*
Sergei I. Zhuk, *Ball State University*

WEST

EXPERIENCE WESTERN CIVILIZATION

BOOK OF THE DEAD OF HUNEFER, NEW KINGDOM, ca. 1295–1186 B.C.E. This scene depicts the ceremony in which the mouth of the embalmed body is "opened" and restored to its ability to breathe and feel. The image shows the priests, female mourners, and jackal-headed mortuary god. The scene also shows the importance of writing in its surrounding hieroglyphs and the wealth of a society that can bury expensive goods (in the lower section) and devote resources to an afterlife.

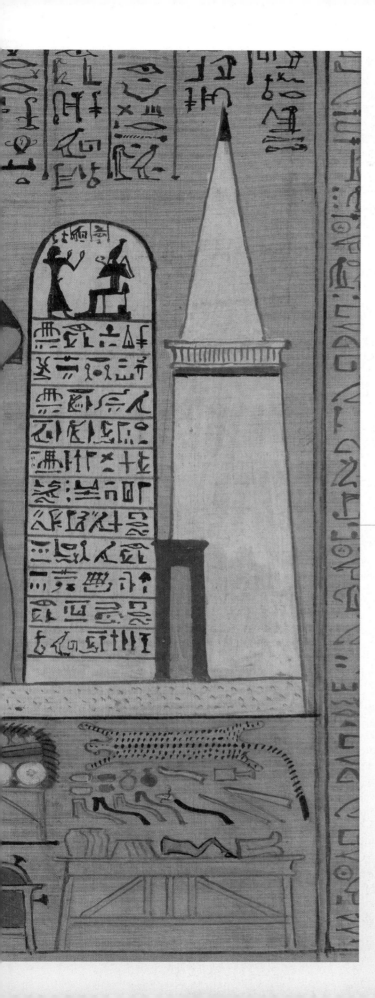

The Roots

of Western Civilization

The Ancient Middle East to the Sixth Century B.C.E.

1

What's to Come

A Struggling Sumerian Schoolboy

In 2500 B.C.E., a Sumerian schoolboy wrote an essay about his struggles to learn reading and writing. He claimed that he practiced these skills in school all day, and he was right. Ancient texts show that children attended classes from sunrise to sunset from the age of about 5 or 6 until they were young adults. Children had to master the difficult task of writing many complex symbols on clay tablets, so their school was called a "tablet-house," and the headmaster was called the "expert" or "father of the tablet-house." ▶▶

Discipline was handled by the "man in charge of the whip," which shows that corporal punishment was a regular feature of the schoolday.

The Sumerian student wrote that in the evenings, he took his writing tablet home to his father, who praised the boy's progress, a pleasing observation since school was expensive and only the rich could send their sons to learn the prized task of writing. Basking in his father's praise, the boy wrote that he ate his dinner, washed his feet, and went to bed. The next day, however, he had a difficult time in school. He arrived late and was beaten for his tardiness and several other offenses, including poor handwriting. In despair, the boy invited the schoolmaster home to dinner. The wealthy father gave the teacher gifts, and the boy began having fewer problems in school. We don't know whether this boy graduated, but we imagine that he did, to become a "tablet-writer" whose future job was secure.

The narrative by the schoolboy, dating from 4,500 years ago, is perhaps most remarkable for its timeless themes. Tardy students, schools, and concerned parents are all a part of life for most of us today. Here in the village of this young boy, we can find the roots of what we have come to call Western civilization, or "the West." ◄◄

"The West" does not define one location but instead refers to a series of cultures that slowly evolved and spread to impact societies all over the world. Even 4,500 years ago, in the village of this Sumerian, we can identify certain characteristics that define Western civilization and that gave it an advantage—for better or worse—over competing cultures. Western civilization began in the Middle East, which enjoyed the striking advantage of having plants for agriculture and animals for domestication native to the region. Then large cities arose with attendant division of labor and social stratification based on relationships other than family. Another dramatic advantage was the development of writing, which gave schoolboys so much difficulty but allowed the preservation and transmission of advantageous developments.

THE WORLD'S OLDEST SCULPTURE, ca. 33,000 B.C.E. This carving on mammoth tusk is the oldest figurative sculpture found to date. Showing a pregnant woman, it probably was a magic talisman for fertility.

BEFORE WESTERN CIVILIZATION

Recorded history represents less than 1 percent of the time that humans have lived on the earth. Hundreds of thousands of years before the day in the life of the young, urban Sumerian described above, life for human beings was completely different. Before we begin the story of the development of Western civilization, we must explore the life of the first humans in the lush lands of sub-Saharan Africa.

The Paleolithic Period
600,000–10,000 B.C.E.

Human beings first appeared in sub-Saharan Africa hundreds of thousands of years ago. Archaeologists have classified the remains of these early humans into various species and subspecies, most of which were evolutionary dead ends. Modern humans belong to *Homo sapiens sapiens* ("thinking, thinking man"), a subspecies that migrated north and northeast from Africa. These earliest ancestors first appeared some 40,000 years ago and ultimately colonized the world. The first humans used tools made from materials at hand, including wood and bone, but the most useful tools were those made of stone. Initial stone tools were sharpened only roughly, but later humans crafted stones into finely finished flakes ideal for spearheads, arrowheads, and other blades. These tools have led archaeologists to name this long period of human prehistory the Old Stone Age, or the **Paleolithic.**

Throughout the Paleolithic, our ancestors were nomadic peoples living off the land as hunters and gatherers. This nomadic life involved small bands of people—about 30 to 40—who moved to follow the animals and the cycles of plant growth. A culture of hunters and gatherers prevents people from accumulating property, for whatever one owns must be portable, and that includes infants and small children. Anything extra is a burden, not a benefit. Paleolithic cultures also enjoyed a good deal of leisure time—indeed, estimates suggest that working four hours a day would usually generate enough food for a group. Of course, the ancient hunters and gatherers also faced famine if they exhausted the resources of a local area.

Our earliest human ancestors were also distinguished by their ability to use symbols to represent not only reality but also their hopes and fears. That is, the earliest humans created and appreciated what we call art. The photograph on page 2 shows a wonderful, tiny carving on mammoth tusk that was discovered in 2008 in Germany. Carbon dating places this figure between 35,000 and 40,000 years ago, making it the oldest piece of figurative sculpture in the world and demonstrating that art was one of the defining characteristics of humans.

By the end of the Paleolithic Age (about 10,000 B.C.E.), the human population of Europe stood at about 20,000. These numbers may seem sparse by today's standards, but they suggest that *Homo sapiens sapiens* had gained a sturdy foothold on the European continent. By the late Stone Age, these early Europeans practiced agriculture and copper metallurgy, but their most enduring remains are huge stone monuments (called *megaliths*), of which Stonehenge in western England is probably the most famous. Whatever the purpose of these stone structures that dot Europe, they all suggest highly organized societies that were able to marshal the labor needed for such complex building projects.

Stone monuments

However, although these early Europeans displayed some characteristics that would mark Western civilization—agriculture, a curiosity about nature, and a highly developed political structure—these great builders in stone lacked a critical component: writing. Although wisdom transmitted solely through memory can be impressive, it is also fragile, and thus engineering skills and astronomical knowledge of the earliest Europeans were lost. The real origins of Western civilization lay in the Middle East, where an agricultural revolution occurred that changed the course of human history, and where writing preserved the story of the developing West.

The Neolithic Period: The First Stirrings of Agriculture

10,000–3000 B.C.E.

Sometime around 10,000 B.C.E., people living in what we call the Middle East learned how to plant and cultivate the grains that they and their ancestors had gathered for millennia. With this skill, humankind entered the **Neolithic** era, or the New Stone Age. Agriculture did not bring complete improvement in people's lives compared to hunting

STONE AGE MONUMENTS FROM STONEHENGE, SOUTHERN ENGLAND, ca. 7000–1500 B.C.E. These huge structures of stone, carefully shaped and moved long distances, testify to early human technical skill. The alignment of the stones suggests knowledge of the heavens gained from many years of observations.

and gathering. Diets were often worse (with a reliance on fewer foods), sewage and animal wastes brought more health problems, and farming was a lot of work. People adopted this way of life because the environment changed, but once people learned how to plant crops instead of simply gathering what grew naturally, human society changed dramatically.

Just as people discovered how to control crops, they also began to domesticate animals instead of hunting them. Dogs had been domesticated as hunting partners during the Paleolithic, but around 8500 B.C.E., people first domesticated sheep as a source of food. Throughout the Middle East, some people lived off their herds as they traveled about looking for pasturage. Others lived as agriculturalists, keeping their herds near stationary villages.

Domestic animals

These two related developments—agriculture and animal domestication—fostered larger populations than hunting and gathering cultures, and gradually agricultural societies prevailed. In large part, the success of Western civilization in eventually spreading throughout the world lay in its agricultural beginnings in the Middle East. Why were people in this region able to embrace agriculture so successfully? The main answer is luck—the Middle East was equipped with the necessary resources.

Of the wealth of plant species in the world—over 200,000 different varieties—humans eat only a few thousand. Of these, only a few hundred have been more or less domesticated, but almost 80 percent of the world's human diet is made up of about a dozen species (primarily cereals). The Middle East was home to the highest number of the world's prized grains, such as wheat and barley, which are easy to grow and contain the highest levels of protein. By contrast, people who

Middle East plants and animals

independently domesticated local crops in other regions did not enjoy the same abundance.

The Middle East maintained the same advantage when it came to animals for domestication. Very few species yield to domestication; beyond the most common—dogs, sheep, goats, cows, pigs, and horses—there are only a few others—from camels to reindeer to water buffalo. Because domesticated animals provide so many benefits to humans—from food to labor—the distribution of animals fit for domestication helped determine which societies would flourish. Most of these animals were confined to Europe and Asia, and seven—including goats, sheep, and cattle—were native specifically to the Middle East. With these resources, the people of the Middle East created civilization, which quickly spread east and west (along with valuable crops and animals).

With the rise of agriculture, some small kin groups stopped wandering and instead slowly settled in permanent villages to cultivate the surrounding land. As early as 8000 B.C.E., Jericho (see map on page 5) boasted about 2,000 people

Population growth who lived in round huts scattered over about 12 acres. Human social forms broadened from small kin groups to include relative strangers. The schoolboy whom we met earlier had to make a point of introducing his teacher to his father. This effort would have been unheard of in the small hunting clans of the Paleolithic.

Agriculture also sparked a major change in values. Since people no longer had to carry everything they owned as they traveled, farming, animal husbandry, and fixed settlement led to the accumulation of goods, including domesticated animals. Consequently, a new social differentiation arose in agricultural villages as some people acquired more belongings than others.

The social stratification that arose in the earliest cities included slavery as part of what people thought of as the natural order of things. There were various ways to become a slave in ancient Middle

Slavery Eastern society. Sometimes economic catastrophe caused parents to sell their children or even themselves into slavery to repay their debts, and children born to slaves were automatically enslaved. Although slavery was part of ancient societies, it was a slavery that could be fairly fluid—unlike the slavery of the early modern world, it was not a racial issue. Slaves could save money to purchase their freedom, and children born of a freewoman and a slave were free. Ancient slavery, while taken for granted, was based on an individual's bad luck or unfortunate birth, so a servile status did not hold the severe stigma it later would acquire.

The accumulation of goods also changed the nature of warfare. Although hunter-gatherers fought over territory at times, the skirmishes tended to be short-lived and small scale because the individuals involved were too valuable to waste through this sort of conflict. The agricultural revolution pushed warfare to a larger scale. With the population increase that the revolution fueled, there were more people to engage in conflict and more rewards for the winners, who could gain more goods and enslave the losers. Excavations have shown that the early settlement of Jericho was surrounded by a great stone wall about 3 yards thick—one of the earliest human-made defensive structures. Indeed, people must have greatly feared their neighbors to invest the labor needed to build such a wall with only stone hand tools. Settlements arose throughout the Neolithic in Europe and in Asia Minor (as well as in many regions in Asia), but the mainstream in the story

New warfare

of the West arose farther east in a river valley where writing preserved the details of the development of even larger and more sophisticated cities.

connect to today

Genetically Modified Foods

The first development of agriculture and animal husbandry in a large part contributed to the success of Western civilization in eventually spreading throughout the world. How do you think modern agricultural innovations such as the development of drought-resistant grains and genetically modified foods affect today's society?

STRUGGLING WITH THE FORCES OF NATURE: Mesopotamia

3000–ca. 1000 B.C.E.

Between 3000 and 1000 B.C.E., people began to cultivate a broad curve of land that stretched from the Persian Gulf to the shores of the Mediterranean (see map on page 5). This arc, the Fertile Crescent, has been

Bronze Age

called the cradle or birthplace of Western civilization. It earned this appellation in part because of its lucky possession of essential plants and animals and its central

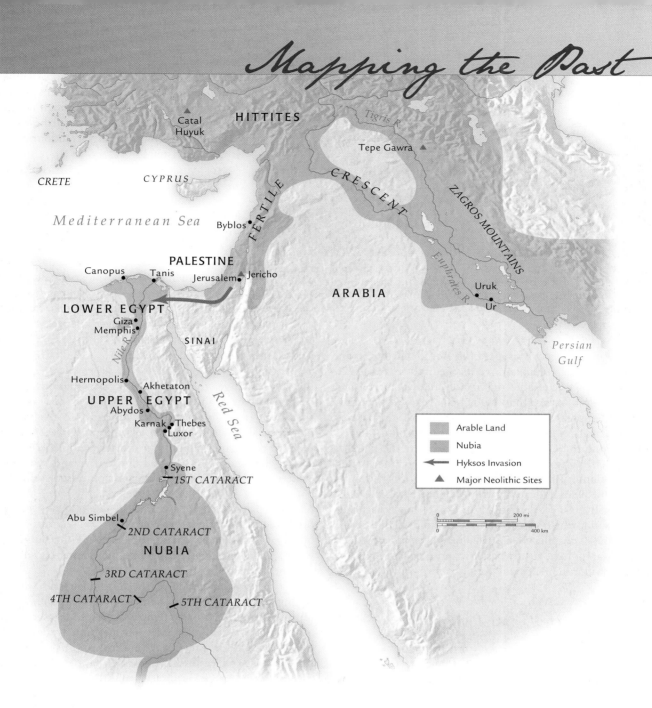

Mesopotamia and Egypt, ca. 2000 B.C.E.

This map illustrates the cradles of Western civilization in Mesopotamia, along the coast of the Mediterranean Sea, and in Egypt. It also identifies this region's major Neolithic sites. **What advantages did the locations of the rivers provide to the growing cultures?**

location, which placed it at a crossroads, for mingling of ideas and peoples. The ancient Greeks called this region Mesopotamia, or "land between the rivers," emphasizing the importance of the great Tigris and Euphrates Rivers to the life of the area. The earliest cities in which civilization took root were located in the southern part of Mesopotamia. During the late Neolithic period, people living

in this region used agriculture; sometime after 3000 B.C.E., they learned to smelt metals to make tools and weapons. By smelting, they developed a process to combine copper and tin to make a much stronger metal, bronze. At last, there was a substance that improved on stone, and archaeologists note this innovation by calling this period the Bronze Age.

ZIGGURAT AT UR, ca. 2100 B.C.E. The great mud-brick temples known as ziggurats rose from the flat landscapes of Mesopotamia. The builder wrote that he was ordered to erect this ziggurat by his god Marduk. The structure shows both the power of religion and the skill of builders in this cradle of Western civilization.

Life in southern Mesopotamia was harsh but manageable. Summer temperatures reached a sweltering 120 degrees Fahrenheit, and the region received a meager average rainfall of less than 10 inches a year. Yet the slow-running Euphrates created vast marshlands that stayed muddy and wet even during the dry season. Villagers living along the slightly higher ground near the marshes poled their boats through the shallow waters as they netted abundant river fish and shot waterfowl with their bows and arrows. Domesticated cattle and sheep grazed on the rich marsh grass while agriculturalists farmed the fertile high ground, which was actually made up of islands in the marshland. The villagers used the marsh reeds as fuel and as material to make sturdy baskets, and they fashioned the swamp mud into bricks and pottery.

The Origins of Western Civilization

In about 3000 B.C.E., a climate change occurred that forced the southern Mesopotamians to alter their way of life. As they did so, they created a more complex society that we call Sumerian—the earliest civilization. Starting around 3200 B.C.E., the region became drier. The rivers no longer flooded as much of the land as before, and more and more of the marshes evaporated. When the rivers flooded, they still deposited fertile soil in the former marshlands, but the floods came at the wrong times of the year for easy agriculture. Fed by the melting snows in the Zagros Mountains (see map on page 5), the Tigris flooded between April and June—a time highly inconvenient for agriculture in a region where the growing season runs from autumn to early summer. Furthermore, the floods were unpredictable; they could wash away crops still ripening in the fields or come too early to leave residual moisture in the soil for planting. Now people began to dig channels to irrigate the dry land and save the water for when they

needed it, but these efforts were never certain because the floods were unpredictable. Mesopotamians developed an intense pessimism that was shaped by the difficult natural environment of the land between the rivers, which could bring seemingly random abundance or disaster.

To manage the complex irrigation projects and planning required to survive in this unpredictable environment, the Sumerians developed a highly organized society to bring order to the chaos that seemed to surround them. Their resourcefulness paid off; by 3000 B.C.E., the valley had become a rich food-producing area. The population of Uruk, shown on the map on page 5, had expanded to nearly 10,000 by about 2900 B.C.E. Neighbors no longer knew each other, and everyone looked to a centralized administration led by priests and priestesses to organize daily life. In exchange, these religious leaders claimed a percentage of the land's produce. With their new wealth, they built imposing temples called *ziggurats* that dominated the skylines of cities like Uruk and Ur. Above is a modern-day photograph of one of those temples.

Administration

Ziggurats also served as administrative and economic centers of cities, with storehouses and administrative rooms housed in the lower levels. They were bustling places as people came to bring goods and socialize with neighbors. Just as religion was at the center of the Sumerian world, these buildings, rising like mountains out of the mud plains, served as the center of city life.

Economic functions

The labor and goods of the local men and women belonged to the deity who lived in the inner room at the top of the temple. In one temple dedicated to a goddess, attendants washed, clothed, and perfumed the statue every day, and servants burned incense and played music for the statue's pleasure. Meanwhile, temple administrators organized irrigation projects and tax collection in the cities to foster the abundance that allowed the great cities to flourish and serve their patron deities. Through these centralized religious organizations, ancient loyalties to family and clan were slowly replaced by political and religious ties that linked devoted followers to the city guarded by their favored deity. This was a crucial step in creating the large political units that were to become a hallmark of Western civilization.

Life in a Sumerian City

In the shadow of the ziggurats, people lived in mud-brick houses with thick walls that insulated them from heat, cold, and noise. Women and slaves prepared the family meals, which consisted mostly of barley (in the south) or wheat (in the north). Vegetables, cheese, fish, figs, and dates supplemented the Sumerian diet. A large portion of the calories people consumed came from ale. Forty percent of all the grain grown in the region was brewed for ale by women in their homes, not only for their family's consumption but also for sale.

Although Mesopotamia offered early settlements the significant advantage of indigenous plants and animals, the area had some severe shortages. The river valleys lacked metal and stone, which were essential for tools and weapons. The earliest settlements depended on long-distance trade for these essential items, and soon the wheel was invented to move cartloads of goods more easily. Materials came from Syria, the Arabian peninsula, and even India, and Mesopotamian traders produced goods for trade. The most lucrative products were textiles. Traders transported woven wool great distances in their quest for stone, metal, and, later, luxury goods. Mesopotamian goods, animals, and even plants moved slowly as far as China as the ancient cultures of the Eurasian land embarked on mass trade. The essential trade routes that marked the whole history of Western civilization appeared at the dawn of its inception.

Trade

Sumerian women worked in many shops in the cities—as wine sellers, tavern keepers, and merchants. Some women were prostitutes, although in time Sumerians came to view this profession as a threat to traditional ties. Late in Mesopotamian history, laws arose that insisted on special clothing to distinguish "respectable" women from prostitutes. Ordinary women were expected to veil their heads in public, whereas prostitutes and slaves were forced to go about their day with bare heads. At the end of Mesopotamian ascendancy, these laws were made extremely strict—any slave woman who dared to wear a veil was punished by having her ears cut off. In this society, in which people did not know one another, city residents strove mightily to distinguish social ranks. City life came with increasing emphasis on social stratification as the cornerstone of urban order.

Women's work

Gods and Goddesses of the River Valley

The men and women of the Tigris-Euphrates river valley believed that all parts of the natural world were invested with will. For example, if a river flooded, the event was interpreted as an act of the gods. People also viewed inter-city warfare as a battle between each city's gods. On a broader level, the Sumerians saw themselves and their deities as combatants locked in a struggle against a mysterious chaos that could destroy the world at any moment—just as sometimes the unpredictable rivers flooded and brought destruction. People viewed themselves as slaves of the gods and provided the deities with everything they needed—from sacrifices to incense to music—to try to keep order in their uncertain world. In spite of their appeasements, however, when disorder appeared in the form of natural disasters or disease, the pessimistic Sumerians were not surprised.

An anonymous Sumerian poem of despair expresses the anxiety that came with this view of religious responsibility. In this poem, a once-prosperous man suffers a reversal of fortune. He laments:

Sumerian pessimism

> My ill luck has increased, and I do not find the right.
> I called to my god, but he did not show his face,
> I prayed to my goddess, but she did not raise her head.

The man seeks out diviners and dream priests, but no one can tell him the omission that brought about his downfall. In his despair, he can only hope that continued devotion to the gods will restore his prosperity, but his tone is not optimistic.

Neither the Sumerians nor their eventual conquerors envisioned an attractive afterlife. They believed that the spirits of the dead went to a shadowy, disagreeable place from where they might occasionally affect the living, usually for ill. Sumerians' only hope for happiness lay in the present life, and that happiness hinged on capricious deities who cared little for humans.

By the third millennium B.C.E., earthly society in the ancient Middle East mirrored the hierarchical heavenly one. Kingship was universally accepted as the correct political order, and castes of nobles and priests were also deemed natural. Inequality among people was seen as normal and theologically justified, and people accepted their place in this highly ordered world with kings on top and slaves on the bottom. Individuals' longings for social justice and hopes for improving their situations all took place within a frame of reality that was very different from ours—one that assumed inequality was natural.

Sometime during the second millennium B.C.E., the Sumerians began to reflect on individuals' relationships with the gods. Instead of being content with a corporate association between a city and its guardian, some men and women looked to a more personal alliance, just as the despairing poet we met earlier cried out for a divine explanation of his plight. This longing led individuals to ponder the concept of immortality, wondering whether death was avoidable. In the celebrated poem *The Epic of Gilgamesh,* the poet articulates this search for meaning in death while telling an engaging story of a Sumerian hero and his fortunes. Gilgamesh was a king who ruled Uruk (see map on page 5) in about 2700 B.C.E. Sometime after 2000 B.C.E., stories about the by-then semimythical king were collected and written down in the epic. In one version of Gilgamesh's adventures, his best friend, Enkidu, is killed and the reality of death strikes home. Gilgamesh refuses to bury Enkidu; in his

Individual longings

CUNEIFORM SCRIPT, ca. 2600 B.C.E. Sumerian writing, made with wedge-shaped indentations in wet clay, revolutionized record keeping, allowing texts to long outlast memory. This tablet records lists of trade commodities.

system called **cuneiform** (named from the Latin word that means "wedge"). Scribes imprinted wedge-shaped characters into wet clay tablets, which became highly durable when dried. The photograph on this page shows a tablet of cuneiform script made in about 2600 B.C.E., which lists quantities of various commodities.

Scribes labored for many years to memorize the thousands of characters of cuneiform script. By 2500 B.C.E., scribal schools had been established to train the numerous clerks needed to serve the palaces and temples. Some surviving cuneiform tablets reveal that these students also studied mathematics and geometry. At first, girls attended these scribal schools, and records testify to a number of successful female scribes. Later, however, the occupation became exclusively male, but the reasons for this change have been lost. The schoolboy described at the beginning of this chapter was one of the lucky few who were trained to read and write. Anyone possessing these skills was assured a prosperous future.

grief he is unwilling to give up his friend. When the reality of decomposition confronts the king, he travels to find the secret of immortality. At the bottom of the sea he finds a plant that will give eternal life, only to see the magic herb stolen by a snake before he can bring it back to Enkidu. Gilgamesh is left facing the reality of death and the equally important reality of the value of finding joy in the present. This pessimistic epic once again reveals the Sumerian assumption that humans are doomed to struggle endlessly in a difficult universe.

The Development of Writing

Although religion dominated Mesopotamian thought, the Sumerians' real impact on the future of Western civilization derived from their more practical inventions. As Mesopotamian cities expanded and grew wealthy, the need arose for a system of keeping records that would prove more enduring and accurate than the spoken word. In response, the Sumerians developed a system of writing. Some scholars believe that writing first emerged from a system of trade tokens. For example, if a merchant wanted to verify the number of sheep someone else was supposed to deliver, he would count out tokens to represent the sheep and seal them in a clay envelope that would be broken open upon delivery. The tokens left an imprint in the clay, and in time people realized that they could omit the tokens entirely and simply mark the clay.

At first, Sumerian writing consisted of stylized pictures of the objects represented—birds, sheep, or bowls to signify food. Soon the characters became more abstract and indicated sounds as well as objects. By 2800 B.C.E., the Sumerians had developed a sophisticated writing

Cuneiform

Laws and Justice

Writing also fostered the emergence of another element that would remain an essential component of Western civilization: a written law code. Recording laws in writing was an attempt to establish order in the land between the rivers that seemed so susceptible to chaos. But these laws also tried to express principles of justice that outlasted the ruler who issued them.

The most famous and complete of the ancient law codes was that of the Babylonian king Hammurabi (ca. 1792–1750 B.C.E.), who ruled the southern Mesopotamian valley. In the prologue to his law code, which is preserved in cuneiform script on a stone column, the king expressed the highest principles of justice: "I established law and justice in the language of the land and promoted the welfare of the people." Studying Hammurabi's code, which was a compilation of existing laws, opens a window into the lives of these ancient urban dwellers. It regulated everything from family life to physicians' fees to building requirements. The king seemed determined to order his society, for he introduced harsh penalties that had been absent from earlier laws. His code literally demanded an "eye for an eye"—one law stipulated that "should a man destroy another's eye, he shall lose his own." Another stated that a son who strikes his father shall have his hand cut off.

Code of Hammurabi

Hammurabi's code clearly expressed the strict social hierarchy that Mesopotamian society counted as natural. The laws specified different penalties for the three social orders: elites, freemen, and slaves. The elites included everyone from officials to priests and warriors. Beneath them were freemen, including artisans, merchants, professionals, and some farmers. Slaves occupied the bottom stratum, but they, too, had some rights under Hammurabi's laws—for example, they might own land and marry free persons. Many of the laws sought to protect the powerless so, as the prologue says, "that the strong may not oppress the weak."

Many laws tried to protect women and children from unfair treatment and limited the authority of husbands over their households. For example, women could practice various trades and hold public positions. Husbands could not accuse their wives of adultery without proof, for the penalty for proven adultery was harsh—the adulterous wife and her lover would be drowned. However, a woman could obtain a divorce from her husband. In spite of these protections, women still remained largely the property of their husbands. For example, a woman could be put to death for entering—without her husband—a facility that served alcoholic beverages. Further-

Women and children

more, a wife's fortunes were so dependent upon her husband that he could even sell her into slavery to pay his debts.

Perhaps one of the most significant things about Hammurabi's code was that the king intended his laws to outlast his own rule. On the tablet, he inscribed: "For all future time, may the king who is in the land observe the words of justice which I have written upon my monument!" Writing, and written law in particular, gave kings and reformers like Hammurabi hope for the establishment of timeless justice and a chance for a kind of personal immortality for the king.

Indo-Europeans: New Contributions in the Story of the West

While the people in the Fertile Crescent developed many of the elements that contributed to the formation of Western civilization—agriculture, writing, and law—the emerging culture remained subject to transformation. As we have seen, one of the advantages of the ancient Middle East was its location, which permitted it to benefit from influences from the far reaches of Asia. Of course, this geographic openness also contributed to instability—ideas often came with invaders and destruction. The region north of the Black Sea and the Caucasus Mountains (see map on page 21) produced peoples living on the steppes who waged war on the peoples of the Fertile Crescent and developed a culture that eventually had a profound influence on the West.

Linguists, who analyze similarities in languages, have labeled these people Indo-European because their language served as the basis for virtually all subsequent European lan-

Indo-European languages

guages (except Finnish, Hungarian, and Basque). This language family separates the Indo-Europeans from most of the original inhabitants of the Fertile Crescent, who spoke "Semitic" languages. The steady

influx of Indo-European invaders (later called Celts, Latins, Greeks, or Germans) formed the dominant population of Europe. Other Indo-Europeans moved east and settled in India or traveled south into modern-day Turkey and Iran.

The Indo-Europeans were led by a warrior elite, who were buried in elaborate graves. Excavations of these graves have allowed scholars to analyze the prized possessions and weapons that were buried with these rulers, yielding many insights into this society. Some archaeologists

Mounted warriors

refer to the Indo-Europeans as "battle-ax people" because of the many axes found in their burial sites. They also rode horses, which they first domesticated for riding in about 2000 B.C.E. Riding on horseback gave Indo-European warriors the deadly advantages of speed, mobility, and reach over the Stone and Bronze Age archers they encountered in their travels.

The warrior elite of the Indo-Europeans excelled in battle and moved their families with them as they journeyed and fought. They carried their belongings in heavy carts outfitted with four solid, wooden wheels. The carts were a significant departure from the Sumerian two-wheeled chariots, which proved too unstable over long distances. The heavy carts traveled best over flat surfaces, and evidence indicates that as early as 2000 B.C.E. wooden roadways were built across boglands in northern Europe to accommodate the movement of people and their goods.

When the Indo-Europeans moved into the Fertile Crescent, they were not literate, but they preserved their values in oral traditions. Later, influenced by the literary traditions of those they conquered, Indo-Europeans developed their own written languages, and many of these tales were written down and preserved. Ideals of a war-

Contributions

rior elite and worship of gods who lived in the sky instead of on the earth continued, as did the Indo-European language. These elements were among the Indo-European contributions to Western civilization. In turn, early in the history of the Indo-Europeans (long before they acquired a written language), they adopted some things from the Mesopotamian cradle of civilization. They acquired many of the grains and other foods that were native to Mesopotamia and spread them widely. The successful culture of the Fertile Crescent was making its impact known far outside the river valleys that spawned it.

Hittites Establish Their Empire

In about 1650 B.C.E., an Indo-European people called the Hittites established a kingdom in Asia Minor (modern Turkey) and set up their capital at Hattusas (see map on page 21). For the next three hundred years, the Hittite people planted crops on the fertile lands north of their capital, irrigated their fruit groves, and mined the ore-rich mountains. Throughout this time, they interacted with their neighbors in Mesopotamia and integrated much of Mesopotamian language, literature, law, and religion into their own Indo-European heritage. The interactions were often violent as the Hittites entered into the stormy politics of the ancient world.

The Hittites introduced a new technology of warfare into the West in the form of powerful—and deadly—war chariots. The oldest reference to chariot warfare in the ancient Near East comes from about the eighteenth century B.C.E., in a text that mentions forty teams of horses at one battle. The wheels of the Hittite chariots, lighter than those for any previous vehicle, made the chariots highly maneuverable, and the axle was set forward for stability.

Fortunately for historians, the Hittites learned the art of writing from the Mesopotamians. At Hattusas archaeologists have excavated about 10,000 cuneiform tablets, which shed much light on this culture that stood at the crossroads of the Middle East for such a long time. Inevitably, Hittite armies clashed with the culture arising to the south and west—along the river valley of the magnificent Nile River.

RULE OF THE GOD-KING: Ancient Egypt

ca. 3100–1000 B.C.E.

The food crops that proved so successful in Mesopotamia spread to Egypt, stimulating another ancient civilization that arose on the banks of a great river—the roots of Western civilization moved farther west. The Nile River in Egypt flows more than 4,000 miles,

Nile Valley from central Africa north to the Mediterranean Sea. Just as in Mesopotamia, a climate change forced dependence on the great river. In about 6000 B.C.E. the prevailing Atlantic rains shifted, changing great grassy plains into desert and forcing people to move closer to the Nile to use its waters.

Unlike the Tigris and Euphrates, the Nile reliably overflowed its banks every year at a time convenient for planting—flooding in June and receding by October. During this flood, the river deposited a layer of fertile black earth in time for a winter planting of cereal crops. In ancient times, the Nile also provided the Egyptians with an excellent communication and transportation system. The river flowed north, encouraging traffic in that direction, but the prevailing winds blew from north to south, helping ships to sail against the current.

Egypt was more isolated than the ancient civilizations to the northeast. The deserts to the Nile's east and west stymied most would-be invaders, and in the southern Sudan a vast marsh protected the area from encroachers.

Potential invaders from the Mediterranean Sea confronted shallows that prevented ships from easily approaching the Egyptian coast. As a result, Egyptian civilization developed without the fear of conquest or the resultant blending and conflict among cultures that marked the Mesopotamian cities. By about 3100 B.C.E., a king from Upper Egypt (in the south), who according to tradition was named Menes, had consolidated his rule over the entire Egyptian land.

Prosperity and Order: The Old Kingdom
ca. 2700–2181 B.C.E.

Ancient Egyptians believed that the power of the gods was visible in the natural world—in the Nile and in the people and animals that benefited from its bounty. Consequently, they worshiped the divine spirit that was expressed through heavenly bodies, animals, and even insects. Over time, some gods were exalted over others, and deities were combined and blurred. However, through most of Egypt's history the most important deities were the sun god Re (or Amon) and the Nile spirits Isis, her husband-consort, Osiris, and their son, the falcon-god Horus. Unlike the Mesopotamians, the Egyptians were optimistic about their fortunes. They believed they were blessed by the gods, who brought such a regular and fertile flooding of the Nile, not cursed by their chaotic whims. This optimism infused Egyptian culture with extraordinary continuity—why change something that brought such blessings?

At the heart of their prosperity was the king, whom Egyptians considered the living embodiment of the deity, and this linking of political power with religion reinforced the stability of the Old Kingdom. While Mesopotamians believed their kings served as priests to their gods, Egyptians believed **Preserving order** their rulers *were* gods, who had come to earth to bring truth, justice, and order—all summarized in the word **ma'at.** In return, the populace was obligated to observe a code of correct behavior that was included in the concept of *ma'at.* For millennia, Egyptians believed strongly that the importance of proper behavior brought prosperity to the land, and such beliefs contributed to a stable society. (The funeral inscription on page 11 shows these enduring values.) This ordered society was ruled by a god-king later called pharaoh (great house), a term that referred to the general institution of the monarchy as well as the ruler.

The Old Kingdom period (ca. 2700–2181 B.C.E.) saw astonishing prosperity and peace, as farming and irrigation methods provided an abundance of crops and wealth to many. Unlike the Mesopotamian valley, Egypt had ready access **Trade** to mineral resources, most importantly copper, which was in great demand for tools. Egyptians refined copper ore at the site of the surface mines, and ingots of copper were transported by caravans of donkeys overland to the Nile. From there, the precious ores were manufactured or used to trade abroad. Egypt was also happily situated to capitalize on trade with Nubia, which gave access to the resources of sub-Saharan Africa. From Nubia, Egyptians gained gold, ivory, ebony, gems, and aromatics in exchange for Egyptian cloth and manufactured goods. With the surpluses of metals and grains, Egyptians could import goods from the Middle East and beyond. In addition to textiles, Egyptians desperately needed wood to make large seagoing vessels for their trade and navy. All this industry generated prosperity for many people, and in the Old Kingdom, people used these resources to support close families, and raise pampered children.

Hieroglyphs: Sacred Writing

Sometime around 3000 B.C.E., Egyptians developed a system of writing. Egyptian writing was not cuneiform, nor was it used primarily for accounting purposes. While Egyptian administrators surely had as much need for clear records as the Sumerians, they primarily used writing to forward religious and magical power. Every sign in their writing system represented a real or mythical object and was designed to express that object's power. The ancient Greeks saw these images on temples and named Egyptian script **hieroglyph,** meaning "sacred writing."

Hieroglyphs were more than a series of simple pictures. Each symbol could express one of three things: the object it portrayed, an abstract idea associated with the object, or one or more sounds of speech from the spoken Egyptian word for the object. (The technical terms for these three uses are *pictogram, ideogram,* and *phonogram.*) Because this writing had ceremonial religious use, it changed little over the centuries as scribes carved it into stone monuments. An example of hieroglyphic writing can be seen in the background of the chapter opening image on page 1.

However, hieroglyphs were too cumbersome for everyday use, so scribes learned two other simplified scripts—called Hieratic and Demotic—to keep records or write literature. Whereas many of the hieroglyphs were carved into stone, everyday records were more often written on papyrus, a kind of paper made from the Nile's abundant papyrus reeds. This versatile, sturdy reed could be reused—much like recycled paper today—and in the dry desert air was very durable. Often in Egypt's history, the lucrative export of papyrus increased the royal treasury.

Scribes studied for many years to master the complicated, varied Egyptian scripts. As in Mesopotamia, there

Scribes are early records of women scribes, but the occupation later became restricted to men. On one surviving papyrus fragment, a scribe praised his occupation: "Writing

An Egyptian Nobleman Writes His Obituary

This document from second-millennium B.C.E. Egypt records the obituary inscribed on the tomb of an Egyptian nobleman named Ameni (or Amenemhet). This excerpt reveals what he counted as his greatest deeds in his years of service during Egypt's Middle Kingdom.

There was no citizen's daughter whom I misused, there was no widow whom I oppressed, there was no [peasant] whom I repulsed, there was no shepherd whom I repelled, there was no overseer of serf-laborers whose people I took for (unpaid) imposts, there was none wretched in my community, there was none hungry in my time. When years of famine came I plowed all the fields of the Oryx nome, as far as its southern and northern boundary, preserving its people alive and furnishing its food so that there was none hungry therein. I gave to the widow as (to) her who had a husband; I did not exalt the great above the small in all that I gave. Then came great Niles, possessors of grain and all things, [but] I did not collect the arrears of the field.

What does this inscription reveal about the values of ancient Egypt?

for him who knows it is better than all other professions. It pleases more than bread and beer, more than clothing and ointment. It is worth more than an inheritance in Egypt, than a tomb in the west."

Pyramids and the Afterlife

Scribes furthered the prosperity of the god-kings by carefully tracking the rulers' finances as they grew rich from state monopolies and taxes on all the products created in the fertile land. Whenever they had excess income, the kings proved their greatness by building pyramids, monuments to their glory that in some cases survive today. Unlike the ziggurats, which were made of dried clay bricks, these pyramids were built of cut stone—a remarkable building innovation.

The Old Kingdom rulers made the pyramids the great symbol of Egyptian power and longevity. An anonymous architect refined early step pyramid design and built the Great Pyramid as a burial tomb for the Fourth Dynasty ruler, Khufu (also known as Kheops), in about 2590 B.C.E. This pyramid became the model for the later Old Kingdom tombs that were built in Giza, which continue to dominate the skyline there. The photograph above shows the pyramids at Giza, with the Great Pyramid of Khufu on the left. Khufu's pyramid covers about 13 acres and is made of more than two million stone blocks. Peasants labored on these pyramids before planting season during the months when the Nile was in flood. Ancient Greek historians later claimed that the Great Pyramid of Giza took twenty years to build and required the labor of 100,000 workers. Modern estimates tend to agree with these calculations. The pyramids—so visible in the ancient skyline—proclaimed the god-king's immortality and the permanence of the order he brought to the land along the Nile.

Pyramids—and later mortuary temples—were built as tombs for the god-kings or, more precisely, as houses for their departed spirits. The departed's soul was sustained in the tomb by the same food and goods that had sustained the living body. The Egyptian notion of immortality marked an important contribution to the

Pyramids

Afterlife

PYRAMIDS, ca. 2590 B.C.E. These burial places for the royal dead had a long history in the Old Kingdom. The most famous pyramids are at Giza, with the Great Pyramid of Khufu on the left.

world of ideas, for the afterlife Egyptians conceived of was dramatically different from the dark world of the Mesopotamian dead. We do not have an exact idea of how the Egyptians visualized the afterlife, but it seems to have been an improved version of this world—a heavenly Nile valley. Some poets even wrote of death as a pleasant release:

Death is before me today
Like a man's longing to see his home
When he has spent many years in captivity.

Upon the death of a king, or in later years a nobleman who could afford a burial, the body was embalmed. Embalmers removed the internal organs through an incision in the abdomen and placed them in a vessel filled with a salty preserving solution. The body cavity was then probably dried in a pile of natron crystals. Later in Egypt's history, embalmers used resin-soaked linen to pack the body cavity. Finally the embalmers wrapped the body in more linen with resin. The wrapped, embalmed body—the mummy—along with a box containing the internal organs, was then placed in a chamber deep within the pyramid. Stocking the tomb with an array of food, household goods, and precious jewels for the pharaoh to enjoy in the afterlife completed the burial process.

Burial rituals

Pyramids from the Old Kingdom contained no images, but later artists painted the interior walls of tombs with scenes of activities that the deceased could expect to enjoy in the afterlife, and these scenes offer us a glimpse of how Egyptians viewed the next world.

"Writing for him who knows it is better than all other professions. It pleases more than bread and beer, more than clothing and ointment. It is worth more than an inheritance in Egypt, than a tomb in the west."

Then & Now

Valuable Trade from Southern Arabia

Frankincense and myrrh are valuable resins that are produced from brush-like trees in Yemen. From as early as 1000 B.C.E., these prized goods were brought across the desert on camels and traded throughout the Mediterranean. They were essential in medicines, perfumes, and religious ceremonies, appearing in the Bible as part of the Queen of Sheba's gifts to King Solomon and Persian wise men's gifts to Jesus. Frankincense remains a popular product today as researchers continue to find medicinal benefits from it in treating chronic inflammatory diseases like osteoarthritis and Crohn's disease. Myrrh remains equally as popular today for its aromatherapeutic qualities and its use in holistic remedies.

Changing Political Fortunes

ca. 2200–1570 B.C.E.

The order and prosperity promised by the pyramids proved less enduring than the Egyptians expected. At the end of the Old Kingdom period, the climate turned against the god-kings. As drought **Famine** in southern Nubia led to a series of low floods in Egypt, crops failed, and people pillaged the countryside in a desperate search for food. There was even one account of cannibalism. Under such pressure, Egypt needed a strong ruler to preserve *ma'at,* but one was not forthcoming. Near the end of the Old Kingdom, one king—Pepi II (ca. 2270–2180 B.C.E.)—reputedly ruled for more than ninety years, which was an extraordinary feat in an age when a decade or two was considered a substantial rule and when 40 years of age was the normal life expectancy. However, the old king was unable to keep a strong rule; during his reign, authority broke down, and he outlived his heirs. After his death a succession of little-known kings with very short reigns followed—a clear indication that all was not well within Egypt. Sources indicate that one of these ephemeral rulers was a woman—Nitocris—who ruled for about two years. During these times of weak central authority, local nobles exerted power, and Egypt suffered a period of social and political instability called the First Intermediate Period (2181–2140 B.C.E.).

A text from the time articulated poignantly the widespread misery experienced during these hard years: "Everything is filthy: there is no such thing as clean linen these days. The dead are thrown into the river. . . . The ladies of the nobility exclaim: 'If only we had something to eat!'

They are forced to prostitute their daughters. They are reduced to sleeping with men who were once too badly off to take a woman."

During these difficult times, people began to hope for a more pleasant afterlife, which many began to believe was possible for more than just the royal family. In the First Intermediate Period, anyone who could afford the appropriate burial rituals and magic spells could expect to achieve immortality. Still, prosperity continued to elude the Nile valley.

In about 2060 B.C.E., Amenemhat I of Thebes finally restored peace to the crippled valley and introduced what has come to be called the Middle Kingdom period (ca. 2060–1785 B.C.E.). Egypt prospered once again, and one pharaoh **Middle Kingdom** wrote: "None was hungry in my years, none thirsted then; men dwelled in peace." During these years, the kings conquered Nubia and grew rich on the gold of that kingdom. This conquest also brought sub-Saharan Africa into closer contact with the Mediterranean world, and continued trade with Nubia integrated African goods and elements of their culture into Egypt's and into the developing Western culture in general. Egypt's rulers also introduced impressive engineering projects that expanded Egypt's amount of irrigated land by more than 17,000 acres. The Egyptians also began engaging in lucrative trade with the peoples of the Fertile Crescent. This practice had a price, however: It drew Egypt into the volatile politics of the ancient Middle East.

In the eighteenth century B.C.E., trouble struck again. The kings at the end of the twelfth dynasty were weak, and local magnates began to claim autonomy. Without a strong central authority, the Nubians in the south revolted and

Egyptian Fresco

ca. 1295–1186 B.C.E.

A fresco is a kind of mural painted on plaster. This **fresco** from Thebes shows Nubians bearing gifts (tribute) of an exotic giraffe, an animal skin draped over a man's arm, a mound of ostrich eggs, and most valuable of all, highly bred cattle, valued for their coloring. What does the fresco suggest about the value of Nubian trade to Egypt?

hated Hyksos and established a new dynasty that introduced what historians call the New Kingdom (1570–1085 B.C.E.). While these kings—now officially called pharaohs—intended to restore the conservative glory of the Old Kingdom, they nevertheless remembered the lesson of the invasion from the north and no longer relied on Egypt's geographic isolation to protect their way of life. Instead, the newly militant god-kings embarked on a series of foreign wars to build an empire that would erect a territorial barrier between Egypt and any potential invaders.

As the Egyptian Empire expanded, it was in turn shaped by Fertile Crescent politics and culture. For example, the riches that poured into the Nile valley from foreign conquests often ended up in the hands of temple priests, who began rivaling the pharaohs in power. Slaves, captured abroad and brought to Egypt, introduced new languages, views, and religions **Egyptian Empire** to the valley. Not surprisingly, the lives of Egyptian soldiers, battling in foreign wars, changed for the worse.

Despite the challenges, the imperial pharaohs successfully built their empire and made Egypt prosperous again. However, such expansion always came with a cost. Rulers had to weigh placing resources into military expansion or into local projects. Hatshepsut's (ca. 1504–1482 B.C.E.) endeavors demonstrated this tension as she ruled the extended Egypt (see Past Lives on page 15). While protecting her borders, Hatshepsut concentrated her resources on domestic developments and commercial enterprises. Her inscriptions claim that she restored temples **Hatshepsut** that had lain in ruins since the Second Intermediate Period, and she engaged in numerous public works, all achievements that made her popular among her people.

Hatshepsut's successors reversed her traditional politics and revived Egypt's imperial ambitions. The New Kingdom reached its apogee in expansion and prosperity under the reign of Amenhotep III (r. ca. 1412–ca. 1375 B.C.E.). This confident pharaoh built huge statues of **Empire building** himself and a spacious new temple. His luxurious lifestyle,

broke away from Egyptian control, taking their gold with them. In 1650 B.C.E., the Hyksos who had settled in the

Egypt conquered

lowland where the Nile poured into the Mediterranean (the Delta) rose to power (see map on page 5). The Hyksos brought with them a new technology of warfare. They fought with bronze weapons, chariots, and body armor against the nearly nude Egyptians, who used only javelins and light copper weapons. The Hyksos established a kingdom in the Delta and this uneasy time, the Second Intermediate Period, extended from about 1785 to 1575 B.C.E.

Political Expansion: The New Kingdom
1570–1085 B.C.E.

In about 1570 B.C.E, the Egyptians adopted the new technology of warfare. With bronze weapons and chariots of their own, they liberated themselves from the

however, took its toll on him. He died at age 38, and his mummified remains reveal a balding, overweight man with rotted teeth.

The Religious Experiment of Akhenaten

ca. 1377–1360 B.C.E.

During the New Kingdom, the traditional relationship between the god-king and his priests began to change. Priests of Amon became almost as powerful as the pharaohs in administering the kingdom. The priests of Osiris grew popular with wealthy people, to whom they offered the possibility of immortal life in return for money. Within this increasingly tense environment arose a reformer who tried to create a religious revolution.

Amenhotep IV (r. ca. 1377–1360 B.C.E.), the son of Amenhotep III, tried to renounce the many divine principles worshiped in all the temples of Egypt and institute worship of a single god whom he called Aten, the sun-disk. The god-king changed his name from Amenhotep (Amon is satisfied) to Akhenaten (useful to Aten, the sun-disk). Then he withdrew

Akhenaten's religion his support from the old temples and tried to dissolve the powerful priesthoods. Akhenaten also departed from tradition by introducing a new naturalism in art, in which he allowed himself to be portrayed realistically, protruding belly and all (see photograph on page 16). However, the artwork in Aten's new temples often featured portraits of Akhenaten's beautiful wife, Nefertiti, without the pharaoh, suggesting that the queen may have played a large role in planning the new cult.

Many scholars have speculated about the motives behind Akhenaten's dramatic innovation of worshiping a single god. Had Akhenaten been influenced by Israelites living in Egypt? Was his declaration of a single god a political move to reduce the power of the priests of Amon? Or was the king a sickly dreamer who merely had a strange spiritual vision? We will never know Akhenaten's motives, but his reign caused turmoil in Egypt.

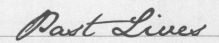

Powerful Female Pharaoh, Hatshepsut (r. 1473–1458 B.C.E.)

In 1504 B.C.E., Pharaoh Thutmose II died, leaving his wife (who was also his sister) Hatshepsut to act as regent for his son (her stepson), who was just a boy when his father died. Hatshepsut wanted to rule by herself, so she had herself declared pharaoh queen. She kept her army strong, allowing no incursions from her powerful neighbors, but she focused most of her efforts on trade and large building projects to legitimize her reign.

HATSHEPSUT, ca. 1460 B.C.E.

To control her image, Hatshepsut had many of her statues and portraits commissioned showing her dressed as a man. For example, in the statue shown here, the queen wears men's clothing and sports a fake beard. These portrayals were designed to convince her subjects that she was fully pharaoh and ruler.

When Thutmose III grew to manhood, he threw off the ties with his stepmother/aunt/mother-in-law. We do not know whether he had Hatshepsut murdered or simply deposed, but he introduced a new political order and erased Hatshepsut's name from most of her monuments.

How did Hatshepsut work to rule within the constraints of her gender? What role does gender play in politics today?

PHARAOH AKHENATEN AND FAMILY, ca. 1340 B.C.E. This limestone carving shows Akhenaten, his wife, Nefertiti, and three of their daughters relaxing in a family pose that departed from the usual formal depictions of the pharaoh. They bask in the rays of Aten, the sun-disk, the new deity they worshiped.

The Twilight of the Egyptian Empire
1360–ca. 1000 B.C.E.

Akhenaten was succeeded by Tutankhaton (r. 1347–1338 B.C.E.), who was only 9 years old at the time of his succession. However, the young Tutankhaton was unable to carry on the unpopular religious reforms of his father-in-law. The priests of the old cults had grown increasingly resentful of Akhenaten—whom they called "the criminal"—and within three years the young king changed his name to Tutankh*amen* as he renounced the old pharaoh's religious convictions. Tutankhamen died at just 18 years of age, and the general who succeeded him as pharaoh—Harmhab—destroyed Akhenaten's temples and restored the worship of the old gods.

Egypt showed a hint of its former greatness during the reign of Ramses II (1279–1213 B.C.E.), who reestablished the imperial frontiers in Syria and restored peace under Egypt's traditional gods. After the hard-fought battle at Kadesh in 1274 B.C.E., Ramses negotiated a treaty with the Hittites that is believed to be the first recorded nonaggression pact. Ramses' success in bringing peace allowed him to free resources for huge building projects, most notably a great temple carved out of the rocky cliffs along the Nile. The tribute portrayed in the fresco on page 14 testifies to the prosperity restored during the New Kingdom.

Subsequent pharaohs, through the end of the New Kingdom in 1085 B.C.E., tried to maintain the fragile empire. However, major challengers arose to confront the god-kings. Libyans to the west and Nubians from the south invaded the Nile valley and took power for a while. Eventually, greater empires to the east and north would conquer Egypt permanently, and the center of Western civilization would move to other lands. However, the advanced culture, ordered life, and intense spirituality of the rich land of the Nile would continue to exert a profound impact on the early peoples of the West.

PEOPLES OF THE MEDITERRANEAN COAST

ca. 1300–500 B.C.E.

Along the eastern coast of the Mediterranean Sea, various civilizations arose and became part of the power struggles plaguing the Middle East. Most of these Mediterranean cultures eventually were absorbed by their neighbors and disappeared. However, two of them—the Phoenicians and the Hebrews—made a lasting impact as they vigorously expanded their fortunes and furthered the worship of their gods.

The Phoenicians: Traders on the Sea

The Phoenicians were successful traders whose culture was based in the coastal cities of Sidon, Tyre, and Byblos (see map on page 20). These seagoing merchants made the most of their location by engaging in prosperous trade with Egypt and the lands in the Fertile Crescent. The Phoenicians controlled forests of cedar trees that were highly prized in both Mesopotamia and Egypt. They also had an even more lucrative monopoly on purple dye made from coastal shellfish. Purple dyes were so rare that cloth of this color was expensive, so it soon became identified with royalty. Phoenician weavers dyed cloth purple and sold it throughout the Middle East and western Mediterranean for huge profits. Throughout the ancient world, nobility was demonstrated by wearing purple clothing.

Explorers from the Phoenician cities traveled widely throughout the Mediterranean Sea. By 950 B.C.E., these remarkable sailors traded as far west as Spain and even into the Atlantic down the west coast of Africa. Like all ancient sailors, they hugged the coast as they | **Trading colonies** traveled so that they could stop each night to beach the ships and sleep. To guarantee safe harbors, Phoenician traders established merchant colonies all along the north coast of Africa; by some estimates there was a colony about every 30 miles. The most important colony was Carthage, which was founded about 800 B.C.E. and would become a significant power in the Mediterranean (see Chapter 4). Through these colonies, the Phoenicians spread the culture of the ancient Middle East—from their trading expertise to their gods and goddesses—around the Mediterranean all the way to Spain.

The enterprising Phoenician sailors left their mark on the Mediterranean world long after neighboring empires conquered the Phoenicians' home cities on the eastern coast. They began their early voyages in search of metals: tin, copper, iron for tools and weapons, and silver and gold for luxury items. This quest even led these intrepid sailors through the Strait of Gibraltar into the Atlantic, where they traded as far as the African coast and Britain. They were skilled at smelting metals—including the difficult-to-forge iron—and their metallurgy talents, along with the trade they fostered, stimulated growth throughout the region.

The Phoenicians' most important contribution to Western culture was their remarkable alphabet. In developing a writing system, the Phoenicians improved on the Sumerian

Phoenician alphabet script by creating a purely phonetic alphabet of only twenty-two letters. This system was simpler than the unwieldy cuneiform and hieroglyph that dominated the rest of the Middle East. The Phoenician alphabet spread rapidly and allowed later cultures to write without the long apprenticeships that characterized the proud scribes like the one shown at the beginning of this chapter. Through adopting a Phoenician-style alphabet, cultures of the West achieved a significant advantage over cultures whose written languages remained the exclusive province of the elite.

The People of the One God: Early Hebrew History

1500–900 B.C.E.

Phoenician society in the Near East ultimately disappeared as an independent state, but not before it had performed an immense service as a transmitter of culture throughout the Mediterranean. The Phoenicians' neighbors, the Hebrews, followed an entirely different course. The Hebrews resiliently withstood both time and conquest and emerged from a difficult journey with their culture intact.

While the Sumerians and their successors in Mesopotamia developed complex civilizations based on irrigation and built ziggurats to their many deities, the seminomadic Hebrews moved their flocks from Mesopotamia into the land of Canaan, comprising much of the modern states of Israel, Lebanon, and western Syria.

OPINION

What do you think was the most significant contribution made by the Sumerians and the Phoenicians to today's society?

Sometime before about 1700 B.C.E., the early leaders of the Hebrews, the patriarchs—Abraham, Isaac, and Jacob—led these seminomadic tribes that roamed the eastern Mediterranean and beyond. Jacob changed his name to Israel ("he who prevails with God"), and this name marked Jacob's followers as having a special relationship with one God. Consequently, historians refer to these tribes as the Israelites. Several clans traveled to Egypt, where Israelite texts claim they were enslaved by the Egyptians, although their status is not clear. They might simply have been employed in the labor-intensive Egyptian work projects, and their position may have changed over time to a more restrictive relationship. Some historians identify the Israelites with a group who helped build the huge projects of the Egyptian pharaoh Ramses II (r. ca. 1279–1213 B.C.E.). According to the Bible, Moses led this same group from Egypt. This Exodus (which means "journey out" in Greek) transformed them into a nation with a specific religious calling.

The details of the history of the Israelites are found in the Hebrew Scriptures (later called the Old Testament by Christians). Made up of writings from oral and written traditions and dating from about 1250 to 150 B.C.E., these Scriptures record laws, wisdom, legends, literature, and the history of **Hebrew Scriptures** the ancient Israelites. The first five books (known as the Pentateuch) constitute the **Torah,** or law code, which governed the people's lives. The Bible contains some information that is historically accurate and can be generally confirmed by archaeological evidence.

Historians must be cautious when using the Bible as a source, because it is basically a religious book that reveals faith, not science. Archaeology and history can illuminate the events of the ancient Israelites, but these sciences can shed no light on the faith that underlies the text. Used carefully, though, the Bible is an important source of information on these early Israelites, for they made a point to record and remember their own history—they wove teachings and morality into a historical narrative. Thus, Hebrew religion was rooted in history rather than myth, and from this text we can begin to re-create the early history of this profoundly influential people.

According to the Bible, the Hebrews from Egypt eventually returned to ancient Palestine and slowly reconquered the land, uniting the other nearby Hebrew tribes in the process. During this period of settlement, between about 1200 and 1050 B.C.E., Israelites experienced a change in leadership. Instead of relying solely on tribal leaders, people turned to "judges"—charismatic leaders who helped unite the people against the threats of their neighbors. In time, the elders of the tribes felt they needed a king to lead the people, declaring, "then we shall be like other nations, with a king to govern us, to lead us out to war and fight our battles" (1 Sam. 8:20). The people insisted that Samuel, the last of the judges, anoint their first king, Saul (r. ca. 1024–ca. 1000 B.C.E.).

Saul's successor, David (r. ca. 1000–ca. 961 B.C.E.), began encouraging the tribes to settle in a fixed location, with their capital at Jerusalem. David's successor, Solomon (r. ca. 961–ca. 922 B.C.E.), brought Phoenician craftsmen to Jerusalem to build a great temple there. Now a territorial power like others in the Fertile Crescent, the Hebrews worshiped their God in the temple overlooking a majestic city. But the costs of the temple were exorbitant, causing increased taxes and the growth of an administrative structure to collect them.

Solomon was a king in the Mesopotamian style. If the biblical account is to be believed, he used marriage to forge political alliances, accumulating hundreds of wives and many hundreds more concubines,

Dividing a kingdom including the daughter of an Egyptian pharaoh. However, the unified kingdom of tribes barely outlasted Solomon's reign. After his death, the northern tribes—particularly angry about Solomon's taxation and administrative innovations—broke away to form the separate kingdom of Israel (see map on page 20). The southern state was called Judah, with its capital at Jerusalem, and at this time the southern Israelites began to be called Jews. Israel was the more prosperous of the two kingdoms and was tied more closely to Phoenicia by trade and other contacts. Judah adhered more rigorously to the old Hebrew laws. The two kingdoms often fought each other as they participated in the shifting alliances of their neighbors. Dominating all politics, however, was their commitment to their one God.

The authors of the Scriptures developed an overriding theme in Jewish history: the intimate relationship between obedience to God's laws and the unfolding of the history of the Jewish people. As these authors recorded their recollection of events, they told of periodic violations of the uncompromising covenant with God and the resulting punishments that God imposed.

A Jealous God

1300–587 B.C.E.

When Moses led his people out of Egypt, they reportedly wandered for forty years in the wilderness of the Sinai Peninsula before returning to the land of Canaan (see map on page 20). During that time, Moses

The covenant bound his people to God in a special covenant, or agreement, through which the Jews would be God's "chosen people" in return for their undivided worship. The ancient Hebrews were not strictly monotheistic, for they believed in the existence of

the many deities of their neighbors. For Moses' people, however, there was only one God, and this God demanded their exclusive worship and the practice of his many laws.

The core of the Hebrew legal tradition lay in the Ten Commandments that the Bible claims God gave to Moses during his exodus from Egypt, and these were supplemented by other requirements listed in the Scriptures. Adhering to these **Hebrew laws** laws defined one as a Jew. While the laws bound the Jewish people together—to "love thy neighbor as thyself"—they also set the Jews apart from their neighbors. For example, boys were circumcised as a mark of the covenant between God and his people. In addition, Jews observed strict dietary laws that separated them from others—for example, they could eat no pork nor any animal that had been improperly slaughtered. But the fundamental commandment that allowed for no compromise with non-Jews was the injunction against worshiping the idols, or deities, of their neighbors.

Around the eighth century B.C.E., Jews were called to even higher ethical standards by a remarkable series of charismatic men—the prophets. These men, such as Amos, Micah, Hosea, Jeremiah, and Isaiah, were neither kings nor priests nor soldiers. Instead, they **Prophets** were common people—shepherds or tradesmen—who cared nothing for power or glory. They were brave men who urged their people to return to the covenant and traditional Hebrew law. In times of social distress, they became the conscience of Israel, and in turn they helped shape the social conscience that was to become part of Western civilization. The prophets reminded the Jews to care for the poor and in doing so, they emphasized the direct ethical responsibility of every individual. Unlike the other religions of the ancient Middle East, Judaism called individuals to follow their consciences to create a more ethical world. Religion was no longer a matter of rituals of the temple, but a matter of people's hearts and minds. The prophets preached a religion that would be able to withstand turmoil and political destruction, and it is fortunate that they did so, for the Hebrews would suffer much adversity, which they believed was a form of testing by their God.

According to the Bible, King Solomon had a weakness that stemmed from his polygamy. (See Exploring the Past on page 19.) Not only did he violate the biblical command not to take foreign wives, but to please them he allowed the worship of other deities (especially the **"God's punishments"** fertility goddess Astarte), even in the holy city of Jerusalem. Prophets claimed that it was his impiety that had divided the kingdom against itself. Later events showed a similar theme. Ahab (r. 869–850 B.C.E.), king of the northern kingdom of Israel, married a Phoenician princess, Jezebel, and erected an altar to her god Baal in order to please her. When Israel was conquered in 721 B.C.E. by the Assyrians, prophets who had predicted its downfall pointed to Ahab's breach of the covenant as the cause of the misfortune. The southern kingdom of Judah fared little better than Israel in trying to escape the aggressions of its neighbors. In 587 B.C.E., the Babylonians captured Jerusalem and destroyed Solomon's magnificent temple. Many Jews were exiled and enslaved in Babylon, and the "chosen people" were once more without a country or a religious center. From then on, there would be substantial numbers of Jews who lived outside Israel or Judah, and they later would be collectively known as the **Diaspora.** Instead of renouncing their God, however, the Jews reaffirmed their covenant in a different way.

Judaism in Exile

Hebrew priests in exile worried that Diaspora Jews living among non-Jews would forget the old traditions and be assimilated into the cultures of their neighbors. Therefore, they carefully compiled and edited the Scriptures to preserve their unique view of religion and history. These written accounts helped Judaism survive without a geographic center. The authors of the Scriptures arranged the history of the Jews to show that, despite hardships, God had always cared for his people. The priests believed that the destruction of the two Hebrew kingdoms had come because people either did not know the laws or had failed to obey them. As a result, Hebrew teachers emphasized the study of and strict adherence to the purity laws to keep their people separate from non-Jews even when they lived in close proximity as neighbors.

Without the temple in Jerusalem to serve as the center of worship, Jewish worship began to convene in more local establishments—synagogues and the home itself. This movement had an important impact on the status of women in Jewish culture. The emphasis on details of purity law to keep the chosen people separate reduced women's roles in formal prayer because the law stressed that anyone worshiping God had to be "clean." Women, seen as sometimes unclean because of menstrual blood or childbirth, were excluded from participating in the formal worship rituals. On the other hand, the experience of exile strengthened the family as a social and religious

King Solomon Secures His Realm's Fortune

This passage from the Book of Kings in the Bible shows that King Solomon, like other ancient leaders, tried to secure the fortunes of his kingdom through marriages with neighboring peoples.

Now King Solomon loved many foreign women: the daughter of Pharaoh, and Moabite, Ammomite, Edomite, Sidonian, and Hittite women, from the nations concerning which the Lord had said to the people of Israel, "You shall not enter into marriage with them, neither shall they with you, for surely they will turn away your heart after their gods"; Solomon clung to these in love. He had seven hundred wives, princesses, and three hundred concubines; and his wives turned away his heart. For when Solomon was old his wives turned away his heart after other gods; and his heart was not wholly true to the Lord his God, as was the heart of David his father. For Solomon went after Ashtoreth the goddess of the Sidonians and after Milcom the abomination of the Ammonites. So Solomon did what was evil in the sight of the Lord, and did not wholly follow the Lord as David his father had done. Then Solomon built a high place for Chemosh the abomination of Moab, and for Molech the abomination of the Ammonites, on the mountain east of Jerusalem. And so he did for all his foreign wives, who burned incense and sacrificed to their gods. And the Lord was angry with Solomon . . . (1 Kings 11:1–9).

What particular challenges do monotheistic Jews face in dealing with their neighbors?

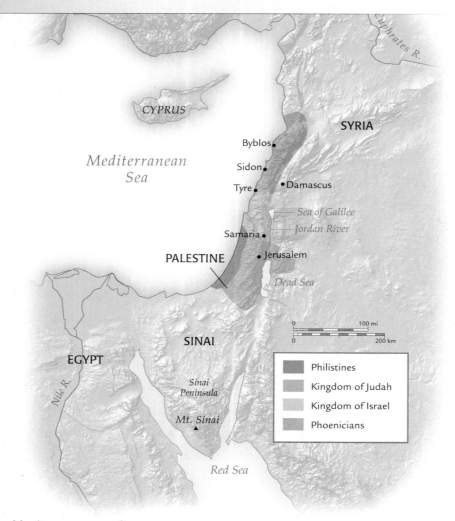

did not return to Israel, and the question of the relationship between Diaspora Jews and the cultures in which they lived would reemerge periodically throughout history as followers of this old covenant interacted with their neighbors.

The ancient Hebrews made a tremendous impact on the future of Western civilization. They believed that Hebrew contributions God created the world at a specific point in time, and this notion set them apart dramatically from their neighbors, such as the Egyptians, who believed in the eternity of the world. The Hebrews' view of history as a series of purposeful, morally significant events was unprecedented in the ancient world. Their concept of ethical monotheism, in which a single God of justice interacted with humans in a personal and spiritual way, offered a vision of religion that eventually dominated in the West. The many deities and demons that ruled the Mesopotamian and Egyptian worlds would in time be rendered insignificant by the God of the Hebrews, who transcended nature. The Hebrews believed that there was a profound distance between people and God, and thus individuals took more responsibility for the events of this world even as they worshiped and held in awe the deity who had made a deep and abiding covenant with the Jewish people.

Mediterranean Coast in the first millennium B.C.E. **This map shows the major kingdoms of the Mediterranean coast, together called the Land of Canaan in the Bible. The kingdoms include those of the Philistines, Hebrews, and Phoenicians.**

unit, a change that improved women's lives in other ways. For example, concubinage disappeared and women presided over the household, upholding the dietary laws and household rituals that preserved the Jewish culture wherever they lived.

In time, however, the Hebrews were able to reestablish their religious center in Jerusalem. After ruling Judah for forty-eight years, the Babylonians were, in turn, conquered by new peoples, the Persians. **"Second Temple" period** The Persians proved much more tolerant than the Babylonians of the varied beliefs of their subject peoples. In 538 B.C.E., the Persian king Cyrus let the Jewish exiles return to Jerusalem. The Jews built a new temple in 515 B.C.E., an event that introduced the "Second Temple" period. Again, the Jews had a temple and center of worship like other Mesopotamian peoples. However, all Jews

TERROR AND BENEVOLENCE: The Growth of Empires

1200–500 B.C.E.

By the second millennium B.C.E., many people could see the value of centralized control over larger territories. The Egyptians were establishing an empire, and the Hebrews had united into a kingdom. Not only did size offer the potential for larger armies, but expansion westward also secured access to valuable seaborne trade (which was making the Phoenicians wealthy) and would secure the strategically important region of Syria and Palestine. Perhaps most important, people wanted to expand their territories

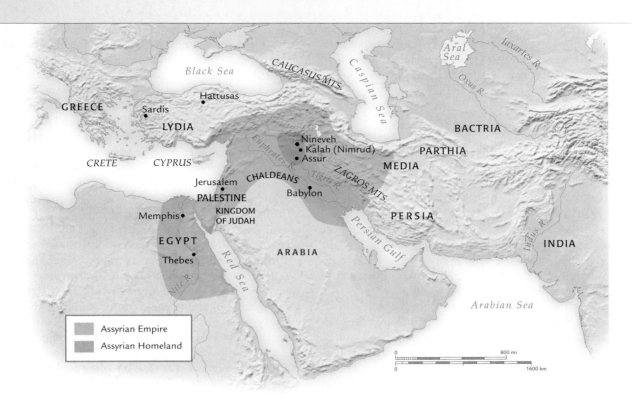

The Assyrian Empire, ca. 662 B.C.E. This map shows the homeland of the Assyrians and their expansion as they conquered the older centers of Western civilization.

to acquire the metals so necessary for military and economic success. These impulses led to the growth of a new political form in the West—huge empires based on a new technology, iron.

The Age of Iron

Before the eleventh century B.C.E., ancient civilizations depended on bronze, an alloy of copper and tin. All across Europe and the Middle East, people used bronze plows to cultivate the land and employed bronze-tipped weapons to make war. While agriculture remained the most important enterprise, the economies of these civilizations were fueled by trade in copper and tin. Initially, these essential metals came largely from Asia Minor, Arabia, and India. Later, sources of these metals were also found in the western Mediterranean.

In about 1200 B.C.E., warfare disrupted the usual trade routes, making tin scarce. Pure copper is a soft metal, and without the tin needed to make bronze, smiths

OPINION

How do you think the Jews were able successfully to maintain their identity while being part of the Diaspora?

could not produce effective tools and weapons. To overcome the tin shortage, Hittite metalworkers in Asia Minor first began to employ iron, an abundant mineral in that region. Unforged iron is not much stronger than copper. However, when it is repeatedly heated in a hot charcoal furnace, carbon molecules combine with iron molecules to form a very reliable metal known as carbon steel. Even low-carbon steel is stronger than bronze, and when it is cold hammered, the strength more than doubles. People—particularly soldiers—gained a huge advantage by using the new metal.

Iron Age

The technology used to create the superior forged iron spread rapidly throughout the Mediterranean world, and from about 1000 B.C.E. on it was used in tools, cookware, and weapons. The use of iron spread to sub-Saharan Africa through Nubia, and ironworking became prominent throughout much of that continent, which was rich in iron ore. Soldiers wielding iron weapons easily vanquished those armed with bronze. The Age of Iron had dawned, and it dominated the world until the late nineteenth century when metalsmiths developed new ways to make iron into steel without the carbon method (Bessemer steel). Iron Age kings in Mesopotamia forged enough weapons and fielded armies so large, their extensive conquests introduced multiethnic empires that dwarfed all that had gone before.

Rule by Terror: The Assyrians

911–612 B.C.E.

The Assyrians, a people living originally in the northern Tigris-Euphrates valley, had traded profitably with their neighbors for centuries. In the early tenth century B.C.E., they began arming themselves with iron weapons and following the one command of their god Assur: Expand the frontiers of Assyria so that Assur finally rules over all. The map on page 21 shows the striking success of the Assyrians as they cut a swath through the civilizations of the ancient Near East.

The Assyrians' success stemmed from the skill of their armies and their willingness to engage in almost constant warfare to follow the command of Assur. Assyrian histories recounting their military campaigns were written as propaganda pieces to instill fear in their enemies. The historians accomplished their goal, and the cold-blooded details cemented the Assyrians' reputation for ruthlessness. King Sargon II's (r. 722–706 B.C.E.) description of his conquest of Babylon is one chilling example of these accounts: "I blew like the onrush of a hurricane and enveloped the city like a fog. . . . I did not spare his mighty warriors, young or old, but filled the city square with their corpses."

Beyond sheer brutality, the Assyrians relied on some of the most advanced military techniques that the ancient world had seen. They employed a corps of military engineers to build bridges, tunnels, and efficient siege weapons capable of penetrating strongly fortified cities. Furthermore, they had a highly trained and well-rewarded officer corps who became the elite in Assyrian society.

The Assyrians were first both to acquire such a large territory and to try to govern it cohesively. In many ways, they proved to be skilled administrators. For example, they built roads to unify their holdings, and kings appointed governors and tax collectors to serve as their representatives in the more distant territories. One of the elements that facilitated governing and trade over large areas was the Assyrians' use of Aramaic as a common language. This was a Semitic language originally spoken by the Aramaeans, successful merchants who lived in Mesopotamia in about 1100 B.C.E. Aramaic remained the official language of subsequent empires—it was even spoken by Jesus.

Governing an empire

Many Assyrian rulers also appreciated the wealth of knowledge and culture that had accumulated in these lands for centuries. The great Assyrian king Ashurbanipal (669–627 B.C.E.) collected a huge library from which 20,000 clay tablets have survived. Within this col-

Preserving learning

lection, the king preserved the best of Mesopotamian literature, including *The Epic of Gilgamesh*. The highly educated Ashurbanipal took pride in his accomplishments: "I acquired the hidden treasure of all scribal knowledge, the signs of the heaven and the earth. . . . I have solved the laborious problems of division and multiplication. . . . I have read the artistic script of Sumer and the obscure Akkadian." This quotation offers an excellent example of how a written language served to preserve and disseminate the culture developing in the ancient Middle East.

Although the Assyrians were skilled in making both war and peace, they still faced the problem that confronted all empire builders: how to keep the empire together when subject peoples resisted. The Assyrians used terror to control their far-flung territories. When individuals dissented, they were publicly tortured; when cities revolted, they were razed to serve as examples to others. To break up local loyalties, Assyrian commanders uprooted and moved entire populations. These methods worked for a while; eventually, however, they catalyzed effective opposition.

Fall of Assyrians

Ashurbanipal ruled from his capital in Nineveh—reputedly so well fortified that three chariots could ride abreast along the top of the walls surrounding the city. However, even those great walls could not save the king's successors. A coalition including Babylonians from southern Mesopotamia; Medes, an Indo-European tribe from western Iran; and Egyptians gathered against the Assyrian domination. Because the empire was so large it overextended the Assyrians' resources, and the provinces gave way quickly. Nineveh itself finally collapsed in 612 B.C.E. after a brutal two-year siege. Assyrian rule came to an ignominious end. However, the Assyrians left an enduring legacy for Western civilization: centralized empires that ruled over extended lands and different peoples.

Babylonian Rule

612–539 B.C.E.

After vanquishing the Assyrians, the Medes left Mesopotamia and returned to their homeland near the Zagros Mountains (see map on page 21). The Babylonians (also called Chaldeans, or Neo-Babylonians, to distinguish them from the earlier kingdom of Hammurabi) remained and ruled the lands of the former Assyrian Empire. The new rulers emulated the Assyrian use of terror to enforce their will on subject peoples. King Nebuchadrezzar (r. 605–561 B.C.E.) kept penalties similar to those in the Code of Hammurabi for civil crimes, but introduced extreme punishments for enemy rulers and their followers. When captured, these people were often flayed or burned alive. It was this severity that led Nebuchadrezzar to destroy Jerusalem in 587 B.C.E. and lead the Jews into captivity. This incident was the formative "Babylonian Captivity" discussed earlier that shaped much of subsequent Jewish history.

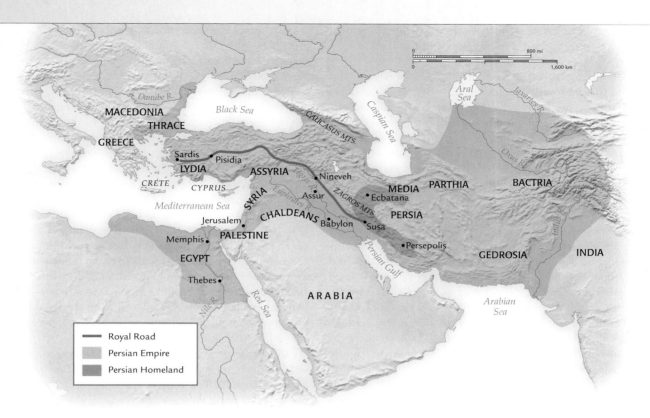

The Persian Empire, ca. 500 B.C.E. **This map illustrates the Persian Empire that replaced and greatly expanded the previous Assyrian domain and highlights the Royal Road, which spanned a large portion of the territory. It also shows the capital of the empire, Persepolis.**

The Babylonians also continued the Assyrian passion for art and education. The king rebuilt his capital city of Babylon in such splendor that it was admired throughout the ancient world. His architects constructed huge ziggurats in praise of the Babylonian god Marduk and fortified the structures with walls more impressive than even Nineveh's had been. Under Nebuchadrezzar, Babylon blossomed into an impressive city graced by gardens, palaces, and temples.

Culture and commerce

The magnificent architecture that marked Babylon cost a fortune, and the Babylonian kings obtained these funds largely through fostering the commerce that often guided their military policies. One king, for example, besieged Tyre for thirteen years, hoping to win control over the Phoenicians' far-reaching trade. Another king established himself in Arabia in an attempt to control a new trade—in incense—that came from southern Arabia to the Mediterranean Sea.

Kings used their new wealth not only to decorate their cities, but also to foster learning. Within the cosmopolitan city, Babylonian priests excelled in astronomy and mathematics. They observed the heavens in an effort to understand the will of the gods, and in the process they charted the skies with impressive accuracy; they could predict solstices, equinoxes, and other heavenly phenomena. Their passion for predictions led them to develop another innovation with which they sought to foretell the future for individuals: astrology. By the fifth century B.C.E., Babylonian astrologers had divided the heavens into twelve signs—including the familiar Gemini, Scorpio, Virgo, and others—and began to cast horoscopes to predict people's futures based on their birth dates. The earliest surviving example of a horoscope was for a child born in 410 B.C.E. and marks the beginning of a long-standing practice.

Astronomy and mathematics

Rule by Tolerance: The Persian Empire
ca. 550–330 B.C.E.

In 553 B.C.E., the fortunes of the Babylonian Empire changed. The Persians, a people from east of the Zagros Mountains, overran the land of their Indo-European relatives, the Medes. Under their wise king, Cyrus the Great (r. 559–530 B.C.E.), the Persians expanded westward to establish an empire even larger than that of the Assyrians (see map above). The Babylonian rulers found few supporters against the invaders even among their own people, and in 539 B.C.E. Babylon fell to the Persians virtually without a struggle.

Cyrus rejected the Assyrian policies of terror and sought to hold his vast empire together by tolerating differences among his many subject peoples. As mentioned earlier, in 538 B.C.E. he allowed the Jewish captives in Babylon to return to Jerusalem and rebuild their temple. At the same time, he appeased Babylonians by claiming he was "friend and companion" to their god Marduk. In the conquered provinces—or satrapies—Cyrus retained local officials but installed Persian governors called **satraps.** He controlled the satraps' power by appointing additional officials who were directly responsible to the king. The Persians required subject peoples to pay reasonable taxes and serve in their armies, but Cyrus's system prevented local officials from abusing their power excessively. Conquered peoples could worship their own gods and follow their own customs, and under Cyrus's reign, the ancient civilizations enjoyed a long period of peace. The Great King (as his subjects called him) was seen as a semidivine figure who ruled benignly from his golden throne.

After Cyrus's death in 530 B.C.E., his son Cambyses II (r. 529–522 B.C.E.) inherited the throne and continued the expansion his father had begun so effectively. The new king extended Persian control to the eastern Mediterranean by conquering Egypt and the Phoenician port cities.

Cambyses was succeeded by Darius (r. 521–486 B.C.E.), a brilliant ruler who was able to consolidate and further organize what Cyrus and Cambyses had hastily conquered. Darius built a new capital city at Persepolis (see map on page 23) moving the center of his empire east, but he also realized how important it was to facilitate travel throughout his empire. To accomplish this, he built and carefully maintained a complex system of roads, and the most famous was the Royal Road, between Susa in the east (in modern Iran) and Sardis (in modern Turkey) in the west. This impressive road, almost 1,700 miles long, fostered the economic life of the empire.

A unified empire allowed the Persians to adopt ideas that had proven successful in the civilizations that preceded them. For example, Persians retained Aramaic as the common language of commerce, making communication easier across many cultures, and they fostered the trade routes that had brought so much wealth to the Babylonians. Persian astrologers learned from their Babylonian predecessors as well. These wise men, or magi, became celebrated for their knowledge of the heavens.

Of all the conventions the Persians borrowed from the inhabitants of their diverse empire, the adoption of coinage had the greatest long-term impact. The Lydians seem to have invented the use of coins in the seventh century B.C.E. Before this time, traders either bartered or used cumbersome bars of precious metals to purchase goods.

Persian administration

Coins

timeline

Paleolithic 600,000–10,000 B.C.E.

Neolithic 10,000–3000 B.C.E.

600,000 B.C.E.

10,000

⫟ This symbol denotes a change in the time scale

For example, in Egypt in 1170 B.C.E., a burial vault that was priced at 5 pounds of copper might have been bought with 2 ½ pounds of copper, one hog, two goats, and two trees. By minting coins with precise, identifiable values, kingdoms greatly facilitated trade. The kings of Lydia were said to have grown fabulously rich after their invention, and the Persians rapidly spread the use of coins throughout their far-flung lands.

While the Persians adopted many novelties of their predecessors, they also made a unique contribution of their own: a new movement in religious thought initiated by the talented prophet Zoroaster (ca. 628–551 B.C.E.). One of the most important religious reformers of the ancient world, Zoroaster founded a new religion (later called **Zoroastrianism**) that contained the seeds of many modern belief systems. Zoroaster experienced a revelation given to him by the one god, Ahura Mazda, the Lord of Light. In this revelation, recorded in a holy book called the Avesta, Zoroaster was called to reform Persian religion by eliminating polytheism and animal sacrifice. In the tradition of those throughout the early history of Western civilization who called for social justice, Zoroaster also urged people to live ethical lives and to show care for others. Finally, the prophet believed that the history of the world was one of ongoing conflict between Ahura Mazda and the forces of the evil god Ahriman. Zoroaster felt confident that Ahura Mazda would ultimately prevail over evil and that eventually the dead would be resurrected. Believers would go to paradise, while evildoers would fall into a hell of perpetual torture.

Followers of Zoroastrianism still exist today, and even in the ancient world many of the prophet's ideas influenced other religions as well. Over time, some believers transformed Zoroaster's monotheism into a dualistic belief in two gods, one good and one evil. Judaism—and, later, Christianity—seem to have been influenced by his vision, for Jewish texts began to write of the power of a devil and of a final struggle between good and evil. Zoroaster was the first prophet whose ideas would spread throughout a large political empire, but he would not be the last.

SUMMARY

In the three thousand years that make up the history of the ancient Middle East, many elements that characterize Western civilization emerged, including great cities, vibrant trade, laws and principles of justice, and systems of writing designed to preserve their accumulated knowledge for future generations including ours.

- The roots of civilizations began in prehistoric times, as humans moved out of Africa, domesticated plants and animals, and began to express their knowledge and dreams by building large stone monuments in Europe.

- Urban life sprang up with the Bronze Age societies of Mesopotamia, where writing developed, laws were recorded, and deeply pessimistic religious impulses ruled the human spirit.

- In the Nile valley, Egyptians created a brilliant civilization that would endure for millennia. Ruled by a god-king, and looking forward to a joyous afterlife, Egyptians left their mark on the Mediterranean world.

- Other peoples on the coast of the eastern Mediterranean contributed much to the future. The great Phoenician traders established colonies as far west as the Atlantic Ocean, and ancient Hebrews contributed their vision of monotheism to the growing story of the West.

- This whole region that was the birthplace of Western civilization was plagued by violence as great empires—the Babylonian, Assyrian, and Persian—arose to unify the prosperous region ruling with both terror and benevolence.

The patterns of interaction and cross-fertilization of goods and ideas that would mark Western civilization from its beginnings through today were established here in the ancient Middle East and Africa. The next developments in the story of the West would come from a different people farther west: the Greeks.

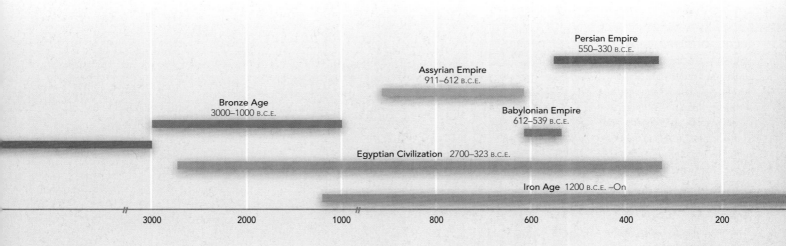

ACROPOLIS OF ATHENS, 448–434 B.C.E.   This hill dominates the skyline of the Greek city-state Athens. It was rebuilt to celebrate Athenians' victories over the Persians, and it proclaimed Athenian control over the prosperous Aegean Sea. The greatest artists and architects built marble temples to the gods, celebrating beauty and mathematical perfection. The most famous temple is the Parthenon, shown prominently at the center of the acropolis.

The Contest
for Excellence

Greece, 2000–338 B.C.E.

2

The Gadfly of Athens

Athens in the fifth century B.C.E. was beautiful. The skyline was dominated by a tall hill—the acropolis—topped by magnificent, brightly painted temples that testified to Athenian wealth and love of beauty and perfection. At the bottom of the hill lay the *agora,* the marketplace where men gathered every afternoon to shop and talk. The only women in the agora were slaves; "respectable women" stayed home. For decades, from about 420 until 399 B.C.E., a short, ugly, bandy-legged man wandered through the agora talking to citizens and humiliating them by showing they were not as smart as he. ▶▶

This man was Socrates, son of a stonemason and a midwife, who became the great philosopher whose ideas changed the course of Western civilization.

Many of his neighbors found Socrates annoying—he called himself the "gadfly of Athens," goading citizens into examining their opinions—but gadflies that sting painfully are seldom appreciated. A comic playwright (Aristophanes) portrayed Socrates as a buffoon who speculated on foolish matters, and his neighbors laughed uproariously at the portrayal. As the play showed, young men gathered around the philosopher, entranced by his ability to demonstrate that their elders were wrong, and looking for the tools they, too, could use to win arguments with their contemporaries.

The small man was not like other Athenians. He said, "I did not care for the things that most people care about: making money, having a comfortable home, high military or civil rank, and all the other activities . . . which go on in our city." He remained poor his whole life, rich only in the life of the mind.

Socrates would have been found annoying anytime, but many Athenians were more angered because Athens was at war—the deadly Peloponnesian war against Sparta dragged on, and Greeks were disillusioned by seemingly endless violence. In 404 B.C.E., Athens lost; the great city was devastated and people were angry. They turned on their gadfly. Then they put him on trial—the most famous trial in history—and accused him of impiety to the gods and corrupting the youth. Socrates' defense was a model argument for living a rational, moral life, but his contemporaries found him guilty. He knew he was innocent of the charges, but knew, too, that he was guilty of annoying his neighbors in the shadow of the acropolis. They sentenced him to be quiet and stop questioning, but he responded: "It is the greatest good every day to discuss virtue . . . for life without enquiry is not worth living for a man."

These words have become a famous articulation of the value of the spirit of inquiry, but the philosopher was sentenced to death, and he drank hemlock poison and died surrounded by his followers. Fortunately, his call for rational inquiry did not die with him, but flourished to become a fundamental characteristic of Western civilization. In this chapter, we'll learn about the world that spawned these revolutionary ideas. ◄◄

THE RISE AND FALL OF ANCIENT HEROES

2000–800 B.C.E.

The Greek peninsula is dominated by striking mountain ranges. Lacking large rivers that would have provided natural communication links, the ancient Greek civilization consisted of separate communities scattered throughout the peninsula and the numerous Aegean islands. The mountain ranges protected the Greeks from large-scale invasions, but the rocky soil made agriculture difficult. The Greeks had to grow their wheat and barley on the scarce lowland, and in time they came to depend on imports for the grain they needed. As the map on page 29 indicates, most places in Greece enjoyed a close proximity to the sea, which allowed overseas trade to become an essential part of ancient Greek society. This orientation toward the sea stimulated the many cultural contacts that marked the development of Western civilization (as discussed in Chapter 1). In fact, the earliest advanced civilization that arose in this region originated on an island that lay at the heart of the eastern Mediterranean.

The Minoans

2000–1450 B.C.E.

By 2000 B.C.E., the islanders living on Crete boasted the wealthiest, most advanced civilization in the Mediterranean. They were not Greek—nor Indo-European—but were probably a Semitic people related to those living in the eastern and southern Mediterranean. At the height of its economic and political power, Crete consisted of a number of principalities, each dominated by a great palace. Knossos (see map on page 29) is the best excavated and thus the most well known of the palaces. Early Greek historians identify the ruler of Crete as King Minos, and thus modern excavators named Minoan society after this legendary king. Minoan prosperity permitted the growth of a relatively large, peaceful population. During the golden age of this culture, the population of Crete reached an impressive 250,000, with 40,000 living in Knossos alone.

By trading with the peoples of the Fertile Crescent, the Minoans learned much of the best of early Western civilization. They learned to make bronze from the Sumerians, and their foundries produced a steady stream of valuable bronze tools and weapons. Minoan ships were the best made in the region. With their heavy

Economic power

Approximate Range of Mycenaean Culture

THRACE

Propontis

Hellespont

Olympus

Ilium (Troy)

CORCYRA

Aegean Sea

ASIA MINOR

Ionian Sea

SYCROS

LYDIA

Delphi
Orchomenus
Eleusis
Athens
ATTICA

IONIA

Miletus

Mycenae
PELOPONNESE

CYCLADES

DELOS

Sparta

Mediterranean Sea

THERA

RHODES

Sea of Crete

Knossos

CRETE

0   50   100 mi
0   100   200 km

The World of the Greeks   **This map shows the Greek peninsula with the surrounding seas. Notice the locations of Asia Minor and the islands of Crete and the Cyclades. Locate the important cities of Troy (in Asia Minor), Athens, and Sparta.**

construction and high front prows, these vessels cut effortlessly through rough seas and proved reliable in conditions that the islanders' shore-hugging contemporaries deemed impossible.

Centers of economic as well as political power, Minoan palaces comprised vast mazes of storerooms, workrooms, and living quarters. These structures were markedly different from the huge buildings in Sumeria and Egypt, where architects of pyramids and ziggurats valued symmetry. Minoan architects preferred to build palace rooms of different sizes that wandered without any apparent design. The Greeks later called these palaces labyrinths. Kings controlling the trade through which wealth poured into Crete stashed goods away in the huge palace storerooms. One room in the palace at Knossos contained clay jars for olive oil that totaled a remarkable capacity of 60,000 gallons.

Like many maritime civilizations, the Minoans learned much from their encounters with other peoples. For example, their artwork reveals the influence of Egyptian

colors and styles. The Minoans also learned writing from the Sumerians, and their script (called Linear A) was also a pictographic script written on clay tablets. As in Sumer, archaeologists have excavated clay tablets in Crete that seem to have been used for accounting and for tracking the movement of merchandise. So far, the symbols of Linear A have not been translated, so to learn about Minoan society, we must rely on archaeological remains, including their riveting artwork.

The Minoans decorated their palaces with magnificent frescoes, created by mixing paint with plaster and crafting the image as part of the wall. These paintings portrayed many of the everyday objects and activities that **Religious ritual** Minoans held dear, including religious rituals. The fresco on page 30 shows a ritual in which men and women performed gymnastic activities with a wild bull.

In the centuries after the Minoans, the ancient Greeks often told their history in the form of myths that recounted

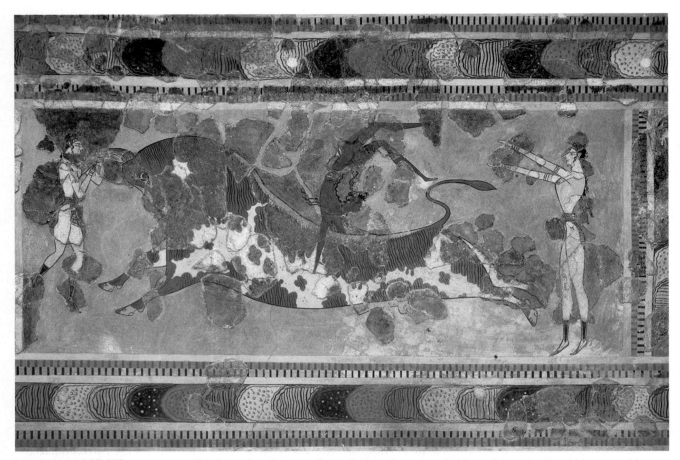

MINOAN ACROBATS, ca. 1500 B.C.E. This fresco from Knossos, Crete, depicts what was probably a religious ritual in which women (shown with pale skin) and a man leap over a charging bull.

heroic acts from the Greek past. Some of these myths recalled the eventual destruction of Minoan society. In their myths, Greeks remembered a time when Greece owed tribute to Crete, including young people to be sacrificed to the Minotaur—a creature that was half human and half bull. One mythical Greek hero, The-

Minoan destruction seus, joined the sacrificial group, killed the Minotaur, and escaped the palace labyrinth by following a thread he had unraveled as he entered. This myth may hold a core of truth, for archaeological evidence shows that the great Minoan palaces were burned by invaders who destroyed the unfortified cities. A man named Theseus may not have killed a minotaur, but it seems that Greeks killed the king of Crete.

Historians have looked further for the cause of the Minoans' downfall. Some suggest that a natural disaster contributed to their decline. In about 1450 B.C.E., a volcanic explosion on the nearby island of Thera (today known as Santorini) caused a tidal wave that may have destroyed the Minoans' protective fleet. However, this explanation is uncertain because other scholars question the date of the eruption, placing it two centuries earlier than the burning of Crete. Whatever the cause, the center of Aegean civilization passed to the earliest Greeks, whom we call the Mycenaeans.

Mycenaean Civilization: The First Greeks
2000–1100 B.C.E.

Sometime after 2000 B.C.E., Indo-European Greek-speaking people settled on the mountainous Greek peninsula. By 1600 B.C.E., they were increasingly influenced by the Minoans and had developed a wealthy, hierarchic society centered in the city of Mycenae (see map on page 29). Excavations of their shaft graves have yielded golden crowns and masks and, as with other Indo-European burials, many weapons, perhaps confirming ancient writers' characterizations of these people as the "war-mad Greeks." Yet, these early Greeks were also traders, and much of their wealth came from the growing commerce in the Aegean. As the Mycenaeans traded with wealthy Minoans, they learned much from them, evidenced by the strong Minoan influences in Mycenaean artwork. Mycenaean Greeks even learned to write from the Minoans, and their script is called Linear B for its similarity to the Minoan script. Because Linear B recorded an early form of the spoken Greek language, linguists have been able to translate Mycenaean tablets.

After Minoan society was destroyed in about 1450 B.C.E., the Mycenaeans took over as the commercial masters of the Mediterranean. As their wealth increased, so did the complexity of their governing system, which had a hierarchy of kings, nobles, and slaves. Powerful kings built palaces of stone so large that later Greeks thought they must have been constructed by giants. Unlike Minoan palaces, these structures were walled, indicating to archaeologists that there was a great deal of warfare, necessitating defensive fortifications. This conclusion is reinforced by written sources claiming that the kings surrounded themselves with soldiers.

Mycenaean states were not self-sufficient. Like the civilizations of the ancient Middle East, they depended on trade for many essentials. For example, there was little copper and no tin on the peninsula, so they had to trade for ore to make bronze weapons and tools. The vast expanse of Mycenaean trade is clear. Mycenaean pottery has been found on the coast of Italy, and after the destruction of Crete, Mycenaean pottery replaced Minoan pottery in Egypt, Syria, Palestine, and Cyprus. These pottery remnants testify to the beginnings of the trade that linked the fortunes of the ancient Greeks intimately with those of their neighbors.

Trade

In about 1200 B.C.E., violence and a wide-ranging movement of peoples disrupted the eastern Mediterranean. A scarcity of sources does not allow historians to detail the exact causes of the upheaval, but we can see the effects on kingdoms and individuals. The Egyptian Empire was besieged and lost territory as Syria and cities all along the coast confronted invaders. Archaeological evidence shows towns sacked and burned throughout the region during these times of trouble. The important trade in copper from Cyprus was interrupted, and as we saw in Chapter 1, this violent era stimulated the dawning of the Iron Age.

Violence and disruption

The Mycenaeans were surely involved in these invasions that disrupted the ancient civilizations. According to later Greek myths, part of this violence included the Mycenaean invasion of Troy (see map on page 29) in about 1250 B.C.E. The Trojan War became the basis of Homer's influential epics. Greek mythology attributes the conflict to a rivalry over a beautiful Greek woman, Helen, who was seduced by the Trojan prince Paris. Less-romantic historians believe the war stemmed primarily from the intensifying economic competition and growing violence in the eastern Mediterranean. Either way, the fighting was relentless and devastating—Homer claimed that the Greeks besieged Troy for ten years. At the end of this ordeal, Troy was destroyed (demonstrated by evidence from archaeological excavations).

Sometime after 1200 B.C.E., Mycenaean civilization itself dissolved. Later Greeks attributed this downfall to the Trojan War, which supposedly kept the Mycenaean leaders and soldiers away from home for so long. Archaeological evidence, however, shows that during and shortly after the Trojan War, the highly structured life on the Greek main-

land broke down. Amid crop failures due to drought and internal instability, more Greek invaders from the north (later called Dorian Greeks) moved into the peninsula, especially the southern part, the Peloponnese. Population dropped dramatically. We do not know exactly what happened, but the flourishing Bronze Age Mycenaean society came to such a complete end that even the valuable art of writing was lost. All the great Mycenaean centers except Athens were destroyed. Life on the Greek mainland now consisted of a smattering of small villages, where people survived largely through subsistence farming.

From Dark Ages to Colonies

The period after the fall of Mycenae is called the Dark Ages (which extend from about 1100 B.C.E. to about 750 B.C.E.), because with the loss of writing, we have no texts that illuminate life during this time. For three centuries, life went on in the small villages, and people told tales that preserved their values. At the end of the Dark Ages, in about 800 B.C.E., Homer brilliantly recast some of these oral tales, and the details he included offer glimpses into life during the previous three centuries. As tantalizing as these bits of literary evidence are, most of our information for this period nevertheless must come from archaeology.

Excavations show that during these years, bronze gave way to iron as the primary metal used in weapons and tools. Archaeological findings also reveal that near the end of the Dark Ages, trade of wine, olive oil, and other goods began to flourish again all over the Mediterranean. By tracing the movement of Greek goods through the remnants of pottery and other artifacts excavated around the Mediterranean, archaeologists have discovered that Greek culture spread through the many colonies Greeks established in the region. At first, Greeks fled the disasters on the peninsula by settling on the numerous islands of the Aegean and the coast of Asia Minor (called Ionia). Later, colonists may have left the peninsula to escape overpopulation and seek new land and prosperity. Some aristocrats in Greek cities used the founding of new colonies as a way to diffuse social unrest by sending the dissatisfied elsewhere. Greek colonies were very different from modern colonial efforts because Greeks in the new settlements arranged themselves in cities that were just as independent as the mother city. The ties to the original cities were ones of emotion, not of colonial control.

Founding colonies

For a time, Greeks in the new colonies remained independent from the other civilizations around them—the neighboring Phoenicians and the Babylonian and Persian Empires. However, while trading with their neighbors, the Greeks participated in the growth of Western civilization by adopting much that had gone before. For example, they derived their systems of weight from Babylonia and Phoenicia and adopted the practice of making coins from the Lydians. Societies transform acquired innovations, and the Greeks were no exception. For their coins, they minted silver (instead of the Lydian white gold) and usually placed secular images on them—sometimes illustrating their exports, like grapes or fish, and sometimes using emblems of civic pride. However, when describing Greek use of other civilizations' inventions, the Greek philosopher Plato (428–348 B.C.E.) characteristically gave the Greeks undue praise, boasting, "Whatever the Greeks have acquired from foreigners, they have in the end turned into something finer."

EMERGING FROM THE DARK: Heroic Beliefs and Values

Through their trade with the Phoenicians, the Greeks acquired and adapted the Phoenician alphabet, and writing reemerged among the Greeks around 800 B.C.E. Once more Greek society was illuminated for historians. The Greeks did not use writing only for trade and contractual agreements—the Phoenician alphabet was simpler than other scripts, so it lent itself to a wider use. Talented Greeks used writing to record and transmit powerful and inspiring poetry that had been preserved for centuries only through human memory, and the ideas of the ancient Greeks once more came to light; the Dark Ages were over.

Heroic Values Preserved

The earliest of this Greek literature preserved a series of values that define what historians call a heroic society, in which individuals seek fame through great deeds and advocate values such as honor, reputation, and prowess.

The most influential Greek poet was Homer, who historians believe lived in the early eighth century B.C.E. Homer's

PERFECTING THE HUMAN FORM, ca. 530 B.C.E.
Greek artists glorified humanity by carving monumental, realistic life-size statues. Sculptors revealed their interest in the human form by depicting the males—called *kouroi* (sing. *kouros*), a word that is Greek for "boys"—without clothing. The females—called *korai* (sing. *kore*), the Greek word for "girls"—are always portrayed modestly clothed.

two greatest epics were the *Iliad,* the tale of Achilles' heroic wrath, and the *Odyssey,* the story of the Greek warrior Odysseus's ten-year travels to return home from Troy.

Homer

The highest virtue for Homer (and subsequent Greeks) was **arête**—manliness, courage, and excellence. *Arête* was best revealed in a "contest," whether sporting, warfare, or activities extending into many other areas of life and recreation. The ancient Greeks believed that striving for individual supremacy enhanced one's family honor, and the hero's name would live in poetic memory. Such beliefs and values helped fuel the greatness of ancient Greece. However, this striving for excellence—for heroism—was not always beneficial. At times it created a self-centered competitiveness that caused much suffering. Harboring such intense competitive spirit, Greeks also held a deep disregard for all cultures other than their own (and they even had disdain for neighboring Greeks from different cities). Greeks distinguished themselves from "barbarians" who "spoke other languages" and felt it demeaned them to work alongside such foreigners. Individuals adhering to "heroic" values brought a combination of good and bad results, and the best of the Greeks from Homer on recognized this ambiguity.

Visual artists in the archaic age also glorified humanity in their increasingly realistic portrayal of the human figure. The carvings to the left show two typical sculptures from the sixth century B.C.E.

In literature, too, poets praised human accomplishments. Hesiod, an early Greek poet who wrote around 750 B.C.E., left almost as

Hesiod

important a mark as Homer. His *Works and Days* describes farm life, wisdom, and values near the end of the Greek Dark Ages.

Hesiod lived in poverty—cheated out of his inheritance by a greedy brother and corrupt officials—yet he still articulated the ideals of heroic individualism. However, he clearly saw that the pursuit of excellence was a two-sided coin. At the end of *Works and Days,* he wrote of two kinds of "strife." One was good—a healthy spirit of competitiveness that Hesiod believed made people work and achieve their best. The other kind of strife, however, was bad and led to some people exploiting others, as happened in Hesiod's own life. This tension within heroic values marked Greek life and values and even their gods and goddesses.

The Family of the Gods

The poems of Homer's and Hesiod's day were populated by an extended family of gods and goddesses, loosely ruled by Zeus and his wife, Hera. This family included ten other main deities, among them Aphrodite, goddess of love; Athena, goddess of wisdom and war; Poseidon, god of the sea; Apollo, god of music, divination, and healing; and Demeter, goddess of fertility. These gods lived on Mount Olympus and periodically interfered in human affairs.

The Greek gods and goddesses resembled humans so much that one Greek critic from the sixth century B.C.E. observed that "Homer and Hesiod ascribed to the gods everything that among men is a shame and disgrace: theft, adultery, and deceiving one another." It is true that the gods shared human flaws, but they also shared admirable human qualities. Like the Greeks themselves, they loved beauty, banquets, processions, athletic competitions, music, and theater. The Greeks therefore infused all these activities with a feeling of worship. Religious rituals, for example, had an intensely festive air, and ancient Greek writings characterize religious activities as "sacrificing and having a good time." Unlike in Egypt and Mesopotamia, powerful religious institutions never developed in ancient Greek society. Each temple had a priest or priestess, but their duties were usually part-time activities requiring little training.

Just as they envisioned their gods with all the qualities and foibles of humans, the Greeks embraced all facets of human behavior, even the irrational. To Homer's list of Olympians, subsequent Greeks added the worship of Dionysus, the god of wine and fertility.

Worship of Dionysus Men worshiped this god during lavish banquets, but the cult had special appeal to women. During worship of Dionysus, women temporarily escaped their domestic confinement and engaged in drinking, ecstatic dancing, and sometimes sexual license as part of the ritual.

Greek religious thought marked a significant departure from the forms of worship of the ancient Middle East. In Greece, the gods were so much like humans that worshiping them encouraged people to aspire to the greatest in human accomplishments and to acknowledge the worst in human frailties. The Greeks did add a cautionary warning in their praise of humanity. If people exhibited excessive pride or arrogance as they tried to become godlike (called **hubris**), the gods would destroy them. Yet they still had a great deal of room to celebrate human accomplishments. As Greek thinkers placed humans rather than gods at the center of their understanding of the

Impact of religious ideas

world, and as they studied reality from a human perspective, they began to transform the Mesopotamian view that had contributed so much to Western civilization. Humans were no longer impotent before a chaotic world ruled by arbitrary deities; instead, they were encouraged to understand and master their world.

Studying the Material World

The Greeks had great confidence in their ability to learn everything about the world. They rejected many earlier explanations and began an objective, almost scientific, approach to comprehending nature. This special search for knowledge was termed philosophy (love of wisdom) and would become the Greeks' most important intellectual invention. The earliest known scholar of this kind was Thales of Miletus (ca. 624–ca. 548 B.C.E.). The location of Miletus on the Ionian coast (see map on page 29) shows how Greek culture and its tremendous influence had moved beyond the Greek mainland itself.

Thales reputedly studied Egyptian and Babylonian astronomy and geometry and brought this knowledge to practical use by measuring pyramids, based on the length of their shadows, and predicting a solar eclipse. Departing from most of his Egyptian and Mesopotamian predecessors, Thales believed in an orderly cosmos that was accessible to human reason. This formed the heart of much subsequent Greek (and Western) inquiry. He sought a single primal element that would explain a cosmic unity and believed that element was water. Although Thales' conclusion was wrong, his assumption of an orderly universe accessible to human inquiry was pivotal to the future of Western thought.

Thales and Democritus

Thales was followed by others who continued the rational approach to the natural world. Democritus (ca. 460–ca. 370 B.C.E.), for example, posited an infinite universe of tiny atoms with spaces between them. Although his ideas were not widely supported in ancient Greece, they were proven by early-twentieth-century physicists.

Pythagoras (ca. 582–507 B.C.E.), who fled from Ionia to Italy, made even greater discoveries in the fields of mathematics and astronomy. He believed that order in the universe was based on numbers (not water), and that mathematics was the key to understanding reality. He developed the Pythagorean theorem, the geometrical statement that the square of the hypotenuse of a right triangle is equal to the sum of the squares of the other two sides. He

Pythagoras

Ezekias, Suicide of Ajax, Athenian Vase

ca. 450 B.C.E.

The famous vase painter Ezekias has portrayed a significant moment in the Trojan War. After the death of Achilles, the hero Ajax expected to be named to lead the army. Instead, the Greeks chose Odysseus. In his humiliation, Ajax commits suicide. The artist shows him preparing for his death, burying the hilt of his sword in the earth so that he can fall on his sword. On the right, the artist shows the all-important hoplite weaponry: the great shield with the head of the mythological monster Gorgon emblazoned on the front, the helmet, and the long spear. Yet, in this contest for excellence the pride of the individual was more important than the strength of the army, and the artist shows this in the vase. Would the Greeks have considered this act heroic or cowardly? What would our society think?

dards, but we would not be who we are without them.

While modern scholars admire these early Greek thinkers, many contemporaries looked with suspicion on those who studied the world while seemingly ignoring the gods. Even though the Greeks worshiped humanlike gods and goddesses, they still revered them, and accusations of impiety always hovered on the borders of scientific inquiry. In 432 B.C.E., **Fears of "impiety"** the democratic assembly of Athens made it a crime to "deny the gods, or disseminate teachings about the things that take place in the heavens." This law was precipitated by the teachings of Anaxagoras (ca. 500–ca. 428 B.C.E.), who claimed that the sun was a white-hot stone instead of a god. Even in the field of rational inquiry, in which the Greeks made such impressive strides, the ambiguities that marked this dynamic society are evident. The same culture that produced impressive thinkers like Anaxagoras and Socrates (whom we met at the beginning of this chapter) sometimes recoiled from the results of their studies. Nevertheless, Greek intellectual accomplishments formed one of their central contributions to Western civilization.

LIFE IN THE GREEK POLEIS

With the brisk trade that comes so naturally to sea peoples, a new prosperity based on commercial expansion emerged, creating an urban middle class of merchants and artisans who owed no loyalty to aristocratic landowners.

By 700 B.C.E., changes in warfare brought about in part by the growth of Greek trade also made aristocratic warriors less important. First, the growing commercial classes became wealthier, **Hoplite armies** and at the same time the increased trade brought down the price of metals. Now more men could afford to arm themselves and go to war. New armies of

went on to explore additional theories of proportion that have contributed to much modern mathematics.

These philosophers, in a dramatic way, changed the direction of thinking about the world. They rejected the mythopoeic approach to understanding the world and made the first attempts to understand and explain the world in a scientific and philosophical way. Because they had little experimental equipment and no prior knowledge to draw upon, their ideas were not necessarily accurate by our stan-

infantrymen (called **hoplites**) dominated the art of making war. Common citizens armed with swords, shields, and long thrusting spears formed a **phalanx**—a tight formation about eight men deep and as wide as the number of troops available. As long as these soldiers stayed tightly pressed together, they were virtually impenetrable. Elite warriors once could rely on their own heroism and on their monopoly of horses and cavalry to ensure victory on the battlefield. Now that a hoplite phalanx could withstand cavalry charges, the aristocracy no longer maintained a privileged position; they needed the support of citizen armies. This dependence further weakened aristocratic rule. The vase painting on page 34 shows the tension between the traditional values of heroic pride on the one hand and the needs of the phalanx-dependent hoplite army on the other hand. Even as the artist immortalized the hero's prideful suicide, he also highlighted the hoplite weaponry that made the phalanx invincible.

The Invention of Politics

Between 650 and 550 B.C.E., civil war broke out in many cities as the lower classes rose to overthrow the aristocracy. This violence led to the rule of men who became rulers by physical force. Although kingship had a

Tyrants long-standing tradition in the West, this was a new form of authority—based on power, not hereditary right. The Greeks called such rulers *tyrants* to distinguish them from more traditional kings. At first the term had no pejorative connotation—one could easily be a kind tyrant, and indeed some were sincere reformers seeking to end aristocratic exploitation. For example, some tyrants gained popular support by such reforms as freeing slaves, eliminating debts, redistributing land. Later, however, as these rulers relied on force to hold power, the term *tyrant* acquired the negative meaning it holds today.

Greek citizens—especially those who controlled the lucrative trade and fought in the successful phalanxes—thus began to take charge of the political life of their cities. A

City-states Greek city-state was called a **polis** (pl. *poleis*). It was a small but autonomous political unit that generated intense loyalty from its citizens, who conducted their political, social, and religious activities in its heart. The poleis frequently included a fortified high ground—called an *acropolis,* the most famous of which is in Athens. They also had a central place of assembly and market, called the **agora** (pl. *agorae*). Surrounding villages began to consolidate and share a political identity, and the word *polis* came to mean the city-state itself and its surrounding countryside. Each city-state was an independent governing entity, but in the view of its residents, a polis was also a state of mind. Unlike in Mesopotamia, Egypt, and Mycenae, polis inhabitants did not think of themselves as subjects of a king or as owing obedience to a priesthood. Instead, they were "citizens" who were

actively responsible for guiding their poleis. Aristotle (384–322 B.C.E.) even characterized humans by their participation in politics (the word *politics* is derived from the word *polis*), arguing that "man is a political animal" (although a more accurate translation is "man is an animal of the polis").

Although Greece's rocky terrain separated the land into many small city-states, they shared certain characteristics. They all developed self-government by male citizens, with variations as to the exact form. All the states relied on hoplite armies, and all used slavery to run their small-scale industries and farming. In all the city-states as well, Greek men who fought together in the hoplite armies gathered daily in the agorae to discuss matters of life and politics.

The Heart of the Polis

The heart of the polis was the household, which consisted of a male citizen, his wife and children, and their slaves. This configuration formed the basis for both the rural and urban economies. In the villages outside the walls of the city itself, household members herded sheep and goats, worked in the vineyards and olive groves, and struggled to plant crops in the rocky ground. Olive trees yielded abundant fruit, but harvesting required a good deal of labor.

In addition to olive harvesting, craftsmanship and trade completed the polis economy. Artisans in the polis labored at their crafts or sold their merchandise in the open market during the mornings. After a large afternoon meal, they napped and then either returned to their shops or (more likely) went to the gymnasium to exercise and talk with other citizens. The gymnasium grew in part out of the Greek belief in cultivating perfection in all things; thus a skilled artisan or philosopher also needed to cultivate his physical prowess as part of his pursuit of excellence. The gymnasium **Men's and women's** proved an enduring feature of life in **roles** the Mediterranean city-states. This was a highly public life for male citizens; work, exercise, and talk were all central activities of the masculine life.

In most city-states, women's lives were more restricted than men's—at least in the ideal. Wealthy, upper-class women were married at puberty and were supposed to stay indoors, teaching female slaves necessary skills, managing the goods brought into the household, and presiding over the spinning and weaving. When men entertained their peers at dinner parties or visited, "respectable" women stayed home and out of sight along with their female slaves and children. (As we will see, life for women in Sparta marked an exception to this pattern.)

In addition to having defined gender roles, Greek society depended heavily on slave labor; virtually every household had a few **Slave labor** slaves. Some slaves worked alongside free men and women in almost every occupation. (There were even slave policemen in Athens.) Some slaves could earn money to purchase their freedom, but others had the misfortune to work in the silver mines, where they were beaten and died young. For the most part, however, slavery was treated as a simple fact of life—an essential tool for getting necessary work done.

Fears and Attachments in Greek Emotional Life

Many Greek writers expressed a great suspicion of women. As one poet, Semonides of Amorgos, wrote: "God made the mind of women a thing apart." The strict segregation of men and women through their lives may have contributed to misunderstandings. Men with little experience with women believed that virtuous women were scarce. Many husbands feared that their wives would escape their seclusion and take lovers, and thereby raise questions about the paternity of their children. These fears permeate many writings by Greek men.

Perhaps as part of their overall praise of masculinity, many ancient Greeks accepted bisexuality, at least among wealthy urban dwellers. The ideal of **Bisexual relations** such a relationship took the form of a mentoring arrangement between a well-connected older man and a "beardless youth" (although school-aged, freeborn boys were protected from such liaisons). As the pair matured, the elder man would marry and take up his family responsibilities, and the younger would serve as a mentor to a new youth.

We have only a few examples of women engaging in homosexual behavior, probably because their lives were conducted in privacy and were not recorded in as many historical documents. However, one sixth-century B.C.E. poet, **Sappho of Lesbos** Sappho from the island of Lesbos, expressed passionate love for the young women in her social circle. Her poetry has since been both highly respected for its beauty and severely criticized for its content. Sappho's poetry was so influential that the word *Lesbian,* meaning a resident of Sappho's island of Lesbos, has become synonymous with female homosexuality.

Not all women were confined to the home. While respectable women stayed carefully indoors, some women—slaves or foreigners—who had no economic resources or family ties became prostitutes and courtesans who shared men's public lives at dinners and drinking parties. Prostitutes were **Courtesans** even registered and taxed in many Greek city-states and thereby became a legitimate part of social and economic life. Men and prostitutes drank freely together from the wine bowls abundantly filled at banquets. These bowls, like the one shown below, were decorated inside and out with exuberant images that not only portrayed scenes from the parties but also were intended to spur people on to greater abandon. Women in ancient Greece, particularly Athens, were thus placed in the peculiar situation of being invisible if they were "respectable," and mingling with and influencing powerful men only if they were not.

All the city-states shared many of these elements of urban life, from work to pleasure. However, each polis had its own distinctive character, as citizens structured their political lives to suit themselves. The two best-documented Greek cities were Athens and Sparta, and yet most of the cities did not match the extremes in art and austerity that marked these two influential states.

Athens: City of Democracy

Theseus founded Athens. The document on page 37 relates the city's founding myth and suggests that participatory democracy was at the heart of its origins. The reality of a developing democratic form of government was more complicated. By 700 B.C.E., Athenian aristocrats had established a form of government—an **oligarchy**—that allowed them to control the growing city. Elected admin-

Oligarchy

A DRINKING GAME, ca. fifth century B.C.E.   This pottery bowl shows a courtesan swirling a wine bowl until the dregs fly out. It reminds us that although respectable women stayed home, prostitutes were a regular part of Athenian social life.

istrators called *archons* ran the business of the city, and the wealthy families controlled these offices. However, this oligarchy proved unable to respond to changing economic fortunes.

By about 600 B.C.E., the economy took a downturn, and small farmers could not produce enough to feed the growing population; many fell into debt and even slavery by offering themselves as security in exchange for food. At the same time, hoplite armies caused the aristocracy to lose its monopoly over the military. A farsighted Athenian aristocrat, Solon, who was elected sole archon in 594, introduced reforms designed to appease the lower classes while keeping aristocrats in power.

Solon was most successful in economic reforms, abolishing debt slavery and stimulating the export of olive oil to alleviate the rural economic crisis. He tried to reform the political structure by breaking up the powerful oligarchy, but his attempts to offer compromise among the contentious social groups in Athens only succeeded in angering everyone. During the resulting civil strife, a succession of tyrants seized power in Athens. This period of tyranny broke the power of the aristocrats and paved the way for full democracy.

In 508 B.C.E., the people rallied to Cleisthenes, a nobleman who stood for popular interests, who offered a constitution that refined Solon's reforms and brought a remarkable degree of direct democracy to the city. He restored the assembly of male citizens (called the *Ecclesia*) that had fallen dormant during the period of oligarchy, and which Solon had tried to reestablish. Cleisthenes' major innovation was to redistrict the city in a way that broke up old alliances of geography and clan, so traditional oligarchs could no longer control the city offices. While the Ecclesia consisted of all citizens, business was conducted by a council of 500—each new tribal unit could select 50 members by lot, instead of by election, so there was no room for bribery or political infighting. The council adopted legislation that was then voted on by the Ecclesia.

Although the Ecclesia offered a new level of participation to the men of the ancient world and a model of representation that has been praised since, it was not a perfect democracy. It still represented only about 20 percent of the population of Athens, for it excluded women and slaves. Also

Theseus Founds the City of Athens

The famous ancient biographer Plutarch (46–120 C.E.) related Athens's founding myth, in which the hero Theseus defeated the Minotaur of Crete and returned to establish a city that would be unlike any that had gone before.

After the death of Ægeus, Theseus conceived a great and important design. He gathered together all the inhabitants of Attica and made them citizens of one city, whereas before they had lived dispersed, so as to be hard to assemble together for the common weal, and at times even fighting with one another.

He visited all the villages and tribes, and won their consent, the poor and lower classes gladly accepting his proposals, while he gained over the more powerful by promising that the new constitution should not include a king, but that it should be a pure commonwealth, with himself merely acting as general of its army and guardian of its laws, while in other respects it would allow perfect freedom and equality to everyone. By these arguments he convinced some of them, and the rest knowing his power and courage chose rather to be persuaded than forced into compliance.

. . . Aristotle tells us that he was the first who inclined to democracy, and gave up the title of king; and Homer seems to confirm this view by speaking of the people of the Athenians alone of all the states mentioned in his catalogue of ships.

How might this myth have influenced the development of Athenian democracy?

excluded were the *metics,* resident foreigners who lived and worked in Athens in manufacturing and commerce

Assessing democracy

and who represented nearly one-third of the free population of Athens. Furthermore, recent scholarship shows that only a minority of the qualified citizens could attend the assembly at any given time—only about 6,000 can fit into the meeting place, a small sloping hillside. It seems that when the meeting place was full, no one else could enter and a quorum was declared. Thus, probably many of the same people (those living nearby) attended the Ecclesia regularly.

However, other parts of the Athenian government made sure the principle of egalitarian democracy prevailed. The Council of 500 was chosen annually by lot from male citizens over age 30, and citizens could not repeat tenure. Choosing representatives by lot (instead of by election or other device) removed much of the influence of wealth and personal power from the political process. The great leader of Athens Pericles, in a famous funeral oration preserved (or paraphrased) by the historian Thucydides, rightly observed: "Our constitution is called a democracy because it is in the hands not of the few but of the many."

The people did recognize that sometimes individuals could threaten the rule of the many, and to protect the democracy, Cleisthenes instituted an unusual procedure early in the sixth century B.C.E.:

Ostracism

ostracism. Once a year, Athenians could vote for the man they considered most dangerous to the state by inscribing his name on a scrap of pottery (called an *ostracon*). If a man received 6,000 votes, he was sent into exile for ten years. Although Athenian democracy was not perfect, it was an extraordinary new chapter in the history of the West, and one that has held long-standing appeal.

Sparta: Model Military State

Sparta's development led to the emergence of a state thoroughly different from Athens, with a markedly different set of values. Whereas Athenians were creative, artistic, and eloquent, Spartans were militaristic, strict, and sparing of words (our word *laconic* comes from "lakonia," the countryside surrounding Sparta). The nature of their state was shaped by an early solution to their land hunger. Instead of sending out colonists or negotiating partnerships with the peoples in their vicinity (as the Athenians had done), the Spartans conquered their neighboring districts and enslaved the local populations. The slaves, called **helots,** were treated harshly. As one Spartan poet observed, they were like "donkeys worn down by intolerable labor." Sparta's helots greatly outnumbered free citizens and always seemed to threaten rebellion. To keep the helots in slavery, the Spartans virtually enslaved themselves in a military state of perpetual watchfulness. They consoled themselves by observing that at least they had chosen their harsh life, whereas their helots had not.

The Spartan constitution—reputedly introduced by the semilegendary Lycurgus in about 600 B.C.E.—reflected their deep conservatism and made a minimal concession to democracy. Authority was carefully kept in the hands of the elders. In this oligarchy, citizen representation was firmly guided by age and experience, and many outsiders admired Sparta's "mixed constitution," which seemed to balance democracy with oligarchy.

Life in Sparta was harsh, although it was much admired by many Greeks who appreciated the Spartans' powers of self-denial. At birth, each child was examined by elders, and if deemed physically deficient, the child would

Spartan life

be exposed—left outdoors to die. At the age of 7, boys were turned over to the state and spent the next thirteen years in training to learn military skills, endurance, and loyalty to the polis. At 20, young men entered the army and lived the next ten years in barracks. They could marry but could visit their wives only by eluding the barracks guards. At 30, men became full citizens and could live at home. Nevertheless, they were expected to take all meals in the military dining hall, where food was sparse and plain.

While their men lived isolated in the barracks, Spartan women had far more freedom than Greek women of other city-states. Because men concentrated on their military activities, women handled most of the household arrangements and had wide economic powers. They attended contests to cheer the brave and mock the losers, but they were not simply spectators. Women, too, trained in athletic endurance, and the fierceness of Spartan women was said to match that of their men. Such dedication to military training made the armies of Sparta the best in Greece, and though the Spartans created no works of art, they probably would have said that their own lives were masterpiece enough.

The Love of the Contest: Olympic Games

Athens and Sparta were only two examples of the many varieties of city-states that developed with fierce independence on the Greek mainland and in the colonies throughout the Mediterranean. But, although there was much rivalry among the poleis, they still shared a certain sense of identity. They spoke the same language, worshiped the same gods, cherished Homer's poetry, and had a passionate love for individual competition. They recognized these affinities, calling themselves *Hellenes* (the

OPINION

How did geography influence the Greek city-states' economic choices?

Romans later called them "Greeks"), and they considered all Hellenes to be better than other peoples. Their love of contest caused Hellenes to gather at many local competitions that included drama as well as sport. The largest and most famous of these events was a religious festival dedicated to Zeus, and Hellenes even stopped their almost interminable warfare to come together and compete.

The first pan-Hellenic Olympic Games were held in 776 B.C.E. At first, the event consisted only of a footrace, but soon the games expanded to include boxing, wrestling, chariot racing, and the grueling pentathlon, which consisted of long jumping, discus and javelin throwing, wrestling, and the 200-meter sprint. Olympic victors brought glory to their home cities and were richly rewarded there with honor and free meals.

Olympic Games

The Olympics were so popular that they served as an inspiration to many artists. The athletes shown below demonstrate the perfection that people expected from their athletic heroes. Critics, such as the playwright Euripides (485–406 B.C.E.), chided Greeks for their adulation of athletes. "We ought rather to crown the good man and the wise man," he scolded. Nevertheless, spectators flocked to the games.

Olympic planners prohibited women from attending the contest, although they could purchase a chariot and horses with which men would compete in their names. Some women conducted games of their own separately from the men's. These games, dedicated to Zeus's wife Hera, involved footraces run by unmarried women of various ages. Women judged and sponsored the games and awarded the fastest competitors crowns of olive branches. However, these winners did not receive the high level of acclaim or wealth accorded to male victors, who brought prestige to their cities and fame for themselves through their athletic prowess. Although the Olympic Games offered a

Women at Olympics

safe outlet for the Greeks' love of competition, Greek history was shaped by more devastating strife in which city-states tried to outdo each other on the battlefields.

The Persian Wars

490–479 B.C.E.

Greek colonists who settled in Asia Minor built their city-states in lands that the Persian Empire had claimed by 500 B.C.E. As we saw in Chapter 1, the Persians were tolerant of the various subject peoples within their territories, so they did not object to the growing spirit of independence that accompanied the prosperity of these successful commercial cities. However, open revolt was another matter.

In 499 B.C.E., the Greek tyrant ruling in the city of Miletus (see map on page 40) offended the Persian rulers. Hoping to avoid retribution, he staged a revolt against Persian rule and asked for help from his compatriots on the Greek mainland. Sparta refused, but Athens sent twenty ships—enough only to anger the Persians but not to save Miletus. The Greek city was sacked, and the Persians turned their attention to the Greek peninsula. They planned an invasion in part to punish Athens for its involvement in the Miletus uprising.

Causes of war

Any forces seeking to invade the Greek mainland had to negotiate the mountainous terrain and the narrow passes that afforded the only access to the interior. Furthermore, an invading land army had to be supplied by a shore-hugging fleet that backed up the infantry while navigating the narrow straits of the Aegean shoreline. In 490 B.C.E., the Persian king Darius I (r. 522–486 B.C.E.), therefore, sailed across the Aegean and landed near Athens. The map on page 40 depicts the route of the invading Persian army and the battle site located on the plain of Marathon.

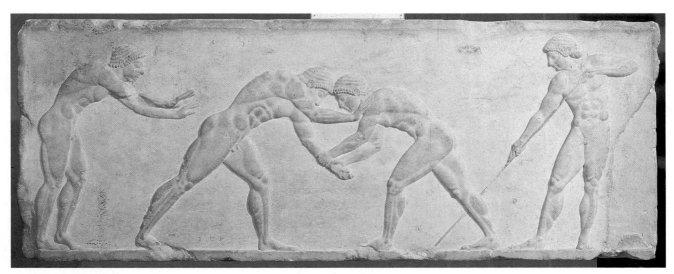

THE OLYMPIC GAMES, late sixth century B.C.E.   As part of their ongoing contest for excellence, the Greeks developed the Olympic Games in honor of Zeus. Here, athletes participate in the footrace, wrestling, and the javelin throw.

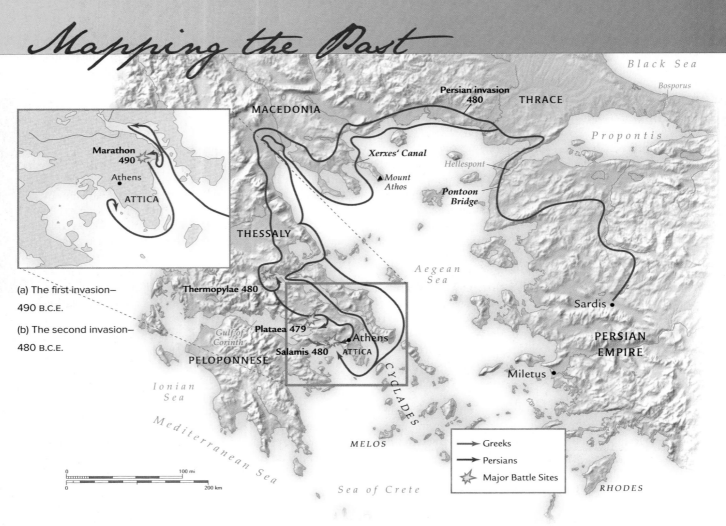

The Persian Wars, 490–479 B.C.E.

The Persian Wars, 490–479 B.C.E. **This map shows the routes of invasions and the major battles of the wars between Persia and the Greek poleis. Map (a) traces the first invasion by sea in 490 B.C.E., and Map (b) illustrates the routes of the second invasion, during which armies marched by land, supported by accompanying ships.   What might have been the particular advantages and disadvantages posed by the land and sea routes?**

At the Battle of Marathon, the Athenians and their allies were far outmatched by the numerous Persians. The worried Athenians asked their Spartan compatriots for reinforcements, but the Spartans replied that they had to complete their religious festival first—then it would be too late to repel the Persians. Athens and its allies had to stand alone. In spite of being outnumbered, the Athenians decided to march from Athens to meet the Persians near their landing site on the plain of Marathon. Confident of an easy victory, the Persians launched their attack. Things did not go as expected for the Persians, however. The Athenian general, Miltiades, developed a clever strategy that helped the Greeks outwit the lightly armed Persians. Weakening the center of their line and strengthening the two wings, the Athenians outflanked the advancing Persian force and inflicted severe damage.

Battle of Marathon

The Greeks also made a running advance, a novelty that surprised and confused their enemy. Athenian innovation and energy won the day, bringing a decisive and stunning victory to the Greeks. According to the texts, 6,400 Persians perished in the battle, compared with only 192 Athenians. This unexpected victory of the polis over the huge empire of Persia earned Athens great prestige, and the Athenian victory also inspired confidence in the newly emerging democracy itself.

Athens had fended off the invaders, but the humiliated Persians were determined to try again. Ten years after the disaster at Marathon, Darius's successor, Xerxes (r. 486–465 B.C.E.), plotted a full-scale invasion of the Greek mainland. Xerxes brought the best of ancient engineering to the invasion to try to avoid the disaster of the first war. To move a large infantry force, he built a pontoon

A second invasion

Then & Now
The First Marathon

After the Athenians' victory at the battle of Marathon, their fastest runner, Philippides, was reputed to have run to Athens to deliver the news of victory to the polis. He died on the spot from his exertions. Modern-day races are called *marathons* in commemoration of Philippides' legendary—and fatal—26-mile run from the plain of Marathon to Athens.

bridge across the Hellespont and marched 180,000 soldiers to Greece. Even more impressive, he ordered his men to build a canal a mile and a quarter long through a peninsula in northern Greece so that his fleet could supply the ground force. Historians have debated for decades about whether the canal existed, but recently, scientists from Britain and Greece proved conclusively that the canal was built. It spanned about 100 feet at the surface, just wide enough for two war galleys to pass. It was an astonishing engineering feat and showed Xerxes' determination. (Both the bridge and the canal are shown on the map on page 40.)

For the Persian army, the gateway to the south lay through the pass at Thermopylae (see map on page 40). Yet the narrow pass, held by a small coalition of Greeks led by Spartans, turned the Persians' greater numbers into a liability. The Greeks held the pass for days against repeated assaults by the best Persian forces. In the end, however, they were betrayed by a Greek who expected to enrich himself by aiding the attackers. The traitor led the Persians around the defended pass, where they could fight the Greeks from the rear. Only the Spartans stayed to fight to the death. Defending themselves from front and back, the Spartans fought fiercely in a long-remembered feat of bravery, and all died with sword in hand. An inscription placed on their graves immortalized their heroic stand: "Tell them the news in Sparta, passer by. That here, obedient to their words, we lie."

Thermopylae

The Persians' success at Thermopylae opened a route for them to march south to Athens itself. The Athenian leader, Themistocles, persuaded the people to take refuge in their fleet and abandon the polis for nearby islands. Many horrified Greeks were close enough to watch as the Persians plundered Athens and burned the temples on the Acropolis as an act of revenge for their previous losses. Yet, as in Marathon, the tide again turned against the mighty Persians, this time in the bay of Salamis (see map on page 40).

Artemisia, queen of Caria in Persia and commander of a squadron of Xerxes' fleet, immediately saw that the Persians would lose their advantage in numbers fighting in a narrow bay and strongly advised the Persian king against it. Her military wisdom proved well founded; the swift Greek vessels rallied and crushed almost the entire Persian fleet. The next year, the Spartans led a coalition that defeated the remnants of the Persian army at Plataea (see map on page 40). The individualistic, dispersed Greeks had triumphed once more over the vast, unified Persian Empire.

Greek naval victory

Herodotus: The Father of History

In a famous work called simply *The History,* the Greek historian Herodotus recorded the great deeds of the Persian Wars with a combination of a broad perspective and an attention to detail. This monumental work—some 600 pages long—was so pathbreaking that he is universally considered the father of Western history. With his first sentence, Herodotus placed himself within the Greek heroic tradition, claiming to have written in order "that the deeds of men may not be forgotten, and that the great and noble actions of the Greeks and Asiatics may not lose their fame." While immortalizing these warriors, Herodotus did not take the traditional approach of converting heroic deeds into godlike myths. Instead, he drew from oral traditions acquired during his extensive travels—the things he had "seen and been told"—and wrote what he intended to be a total picture of the known world. This was an account not simply of a war but of a heroic-scale conflict between two types of societies, the poleis and the Asian empire—or, for Herodotus, between freedom and despotism.

Herodotus did much for the discipline of history by striving to record historical events as accurately as possible and separating fact from fable, but his efforts marked only a beginning in the quest for historical objectivity. He clearly shared the Greeks' belief that their culture was far superior to that of the "barbarians," and these preconceptions biased his conclusions.

Although Herodotus wrote a lively, fascinating history, as we will see, he was wrong in identifying the Persians as the Greeks' worst enemies. Just as a Greek had betrayed the Spartans at Thermopylae, the Greeks themselves would one day bring about their own downfall. But for the time being, they gloried in their astounding victory over Persia, the great power of Asia.

GREECE ENTERS ITS CLASSICAL AGE

479–336 B.C.E.

Victory over the mighty Persian Empire launched the Greeks into a vigorous, creative period that later historians and art critics admired so much they named it the classical age. This period was marked by stunning accomplishments in art, architecture, literature, philosophy, and representative democracy in Athens. This same age that saw such impressive artistic innovations ended as the contest for excellence among the city-states plunged them into devastating wars. At the beginning of the period, however, Athens, which took the lead in guarding Greece from Persian incursions, began to flex its muscles.

Athens Builds an Empire

477–431 B.C.E.

The Greeks' defeat of the Persians, though sweet, presented the fiercely independent poleis with a new dilemma. The Persian Empire was still powerful. How would the Greek city-states work together to remain vigilant in the face of this threat, and who would lead them? The most effective defense of Greece lay in controlling the Aegean, and the Athenians possessed the strongest fleet.

In 477 B.C.E., most maritime poleis on the coasts and the islands of the Aegean finally decided to form a defensive league. Each member of the league contributed money to maintain a large fleet for the defense of them all, and the alliance decided to establish their treasury on the island of Delos. The coalition was thus called the Delian League. Theoretically, all league members were entitled to an equal voice in decision making, but Athens was the strongest member and began to dominate league policy.

Delian League

As early as the 470s B.C.E., some members took offense at Athens's prominent role and sought to withdraw from the arrangement. But the Athenians swiftly made the situation clear: This was not a league of independent states

after all, but an Athenian empire with subject cities. In 454 B.C.E., the Athenians dropped any pretense of the member states' autonomy and moved the league's treasury from Delos to Athens. It is hard to imagine how deeply the Athenian actions horrified the Greek world, but consider that it was a sacrilege to raid the shrine that had been safe under Apollo's protection for centuries. It is also hard to grasp how vast were the stores of money on Delos. The Athenians would use this wealth to rebuild the Acropolis and to fund Athens's Golden Age, which included dressing the cult statue of Athena in astonishing amounts of gold.

During the Persian Wars, the Athenian military commanders had understandably acquired a good deal of power. Officials called **strategoi** (sing. *strategos*) were elected as commanders of the tribal army units, and during Athens's imperial age, a particularly strong strategos came to wield considerable power for a time. The political architect of Athens's Golden Age was the statesman Pericles (495–429 B.C.E.), who was elected strategos every year from 443 B.C.E. to his death in 429 B.C.E. He so dominated Athenian affairs that many compared him to a tyrant, yet this powerful aristocrat eloquently championed democracy in the assembly of Athens and encouraged democratic principles within the states of the league. However, he did not permit independent action by subject states. Thus, Pericles supported Athens's removal of the league treasury. As he pointed out, it was only right that Athenians enjoy the money, given that they had led the victory over Persia in the first place and their city had been burned in the process. Pericles followed up this argument by playing an instrumental role in plans for spending the money.

Pericles

Pericles forwarded democracy within Athens by trying to ensure that even poor citizens could participate fully in Athenian politics and culture. His most significant contribution was to pay the people who served as jurors or on the Council of 500. Now all male citizens—not just the rich—could participate in the democracy. Equally important, he used much of the treasury to employ citizens on a project designed to beautify the public spaces of Athens. He organized armies of talented artists and artisans and paid thousands of workers to participate in the project. Finally, he put about 20,000 Athenians on the municipal payroll, a move that stimulated widespread involvement in the democratic proceedings of the city.

Pericles' democracy

Artistic Athens

Pericles' leadership made Athens the political and cultural jewel of Greece. At the heart of the reconstruction program lay a plan to rebuild the Acropolis, which the Persians had destroyed. The restored Acropolis consisted of several temples and related buildings. As they designed the buildings, architects drew from the best of Greek tradition to make a political as well as an artistic statement. Design came first: Greek temples had always been constructed of *post and lintel* form, in which columns supported the roof. By 600 B.C.E., Greeks had developed "orders" of architecture to describe the various designs of the columns (and buildings), and these orders have influenced architecture down to the modern day. There were three orders of classic Greek buildings—Doric, Ionic, and Corinthian. **Doric,** the oldest order, developed on the Greek mainline, has a simple capital on top of a fluted column. The **Ionic** order, developed in Ionia on the eastern Mediterranean, features taller, more slender columns topped with elegant scroll shapes. The **Corinthian** order was a later development (probably from the fifth century B.C.E.) and was not used on the Acropolis, but its columns, topped with an acanthus-leaf capital, were extremely popular in later architecture. The sketches below show the major elements of these three orders that make them recognizable. The architects of the buildings on the Acropolis used both Doric and Ionic columns in the temples.

In effect, these structures were nothing less than a political statement. Indeed, visitors to the Acropolis could see the empire's might in the majestic columns, which proclaimed Athenian control over the mainland to the Ionian coast. Although people would forget that political statement over time, the architectural elements would constantly be duplicated.

The largest temple in the Acropolis was the Parthenon (shown in the chapter opening photo), located on the highest point and dedicated to Athena, the patron goddess of the city. The temple had a magnificent statue of the goddess (now lost) created by Phidias, the greatest sculptor of the day, whose reputation for excellence continues today.

The Athenians adorned the Parthenon with many sculptures and statues of both gods and humans. (Today, few statues remain in Athens—most are in museums

GODS ON THE PARTHENON, ca. 440 B.C.E.   Every four years, Athenians staged a major festival, the Panathenaic procession. The frieze along the Parthenon's inner colonnade memorializes the event. In this detail, the humanlike gods are shown reclining and enjoying their tribute.

elsewhere.) These statues, which all bear a strong resemblance to one another, echo the Greek belief that gods and humans had much in common.

The photograph above shows gods and a goddess from a frieze on the Parthenon. They are seated, waiting for the procession of the Athenians to begin, and are shown posed and dressed as Athenian citizens. By blurring humanity and divinity in their visual arts in this way, the Greeks explored the highest potential of humanity in their artwork.

Greek Theater: Exploring Complex Moral Problems

In addition to their architecture and sculpture, the Athenians' theatrical achievements set new standards for Greek culture. Greek theater grew as part of the religious celebration of Dionysus, held in the late spring. Every year, Athens's leaders chose eight playwrights to present serious and comic plays at the festival in a competition as fierce as the Olympics. The plays were performed in open-air theaters with simple staging. Men played both male and female parts, and all actors wore stylized masks. The themes of these plays centered on weighty matters such as religion, politics, and the deep dilemmas that arose as people grappled with their fates. During Athens's Golden Age, playwrights reminded the Athenians that, even at the height of their power, they faced complex moral problems.

One of Athens's most accomplished playwrights was Aeschylus (ca. 525–456 B.C.E.), who had fought at the Battle of Marathon. His earliest play, *The Persians,* added thoughtful nuance to the celebrations that the Athenians

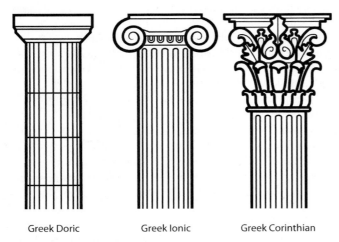

Greek Doric	Greek Ionic	Greek Corinthian

ARCHITECTURAL ORDERS The magnificent Greek architects developed *orders*, conventional architectural styles most readily identified by the tops of the columns. The Doric, Ionic, and Corinthian orders are shown here. The Greeks' orders have influenced architecture into modern times.

A Playwright Reflects on the Meaning of Life

The tragic playwright Sophocles wrote *Oedipus the King* in about 429 B.C.E. at the beginning of the Peloponnesian War and at the height of Athenian power. The following passage, from the chorus, reminds all of Athens never to be prideful and complacent.

Chorus: Men of Thebes: look upon Oedipus. This is the king who solved the famous riddle and towered up, most powerful of men. No mortal eyes but looked on him with envy. Yet in the end ruin swept over him. Let every man in mankind's frailty consider his last day; and let none presume on his good fortune until he find life, at his death, a memory without pain.

How do you think the Athenian audience would have reacted to Sophocles' warning against pride just as Athens was beginning a war against Sparta?

had enjoyed after their victory. Instead of simply praising Athenian success, Aeschylus studied Persian loss, attributing it to Xerxes' hubris at trying to upset the established international order. This also subtly warned the Athenians not to let their own arrogant pride bring about their own destruction.

The most revered playwright of this period, however, was Sophocles (ca. 496–406 B.C.E.), who is best known for *The Theban Plays,* a great series about the mythological figure Oedipus and his family. All Athenians would have known the story of Oedipus, an ill-fated man whose family was told by a soothsayer at his birth that he was doomed to kill his father and marry his mother. The family exposed the baby to die, but he was rescued by a shepherd and raised as a prince in a faraway land. When he was grown, a soothsayer in his new land repeated the prediction, and when Oedipus fled to avoid killing the man he believed was his father, he returned to his original home, where he unintentionally fulfilled the prophecy. In Sophocles' hands, the play became a study in the range of human emotions measured by how man responds to tragic fates. (See Exploring the Past.) Oedipus moves from pride in his own position as king to deep agony and humility as he discovers the horrifying truth of his life. The play concludes with a reminder to all spectators not to feel complacent in their own lives.

Aeschylus and Sophocles

DESTRUCTION, DISILLUSION, AND A SEARCH FOR MEANING

Sadly for the Athenians, they failed to heed Sophocles' warnings about pride and impiety. Their era of prosperity came to a violent end with the onset of the Peloponnesian War, a long, destructive conflict between Athens and Sparta and their respective allies. Like the Persian Wars, this new contest generated its own historian. Thucydides (460–400 B.C.E.), an even more objective historian than Herodotus, wrote: "I began my history at the very outbreak of the war, in the belief that it was going to be a great war. . . . My belief was based on the fact that the two sides were at the very height of their power and preparedness." Historians today share his desire for intellectual analysis of the facts but might come to different conclusions about the results. In any case, as a result of Thucydides' *History of the Peloponnesian War,* we now have the earliest, most carefully detailed record of a war—and of the destruction of a way of life.

Thucydides

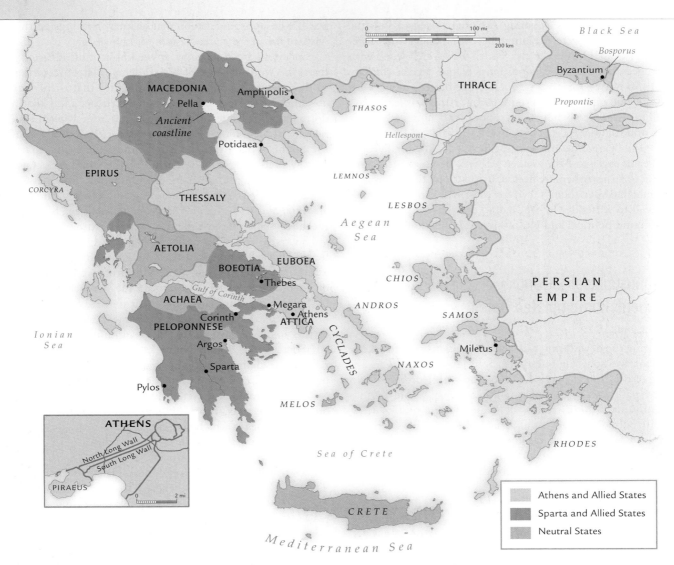

The Peloponnesian War, 431–404 B.C.E. This map shows Athens and Sparta and their allies during the Peloponnesian War. The inset illustrates the "long walls" that joined Athens to the sea at its port of Piraeus.

The Peloponnesian War

431–404 B.C.E.

To counter growing Athenian power, Sparta gathered together allies—the Peloponnesian League—to challenge the power of the Athenian Empire. While the flash point of the conflict was a dispute between two poleis, Thucydides recorded the Spartan viewpoint: "What made war inevitable was the growth of Athenian power and the fear which this caused in Sparta." At its core, this was a war to preserve the independence of each city-state and the unique brand of competitiveness among all the poleis. Athens had grown too strong, and the contest too uneven. Sparta felt compelled to take action when Athens increased its imperial ambitions.

The actual fighting proved awkward and difficult, for Athens and Sparta each had differing strengths and military styles. Athens was surrounded by long walls that extended to the shore (see inset in the map above). Therefore, as long as the Athenian navy controlled the sea, Athens could not be successfully besieged. Thus Athens preferred to conduct battle with its navy and harried Spartan and allied territories from the sea. Sparta, on the other hand, put its trust in its formidable infantry. Bolstering their individual strengths, Athens's allies surrounded the Aegean Sea, while Sparta's allies were largely land based, as the map shows. As the Spartans marched across the isthmus near Megara to burn Athens's crops and fields, Athenians watched safely from behind their walls and supplied their needs with their massive fleet. However, there were bloody clashes as young Athenians tried to stop the Spartans, who were ravaging the countryside, and Athenians suffered inside the city, which was overcrowded with refugees. Under these conditions, plague struck the city in 430–429 B.C.E. Even Pericles succumbed, along with about one-quarter of the population. Athenian leadership fell to lesser men, whom contemporaries denounced as selfish and impulsive.

The Peloponnesian League's fleet, partially financed by a Persia eager to help weaken Athens, destroyed the remnants of the Athenian fleet. Cut off from the trade that would have let them survive a siege, the Athenians were forced to surrender in 404 B.C.E. Their defeat would have profound political and philosophic ramifications.

Philosophical Musings: Athens Contemplates Defeat

During the devastating war, some Athenians started asking themselves sobering questions about justice and the meaning of life. The answers they came up with led them down new pathways of thought—pathways that would permanently alter the direction of Western philosophy. Athenian politicians had promulgated the principle of moral relativism—whatever was good for them was right. At the time, some philosophers in Athens shared this belief. These Sophists (or "wise ones") doubted the existence of universal truths and, instead, taught their followers how to influence public opinion and how to forward their own fortunes. Rather than seeking truth, the Sophists argued that "man is the measure of all things" and that people should therefore act in accordance with their own needs and desires.

Socrates (ca. 470–399 B.C.E.), the first great philosopher of the West, developed his ideas as a reaction against the Sophists' moral relativism. Supposedly, the Delphic oracle had reported that there was "no man wiser than Socrates." After this revelation, the philosopher spent the rest of his life roaming the streets of Athens, questioning his fellow citizens in an effort to find someone wiser than

connect to today

Free Speech

The trial of Socrates raised issues of freedom of speech and thought that persist today. How do you think his trial might apply to contemporary issues such as hate speech and political postings on Internet sites such as Facebook and YouTube?

he. His questions took the form of dialogues that forced people to examine their beliefs critically and confront the logical consequences of their ideas. Socrates came to the conclusion that, indeed, he was the wisest man

Socrates

because he alone understood that he knew nothing and that wisdom lies in the endless search for knowledge.

Socrates left no writings, so we know of his ideas only from the words of one of his students, Plato. According to these texts, Socrates expressed the idea that there were absolutes of truth and justice and excellence, and that a dormant knowledge of these absolutes rested within all people. In these inquiries, Socrates departed not only from the Sophists but from the early philosophers like Thales who wanted to know the nature of the world—Socrates wanted to explore the nature of right action. The method he employed was that of questioning and refuting students' answers, and with this method—now called the **Socratic method**—he brought students to see the truth.

Socrates began his inquiries in the dynamic period before the Peloponnesian War, but in the times of disillusionment after the war, Athenian jurors were suspicious of anyone who seemed to oppose the democracy—even by pointing out humankind's inadequacies. Socrates was brought to trial and accused of impiety and corruption of the young. As we saw at the beginning of this chapter, Socrates was found guilty, even though he shrewdly refuted the charges during his trial. He received the death penalty and drank a cup of the deadly poison hemlock.

Socrates' ideas, however, did not die with him but lived on in his students. Plato, his best-known follower, wrote many dialogues in which he seems to have preserved his teacher's ideas, although historians are uncertain where Socrates' teachings end and Plato's begin. Plato

Plato

believed that truth and justice existed only as ideal models, or forms, but that humans could apprehend those realities only to a limited degree. Real people, he argued, lived in the imperfect world of the senses, a world that revealed only shadows of reality. This was his answer to the relativist Sophists, who saw the imperfect world as the true measure of right and wrong. For Plato, the goal of philosophical inquiry was to find the abstract and perfect "right" that was so elusive in this world. He established a school in Athens called the Academy to educate young Greek men in the tenets of virtue, for he believed that only through long training in philosophy could one learn to understand the ideal forms that exist outside the human world.

Plato was disillusioned with the democracy that had killed his teacher, Socrates, and admired Sparta's rigorous way of life. This political affinity shaped what is perhaps Plato's best-known work, *The Republic,* in which he outlined the ideal form of government. Instead of encouraging democracy, he explained, states should be ruled autocratically by philosopher-kings. In this way, the world might exhibit almost perfect justice. In some respects, this work expresses an articulate disillusionment with the failure of Athenian democracy to conduct a long war with honor or to tolerate a decent man pointing out citizens' shortcomings.

Plato's perfect state was never founded, but his ideas nevertheless had an enduring impact on Western civilization. Subsequent philosophers would confront his theory of ideal forms as they created other philosophic systems. His call for introspection and an awareness of self as the way to true knowledge would also have profound intellectual and religious implications.

Plato's ideas were not accepted universally in the Greek world. The career of his student Aristotle is one example. The son of a physician, Aristotle studied at Plato's Academy

Aristotle

and then spent another twenty years refining his thinking, debating his ideas, and writing. As much as Aristotle valued his teacher, he departed from Plato's theory of "perfect forms" and declared that ideas cannot exist outside their physical manifestations. Therefore, Aristotle concluded, to study anything—from plants to poetics to politics—one had to observe and study actual entities. He approached these studies through logic, which, in his hands, became a primary tool of philosophy and science. Aristotle's approach represented a major departure from the perspective of Plato, who argued that one should think about ideals instead of studying the imperfect nature of this world.

Aristotle also departed from his teacher on the subject of politics. As was his custom, the philosopher studied the different kinds of governments—monarchies, aristocracies, and republics—and discussed how each style could degenerate into corruption. He thought the ideal state was a small polis with a mixed constitution and a powerful middle class to prevent extremes. Aristotle recoiled from extremes in all aspects of life and argued for a balance—in his famous phrase, a "golden mean"—that would bring happiness. The philosopher extended his idea of moderation to the realm of ethics, arguing that the lack of excess would yield virtue.

Tragedy and Comedy: Innovations in Greek Theater

Athens's disillusioning war with Sparta had prompted philosophers to explore challenging questions of justice and virtue. Athenian theater, too, underwent change during the conflict. The playwright Euripides

Euripides

(485–406 B.C.E.) wrote tragedies in which people grappled with anguish on a heroic scale. In these plays, he expressed an intense pessimism and the lack of a divine moral order that marked Athens after the Peloponnesian War. In *Women of Troy,*

Euripides explored the pain of a small group of captured Trojan women. Though set in the era of the war immortalized by Homer, *Women of Troy* also had a strong contemporary message. When a character mused, "Strange how intolerable the indignity of slavery is to those born free," Euripides was really asking the Athenians to reflect on their own actions. In foretelling destruction to the Greeks who abused the women of Troy, Euripides predicted the eventual downfall of Athens.

Tragedy was not the only way to challenge contemporary society; talented playwrights also used comedy. As Greeks laughed at the crudest of sexual jokes and bathroom humor, they criticized public figures and conquered their own anxieties. These plays appeal less to modern audiences than do the Greek tragedies, for in their intense fascination with human nature, Greeks embraced even our basest inclinations.

While people laughed at comic portrayals, the greatest of the comic playwrights also used humor for serious purposes. Aristophanes (455–385 B.C.E.), for example, used costumes and crude humor to deliver biting political satire. This esteemed Athenian playwright delivered a ruthless

Aristophanes

criticism of contemporary Athens. Like many citizens, Aristophanes longed for peace. In 411 B.C.E.—at the height of the Peloponnesian War—he wrote *Lysistrata,* a hilarious antiwar play in which the women of Athens force their men to make peace by refusing to have sexual intercourse with them until they comply. With *Lysistrata,* Aristophanes reminded people that life and sex are more important than death and war.

Hippocrates and Medicine

While philosophers and playwrights mulled over abstract notions of life and human nature, Greek physicians turned to a practical study of the human body, influencing subsequent opinions of medicine. Previous ancient societies had made a number of strides in medical knowledge—the Babylonians and Assyrians kept catalogs of healing herbs, and the Egyptians were famed for medical treatments such as setting fractures, amputating limbs, and even opening skulls to relieve pressure on head injuries. However, most of the medical knowledge that influenced the West for centuries came from the Greeks, whose systematic treatises really began to separate medicine from the supernatural. Hippocrates (ca. 460–ca. 377 B.C.E.), considered the father of modern Western medicine, supposedly claimed that "every disease has a natural cause, and without natural causes nothing ever happens." With this statement Hippocrates rejected the ancient belief that spirits were responsible for human ailments.

Hippocrates was a highly respected physician and gave his name to a body of medical writing known as the *Hippocratic Collection,* compiled between the fifth and third centuries B.C.E. The *Collection* established medicine on a rational basis devoid of supernatural explanations of disease—a major innovation in Western culture. Consistent with other Greek thinkers from Thucydides to Aristotle, Hippocrates also emphasized careful observation. This body of writings contains more than four hundred short observations about health and disease—for example, "People who are excessively overweight are far more apt to die suddenly than those of average weight," or "Extremes in diet must be avoided." Overall, this new approach to medicine put human beings, rather than the gods, at the center of study. The human-centered outlook of Greek medicine culminated in a long-standing idea expressed in the Hippocratic Oath. Modern physicians still take this oath, in which they vow first to do no harm to their patients.

Though Athens suffered some dark days of war and disillusionment, this difficult era also witnessed the rise of geniuses who used the hard times as a backdrop for exploring the complex nature of humanity. Greek philosophers, playwrights, and physicians created brilliant works and conceived of ideas that transcended their time despite the turmoil of the age.

The Aftermath of War

404–338 B.C.E.

As a condition of its surrender at the end of the Peloponnesian War, Athens agreed to break down its defensive walls and reduce its fleet to only twelve ships. These harsh measures not only ended the Athenian Empire but also erased any possibility for a politically united Greece. The Spartans left a garrison in Athens and sent the rest of their troops home to their barrack state to guard their slaves. Sparta's subsequent attempts to assemble a political coalition foundered on its high-handed and inept foreign policy. Sparta's major allies, especially Corinth, opposed the Peloponnesian peace treaty, accusing Sparta of grabbing all the tribute and objecting to what they saw as lenience toward Athens. The generous treaty also stipulated that the Greek states in Asia Minor be given to Persia as the price for Persia's aid to Sparta, further eroding Greek unity.

All these postwar developments heightened competition among the poleis in the years after Athens's loss. For example, Corinth and Thebes fought wars to earn control of other Greek city-states, while Sparta ineptly struggled to preserve some leadership. Persia remained **Power struggles** involved in Greek affairs, shrewdly offering money to one side and then another so that the Greeks would continue to fight one another. In this way, Persia kept the poleis from marshaling their strength against their longtime imperial enemy.

These wars among the poleis only aggravated serious weaknesses within each city. Democracy in Athens as a political form, for example, had been deeply threatened by the long, devastating war, especially since decisions made by the citizens led to failure. Antidemocratic feelings expressed in the works of Plato erupted as Athens fell. As Thucydides had noted, democracy was not safe dur-

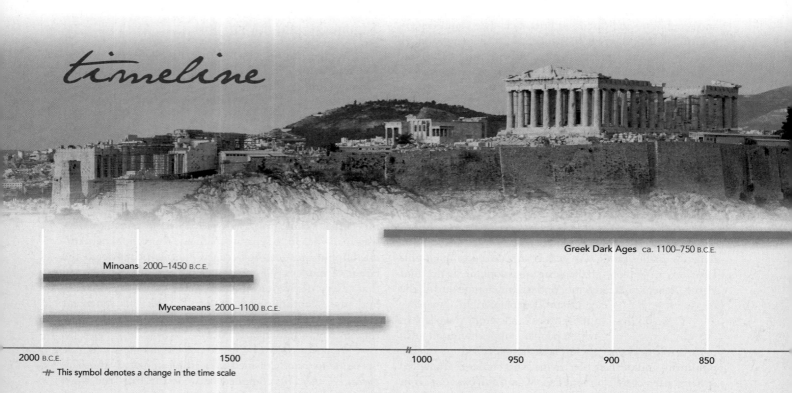

timeline

Greek Dark Ages ca. 1100–750 B.C.E.

Minoans 2000–1450 B.C.E.

Mycenaeans 2000–1100 B.C.E.

2000 B.C.E.   1500   1000   950   900   850

⊬ This symbol denotes a change in the time scale

ing turbulent times. As the war came to an end in 404 B.C.E., Sparta imposed an oligarchy of 30 men over Athens, a brutal tyranny that tried to stamp out the vestiges of democracy. Fifteen hundred democratic leaders were killed in the coup, and 5,000 more were exiled. This oligarchy lasted only eight months before democracy was restored, but the revived government had only a shadow of its former vigor. Fed by an involved citizenry, democracy had flourished in Athens. Now, without its empire and large fleet, fewer citizens became wealthy and political involvement waned.

Traditional participatory government in all the poleis unraveled further with innovations in military tactics. Under skillful generals, lightly armed javelin throwers, slingers, and archers began to defeat the heavily armed citizen hoplite armies that had once been the glory of Greece. Moreover, in the century following the Peloponnesian War, more and more Greeks served as mercenaries. These paid soldiers, owing allegiance to no city, added further disruption to an already unstable time, finally breaking the link between the poleis and the citizen-soldiers who defended them. In this period of growing unrest, every major Greek polis endured at least one war or revolution every ten years.

The nascent collective power of the Greek city-states also deteriorated during the postwar era. None of the poleis had succeeded in forging a lasting Hellenic coalition. The sovereignty of each city remained the defining idea in Greek politics. With this principle as a backdrop, individualism and loyalty to one's own city overrode any notions of a larger civic discipline. This competitive attitude had fueled the greatest of the Greeks' accomplishments in the arts, athletics, and politics, but it also gave rise to men who could not see beyond their own self-interests. In the midst of the troubled fourth century B.C.E., many Greeks feared that Persia would return to conquer a weakened Greece. As we will see in the next chapter, they should have worried about the "backward" people to the north instead.

SUMMARY

Small city-states nestled in the mountains of the Greek peninsula rerouted the course of Western civilization by their political ideas, artistic innovations, and philosophical musings.

- Two early civilizations arose in the eastern Mediterranean Sea: the Minoan on the island of Crete and the Mycenaean on the Greek mainland. These cultures were destroyed, but they laid the groundwork for the Greek culture that would emerge.

- Greeks living on the Ionian coast of Asia Minor preserved ideals of a heroic culture and memories of Mycenaean greatness as they expanded scientific inquiry and sent out colonists to establish city-states around the Mediterranean.

- These city-states developed varied political forms, from Athenian democracy to Spartan militaristic oligarchy, and everything in between. They began the Olympic Games that celebrated a spirit of contest, and managed to fight together to beat invading Persians.

- Athens emerged victorious after the Persian Wars and used this position to build an empire. Using imperial funds, Athens developed an artistic heritage that shaped ideals of beauty for millennia to come.

- Sparta assembled allies to challenge Athenian ascendancy and the destructive thirty-year Peloponnesian War ensued. During this time, Greek philosophy blossomed, but the traditional life of the poleis declined.

The future leadership of the eastern Mediterranean would come from a people to the north, the Macedonians, who took the greatness of Greek culture and spread it as far east as India as they forged a new empire.

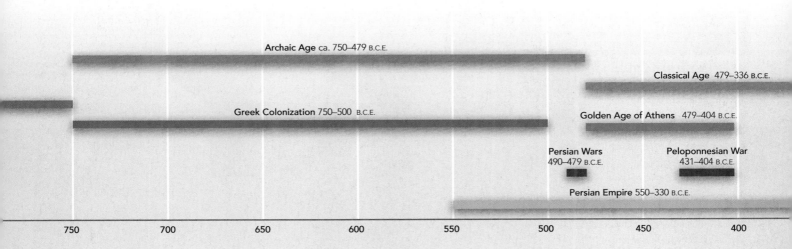

Archaic Age ca. 750–479 B.C.E.

Classical Age 479–336 B.C.E.

Greek Colonization 750–500 B.C.E.

Golden Age of Athens 479–404 B.C.E.

Persian Wars 490–479 B.C.E.

Peloponnesian War 431–404 B.C.E.

Persian Empire 550–330 B.C.E.

750   700   650   600   550   500   450   400

ALEXANDER IN BATTLE, fourth century B.C.E. This magnificent marble sarcophagus (burial casket) found in Sidon (present-day Lebanon) shows a victorious Alexander defeating the Persians at the Battle of Issus. Originally painted in brilliant colors, the coffin reveals the tremendous influence of the conquests of Alexander the Great, who brought Greek culture into Asia.

The Poleis Become
Cosmopolitan

The Hellenistic World, 336–150 B.C.E.

3

What's to Come

A Disobedient Daughter

In 220 B.C.E. a young Egyptian girl, named Nice, went to the theater and fell in love with a comic actor named Dionysus. She quit her job to frolic with the charismatic actor, drinking wine and making love without worrying about what family and neighbors thought of her behavior. Her distraught father didn't know what to do with her. They did not live in a small city-state in which everyone knew everyone else's business, and if they didn't like some behavior they could take strong measures, as Athenians had done with Socrates. ▶▶

A hundred years earlier, the world had changed when the brilliant young general, Alexander of Macedon, conquered Persia and introduced a period of time historians have called "Hellenistic" (meaning "Greek-like"). During this time, the ideal Greek poleis changed from scattered, independent city-states into large, multiethnic urban centers—what the Greeks called "world cities," or cosmopolitan sites—firmly anchored within substantial kingdoms. Within these large, anonymous urban centers, who could help a father control his wayward daughter?

The father turned to the king, Ptolemy IV, and wrote him a letter.

According to the father, Nice had promised to get a job and pay him a pension out of her wages every month. Now that Nice had run off neglecting her filial duties, the father had no support in his old age. His letter pleaded, "I beg you O king, not to suffer me to be wronged by my daughter and Dionysus the comedian who has corrupted her."

Sadly, we do not know how this family drama was resolved, but it reveals several interesting points about Mediterranean life in the Hellenistic era, which we will explore in this chapter. It suggests that women worked and earned money instead of staying carefully guarded within the home. It also shows a loosen-

ing of the tight family ties that had marked the Greek poleis and the ancient Middle East civilizations—a father could no longer exert authority over his rebellious daughter and could no longer count on his children to care for him in his old age. Finally, it indicates people's view of their king as the highest authority in redressing personal problems. These were dramatic changes, and to trace their origins, we must look to Macedonia, a province on the northwest border of Greece. There, in a land traditionally ruled by strong monarchs, a king arose who would redefine life in the ancient world. ◄◄

THE CONQUEST OF THE POLEIS

Although Macedonia was inhabited by Greek-speaking people, it had not developed the poleis that marked Greek civilization on the peninsula. Instead, it had retained a tribal structure in which aristocrats selected a king and served in his army bound by ties of loyalty and kinship. The southern Greek poleis—populated by self-described "civilized" Greeks—had disdain for the Macedonians, whom they saw as backward because they did not embrace the political life of the city-states.

The Macedonian territory consisted of two distinct parts: the coastal plain to the south and east, and the mountainous interior. The plain offered fertile land for

Geography

farming and lush pastures in which fine warhorses grazed along with sheep and oxen. The level land of the coastline bordered two bays that afforded access to the Aegean Sea. The Macedonian interior, by contrast, was mountainous and remote and posed the same problems for rulers that the Greek landscape presented. Kings struggled to exert even a little authority over the fierce tribes in the hills. Yet, concealed within the mountains were precious reserves of timber and metals, including abundant veins of gold and silver in the more remote locations.

For centuries, the weak Macedonian kings failed to take full advantage of such treasures, in large part because they could not control the remote tribes. Repeated invasions of Macedonia by its neighbors to the north only

added to the problem. Throughout this turbulent period, the southern Greeks thought of Macedonia only as an area to exploit for its natural resources. The Greeks neither helped nor feared their beleaguered relatives to the north and instead focused on keeping their old enemy, Persia, at bay. Nevertheless, eventually a Macedonian

Uniting the tribes

king arose who not only succeeded in marshaling the resources of his land but also rerouted the direction of Greek history.

This great king, Philip II (r. 359–336 B.C.E.), had participated in some of the many wars that disrupted Greece during the fourth century B.C.E. (see Chapter 2) and, as a result, had been held hostage as a young man in the Greek city-state of Thebes for three years. During his captivity, he learned much about the strengths and weaknesses of Greek politics and warfare. When he returned to Macedonia, he used his new knowledge to educate his people.

Philip II: Military Genius

The pride of the Macedonian army was the cavalry, led by the king himself and made up of his nobles, known as "companions." Yet Philip showed his military genius in the way he reorganized the supporting forces. The shrewd monarch changed the traditional Greek phalanx, already threatened by a new fighting style that favored lightly armed—and therefore more mobile—foot soldiers. Philip strengthened the phalanx by arming his soldiers with pikes 13 feet long or longer instead of the standard 9-foot weapons. Then he instructed the infantry to arrange themselves in a more open formation, which let them take full advantage of the longer pikes. Philip also hired lightly armed, mobile mercenaries who could augment the Macedonian phalanx with arrows, javelins, and slings.

In battle, the long Macedonian pikes kept opponents at a distance, while the cavalry made the decisive difference in almost every battle. The mounted warriors sur-

Military innovations rounded the enemy and struck at their flank, leaving the lightly armed mercenaries to move in to deliver the final blow. This strategy, which combined traditional heavily armed foot soldiers with the mobility of cavalry and light troops, would prove virtually invincible.

Philip also developed weapons for besieging walled cities. During the Peloponnesian War, even mighty Sparta's only strategy against the sturdy walls of Athens had been to starve the inhabitants to death—a slow and uncertain method. Philip is credited with using a torsion catapult that twisted launching ropes to gain more force than the older models that used counterweights could exert. With this new device, his forces could fire rocks at city walls with deadly force. Although Philip is credited with developing these siege weapons, his son would be the one to successfully use them against many fortified cities.

With his forces reorganized and equipped with the latest weapons, Philip readied himself to expand his kingdom. First, he consolidated his own highlands and the lands to the north and east. These conquests allowed him to exploit the gold and silver mines in the hills, which yielded the riches he needed to finance his campaigns. With his northern flank secure and his treasury full, the conqueror then turned his attention to the warring Greek cities to the south.

Philip dreamed of uniting the Greek city-states under his leadership. Some southern Greeks shared this dream, looking to the Macedonian king to save them from their own intercity violence. Isocrates (436–338 B.C.E.), an

Greek responses Athenian orator and educator, made eloquent speeches in which he supported Philip's expansionist aims. Expressing a prevalent disillusionment with democracy, Isocrates argued that the Greeks were incapable of forming a cohesive union without a leader like Philip. In his view, this form of participatory governance had become so corrupt that "violence is regarded as democracy, lawlessness as liberty, impudence of speech as equality." Isocrates believed that only Philip could unify the Greeks and empower them to face Asia as one people finally to vanquish their ancient enemy, Persia.

Isocrates' words were compelling. But Athens had another great orator who opposed Philip and who proved

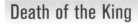

OPINION

What do you think was most important in Macedonia's conquering of the Greek city-states— the weakness of the poleis or the strength of Macedonia?

more convincing than Isocrates. Demosthenes (384–322 B.C.E.) argued brilliantly for a position that rejected union under a tyrant like Philip in order to preserve Athens's traditional freedom and the self-government of the polis. As we saw in Chapter 2, the classic polis had eroded in the aftermath of the Peloponnesian War, but the orator was looking backward to a golden age of democracy. Historians have characterized Demosthenes as everything from a stubborn, old-fashioned orator to the last champion of the lost cause of Athenian freedom. Ultimately, however, the spirited debate about Philip became moot. The question of freedom was answered not in the marketplace of Athens but on the battlefield.

In 338 B.C.E., Philip and his armies marched south toward the peninsula, where they confronted a Greek coalition led by Athens and Thebes, long-time rivals who at last joined in **Greece conquered** cooperation. The belated cooperation among the Greeks came too late. At the Battle of Chaeronea near Thebes, the powerful left wing of Philip's phalanx enveloped the approaching Greeks. The Macedonian cavalry, led by Philip's talented son, Alexander, slaughtered the surrounded Greeks. The victory paved the way for Philip to take control of the Greek city-states (except Sparta).

Philip proved a lenient conqueror; he charged the Greeks no tribute but, instead, united them in a league under his command, so they were technically allies with Macedonia. No longer allowed to wage war against one another, the poleis joined the combined army of Greeks and Macedonians. Isocrates' hope was fulfilled, and the Greeks reluctantly renounced internal warfare. Now they prepared to follow Philip to attack the Persian Empire, which extended far beyond the borders of the Persian homeland into Asia.

Death of the King

Philip's brilliance on the battlefield exceeded his judgment in domestic matters. In the tradition of Macedonian kings, Philip had taken at least six wives. The most important was Olympias, daughter of the king of Epirus (which was southwest of Macedonia and bordered the Greek city-states) and mother of Alexander. According to Plutarch, who drew from earlier sources, Olympias and Alexander were highly insulted when Philip, in his forties, took a young bride, Cleopatra. At the wedding, Cleopatra's uncle made a toast implying that he hoped Philip would disinherit Alexander.

Political and personal resentments came to a head in 336 B.C.E. at the wedding of Alexander's sister, also named

Then & Now

Armor Made of Cloth

Alexander the Great's armies were clad in lightweight armor that was made of layers of linen fastened together with glue made from boiled rabbit bones. This armor—called *linothorax*—was surprisingly effective at deflecting arrows. Modern bullet-resistant vests are also made of fabric—woven nylon-like material stitched and coated with glue-like resin to deflect bullets in exactly the same way as linothorax did.

Cleopatra. On the morning of the wedding, one of the king's companions stepped in and stabbed Philip to death.

Philip murdered Alexander killed anyone who might have been involved, and even killed Philip's wife Cleopatra and their infant child. Alexander was now securely king, and the Mediterranean world would change dramatically.

Alexander's Conquests

The brilliant king was dead, but Philip's son, Alexander, would make an even greater mark on the world than his father had. Alexander (r. 337–323 B.C.E.) was born in 356 B.C.E. and raised by his parents expressly to rule. Philip diligently taught the young boy the arts of Macedonian warfare, including horsemanship, an essential skill for service in the cavalry. Philip and Olympias also encouraged Alexander's intellectual development. They appreciated the accomplishments of the classical Greeks and hired the revered philosopher Aristotle (384–322 B.C.E.) to tutor their promising heir. We cannot know the exact influence of the philosopher on his young student, but Aristotle certainly imparted a love of Greek culture and literature to Alexander. Moreover, he may well have cultivated Alexander's curiosity about the world, which would fuel the young man's later urge to explore. However, Alexander seems to have rejected Aristotle's prejudice against non-Greek "barbarians." Philip's son imagined a world much wider than that of Aristotle's ideal, small city-state.

As soon as Alexander ascended the Macedonian throne, he needed to be recognized as the legitimate king, so he consolidated his rule in the region with a decisive ruthlessness that marked all his subsequent campaigns. For example, when the Greeks revolted after hearing false rumors of Alexander's death, the king promptly marched south, sacked the city of Thebes, and slaughtered or enslaved the inhabitants. With the Greeks subdued, he

Military exploits

then turned to implementing Philip's planned war against the Persian Empire. In 334 B.C.E., Alexander advanced into Asia Minor with a large army of hoplites and cavalry.

After several decisive victories in Asia Minor, Alexander engaged the full power of Persia at the Battle of Issus (see map on page 55), where he matched with Persian forces and Greek mercenaries led by the Persian Great King Darius III. Through skillful deployment and swift action, Alexander's armies defeated a force more than twice as large as their own. Darius fled the battle, leaving his mother, wife, and children. The young king captured Darius's family but treated them with respect and courtesy. In this way, he showed his belief that savagery should be reserved for the battlefield.

Before driving deeper into Asia, Alexander turned south along the Phoenician coast, shrewdly recognizing the problem of the superior Persian fleet, which was reinforced by Phoenician vessels. He captured the great coastal cities of Sidon, Tyre, and finally Gaza, thus rendering the fleet useless without ever engaging it. The brilliant young strategist also perfected the art of siege warfare, improving on Philip's catapults and adding siege towers erected next to the defensive walls that allowed attackers to penetrate the fortresses. As the proud cities fell one by one, Alexander gained a reputation for brutal warfare but generosity to subject peoples. Subsequent cities surrendered quickly and joined the rapidly growing Macedonian Empire.

After conquering Gaza, Alexander swept into Egypt virtually unopposed in 332 B.C.E. The Egyptian priests declared Alexander the incarnation of their god Amon, treating him as pharaoh. Now the god-king of Egypt, the young Macedonian founded a new city, Alexandria, on the Delta. This development brought Egypt more fully into Mediterranean economy and culture than it had ever been before, as the new northern, coastal capital encouraged trade and attracted colonists from elsewhere—a cosmopolitan center was founded in Egypt. With his western flank thus secured, Alexander once again headed for Asia to revive his pursuit of the Persian Great King, Darius.

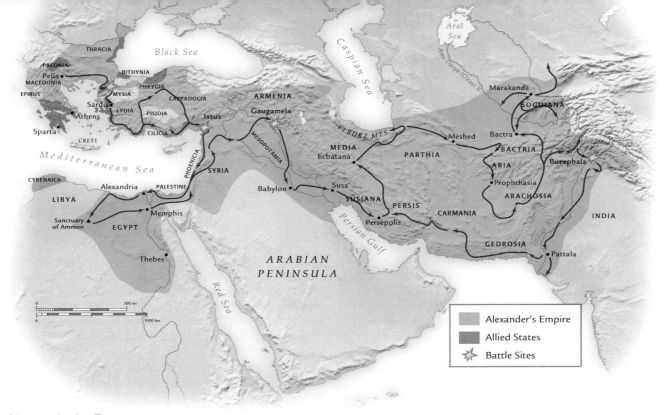

Alexander's Empire

This map shows the vast territory Alexander conquered, the route he took, and the major battle sites.

After crossing the Euphrates and Tigris rivers, Alexander encountered Darius at Gaugamela in 331 B.C.E. The Persian ruler had fitted chariots with sharp scythes to cut down the Macedonian infantry, and his forces far outnumbered Alexander's army—by about 250,000 to 47,000 (although these figures are certainly exaggerated). Despite the Persian strength, Alexander's superior strategy vanquished the Persian warriors yet again. He forced the Persians to turn to confront his wheeling formation and thus opened fatal gaps in the long Persian line. His cavalry set upon the trapped Persian infantry. In the ensuing slaughter, a reputed 50,000 Persians died. Alexander entered Babylon and was welcomed as a liberator. He then turned southeast to Persepolis, the Persian capital. Despite fierce resistance, in 330 B.C.E. Alexander captured the city and plundered it ruthlessly, acquiring enough wealth to fund his future military ambitions. Then he burned it to the ground. Alexander never met Darius on the battlefield again, for the Persian king was assassinated by one of his own guards. After this, no one could doubt that the mighty Persian Empire had a new master—Alexander, who was crowned Great King.

The war against Persia had finally ended, but the young conqueror was still not satisfied. Having studied world geography as documented by the ancient Greeks, Alexander yearned to push his conquests to the edge of the known world. He mistakenly believed that this enticing frontier lay just beyond the Indus River in India. A last

India

major battle against an Indian king eliminated opposition in northern India, and Alexander made plans to press farther into the subcontinent. However, his Macedonian troops had had enough and refused to go on. Alexander wept in his tent for days at the mutiny of his beloved troops, but he finally conceded and turned back. However, instead of returning along the northern route, he led his troops south to explore the barren lands at the edge of the Arabian Sea (see map above). His exhausted, parched army finally reached the prosperous lands of Mesopotamia. Yet their relief was marred by an ironic tragedy: Alexander, seriously weakened by ever-growing alcohol abuse, caught a fever and died in Babylon in 323 B.C.E. He was just 32 years old. Others would have to rule the lands conquered by Alexander the Great.

A Young Ruler's Legacy

The Greek biographer Plutarch (46–119 C.E.) wrote that Alexander had a radical new plan: He claimed that the king "wanted to make all mankind a single people." Was he right? This ideal, which marked a radical departure from traditional Greek attitudes, has provoked intense historical debate virtually from the time of Alexander's life to the present. The Macedonian conqueror implemented several policies that some scholars have interpreted as his desire to rule over a unified rather than a conquered people. One such policy, and certainly the most influential, was his founding of cities. In all his conquered territories, Alexander established an array of new cities. He intended these urban centers in part to recreate the Greek city life that he and his father had so admired. To this end, the conqueror helped settle numerous Greek and Macedonian colonists in the new cities. Hundreds of thousands of Greeks emigrated to the newly claimed lands in Asia, taking privileged positions. We will see that as they introduced their culture into Asia, these colonists inevitably influenced and were changed by the subject peoples. These culturally rich cities rank among Alexander's most enduring legacies.

Meanwhile, in Asia, Alexander strongly supported the intermarriage of Greeks and Macedonians with Asians. He himself married the daughter of Darius and Roxane, the daughter of an Asian tribal king who ruled near modern-day Afghanistan. Alexander also presided over the weddings of hundreds of his generals to highborn Persian women. As Plutarch said, he "joined together the greatest and most powerful peoples into one community by wedlock." Ten thousand more of Alexander's soldiers also married Asian women. Alexander might well have imagined that the offspring of these marriages would help seal the union of the two populations.

Intercultural marriages

Finally, Alexander had a constant need for additional soldiers to support his campaigns, and he obtained these men from the conquered peoples. He accepted both Persian soldiers and commanders into his companies. Preparing for the future, he also chose about 30,000 Asian boys whom he slated to learn the Greek language and the Macedonian fighting style. These boys would become the next generation of soldiers to fight for the king in a combined army.

Alexander's cultural blending disturbed those upper-crust Greeks and Macedonians who saw themselves as conquerors rather than as equals among the subject peoples. Indeed, while in Persia, Alexander adopted Persian robes and courtly ceremonies, including having his subjects prostrate themselves on the ground in his presence. Without a doubt, this ritual helped Persians accept their new king—but it also offended the proud Macedonians. Alexander's inclusion of Asians in the military elite only intensified Macedonian resentment. At one point, an outcry arose among Alexander's soldiers when the king apparently sought to replace some of them with Asians. Alexander squelched these objections decisively, executing 13 leaders and suggesting that the rest of them go home so that he could lead the Asian troops to victory. The Macedonians backed down, pleading for their king's forgiveness. Alexander resolved the

Resentments

> Legends preserve the probably false tale that as Alexander lay dying, he told his comrades that the kingdom should go "to the strongest."

incident with a lavish banquet of reconciliation, at which Asians and Macedonians drank together and Alexander prayed for harmony (sometimes mistranslated as "brotherhood") between them.

Alexander died too soon for historians to be certain of his exact plans for ruling his vast, multi-ethnic empire. For all we know, he might well have intended that Greeks and Macedonians would remain a ruling elite. The cities and colonies guaranteed a continued Greek presence, as did the invaders' weddings to local women. The conqueror's inclusive army might have been simply a practical means of ensuring a large enough force to fulfill his ambitions. Whatever his intentions, Alexander created a fertile combination by joining the cultures of the ancient Middle East and classical Greece.

Alexander's legacy included more than his political conquests—which in some regions hardly outlasted the young king himself. The memory of his accomplishments has endured in an embellished way far beyond even his most impressive victories. For example, Plutarch's interpretation of Alexander's desire for a blending of peoples made this notion a foundational characteristic of Western culture, regardless of whether the king truly held this ideal. Moreover, a highly imaginative version of Alexander's accomplishments, titled *The Alexander Romance,* was translated into twenty-four languages and found its way from Iran to China to Malaysia. The idea of a great empire ruled by one king may have exerted an influence as far as the Han dynasty in China. It certainly shaped Mediterranean thinking, where would-be conquerors reverently visited Alexander's tomb in the spectacular Egyptian city of Alexandria that he founded.

Alexander's memory

THE SUCCESSOR KINGDOMS

323–ca. 100 B.C.E.

Admirers across the world may have romanticized Alexander's supposed dream of a unified kingdom. In reality, however, brutal politics sullied the picture soon after the Great King's death. Legends preserve the probably false tale that as Alexander lay dying, he told his comrades that the kingdom should go "to the strongest." Even if Alexander never said this, the story reflects the reality of the violent fighting that broke out among the Macedonian generals shortly after the king died. Alexander's wife, Roxane, was pregnant when he succumbed, and presumably

The Successor States After the Death of Alexander, ca. 240 B.C.E. **This map shows the breakup of Alexander's empire into three states and illustrates the relative sizes of the successor kingdoms. Based on your analysis of previous maps, as well as the information in the text, what were the historical and geographic reasons for the differing sizes of the successor kingdoms?**

the empire should have gone to his infant son, Alexander IV. But within thirteen years of Alexander's death, both Roxane and her young son had been murdered. Moreover, the Macedonian generals had carved up the great empire into new, smaller kingdoms that became the successors to Alexander's conquests.

Egypt Under the Ptolemies

Upon Alexander's death, one of his cavalry "companions," Ptolemy, moved toward Egypt with his own loyal troops to take control of that wealthy region. Ptolemy diverted the king's corpse, which was being returned to Macedonia for burial, and took it to Alexandria, where he erected an imposing tomb for Alexander. It seems that Ptolemy believed the presence of the conqueror's remains would help legitimize his own rule. Fending off attempts by Alexander's other generals to snatch the rich land of the Nile, Ptolemy and his successors ruled as the god-kings of Egypt for the next three hundred years.

The **Ptolemies** inherited a land with a long tradition of obedience to authority. Accordingly, the new kings wisely struck a bargain with the Egyptian priests, promising to fulfill the traditional duty of the pharaohs to care for the temples (and the priests) in exchange for protection of their legitimacy. Through most of their history, the **Continuity of life** Ptolemies lived in luxury in Alexandria, conducting official business in Greek while Egyptian peasants continued to obey the age-old dictates of the Nile, the priests, and the tax collectors. Life away from the court under the new order changed very little, which made it easier for the new dynasty to rule. The parallel practicing of both Egyptian and Greek ways continued throughout most of the Ptolemaic rule. In fact, the majority of these Greek kings rarely carried out traditional ritual functions, and some were probably not even formally crowned. For their part, the priests honored the Ptolemies while still governing in the traditional way.

However, in one significant way the Hellenistic rulers departed from their Egyptian predecessors—their queens took a more prominent role. Many of the Ptolemaic rulers engaged in brother-sister marriages as the ancient Egyptians had **Hellenistic queens** done, but many women were able to exert considerable power. Hellenistic queens derived much of their authority from controlling substantial wealth and spending it on public works (and on hiring large armies). The height of the Hellenistic queens of Egypt came with the last one—Cleopatra VII—who challenged the growing power of Rome (discussed in Chapter 4).

Under the Ptolemies, the port city of Alexandria became the premier city of the Hellenistic world. It was a dynamic cosmopolitan city that by the end of the first century B.C.E. boasted almost one million inhabitants. Alexandria was a bustling port city where the main enterprise was the pursuit of wealth. The harbors were busy and the markets thronging, and international banks grew up to serve the people. To make sure ships could enter the port safely, Hellenistic scientists built a huge lighthouse on an island (Pharos) outside the harbor. The structure was 440 feet high, and the light from the lantern at the top was intensified by a system of reflectors. Ships approaching the harbor were guided by the beam of the lantern. This lighthouse came to be regarded as one of the seven wonders of the ancient world.

For all its commercial value, Alexandria under the Ptolemies also became an intellectual and cultural center. The rulers established a world-famous museum (the word *museum* means "temple to the muses," the Greek goddesses who served as inspiration to creativity). At the museum, scholars from around the Mediterranean and Asia gathered to study texts and discuss ideas. The Greek rulers founded a great library as part of this museum and ambitiously designed it to stand as the West's first complete collection of published works. Well established by 280 B.C.E., the library boasted more than 700,000 volumes just one century later, making it the largest collection the ancient world had seen.

Eventually, however, the Ptolemies encountered both internal and external pressure to change. Under the reign of Ptolemy V (r. ca. 205–ca. 183 B.C.E.), a boy not yet in his teens, priests began demanding that the young king be more involved in religious rituals. The boy-king's problems only worsened when sub-Saharan Nubians, detecting his weakness, clamored for their own pharaoh. In addition, the armies of Alexander's successor in Asia were threatening Egypt's borders. Pressured on all sides, Ptolemy offered concessions to the powerful priests in return for their support in rallying the Egyptians to his cause. The young ruler reduced taxes on the peasants and increased payments to the priests. In return for his cooperation, the priests brought Ptolemy to Memphis, the traditional capital of the pharaohs, where they placed the great double crown of Egypt—the sign of royalty—on his head. Finally, they ordered that Ptolemy V be worshiped in every Egyptian shrine. To make good on this policy, they demanded that scribes write all the accomplishments of Ptolemy V "on a slab of hard stone, in the writing of the words of god, the writing of documents and the letters of the Northerners, and set it up in all the temples."

The **Rosetta Stone** (see page 59), the tablet that resulted from this decree, was unearthed in 1799. Demonstrating the presence of both Greeks and Egyptians in the kingdom of the Ptolemies, the stone records Ptolemy's deeds in three written versions: the sacred hieroglyphics at the top, Egyptian cursive administrative script at the center, and Greek ("the letters of the Northerners") at the bottom. The Rosetta Stone provided the key that finally let nineteenth-century scholars decipher hieroglyphic writing. Without the stone, the meaning embedded in the great carvings of the ancient Egyptians might still remain a mystery.

Rosetta Stone

The Seleucids Rule Asia

In the violent political jockeying that broke out after the death of Alexander, one of Ptolemy's lieutenants, Seleucus, entered Babylon in 311 B.C.E. and captured the imperial treasure there. With this money, Seleucus laid claim to the old heartland of the Persian Empire. Yet the extensive eastern lands that Alexander had conquered eluded his grasp. As early as 310 B.C.E., Seleucus gave northwest India back to its native rulers in return for five hundred war elephants, and by the third century B.C.E., eastern Asia Minor had fallen away. Nevertheless, Seleucus founded a long-standing kingdom that continued the Hellenizing process begun by Alexander.

Like Alexander, the **Seleucids** founded cities and populated them with imported Greek and Macedonian bureaucrats and colonists. Seleucia, about 50 miles north of Babylon, was established as the new capital of the kingdom, and Dura Europus, near the midpoint of the Euphrates River, was another important center. Their locations reveal that the Seleucid kings recognized the crucial role of eastern trade in the prosperity of their kingdom. These cities controlled the trade routes through the Tigris-Euphrates valley and the caravan trails that crossed the desert from Damascus and, along with Antioch, became vital political and economic centers within the former Persian lands (see map on page 57).

Commercial cities

While the Ptolemies could depend on an established Egyptian priesthood to facilitate their control of their kingdom, the Seleucids had no such ready-made institution. Instead, they relied in part on Macedonian and Greek colonists to secure their hold on their Asian lands. After Alexander's death, the Seleucids settled at least 20,000 Macedonian colonists in Syria and Asia Minor. This number was supplemented by others from Macedonia who came looking for riches and privileges.

Seleucid colonists

Although Greek sovereignty faded quickly in the easternmost edges of the Seleucid lands, evidence remains of the impact of the Greek presence there. To illustrate, con-

Alexandria

ROSETTA STONE, 197 B.C.E. Greek-speaking Macedonian rulers had to communicate with Egyptians. Fortunately, the Macedonians wrote an edict in Greek and translated it into two Egyptian scripts on this famous stone. This translation provided the key to scholars' ability to read Egyptian hieroglyphs.

sider the famous king of northern India Aśoka (r. ca. 268–ca. 233 B.C.E.). Aśoka is perhaps most remembered for spreading the ideals of Buddhism through inscriptions on stones. Like the Rosetta Stone, these Rock Edicts testify to the Hellenic presence in India, because Aśoka's sayings were preserved both in the Indian language of Prakrit and in Greek. In wise phrases such as "Let them neither praise themselves nor disparage their neighbors, for that is vain," the ideas of Buddhism met the language of Hellenism in the farthest lands of Alexander.

Antigonids in Greece

The Seleucid kings concentrated on ruling the western portions of their Asian provinces, ever watchful for opportunities to gain advantage over the Ptolemies or the Macedonian leaders who now ruled in Macedonia and Greece. These kings, known as the **Antigonids,** were descended from Antigonus the One-Eyed (382–ca. 301 B.C.E.), a general who had joined in the struggle for succession after Alexander's death. Antigonus failed to score a decisive military victory, however, and died on the battlefield at the venerable age of 80, still trying to win control of the entire Macedonian Empire. Nevertheless, his descendants eventually took power in Macedonia and Greece and introduced the Antigonid dynasty.

In the short run, Alexander's conquests profoundly affected Macedonian society and economy. At first, wealth poured from the east into the young king's homeland. Indeed, near the end of his life, Alexander sent home one shipment of booty that proved so large that 110 **Life in Macedonia** warships were needed to escort the merchant vessels on their return journey. Numismatic evidence also confirms the volume of wealth that initially flowed into Macedonia, for its mint churned out about 13 million silver coins immediately after Alexander's reign. Much of this coinage came into wide circulation, for officials used it to pay troops and provide stipends for veterans' widows and orphans. Yet the money did not profoundly alter Macedonian society. By the reign of Antigonus's great-grandson, Demetrius II (r. 239–229 B.C.E.), life in Macedonia had changed little from even as far back as Philip II's time. The army still consisted mainly of Macedonian nobles, who fought as companions to their king. Invaders from the north still threatened; indeed, in the 280s B.C.E. the Gauls, a tribe on the Macedonians' northern border, launched an attack that cost Macedonia dearly. To make matters worse, the Greeks to the south, who had never really accepted Macedonian rule, kept revolting.

The Greek city-states experienced more change than Macedonia did, for the traditional democracy of Athens and the other poleis had evaporated. The poleis relaxed their notions of citizenship, so many immigrants and freed slaves became **Changes in Greece** citizens, but at the same time people had less attachment to their cities. Many jobs—from soldier to athlete—became the province of specialists, not citizens, and thus international professionals replaced the native competitors who brought glory and wealth to their cities. Furthermore, the new economy of the Hellenistic world widened the gulf between rich and poor, and the disparity undermined participatory government: Rich Greeks took over governance and frequently forgot that they had any responsibility to the poor.

Despite these tensions, outright revolution never materialized. The relentless warfare plaguing the poleis simply proved too distracting. In addition, Greeks from all walks of life continued emigrating to the other Hellenistic kingdoms in search of a better life, and this exodus helped ease population pressures at home. Bureaucrats and scientists headed for the Greek colonies to take advantage of the tempting opportunities there—for example, a talented mathematician, Apollonius, first worked in Alexandria, Egypt, and then was lured to the Seleucid kingdom in the east. The poleis, which in the old days had claimed people's loyalty, had given way to cosmopolitan cities. Now individuals sought to enhance their own fortunes in a wider world.

EAST MEETS WEST IN THE SUCCESSOR KINGDOMS

The vast breadth of the Hellenistic kingdoms stimulated the West's economy to new heights. Trade rhythms quickened, and merchants raked in unprecedented wealth. Under Alexander and his successors in the various kingdoms, Greek became the universal language of business. Now traders could exchange goods across large distances without confronting confusing language barriers. The Greeks also advanced credit, a business practice that let merchants ply their trade without having to transport unwieldy quantities of hard currency.

Money in the New Cosmopolitan Economies

The Hellenistic kings standardized currency as well, another boon for trade. These standards helped merchants buy and sell with ease throughout the extensive region. The coins in the photograph below show that the Hellenistic kingdoms had much in common. Both coins show the **Coinage and trade** monarchs in the style of Macedonian rulers, wearing the simple diadem that since Philip II's time had marked Macedonian kingship, and both are based on the standard weight called the drachma. They also graphically represent both the wealth that the Macedonian conquests generated and the spread of Greek cultural influence throughout the region as trade intensified.

Goods moved briskly through the Hellenistic kingdoms, reshaping old patterns of trade and consumption. Athens initially benefited from the widespread demand for Greek goods like pottery and weapons, but a century after the death of Alexander, Alexandria had replaced Athens as the commercial capital of the eastern Mediterranean. The small islands of Rhodes and Delos also rose to prominence because of their advantageous locations along the routes that connected the north and southeast areas of the Mediterranean with Greece and Italy.

Heightened trade led to new approaches to agriculture as people rushed to develop and sell novel delicacies. As one example, Greek farmers began planting their precious olive trees and grapevines in the eastern kingdoms, permanently altering the ecosystems in those regions. In turn, eastern spices transformed cooking on the Greek mainland and in Egypt. Agricultural crossbreeding also became common, though it failed in some cases—even seeds imported from Rhodes to cross with Egypt's bitter cabbage could not sweeten that pungent vegetable of the Nile valley.

While commerce made countless merchants rich, the individual kingdoms also benefited—mainly by taking control of economic activity. In Egypt, where pharaohs traditionally controlled much trade and industry—a system called a command economy— the Ptolemies increased their controls to funnel the riches of the Nile **Command economies** valley into the royal treasury. They converted the most successful industries into royal monopolies, controlling such essentials as sesame oil, salt, perfumes, and incense. Their most successful venture, however, was the beer industry, which had been a royal monopoly since the Old Kingdom. The Ptolemies insisted that the millions of gallons of beer consumed each year in Egypt be manufactured in the royal breweries, though many women doubtless continued to brew the beverage for household consumption as they had always done.

Kings also levied taxes on imports and exports, such as grain, papyrus, cosmetics, timber, metals, and horses. These policies required a complex administrative system, which in turn led to the proliferation of Greek-speaking bureaucrats. Equally important, the kings used their new riches not only to live lavishly, but also to fund the expensive wars that ravaged the Hellenistic world.

(a) (a) (b) (b)

HELLENISTIC COINS Standardized currency facilitated trade among all the Hellenistic kingdoms and serves as fine historical evidence. Coin (a) is an eight-drachma coin of Ptolemy II of Egypt (r. ca. 284–ca. 247 B.C.E.). Coin (b) is a silver coin of King Orophernes (2nd century B.C.E.) from Cappadocia in the Seleucid kingdom.

Armies of the Hellenistic World

The Macedonian kings thought of themselves as conquerors and derived their legitimacy in large part from their military successes. Like Alexander, whom they strove to emulate, these monarchs fully expected to participate in the hardships of battle and the dangers of combat. Consequently, they regularly made war on one another in hopes of gaining land or power. The ideal of conquest thus persisted after Alexander's death. However, the scale of warfare had broadened.

This broadening occurred partly because of the larger territories in dispute. Some boundaries now far surpassed the dimensions of the earlier Greek poleis. To cover these daunting distances, monarchs accumulated vast armies. Philip had conquered Greece with a force of about 30,000 men, and Alexander had increased the numbers significantly as he moved east. Alexander's force in India may have exceeded 100,000—exceptional for ancient armies. The Hellenistic kings, however, regularly fielded armies of between 60,000 and 80,000 troops. These large armies consisted no longer primarily of citizen-soldiers but of mercenaries—who were loyal only to their paymaster and who switched sides with impunity. Tellingly, Hellenistic theater often featured mercenary soldiers who returned home with lots of money to spend and a newly cynical outlook.

Mercenary armies

The Macedonian armies were also influenced by their contact with the far eastern provinces. For example, in these distant lands they encountered war elephants for the first time. Just as horses had offered mounted warriors advantages of mobility and reach over foot soldiers, soldiers mounted on elephants had an even greater military advantage. Furthermore, elephants participated in the fray, trampling men and using their trunks as weapons. The Seleucids tried to breed elephants in Syria but had to keep trading with India for more elephants when their efforts failed. To retain their advantage, the Seleucid kings cut off the Ptolemies' trade in Asian elephants, forcing the Egyptians to rely on the smaller, less effective African breed. The Greek historian Polybius (ca. 200–ca. 118 B.C.E.) described a confrontation between the two classes of pachyderms: The African elephants, "unable to stand the smell and trumpeting of the Indian elephants and terrified, I suppose, also by their great size and strength, . . . at once turn tail and take to flight." As impressive as the Asian elephants were, foot soldiers learned to dodge the beasts and stab or hamstring them.

War elephants

OPINION

What do you think were the greatest advantages and disadvantages of the changes to women's opportunities under the Hellenistic monarchies?

However, the massive animals remained a valuable tool for moving heavy siege engines to walled cities and attacking fortified positions.

Large, wealthy, and well-equipped armies now routinely toppled defensive walls, and kings followed Alexander's ruthless model of wiping out any city that showed even a hint of defiance. Mercenaries, too, cared little for civilians, and historical sources describe soldiers drunkenly looting private homes after a conquest. The countryside also suffered from the warfare, and peasants repeatedly petitioned kings to ease their burdens. Peasants faced increased taxes levied to fund expensive wars and then frequently confronted violence from marauding mercenaries. To an unprecedented level, civilians became casualties in wars waged between kings.

The incessant warfare also changed the nature of slavery in the Greek world. As we have seen, during the classical Greek period—as throughout the ancient world—slavery was taken for granted. Every household had one or two domestic slaves, and most manufacturing and other labor was done by slaves. Alexander's immediate successors generally avoided mass enslavement of prisoners, but traditionally it was customary to enslave losers in battle. Therefore, by the late third century B.C.E., prisoners began to be enslaved in huge numbers. This changed the scale of the institution of slavery and, ultimately, the treatment of the slaves themselves. By 167 B.C.E., the island of Delos in the Aegean Sea housed a huge slave market. Claiming that 10,000 slaves could arrive and be sold in a day on Delos, the Greek historian Strabo quoted a contemporary saying about the slave markets that suggested how quickly the slave-traders sold their human cargo: "Merchant, put in, unload—all's sold." Although these large numbers are surely an exaggeration, they testify to the huge increase in numbers of slaves that began to be moved around the eastern Mediterranean. Wealthy households now could have hundreds of slaves, and others worked in gangs in agriculture and mining. This new scale of slavery further dehumanized those who had been taken, and slaves joined civilians as a population suffering under the new kingdoms.

Slavery

A True Cultural Blending?

Whether or not Alexander had envisioned a complete uniting of east and west, in reality a full blending of peoples never occurred in the lands he conquered. The Hellenistic kingdoms in Egypt and Asia consisted of local native populations ruled by a Greek/Macedonian elite who made up less than 10 percent of the population. However, this elite was not limited to people of direct Macedonian descent; it also included those who acquired Greek language and culture through formal or informal education. Alexander's conquests opened opportunities for people from many ethnic backgrounds to join the elite—a development that inevitably transfigured Greek culture itself.

The intermingling of East and West intensified with the movement of travelers, which the common use of the Greek language and the size of the kingdoms facilitated. Travel-

Travelers ers included merchants and mercenaries and diplomats seeking political and economic advantages or opportunities to spy. Perhaps most instrumental in blending cultures were the artists and artisans who journeyed widely in search of patrons and prizes.

In this new, cosmopolitan world, even women traveled with a freedom unheard of in the classical Greek poleis. Female musicians, writers, and artists embarked on quests for honors and literary awards. One inscription on a commemorative stone recalls "Aristodama, daughter of Amyntas of Smyrna, an epic poetess, who came to the city and gave several readings of her own poems." The citizens were so pleased with this poet's work that they granted her citizenship. During such readings, authors shared experiences from one part of the world with the people of another, enhancing the diversity that marked this vibrant time.

Such diversity showed up vividly in the art of the period. For example, classical Greek artists had sometimes depicted black Africans in their works. In the Hellenistic age such portrayals grew more frequent. The sculpture of the African musician exemplifies the cultural blending that occurred in the visual arts of this period.

All travelers left some evidence of their visits in the farthest reaches of the Hellenistic world. In the third century B.C.E., for example, the Greek philosopher Clearchus discovered a Greek-style city, complete with a gymnasium at the center, on the northern frontier of modern Afghanistan. In the gymnasium, Clearchus erected a column inscribed with 140 moral maxims taken from a similar pillar near the shrine of Apollo at Delphi. Like the Rock Edicts of Aśoka, the pillar of Clearchus preserves in stone the mingling of ideas at the fringes of the Hellenistic world.

AFRICAN MUSICIAN, second century B.C.E. The Hellenistic kingdoms were characterized by a movement of peoples and a resulting cultural blending, exemplified by this African musician playing a Greek musical instrument.

Struggles and Successes: Life in the Cosmopolitan Cities

The new cities founded by Alexander and his successors were in many ways artificial structures—they did not grow up in response to local manufacturing or commercial needs. Instead, they were simply created by rulers as showcases of their wealth and power. Expensive to maintain, these cities burdened local peasants with extra taxes and produced little wealth of their own. However, they played a crucial role as cultural and administrative centers, and they became a distinctive feature of Hellenistic life. Modeled on the Greek city-states, these cities still differed markedly from the poleis in several important ways, including the opportunities for women.

The travelers and the diversity of the cities helped loosen the restrictions of family life and female seclusion that had marked traditional Greek cities. Women were more free to move about in public than in earlier times. Furthermore, many texts indicate that Hellenistic women had more indepen- **Women** dence of action than their Greek counterparts. For example, a marriage contract explicitly insists that a couple will make joint decisions: "We shall live together in whatever place seems best to Leptines and Heraclides, deciding together." These new opportunities for independence made possible the situation at the opening of this chapter, when the young working woman ran off with her lover.

The Hellenistic cities also differed from their Greek counterparts in that they owed allegiance to larger political entities, the kingdoms. Now Greek monarchies had replaced Greek city-states as the influential political form in the developing history of the West. The relationship between the Hellenistic kings and the new cities derived from both Macedonian and Greek traditions. For example, during and **Cities and kings** after Alexander's reign, monarchs advocated democracy within the cities they founded. Cities were governed by magistrates and councils, and popular assemblies handled internal affairs. In return, the kings demanded tribute and special taxes during times of war. However, these taxes were not onerous, and a king might even exempt a city from taxation. In response, many cities introduced a civic religious cult honoring their kings. As one example, to show this dual allegiance to both their king and city, citizens of the city of Cos had to swear the following oath: "I will abide by the established democracy . . . and the ancestral laws of Cos, . . . and I will also abide by the friendship and alliance with King Ptolemy."

These cities flourished under the patronage of their kings, but they also struggled with all the problems endemic in any urban area. To feed the towns-

Urban problems

people, city officials often had to import supplies from distant sources. Following Hellenistic ideas of a command economy, these urban leaders set grain prices and sometimes subsidized food to keep the costs manageable. They also regulated millers and bakers to prevent them from making large profits from cheap grain. Finally, the cities suffered the unavoidable problems of what to do about sewerage and water drainage; the largest urban centers had drainpipes under the streets for these purposes. Gangs of slaves owned by the city maintained the drainage system and cleared the streets.

City leaders gave little attention to public safety. They hired a few night watchmen to guard some public spaces, but for the most part, they considered safety a personal matter. Consequently, people mingling in the crowded markets or venturing out at night were often victims of robberies, or worse. Danger lurked everywhere, but especially in the many fires that broke out from residents' use of open flames to cook and heat their wooden homes. Despite the perils of fire, crime, and lack of sanitation, however, cities still offered the best hope of success for enterprising people.

The greatest of the new cities—Alexandria, Antioch, Seleucia—drew people from around the world. No longer connected to the original Greek city-states, such newcomers felt little obligation to participate in democratic politics or to profess loyalty to a clan or polis. Greeks, Phoenicians, Jews, Babylonians, Arabs, and others gathered in the cosmopolitan centers to make their fortunes. As the most ambitious among them took Greek names, the old divisions between Greek and "barbarian" blurred. Traditional family ties dissolved, too, as we saw in the story that opened this chapter.

City dwellers improved their lot in several ways, some of them advancing through successful military activities. The Greek Scopas, for example, unable to find work in his

New opportunities

home city, "turned his hopes toward Alexandria," where he got a job in the army. Within three years, Scopas had risen to command the armies of Ptolemy V. Women, too, had opportunities to participate in the public sphere. The document to the right offers examples of women who were remembered for their contributions to their cities.

Though cities opened up new opportunities, they also spawned miseries. Many poor people were forced to continue working well into their old age; the father in the chapter's opening story looked to his king to spare him an impoverished old age. His pleas probably went unheard, however; cities and their royal patrons tended to ignore the

Cities Celebrate Professional Women

Throughout the Hellenistic age, there is evidence of women whose public service brought them to the attention of their communities. The following inscriptions commemorate women who served as a physician and a public official.

1. Physician and Midwife: Phanostrate of Athens, fourth century [B.C.E.] Funeral inscription

Phanostrate. . . , the wife of Melitos, midwife and doctor, lies here. In life she caused no one pain, in death she is regretted by all.

2. Public Servant: Phile of Priene, first century [B.C.E.] Public inscription

Phile daughter of Apollonius and wife of Thessalus, the son of Polydectes, having held the office of stephanephoros [city magistrate], the first woman [to do so], constructed at her own expense the reservoir for water and the city aqueduct.

What aspects of Hellenistic cities allow women to become prominent?

mounting problems of poverty. Slums cropped up, becoming just as characteristic of Hellenistic cities as the palaces of the wealthy and the libraries of the wise.

In some cities, destitute people designed institutions to help themselves. Artisans' guilds, for example, offered a sense of social connection to people bewildered by the large, anonymous cosmopolitan cities. Some people organized burial clubs, in which members contributed money to ensure themselves a decent interment at the end of lives that had little material security. Historical evidence suggests that some rich city dwellers worried about the possibility of social revolution. As one illustration of this fear, the citizens of a city in Crete were required to include the following statement in their oath of citizenship: "I will not initiate a redistribution of land or of houses or a cancellation of debts."

Patronage, Planning, and Passion: Hellenistic Art

The monarchs who were becoming fabulously wealthy did not spend much money on the urban poor. What did they do with the mounds of coins that filled their coffers? In part, they spent fortunes as patrons of the arts, commissioning magnificent pieces that continue to be treasured today. However, not all critics have admired the products of the Hellenistic artists. For example, early in the first century C.E., the prolific Roman commentator Pliny the Elder (23–79 C.E.) energetically discussed Greek art. A passionate admirer of classical Athenian art, Pliny claimed that after the accomplishments of Lysippus (ca. 380–ca. 318 B.C.E.), "art stopped." His dismissal of the Hellenistic world's artistic contributions has since been shared by many observers who admire the idealized poses of classical Greek works. But art did not stop with Lysippus; it merely changed as its center migrated from Athens to the great cosmopolitan centers of the East.

Classical Greek artists had been supported by public funding by democratic poleis. By contrast, Hellenistic artists received their funding from wealthy kings seeking to build and decorate their new cities. **Royal patrons** Royal patronage began with monarchs who wanted their newly established cities to reflect the highest ideals of Greek aesthetics. At the same time, this policy served the political agenda of promoting Greek culture. These rulers hired architects to design cities conducive to traditional Greek life, with its outdoor markets and meeting places, and employed artists to decorate the public spaces. Pergamum posed a special challenge to architects: Its center was perched on a high hill, so city planners had to take the steep slopes into account in designing the city. In the end, they arranged the royal palaces at the top of the hill—visibly proclaiming the king's ascendancy—and the markets at the bottom. The layout of this magnificent city is typical of many Hellenistic urban centers.

After cities were designed, kings commissioned sculptors to decorate the great public buildings, especially temples. Throughout **Sculpture**

RESTORED MODEL OF PERGAMUM Hellenistic rulers built great new cities such as Pergamum in what today is the country of Turkey. The city spread over a high hill, from the royal palace at the top to markets at the bottom and a theater at the left.

the Hellenistic period, sculptors also found a market in the newly wealthy, who hired these artists to create works of beauty to decorate their homes. Hellenistic sculpture built on classical models in the skill with which artists depicted the human form and in the themes that harked back to the age of Greek heroes and the Trojan War. Still, Hellenistic artists departed from the classical style in significant ways. Classical Greek sculptors sought to portray the ideal—that is, they depicted scenes and subjects that were above the tumult and passion of this world. By contrast, Hellenistic artists faced passion and emotion head-on. Their works exhibit a striking expressiveness, violence, and sense of movement, along with contorted poses that demonstrate these artists' talents for capturing human emotion in marble.

Laocoön and His Two Sons

25 B.C.E.

This marble sculpture is a first-century C.E. copy of a Hellenistic statue showing a moment from the Trojan War when Laocoön tried to warn the Trojans to ignore the horse statue that was filled with hidden Greek soldiers. Athena, who favored the Greeks, sent serpents from the sea to kill the informers, leading to the fall of Troy. Notice the artists' style—the emotions expressed, and the tension shown by the twisted figures—and discuss what you think the sculpture reveals about the aesthetic values of the Hellenistic societies. What do you like or dislike about the work, and what do your reactions say about modern artistic values?

Resistance to Hellenism: Judaism

323–76 B.C.E.

Much of Hellenistic art and life in the cosmopolitan cities reflected a deep and, in many ways, successful blending of classical Greek culture with that of the ancient Middle East and Egypt. Yet Alexander's desire to make "all mankind a single people" did not appeal to everyone in the Hellenistic world. Throughout their history, Jews had worked to preserve their distinctive identity, and this desire came directly into conflict with spreading Hellenism (ancient Greek culture). Although Judea remained an independent political unit under Alexander and the Ptolemies, the successor kingdoms offered opportunities for Jews from Palestine to trade and settle throughout the Hellenistic world. In the new multiethnic areas, urban Jews struggled to clarify and sustain their sense of identity. The most pious among them lived together in Jewish quarters where they could observe the old laws and maintain a sense of separate community. Alexandria and Antioch had substantial Jewish quarters, and most large cities had a strong Jewish presence.

Some Jews compromised with Hellenism, learning Greek and taking advantage of the opportunities available to those who at least had the appearance of Hellenism. As they learned to speak and write in Greek and studied the classical texts, some of their traditional beliefs changed, especially where they sought to reconcile Judaism with Hellenism. Sometime in the third century B.C.E., the Hebrew Scriptures were translated into Greek, in the

Hellenized Jews

influential document known as the **Septuagint.** (The name derives from the Latin word for "seventy," recalling the legendary group of 72 translators who were credited with the accomplishment.) In great cities like Alexandria, Jews gathered in synagogues to pray in a traditional fashion, but in many of these centers of worship, the Scriptures were read in Greek.

In Palestine, too, Jews and Gentiles, or non-Jews, met and mingled. Palestine had many Greek settlements, and even in Jerusalem Jews faced the question of what it meant for them to compromise with Hellenism. Jesus Ben Sirach, a Jewish scribe and teacher in Jerusalem, wrote a text called *Ecclesiasticus* (ca. 180 B.C.E.) in which he scolded believers who had turned away from the traditional Jewish Law of Moses and warned them that God would exact vengeance for their impiety. In an ironic twist, his text was translated into Greek by his grandson.

These uncertainties within the Jewish community came to a head when the Seleucid kings wrested Palestine from the Ptolemies in 200 B.C.E. The pace of Hellenization quickened after this pivotal event. Both Jewish and pagan historical sources claim that the Seleucid king Antiochus IV (r. 175–163 B.C.E.) intended to change Jewish observance in order to "combine the peoples"—that is, to Hellenize the Jews. According to an early Jewish text, even the high priest of Jerusalem supported the king and "exercised his influence in order to bring over his fellow-countrymen to the Greek ways of life." Antiochus established Greek schools in Jerusalem and went so far as to enter Jewish contestants in the Greek-style athletic games celebrated at Tyre. In 168 B.C.E., he ordered an altar to Zeus to be erected in the Temple of Jerusalem and sacrifices to be offered to the Greek god. The Roman historian Josephus (75 C.E.) later described the sacrilege: "He sacrificed swine upon the altars and bespattered the temple with their grease, thus perverting the rites of the Jews and the piety of their fathers."

Antiochus's policies proved too much for pious Jews, and in ca. 166 B.C.E., Judas Maccabeus (Judas the Hammer) led an armed revolt against the Seleucids. (See Exploring the Past on page 67.) The account of the **Maccabean Revolt** is preserved in a text titled *The First Book of the Maccabees,* probably written in 140 B.C.E. by a Jew in Judea. The author articulated the goal of Antiochus clearly: "Then the king wrote to his whole kingdom that all should be one people, and that each should give up his

Maccabean Revolt

→ **connect to today** ←

Evolving Global Cities

Throughout the Hellenistic kingdoms, people wrestled with the question of how to preserve their identity while adapting to a cosmopolitan world that blends many cultures. How do we in America confront constantly evolving culture brought by immigrants and travelers in an increasingly global world?

customs." This decree of Antiochus confirms the differing, intensely felt opinions that people often have about cultural blending.

In the end, the Maccabeans prevailed. In 164 B.C.E. the Jewish priests rededicated the Temple, and the Jews celebrated the restoration of their separate identity. The historian of *First Maccabees* wrote that "Judas and his brothers and all the assembly of Israel determined that every year at that season the days of the dedication of the altar should be observed with gladness and joy for eight days." This declaration instituted the feast of Hanukkah, which Jews continue to celebrate today.

The Maccabean revolutionaries established a new theocratic state of Judea, which the Seleucids were too busy with war on their eastern borders to challenge. The reinvigorated Jewish state continued its conquests of neighboring states, including Greek cities in Galilee, and by 76 B.C.E. the Jews had established a kingdom almost as extensive as that of Solomon (r. 970–931 B.C.E.) (see Chapter 1). Though they had revolted to preserve their cultural and religious purity, the new rulers proved intolerant of their Gentile subjects, forcing many to convert and insisting that non-Jewish infant boys be circumcised. These practices worsened the instability already plaguing the region.

Independent Judea

THE SEARCH FOR TRUTH: Hellenistic Thought, Religion, and Science

Hellenistic rulers from Alexander on consciously spread Greek ideas and learning. To do this, they vigorously supported education, which they saw as key to the preservation of Greek ideals and the training ground for new Hellenized civil servants. Within these educated circles occurred most of the intellectual and cultural blending that created the brilliance of Hellenistic art as well as the struggles of cultural identity. However, these communities of the educated also proved a fertile ground for intellectual inquiry in which great minds eagerly sought truth about the world, religion, and the meaning of life.

A Life of Learning

Great speculations, however, began first in the schoolrooms. Families who wanted their boys to succeed invested heavily in education. At the age of 7, boys attended privately funded schools and practiced Greek and writing. The parchment samples of their assignments reveal a strong anti-"barbarian" prejudice in which the culture of all non-Greeks was dismissed. Thus, even early schooling aimed to inculcate Greek values among non-Greek peoples. This indoctrination was reinforced by an emphasis on Homer's works as the primary literary texts.

At 14, boys expanded their education to include literary exercises, geography, and advanced studies of Homer. Successful students then continued their studies in the gymnasium, the heart of Hellenistic education and culture. Most cities boasted splendid gymnasia as their central educational institutions. Often the most beautiful building in the city, the gymnasium sported a running track, an area for discus and javelin throwing, a wrestling pit, and baths, lecture halls, and libraries. Here, Greek-speaking boys of all ethnic backgrounds gathered, exercised naked, and finished an education that allowed them to enter the Greek ruling class.

Hellenistic kings cultivated education just as they served as patrons of the arts. They competed fiercely to hire sought-after tutors for their families and schools and to purchase texts for their libraries. The best texts were copied by hand on Egyptian papyrus or carefully prepared animal hide called parchment. (The word *parchment* derives from *Pergamena charta*, or "Pergamum paper," which refers to where the best-quality parchment was made.) Texts were prepared in scrolls rather than bound in books and were designed to be unrolled and read aloud.

This advocacy of education yielded diverse results. Many scholars produced nothing more than rather shallow literary criticism; others created literature that captured the superficial values of much of Hellenistic life; and some created highly sophisticated philosophy and science. The range of these works, however, contributed important threads to the tapestry of Western civilization.

Theater and Literature

The tragedies and comedies of classical Greek theater had illuminated profound public and heroic themes ranging from fate and responsibility to politics and ethics. Theater proved extremely popular in the Hellenistic cities as well. Though some cosmopolitan playwrights wrote tragedies, few of these works have survived. We do have many comedies from this era, which contrast so starkly with the classic Greek examples of this genre that this body of work is called New Comedy. Hellenistic plays were almost devoid of political satire and focused instead on the plights of individuals.

Judas Maccabeus Liberates Jerusalem

In the first century C.E., the Jewish historian Josephus wrote a history of the Jews in which he described the revolt of Judas Maccabeus against the Hellenistic king Antiochus in ca. 166 B.C.E.

And [the Jews] avoided to defend themselves on that day because they were not willing to break in upon the honor they owed the Sabbath, even in such distresses; for our law requires that we rest upon that day.

There were about a thousand, with their wives and children, who were smothered and died in these caves; but many of those that escaped joined themselves to Mattathias and appointed him to be their ruler, who taught them to fight even on the Sabbath day, and told them that unless they would do so they would become their own enemies by observing the law [so rigorously] while their adversaries would still assault them on this day, and they would not then defend themselves; and that nothing could then hinder but they must all perish without fighting. This speech persuaded them, and this rule continues among us to this day, that if there be a necessity we may fight on Sabbath days.

How did this conflict resemble modern controversies regarding fighting during Ramadan or Christmas?

The best-known playwright of New Comedy is Menander (ca. 342–ca. 292 B.C.E.), whose works often centered on young men who fell in love with women who were unattainable for some reason.

New comedies Most of these plots ended happily with the couples overcoming all obstacles. In general, New Comedy characters were pre-occupied with making money or indulging themselves in other ways. This focus on individual concerns reflected the realities of cosmopolitan life—ruled by powerful and distant kings, individuals had limited personal power. Menander and the other playwrights of the age shed light on this impotence by focusing on the personal rather than on larger questions of good and evil.

A new genre of escapist literature—the Hellenistic novel—also emerged in this environment. The themes in these novels echo those of the plays: Very young men and women fall in love (usually at first

Hellenistic novels sight), but circumstances separate them. They must endure hardships and surmount obstacles before they can be reunited. Surprisingly, most of these novels portray young women as resourceful and outspoken individuals. For example, a remarkable heroine in the novel *Ninos* dresses in gender-ambiguous clothing and leads a band of Assyrians to capture a fortified city. Although wounded, she makes a brave escape while elephants trample her soldiers.

Both the New Comedy and the Hellenistic novel sought to provide an escape from the realities of cosmopolitan life. Yet they also reflected new ideals in this society that often looked to the personal rather than to the polis for meaning. For example, unlike the writings of classical Greece, Hellenistic texts expressed an ideal of affection within marriage. The philosopher Antipater of Tarsus wrote, "The man who has had no experience of a married woman and children has not tasted true and noble happiness." The literature of the day also revealed an increased freedom of Hellenistic women to choose their partners. While families still arranged most marriages, some women (and men) began to follow their hearts in choosing a spouse. Women also gained more freedom in divorce laws. Like men, they could seek divorce if their husbands committed adultery. One marriage contract from as early as 311 B.C.E. included clauses forbidding the husband to "insult" his wife with another woman. Taken together, all these themes expressed a new emphasis on love within the family.

Cynics, Epicureans, and Stoics: Cosmopolitan Philosophy

Like their literary counterparts, Hellenistic philosophers also narrowed the focus of their inquiry. Most of them no longer tackled the lofty questions of truth and justice that had preoccupied Socrates and Plato. Instead, they considered how an individual could achieve happiness in an age

in which vast, impersonal kingdoms produced pain and weariness.

The sensibilities of the Hellenistic age had been first foreshadowed by Diogenes (ca. 400–ca. 325 B.C.E.), an early proponent of the philosophic school called **Cynicism.** Diogenes was disgusted with the hypocrisy and materialism emerging around him in the transformed life **Cynics** of Athens as traditional polis life deteriorated. Diogenes and his followers believed that the only way for people to live happily in a fundamentally evil world was to involve themselves as little as possible in that world. The Cynics therefore claimed that the more people rejected the goods and connections of this world—property, marriage, religion, luxury—the more they would achieve spiritual happiness. To demonstrate his rejection of all material things, Diogenes reputedly lived in a large tub.

Although Plato had dismissed Diogenes as "Socrates gone mad," Cynicism became popular during the Hellenistic period as people searched for meaning in their personal lives, rather than justice for their polis. Some men and women chose to live an ascetic life of the mind instead of involving themselves in the day-to-day activities of the Hellenistic cities. However, most found it difficult to reject material goods completely.

Other Hellenistic philosophies offered more practical solutions to the question of where to find personal happiness in an impersonal world. Epicurus (ca. 342–ca. 270 B.C.E.), for example, founded a school of philosophy that built on Democritus's (460–370 B.C.E.) theory of a universe made of atoms (described in Chapter 2). Envisioning a purposeless world of randomly colliding atoms, Epicurus proclaimed that happiness came from seeking pleasure while being free from pain in both body and mind. From a practical standpoint, this search for happiness involved pursuing pleasures that did not bring pain. Activities such as overeating or overdrinking, which ended in pain, should thus be **Epicurus** avoided. In Epicurus's view, the ideal life was one of moderation, which consisted of being surrounded by friends and free of the burdens of the public sphere. His circle of followers included women and slaves. The Roman **Epicurean** Lucretius Carus (ca. 99–ca. 55 B.C.E.) articulated Epicurus's ideal: "This is the greatest joy of all: to stand aloof in a quiet citadel, stoutly fortified by the teaching of the wise, and to gaze down from that elevation on others wandering aimlessly in a vain search for the way of life." Of course, this "greatest joy" required money with which to purchase the pain-free pleasures that Epicurus advocated. His was not a philosophy that everyone could afford.

While Epicurus honed his philosophy in his private garden, the public marketplace of Athens gave rise to a third great Hellenistic philosophy: **Stoicism.** Named after *stoa,* the covered walkways surrounding the marketplace, the school of Sto- **Stoics** icism was founded by Zeno (ca. 335–

ca. 261 B.C.E.). Zeno exemplified the cosmopolitan citizen of the Hellenistic world, for he was born in Cyprus of non-Greek ancestry and spent most of his life in Athens.

At age 22, Zeno was a follower of Crates the Cynic, but later he abandoned his early connection to Cynicism, arguing that people could possess material goods as long as they were not emotionally attached to them. Indeed, the Stoic philosophers advocated indifference to external things. While this attitude paralleled Epicurus's desire to avoid pain, Zeno and the Stoics did not frame their philosophy in terms of the materialism of an atomic universe. Instead, they argued for the existence of a Universal Reason or God that governed the universe. As they explained, seeds of the Universal Reason lay within each individual, so everyone was linked in a universal brotherhood. In quasi-religious terms, this belief validated Alexander's supposed goal of unifying diverse peoples.

The Stoics' belief in a Universal Reason led them to explain the apparent turbulence of the world differently than the Epicureans. Stoics did not believe in random events but instead posited a rational world with laws and structures—an idea that would have a long history in the West. While individuals could not control this universe, they could control their own responses to the apparent vagaries of the world. Followers were implored to pursue virtue in a way that kept them in harmony with rational nature, not fighting it. The ideal Stoic renounced passions (including anger) even while enduring the pain and suffering that inevitably accompany life. Through self-control, Stoics might achieve the tranquillity that Epicureans and Cynics desired.

Cynicism, Epicureanism, and Stoicism had many things in common. Arising in settings where individuals felt unable to influence their world, they all emphasized control of the self and personal tranquillity. Whereas the classical Greeks had found meaning through participation in the public life of their poleis, Hellenistic philosophers claimed that individuals could find contentment through some form of withdrawal from the turbulent life of the impersonal cosmopolitan cities. Moreover, all three philosophies appealed primarily to people with some measure of wealth. The indifferent, pain-free life of both the Epicureans and the Stoics required money, and the self-denial of the Cynics seldom appealed to really destitute people.

New Religions of Hope

For most ordinary people, the philosophies of the Hellenistic age had little relevance. These people looked instead to new religious ideas for a sense of meaning and hope. During this period, the gods and goddesses of the poleis gave way to deities that had international appeal and that were accessible to ordinary individuals—two features that marked a dramatic departure from previous religions of the West. Furthermore, the new religions offered hope in an afterlife that provided an escape from the alienation of

DIOGENES AND ALEXANDER Diogenes, the advocate of Cynicism, argued that people should live a simple life, much like the dog shown sitting on the barrel in which the great philosopher lived. The artist included in this scene Alexander the Great, who reputedly admired the simple lifestyle that was so rare in the Hellenistic kingdoms.

the Hellenistic world. The international component paved the way for a blending of religious ideas—syncretism—and individuals felt a deeply passionate spiritual connection to their deities. The most popular new cults were known as **mystery religions** because initiates swore not to reveal the insights they received during the highest ceremonies. The historical roots of these cults stretched back to early Greece, Egypt, and Syria, but they acquired a new relevance throughout the Hellenistic era.

Mystery cults included worship of fertility goddesses like Demeter and Cybele, and a revitalized cult of Dionysus. However, the most popular was that of the Egyptian goddess Isis, who achieved a remarkable universality. Inscription stones offering her prayers claim that Isis ruled the world and credited her with inventing writing and cultivation of grain, ruling the heavenly bodies, and even transcending fate itself—the overarching destiny that even the old Homeric gods could not escape. Isis reputedly declared: "I am she who is called Lawgiver. . . . I conquer Fate. Fate heeds me." In other inscriptions, worshipers claimed that Isis was the same goddess that other peoples called by different names: "In your person alone you are all the other goddesses named by the peoples."

Mystery religion

Men and women who wanted to experience the mysteries of these new religions believed that they had been summoned by a dream or other supernatural call. They took part in a purification ritual and an elaborate public celebration, including a procession filled with music and, sometimes, ecstatic dance in which people acted as if possessed by the goddess or god. Finally, the procession left the public spaces and entered the sacred space of the deity, where the initiate experienced a profound connection with the god or goddess. Many mysteries involved sacred meals through which people became godlike by eating the flesh of the deity. Such believers emerged from this experience expecting to participate in an afterlife. Here lay the heart of the new religious impulses: the hope for another, better world after death. The mystery religions would continue to draw converts for centuries, and perhaps paved the way for Christianity—the most successful mystery religion of all.

Hellenistic Science

The philosophic and religious longings of the Hellenistic world bred long-standing consequences for the future. People living in later large, impersonal cities turned to the philosophies of indifference and religions of hope. Equally impressive were the improvements on classical Greek science and technology that emerged in the Hellenistic learning centers. This flourish of intellectual activity was fostered in part by the generous royal patronage that made Alexandria and Pergamum scholastic centers, and in part by the creative blending of ideas from old centers of learning.

One scholar who benefited from the new Hellenistic world of learning was Herophilus (ca. 335–ca. 280 B.C.E.), who traveled to Alexandria from the Seleucid lands near the Black Sea to study medicine. **Medical advances** The first physician to break the strong Greek taboo against cutting open a corpse, Herophilus performed dissections that led him to spectacular discoveries about human anatomy. (His curiosity even reputedly led him to perform vivisections on convicted criminals to learn about the motion of living organs.) His careful studies yielded pathbreaking knowledge: He was the first to recognize the brain as the seat of intelligence and to describe accurately the female anatomy, including the ovaries and fallopian tubes. However, all physicians were not as willing as Herophilus to treat the human body as an object of scientific study. Even in intellectually advanced Alexandria, dissection became unpopular, and subsequent physicians focused on techniques of clinical treatment rather than on anatomy. However, they made major strides in pharmacology, carefully studying the influence of drugs and toxins on the body.

In spite of these noteworthy advances, the most important achievements of the Hellenistic scientists occurred in the field of mathematics. Euclid (335–270 B.C.E.), who studied in Alexandria, is considered one of the most accomplished mathematicians of all time. In his most famous work, *Elements* (ca. 300 B.C.E.), Euclid presented a geometry **Mathematics and astronomy** based on increasingly complex axioms and postulates. When Euclid's patron, King Ptolemy, asked the mathematician whether there was an easier way to learn geometry than by struggling through these proofs, Euclid replied that there was no "royal road" (or shortcut) to understanding geometry. Euclid's work became the standard text on the subject, and, even today, students find his intricate proofs both challenging and vexing.

Euclid's mathematical work laid the foundation for Hellenistic astronomy. Eratosthenes of Cyrene (ca. 275–ca. 195 B.C.E.), for example, used Euclid's theorems to calculate the circumference of the earth with remarkable accuracy—he erred only by about 200 miles. Aristarchus of Samos (ca. 310–ca. 230 B.C.E.) posited a heliocentric, or sun-centered, universe (against prevailing Greek tradition) and attempted to use Euclidean geometry to calculate the size and distance of the moon and sun. Although Aristarchus's contemporaries rejected his work, he and other astronomers introduced a striking change into the study of the heavens: They eliminated superstition and instead approached their work with mathematics.

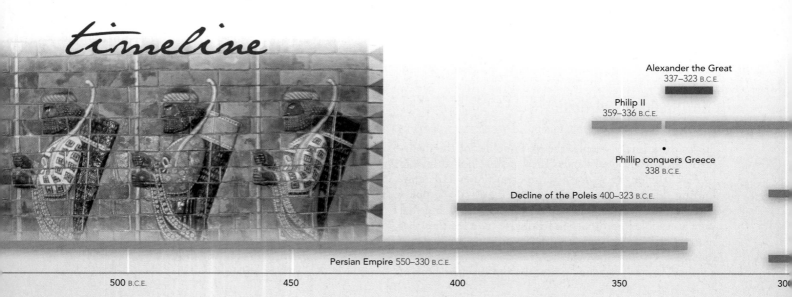

timeline

Alexander the Great
337–323 B.C.E.

Philip II
359–336 B.C.E.

Phillip conquers Greece
338 B.C.E.

Decline of the Poleis 400–323 B.C.E.

Persian Empire 550–330 B.C.E.

500 B.C.E.   450   400   350   300

Many Greek thinkers combined theoretical science with practical applications. One of the most influential in this regard was Hipparchus of Nicaea (160–125 B.C.E.). A brilliant mathematician, Hipparchus invented trigonometry—the mathematics of measuring angles—and applied these insights to measuring the heavens and the earth. His accomplishments demonstrated once again the benefits of cultural blending, for he introduced into Greece the Babylonian mathematical convention of measuring the circle in terms of 360 degrees, the method by which we continue to measure the globe. Among Hipparchus's other practical applications were measuring the length of the lunar month within an error of one second, a stunning achievement, and being the first to use the ideas of latitude and longitude consistently to measure the earth.

Another beneficiary of Greek mathematics was Archimedes (ca. 287–ca. 212 B.C.E.), often considered the greatest inventor of antiquity. Like so many cosmopolitan scholars, Archimedes, who was born in Syracuse, traveled to Alexandria to study. He later returned to Syracuse, where he worked on both abstract and practical problems. He built further on Euclid's geometry, applying the theorems to cones and spheres. In the process, he became the first to determine the value of pi—essential in calculating the area of a circle. He also applied geometry to the study of levers, proving that no weight was too heavy to move. He reportedly coined the optimistic declaration "Give me a place to stand, a long enough lever, and I will move the earth."

Archimedes

Archimedes did more than advance theoretical mathematics: He also had a creative, practical streak. For example, he invented the compound pulley, a valuable device for moving heavy weights. His real challenge, however, came at the end of his life. As we will see in Chapter 4, Syracuse, the city of Archimedes' birth, was besieged by Rome, a rising power in the Mediterranean. Throughout the siege, Syracuse used both offensive and defensive weapons that Archimedes had invented. Yet the great man's inventions could not save the Sicilian city. The Romans ultimately prevailed, and in 212 B.C.E. Archimedes was struck down by a Roman soldier as he was drawing a figure in the sand.

Archimedes serves as an apt symbol for the Hellenistic world that produced him. He was educated with the best of Greek learning and combined it with the rich diversity of Asia and the Mediterranean lands—a blending that gave Western civilization dramatic impetus. The Hellenistic scientist died at the hands of a new people—the Romans—who embraced the practical applications of men like Archimedes and who next took up the torch of Western culture.

SUMMARY

The Macedonian kings Philip and Alexander permanently transformed the life of the polis that had marked the glory of Greece. Their conquests created a unique blend of Greek, Egyptian, and Persian cultures.

- Philip of Macedon developed military innovations that allowed him to conquer the Greek city-states. His son Alexander continued his expansion eastward and conquered the vast Persian Empire and Egypt.

- After Alexander's death, his empire broke up into successor kingdoms ruled by dynasties formed of his generals.

- The Hellenistic kingdoms established a cosmopolitan culture dominated by international trade, huge mercenary armies, diverse populations, and an increased disparity of wealth. Notice how Jews rebelled against this new blending of cultures.

- New schools and a vigorous commitment to education fostered learning in the Hellenistic kingdoms. This led to new theater and literature; highly influential schools of philosophy: Cynics, Epicureans, and Stoics; and innovations in science and medicine. There also arose new "mystery religions" offering spiritual solace to many.

In spite of the power of these kingdoms, a new force was gathering momentum in Italy, one that would profoundly impact the fate of Hellenistic civilization and the future of the West.

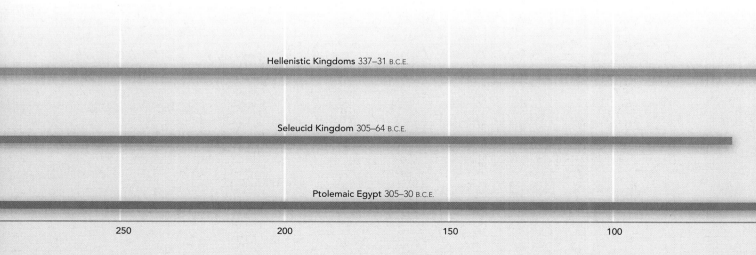

Hellenistic Kingdoms 337–31 B.C.E.

Seleucid Kingdom 305–64 B.C.E.

Ptolemaic Egypt 305–30 B.C.E.

250   200   150   100

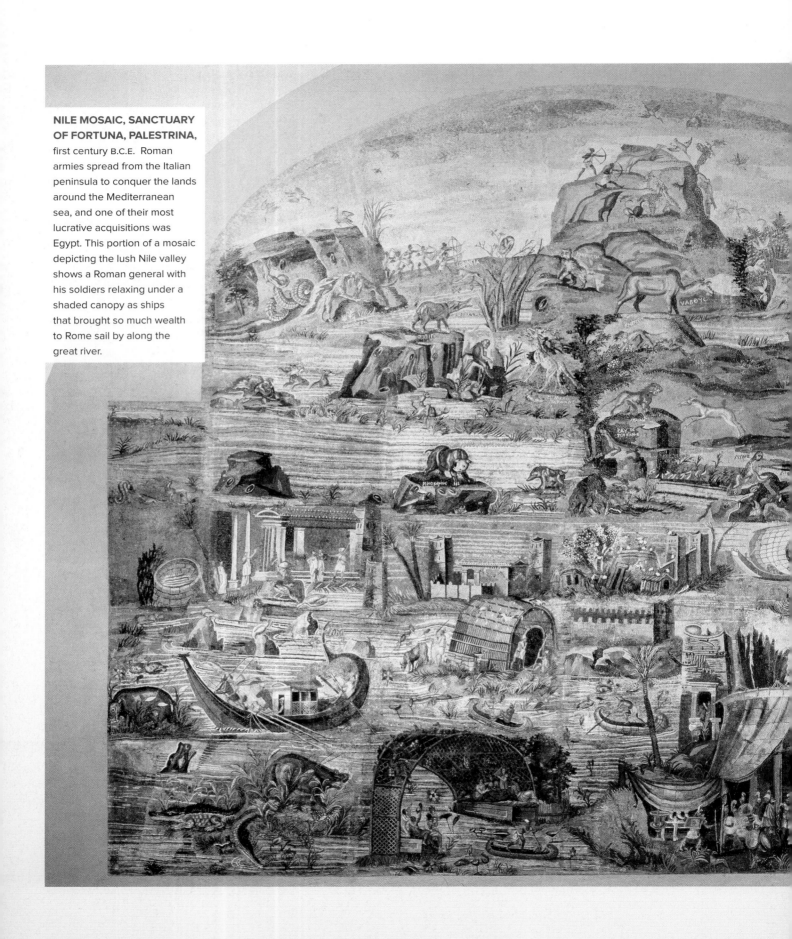

NILE MOSAIC, SANCTUARY OF FORTUNA, PALESTRINA, first century B.C.E. Roman armies spread from the Italian peninsula to conquer the lands around the Mediterranean sea, and one of their most lucrative acquisitions was Egypt. This portion of a mosaic depicting the lush Nile valley shows a Roman general with his soldiers relaxing under a shaded canopy as ships that brought so much wealth to Rome sail by along the great river.

Pride
in Family
and City

Rome from Its Origins
Through the Republic,
753–44 B.C.E.

4

Rome Saved by a Farmer

On a warm spring day in 458 B.C.E., a Roman farmer named Cincinnatus was plowing the land adjacent to his small, round hut. In the capital, a few horsemen galloped toward the Senate House to warn the senators that the Roman army had been trapped and the warring neighboring tribes were threatening the city. The senators realized they needed a great leader at this critical moment. The senators remembered Cincinnatus's skill as a general and swiftly voted him "dictator," a title that gave him full authority for six months, and a delegation went to his farm and called him from his plow. ▶▶

Cincinnatus told his wife to bring him his toga—a long cloth of bleached wool that set a man apart as a patrician, or noble of Rome.

The farmer-turned-general set off for Rome, raised an army of Roman citizens, and then marched to war. He led the infantry in person as they marched with the discipline that marked the Roman army and confronted the enemy with the courage that defined Rome's generals. Cincinnatus won a swift victory, and the vanquished begged him for mercy, which he granted in exchange for their capitulation. A mere sixteen days after the war began, the victorious Cincinnatus was back in Rome. The grateful people urged him to continue his leadership after the crisis had passed, but he refused, preferring to return to his plow.

Throughout the next centuries, this story of the strong, unassuming farmer Cincinnatus was told and retold by conservative Romans who looked back to the "ways of the fathers," *mos maiorum,* for models of virtue. (The American city Cincinnati was so named to honor George Washington, another savior farmer-general.)

Here in the story of Cincinnatus, we can see the beginnings of the greatness of the Romans: an unassuming love of duty and tradition, a pride in discipline, and a stunningly victorious army. At the same time, we can get a hint of transformations that would come to this city-state. Conquests funneled untold wealth and numerous slaves into Rome, and contact with Hellenistic civilization brought new culture, ideas, and values, causing the Roman historian Livy to lament the decline of "plain living" that had made the Romans great. But we will see in this chapter that their very success would fuel the demise of the Republic that voted to offer leadership to a modest farmer. ◄◄

THE RISE OF ROME

753–265 B.C.E.

The historian Livy did not mind mixing history with myth, for he said: "There is no reason to object when antiquity draws no hard line between the human and the supernatural; it adds dignity to the past." Romans regularly remembered their history in terms of legends. Perhaps the most beloved of these stories told Romans how their city was founded. Like the story of Cincinnatus, the tale of the birth of Rome is filled with drama, conflict, heroes, and values. The tale begins with Aeneas, a Trojan hero who escaped from the destruction of his city after the Trojan War (described in Chapter 2). A royal female descendant of Aeneas decided to dedicate her life to serving the gods. She became pregnant by the god Mars and bore twin boys, Romulus and Remus. The princess's uncle did not believe in the miraculous conception, nor did he want her sons to threaten his rule, so he threw the infant boys in the Tiber River. Soon a shepherd found them being suckled by a wolf and raised them as his own sons. Many years later, after the boys had grown up, Romulus killed his brother during a quarrel and became the first king of the newly founded city of Rome. The traditional date of the founding of the city is 753 B.C.E., and archaeological evidence confirms the existence of a settlement there by this time. Reflecting a sense of destiny and heroic action shown in the myth, Livy concluded that "with reason did gods and men choose this site for our city—all its advantages make it of all places in the world the best for a city destined to grow great."

Rome was located on hills overlooking a fertile, low-lying plain and the Tiber River, which afforded access to the Mediterranean Sea and to the inland regions. The geography of the surrounding Italian peninsula offered a number of advantages that would ultimately favor the growth of the young city. In contrast to Greece, whose mountainous terrain discouraged political unification, the large plains along Italy's western and eastern shores fostered trade, communication, and agriculture. The Apennine mountain range that marches down through the peninsula also creates abundant rainfall on the western plain. Therefore, Rome's fields were better situated for large-scale agriculture than had been possible for the Greek city-states. In addition, calm, accessible harbors along the western coast opened avenues for trade throughout the Mediterranean, which was further enhanced by Italy's central location in that important sea.

Geography

The initial settlers of Rome, like many of the other tribes in the region, were Indo-Europeans, those ubiquitous migrants from near the Black Sea whom we first saw in Chapter 1. They farmed, living in round huts and plowing their land. Cato the Elder (234–149 B.C.E.), a Roman political leader known for expressing traditional Roman values, summarized the Romans' pride in this way of life: "From farmers come the bravest men and sturdiest soldiers." Yet Rome also grew stronger through absorbing some of the culture and ways of its particularly talented neighbors. Greek colonies were well established in southern Italy and Sicily; Phoenician colonies prospered along the coast of North Africa. Most influential, however, were the Romans' immediate neighbors to the north, the Etruscans.

The Etruscan Influence

The Etruscans had appeared in Italy by 800 B.C.E., and for millennia historians argued about the origin of these peoples who did not speak an Indo-European language.

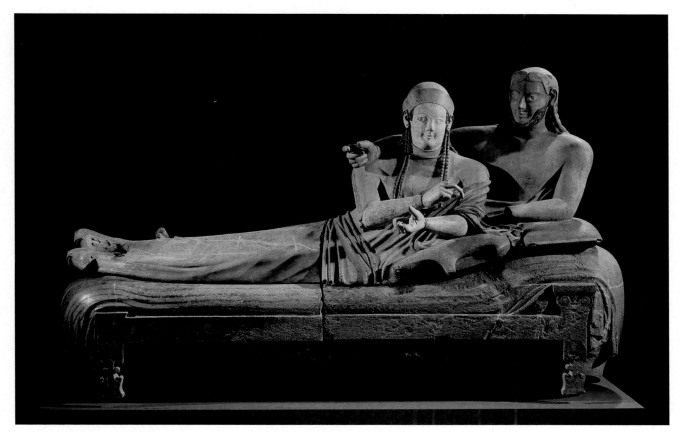

ETRUSCAN SARCOPHAGUS, ca. 520 B.C.E. This sarcophagus (stone burial casket) was designed to hold cremated remains. The decoration celebrates the couple's life. They are shown reclining at dinner, an activity in which the wife and husband shared equal status.

Did they come from northern Europe, Italy, or North Africa? Modern DNA testing has confirmed the ancient historian Herodotus's claim that they arrived from Lydia in Asia Minor. The DNA evidence demonstrates that not only did the people come from modern Turkey, but they also brought their own cattle, setting that breed apart from the indigenous Italian cattle. The Etruscans settled the land and prospered. They traded all over the Mediterranean, importing luxury items and enjoying a good life.

Etruscan kings ruled Rome for a time, and the Romans learned a good deal from their civilization; indeed, much that we define as Roman was in fact Etruscan. For example, the Romans adopted Etruscan engineering and used their newfound skills to drain their lowland marsh, which formed the center of the growing city of Rome, and to build the great sewers that drained water from the city. They also adopted Etruscan architectural features— among them, the arch and vault construction—and modeled their temples on those of the Etruscans. Inside the temples, Romans learned to rely on divination—interpreting the will of the gods in the entrails of sacrificial animals—from Etruscan priests. Romans also adopted the toga, the white woolen robe worn by citizens, as well as the *fasces,* a bundle of rods surrounding an ax that was the powerful emblem of Roman authority.

Finally, the Romans acquired the Etruscan alphabet and began using it to write in their own Latin language. The Italian region of Tuscany is named after this early people who exerted an enduring influence on the growing culture of Rome.

The Roman Monarchy

ca. 753–509 B.C.E.

Like other ancient civilizations, the early Romans were ruled by kings, but to work out the details of the monarchy, historians have to struggle with combinations of history and legend. Romulus (ca. 753–ca. 715 B.C.E.) was the first king, and more unverifiable legends claim he was followed by four more monarchs. By the seventh century B.C.E., it seems, Rome was ruled by an Etruscan dynasty that governed for almost a century, from about 616 to about 509 B.C.E.

By the end of the sixth century B.C.E., the Roman aristocracy had come to chafe against the Etruscan kings' authority. Roman tradition holds that rebellion against the Etruscans erupted in response to the violation of Lucretia, a virtuous Roman matron. According to Livy, Sextus, son of the Etruscan

Overthrow of Etruscans

king Tarquin the Proud, raped Lucretia at knifepoint. Her husband, Collatinus, told her not to blame herself, but after extracting her husband's promise to exact vengeance, she committed suicide. She was remembered as a chaste, heroic woman who chose death over dishonor. After her death, Romans rallied around the leadership of an Etruscan nobleman—Brutus—who joined Collatinus in a revolt that toppled the monarchy. The story of Lucretia illuminates the values of bravery and chastity held by early Roman men and women, but it also became a symbol of Romans' revulsion against kings, which would be a continuing theme throughout their history.

The legend accurately concluded that the Etruscan monarchy was overthrown, but the historical reality was more complex. All Romans did not support the overthrow of the monarchy—many in the lower classes relied on the monarchy to control the power of the noble families (the **patricians**), and some patricians who were related to kings also supported the monarchy. With these competing social forces, simply overthrowing a monarchy would not resolve social issues. However, just as the Greek poleis had overthrown their own kings and replaced them with oligarchies of nobles during their early history, the situation was repeated in Rome. The erection of a stable governmental form would require time and struggle.

Governing an Emerging Republic

509–287 B.C.E.

With the overthrow of the Etruscan monarchy, the Romans established a republic, a Latin word that meant "public matter" (often rendered "public realm" or "commonwealth" in English), which they distinguished from the "private realm" of the Etruscan kings. For Romans, this meant that power rested with the people assembled together and that magistrates served the state. This influential vision of government was in striking contrast to that of the Hellenistic kings, who generally viewed their kingdoms as their own property, their spoils of war, their private realm.

In practice, the Republic consisted of three parts—consuls, the Senate, and the assemblies. Executive authority rested with two male **consuls** who were elected annually by an Assembly of Centuries organized by army groupings of 100 men, or "centuries." The consuls were advised by a body of elder statesmen, the **Senate.** Finally, adult male citizens met in **assemblies,** outdoor public gatherings in which the participants voted—by group, not as individuals—on issues that had previously been presented to them by leading statesmen. Beyond this governmen-

> Many abused their power and oppressed the commoners in their charge, even enslaving many because of debts they incurred.

tal structure, the Roman people were separated by two general social distinctions into groups called patricians and plebeians. The patricians, old families who composed about 6 percent of the population, were recognized as socially and legally superior to everyone else. The **plebeians,** who made up the majority of the population, were the Republic's working people; their numbers, however, did not include slaves. Although the republican system seemed to offer a balance of power, in reality authority rested with the patricians, who sat in the Senate, and with the wealthy men who dominated the Assembly of Centuries.

Perhaps not surprisingly given that so few dominated the many, some individual patricians found ways to enrich themselves and their families. Many abused their power and oppressed the commoners in their charge, even enslaving many because of debts they incurred. By the fifth century B.C.E., social relations between patrician and plebeian had deteriorated enough that a social revolution occurred, which historians have called the **Struggle of the Orders.** Two main issues fueled this controversy: First, the poor wanted guarantees against the abuses of the powerful, and second, the wealthy plebeians wanted a role in government. This struggle was not a civil war, but instead a series of political reforms forced on the aristocracy from about 509 to 287 B.C.E.

Struggle of the Orders

Plebeians began their revolution by establishing themselves as a political alternative to the patricians. They withdrew from the city, held their own assemblies, established their own temple to counter the patrician cults, and even elected their own leaders, called **tribunes,** who were to represent plebeian interests. Tribunes could veto unfavorable laws and represent plebeians in law courts, for example. Patricians also had a practical reason to listen to the voice of the people through their tribunes, because they needed the plebeians to fight in the infantry. Just as Greek citizens forced concessions from aristocrats who needed armies, Roman citizen-soldiers threatened to refuse military service unless some of their demands were met. This was an effective threat; slowly, plebeians gained in political skill and, through the pressure of their tribunes, extracted meaningful concessions.

Plebeians won a number of important rights: First, they gained a written law code that could be consistently enforced. Between 451 and 449 B.C.E., the laws were written down and displayed in a form called the **Twelve Tables.** Subsequent Romans looked back proudly to this accomplishment, which established a Roman commitment to law that became one of Rome's most enduring contributions to Western culture. To mark the importance of the establishment of written law, Roman children continued to memorize the Twelve Tables for up to four centuries later. Plebeians also won the right to hold sacred and political offices. Although, in practice, offices more readily went to the wealthy, upward mobility was possible. Perhaps the greatest concession the plebeians eventually won was the right to marry patricians. This removed birth as the most serious impediment to the rise of talented and wealthy plebeians.

The plebeian struggle for representation culminated in 287 B.C.E., when the Tribal Assembly became the principal legislative body. This group was named because the assembly was organized in "tribes" or regions, urban and rural, where plebeians lived. Laws

Governing the Republic

passed by the Tribal Assembly did not need Senate approval, but bound everyone—rich or poor. The resulting society in Rome contained three main social classes: patricians, wealthy plebeians—later called **equestrians** (or knights) because they could afford to be in the cavalry—and the poorer plebeians. Money and connections dominated Roman politics as patricians and equestrians fought to increase their power. In spite of these problems, Polybius believed the people retained important powers, as the document to the right describes. The Roman system probably worked in part because most of the political life took place within an informal system.

Informal Governance: Patrons and Clients

From the earliest years of the Republic, Romans relied on semiformal ties to smooth social and even political intercourse. Powerful members of society, called patrons, surrounded themselves with less powerful people—clients—in a relationship based on informal yet profoundly important ties. Patrons provided clients with what they called "kindnesses," such as food, occasional financial support, and help in legal disputes. Clients consisted of people from all walks of life: aristocratic youths who looked to powerful patrons for help in their careers (or hoped to be remembered in a rich patron's will), businessmen who wanted to use a patron's

The Power of Public Opinion

The Greek historian Polybius (ca. 200–ca. 118 B.C.E.) was a great admirer of the Roman constitution, which he described in his *Histories*. After he described the roles of the Senate and all the officers of the state, he turned to the more informal power of the people of Rome.

After this one would naturally be inclined to ask what part is left for the people in the constitution. . . . There is, however, a part left for the people, and it is a most important one. For the people is the sole fountain of honour and of punishment; and it is by these two things and these alone that dynasties and constitutions and, in a word, human society are held together. . . . The people then are the only court to decide matters of life and death; and even in cases where the penalty is money, if the sum to be assessed is sufficiently serious, and especially when the accused have held the higher magistracies. . . .

Again, it is the people who bestow offices on the deserving, which are the most honourable rewards of virtue. It has also the absolute power of passing or repealing laws; and most important of all, it is the people who deliberate on the question of peace or war. And when provisional terms are made for alliance, suspension of hostilities, or treaties, it is the people who ratify them or the reverse. These considerations again would lead one to say that the chief power in the state was the people's, and that the constitution was a democracy.

What powers does Polybius attribute to the people? Do you think he's right that these powers are substantial?

political influence to profit in their enterprises, poets who needed money, or freed slaves who remained attached to their former owners. Because Rome remained overwhelmingly an agricultural society, the largest group of clients was small farmers, who depended on their patrons to help them survive in a land that was becoming dominated by powerful aristocratic landowners. Clients owed their patrons duties, such as financial and political support.

Many clients gathered at their patrons' doors every morning as the cock crowed—failure to appear would jeopardize one's tie of clientage. This **Clients' role** mixed crowd numbering in the tens to hundreds received ritual gifts, ensuring that the poorest would eat and the richest were remembered, and everyone was invited into the patron's home to greet him. The patron was supposed to exert a moral authority over his clients, helping them to be good citizens. As the Roman poet Horace (65–8 B.C.E.) wrote, "A wealthy patron governs you as a good mother might do and requires of you more wisdom and virtue than he possesses himself."

In the public world of Mediterranean society, clients provided patrons visible proof of their authority. After the morning greeting, clients accompanied their patron to the center of the city, where the day's business took place. A patrician surrounded by hundreds of clients was a man to be reckoned with. Political life of the Republic was conducted in the **Forum,** a large gathering area surrounded by temples and other public buildings. The Forum included the Senate chamber, the people's assembly, and a speaker's platform—called the Rostra—where politicians addressed the Roman people. The map on page 79 shows the City of Rome with its important public spaces, including the Rostra and the Senate chamber. Clients would cheer their patron, shout down his opponents, and offer their votes to his agenda. An aristocrat who abandoned this public life that gave him stature and dignity was described sadly: "He will have no more entourage, no escort for his sedan chair, no visitors in his antechamber."

The Struggle of the Orders created a republic in which rich and poor both had a voice. In fact, it was a system dominated by wealth and an aristocracy that used its influence in the Senate and the Forum to preserve traditional privileges. However, the wealthy never forgot they needed the support of the Roman clients who gathered at their doors in the morning, shouted their support in the Forum, and manned Rome's armies.

Dominating the Italian Peninsula

As the Republic gathered strength, territorial wars between Rome and its neighbors broke out almost annually. What led Rome into these repeated struggles? Romans themselves claimed that they responded only to acts of aggression, so their expansion was self-defensive. The reality, however, was more complicated. Rome felt a continual land hunger and was ever eager to acquire land to establish colonies of its plebeians. Roman leaders also had a hunger for glory and plunder that would let them acquire and reward clients—victorious generals were well placed to dominate Rome's political life. Thus, farmers often had to drop their plows, as Cincinnatus did, to fight.

By the beginning of the fourth century B.C.E., Rome was increasingly involved in wars in the Italian peninsula. From an early period, Romans identified themselves with fellow Latin tribes as they fought together against surrounding hillside tribes. By the early Republic, this alliance was known as the Latin League. Under Rome's leadership, the Latin League successfully defended its borders during the fifth and fourth centuries B.C.E. However, Rome's allies became increasingly resentful of Rome's leadership and revolted in 340 B.C.E. Two years later, Rome decisively defeated the rebellious allies and dissolved the League. Here, however, Rome showed its genius for administration. Instead of crushing the rebellious states, Rome extended varying degrees of citizenship to the Latins. Some received the rights of full Roman citizenship, while others **Italian wars** became partial citizens who could earn full citizenship by moving to Rome. This benign policy allowed Rome with its allies to confront and conquer other peoples of the peninsula.

In the third century B.C.E., Rome acquired territories to the south and north. This was not a time of endless victories, however. In 390 B.C.E., the Gauls of northern Italy (a Celtic tribe) sacked much of the city before being bribed to

→ connect to today ←

Political Participation

The Forum was the center of political life in the Republic, where both the rich and the poor had a voice. Politicians addressed the Roman people from the Rostra, while clients cheered their patron, voted for his agenda, and criticized his opponents. How does the Forum compare with today's political system? Do the rich and the poor have an equal voice?

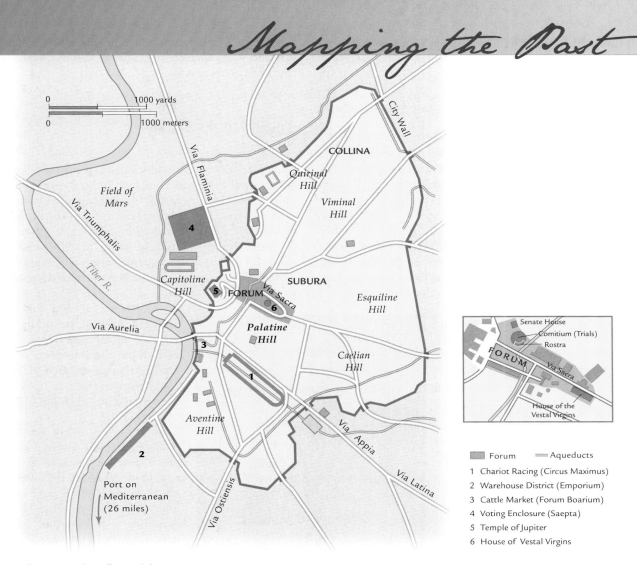

0   1000 yards

0   1000 meters

COLLINA

Via Flaminia

City Wall

Quirinal Hill

Field of Mars

Viminal Hill

Via Triumphalis

4

Tiber R.

SUBURA

Capitoline Hill

5 FORUM

Via Sacra

6

Esquiline Hill

Via Aurelia

Palatine Hill

3

Caelian Hill

1

Via Appia

Aventine Hill

Via Latina

2

Port on Mediterranean (26 miles)

Via Ostiensis

Senate House

Comitium (Trials)

Rostra

FORUM

Via Sacra

House of the Vestal Virgins

■ Forum   ══ Aqueducts

1   Chariot Racing (Circus Maximus)
2   Warehouse District (Emporium)
3   Cattle Market (Forum Boarium)
4   Voting Enclosure (Saepta)
5   Temple of Jupiter
6   House of Vestal Virgins

Rome During the Republic

This map shows the city of Rome during the late Republic. The inset pinpoints the locations of the important features of the Forum. **Which elements in the Forum and at the center of the city show how political life and religious institutions dominated life in Rome?**

leave with a large tribute payment, but it would be another eight hundred years before a foreign army once more set foot in the city. However, their invasion had weakened the Etruscan cities of the north, so by 295 B.C.E., Roman armies controlled the north of the peninsula. By the middle of the third century B.C.E., Rome dominated most of the Italian peninsula.

The Romans' successful expansion in part stemmed from their renowned courage and tenacity in battle. Most of their success, however, came from their generosity in victory, because the Romans chose not to control the conquered territories directly. In fact, the peninsula remained a patchwork of diverse states allied to Rome by separate treaties. These treaties were varied, but all were

Foreign policy

generous to conquered peoples. Romans allowed all the tribes to retain full autonomy in their own territories and to elect their own officials, keep their own laws, and collect their own taxes. These peoples were required to supply troops for Rome's armies and to avoid pursuing independent foreign policy. Many of the conquered peoples did have to give up some territory for Rome to use as colonies to feed their land hunger, but the colonies served to help Rome watch over and control its ever-widening borders of influence. As a result of Rome's leadership, the conquered territories at times enjoyed more peace and freedom than they ever had. Rome's sensible policy toward the territories bought the loyalty of many states and created a relatively cohesive unit that would fuel further imperial expansion.

FAMILY LIFE AND CITY LIFE

The great Roman orator Cicero (106–43 B.C.E.) wrote that the Romans were like other peoples except in their religious fervor: "In reverence for the gods, we are far superior." Perhaps more than other ancient civilizations, the Romans saw the world as infused with spirits; in their view, almost every space was governed by some divinity. Rome itself was guarded by three deities that protected the state—Jupiter, Juno, and Minerva—but there were gods for even smaller spaces. There were goddesses for the countryside, for the hills, and for the valleys. There were three gods to guard entrances—one for the door, another for the hinges, and a third for the lintel, the door's upper supporting beam. The remaining spaces within the home were equally inhabited by spirits that demanded worship and sacrifice.

A Pious, Practical People

Formal worship of the many gods and goddesses took place at the temples, where priests presided over sacrifices and divination officials looked for favorable omens in the entrails of sacrificial animals. The Vestal Virgins, six priestesses who presided over the temple of Vesta, goddess of the hearth, kept the sacred fire of the state hearth burning.

According to the Roman people, their success hinged on proper worship, which meant offering sacrifices. Sacrifices could be as small as a drop of wine or a honeycake, or as large as an ox, but the Romans believed their destiny was deeply tied to their proper observation of religious rituals. When Rome was sacked by the Gauls in 390 B.C.E., Livy reported, one Roman general supposedly said, "All things went well when we obeyed the gods, but badly when we disobeyed them."

In addition to piety, Romans valued moral seriousness. These hardworking men and women prized duty to family, clients, patrons, and the Republic itself. They rejected the individualism of the Greeks and

ROMAN PATRICIAN, first century C.E. The conservative Romans took great pride in their ancestors, whose lives, they believed, gave legitimacy to their descendants. Romans venerated busts of their ancestors, as this statue of a Roman holding two busts of his forebears shows.

stressed collective responsibility and obedience to both secular and religious authority. They would one day rule the entire Mediterranean world.

Loyalty to the Family

Roman religion, duty, and loyalty began in the family. A father, in theory, had complete authority over everyone in his household, including his wife, children, slaves, and even ex-slaves. The father served as guardian of the family's well-being and shared with his wife the responsibility for venerating the household gods. In addition to recognizing all the spirits who guarded the home, families worshiped their ancestors, whom they considered the original source of their prosperity.

Marriages in early Rome were arranged, to make politically advantageous alliances between families and ensure the continuation of the family through children. A woman could be given in marriage in two ways. Her **Marriage patterns** family of origin might transfer her to her husband's control, in which case she became part of his family and participated in the worship of his ancestors. Or she might remain under her father's "hand," never becoming a full part of her husband's family. In this case, the woman's family of origin kept more political and financial control of her resources.

Despite the authority of husbands, women still played an important role in the family. They instilled the values of Rome in their children and raised them to be responsible and obedient citizens. Historical evidence such as letters indicates that mothers exerted as much stern authority as fathers and therefore wielded some political power through their sons.

Life in the City

By the late Republic (ca. 50 B.C.E.), the population of Rome had reached an astounding 1,000,000. The richest Romans lived on the hills (shown in the map on page 79), aloof from the bustle of the crowds and the

Roman soldiers ate only wheat bread and drank only water while at war. In hot weather, they added some vinegar to their drink. Sometimes during campaigns in which the wheat ran out, the soldiers had to eat meat, but they feared the meat would "soften" them and erode their invincibility. They sneered at their opponents who slept heavily on wine and food. Today's troops eat balanced meals. When deployed they often eat what's called an MRE, or meals ready-to-eat, which is a packaged ration that provides a well-balanced diet without requiring cooking or refrigeration.

smells of the lower city. They surrounded themselves with elegance and beauty and often decorated their houses with wall paintings called frescoes.

Below the hills, most city dwellers lived in small houses or crowded, multistoried tenements. The region of the city called Subura was the most notorious. It was near the Forum and at the foot of the most prestigious house on the Palatine Hill. People brought water from the public fountains and heated their homes with open flames or burning charcoal. Waste ran down sewers and washed out of the city, but never with the efficiency that modern hygiene requires. Townspeople dumped garbage just outside city walls near the cemetery for the poor, where shallowly buried corpses rotted and carrion crows circled endlessly. Wealthy urban men and women carried little bouquets of fragrant flowers that they held to their noses to protect themselves from the smells of the city.

In addition to being the political center of Rome, the Forum was the economic and social center. Two rows of shops lined the large square, and merchants shouted, hawking their wares as slaves

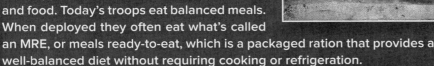

Life in the Forum shopped for the household needs. In the afternoon, work ceased and the men headed for the baths. (Women, too, probably had public bathing time set aside for them as well, but the historical evidence for the Republic does not explicitly discuss it.) The baths served much as a modern health club. People exercised or played ball, swam, took steam baths, had massages, got their body hair plucked, and socialized. Then, in the late afternoon and evening, it was time for leisure. The crowds in the Forum strolled, chatted, and gossiped. Romans always included a political dimension in this informal talk, for here politicians gained nicknames like "knock-knees" or more obscene appellations. In the course of passing on rumors and jokes, Romans helped set future political fortunes.

In the afternoon and at home, men abandoned their togas (a huge length of unbleached wool, carefully wrapped around the wearer) and wore their undergarments: usually a tunic that came down to the thighs. Men who wore sleeves or long tunics were considered effeminate. Women, on the other hand, covered themselves with long, sleeved tunics that they wore under their dresses.

As in cities today, life in the urban heart of Rome was a mixture of ease and hardship, and of excitement, fellowship, and danger. Yet this complex, vibrant center marked the ideal of the Republic: a place where citizens met and mingled in a public setting, and where political and economic dramas unfolded. Unfortunately for the Romans, this appealing way of life could not last. As Rome expanded, its spectacular military successes brought changes that undermined the Roman civic ideal.

EXPANSION AND TRANSFORMATION

265–133 B.C.E.

The Romans who enjoyed and contributed so much to the good life of the city represented only a part of the population. Rome's success derived primarily from its army. Over time, the army began to define the very structure of what was becoming an empire. As we saw in the example of Cincinnatus, the army of the Republic was made up of citizen-soldiers who set aside their work to fight for a season. When Rome's leaders believed they were threatened by foreign invaders, the consuls raised a red flag in the Forum. Then free householders

Weapons and discipline

Trajan's Column

This relief carving is a detail of one of the winding panels from Trajan's Column, which was dedicated in 113 C.E. to celebrate the emperor Trajan's victories in war. The full column is shown on the right. Even though this column is from later than the republican period, it remains one of the important historical sources for Roman military life. The scene highlighted here depicts soldiers, dressed in battle armor (except their helmets), building a camp—a common daily activity for soldiers while they were on campaign. Why do you think the artists included soldiers' tasks on a column celebrating a military victory?

practiced decimation, in which one soldier in ten was killed if a unit disobeyed an order or failed badly. Traditionally, warfare in the Mediterranean was governed by informal rules that allowed surrender before either side suffered extensive losses. The Roman soldier, however, hated to return home defeated. The shame of it would prevent him from resuming his life in the city where everyone met face-to-face in the Forum.

The Roman army was an obedient, iron-willed fighting machine under the strict command of its leaders. The harsh discipline extended to camp life, because soldiers could not rest until they had fortified their camp to make them impregnable to surprise attack.

The victorious republican soldier returned after a season of fighting with only a few gold coins in his hand and the pride of victory in his heart. Through a relentless series of such victories, by 265 B.C.E. Rome had unified virtually the whole Italian peninsula. However, the Republic's growing wealth and power clashed with new foes outside the peninsula. These contests would transform the army, the Republic, and the Romans.

Wars of the Mediterranean

After Rome consolidated its hold on the Italian peninsula, it confronted Carthage, the other great power in the western Mediterranean. Carthage was founded around the same time as the city of Rome (ca. 800 B.C.E.) by a group of colonists from Phoenicia. The colony profited from its trade, prospered, and became a diverse and cosmopolitan city as great as those of the Hellenistic kingdoms. At the height of its power, the population of Phoenician Carthage probably approached 400,000, of whom no more than 100,000 were of fairly pure Phoenician heritage. In the busy shops, merchants spoke Greek and many other languages of the Mediterranean as they sold wares drawn from the farthest reaches of the Hellenistic kingdoms.

The skillful Phoenician sailors even ventured outside the Mediterranean basin, trading along the western coast of Africa. The Greek historian Herodotus (ca. 484–ca. 424 B.C.E.) described how Carthaginian merchants traded with African tribes, relying on mutual trust instead of language

throughout the territory—that is, tax-paying men between the ages of 17 and 46—had to report to the capital within thirty days. From this large group, the consuls and military tribunes chose their army.

The Romans' Victorious Army

By the early Republic, the army was organized in legions of about 4,000 men—about 40 companies of 100 men each, although the actual numbers that constituted a legion or a company varied over time. These were mostly foot soldiers fighting bare-legged in their tunics. All soldiers took an oath binding themselves to the army until death or the end of the war. The remarkable strength of this citizen army lay in its unequaled discipline. For example, commanders

skills. The merchants unloaded their cargo on the African shore, summoned local tribesmen by smoke signals, and then returned to their ships. The Africans approached and laid out what they thought would be a fair amount for the goods and then withdrew without taking the goods until the Carthaginians indicated their agreement on the price. As Herodotus wrote, "They say that thus neither party is ill-used; for the Carthaginians do not take the gold until they have the worth of their merchandise, nor do the natives touch the merchandise until the Carthaginians have taken the gold." By the third century B.C.E., the wealthy, enterprising Carthaginians had gained control of many territories in the western Mediterranean and confronted the growing power of the Roman Republic.

Rome's expansion and growing alliances began to encroach upon the Carthaginians, who had controlled the western Mediterranean for centuries, and it was only a matter of time before tensions came to a head. Rome's clash with Carthage began over who would control the Sicilian city of Messana, an area that the Romans saw as strategically vital to the security of southern Italy because it was on the straits between the island and the mainland. Carthage, for its part, resented the idea of Rome as a presence in Sicily. In 264 B.C.E., both sides sent troops in an effort to conquer the disputed island. This confrontation began the first of three hostile encounters between Rome and Carthage, called the Punic Wars. *Punic* meant "Phoenician," by which the Romans recalled the origins of the Carthaginians.

First Punic War

But to broaden their military efforts beyond Italy, the Romans needed ships. The city managed to raise some money and build a fleet, yet it had trouble finding admirals who had any solid seafaring experience. The Romans nevertheless demonstrated their famous tenacity and designed a new warship that would change the nature of naval battles. Before the Romans, the basic tactic at sea was ramming one ship into another, thus sinking the second. Sometimes sailors would board the opposing ship to engage the enemy, but not often. The Romans changed this. They developed a new vessel that featured a special platform that allowed many infantrymen on board. When they approached an opposing ship, Roman soldiers could then board the enemy vessel and fight hand to hand, a style that was their specialty. In the Punic Wars, Carthaginian naval commanders did what usually brought them success—they rammed the Roman ships. Before the Carthaginian vessel could pull away, however, a platform descended and Roman troops swept across, taking the lightly manned Carthaginian ship. The Romans would then simply scuttle their own destroyed ship and seize the Carthaginian one.

New Roman navy

In 241 B.C.E., Rome finally won a decisive sea battle against Carthage, and the First Punic War ended with a Roman victory. The Republic received control of Sicily and a large financial indemnity from the Carthaginians.

ROMAN WARSHIP The Roman infantry was unbeatable, but when Romans challenged Carthage, they had to learn to fight at sea. Instead of ramming an opponent's ship, Romans lowered a gangplank so that their infantry, shown here, could board the enemy ship and fight by hand.

But the larger question of who would control the western Mediterranean remained unresolved. A second contest seems to have been inevitable.

The Second Punic War (218–201 B.C.E.) began in Spain, where Rome and Carthage had signed a treaty dividing the spheres of influence at the Ebro River (see map on page 84). However, the treaty left one issue unresolved: Who would control the city of Saguntum, which lay south of the Ebro? Under the terms of the treaty it was in Carthaginian territory, but Rome had an alliance with Saguntum that predated the treaty. The Carthaginian general, Hannibal Barca, attacked Saguntum and in the process began the Second Punic War. This war was different from the first one, for when war was declared, the Romans had control of the sea, so Carthaginians knew victory would come only if they brought war to Rome itself.

Second Punic War

The Carthaginians may have lacked a fleet, but in their general Hannibal they possessed one of the greatest military strategists in history. The confident general surprised the Romans by taking the war to Italy, moving his large Hellenistic-style army overland from Spain into the peninsula. Now Roman legions had to confront the military power of armies that included war elephants. Crossing the Alps with 30,000 to 40,000 men, 6,000 horses, and about 35 elephants was a difficult feat; many men and elephants fell and died in the dangerous passes. However, Hannibal emerged in northern Italy with enough of an army (complete with a dozen or so elephants) to shock the local population and win many victories.

Hannibal expected Rome's subject peoples to rise up in his support, and while some did, the inner core of central Italy stayed loyal. The strong alliance system that Rome had built gave it a huge advantage. Nevertheless, the astonishing general handed Rome its worst defeat ever at the Battle of Cannae in 216 B.C.E., in which approximately 30,000

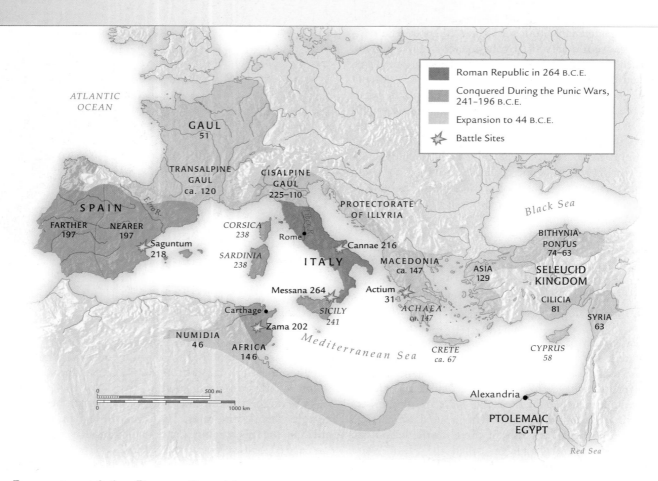

Expansion of the Roman Republic, 264–44 B.C.E. **This map shows the expansion of the Republic as it fought victorious wars against Carthage and the Macedonian and Seleucid kingdoms in the East.**

Romans died (see map above). Romans were shocked and frightened—for years Roman mothers would scare naughty children with the threat "Hannibal will get you"—and yet the Romans would not surrender. They adopted a defensive attitude of delay and refusal to fight while the Carthaginian forces marched up and down Italy for almost seventeen years—wreaking havoc along the way.

Finally, Rome produced a general who could match Hannibal's skill. Publius Cornelius Scipio (236–183 B.C.E.) had studied Carthaginian battlefield tactics and had the skill to improve on them. Scipio took Carthage's Spanish lands and then sailed to North Africa, bringing the war to Carthage. Hannibal had to leave Italy to defend his homeland, and he had to face the Romans virtually unaided. The Roman control of the sea prevented the Carthaginian ally Philip V of Macedonia (of the Hellenistic Macedonian kingdom discussed in Chapter 3) from helping, and Carthaginian support in North Africa was weak. Scipio decisively defeated Hannibal at the Battle of Zama in 202 B.C.E. (see map above) and won the surname "Africanus" to commemorate his great victory that saved Rome. Carthage again sued for peace—giving up Spain and promis-

ing not to wage war without Rome's permission. But peace would prove temporary.

Carthage was placed in a difficult position, for Numidia, one of Rome's allies in North Africa, was encroaching on its territory. Yet Carthage could not wage war against Numidia without Rome's permission, and Rome withheld it. The Senate was led by Cato the Elder (234–149 B.C.E.), who was virulently anti-Carthaginian. Plutarch recorded his famous rousing speech in 150 B.C.E. as he tried to spur his countrymen to resume the fighting against Car- **Third Punic War** thage. He reminded the Senate that Carthage was "only three days' sail from Rome," and he ended all his speeches with the phrase "Carthage must be destroyed." Cato spoke for many Romans who wanted to take on their old enemy again. The inflammatory language worked, and the Third Punic War began. After a long siege of the citadel at the top of the hill overlooking the town, Rome crushed the city of Carthage in 146 B.C.E. The Carthaginian general surrendered, and his wife, accusing him of cowardice, committed suicide by leaping with her two children into the flames of the burning city. The Roman general—another Scipio called

Aemilianus—reputedly shed tears at the sight of the ruin of the great city. The once-shining city of Carthage would lie in ruins for a century until Rome itself recolonized it.

The wars against Carthage drew the Romans into battling in the eastern Mediterranean, leading to three wars against Macedonia between 215 and ca. 168 B.C.E. Romans

Macedonia and Greece felt drawn into the first war because the Macedonian king, Philip V (221–179 B.C.E.), had allied with Hannibal after the Roman defeat at Cannae. Following this indecisive war, Rome was again drawn into eastern affairs as some of the Greek poleis solicited Rome's help against a coalition between the Macedonian and Seleucid kings. This time Rome won decisively and Macedonia agreed to stay out of Greek affairs. The third war arose when Macedonia again tried to reassert control over Greece. As a result of this war, Rome ruthlessly divided up Macedonia and eliminated any opposition.

At first, Rome left the Greeks "free," but there quickly arose a difference of opinion about the meaning of this term. The Greeks believed freedom meant to do as they liked; Romans believed it meant to act as obedient Roman clients. The Roman Senate finally ran out of patience and decided to annex the Greek mainland. To set an example to the recalcitrant Greeks, a Roman commander burned the city of Corinth, enslaved its inhabitants, and brought rich plunder back to Rome. The expansion eastward had begun, and it continued with the establishment of the province of Asia in 137 B.C.E., when the last king of Pergamum died, willing his land to Rome. Money, art, and slaves now flowed from the east to Rome, and the Republic had to decide how to govern its new far-flung conquests.

Historians still disagree about Rome's motives for continuing the warfare. Rome often marched to protect its allies—waging what they called "just wars." At the same time, some Romans were becoming rich in these enterprises, and Roman generals saw war as the road to upward mobility. Now the path to success for an ambitious Roman lay not in impressing his fellow citizens in the Forum, but in leading victorious armies.

Rome did not always annex territories outright. Sometimes it operated through client states, leaving local rulers in place. Sometimes victorious Romans established the

Administering provinces conquered territories as provinces—one in Africa, one in Asia, and later across the Alps in Gaul (southern France) in an area that is still called Provence. Within the provinces, people lived as they had in the past, but Rome's leaders expected these states to conform to their wishes (which at times caused friction). Governors were appointed by the Roman Senate to preserve

peace and administer justice to Roman citizens. Other duties were given to private individuals, who could make fortunes performing administrative duties. For example, tax collectors received a contract to collect a certain amount of taxes, and they could legally keep some profits they squeezed from local populations. The governors were supposed to make sure tax collectors did not abuse their privilege, but, not surprisingly, many of them took full advantage of this system and extracted huge amounts of money from helpless residents. The conquests in Italy had yielded most profits from land. In the provinces, on the other hand, people made money from land, slaves, and graft. In the process, the Roman Republic itself was transformed in various ways by its military success abroad.

An Influx of Slaves

In the ancient world, successful military campaigning earned a victor not just new territory and riches but also slaves. As Rome expanded, it accumulated more and more bondsmen and bondswomen. After the Second Punic War, more than 200,000 men and women were captured as prisoners of war and brought to Italy as slaves. Numbers like these changed the nature of Roman society. Now, instead of each small householder having one to three slaves (as we saw was the pattern in ancient Greece), rich households might have hundreds of domestic slaves. By the end of the Republic, there were between two and three million slaves in Italy, an astounding 35 to 40 percent of the population.

Thousands of slaves labored in agriculture or mining, working in large anonymous gangs. However, in the cities, slaves and citizens often worked in the same occupations, and all could earn money through their labor. The most undesirable jobs—garbage collection, mining, acting, and prostitution—were generally reserved for slaves, although freed men and women, while technically citizens,

Slave occupations were willing to do the most lucrative of these jobs. Often slaves dominated some of the higher-status jobs. After Rome's conquest of Greece (ca. 148 B.C.E.), most of the tutors and teachers to Roman children were Greek slaves. Most physicians were either Greek or trained in Greece, and it was not unusual for physicians to be succeeded by their Greek slaves, whom they had trained and then freed to take their place.

Perhaps not surprisingly, Romans often feared their slaves. The Stoic philosopher Seneca (4 B.C.E.–65 C.E.) wrote that "the **Slave revolts** least of your slaves holds over you

> The Greeks believed freedom meant to do as they liked; Romans believed it meant to act as obedient Roman clients.

An African Playwright

T.VI.ᵉ P.ⁱᵉ I.ʳᵉ   P.ᵉ CXI.

P.
TERENTIUS
AFER.

J.D. Dugourc del.   Legorof Junior Sculp.

TERENCE.

TERENCE, ca. 190—159 B.C.E.

During the peaceful interlude between the First and Second Punic Wars, a slave trader in Carthage purchased a young man named Terence, whose surname, "Afer," means "the African." Like many young slaves from the great conquered cosmopolitan cities, Terence was educated and talented. His owner recognized the youth's promise and granted him his freedom to pursue his artistic talents.

Terence gained fame as a playwright by transforming classic Greek works to give them a new vibrancy, while other playwrights simply translated classic plays into Latin, which Terence said "turned the best Greek plays . . . into Latin flops." Sadly, Terence died in his prime, from either illness or shipwreck, but he left a body of work that people still enjoy today. Terence exemplified the kind of upward mobility available to educated slaves during an age when Rome fell in love with Greek intellectual life.

How might Terence's life story foreshadow the ways in which modern artists and dramatists transform global art into work that is relevant to their own country? (Consider world music or the export of rap music for some examples.)

the power of life or death." As the numbers of slaves increased, Romans had more and more reason to worry, and they passed laws to try to protect themselves. For example, the punishment for murdering one's master was severe—all the slaves in the household were to be executed. Not only did individual instances of slave treachery crop up, but large-scale slave rebellions broke out as well.

Three great slave uprisings disrupted Italy and Sicily between 135 and 71 B.C.E. The most famous was led by the gladiator Spartacus between 73 and 71 B.C.E. Spartacus escaped his master with 70 of his fellow gladiators. Many other slaves joined them as the army of almost 70,000 slaves ravaged portions of Italy. They succeeded in defeating many of the soldiers sent after them. Some sources suggest that Spartacus even tried to take his army to Sicily to rally the slaves there but could not gather enough ships to cross the sea. Spartacus was finally killed and the rebellion crushed. Six thousand of Spartacus's followers were crucified—the brutal form of execution reserved for slaves. This revolt was suppressed, but Rome did not forget the potential for violence that simmered within the many men and women they had enslaved in their imperial expansion.

Economic Disparity and Social Unrest

Just as the expansion of Rome altered the nature of slavery, it transformed many other aspects of life in the Republic. These changes were noted sadly by many conservative Romans who watched their traditional way of life fade. One Roman (Silius Italicus) lamented the aftermath of Rome's victory in the Punic Wars: "[I]f it was fated that the Roman character should change when Carthage fell, would that Carthage was still standing." But such qualms were too late; the Republic was transmuting into something else entirely, even as some Romans mourned it.

One of the most noticeable changes came in the form of increasing disparity between rich and poor. Many of the upper classes had grown very rich indeed.

Governors of provinces had the opportunity to make fortunes undreamed of in the Republic's earlier years. Other enterprising Romans made fortunes in ship-building contracts, banking, slave trading, and many other high-profit occupations. Rome had become a Hellenistic state like the successor states of Alexander the Great (see Chapter 3), with a growing distance between the rich and the poor.

While some Romans amassed great fortunes, others suffered a worsening of their economic situations. The example of Cincinnatus, who fought for only one season and then returned to his plow, was impossible to repeat when foes were far away and wars long. During the Punic Wars, military time was extended. As a result, more than 50 percent of adult males spent over seven years in the army, and some spent as long as twenty years. Throughout most of the Republic, the army was not formally paid, and this caused both some hardship and a particularly strong relationship between soldiers and their generals. By right, generals controlled all booty taken in war, and they distributed some of it to their troops. Thus generals acted as patrons to their client soldiers, who increasingly owed loyalty to their general rather than to Rome itself. Meanwhile, as soldiers stayed longer in the army, their family fields remained unplowed. Numerous farmers went bankrupt, and soldiers returned to their homes to find them sold and their wives and children turned out of the family farm.

Newly rich men and women eagerly purchased these neglected lands, and small landholders were replaced by large plantations worked by gangs of new slaves. Fields that had cultivated wheat were slowly transformed to produce olives and wine grapes, much more lucrative crops. Other great landowners in Italy grew rich on ranches that raised animals for meat, milk, or wool. Now Romans had to import their wheat from abroad, particularly North Africa.

Spurred by economic hardship, the displaced citizens flocked to the city. The population swelled with a new class of people—propertyless day laborers who were unconnected to the structures of patronage and land that had defined the early Republic. **New poverty** These mobs created more and more problems for the nobility because they always represented a potentially revolutionary force in the Forum. Aristocrats tried to keep them happy and harmless by subsidizing food, but this short-term solution could not solve the deeper problem of lost jobs taken by newly captured slaves and land seized by the newly rich. The situation had become volatile indeed.

As if these social tensions were not disruptive enough, new intellectual influences further modified Rome's traditional value system. As the Republican armies conquered some of the great centers of Hellenistic culture from Greece to North Africa, Romans became deeply attracted to many of the Hellenistic ways. As the Roman poet Horace (65–8 B.C.E.) observed: "Captive Greece took her Captor Captive." With the capture of slaves from Greece, Greek art, literature, and learning came to Rome, and many in the Roman aristocracy became bilingual, adding Greek to their native Latin. Rome became a Hellenized city, with extremes of wealth and poverty and a growing emphasis on individualism over obedience to the family.

OPINION

When the Romans conquered the Hellenistic kingdoms and new ideas, goods, and slaves entered the city, what do you think caused the greatest transformation to the traditional Roman way of life?

Cato the Elder (234–149 B.C.E.)—the anti-Carthaginian orator—was one Roman who feared the changes that came with the increasing wealth and love of things Greek, and when he held the office of censor, he tried to stem the tide of Hellenization. The office of censor had come to be an influential one. During the early Republic, censors **Resisting change** had made lists of citizens and their property qualifications, but in time the censors became so powerful that they revised the lists of senators, deleting those whose behavior they deemed objectionable. To preserve the old values, Cato tried taxing luxury goods and charging fines to those who neglected their farms, but his efforts were in vain. Romans had added an appreciation of Greek beauty to their own practical skills, and they adopted a new love of luxury and power that seemed to erode the moral strength of old Rome. To men like Cato, the Republic was becoming unrecognizable, but Greek designers changed even the look of the city of Rome itself.

Concrete: A New Building Material

In the late third century B.C.E., Roman architects discovered a new building material that opened even more architectural possibilities than the perfection of the arch. Masons found that mixing volcanic brick-earth with lime and water resulted in a strong, waterproof building material—concrete. With this new substance, architects could design large, heavy buildings in a variety of shapes.

Combining concrete construction with the knowledge of the arch allowed for even more flexibility than before. After they had mastered the arch, Romans built with barrel vaults, a row of arches spanning a large space. As early as 193 B.C.E., builders constructed a gigantic warehouse in Rome using this technique. Concrete and barrel vaults also made possible the design of large bathhouses, for the concrete was strong enough to withstand the heat of steam

THE PANTHEON, 125 c.e. The Romans' use of concrete permitted the construction of stunning, enduring structures such as the Pantheon, a temple devoted to all the gods. The dome's circular hole, called the *oculus* (eye), reminded visitors of the eye of Jupiter that watched them continuously.

rooms. Finally, the new technology permitted the design of the oval amphitheaters that so characterized Rome.

Of course, people as religious as the Romans applied their architectural skills to their temples as well. Although most structures in Rome were made of brick or concrete covered with stucco, the growing Hellenization began to influence architectural tastes. Marble columns would soon grace the traditional buildings. In this new architecture, we can see the degree of the Greek slaves' influence on the Romans and Rome's own growing appreciation of Hellenistic art.

The fullest development of this temple construction took place early in the empire. The outstanding example of Roman religious architecture is the **Pantheon,** a temple

Pantheon dedicated to all the gods, shown above. It was built in 125 c.e. on the site of a previous temple that had been constructed during the late Republic. The structure is a perfect combination of Roman and Hellenistic styles and thus embodies the transformation of republican Rome imposed by Hellenistic influences. The front of the temple has a classical rectangular porch with Corinthian columns and a pediment, the triangular structure on top of the columns. From the front, the Pantheon resembles the Greek temples we discussed in Chapter 2. Inside the temple, however, any resemblance to Hellenistic architecture disappears.

The interior of the Pantheon consists of a massive round space (visible in the photograph above) covered by

"Our leaders ought to protect civil peace with honor and defend it even at the risk of life itself."

a high dome, revealing the Romans' engineering skills. A heavy concrete base supports the weight of the whole, while the upper walls are constructed of a lighter mix of concrete. The center of the dome has an opening that lets in natural light—and rain, though drainpipes beneath the ground (which still function today) took care of flooding problems.

Latin Literature

240–44 B.C.E.

In the third century B.C.E., Roman literature emerged. Written in Latin, it reflected the elements we have discussed throughout this chapter: Roman values, society, and the influence of Hellenistic culture. The earliest surviving examples of Roman literature are comic plays. Latin comedy flowered with the works of Plautus (205–185 B.C.E.) and Terence (190–159 B.C.E.), who wrote plays based on Hellenistic models but modified them for their Italian audience. Plautus and Terence wrote in verse, but unlike their Greek predecessors, they added a good deal of music, with flutes and cymbals accompanying the productions.

The Latin prose literature of the Republic emphasized the serious side of Roman character. The best of the prose writers were men who combined literary talent with public service—for example, Cicero and Julius Caesar.

Latin literature was shaped—indeed defined—by the writings of Cicero, whose career coincided with the decline of the Republic. His skillful oratory and strong opinions about Roman **Cicero** values placed him in the center of public life, but his long-standing influence derived from his prose, not his political involvement. His writings cover an extraordinary range of topics, from poetry to formal orations to deeply personal letters. From his more than nine hundred letters, we get a revealing picture of the personality of this influential man. He was deeply concerned about public affairs and political morality, writing, "our leaders ought to protect civil peace with honor and defend it even at the risk of life itself." At the same time, his letters reveal him to be vindictive, mercurial of mood, and utterly self-centered. Although scholars are ambivalent about the character of this complex man, there is no doubt about his influence. Cicero's writings defined the best use of Latin language, and his works were used as textbooks of how to construct elegant prose.

Julius Caesar's literary legacy also grew out of his active political life. As Caesar rose to power, he used literature to enhance his reputation in Rome. His accounts of his dazzling military campaigns in Gaul (across the Alps in modern France), vividly told in his *Commentaries,* intensified his popularity and have fascinated generations ever since. His Latin is clear and accessible, and his narrative vivid and exciting.

Caesar's writings

By the middle of the second century B.C.E., the Roman Republic had reached a crucial threshold. Vibrant, wealthy, and victorious in war, the Republic had established political and social structures that steadily fueled its success. But in crafting their society, the Romans had unwittingly planted the seeds of their own undoing. Their much-loved precepts, established in a simpler age, would prove unsustainable in a future where Rome boldly sought to extend its reach farther than ever before.

THE TWILIGHT OF THE REPUBLIC
133–44 B.C.E.

In the mid-second century B.C.E., Rome suffered a sudden economic downturn. The wars of expansion had brought vast riches into Rome, and this wealth drove prices up. When the wars ended, the influx of slaves and wealth subsided. Furthermore, an unfortunate grain shortage made grain prices skyrocket. This shortage worsened in 135 B.C.E. with the revolt of the slaves in Sicily. Half of Rome's grain supply came from Sicily, so the interruption of grain flow threatened to starve the masses of people who had fled to Rome when their own small farms had been taken over. To stave off disaster, two tribunes of the plebeians, Tiberius and Gaius Gracchus, proposed reforms. (The brothers were known as the Gracchi, which is the plural form of their name in Latin.)

The Reforms of the Gracchi
133–123 B.C.E.

The Gracchi brothers came from a noble family, yet they devoted their lives to helping the Roman poor. They credited their mother, Cornelia, with giving them the education and motivation they needed to use their privilege

Tiberius Gracchus Cries Out Against Injustice

The Greek historian Plutarch (ca. 46–120 C.E.) wrote a biography of Tiberius Gracchus. This excerpt contains Tiberius's most famous speech that became a rallying cry for the poor in Rome and precipitated Tiberius's murder.

For Tiberius . . . took his place, and spoke in behalf of the poor. "The savage beasts in Italy, have their particular dens, they have their places of repose and refuge; but the men who bear arms, and expose their lives for the safety of their country, enjoy in the meantime nothing more in it but the air and light; and, having no houses or settlements of their own, are constrained to wander from place to place with their wives and children." He told them that the commanders were guilty of a ridiculous error, when at the head of their armies, they exhorted the common soldiers to fight for their sepulchers and altars; when not any amongst so many Romans is possessed of either altar or monument, neither have they any houses of their own, or hearths of their ancestors to defend. They fought indeed and were slain, but it was to maintain the luxury and the wealth of other men. They were styled the masters of the world, but in the meantime had not one foot of ground which they could call their own.

What traditional Roman values does Tiberius say have been violated? What might the response have been to his speech?

for the good of the Roman people. The Gracchi seemed to many Romans to represent the best of republican men—devoted to a public life. Of course, many modern historians have observed that helping the poor would increase their own clients and prestige. Regardless of the motivations of the brothers, they set themselves apart from many aristocrats who no longer obeyed the rigorous demands of public service, preferring private pleasures instead. There were too few nobles willing to sacrifice their own interests for those of Rome when Tiberius became tribune of the plebeians in 133 B.C.E.

In Tiberius's view, Rome's problems came from the decline of the small farmer, which in turn prompted migra-

Tiberius's reforms

tions into the city and a shift to large-scale and cash-crop agriculture. Tiberius also recognized an additional problem with the growing landlessness—Rome did not have a pool of soldiers, for men had to meet a property qualification to enter the army. Thus, the newly poor could neither farm nor serve in the army—Rome had moved a long way from the days of the farmer-soldier Cincinnatus.

Tiberius proposed an agrarian law that would redistribute public land to landless Romans. The idea may have made a difference, but it alarmed greedy landlords. The law passed, but the Senate appropriated only a tiny sum to help Tiberius administer the law. Many senators were particularly worried when Tiberius announced he was running for reelection. Although in the distant past, tribunes had run for a second term, that had not been done for a long time, and Tiberius's opponents argued that it was illegal. In the ensuing turmoil, a riot occurred at an assembly meeting, and some senators with their followers beat Tiberius and 300 of his followers to death. With one stroke, a new element emerged in Roman political life: political murder.

Tiberius's land law continued to operate for a time, but not very effectively. In 123 B.C.E. Tiberius's brother Gaius became tribune in an effort to continue his brother's work, and he wisely appealed to a broad sector of the Roman people. He built granaries, roads, and bridges to improve the distribution of grain into the city, and these projects created jobs for many Romans. Gaius also tried to fix the price of grain to keep it affordable, and he appealed to the equestrian order by giv-

Gaius's reforms

ing them more influence in the wealthy provinces. Gaius opened the new Asian provinces to equestrian tax collectors and placed equestrians in the courts that tried provincial governors accused of abusing their powers. Many senators believed these reforms were politically motivated to destroy the Senate (which had destroyed Tiberius), and it was true that cheap grain might weaken the patron-client relationship that represented the backbone of senato-

rial power. The Senate moved to undo his reforms as soon as Gaius was out of office, and he and some 250 supporters were murdered in 122 B.C.E.—their deaths were arranged by one of the consuls supporting the Senate.

The Gracchi's sacrifices did not solve the Republic's problems. Their careers focused Rome's attention on its worries, but the brothers had also established a new style of republican government. From their time on, a struggle unfolded in Rome between men like the Gracchi, who enjoyed popular support (**populares**), and **optimates,** who intended to save the Republic by keeping power in the Senate. The old image of a nobility surrounded by and caring for its clients became supplanted by a much more confrontational model. The Gracchi were only the first to die in this struggle, and perhaps the greatest legacy of the Gracchi was the subsequent violence that descended upon the political arena. Roman public life would not be the same again.

Populares vs. *Optimates:* The Eruption of Civil Wars

123–46 B.C.E.

Even as Rome experienced violence in its political life, life in the provinces, too, seemed threatened. In North Africa, Rome's old ally Numidia caused trouble, and the Gauls threatened Italy from the north. Just as the military emerged as a primary instrument of political power, the generals, especially, had new opportunities to play a role in internal politics. The political struggle between the *populares* and the *optimates* catalyzed by the Gracchi was continued by popular generals.

The first general to come to power based on the support of the army was Gaius Marius (ca. 157–86 B.C.E.). An equestrian tribune, Marius took up the cause of the *populares*. To address the problem of the African wars and the shortage of soldiers noted by Tiberius, Marius initiated a way of enlisting new soldiers that would redefine the Roman military. He created a professional army, eliminating the previous requirement that soldiers own property. In addition, he formally put the soldiers on the payroll, making official the previous informal patron-client relationship between generals and their troops. Marius also prom-

Marius

ised them land after their term of service. In this way, he cultivated an army with many rootless and desperate men who were loyal only to him. Although Marius could not foresee the results, his policies established a dangerous pattern that continued through the rest of Roman history. With his new army at his back, the

OPINION

What do you think was the major reason the Roman Republic failed?

victorious general decisively defeated first the Numidians in Africa and then the Celts to the north. In his battles against Africans and Celts, Marius was accompanied by a brilliant young second-in-command, Lucius Cornelius Sulla (ca. 138–78 B.C.E.). In these wars that brought Marius so much power, Sulla felt that his brave exploits deserved some of the credit that Marius took, and he seethed with resentment.

New crises paved the way for the *optimates* to restore their own power under the aristocrat Sulla, who had learned warfare and resentment from Marius. The first threat to Rome's safety came from within Italy itself—the Italian allies who had first been conquered wanted a greater share in the prosperity that Rome's conquests were bringing. The violent fighting that took place between 90 and 88 B.C.E. finally forced Rome to give full citizenship to the Italian allies. This revolt by the Italian allies is called the "Social War" (from the Latin word *socii,* which means "allies"). The violence that devastated much of the countryside further weakened the Republic. As one of the consuls for 88 B.C.E., Sulla commanded six legions in the final stages of the Italian wars, and his successes earned him a

Sulla

governorship in Asia, where he was given the command to lead the armies against a second threat to Rome—Mithridates (120–63 B.C.E.), a king in Asia Minor who was threatening Rome's borders. However, fearing Sulla's growing strength, the assembly called Marius out of retirement and tried to give him control of Sulla's army. Perhaps Sulla's most dramatic moment came when he marched his army directly into Rome to confront Marius. The hostilities between the two generals made a permanent mark on the city, changing the peaceful Forum into a war zone. After defeating Mithridates, Sulla returned to Rome in 83 B.C.E. to take up the cause of the *optimates.*

Sulla assumed the long-dormant office of dictator but violated tradition by making the term unlimited. He also repealed laws that favored equestrians, and he killed off his political opponents. He buttressed the power of the Senate by passing laws to guarantee it, instead of allowing the tradition of Senate leadership to suffice. The venerable Roman constitutional system was becoming changed, and power politics began to fill the vacuum.

With the wars of Marius and Sulla, a new question confronted Roman politicians: how to protect the citizens from people seeking power and personal gain. Clearly, the old system of checks and balances no longer worked. The next group of popular leaders bypassed most of the formal structures and made a private alliance to share power. Modern historians have called this agreement the First **Triumvirate,** or the rule by three men. A contemporary called it a "three-headed monster."

The First Triumvirate (60–49 B.C.E.) was made up of three men who appealed to various sectors of Roman soci-

First Triumvirate

ety. Pompey, beloved of the *optimates,* was a brilliant general who had won striking battles in the east against Sulla's old enemy, Mithridates, and Mediterranean pirates.

Julius Caesar was probably an even more talented general and brilliant orator, who won wars in Gaul and Britain and had the support of the *populares.* The third man was Crassus, a fabulously rich leader of the business community who had also led armies (including defeating the rebel slave Spartacus). In keeping with tradition in Roman society, the political alliance was sealed by marriage between Pompey and Caesar's daughter, Julia. Instead of bringing peace, however, the triumvirate simply became an arena in which the three powerful figures jockeyed for control.

Events soon came to a head. Crassus perished leading armies to confront a new threat in Rome's eastern frontier. Julia died in childbirth, along with her infant. With her death, little remained to hold Caesar and Pompey together. *Optimates* in the Senate co-opted Pompey in their desire to weaken the popular Caesar, and they declared Pompey sole consul in Rome. Pompey accepted this command from the Senate, breaking his agreement with Caesar, ensuring retribution from the popular general. Caesar defied the Senate, which had forbidden him to bring his army into Italy, and in 49 B.C.E. marched across the Rubicon River into Italy. There was no retreating from this defiant act—a new civil war had erupted.

Julius Caesar

100–44 B.C.E.

Julius Caesar came from one of the oldest noble families of Rome. As with the Gracchi, his family associated itself with the *populares.* In the civil wars to come, Caesar enjoyed a high degree of support from the plebeians, but before he could take power, he needed the backing of an army. This he achieved in his wars of conquest in Gaul. Both his military successes and his captivating literary accounts of them won him broad popularity. According to the ancient writers, this accomplished general was tall with a fair complexion and piercing black eyes. Clearly a brilliant man in all fields, he enthralls historians today much as he fascinated his contemporaries.

The civil war between Caesar and Pompey that began in 49 B.C.E. was not limited to Italy; battles broke out throughout the Roman world. Caesar's and Pompey's armies clashed in Greece, North Africa, and Spain. After losing a

Civil war

decisive battle in Greece in 48 B.C.E., Pompey fled to Egypt, where he was assassinated. When Caesar followed Pompey to Egypt, he became involved with Queen Cleopatra VII (r. 51–30 B.C.E.) (also discussed in Chapter 5), who was engaged in a dynastic struggle with her brother. Caesar supported her claims with his army, spent the winter with her, and fathered her child; then he left in the spring to continue the wars that consolidated his victory over Pompey's supporters. In 46 B.C.E., Caesar returned to Rome.

Cleopatra joined Caesar in Rome as he took up a task harder than winning the civil war: governing the Republic.

The new leader faced two major challenges. First, he had to untangle the economic problems that had plagued the Republic since before the Gracchi attempted reform. Second, Rome needed a form of government that would restore stability to the factions that had burdened the city with so much violence.

Caesar applied his genius for organization to these practical tasks. He reformed the grain dole and established an ambitious program of public works to create jobs for the unemployed. To help displaced peasants, he launched a program of colonization all around the Mediterranean. Caesar's policies extended widely. With the help of an Egyptian astronomer who had accompanied Cleopatra to Rome, Caesar even reformed the calendar. The new "Julian calendar" introduced the solar year of 365 days and added an extra day every four years (the prototype of the "leap year"). With modifications made in 1582, the Julian calendar has remained in use throughout the West.

Despite his organizational skill, Caesar could not solve the problem of how to govern the Republic. In 48 B.C.E., he accepted the title of dictator, the venerable title Romans reserved for those who stepped in during a crisis. Unlike Cincinnatus (the Roman with whom we began this chapter), Caesar did not renounce the title when the emergency was over, but ultimately proclaimed himself dictator for life, a shocking departure from the traditional six-month tenure. He reportedly refused the title of king to avoid offending the republicans, yet he took on many of the trappings of a monarch. He wore royal regalia and established a priesthood to offer sacrifice to his "genius"—what the Romans called each person's spirit. In 44 B.C.E.,

Political titles

Caesar had his image placed on coins—perhaps the first time a living Roman was so honored. (Some historians believe Pompey may have beat Caesar to that distinction.) Some people began to question whether the Republic of Rome was changing too radically.

The Roman Republic Ends

The peace and order that Caesar brought to Rome pleased many, particularly the *populares* whose support had lifted Caesar to power. However, many Romans, even among his supporters, were outraged by the honors Caesar took for himself. He had shrunken the role of the *optimates,* and peace seemed to come at the price of the traditional Republic and at the expense of the old power structure. Some conspirators were simply self-serving, hoping to increase their own power. Sixty senators with various motives entered into a conspiracy to murder their leader. Even Brutus, a friend and protégé of Caesar, joined in the plot. He would be like the Brutus of early Rome who had avenged Lucretia and freed Rome from the Etruscan kings. This Brutus would save Rome from a new king—Caesar.

Conspiracy

Caesar was planning a military campaign for March 18, 44 B.C.E., so the assassins had to move quickly. On March 15, the date the Romans called the "ides," or middle of the month, they surrounded the unwary dictator as he approached the Senate meeting place. Suddenly they drew knives from the folds of their togas and plunged them

Caesar's murder

timeline

Struggle of the Orders 509–287 B.C.E.

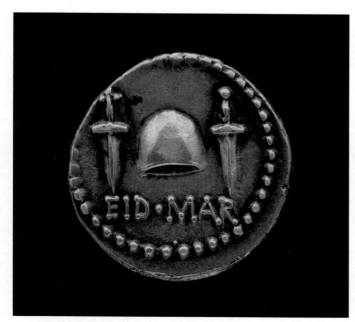

COMMEMORATIVE COIN Coins were struck to memorialize famous people and important events. Caesar's assassins produced this coin, marked with the Ides of March, the date of Caesar's murder, as well as the dagger that killed him.

into his body. He died at the foot of the statue of Pompey, his old enemy. Most of the killers seem to have genuinely believed they had done what was best for Rome. They saw themselves as "liberators" who had freed Rome from a dictator and who would restore the Republic. In 43 B.C.E., they issued the coin shown above. The coin depicts the assassins' daggers and reads "Ides of March." On the other side of the coin is a portrait of Brutus.

This attempt to celebrate a great victory on the coin was mere propaganda. The conspirators had no real plan beyond the murder. They apparently had made no provision for control of the army, nor for ensuring peace in the city. In the end, their claim to "save the Republic" rang hollow. After Caesar's death, one of his friends supposedly

lamented, "If Caesar for all his genius, could not find a way out, who is going to find one now?" The republican form of government so carefully forged during the Struggle of the Orders crumbled under the stress of civil wars and murder.

SUMMARY

The Republic of Rome, with its emphasis on family and city, began as a small village in central Italy and expanded until it controlled the Mediterranean basin, transforming the whole region.

- Early Romans founded their city near land occupied by the talented Etruscans and learned much from them as they moved from a monarchy to a Republic in which all citizens had a voice. They slowly expanded until they dominated the Italian peninsula.

- Romans were very different from the individualistic Greeks as they valued duty, family, and piety above all else, and prided themselves on their public reputations.

- With its disciplined armies, Rome began to expand beyond Italy, fighting the Punic Wars against Carthage in North Africa and conquering Greece and parts of Asia Minor. These conquests brought riches and slaves into Rome, transforming its traditional society, making it more like a Hellenistic state.

- The changes brought violent power struggles that tore at the traditional social fabric, bringing civil wars to the Republic. In the late Republic, Julius Caesar became a dictator, but he was murdered, plunging the Republic again into chaos of political strife.

Despite the assassins' confident claims, Caesar's murder did not solve anything. More violence would ensue until a leader arose who could establish a new form of government—and empire—that would endure even longer than the Republic.

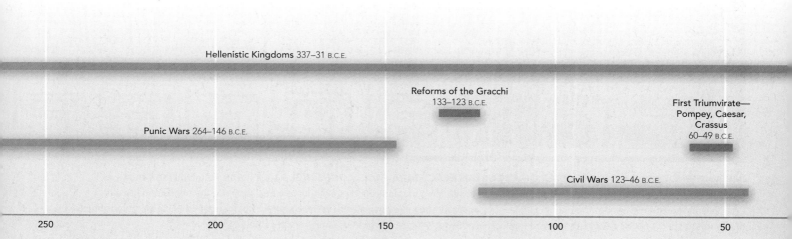

Hellenistic Kingdoms 337–31 B.C.E.

Reforms of the Gracchi 133–123 B.C.E.

First Triumvirate— Pompey, Caesar, Crassus 60–49 B.C.E.

Punic Wars 264–146 B.C.E.

Civil Wars 123–46 B.C.E.

250   200   150   100   50

IMPERIAL PROCESSION ON THE ALTAR OF AUGUSTAN PEACE (*ARA PACIS AUGUSTAE*), 9 B.C.E.   This sculptural relief shows a procession of the imperial family and their senatorial friends attending the dedication of a monument built to praise the peace and prosperity that Caesar Augustus brought to the Roman Empire. The portrayal shows Augustus with his head veiled as he performed ancient religious rituals to ensure prosperity for his people; the children reveal his hope for a future in which his family would continue to rule Rome.

Territorial and Christian Empires

5

The Roman Empire,
31 B.C.E.–410 C.E.

A Devoted Wife Protects Her Husband

During the years of civil war in Rome, when the Republic fell into violence as Julius Caesar fought with Pompey, took power, and was assassinated, many lesser Romans were swept up into the violence. Even after Caesar's death, the violence continued until his successor, Caesar Augustus, established an empire and brought about peace in the land. The life of one young couple reveals the struggles in this time of troubles. ▶▶

In 49 B.C.E. just as Julius Caesar was invading Rome, a young patrician couple married. Vespillo and his bride, Turia, paused during the happy ceremony to remember Turia's parents, who had been killed the day before during the wars between Caesar and Pompey. Turia's troubles were only beginning, because Vespillo had supported Pompey against Caesar, so he had to flee to Greece immediately after the wedding, leaving Turia and her sister to handle the family estate. When his escape seemed to fail, Turia hid him and made plans to help him slip away safely. She sold all her gold and pearls to fund his exile and continued to secretly send him money, even though such loyalty endangered her own life.

After Caesar's murder, Vespillo was pardoned by Caesar's successor, Augustus, but his troubles didn't end. Augustus's colleague, Lepidus, opposed the pardon. Brave Turia threw herself at his feet pleading for mercy for her husband, but that only made Lepidus more angry. He grabbed her, dragged her across the floor, covering her with bruises, but she never relented. She engaged sympathy from other patricians by showing off her bruises to all who would look, and shaming Lepidus in the process. Vespillo finally received his pardon, and he and Turia survived the civil war to enjoy the long years of peace—the *Pax Romana*—that Augustus introduced to Rome as he established an empire that was to endure for centuries.

The couple were married for forty-one years, and Vespillo's eulogy at Turia's death chronicled his appreciation of her resilience that had kept him alive during the wars. The couple's only disappointment in their marriage was their lack of children—a problem that repeatedly confronted the Romans during the empire.

While many like Turia and Vespillo praised Augustus as the savior of Rome, they did not realize that another child, Jesus, who had been born in the time of Augustus would eventually offer even greater promises of peace and salvation. Two empires grew up during this pivotal age—the Roman and the Christian—and both transformed the history of the West. ◄◄

THE *PAX ROMANA*

27 B.C.E.–180 C.E.

In 43 B.C.E., three powerful men emerged who established a new triumvirate to rule the Republic. Unlike the first, the Senate legitimized this Second Triumvirate, which ruled from 43 to 33 B.C.E. and seemed to offer a way to bring peace to the turbulent land. Marc Antony, who managed Caesar's vast fortune, was a strong general who seemed to challenge senatorial power. To balance his power, the Senate turned to Julius Caesar's grandnephew and adopted son, Octavian—a remarkably talented 19-year-old who played on popular sympathy for the murdered dictator by calling himself Caesar. The young Octavian offered respect to the Senate as he jockeyed for position against Marc Antony. The two brought into their partnership one of Julius Caesar's loyal governors and generals, Lepidus. At first, the three men controlled various parts of the empire: Octavian based his power in Italy and the provinces to the west; Lepidus held North Africa; and Marc Antony governed Egypt, Greece, and the provinces to the east. However, like the First Triumvirate, the second soon deteriorated into a power struggle among the three rulers. Octavian forced Lepidus into retirement in 36 B.C.E., and he and Antony vied for sole control of the empire.

As was traditional in Rome, politics was intimately bound up with family and with the women who, through childbearing, held the key to future family alliances. Not surprisingly, the political struggles between Octavian and Antony were to some degree played out in the bedroom.

Having lost Julius Caesar, Cleopatra sought to continue her ruling dynasty through a new alliance with a new ruler of Rome. She seduced Antony with the wit and charm that had so impressed the ancient biographers and bore him twins. Antony, however, was not yet committed to an alliance with Egypt's ruling house. Octavian's popularity in Rome was too high for Antony to risk offending the Roman people. Rumors already circulated in Rome's Forum that Antony wanted to move the Roman capital to Alexandria, so Antony had to negotiate a marriage that would be more acceptable to the public.

Antony and Octavian finally negotiated a peace that was to be secured by Antony's marriage to Octavian's sister, the young, beautiful Octavia. Octavia soon became pregnant, so the two families had the opportunity to seal their agreement permanently. But Antony left **Civil war** Octavia and traveled to Egypt. It is uncertain whether he decided that a strong political ally like Cleopatra afforded better security against Octavian than marriage to his rival's sister, or whether he was driven by the Egyptian queen's allure. In either case, the alliance bound through marriage dissolved. Octavian and Antony resumed their battle over who would rule all of Rome.

The war between the two leaders finally came to a head in 31 B.C.E., when Antony and Cleopatra, surrounded by Octavian's forces, risked all on a sea battle near the city of Actium, off the western coast of Greece. During this famous battle, Cleopatra and Antony proved less determined than Octavian, for Cleopatra's squadron left for Egypt in the course of the battle, and Antony followed her. They abandoned their navy and about twenty legions of their troops. Octavian's navy destroyed the Egyptian fleet, and his land forces quickly occupied Egypt.

Antony committed suicide, and Octavian personally inspected his corpse to be sure his rival was dead. Cleopatra refused to be taken prisoner and, according to legend, ordered her servant to bring her a poisonous snake. She committed suicide by its bite. Although robbed of an imprisoned Egyptian queen, Octavian stood as sole ruler of Rome. With Cleopatra's death in 31 B.C.E., the last Macedonian kingdom fell, ending the Hellenistic age that had begun with the empire of Alexander the Great. Now the new empire of Rome dominated the Mediterranean world.

A New Form of Governing

Unlike his uncle, Julius Caesar, Octavian successfully established a form of government that let him rule without offending the traditions of conservative Romans. This delicate balance between his leadership style and the old ways earned him widespread popularity. On January 1, 27 B.C.E., the young general appeared before the Senate and claimed that he had brought peace and was thus returning the rule of the state to the Senate and the people of Rome. Octavian acted in the spirit of Cincinnatus (see Chapter 4), the general who gave up rule to return to his plow, and the tradition-loving Romans appreciated his gesture. The Senate showed its gratitude by giving him the title Augustus, a name that implied majesty and holiness. It is by this informal title that his people addressed him and historians remember him. Augustus, however, modestly referred to himself as the *princeps*—that is, the "first citizen." The government he established was in turn called the **principate,** after the first citizen upon whom everyone depended.

The principate

The principate transformed the republican form of government, and historians roughly date the beginning of the Roman Empire from 27 B.C.E.—the date of Augustus's famous renunciation and acceptance of power. Under this new imperial form, the traditional representatives of government—the

Governmental structure

Augustus Tallies His Accomplishments

Shortly before he died in 14 C.E., Augustus left an account of his accomplishments that he wanted inscribed on bronze pillars to be installed in front of his mausoleum. Excerpts of this document give us a glimpse into this early period of the principate, which set the stage for subsequent imperial success.

5. The dictatorship offered to me in the consulship of Marcus Marcellus and Lucius Arruntius by the people and by the senate, both in my absence and in my presence, I refused to accept. In the midst of a critical scarcity of grain I did not decline the supervision of the grain supply, which I so administered that within a few days I freed the whole people from imminent panic and danger by my expenditures and efforts. The consulship, too, which was offered to me at that time as an annual office for life, I refused to accept.

17. Four times I came to the assistance of the treasury with my own money, transferring to those in charge of the treasury 150,000,000 sesterces. And in the consulship of Marcus Lepidus and Lucius Arruntius I transferred out of my own patrimony 170,000,000 sesterces to the soldiers' bonus fund, which was established on my advice for the purpose of providing bonuses for soldiers who had completed twenty or more years of service....

Why was Augustus so popular with the Roman people?

Senate and the Roman people—continued to exist and appoint the traditional magistrates to carry out their public business. The Senate continued to make disbursements from the traditional treasury and, in fact, slowly increased its power as it began to take over elections from the popular assemblies. The Senate also maintained control over some of the provinces—the older ones that did not require so many soldiers to guard the borders. In these ways, Augustus avoided offending the senators as Julius Caesar had done.

However, the vast extent of the empire and the increased complication of public affairs required a special magistrate—the princeps—to coordinate the administration of the empire and, more importantly, to control the army. By 70 C.E., the princeps was more often called emperor, a title with which troops had customarily hailed their generals. Building further on military precedent, Augustus established an imperial legion in Rome as his personal bodyguard. Known as the **praetorian guard,** this new body was named after the headquarters of the legion, or the *praetorium.* Roman generals had always had their own elite bodyguard, but because of its close association with the emperor, the praetorian guard, led by the praetorian prefect, became a powerful force on its own. The guard was unquestionably loyal to Augustus and worked to avert civil war such as the strife that had torn apart the Republic, but after his death a new political force had been created in Rome.

With these efforts, Augustus created a new structure on the remnants of the traditional Republic. In 2 B.C.E., the Senate awarded Augustus the title Father of the Fatherland. In a culture that depended on the father to guard his family's prosperity and honor, perhaps no other title could convey greater respect.

Of course, all these titles and honors, though significant, had little to do with the day-to-day practical problems of managing a large empire. Like any good father, Augustus ran the empire as one would run a household. He kept authority for himself, but the everyday business was handled by freed-

Administering an empire

AUGUSTUS OF PRIMA PORTA, ca. 20 B.C.E. This idealized portrait of Augustus shows the first Roman emperor as a divine guardian of Rome.

men and slaves in his household. Although Rome itself remained governed largely by the traditional forms, Augustus made dramatic changes in governing the provinces.

Augustus kept about half of the provinces—including wealthy Egypt—under his direct control, sending out representatives to govern there in his name. He began to create a foreign service drawn from the equestrian class (wealthy, upwardly mobile nonnobles), whose advancement depended upon their performance. This reform eliminated some of the worst provincial abuses that had gone on during the late Republic—for example, Augustus began eliminating private tax collectors. To keep the peace on the borders, Augustus stationed troops permanently in the provinces; the empire began to maintain fixed borders with military camps along the frontiers.

For all these reforms, even by ancient standards, the empire was astonishingly undermanaged—a few thousand individuals controlled some 50 million people. The genius of the system lay in a combination of limited goals on top—maintain peace, collect taxes, and prevent power from accumulating—with actual power exerted at the local level. Through its relative simplicity, the principate established by Augustus continued to function efficiently even during years of remarkably decadent rulers.

The Roman people recognized Augustus's accomplishments by according him a level of respect almost suiting a god, and this veneration would dramatically shape the future of the principate.

The image of Augustus as a divine being was reinforced in the great literature produced under his patronage. Virgil's famous epic, the *Aeneid* (ca. 29–19 B.C.E.), is a mythological tale of the wandering of the Trojan hero Aeneas, who founded the city of Rome. However, in spite of the book's echoes of Homer, Aeneas was a kind of hero different from Achilles, and in this portrayal, Virgil was able to show that the virtues of the past could work in the new age of the principate. Aeneas refuses to yield to his weaknesses or his passions and is rewarded

Virgil's *Aeneid*

with a vision of the future in which his descendants will extend Rome's rule "to the ends of the earth." In his epic, Virgil promises:

> . . . *yours will be the rulership of nations. Remember Roman, these will be your arts: to teach the ways of peace to those you conquer, to spare defeated peoples, tame the proud.*

The *Aeneid* did for Rome what Homer had done for classical Greece: It defined the Roman Empire and its values for subsequent generations, and in the process it contributed to the deification of Augustus. It was also a fine example of Augustus's talent for propaganda.

What Virgil did for Roman literature, Livy (59 B.C.E.– 17 C.E.) did for the empire's recorded history. In his long, detailed work, *The History of Rome* (ca. 26 B.C.E.–15 C.E.), **Livy's *Historia*** Livy recounted the development of his city from the earliest times to the principate, and he included many speeches that brought the past to life. Like Virgil, Livy emphasized Roman religion and morality, looking nostalgically back to republican values. And again like Virgil, the historian recognized that the future lay with the new imperial form of government. His history strongly influenced subsequent ancient historians and has remained a central source of information today.

The system established by Augustus was not perfect, but Augustus lived for so long that the principate became tradition. The Roman historian Tacitus (56–120 C.E.) wrote that by Augustus's death in 14 C.E., no one left alive could remember any other way to govern. For the next two centuries his successors ruled with the benefits of the imperial system that Augustus had established. But they also inherited major problems he left unresolved—Who should succeed the "first citizen"? How should one best govern such a large empire, and how would rulers handle such power?

Challenges to the Principate

69–193 C.E.

Augustus's long tenure as emperor postponed the problem of imperial succession, but this weakness in the principate showed up soon after his death. The next four **Augustus's successors** emperors all ascended the throne based on their ties to Augustus's family, and this succession showed how flimsy the concept of "first citizen" really was. An imperial dynasty had been established, and it did not matter that the rulers lacked the moral stature of Augustus or traditional republican virtues. During the Republic, leaders regularly confronted the Roman people in the

Forum and yielded to the pressure of scorn or applause. However, the new rulers of the empire experienced no such corrective public scrutiny, and the successors of Augustus immediately proved that power corrupted. The historian Suetonius (69–130 C.E.) recorded the popular scandalous rumors that circulated about the decline of Augustus's successor, his stepson Tiberius (r. 14–37): "No longer feeling himself under public scrutiny, he rapidly succumbed to all the vicious passions which he had for a long time tried, not very successfully, to disguise." Tiberius "made himself a private sporting house where sexual extravagances were practiced for his secret pleasure," and in his isolation, Suetonius claimed, his paranoia grew. He even executed people for insulting his stepfather's memory if they carried a coin bearing Augustus's image into a lavatory or brothel. The Roman people believed that such excesses continued throughout the dynasty of Augustus's heirs.

One of the heirs in this dynasty was Caligula (r. 37–41), an irrational—if not insane—ruler who wanted to be worshiped as a god. The praetorian guard took matters into its own hands and assassinated Caligula. The guard then found Claudius, a retiring, neglected relative of Augustus,

"How ugly and vulgar my life has become!"

hiding in the palace and promptly declared him emperor. Claudius (r. 41–54) was regarded by many Romans as an imbecile subject to the whims of his wives, but the power of the connection to the family of Augustus prevailed to solidify his rule.

Suetonius's history of those years tells of a series of murders within the family as members vied for the power of the princeps. Nero (r. 54–68) marked the most excessive of the murderers, for he killed many of his family members, mostly using his favorite means, poison. He even killed his mother, although it was not easy. He poisoned her three times, but she had taken a preventive antidote. Nero then tried to arrange for the ceiling of her room to collapse on her and for her boat to sink. When all these techniques failed, he simply sent an assassin to kill her and make it appear that she had committed suicide.

Nero was so despised that even his personal guard deserted him, and to avoid being captured and publicly executed, Nero commanded his slave to slit his throat, saying, "How ugly and vulgar my life has become!" It is not surprising that there were no more members of **A new dynasty** Augustus's family left to claim the succession, and the armies and the praetorian guard fought a bloody civil war to see which family would succeed to the imperial throne. Fortunately for Rome, Vespasian took power in 69 C.E. and restored some order to the empire, but even so fine an emperor could not ensure that his son would be equally competent. Each subsequent dynasty would eventually end through the weakness or corruption of one of the rulers,

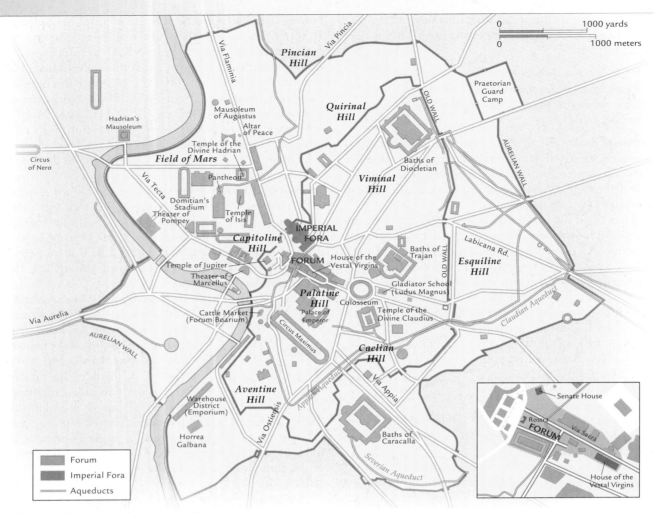

City of Rome During the Empire

This map shows the city of Rome during the empire and identifies the new buildings constructed by the emperors. Notice how monuments of imperial power and establishments for entertainment dominated the city during the empire.

and the flaws in the succession policy were repeatedly highlighted. The assassination of Vespasian's murderous son Domitian (r. 81–96) introduced a new period, that of the "Five Good Emperors" (96–180). These rulers increasingly centralized their power at the expense of the Senate, but they ruled with a long-remembered integrity. From Nerva (r. 96–98) to Marcus Aurelius (r. 161–180), these emperors established a tone of modest simplicity and adherence to republican values.

Marcus Aurelius represented the highest expression of a ruler whose political life was shaped by moral philosophy. He was highly educated in law, poetry, and philosophy, but the latter was his greatest love. When he was only 11, he adopted the coarse dress and sparse life of Stoic philosophers (discussed in Chapter 3), and when he became emperor, he continued to act based on the self-containment embodied in Stoic principles. Unfortunately, too many emperors did not share Marcus's wise self-containment.

Through these years, the City of Rome was transformed from a center of republican power to a glorification of imperial power. As the map above shows, the entertainment centers—baths, games—offered by the emperors began to dominate the city, and temples to divine emperors sprang up.

Throughout the reigns of emperors good and bad, the borders had to be guarded. Armies fought in the east and as far away as Britain. Centuries of Roman military presence along the frontiers had brought Roman-style **Provincial defense** cities and agriculture—indeed, Roman civilization—to the edges of the empire. This long-term presence of Rome in lands far from Italy served to add Roman culture to the growing Western civilization in the north of Europe as well as the Mediterranean.

However, holding such extensive lands caused many of these soldier-emperors to be away from Rome for extended periods. Hadrian (r. 117–138) spent twelve of his twenty-

The Roman Empire, 44 B.C.E.–284 C.E.
This map shows the greatest extent of the Roman Empire. Notice how much of this territory was acquired during the Republic, before Augustus's rule. The key also shows the major trade goods from the various parts of the empire. **Which territories brought the most essential or expensive trade goods?**

one ruling years traveling around the provinces, establishing fortifications and checking on provincial administration. However, it was one thing to establish definite borders and quite another to hold them. The Stoic emperor Marcus Aurelius spent the better part of thirteen years in fierce campaigns to keep the border tribes out of the empire, and he died while on campaign. His death brought an end to the era of the "good emperors," caused once again by a decadent son.

The long rule by good emperors may have been more the result of biological accident than anything else: Four of the emperors had no sons, so each of them adopted as his successor a man he thought best able to rule. However, Marcus Aurelius fathered a son, Commodus (r. 180–192), who unfortunately brought the age of the Five Good Emperors and the *Pax Romana* to an ignoble end through his cruel reign. Commodus seems to have been a simple-minded man who loved the games. He even shocked Rome by fighting in the arena as a gladiator. With Commodus's murder (he was strangled by his wrestling partner), peace ended in Rome in a fresh outbreak of civil war.

A Vibrant, Far-Flung Empire

One must credit the genius of Augustus's political system and the steadfastness of the Roman administrators for the empire's ability to flourish even during years of imperial decadence. In our age of rapid communication and many levels of administrators and financial managers, it is difficult to imagine how hard it must have been to govern, with a small bureaucracy, an area as large as the Roman Empire. The map above shows the extent of the empire through 284 C.E. Although this map looks impressive, it still requires some imagination to understand the meaning of these distances in the third century. For example, in good sailing weather, it took three weeks to sail from one end of the Mediterranean Sea to the other, and travel overland was even harder. Hauling goods by wagon train with escorts armed against bandits took so much time and manpower that it was cheaper to send a load of grain all the way across the Mediterranean than to send it 75 miles overland. Information moved almost as slowly as goods.

What could hold the empire together against the centrifugal force of these distances?

The empire found a partial answer in Romanization. From the time of the Republic, Romans had established colonies for military veterans in the provinces, and such colonial expansion continued under the empire. Furthermore, to boost the strength of his army, Augustus recruited auxiliary troops from the noncitizen population all over the empire. After serving twenty-four years, these veterans were awarded with citizenship and land in the colonies. These auxiliary troops also served to spread Roman culture. Colonies became the cities that grew up in Britain, North Africa, Germany, and the East, bringing Roman culture to the most distant corners of the empire. The cities boasted all the amenities that Romans had come to expect: theaters, baths, a colosseum, roads, and townhouses. These urban communities had so much in common that they seemed to erase the huge distances that separated them.

In these scattered, Romanized centers, local officials ruled. Town councils, for example, collected taxes and maintained public works, such as water systems and food markets. To collect taxes, officials maintained census figures on both the human population and agricultural produce and reported all to their superiors in Rome. This combination of local rule, Romanization, and some accountability to the central authority helped hold the fabric of the huge empire together.

The provinces depended not only on the administrative skills of local officials but also on their philanthropy. In the best tradition of ancient Rome, men and women used their private resources for the public good. Inscriptions recalling private contributions survive in towns and cities all over the empire and reveal how essential such charity was to the maintenance of the Roman Peace. One woman in central Italy bequeathed one million coins in her will for the town to use to provide monthly child-assistance payments for all children until boys reached 16 years of age and girls 14. Philanthropists ensured that Roman life prospered all over the empire by contributing funds for baths, libraries, relief of poverty, and even public banquets.

The empire also remained unified through the marvels of Roman engineering. Fifty thousand miles of roads supplemented the great rivers as primary means of transportation. As is true today, the upkeep of roads posed a constant challenge and expense, and the empire used public and private means to fund them. The government collected tolls on goods in transit to fund road maintenance, but the toll payments seldom generated enough income. When in need, the empire turned to traditional philanthropy to make up the difference, asking local individuals and businesses to sponsor the upkeep of a particular portion of the road and erecting stones acknowledging their contribution. Such stones remain today in silent testimony to the philanthropy and organization that helped tie together the vast imperial lands.

Roman authorities also established a transportation system that provided travelers with horses and carriages and that monitored the movement of heavy goods. Regulations established maximum loads but were frequently ignored by inspectors, who often took bribes. With these elaborate networks of roads, lightly burdened travelers could cover an astonishing 90 miles a day—an extraordinary feat in ancient times.

During the early centuries of the empire, goods moved over great distances not only along the road network, for there was also a great deal of shipping. For the first time in the ancient world, the Roman navy kept the Mediterranean Sea relatively free of pirates, so shipping flourished. The sea had become a virtual Roman lake, and the Romans confidently called it Mare Nostrum (our sea) to show the degree to which the Mediterranean world was united under Rome.

The peace and unity of the empire allowed merchants to increase trade with the farthest reaches of Asia. The fabulous Silk Road brought spices and silks from as far away as China and only whetted the appetite of wealthy Romans for exotic goods from the East.

Finally, the movement of people and armies also held the empire together. The Roman Empire boasted a remarkably multiethnic and multicultural population. Many educated provincials, for example, spoke at least three languages: Greek, Latin, and a local dialect. The imperial lands included a bewildering array of climates and geological features as well. The northern outpost of the empire in Britain was the 80-mile-long wall of Hadrian, built in the early second century. Here, Roman forts dotted the wall at 1-mile intervals. Roman soldiers peered into the damp fog, on alert against the fierce northern tribes who threatened to swarm across the imperial boundary. In the photograph on page 103 of the ruins of Dougga, a Roman city in North Africa, you can see in the background the desert that marked the southern border of the empire. Beyond the great groves of olive trees that, together with abundant fields of grain, produced much of the agricultural wealth of North Africa, Roman legions stood watch against the Bedouin tribesmen who came galloping out of the desert to menace the edge of the empire.

With this remarkable diversity came the constant movement of people. Merchants traveled with their goods, and just as in the Hellenistic world, enterprising people moved about to seek their fortunes. Furthermore, to

Colonies

Provincial administration

Roads and transportation

OPINION

Why do you think Romans found it fairly easy to conquer huge territories, but harder to manage them?

Imperial diversity

ROMAN RUINS The southern boundary of Rome was marked by a desert. These Roman ruins in the city of Dougga in modern Tunisia show how Roman culture extended to the dry southern lands.

defend the empire's 6,000 miles of border, Roman authorities moved approximately 300,000 soldiers to wherever they were needed. The armies usually did not patrol their own regions. A garrison of black sub-Saharan Africans, for example, was stationed in the foggy north along Hadrian's Wall, and Germans from the north patrolled the desert. At the height of the *Pax Romana,* this flexible system seemed to ensure peace within Rome's borders.

As we will see, in time the centrifugal forces began to work against the ability of such a far-flung empire to hold together. The expense and difficulties of long-distance trade caused more and more provinces to produce their goods locally. Outside the empire itself, more tribes wanted to enter and share Rome's prosperity, and the borders would become all too permeable. But for the first two hundred years of the empire, it seemed as if the promise of a glorious new age had been fulfilled.

LIFE DURING THE PEACE OF ROME

Just as Augustus wanted to return politics to the traditional morality of the Roman Republic, he also tried to revive the old morality in the private lives of Rome's citizens. However, the new wealth that poured into the pockets of well-placed Romans made the old morality seem quaint and antiquated.

A New Decadence

Although the growing separation between rich and poor that began under the Republic continued through the empire, those getting more wealthy began to flaunt their riches. Silks and embroidery replaced the rough wool of republican virtue, and satirists wrote scathingly of women sporting makeup, high heels, elaborate hairstyles, and lots of jewelry. Men, too, indulged in similar excesses to ensure their appearance reflected their wealth and status. Augustus and subsequent moralists would fight a losing battle against such decadent displays.

The Problem with Population

During the Republic, marriage and family ties were central values of the Roman people, and Augustus used his power to support those values. The princeps promoted legislation that assessed penalties on people who remained unmarried and instituted strong laws against adultery. These laws, though intended to strengthen the family, fell far short of their mark. Morality is singularly hard to legislate, and the Roman historian Tacitus observed that many people simply ignored the laws. Augustus himself experienced this phenomenon firsthand: Unable to control his own daughter's behavior (which he perceived as inappropriate), he ended up exiling her.

Then & Now
Gym Habits

At Roman baths men and women (in separate accommodations) lifted weights, ran on tracks, swam, and enjoyed massages and soaking in hot tubs. These baths also offered the services of a hair plucker, whose job was to remove the body hair of men and women one hair at a time. This was not only for appearance, but also to make sure no body lice could attach. Although today's gyms don't host "pluckers," they have borrowed many amenities from the Roman baths. They also offer popular spa treatments, such as facials and mud baths, that Romans might find as peculiar as we find the concept of a plucker today.

 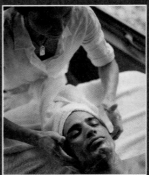

At heart, however, the laws were probably as much about children as about morality. The future of Rome, like the succession of the emperor, depended on offspring to carry on the family and other cultural traditions. Yet, throughout the empire, Romans had a particularly hard time reproducing. Augustus even promoted a law that exempted women from male guardianship if they bore three children (four children for a freed slave). These numbers are a far cry from those in earlier times; Cornelia, mother of the Gracchi, earned praise for bearing 12 children! Fecundity in the empire certainly had plummeted to alarmingly low levels.

Birthrates

This phenomenon had cultural as well as physical causes. Wealthy Roman men and women often wanted few children, so as to preserve their inheritance intact. Yet, Augustus's law specifically tried to influence women. This law is particularly interesting in its assumptions: It recognized women's desire for freedom, and it assumed that women controlled their own fecundity. The former assumption may have been accurate, but the latter was only partially so. Sometimes women used birth-control methods based on herbs, spermicidal drugs, or douches. The texts also refer to abortion, although drugs strong enough to abort a fetus often endangered the life of the mother. The causes of Roman infertility lay in a full complex of medical misunderstandings combined with cultural practices.

Sexual and Medical Misunderstandings

Despite the scandalized commentary lamenting the sexual excess of "loose" women and decadent emperors, Romans in fact were very circumspect about sex. Medical wisdom warned men against the fatiguing effects of sexual activity, which they thought deprived the body of vital spirit. Roman physicians believed semen was made of brain fluid, and urged men to conserve it carefully.

By contrast, physicians did not believe that sexual intercourse weakened females. Indeed, medical advice for women focused on helping them to bear as many children as possible. Yet, medical misinformation actually contributed to Rome's falling birthrate. Physicians concluded, incorrectly, that women were most fertile soon after their menstrual periods, so they recommended reserving intercourse for that time. Furthermore, some doctors thought that women had to have intercourse before puberty in order to mature correctly. Medical misunderstanding about women's bodies and children's health care contributed to a low birthrate. These factors combined with other cultural issues—the desire to restrict children to keep from reducing inheritances, for example—help explain why Rome had so much trouble maintaining its population.

Despite the confusion regarding human reproduction, Roman medicine proved highly influential for the next 1,500 years. In particular, the physician Galen (131–201) popularized views that have prevailed even into modern times. Galen used some modern scientific techniques—for example, he performed vivisections on pigs to see the process of digestion—but his conclusions were strongly rooted in the classical world. He embraced the notion of moderation that was so central to ancient thought and therefore saw disease as the result of an imbalance, or excess. Galen believed that good health resulted from a balance among the four "humors," or bodily fluids—blood, bile, urine, and phlegm. He argued that each of these humors had its own properties—warm, cold, dry, and moist—and when a person was out of balance—that is, when one

Galen

humor dominated—the cure was to restore an appropriate equilibrium. For example, if a person was feverish and flushed, he or she was considered to have an excess of blood. An application of blood-sucking leeches or the initiation of bleeding would reduce the blood and restore the balance. These ideas may not have improved people's health, but they formed the subsequent basis for medical treatment.

The Games

Families may have formed the basis of Roman society, but as we saw in Chapter 4, during the Republic, men forged critical ties in the world of civic affairs centered in the Roman Forum. Under the empire this focus changed; real power moved from the Forum to the emperor's household. Yet the Roman people still needed a public place to gather and express their collective will. Over time, they began satisfying this need at the great games and spectacles held in the amphitheaters across the empire. During the late Republic, wealthy men who craved the admiration of the people, and politicians who sought the loyalty of the crowd, spent fortunes producing chariot races in the Circus Maximus and hunts and gladiator games. After the time of Augustus, the emperors had a virtual monopoly on providing entertainment in Rome, although in the provinces others could produce spectacles. These games always had a religious significance to the Roman people, ritualizing Roman power and authority.

The Roman Colosseum, shown in the photographs on page 106, was built by Emperor Vespasian (r. 69–79) as a gift to his subjects. The map on page 100 shows its location within the city. This structure was the largest of its kind in the Roman world and held about 50,000 people. The photograph on the right on page 106 shows what remains of the interior,

From Forum to arena

Art Investigation

Wall Painting from a Baker's Shop in Pompeii

ca. 70 C.E.

This painting is from a baker's shop in the city of Pompeii, which was destroyed by the volcano Vesuvius in 70 C.E. Pompeii's preservation of small elements of Roman daily life makes it an important source of information about the past. The painting shows a prosperous, middle-class couple; the woman holds writing implements—a stylus and wax tablet—and the man holds a scroll (equivalent to an ancient book) with a label that identifies its contents. Notice how realistically the couple is portrayed.   What does the image suggest about the woman's role in business, and in urban economy more generally?

including subterranean passages that held animals and prisoners. The photograph on the left shows the exterior, which dominated the skyline of Rome. Men and women flocked to the arena in the mornings to watch men hunt

THE COLOSSEUM This magnificent building was inaugurated in 80 C.E. The concrete foundations were 25 feet deep to support the structure of concrete and marble. More than 50,000 spectators entered through numbered gates to their seats.

exotic animals that had been transported to Rome from the farthest reaches of the empire. Augustus proudly claimed to have provided a total of 3,500 animals in these hunts; other emperors were equally lavish in their displays.

The crowds then witnessed the public executions of criminals who were either set aflame or put in the path of deadly wild animals. Through such rituals, Rome displayed its power over its enemies. The image below shows a criminal being attacked by a leopard in the arena. The very existence of the mosaic, which was displayed in a private home, reveals the Romans' pride in the empire's dominance over its perceived enemies. As we will see, these enemies would eventually include Christians.

CONDEMNED TO THE BEASTS, ca. second century C.E. During the mid-afternoon at the games in the amphitheaters, criminals sentenced to death were attacked by beasts. This mosaic from a private home was designed to celebrate Rome's victory over its enemies.

Afternoons at the Colosseum were reserved for the main event, the gladiator contests. Gladiators were condemned criminals who were trained in the gladiator school near the Colosseum (see map on page 100). They then received the right to live a while longer by fight-

Gladiators

ing against each other in the arena. In time, the gladiatorial ranks were increased by slaves who were specifically bought and trained for this purpose. Gladiators armed with weapons were paired to fight until one was killed, and the winner won the right to live until his next fight. At first, gladiator contests were part of funeral rites, and the death blood of the losers was seen as an offering to the recently departed. Later, however, emperors sponsored contests featuring hundreds of gladiators. At the end of a gladiator contest, the man who had been overpowered was supposed to bare his throat unflinchingly to the killing blade of the victor. Not all defeated gladiators were killed; those who had fought with extreme bravery and showed a willingness to die could be freed by the emperor's clemency.

It is easy to judge these activities as wanton displays of brutality. Yet, from the Roman perspective, these rituals actually exemplified and perpetuated Roman virtue. In the arenas, private honor and public good intersected: The private generosity that funded the games served the community's need for ritual, and the emperor's sponsorship strengthened the community's loyalty to its leaders. Finally, individuals learned to face death bravely by watching people die; as the historian Livy (59 B.C.E.–17 C.E.) wrote: "There was no better schooling against pain and death." Nevertheless, all these demonstrations of Roman largesse, prowess, and courage could not stave off the threats to the empire that came at the end of the *Pax Romana*.

CRISIS AND TRANSFORMATION

192–ca. 400 C.E.

The violence that accompanied the assassination of Marcus Aurelius's decadent son Commodus in 192 transformed Augustus's principate. The armies had grown strong under the military policy of the Five Good Emperors, so armies even beyond the praetorian guard became the king makers. Septimius Severus (r. 193–211) was a new kind of emperor—a North African general who came to power because of his army's support. A military man to the core, he also embodied the multicultural elements of the empire. He spoke Latin with a North African accent and seemed to feel more at home among provincials than among the old, wealthy families of Rome.

The Military Monarchy

Septimius transformed the political base for Roman rule. Under the principate as established by Augustus, the empire was ruled by a partnership between the emperor and the Senate; Septimius and his successors ruled with the support of the army, creating a military dictatorship. Septimius enlarged the army until it contained several legions more than the army of Augustus. He also raised soldiers' pay, ensuring their loyalty. Septimius militarized the civil government as well, by making extensive use of generals in positions of power. With these changes, the route to high office lay through the emperor's army instead of the *cursus honorum*. Rome had changed indeed.

Severan dynasty

Septimius established a dynasty (the Severan) that uneasily held power until 235. His son Caracalla (r. 211–217) was ruthless and was murdered while on campaign. Strong women in the Severan family—Julia Maesa, Caracalla's aunt, and her two daughters—managed to ensure that two more incompetent boys took the throne, but both Elagabalus (r. 218–222) and Alexander (r. 222–235) were murdered.

In the fifty years that followed Alexander's death, Rome was beset with chaos. During this period, legions in various parts of the empire put forth their own claimants to the throne. This era of conflict—from 235 to 285—was dominated by what has come to be called "barrack-room emperors," men who had little allegiance to the ancient values of the city of Rome. From 235 to 285, the number of claimants to the throne exploded. In one nine-year period, the emperor Gallienus fought off as many as 18 challengers. A unit whose general became emperor increased its own status, so armies fought for the throne.

While armies were busy trying to create emperors, Rome's borders were threatened on all fronts. In the north, Germanic tribes (discussed more fully in Chapter 6) began to penetrate across the Rhine and Danube defenses. Soldiers and resources had to be moved north to try to stem the tide. Meanwhile in the east, Rome seemed so weakened that Zenobia, a powerful queen of Palmyra (a city in Syria), declared independence from Rome and led armies against the legions. Emperor Aurelian (r. 270–275) crushed Palmyra after two wars and brought Queen Zenobia in chains to Rome. The resourceful queen ended up living out her life in an extravagant villa near Tivoli in Italy, but her city was destroyed. Rome was not as successful in other eastern campaigns, as the Persian Empire encroached on Rome's eastern provinces. A Persian rock inscription celebrates a Persian victory and indicates the stress on the empire during these dark days: "We attacked the Roman Empire and annihilated . . . a Roman force of 60,000."

Border wars

This whole military era demonstrates the centrifugal force that had marked Rome's growth from the beginning. Emperors were created in barracks far from Rome, and territories on the edges of the empire were slipping from centralized control. As if these internal and external pressures were not enough, a severe economic downturn loomed.

Ravaged by Recession, Inflation, and Plague

At the height of the empire, certain families accumulated astonishing wealth. Even though they gave some of it back to the public in the form of monuments or games, they still lived lavishly. Not only did they buy jewels and fine silks, but they gave banquets featuring exotic (and expensive) imported foods. One menu from a Roman cookbook recommends rare dishes from the far reaches of the empire: sow's udders stuffed with salted sea urchins, Jericho dates, boiled ostrich, roast parrot, boiled flamingo, and African sweet cakes.

Economic recession

This kind of luxury spending seriously damaged an already weakening economy for two reasons: It drained hard currency from the West and transferred it to the Far East, which supplied many of the luxuries; and it kept money from circulating, thus limiting the avenues for the growth of a prosperous middle class. As the poor in Rome received more and more food subsidies, the city had to spend more

> "We attacked the Roman Empire and annihilated . . . a Roman force of 60,000."

money on imported grain, further reducing the treasury. With the increase in imports from the East, the western centers of the empire began to suffer a shortage of hard currency, as money flowed to the great eastern centers that supplied most of the imports. As we will see, this shifting of wealth to the East had profound ramifications for the governing of the empire.

There was a further inherent weakness in the imperial economy: When territorial expansion stopped, there was little to bring new wealth into the empire. Instead, a growing bureaucracy, increased military expenses, and costly military rivalries served to drain money. The economy stagnated while expenses increased.

Emperors throughout the centuries tried to address the problem of a shortage of hard currency by debasing the coinage, which meant that plenty of money still circulated, but it was not worth as much as it had been before. Gold coins virtually disappeared from cir-

Inflation

culation, and by the mid-third century the silver content of coins had dropped to a negligible 1 percent. Not surprisingly, inflation struck. The price of grain climbed so much that a measure that cost two coins in 200 C.E. cost 330 coins just a century later. Inflation always hits the poor hardest, and many people turned to banditry out of desperation. The resulting fear and unrest further rocked life in the empire.

To worsen matters, plague from China spread through the empire along with the luxury goods that came along the Silk Road. Just as in China, the disease caused intense suffering and depleted the already low Roman population. Labor became as scarce as hard currency. The Roman government turned to the tribes outside its borders to replenish its armies. Mercenaries crossed the borders to fight for Rome, and the legions of Rome increasingly came to resemble the "barbarians" from the outside. Structures like Hadrian's Wall no longer clearly separated the "civilized" from the "uncivilized."

All the problems of the late second and third centuries demonstrated that the Roman Peace was over. The borders between Roman and non-Roman had dissolved, and hungry, restless residents agitated within the empire. Medical knowledge was helpless in the face of pandemics like the mid-third-century plague, and Roman families could no longer populate the empire. The empire seemed to teeter on the brink of collapse.

The Reforms of Diocletian

285–305 C.E.

Considering the many disasters facing the empire in the mid-third century, it is a wonder that the empire did not fall then. In fact, it was the dramatic measures of Diocletian, an autocratic new emperor, that helped Rome avert ultimate disaster—at least for the time being. Diocletian (r. 285–305) was a general who rose from the ranks

to wear the imperial purple. Not content to be called emperor, he assumed the title "lord" and demanded that his subjects worship him as a living god. The change in title marked the formal end of the principate founded by Augustus—from then on, emperors were no longer "first citizens." Diocletian had a shrewd, practical side and used his considerable administrative talents to address the problems plaguing the empire. The new Roman lord was up to the task and stopped the decline.

Turning to the problems of communication, administration, and succession, Diocletian organized the government into a **tetrarchy,** or rule by four men. Diocletian ruled in the wealthier eastern region of the empire, while assigning his partner, Maximian, to rule in the

Tetrarchy

West. To address the issue of succession, each of these "augusti" adopted a "caesar" who would succeed him. In the Roman tradition dating back to Octavian, each caesar

TETRARCHS, ca. 305 C.E. Diocletian's division of the Roman Empire's administration among four men might have seemed to some people to fragment it. This statue from Venice shows the four tetrarchs embracing and thus strongly linked as one, assuring the viewer that the empire still stood united.

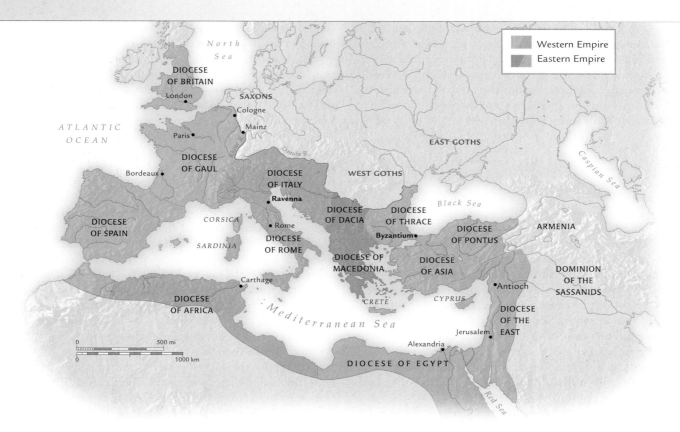

Diocletian's Division of the Empire, 304 C.E.

This map shows Diocletian's administrative reform of the empire and its division into four parts that would be governed by a tetrarchy (four men). Notice the primary division into east and west, with each unit ruled by an augustus.

married his augustus's daughter, sealing the alliance through family bonds. The map above shows the territorial division of the tetrarchy.

Diocletian then turned his administrative talents to problems other than succession. He recognized that the military that had created so many emperors from the time of Septimius Severus onward was a threat to political stability. He brought the army under control in part by reversing Septimius's policy of uniting civil and military offices. He separated the two so that provincial governors could not command armies, thus making it harder for generals to aspire to the purple. To address the problem of incursions along the imperial frontiers, Diocletian rearranged the armies.

Military reforms

Instead of placing his greatest martial strength along the borders, he stationed mobile legions deep inside the empire. That way, they could move quickly to meet a threat rather than just react as outsiders encroached. The Germanic tribes on the northern borders were particularly eager to enter the empire, looking for wealth. Diocletian recruited many of these Germans to serve in this new army, further diluting its traditional Roman character even as he made it more effective.

Finally, Diocletian turned to the severe economic problems troubling the empire. In the same way Augustus had tried to improve morality by decree, Diocletian issued economic edicts. He addressed the rampant inflation by freezing prices and wages, but these policies simply led merchants to withdraw goods from the **Economic reforms** open market to participate in informal black market exchanges. The emperor also raised taxes to pay for an expanding army, but he reformed the tax system so that it was partially based on payment in goods instead of in the inflated, scarce coins. This kind of authoritarian approach could not solve the empire's most deep-seated economic troubles, but it kept the economy from collapsing altogether.

The last problem that Diocletian addressed was the simple shortage of people to perform the tasks needed to keep the empire running. Again, he sought solutions in decrees. He identified "essential" occupations—ranging from soldier to farmer, baker, and tax collector—and froze people in these jobs. Furthermore, he made these occupations hereditary. His decrees had a serious unintended consequence: They weakened the willingness of well-off locals to contribute to the public works and the games that had so defined imperial life. Instead, great estates became more self-contained, pulling away from the central authority and maintaining their own mercenary armies. People increasingly complained about the tax collectors and the central government that seemed to ask more and more of its citizens while providing less and less.

The Capital Moves East

Diocletian's attempts to stabilize the succession barely outlasted him. He and his co-augustus stepped down in 305 as planned, leaving the empire to be ruled by their two caesars, but Diocletian's hopes for a smooth transition proved overly optimistic. There were years of intrigue and civil war as several rulers fought for the throne. Finally, one of the caesars was succeeded by an ambitious son, Constantine (r. 306–337), who defeated his rivals to assume sole control of the empire. The new emperor finally disbanded the powerful praetorian guards, who had backed his rival. Beyond that, he kept Diocletian's economic and military reforms but put his own unique stamp on the empire.

In 330, Constantine made a momentous decision for the future of the empire: He built a new urban center on the site of the old Greek city of Byzantium. Later the city would be called Constantinople, **Constantinople** after its founder, and become a second capital to the empire, eclipsing Rome itself in power and grandeur. Rome was no longer a practical site for the capital of the empire because it was too far from the center of the military actions on the borders, and the conservative old Roman nobility made it very difficult for emperors to implement vigorous new ideas. Constantine could not have chosen a better site for a new capital city, which he called his "new Rome." It was easily defended and located along the rich eastern trade routes. Since Diocletian, when emperors ruled autocratically based in cities away from Rome, the great Roman Senate that had governed in concert with Augustus had shrunk to no more than a city council. The Roman Empire seemed to have little to do with Rome anymore and bore scant resemblance to the principate created by Augustus.

As the capital moved east, the western provinces came under increasing pressure from the Germanic tribes outside the empire. Great estates in the provinces—called *latifundia*—became more self-sufficient, needing nothing from the central authority.

After the death of Constantine in 337, emperors reacted to Germanic invaders by inviting some tribes into the empire to settle and become allies. The borders had already proved permeable, and with the continued population decline within the empire, there seemed to be enough space for everyone. This influx, however, carried the seeds of the empire's eventual disintegration. The Visigoths (more fully described in Chapter 6) were one of the tribes the Romans invited across the border to settle. However, the Romans treated them abysmally, giving them land they could not farm, raping their women, and forcing them to sell their children into slavery in return for food. The warlike tribe went on a rampage.

In 378, Romans under Emperor Valens (r. 364–378) confronted Gothic troops, and the resulting battle marked a change in military tactics. The Goths were heavily outnumbered by the heavy Roman infantry that had always seemed invincible. The Romans pushed the Goths back to their circled wagons, and defeat seemed imminent. Just then, Gothic cavalry dashed from the hills, smashing the Roman line. The infantry was no match for mobile cavalry, and the Roman army was destroyed. Emperor Valens was killed on the field. This battle dispelled the aura of invincibility that had surrounded the Roman legions for centuries and demonstrated the military importance of cavalry. It seemed that military might now lay in the hands of the "barbarians" rapidly pouring through the borders.

Even Rome itself was no longer the center of the empire, for by the fourth century, the emperors in the West had made Milan their capital. Then, in 402, Emperor Honorius fled from the invading Visigoths to create a new capital in Ravenna, behind defensible marshes. Ravenna was safe, but Rome was not, and in 410, the Visigoths plundered the "eternal city," Rome itself. Masses of panicked Romans fled to Africa and the East.

It seemed that an era had passed and that the empire had finally fallen—but the end had not come quite yet. The Visigoths left Italy and settled in Spain as allies of the empire, just as many other tribes had done in other provinces. An **Twilight of the empire** emperor remained in the west, ruling from Italy, and a co-ruler continued to govern in the east, from Constantinople. But by 410 the western region had disintegrated so much that there seemed to be no point in referring to a Roman Empire in the West at all.

For the last few centuries, historians have spent a great deal of thought (and paper) exploring what has come to be known as the "fall" of the Roman Empire that began in the turmoil of the third century. Historians point to dwindling population, economic problems, reliance **Rome's "fall"** on slave labor, civil warfare, and moral decay as the causes of the decline. All of these factors contributed to the transformation of the old Roman world, but perhaps more important than anything else was the great influx of peoples from the north who invaded the empire. These invasions (which we will explore in more detail in Chapter 6) caused the breakup of the huge empire that had dominated the Mediterranean world since the time of Augustus. The territorial empire was ending, but throughout these years of power and turmoil a religion arose that would give a new source of unity to the Mediterranean world.

THE LONGING FOR RELIGIOUS FULFILLMENT

As we saw in Chapter 4, the Romans were a deeply religious people who carefully linked their deities to cherished spaces. As the empire controlled more and more land, its subjects seemed increasingly distanced from their traditional gods. In part, worship of the emperor served as a unifying religious cult. By the middle of the third century, some twenty festival days honored deified emperors or their families each year. However, for all the reverence given to the emperors, a spiritual dissatisfaction still gnawed at the Roman people. Many Romans seemed to long for a closer relationship to a truly transcendent divinity, and Romans expressed this longing through a rise in various philosophic and religious movements.

We can see this attempt to bring the gods a little closer to earth in the increasing numbers of spells and charms that Roman men and women purchased. People tried everything from healing and love charms to curses placed on chariot racers. Prophets, magicians, and charlatans also proliferated. One late-second-century writer described a man who made a fortune by pretending to prophesy through a giant serpent that he wrapped around himself. However, all the religious movements of the Roman world were not as superficial as magical curses and false prophets.

Stoicism and Platonism

The Hellenistic philosophies (Chapter 3) all continued to offer religious satisfaction to some educated Romans. The great Roman Stoic Seneca (ca. 4 B.C.E.–65 C.E.) wrote that by focusing on their own ethical behavior, people could locate the divinity that dwells within each person. As mentioned earlier, the Stoic emperor Marcus Aurelius used this philosophy to bring meaning to the challenges of his life. Like the reflective emperor, many people found in Stoicism ethical principles to help guide their lives, and Stoicism exerted an important influence on both Christianity and Western ideas in general.

The most influential philosophical system, however, came with a new form of Platonism, **Neoplatonism,** that emerged during the late empire. In the third century, these Neoplatonists created a complex system that offered an explanation for the link between the divine and the human. Like Stoics, Neoplatonists believed that each person contained a spark of divinity that longed to join the divinity that had created it. Through study, contemplation, and proper living, people could cultivate that bit of divinity within themselves and thereby reduce the distance between the human and the divine.

These philosophies, though intriguing, had limited appeal. Just as they had in the earlier Hellenistic kingdoms, they attracted people with leisure, education, and a respectable income. Most people instead tried to satisfy their spiritual desires through one or more of the mystery cults that gained popularity in the second century.

Mystery Cults

The mystery cults that had become popular during the Hellenistic world (Chapter 3) had an even stronger appeal in the difficult times of the late empire. These cults had always offered hope to individuals seeking meaning in their lives and ecstatic celebrations that seemed to transport individuals outside themselves into the world of the gods. Some cults claimed to offer a universality lacking in many of the Roman deities, and many offered hopes of a better afterlife to people disenchanted with their current existence.

The cult of Isis, the Egyptian goddess of fertility, enjoyed remarkable popularity throughout the empire. Septimius Severus and his wife portrayed themselves as Isis and her consort, Serapis. As we saw in Chapter 1, the ancient Egyptians called Isis's husband Osiris, but in the Hellenistic period, when many of the Egyptian deities were assimilated into the Greek pantheon, Osiris began to be called Serapis. As the noted Greek biographer Plutarch (ca. 46–ca. 120 C.E.) explained, "Serapis received this name at the time when he changed his nature. For this reason Serapis is a god of all peoples in common." In his new form as Serapis, the old god Osiris left his traditional home of the Nile and brought protection to wide areas of the empire. Thus, Serapis was an appropriate incarnation for Septimius, a North African emperor who wanted to combine imperial worship with that of a popular mystery religion to try to overcome Rome's lack of a single, unifying religion.

While some cults, like that of Serapis, strove for universal appeal, the worship of other deities was not intended to be for everyone. Instead, initiates prided themselves on participating in an exclusive and difficult worship. For example, some men and women celebrated the mystery of the Great Mother, the female goddess who brought fertility and comfort. In frenzied rituals, celebrants flogged themselves until their blood flowed, and some men castrated themselves as an ultimate sacrifice to the goddess. In another example, imperial soldiers felt particularly drawn to the mysteries of Mithraism, whose followers were exclusively men, and the religion's emphasis on self-discipline and courage made it very popular with the armies of Rome. These soldiers gathered in special buildings, ritualistically ate bread and water, and awaited salvation.

These different mysteries practiced throughout the Roman world reflected the multicultural nature of the empire. People were willing to partake in mysteries of any origin, whether Egyptian, Syrian, or Persian.

The Four Faces of Judaism

Although Palestine had struggled for religious purity while under the Hellenistic kings, the Jews under Roman rule were not exempt from the religious angst that swept the empire. At the time of Julius Caesar, the kingdom of Judah had been ruled by descendants of Judas Maccabeus (see Chapter 3), but the kingdom was swept into the turmoil of Rome's civil wars following the death of Julius Caesar. Finally, Herod, a member of a prominent family in Hebron, south of Jerusalem, rose to power and, with the support of Octavian, was made king of Judea and subject to Rome by the Senate of Rome. Herod was unpopular with the Jews, and during this kingdom, controversies grew. The struggles of four main Jewish groups shaped the religious and political future of this region and beyond.

The **Sadducees** largely comprised members of priestly families. They emphasized Jewish worship at the Temple in Jerusalem, which they saw as the cult center of the Israel-ites. (In Chapter 3 we saw that the Temple had been rebuilt in the sixth century B.C.E., and this structure—which had been further rebuilt in 19 B.C.E.—is known as the Second Temple.) The Sadducees were religious conservatives who rejected any "new" ideas that they did not find in the Torah—the first five books of the Bible. These innovations included the ideas of angels and resurrection of the dead, both of which began to win more adherents. The Sadducees were also willing to compromise with the Hellenized world and the Roman rulers as long as the Temple cult remained secure. However, the Sadducees would not continue as a viable force after Titus destroyed the Temple in 70 C.E.

The **Pharisees,** on the other hand, emphasized Jewish purity laws. They refused all compromise with the Hellenized world and adhered strictly to dietary rules and rituals to reinforce their separateness from all non-Jews. However, the Pharisees did accept new ideas such as the resurrection of the just and the existence of angels. For Pharisees, Judaism centered not on public worship in the Temple but on the private observances of Jews all over the Roman world. The Pharisees also supported sayings and interpretations of Jewish scholars, such as the influential Hillel the Elder (ca. 30 B.C.E.–ca. 10 C.E.),

that later became part of the Jewish tradition. It was the work of the Pharisees that would ultimately lead to the expanded writings that updated the practice of the Torah.

Although the Pharisees believed strongly in separating themselves from the surrounding non-Jewish world, they avoided political revolution. Another group in Palestine, the **Zealots,** took a different approach. This group looked back to the successful revolt of the Maccabees against Seleucid rule and urged political revolt against Roman rule as a way to restore Israel to an independent state. Not surprisingly, clashes between the Zealots and Roman troops broke out throughout the early first century C.E.

Despite their differences, all these groups were struggling in some way with the same question that had plagued Jews since the first Hellenistic conquest: how to maintain a separate identity within the Roman world. A fourth group, the **Essenes,** tried to avoid the problem altogether by withdrawing from the social world. The Essenes moved to separate communities and attempted to live pure lives, seemingly alienating themselves from the Temple cult. The Essenes have drawn much scholarly attention because they probably authored one of the most exciting archaeological finds in biblical history, the Dead Sea Scrolls.

In 1947, a shepherd boy discovered a deep cave containing ancient pottery jars holding hundreds of scrolls of texts dating from as early as 250 B.C.E. The scrolls include such valuable works as the oldest version of portions of the Hebrew Bible and other documents revealing the historical context of the biblical texts. Most of the works are severely damaged and have been reconstructed from hundreds of tiny fragments, which leaves a lot of room for differing interpretations. Although many of the texts have been studied since the 1950s, there is still no scholarly consensus surrounding these precious scrolls.

Most scholars believe these texts were produced by the Essenes in their mountain retreat in Qumran—a desert community 15 miles from Jerusalem, near the Dead Sea—and hidden in the cave during the turbulent times when Rome was exerting its dominance in the region. All the writings were completed before 68 C.E., when the Romans destroyed the settlement at Qumran. Some scholars believe the writings came from a large library of various Hebrew documents, and thus they may reveal the origins of the many strains of Judaism, perhaps even the early Jesus movement. It is certain that continued analysis of these texts will shed a good deal of light on these early centuries that were so fertile to spiritual impulses.

In this time of spiritual longing, many Jews believed that a savior—a Messiah—would come to liberate them. Some believed that he would be a political figure who would liberate the Jews from foreign domination, and peo-

> People were willing to partake in mysteries of any origin, whether Egyptian, Syrian, or Persian.

ple like the Zealots were poised to fight for this political leader. Others, however, expected a spiritual savior—a Chosen One who would bring a kingdom of righteousness to earth. The Essenes may have withdrawn to the desert community to wait for the spiritual Messiah— their "Teacher of Righteousness." It was into this volatile religious time that Jesus of Nazareth was born.

The Messiah

The Jesus Movement

During the reign of Augustus (r. 27 B.C.E.–14 C.E.), at the beginning of the empire, a child named Jesus was born in about 4 B.C.E., possibly in Bethlehem (about 10 miles southeast of Jerusalem). This event dramatically influenced the empire by the fourth century. Thus, we must return to the time of Augustus to trace the fortunes of a small religious sect in Judea that would ultimately conquer Rome itself.

The information we have on Jesus' life and teachings is drawn largely from the Gospels of the New Testament of the Bible, which were written sometime after his death, probably by people who never knew him. (Estimates on the time of the composition of the Gospels range from thirty to ninety years after Jesus' death.) The Gospels offer little information about the first thirty years of Jesus' life. They do tell us that he was the son of a woman named Mary and a carpenter named Joseph and that he excelled in his religious studies, for he confounded the priests of the Temple with his knowledge of matters of faith.

According to the limited historical information available, Jesus drew from the rich religious environment in the Jewish lands. Like the Pharisees, he appealed to the poor, and many of his sayings resembled those of Hillel the Elder. His teachings also had some qualities in common with those of the Essenes, who had written of a coming Teacher of Righteousness. Unlike the Zealots, Jesus spoke of a heavenly kingdom rather than a violent revolution and attracted a large following of those who longed for a better life. Jesus began his ministry after being baptized by John the Baptist, and the Gospels tell the story of his activities after this defining event in some detail. For many, Jesus was the awaited Messiah who would save and transform the world. Many called him Christ—the Lord's Anointed, the Messiah.

Jesus' ideas

While Jesus' ideas resembled those of some of his contemporaries, the totality of his message was strikingly new and changed the course of Western civilization. For about three years, Jesus preached in Judea and Galilee, drawing huge crowds to listen to his message of peace, love, and care for the poor and suffering. He was accompanied by a small group of devoted followers—the apostles—who carried on his message after his death. Many people also believed that he performed miracles and cures. His grow-

ing popularity alarmed both Jewish leaders and Roman authorities, who constantly watched for uprisings in Judea. In about 29 C.E., the Roman governor, Pontius Pilate, sentenced Jesus to crucifixion, the cruel death reserved for many of Rome's enemies. The Romans nailed a sign on Jesus' cross identifying him as the "king of the Jews," perhaps mistranslating the powerful notion of Messiah as king, and certainly underestimating the nature and appeal of Jesus and his message.

Jesus' brief, three-year ministry had come to an end. However, three days later, Jesus' followers believed they saw him risen from the dead and subsequently taken into heaven. They believed this proof of Jesus' divinity promised a resurrection for his followers, and the apostles wanted to spread this good news to other Jews.

A small group of Jesus' followers led by the apostles Peter and James formed a Jewish sect that modern historians call the Jesus movement to identify the period when followers of Jesus continued to identify themselves as Jews. The apostles appealed to other Jews by preaching and praying at the Temple and at small gatherings of the Jewish faithful. The earliest history of this Jesus movement is recorded in Acts in what Christians call the New Testament of the Bible. Like others throughout the Roman world, these Jews believed that prophecy and miracles marked the presence of the divine. Thus, the apostles, the followers who had known Jesus personally, began traveling to bring his message to others. They spoke in prophetic tongues and appeared to work miracles. They also began preaching in Jewish communities around the Mediterranean world.

Apostles

The early Jesus movement could have taken various different directions. Would Jesus' followers withdraw from society like the Essenes and John the Baptist had done? The apostle James moved to Jerusalem and centered his leadership of the church there, thus choosing not to lead a sect in the wilderness. A more thorny issue was the question of accepting Gentiles—non-Jews—into the new religion. James took a position of conservative Judaism, insisting that Christianity required its adherents to follow the circumcision and strict dietary laws that had marked the Jewish people. The apostle Peter seems to have been more willing to preach to Gentiles, particularly "God-fearing" Greeks who were interested in the ethical monotheism of the Jews. Peter believed they would not have to be circumcised or keep all the Jewish festivals, but they would have to follow the dietary restrictions.

However, the man who would be remembered as the Apostle to the Gentiles had not known Jesus before his crucifixion. Saul of Tarsus (ca. 5–64 C.E.), whom we remember by the name of Paul, was a Hellenized Jew and a Roman citizen who had at first harassed Christians. After he experienced a vision of the risen Jesus, he converted and took up the mission of bringing the Christian message beyond the particularity of the Jewish communities to the

Paul of Tarsus

wider world of the Roman Empire and beyond. He moved beyond Peter by eliminating all dietary restrictions on Christians, and he traveled widely through the eastern portion of the empire establishing new Christian communities. The map on page 117 shows where Paul journeyed and how the Christian message slowly spread throughout the Roman world. Paul's influence on the young church was immense, and his letters became part of the Christian Scriptures.

Religious tensions between Jews and Roman authorities in Palestine culminated shortly after the deaths of

Destruction of the Temple

Peter and Paul. Rome finally decided to take strong action against those in Judea, including Zealots, who were rebelling against Roman rule. In the course of the suppression, the Essene community at Qumran was destroyed (but not before they had buried

their precious scrolls, which we call the Dead Sea Scrolls), and then the armies proceeded against Jerusalem. In 70 C.E., the son of Emperor Vespasian, Titus (who later became emperor in his own right), led Roman legions into Jerusalem, burned the city, and destroyed the Second Temple. All that seems to have remained of Herod's great temple was the western wall. For many years it was called the Wailing Wall, so designated to mark it as a mourning space for the destruction of the Temple. In the twenty-first century, it is more often called the Western Wall, and in Hebrew, it is simply called the Wall. The Temple was never rebuilt. Many Jews were scattered from Judea all over the Mediterranean after this devastation, and with them traveled numerous followers of the Jesus movement.

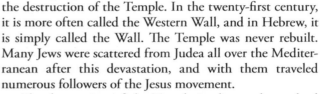

OPINION

How do you think the political and cultural complexities in Judea at the time of Jesus' life affected the growth of Christianity and the transformation of Judaism?

The destruction of the Temple inadvertently resolved the tensions within Judaism. The Sadducees, Essenes, and Zealots were all destroyed, and the Pharisees made peace with the Romans and recentered Judaism on synagogue worship. An emphasis on prayer and the law

Dispersion of Jews

replaced sacrifices at the Temple. After 70 C.E., the Hebrew canon of scriptures came to be closed and the Hebrew Bible—what the Christians would call the Old Testament—was completed. Followers of the great teacher Hillel reached a compromise with the authority of Rome that let Jews maintain an identity within the empire, and future rabbis would study scripture and interpret the ways Jews should act while living among Gentiles.

The conquest of Jerusalem also settled any question about whether Christianity was to be centered in Jerusalem. Early Christianity, like Diaspora Judaism, was to be a religion that was not bound to one city, and it began to claim universality. The Jesus movement within Judaism was transformed and was now more accurately called the early Christian church.

Early Christian Communities

The spread of Christianity was slow. Small groups of converts in the major cities of the empire gathered in one another's houses because there were no designated churches for the new movement. The culmination of the worship service was the Eucharist—the commemoration

WESTERN WALL, ca. 19 B.C.E. When the Romans destroyed the Jewish Temple in Jerusalem, all that was left standing was the western wall. This architectural remnant was called the Wailing Wall for centuries as Jews visited the site and lamented the loss of the Temple. Now people often refer to it simply as the Wall.

of Jesus' last supper—in which the faithful shared cups of wine and pieces of bread. Members then offered prayers of thanksgiving for Christ's sacrifice and death, which the faithful believed offered them salvation and eternal life.

The relatively small numbers of Christians grew consistently throughout the first few centuries after the death of Jesus. Some estimates suggest that the total number of Christians at the beginning of the third century C.E. was about 200,000, or less than 0.5 percent of the total population. Although this is a small percentage, the actual number is significant—Christians were slowly becoming more visible. This small but growing number would periodically come into conflict with the power of Rome.

FROM CHRISTIAN PERSECUTION TO THE CITY OF GOD

64–410 C.E.

Conservative Romans looked askance at any innovations, particularly religious novelties. It was one thing for Christians to worship someone who had died within living memory as a divinity, but it was quite another for them to reject the traditional Roman assortment of gods. Furthermore, early Christians seemed to violate the traditional Roman social order by including the poor, slaves, and women as equals in their congregations.

Looking for Christian Scapegoats

To quell accusations that he was responsible for a devastating fire in Rome, Emperor Nero looked for scapegoats and implemented the first large-scale persecution of Christians in Rome in 64 C.E. He executed hundreds of Roman Christians, possibly including the apostles Peter and Paul, and set a precedent that would be repeated periodically over the next two centuries. During the contentious years, provincial officials played a leading role in the persecutions. Some of these authorities chose to harass Christians; others

Titus Destroys Jerusalem

In the first century C.E., the Jewish historian Josephus wrote a history of the Jews in which he described the violent destruction of Jerusalem in 70 C.E. by Titus. In this excerpt, Josephus describes the internal dissensions among the Jews (whom he calls the "seditious").

Now, when hitherto the several parties in the city had been dashing one against another perpetually, this foreign war, now suddenly come upon them after a violent manner, put the first stop to their contentions one against another; and as the seditious now saw with astonishment the Romans pitching three several camps, they began to think of an awkward sort of concord, and said one to another: "What do we here, and what do we mean, when we suffer three fortified walls to be built to coop us in, that we shall not be able to breathe freely? While the enemy is securely building a kind of city in opposition to us, and while we sit still within our own walls and become spectators only of what they are doing, with our hands idle, and our armor laid by, as if they were about somewhat that was for our good and advantage. We are, it seems (so did they cry out), only courageous against ourselves [in mutual argument], while the Romans are likely to gain the city without bloodshed by our sedition." [After a long and bloody siege, the Romans finally entered the city.]

Now the number of those that were carried captive during this whole war was collected to be ninety-seven thousand; as was the number of those that perished during the whole siege eleven hundred thousand. . . .

How do the Jews' internal problems impede their defense of Jerusalem?

ignored the new religion. Whatever their policy, however, the texts make it clear that when Christian men and women were brought to the arena, many died so bravely that some Roman spectators promptly converted.

During the third century when the empire confronted many internal and external problems, its policy toward Christians grew harsher. Under Emperor Decius (r. 249–251) and then again under Emperor Diocletian (r. 285–305), all imperial residents were to sacrifice to the emperor and receive a document recording their compliance. Diocletian, the autocratic emperor who legislated wages, prices, and military matters, thought he could decree religious beliefs as well. But this wide-scale demand for conformity only provoked many more Christians to die for their beliefs. The map on page 117 reflects the extent of Christian strength after the persecutions of Diocletian had ended.

Constantine: The Tolerant Emperor

In the long tradition of Roman emperors, Constantine looked for supernatural help in his wars with his rivals. According to the Greek historian Eusebius (ca. 260–ca. 340), as Constantine prepared for a crucial battle he saw in the sky a vision of a cross with Greek writing reading, "In this sign, conquer." That night he had a prophetic dream explaining that soldiers would triumph only if they fought under Christian symbols. He obeyed the dream and won a decisive victory. To the Romans, dreams and omens carried crucial religious messages, and Constantine's nighttime message convinced him of the power of the Christian God. In 313, he issued a decree of toleration (the Edict of Milan) for all the religions of the empire, including Christianity, and the martyrdoms ended.

Constantine did more than simply tolerate Christians. He actively supported the church. He returned property to Christians who had been persecuted, gave tax advantages to Christian priests, and let Christian advisors play a role in his court's inner circle. Constantine's support of Christians probably derived in part from his military victory under the sign of the cross. The women in his family exerted a strong influence on him as well. His half-sister Constantia and his mother, Helena, were both Christians. Whatever religious motives Constantine had for his support of Christianity, the emperor remained a shrewd politician. In fact, his support of the new religion included a practical political basis. For one thing, there were so many Christians in the empire that it would have been unwise to continue to marginalize them. Furthermore, Constantine's withdrawal of support for traditional pagan shrines permitted him to confiscate their gold to help standardize his currency.

Under Constantine's patronage, the Christian movement grew rich and powerful, and the emperor built beautiful churches in support of the religion. As part of the emperor's respect for Christianity, he decided to restore the Holy Places at Jerusalem and Palestine to Christian worship. Helena toured the region to identify the sacred spaces, but this was quite a feat, for since the destruction of the Temple, Jerusalem had become a Roman city that had lost all identification with its Jewish past. Nevertheless, Helena located what she believed were key sites in the life of Jesus, building great churches where he was born and where he died. With the backing of Constantine and his family, Jerusalem was revived as a holy place, and Christians began to make pilgrimages there. These journeys began a tradition of Christian claim on that land that would continue throughout the Middle Ages.

Constantine supports church

Constantine's support of Christianity throughout his life established a relationship between church and state that moved Christianity in a new direction: It would continue to flourish and grow in the shadow of the imperial throne.

→ connect to today ←

Religious Conflicts

During the late Roman Empire, the spread of Christianity brought violence and disruption. What do you think people of opposing religious views today can learn from the religious struggles experienced by imperial Romans?

The Empire Adopts Christianity

Theodosius I (r. 379–395) put the final cap on the movement toward Christianity by forbidding the public worship of the old Roman cults. With this mandate, Christianity became the official religion of the Roman Empire. Of course, everyone did not immediately convert to Christianity; Judaism remained strong, and those who clung to traditional Roman religious beliefs came to be called pagans. This word came from *pagani,* a derogatory term for backward peasants, and its etymology shows how Christianity spread first from urban centers.

This merging of a political and Christian empire irrevocably changed both Rome and Christianity. After the

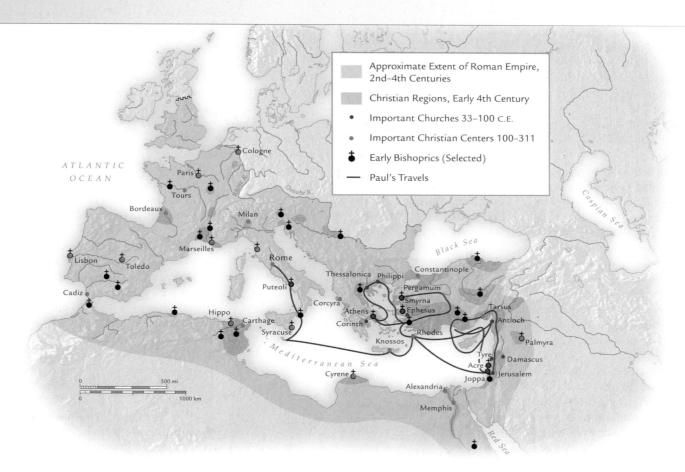

The Spread of Christianity, to 311 C.E. **This map shows the areas of Christian strength by the fourth century and traces Paul's journey as he conducted his missionary work.**

fourth century, Christian communities looked very different from those of two centuries earlier. Instead of gathering secretly in one another's homes, Christians met

Christianity changes publicly in churches that boasted the trappings of astounding wealth. Indeed, where once people converted to Christianity in spite of the danger of persecution, the influential church father Augustine (354–430) complained, some people now converted only to impress the rich and powerful. Artistic portrayals of religious figures also show the growing wealth and power of the church. The images of Christ on pages 118 and 119 reveal this shift from a poor shepherd to the lord of the universe.

As the empire embraced Christianity, the organization of the church began to duplicate the civil order of Rome.

Christian organization The emperor Diocletian had clustered provinces into larger units, called dioceses, for ease of administration. The church retained these divisions and placed bishops in charge of the major communities. Bishops were

in charge of all aspects of church life, from finances to spiritual guidance, and as early as the third century in most regions they were paid by a church depending increasingly on their administrative skills. For example, by 245 C.E. the province of North Africa had 90 bishops, and each was served by a well-developed hierarchy of priests and deacons. The ecclesiastical structure of the dioceses was divided into parishes, presided over by priests who reported to the bishops.

With Constantine's support, the church had become powerful, and as leaders began to look to a hierarchical organization for guidance in religious matters, it was perhaps inevitable that questions would arise over who should lead—religious or secular leaders. Ambrose (r. 374–397), the bishop of Milan in Italy, was one of the earliest bishops to challenge the power of the emperors and set a precedent for later bishops. In 390, Ambrose reprimanded Emperor Theodosius for massacring some rebellious citizens: The bishop excommunicated the emperor, forbidding him to participate in church services until he repented. Theodosius acceded to the bishop's demands, and later bishops of

Rome (who came to be called popes) looked to this example of the church leading the state.

In the eastern part of the empire, the relationship between bishops and emperor took a different turn. Beginning with Constantine, emperors in the East had involved themselves directly in religious disputes. Since the early third century, for example, Christians had quarreled over the nature of Christ. "Had he always existed," they asked themselves, "or did God bring him forth at a particular time?" In about 320, Arius, bishop of Alexandria, raised a furor when he argued that Jesus had been created by God. Arius's teachings polarized believers all over the empire, and Constantine did not want such a dispute raging in his lands. Therefore, he called a meeting that was the first "ecumenical" council—purportedly with representatives of the whole inhabited world. In 325, Constantine vigorously presided over the bishops he had summoned to the Council of Nicaea to resolve Arius's dispute over the nature of Christ. With the formulation of the Nicene Creed, which stated that Christ had always existed, Constantine and his bishops hoped to put that controversy to rest. However, as we shall see in Chapter 6, Arius's beliefs had already spread, and the church would have to face the problem of **Arianism** again. The council also set the precedent that orthodox Christians could exert their authority over those who believed otherwise.

Religious disagreements

The many religious quarrels that spilled into secular politics raised the question of the relationship between church and state. In the early church, the relationship had been simple—Christianity focused on the next world while enduring an antagonistic earthly relationship with an unsympathetic state. Now, with church and state combined, the situation had become exceedingly complex. Many Christians felt ill at ease with all the resulting uncertainty. In his influential work *City of God* (413–427), Augustine tried to address these very complexities. Writing after the Visigoths

had sacked Rome and terrified Romans had fled the city in waves, he explained that Christians should not look at the current disasters with despair, nor see in them divine punishment. Instead, the church father drew from his strong background in Neoplatonism to explain worldly pain much as Plato had (described in Chapter 2), but with a Christian understanding. Augustine claimed that the world—and worldly cities—were made up of individuals who were constantly in struggle between their spiritual and earthly selves. Those people in whom the spiritual dominated belonged to a City of God, and those in whom the earthly dominated belonged to an earthly city. The perfect community of the faithful—the City of God—could exist only outside this world and would dominate at the end of time. In the meantime, all communities were mixed with members of both cities. Therefore, people ought to obey the political order and focus on the worthiness of their own souls rather than the purity of the reigning political institutions. They need not worry even when the city of Rome was sacked.

City of God

For Augustine and other religious thinkers, church and state were not incompatible. In fact, these men believed that the state should play an active role in ensuring the health of the church. In the early centuries of Christianity, **heresy** (expressing opinions that differed from official church doctrine) could be considered treason punishable by civil sanctions. As the ultimate power of the empire was brought to issues of conscience by these sanctions, church members learned that the path to salvation lay in obedience. Inevitably, there were Christians who objected to this direction, but the majority saw in this Christian order a fulfillment of God's plan—a victory for the earthly church.

CHRIST AS THE GOOD SHEPHERD, second century C.E. The earliest centuries of Christianity were marked by slow missionary work to gather new converts. The predominant image for this time and initiative was that of Christ the Good Shepherd gathering his flock.

The New Roman

Like political institutions and the church itself, everyday Roman life was also transformed with the burgeoning strength of Christianity.

CHRIST AS THE GOOD SHEPHERD, ca. 450 C.E. After the Roman Empire became Christian, artists began to portray Christ with more imperial majesty. Here, Christ the Good Shepherd is shown clothed in gold and royal purple and presiding over his flock rather than working with his hands.

As church fathers in many regions of the empire wrote on matters of religion, they also addressed the larger question of how the new Christian Roman was to behave. In some areas of life it was easy simply to prohibit certain behaviors. For example, the church fathers wrote that Christians should not attend gladiator shows or arena games. Over time, the great amphitheaters fell out of use. Instead, Christian Romans satisfied their appetite for spectacle with chariot races, which remained hugely popular for centuries. In other areas, religious leaders and the populace reached a compromise—Christians could read the beloved traditional literature, such as Virgil or Homer (even though it praised pagan gods and suspect morality), but they were to try to extract a Christian message from it. (This is a major reason why such literature has survived.)

Christians also reshaped the social fabric of Roman life. For example, they did not believe in exposing unwanted children. Indeed, through the early centuries, they actively rescued foundling infants and raised them as Christian. Furthermore, they placed enormous priority on caring for the poor and needy. By the middle of the third century,

church records show, in Rome alone the bishop provided charity for more than 1,500 widows and others in need.

Views on sexuality also shifted with the influence of the church fathers. As we have seen, although the Romans showed a certain cautiousness in their sexual lives, they also passionately believed that people had a duty to marry and procreate. Some Christian leaders, on the contrary, strongly advocated celibacy as the ideal life. Numerous Roman men complied with this recommendation, and many women used Christian celibacy as a way to free themselves from the expectations that they would marry and bear children.

Christian sexuality

The most influential writer on sexuality was Augustine. In his widely read work *The Confessions,* he described his inability to give up his mistress and his "habit" of lust. As he explained, only with God's help was he able to summon the resolve to renounce these vices. This experience convinced Augustine that human beings were born with original sin and that this sin was passed to subsequent generations through semen during sexual intercourse. Because of original sin, Augustine concluded, people had to keep constant vigil against the force of lust—even marital intercourse was somewhat suspect. Through this kind of thinking, religious leaders involved themselves in people's private lives, and this watchfulness continued for centuries through a growing body of church law. Hardly any aspect of Roman life was left untouched by the Christianization of the empire.

Perhaps surprisingly, some highly influential Christians were those who fled society and sought to live in solitude in the wastelands of the empire. Some Christians fled into the desert to escape the persecutions and chaos of the mid-third century. Others left during the fourth and fifth centuries because they objected to the union of church and state that developed after Constantine's rule. Still others fled the tax collectors. Whatever the reasons, the popularity of this movement reached enormous proportions. Historians estimate that by 325, as many as 5,000 men and women lived as hermits along the banks of the Nile, each in his or her own small cell. The fame of these holy people spread.

Flight to the desert

Many of these holy men and women survived extraordinary feats of self-denial—enduring lack of food, sleep, and other basic necessities. Some people insisted on living for decades on platforms perched high on poles. Women in particular sealed themselves into tombs that had only a tiny opening through which they could receive a small loaf of bread, and they eked out their lives in cramped, filthy solitude. These people's contemporaries found their behaviors so unusual that they concluded that to endure such hardships, the holy men and women must be recipients of God's power.

Of course, the extreme deprivation of heroic abstinence was not for everyone. Some people wanted simply to withdraw from the distractions of the world so as to worship God without enduring the rigors of the desert hermits. Communal monasticism developed as a parallel movement to the hermit life and offered an appealing alternative to life in the thick of Roman society. Discipline was strict in these pious oases, but participants had contact with other people, and conditions were not as harsh as those in the desert. In time, communal monasteries were brought into the overall structure of the church. Monks and nuns took vows of obedience to the monastery head (the abbot or abbess), and the monastic leader answered to the local bishop.

Monastic communities

The Influence of Holy People

The earliest holy people had been the Christian martyrs. Faithful observers witnessing their brave deaths concluded that God had invested their bodies with the power to withstand torture. People believed that martyrs' remains contained sacred power and saved and venerated their bones, or **relics.** Christianity thus became a religion that accepted the body. Believers wanted the holy dead to be buried near them, and by the fourth century, most altars included relics. In a very short time, the faithful and the enterprising began to engage in a brisk trade in relics that would be lucrative and influential throughout the Middle Ages.

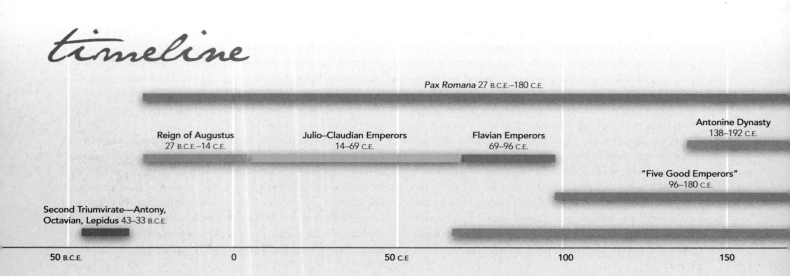

timeline

Pax Romana 27 B.C.E.–180 C.E.

Antonine Dynasty
138–192 C.E.

Reign of Augustus
27 B.C.E.–14 C.E.

Julio–Claudian Emperors
14–69 C.E.

Flavian Emperors
69–96 C.E.

"Five Good Emperors"
96–180 C.E.

Second Triumvirate—Antony, Octavian, Lepidus 43–33 B.C.E.

50 B.C.E.　　　　　　　0　　　　　　　50 C.E　　　　　　　100　　　　　　　150

Relics were preserved, treasured, and displayed in reliquaries—containers, often covered in precious metals and jewels, that displayed the precious bones that lay within. These reliquaries spread all over

Saints' cults

Europe and became a visible feature of the growing religion. Exquisite jeweled containers were supposed to express both the power of the relic and the incorruptibility of heaven, where people believed the saint dwelled.

Saints gained reputations for doing everything from raising the dead and healing the sick to extending a too-short wooden beam so an overworked carpenter would not have to cut another. The conversion of the northern European countryside was inspired largely by living and dead holy people who had brought God's power down to the community.

The ascetic practices of the monasteries also shaped the lives of everyday Christians. Even for people who did not adhere to the strict rules of the monasteries, the luxuries of the Roman world seemed shameful when compared with the purity of the monasteries. Over time, people concluded that the ideal Christian life should be simple, and some Christians looked with disdain at those who surrounded themselves with comfort and pleasure. This tendency of monastic rigor to influence Christian life continued throughout the Middle Ages.

Monasteries always served both as havens during stormy political times and as outlets for those who sought a highly spiritual life. For centuries, these communities rejuvenated the Christian world and helped the church meet people's changing spiritual needs. Men and women in search of personal spiritual perfection would ultimately become powerful social forces for the medieval world.

SUMMARY

The conservative Romans who mourned the death of Julius Caesar and celebrated the victory of his young nephew Octavian (Augustus) would hardly have recognized the world of the late fourth century. Rome had been transformed.

- Caesar Augustus introduced the *Pax Romana* (the Roman Peace) by establishing a new form of governance—the empire—that preserved the institutions of the Republic while keeping real power centralized in the person of the emperor. Instead of voting in the forum, Romans cheered in the amphitheaters of the empire.

- Beginning in the second century, the institutions established by Augustus were no longer up to the challenge of the huge empire. In the crisis, Diocletian transformed the empire significantly.

- Even while Augustus founded his empire, a religious revolution was slowly taking place as Christians began to spread their message, and Jerusalem was destroyed.

- Christians were killed as Romans became suspicious of the new religion, but by the fourth century, Roman emperors converted, and the empire itself became Christian. In the process, Christianity changed the culture of Rome itself.

The empire would soon split into cultural and political divisions, but the glory and accomplishments of Rome would remain in the West's memory and periodically inspire people to try reviving its greatness.

Severan Dynasty
193–235 C.E.

Diocletian
285–305 C.E.

Constantine
306–337 C.E.

Persecution of Christians 64–304 C.E.

200   250   300   350

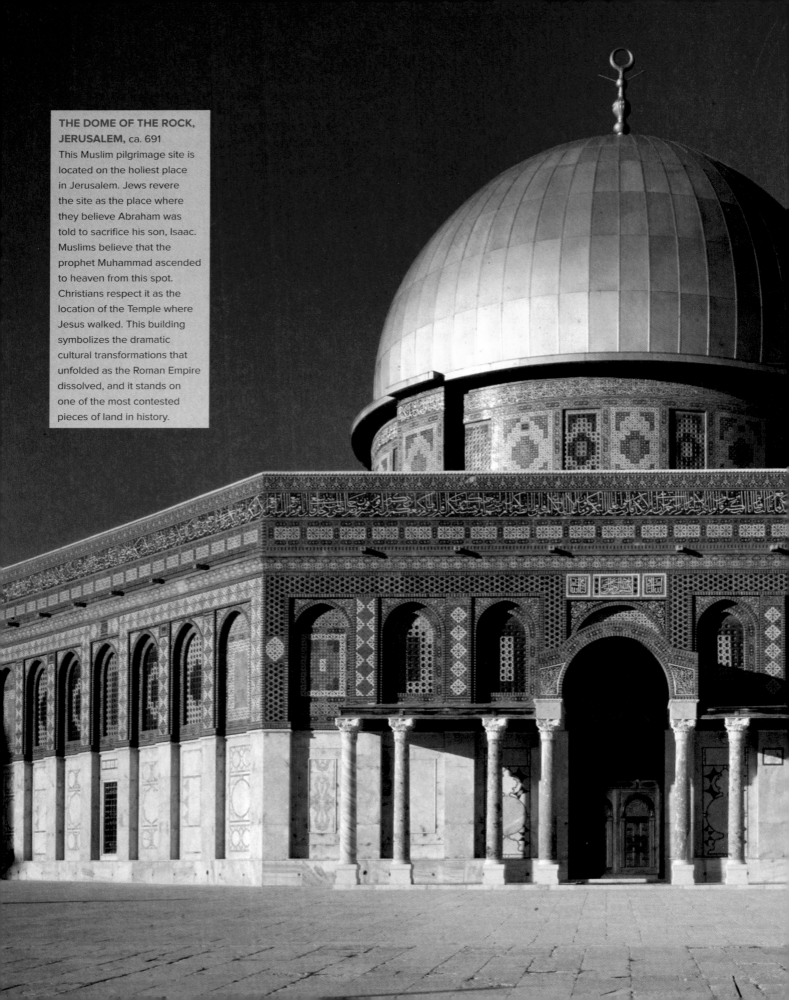

THE DOME OF THE ROCK, JERUSALEM, ca. 691
This Muslim pilgrimage site is located on the holiest place in Jerusalem. Jews revere the site as the place where they believe Abraham was told to sacrifice his son, Isaac. Muslims believe that the prophet Muhammad ascended to heaven from this spot. Christians respect it as the location of the Temple where Jesus walked. This building symbolizes the dramatic cultural transformations that unfolded as the Roman Empire dissolved, and it stands on one of the most contested pieces of land in history.

A World Divided

Western Kingdoms, Byzantium, and the Islamic World, ca. 376–1000

6

The Besieged Bishop

"Our town lives in terror of a sea of tribes which find in it an obstacle to their expansion and surge in arms all round it." This letter written by Sidonius Apollinaris in the fifth century captured the violence that accompanied the large-scale invasions that left much of the glory of the Roman Empire in ashes and transformed the West. Sidonius, who left many letters, was a perfect witness to this violent transformation. ▶▶

Sidonius was born in Gaul—southern France—into a family who had long served the Roman emperors as administrators. He was a scholar of note, and had risen to the post of senator of Rome, and even married the daughter of an emperor. His early letters elegantly describe the gracious life of a highborn Roman, surrounded by fine literature, good food, and leisure to enjoy them. Sidonius was not a religious man, but because of his political connections, he was made bishop of Clermont in France. He expected to live out his life in comfort in this position, but the Visigoths invaded.

Sidonius led the defense of his walled city for three years as the Visigoths besieged it. When the city finally fell in 474, he was imprisoned by the invading king, but eventually he was released and reinstated as bishop. In his later letters, Sidonius described the new world of an empire that had fallen but did not disappear. He wrote of blue-eyed Saxons and tall Burgundians dressed in exotic bristly hide boots with large swords hanging across their backs. He wrote of the spread of the German language and praised one of his friends for his skill in acquiring the new tongue. At the same time, Sido-

nius continued to exchange Latin literature with friends back in Rome and care for his Christian congregation as he lived out the rest of his days tranquilly, serving as bishop in a town now governed by Visigoths. His Roman world had been reshaped, but not obliterated. To understand the changes that Sidonius experienced, we must first meet the Germans, who played such a major role in the remaking of the Roman Empire. ◄◄

THE MAKING OF THE WESTERN KINGDOMS

ca. 376–750

Who were these "Germani" that the Romans called "barbarians"? In about 500 B.C.E., when the earliest Romans were settling on the seven hills of their city and beginning their republic, groups of Indo-European Scandinavian people began to migrate south into the Baltic states and Germany and east into Ukraine. As they fanned out across the land, their tribes took on a bewildering array of separate names: East Goths (Ostrogoths), West Goths (Visigoths), Burgundians, Franks, Saxons, and so forth. These tribes traded with Rome and sometimes threatened its northern borders throughout the history of the empire. Whereas Chapter 5 focused on life within the empire, here we will move back in time to describe the culture of the early Germans and follow the fortunes of the tribes as they entered the empire.

Because the Germanic tribes had originally come from a small region in Scandinavia, they shared many cultural similarities. Their settlements were based on clans—families joined in kinship groups. A whole tribe made up of many clans might number no more than 100,000 people, including only about 20,000 warriors. Historians studying their early history are hampered by the fact that they did not write and thus left no written records. Instead, we must piece together their history from archaeology, Roman descriptions of the tribes, and texts based on imperfect memories written centuries later.

The earliest descriptions by Romans are not objective. Some Roman accounts depict the Germans as "barbarians" (outsiders) whose language sounded like babbling

and whose personal hygiene was objectionable. One Roman wrote, "Happy [is] the nose that cannot smell a barbarian." However, the earliest and most famous text, Tacitus's *Germania,* written at the end of the first century, praises the Germans in order to criticize Roman society by contrast. Therefore, Tacitus portrays the Germans as strong and brave people who cared for their families and raised sturdy children.

Roman sources

Tacitus praised the Germans' devotion to marriage—"This they consider their strongest bond"—and the children it produced. Although Tacitus somewhat romanticized the marriage bonds, without a doubt they forged the essential ties that bound society together. Within marriages, men and women had clearly defined and equally essential roles. Men cared for the cattle (a clan's greatest measure of wealth) and took primary responsibility for crop tending, iron working, and war making. Women owned property and received a share of their husbands' wealth upon marriage. Women also performed agricultural labor, but they were mainly responsible for pottery and textile production and household care. In addition, they brewed the all-important alcoholic beverages—honey-sweetened ale and mead, a fermented concoction of honey and water—that provided much of the caloric intake needed for survival. Preserving knowledge of herb lore, women also cared for the sick and injured members of the clan. Perhaps in part because of their knowledge of brewing and healing, women were reputed to have a gift for prophecy, so men often consulted their wise female elders regarding important forthcoming enterprises.

Marriage patterns

Tacitus claimed adultery was rare because it deeply threatened the strong kinship ties that marriage forged and

Archaeologists have excavated surprisingly well-preserved ancient Germanic corpses that had been buried in peat bogs. These naturally mummified bodies allow scientists to study the contents of their stomachs and note that they ate only a cereal gruel that included wild grasses and weeds. This was probably not only the last supper of the executed. The average woman at that time stood just under 5 feet; the average man, 5 feet 6 inches. Today, Scandinavians coming from the same genetic heritage average 5 feet 10 inches—a towering difference—which gives researchers a better idea of how a diet rich in protein impacts growth and wellness.

was severely punished. The image below shows the corpse of a 14-year-old girl who was executed in the first century C.E. by drowning, probably for committing adultery. Such bodies—well preserved by the northern European bogs—offer a wealth of information about the lives of these early Germanic peoples. The corpse of this girl offers eloquent, though silent, testimony to the importance of the marriage ties holding Germanic communities together, and the gruesome penalty for violation.

GERMANIC GIRL'S CORPSE, first century C.E. In the peat bogs of the north, corpses were mummified. The well-preserved bodies provide detailed information about ancient life. When this girl was killed, her right hand was frozen in an obscene gesture toward her executioners.

Germanic Clothing and Food

Germanic peoples differed from the more southerly Romans in more ways than family traditions. Their clothing styles and diets also set them dramatically apart. Germanic men wore trousers, a long-sleeved jacket, and a flowing wool or fur cape secured by a large brooch or pin (or even a thorn if the wearer was impoverished). With their elaborate, luxurious detail, some of these brooches signified wealth and prestige.

Germanic women wore ankle-length dresses of linen or woven wool, which they colored with vegetable dyes. Like the men, they wore capes for warmth. They also dressed their hair with elaborate combs and hairpins and wore patterned jewelry as marks of wealth and prestige.

The Germans' diets were not as elaborate as their fashion accessories. The German peoples raised cattle but seldom ate the meat—the animals were too valuable for the milk and labor they provided. Instead, most of the clans were primarily agricultural. They apparently invented a large, wheeled plow that only a team of six to eight oxen had the strength to pull. Unlike the small plows of the south that merely scratched the surface of the sandier land there, this plow could turn over the heavy clay soils of the north. Furthermore, it encouraged cooperation—for to use a plow of this size, members of the community had to work together. But even this technol-

Agriculture and diet ogy did not yield enough grain for a healthy diet, for the northern growing season was short. In addition, the disruptions of wars—even raids—upset agriculture and led to frequent hunger.

Heroic Society

Like the ancient Greeks, the Germanic tribes of the north cherished the heroic ideals. Warfare played a central role in this society. Through raiding and plundering, they acquired both wealth and fame. In the evening gatherings after a day of war making, a poet might praise a particularly heroic deed, and the warrior's name would be permanently preserved in the "word-hoard" or poetry of his people.

Just as Homer had recorded the dramatic deeds of Achilles and Odysseus, anonymous Germanic poets composed works remembering the heroes of the north. The Anglo-Saxon poem *Beowulf* is a written version of one such heroic account. *Beowulf* not only tells of the accomplishments of the monster-killing hero but also gives us a glimpse into traditional Germanic society: The warriors gather in the hall to boast, drink, and prepare for their military feats; the women serve in the hall but also speak their minds; and the king takes responsibility for guarding his people and doling out gifts to ensure their loyalty.

A stunning hoard of Anglo-Saxon gold and silver objects dating from about 675 was excavated in 2009 in Staffordshire, England. This collection offers a recent confirmation of the accuracy of the accounts of the heroic society in *Beowulf.* The huge size of the collection—the gold alone weighs 11 pounds—suggests that Anglo-Saxon England was extremely wealthy. Most of the artifacts are war gear such as sword fittings, pommels, and helmets, and they may represent a victory hoard of the kind *Beowulf* refers to in documenting how warriors stripped the weapons of the defeated. The gold was probably buried to hide it from competing tribes and subsequently lost for over a millennium. Future archaeological finds will continue to fill in the gaps in the history of these elusive tribes who fought for gold and glory.

Each clan within the larger tribe was led by its own chieftain, who served as priest, main judge, and war leader. However, this was no absolute ruler, for the warrior elite

Warrior bands (comitatus) was continually consulted in the decisions made for the whole clan. At times, small groups of warrior bands (usually less than 35 strong) set out to raid neighboring villages and bring back booty and tales of bravery. Sometimes the whole tribe decided to move, bringing along all the related clans and escorting their women and children. According to Tacitus, women traveling with these fighting tribes stayed behind the battle lines, probably within a protective circle of ox carts. If their men seemed to be losing, the women goaded the warriors to victory by baring their breasts behind the battle lines to remind them of their responsibility to protect their dependents.

Infiltrating the Roman Empire

376–476

While there was periodic, fierce fighting on the borders of the empire between the German tribes and the Romans, there was also a growing relationship based on mutual advantage. After the third century, Rome relied more and more on mercenaries to guard the empire's borders (described in Chapter 5). By the late fourth century, then, many tribes had a great deal of contact with the empire. Numerous young Germanic warriors no longer farmed but instead used Roman pay to support their families. Nearby tribes had learned to value Roman coins as much as cattle and jewelry (their traditional forms of wealth), and Rome had come to depend on the Germans' impressive skill in war.

This mutually satisfying relationship changed in the late fourth century when a Mongolian tribe originating in northern China came sweeping out of the steppes of Asia. These Huns (known as Hsiung-hu in their homeland) struck terror in **The Huns** the hearts of the Germanic tribes in their path. The map on page 127 shows the route of the Huns as they galloped out of the east beginning in about 375. The Huns were a fierce people (even by Germanic standards) who charged across the continent on small ponies that seemingly needed no rest. Contemporary descriptions of the Huns reveal the dread and disgust generated by this wild and remarkably successful people. For example, the Roman historian Ammianus Marcellinus (ca. 354) wrote: They "are so prodigiously ugly and bent that they might be two-legged animals. Their shape, however disagreeable, is human." Some Germanic tribes fled across the boundaries of the empire in search of safer territory. One such tribe, the Visigoths, crossed into the empire looking for land and ended up sacking Rome itself in 410 (discussed in Chapter 5). As the map reveals, the Visigoths were only one of many Germanic peoples who crossed into the empire in the early fifth century.

As we saw in Chapter 5, by the late third century, the Romans faced severe economic problems that kept them from successfully defending their borders against these new encroachments. They could not even afford to pay for the minimum **Federate treaties** defense, for the empire spent about thirty gold pieces a year for each soldier. An army of only 30,000 would have cost the entire annual budget of the western empire, so the Romans had to develop a new, less expensive way to defend its borders. To address this need, the Romans offered some encroaching tribes a treaty that

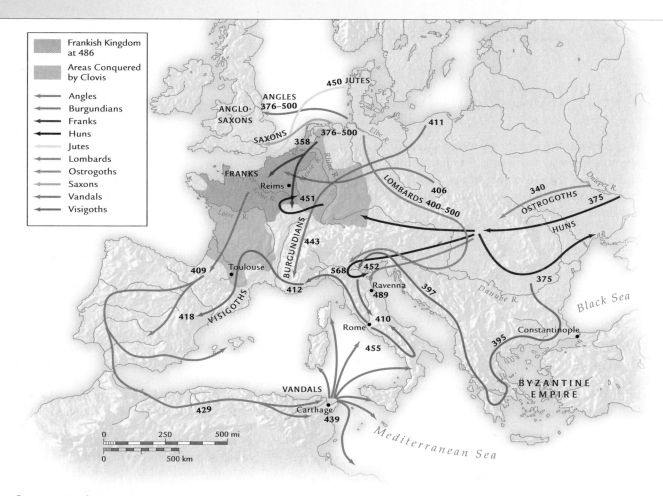

Germanic Invasions, fifth century This map shows the routes of the various Germanic tribes as they invaded the Roman Empire and gives the dates of their invasions.

made them **federates,** or allies, of Rome. Through this treaty, the warrior tribes received permission to live within the borders of the empire, and in exchange, they agreed to fight the enemies of Rome. The Visigoths became federates for enough grain to feed their warriors and families; in return they agreed to fight their traditional enemies, the Germanic Vandals. The Visigoths were later called north to protect the Italian borders. As more tribes were awarded federate status, the western empire began to be transformed by the blending of peoples.

The federate treaties allowed the Germanic tribes to live within the empire and govern themselves by their own laws and customs, using their own leaders. This model of separate, coexisting cultures almost immediately proved to be utopian. In most of the territories, such as Spain or North Africa, the Germans were very much in the minority, so their culture was transformed by contact with neighboring Romans. For example, tribal leaders began to be called and treated as kings, although competing German noblemen consistently resorted to assassination to maintain their traditional voice in tribal affairs.

In many cases, two religions also existed side by side. Some pagan tribes (Anglo-Saxons, for example) restored paganism to parts of the nominally Christian empire. Other tribes (Visigoths and Ostrogoths) were Christian but had been converted by a missionary named

Arian Christianity

Ulfila (ca. 310–ca. 381), whose Christian ideas had been shaped before Arius's teachings had been condemned at the Council of Nicaea in 325 (see Chapter 5). Ulfila's parents had been captured by Goths, and he grew up speaking the early Germanic language, so he was the natural candidate to convert the Germans. In the settlements established in the fifth century, the Arian tribes associated their religious beliefs with their ethnic identity, and this impeded their relationship with the orthodox Catholics living in the disintegrating empire.

In addition to having disputes with the federate tribes, the empire lost some provinces altogether. In about 407, Rome recalled legions from Britain to help defend Italy against invaders. This left the Celtic Britons, who were

Loss of provinces

The Huns Menace Rome

The mid-fourth-century historian Ammianus Marcellinus wrote a history of the later Roman Empire, including the invasions of the Germanic tribes. In this excerpt, he pointedly describes the Huns as strikingly different from the "civilized" Romans.

At the very moment of their birth the cheeks of their infant children are deeply marked by an iron, in order that the usual vigor of their hair, instead of growing at the proper season, may be withered by the wrinkled scars; and accordingly they grow up without beards, and consequently without any beauty, like eunuchs, though they all have closely knit and strong limbs and plump necks; they are of great size, and bow-legged, so that you might fancy them two-legged beasts, or the stout figures which are hewn out in a rude manner with an axe on the posts at the end of bridges.

They are certainly in the shape of men, however uncouth, but so hardy that they neither require fire nor well-flavored food, but live on the roots of such herbs as they get in the fields, or on the half-raw flesh of any animal, which they merely warm rapidly by placing it between their own thighs and the back of their horses.

They wear linen clothes, or else garments made of the skins of field-mice. . . .

How might this description have shaped Roman policy toward the Huns?

Christian and lived in the Roman manner, alone to defend themselves against invaders from Scotland and from the Scandinavian countries. As the map on page 127 shows, tribes of Angles, Saxons, and Jutes entered and settled the eastern portions of Britain, pushing most of the Celtic Britons to Wales and Ireland, the western edges of the British Isles. In the midst of these invasions, one British war chief won a great victory at the Battle of Badon (about the late fifth century) over the Anglo-Saxons. This victory stemmed the tide of the invasions, but only for a while. The deeds of this war chief, Arthur of Britain, were nevertheless remembered in the western Celtic lands and formed the basis for the famous Arthurian romances composed in the twelfth century (see Chapter 8). Britain was lost to Rome and became a mosaic of small Germanic kingdoms.

North Africa also fell away from the empire. At first the Vandals were settled as federates in the northern lands of Africa, but they soon broke off their allegiance to Rome and created a separate kingdom with their capital in Carthage. By the middle of the fifth century, Rome had lost the rich tax shipments of grain and oil that had come in a steady stream from North Africa. Struggling with this and other territorial losses, the empire in the West was slowly disintegrating.

Did Rome "Fall"?

By the fifth century, the provincial armies in the West were dominated by Germans, so it is not surprising that many rose to military power in Rome itself. When the Visigoths invaded Italy, the Roman defense was led by a Vandal general, which shows how ineffective the Roman emperors in the West had become. During the invasion, the Visigoths' leader even captured Emperor Honorius's (r. 395–423) sister, Galla Placidia, and took her with him as he sacked Rome itself.

Finally, in 476, the military leader Odovacar deposed the last western emperor. Odovacar disdained the practice of dual emperorship that the Romans had established and shipped the imperial regalia off to the east. He then appointed himself regent in Italy.

The western empire did not fall with a cataclysmic crash. People like Sidonius in Gaul probably did not even use words such as "fall" to describe the times. After all, the eastern regions still had an emperor to whom people could give their allegiance if they wished, and in fact, many in the east celebrated the fact that there was once again one emperor who ruled the Mediterranean world. However, Sidonius and his contemporaries knew that the Roman Empire overall had undergone a major shift.

Transformation, not "fall"

The empire's declining population played a key part in this transformation. The shrinking populace left plenty of room for the Germanic tribes to settle without severely dislocating residents. Even after the Germanic settlements, as much as 20 percent of the arable land was abandoned in some areas of the empire. As we saw in Chapter 5, economic and social problems had also eaten away at the empire for centuries. Finally, plagues and warfare had decimated the already fragile population. The empire, therefore, did not fall; instead, it was transformed as new people moved into the territory that the Romans failed to populate.

The urban life that had so characterized Roman culture was the first thing to go. The violence of the times crippled the towns, and the Germanic preference for rural living shifted attention to the countryside. The urban tax base shriveled as powerful Romans began to refuse to pay taxes to Rome. The Germans, for their part, were not often vigilant in collecting them. The roads and bridges that connected the empire fell into disrepair, and people's focus narrowed to the local level.

There were always Romans like Sidonius who continued their correspondence with Romans elsewhere, but they became fewer and fewer. Even Roman clothing changed; the toga that had symbolized the civilized life of the city was abandoned in favor of trousers more suited to country life. (Churchmen continued to wear traditional Roman robes. Indeed, to this day, Catholic vestments resemble the clothing of the ancient Roman upper class.)

Of course, change happens in both directions when different peoples intermingle. The Germans were as much influenced by the Romans as the Romans were by Germanic culture. Slowly, the Germanic pagans and Arians converted to orthodox Christianity and began to intermarry with resident Romans. In southern Europe, Germans began to speak the local Latin-derived dialects instead of their native Gothic. This is why the southern European languages (French, Spanish, Portuguese, Italian, Romanian) are called Romance languages—they are based on the language of the Romans. The Germans also became literate and began to produce written texts.

Germans transformed

The Germans and the Romans, through their mutual influence, were creating a whole new culture—that of the medieval west. After invading, the Germanic tribes settled down and created new political entities—kingdoms instead of tribal units. These new entities formed the basis for the medieval kingdoms that defined the West in the centuries to come.

ILLUSTRATION FROM THE GOSPEL OF MATTHEW, ca. 660
This manuscript illustration of Matthew, Jesus' disciple, was probably created in Ireland. It reveals the Germanic love of intricate patterning, as well as discomfort with portraying the human form.

Rise and Fall of a Frankish Dynasty
ca. 485–750

In the sixth century, the Germanic Franks established a powerful kingdom in the old Roman province of Gaul (see map on page 127). The Franks were ruled by the Merovingian family (named after a legendary ancestor, Merovech). The most famous Merovingian was Clovis (r. 485–511), a brutal man who murdered many of his own relatives to consolidate his rule. Clovis's descendants were no less brutal, and the accounts of subsequent reigns tell of feuds and assassinations involving Merovingian princesses as well as princes.

Clovis is significant not only because he unified large portions of the Frankish kingdom but also because he converted to Roman Christianity. According to Gregory, Clovis's wife, Clotilda, was a Christian and was influential in persuading the king to convert. In the tradition of Constantine before him, Clovis reputedly vowed to convert if he won a significant battle. He won and fulfilled his vow around the year 500 (although the date is controversial). Unlike the Visigoths and other Germans, Clovis converted to orthodox, not Arian, Christianity, and this began a long relationship between the popes and the Frankish kings. As was traditional with the German tribes, the conversion of the king meant the conversion of his people, which paved the way for the slow transformation of Germanic culture through the influence of the Roman church.

Christian Merovingians

Although Clovis had been highly skilled in forging a Christian kingdom from the ashes of the Roman Empire in Gaul, the subsequent Merovingians were not as competent. By the seventh century, the authority of these kings had deteriorated—frequently, children inherited the throne and in turn died young, leaving the throne to another child. Real power began to be exerted by the "mayors of the palace," an office controlled by another noble family, the Carolingians. This enterprising family included a number of skilled leaders, and as we will see, the Carolingian Charles Martel won a great victory in 732 to save the land. His son, Pepin the Short (r. 747–768), forwarded the for-

Fall of Merovingians

tunes of the family. Pepin wanted more than just to rule; in fact, he craved the royal title as well. Just as Clovis had enhanced his authority through Christian ritual, Pepin looked to the spiritual leader of Christendom for help. The shrewd Carolingian wrote to Pope Zachary (r. 741–752), asking him who should hold the title of king: he who actually exercised the power or he who had the name of king but no actual authority. The pope favored Pepin, and the mayor of the palace then gathered all the Frankish bishops and nobles, who promptly proclaimed him their king. The last of the ineffectual Merovingian kings was forced to cut his long hair (a symbol of his power) and lived out his days in a monastery. Armed with the support of the church, the vigorous new dynasty was now in a position to bring centralized order to western Europe. We will follow the fortunes of the Carolingians in Chapter 7.

Accomplishments and Destruction in Italy

ca. 490–750

As the Franks established their kingdom in the sixth century, another Germanic kingdom took shape on the Italian peninsula. The story began when Theodoric (r. 493–526), an Ostrogothic leader, ousted Odovacar (who had deposed the last Roman emperor) and declared himself ruler of Italy. Theodoric had received a Roman education and proved a talented and balanced ruler—at first. The Ostrogoths were Arian Christians, so Theodoric had difficulty uniting Goths and Romans in Italy. Nevertheless, he seems to have exhibited a surprising religious toleration in an age that had little.

Theodoric fostered learning at his court and supported a number of scholars who had a profound influence on Western culture. Boethius, for example—a high official in Theodoric's court—was a man of great education. He translated works of Aristotle from Greek to Latin, and these translations became the basis for the study of logic for centuries. He also had an inventive streak and built a water clock for his patron. But Theodoric's court was plagued with intrigue, and Boethius was unjustly accused of treason and jailed. He wrote his most influential work, *The Consolation of Philosophy*, while in prison. In *The Consolation*, Boethius thought about the injustices of life and found comfort in philosophy. This profound and sensitive work

Fostering learning

KING CLOVIS The violent Merovingian king Clovis is shown here as a model of piety at the moment of his baptism, which drew together church and state in the lands of the Franks.

remains much studied today. However, it did not save Boethius, for Theodoric had him executed.

Dionysius Exiguus, a Greek-speaking monk, was another respected scholar in Theodoric's Italy. A skilled mathematician, the monk calculated the date of Easter (which changes each year) and was apparently the first to suggest that calendars be dated from his estimation of when the Incarnation of Christ occurred (originally the B.C./A.D. system, which has turned into B.C.E./C.E.). Although modern scholarship shows that his dates were slightly wrong—Christ was probably born about 4 B.C.E.—Dionysius's dating system remains the basis of our Western dates.

Theodoric was succeeded by his daughter, Amalasuintha, who ruled at first as regent for her young son and then as queen after the boy's death. She

Fall of Ostrogoths

was well educated and well suited to rule, but the unruly Germans were unused to being governed by a woman. Amalasuintha corresponded with the Byzantine emperor Justinian to gain support for her rule, writing: "We hope that the peaceful relations that you maintain toward us . . . may be extended." However, all her diplomatic skills could not save her from internal intrigue. In 535, she was murdered—according to Gregory of Tours, locked in an overheated steam bath where she was scalded to death.

Justinian used her death as an excuse to begin his reconquest of Italy as part of his ambitious plan to retake the western portions of the empire. The emperor's forces crushed the Ostrogothic kingdom. The scholar Boethius's widow seems to have received some satisfaction after the reconquest, for the emperor gave her permission to destroy statues of Theodoric as revenge for her husband's death. But few others celebrated the conquest that brought down the religiously tolerant and impressive rule of the Ostrogoths.

> "We hope that the peaceful relations that you maintain toward us . . . may be extended."

Justinian had overextended his resources, and the reconquest of Italy did not last long. A Germanic tribe that had fought as allies of the Byzantine army learned about the riches of Italy during the campaign against the Ostrogoths. In 568, these Lombards (longbeards) moved south and took over most of the peninsula. Italy would now be ruled by a tribe much less Romanized than the Ostrogoths, and the

Lombards

slow struggle to achieve a synthesis between Germans and Romans began again. The fierce Lombards ruled the northern part of the peninsula until they confronted the growing power of the Franks in the north. Pepin conquered the Lombards in the mid-eighth century, and northern Italy came under the rule of the Frankish Carolingians.

Pepin did not forget his debt to the papacy that had supported his coronation, and when the Byzantines demanded that he return the Italian conquests to them, Pepin angrily refused. He said he had fought his war for St. Peter, and it was to Peter (that is, the papacy) that he would hand over his conquests. From this time onward, the pope ruled in central Italy as an independent monarch, and the "Donation of Pepin" marked the beginning of the Papal States, which endured until the nineteenth century.

The Visigoths in Spain

418–711

The history of the Visigoths in Spain resembles that of the other growing kingdoms. Like the Ostrogoths, Visigoths were Arian Christians when they became federates of Rome, and the two cultures, Roman and Goth, lived separate though parallel lives in Spain. However, in the 580s the Visigothic kings converted to Roman Christianity and paved the way for a close church and state rule. Like the Ostrogoths, Visigothic kings fostered learning in their land. The most famous Visigothic writer was Isidore of Seville (ca. 560–636), who compiled collections of Roman works that preserved classical knowledge for subsequent generations.

Two flaws marred Visigothic civilization, however. The first was a delight in political assassination, which even the violent Franks called the "Visigothic curse." Church and state repeatedly condemned people who "turned their hand against the king," but the assassinations contin-

Visigothic weaknesses

ued, weakening the kingdom. The second problem was Visigothic persecution of Jews. Kings passed strict laws against the many Jews living in Spain, undermining their communities and dampening their loyalty.

The Visigothic kingdom was ultimately destroyed by invasions of Muslims from North Africa. As we will see later, followers of the new religion of Islam swept across North Africa, crossed the narrow straits known as the Pillars of Hercules (now the Strait of Gibraltar), and in 711 conquered most of the Iberian Peninsula.

The only remaining Christian territory on the peninsula lay in the northwest hills. From there the Iberians would spend the next seven hundred years reconquering their land. The invasion, the interaction between Christians and Muslims, and the long era of reconquest left the Visigothic kingdom in ruins and shaped the subsequent history and culture of Spain.

The Growing Power of the Popes

As central authority fell away in western Europe, some people—especially in the cities—looked to their local bishops to handle things previously left to secular authorities. Bishops sometimes organized aqueduct repair or food relief, and perhaps not surprisingly, the bishop of the most prestigious city—Rome—began slowly to come to the fore. In these tumultuous centuries, the bishops of Rome began to claim earthly as well as spiritual authority and, in doing so, established precedents that would reach well into the future.

All Christian bishops were believed to be the successors of the original apostles and as such held the authority to guide the faithful. However, as early as the fourth century, the bishops of Rome began to assert their supremacy over all the other bishops. Many bishops during the early church period were called popes, based on the Latin word for "father," but the bishops of Rome slowly began to claim exclusive use of that title to set themselves apart from other bishops. On what did the popes base their claims of leadership? In part, the early-fourth-century popes claimed primacy because Rome had been the capital of the empire. However, as the imperial city faded in importance, the popes began pointing to biblical writings to justify their leadership of the church. They based their claim mainly on a passage from the Book of Matthew (Matt. 16:18–19) in which Christ said: "And I tell you, you are Peter, and on this rock I will build my church. . . . I will give you the keys of the kingdom of heaven. . . ." The early popes had

claimed that Peter was the first bishop of Rome, so each subsequent pope claimed to be the spiritual descendant of Peter—thus also controlling heaven's keys.

The claim that the supremacy of the pope is based on Christ's words to Peter is called the **Petrine doctrine** of papal supremacy. Not surprisingly, some people—especially the emperors in the east and some other bishops—disagreed with this interpretation of the Bible.

Petrine doctrine

Since the fourth century, some popes had involved themselves in politics. As we saw in Chapter 5, Bishop Ambrose had forced Emperor Theodosius to bend to his will, and in the following century, Pope Leo I (r. 440–461) successfully negotiated with invading Huns and Vandals to spare Rome. At the end of the fifth century, Pope Gelasius (r. 492–496) tried to resolve this issue of who had power by describing authority on earth as two swords: one wielded by kings and the other by the church. In Gelasius's view, the church's sword was the greater because it was spiritual—popes were responsible for the souls of kings. In a metaphorical sense, then, Gelasius converted St. Peter's keys to heaven into an earthly blade.

However, these early popes could exert only sporadic authority, and they had little real power. It was Pope Gregory the Great (r. 590–604) who dramatically forwarded the case for papal supremacy, as much through his actions as with his words. A talented, energetic administrator, he defined the role of the pope in broad terms. For example, he took over the day-to-day administration of Rome, reorganizing estates and managing them in such a way as to generate extra revenue to feed the poor. When the Lombards invaded the peninsula, Gregory directed the defense of the city and negotiated the truce. Acting the part of a territorial ruler, he even exerted his authority outside Italy, writing letters to settle disputes and offering financial assistance to distant churches. Gregory's influence extended far beyond sixth-century Italy: In the ninth century, when the Anglo-Saxon king Alfred (see Chapter 7) selected seminal works to translate from Latin to Anglo-Saxon, Gregory's writings were prominently featured. With Gregory's precedent, popes of the eighth century and beyond were prepared to claim influence throughout western Christendom, although it would take until the thirteenth century for them to fully wield such authority over a Christian world.

Gregory the Great

PAPAL SUPREMACY, ca. 1007 To argue for the supremacy of the popes over other bishops, some Christians looked to the biblical account of Christ giving the keys of heaven to his apostle Peter, an event that is shown in this colorful manuscript illustration.

Monasteries: Peaceful Havens

As the Germanic tribes were spreading into the western empire, many men and women sought refuge from the chaotic times in monasteries, where they could concentrate on their spiritual growth. As we saw in Chapter 5, communal monasticism began to appeal to many Chris-

Benedict of Nursia

tians throughout the empire. In the west, the most influential founder of communal monasticism was the Italian Benedict of Nursia (ca. 480–543). His twin sister, Scholastica, shared his calling and founded monasteries for women. Like many other churchmen, Benedict disapproved of people who lived independently. He feared that without guidance, such individuals might go astray, and he complained of wandering holy men, saying: "Whatever they think of or choose to do, that they call holy; what they do not like, that they regard as illicit." Instead, Benedict wrote a book of instruction—a *rule*—to guide monks and nuns in their communal lives.

Benedict eschewed the extreme fasts and bodily mortifications that had marked the eastern holy men and women, writing: "We hope to ordain nothing that is harsh or heavy to bear." Benedict's *Rule* required that people spend a balanced day divided into work and prayer, with moderate and regular meals. The requirement to work encouraged monks and nuns to study and copy the precious manuscripts that preserved classical learning. Benedict himself called his monastery a "schoolhouse for the Lord," which was an apt description for an institution that served a central role in education throughout the Middle Ages.

Although Benedict did not require heroic asceticism, the monk insisted that individuals ignore their own desires—whether for extra food, different work, or even extra hardships—and live in strict obedience to the head monk or nun. These monastic leaders, called abbots or abbesses, eventually became powerful figures in medieval life, extending their influence far outside monastery walls. By requiring a vow of obedience from monks and nuns, Benedict created an effective mechanism for bringing otherwise independent religious people into the Christian hierarchy.

Monasteries formed an effective avenue through which Christianity spread to the pagan outposts. In the early fifth century, a Romano-British Christian named Patrick (ca. 390–461) was kidnapped by **Irish Christianity** Irish raiders and enslaved in Ireland. He later escaped to Britain, where he became a bishop. However, he decided his calling was to return to Ireland to convert the pagan Irish. He established monasteries in Ireland, and the Irish consider him the founder of Irish Christianity. The strong monastic tradition in Ireland created monks who made great strides in preserving learning and stimulating ideals of asceticism in the West. Furthermore, some Irish monks became missionaries to the pagan Anglo-Saxons in Britain. In fact, scholars give the Irish monks a great deal of credit for preserving the classical wisdom and transmitting it on to subsequent civilizations of the West.

Pope Gregory the Great—a monk himself—was also interested in converting the Anglo-Saxons and bringing them into the orbit of Roman Christianity. The pope sent monks to Britain in 597 to convert **Conversion of Britain** the natives—a task they slowly, but successfully, achieved. However, the monks sent from Rome came in contact with those sent from Ireland, and it became clear that the two strands of Christianity had developed differing opinions on certain points (the most important was the date of Easter). In 664, the Anglo-Saxon king called a council in Whitby to resolve the discrepancy. After ascertaining that all the monks agreed on the primacy of the apostle Peter, the king decreed that Peter's heir in Rome should prevail. Thus, the practices of Roman—instead of Irish—Christianity prevailed throughout Europe.

Beyond their missionary roles, monasteries served as quiet havens from a tempestuous world. In these retreats, men and women worked, prayed, and studied—keeping ancient texts alive for a time when learning could again emerge from behind monastery walls.

THE BYZANTINE EMPIRE

ca. 400–1000

As early as the beginning of the fourth century, Roman emperors had recognized the unique strategic and economic advantages of the eastern portion of the empire. During the turbulent fifth and sixth centuries, the eastern Roman Empire with its capital in Constantinople held firm as the western provinces fell away to the Germanic tribes. However, the eastern empire did not remain unchanged; instead, Constantine planted seeds that would later flower into a dramatically different empire. By the eighth century, the eastern Roman Empire had changed so much that historians call it the Byzantine Empire, or Byzantium, to distinguish it from the Latin Roman Empire that it succeeded. As with the emergence of the western Germanic kingdoms, the rise of the Byzantine Empire represented not a sudden break from the past but simply another aspect of the Roman Empire's transformation.

When the Visigoths sacked Rome in 410, the eastern emperor, Theodosius II, began to build a great wall to protect Constantinople from a similar fate. This structure stood firm even during the violent fifth and sixth centuries—inhabitants of Constantinople watched from the safety of the top of the wall as smoke rose from villages set aflame by the Germanic tribes and the Huns surging westward. The wall continued to protect the new capital for almost a thousand years.

The wave of invasions separated the eastern and western portions of the old Roman Empire. While the western portion adopted some aspects of Germanic culture, the easterners consciously rejected such changes. For example, at the end of **A separate empire** the fourth century, residents of Constantinople were forbidden to wear Germanic clothing, such as pants and anything made from furs. Between 400 and 1000 C.E., the Byzantine Empire distanced itself more and more from the concerns of the west and turned its focus north and east instead. One eastern emperor stood out as an exception to this tendency and turned his attention again to the west.

Justinian and Theodora

r. 527–565

Justinian was born in 483 to peasant parents living in a province near Macedonia. A promising youth, he was adopted by an uncle in the royal court. His uncle became emperor, which paved the way for Justinian to take the crown at his uncle's death in 527. The most influential person in Justinian's court was his wife, Theodora. She, too, had come from a humble background. She had been an actress, and according to the Byzantine historian Procopius (d. 562) (whose *Secret History* is biased against Justinian, so it may not be fully accurate), Theodora won the emperor's heart with her skill as an erotic dancer.

Early in Justinian's reign, Theodora established her role in the emperor's court when a violent riot (remembered as the Nika riot for the rioters' rallying cry "Nika," which means "victory") broke out in Constantinople between two rival political factions who supported different chariot racing teams. In an uncommon alliance, they joined forces to try to oust Justinian. When the rest of his advisors urged Justinian to flee the city, Theodora insisted that Justinian confront the rioters, saying, "For one who has been an emperor it is intolerable to be a fugitive." Justinian's forces brutally squelched the riot—probably 30,000 were killed—and this victory broke any political opposition.

Nika riot

During the Nika riot, much of Constantinople was burned, so Justinian and Theodora embarked on an ambitious reconstruction plan. The most impressive outcome of this effort was the design and construction of a massive church, the Hagia Sophia (Holy Wisdom). The central dome, with its diameter of 101 feet, is the largest such structure in the world. Two half-domes double the interior length of the church to 200 feet. After the Muslims captured the city in 1453, the church became a mosque, and today the magnificent structure is a museum, but it still showcases the impressive Byzantine engineering along with the blend of cultures that marks this region.

Rebuilding the city

Besides the Hagia Sophia, Justinian left another enduring contribution: the codification of Roman law. From the earliest codification—the Twelve Tables (Chapter 4)—Roman law continued growing and changing.

HAGIA SOPHIA, 537 The Byzantine emperor Justinian commissioned this huge church in Constantinople. The structure's expansive domes and flowing lines long remained the wonder of the world. Builders added the four minarets in 1453 when they converted Hagia Sophia into a mosque.

Emperors and senators had passed decrees, judges had made precedent-setting decisions, and jurists had written complicated legal interpretations. By Justinian's time, the collections were full of obscurities and internal contradictions, and the emperor wanted them organized and clarified. The enterprise was immense, as

Legal codification

Justinian himself noted: "We turned our attention to the great mass of venerable jurisprudence and, as if crossing the open sea, we completed a nearly hopeless task." The results of this formidable project were published in fifty books called the *Corpus Iuris Civilis* (the *Body of Civil Law*) (ca. 533). In this form, Roman law survived and was revived in western Europe in about the thirteenth century. From there it has influenced Western legal codes through today.

Finally, as we have seen, after the murder of the Ostrogothic queen Amalasuintha, Justinian tried to reconquer the western territories that had fallen to Germanic tribes. In part, he wanted to recapture lost

Reconquering the west

tax revenues, but probably the ambitious emperor also hoped to resurrect the Roman Empire to its past glory. However, he succeeded only in taking North Africa from the Vandals and Italy from the Ostrogoths.

Under the newly established control of Justinian, a great church was built in the imperial capital of Ravenna, in the north of Italy. The images on page 136 are sixth-century mosaics of Justinian and Theodora that adorned this Church of San Vitale, and they reveal much about how people perceived the royal couple. The mosaics were a worthy celebration of the victorious conquest of Italy, but the accomplishment proved more ephemeral than the magnificent mosaics.

The map on page 137 shows the extent of Justinian's reconquest. As impressive as it looked, it was destructive and costly. While the North Africans welcomed the rule of the orthodox emperor over the Arian Vandals, the Italians, who were governed by the tolerant Ostrogoths, were less thrilled. The new regime brought more violence and taxation. Worse, Justinian had to rely on German mercenaries to win these battles, and this strategy paved the way for the Lombards to conquer Italy in 568. Although Justinian temporarily accomplished some of his goals, the reconquest led only to failure in the long run. He could not maintain a firm grip on the western provinces, and the constant battling drained the eastern empire of needed resources. Justinian's dream of reuniting and reconnecting with the empire's old homeland in Rome would vanish forever.

Constantinople: The Vibrant City

Constantinople not only was the administrative and cultural center of the east but also served as the economic hub. The great city's wealth stemmed in part from commerce: Trade

routes to the Far East all passed through Constantinople, so spices, silks, rare woods, and perfumes poured into the Byzantine capital. These luxury items brought a fine profit to the men and women who resold them. Streets thronged with shopkeepers displaying their wares: goldsmiths, silversmiths, furniture makers, textile merchants, and so on. Shoppers bargained at the booths, and the sounds of commerce rang through the streets.

The Byzantine Empire also grew rich producing luxury items. Artisans in Constantinople and the other major cities of the east crafted expensive fabrics, fine jewelry, glassware, and ivory works. The empire imported silkworms from China in

Lucrative industries

the sixth century, which opened a new, lucrative industry. The royal court held a monopoly on silk production, and the finest silk was made in the emperor's palace itself. The court also controlled the profitable industry of purple dye, which was produced from mounds of shellfish left to rot on the shores of the eastern Mediterranean. As we saw in Chapter 1, everyone, from east to west, who wanted to demonstrate their nobility or royalty had to have purple dye. The long purple robes worn by Justinian and Theodora in the mosaics testify to more riches than the couple's gold and jewels.

While great wealth was available in the bustling city, it came to only a few. The Byzantines had abandoned the ancient Roman tradition of offering free food to the urban poor, but officials offered food to those who worked in imperial bakeries or on aqueduct repair. The palace also established a number of charitable institutions for the needy, including poorhouses, hospitals, and the first orphanages recorded in Western tradition.

Prosperity brought temptation, and emperors and other highly placed officials began to favor eunuchs (castrated men) as a way to control corruption. Easterners from the time of the ancient Persian Empire believed that eunuchs were less prone to corruption than other men. Because eunuchs had no children, they were expected to have little motivation to acquire wealth to pass along to subsequent generations. As eunuchs gained favor in high places, some poor families even had a son castrated to prepare him for a prosperous career. In addition to the emperor's closest aides, highly placed bureaucrats, some army and navy commanders, and some high church officials were eunuchs. Doctors who were eunuchs were allowed to treat women, though some women's hospitals insisted on letting only female doctors attend to their patients.

A society and economy that so prominently featured eunuchs would have been unthinkable in the Roman Empire of Augustus. Yet, the Byzantines did retain some Roman characteristics. For example, the Roman tradition of public political involvement continued in Con-

Chariot races

stantinople, as Justinian and Theodora discovered during the riots. In this vibrant city, people argued about the great religious questions, political issues, and the ever-intriguing chariot races. In Rome, men and women had gathered in

Art Investigation

Mosaics in San Vitale, Ravenna, Italy

548

In 540, Emperor Justinian's troops conquered Ostrogothic Italy, restoring the peninsula and its capital, Ravenna, to Byzantine control. As part of the celebration of this victory, the mosaics shown here were added to the Church of San Vitale in time for its consecration in 548. The images depict Emperor Justinian with his attendants (top) and his wife, Theodora, similarly accompanied (bottom). These works of art were brilliant propaganda pieces, intended to show the faithful a new order—one in which church and state were combined, with the imperial family at the head. Why are Justinian and Theodora shown bringing gifts to the church? He carries a golden plate for communion wafers, and she brings a golden cup for the wine.

the Forum or the Colosseum to express their collective opinion; in Constantinople they flocked to see the chariot races. The great race track—the hippodrome—could seat 40,000 people, and the emperor frequently addressed his people there. The two chariot teams, the Blues and the Greens, signified much more than simply a love of sports. People aligned themselves with the teams as we do with political parties—by wealth, religion, social class, and political inclination.

Military Might and Diplomatic Dealings

Constantinople's walls kept the empire safe from the Germanic tribes heading west, but external enemies still posed a threat. The Byzantines clashed regularly with the powerful Persians and kept a vigilant eye on the tribes to the north. As we will see, the Muslim people to the south also represented a constant danger. To withstand these challenges, the Byzantines carefully considered both military and diplomatic science.

While the emperors kept the administration of Constantinople in civilian hands, they entrusted the care of the provinces to military men. Rulers divided up their empire into about twenty-five provinces, called **themes,** governed by military commanders. Assemblies composed of "heads of households" empowered to make judicial and financial decisions administered the villages within each theme. Governors designated most village families as "mili-

Provincial organization

tary households," which meant they owed one fully equipped man to the empire's army. In this way, the provinces were guarded by armies made up of local residents who had a strong stake in the protection of their homes.

The Byzantine army was disciplined, well paid, and thoroughly

Justinian's Conquests, 554

This map shows the size of the Roman Empire in 527 C.E. after the western provinces had fallen away, and it illustrates the extent of Justinian's reconquest. **What was the extent of Justinian's conquest? How expensive do you think it was to control all that territory? Why?**

armed. Its backbone, the heavy cavalry, provided the army with extraordinary flexibility. Protected by mail armor and outfitted with lances and swords as well as bows and arrows, these fighters could shoot from a distance as archers or do battle at close range while heavily armed. The cavalry in turn was supported by an efficient infantry. Though only about 120,000 men at its height, this standing army was supplemented by a large number of camp followers. Slaves and engineers accompanied the infantry everywhere. Unlike the Roman legions, who constructed their own camps every night, the Byzantines depended on camp slaves to carry out such tasks. The army also developed a finely tuned medical corps, complete with ambulance carts that moved the wounded to safety.

The army

In addition to its land army, the empire continued the Roman tradition of maintaining a strong navy. In the seventh century, Byzantine scientists invented "Greek fire," a deadly new weapon that gave the navy a crucial competitive edge. The substance was made of combustible oil that was pumped through tubes or placed in containers to be launched from a catapult. The liquid then burst into flames on contact with the target. This weapon proved particularly effective at sea; because the oil floated, it kept burning on the water. Not surprisingly, the Byzantines closely guarded the secrets of Greek fire.

The Byzantines' military success stemmed from more than strategic and technical innovations. Unlike their western counterparts, the easterners continued and improved the ancient Romans' highly developed diplomatic techniques to protect their empire. Many Byzantine emperors considered diplomacy as important as war and therefore worthy of just as much investment. As a matter of policy, these rulers used spies, lies, and money to weaken their enemies, and

OPINION

What do you think were the most striking strengths and weaknesses of the Byzantine Empire and the western kingdoms?

GREEK FIRE The Greeks invented a combustible liquid that they pumped through tubes onto enemy ships. The liquid ignited the wooden hulls on contact and also floated on the water, killing sailors who attempted to escape. One enemy observed that the Greeks possessed lightning from the heavens to burn their enemies.

sometimes even turned their enemies against each other. Indeed, today the term *Byzantine diplomacy* still connotes expedient and tricky negotiations. However, such complex diplomacy needed money to succeed. As long as the empire was wealthy enough to keep funding bribes, spies, and counterintelligence efforts, it stood firm. Later in the Middle Ages, the empire's diplomatic powers faded after an economic downturn. Nevertheless, the world learned much from the Byzantines about using diplomacy instead of war as a way to resolve conflict.

Diplomacy

Breaking Away from the West

Emperors in the east saw themselves as heirs to the Roman Empire and frequently used images to demonstrate this continuity. However, it soon became apparent that the east was moving ever farther from the west.

Justinian was the last eastern emperor to use Latin as the official language. After the seventh century, the language of the Byzantine bureaucracy changed to Greek. This made sense given that the native language of most educated people in the east was Greek rather than Latin, but it accelerated the east's drift away from the west. The split became even more pronounced after people living in the Germanic kingdoms gradually forgot how to speak and read Greek. Men and women living in the two sections of the old Roman Empire could no longer converse except through interpreters.

During the late Roman Empire, Christianity had linked the faithful of many regions and backgrounds together in one worship. Greek was the language of scripture and worship in earliest Christianity, and as Christianity spread, people worshiped in their local languages. Usually that meant Latin in the west, and Greek, Syriac, Coptic, Armenian, and other languages in the east.

As people in the western portion of the old empire forgot how to speak Greek, the western church began to use Latin exclusively in worship services, while in the east church services continued to be conducted in local languages. Over time, these language differences drove the churches apart.

The question of who should lead the church posed another problem. As we have seen, the power vacuum caused by the invasions allowed the popes to emerge as independent political leaders. In the east, however, the self-styled sacred emperors were **Caesaropapist**; that is, they led both church and state. Note, for example, how the images of Justinian and Theodora on page 136 include religious symbols in addition to emblems of their secular offices. Emperors led the church, appointed the patriarchs (the eastern equivalents of the highest-ranking archbishops), led church councils, and involved themselves in theological controversies.

Religious controversy

Just as Constantine had called the Council of Nicaea in 325 to discuss the origin of Christ (see Chapter 5), the Byzantine emperor Marcian called the Council of Chalcedon in 451 to resolve questions about the human and divine natures of Christ. The council decided that Jesus was both fully human and fully divine. This position seemed eminently logical to the pope in the west. Yet some men and women in portions of the east were shocked by this conclusion. In their view, this statement seemed to reduce the power of God by acknowledging that Jesus remained human. The anger catalyzed by this resolution further separated portions of the eastern empire from the west.

In the eighth century, another religious controversy convulsed the east and brought the growing differences between the Latin and Greek churches to the forefront.

Iconoclasm

From the fifth through the sixth centuries, the worship of the faithful in the eastern church had focused on icons—images of Jesus, Mary, and the saints. People viewed these depictions as more than simple portrayals; they believed that the images contained spirituality that had become material and thus could bring divine help. Byzantine monasteries in particular had amassed huge wealth by painting and selling icons. In the west, men and women also venerated images of saints, but not to the same degree.

The Byzantine emperor Leo III (r. 717–741) ordered all icons destroyed, and in an autocratic style, he intended for his decree to apply to all of Christendom, east and west. In part this dictate represented a belief common in the Asiatic provinces, that veneration of icons amounted to worshiping idols. Leo's policy also had a political side. The eastern emperors wanted to challenge the growing power of the monasteries that were producing most of the icons. This **iconoclasm** (icon breaking) controversy raged for a century in the east, during which time many mosaics in Constantinople and Asia Minor were destroyed, leaving Ravenna as the most important repository of the old mosaics. Finally, less controversial emperors withdrew their support from the iconoclasts (icon destroyers). In the meantime, however, the western popes did not acknowledge the emperor's authority, and Pope Gregory II (r. 715–731) defied Leo's edict. The tensions resulting from this struggle strained relations between the eastern and western churches even further.

Over the centuries, two branches of Christianity grew more and more apart until they became two separate churches—the Catholic west and the Orthodox east. The

Orthodox church

Orthodox church rejected the concept of papal supremacy that was growing in the west and preserved the idea that the church should be led by five bishops (called patriarchs) who presided in the five major cities: Rome, Constantinople, Jerusalem, Alexandria, and Antioch. Each of the five patriarchs—called the Pentarchs—exerted jurisdiction in his own area and met with the other patriarchs in council to regulate matters of dogma and church discipline. Over time, they rejected decisions made outside these councils by the popes alone. Questions of language, theology, hierarchy, and the wording of the creeds finally severed ties between east and west.

In 1054, the two churches broke apart. The pope and the patriarch of Constantinople excommunicated each other, and the unified Christian church became two. (The

mutual excommunications were finally withdrawn, but not until 1965.) Both the Roman Catholic and Greek Orthodox churches would grow and find adherents all over the world into the twenty-first century.

Converting the Slavs

560–ca. 1000

Starting in the sixth century, the several Slavic groups settling along the Danube River, which had once formed the northeastern boundary of the Roman Empire, represented yet another challenge to Byzantine unity. These pagan tribes included Serbs, Croats, and Avars. In 679, the Bulgars, a Turko-Mongolian people, came out of the steppes of Russia and built a powerful kingdom just north of the Danube. In the ninth century, Scandinavian traders (and raiders) established a kingdom in Kiev (modern Ukraine) made up of Slavic people ruled by Scandinavian princes. (This principality, called Kievan Rus, became the origin of the name "Russia.") All these peoples alternately raided and traded with the eastern empire and personally experienced the famed Byzantine diplomacy. Some tribes were bribed into peace, some kings were offered Byzantine brides, and occasionally tribes were tricked into fighting each other.

The Byzantines sought a way to bring these peoples within the eastern empire's influence by converting them to Christianity. In 863, the Byzantine emperor Michael III (r. 842–867) sent two missionaries, Cyril and Methodius, to the Slavs. The missionaries realized that conversion depended in part on literacy. The Slavs, who had no written language, could not read the church services. Therefore, Cyril and Methodius developed a Slavonic written language based on the Greek alphabet.

Cyril and Methodius

Their mission was successful. Serbs and Russians embraced Greek Christianity, and the alphabet that Cyril and Methodius developed to transmit the religion became known as the **Cyrillic alphabet** (named after St. Cyril). It is still used in Russia and in portions of the Balkan peninsula today. The Bulgar leader also converted to Othodox Christianity in the 890s and adopted the Cyrillic alphabet.

The state of Kievan Rus was brought to Christianity by a bargain struck between the reputedly ruthless prince of Kiev, Vladimir (r. 978–1015), and the Byzantine emperor Basil II (r. 976–1025). Basil wanted to secure Vladimir's military assistance and bring the growing eastern

Conversion of Russia

Slavic state into Byzantium's sphere of influence. Vladimir agreed to convert to Greek Orthodox Christianity and help Basil if the emperor would give his own sister, Anna—a princess "born to the purple"—as Vladimir's bride. The Kievan prince already had several wives, but Basil had little choice. Anna went north and Vladimir established churches along the Byzantine model. Vladimir's "conversion" in 989 marks the traditional date for the beginning of Christianity in Russia.

Like its Byzantine counterparts, the Catholic church also sent missionaries who successfully converted tribes in portions of the east. The Poles, Bohemians, Hungarians, and Croats adopted Catholic Christianity and the Latin alphabet that came with it. These divisions in religion, loyalty, and alphabet divided eastern Europe, and, indeed, cultural divisions established during this period have continued to color the politics of the region into the twenty-first century.

By the tenth century, the Byzantine Empire had entered a sort of golden age. It had occupied and assimilated the strong Bulgarian kingdom, and the eastern emperor exerted his authority from the Adriatic to the Black Sea. The empire was prosperous and secure. The Byzantine culture and the western kingdoms would interact for centuries, during which time the West gained a great deal from Byzantium. The western legal system owed much to Justinian's codification, western scholars would gain from the Greek texts preserved in the east, and western kingdoms owed their survival to Byzantium's serving as a buffer state against incursions from the east. The eastern empire and the Orthodox church left an enduring cultural influence in eastern Europe that continues to affect political life today. In the seventh century, the Mediterranean world grew even more complex: A third great power was rising in the south and this new civilization would come to challenge both the west and Byzantium.

ISLAM

600–1000

In the early seventh century, the Arabian peninsula was part of neither the Byzantine nor the Persian Empire. The region contained both oases with settled populations and great reaches of desert. In the desert, nomadic Bedouin tribes roamed, living on milk, meat, and cheese from camels and goats; dates; and some grain from the oases. These tribes emphasized family and clan loyalty and fought, raided, and feuded with one another to protect their honor and their possessions. The Arabs were pagan, worshiping natural objects such as stones, springs, and a large ancient meteor that had fallen into the Arabian desert long before human memory.

The success of Bedouin life stemmed in large part from the use of domesticated camels. These magnificent desert animals could carry heavy loads for many miles without water and proved a speedy form of transportation in the raids of desert warfare. The Bedouins sold camels to the Arabs of the oases, who in turn used them for the long-distance trade that brought prosperity to the small cities of the oases.

During the wars between Byzantium and Persia (540–ca. 630), the land route to the Far East through Mesopotamia became dangerous. For safety's sake, some traders from Constantinople and Egypt decided to travel through Mecca in Arabia to reach a water route through the Red Sea. Others crossed the Arabian peninsula to leave by sea from the Persian Gulf. This trade brought even more wealth to the thriving oasis cities, the most important of which was Mecca. Mecca housed an important pagan shrine, the Ka'bah, containing the ancient meteorite, which drew Bedouins and other Arabs to gather in peace for trade. But trading had another consequence beyond stimulating commerce: It brought Arabs in contact with Christians and Jews, and, as a result, new ideas filtered into the Arabian peninsula.

OPINION

What do you think was the most important reason for the rapid spread of Islam?

The Prophet

The new ideas generated by Arab, Christian, and Jewish interaction came to be embodied in the person of a man named Muhammad. Muhammad (570–632) was an orphan who grew up in Mecca in the care of his uncle. He became a merchant and made an excellent marriage to a wealthy widow and businesswoman, Khadijah. The couple had seven children and lived a prosperous life. As a merchant, Muhammad earned a reputation for being a good and honest man. His nickname was "al-Amin"—"the trustworthy."

In his fortieth year, Muhammad began to have visions. First an angel appeared to him while he was sleeping and said: "Recite! Thy Lord . . . taught by the pen, taught that which they knew not unto men." When Muhammad awoke from this vision, he saw a huge man with his feet astride the horizon. This man claimed to be the angel Gabriel and told Muhammad to be the apostle to his people. According to Islamic tradition, Muhammad received an additional 114 revelations over the next twenty years. These revelations were recorded as the word of Allah (God) given in the Arabic language. Accounts of the revelations were collected after Muhammad's death and became the book of inspired scripture of the new religion. This scripture is called the Qur'an (sometimes written in English as "Koran").

Muhammad believed the God who spoke through him was the same God worshiped by Jews and Christians. Muhammad said that five major prophets had come before him: Adam, Noah, Abraham, Moses, and Jesus. Muhammad said each had brought truth, but Christians and Jews had departed from the prophets' messages—the Jews had ignored Jesus, and Christians had embellished the simple message of the Gospels by adding theological complexities. Therefore, Allah had decided to speak through Muhammad, who is known simply as the Prophet. The religion he founded is called Islam, and its followers are known as Muslims.

The Religion

The nature of Islam is as clear and stark as the Arabian desert itself. *Islam* means "surrender to God," and this idea lies at the heart of the religion, for a follower of the religion is called a Muslim—"one who submits." Christians had to study for years before converting and had to understand the subtlety of various creeds. For a man or woman to convert to Islam, he or she merely needed to testify, "There is no God but Allah and Muhammad is his prophet." Whenever children were born in Muslim lands, midwives and parents whispered this creed into their ears so that they would grow immediately into faith. After this simple creed, Muslims were to follow the Five Pillars of Faith.

The first pillar of faith is the profession of faith itself. Believers adhere to a strict monotheism. (For example, Muslims believe that the Christian belief in the Trinity of the Father, Son, and Holy Spirit signaled a departure from the command to have only one God.) Further, Muslims believe that the Qur'an represents the word of God. The power of the spoken and written word had come to light in Muhammad's first vision, which emphasized the importance of God's words brought through the Prophet. Many of the faithful memorize and recite the entire Qur'an (which is about as long as the Christian New Testament).

Faith

The first pillar concerned private behavior, indicating the faith within, but the next four reinforced the first through public actions of all believers. The second pillar of faith is prayer, an activity that the faithful perform five times a day. In addition, every Friday, Muslims gather to pray together at the local mosque, called there by a human voice beckoning from the mosque towers, or minarets. (Christians are called by bells, and Jews by horns. Muslims believe the angel Gabriel told Muhammad to use the human voice to call his followers to prayer.)

Public rituals

Unlike Christian churches, mosques display no images of God. Muslims take the biblical prohibition against the idolatry of graven images literally. It may be that the Byzantine iconoclast movement was influenced by the example of the strict interpretation of the Muslims. Instead of images of God, mosques are decorated with beautiful geometric patterns. These designs are intended to help the faithful in their prayers by focusing their attention on the divine pattern of the universe. An example of mosaic patterning appears on the photograph of the Dome of the Rock shown at the opening of this chapter.

The third pillar of faith is almsgiving. Muslims are to donate a portion of what they earn to the needy, and this

THE QUR'AN Because images are forbidden to Muslims, writing became the most honored art in the Islamic world. Muslims considered beautiful calligraphy to be part of the revealed word of God, as shown in this manuscript page from the Qur'an.

giving purifies the rest of their earnings. The fourth pillar of faith is fasting. All Muslims fast during the month of Ramadan, a time based on the lunar calendar that comes at a different point every year, which commemorates the month Allah revealed the Qur'an to Muhammad. During this month, the faithful ingest no food or drink and do not engage in sexual relations during the day, but eat and celebrate every night after sundown. This month is much loved by Muslims because it lets them attend to spiritual matters and family in a concentrated way.

The last pillar of faith is pilgrimage. All Muslims try to make a journey to Muhammad's holy city of Mecca once in their lifetime. This trip—called the **Haj**—is made during a designated pilgrimage month, so the city throngs with Muslims from all over the world during this special time. Muslims today continue to follow all the pillars of faith, including the Haj.

The Spread of Islam

When Muhammad began to speak of his visions, his wife Khadijah became his first convert. However, aside from her and some close friends, few people living in the market city of Mecca paid any attention to his message. This city had grown prosperous in part because of pilgrims coming

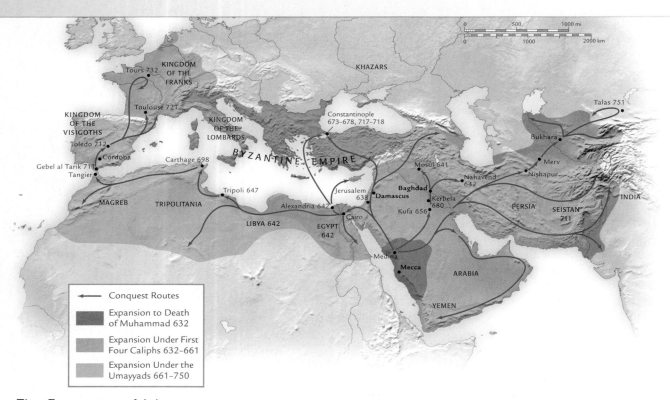

The Expansion of Islam, to 750

This map shows the expansion of Islam from the Arabian peninsula to the southern and eastern Mediterranean, with the dates of the expansion. It includes the cities of Mecca, Damascus, and Baghdad—each of which, in turn, would become the capital of the Muslim world.

to worship at the pagan shrine of the Ka'bah, so the city leaders had little interest in the words of a new prophet.

In 622, Muhammad and his small group of followers fled Mecca to another city 250 miles to the north. This city was later named Medina, which simply means "the city." Muslims consider this flight, called the ***Hijra*** (or *Hegira*), the turning point in the acceptance of the new religion. Just as Christians mark the birth of Christ as a turning point by dating the calendar from that year, Muslims remember the Hijra by using the year 622 as the year 1 in their calendar. The dating system uses A.H. (*anno Hijrah*) instead of C.E. (common era).

From his new base in Medina, Muhammad spread his ideas to the desert Bedouins. Tribe by tribe, the Arabians converted and began to focus their warfare on "unbelievers" instead of on each other, eventually coalescing into a unified group. In 628, Muhammad returned victorious to Mecca, where the large numbers of his followers persuaded the urban dwellers that his message was true. He kept the great shrine at the Ka'bah, convinced that the large meteor within it was sacred to Allah. Pilgrims still journey to this holy place and it is the focal point of the prayer of Muslims worldwide.

The map above shows the extent of Islam at the death of the Prophet in 632. At first, Muhammad's closest followers proclaimed themselves **caliphs** ("deputies" or "suc-

cessors") of the Prophet. The map shows how rapidly the first four caliphs spread the new religion. These successes continued, and only a century after Muhammad's death, Islam held sway in an area stretching from India to Spain. After this remarkable spread, many people who were not Arabs became Muslims, and although all learned to speak Arabic so that they could read the Qur'an, sometimes tensions emerged between Arab and non-Arab believers. Nevertheless, the spectacular growth of this new creed obliterated the Persian Empire, shrank the Byzantine Empire, and conquered the Vandal and Visigothic kingdoms.

In the summer of 732, the forces of Islam drove through the passes of the Pyrenees into the Merovingian kingdom of the Franks. The army was made up of a large body of light cavalry and was a formidable force.

Battle of Tours

Muslim generals were confident of their ability to conquer the less-organized Franks. They easily swept through the southern lands, destroying the opposition and taking great plunder. As the Arab chronicler relates, "All the nations of the Franks trembled at that terrible army." The retreating forces approached the Merovingian household for help, and the great general Charles Martel (Charles the Hammer) led a force to a large grassy plain near Tours (see map above). The Arab chronicler recognized the momentous nature of this meeting: "The two great hosts of the two languages and the two creeds were set in array against each other." The battle was fierce and tens of thousands died, but Charles won a decisive victory. The remaining Muslim force retreated across the Pyrenees, and the storm of Islamic conquests in the west was halted.

In spite of Charles's victory, the Islamic conquests were impressive. Why did Islam spread so quickly? There are a number of reasons. In part, its success came from the military strength of

Reasons for success

the recently unified Bedouin and oasis Arabs. Forming a new "tribe" based on religion, these formerly separate groups now made an effective fighting unit. Islamic armies also benefited from believing that God supported their military expansion, for the Qur'an urged warriors to fight vigorously in the cause of monotheism: "Fight in the path of God with those who fight with you . . . kill them; such is the reward of the infidels. . . . Fight them till there be no dissent, and the worship be only to God." As Muslim armies swept to victory in what they believed was a holy war, or **jihad,** they may have forced pagans to convert or be killed.

The concept of jihad is a complicated one because the word has several meanings that have allowed for differ-

Jihad

ent interpretations and emphases over time. From the beginning, Muslims identified two kinds of jihad: The "greater jihad" is the ongoing struggle within each individual to strive against base desires. This inner struggle is more meritorious than warfare, and many scholars emphasize this greater jihad when discussing the concept. The "lesser jihad" is a military struggle conducted against infidels.

In the early Islamic expansion, the jihad against polytheism established Islamic territories, which were called the House of Islam. In theory, non-Muslim states were called a House of War that existed until they were subjugated or converted. Under early Muslim laws, jihad was to be a constant state of war against the infidels, but as we will see, this idea would change over time.

The expansion of Islam also drew strength from the relatively benign attitude of the Muslim conquerors. Christians and Jews, whom Muslims called "people of the Book" because they all shared the same scriptural tradition and worshiped the same God that Muslims venerated, had only to pay taxes to the Muslim rulers. In one of the earliest political documents of Islam,

Christians Accept Caliph Umar's Terms

The following letter from the Christians in Syria to Caliph Umar (r. 634–644) outlines the agreed-upon terms and indicates what kinds of things Christians were forbidden.

We shall not build, in our cities or in their neighborhood, new monasteries, churches, convents, or monks' cells, nor shall we repair, by day or night, such of them as fall in ruins or are situated in the quarters of the Muslims. We shall not give shelter in our churches or in our dwellings to any spy, nor hide him from the Muslims. We shall teach the Qur'an to our children. We shall not manifest our religion publicly nor convert anyone to it. We shall not prevent any of our kin from entering Islam if they wish it. We shall show respect toward the Muslims, and we shall rise from our seats when they wish to sit. We shall not seek to resemble the Muslims by imitating any of their garments, the headgear, the turban, footwear, or the parting of the hair. We shall not mount our saddles, nor shall we gird swords nor bear any kind of arms nor carry them on our persons. We shall not engrave Arabic inscriptions on our seals. We shall not sell fermented drinks. . . . We accept these conditions for ourselves and for the people in our community, and in return we receive safe-conduct. . . .

What prohibitions do you think might have eventually encouraged many Christians to convert to Islam?

Muhammad wrote a "constitution" for Medina in 622 outlining the policies of the new religion. In this document, he laid out the principle of toleration and mutual aid: "The Jews must bear their expenses and the Muslims their expenses. Each must help the other against anyone who attacks the people of this document." However, such toleration did not mean equality; it came with conditions, as shown in the document on page 143.

Many Christians, especially in Syria, Egypt, and North Africa, had rejected the policies of the Byzantine emperors and tolerated Islam. Within Byzantium, men and women whose beliefs had been declared heretical had been forbidden to continue in their beliefs. Under the Muslims, who cared little about the subtleties of Christian theology, they could believe as they liked as long as they submitted to the conquerors. Jews, too, were free to practice their religion without the pressure they had experienced before, particularly under the Visigoths. In time, many Christians converted to Islam. The rise of Islam had created a whole new culture in the Mediterranean world.

Creating an Islamic Unity

The Muslim armies not only conquered large expanses of land but also quickly transformed the society and culture of these territories. Anyone traveling in the Mediterranean world today can see immediately that life in Algeria is strikingly different from life in Italy. This was not so during Roman times.

What was it about Muslim rule that made Islamic culture take root so powerfully in these formerly Christian regions? Language played a large role. Because the Qur'an was not to be translated, believers of Islam had to learn Arabic. Therefore, Arabic became the language of business, government, and literature in Islamic strongholds. Prayer and pilgrimage also served to solidify the Muslim world. As the faithful all looked to Mecca five times a day during prayer and made pilgrimages to the holy places, men and women broadened their attention and loyalties beyond their local kingdoms. Over time, they began to think of themselves as part of a larger group.

Unifying elements

Law was another important unifying force. The Islamic governments were ruled by Muslim law based on the Qur'an and the Sunna, which is a collection of cultural traditions based on the life of the Prophet. These laws, administered by Muslim judges, governed most aspects of Islamic life. Uniform enforcement of the laws contributed to a growing cultural homogeneity.

Finally, the great Muslim trade network that extended from India to the Mediterranean powerfully united the Islamic world. The freedom that Muslim rulers allowed merchants and artisans fueled economic development. Arabic coins, dinars, began to replace Byzantine or Persian coins as the main trade medium, and the Muslims developed advanced banking techniques to facilitate trade. For example, they initiated the use of bank checks, which would not be employed in the West for another eight hundred years.

The Gracious Life

With large-scale trade came dramatic changes in Muslim society. The conquerors adopted the best of both the Persian and Hellenistic worlds and created a way of life that was comfortable and pleasant, at least for the wealthy. Muslim households built on traditions drawn from the Bedouin tribes combined with practices from the Persian Empire. Previously, men had been allowed to have an unlimited number of wives, as in the Persian harems. However, the Qur'an limited a man to four wives, and this only if he could demonstrate that he had enough money to provide each wife with her own quarters and her own slaves. If husbands and wives did not get along, they could appeal to a judge who acted as an arbiter. If arbitration failed to resolve a conflict, either the man or the woman could obtain a divorce. Women's status under Islam improved in other ways as well: They were no longer treated strictly as property as they had been in pagan Arabic tribal society, and under Islamic law, Muslim women could inherit and keep their property even after marriage.

Women

Within the household, women were separated from the company of men, and this seclusion continued when they went outdoors. Muslim women continued an age-old Middle Eastern practice of wearing heavy veils to cover themselves, and this practice continues in many Muslim countries today. Within the households, women presided over the many slaves generated from the conquests and subsequent trade and created a lifestyle that was the envy of many in the Mediterranean world.

Persians taught the Arabian Muslims to play chess and backgammon; from Syria, Muslims learned to wear wide trousers instead of the traditional Arab robes. They also began to eat at tables instead of sitting cross-legged on the floor. These seemingly small matters, when taken together, reflected a prosperous, relatively homogeneous society.

Daily life

The image on page 145 reveals several unique aspects of Islamic society. In this illustration, two wealthy Muslim men are served wine by a Christian slave probably captured in Spain. (Islamic society depended heavily on slavery, just as the Persian and Roman cultures had.) This picture also captures Muslim attitudes toward alcohol. The Qur'an forbids drinking of wine, but many Muslims routinely violated this prohibition. Indeed, some beautiful Arabic poetry even extols the pleasures of good wine. As this illustration indicates, Muslim culture was developing into something very different from life in western Europe and Byzantium.

Forces of Disunity

For all its cultural commonalities, the Muslim world was not without strife. Two related problems led to conflict within the Muslim territories. One problem centered on ethnicity—specifically, relations between Arabs and other Muslim peoples. The other involved a pressing political question: Who would rule after the death of the Prophet?

Some Muslims believed that the caliphs should be spiritual leaders who based their authority on the Prophet's family. In the mid-seventh century, amid much controversy over the succession, the Prophet's son-in-law and cousin, 'Ali, became the caliph. 'Ali promoted the idea of equality for all believers, rather than privileged status for Arabs who had initially spread the Prophet's message. Although he hoped to serve less as a governor and tax collector than as a spiritual leader, 'Ali had to devote much of his reign to fighting political rivals.

Shi'ite Muslims

In 661, as 'Ali was entering a mosque to pray, an assassin supporting another political faction plunged a dagger into the caliph, but 'Ali's notion of the caliphate remained alive. Men and women who followed his ideal were called **Shi'ites.** They continue to believe that the Islamic world should be ruled by **imams,** men descended from 'Ali who act as true spiritual heads of the community. The Shi'ite faithful proclaimed 'Ali's two sons, Hasan and Husayn, the second and third Imams. Husayn is particularly revered by Shi'ites today because followers of the caliph killed him and his infant son. Although Shi'ites look upon the usurpation of 'Ali's rights to rule as the beginning of their movement, Husayn's death—which they saw as a martyrdom—served as the emotional rallying point for the Shi'ites. To this day, the death of Husayn is the most fervently celebrated event in the Shi'ite calendar. From these early centuries on, Shi'ites have believed that imams are endowed with the Divine Light Wisdom, which enables them to interpret complicated passages in the Qur'an. Shi'ites today are a significant minority in the Muslim world and continue to disagree with the Sunnis, who advocate a political, rather than purely spiritual, caliphate. In southern Arabia (modern Yemen), even the Shi'ite communities split. One branch, called the Zaydi sect, established a separate state in Yemen's mountainous region in 901. These early religious tensions in Yemen have continued to the present day, influencing modern terrorist struggles.

After the murder of 'Ali, the caliphate was taken over by the Umayyad family, who established a dynasty that lasted almost a century. The Umayyads located their capital in Damascus and created a government that favored Arabs. This dynasty represented the traditional military and economic leaders of the Arabs. Nevertheless, dissent

SPANISH MUSLIMS Muslim life included the enjoyment of many things, including a good game of chess. The game was probably developed in India and spread rapidly through Muslim lands into the West, where it was much beloved in the courts of Europe.

stirred even within the Umayyad caliphate. The Dome of the Rock (shown at the beginning of this chapter) was built by an Umayyad caliph in 691 who wanted to de-emphasize Mecca. He encouraged the faithful to visit the rock in Jerusalem from where Muslims believed Muhammad had ascended to heaven. He was successful; the Dome of the Rock today is a much-loved shrine. Unfortunately, it stands on land that Jews and Christians also venerate, and the site continues to generate controversy.

Umayyad caliphate

In 750, the 'Abbasids overthrew the Umayyad caliphate. They intended to restore more spiritual authority to the caliphate and to broaden authority from the Arabs to other believers, but most important, they moved the capital from Damascus to Baghdad. This newly built city, located on the banks of the Tigris River, was perfectly suited to take advantage of the rich trade from the Far East. Its land was rich, and the caliph was particularly impressed with its cool nights and freedom from mosquitoes. The founder claimed, "It will surely be the most flourishing city in the world," and he was not wrong. The great city, fortified by three concentric round walls, was the administrative center of Islam and by the tenth century had a population of about 1.5 million people. This extraordinary city helped the Muslim world focus toward the old Persian provinces, with their rich trade routes to the east. Seen from this magnificent cosmopolitan city, rivaled only by Constantinople, western Europe seemed very primitive indeed. However, the move to the east did not help the 'Abbasids eliminate political dissension. The Umayyads continued to hold power in Spain, and the Shi'ites refused to support the 'Abbasids.

'Abbasid caliphate

Beyond the disunity percolating within the ruling dynasties, there was the ever-present tendency toward local control. Caliphs in Baghdad growing rich on eastern trade had little authority over commanders as far away as Spain, and by the tenth century (fourth century of the Islamic calendar), military commanders, called **emirs,** were taking power in their local areas. Although they theoretically followed the rule of the caliphs, they frequently acted with a good deal of autonomy.

The many divisions within the House of Islam that had emerged by the tenth century led to a transformation of the idea of jihad. During the early expansion years, there had been a clear, twofold division of the world—the House of War and the House of Islam. Now, complex realities of political alignments caused some Muslims to argue for an intermediate area—a House of Peace—in which non-Muslim states could be exempt from attack. This legal device permitted travel and trade between Muslim and non-Muslim regions, and through the tenth century there was often a relationship of mutual tolerance established between the Muslim world and regions outside its borders.

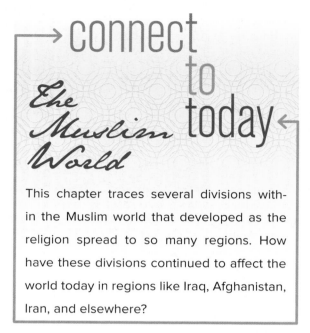

connect to today

The Muslim World

This chapter traces several divisions within the Muslim world that developed as the religion spread to so many regions. How have these divisions continued to affect the world today in regions like Iraq, Afghanistan, Iran, and elsewhere?

Heirs to Hellenistic Learning

Despite all the political tensions, the Muslim world still managed to make astonishing gains in the arts and sciences, and in fact remained the intellectual center of the Mediterranean world for centuries. By the eighth century, the caliphs had collected Persian, Greek, and Syriac scientific and philosophical works and had them translated into Arabic. In the ninth century, the 'Abbasids ruling in Baghdad maintained this support of science. They built the House of Wisdom in Baghdad, which included a library, a translation center, and a school. This careful cultivation of learning and the blending of so many traditions led to remarkable accomplishments. Muslim scientists and physicians were by far the best in the Western world.

Muslim doctors did not slavishly follow the great classical physicians Hippocrates and Galen, even though the works of these men circulated widely. Instead, they combined this ancient wisdom with practical and empirical observation. Islamic rulers required doctors to be licensed, so the practice of medicine was well regulated. Some Islamic physicians wrote extensively and exerted a profound influence on Western medicine. Razi (865–925) (called Rhazes in the West) authored more than one hundred books on medicine. He was the first to diagnose smallpox and prescribe an effective treatment for it. Ibn Sina (980–1037) (known as Avicenna in the West) wrote *Canon of Medicine,* an encyclopedia of medicine that laid the foundation for experimental science.

Medicine

Muslim surgeons performed remarkably complex operations. They practiced vascular and cancer surgery and developed a sophisticated technique for operating on cataracts of the eyes that involved using a tube to drain

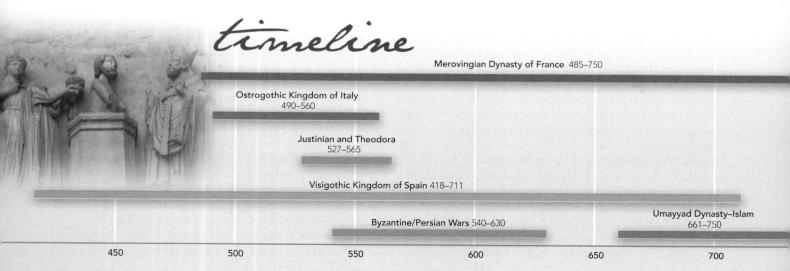

timeline

Merovingian Dynasty of France 485–750

Ostrogothic Kingdom of Italy 490–560

Justinian and Theodora 527–565

Visigothic Kingdom of Spain 418–711

Byzantine/Persian Wars 540–630

Umayyad Dynasty–Islam 661–750

450 500 550 600 650 700

the fluid from the cataract. This technique was employed even in modern times, until physicians developed procedures for removing the cataracts completely. A wide range of anesthetics, from opium mixed in wine to more sophisticated drugs, made surgery tolerable for Muslim patients. Hospitals, too, sprang up throughout the Muslim world and included outpatient treatment centers and dispensaries for the many medicines being developed. Thanks to the careful sharing of knowledge and the development of advanced procedures and study, Muslim physicians provided outstanding medical care between the seventh and twelfth centuries.

Scientists made dramatic progress in other areas as well. Mathematicians brought the use of "Arabic" numerals from India, and these replaced the Roman numerals that had been used throughout the former empire. The major advantage of Arabic numerals was that they included the zero, which makes complex calculations manageable. By the tenth century, Muslim mathematicians had perfected the use of decimals and fractions and had invented algebra. The word *algebra* comes from Arabic and means "the art of bringing together unknowns to match a known quantity." Today students all over the world continue to learn this art.

Mathematics

Even the religious architecture developed by the Muslims put a unique imprint on the appearance of the southern Mediterranean cities. Whereas Christians emphasized religious images based on the human form, Muslims developed exquisite patterning designs. Domes and minarets gracing impressive mosques gave the skylines of eastern and southern cities their own distinct character.

Islam and the West

Before the seventh century, the story of the West unfolded rather organically from the Fertile Crescent around the Mediterranean basin and into northern Europe. After Muhammad's visions and the spread of Islam, that experience changed. The Mediterranean world was split into two separate cultures. Historians have argued over the degree to which trade and travel were interrupted by the division, but none questions the cultural divide. From the seventh century on, Islam and the West would take two different paths, always interacting at some level, but always conscious of the difference between them.

SUMMARY

After the sixth century, the Mediterranean world of the old Roman Empire underwent a dramatic transformation: In the west, it dissolved in the face of the rising Germanic kingdoms; in the east, it was changed into the Byzantine Empire; and in the south, armies of the new religion of Islam conquered vast territories.

- In the west, tribes of Germanic peoples, who had different lifestyles and values from the Romans, invaded the old empire and established kingdoms. As they settled, they acquired characteristics from Rome and converted to Christianity. The resulting kingdoms—Franks in France, Ostrogoths and Lombards in Italy, and Visigoths in Spain—established new civilizations that marked the west. The Catholic Church also strengthened in the west, fostered by strong Popes and the spread of monasteries.

- In the east, emperors considered themselves the heirs of Rome. Under the rulers Justinian and Theodora, Constantinople grew into a huge city dominated by the great church, Hagia Sophia. They briefly reconquered western lands, but could not hold them for long. The Orthodox Church in the east separated from the Catholics in the west, creating a long-lasting split.

- In the early seventh century, a new religion grew out of the Arabian desert and spread rapidly. Followers of Islam conquered as far west as Spain and as far east as India creating a vast new civilization that led the world in medicine and science.

From this time forward, the interactions among these three great cultures—western European, Byzantine, and Muslim—would profoundly shape the history of the West.

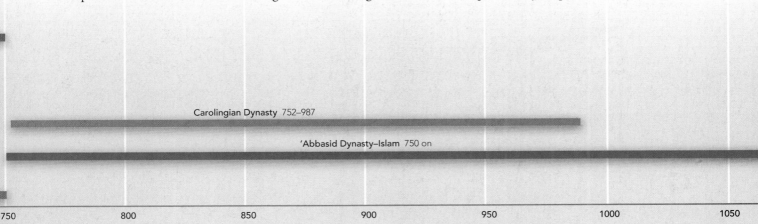

Carolingian Dynasty 752–987

'Abbasid Dynasty–Islam 750 on

750   800   850   900   950   1000   1050

OSEBERG VIKING SHIP,
ca. 800   Beginning in the ninth century, Vikings from Scandinavia traveled from Russia to Newfoundland on magnificent ships built of oak and designed to flex with the rough waters of the North Atlantic. This is the Oseberg ship, buried as part of a funeral ceremony, with two women and their precious goods interred with the ship. Carried in these ships, Viking warriors disrupted and transformed western Europe.

The Struggle to Bring Order

7

The Early Middle Ages,
ca. 750–1000

A Carolingian Family Tragedy

In 824, a wedding took place in the palace of Emperor Louis the Pious between Dhouda, a highborn woman, and Bernard, a knight and relative of the emperor. Dhouda's family was proud of this marriage, certain it would secure their family's place in the ordered Carolingian Empire, but the violence and instability of the age—not to mention Bernard's incompetence— swept the family into tragedy. Dhouda and Bernard had two sons: ▶▶ William, born in 826, and Bernard Jr., born in 841. ▶▶

But Bernard was restless. He sent Dhouda away to live in a small town in the south of France, visiting her periodically, then proceeded to involve himself in political and personal intrigue.

Bernard was accused of committing adultery with Emperor Louis' wife and engaging in other unmentioned treasonous activities. Bernard escaped from the king, who then took out his wrath on Bernard's family. Louis arrested Bernard's sister, a nun, accused her of sorcery, sealed her in a wine cask, and threw her in a river to drown. The king then turned to Bernard's brother, and blinded and imprisoned him. In the Middle Ages, families were linked in innocence and guilt, and even the life of a nun could be jeopardized by the misbehavior of her brother.

After Louis the Pious's death in 840, things only got worse. When civil wars erupted among Louis' sons, Bernard got involved, giving his 14-year-old son, William, to Charles the Bald as hostage. Dhouda, who had received a good education, wrote a book of instructions for her son William, hoping to guide him to a life of more integrity than his father's, and her book reflects the central values of the ninth century. Dhouda urged William to have faith in God and in the feudal ties that bound men together. She warned, "Never let the idea of disloyalty against your lord be born or thrive in your heart." Her advice could not save her family.

Bernard was publicly beheaded after he switched sides, betraying his lord, and William was also executed.

This tale of ninth-century violence shows that while early medieval kings began to bring order to their societies with law and learning, these efforts failed by the ninth century. What was left were ties of loyalty between individuals, as men joined their fortunes to each other and women were swept into these mutually binding contracts. However, everything was not lost. Legal structures would reassert themselves, and the learning that Dhouda showed in her book would come to the fore again. The story of the development of the West grew from the kind of destruction that devastated this Carolingian family. ◄◄

BRINGING ORDER WITH LAWS AND LEADERSHIP

Long before their penetration into the Roman Empire, the Germanic tribes had valued the force of law. Laws were not written down, however, nor legislated by king or council. Instead, laws constituted the customs of the past enforced by individuals and families. Traditionally, kings could arbitrate between conflicting parties, but people believed the law transcended any individual ruler, and law was administered by assemblies of the people. The German assemblies had developed some unusual means to help determine the truth in disputed cases. For example, they might consider the character (or value to the community) of the accused, and in a practice called **compurgation,** 12 honorable men testified to the character of the accused (without any necessary knowledge of the facts of the incidents under discussion). Or the assembly might appeal to the supernatural, in a process called **ordeal** (the word originally meant "judgment"). In an ordeal, the accused might pick up a red-hot iron or immerse his hand in boiling water. If the hand was not severely burned, the accused was judged innocent. Later in the Middle Ages, ordeals by battle would also be used to determine guilt, and in late witchcraft trials, women were thrown into the water to see if they sank. Floating—an indication that the water rejected the woman—was seen as a sign of guilt.

In the late fifth century, the kings from the western Germanic kingdoms—who inherited the Roman traditions of the lands they held—began to codify their people's laws, and they were helped by their Roman subjects trained in classical law. The ancient laws of the Germanic peoples were written down in Latin and began to incorporate some of the principles of Roman law. The laws of the land **Legal codes** became yet another example of the slow blending of cultures that shaped the medieval world. The codes of the Franks, Lombards, Visigoths, and Anglo-Saxons offer historians important insights into these early kingdoms. The prologues of these codes continued to insist that the kings were not making laws, but simply recording the people's will—the old Germanic tradition of law was preserved.

In villages (which might have as few as a dozen families), the most respected people in the community assembled periodically to administer their local affairs. In many ways, these day-to-day decisions, made by people gathering together at a crossroads in the village, were more important to these people's lives than the larger policies set by kings. These villagers were participating in an ancient custom of self-governance at the most local level.

Like the villagers, the nobles of the Germanic tribes also had traditions for resolving disputes; they depended upon private vengeance for justice. According to the recorded laws, the principal preoccupation was to find ways to stop the bitter feuds that broke out between extended families who cherished their ability to protect their people and their honor above all else. The written law codes became a first step toward regularizing and perhaps controlling the violence to bring order to the growing kingdoms.

Feuding was slowly regulated by placing limits on the occasions where vengeance was allowed. For example, a family was not permitted to seek revenge if one of their number was killed while committing a crime. Nor could a family strike back before an offender from another family was proven guilty. However, the

Wergeld

most important mechanism for regulating violence was persuading family groups to accept compensation (in money or goods) instead of vengeance. If a member of one's kin was killed or injured, for example, the guilty party had to restore the victim's monetary worth to his or her family. This amount of money was called **wergeld,** or "man gold"—in other words, the worth of a man. A free peasant was worth about 200 shillings; a nobleman, six times that. The Germanic laws used the techniques of ordeal and compurgation to determine who should pay wergeld.

The intricate system of fines that formed the basis of wergeld included outrages committed against all members of the tribe, from women and children to livestock. Wergeld was assessed for the rape of young women or nuns, for adultery committed with a married woman, and even for crimes as specific as watching a woman who was modestly hiding behind a bush to urinate. The early laws of the Franks penalized anyone who hit a pregnant woman, and the penalty was increased if the woman died, thus killing the unborn child. The laws recognized that part of a woman's value included her potential for bearing children; if someone killed a postmenopausal woman, he had to pay one-third of the fine for killing a woman during her childbearing years.

These law codes that so precisely reveal the details of life in the early Germanic kingdoms may appear strange to us because they put a price on everything from an insult to a toe injury. However, they represented an important step in the emerging synthesis between Germanic and Roman societies, as kings began to record the customs of the people. These records were intended to bring peace and order to the kingdoms, but in this they were only partially successful: The early medieval kings never succeeded in weaning their subjects completely from their need for vengeance. In spite of the efforts of kings, the eighth and ninth centuries remained an era of rampant lawlessness, largely because these laws were too difficult to enforce. However, important seeds were planted in the legal traditions that we have come to identify with Western civilization.

The eighth-century monarchs slowly insinuated themselves and their royal officers between feuding families, and written law codes became an instrument by which royal power could be slowly increased. Wergeld, compurgation, and trial by ordeal became major legal pillars of the early Middle Ages, adding to the judicial tradition left by the Romans. The Germanic custom of trial by assemblies became an important base for the growth of representative institutions that would emerge in the Middle Ages. The concept of the rule of law—in which law superseded individual inclination and played a central role in keeping order—proved highly resilient and helped consolidate these early monarchies.

ANGLO-SAXON ENGLAND: Forwarding Learning and Law

As the eighth century opened, Anglo-Saxon England consisted of several kingdoms (shown on map on page 153). The most powerful were Northumbria, Mercia, and Wessex. At this time, these kingdoms were separate and struggling to integrate their new Christianity and the new learning they inherited from the Roman texts that Christian leaders brought to the island.

The Anglo-Saxons had been converted to Christianity in the seventh century, and after the Synod of Whitby in 664 (discussed in Chapter 6), the English church began to be organized along the Roman model—with a clearer hierarchy of bishops and priests—instead of as a monastic, missionary organization. In 669, Pope Vitalian sent Theodore of Tarsus to be the archbishop of Canterbury, and this erudite man from the eastern Roman Empire significantly forwarded learning in Britain. He established a school at Canterbury and brought other scholars with him who founded Benedictine monasteries in the north of England—at Wearmouth-Jarrow—that also became centers of learning. By the end of the seventh century, England was poised to be a center of intellectual activity.

The illustration on page 154 was produced at Jarrow and shows the intellectual skill that had grown in this island outpost of Christianity. *Beowulf,* the most famous Old English poem that has immortalized the heroic values of the Germanic tribes (described in Chapter 6), was probably written down during this period of monastic scholarship. Although the English monastic schools created valuable manuscripts, their proudest creation was probably the greatest scholar since the decline of the Roman world: the Venerable Bede (ca. 672–735).

The Venerable Bede: Recording Science and History

In the early eighth century, Bede studied in Jarrow, and the young scholar mastered all the texts available to him. His writings interpreted the ancient works and made them accessible to his contemporaries. As a product of the monasteries, he wrote in Latin—the language of the church and of the educated—and his writings became essential to generations of subsequent Latin scholars. Bede was primarily a teacher who wrote a number of works intended as educational tracts. In these works he drew from previous scholars, thus preserving and expanding upon knowledge from previous centuries. For example, in an influential text—*The Nature of Things*—Bede incorporated much from the Roman encyclopedist

The Visigoths Lay Down the Laws

In about the seventh century, Visigoths began to write down their customary laws, which are excellent sources of information about ancient village life. The laws use the principle of wergeld, monetary compensation, to resolve conflicts between neighbors.

I. Where a Horse, or Any Other Animal, Which Has Been Tied Up, Is Removed, or Injured, in Any Way.

If any person should free a horse, or any other animal belonging to another, from its halter, or from its hobbles, without the knowledge of the owner, he shall pay him a *solidus*. If said horse, or other animal, should die, in consequence, said person shall give its owner another of equal value.

XIX. Where a Dog . . . Is Proved to Have Injured or Killed Anyone.

Where a dog bites another person not his owner, and said person is known to have been crippled or killed, in consequence thereof, no responsibility shall attach to the owner of the dog, unless it shall be proved that he caused said dog to make the attack. If, however, he should encourage his dog to seize a thief, or any other criminal, and the latter should be bitten while in flight, and should be crippled, or die from the effects of the bite, the owner of said dog shall incur no liability therefor. But if he should cause said dog to injure an innocent person, he must render satisfaction according to law, in the same manner as if he himself had inflicted the wound.

What kinds of problems arose among neighbors, and how were they resolved?

Pliny the Elder (23–79) and the Visigothic scholar Isidore of Seville (ca. 560–636), but he added his own interpretations. For example, *The Nature of Things* attempted to explain the orbits of the earth, heavens, stars, and planets. In this widely copied and read work, Bede described the earth as a globe and discussed its geography, and this tract was counted among the most important scientific texts of the early Middle Ages.

Bede's most famous work, however, is the *Ecclesiastical History of the English People*, in which he tells the history of early Anglo-Saxon England to ca. 731. This enterprise was pathbreaking in that he took as his canvas an entire nation—not just a local region, as was customary. This was all the more remarkable from a man who probably never went farther than 7 miles from the place where he was born. But his vision helped shape the English into a cohesive entity. Bede drew from sources that are now lost, so his work is invaluable to our understanding of this early period of the Middle Ages. Further, Bede was careful to distinguish between knowledge and rumor, so he established principles of historical writing that had been virtually forgotten since the Roman historians. Perhaps the most influential aspect of Bede's history was that he adopted Dionysius Exiguus's B.C./A.D. (now B.C.E./C.E.) dating system (described in Chapter 6). Not many people had read Dionysius's tract, but Bede's was read and translated for centuries, and our adoption of Dionysius's historical dating system can be largely attributed to Bede.

Bede's *History*

Centuries of readers were not captivated by these technical details. Instead, they were drawn to his powerful prose that brought to life the centuries in which the Germanic tribes seemed very foreign to Roman Christian missionaries. He wrote of how the first missionaries ordered to go to England in 596 by Pope Gregory recoiled at the prospect: "For they were appalled at the idea of going to a barbarous, fierce, and pagan nation, of whose very language they were ignorant." Readers followed these timid missionaries as they slowly converted the Anglo-Saxon kings and established monasteries that by the late seventh century could spawn a scholar of Bede's stature. The missionaries had done their work so well that when royal courts were ready, learning could leave the monasteries and enter secular life.

Governing the Kingdom

Like the other Germanic kings, the Anglo-Saxon kings developed detailed law codes that combined wergeld with some principles of Roman jurisprudence. Indeed, the small island developed an enduring legal tradition that has become known as **common law,** which differs from the **statutory law** that is based on mandates passed by a legislative body. The common-law tradition preserves a vestige of the Germanic tradition in which the customs of the people are law.

The Christian kings claimed to rule by the grace of God, but they did so with the approval and advice of the powerful men in their court. A king could succeed to the throne only with the approval of the witan, or circle of wise men of the realm. (The full assembly was called the *witenagemot.*) In addition, the king

Witan periodically called the witenagemot to meet with him and discuss matters important to the governing of the realm. Like the laws themselves, the assembly had arisen through custom and tradition rather than from any constitutional authority. Moreover, its power ebbed and flowed in accordance with the king's power. For example, if a monarch were weak (or young), the witan exerted a great deal of influence. A strong monarch, on the other hand, might call his lords together merely to confirm his decision. Over time, however, all kings governed with the assistance of this body of powerful men.

In an age of slow communication, kings depended on other officials as well to govern their realms. Monarchs divided their kingdoms into shires (roughly the size of modern counties) and appointed royal representatives to govern in their name. These aristo-

Royal offices cratic earls had many responsibilities, including mustering the local men into armies if the king needed them and leading warriors into battle. Earls also served as the principal judges, presiding over shire courts and executing royal commands.

Some earls amassed so much power that they governed several shires. This tendency might have weakened royal authority and essentially created new kingdoms had not the Anglo-Saxon monarchs moved to name additional royal officials. For example, kings appointed shire reeves (who later were called sheriffs) to help the earls fulfill their duties, but the sheriffs answered only to the kings, not to the earls. In this way, rulers kept a firm grip on power, even down to the shire level.

Yet, in this preindustrial world, in which people had no mail system or telephone network to connect them, kings had to do more than just appoint earls and sheriffs to keep order. For instance, collecting taxes and resolving legal disputes were matters for face-to-face contact. These emerging kingdoms struggled to provide the means for such contact and the ways by which to control it. The Anglo-Saxons accomplished this feat not only by assigning royal repre-

Anglo-Saxon Kingdoms, ca. 700 **This map shows the seven Anglo-Saxon kingdoms that had emerged by the eighth century. It also locates the major intellectual centers—Canterbury and the monasteries at Wearmouth-Jarrow.**

sentatives to govern at the shire level, but also by recognizing that some tasks were best handled at the local village level. Village laws enforced by community elders formed the basic level of administrative order, and parish priests and local tax collectors joined sheriffs and earls in structuring a network that could govern the new kingdoms.

Alfred the Great: King and Scholar

The administrative organization and the patronage of the arts flourished in England under the reign of King Alfred the Great (r. 871–901) of Wessex. Alfred is the only English king who has been called "the Great," in memory of his military victories and his support of learning and culture in his realm.

Alfred's contemporary biographer, Asser, offered an engaging picture of the young prince and emphasized his early love of learning: "As he passed through his childhood and boyhood he appeared fairer in form than all his brothers, and more pleasing in his looks, his words and his ways. . . . From his cradle, Alfred had been drawn to wisdom." Despite his intelligence, Alfred did not learn to read until he was 12 years old. In adulthood, he would make up for lost time. He studied Latin, collected books, and invited scholars to his court. His interests extended to the arts, for he encouraged singers to fill his court with sacred music and traditional folk songs.

By the time Alfred became king, the political divisions shown in the map above had been shaken by a wave of outside invaders—the Danes from across the North Sea. As early as the late eighth century, raiders from the

Saint Matthew, from a Gospel Book

ca. 700

Medieval patrons from western European courts and monasteries commissioned colorfully decorated Gospel books. This illustration of Saint Matthew was part of a Gospel book made in Anglo-Saxon England in about 700. How effective is this work in showing the synthesis of Germanic, Roman, and Christian culture that marked the Middle Ages?

ultimately make it easier for the peoples to share the land). The treaty also paved the way for Alfred to forge a unified kingdom in the south and to focus on the laws and learning that were his passions.

Alfred worked to bring southern England into the intellectual world of wider Europe through literature. From his own educational experience, Alfred knew that Latin texts were not accessible to many inquiring minds. In a letter to one of his bishops, **Alfred's translations** Alfred expressed the opinion (highly unusual in his time) that intellectual ideas should be available to everyone. He wrote, "It seems better to me for us also to translate some of the books which are most needful for all men to know into the language which we can all understand." The wise king followed his own advice and translated, or helped to translate, some of the great books of literature into Old English so that his own people could read them.

The rule of Alfred the Great marked the high point of the accomplishments of Anglo-Saxon England. Much of the southern portion of the island was ruled by this skilled king who brought the benefits of law and learning to his land. However, a century before Alfred's reign, across the English Channel, comparable developments had taken place on the Continent, where an even more powerful king had unified the lands of western Europe and established an empire that shone even more brightly than that of Alfred.

Scandinavian countries had begun raiding northern England. The great monastery of Jarrow had been looted and destroyed, and the intellectual flowering in the north that had produced Bede came to an end. A Danish raid with some 350 ships plundered London, and it looked as if the Anglo-Saxon kingdoms would all fall to the Northmen.

However, King Alfred had reorganized the military to confront the invaders, and he built the first English navy to patrol the coast against the raiders. After some English victories, the Danes and the English **Danelaw** signed a treaty in 886. Under its terms, Alfred and the Danish king Guthrum agreed to divide England between them. The northern lands later became known as the Danelaw to recognize that they were governed by laws different from those in the southern parts of the land. As part of this settlement, Guthrum agreed to convert to Christianity (which would

CHARLEMAGNE AND THE CAROLINGIANS: A New European Empire

The Carolingian king Charles (later known as Charles the Great, or Charlemagne) earned that accolade by the force of his personality and the breadth of his talents. About 6 feet tall and physically powerful, he boasted a full head of red hair and a prominent belly. Charlemagne represented the high point in the process of the combining of classical, Germanic, and Christian cultural elements that we saw beginning in Chapter 6.

Charlemagne's Kingdom

This impressive warrior undertook fifty-three campaigns throughout his reign—and won most of them. A pious man as well, Charlemagne established himself as a leader and reformer of the church. Finally, he had a deeply curious intellect. He knew the importance of education, recognized the worth of scholars, and energetically sponsored learning by establishing schools and hiring scholars. The political, ecclesiastical, and intellectual order that Charlemagne brought to the Continent has been called the Carolingian Renaissance, to emphasize the rebirth of learning that he initiated. As was the case in England, publicly fostered intellectual life depended upon a relatively ordered society, and in the early Middle Ages, this stability was purchased by military victories.

The map of Charlemagne's realm on page 156 shows the vast span of territory—from northern Spain to the North Sea, from the English Channel well into Germany,

Administering the realm

and across the Alps into northern Italy—that this accomplished leader brought under his control. If we contrast this area with the smaller Anglo-Saxon kingdoms shown on the map on page 153, we can imagine the challenges Charlemagne faced in administering this territory.

Like his English counterparts, Charlemagne put noblemen in charge of the various provinces he controlled and tried to use laws to bring order to his lands. However, his approach differed from that of the Anglo-Saxons in that, instead of having fixed sheriffs at his command, Charlemagne sent traveling agents (called *missi dominici*) throughout his territory to examine conditions in his name and to redress certain abuses. These royal representatives traveled in pairs—a bishop and a nobleman, representing both the secular and religious arms of Charlemagne's realm.

An edict issued by Charlemagne in 802 describes the high expectations he had for his officials, who were sent "throughout his whole kingdom, and through them he would have all the various classes of persons . . . live in accordance with the correct law . . . and let no one, through his cleverness or craft, dare to oppose or thwart the written law, as many are wont to do." The king knew that his rule depended upon his subjects obeying his laws.

Charlemagne enhanced his authority further by requiring his nobles to attend two assemblies a

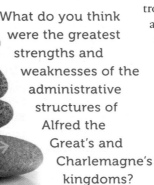

OPINION

What do you think were the greatest strengths and weaknesses of the administrative structures of Alfred the Great's and Charlemagne's kingdoms?

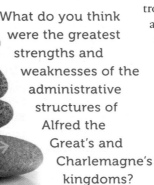

CHARLEMAGNE This bronze statue of the emperor portrays him in the pose of ancient Roman emperors, crowned and holding the orb of empire. The artist's intent was to communicate boldly that a new emperor reigned in the West.

year. As the men gathered in the outdoor meeting fields, they listened to the emperor's latest decrees and offered some opinions—but then went home and obeyed their ruler. In this way, Charlemagne moved from the original Germanic legal practice of the king simply recording the customs of the people; the Frankish king actually issued legal commands, and these carefully recorded capitularies serve as rich historical sources of his times.

In all these ways, Charlemagne departed from the Anglo-Saxon model and, in a strikingly new departure from traditional Germanic practice, sought to maintain a personal, centralized control over his unwieldy kingdom without appointing local administrators. Of course, personal rule hinges on the ruler's physical presence. Charlemagne met this requirement by traveling frequently throughout his lands, enjoying the hospitality of his noblemen. It is to Charlemagne's credit that this system worked as well as it did during his lifetime. As we will see, his administrative structure would not survive the loss of his personal attention.

The Empire of Charlemagne, ca. 800

This map shows the impressive kingdom of Charlemagne, with the dates of his conquests. **What strategic advantage did the tributary peoples on Charlemagne's eastern border offer to the emperor?**

Linking Politics and Religion

Charlemagne's political order had close links to his religious policies. He followed his father's lead in ensuring that his success as emperor was firmly tied to the fortunes of the church. This religious policy manifested itself in his treatment of the Saxons, a fierce people living on the northern borders of the empire. The Saxons had raided Frankish territory for generations. Charlemagne marched north in 772 and again in 775 and won decisive victories against the ferocious Saxons, but each time he left, they rose in revolt again. The emperor surmised that only by forcibly Christianizing the Saxons could he make them permanent members of his kingdom. In 785, after a particularly punitive campaign in which Charlemagne crushed the Saxon armies, the emperor forced the Saxon leader to convert to Christianity. Then Charlemagne established priests and monks in the conquered lands and punished relapses into paganism or other religious disobedience as treason. After some thirty years of religious coercion, Charlemagne's program worked—Christian Saxony no longer rebelled, again demonstrating how the church could serve his political ends.

As Charlemagne grew more powerful in the West, perhaps inevitably the question came up about his relationship with the Byzantine emperor in the East, and the two powers jockeyed for position. Charlemagne began to enter into many diplomatic contacts with the Byzantine court—he and Empress Irene of Byzantium engaged in ultimately unsuccessful negotiations to arrange a marriage between Charlemagne's daughter and Irene's son, the future emperor Constantine VI. However, in 797 Irene blinded and deposed her son Constantine, an act that made her the sole ruler. Charlemagne reputedly then proposed marrying Irene, thereby becoming the emperor himself, but these negotiations bore no fruit either. Instead, many wondered if Irene, a woman, could rule as emperor. If not, perhaps there was no emperor at all, and a new one should be named.

The turmoil in Byzantium contributed to one of the pivotal incidents in Charlemagne's reign, which showed his penchant for joining church and state. The event took place on Christmas Day in the year 800. The Carolingian king was in Rome; he had journeyed there at the request of Pope Leo III (r. 795–816), who had been attacked and brutally beaten while he conducted a procession through the streets of Rome. Charlemagne's armies restored the pope to power and calmed the violence in the city.

Charlemagne's coronation

POPE AND EMPEROR Charlemagne's crown did not resolve the question of who was superior: pope or emperor. This image tries to strike a balance, showing the two as equals as they kneel before Saint Peter.

When Charlemagne went to church in Rome on Christmas Day in 800, the relationship between pope and king was dramatically transformed. As the king of the Franks rose from prayer, the pope produced a crown and set it on Charlemagne's head. The watching crowds jubilantly proclaimed Charlemagne emperor. This event was of immense importance, for once again, a Roman emperor ruled in the West (independent of Byzantium), and he reigned by the might of his armies and with the blessing of God. The coronation reaffirmed the central alliance between the papacy and the Frankish kings. A new prominence of the northern kingdom had begun. In his political activities and his personal life, the Frankish emperor personified the artful integration of God and politics.

Negotiating with Byzantium and Islam

As Charlemagne forged a new empire out of the fragmented kingdoms in the West, he naturally attracted the notice of the neighboring Byzantine and Islamic leaders. Not surprisingly, his taking the title of emperor irked the Byzantine court, but Irene ran out of time to object strenuously. She was overthrown in 802 by Nicephorus, a Byzantine aristocrat, who continued the diplomatic negotiations over the status of the Frankish ruler's title. Finally, in 813, both parties agreed that Charlemagne could be emperor of the Franks and the Byzantine emperor would be emperor of the Romans. This decision solved the immediate dispute, but the political split between East and West continued to widen.

Charlemagne had more promising relations with the Islamic caliph in Baghdad, Harun al-Rashid (r. 786–809). There were many diplomatic exchanges between the two courts, as it was in both their interests to forge a friendly bond against their mutual enemy, the Byzantine Empire. The Frankish sources say Harun even gave Charlemagne jurisdiction over the Christian holy places in Palestine, certainly a gracious, though empty, diplomatic gesture—Harun reportedly said, the holy land is "so far away that [Charlemagne] cannot defend it from the barbarians. . . . [Therefore] I myself will rule over it as his representative." Nevertheless, the two rulers exchanged many more tangible gifts to seal their friendship—among them an elephant that Harun gave Charlemagne in 802. The elephant lived eight more years and traveled with Charlemagne as he patrolled his kingdom, causing quite a stir among his subjects who had never seen such a beast.

Charlemagne's negotiations and the relative peace that came within his lands (in spite of almost incessant warfare on the borders) served to stimulate trade, which had declined during the previous tumultuous centuries. Through the ninth century, Venice, in Italy, had assumed a leading role in the southern Mediterranean trade. Venetian merchants sent grain, wine, and timber to Constantinople in exchange for silk cloth and other luxury goods. Other Italian cities also joined in the growing trade, and the Mediterranean trade that had been one of the hallmarks of the West continued to link the region and its varied peoples. More trade brought increased prosperity into Charlemagne's lands, and the great emperor used a portion of it to forward intellectual endeavors.

An Intellectual Rebirth

As memorable as Charlemagne's political and diplomatic victories were, his most enduring impact came in the area of intellectual achievement. Although Charlemagne himself had never learned to write, he had always shown a wide-ranging intellectual curiosity that as a powerful ruler he was able to indulge. Like the Anglo-Saxon cultural revival, the Carolingian rebirth built upon learning that had been preserved in monasteries.

Charlemagne's motivation for fostering learning stemmed primarily from his concern for the religious health of his kingdom. The emperor had observed that even many of the priests serving in his parishes could not read well enough to recite the proper form of the liturgy. Nor were they sufficiently educated to guide their parishioners to what the emperor considered the correct understanding of a Christian life. To address these matters, Charlemagne issued an edict ordering that "in the villages and townships the priests shall open schools," and that the clergy must accept all interested children without charging them fees—although he did allow teachers to accept "the small gifts offered by the parents." Dhouda, the young wife we met at the beginning of this chapter, benefited from the educational support introduced by Charlemagne. From this pool of literate children, Charlemagne expected to produce a clergy educated, as one of his edicts said, "in the psalms, musical notation, chant, the computation of years and season, and in grammar."

Establishing schools

Providing schools was not enough; Charlemagne noted that this education depended upon the proper books, ordering "all books used shall be carefully corrected." To accomplish this, the emperor gathered scholars from all over Europe to assemble a canon of corrected readings.

These scholars revived a curriculum (originally proposed by fifth-century scholars) that would dominate medieval universities and profoundly influence modern liberal-arts education. To create this course of study, they divided knowledge into seven liberal arts. The most basic of these were the **trivium,** in which students learned grammar, rhetoric, and logic. With these tools, students could read texts, explain them, and understand the way to think about them. Next came the more advanced curriculum, the **quadrivium:** arithmetic, music, geometry, and astronomy. Whereas to us these four subjects may not seem obviously related, to medieval thinkers they all shared one characteristic: They involved the patterns by which God organized the world. Because scholars of the Middle Ages saw this organization as consistent, they believed they could study music, for example, to understand mathematics or the movement of the heavens.

The scholars also contributed much to text reform. Before the invention of the printing press, scribes copied books laboriously by hand onto animal skins (called parchment or vellum) with quill pens and ink. Copyists sometimes needed a full day to copy just six to ten manuscript pages. Moreover, there was a shortage of these scribes. Today, we learn to read and write at the same time. During the Middle Ages, however, these two skills were considered separate. Although many people could read, not so many could write.

Correcting texts

The problems associated with handwriting only compounded these difficulties. Handwriting was not standardized, and copyists ran words together and employed contractions in an effort to use as little of the precious parchment as possible. Copyists not fluent in Latin (as few were) also made many mistakes. By the eighth century, these errors had been multiplying for several hundred years.

The scholars who gathered at Charlemagne's court school attacked these problems in two ways. First, they compared many versions of the same text to prepare a correct rendition. Second, they developed a standardized handwriting so that future copyists could accurately preserve the corrected text. This reformed handwriting style reduced errors, thus saving much wisdom for future generations. Moreover, the Carolingian handwriting style formed the basis for our own lowercase letters and the printing-press letters invented 600 years later. The scholars carefully working on texts played a crucial role in preserving the intellectual contributions of the classical world.

STRUGGLE FOR ORDER IN THE CHURCH

Established long before the Roman Empire disintegrated, the church had adopted the Roman administrative system in which bishops presided in dioceses (see Chapter 5). At the local level, priests in parishes cared for their flocks in manorial villages. Parish priests were accountable to their bishops, who in turn were accountable to archbishops, ruling in the largest urban center of the region. Archbishops called their subordinates together periodically to discuss church issues. During these meetings, bishops also learned about new church rules or ideas, which they then took back to their dioceses and communicated to their priests. This whole structure was designed to weave the Christian world and its administrators into a tight fabric of personal ties.

However, this structure sounds better on paper than it worked in practice during these tumultuous early medieval centuries. Communication among churchmen was always disrupted during warfare, and there was no certainty that competent priests and bishops would be appointed when a church office became vacant. Nor did the theoretical structure mean that the church operated independently of local warlords. Even during the years of relative peace under strong Carolingian kings such as Charlemagne, the church was dominated by monarchs, who felt responsible for bringing order to their churches. Nevertheless, during the eighth and ninth centuries, the church planted seeds of order that would fully flower in the High Middle Ages (see Chapter 8).

Monasteries Contribute to an Ordered World

Bringing structure to the ecclesiastical order was not limited to priests, bishops, popes, and kings. As we saw in Chapter 6, Benedict of Nursia (ca. 480–543) had established a monastic rule that brought men and women into obedience to their monastic leader, who in turn obeyed the local bishop. This kind of monastic structure had proved immensely popular. By the late seventh century, monasteries had sprung up throughout the northern regions of Europe, including Anglo-Saxon England. Monasteries for men and women provided one of the few avenues for social mobility for promising individuals, and for women, the monastic life offered the possibility of a voice in church affairs.

Monasteries performed an essential service in copying and preserving texts and learning. Numerous men and women excelled in scholarship in an age that valued warfare more. The manuscript painting on this page emphasizes the importance of this monastic learning.

Monasteries also became involved in the growing political issues of the day. As we have seen, nobles and kings exerted control over priests and bishops in their lands, and they believed they could exert the same authority over monasteries. To many spiritual reformers this seemed to subordinate spiritual values to secular politics, and in the early tenth century, reformers took a step to correct this imbalance.

Cluniac reform

In 910, a group of monks persuaded a duke in southern France to found a new monastery at Cluny. The Cluniac founding charter refined the Benedictine rule by insisting that the monastery was exempt from local control—owing only prayers for the donor and, as Duke William wrote in the founding charter, "subject neither to our yoke, nor to that of our relatives, nor to the sway of royal might, nor to that of any earthly power." To do this, Cluny was established to be directly subordinate to the pope, and all subsequent Cluniac foundations were to be accountable to the abbot at Cluny and, through him, the pope. This tenth-century movement established a strong, reinvigorated monasticism that helped increase papal authority (as we will see in Chapter 8). However, all these developments establishing order and hierarchy in the church would be shaken—and almost destroyed—by a new cycle of violence that engulfed western Europe.

ORDER INTERRUPTED: Vikings and Other Invaders

Although Charlemagne valued much of classical culture, such as education and even the title of emperor, his imperial rule was different from that of an early Roman emperor. His sense of empire remained highly personal. Like the innumerable German kings before him, he saw his kingdom as consisting of subjects loyal to him and to his family, not to an abstract political entity. He viewed his realm as his to divide up among his sons, not as an entity separate from himself and his family. This perception put him firmly in the Germanic tradition. However, in the end it undermined the order that he had built, as the emperor's descendants vied for control of the lands he bequeathed them.

LITERATE NUNS Women played a vital role in the preservation of learning in the monasteries as they copied precious manuscripts. Women's valuable contribution is shown in this illustration of Abbess Hitda presenting a manuscript to Saint Walburga.

Competing for the Realm: Charlemagne's Descendants

Charlemagne's only son, Louis the Pious (r. 814–840), inherited the empire, but during the course of his reign problems began to appear. However, the final disintegration of Charlemagne's empire took place after Louis' death, when his kingdom was divided among his surviving three sons: Charles the Bald (r. 843–877), Lothair I (r. 840–855), and Louis the German (r. 843–876). The three brothers succumbed to the Germanic tendency toward civil war, each seeking to increase his power at the expense of the others. Their violent clashes struck at the foundation of what Charlemagne had constructed, and they brought untold hardship to the subjects of the once-unified kingdom. The map on page 160 shows the division of the lands established in the Treaty of Verdun in 843, which effectively destroyed Charlemagne's creation of a united western Europe.

Treaty of Verdun

The Treaty of Verdun anticipated some important nationalistic developments in western Europe, because for the first time, linguistic differences that would divide the lands seemed to be solidifying. When Charles the Bald and Louis the German took oaths (called the Strasbourg Oaths) to support each other in this division, the oaths were recorded in two languages so that the subjects of each would understand them—Charles pledged in a Romance (Latin-derived) language, and Louis spoke in an early Germanic tongue. This showed how the two sections of Charlemagne's empire were already separating culturally and linguistically.

Battered by the disruptions of war, the already local economy became even more isolated. The long-distance trade that had begun to enrich the Italian cities as well as the Carolingian kings virtually evaporated, and money went out of circulation. If it had even a brief respite from this dynastic turmoil, the Carolingian Empire might have recovered from mismanagement by Charlemagne's grandsons—but this was not to be. Instead, the weakened empire would succumb to new invaders from the north, south, and east.

The map on page 161 shows the impact of these invasions on Europe. Part of the pressure came from the south, as Muslim maritime raiders sailed across the Mediterranean Sea and penetrated most of the southern coasts of Europe. Sicily fell to the forces of Islam, as did the islands in the western Mediterranean. In spite of Charlemagne's foresight in establishing protective tributary peoples on his eastern flank, eastern Europe reeled from a serious blow with the invasion of the Magyars (now known as Hungarians, a name derived from one group of Magyars). Magyar warlords led their people in raids across Germany, France, and Italy before they settled down and established the kingdom of Hungary. The influx of Muslims and Magyars left an indelible imprint on Europe. However, the invaders who wreaked the most violence, and ultimately settled the most widely, came from the north—bands of Scandinavian warriors known as Vikings.

New invaders

Partition of the Carolingian Empire, 843—Treaty of Verdun
This map shows the division of Charlemagne's lands under his grandsons.

"The Wrath of the Northmen": Scandinavian Life and Values

Back when Charlemagne had forcefully converted the Saxons to Christianity, the people living farther north, in what we know as Denmark, Norway, Sweden, and Finland, remained pagan. For the most part, these Scandinavians lived on farms rather than in communal villages; they grew crops and kept cows and sheep. The short growing seasons of the north made agriculture especially challenging, and the people supplemented their produce by fishing in the cold, stormy waters of the North Sea. Over time they became skilled seamen and even engaged in long-distance commerce. They traded furs, amber, and honey for finely wrought jewelry, glass, cloth, and weapons. These rugged seamen from the north drew a fine line between trading and pirating and crossed it often. Still, their activities prompted the spread of goods from all over Europe to Scandinavian farms.

Who were these northern peoples? The Scandinavians were Germanic, so their way of life resembled that of the Germanic tribes who had earlier invaded the Roman Empire. The Scandinavians cherished heroic values and sought fame in notable deeds and through the works of poets who recorded those deeds. In their literature—both the poetry and the old Norse prose narratives called **sagas** that preserve their history—we can detect a people who valued words and wit as much as strength and courage. They worshiped gods similar in function to those of the ancient Greeks and Romans, but with different names—Wodin, Thor, and Freya are three deities whose names have been preserved in the English days of the week: Wodin's Day (Wednesday), Thor's Day (Thursday), and Freya's Day (Friday).

The powerful and violent Scandinavians shared another trait with the early Germanic people: a passion for revenge.

OPINION

After Charlemagne's death, his empire experienced many challenges from fighting siblings to invading Vikings. What do you think contributed most to the breakup of the empire?

Although these northerners tried to control their feuding through a system of compensation involving wergeld, they had much less success stemming their tendency toward violence than even the Anglo-Saxons had. Indeed, it may have been this very violence that prompted numerous Vikings to leave Scandinavia in search of new, more peaceful lands overseas. Some may have left to avoid feuds, and the sagas suggest that others emigrated to escape the growing power of kings who tried to impose peace on many violent men who did not want to submit to authority.

All Northmen did not emigrate to avoid or seek violence. Many were drawn by the wealth that had accumulated in Europe during the prosperous years of the Carolingians and Anglo-Saxons. All these

Viking ships

movements during the ninth and tenth centuries—raids, trading, and settlements—left a deep impact on European life. The map to the right shows the Northmen's movements to the western and eastern edges of Europe. Their success in these campaigns stemmed largely from their innovative ships and their skill in navigating them. The ships were highly valued possessions, guarded with honor and praised in Scandinavian poetry. Often built of oak and designed to flex with the rough waters of the North Atlantic, the vessels each carried between 50 and 100 men who manned oars on either side. A large sail, usually decorated in bright colors, completed the propulsion system.

These ships also had a shallow keel, the long timber that extended the length of the ship and supported the frame. This feature allowed the Vikings to pilot their ships up rivers during raids. It also let them beach the crafts easily and launch them back out to sea before their surprised victims could mount an effective counterattack. The ships and the ferocity and bravery of the men who sailed them earned the Scandinavians a widespread, fearsome reputation. Many a European repeated the oft-quoted Anglo-Saxon prayer for God to "save us from the wrath of the Northmen."

Viking Travels and Conquests

As the map above suggests, the unmatched navigational skills of the Vikings gave them access to many parts of Europe. Some Northmen traveled east down the Dnieper River to the Black Sea and the rich city of Constanti-

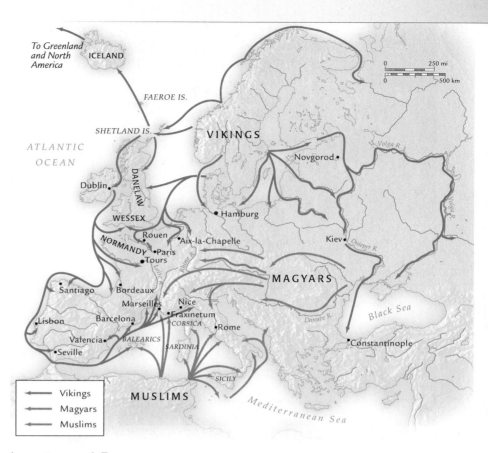

Invasions of Europe, ninth and tenth centuries **The arrows on this map show the invasion routes of the major peoples who threatened Europe during the ninth and tenth centuries, along with the dates of their invasions.**

nople, at times settling along this rich trade route. The oldest Russian chronicle contains the story of an invitation to the Northmen to come and rule, for there was no order in their land. As we saw in Chapter 6, the Scandinavians established a strong state centered in Kiev. Other Vikings traveled to Constantinople and served as soldiers of fortune in the Byzantine emperor's service. Throughout the tenth century, the emperor's personal guard—the Varangians—was composed entirely of Scandinavians. The most famous of these—Harald Sigurdson of Norway (r. 1046–1066)—grew so wealthy while serving in Constantinople that when he returned to Norway he became a great king. Archaeologists have discovered early-eleventh-century Byzantine coins in Norway that may have come from the hoard that Harald shipped home.

Harald's hoard of coins was not unique. Archaeologists have found some 1,700 treasure hoards, each containing on average about three hundred coins. These (primarily silver) coins were mostly eastern—Byzantine or Islamic. Great piles of treasure like these continue to draw our imagination, but the fact that so many were simply buried tells us that the Scandinavian eastern trade in the eighth and ninth centuries did not contribute much to the overall European economy. Most gold was not circulated; it was

VIKING JEWELRY For a long time the Vikings, like the Germanic tribes, treasured precious metals like gold and silver and wore them as signs of status. This hoard reveals that even when the Vikings acquired gold and silver coins, they fitted them with clasps and wore, rather than spending, them.

Because they considered these natives inferior, they called them by the contemptuous term *Skraelings,* which defies exact translation. They used this term to refer to Eskimos in northern Greenland and tribes they encountered in North America. The Scandinavians who settled in southern Greenland mostly ignored their neighbors to the north. In North America, the encounter proved more dramatic. At first, these tribes and the Scandinavians engaged in some trading. Amerindians especially valued the Vikings' red cloth and milk. They also coveted the Scandinavians' weapons, but the newcomers refused to give them up.

Relations between the two peoples soon soured. Several confrontations occurred in which parties on both sides were killed. The sagas described one incident in which Amerindians in skin-covered boats and armed with arrows and catapults attacked. In another case, only the courage of a pregnant Scandinavian woman saved the day for the Vikings. According to the story, the woman picked up a sword and slapped it on her bare breast as the natives charged her. Unnerved by this odd sight, the attackers fled, and the woman won praise for her bravery. After this confrontation, the Vikings concluded that, although the North American land was bountiful, they could not live there safely because of the ferocity of its inhabitants. They abandoned North America and returned to Greenland, Iceland, and other areas where they could settle more easily.

Within western Europe, Vikings (or their descendants) made permanent conquests in northern France (Normandy), Sicily, and England. As previously mentioned, one group of Vikings, the Danes, had conquered most of northeast England by the middle of the ninth century, until **European settlements** they were stopped by Alfred the Great in 886. However, the British Isles remained a tempting target for the Northmen. In the summer of 1016, a great fleet led by King Swein of Denmark and his son Canute sailed for England. The Anglo-Saxon king Edmund Ironside (r. 1016) was beaten, and Canute became king of a united England. He was an able ruler and was one of many who demonstrated that the Northmen were effective administrators as well as skilled warriors. In 1066, the Norwegian king Harald Sigurdson— the enterprising Varangian who brought a fortune back from Constantinople—set himself a final goal of conquering all of England. He died in the attempt, and the sources say that the only English land he claimed was the "seven feet of soil" required to bury this tall warrior.

either hidden during the violence that dominated the age or used as jewelry to show status.

Still other Scandinavians sailed west across the North Atlantic, seeking other lands and wealth. Although some Europeans may have imagined the world as flat, people who sailed westward out of sight of **Western explorations** land and who watched ships return from the eastern horizon knew better. Like many ancients, Scandinavian sailors perceived the world as round. With these views, Scandinavians sailed confidently into the open seas in their sturdy, versatile ships. They established permanent settlements in Iceland and a settlement in Greenland that lasted for centuries. In the late tenth century, an expedition led by the Norwegian Leif Erikson (970–1035) traveled all the way to North America, which Erikson dubbed Vinland. Although the Vikings did not establish a permanent settlement there, their arrival on this distant coast counts as one of history's most extraordinary feats of sailing, and the difficult passage earned the captain the name "Leif the Lucky."

As the Vikings explored Greenland and North America, they naturally encountered peoples who already lived there.

An Age of Invasions: Assessing the Legacy

The invasions from the north, south, and east brought sporadic violence to western Europe for about two hundred years. With this kind of pressure, Viking, Magyar, and Muslim conquests all disrupted the newly established order that had reigned in Europe for more than a century. In Charlemagne's Frankish Empire, the onslaughts from many foreign fronts accelerated the disintegration initiated by the emperor's feuding descendants, and the central authority envisioned by Charlemagne could not hold.

Learning also suffered as people devoted more and more attention and resources to war. Charlemagne's great palace school in Aachen, which had drawn scholars from all over Europe, ceased functioning. Again, learning took place primarily behind monastery walls. However, this time monks and nuns had the benefit of texts that had been corrected during Charlemagne's rule. In time, these carefully preserved sources of knowledge would once more play a role in centers of learning, but not until peace returned to western Europe.

Finally, order in the church crumbled under the tenth-century turmoil. In Ireland and on the western coasts of Britain, the magnificent Celtic monasteries were almost completely destroyed by Vikings looking for plunder. The invaders damaged monasteries in France as well. This violence took a massive personal toll on men and women seeking God. As just one example, texts tell of houses of women who feared that the Vikings would rape them and thus violate their vows of virginity. To avert this disaster, the women cut off their noses and lips as the Vikings approached their gates and greeted the invaders with mutilated faces.

The church structure of parishes and bishops under the control of the pope also deteriorated. Bishops and priests placed themselves under the protection of local lords instead of looking to Rome for help. Sometimes lords simply took over church lands, as a Frankish law declared: "because of threats of war and the invasions of some of the border tribes, we shall . . . take possession of a part of the land belonging to the church . . . for the support of our army." The church itself became fragmented in the service of war. In the end, the notion of a Christian Europe with both a pope and an emperor at its head disappeared into the wreckage of lives and property as the invasions dragged on.

In the eleventh century, the violence at last spent itself. The traditional Scandinavian farming and trading life was easier to conduct in peace than in war. And as the invaders settled in newly conquered territories, they absorbed some of the structures already in place

Vikings convert

there. The Scandinavians also eventually converted to Christianity and thus became fully integrated into Christian Europe. Harald Sigurdson's brother, Olaf (r. 1016–1030), for example, converted the Norwegians by force of arms and his own charisma in the early eleventh century. Leif Erikson "the Lucky" introduced Christianity to Iceland and Greenland around the same time. Canute, who ruled England, Denmark, and Norway, converted to Christianity and brought priests from England to complete the conversion of the Northmen.

The Vikings may have settled down, but the centralization that had unraveled through the centuries of chaos would not be restored easily. However, throughout this time people had created another kind of order—one that was not imposed by royal officials, like Charlemagne's *missi dominici,* traveling through the land. Instead, people bound themselves to each other in solemn contracts. These local ties formed a new order from which the medieval world would build again.

→ connect to today ←

Fragmentations of War

This chapter recounts the horrors and social fragmentations of war. How are modern disruptions of war in places such as Iraq and Afghanistan similar to those experienced in the early Middle Ages? What are the differences?

MANORS AND FEUDAL TIES: Order Emerging from Chaos

As early as the eighth century, Carolingian nobles began to develop mutual contracts that bound people together in personal relationships. In a modified version of the ties that bound the Germanic tribes, these structures were personal, tying each person to a superior. In the modern West, we often judge a society in terms of the freedom of its citizens, but in the Middle Ages, social order was defined by connections rather than degree of freedom. All men and women—from the peasantry all the way up to the king—were connected to someone above or below them in a contractual system of mutual obligations. The obligations did not fall equally on everyone, but each person had explicitly defined commitments to someone else. Everyone in society expected to live within a hierarchy that ordered nature, the church, and society. This social order was not a product of rational planning but instead developed slowly over centuries—and the chaos of the tenth century escalated the development.

Peasants and Lords: Mutual Obligations on the Medieval Manor

Manors developed from the agricultural estates of the old Roman Empire (described in Chapter 5) and the new divisions of the land made by early medieval kings. In various forms, manors existed throughout the Mediterranean world, including the Byzantine and Islamic empires. In western Europe during the Carolingian Empire, manors developed a characteristic pattern of **serfs** and lords that marked the medieval West for almost the next millennium. Virtually all manors consisted of the lord's home and outbuildings (barn, mill, etc.) and at least one village in which the peasants resided and worked.

The drawing on this page shows the layout of a typical manor. Notice that unlike in today's farm communities, where farmers live on their cropland and travel into the village, medieval peasants lived close together in the village and traveled out to their fields. The fields were organized in strips, with each **Manor layout** peasant family using some and the lord owning a large number himself. The church, too, owned some strips for the priest's support. However, the pasture, woodlands, and water were as important as the cultivated land, because they supported the village's animals.

The survival of the peasants depended not only on the crops they grew on their plowed strips but also on their wise use of the other spaces identified in the drawing. Serfs grazed their oxen and working horses, as well as their sheep and goats, on the common pastureland. They relied on the large draft animals to help with the hard labor of plowing, especially in the heavy, clay soils of northern Europe. The animals also provided essential leather and wool for clothing and other uses. In our age of cotton and synthetic fabrics, it is easy to forget how important animals were for medieval clothing. Farm animals supplemented a grain diet as well, with milk and cheese (especially from goats) and some meat. Peasants ate very little meat because their animals were too valuable to be disposed of in this way. However, sometimes the lord gave the peasants his unwanted portions of meat (tails, hooves, or entrails) to make soup.

The forests of the manor also played a key role in village life. Although the trees and the game animals belonged to the lord, peasants were allowed to gather fallen branches as firewood. Pigs could browse in the forest as long as the lord got a share of the pork. Finally, in times of hunger, villagers gathered acorns in the oak forests and ground them into flour to make bread.

Medieval European peasants were at the bottom of the social order in that they had obligations to people above them, but no one below them owed them any commitments. Most medieval peasants were personally free (that

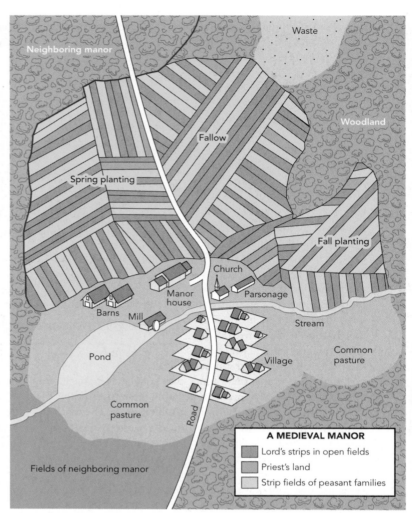

MEDIEVAL MANOR This drawing of a hypothetical medieval manor shows how peasants lived in villages and worked strips of cultivated land. Notice all the important features of the manor, including pastures, mill, church, and woodlands.

is, they were not slaves), but they were bound to the land. When a lord received a land grant from the king, he also gained the service of the peasants who worked the land. Peasants who were semifree in this way—that is, personally free yet not free to move from their village—were called serfs.

Beyond their obligation to remain on the land, serfs owed their lords many other things—roughly divided into goods and labor. For example, they had to give the lord a percentage of their crops or whatever livestock they raised—perhaps a **Serfs' obligations** tenth of their grain, a piglet, a number of eggs from their hens, or some of the cheese made from the milk of their goats. They also owed him their labor. On some manors, serfs had to work as many as three days a week on the lord's demesne lands, those set aside for his own consumption and use. Serfs had to plant his crops, build roads, erect walls or buildings, dig ditches, and do anything else the lord ordered. Serfs did not owe military service—fighting was the privilege of the nobility.

Peasant women worked as hard as the men. They did all the domestic chores, toiled in the fields, tended vegetable gardens, and fed the animals. In addition, they performed the time-consuming task of producing cloth. Women sheared the sheep, cleaned and prepared the wool, spun it into thread, and wove it into cloth. As serfs, women also shared the labor obligations of their husbands. They, too, owed the lord a portion of what they produced (from cloth to garden vegetables) and owed the lord and lady of the manor a certain amount of their labor for domestic chores, spinning, and weaving. Peasant children bore obligations as well. Children as young as 6 were responsible for the care of their younger siblings, and older children worked in the fields alongside their parents.

In exchange for peasant services, lords provided things that required a large investment of capital: mills, barns, ovens, large draft animals, and the like. However, the lords primarily offered justice and protection to their serfs. In times of war, for example, the presence of a well-armed warrior and his followers could make the difference between a village's survival and its destruction. When an attacking army neared the vicinity, peasants with their flocks rushed inside the armed fortress of the lord to stay until the battle ended. However, they often had to watch as their crops and villages were raided and burned, and when the war ended they were left to begin again.

All serfs did not enter voluntarily into this contract in which they exchanged their labor for safety (especially since safety was never absolutely ensured). Sometimes armed lords who needed their lands cultivated forced peasants into servitude on their estates. Late in the Middle Ages, as we will see in Chapter 9, many serfs decided the benefits of protection were not worth the price. However, the newly restored order that established the medieval structure was built on the labor of peasants bound to work the land, which was divided up into manors—agricultural estates under the control of a lord.

Noble Warriors: Feudal Obligations Among the Elite

The medieval manors were structured and organized to provide food for everyone. However, in the medieval mind these manors served an additional function: They were the economic and agricultural base which supported the fighting forces that allowed rulers like Charlemagne and Alfred to conduct their campaigns. Armies were expensive. It took about ten peasant families to support one mounted soldier, so an efficient manorial organization was essential to produce an army. However, the Carolingians developed a way to organize the fighting men as well. Like the serfs, noble warriors were also bound to their lord in a system of mutual obligation. This system was a fluid one—each contract could be different, and some men might be bound to more than one lord. Nevertheless, a general system slowly

developed that was based on the exchange of land for military service. In its most general sense, this system—which historians in the sixteenth century called feudalism—formed the political structure of the elites in medieval society. Many historians today prefer to avoid the term *feudalism* because it seems to suggest a clearly organized structure instead of the loose system that varied from place to place. Regardless of modern disagreements, it is clear that medieval people saw themselves linked in a chain of mutual obligation; only the forms of those obligations were varied.

As we saw in Chapter 6, men in the Germanic tribes saw themselves as linked in loyalty to their chief. This was a personal tie that bound fighting men together. Charlemagne's grandfather, Charles Martel (r. 714–741) (who defeated the Muslims at the Battle of Tours), had seen the virtues of having an army made up of heavily armed men on horseback to replace the more lightly armed citizen foot soldiers that made up the Anglo-Saxon armies. But armed, mounted knights were expensive. Instead of trying to raise money to support an army of this kind, Charles drew from what he had in abundance: land. He granted huge tracts of land, including the serfs who lived on them, to his followers in exchange for their military service. This process laid the foundation for a complex system that later brought order to the fighting men of the land.

The feudal system that grew out of Charles Martel's innovation bound men together in a series of mutual obligations, but what set it apart from other bonds of loyalty was the linking of loyal service with land. When a nobleman bound himself in service to a lord, he swore **Lords and vassals** a solemn oath of fealty (that is, to be faithful to his vows and his lord) by placing his hands between those of his lord. The nobleman now became the lord's **vassal**—bound to him for life. In return, the vassal would receive his **fief**—usually land, but it might be something else that would generate enough income to support the vassal.

The lord (who could be a king or any other man with land to bestow) gave away enough land to support the lifestyle of his noble vassals. These nobles' main function was warfare; they did not work the land as serfs did. Later, vassals took on other titles, like baron or duke, that showed their position relative to other greater or lesser vassals, but the word *vassal* remained a general term that applied to all noblemen bound in contract and loyalty to a lord. Theoretically, a vassal held his fief only as long as he was able to fight for his lord, but in fact, by the ninth century, vassals expected to be able to pass their fiefs on to their sons. A son was expected to place his hands between those of his lord and renew his father's vows before he took full possession of the fief, but as fiefs became hereditary possessions, the lord's control over his fiefs was reduced.

Each party owed something to the other. Lords owed their vassals "maintenance" (usually land) and military protection. In recalling the old Germanic legal principle of compurgation, the lord was also to act as his vassals' advocate in public court. Vassals owed lords "aid and counsel."

VASSAL RECEIVING FIEF This intricate drawing captures the complexities of the relationship between vassals and lords. The vassal points to the grain as a symbol of the land he receives in exchange for his loyalty, which he demonstrates by placing his hands between his lord's palms. The vassal points to his lips acknowledging the formal kiss that sealed the contract.

The primary aid took the form of military service. Just as serfs owed their own lords labor, nobles owed their superiors specified periods of fighting time; these varied, but an average length of service might be forty days a year. Vassals also owed monetary aid. When a lord incurred certain expenses, such as for his daughter's wedding or his son's knighting, the vassals paid extra taxes to fund the event. In addition, vassals owed their lord counsel, or advice at the lord's command. This obligation, along with the witenagemot, paved the way for the parliamentary system that developed later in the Middle Ages (see Chapter 8). Both parties owed the other fealty—that is, good faith to do the other no harm—and this was granted by a solemn kiss that sealed the pact.

Because this was a system of mutual obligation, if either party breached the contract, the arrangement could be rendered null. For instance, if a vassal failed to fight or give counsel, the lord could declare his land forfeit and give it to someone else. Of course, enforcement became complicated when armies of men were involved, but the system did establish the idea of the primacy of contract law that bound people together in a more ordered society. However, because the feudal system varied from place to place and across time, historians disagree on exactly how formal or influential these contractual bonds were. Nevertheless, in the most general sense, feudal ties joined older kinship bonds in linking medieval warriors and their families together.

In this system, a nobleman could be both a vassal to someone over him and a lord to someone under him. A powerful vassal who had received large tracts of land from his overlord might offer portions of it to other nobles

Feudal complexities

who, in turn, would become his vassals. The lowest vassal in this structure was still a lord to the serfs who worked the land (who were lords to no one). Medieval people did not find ambiguity in these flexible terms, because the words *lord* and *vassal* were not absolute—they expressed a legal condition that defined one person's relationship with another.

These feudal bonds were remarkably flexible because they were adapted to each place, time, and individual. Furthermore, the feudal ties kept society from disintegrating altogether in the face of the invasions and decentralization of the ninth century. In spite of these benefits, feudal ties also had features that further decentralized society and even contributed to increased violence. In most cases, the vow of fealty was not necessarily exclusive, and in time the notion of personal loyalty became secondary to the idea of acquiring more property. Many vassals would serve different lords in exchange for different fiefs.

Of course, one can readily see the potential for divided loyalties built into this structure. What if both lords of one vassal were at war? Sometimes—very practically—a vassal followed the lord who gave him the largest fief. At other times, the vassal's first vow was the one that bound. Other vassals probably just tried to back the lord most likely to win the engagement. Beginning in the eleventh century in France and spreading from there over the next centuries, kings tried to establish the concept of **liege lord**—that is, the lord who could claim unreserved loyalty. Kings were able to enforce this with mixed success—the kings in England were successful, but in Germany they were less so. These systems of divided loyalty strained attempts to exert central authority in western Europe, so while feudal ties reduced the chaos, they still preserved some measure of violence. No doubt most people did not reflect upon these abstract considerations as they lived their lives. Feudal ties became simply one more reality of life in the Middle Ages.

Merriment, Marriage, and Medicine: A Noble's Life

The daily life of the nobility revealed the sense of community engendered by the feudal system. The feudal lords with their wives and children lived together with crowds of their own vassals and their servants. All ate together at long tables in the common hall of the manor house.

The nobles amused themselves with music, dance, and games like backgammon, chess, and dice. Archaeologists have even found loaded dice in an Anglo-Saxon excavation, so cheating at such games is not a modern invention. In times of peace, both noblemen and noblewomen indulged their passion for hunting with hawks, horses, and hounds. Hunting was intended to keep their skills sharp for their real purpose: warfare.

Just as in the Germanic tribes, noble families in the feudal system were bound to each other by the important ties of marriage. Yet, the institution of marriage changed during the Carolingian years.

Marriage ties

In the tradition of the Germanic tribes, Charlemagne had taken a number of wives—renouncing the marriage ties with one in order to marry another—and he even kept a number of concubines at the same time. However, under his religious son Louis the Pious, churchmen began to regulate the marriage bond, emphasizing monogamy and urging married men to give up their concubines. Although the church intruded more and more into the marriage relationship, it never persuaded all noblemen to make this sacrifice. Nonetheless, the church's interventions enhanced the status of the legal wife and made it essential that she, and only she, produce an heir. As a new bride came to the wedding with great ceremony, and as she emerged from the nuptial bedroom in the morning, crowds cheered the consummation of a marriage that everyone hoped would produce offspring. As highly placed wives, noblewomen exerted a significant degree of autonomy. Many texts suggest that such women were responsible for managing the royal treasury. Furthermore, when their husbands were away on military campaigns, noblewomen managed all the affairs of the manors—including defending the castles from hostile invaders when necessary.

Noble girls married young, many of them between the ages of 12 and 14, if not younger. A girl who was betrothed early might be raised in the household of her fiancé's family until she was deemed old enough for the marriage to be consummated. As they awaited their wedding day, girls learned household management, cloth making, and often reading and writing. Women could also inherit and hold land, but they still owed the feudal obligations that structured this society. If an unmarried girl's father died, she was

Feudal Relationships Grow Complex

The following documents describe some legal contracts that created feudal ties. The first presents a legal form that arose in the mid-eighth century and that shows the establishment of the feudal relationship. The second entry, from the early fourteenth century, describes the later stages of the relationship in which a vassal held lands from four different lords.

1. To my great lord, (name), I, (name). Since, as was well known, I had not wherewith to feed and clothe myself, I came to you and told you my wish, to commend myself to you and to put myself under your protection. I have now done so, on the condition that you shall supply me with food and clothing as far as I shall merit by my services, and that as long as I live I shall perform such services for you as are becoming to a freeman, and shall never have the right to withdraw from your power and protection, but shall remain under them all the days of my life.

2. I, John of Toul, make known that I am the liege man of . . . Theobald, count of Champagne, against every creature, living or dead, saving my allegiance to lord Enjorand of Coucy, . . . the count of Grandpré. If it should happen that the count of Grandpré should be at war with the . . . count of Champagne on his own quarrel, I will aid the count of Grandpré in my own person, and will send to the count . . . of Champagne the knights whose service I owe to them for the fief which I hold of them.

What were the mutually binding obligations that joined the parties to the relationship?

Then & Now
Testing Urine Samples

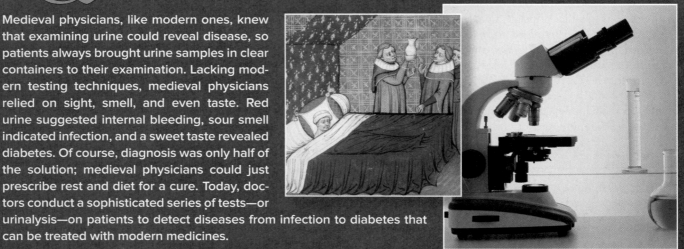

Medieval physicians, like modern ones, knew that examining urine could reveal disease, so patients always brought urine samples in clear containers to their examination. Lacking modern testing techniques, medieval physicians relied on sight, smell, and even taste. Red urine suggested internal bleeding, sour smell indicated infection, and a sweet taste revealed diabetes. Of course, diagnosis was only half of the solution; medieval physicians could just prescribe rest and diet for a cure. Today, doctors conduct a sophisticated series of tests—or urinalysis—on patients to detect diseases from infection to diabetes that can be treated with modern medicines.

placed under the wardship of the lord her father had served, because her future husband would become that lord's vassal. Widows, too, became wards until their lord arranged another marriage for them, but lords at times relinquished their rights of wardship in exchange for money, so wealthy widows might well control their own lives. Orphans were under the lord's control until they grew old enough to take their place in the lord's army or marry someone who could do so.

Germanic women had traditionally been responsible for medical care, and this continued through the early medieval period. Medicines consisted primarily of herbs, as suggested by the manuscripts from this era that preserve what are probably long-treasured medical recipes. Nasturtium, for example, was recommended for indigestion, wormwood for sleep disorders, and frankincense and oil for sore hands and fingers.

Medicine

timeline

Charlemagne's Kingdom
768–814

Viking Invasions 800–950

Alfred the Great of England
871–901

Muslim Assaults 850–950

Growth of Feudal Ties 818–1000

775   800   825   850   875   90

Even food was considered medicinal if prepared properly; therefore, women were also in charge of designing a healthful diet. Just as our notion of a balanced diet changes with the latest research, early medieval ideas about nutritious eating relied on contemporary understanding of health. For example, people during this period continued to hold the classical idea that health depended on a balance between the body's "humors": wet, dry, cold, and hot. A proper diet must be "tempered"—that is, feature a balance of foods in each category of humor. For example, beans were considered "cold," so they were supplemented by "hot" spices to balance them. Likewise, illness was treated by correcting an imbalance of the humors. For example, if a person was considered too hot, the patient was given predominantly "cold" foods to bring his or her humors back into balance. This system also applied to the preparation of food. Charlemagne's biographer tells about the emperor's growing "dislike" of his physician after Charlemagne was forced to forgo his beloved roast meat in favor of boiled fare. Food and medicine were considered interchangeable in this era, and knowledgeable men and women alike prescribed medicinal diets.

By the year 1000, peace came slowly back to the manors and fortified houses of the nobility, and medieval life was established. In the coming years, rulers, churchmen, philosophers, and merchants brought the West into a flourishing expansion that is known as the High Middle Ages.

SUMMARY

At the beginning of the eighth century, the Germanic tribes that had precipitated the collapse of the Roman Empire in the West established kingdoms and converted to Christianity. Yet, that did not ensure an orderly society.

- The rule of law had been valued in different ways by the Romans and the tribal Germans. In the early Middle Ages, Germanic kings recorded laws that brought a synthesis of these traditions, including Germanic principles of wergeld. Kings began to use these laws to bring centralized control to their kingdoms.

- Anglo-Saxon England was made up of several kingdoms until it was largely united under the great scholar and king Alfred. Yet, a large portion of the island remained under the control of Danes from the north.

- On the Continent, Charlemagne was able to unify most of western Europe, creating an empire in the West again, and his reign introduced a flourishing of learning and a temporary peace.

- The church, too, struggled to bring order to European Christendom, reforming monasteries and using them to strengthen a centralized rule. However, society did not resolve the question of whether church or kings should rule.

- Charlemagne's empire fell apart under the pressures of rival heirs and new invaders. Vikings from the north, Muslims from the south, and Magyars from the east brought new violence.

- The decentralization resulting from the violence brought forth new structures to bring order to local territories. Personal relationships tied people together whether on the manors that produced the food or in the feudal noble households that ruled and fought.

In the late eleventh century, kings, emperors, and popes would once again try to take charge and bring about a flourishing of medieval civilization in the West.

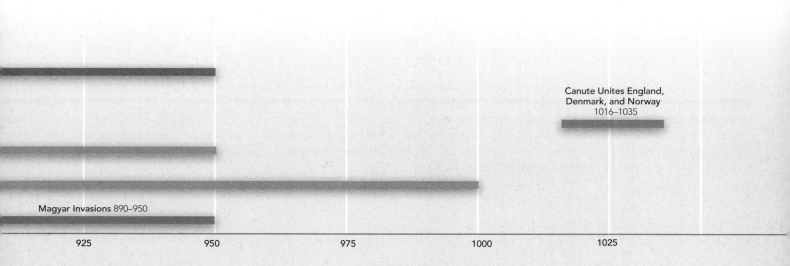

Canute Unites England, Denmark, and Norway 1016–1035

Magyar Invasions 890–950

925 950 975 1000 1025

NORMAN CONQUEST OF ENGLAND, BAYEUX TAPESTERY,

ca. 1070–1080   This embroidery was commissioned by the victorious Normans to celebrate William the Conqueror's victory over the Anglo-Saxon kingdom of Harald. It shows armies of mountain knights in chain mail, with dismembered dead in the border. Order would come to western Europe slowly by regulating the violence of mounted warriors.

Order
Restored

8

The High Middle Ages, 1000–1300

A Chivalrous Knight

In the late twelfth century, a noble knight, William Marshall, rested in the woods while on a journey accompanied only by his squire. He was awakened from his sleep by the sound of a woman's voice saying, "Ah, God, how weary I am." Opening his eyes, William saw a well-dressed couple riding along. William quickly mounted and rode to introduce himself and offer help, but the man was not pleased to see the knight. As the stranger drew his sword, his hood fell off and William saw by his tonsured hair that he was a monk—the handsomest one that he had ever seen. Filled with shame, the monk confessed he had run from his monastery with his lady love: "I have carried her off from her own country." ▶▶

William reprimanded the young woman and offered to escort her back to her brother so she would avoid the shame of the path she had chosen. She refused, and William did not persist.

The knight did show continued concern, asking the couple how they would live. The monk showed a belt bulging with coins and said that they would lend money and live off the interest. The good knight William was horrified. "Upon usury? By God's sword, you shall not." He told his squire to take the money to save the couple from falling into the additional shame of moneylending. He sent the couple on their way (penniless) and took the money to the local inn, where William generously treated his friends to abundant food and drink with the purloined coins.

In this story of a noble knight—preserved in a long poem written by his son—we can see the Middle Ages coming into full flower. Knights acted with courtesy to help women who may have been in distress. (At least they claimed to do so within a code of chivalry, even though they actually seldom behaved so nobly.) Knights were also generous with money, even if it wasn't their own. Wealth and love were to be had, and some people—even monks and women—began to explore new ways to live their lives. This ideal knight also revealed a disdain for banking principles, little noticing that the new wealth grew on a growing commerce. Like the prosperous knight, however, the West was expanding and thriving after the turn of the new millennium. ◄◄

THOSE WHO WORK:
Agricultural Labor

"From the beginning, mankind has been divided into three parts—men of prayer, farmers, and men of war." These words written in the eleventh century capture the social order as the people of the High Middle Ages understood it. In this highly organized world, everyone was expected to keep his or her place, or "order." And these orders were arranged by their function—prayer, warfare, and labor on the land. This understanding of the world ignored the important role of commerce in the growing cities, but it quite rightly noted that the booming times began with an agricultural revolution.

developed ways to bring mechanical power to regions without rivers to drive water mills.

In many parts of Europe, medieval peasants used windmills to generate power from wind. Although people had harnessed the wind much earlier in Asia and the Middle East, European engineers evidently invented these mills based on water mills. In addition, enterprising engineers managed to tap power from tides. As evidence, in 2009, archaeologists excavated a well-preserved tidal mill in Greenwich, near London, that had been built of huge oak trees cut down in 1194. The wheel diameter of this monumental engineering project is 16 feet. This huge mill drew water in as the tide rose and released it as it fell, powering the adjacent mill. This new find, which supplements excavations around the North Sea, demonstrates an early and wide use of tidal mills.

Harnessing all this power accomplished what technology in the ancient world had never achieved: It released human power for other uses.

Harnessing the Power of Water and Wind

After 1000, Europeans used more mechanical power than any previous society had; and this power helped fuel the expansion of population, commerce, and political power in western Europe. Water mills provided the major source of mechanical power. In England in 1086, there were often as many as 3 mills for every mile of river. Water mills ground grain with extraordinary efficiency, and their technology spread rapidly across Europe.

How did the mills actually work? A cam, projecting from the axle of the waterwheel, converted rotary motion to vertical motion, which let mill workers accomplish tasks from forging iron to softening wool cloth to making beer and paper. By the twelfth century, creative builders had

New Agricultural Techniques

Peasants supplemented water power with effective use of animal muscle. In the early Middle Ages, as in the ancient world, people harnessed horses with the same kind of yoke they used on oxen. This device was highly inefficient on horses, however, because the yoke rested on their necks and impeded their breathing when they lowered their heads to pull. By the eleventh century, a new padded horse collar that had been developed in China appeared in western Europe. This harness rested on the animal's shoulders, making it possible for people to use horses for heavy plowing and pulling. Because horses can work 50 percent faster and two hours a day longer than oxen, the advantages were huge. Of course, now the peasant walking behind the team of horses also had to work longer and harder. Not surprisingly, the improvement was not as popular with workers as it was with their lords. Nevertheless, the amount of land under cultivation expanded dramatically with increased use of the horse.

The increased use of animal power required peasants to cultivate more land for fodder and hay. Traditionally—since Roman times—most peasants had used what is

Three-field cultivation

called a two-field system, in which half the land was left fallow (unplanted) while half was planted. The fertility of the fallow land was restored to yield more crops the following year. However, to accommodate the need to cultivate more land, manors slowly adopted a three-field system that further increased agricultural yields. In this system, plots of land were divided into thirds: One-third was planted in the spring and another in the fall, and the remaining third was left fallow. The three-field system also stimulated the growth of new crops that boosted production. Villagers began to plant legumes, such as peas and beans, which add nitrogen to the soil, thus fertilizing the subsequent grain crop. Legumes also provided an excellent source of protein, which vastly improved the villagers' diets.

The Population Doubles

These agricultural improvements (and the declining violence after the ninth and tenth-century invasions

King Oswald with His Bishop Aiden
ca. 1200

This illustration shows the hierarchy of medieval society: The king and his bishop talk at the table while the poor sit at the great men's feet soliciting charity. A fortified castle frames the whole picture. Notice the strong vertical composition of the image that reinforces the hierarchic nature of the medieval order. How does this image express late-medieval society? What significance might you attach to the lack of women in the image?

ended) led to unprecedented population growth. Although it is impossible to get exact figures, estimates of population growth indicate that from the eleventh through the thirteenth century, the population of Europe approximately doubled—from about 37 million to 74 million. Women in particular benefited from the addition of legumes to their diet because the iron in these foods helped replenish blood lost through menstruation and childbirth, and it enabled healthy women to have fewer miscarriages and nurse stronger babies. With such improvements, women began out-numbering men during these centuries, and even some medieval commentators noted this disparity, considering it a "problem."

To accommodate the ballooning population, western Europeans expanded their settlements. Hardworking villagers on the northwest coast (later the Low Countries) built dikes to hold back the ocean itself to expand their agricultural lands. Sometimes groups of villagers left an overcrowded area and cultivated new land, a process called assarting. The resulting "assart" was great open fields that

European expansion brought dire environmental consequences. Fields were cleared by slash-and-burn techniques that left clouds of smoke and ash hanging in the air. Great forests disappeared in the insatiable demand for wood. One castle alone caused four thousand oak trees to be felled for lumber. Then, as now, population expansion comes with environmental consequences. Even today a 2,000-square-foot house takes between eleven and thirty trees to build. However, environmental issues are now a global priority. In 1997, countries came together to adopt and sign the Kyoto Protocol, an agreement to reduce their emissions of carbon dioxide and other dangerous greenhouse gases significantly by 2012.

the peasants divided into strips as they established new villages and manors. Primarily they moved eastward. Probably as many as three thousand new villages were established in lands east of the Elbe River in modern-day northern Germany. As they migrated east, settlers spread western European culture into the lands of the Slavs.

Why would peasants leave their established villages to go east and do the hard work needed to clear new agricul-

New freedoms

tural lands? The texts show that people had two motivations: the possibility of better lands and more freedom. The twelfth-century chronicler Helmod of Bosau described how Count Adolf II of Holstein (1128–1164) attracted settlers to his new lands: He insisted that "whoever might be in difficult straits because of a shortage of fields should come with their families to accept land which was excellent, spacious, fertile with fruits, abounding in fish and meat, and favorable to pastures." Still, the peasants drove a hard bargain—many surviving charters show that the new settlers gained many freedoms from the feudal obligations of serfdom. With such incentives, the spread to new lands blossomed, and western European culture flourished.

Few expansions offer unmixed blessings, and the population growth had dire environmental consequences. To build their new settlements, people clear-cut huge swaths

Environmental consequences

of forest, and also dumped human waste and the remains of slaughtered animals in the rivers. In the cities, coal burning poured clouds of dangerous pollutants into the air. Still, the population kept expanding, and more and more people appreciated being freed from the land to populate the burgeoning cities and towns.

THOSE OUTSIDE THE ORDER: Town Life

When medieval writers identified an ordered world of "those who work," they imagined agricultural laborers providing for the lords who ruled and the clergy who prayed. Yet, there were others who labored outside this well-defined hierarchy who did not fit medieval understandings based on a rural society. It was in these towns that people forged the real future of modern urban western European culture.

The few towns of the early Middle Ages were primarily administrative centers, serving as the residences of bishops or occasionally of a nobleman. These towns were walled for protection from the surrounding violence of the feudal world. After 1000, more cities grew up and began to take on more commercial roles. In the process, they grew not only larger, but wealthier as well, and they developed new ways to govern their increasingly prosperous lives.

Communes and Guilds: Life in a Medieval Town

People moved to towns that offered work in a thriving trade and a lively demand for goods. By present-day standards, most medieval towns were small. For example, of the 3,000 identified "towns" in late medieval Germany, 2,800 had populations of only about 1,000. Europe did have a few great cities, however. Cologne was home to some 40,000 people, and London's population approached that figure by the fourteenth century. The Italian cities of Florence and Venice boasted almost 100,000 residents each.

Men and women living in these small towns shared many ideas with the feudal society that surrounded them, like a belief in hierarchy and a sense of mutual ties. However, they expressed these ideas in ways that dramatically shaped urban life. To escape the many requirements imposed on village serfs, towns negotiated charters with the lords on whose lands the town stood. These charters granted townspeople freedom from labor obligations and freedom to travel at will. They also protected the growing town profits from unreasonable taxation and seizure, and some charters allowed the towns to run their own law courts. All these rights made towns islands of freedom in a tightly ordered world, and in return, the lords received money from the prosperous burgs. Towns also served as magnets drawing those who wished to escape from the ordered constraints of the feudal world. In most towns, if a serf could live for "a year and a day" without being caught, he had earned his freedom to stay in the town.

Sometimes townspeople could not peacefully obtain the liberties they desired, and they joined together in sworn associations called **communes** and staged violent revolutions to take communal liberties

that they believed came with urban life. The communes elected their own officials, regulated taxation within the town, and generally conducted the business of running the urban centers. These communes were not democratic, for most people accepted it as natural that the rich citizens would govern the town. In Italy, the communes became so strong that the cities developed into independent city-states. In the French and English lands, by contrast, all the towns remained subject to the political authority of the king. In all cases, however, towns encouraged people to develop their skills, learn a trade, and make money.

Tradesmen within towns formed **guilds,** or organizations to protect their interests and control the trade and manufacturing within the towns. These guilds regulated the quality of such products as gold work, shoes, bread, and so forth; they managed their own membership and set prices. In part because urban women outnumbered men, they participated in the guilds, and families arranged marriages to cement bonds of loyalty and control of commerce. Widows in particular ran businesses and took their husbands' places in the trade organizations. Boys and girls served as apprentices in the shops until they learned their trade. Then they could work as "journeymen"— paid employees under the guidance of a master. Finally,

journeymen would present a sample of their best work— whether a gold piece or a loaf of bread—to the guild masters to see if this "masterpiece" would qualify them to become full guild masters. In these ways, the guild could control both the quality of the products and the number of guild members involved in the trade.

For other groups, town life offered a more mixed set of opportunities and limits. Since the time of the Roman Empire, many medieval towns had a significant population of Jews. For centuries, Jews had played a vital role in town life as merchants, artisans, and members

Urban Jews

of many other professions. By the eleventh and twelfth centuries, however, Christian merchants and craftspeople began to view the Jewish community as competition. Slowly, they excluded Jews from guilds and, in some places, kept them from owning land. However, Jews still engaged in commerce and many Christians found them valuable—although separate—members of the town. For example, a late-eleventh-century charter was granted by a bishop (Rudgar) to Jews who were willing to settle in the German town of Speyer. He wrote that he thought "it would greatly add to its [Speyer's] honor if I should establish some Jews in it." He gave them a section of the city for their use (and walled it off to provide protection from less-enlightened Christians) and offered them special concessions for trading.

The bishop of Speyer also gave Jews the right to freely change coins, and, slowly, urban Jews such as those in Speyer began to enter into moneylending, which is essential to commercial enterprises. The Christian religion forbad its followers to collect interest on loans, for they believed that it was unseemly to make money from time, which belonged to God. While many Christians continued to engage in the lucrative practice of moneylending, slowly through the late Middle Ages, Jewish bankers increasingly began to take over the practice because Judaic practice contained no such strictures against lending money. The two urban groups thus depended on each other in an uneasy coexistence throughout most of the Middle Ages.

OPINION

As commerce began to expand, how do you think communes and guilds changed daily life for townspeople?

The Widening Web of Trade

The impetus for the growth of towns and wealth in the Middle Ages came not from manufacturing but from trade. Therefore, the most important towns were those that served as bustling centers for moving goods—throughout the Middle Ages most of the trade centered on luxury goods. Northern Italy, especially, became a significant

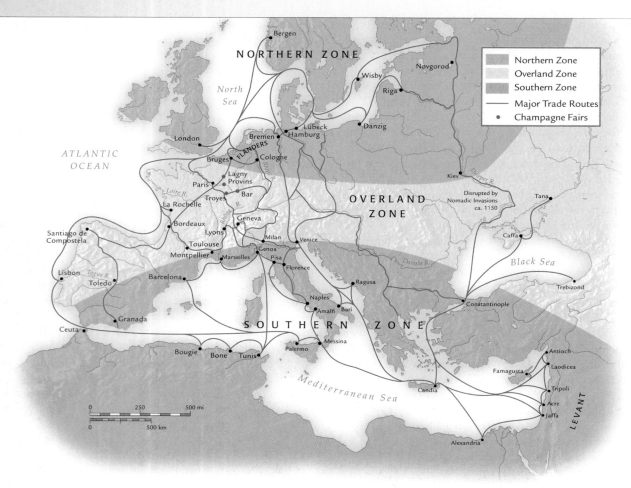

Trade Routes, twelfth and thirteenth centuries This map illustrates the major trading areas of the High Middle Ages, including the three principal zones of trade. It also shows the importance of sea and river routes and the Champagne fairs.

nexus in southern Europe, and Venice, Pisa, and Genoa took the lead. As early as 998, Venetians had received charters from the Byzantine emperor that gave them complete freedom in Byzantine waters, and Pisa and Genoa had negotiated treaties with Muslim rulers that opened new markets. Thus, the way was paved for merchants to sail to the eastern Mediterranean and buy silks and spices passing through the great Muslim bazaars in Baghdad. They then brought the goods westward to Spain and southern France. Whereas the Mediterranean trade had been the commercial center during the Roman Empire, the medieval world opened a new trading hub in the north.

Cities in Flanders (particularly Bruges and Ghent) joined the Italian cities as commercial centers. They supplied fine wool cloth to all of northern Europe and acted as a supply center for Scandinavian products—particularly furs and hunting hawks—that were in demand all over Europe. The growth of the cloth industry, and the handsome profits to be made, led many northern men to replace at the looms the women who had dominated the industry. The map above shows the three major trade zones—

northern, southern, and the central overland route—that distributed goods. However, through the eleventh century, there was no easy mechanism for joining the three zones.

Early in the twelfth century, the French count of Champagne saw an opportunity to make a large profit by hosting fairs in his lands at which merchants could sell goods from the three zones. He granted the right to various towns in his county to organize such gatherings. The counts of Champagne provided the space, set up booths, arranged for police to keep order, and invited moneylenders. Each day, the trade featured a different product, and the counts collected a sales tax from all the transactions made.

Champagne fairs

In the late thirteenth century, many cities in northern Germany united to create the Hanseatic League, an association to capitalize on the prosperous northern trade. The cities formed a political as well as an economic power, and they were able to acquire a monopoly on the Baltic trade, replacing Flanders as the center of the northern

Hanseatic League

trading zone. At its height, the Hanseatic League included seventy or eighty cities, led by Lubeck, Bremen, Cologne, and Hamburg. By the fourteenth century, these cities offered their own great fairs, which replaced the French fairs.

The Glory of God: Church Architecture

With the wealth that came pouring into the cities, townspeople built great churches to celebrate the glory of God and express their pride in their own towns. From about the tenth century until the twelfth, church architecture was dominated by the **Romanesque** style. Mostly monastic structures, these buildings were large and dark with long, central aisles made of barrel vaults and round arches. They seemed so solid and formidable, people often called them "fortresses of God."

In about 1140, Abbot Suger of the Church of St. Denis near Paris decided to change all this. He envisioned a majestic church built in a new style—a church that reached up toward the heavens and that was filled with light. Architects and builders set about making this vision a reality, and to do so, they adopted innovative techniques that came to be called the

Gothic architecture

Gothic style. Instead of round arches, they used pointed ones. The new arch style directed the weight of the roof down the building's massive columns instead of its walls. But such tall walls were vulnerable to cracking under the pressure of high winds. To guard against this danger, architects developed "flying buttresses," large braces that supported the outside of the building.

With these innovations, the walls no longer needed to be thick to provide the support for the church. Builders could therefore add large windows that let light fill the

Stained glass

interior. Glassmakers gathered in nearby forests to burn the hardwood needed to blow glass, and they added metallic oxides to make rich primary colors. Artists fitted the colored glass into intricate lead webs to form magnificent pictures showing everything from biblical stories to scenes of medieval life. Abbot Suger himself contracted the stained-glass windows for his new church. Delighted with the result, he wrote, "The entire sanctuary is pervaded by a wonderful and continuous light."

Beginning in the mid-twelfth century, these immense Gothic cathedrals, with their pointed arches, stained-glass windows, and flying buttresses, began appearing in all the great cities of Europe. Designed to accommodate

MEDIEVAL FAIR IN FRANCE Merchants gathered at periodic fairs to sell their wares, and these fairs stimulated long-distance trade. Local people found goods and excitement at the fairs' temporary stalls.

the entire population of a city (some can hold as many as 10,000 people standing during mass), they were also designed to attract admiring pilgrims. The cathedrals vied to acquire and feature relics of famous saints that drew the faithful seeking solace and miracles. These pilgrims brought money to both the church and the city and helped stimulate movement throughout medieval Europe. The skylines of medieval Europe were reshaped by the towers of these striking new cathedrals.

The Rise of Universities

The cathedrals became more than just centers of worship and pilgrimage; they began serving as places of learning. Scholars and students gathered at cathedrals to study, and these cathedral schools became vibrant centers. It soon became clear that the informal organization of these schools was inadequate. Townspeople frequently protested to the bishop against the students, who were often rowdy and sometimes violent. Students, on their part, resented the high prices that townspeople charged for rooms, food, and drink, and they needed protection against incompetent teachers. By the twelfth century, new structures were emerging to address some of these problems, establishing the beginnings of universities.

Just as townspeople founded guilds and used charters to protect their interests, students and scholars did the same. In some places (like Paris), masters grouped themselves into guilds, and in other cities (like Bologna), students organized themselves. These organizations were called universities—from the Latin word *universitas,* which means "guild." These universities received charters that confirmed the guild's autonomy and authority to license teachers.

Young men (some only 14 years old) from all social classes attended universities; wealthy younger sons of the nobility and promising young village boys could eventually hope for lucrative jobs in the church or courts. (Women were not permitted to attend universities.) Students completed the traditional course of study that had been established centuries before at Charlemagne's (r. 768–814) court. They studied the trivium—grammar, rhetoric, and logic—first and then the quadrivium—arithmetic, geometry, music, and astronomy. Upon completion, they would receive first a bachelor's degree and then a master's degree.

Advanced students interested in focusing on a specialized course of study could continue their studies and receive a doctorate degree. Students might study medicine in Salerno, where masters taught Arabic medicine and sometimes dissected human cadavers. Others might go to Bologna to study law based on Justinian's *Corpus* (discussed in Chapter 6) or study theology—the "queen of all the sciences"—in Paris.

Advanced degrees

The universities gave rise to a new kind of life for the young men who attended them. Many students eagerly devoured the ideas and knowledge that percolated at these centers of learning. The less serious students deeply enjoyed the freedom of university life, drinking in the local bars and brawling in the streets, raising the townspeople's ire. In Paris, a law was passed forbidding students to gamble with dice on the altar of the cathedral while mass was being said! All this freedom cost money; many letters in which students ask their parents to send more cash survive from this era. Yet, despite the occasional disruptions and distractions of life in the universities, students and teachers managed to engage in stimulating dialogues that led to exciting new ideas.

ROMANESQUE AND GOTHIC ARCHITECTURE Medieval church architecture reflected two main styles. (a) Romanesque design, with thick walls and round arches like those in La Madeleine at Vézeley (ca. 1104), shown here, was the earlier style. (b) Gothic style, featuring pointed arches and soaring heights as exemplified in Amiens Cathedral (begun in 1248), shown in this photograph, came later.

STAINED-GLASS WINDOWS, ca. 1245 In the Gothic style, strong stone columns supported the weight of the cathedral's roof, thus freeing the walls from weight-bearing function. Skilled artisans installed stained-glass windows into those walls, such as these examples from the magnificent Sainte-Chapelle, Paris.

Scholasticism: The Height of Medieval Philosophy

The main goal of medieval philosophy was to reconcile faith with reason—that is, to understand with one's mind what one believed in one's heart. This philosophy was called **scholasticism.** The medieval thinkers applied a particular form of logic, called dialectic, which involves using logic to explore various sides of an issue, and these writings often take the form of questioning. The greatest thinkers drawn to the new universities in the twelfth century wrestled constantly with this problem and, in doing so, shaped both knowledge and faith.

The earliest medieval philosopher to explore the religious applications of dialectic was Anselm of Canterbury (1033–1109). Anselm's motto was

Anselm and Abelard "faith seeking understanding," and his most famous effort involved showing a logical connection between the belief that God

is a perfect being and a proof (by the rules of logic) that God exists. He argued that because God was perfect he *must* exist, or else he would not be perfect (for Anselm, perfection demonstrated a real existence). Anselm established the exciting possibility that human reason could be brought to study the deep mysteries of Creation.

One of the most esteemed scholastic scholars was Peter Abelard (1079–1142), who taught in Paris. In his mid-thirties, Abelard was hired to tutor Heloise (ca. 1100–1163), the talented 17-year-old niece of a local church official. Teacher and student were soon lovers, and Heloise became pregnant. The couple married secretly because Heloise feared that a traditional marriage would hurt Abelard's reputation as a teacher, but her infuriated uncle had Abelard castrated. Leaving their child to be raised by relatives, both Heloise and Abelard entered monasteries, where they each continued brilliant careers of learning and influence.

Abelard established a method of applying critical reason to even sacred texts. His most famous work, *Yes and No* (*Sic et Non*), assembled a variety of authoritative sources, from the Bible to church fathers, that seemed to contradict one another. From these, the scholar compiled 150 theological questions and the passages relevant to each question, which allowed scholars to consider the full range of the questions. Although his book has such provocative chapters as "Is God the Author of Evil, or No?" Abelard had no desire to undermine faith; on the contrary, he believed that this kind of inquiry would strengthen faith through the discovery of truth. This was an academic exercise in which students were expected to reconcile apparent contradictions.

Throughout the Middle Ages, there had always been people who believed that it was not possible or even desirable to reach God through reason. Abelard's adversary Bernard of Clairvaux (1090–1153) condemned many of Abelard's writings, primarily because he disapproved of the process of inquiry. Bernard wrote passionately: "I thought it unfitting that the grounds of the faith should be handed over to human reasonings for discussion." Although Bernard approved of rational inquiry in nonreligious areas, he firmly believed the way to God lay in faith and love—in other words, in emotion, not intellect. He wrote beautiful tracts on the mystic approach to God through feeling and faith, and many men and women chose to seek God through this mystic path rather than through logic.

Through the twelfth century, Islamic scholars also continued the great intellectual strides that had been begun by scholars like Avicenna (980–1037). Muslim scholars from centers as far apart as Baghdad in the east and Toledo in Spain studied the classical works of Aristotle and others with a sophistication lacking in the western kingdoms. The Muslim scholar Averroës (1126–1198) and the eminent Jewish scholar Maimonides (1135–1204) interpreted Aristotle's works and left extensive commentaries on the sophisticated ideas. These texts were discovered in Arabic libraries in Spain as Christians slowly reconquered Muslim territory, and the emergence of these commentaries

MEDIEVAL UNIVERSITIES Universities were first founded in the Middle Ages. Scholars gathered at these new institutions to listen to lectures from famed masters. This image shows the youthfulness of many of the students as well as some lack of attention: students talking and sleeping.

along with the advanced logic of Aristotle generated much intellectual excitement in the university communities of western Europe.

The scholastic enterprise reached its height in the thirteenth century with the works of Thomas Aquinas (1225–1274), an Italian churchman whom many regard as the greatest scholar of the Middle Ages. Aquinas wrote many works, from commentaries on biblical books and Aristotelian texts to essays on philosophical problems. However, his most important work was the *Summa Theologiae* (*Summary of Theology*), which was intended to offer a comprehensive summary of all knowledge available at the time.

Thomas Aquinas

Aquinas taught that faith and reason were compatible paths to a single truth, but that the mind by itself could grasp only the truth of the physical world. Faith (given by God's grace), however, could help reason grasp spiritual truths such as the Trinity. This central understanding—that faith and nature cannot contradict each other and that each can inform the other—has remained one of Aquinas's most important contributions.

Aquinas's *Summa* remains one of the masterpieces of philosophy, but not all medieval thinkers found it satisfying. For some, it was too speculative and abstract. For all Aquinas's emphasis on using the natural world as a path to truth, he did not study the natural world very much. Instead, he read Aristotle's views on the natural world. Yet some of the great minds of the age turned directly to matters of the physical world. In this area, they would find plenty to think about.

Discovering the Physical World

The passion with which university scholars read Aristotle and the other ancient writers led them to adhere to classical views of physics and medicine. The educated man or woman of the thirteenth century held the same view of the physical universe as the ancient Greeks had: a motionless world made of earth, water, air, and fire.

Scientific advances came (albeit slowly) in the fields of medicine as physicians built on the works of Galen and Avicenna. Physicians studying at the medical school in Salerno learned Galen's theory of the four "humors" (discussed in Chapter 5) and studied how to bring the body back into balance.

Since classical times, the study of women's health had been limited by the fact that midwives did not write medical texts. Yet, male physicians, who did write the texts, frequently misunderstood women's bodies. In the Middle Ages, a few women wrote books that in part corrected this problem and thus contributed much to the field of women's health. The best known was Hildegard of Bingen (1098–1179), an abbess and mystic in Germany. She wrote compelling accounts of her visions, which showed the same blend of faith and scholarly knowledge that marked the university-trained scholastics. Perhaps most interesting, however, Hildegard authored a medical tract, *Of Causes and Cures.* In this important work, she took the classical view of human beings as consisting of either hot, cold, wet, or dry "humors," and applied it to women's health. In addition, she included in her text the popular cures she practiced as she ministered to the sick in the community, and she gave German and Latin names for drugs—all things that were not part of traditional scholarly writings. Hildegard's work pointed to the possibility of combining women's practical wisdom about women's health with traditional medical knowledge.

Hildegard of Bingen

Some scholars noticed the loss in wisdom that accompanied the separation of practical experience from the universities. One Oxford master, Robert Grosseteste (1168–1253), challenged his students to develop an experimental method to question the ancients. His most famous student, Roger Bacon (ca. 1214–1292), continued Grosseteste's work and is usually credited with popularizing his teacher's movement toward a scientific method. Bacon's greatest practical contribution came in the field of optics,

Experimental science

Ramón Lull (ca. 1232–1316)
Scholar and Overzealous Missionary to the Muslims

Ramón Lull was born in about 1232 on Majorca, an island off the east coast of Spain. As a young man, Ramón devoted his life to converting Muslims to Christianity, learning Arabic, and attending the University at Paris to study theology and logic.

RAMÓN LULL, Majorca

When he was 60 years old, he traveled to North Africa to begin his missionary work. In Tunis, Ramón invited all the local Muslim scholars to debate with him the merits of the two religions, but he soon discovered that logic could not make people change the faith they held in their hearts. Tired of his preaching, the Muslims placed Ramón on a ship to Italy, but a great storm sank the vessel. The robust 76-year-old lost his belongings but managed to swim ashore.

He returned to Tunis when he was 83 years old, and roamed the streets preaching. Tunisian authorities finally lost patience with him in 1316 and executed him.

What techniques do people today use to foster interfaith understanding in order to avoid the animosity generated by Ramón Lull?

when he discovered how to make glasses by grinding lenses. Perhaps more important than any specific invention, Grosseteste and Bacon demonstrated the value of experimentation over pure logic, thus challenging the ancient scholars who formed the core of the traditional courses of study at the universities. In the centuries to come, the major discoveries in the physical world would come from people like Bacon, who had the courage to think for themselves instead of simply looking to ancient experts.

This intellectual expansion was one of many measures of the vitality of medieval life. The cities and the universities were growing in ways the medieval world hardly understood, much less expected, but this was not the only expansion of the Middle Ages. The world of "those who fight" began to see a dramatic growth.

THOSE WHO FIGHT: Nobles and Knights

The multiplication of the population of Europe in the eleventh century prompted a surge of construction of homes for the nobility. The aristocracy required fortresses and towers to "keep the peace" (and to collect the taxes paid by the peasantry). The characteristic defensive structure of the nobility was the castle, which came to define the landscape of the medieval world.

Castles: Medieval Homes and Havens

In the tenth century, castles were actually private fortresses made of timber and earth that were built on mounds. By the thirteenth century, they had become large, defensive structures of wood and stone and were virtually impregnable.

Living quarters Many castles consisted of a large exterior wall surrounded by a moat filled with water, and an interior fortified structure that served as the noble family's home and an extra line of defense should invaders breach the outer wall. The inner fortress contained a deep well, for the castle's ability to endure a long siege depended on the availability of food and water as well as a strong defense. Protected by such features, a few people could withstand the assault of many.

The main household of a castle consisted of a large public hall where the castle residents ate, played games, and entertained themselves while gathered around the open hearth in the center of the room. There were also smaller, private chambers where the lord and lady slept, the women of the household did the weaving and sewing, and children were born. In such a private chamber, the lord also stored a strongbox filled with coins and other valuables. In an age with no banking, most nobles guarded their wealth themselves.

The Ideals of Chivalry

The contractual form of feudalism (see Chapter 7) persisted throughout the Middle Ages as a way to provide armies for lords and kings. However, the mutual contract did nothing to reduce the violence that continually plagued medieval society. Early in the eleventh century, churchmen meeting in councils tried to reduce the violence by advocating a Peace of God, which would impose rules of war—for example, exempting the poor and the clergy from the violence. In the middle of the eleventh century, churchmen tried to add a related concept, the Truce of God, which forbad fighting on Sundays and other holy days. Neither of these worthy movements fully quelled the violence.

By the twelfth century, the feudal tie had become interwoven with an elaborate code of values and symbolic rituals that served somewhat to tame the violent world of warriors. This code and culture of the ruling class was called **chivalry,** and its values became evident in church writings, romantic literature, and treatises. Ramón Lull, whose life is described in Past Lives on page 181, wrote *The Order of Chivalry,* one of the most famous of such treatises.

JOUST Knights honed their skill in warfare by fighting in periodic mock battles such as the joust shown here. Elaborate heraldic markings conveyed the knights' noble lineage. The ladies who watched served as an admiring audience spurring on the combatants.

According to the texts, a knight should be strong and disciplined yet use his power to defend the church, the poor, and women in need. Knights were expected to possess the virtue of military prowess, but they also had to be loyal, generous, courteous, and "of noble bearing." In reality, knights probably violated these ethics as often as they adhered to them; the code of chivalry provided only a veneer of symbols and ceremonies that overlay the violence at the heart of "those who fight."

One activity required of chivalrous knights was participation in mock battles called jousts or tournaments. These were only mock battles, yet many combatants came away from them with debilitating—and sometimes fatal—injuries. The church repeatedly tried to ban tournaments, but the code of chivalry proved too powerful. Tournaments and jousts not only satisfied a profound social need but also provided a practical

Jousts and tournaments

way for young men to win horses and armor—the victors in these contests took the equipment of the losers.

The very vehemence with which the aristocracy clung to demanding rituals of behavior points to a weakness in their rule. As the Middle Ages wore on, the public role of the nobility—defending and administering Europe—was weakening. Merchants had more wealth, so chivalry was in part a way to hold on to privileges that were eroding. Yet, the nobility convinced itself of its special place in the world through elaborate ceremonies, proper dress, staged battles, and a mania for genealogy.

In Praise of Romantic Love

In the twelfth century, a new kind of poetry appeared in southern France that changed the social code between men and women—the poetry of the **troubadours,** or court poets. Historians are divided on why this new sensibility emerged at this time. Some postulate an influence of Arabic love poetry from Spain; others emphasize the patronage of wealthy noblewomen. Whatever its origin, the new poetry was highly influential in shaping people's ideas of love. In these works, the poets praised love between men and women as an ennobling idea worthy of being cultivated. Troubadour poetry is diverse, but from it

→ connect to today ←

The Nature of Romantic Love

In the twelfth century, noblemen and noblewomen began to aspire to exciting, romantic love outside of marriage. The poetry of the troubadours told of a love where a man became more noble by loving and serving a highborn woman, who wasn't necessarily his wife. How have these notions influenced our modern views of love and marriage?

we can distill some basic characteristics of this new romantic love. The ideal love was one in which a man grew more noble by loving and serving a highborn woman (not necessarily his wife and often somebody else's). Knights who pledged this kind of service hoped to be rewarded ultimately with sexual favors. This kind of love was meant to be difficult to attain, secret, and highly exciting.

In the twelfth century, Andrew the Chaplain wrote a book titled *The Art of Courtly Love* that paralleled earlier treatises on knightly chivalry. In this work, Andrew described how lovers must always turn pale in the presence of the beloved and stressed that secrecy and jealousy were essential for intensifying feelings of love. The ideal of courtly love was as much the exclusive property of the nobility as the ideals of chivalry had been. For example, Andrew wrote that if a nobleman fell in love with a mere peasant woman,

Courtly love

"do not hesitate to take what you seek and to embrace her by force." Andrew and his noble patrons believed that only the nobility could love properly—that is, possess the leisure and money to engage in this elaborate game.

Historians have argued about whether the ideal of courtly love improved the actual treatment of women, given that men supposedly bettered themselves in order to win women's hearts. Certainly Andrew's advice about raping peasant women helps answer this question. The poetry written by women troubadours also reveals something about women's experience of this kind of love. Some of this poetry describes the tension between women and the men who claimed to love them but then left to embark on great deeds. The women's poetry shows a desire to have men remain present and attentive.

Troubadour poetry spread beyond France to other areas of Europe. Poets also wrote long romances describing the courtly love tradition. The earliest of these writers, Chrétien de Troyes, penned a number of romances set in the court of the imagined hero King Arthur. (The historical Arthur was the Celtic Roman general described in Chapter 6.) These works told of love, loyalty, and great deeds, and served to entertain a nobility that was as enthralled with courtly love as it was with chivalry. These stories and the ideal of romantic love profoundly influenced modern notions of the nature of love between men and women.

THE RISE OF CENTRALIZED MONARCHIES

While noblemen and noblewomen cultivated ideals of war and love, real warfare struck with relentless regularity. Kings were constantly trying to reestablish control over provinces that had drifted away during the turbulent tenth century. At the same time, nobles struggled to keep and even increase their own power. The repeated conflicts between monarch and aristocrat transformed the political map of Europe.

England: From Conquest to Parliament

In the early eleventh century, England had been ruled by the able Danish king Canute (r. 1016–1035) (see Chapter 7), but after his death his Scandinavian empire did not hold together. Before his death, Canute and the English nobility turned to a surviving member of the family of the Anglo-Saxon king Alfred. Thus, Edward the Confessor (r. 1042–1066) reestablished the Anglo-Saxon monarchy. However, a dynasty requires heirs to be stable, and Edward did not have any children. A new succession crisis would lead to the conquest of England.

In 1066, when Edward the Confessor died without an heir, the Anglo-Saxon witan crowned one of their own—Harold Godwinson—as king, and the Anglo-Saxon kingdom was poised to continue as it had before. However, two men believed they had better claims on the English crown. First, Harold Hardradi of Norway landed in the north of England. Harold Godwinson defeated him at the Battle of Stamford Bridge, but that was to be the last battle won by an Anglo-Saxon king. As Halley's comet streaked across the skies that year, seeming to predict disaster, the other claimant, Duke William of Normandy, prepared to sail. William was Edward the Confessor's cousin, and he also claimed that the Anglo-Saxon king had promised him the throne; he aimed to take what he believed was his right. William sailed a fleet across the English Channel and engineered the last successful large-scale invasion of England. The Anglo-Saxon king was killed at the Battle of Hastings and henceforth Duke William reigned as William the Conqueror (r. 1066–1087).

Conquest of England

William brought a highly controlled feudal system to the island as he redistributed the Anglo-Saxon nobles' lands to his Norman followers. Although he allowed them to have subvassals, he required everyone to take an oath to him as liege lord (see Chapter 7), so the future Anglo-Norman kings could avoid some of the decentral-ization implicit in feudalism. William wanted to know exactly what lands he ruled, so he sent out royal officials to make a record of his holdings. The resulting text—the *Domesday Book*—is an invaluable historical record of the times. While William kept the local officials (like sheriffs) that had been so effective in Anglo-Saxon times, he replaced the Anglo-Saxon witan with his own assembly of vassals—the *curia regis*. In this assembly, or Great Council, vassals satisfied their feudal obligations to give the king advice and help him pass judgment. This advisory council would become one of the precedents for the growth of Parliament.

The Norman conquest of England had implications for the French monarchy as well, for now the king of England held lands in France—Normandy—as vassal to the king of France. However, this English vassal was stronger than the French kings, and this ambiguous situation would lead to repeated tensions between the English and French royalty over these possessions in France (see Chapter 9).

Henry I (r. 1100–1135) was as able an administrator as William I. To make the *curia regis* more efficient, Henry created separate departments. The financial department—known as the exchequer—with a chancellor at its head, became extremely important in making sure the crown remained fiscally solvent. Wealth remained the mainstay of power for the medieval monarchies; the other source was the law. Henry **Henry I and II** I used the law courts to maintain royal control over his vassals. However, a civil war over succession erupted after Henry's death, and during this time of troubles, the monarchy was weakened at the expense of strong nobles. It would take another strong monarch to restore the power of the kings. England found this monarch in Henry II (r. 1154–1189).

Henry II (who introduced the Angevin dynasty of English kings) left a permanent impact on the government and law of England. He continued Henry I's fiscal policies and expanded royal control of justice in the land. He sent traveling justices (called Justices in Eyre) empowered with royal authority around the countryside. They traveled regularly to the courts of the shire investigating and punishing crimes. Henry's legal reforms led to controversies with church courts (described later in this chapter), but they strengthened the power of the king.

Primarily through his marriage, Henry II greatly increased the English holdings in France. In 1152, Henry married Eleanor of Aquitaine, a great heiress (whose first marriage, to the king of France, had been annulled). She brought to the marriage her extensive family estates in France, and the map on page 185 shows how much of France was under English control. This great English empire was increasingly threatening to the French kings, and it would have been even more so, but Henry and Eleanor's sons dissipated much of the royal wealth and power.

Henry's eldest son, Richard I (r. 1189–1199)—known as "the Lion-Hearted"—much preferred fighting to administering the land, and he spent all but ten months of his reign on campaign outside England. He died from a neglected wound received when he was besieging a castle, and the crown went to his younger brother, John.

The reign of John (r. 1199–1216) was marked by a series of humiliations. He fought costly wars in Normandy to try to defend his possessions against the French king's intrusions. To raise money, John departed from feudal custom in many regards; for example, he married heiresses to the highest bidders and even extorted money from his subjects.

Finally, in the spring of 1215, the barons, disgusted by John's high-handed behavior, staged a rebellion. They even took over Lon-

Magna Carta

don, forcing the king to retreat to a broad field south of the city. There, under duress, John signed the **Magna Carta** (the Great Charter), which asserted that kings were not above the law. Beyond establishing this general principle, the charter was a feudal document that promised the king would not impinge on noblemen's traditional rights. However, the charter also included two principles that shaped the future of English (and North American) law: The king would impose no new taxes without the consent of the governed and would not violate the due process of law. This document is treasured as one of the precedents of constitutional law.

Another central institution that arose in the Middle Ages with special implications for England was **Parliament.** As part of their feudal obligations, nobles were to give advice to their lords, and kings all over Europe gathered their vassals and wealthy townspeople in councils—called parliaments—to discuss matters of the realm, which included every-

Parliament

thing from justice to collecting new taxes. In England in the thirteenth century, this council took a signifi-cant turn and became an institution that was able to restrict the power of the king.

The English king Edward I (r. 1272–1307) desperately needed new taxes to finance his wars. Ordinarily, English kings asked their nobles in parliament to give additional aid and then sent their agents to cities throughout the land asking for additional money from wealthy merchants. Edward simplified this process by calling for two knights from every county and two burgesses, or townsmen, from every city "to be elected without delay, and to . . . come to us at the aforesaid time and place."

This body with its expanded representation was called the Model Parliament, and it became precedent setting. As

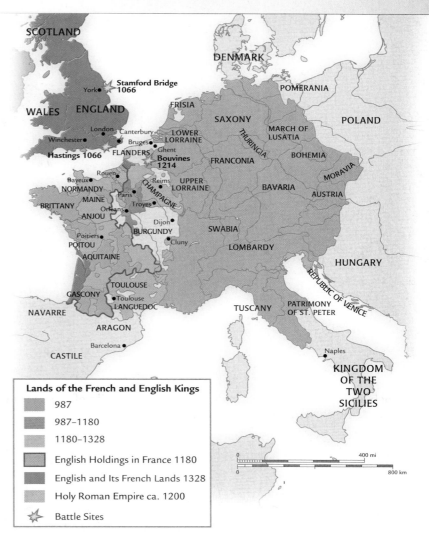

Medieval France, England, and Germany, tenth through fourteenth centuries
This map shows England, with the major cities and battles of the eleventh century, and the patchwork of lands that made up France and Germany. It also traces the slow centralization of royal control in France.

they gathered, the knights and the lower nobility sat with the burgesses and began to act together for their mutual benefit, while the clergy sat with the upper nobility. In time, the nobles would become the House of Lords, and the burgesses with the lower nobility, the House of Commons. At first, the House of Commons did little more than approve the rulings of the lords, but in time this institution came to rule England.

The Spanish Reconquer Their Lands

On the Iberian Peninsula, kings and nobles still fought over the issue of centralization, but a larger political prob-lem—the reconquest of Muslim lands—overshadowed

Christian Expansion in Iberia

This map shows the location of the Christian kingdoms on the Iberian Peninsula, tracing their expansion southward into the Muslim territories, with dates. **How might the location of Santiago de Compostela have stimulated the reconquest?**

Map legend:
- Christian Territory, ca. 900
- Reconquista, ca. 900–1150
- Reconquista, ca. 1150–1250
- Muslim Holdings, ca. 1250

this concern. Land that in other countries might have been held by the nobility emerged as small individual kingdoms—Aragon, Leon-Castile, and Navarre (see map above). These kingdoms sometimes presented a united front to the Muslims and other times fought each other to increase their power. With the threat of the Muslims constantly lurking on their borders, they simply could not afford to focus on unifying the Iberian kingdoms. In the twelfth century, Portugal continued the forces of decentralization when it emerged as a separate kingdom. Portugal had once been part of Leon, but King Alfonso VI (r. 1065–1109) gave it as an independent country to his illegitimate daughter and her crusader husband.

The map above shows the Iberians' slow reconquest of the peninsula from the Muslims. As the map indicates, each Iberian kingdom pursued its expansion southward at the expense of the Muslims. Kings then consolidated their hold on the new lands by establishing Christian settlers and building castles on the border lands. To encourage town settlements, which brought in profitable taxation, kings often gave privileges to Muslim and Jewish artisans and merchants. With this policy, the Iberian Peninsula became a hub for the fertile exchange of ideas among the three religious cultures.

The reconquest

The miraculous tenth-century discovery of the bones of Saint James the Elder stepped up the crusading zeal of the Iberian Christians. A peasant discovered the relics after a vision of brilliant stars shining over a field revealed their location to him. A great shrine—Santiago de Compostela (St. James of the Starry Field)—was built to house the bones. This shrine became a renowned pilgrimage site, attracting the faithful from as far away as Scandinavia. Such pilgrims brought both money and arms, which supported the Iberians' battle against the Muslims. Visitors to the shrine also brought artistic talent, and traveling builders designed and built great Gothic churches along the pilgrimage route. Christian warriors believed that Saint James appeared on a white horse at the front of Christian armies. Their faith seems to have spurred on their efforts.

The Iberian armies fighting in the culturally diverse land made a significant contribution to the intellectual life of western Europe, for in 1085, King Alfonso VI retook the important city of Toledo, which dominated the peninsula's central plateau. There, churchmen following Alfonso's army recovered the precious manuscripts of Aristotle and the Muslim and Jewish scholars (discussed earlier) that made such an impact on the universities of Europe. As the map shows, by the late thirteenth century, the Muslim lands had dwindled to the city of Granada in the south and the surrounding countryside.

France and Its Patient Kings

Late in the tenth century, the Carolingian family finally lost the royal title west of the Rhine. The descendants of Charlemagne had not exercised effective control of the great feudal princes for a hundred years, yet the title of king still brought some measure of prestige. In 987, Hugh Capet, the lord of the Île-de-France (the region surrounding Paris), was elected by the nobles to the French throne. The church legitimized his rule and a new dynasty was in place in France. The rule of the Capetians involved a long history of slowly reasserting control over the great nobles of their lands. As the map on page 185 shows, the kings had to wrestle with the problem of the extensive English holdings in France.

The history of France from the tenth through the fourteenth century suggests the patience of the French kings. The map shows how they gained control over one province after another. These monarchs seldom resorted to war and conquest, but used the means provided under feudal contract law to bring regions back under their control. They also made prudent marriages with wealthy heiresses who brought their inheritances back into royal control. Perhaps most important, the Capetians were fortunate enough to produce sons to inherit their throne.

Philip II Augustus (r. 1180–1223) made great strides in centralizing his lands by directly addressing the English holdings. In wars against the English, Philip finally defeated King John and took over the English lands of Normandy, Maine, and Anjou (see map on page 185). Through these conquests, Philip quadrupled the income of the French monarchy. This talented king recognized the need to develop new ways to maintain his control over the widely dispersed patchwork that was France. Instead of relying on the feudal hierarchy to govern locally, he appointed salaried officials—bailiffs—to collect taxes and represent his interests. These ambitious men, most well educated at the University of Paris, did much to strengthen royal power at the expense of the feudal nobility.

| Capetian dynasty |

The fortunes of the Capetians were dramatically forwarded by Louis IX (r. 1226–1270), whom many consider the greatest of the medieval kings.

| Louis IX |

He was a pious man who went to church at least twice a day and cared for the poor and sick, and he achieved a distinction highly unusual for a king: he was proclaimed a saint by the church.

For all his piety, Louis did not neglect matters of the realm. Although he did not try to extend the royal domain, he nevertheless expected his nobles to be good vassals. He also took an interest in law and justice and wanted royal justice to be available to all his subjects, dispensing it personally. However, Louis did more than dispense justice; his advisors began to codify the laws of France, and he was the first king to legislate for all of France. Finally, Louis confirmed the Parlement of Paris—a court, not a representative assembly—as the highest court in France. (It held this position until 1789.) Saint Louis died while on crusade, and his successors continued to ride the Capetian momentum, slowly centralizing their authority.

King Philip IV "the Fair" (r. 1285–1314) believed that the greatest obstacle to his power was Edward I of England and his extensive French fief of Gascony (see map on page 185). Philip engaged in intermittent wars against Edward from 1294 to 1302 and even tried to attack the

| Philip IV |

important English wool industry by blocking importation of English wool into Flanders, but the Flemish towns revolted against him. All these wars were expensive and drove Philip to look for additional funds. The king tried to collect money from the church, which led to a protracted struggle with Pope Boniface VIII (described fully in Chapter 9).

In 1302, Philip needed the support of the realm in his struggles against the pope and to raise money, so he summoned representatives from church, nobility, and towns to the first meeting of the **Estates General.** As these men gathered to advise their king, they sat according to the medieval order—those who prayed, fought, and worked (including townsmen) deliberated separately. This triple arrangement, so different from the two houses of Parliament that grew up in England, helped diffuse each group's power, allowing kings to maintain tight control. This had dramatic consequences for the future of France.

By the end of the thirteenth century, the French monarchy was the best governed and wealthiest in Europe. It was a power to be reckoned with, but there were clouds on the horizon. The Flemish towns remained defiant, England continued to hold and contest lands in France, and the religious struggles had just begun. Philip's successors would face great difficulties.

The Myth of Universal Rule: The Holy Roman Empire

The map on page 185 depicts a large, seemingly powerful neighbor—the Holy Roman Empire—looming to the east of France. But that empire was not as potent as its size might suggest. Early in the tenth century, the last direct descendant of Charlemagne died. The German dukes recognized the need for a leader and, in 919, elected one of their number (Henry of Saxony) to be king. His descendants held the German monarchy until 1024.

The most powerful of this line of kings was Otto I (r. 936–973), who restored the title of emperor. Otto in many ways resembled Charlemagne. He was a warrior king who stopped the advance of the Magyars in 955

| Saxon dynasty |

and won further conquests in northern Italy. Also like Charlemagne, Otto fostered a revival of learning in Germany in which literature and art flourished. (Otto had married a Byzantine princess, and she brought artists from Byzantium to enhance the German court.) Finally, the German king marched into Rome to receive the crown of the Roman emperor from Pope John XII, much as Charlemagne had done a century and a half earlier. For hundreds of years after this ceremony, an emperor would be proclaimed in German lands—later to be called the Holy Roman Empire. However, it is one thing to claim a far-flung empire and quite another to exert consistent control over it. Like other rulers in the west, Otto and his successors faced repeated challenges from the strength of the independent nobles within their lands.

The Ottonian dynasty ended in 1024, and the German nobles selected Henry III (r. 1039–1056) from another branch of the Saxon family. Henry began the Salian dynasty of Germany. He was an able

Salian dynasty king who looked for ways to exert more control in his lands, and he increasingly used bishops and abbots that he appointed as his administrators. When his son Henry IV (r. 1056–1106) tried to continue that policy, he ignited a firestorm of debate called the investiture controversy (see page 189).

The Emperor Frederick I (r. 1152–1190), known as Barbarossa, or "red-beard," elected from the house of Hohenstaufen, came close to establishing a consolidated German empire. He planned to exert tight

Hohenstaufen dynasty control over three contiguous regions that could form the core of royal lands. He had inherited Burgundy and Swabia and invaded Italy to subdue Lombardy in the north. However, while this policy was theoretically sound, it proved ill conceived, and the German emperors were weakened by their continued involvement in Italian politics. Italy's city-states and a strong papacy refused to submit to German rule. The resulting, almost incessant, wars in Italy drained rather than strengthened the emperors' resources.

The rule of Emperor Frederick II Hohenstaufen (r. 1215–1250) effectively ended any chance of a unified German monarchy. Frederick was a brilliant ruler and patron of the arts, who had been raised in Sicily and had come to love the diverse Muslim and Christian cultures that coexisted in that sunny land. His policy was to confer upon the German princes and nobility virtual sovereignty within their own territories—he retained only the right to set the foreign policy of the empire. His goal was to take as much profit as possible from the German lands but focus his rule in Italy—particularly the Kingdom of the Two Sicilies in the south.

In southern Italy, Frederick rigorously centralized his administration and imposed a monetary tax on all his subjects. He used Muslims as soldiers and was reputed to have a harem of Muslim women. He turned Sicily into a highly organized and culturally exciting monarchy, guided by his firm rule. Although many historians praise Frederick as the first modern ruler—highly organized and practically

calculating—the pope and the northern Italian towns feared his expanding policies in Italy. Their fears were well founded, for he led a campaign against the cities of northern Italy (the Lombard League) and scored some victories in 1237. The popes and the towns feared Frederick's encirclement. The pope excommunicated him, and both sides conducted public relations campaigns to discredit the other. Frederick's attempts to unify Italy ended with his death in 1250.

The German princes wanted to preserve the freedoms they had acquired under Frederick II, so they elected a man they considered a weak prince— Rudolph of Habsburg—as emperor. **Habsburg dynasty** Eventually, the Habsburgs acquired the duchies of Austria, which became the chief foundation for the powerful Habsburg dynasty (see Chapter 11). Burdened by independent nobles and worn down by political trouble in Italy, medieval German emperors had little hope of holding their so-called empire together.

THOSE WHO PRAY: Imperial Popes and Expanding Christendom

Like the monarchies that had seen their political power fragment during the tumultuous tenth century, the church, too, had decentralized. Local lords saw the churches on their manors as their own property and priests as their own vassals. Nobles sometimes treated bishoprics as rewards for loyal subjects rather than as religious positions. Critics of these practices began to voice demands for reform; and reformers sought an authentic leader who could preside over a universal Christendom.

A Call for Church Reform

One obvious candidate to reform the church was the Holy Roman Emperor. In 1046, when the German Henry III (r. 1039–1056) traveled to Rome to receive the imperial crown, he found the papacy dominated by Roman aristocrats and interfamilial disputes. When he arrived, three rival popes were vying for power. He deposed them all and established a pope (Clement II) loyal to Henry and a strengthened papal court. In the search for order in the Christian world, it seemed that the German emperors might preside over a unified Christendom.

But the eleventh-century popes also began to step forward as a force for reform. Pope Nicholas II (r. 1058–1061) began to free the papacy from military dependence on the

German emperor by allying himself with the Normans in southern Italy. However, he also recognized that the church as a whole needed to be free from lay intervention. He was the first pope who expressly condemned the practice of lay investiture: Popes disapproved of a layperson (a secular ruler) giving a churchman the symbols of spiritual office (the ring and staff) because it appeared that the ruler was the source of spiritual authority. Nicholas was not able to stop that long-standing practice, but his voice would not be the last on this subject. However, he was able to move the selection of popes from lay interference, for he called a Roman council in 1059, which defined the principles by which popes were chosen by a college of cardinals, a practice that continues today. It seemed as if the popes might be able to preside over a unified Christendom.

Calls for church reform also came from another source: The ecclesiastical network of Cluniac monasteries that had been established in the early tenth century (see Chapter 7) began to raise its voice. From their foundation, Cluniacs had supported a strong papacy, and their influence increased even further when a cardinal highly sympathetic to the Cluniac order became Pope Gregory VII (r. 1073–1085). Gregory decided that popes, not kings or emperors, should guide Christendom. This outlook led him directly into conflict with the Holy Roman emperor Henry IV (r. 1056–1106).

The Investiture Controversy

The controversy between Gregory and Henry was triggered by the question of who should appoint or invest bishops in Germany, a matter that was as much political as religious. As we have seen, the emperors had used their right to choose bishops to appoint men to act as royal representatives throughout the lands of their independence-hungry nobles. The pope also understood the importance of having allies in distant lands, and he wanted his loyal men in the German churches. This controversy arose out of the dual allegiances bishops faced—to whom did they owe their principal loyalty, pope or king? Through the struggle, the two sides liberally wielded their weapons: Henry sent his armies marching into Italy; Gregory threatened to excommunicate the emperor (and indeed later did so), claiming that this action could free the ever-rebellious vassals from their feudal obligations. Gregory also had the support of a powerful patron, Matilda,

OPINION

Kings and popes struggled to rule Christian Europe. What do you think were the advantages and disadvantages of each faction's position?

Countess of Tuscany. This skilled tactician promptly challenged Henry's military strength, leading her own armies into battle against him. In a dramatic incident at Canossa, Henry waited three days in the snow dressed in the sackcloth of a penitent begging the pope's forgiveness. Gregory as a priest was obliged to forgive a sinner professing sorrow, so the two temporarily made peace.

Within three years, pope and king were again locked in combat. This time, however, when Henry invaded Italy, Gregory's Norman mercenaries caused so much damage in Rome that the outraged citizens forced the pope to abandon the city. He died in exile in 1085, bitterly convinced he had failed in forwarding papal authority. But Henry was unable to secure a decisive victory, either, and spent the remainder of his life trying to recover his authority in Germany. The issue of investiture was left for a later king and pope to resolve.

In 1122 the new emperor, Henry V, negotiated a compromise in the investiture controversy, the Concordat of Worms. Pope and emperor decided the pope could present new bishops with their symbols of office, indicating the priority of the church over its churchmen. However, the emperor could be present at and influence the elections of bishops. This compromise actually represented a victory for the popes, who now had an opening for exerting authority within the rising national monarchies all over Europe. But the papal victory would not come easily or unopposed.

Concordat of Worms

Such tensions persisted between clergy and lay rulers who wanted to strengthen their own rule in their home territories. In England, the struggle took the form of a deadly clash between King Henry II (r. 1154–1189) and his archbishop and once best friend, Thomas Becket. Becket wanted to preserve the church's right to be exempt from the legal authority Henry was using to consolidate his power over his land. One day, a small group of knights seeking to please their king surprised Becket in his church at Canterbury and split his head with their swords. Becket died on the altar he had served so well. Their plan to eliminate the influence of the archbishop backfired, however: Becket quickly became a martyr in the battle for church autonomy. In the face of popular revulsion for the crime, Henry was forced to compromise with the pope to gain forgiveness for his archbishop's murder. Henry had to allow the papacy to be the court of appeal from English ecclesiastical courts, and this concession brought the English church more closely into the sphere of Rome.

Thomas Becket

The power of the popes grew; the example of Becket showed that their weapons of excommunication and spiritual leadership were impossible to fight with swords. As church power grew, the papacy developed structures that increasingly resembled the powerful medieval monarchies. Just as monarchs began to rely on bureaucracy, court systems, and money to consolidate their power, the

HENRY IV AND MATILDA OF TUSCANY, twelfth century This image captures the importance of the noblewoman Matilda of Tuscany in the investiture controversy, for it shows Holy Roman emperor Henry IV being forced to kneel before her and ask for her intercession. The stylized castle surrounding Matilda symbolizes her power.

pope created a papal curia—an administrative unit—to handle financial matters. He also created a branch to handle legal appeals with the growing body of canon law, which was the compilations of religious laws that slowly came to govern much of medieval life.

By the beginning of the thirteenth century, popes could with some accuracy claim that they presided over a universal Christendom, and one of the most powerful was Innocent III (r. 1198–1216). Innocent was able to exert leadership over princes of Europe: He reprimanded

| Innocent III | the kings of England, Aragon, Portugal, France, Poland, and Norway and insisted that they obey him. He

vigorously fought heretics and wanted to clarify Christian belief. To accomplish the latter, he called the Fourth Lateran Council, which met in 1215. Among other things, this council identified exactly seven sacraments and reaffirmed their essential role in reaching salvation. The council also pronounced on many other matters, from qualifications for the priesthood to monastic life and veneration of relics. With the clarity expressed by the council, the medieval church was firmly defined. In effect, the church had become an empire that superseded all other empires.

The Byzantine Empire Struggles

The Byzantine Empire had reached the height of its expansion and power in 1056, but in the late eleventh century troubles flared up. The Byzantine army had deteriorated, and the emperors had begun to use mercenary soldiers, who were expensive to maintain. When the empire became vulnerable on several fronts in the late eleventh century, neither the army nor the treasury was prepared. The Normans threatened Byzantine provinces in southern Italy, and the Muslims menaced in the east.

Islam had gained strength from the movement of the Seljuk Turks, a fierce central Asian tribe whose members had converted to Islam and reinforced the Muslim armies threatening Byzantium. In the midst of succession problems, Byzantium elected a strong soldier—Ramonos Diogenes (r. 1068–1071)—as emperor. Diogenes led an army east in 1071 and challenged the Turks. However, he experienced a crushing defeat at the Battle of Manzikert, and this loss triggered another succession crisis in the capital. Meanwhile, the victorious Turks drove deeper into the empire, capturing all of Asia Minor and taking control of some of the Byzantines' richest lands.

In Byzantium's darkest days, a strong new emperor, Alexius Komnenus (r. 1081–1118), emerged and managed to halt the imperial disintegration. Alexius built a new army based on feudal ties, raised taxes, and desperately cast about for ways to check the Turkish advance. Remembering the skilled knights whom his forces had fought in Sicily, Alexius looked to the West for help. His appeal found fertile ground with a papacy looking for a cause.

Christians on the March: The Crusades

1096–1291

From as early as the fourth century, Christians had begun to visit holy places, and with the prosperity of the eleventh century, these pilgrimages became even more popular. One of the favorite pilgrimage destinations (along with Santiago de Compostela, described earlier) was Palestine, where Jesus had lived. Sometimes bands of thousands traveled, and when they journeyed to the Holy Land, they passed through Byzantine lands to reach the Muslim territories that included the holy places. For centuries, these trips—albeit hazardous—were possible.

The Turks, who now controlled Jerusalem, did not consciously stop the pilgrim traffic, but they did impose taxes on travelers, and to many Christians it seemed that the Holy Land should not be controlled by these Turks. When Emperor Alexius sent an appeal to Pope Urban II (r. 1088–1099) pleading for help to supplement his forces, the pope was ready to respond. In 1095, Urban called for Christians to begin a holy war against the newly strengthened Muslims.

Pope Urban's call

The text of Urban's speech was preserved by several (sometimes conflicting) chroniclers, yet all agree that it shows a clear perception of the needs of the West and the motives of crusaders. Urban reminds his audience that western Europe is becoming too confining: "For this land which you inhabit, . . . is too narrow for your large population; nor does it abound in wealth; and it furnishes scarcely food enough for its cultivators." He further promised crusaders remission of sins if they undertook this journey. Urban's call was spectacularly successful, and members of the aristocracy began to plan the journey to the Holy Land.

Urban told departing soldiers to wear the sign of the cross on their breasts and encouraged them to earn the right to wear the symbol on their back when they returned, a symbol proving they had successfully fulfilled their vow to fight in this holy cause. The series of military engagements against the Muslims that continued for two hundred years are called the **Crusades,** named for the cross under which the Christians fought. People went on crusade for a number of reasons. Many were driven by sincere religious motivation, although their lofty purposes frequently deteriorated in the heat of battle. Some propertyless nobles hoped to find some land of their own, and other people sought wealth to bring home.

People responded to Urban's call with a fervor that surprised even the planners of the crusade. The first to respond included large numbers of peasants who followed two self-appointed leaders—Peter the Hermit and Walter the Penniless—to the east to free the Holy Land. Long before they reached the Holy Land, their zeal led to violence in the West. They terrorized local people, looting for food and supplies to take on their way. A contemporary chronicler also told how their religious fervor led to other violence: "Led by their zeal for Christianity, they persecuted the hated race of the Jews wherever they were found and strove either to destroy them completely or to compel them to become Christians." These early excesses would mark many of the subsequent crusades. When these peasants arrived in Constantinople, the emperor quickly shipped them over to Asia Minor, where they were massacred by the Turks.

The earliest crusaders were vividly described by the Byzantine emperor's daughter Anna Komnene in *The Alexiad,* a history

Princess Anna Komnene Writes of Byzantium's Troubles

The Byzantine emperor Alexius's daughter Anna wrote *The Alexiad*, a history of her father's reign. In this excerpt, she describes the growing animosity between western Europeans (whom she called Franks) and the Byzantines.

Book 3: X   Before [Alexius] had enjoyed even a short rest, he heard a report of the approach of innumerable Frankish armies. Now he dreaded their arrival for he knew their irresistible manner of attack, their unstable and mobile character and all the peculiar natural and concomitant characteristics which the Frank retains throughout; and he also knew that they were always agape for money, and seemed to disregard their truces readily for any reason that cropped up. For he had always heard this reported of them, and found it very true.... And indeed the actual facts were far greater and more terrible than rumor made them. For the whole of the West and all the barbarian tribes which dwell between the further side of the Adriatic and the pillars of Heracles, had all migrated in a body and were marching into Asia through the intervening Europe, and were making the journey with all their household.

What characteristics does Anna Komnene attribute to the Franks?

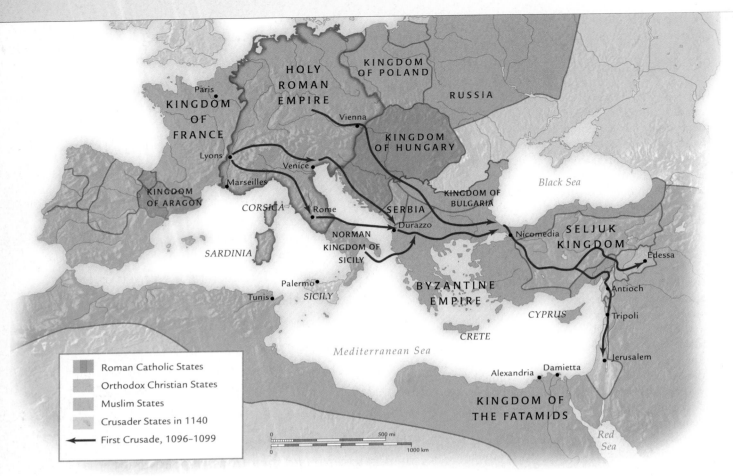

The First Crusade, 1096–1099 This map shows the route of the First Crusade and the crusader states that were established in 1140.

of her father's reign. In addition to offering a first-person account of the crusaders, Anna sheds light on the mutual suspicion and ill will that divided Byzantines from westerners (whom she called Franks) and forecasts a future deterioration of the crusading ideal. In contrast to Komnene, western sources describe the crusaders as fulfilling a high purpose: "The Franks straightway began to sew the cross on the right shoulders of their garments, saying that they would all with one accord follow in the footsteps of Christ." These contrasting accounts underscored the widening split between East and West, which was fueled by a fundamental misunderstanding: The crusaders wanted land in exchange for their military service (western-style feudalism), but Alexius just wanted to pay them and have them turn over the land to him. The Muslims wanted them all to stay away from their lands.

The crusaders were highly skilled and successful warriors, and they relentlessly swept the Muslim forces out of the Holy Land. In 1099, when they took Jerusalem after a five-week siege, the carnage was brutal. The eyewitness Fulcher of Chartres tells of the bloodshed: "Within Solomon's Temple, about ten thousand were beheaded. If you had been there, your feet would have been stained up to the ankles with the blood of the slain." When the violence died down, the crusaders took the Holy Land and established kingdoms there.

The crusader principalities served as outposts of western European culture in the East. They entertained pilgrims, fought skirmishes on their borders, and learned about life in the eastern Mediterranean. Generations of western Europeans living in proximity with Muslims were changed somewhat by the interactions. They learned to eat different foods, began to value bathing, and acquired a taste for urban life, unlike their rural cousins at home. Even a Muslim chronicler noticed the transformation: "Everyone who is a fresh emigrant from the Frankish lands is ruder in character than those who have become acclimatized and have held long association with Muslims."

Crusader states

However, the official relationship between crusader and Muslim was not friendly. On the Muslim side, the appearance of Christian soldiers reawakened the spirit of jihad that had receded from political policy. (See Chapter 6.) For example, a Syrian legal scholar in the twelfth century wrote a work called the *Book of Holy War,* in which he argued that it was the neglect of jihad that allowed the crusaders to conquer

Jerusalem and surrounding areas. His solution was to call for a moral and military resurgence to respond to the crusading movement. But this work was not widely circulated; it established an ideal, but it took until later in the twelfth century for Muslims to rally against crusaders in the spirit of jihad.

The most important determinant of the relations between the two groups was probably geographic. The map on page 192 shows the precarious location of the crusader states, surrounded by the Muslim world. These states would need constant support from the West to keep them from being retaken by the Muslims.

As early as the 1120s, the Muslims had begun to strike back, and Edessa fell in 1144. Christians in the west mounted further Crusades to support their fellows in the Holy Land, but the subsequent crusades were not as successful as the first, even though some illustrious western kings participated.

The Second Crusade was urged on by Bernard of Clairveaux (Peter Abelard's foe, described earlier), but the two leaders—King Louis VII of France and Emperor Conrad III of Germany—could not coordinate their efforts enough to make any difference.

Subsequent crusades

Things became worse for the crusader states: The Muslims of Syria produced a vigorous leader named Saladin, who controlled Syria and Egypt. Using the newly invigorated spirit of jihad, Saladin conducted a coordinated force that retook Jerusalem in 1187. Saladin did not permit a massacre of civilians, and he even tolerated a continuation of Christian services, but the West was ablaze with calls for a new crusade. Three major monarchs responded: Emperor Frederick Barbarossa, Richard the Lion-Hearted of England, and Philip II of France. Everyone thought these pillars of chivalry could retake the Holy City, but they, too, had problems coordinating their efforts. After some stunning successes, Frederick Barbarossa drowned while swimming and his army went home. The French king also retreated after some losses, leaving Richard and Saladin to negotiate a settlement whereby Christian pilgrims could have free access to Jerusalem. However, these concessions seemed humiliating to Christians in the West who unrealistically hoped for a decisive victory.

The Crusades spurred the emergence of new religious orders that followed a monastic rule and that served as a crucial part of the permanent garrison guarding the Holy Land. Their principal function was to serve God by fighting Muslims, and Muslims and Christians alike respected their military accomplishments. The Knights Templars, the most famous of these orders, protected pilgrims and served as bankers for those traveling to the Holy Land, but they grew so powerful that many began to resent

Knights Templars

> After some stunning successes, Frederick Barbarossa drowned while swimming and his army went home.

their strength and organization. Saladin hated the Templars, saying, "Let us rid the earth of the air they breathe," but they remained a central force in the Holy Land. Again, the medieval social order blurred, as one group of those who prayed also began to specialize in warfare.

The noble ideal of crusading deteriorated over time as Christians began to focus less on the Holy Land itself and more on Christendom's perceived enemies. For example, crusading fervor led Christians in Europe to conduct more pogroms (massacres) against Jews in Europe.

Crusading armies also turned on Byzantine Christians as relations between them had continued to deteriorate. In 1182, the man who would become the Byzantine emperor Andronikos (r. 1183–1185), the last of the Komnenian dynasty, allowed a massacre of Latins in Constantinople. Westerners reacted to the slaughter with rage. Andronikos's death ended the strong Komnenian dynasty, and the Byzantine royalty once again was roiled by family feuding, negligence, and corruption. In 1204, crusaders were drawn into Byzantine politics and took advantage of the Byzantine disarray. The Fourth Crusade, short of money, first attacked the Christian city of Zara for the Venetians in exchange for their passage to the Holy Land. Then a pretender to the Byzantine throne offered crusaders money to place him in power, and crusaders attacked Byzantium itself. Successful in their mission, they sacked the great city, raping women (some of them nuns) and defiling altars. Despite the pope's condemnation, the westerners divided the empire among themselves and abandoned their plan to go to Jerusalem. They held Byzantium for fifty-seven years—until the Byzantines managed to retake it—but this interim badly weakened the empire, as well as the crusading ideal.

The Seventh and Eighth Crusades, led by the saintly French king Louis IX (r. 1226–1270), went to North Africa, where the crusaders failed miserably. Louis died in Tunis.

Perhaps the height of misplaced religious zeal took place during the Children's Crusade (1212–1213), when some preachers argued that crusaders had lost God's help through their misdeeds, and only the innocent might save the Holy Land. The sources say thousands of innocent children died or were sold into slavery during this fiasco. (Some modern historians question whether this appalling incident really occurred.)

Finally, in 1291, the Muslims seized the last crusader outpost on the Asian mainland when the fortified city of Acre fell. This was a terrible military disaster for the West, and the last frightened Christians in the Holy Land paid ship masters fortunes for passage out of the doomed city. Knights Templars died courageously while

Crusaders expelled

A Professor Advertises His Law Lectures

Odofredus taught law at the University of Bologna beginning in 1228 and was popular for his personal interest in his students. Medieval students would not have had textbooks; they needed to learn everything from lectures. Here, Odofredus announces his lectures in hopes of gathering an audience—the only way he would be paid.

For I shall teach the unskilled and novices but also the advanced students. For the unskilled will be able to make satisfactory progress in the position of the case and exposition of the letter; the advanced students can become more erudite in the subtleties of questions and contrarieties. I shall also read all the glosses, which was not done before my time.

For it is my purpose to teach you faithfully and in a kindly manner, in which instruction the following order has customarily been observed by the ancient and modern doctors and particularly by my master, which method I shall retain. First, I shall give you the summaries of each title before I come to the text. Second, I shall put forth well and distinctly in the best terms I can the purport of each law. Third, I shall read the text in order to correct it. Fourth, I shall briefly restate the meaning. Fifth, I shall solve conflicts, adding general matters . . . and subtle and useful distinctions and questions with the solutions, so far as divine Providence shall assist me. And if any law is deserving of a review by reason of its fame or difficulty, I shall reserve it for an afternoon review.

What would have made Odofredus's lectures popular? What do you think of his class outline? What might or might not make it effective?

guarding the evacuation of Christians from the burning city. Two centuries of Christian expansion into the eastern Mediterranean ended with few concrete results. Islam was as strong as ever; Byzantium had only weakened further. For centuries, however, the image of knights galloping across Europe to reclaim the Holy Land from the Muslims continued to captivate Christians throughout the West. The church lost prestige as crusaders lost the Holy Land, but even more devastating criticism emerged in western Christendom itself.

Criticism of the Church

In the West under the guidance of many skilled popes, the church had established a strong organization and wielded much authority. Yet some Christians, called heretics by the orthodox, disagreed with established doctrine and criticized the direction the church had taken. Some of these people believed that the church had erred in becoming rich as early as the reign of the Roman emperor Constantine (r. 306–337) (discussed in Chapter 5). These critics wanted to follow the example of the apostles described in the Bible and live a simple life by being poor, preaching, and reading the sacred text. This criticism also reflected a new reality in the West—there now existed a richer and increasingly urban world with the kind of visible inequities that seemed worth rejecting.

The best-known proponent of the simple life was Valdes of Lyons. (Later he became incorrectly called Peter Waldo, and he is often remembered by that name.) A rich merchant in his younger years, Valdes gave up all his material posses-

Waldensians

sions in order to wander, beg, and preach. Many ordinary Christians were drawn to the holy simplicity of his life, but churchmen were threatened by his implicit criticism of churches decorated with gold. The pope condemned Valdes and his followers as heretics in 1181, but many of his supporters, called Waldensians, stayed loyal to their beliefs, and, in fact, Waldensian churches exist today.

Several similar sects arose that advocated the apostolic life (called *vita apostolica*). Indeed, numerous men and women throughout the Middle Ages continued to consider wealth and Christianity incompatible. Taken together, such movements represented a growing discomfort with a church that seemed too powerful and too embroiled in the gritty details of the physical world to fulfill the spiritual needs of men and women. The thirteenth-century church met these criticisms with both accommodation and repression.

The Church Accommodates: Franciscans and Dominicans

New monastic movements had always been a source of reform for the church and an outlet for men and women who sought different ways of expressing their religious impulses. In the thirteenth century, popes approved two such movements, the Franciscans and the Dominicans, that promised to address the criticism that had arisen so strongly against the church. In previous monastic movements, men and women isolated themselves behind great walls to devote themselves to God. By contrast, the new religious impulses called for holy men and women to mingle among the people in the growing towns of Europe and help alleviate the new problems of urban poverty and suffering. Therefore, Franciscans and Dominicans did not retire from society as monks but were called **mendicant orders** (literally "begging orders," which alludes to their poverty) and served God by helping the needy within their villages and towns.

The Franciscan movement was founded by Francis of Assisi (1182–1226), the son of a wealthy Italian merchant. Like Valdes of Lyons, Francis had a conversion experience that inspired him to give up all his earthly goods to live in poverty. He survived by begging, and he helped care for the poor people of Assisi and other nearby towns. His gentle demeanor and charismatic preaching had broad appeal. Francis attracted a number of followers among the young in Assisi. One young woman, Clare, heard him speak, and in 1212 she followed him into a religious life. She established a mendicant order for women and presided over a group of women dedicated to the same ideals she had embraced. These Poor Ladies of Assisi, sometimes called Poor Clares, became the female counterparts of the Franciscans, but soon their lives were structured differently from the lives of their male counterparts: Instead of wandering and preaching, they lived in silence in enclosed convents. In spite of this change, this spiritual life still attracted many followers.

Francis of Assisi

> [T]he new religious impulses called for holy men and women to mingle among the people in the growing towns of Europe and help alleviate the new problems of urban poverty and suffering.

Although Franciscans in some ways resembled the Waldensians, who had been condemned as heretics, they differed in one significant respect: They believed in obedience to the pope. Because of this humility, Francis received papal dispensation to establish a new order of "friars," who would live in poverty and preach.

The Franciscans appealed to those who believed in a poor and humble church, but their work did not satisfy all the critics. Many people thought that the church had fallen into error because of ignorance. Another new mendicant order, the Dominicans, arose to address this problem. The Dominicans were led by the Spanish priest Dominic de Guzmán (1170–1221), an intellectual who believed that heresy could be fought through preaching. In 1215, Pope Honorius approved the Order of Preachers, or the Dominicans, who, like the Franciscans, took an oath of poverty and lived among the townspeople instead of in monasteries. However, they emphasized preaching rather than poverty and stressed study at universities to ensure that their preaching was strictly orthodox. The Dominicans thus appealed to people's minds, whereas the Franciscans spoke to their hearts. Through permitting both of these orders, the church had responded to the spiritual needs of its followers by authorizing dedicated men and women to teach and practice among the people. Christians hungering for a more profound sense of spiritual connectedness welcomed the lessons they received from these pious teachers.

Dominican order

The Church Suppresses: The Albigensian Crusade and the Inquisition

The church did not always prove so accommodating in the face of criticism. In the late twelfth century, a heretical movement became very popular, particularly in southern France. This movement, called Catharism (from the Greek word for "pure"), was similar to Zoroastrianism (described in Chapter 1) in that it professed a system of two principles (or two deities)—light and darkness—fighting for supremacy. Adherents identified the god of darkness with the Old Testament deity who created the world and the god of light with the New Testament and spiritual salvation. They believed that people had to struggle to help the good principle trapped in everyone escape the evil world of the flesh. Because a center of this group was in Albi in southern France, they are also commonly known as Albigensians.

Albigensians were particularly threatening to the church because their ideas struck at the very heart of Christian belief, which considered the material world as good.

Albigensian Crusade

Pope Innocent III first sent preachers to Albi to show people the error of their ways. However, in 1209, after some violence against papal representatives, the pope lost patience and called a crusade against the heretics. Northern French nobles, eager to break the power of the strong southern lords, participated avidly in the savage campaign. During the crusade's twenty years, thousands of people were massacred. In one especially tragic example, 7,000 men, women, and children of the town of Béziers took refuge from the crusaders in the local cathedral. When soldiers asked the papal representative how they could distinguish between heretics and the faithful, he reportedly replied, "Kill them all; God will know his own." All 7,000 of the townspeople—heretic and orthodox alike—died that day in the church's attempt to stamp out heresy.

Even after such brutal displays of power, church leaders still felt endangered by diversity of beliefs. In the mid-thirteenth century, the church established a new court—the **inquisition**—designed to ferret out and eradicate threatening ideas. Unlike secular courts, which determined the guilt or innocence of actions, the inquisition aimed to detect wrong beliefs. The court recognized the difficulty in examining people's ideas and developed special means by which to determine what people were thinking.

The inquisition

Often it relied on the Dominicans, with their training in understanding heresy, to serve as the inquisitor generals. These generals used questioning, starvation, and other forms of torture to force people to reveal their beliefs. Many unfortunate victims "confessed" to escape further torture or execution, and although they were released, many faced extreme "penances," such as renunciation of property or imprisonment. All self-confessed heretics faced severe social repercussions from their neighbors, who no longer wanted to associate with the "guilty." Those who were deemed guilty and unrepentant were turned over to the secular authority to be executed, usually by burning.

The inquisition swept through much of Europe, inflicting more damage in some communities than in others. Perhaps the only way to understand this phenomenon is to remember that people in the Middle Ages were deeply concerned about the state of their souls and their own salvation. They believed that exposure to incorrect religious ideas could jeopardize that salvation, and this was a risk they simply could not take. In their emphasis on community over the individual, they did not share modern beliefs that efforts to save one another from "wrong" ideas potentially put all ideas in peril.

By 1300, many in medieval Europe were convinced that order was established in the world. Bishop Gerard of Cambrai elaborated on the three-part structure of this perfectly ordered society: Those who pray are able to enjoy this "holy leisure" because of the efforts of those who fight, who guarantee their security. Both of these groups are able to fill their functions because those who work see to the needs of their bodies. The world seemed perfectly appointed.

timeline

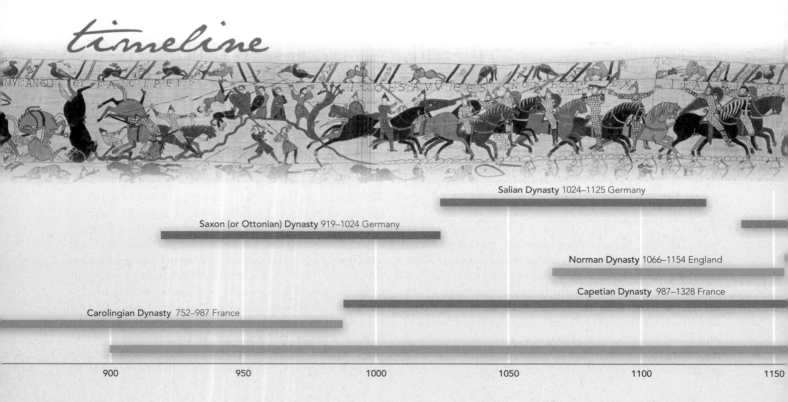

Salian Dynasty 1024–1125 Germany

Saxon (or Ottonian) Dynasty 919–1024 Germany

Norman Dynasty 1066–1154 England

Capetian Dynasty 987–1328 France

Carolingian Dynasty 752–987 France

900   950   1000   1050   1100   1150

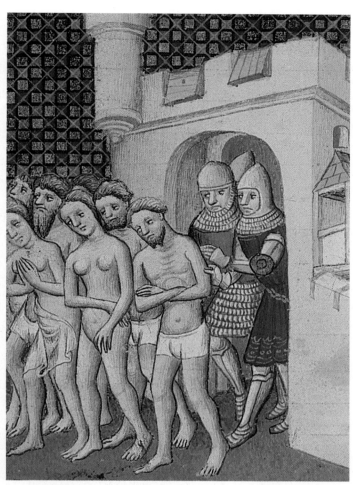

ALBIGENSIAN CRUSADE The church turned the power of crusade against heretics in southern France, centered in Albi. This illustration documents the expulsion of the Albigensians from the town of Carcassone in 1209; their nudity symbolizes how they lost all their goods.

SUMMARY

At the turn of the first millennium C.E., western Europe began to flourish and expand. This century introduced the high point of the Middle Ages, expanding politically and intellectually.

- Medieval engineers began building wind and water mills that saved people many hours of labor. In addition, agricultural innovations brought more food and the population of western Europe doubled.

- Towns grew up expanding trade and commerce and stimulating the building of great cathedrals that served as centers of piety and learning. Universities, too, were established, stimulating education and philosophical and scientific innovations.

- Society was ruled by noble families, whose role was warfare and serving new powerful kings. These rulers built powerful centralized kingdoms in England, France, and Spain, leaving the Holy Roman Empire weak and fragmented.

- Popes also consolidated their power establishing leadership over Christian Europe. The powerful church was then able to call for a series of crusades to wrest rule of Jerusalem and its environs from the Muslims. Finally, criticism of the strong church led to the founding of new monastic movements and repression of some new ideas by the new court—the inquisition.

The fourteenth century would bring dramatic challenges, when disasters struck from many fronts. Would medieval structures prove resilient enough to withstand the pressure?

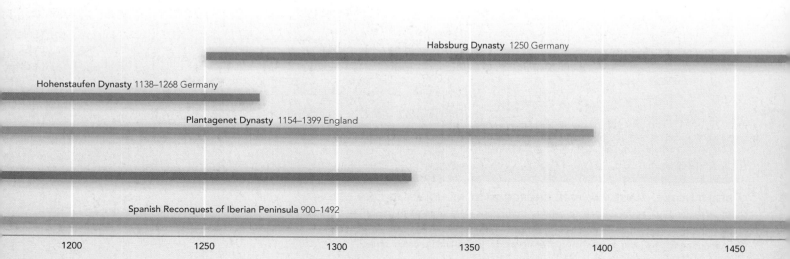

Habsburg Dynasty 1250 Germany

Hohenstaufen Dynasty 1138–1268 Germany

Plantagenet Dynasty 1154–1399 England

Spanish Reconquest of Iberian Peninsula 900–1492

| 1200 | 1250 | 1300 | 1350 | 1400 | 1450 |

BERNT NOTKE, *DANSE MACABRE,* **CHURCH OF ST. NICHOLAS, TALLINN, ESTONIA,**

fifteenth century   In the fourteenth century, Europeans were struck with a series of disasters from famine to plague to warfare. One of the most popular artistic themes of the age was the "Dance of Death," shown in this image, in which skeletal death takes everyone from noble to commoner. The leveling of death and destruction destroyed the medieval order.

The West Struggles and Eastern Empires Flourish

The Late Middle Ages,
ca. 1300–1500

9

Agnolo the Fat Survives the Plague

"I do not know where to begin to tell of the cruelty. . . . It seemed to almost everyone that one became stupefied by seeing the pain." Agnolo di Tura del Grasso, known as Agnolo the Fat, wrote these words in Siena, Italy, when the plague struck in 1348. Diseases had come and gone before, but no one had witnessed the scale of devastation that followed as the bubonic plague, or "Black Death," swept through the city. According to Agnolo, people's armpits and groins would swell and blacken causing much pain; for most, death followed swiftly. ▶▶

In the wake of such death, traditions and families broke apart. Husbands and wives abandoned each other; work remained undone, the living stole from the dead and dying. There was no time for proper funerals, and great pits were dug and piled deep with the dead. To the horror of the living, many of the graves were too shallow, and dogs dug up the corpses, dragging remains through the streets.

Agnolo watched his five children die of the disease, and he dug their graves himself, trying to save their bodies from the common graves that sprang up everywhere in the city. The distraught father wrote: "There was no one who wept for any death, for all awaited death." But Agnolo the Fat did not die; he served as the witness of his city's devastation when the plague subsided. The city was almost empty, and the survivors gave themselves over to pleasure. Even monks and nuns who had survived devoted themselves to love, drink, and gambling, for there seemed no reason to maintain the old ways—the old world seemed to have come to an end.

Agnolo's experience was multiplied all over Europe. The fourteenth century brought so many disasters—famine, plague, revolts, warfare, and religious turmoil—that the medieval order that had seemed so perfected and entrenched was swept away. At the end of the century, the survivors would move the West in exciting new directions. However, that rebirth would come only after a century and a half of suffering, death and destruction. ◄◄

ECONOMIC AND SOCIAL MISERY

The growth of European society stemmed mostly from agricultural innovations that had generated the boom of the eleventh century. By 1300, however, the burgeoning population began to put a strain on medieval technology. People were cultivating poorer lands, and crop yields were dwindling; on some marginal lands, farmers might harvest only three bushels for every one planted. After setting aside one bushel to plant the following year, the remainder was hardly enough to maintain a fixed population.

As the population grew, people tried to bring more and more lands into cultivation to make up for the scarcities, and this often resulted in plowing the common fields on which villagers grazed their animals. Unable to feed their livestock, people were forced to kill many of their animals—from one-quarter to one-third of their animals were slaughtered. This significant reduction of livestock also reduced the amount of manure for fertilizer, and yields fell again. By the beginning of the fourteenth century, farmers faced increasing difficulties accumulating a surplus of food—and then the weather worsened.

Famine

A series of years with too much rain began in 1310; lands were drenched. Chroniclers all over Europe wrote that the rains—with unusually deafening thunder and terrible lightning—were steady from April throughout the summer. The winds and overcast skies made the whole growing season abnormally cool. The rains came when the seed had just been scattered—washing much of it away—and continued to fall through the summer, flooding the lower croplands. When farmers tried to harvest the meager crops, the rains came again. Rivers flooded, bridges were swept away, and the crops, with previously low yields, failed.

Famine began in 1315 and, in some parts of Europe, lasted until 1322. During these years, cold winters followed by cool and extraordinarily wet summers brought disastrous harvests. Aching hunger drove peasants from their lands in search of food, and according to some reports, starving farmers at times even resorted to cannibalism. Still, the disasters of this century were only beginning. Many who did not starve suffered from malnutrition and were susceptible to infection. Respiratory illnesses and intestinal ailments reached epidemic proportions in this century, but an even greater threat appeared.

The Black Death: A Pandemic Strikes

In the fourteenth century, a horrible pandemic swept in from the east and devastated Europe. The disease spread over vast areas, helped by increased trade from ships moving through the Mediterranean and by the expansion of the Mongol Empire. There is general agreement that the plague arrived in Europe in about 1348 on ships of Genoese merchants who traveled between Sicily and the Middle East, but the historical consensus about this pandemic ends here. What was this terrifying disease that people in the Middle Ages called the **Black Death?**

Medieval descriptions of the disease cause most historians to identify it as bubonic plague, caused by a virulent bacterium (*Yersinia pesta*) that infected rodents in Manchuria, then spread to black rats. As we saw in Chapter 1, some of the most devastating diseases have been those that move from animals to humans, and this rodent disease was

The disease

passed to humans from the bites of infected fleas. Bubonic plague can also reach a person's lungs, becoming pneumonic plague, which spreads rapidly through sneezing and coughing. Estimates are that between 30 and 70 percent of people who catch bubonic plague die, but almost 100 percent of those with pneumonic plague die.

In modern times, bubonic plague does not spread quickly, which causes some historians to question whether it was indeed the Black Death that brought such destruction. Some argue that this virulent form spread quickly to the lungs, becoming the deadly pneumonic form. Others suggest that several diseases—like smallpox—might have joined bubonic plague in sweeping through a population already weakened from famine. However, recent DNA studies confirm the presence of *Yersinia pestis* in plague cemeteries; so, although other diseases may have joined forces with the plague in killing a weakened population, the Black Death did cause the devastation.

Whatever the exact disease, the pandemic raced through Europe. It spread quickly in the summer and declined in the winter months—the cold, wet summers helped the plague spread. The pandemic killed a shocking one-third to one-half of the population, but historians are uncertain of the

The impact

exact numbers of the dead. Modern estimates agree that one-third of the population died, but they disagree on what that fraction means in actual numbers—estimates range from 20,000,000 to 35,000,000 dead. Disease hit the crowded cities hardest: Paris may have lost half its population and Florence as much as four-fifths. These staggering numbers mean that everyone—especially in the cities where death rates were highest—saw neighbors, friends, and family members die. The psychological impact of so great a plague was perhaps even more important than the actual loss of life. Law and tradition broke down, and many survivors saw no point in trying to preserve medieval customs.

At the time, people did not realize that the disease was caused by bacteria and transmitted by fleas. Theories of the Black Death's etiology ranged from punishment by God to "bad air." Victims could expect only traditional treatments from physicians, who applied leeches, used on previous patients, to remove excessive blood—a lethal practice that is equivalent to sharing needles between patients who have a blood-borne disease.

→ connect to today ←

Pandemic

The Black Death pandemic severely disrupted society and ushered out the medieval order. What are some recent instances in which pandemics have disrupted (or have threatened to disrupt) societies, and how have people responded to such frightening diseases?

As medicine failed to offer solace for this horrifying disease, many could only conclude that God's wrath brought the devastation. Responding to this notion, some people resorted to extreme measures to try to bring God's aid against the plague. One group—the flagellants—thought that by inflicting pain on themselves, they could

Flagellants

ask God to relieve the suffering of others. Flagellants beat themselves three times a day with leather thongs tipped in lead. They marched from town to town "splashing the church walls with their blood," according to contemporary witnesses. This movement reflected the desperation of people searching for ways to appease a seemingly angry God.

In their fear, some people turned against their neighbors, and in many cities, Jews were accused of bringing the plague by poisoning wells. The persecutions fell particularly heavily on Jewish communities in Germany because periodically throughout the thirteenth century, the English and French kings had forced Jews out of their lands and many had moved eastward. Because there was a larger presence of Jews in Germany, their Christian neighbors used them as a focus of their fears. A contemporary chronicler (Jacob von Konigshofen) described a pogrom in Strasbourg that killed thousands of Jews accused of causing the plague: "On Saturday . . . they burnt the Jews on a wooden platform in their cemetery. There were about two thousand people of them. Many small children

Attacking Jews

were taken out of the fire and baptized against the will of their fathers and mothers." In a practical aside, Jacob noted that the persecutors also had money on their minds, because they confiscated the property of the Jews: "The money was indeed the thing that killed the Jews. If they had been poor and if the feudal lords had not been in debt to them, they would not have been burnt."

In spite of the foolishness of blaming people who were also dying from the plague, anti-Jewish persecutions spread. More than sixty major Jewish communities in Germany had been destroyed by 1351. Many Jews fled to eastern Europe—to Russia and Poland—where they received protection, and slowly many Jewish communities moved their homes even farther east. Popes would later condemn this irrational persecution.

The plague continued to ravage Europe in waves into the seventeenth and even early eighteenth centuries. These subsequent visitations of the disease also took a large toll on the population. It seems that the plague finally abated

FLAGELLANTS, fifteenth century Many people of the time believed that the plague was caused by the wrath of an angry God. Flagellants—individuals who beat themselves—tried to appease God by staging ritual parades of self-punishment.

when the larger, meaner Norwegian brown rat (today's urban rat) displaced the European black rats. The brown rats had thicker fur, which resisted the flea bites of the black rat fleas, so the bacterium that caused the disease slowly lost its host pool. Even though the disease eventually disappeared, it left a legacy of fear and despair that haunted Europe for centuries.

Peasants and Townspeople Revolt

As an immediate result of the plague, the European countryside suffered a disabling shortage of labor. Desperate lords tried to increase their customary—and already excessive—labor requirements in an effort to farm their lands. Free laborers, detecting an opportunity, began to demand higher wages, prompting some countries to pass laws freezing earnings. This policy enraged peasants across Europe. Determined to resist, they roamed the countryside, burning manor houses and slaughtering the occupants.

In some of these uprisings, popular preachers arose as leaders who combined social reform with religious hopes. Living in an age crippled by plague and famine, many believed that these "times of troubles" presaged a better world in which Christ would return. The most famous of

John Ball

these preachers was John Ball of England, who rallied listeners by calling for the overthrow of the social order. His most famous couplet attacked the very hierarchical privilege that had marked the three orders of medieval society. He said simply: "When Adam delved and Eve span, where then were all the gentlemen?" When Adam and Eve lived in the Garden of Eden, both worked the soil and no one was a noble "gentleman."

In the ensuing revolt, the peasants had the support of well-armed and disciplined soldiers who had been trained to defend the English coast. The rebels blamed the king's advisors and the local nobility for their misery. Their loyalty to the king made no difference in the outcome—the king joined in repressing the revolt.

French peasants, too, rose up against their lords, in a revolt called the **Jacquerie.** French chroniclers told in horror of peasants storming manor houses and brutally killing noblemen and their families. English peasants burned houses of aristocrats, lawyers, and government officials, at times burning the records that they believed contributed to their oppression. However, the peasants in all regions could not hold out for long against the aristocracy and its superior arms. Eventually, all the revolts were suppressed, with many peasants and their leaders massacred. Yet the violence, the labor shortages, and the prevailing belief that things were changing had begun to erode the old medieval manorial system. Over time, peasants who owed only rent gradually replaced serfs who had owed labor as well as rent. For these new peasants, their labor was now their own, giving them more freedom and opportunities to work for their own profit. Although the condition of many peasants improved, the trend was not uniform throughout Europe. The situation of peasants in western Europe

PEASANTS' REVOLT, 1381 The English preacher John Ball, shown on horseback, led peasants and knights in a revolt for better conditions for the peasantry. Although the uprising failed, rural conditions nevertheless improved.

improved more quickly than that of those in eastern Europe.

The unrest was not limited to the countryside. As population dropped, the declining demand for goods led to falling prices, and some industries suffered. Merchants and manufacturers responded by trying to limit competition and reduce the freedoms of the lower classes in the towns. **Urban revolts** Revolts broke out in many towns throughout Europe. In addition to Douai, violence erupted in Ghent, Rouen, and Florence. (This last was the famous Ciompi revolt in 1378—named for the wooden shoes worn by wool workers who rioted.) While some of these revolts led to short-term gains, most were crushed. Improvements for urban workers would eventually come with the labor shortages caused by the high death rates. But the rural and urban revolts of the fourteenth century set off social conflicts that periodically resurfaced throughout Western history.

IMPERIAL PAPACY BESIEGED

Throughout these troubled times, many medieval men and women looked to the church, especially the papacy, to guide them. Yet the popes were grappling with their own problems, and these very troubles undermined people's confidence in the church. Early in the fourteenth century, the issue of the relative sovereignty of kings and popes resurfaced once more over the taxation of church lands and the clergy's claim to immunity from royal courts. This time, the French king proved stronger than the popes. In the course of this dispute, the French king, Philip IV (r. 1285–1314), ordered his troops to arrest Pope Boniface VIII (r. 1294–1303). Although the elderly pope was quickly freed by his supporters, he died soon afterward as a result of the rough treatment. Unlike Henry II of England after the death of Becket (described in Chapter 8), Philip IV was able to capitalize on the violence against the church. He brought pressure on the college of cardinals—which had elected popes since 1059—and they elected his favored French cardinal as pope.

Cannibalism in the French Countryside

In 1358, French peasants rose up in an angry revolt against the nobility. The chronicler Froissart (1337–1410) describes the event.

One of them got up and said that the nobility of France, knights and squires, were disgracing and betraying the realm and that it would be a good thing if they were all destroyed. At this they all shouted: "He's right! He's right! Shame on any man who saves the gentry from being wiped out!" They banded together and went off, without further deliberation and unarmed except for pikes and knives, to the house of a knight who lived nearby. They broke in and killed the knight, with his lady and his children, big and small, and set fire to the house. Next they went to another castle and did much worse; for, having seized the knight and bound him securely to a post, several of them violated his wife and daughter before his eyes. Then they killed the wife, who was pregnant, and the daughter and all the other children, and finally put the knight to death with great cruelty and burned and razed the castle. . . . But, among other brutal excesses, they killed a knight, put him on a spit, and turned him at the fire and roasted him before the lady and her children. After about a dozen of them had violated the lady, they tried to force her and the children to eat the knight's flesh before putting them cruelly to death.

What does the particularly violent aspect of this revolt tell you about the breakdown of society in the fourteenth century? How do you think readers reacted to the account?

Popes Move to Avignon

Philip expected this pope to support French interests, and to forward this aim, the king persuaded the pope to rule from Avignon, on the east bank of the Rhône River. Although the city was in the Holy Roman Empire, the French influence there was strong. The new pope, Clement V (r. 1304–1314), complied and set up his court in Avignon. The popes never again tried to exert authority of taxation and legal immunity over the French kings. However, the pope's absence from Rome raised serious issues. After all, the pope was the bishop of Rome and was obligated to be there to guide the faithful in his charge.

For seventy-two years after the election of Clement V, the popes ruled from Avignon—in the shadow of the French king. Many Christians objected to this **"Babylonian Captivity,"** as the Italian Petrarch (1304–1374) called it. Some people believed this shocking breach of tradition contributed to the subsequent plague, famine, and violence that accompanied the popes' residence in Avignon, and they urged the popes to resume ruling from Rome. The Avignon popes also expanded their administration, and they streamlined and made more efficient their collection of ecclesiastical taxes because they could not depend on the income from their lands in Rome. To many people, it seemed that the church had become all too secular when the world was in desperate need of spiritual leadership.

An influential mystic, Catherine of Siena (1347–1380), felt called by God to intervene in this situation. Catherine had experienced a number of visions and was highly respected in her home city in the mountains south of Florence, in Italy. Catherine wrote a series of letters to Pope Gregory XI (r. 1370–1378) in which she urged him to return to Rome, and in 1376 she traveled to Avignon to urge him in person. He was persuaded, and in that year he tried to correct the decline in the papal prestige by returning to Rome. But the church's problems only increased.

Return to Rome

Things Get Worse: The Great Schism

Gregory XI died in Rome in 1378, and the situation was volatile. The citizens of Rome feared that the college of cardinals would choose another French pope who would return to Avignon. Indeed, the guard of the cardinals warned them that they "ran the risk of being torn in pieces" if they did not elect an Italian. The fearful cardinals elected an Italian, Pope Urban VI (r. 1378–1389). Urban almost immediately indicated his plans to reduce the French influence in the college of cardinals, and, not surprisingly, the French cardinals—claiming that the election of Urban VI was invalid because they had been coerced by the Roman mob—left Rome. The dissenting cardinals elected a Frenchman—Pope Clement VII (r. 1378–1394)—who took up residence in the papal palace in Avignon. Now there were two popes, initiating what has been called the **Great Schism** of the church. (This is not to be confused with the schism of 1054, which divided the church into the Latin west and the Greek Orthodox east. See Chapter 6.)

Many people chose to follow one pope over the other based on political rather than religious motivations, and the map on page 205 shows the respective alliances. Each pope denounced the other as the anti-Christ, and each tried to increase the revenues that now were split in half as Christians were divided in their loyalties. Many people began to criticize the church for its seeming concern for money over spiritual matters, and they advocated restoring a unified leadership to the divided Christendom. As the Black Death plundered Europe, the papacy lost its moral authority as the ruler of a united Christendom. Who could restore unity?

OPINION

What do you think most undermined the ability of the papacy to provide leadership over a unified Christian Europe?

The Conciliar Movement

Church theorists had long speculated on who might rule the church if the pope should become incompetent. Some suggested the college of cardinals would be the logical body, but the college was split in two, so some theologians suggested that a general council of bishops might be able to restore the order and reform the abuses of the church. There was ample precedent for church councils to meet to resolve controversies, for as early as the fourth century, Emperor Constantine had called the bishops together at Nicaea (see Chapter 5). However, these new "conciliarists" wanted to convert the church to a kind of constitutional monarchy in which the power of the popes would be limited. This would be a dramatic step, but the times seemed to call for radical measures.

The first test of the **Conciliar movement** came at the Council of Pisa, convened in 1409 by cardinals of both Rome and Avignon. This council asserted its supremacy by deposing the two reigning popes and electing a new pope. Although this should have solved the problem, it only exacerbated it—the two previous popes would not step down, so now *three* popes reigned.

Finally, a second council was called. Some 400 churchmen assembled at the Council of Constance (1414–1418), which was the greatest international gathering in the Mid-

The Great Schism, 1378–1417 This map shows how countries' loyalties were divided between the competing popes in Rome and Avignon.

Map legend:
- Catholics Recognizing Pope at Rome
- Catholics Recognizing Pope at Avignon
- Areas of Shifting Obedience
- Catholics and Eastern Orthodox
- Eastern Orthodox
- Muslim
- ● Council Cities

dle Ages. This august body deposed all three of the popes and elected a Roman cardinal—Martin V (r. 1417–1431). The Great Schism was finally over and the Western church was once more united under a single head. However, never again did the popes have the power that the medieval popes had, and church councils gathered periodically to address changes in the church.

New Critics of the Church

Not surprisingly, as men and women became disenchanted with the established church, they sought new ways to approach God so as to address the pressing challenges of the age. Criticisms of the church that had been expressed periodically throughout the Middle Ages appeared with more urgency in this age of crisis. The preacher John Ball was simply one of many who offered a different view of religion, and even the dreaded inquisition could not silence the new critics.

The Englishman and Oxford theologian John Wycliffe (ca. 1320–1384) offered a serious critique that struck at the heart of the organized church. Wycliffe argued that there was no scriptural basis for papal claims of earthly power and that the Bible should be a Christian's sole authority. In the course of his writings, he attacked many of the practices of the medieval church (such as pilgrimages, the veneration of saints, and many of the rituals that had grown up over the centuries). Furthermore, Wycliffe argued that the church (and the popes in particular) should renounce earthly power, leaving it to kings. As he put it, "the pope [should] leave his worldly lordship to worldly lords." Wycliffe wanted a more simple church, led by a clergy that rejected all wealth. This would have been a major renunciation because the church was by far the greatest landlord in Europe. There was a great deal at stake.

John Wycliffe

Though Wycliffe's ideas were profoundly threatening to the established church, he had powerful protectors in the English court, who kept him unharmed until he died. Many of his followers (called **Lollards**) were condemned, but not until the early 1400s, when his ideas seemed to stimulate treasonous acts. One of the most famous proponents of some of Wycliffe's ideas was Jan Hus (ca. 1373–1415), a popular preacher and rector of the university in Prague. Hus and his followers demanded a reform of the church, and his ideas were joined to a desire for Bohemian freedom from German dominance. Hus was certain that

Jan Hus his beliefs were correct and defended them before the influential Council of Constance. However, the Czech scholar was found guilty of heresy and was burned. An eyewitness to the execution wrote that Hus died bravely with the words of the Lord's Prayer on his lips. Many Czechs remembered Hus as a martyr both to conscience and to a growing desire for Czech independence. While the council could silence Hus, it could not silence the growing numbers of voices calling for a significant transformation of the medieval church. As we will see in Chapter 11, these calls for reform would eventually be heard.

MORE DESTRUCTION: The Hundred Years' War

1337–1453

As if famine, plague, revolts, and religious controversy weren't enough, England and France entered into the **Hundred Years' War**—a century-long conflict that became the closing chapter in an age in which long-standing traditions and social contracts crumbled. The issue that triggered the conflict was the succession to the throne of France—the Capetians' good luck in producing male heirs finally ran out in 1328, when the last Capetian died. The nearest male relative was King Edward III of England, son of a Capetian king's (Philip IV) daughter (Isabel). The Parlement of Paris (the supreme court of France) claimed that a woman could not transmit a claim to the crown, so Philip VI of Valois, a first cousin of the previous ruler, became king. Edward at first did not dispute this decision, but he soon found cause to do so.

England vs. France

There were two other reasons for the two kings to clash: one was economic—urban revolts in Flanders gave Philip VI an excuse to interfere in the lucrative wool trade between England and Flanders. The Flemish asked Edward to assert his claim to the French crown so the rich trade could continue unimpeded. The second cause was feudal—the French king wanted to claim the status of liege lord over the lands in southern France held by Edward III. Edward, as a king himself, did not believe he should accept Philip as his liege lord. In response, Philip declared Edward's lands forfeit

[T]he times seemed to call for radical measures.

and Edward decided to exert his dynastic claim to be king of both England and France.

The long struggle began with some stunning English victories. The English first secured their communications across the channel with a naval victory at Sluys in 1340 (see map on page 208); they then could turn to a land invasion of **New weapons** France. Although the French outnumbered the English, the English skillfully used new tactics and new weapons to supplement their mounted knights. In their wars against the Scots in the thirteenth century, the English learned of the effectiveness of the Welsh longbow and brought archers to fight against the French cavalry. The longbow was a simple yet highly effective device that had a greater range than the crossbow and could be fired with unprecedented speed. A longbowman could loose up to ten arrows a minute, compared with the crossbowman's two.

The English armies also took advantage of the pike—a weapon developed in Switzerland and used to good effect against the mounted armies of the Holy Roman Emperor. Foot soldiers wielded the long spears and braced them on the ground to fend off the charge of mounted knights. Some English foot soldiers brought pikes to France to support England's horsemen, who were outnumbered by the French cavalry.

While longbows and pikes challenged the ascendancy of mounted knights, their obsolescence was sealed with the spread of gunpowder from China. Iron shot appeared in England as early as 1346 and Italy in 1341, but the powder was unstable and did not explode immediately. Throughout the war, desperate soldiers used new (and frequently unreliable) guns to bring down knights, and equally desperate armorers tried to make plate armor stronger and curved so that it could deflect bullets. However, the mounted knights simply grew too expensive and ineffective for the new warfare; the future lay with the infantry.

The English, led by Edward III, forged across the channel to confront the superior force of French mounted knights. Edward brought a strong infantry, loud guns, and lethal longbows, which eyewitness accounts of the Battle of Crécy in **English victories** 1346 described as blackening the sky with English arrows. By the end of the battle, the flower of French knighthood lay crushed, which struck a blow against feudalism itself when "those who fought" lost. In this victory, the English had secured Flanders and the important port of Calais. The strategy was repeated at Poitiers in 1356, and the exhausted French were forced to sue for peace (the Peace of Bretigny) in 1360. By the terms of this peace, King Edward renounced his claim to the French throne in exchange for Calais and enlarged holdings in Aquitaine.

The French were not willing to allow so much of their land to remain in English hands, so the war was reopened in 1369 under the French king Charles V (r. 1364–1380).

Peasant English longbowmen defeated mounted French knights in a shocking blow to noble privilege. The new bows they wielded were fearsome weapons: 6-foot bow staff made of yew wood that could fire up to ten yard-long arrows a minute, darkening the sky with a lethal rain of missiles from a range of 200 yards. Modern rifles have a longer effective range: 440 yards for the M1 rifle; 550 yards for the M16. From the fourteenth century onward, warfare is about shooting the enemy from farther and farther away. Today, in the twenty-first century, the use of drones—or unmanned aircraft—to fire on targets has stirred ethical debate, as they often kill innocent civilians during their attacks from high above.

He introduced a wise strategy of avoiding major military confrontation and, instead, wearing down the English forces on the Continent. During this phase of the war, soldiers on both sides devastated the countryside, plundering villages and ruining crops and vineyards. This sort of civilian destruction contributed to the misery of the fourteenth century.

Edward III died in 1377, and Charles V in 1380. At this point, the English had almost been pushed out of France—they held only Calais and a small strip of land between Bordeaux and Bayonne. At first no formal peace was signed, but in 1396 a long truce ended this phase of the Hundred Years' War, and the monarchs turned their attention to internal affairs for a while.

Henry V (r. 1413–1422), who succeeded to the English throne in 1413, was an able soldier, eager to reopen the long-suspended war against France. His timing was good, because the powerful duke of Burgundy had used the turmoil to increase his own land at the expense of the French kings (see map on page 208). The Burgundians leapt into the fray on the side of the English, and with this new ally, Henry reasserted his claims to the French throne. In August 1415, he landed in Normandy with a substantial force of knights and about 6,000 archers, but his men were soon exhausted by casualties and dysentery. The bold king heard that the French army was marching against him, and he had to prepare for battle. Henry chose a troop formation in which the flanks were protected by gardens and orchards of two villages, and he arranged his men forming solid blocks flanked by the archers. The French knights repeated the same tactics that had failed at Poitiers in 1356—a small body of dismounted men-at-arms took the center, followed by mounted knights and supported by crossbowmen, who were placed too far back to be useful. The English slaughtered the French knights in great numbers.

Agincourt

The French king was forced to sue for peace and declare his heir (called the **Dauphin**) illegitimate. England got direct control of northern France as far south as the Loire River and the promise that Henry's son would inherit the throne of France. For all practical purposes, France was defeated. The Dauphin could not accept these terms, but he seemed unable to rally any systematic resistance. In 1428, the English laid siege to Orléans, and its fall would have ensured English control of all the lands north of the Loire River. It seemed it would take a miracle to restore the French monarchy, and many people believed they got one.

PILLAGING SOLDIERS This illustration of rampaging soldiers during the Hundred Years' War shows them searching for valuables in a home and carrying them off. The war and its attendant plunder contributed to the woes of a society already beset by famine, plague, revolts, and religious controversy.

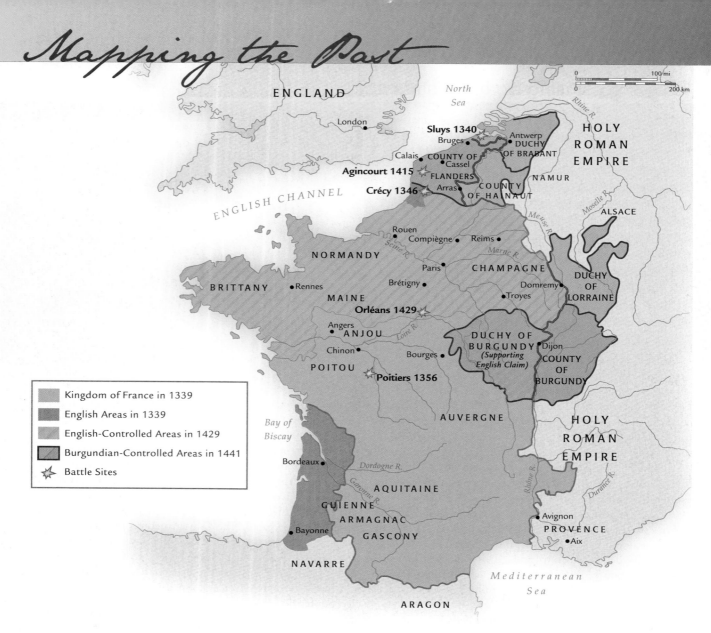

The Hundred Years' War, 1337–1453

This map illustrates the Hundred Years' War between England and France. It shows that the major battle sites and areas of combat were in the north, even though the English claims in France lay in the south. Why do you think the location of Orléans (along the Loire River), where Joan of Arc made her decisive victory, proved to be strategically significant?

Joan of Arc

During these darkest days of France, a young peasant girl—Joan of Arc (1412–1431)—believed she saw visions in which angels urged her to lead the French troops to victory. She persuaded the Dauphin of the authenticity of her mission, and he gave her command of an army. Joan donned armor and almost miraculously stirred the determination of France's armies and lifted the siege at Orléans. Some accounts attribute her success to a skill in placing artillery, the new weapon of warfare. After this victory, she escorted the Dauphin to Reims—the city where French kings were traditionally crowned—where he received the crown of France, thus renouncing the previous treaty. The French embraced the cause of their new king and the new national spirit seemed to revitalize the French armies. They rallied, and by 1453 only Calais was left in English hands.

However, Joan did not live to see the victory. She was captured in 1431 by the Burgundians, who turned her over to their English allies, who put her on trial for witchcraft and her—

Joan executed

esy. The Dauphin did not try to intervene, and his champion was put on trial. The record of her trial provides a fascinating glimpse into the experience of this extraordinary woman. She repeatedly restated her conviction that her voices were from God and that she was following a just cause. Ultimately, she refused to abandon her men's clothing and acknowledge that she had been wrong, so she was condemned to be burned at the stake. The French honored Joan of Arc as a savior of France, and in 1920 she was declared a saint of the Catholic Church.

Results of the War

The new weaponry that was used during the Hundred Years' War set European armies on a new course. Indeed, the weaponry and violence against civilians have caused many scholars to call this the first modern war. The feudal system that demanded knights' military service began to break down, and lords increasingly accepted money (called scutage) instead of military service. Now lords could hire professional armies—called **free companies** because they had no feudal ties and sold their services to the highest bidder—which were becoming more effective than traditional knights. (The knights continued to fight in their beloved tournaments long after they were less welcome on the battlefields.) Many kings had repeated difficulties paying their free companies, and soldiers ravaged the countryside in lieu of their pay. Under these pressures, the deterioration of the feudal system accelerated into what is sometimes called bastard feudalism, in which the old ties of loyalty were replaced with cash payments. Nobles, like kings, simply hired soldiers, dressed them in elaborate uniforms sporting the special colors of the noble families, and created their own private armies.

As a result of the Hundred Years' War, the English were expelled from French soil; the French king emerged more powerful than all his vassals, and the slow consolidation of royal rule was effectively complete. The monarchy had a permanent army, a strong tax base, and a great deal of prestige among people who were coming to see themselves as "French."

England had a longer struggle after its loss in the war. England's monarchy was seriously weakened as Parliament took more control of the purse strings after the wartime excesses. During the turmoil, the Lancaster and York families | **Wars of the Roses** | unleashed a civil war as they competed for the throne. Each family had a different color rose as its emblem, so this sporadic conflict was called the Wars of the Roses (1455–1485). The fighting perpetuated the worst aspects of

> Philosophers, writers, and artists, too, produced works that dramatically changed the direction of Western thought.

feudal life as it degenerated into local skirmishes orchestrated by the nobility. The situation was made worse by mercenary soldiers unemployed after the end of the Hundred Years' War, who returned to England and sold their services to feuding families. Many old noble families were decimated in the course of this war.

Richard III (r. 1483–1485) took the throne from his 12-year-old nephew, Edward V, and had the young king and his brother imprisoned in the Tower of London, where they were murdered. This long-remembered act of cruelty stimulated a final resistance. Nobles rallied to the banner of Henry Tudor, a Lancastrian, and he finally vanquished Richard III at the Battle of Bosworth Field in 1485. He was crowned Henry VII (r. 1485–1509). To try to heal the breach between the noble factions, he married Elizabeth of York; at last the civil war was officially ended, but Henry needed all his skill to restore solid centralized control. He confiscated the lands of rebellious nobles and prohibited private armies. At the end of his reign, England was strengthened; and by the time of his granddaughter's rule, it was poised to expand beyond the seas (see Chapter 12).

RESPONSES TO THE DISRUPTION OF MEDIEVAL ORDER

As war and revolt have shown, one of the ways people responded to the fourteenth-century disasters was to consider new approaches to old problems. Wycliffe and Hus questioned church practices; Edward III of England thought of new battle strategies to confront French knights. These are only three of many famous and anonymous people who changed their world with creative new ideas. Philosophers, writers, and artists, too, produced works that dramatically changed the direction of Western thought.

William of Ockham Reconsiders Scholasticism

Within a century after Thomas Aquinas's synthesis (described in Chapter 8), a new breed of thinkers challenged the premises of scholasticism and questioned the

DOMENICO DI MICHELINO, *DANTE AND HIS POEM, THE DIVINE COMEDY* This illustration of the Italian poet Dante's famous *Divine Comedy* was painted on the walls of Florence's cathedral. In addition to depicting Dante, it shows hell (on the left), a mountain of purgatory, and a celestial heaven.

ties between faith and reason. William of Ockham (ca. 1285–1349) was the most prominent of these thinkers. Scholasticism was based on the idea that thinkers could extract general truths (or universals) from individual cases. Ockham was an English philosopher who argued that universals had no connection with reality, and this philosophy was called New Nominalism. (Ockham used **nominalism,** derived from the Latin word for "name," because he said that universals, or categories, were only convenient names for things.) New Nominalists believed that it was impossible to know God or prove his existence through reason—because God was all-powerful, he did not have to act logically.

So what should philosophers do? Ockham's studies spawned a decline in abstract logic, but a rise in interest in scientific observation that would bear much fruit in later generations. Ockham also discovered a fundamental principle that remained the basis of much scientific analysis. Called **Ockham's razor,** this principle says that between alternative explanations for the same phenomenon, the simpler is always to be preferred. People who have studied the material world ever since have looked to simple, elegant explanations to satisfy Ockham's razor. New Nominalism became popular in universities, and Ockhamite philosophy became known as the *via moderna* (modern way). Indeed, intellectuals were beginning to reject the old and look at the world in a new way.

New Literary Giants

In the fourteenth century, more authors began to write in the vernacular, their national languages, instead of Latin, which had been the language of great literature throughout the Middle Ages. (Latin still remained the language of the church and of official government documents.) In the Middle Ages, romances and other poetry had been written in the vernacular, but in fourteenth-century Italy in particular, a new kind of literature emerged that explored people's place in the world. Italian poets from Tuscany made Italian a literary language and composed some of the greatest literature of all time.

The first of these writers was Dante Alighieri (1265–1321), who was born in Florence. In 1302, he became embroiled in the turbulent political situation of his city and was exiled. He always hoped to return to his beloved city but never succeeded, and he grew to be a bitter, disillusioned man wandering from city to city until he died in 1321.

Dante

While in exile, he composed his masterpiece, now called the *Divine Comedy*. The work became so popular that a century after his death, Florence recognized his genius and commissioned the painting shown on page 210 to honor the man they had exiled.

The *Divine Comedy* is a magnificent allegory of a soul's journey through despair to salvation. The lengthy work is divided into three sections—Hell, Purgatory, and Paradise—and the poet journeys through them all. He is first led through Hell by Virgil, the Roman poet whose works still formed the basis of a good education. Dante described the punishments of the damned in gruesome detail: In one location he saw "long lines of people in a river of excrement that seemed the overflow of the world's latrines," and in these pits Dante placed his contemporaries (as well as historical figures) who deserved punishment. Dante then leaves Hell and climbs the mountain of Purgatory, where sinners who would ultimately be saved were doing penance for their sins. Finally, Dante was led into Paradise by a mysterious woman—Beatrice—who was reputed to be the love of the poet's life.

Some scholars consider the *Divine Comedy* a perfect medieval work: It incorporates Aquinas's theology and Aristotle's science, and the whole work has the complexity

Illumination from a Book of Hours

fifteenth century

This painting in a prayer book imagines a peaceful world with a well-ordered hierarchy: The castle presides under a well-ordered heaven with hardworking peasants tending flocks in a prosperous field. The artist offered the patron a vision of a world that no longer existed after the disasters of the fourteenth century. Why might an artwork of such a fantasy have been particularly satisfying in the midst of disasters, and can you think of modern examples of escapism in the face of troubles?

of a Gothic cathedral or a *Summa Theologiae* (the philosophic summaries described in Chapter 8). Other scholars see in the work something new—a departure from the medieval world that shaped the poet. Dante, after all, was a layman who presumed to express theology of salvation.

Furthermore, he articulated the growing criticism of the medieval church by placing many popes in Hell. Finally, his beloved guide through Hell and Purgatory was a classic poet—Virgil, who represented reason. His final tour through heaven was conducted by Beatrice, who was an allegory of faith. As we will see in Chapter 10, many thinkers who like Dante struggled with the despair of the age would find solace in pagan classics and faith in God's grace.

Another Florentine who had a profound impact on literature was Giovanni Boccaccio (1313–1375), who witnessed the devastating plague as it swept through his city. In his most famous work, *The Decameron,* Boccaccio offers a poignant eyewitness description of the plague, with insights into how various people responded to catastrophe, for he said some shut themselves off from **Boccaccio** everyone else, others prayed diligently in hopes of avoiding early death, and still others denied themselves nothing, "drinking and reveling incessantly from tavern to tavern." This description sets the stage for the heart of the book, in which ten young people escape to a villa outside Florence and decide to amuse themselves by telling stories. *The Decameron* is the collection of the stories they tell, and most are highly entertaining.

The stories reflect a new, permissive attitude that arose in the wake of the plague, for the stories talk frankly of sex, lies, and ordinary people. The heroes are not knights or philosophers, but clever men and women who live by their wits, and their stories were intended more to amuse than to teach moral lessons. In his later years, Boccaccio became uneasy with his lighthearted works, and in a letter written in 1373 he urged someone to not let women read his stories, warning, "You know how much in them is less than decent and opposed to modesty." However, there was no return to a more modest, conservative age—the fourteenth century had disrupted much that was traditional, and many people welcomed a new way to look at life. In these dark times, many found a lighthearted tribute to pleasure particularly satisfying.

One typical way to react to disaster is to look back longingly to a "golden age"—in this case, to an imagined tightly ordered medieval world. The image on page 211 shows one such idealized world.

One of the world's most gifted poets—the Englishman Geoffrey Chaucer (ca. 1340–1400)—also looked longingly backward. Chaucer drew from tales **Chaucer** like Boccaccio's to offer a different view of the turbulent fourteenth century. His most famous work, *The Canterbury Tales,* was written in English and tells of a group of 29 pilgrims who journey from Southwark (outside London) to Canterbury to the shrine of Thomas Becket. Like Boccaccio's youths, Chaucer's pilgrims tell tales to pass the time on their journey, but unlike Boccaccio, Chaucer draws each pilgrim vividly, with a clear personality so each stands out as an individual. The stories are varied, from knightly romances to bawdy tales, and they still delight readers today.

Chaucer's descriptions of the pilgrims offer a subtle, yet revealing, look at fourteenth-century society. He criticized corruption in the church by commenting on monks who would rather hunt than pray and friars who were not interested in the poor: "He knew the taverns well in every town. / The barmaids and innkeepers pleased his mind / Better than beggars and lepers and their kind." However, Chaucer was also a medieval man who looked back to what he imagined was a golden age when knights were virtuous crusaders, priests cared nothing for money, and scholars loved only knowledge. If that golden age ever existed, it was gone by the fourteenth century—money was rapidly becoming the measure of success, and the future belonged to bright individuals with as much character as Chaucer's pilgrims.

The disasters of the long fourteenth century had caused many to question their traditional views and values. As the ordered world they had known was crumbling, however, room was being made for new ideas and new approaches. As we will see in the next chapter, the West would take a fresh and exciting path.

> He criticized corruption in the church by commenting on monks who would rather hunt than pray and friars who were not interested in the poor[.]

EMPIRES IN THE EAST

As the West struggled with disasters that fractured the medieval order, winds of change also blew from the Far East into Europe. New empires were forming in the East that dominated the political landscapes of the regions for the next few centuries, and the West was brought into a new global relationship with lands as far away as east Asia.

Eastern Universalism: The Mongols

As early as the thirteenth century, while the West struggled between localism and centralization, dynamic conquerors swept out of Mongolia and established a new, unified

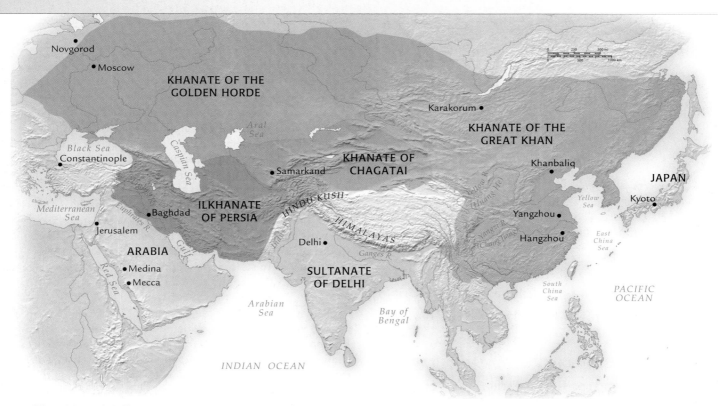

The Mongol Empire, ca. 1300 **This map shows the greatest expanse of the Mongol Empire as it extended from the Pacific Ocean to the Black Sea. The scale indicates the vast distances of the empire.**

empire extending from eastern Europe across Asia to the Pacific Ocean. In 1206, Genghis Khan (r. 1206–1227) united diverse nomadic groups and forged a formidable army that he led with consummate skill. He was an extraordinary figure who is remembered for his appalling cruelty as well as for his wisdom and talent as a leader, for after the violence of his initial conquest, he established a peaceful, tolerant rule. He implemented the first Mongol written language and promulgated the first law code for his nomadic people. His grandson, Kublai Khan (r. 1260–1294), was an equally powerful ruler, whose wealthy empire, centered in China, offered a tantalizing lure to travelers from the West.

The map above shows the remarkable extent of the Mongol Empire in about 1300—from China and Korea in the east to Moscow and Ukraine in

Mongol Empire

the west. The rulers of the Scandinavian/Slavic state centered in Kiev had already moved their capital to the far north in Novgorod, and this Russian state had to pay tribute to the Mongol Empire to its south. This empire encompassed an extraordinary diversity of peoples and religions—from Muslims to Christians to Buddhists—and it accommodated them seemingly without conflict. The popes were eager to convert the Mongols to Christianity and sent missionaries to China.

This unified empire also created a huge trade area through which goods and ideas traveled easily. It is likely that Europeans learned the recipe for gunpowder from travelers through the Mongol Empire. As we saw in Chapter 8, the Venetians in particular were well placed to take

VENETIAN TRADERS With the rise of the Mongol Empire came the facilitation of trade across the old Silk Road. Venetians such as Marco Polo and his family were well placed to take advantage of this lucrative business. Here, Venetian merchants trade cloth for spices.

A Franciscan Missionary Goes to China

John of Monte Corvino (1247–1328) was a Franciscan priest sent to convert the Mongols in China (called Cathay here). He wrote this letter in January 1305.

I proceeded on my further journey and made my way to Cathay, the realm of the Emperor of the Tartars who is called the Great Khan. To him I presented the letter of our lord the Pope, and invited him to adopt the Catholic Faith of our Lord Jesus Christ, but he had grown too old in idolatry. However he bestows many kindnesses upon the Christians, and these two years past I am abiding with him. . . .

I have myself grown old and grey, more with toil and trouble than with years; for I am not more than fifty-eight. I have got a competent knowledge of the language and character which is most generally used by the Tartars. And I have already translated into that language and character the New Testament and the Psalter, and have caused them to be written out in the fairest penmanship they have; and so by writing, reading, and preaching, I bear open and public testimony to the Law of Christ. . . .

What strategies did John use to convert the Mongols, and how effective do you think these strategies might have been?

advantage of this trade. By the fourteenth century, the Venetians had established many trading posts where they could engage in a lucrative commerce.

Certainly the most famous western Europeans who took advantage of the Venetian experience in trade were the Venetians Marco Polo (1254–1324) and his father and uncle, who traveled to the far reaches of the Mongol Empire. During several trading journeys, the Polos traveled all the way to the court of the great Kublai Khan in Khanbaliq. The journey took them three and a half years by horseback. The Polos stayed at the khan's court for seventeen years, and Marco apparently served as an emissary of the khan himself. When the Polos returned home to Venice, they brought back a wealth of spices, silks, and other luxurious curiosities. The extravagant items were so impressive that other merchants followed; by 1300 there was even a community of Italians living in China.

Marco Polo

Perhaps Marco Polo's most important contribution was a book about his voyages, which has been translated into English as *The Travels of Marco Polo*. His writings told of things that people in the West found unbelievable. For example, the merchants found it extraordinary that the Chinese used paper money; as Marco wrote: "The coinage of this paper money is authenticated with as much form and ceremony as if it were actually of pure gold and silver." Even more astonishing, Marco described "a sort of black stone, which they dig out of the mountains. When lighted it burns like charcoal." The Chinese had been burning coal since about 100 B.C.E., but in the West such a feat seemed implausible. Few people believed the exotic tales of the traveler, but the book did excite the imaginations of adventurers. It fueled the great age of exploration that followed—Christopher Columbus carried a well-marked copy of the book through his voyages.

The Ottoman Empire
1300–1566

The political situation in eastern Europe changed permanently with the establishment of a new empire at its borders. In the thirteenth century, a group of Asiatic nomads (later called Ottoman Turks) migrated westward from the expansive Asian steppes. Along the way, they converted to Islam and brought new vigor to Muslim expansion. The Turks were ruled by sultans, who were supposedly the successors of Muhammad and therefore empowered to interpret Muslim law. In this way, the sultans drew on seven hundred years of history to legitimize their authority.

As the map on page 215 shows, the Ottoman Turks expanded slowly but steadily around the eastern Mediterranean. As they moved through the Balkans, the con-

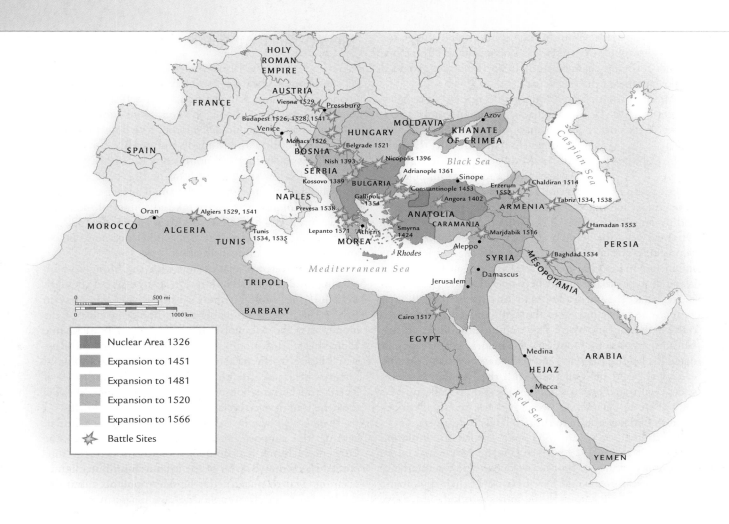

The Ottoman Empire, 1300–1566 This map shows the spread of the Ottoman Empire and identifies the major battles that marked its expansion.

Map legend:
- Nuclear Area 1326
- Expansion to 1451
- Expansion to 1481
- Expansion to 1520
- Expansion to 1566
- ✦ Battle Sites

querors added to the diversity of the region's population. Even before the arrival of Muslim conquerors, the Balkans had been divided by culture and religion. Some countries, among them Hungary, were Catholic and used the Latin alphabet. Others, such as Serbia, were Greek Orthodox and used a Cyrillic alphabet. The Muslim invaders brought a new religion and a new alphabet into the already culturally diverse region, thus setting the stage for problems that would continue into the twenty-first century.

The Ottoman expansion was powered by a formidable military at whose heart was an elite force called the janissaries. The janissaries were slaves who had been raised from boyhood and trained to fight for the sultan. As the Turks took over the Balkans, they forced the occupied peoples to pay a tribute of boys. These youths would be enslaved, converted to Islam, and trained to fight using the latest weapons, including artillery and guns.

By 1355, the Ottomans had effectively surrounded the Byzantine Empire, which had stood for so long as a powerful state and a buffer for the West. Finally, a powerful sultan, Mehmed II (r. 1451–1481), committed his government to a policy of conquest.

Conquest of Constantinople

The sultan turned to new technology to breach the walls surrounding Constantinople; he commissioned a gunner to craft an oversized cannon and smelted smaller weapons for the metal. The barrel, 26 feet long, could launch a stone ball weighing more than 1,000 pounds. Fifty yokes of oxen were needed to move the gun, and 700 men manned it. Constantinople's massive walls shook with the impact of the bombardment. The heavy stones that had provided an impregnable defense for so many centuries cracked. The city fell in 1453, and the last emperor, Constantine XI Palaeologus, died in the battle. Mehmed, now known as the "conqueror," made Constantinople his capital under the name of Istanbul, by which it is known today. (The name was not formally changed until 1930.) Mehmed extended his power around the Black Sea.

Almost a century later, the sultan Suleiman I the Magnificent (r. 1520–1566) brought the Ottoman Empire to the height of its power. As the map on page 215 shows, the Ottoman Empire extended throughout the Middle East and into North Africa. In order to secure his holdings in the eastern Mediterranean, Suleiman made the Ottomans into a major naval power. Suleiman's newly expanded navy had to confront the last Christian outpost in an otherwise Ottoman sea—the island of Rhodes, a highly fortified location held by the crusading order Knights of Saint John. The sultan lost many men in repeated assaults on the fortified island, but eventually his artillery prevailed and the knights surrendered. They were allowed to leave the island with their weapons and they moved to the island of Malta in the central Mediterranean, where they continued to fight against Muslim expansion. However, Suleiman's victory consolidated his hold in the East, and Christian merchants seeking to capitalize on the rich trade with the East found themselves confronted by the sultan's ships and tax collectors. As we will see in Chapter 12, westerners became highly motivated to find new routes to the rich lands of east Asia.

With the sea secure, Suleiman turned his attention northward, and in 1529 he even threatened Vienna, in the heartland of Europe. From now on, the new monarchies of western Europe would have to conduct their diplomatic and military escapades with the Turks in mind, and, as we will see in the next chapters, the Turkish presence posed a significant threat to the West.

Suleiman I

Russia: The Third Rome

At the beginning of the fourteenth century, Russia was divided into many principalities, each self-sufficient and independent. All of them, however, were subject to the Mongol khan of the Golden Horde, to whom they owed tribute and loyalty. The Mongols did not like the forested land of Russia, so they did not occupy it directly. Instead, they stayed in the steppes north of the Black Sea and simply collected tribute. One of the small principalities, the Duchy of Moscow, was able to take advantage of the Mongol overlords' absence to rise to a great empire. In 1322, an enterprising prince, Ivan I (r. 1328–1341), came to power and changed the political situation.

Ivan cultivated a relationship with the Mongol khan, offering loyalty and gifts. In return, Ivan received the right to collect the Mongol tribute within Russia. He grew so rich in the process (probably by withholding most of the money due the Mongols) that he earned the nickname Moneybags. This money fostered the growth of the Russian Empire in the fifteenth century, when the Mongols' fortunes declined. The khanate's hold on the territories of Russia and Ukraine loosened, and the Duchy of Moscow took the lead in overthrowing the last of Mongol rule.

Ivan I also wisely cultivated the Orthodox Church, gaining the support of that venerable institution. The Orthodox Church had flourished in Russia with the support of the Mongols, who gave the church immunity from taxation. Ivan I encouraged the Metropolitan Bishop of the Russian Church to make Moscow his permanent residence, so that city was well placed to lead the Orthodox Church when Constantinople fell in 1453.

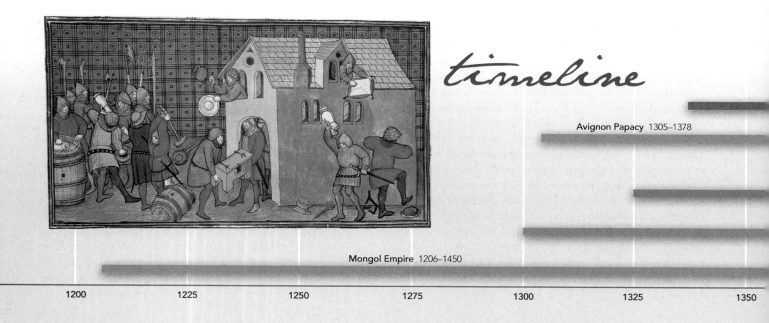

timeline

Avignon Papacy 1305–1378

Mongol Empire 1206–1450

| 1200 | 1225 | 1250 | 1275 | 1300 | 1325 | 1350 |

Ivan III ("the Great") (r. 1462–1505) pushed back the final Mongol advance on Moscow in 1480 and established himself as the first ruler of the new Russian state. Ivan had

Ivan III

married a niece of the last Byzantine emperor, so the Russian declared himself the heir to the Byzantine Empire—he proclaimed Moscow the Third Rome and took the title caesar, or tsar. The tsar strove to reestablish the greatness of the Byzantine Empire, and like the Byzantines, he closely allied with the Orthodox Church in his land. In 1589, the bishop of Moscow was proclaimed a patriarch—one of the five who presided over the eastern Orthodox Church. (See Chapter 6 for the origins of this church.) The Orthodox Church supported the tsar's claim that Moscow was the spiritual heir to Constantinople. Thus, religion and tradition supported the tsar's claim for absolute and universal authority.

OPINION

Which eastern empire that came to power by the end of the fifteenth century do you think was best poised to prosper in the subsequent years?

Russia's empire stretched from Europe into the steppes of Asia, creating what would be a long-standing question in Russia: Where does its identity lie? Is it Western, Asian, or something else? Ivan III did not resolve this question by claiming the mantle of the Byzantine Emperor, and future Russian leaders would continue the discussion as they ruled the new conservative empire that had arisen in the East.

SUMMARY

Events in the fourteenth century transformed western and eastern Europe, although in different ways. Disasters in the west broke down medieval structures, while powerful autocratic empires arose in the east. Europe and Asia confronted a new configuration of power.

- Famine, plague, and popular revolts broke down the hierarchic medieval society as people noticed that disasters were great levelers.

- The imperial papacy, too, was attacked as the bishop of Rome moved to Avignon, and the Great Schism offered two then three popes as simultaneously legitimate. Finally, church councils restored order, claiming that they, not popes, ruled Christendom.

- One hundred years of warfare between France and England destroyed the feudal relationship as mercenary armies, guns, and money dominated mounted knights.

- These disasters stimulated new intellectual movements in philosophy, literature, and art that foreshadowed new western developments.

- In the east, the Mongol Empire swept from China to the edge of Europe; the Muslim Ottoman Empire captured Constantinople and established a frightening presence in the Balkans, and the Russian Empire arose in the north.

The West was weakened by these internal and external threats, but a new spirit would arise that would move Western civilization in a striking new direction.

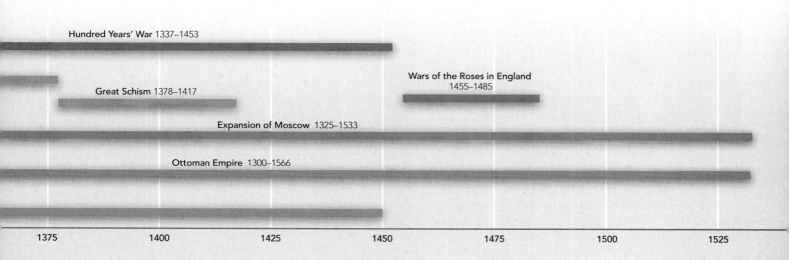

Hundred Years' War 1337–1453

Great Schism 1378–1417

Wars of the Roses in England 1455–1485

Expansion of Moscow 1325–1533

Ottoman Empire 1300–1566

| 1375 | 1400 | 1425 | 1450 | 1475 | 1500 | 1525 |

GENTILE BELLINI, *PROCESSIONS OF EUCHARIST,*

1496 This painting of a religious festival in the great St. Mark's Square of Venice shows the dynamic urban life in Italy that fostered new ideas we call the Renaissance. Pilgrims gathered to celebrate the relics of the saint while stimulating the economy of Venice.

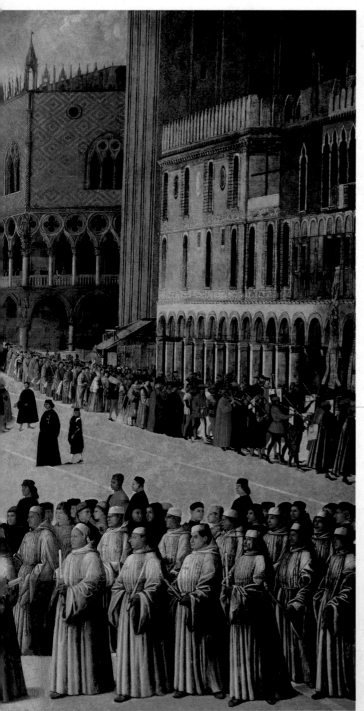

A New Spirit in the West

The Renaissance, ca. 1300–1640

10

A Shepherd Learns to Paint

Shepherds grazed flocks in the hills around the Italian city of Florence in the mid-thirteenth century, and the children stayed all day in the hills guarding the flocks. Giotto was one of these children. He was merry, intelligent, and beloved by all who knew him. Like the children in uncounted generations before him, Giotto was expected to grow up to take his father's place in the Tuscan sheepfolds. ▶▶

However, a new age was dawning in Italy at the beginning of the fourteenth century, and people's talent, not their birth, began to dictate their success. The cheerful shepherd boy would become an early forerunner of this talent-driven epoch that we have come to call the *Renaissance,* which means rebirth.

As Giotto was watching his sheep, he passed his time using bits of rock-chalk to sketch the animals on rocks; the drawings were so realistic, the sheep almost seemed alive. One day, an important painter from Florence named Cimabue walked by and recognized the boy's talent. He immediately asked Giotto's father if the boy could become an apprentice to him to learn to be a painter. His father agreed and Giotto entered Cimabue's workshop to begin learning this trade.

The young shepherd flourished under his master's tutelage, and stories arose about the youth's talent for realistic painting, as well as his independent spirit. He was said to have once painted a fly on the nose of a face that Cimabue was painting, and the fly was so lifelike that the master tried to brush it off several times before he grasped his student's joke. Giotto soon surpassed his master and began to get commissions from churches and cities all over Italy. Giotto created paintings of such realism and emotional honesty that they helped change the direction of painting.

The new spirit that arose in Italy in the fourteenth century was created by individuals with a strong sense of realism and drive, a love of the glory of ancient Greece and Rome, and a talent and confidence that fostered individual achievement. The shepherd boy Giotto was able to thrive in this world, but everyone did not benefit equally. The Renaissance brought excitement and talent to the fore, but often worsened the lot of the poor and the powerless. Nevertheless, it was an exciting, vibrant time that ushered Europe from the medieval world toward modern life. ◄◄

A NEW SPIRIT EMERGES:
Individualism, Realism, and Activism

For centuries, historians have struggled with the very idea of whether this age beginning in the fourteenth century in Italy constituted a turning point—the **Renaissance.** People living in fourteenth-century Italy themselves identified this era as characterized by a return to the sources of knowledge and standards of beauty that had created the great civilizations of classical Greece and Rome. (Classical literature, as they defined it, covered a period from about 800 B.C.E. to about 400 C.E.) Francesco Petrarch (1304–1374), an Italian writer who studied the classics and wrote poetry, was an early proponent of Renaissance ideas. Petrarch even wrote letters to ancient figures, and in one such letter to the Roman historian Livy, he wrote: "I only wish, that I had been born in your time or you in ours. . . . I have to thank you . . . because you have so often helped me forget the evils of today." Later Renaissance thinkers would follow Petrarch's example and see in ancient Greece and Rome the models to shape a new world.

Yet, they overstated their case—medieval scholars had never lost touch with the Latin texts, and no one gazing at the Gothic cathedrals and the magnificent illuminated manuscripts of the Middle Ages can doubt that medieval people had an exquisite sense of beauty. Indeed, most of the qualities that we identify with the Renaissance had existed in some form throughout the Middle Ages. For this reason, some modern scholars have suggested that the Renaissance should not be considered a separate historical era. Some see this era as part of a succession of "renaissances" that spurred the intellectual history of the West. Others argue that a different spirit clearly emerged during the period that we have come to call the Renaissance.

Medieval antecedents

In its simplest sense, the Renaissance was an age of accelerated change that began in Italy and that spread new ideas more rapidly than ever before. Many people, especially urban dwellers, questioned medieval values of hierarchy, community, and reliance on authority and replaced them with a focus on ambitious individualism and realism (both of which had to some extent existed in the Middle Ages but received new emphasis). Some no longer used the classic texts to reinforce the status quo, as had become common in the medieval universities; instead, they studied to transform themselves. As they strove for excellence, the men and women of the Renaissance ushered in a new age.

> "I only wish, that I had been born in your time or you in ours. . . ."

Thus, many historians identify the Renaissance as a unique state of mind or set of ideas about everything from art to politics. Having first sprouted in Italy in the fourteenth century, these ideas slowly spread north as the prevailing medieval culture was rocked by the disasters of the fourteenth century. Just as historians disagree about the nature of the Renaissance, they also differ on exactly why these new ideas took root in Italy. What was it about the Italian situation in the early fourteenth century that made that land ripe for fresh ideas about individualism and realism and that fostered the rise of enterprising people?

Why Italy?

Because the people of the Renaissance themselves believed the heart of their rebirth was a recovery of the spirit of classical Greece and Rome, the ancient ruins provided a continuing stimulus for such reflections. For Petrarch and other Italians, these ruins were an ever-present reminder of an age that they believed was dramatically different from their own—an age they sought to recapture.

A fresh reading of the classics certainly stimulated in some literate Italians a desire to recover a spirit of classical greatness, but were readings alone enough to change a culture's sensibilities so dramatically? Some historians argue instead that the tumultuous politics of the Italian city-states particularly favored the growth of new ideas. Incessant warfare among the states opened the door for skilled, innovative leaders to come forward. These leaders in turn surrounded themselves with talented courtiers who willingly broke from tradition to forward their own careers as they pleased their princes. A new spirit found fertile ground in these ambitious, upwardly mobile men.

Other historians point to the Black Death, which entered Italy in 1348, as the catalyst that transformed the old order (see Chapter 9). The plague's drastic reduction of the population engendered huge economic changes. Prices plummeted, and trade in luxuries such as silk, jewelry, spices, and glass quickened. Italy was ideally placed to profit from this commerce, for throughout the Middle Ages, the Italian city-states had dominated trade in the eastern Mediterranean. During the fourteenth century, individuals, families, and institutions accumulated a good deal of capital, and men and women used some of this money to support the arts. Some have vividly suggested that the Renaissance became one long shopping spree that supported the talented artists whose vision helped define this controversial era—the bridge that began to move Western history from the Middle Ages to modernity.

Plague disruptions

A Multifaceted Movement

At its core, the Renaissance emphasized and celebrated humans and their achievements. It thus revived an advocacy of individualism that the West had not seen since the time of the ancients. As the Italian writer Giovanni Pico della Mirandola (1463–1494) optimistically wrote in his *Oration on the Dignity of Man,* "Man is rightly . . . considered a great miracle and a truly marvelous creature," and in addition to this, Pico said that people could determine their own destiny. This optimistic faith in the human potential was an exciting new idea. Renaissance thinkers asserted a powerful belief in the human ability to choose right and wrong and to act on these choices.

Individualism

MICHELANGELO, *CREATION OF ADAM,* 1508–1512 Michelangelo was commissioned to paint frescoes on the ceiling of the Sistine Chapel, the pope's personal chapel in the Vatican, Rome. This famous scene depicts God shaping Adam in His image, and Adam sharing the act of creation by reaching up to meet God halfway.

Renaissance men and women also prided themselves on their accurate view of the world. This form of realism appears

Realism vividly in the art of the period. Throughout the rest of this chapter, the various examples of artwork from these centuries show a realistic portrayal of the world.

Another prevailing theme in the Renaissance came with the emergence of activism. Petrarch himself succinctly

Activism expressed the energetic spirit of the age, writing, "It is better to will the good than to know the truth." In other words, being wise was not enough; one had to exert one's will actively in the world to make a difference. Leon Battista Alberti (1404–1472) expressed the same sentiment: "Men can do all things if they will." As we see, Michelangelo's Adam in the image on page 221 participates in his own creation by reaching up to receive the spark of life, and people were encouraged to imitate this active involvement.

A secular spirit A final characteristic of this new spirit was that it was secular—that is, it did not take place in the churches, monasteries, or universities that were dominated by religious thought. That is not to say Renaissance thinkers were antireligious, for they were not—Petrarch explained quite clearly: "Christ is my God; Cicero is the prince of the language I use." While most believed deeply in God and many worked in the church, their vocation was to apply the new spirit to this world, not the next.

Renaissance thinkers felt that the spirit of the classical worlds of Greece and Rome had been reborn before their very eyes. In part, they were right. This vital new age witnessed a renewed belief in human beings' capacity to perfect themselves, to assess the world realistically, and to act vigorously to make an impact on their society. The key to this transformation was education.

Humanism: The Path to Self-Improvement

The urban dwellers of the Italian cities knew that education was the key to success. Men entering business had to be trained at least in reading, writing, and mathematics. In Florence at the beginning of the fourteenth century, the number of students enrolled in private schools testifies to the value practical Florentines placed on education:

Out of a total population of about 100,000, some 10,000 youths attended private schools to obtain a basic education. Of those, about 1,000 went to special schools to learn advanced business mathematics. However, another 500 pursued a more general liberal education. From these latter emerged an educational movement that defined and perpetuated the Renaissance spirit and changed the course of Western thought.

Petrarch departed from the traditional medieval course of study and from his father's desire that he prepare for a career in law. Instead, he pursued a general study of classical literature. The cities of Italy spawned **Humanist curriculum** many young men like Petrarch, who wanted an education separated from the church-dominated universities that had monopolized learning for centuries. Such students sought to understand the causes of human actions through the writings of the ancients and, in turn, to improve themselves. After all, if they believed they were created in God's image, they had a responsibility to cultivate their capabilities. The humanities—literature, history, and philosophy—thus formed the core of the ideal Renaissance education, which aimed to shape students so that they could excel in anything. Proponents of this teaching method were called **humanists.**

Humanists stressed grammar (particularly Latin and Greek so that students could read the classics), poetry, history, and ethics. Following the ancient Roman model, humanists capped off their education with rhetoric, the art of persuasive speaking, which prepared men to serve in a public capacity. Although this course of study may not appear revolutionary, it proved to be.

The early humanists' passion for classical texts led them to search out manuscripts that might yield even greater wisdom from the ancients. As they read and compared manuscripts, they discovered that mistakes had crept into texts that had been painstakingly copied over and over in the medieval monasteries. So the early humanists carefully pored over the many copies of texts to compile accurate versions. These techniques established standards for historical and literary criticism that continue today. Our debt to these literary scholars is incalculable as we enjoy accurate editions of works written thousands of years ago.

Urban families who prized education for their sons also expected their daughters to be educated, but not to the same degree. The eminent Italian humanist Leonardo Bruni (1374–1444) wrote an oft-quoted letter praising a humanist—but not a full—education for women. For

→ **connect to today** ←

Value Systems

Key values of the Renaissance included individualism over community, realism over faith, and activism over obedience. In what ways do you think contemporary society and culture still exhibit the values of the Renaissance?

example, he argued that rhetoric in particular was inappropriate for women: "For why exhaust a woman with the concerns of . . . [rhetoric] when she

Women humanists

will never be seen in the forum?" His comments reveal the crux of the matter: Women could be educated, but they were not to use their education in a public way, and since rhetoric was central to the humanists, educated Renaissance women were caught in a paradox.

As one example, Isotta Nogarola (1418–1466) earned much recognition from her family and some family friends for her learning. However, as soon as she tried to engage in a public dialogue (through letters), male humanists reprimanded her and deemed her immoral for her public display. She retired into the seclusion of her study, just as other women took refuge in convents to pursue their research.

Rulers, of course, were exempt from such prohibitions of public use of education, and royal women made good use of the latest Renaissance notions of study. Queens such as Elizabeth I of England (r. 1558–1603) and Isabella of Castile (r. 1474–1504) employed their education to rule effectively, support the arts, and encourage the new educational methods.

Humanists applied their skills in many areas of life. Some—called **civic humanists**—involved themselves in politics, treating the public arena as their artistic canvas. Others applied their skills at literary criticism to the Bible and other Christian texts. The most influential of these **Christian humanists** came from outside Italy. As we will see in Chapter 11, men such as the Spanish cardinal Ximénez de Cisneros (1436–1517) and the Dutchman Desiderius Erasmus (ca. 1466–1536) transformed the study of the Bible and paved the way for dramatic changes in religious sensibilities.

Humanist scholarship was crucial in shaping the new spirit of the Renaissance, but it was not sufficient in itself. Scholars and artists and talented young men would have made little impact without the generosity of patrons who supported the new talent and assiduously purchased their productions. The spirit of the Renaissance thrived on the money that flowed abundantly (albeit unevenly, as we will see) in the Italian cities.

> "For why exhaust a woman with the concerns of . . . [rhetoric] when she will never be seen in the forum?"

The Generosity of Patrons: Supporting New Ideas

The talented writers and artists of the Renaissance depended on generous patrons to support them. During the early Renaissance, cities themselves served as artistic patrons, stimulating the creation of art by offering prizes and subsidies for their talented citizens. Guilds, too, served as artistic patrons, commissioning great public monuments to enhance the spaces of their cities. The public art that graced the streets and squares enhanced the reputation of the city itself and in turn forwarded the new ideas of the gifted artists.

In time, warfare and internal strife caused cities to have less money to use in support of art, and patronage was taken over by wealthy individuals. Rulers, such as the Medici in Florence and the Sforza in Milan, used their wealth to stimulate the creation of spectacular works of art. In return, patrons gained social and political status by surrounding themselves with objects of beauty or intellect.

Not only rulers, but rising bourgeoisie as well, could enhance their social status by owning works of art, and this activity served to spur the production of art.

The church also supported the arts. Religious fraternities commissioned many paintings, and popes financially backed numerous artists. Like cities and individuals, churches gained status through their patronage, but churches also recognized a religious purpose of art. Many people attributed miraculous power to visual portrayals of religious

Religious patronage

themes, and churchmen supported this belief. For example, the Florentines customarily brought an image of the Virgin Mary (called the *Madonna of Impruneta*) down from the hills to Florence in times of crisis, and in 1483, a procession of the Madonna was credited with stopping a destructive, monthlong rainfall.

Thus, dynamic city life and a new emphasis on education stimulated new ideas, and generous patronage helped them grow. However, the new spirit spread rapidly by the late Renaissance owing to a revolutionary advance in technology.

The Invention of the Printing Press: Spreading New Ideas

Throughout the Middle Ages, precious texts had to be laboriously copied by hand, making books relatively scarce and expensive. As we saw in Chapter 1, one of the significant advantages to the growth of civilization is the ability for more people to read and have access to the written word. In Asia (China and Korea), inventors had developed a way to reproduce texts and pictures more quickly—wood-block printing. With this technique, images and some text were carved into wooden blocks and then could be mass-produced by printing. This technique had spread to the West by the late fourteenth century. By the early fifteenth century, Asian printers had replaced wooden type with bronze type, which was much more durable and offered a more consistent print. This method, too, rapidly spread to the West.

In the 1440s, these early printing techniques reached their culmination with the development of movable type and the adaptation of an oil press to print pages more rapidly. A German silversmith named Johannes Gutenberg (ca. 1400–1470) is credited with bringing all these innovations together to produce the first printed Bible in 1455. Suddenly, literature became more available, thereby ultimately affecting all of Western civilization.

The development and proliferation of the printing press were a testimony to the growing confidence that there was a market for books. In addition to a demand for their product, print shops also needed something to print on. Paper technology gave them the necessary cheap medium to replace the expensive parchment used during the Middle Ages. The technique of papermaking came to Europe from China through the Muslim world. By the fourteenth century, Italian paper mills were using old rags to make inexpensive, yet high-quality, paper. Although some wealthy patrons often preferred the more traditional parchment, the future lay with the new paper.

Printing presses spread rapidly through Europe—by the 1480s many Italian cities had established their own presses, and by 1500 there were about a thousand presses all over the continent. Previously, valuable books, painstakingly copied by hand, belonged to the patron who paid for the copy. Now the literary world looked to a broader reading public for support, consequently igniting a rapid spread of ideas that carried the new spirit throughout Europe. Subsequent notions—from the excitement of international discoveries to intellectual challenges to religious ideology—also spread rapidly. The pace of change in Western civilization quickened as the European presses circulated ideas with unprecedented speed.

All the elements were in place for the transformation of thought that we have come to know as the Renaissance. The study of classical texts had helped change people's views of themselves and their approach to the world. Money flowed in support of talented and enterprising individuals, and technology helped spread the ideas rapidly. Finally, men actively implemented these ideas in many fields, from art to business to politics.

THE POLITICS OF INDIVIDUAL EFFORT

The medieval power struggle between emperors and popes left an enormous power vacuum in northern Italy. This vacuum allowed small city-states, or cities that controlled the surrounding countryside, to become used to independence. As the fourteenth century opened, most of the northern cities were free communes with republican forms of government, but as the fourteenth century progressed, changes occurred.

The Italian City-States

These city-states engaged in almost constant warfare over their borders and commercial interests, and within the cities, classes and political factions fought for control of the government. In such unstable times, most of the republican governments were under pressure, and strong men with dictatorial power took over. As we saw in Chapter 9, mercenary armies had become a significant feature of warfare, and they also became a force in Italian politics as city-states hired army captains (called **condottieri**) with their armies to come fight their wars. These mercenaries frequently ravaged the countryside, bringing more misery than protection to the population. Through the fourteenth and fifteenth centuries, city-states would see repeated internal and external strife as they wrestled with their neighbors and with internal governing. These turbulent times brought misery to many but opportunity to others. Sometimes strong, talented individuals rose to positions of authority without constitutional or hereditary legitimacy. These rulers introduced a new kind of politics and perhaps inadvertently stimulated the new spirit of the Renaissance.

The map on page 225 shows Italy in 1454. Notice that the northern areas consisted of a patchwork quilt of city-states. Among these, Venice, Milan, and Florence were the largest and most powerful. Popes controlled the large, central strip of the peninsula, and the Kingdom of Naples dominated the south. It was the competition among the northern states that fueled the politics of individual effort that so influenced Renaissance ideas such as individualism and activism.

The Italian city-states fell into two general categories: republics and principalities. Republics featured the institutions of the medieval city communes, in which an urban elite governed. For the most part, Venice and Florence preserved the republican form of government during most of the Renaissance. Principalities, on the other hand, were ruled by one dynasty. Milan and Naples were the most notable examples of this form of government.

Florence: Birthplace of the Renaissance

Florence at the beginning of the fourteenth century was a vibrant republic where Renaissance ideas seem to have been first fostered. Florence prided itself on its republi-

Italy, in 1454 **This map shows the political divisions of Italy in the fifteenth century. It also includes the locations of the major city-states of the north. What contributed to Naples's relative isolation from the politics of the northern states, and do you think this was advantageous? Why or why not?**

can form of government, in which eligible men held office by random selection. But the city was an uneasy republic indeed, fragmented by local rivalries that always threatened to break out into violence within the urban spaces themselves. Only guild members could participate in the government, and an oligarchy of the leading families was frequently able to control it. Florence was badly hit by the plague—in 1348 alone, almost 40 percent of its population was killed, and its economy, too, was badly damaged as cloth production declined. Warfare with Milan in the early fifteenth century bankrupted many of the city's leading commercial families and created a massive public debt. In their troubles, the Florentines turned to the wealthiest banking family in Europe—the Medici. The republic got more than it bargained for.

In 1434, Cosimo de' Medici took control of the Florentine oligarchy and exiled his rivals. In the tradition of Caesar Augustus, whom he admired, Cosimo concentrated power in his household while ostensibly keeping a republican form of government. Under this shrewd family, Florence and the arts flourished. Cosimo's grandson, Lorenzo the Magnificent (r. 1469–1492), epitomized the ideal Renaissance ruler. A great statesman, he was also a patron of the arts, a poet, and an athlete.

The Medici

Yet even Lorenzo could not bring peace to the contentious Florentine people. During his life he faced intrigue and assassination attempts and had to use all his diplomatic skills to preserve Florence from foreign foes. Late in his tenure, voices began to be raised against the

Friar Savonarola Ignites a "Bonfire of the Vanities"

This diary excerpt from 1497 describes the notorious incident in which the reforming friar Savonarola (whom Landucci calls Fra Girolamo) ordered his followers—young boys—to collect Florentine artworks and burn them in the square.

27th February (the Carnival). There was made on the *Piazza de' Signori* a pile of vain things, nude statues and playing-boards, heretic books, Morganti [poems], mirrors, and many other vain things, of great value, estimated at thousands of florins. Although some lukewarm people gave trouble, throwing dead cats and other dirt upon it, the boys nevertheless set it on fire and burnt everything, for there was plenty of small brushwood. And it is to be observed that the pile was not made by children; there was a rectangular woodwork measuring more than *12 braccia* [about 23 feet] each way, which had taken the carpenters several days to make, with many workmen, so that it was necessary for many armed men to keep guard the night before, as certain lukewarm persons, specially certain young men called *Compagnacci* wanted to destroy it. . . .

What kinds of objects did the friar's followers collect, and do you think any of these might be condemned today?

Renaissance ideals that he so actively supported. Shortly after Lorenzo's death, the rule of the Medici could not withstand the growing pressures from outside and within the city.

In 1494, French armies invaded the countryside around Florence, and the city-state was again buffeted with financial and material woes. The French armies found an ally within the city in the person of a fiery preacher who had objected to the rule of the Medici and to the passionate acquisition of money and art that had dominated the early Renaissance.

Savonarola

Girolamo Savonarola (1452–1498) was a courageous, yet uncompromising, man who had resented the rule of the Medici and accused the clergy of corruption from the papacy on down. He argued vigorously against the lust for money that motivated citizens in the high-tempo Florentine economy. Perhaps most of all, he despised humanism, which he believed poisoned everything from art to religion by placing humans in the spotlight. The passionate preacher clearly recognized the changing times, but he advocated a different response to these changes.

Helped by the disruptions caused by the French invasions, Savonarola was able to arrange for the Medici to be expelled from the city and for a republic to be reintroduced. But Savonarola also wanted to return people's sensibilities to those of what he perceived to be a more pious age. He preached against nude paintings and sculptures and in 1497 presided over a public "burning of the vanities"—a huge bonfire into which people tossed ornaments, pictures, cards, and other "frivolous" items.

Eventually, the monk's zeal sparked opposition. The pope chafed at Savonarola's attacks and finally excommunicated him and forbad him to preach. Savonarola himself came to an ironic, fiery end: He was condemned and hung, and his body was burned in the public square of Florence—exactly where the "vanities" had been burned.

Like the other great figures of the age, Savonarola was a product of the Renaissance—he felt the same civic pride and shared the same love of education. But, instead of responding to these forces with a sense of humanism and realism, he looked for a spiritual reaction, a religious renewal that he believed should shape the future. In time, northern Europeans picked up Savonarola's call for religious renewal, but not yet. In Florence the Medici were restored in the sixteenth century, and the republic was formally dissolved in 1530.

At first glance, it may seem incongruous that the stormy political history of Florence spawned the creative ideas that we have come to identify with the Renaissance. However, the very environment that made people feel they had to be actively involved in their city and fight for their own interests stimulated the driving individualism that characterized this age. Politicians vied to prove themselves superior to their rivals, often by supporting artists whose products contributed to their own status. In the republican turmoil, the Renaissance was born.

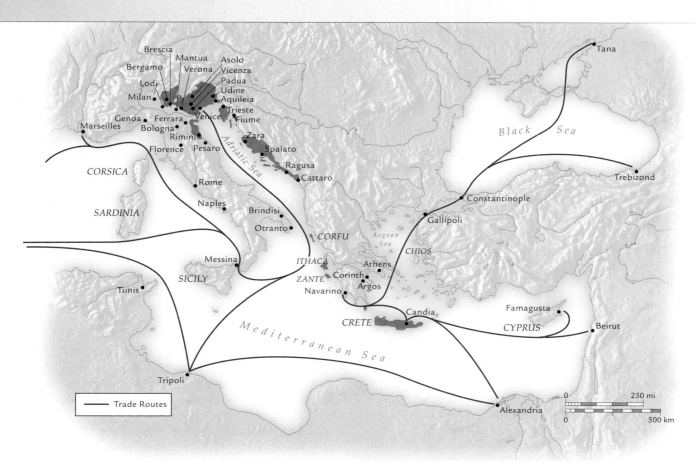

The Venetian Empire, in the fifteenth century This map shows the Venetian Empire, with the red lines indicating the main trade routes of Venice's prosperous commercial ventures.

Trade Routes

Venice: The Serene Republic?

Venice preserved its republic with much less turmoil than Florence, although there, too, an oligarchy ruled. Venice's constitution called for only its aristocratic merchant families—numbering about 2,000—to serve in its Great Council. From among this number, they chose one man to serve as the council leader, or *doge,* for life, but most men were in their 70s before being elected to this office. This rule by the elders made political life in Venice remarkably stable—indeed, the city called itself the "Most Serene Republic." This title underplayed the ever-present factional strife that plagued the Italian cities, but Venetians were able to suppress the strife, and many believed their self-proclaimed myth of serenity.

This peace also stemmed from the prosperity generated by overseas trade, which Venice dominated owing to its advantageous location on the Adriatic Sea. The map above shows how Venice's location perfectly situated it to take advantage of the lucrative trade in the eastern

Overseas trade

Mediterranean. From Venice's earliest history, it enjoyed a privileged position in the trade with Byzantium, and as we saw in Chapter 8, during the Fourth Crusade in 1204, the Venetians led in the conquest of Constantinople itself. The end of the crusader kingdoms did not end the Venetian dominance of trade, and at the beginning of the Renaissance, wealth continued to pour into the Serene Republic. To consolidate its hold on the eastern Mediterranean, Venice built an empire of coastal cities and islands—as shown on the map.

Venice was built on a collection of islands in a lagoon, and the Grand Canal that continues to mark its main thoroughfare is a perfect representation of the city's maritime orientation. Of the city-state's total population of about 150,000 people, more than 30,000 were sailors. Venice's navy boasted forty-five galleys—large warships with sails and oars—and three hundred hefty sailing ships.

In the beginning of the fifteenth century, Venice began to engage in a policy of expanding into the Italian mainland—the city-state wanted to secure its food supply as well as its overland trade routes. The map above shows the cities that became Venetian dependencies. Although this expansionist policy made sense to the Venetians, it understandably upset the neighboring states of Milan and Florence.

The Venetians perhaps should have looked more carefully at their maritime holdings, for Turkish expansion in the eastern Mediterranean (with the capture of Rhodes) seriously challenged Venetian supremacy in the seas. (See Chapter 11 for the subsequent confrontation.)

Through the Renaissance, however, this calm republic helped forward the progress of the new spirit. Its leaders wanted to grace their city with the magnificent new art, so their patronage brought talent to the fore, and their ships helped disseminate the new ideas along with the Italian trade goods.

Milan and Naples: Two Principalities

Milan's violent history mirrored that of Florence, but this city-state more quickly moved from a republican form of government to a hereditary principality. During the thirteenth century, rival political factions in the city had constantly vied for power. In desperation, the commune invited a soldier from a family named Visconti to come in and keep the peace; he stayed on to rule as prince and established a dynasty that reigned in Milan from 1278 to 1447. The Visconti family recognized the volatility of Italian politics and focused on the military strength that had brought them to power in the first place. After fending off attempts to establish a republic, the Visconti established a principality that coveted the lands of the rest of northern Italy. Only the diplomatic and military talents of Florence, Venice, and its other neighbors kept this aggressive principality in check. Finally, in 1447, the Visconti dynasty ended when the prince died without an heir—the door was open for a new power struggle in Milan.

In 1450, another strong dynasty took power. The Sforza family kept the city-state's proud military tradition, yet also served as patrons of the arts to enhance their own political reputations. The Sforza continued to rule until the early sixteenth century, though always under the pressure of growing republican aspirations.

The Kingdom of Naples in the south was the only region of Italy that preserved a feudal form of government ruled by a hereditary monarchy. In the early fourteenth century, Naples was ruled by Angevin kings who were descendants of the king of France. Under these kings, the ideas of the Renaissance came to the feudal and rural south. Giotto (the shepherd-painter whose story opened this chapter) and Boccaccio (see Chapter 9) spent time in Naples under the patronage of King Robert (r. 1309–1343), and even Petrarch called Robert "the only king of our times who has been a friend of learning and of virtue." However, after Robert's rule, Naples became a battleground with claimants from the Angevins and the Spanish Aragonese competing for the throne.

In 1435, the king of Aragon, Alfonso the Magnanimous (r. 1435–1458), was able to reunite the crowns of Naples and Sicily. He worked to centralize his administration but was unable fully to subdue his barons, and Naples remained a feudal kingdom. Alfonso was a passionate devotee of Italian culture and served as a patron of the Renaissance. However, the dynastic claims on this throne by other kings in Europe would disrupt Italian politics in years to come.

The Papal States

The Great Schism ended in 1417, when some 400 churchmen gathered at the Council of Constance and elected a Roman cardinal to be Pope Martin V. When he returned to Rome after the papal sojourn in Avignon (see Chapter 9), Martin found traditional papal lands under the control of neighboring states and the city in sad disrepair. How was he to restore papal prestige? Should he focus on spiritual or secular leadership? These were the weighty questions that confronted the new pope, and his responses would shape the history of the church.

Martin's first decision was to take political control over central Italy. As one supporter of papal rule said, "Virtue without power would be ridiculous." The map on page 225 shows the extensive Papal States, which spanned the peninsula. As rulers of central Italy, the popes had a particular advantage in that their rule was a **theocracy** that derived its legitimacy from God (and election by the college of cardinals), so issues of republicanism and tyranny did not apply. However, their religious role also brought complications. For example, as worldly rulers in the Italian tradition, they were expected to improve the fortunes of their families, so they frequently (and accurately) fell prey to the charge of nepotism as they created positions for their relatives. The popes also looked backward to their medieval struggles with the Holy Roman Emperors to control Italy (see Chapter 8), so many felt they had a right—indeed, an obligation—to expand papal lands on the peninsula. All these factors helped propel the popes into the frequently violent sphere of Italian politics. But they also leaped into the exciting, brilliant world of Renaissance creativity.

Martin V determined that the city of Rome itself should be a place of beauty and a beacon of papal power. Just as the Italian princes used art to enhance their prestige, popes began an ambitious—and expensive—building program that would underscore their authority. The culmination of this effort was the construction of the new St. Peter's Church in the later 1400s. Money flowed from all over Europe to build the new Rome, a development that angered many northern Christians.

With these contributions, the popes transformed Rome into one of Europe's major cultural centers.

To increase (or even maintain) their secular power, the popes waded into the quagmire of Italian politics, and at the end of the Renaissance, a pope was elected from an influential family—the Borgia. Like many other Renaissance princes, the Borgia pope Alexander VI (r. 1492–1503) tried to reclaim his lands from his acquisitive neighbors. Alexander also proved worldly in his personal life; gossips gleefully circulated accounts of his sexual escapades. He still upheld the tradition of Renaissance family life, however, favoring his illegitimate children by placing them in advantageous positions. The pope's warrior son, Cesare Borgia (ca. 1475–1507), seemed a candidate for uniting Italy under Alexander's authority. For his daughter Lucrezia, Alexander arranged three marriages designed to advance the family's dynastic aims. All these manipulations came to nothing, however: Alexander died suddenly, and the family's ambitions failed. The reputation of the papacy as a spiritual authority also declined.

One of the most memorable of the Renaissance popes, Julius II (r. 1503–1513) embodied the ambitious values of the times, but without the scandals that had plagued Alexander. Julius was as perfect a Renaissance ruler as Florence's Lorenzo de' Medici. A patron of the arts, he made Rome a cultural hub on a par with the greatness of Florence. He was also an experienced warrior, personally leading his armies into battle as he carried on Alexander's expansionist policies. Julius II summoned Michelangelo to Rome and commissioned him to decorate the ceiling of the Sistine Chapel (see image on page 221). Michelangelo also worked on the new St. Peter's Church in Rome that was being built at the time. Although Julius and Michelangelo had a stormy relationship, the patron helped his artist produce some of the most beautiful work of the Renaissance.

The Renaissance popes achieved their ambitious agenda: They were powerful earthly rulers living in a magnificent city. As the papacy proved to be a stronger institution than the church councils, efforts were ended to give supreme authority to bishops meeting in councils. However, over time, the popes' territorial power would under-

MELOZZO DA FORLÍ, *SIXTUS IV RECEIVES PLATINA, KEEPER OF THE VATICAN LIBRARY,* 1477 The popes were powerful patrons of the arts. This painting commemorates the founding of the Vatican library, which remains a major center of learning today.

mine papal claims of universality, as many people began to question why Italian princes should have authority over lands outside Italy. As we will see in Chapter 11, these same people would begin to criticize the popes for what some called worldly extravagance.

The Art of Diplomacy

The wars, shifting alliances, and courtly intrigue of Italian politics sparked a new interest (and expertise) in the art of diplomacy. Not since the early Byzantine state had courtiers devoted such attention to the details of successful diplomacy. States exchanged ambassadors to facilitate official communication and sent spies to maintain advantages.

The most noted writer on political skill and diplomacy was Niccolò Machiavelli (1469–1527), whose book *The Prince* still influences many modern-day political thinkers. Machiavelli recognized the danger confronting Florence in the fifteenth century as French armies threatened the independence of the city-states, and he

Machiavelli wrote to offer advice about how to survive—indeed prevail—in these turbulent times. His was an eminently practical guide that looked at politics with a cold-blooded realism that had not been seen before. For Machiavelli, the most important element for a successful ruler (the prince) was his strength of will. He insisted that while princes might appear to have such traditional virtues as charity and generosity, they could not rely on these traits to hold power. They must actually be ruthless, expedient, strong, and clever if they were to maintain their rule. As he said, "It is better for a ruler to be feared than loved."

Machiavelli's blunt description of political power articulated a striking departure from medieval political ideals. During the Middle Ages, the perfect ruler was Louis IX of France (r. 1226–1270) (described in Chapter 8), who proved so virtuous that he was made a saint. With the Renaissance, men like Cosimo de' Medici and Cesare Borgia—self-made rulers who methodically cultivated their talents and grasped power boldly—took power. Machiavelli's book captured the new statecraft and showed that realistic politics often meant a brutal disregard for ethics. Indeed, many Europeans living during the Renaissance showed a social indifference and personal immorality that we might find dismaying today.

INDIVIDUALISM AS SELF-INTEREST: Life During the Renaissance

In spite of efforts to hone their diplomatic skills to a fine art, many Italians still resorted to brute force to get what they wanted. In all the city-states, some individuals came to power by stimulating social strife among competing factions or even using violence to vanquish their rivals. Those who were struggling to better themselves politically and economically often did so at the expense of their neighbors.

Aside from offering the occasional opportunity to improve one's social position, Renaissance cities still had a clearly defined social hierarchy. The Florentines referred to these divisions as the "little people" and the "fat people." The "little people" consisted of merchants, artisans, and workers and made up about 60 percent of the population. Slaves and servants assumed even lower status, beneath the "little people." The "fat people" included well-to-do merchants and professionals and made up about 30 percent of the population. The wealthiest elite—bankers and merchants owning more than one-quarter of the city's wealth—made up only 1 percent of the population.

Whenever there is a great disparity between rich and poor in a situation of some social mobility, crime tends to run high. This was true throughout Renaissance Europe. Many people blamed wanderers for the alarming rise in crime. According-

Rising crime ing to such observers, soldiers discharged from mercenary armies, the poor fleeing poverty in cities and countryside, and other displaced persons made the highways more dangerous than ever. Italy and other states tried to control crime, but their methods were usually ineffective as well as misplaced. As in other times of rapid social change, rulers increased the regulation of social behavior. For example, in England in 1547 a new law stipulated that vagabonds be branded and enslaved for two years. The law tells us a great deal about Renaissance society's intense fear of crime and strangers.

Growing Intolerance

Renaissance governments enacted harsh legislation on people they found threatening, from prostitutes to paupers. This same impulse contributed to an increasing intolerance of other religions and cultures, as evidenced by an intensifying prejudice against Jews. In Italy, Christians passed laws against sexual relations between Christians and Jews, and authorities in Rome reputedly burned 50 Jewish prostitutes to death for having intercourse with Christian men. Laws also restricted Jews to certain parts of cities and required them to wear identifiable clothing. In some instances the clothing included colors that had been set aside for prostitutes. This cruel association left Jewish women open to ridicule, criticism, and sometimes abuse from non-Jewish neighbors.

Persecution of Jews existed during the Middle Ages—thirteenth-century kings of England and France had expelled Jews from their lands, and communities of Jews had experienced periodic violence. (As we saw in Chapter 9, Jews were subjected to particular violence in the wake of the bubonic plague.) However, increasing prejudice in the fifteenth century led to large-scale expulsions of Jewish communities from many cities and countries. Vienna began expelling Jews in 1421, and many other German cities followed. Most German Jews moved eastward into Poland and Russia, and the center of Judaism shifted from western to eastern Europe.

Ferdinand and Isabella forced all of Spain's Jews to leave in 1492, causing one of the largest movements of peoples in the era. Portugal did the same in 1497. Many Iberian Jews fled to the Muslim lands in North Africa, and some people today still trace their ancestry back to this exodus. As a result of this intolerance, western Europe lost the talents of the many Jews who had inhabited these lands for centuries.

Economic Boom Times

The new ideas of the Renaissance (both good and bad) developed against the backdrop of the fourteenth century crises but were fostered in the fifteenth century by a vigorous economic life. Individualism was stimulated by the economic potential, and excess money made the all-important patronage possible. Growing commerce and industries brought money into Italy, stimulating the local economy and allowing wealthy people to indulge their desire for beauty and comfort.

Venice shone as the greatest merchant city in the world, importing tons of cotton, silk, and spices every year and exporting woolen cloth and mounds of silver coins to pay for their imports. As the sixteenth century opened, 1.5 million pounds of spices came through Venice alone every year. Venetians did not simply rest on their commercial wealth; some enterprising citizens developed and manufactured new products—most prominently, forks and windowpane glass—that would in time sweep through the world.

By contrast, Milan and Florence were craft-industrial cities. Florence, with its 270 workshops, led the way in wool cloth making. Renaissance Italy also profited from another new industry: silk. As early as the twelfth century, travelers had smuggled silkworms into Italy from China so that Italians could begin to produce the precious fabric locally. But the industry really blossomed after the thirteenth century, when the Chinese silk loom appeared in Italy. Italians powered the looms with waterwheels and produced large amounts of silk cloth. In the fourteenth century, one city had a silk mill employing 480 spindles rapidly spinning the precious silk. By the fifteenth century, Florence boasted eighty-three workshops devoted to silk production. The wealth let Florence take part in the thriving economy generated by the cloth trade network that connected countries like Italy and the Netherlands all the way to the New World. In the wake of this prosperous trade, even a shopkeeper in Florence wrote excitedly about his first taste of sugar brought in from overseas.

Wool and silk

But the most profitable industry was banking. Throughout the Middle Ages, the development of banking and commerce had been impeded by the Christian belief in the immorality of usury, or charging interest, but enterprising merchants found ways around the prohibition. Some people offered gifts in gratitude for a loan of money, thus effectively paying back more than they borrowed. However, the easiest way to collect interest was by changing money and making a profit on the exchange rate. By the thirteenth

Banking

century, Christians all over Europe began to engage in the lucrative trade of moneylending, but it was the Italian bankers of the Renaissance who really first perfected the art of using money to make money. In the process, many raked in fortunes—for example, the rich families in Florence purchased state-guaranteed government bonds that paid over 15 percent interest. It is not surprising that the "fat people" got even "fatter" as the Renaissance rolled on.

Slavery Revived

The booming economy of the Renaissance led to new institutional oppression—the revival of slavery in Europe. Why was slavery reintroduced precisely when even serfs were being freed from their bondage? Some historians suggest that the labor shortage of the late fourteenth century caused by the bubonic plague drove people to look for fresh hands. However, this explanation is not satisfactory, because the new slaves were by and large not used in agriculture or industry. Instead, it seems that newly wealthy

ALBRECHT DÜRER, *PORTRAIT OF KATHARINA*, 1520 This etching was commissioned by a Portuguese commercial agent living in Antwerp and is silent testimony to the enslavement of peoples in the early modern period.

people trying to make their lives more comfortable looked to new sources for scarce domestic help.

Slavery had some complex facets. Renaissance families, for example, often considered slaves part of the household. One Florentine woman in 1469 wrote a letter to her husband asking him to acquire a slave girl to care for their young child or a "black boy" to become the child's playmate. Occasionally slaves bore children fathered by their owners, who sometimes raised them as legitimate heirs.

The Venetians, positioned near the eastern Mediterranean, capitalized on this trade first, dealing mostly in Muslim and Greek Orthodox slaves obtained through warfare or simply taken captive. Between 1414 and 1423, Venetian traders sold about 10,000 slaves in their markets. Most of these slaves were young girls sold into service as domestic servants. The fall of Constantinople to the Turks in 1453 (see Chapter 9) led to a decline in slaves from eastern lands, and Europeans began to look for new sources of captives. In the early fifteenth century, the Portuguese conquered the Canary Islands off the western coast of Africa, and what had been a trickle of African slaves into Europe swelled. In the following decades, Portuguese traders eager to compete with the wealthy Venetians brought some 140,000 sub-Saharan African slaves into Europe.

Sources of slaves

Many people questioned the reestablishment of slavery in Europe. The church disapproved of it, and numerous slaveowners considered it too expensive in the long run. Slavery gradually disappeared in Europe by the end of the Renaissance. However, the precedent had been reestablished, and traders would later find a flourishing slave market in the New World (see Chapters 12 and 15).

Finding Comfort in Family

In the rugged world that emphasized individual achievement, the family assumed central importance as the one constant, dependable structure in Renaissance society. Men and women believed they could count on their kin when all else failed and highlighted these connections in art, literature, and the decisions they made in their daily lives. The emphasis on family loyalty was not limited to the upper classes. Artisan workshops, for example, were family affairs in which fathers trained sons and sons-in-law to carry on the family business.

Plans for beneficial alliances began as early as the birth of a girl, when wealthy Florentine fathers would open an account with the public dowry fund, which paid as much as 21 percent interest. Family alliances depended on both parties bringing resources to the match. Wealthy families with sons wanted to be certain that their resources would not be diminished by marriage. Thus, parents of girls

Marriage alliances

had to ensure that their daughters could bring enough money to an alliance to ensure a match with well-placed families. The dowry fund was implemented to guarantee that a girl had a sizable dowry when she reached marriageable age. Some Renaissance families could not afford dowries for all their daughters and encouraged some to enter convents (which required smaller dowries). Indeed, the number of convents in Florence increased from only five in 1350 to forty-seven in 1550.

Children's Lives

Though idealized visions of women signaled the importance of the continuity that families provided, and Renaissance families wanted and loved their children, child-rearing practices undermined the hopes of many a proud parent. Privileged families of the Renaissance believed that it was unhealthy (and perhaps even unsavory) for women to breast-feed their infants. Therefore, they customarily sent their newborns to live with peasant women, who were paid to serve as wet nurses until the children were weaned. Some nurses took meticulous care of these infants; others were less attentive. Peasant mothers suffered from poor diets themselves and often had insufficient milk to nurse a fosterling along with her own infants.

Wealthy urban parents reclaimed their children when they were weaned, at about 2 years old. These young strangers then had to fit into large households teeming with older children, stepchildren, and a host of other relatives. With busy parents and stepparents, children often formed their principal attachment with an older sibling or aunt or uncle.

Child-rearing experts warned parents against pampering their offspring, and in general the parents obeyed. Ironically, in this culture of wealth and luxury, people raised their children with a degree of strictness that may seem extreme to us today. One writer (the Dominican Giovanni Dominici), for example, urged mothers to prepare children for hardship by making them sleep in the cold on a hard chest instead of a bed. To toughen them, parents fed children bitter-tasting objects such as peachstones and sometimes gave them "harmless" nausea inducing herbs so as to accustom them to illness. A humanist (Filarete) writing about an ideal school recommended that children be fed only tough meat so that they would learn to eat slowly. This same writer recommended that children eat standing up until they were 20 years old. Many parents let their children sleep only six to eight hours a night to keep them from getting lazy.

Strict upbringing

Within these strict guidelines, boys and girls were treated quite differently. One humanist (Paola da Certaldo) advised feeding and clothing boys well. For girls, he recommended: "Dress the girl well but as for eating, it doesn't matter as long as it keeps her alive; don't let her get fat."

AN AGE OF TALENT AND BEAUTY: Renaissance Culture and Science

Renaissance life had its unsavory side—as rich men struggled to get richer, powerful men worked for more power, and small children sometimes suffered. But at the same time, Renaissance society produced some astonishingly talented people whose works have transformed not only our ideas about beauty but also the very appearance of the world we live in today. During the Renaissance—as in classical Athens—people expected art to be a public thing, to be available to and appreciated by people as they strolled through the cities. Public art nurtured civic pride.

Artists and Artisans

During the Renaissance, many upper-class boys pursued humanistic literary studies to prepare for the day they would play a public role in city life, but their families generally discouraged them from following careers in the visual arts. Filippo Brunelleschi (1377–1446), for example, greatly displeased his father when he declared his interest in sculpting and architecture; his family had fully expected Filippo to become a physician or a notary. Michelangelo's father dismissed his son's interest in art as "shameful."

The majority of Renaissance artists came from artisan families. As boys worked as apprentices in artisan workshops, masters recognized and supported genius. Botticelli, the great Florentine painter, was apprenticed at age 13, as was Michelangelo. These examples were typical—a boy entering adulthood had to learn to take his place in the world, and that place often began in the artisan workshops. As a young man developed his skill, people began to recognize that he was no longer a simple craftsman, an artisan, making goods, but instead an artist, a creator of beauty.

Women ordinarily were excluded from taking this path. Yet, in spite of this lack of official acceptance, a number of female artists won renown during the Renaissance. Two, in particular, were highly respected by their contemporaries. Sofonisba Anguissola (ca. 1532–1625) achieved fame as an artist through her skill and the support of her wealthy, aristocratic father. More typical was the case of Lavinia Fontana (1552–1614), the daughter of an artist who trained in her father's workshop. Despite these successes, the public role of artists precluded many women from active careers in art. For example, Anguissola delayed marriage until she was in her late 40s so that she could paint—a privilege that most Renaissance fathers did not grant.

ANDREA MANTEGNA, *THE CARDINAL FRANCESCO GONZAGA RETURNING FROM ROME,* 1474 The painter was commissioned by the Marquis of Mantua to decorate a room with frescoes. The scenes show the marquis' family and the children who rely on older siblings for comfort in a busy household.

At about 7 years old, middle-class boys were sent to school to learn reading and mathematics and to ready themselves for the complex world of Renaissance economics. As the boys prepared for careers, fathers arranged marriages for their young daughters. Girls were married relatively young—between 17 and 20 years old (although sometimes younger)—to bridegrooms in their 30s who had established their careers.

The harshness of childhood took its toll on many boys and girls; mortality among children reached astonishing rates. In fifteenth-century Florence, 45 percent of children died before the age of 20, most of them girls. The 1427 census in Florence showed a surprising gender ratio: 100 women to every 110 men. This statistic reversed the situation that had prevailed through the High Middle Ages, when women outnumbered men.

Late in the Renaissance, artists overall gained new respect—wealthy patrons stopped viewing them as simply manual laborers and began to recognize them as artists. Michelangelo even earned the title Il Divino, the Divine One. Europeans during the Renaissance valued genius, and these artistic geniuses obliged by creating magnificent works.

Architecture: Echoing the Human Form

The most expensive investment a patron of the arts could make was in architecture, and artists competed for these lucrative contracts. In the process, they designed innovative churches and other buildings that contributed to the prestige of their cities. Where did architects learn these new ideas? Part of the answer comes from the training of architects. Artisans did not consider architecture a separate craft, so there was no direct apprenticeship for this profession that rigidly inculcated old design ideas. Indeed, the greatest architects had all trained for other fields: Brunelleschi, for example, was a goldsmith, and Alberti a university-trained humanist. The Renaissance passion for the glory of classical Greece and Rome led would-be architects to look carefully at the old ruins that had stood for so long; their love of the individual caused them to put humans at the center of their enterprise. The resulting architecture, while looking back to classical models, was strikingly and beautifully new.

Instead of creating soaring Gothic cathedrals dominated by vertical heights, architects followed classical models of balance and simplicity and combined circular forms with linear supports to break up the monotony of vertical lines. Instead of creating structures that made humans seem small and insignificant before God, they built to glorify the human form and proportions. The fifteenth-century architectural drawing above shows the ideal of buildings designed along human proportions. The drawing shows a front view of a building with a man standing to indicate the proper proportions.

The most influential architectural treatise, *On Building* by Alberti, dominated the field for centuries and expressed an architectural aesthetic that echoed that of the ancient Greeks. Alberti argued that buildings should mirror the human body in their supports and openings, and this sentiment is shown in the drawing above. Repeating the same principle, Michelangelo claimed that

Human architecture

FRANCESCO DI GIORGIO MARTINI, *TRATTATO DI ARCHITETTURA*, 1480 As theoreticians of architecture considered the best proportions for designing pleasing buildings, they looked to the human form to determine the proper ratios. This drawing shows these ratios superimposed on the front of a building.

anyone who had not mastered anatomy and painting of the human form could not understand architecture. "The different parts of a building," he explained, "derive from human members." Thus, much of the architecture of the Renaissance was created in the image and likeness of the human form.

It is easy to miss the subtleties of human proportion within architecture as we look at the graceful buildings, but there is no overlooking one of the architects' debts to Rome—domes instead of Gothic spires now began to rise with more frequency over the skylines of Renaissance cities. The image on page 235 shows the cathedral of Florence, with its dome designed by Brunelleschi. The architect had admired the Pantheon dome in Rome (see Chapter 4), and he wanted to erect

OPINION

How were ideas like individualism and realism expressed in different areas of Renaissance life, such as painting and politics?

a massive dome to span the huge base of the new cathedral in Florence. Many Florentines predicted that the dome would collapse, yet Brunelleschi's handiwork continues to dominate the skyline of Florence.

Domes

The Renaissance study of architecture also extended beyond individual buildings to town planning in general. In the fifteenth century, planners began to dream of laying out towns in the simple and logical grid pattern that characterizes our modern cities. Indeed, older European cities still feature a medieval center with curved and random streets surrounded by tidy, post-Renaissance grids. All these new ideas about buildings and street planning reshaped the cities of the West.

Town planning

Sculpture Comes into Its Own

Just as Brunelleschi's admiration of the ancients led him to re-create domed architecture, sculptors also drew from classical models. Italians, who had admired freestanding images from the ancient world, began to demand similar beauty for their cities. City communes and individuals commissioned life-size figures to stand free in the public spaces of cities.

FLORENCE CATHEDRAL, 1420–1436 Brunelleschi's dome for the Cathedral of Florence was an architectural wonder.

The image below shows Michelangelo's widely admired statue of David, the biblical figure who killed the giant Goliath. The work exhibits all the innovations of Renaissance sculpture: It is a huge, free-standing nude that depicts the classical ideal of repose, in which the subject rests his weight on one leg in a pose called ***contra posto.*** The figure exemplifies the confidence and the glorification of the human body that marked Renaissance pride.

Michelangelo's *David*

Michelangelo's statue shows another hallmark of Renaissance spirit—an exuberant praise of realism; the sculptor

MICHELANGELO, *DAVID,* 1504 This spectacular sculpture, more than 14 feet high, was in its day the largest marble nude created since antiquity. It was commissioned by Florence to symbolize how the Florentine republic would stand—like David the "giant killer"—against neighboring political giants.

Art Investigation

Raphael, *School of Athens*

1510–1511

Pope Julius II commissioned the painter Raphael to create a fresco for his library. The artist portrayed famous ancient philosophers, such as Euclid, Pythagoras, and Socrates, along with Plato and Aristotle in the center. Plato (looking remarkably like Leonardo da Vinci) is on the left, with his hand pointing in the air to remind viewers of the realm of ideas. He is speaking to Aristotle, whose hand presses downward, reminding viewers of his more earthly approach to knowledge. Raphael also included a self-portrait on the right (in the black hat) and a depiction of a brooding Michelangelo sitting in the center foreground, leaning his head on his hand. Identify the following characteristics of the Renaissance in this image: individualism, appreciation of the classics, and perspective. Would viewers today appreciate the same characteristics?

was led to an appreciation of realism through admiring the great sculptures that graced the public areas.

Painting from a New Perspective

The shepherd Giotto di Bondone (ca. 1267–1337), whose artistic talents were recognized by a Florentine master, was to revolutionize painting for Florence and the West. The young apprentice who fooled his master with a painting of a fly turned his talents to magnificent religious paintings, and he created realistic figures that showed a full range of human expression. For example, his images of the Virgin Mary were not done as remote queens of heaven but, instead, painted as realistic young girls struggling to be caring mothers.

Like architects and sculptors, Renaissance painters developed striking new techniques, including oil painting on canvas and the perfection of portraiture. However, perhaps their best-known innovation was **linear perspective,** which allowed painters to enhance the realism of paintings by creating the illusion of three-dimensional space on a two-dimensional surface. The Florentines—and Brunelleschi in particular—proudly claimed to have invented this technique of painting. Whether they did or not is probably irrelevant; regardless of who invented linear perspective, the Florentines perfected it.

Linear perspective

Before beginning to paint, Brunelleschi organized the painting around a central point and then drew a grid to place objects precisely in relation to each other. His real innovation, however, came when he calculated the mathematical ratios by which objects seem to get smaller as they recede from view. In this way, he knew exactly how big to paint each object in his grid to achieve a realistic illusion of receding space. In commenting on Brunelleschi's creations, Alberti asserted that a painting should be pleasing

knew anatomy and realistically portrayed the human body. Renaissance sculptors had to look at life carefully in order to reproduce it with such accuracy, and the audience, too,

to the eye but also should appeal to the mind with optical and mathematical accuracy. And here is the essence of these complex works: They used all the intellectual skill of the artists to create images profoundly appealing to the senses.

The painter Raphael (1483–1520) was widely regarded as one of Italy's best painters of the High Renaissance (the late fifteenth and early sixteenth centuries). During his life-

Raphael

time, he was much acclaimed as an artist who could portray transcendent themes with all the realism of fifteenth-century Italian life, and modern critics agree. His reputation gained him the coveted commission to paint a fresco for Pope Julius II's library, and the image on page 236 shows that fresco—*School of Athens*—that demonstrates his command of perspective. Raphael created this fresco just as Michelangelo was painting the Sistine Chapel ceiling (see image on page 221).

Celestial Music of Human Emotions

Renaissance thinkers turned their attention to music in a quest to carry that art into the new age. Early humanists at first thought that music should imitate classical forms, but no one really knew what ancient Greek music sounded like. However, people did look to ancient mathematics to inform musical composition, for Pythagoras (ca. 569–475 B.C.E.) had postulated harmonious relationships among planets, and music intervals were supposed to echo the ratios of those relationships, creating what the ancients called a "music of the spheres." This search for heavenly music helped to standardize musical notation during the Renaissance and would continue into the seventeenth century.

On a practical level, composers drew from humanistic studies and put human feelings at the center of a piece so that the music itself would reflect the emotions of the lyrics. For example, if the lyric was sad, the pitch should descend and the tempo should slow down. Music also moved from the church to the courts in these centuries, and perhaps the best-known secular, emotional music was the **madrigals,** poetic songs usually about love. The attempt to link music, narrative, and emotion led to the invention of opera at the end of the sixteenth century.

Music became part of a well-rounded education. Castiglione, in his *Book of the Courtier,* wrote, "I am not pleased with the courtier if he be not also a musician." Music came into the households as well as the courts, and new instruments were developed to serve the home market. Noble households resonated with the sounds of instruments such as the viola da gamba (a bowed, stringed instrument), the whistle-like recorder, and the harpsichord (an instrument, like the piano, with strings that are plucked). The printing press helped to advance this popularization of music, as it allowed for the wide distribution of sheet music after the 1470s. Despite all the new instruments and the new tech-

nology of printing, however, the human voice, so expressive of human emotion, remained the central instrument of Renaissance music.

Science or Pseudoscience?

The Renaissance passion for direct observation and realistic assessment that led to such magnificent achievements in the visual, musical, and literary arts catalyzed a process that ultimately led to the scientific accomplishments of the seventeenth century. During the fourteenth and fifteenth centuries, however, much scientific inquiry was shaped by a desire to control as well as understand the world. This combination led to the pursuit of what we consider pseudoscientific studies.

Astrology was extremely popular during these centuries. Even some popes hired their own astrologers. The bright appearance of Halley's comet

Astrology and alchemy

in 1456 provoked a flurry of both dire and inspiring prophecies. For example, one humanist physician explained the outbreak of syphilis in Europe in terms of a conjunction of the planets Saturn, Jupiter, and Mars in the sign of Cancer. **Alchemy** was the early practice of chemistry, but the alchemists' interests were dramatically different from those of modern scientists. Their main goal was to find a "philosopher stone" that would turn base metals into gold. This science was perhaps even more popular than astrology.

Such pseudoscience aside, the Renaissance did succeed in combining visual arts with scientific observation. The study of linear perspective, for exam-

Mathematics and anatomy

ple, depended on an understanding of mathematics, and scholars spread the use of Arabic numerals to replace the Roman numerals that had previously dominated the West. The use of these numbers facilitated higher orders of calculations, like algebra, which was also learned from the Muslims. Musicians explored ratios and fractions to try to re-create celestial proportions. Realistic sculpture and painting required a study of anatomy (see drawing on page 234), and this science also progressed. Amid these advancements, the Renaissance saw the birth of a man who came to represent the entire range and combination of talents that so defined this age.

Leonardo da Vinci: The "Renaissance Man"

Leonardo da Vinci (1452–1519) personifies the idea of the "Renaissance man"—the person who can supposedly do anything well. As a young man, he contributed to the architecture of Florence by helping to make the golden ball that topped Brunelleschi's dome (see image on page

235), but he excelled in much more than architecture and sculpture.

This multitalented Italian served in the courts of a number of patrons, from the Medici to the Sforza of Milan. At these courts, Leonardo painted magnificent portraits and beautiful religious works, including the celebrated *Mona Lisa,* probably the most famous portrait from the Renaissance. Although Leonardo's skill as a painter would have satisfied most men longing for greatness, he saw this medium only as a beginning, a means to a larger end. "Painting should increase the artist's knowledge of the physical world," he explained.

Painting

Leonardo left a collection of notebooks that showed his intense interest in the world. His drawings of plants revealed a skill and meticulousness that any botanist would envy, and his sketches of water in motion would have impressed the most accomplished of engineers. Leonardo's imagination seemed boundless—his sketches included tanks and other war machines, a submarine, textile machines, paddle boats, a "horseless carriage," and many other inventions that lay in the future.

Scientific notebooks

Leonardo also took an interest in the inner workings of the human body. Although some medieval physicians conducted dissections, the practice was not common. During the Renaissance, however, physicians and scholars began to approach the study of the human body empirically by regularly dissecting cadavers. At the time, both artists and physicians saw dissection as a way to improve their portrayal of the human form. Like many other artists, Leonardo dissected cadavers to understand anatomy and thereby make his paintings as realistic as possible (as well as to satisfy his insatiable curiosity).

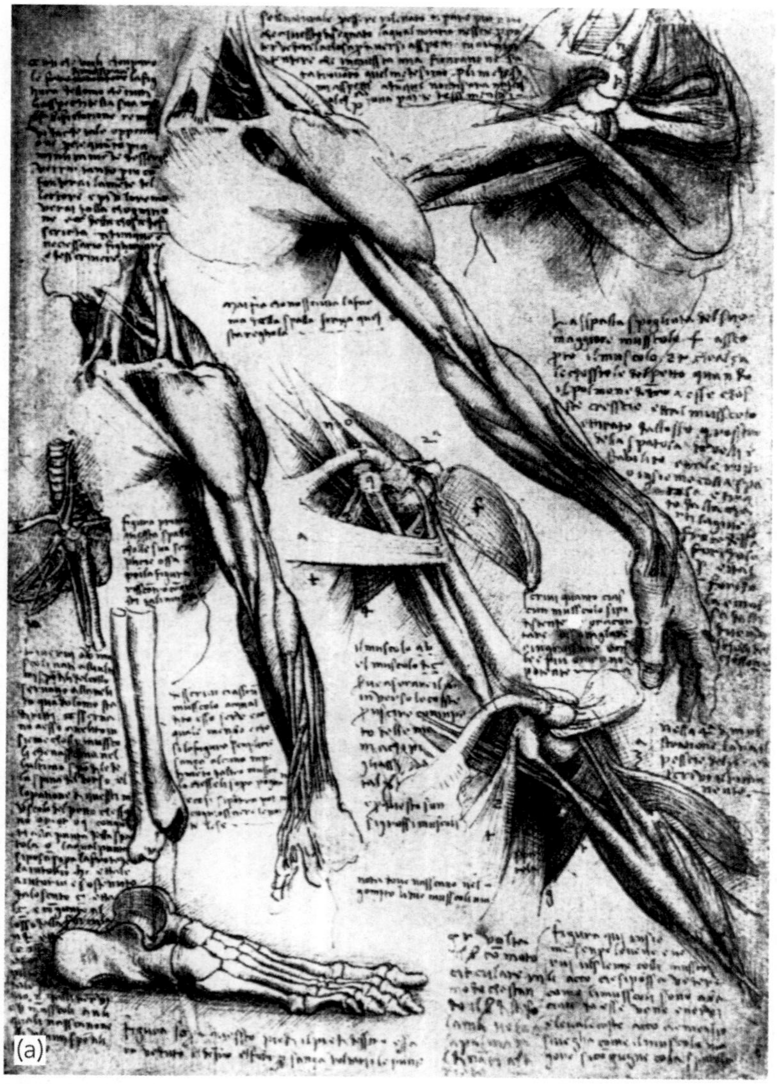

King Francis I of France (r. 1515–1547) once said of Leonardo, "No other man had been born who knew so much." Unfortunately for the future of science and engineering, Leonardo's voluminous notebooks were lost for centuries after his death. In retrospect, perhaps Leonardo's greatest achievement was that he showed how multitalented human beings could be. He proved the humanists' belief that an educated man could accomplish anything in all fields. Leonardo died at the court of Francis I, who had proudly served as his patron.

LEONARDO'S NOTEBOOKS, ca. 1510 Leonardo, like many other artists at the time, studied dissections of cadavers to learn about humans and in doing so forwarded science as well as art. This drawing shows his study of a shoulder and arm.

RENAISSANCE OF THE "NEW MONARCHIES" OF THE NORTH

1453–1640

As we saw in Chapter 9, the medieval political structures of Europe began to fall apart under the pressures of the many disasters of the fourteenth century. The monarchies of the fifteenth century could no longer rely on feudal contracts and armies of mounted knights and began to search for new ways to rule their countries. To bypass their sometimes unreliable nobility, monarchs concentrated their royal authority by appointing bureaucrats who owed their status only to the will of the king or queen. As they looked for new sources of income to pay growing mercenary armies, kings and queens kept imposing new taxes and, in general, were receptive to new ideas to help them consolidate their power. Many hired Italians trained in the humanist tradition to work in their courts, and slowly and fitfully from the late thirteenth through the sixteenth century, the ideas of the Renaissance spread to northern European countries. As Renaissance notions traveled north and bore fruit in the courts of powerful rulers, the ideas were further transformed. This migration of ideas also accelerated the changes triggered by the disasters of the fourteenth century.

France: Under the Italian Influence

France offers a case study in how slowly and sporadically Renaissance ideas moved and how much this new spirit depended on the patronage of monarchs. The French king Charles V (r. 1364–1380), known as "the Wise," encouraged Renaissance learning among his subjects, gathering a circle of intellectuals around him. However, this early flowering of learning withered when his mentally unstable son, Charles VI (r. 1380–1422), took power. Integration of Renaissance ideals in this northern court would have to wait until the end of the Hundred Years' War in 1453 (discussed in Chapter 9).

France eventually triumphed in the Hundred Years' War, but a new threat from the neighboring state of Burgundy immediately arose. The rulers of Burgundy were trying to forge a state between France and the Holy Roman Empire, and their hundred-year expansion represented a real threat to France. Instead of leading armies in the old chivalric manner, however, the French king Louis XI (r. 1461–1483) skillfully brought a new kind of diplomacy to bear in confronting this next challenge. His contemporaries called him "Louis the Spider" because he spun a complex web of intrigue and diplomatic machinations worthy of Machiavelli—bribing his allies and murdering his enemies. Louis subsidized Swiss mercenaries, who eventually defeated the Burgundian ruler. France then seized the Duchy of Burgundy and added the sizable new territory to its

Louis the Spider

A Courtier Describes a Suspicious King— Louis the Spider

Philippe de Commynes (ca. 1447–1511) served Louis XI and wrote an account of the king's reign shortly after Louis' death in 1483. Commynes had been raised at the court of Burgundy, so he was well placed to view the king with the eye of an outsider as well as a courtier.

. . . [Other princes] might too, probably, have been tyrants, and bloody-minded; but our king never did any person a mischief who had not offended him first, though I do not say all who offended him deserved death. I have not recorded these things merely to represent our master as a suspicious and mistrustful prince; but . . . that those princes who may be his successors, may learn by his example to be more tender and indulgent to their subjects, and less severe in their punishments than our master had been: although I will not censure him, or say I ever saw a better prince; for though he oppressed his subjects himself, he would never see them injured by anybody else. . . .

He was involved [in warfare that] . . . lasted till his death, and many brave men lost their lives in it, and his treasury was exhausted by it; . . . When his body was at rest his mind was at work, for he had affairs in several places at once, and would concern himself as much in those of his neighbors as in his own, . . .

What qualities do you think made Louis a successful or unsuccessful monarch?

lands. Louis left France strong and prosperous and well placed to play a powerful political role in the coming centuries.

The French kings succeeded in slowly taking the lands from the nobles who had retained their holdings since the Middle Ages. With its increasing strength, France next began expanding across the Alps into Italy to assert dynastic claims in Naples, because, as we saw previously, the French royal family was related to the rulers in Naples. However, the French came back with much more than wealth. Nobles leading mercenary armies in the Italian campaigns of 1494 came in search of land and left feeling dazzled by the cultural accomplishments of the Italian Renaissance. In a letter to his courtiers back home, the French king Charles VIII (r. 1483–1498) gushed about discovering the "best artists" in Italy. He returned home with some 20 Italian workmen whom he instructed to build "in the Italian style." The aesthetic ideals of Italy thus moved north with the retreating French armies, and the early Renaissance spirit in France was reawakened.

Italian influence increased further with the substantial growth of the French court, which opened positions to Italian humanists and diplomats. France's kings employed more officials than any other state in Europe—one estimate places the number of bureaucrats at more than 4,000 during the reign of Francis I (r. 1515–1547). (Leonardo da Vinci was among those brought to France by this powerful and sophisticated patron.) Under Francis's rule, humanist literature flourished, and the new learning influenced university curricula from languages to mathematics to law.

Italians in France

The French Renaissance did not merely copy the Italian movement. Indeed, many works by French artists and writers during this period show a unique blend of humorous skepticism and creative power. The imaginative humanist François Rabelais embodies this unmistakable French version of Renaissance ideals. His books *Pantagruel* and *Gargantua*—bawdy tales about giants with enormous appetites—are masterpieces of satire. Both stories continue to captivate modern readers. France had left its own mark on the Renaissance spirit.

English Humanism

When Henry VII (r. 1485–1509) became king in England after the Wars of the Roses (see Chapter 9), he succeeded in taming the rowdy and independent nobility and established a strong, centralized monarchy. Under the dynasty that he initiated, England again prospered. The English monarchs now turned their attention to the new spirit emanating from the south as they began to surround themselves with courtiers and art that served as the hallmarks of the courts of new monarchs. Delayed because of internal strife, the English Renaissance (1500–1640) gained momentum just as the Italian movement waned.

OPINION

As the Renaissance ideas spread northward, how do you think they changed in France and England?

During the reign of Henry VII, English scholars intrigued by Renaissance thought traveled to Italy and studied under noted humanists. They frequented the newly established Vatican library and consulted with Platina, the papal librarian shown in the image on page 229, and then returned home brimming with new ideas. By 1500, these scholars had so transformed the curriculum at Oxford that England could offer as fine a classical education as Italy. The forward-thinking English monarchs also brought back technological innovations. They embraced new artillery and set English engineers to work making gunpowder. Henry VII included a fireworks display at his wedding, in so doing importing this Italian skill into England and beginning a long tradition of English pyrotechnics.

Henry VIII (r. 1509–1547) proved an even more vigorous patron of Renaissance learning than his father. Henry met the French king Francis I and tried to outdo that Renaissance prince in splendor and patronage. The English king cultivated interest in astronomy, literature, and music—all the fields advocated by the humanists. Still, the talented monarch was outdone by his Lord Chancellor, Sir Thomas More (1478–1535).

More published a biography of the humanist Pico della Mirandola that revealed the author's debt to the Italian movement. The English scholar mastered classical learning and the humanist curriculum and applied his skills in public life in the best tradition of civic humanism.

Thomas More

More's masterpiece, however, was *Utopia,* a work that commented on contemporary evils while offering a vision of a society free of poverty, crime, and corruption. More's work, with its visions of exploration and decidedly political orientation, points to distinct characteristics of the English Renaissance. More's studies gave him strong views on religion, which, as we will see in Chapter 11, led to a fatal conflict with his king.

Many Englishwomen also wrote during this Renaissance. The first wife of Henry VIII, Catherine of Aragon (1485–1536), had grown up with a love of the new learning encouraged

Renaissance queens

Then & Now
Pyrotechnics in the Theater

Shakespeare used music and fireworks to excite audiences who attended his popular plays. In 1613, theatrical cannons filled with gunpowder and fireworks misfired, catching the thatched roof and wooden beams on fire, burning the theater down. Today, despite fire safety rules to prevent similar fire hazards, performers still find pyrotechnics the most dramatic way to get their audiences' attention. But just like in Shakespeare's time, injuries are unavoidable. In recent years, performers like Michael Jackson, Metallica, and Mötley Crüe have all suffered injuries when fireworks on stage went awry.

by her mother, Isabella of Castile. When Catherine came to England, she stimulated interest among courtiers and scholars in the proper education of women. Consequently, Englishwomen wrote more publicly than their Italian counterparts. In fact, Italian travelers to England wrote disparagingly of the "brazen and violently assertive" Englishwomen. This tradition of education strongly influenced Queen Elizabeth I (r. 1558–1603), under whose rule England prospered and the Renaissance flowered.

Renaissance London: A Booming City

Sixteenth-century London—a vibrant city—scintillated during the English Renaissance, expanding physically and intellectually. Between 1560 and 1603, the population almost doubled, from 120,000 to more than 200,000, and travelers flocked there to see its wonders. The image here shows a 1616 painting of London by Claes von Visscher. In this cityscape, the great sailing ships that made London a bustling commercial hub waft by, along with small vessels that supplied the city's growing

The south bank

CLAES VON VISSCHER, *MAP OF LONDON* (detail), 1616 The south bank of the Thames is shown in the foreground of the image. In this seedy part of town, patrons came to see bear baiting and dog fights. But also here, in the circular theaters, Shakespeare and other playwrights created masterworks of English drama that have come down to us through the ages.

population. Rows of houses stand in front of St. Paul's cathedral, which dominates the skyline. In the foreground of the painting is the south bank of the Thames, which had been a center of prostitution from the time of the Roman settlement of London. The south bank remained the unseemly quarter of the city, inhabited by criminals and prostitutes, and notorious for its violent forms of entertainment, such as bear baiting and dog fights. The south bank also housed private prisons, including the infamous "clink" that housed some of the fiercest criminals. Yet, the south bank was also home to the theaters where crowds gathered to watch the plays of the great Renaissance dramatists. The two tall, round structures in the foreground of the painting are examples of these theaters. The one on the right is inaccurately labeled "The Globe." Known as Shakespeare's theater, the building had burned down in 1613. This took place before Visscher painted his London scene. During the late sixteenth century, however, the Globe served as a backdrop for the work of the greatest writer England has ever produced, and crowds today gather to see plays performed in a newly rebuilt Globe Theater on the south bank of the Thames.

England's Pride: William Shakespeare

The new social mobility of the Renaissance permitted William Shakespeare (1564–1616) to rise to prominence. William's father, a modest glove maker, married a woman above his station, the daughter of a wealthy landowner. Shakespeare probably attended the local school in Stratford-upon-Avon and received a humanist education. At the age of 18, the young scholar married Anne Hathaway, about eight years his elder, who was pregnant with their first child. In 1592, William journeyed to London, where he worked as an actor and wrote comedies, histories, and tragedies.

This master of the English language articulated all the Renaissance ideals: Shakespeare's love of the classics showed in his use of Roman histories in his plays (*Julius Caesar*) and in his study of Roman playwrights that offered him models of theater. Furthermore, Hamlet's words "What a piece of work is man" expressed Renaissance optimism in human accomplishment; *Romeo and Juliet* re-created the story of "star-crossed lovers" (a reference to the Renaissance love of

timeline

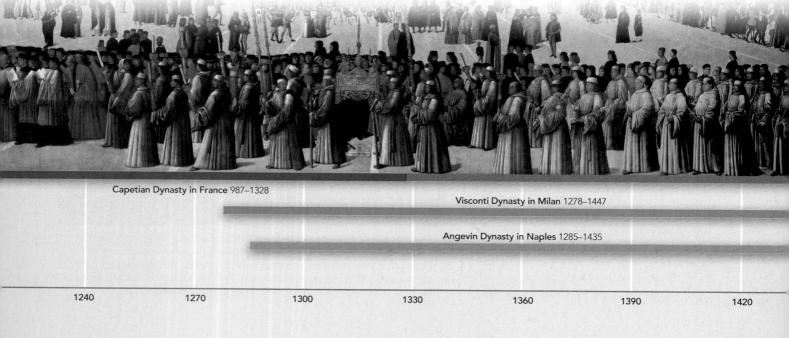

Capetian Dynasty in France 987–1328

Visconti Dynasty in Milan 1278–1447

Angevin Dynasty in Naples 1285–1435

1240   1270   1300   1330   1360   1390   1420

astrology) in the streets of Italy. *The Tempest* featured Renaissance magicians, and Shakespeare's histories described the fortunes of princes as surely as Machiavelli's analysis of history and politics had. His plays incorporated Renaissance music and modern warfare with cannons and fireworks. In Shakespeare's hands, the ideals of the Renaissance were given a new, enduring form—popular theater that reached the masses. However, some modern literary critics believe the great playwright accomplished much more than perfecting Renaissance ideas. Some claim that by expressing complex human emotions in magnificent language, Shakespeare created an understanding of humanity for the West. In this, perhaps, we can see the ideals of the Renaissance come full circle—the early humanists in Italy transformed themselves by the texts they read, and Shakespeare used the written word to shape our understanding of who we are. Western civilization was dramatically transformed.

SUMMARY

In the midst of the disastrous fourteenth century—in which plague, famine, warfare, and religious instability swirled—new ideas percolated in the turbulent Italian city-states. Historians have called this new spirit the Renaissance.

- The characteristics of the Renaissance included individualism, a spirit of realism, a desire for activism to make one's mark on the world, and a secular spirit—that is, it took place in the world, not the church. These ideas were fostered by generous patrons and spread by the new printing press.

- The new spirit arose in the unstable political system of the Italian city-states, where each city—including the Vatican—jockeyed to gain more power over its neighbor.

- The Renaissance led to booming economies but also to new intolerance and suffering, as slavery was reintroduced, Jews were persecuted, and crime increased.

- Artists expressed their creativity in vibrant new art forms in architecture, sculpture, painting, music, and a new realistic view of science.

- Renaissance ideas spread from Italy and changed the courts of the north. French kings practiced a new realistic politics, and in England humanism and theater flourished in ways that profoundly influenced Western culture.

Spain and Germany, too, would mold the praise of individualism and study to their own interests, bringing an upheaval in religion as great as the Renaissance revolution in art and ideas.

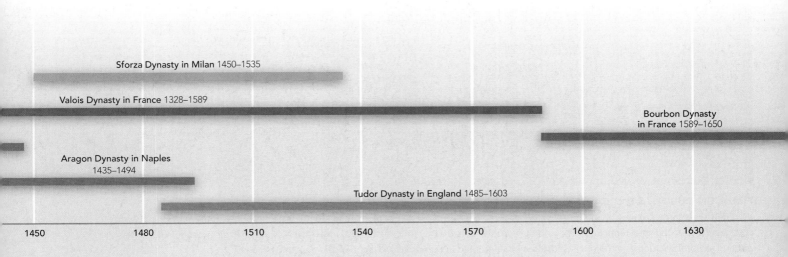

Sforza Dynasty in Milan 1450–1535

Valois Dynasty in France 1328–1589

Bourbon Dynasty in France 1589–1650

Aragon Dynasty in Naples 1435–1494

Tudor Dynasty in England 1485–1603

1450   1480   1510   1540   1570   1600   1630

FRANÇOIS DUBOIS, *SAINT BARTHOLOMEW'S DAY MASSACRE,*

ca. 1576   The spread of new religious ideas did not come easily, and many people died in the resulting struggles. This painting shows the massacre of French Protestants that began on Saint Bartholomew's Day (August 24, 1572) and lasted six days. Even violence such as this did not end the brutal struggle for religious supremacy that erupted in Europe and killed men, women, and children.

"Alone Before God"

Religious Reform and Warfare, 1500–1648

11

A Woman Preacher in Geneva

Marie Dentière was a Roman Catholic abbess in a convent in Tournai, Belgium, when in the 1520s she read some of Martin Luther's works. She was immediately captivated by those in which he denounced monasticism, urging the faithful to leave the monasteries and enter the worlds of marriage, work, and spreading the word of God. Marie took his words to heart, packed her small bag, stole money from the abbey, and left the convent that had been her home for so long. She had to flee to Strasbourg in northeastern France to avoid religious persecution. ▶▶

There she married a Protestant minister, Simon Robert, who had once been a Catholic priest in Strasbourg, and the two traveled together spreading the new religious ideas. The couple had five children.

Marie journeyed to other convents to try to persuade the nuns to follow her example, claiming, "If only you knew how good it was to be next to a handsome husband, and how God considers it pleasing! . . . Thanks to God I have five handsome children and I live wholesomely." This was a dramatic shift in religious values, in which sexuality within marriage was considered a religious gift.

Marie and her husband (and, after she was widowed, a second husband) took their message to the city of Geneva in Switzerland. She spoke out in public taverns and on street corners, and helped stir a revolution that finally culminated in Geneva in 1536, when a Protestant army deposed the Catholic prince and made Geneva into a Protestant city-state. Marie was an eyewitness to these events and described them in her booklet, *The War for and Deliverance of Geneva*.

While Marie celebrated these successes, she failed in one of her deeply held causes—the authorities in Geneva rejected women's participation in preaching and writing, and refused to publish women's voices in their Protestant city. Marie recorded her objections in a letter to the enlightened Queen Marguerite of Navarre (Spain), writing: "If God has given graces to some good women, revealing to them something holy and good through His Holy Scripture, should they, for the sake of the defamers of the truth, refrain from writing down, speaking or declaring it to each other?"

Sadly, Marie was silenced and no longer played any public role in the Reformation she had worked so hard to bring about.

These were dramatic years indeed, when new religious ideas clashed, when men and women died for their beliefs, and warfare brought devastation to Europe. Yet at the end, new ideas of love, marriage, education, and charity were transformed as some people rethought their relationship to God. The West was irrevocably changed. ◄◄

THE CLASH OF DYNASTIES

1515–1555

The kings of France and England ruled strong, unified states, but at the beginning of the sixteenth century, nation-states were not necessarily the ideal political form. Indeed, kings sought to extend their reach even further and acquire multinational empires like that held by the Holy Roman Emperor, Charles V. Ignoring considerations of common culture or the difficulties of holding large empires, each king believed simply that bigger was better.

Charles V was the grandson of Ferdinand and Isabella of Spain. Thanks to the prudent dynastic marriages of his ancestors, he had inherited a sprawling, multinational empire. The map on page 247 shows the Habsburg lands of Charles V, which included the Netherlands, Spain, and lands in Austria, and highlights all the battles to indicate how warfare dominated Charles's reign. The map also shows the extensive empire of the Ottoman Turks, which threatened Charles in the East.

As we saw in Chapter 9, events in the eastern Mediterranean had complicated western European rivalry, for the empire of the Ottoman Turks had gained strength. After the Turks conquered Constantinople in 1453, they consolidated their rule and developed a sophisticated administration and a well-trained military. Under Suleiman I the Magnificent (r. 1520–1566), the Turks began to advance again, this time toward the very heart of Europe.

Turkish expansion

In 1521, the Turks marched up the Danube valley and seized Belgrade and Hungary, creating a panic throughout central Europe. By 1529, they were outside the walls of Vienna, the core of the Austrian Habsburg lands. At the same time, Turkish ships proved so effective in the eastern Mediterranean that all the western rulers wondered how long they could hold on to their share of the lucrative sea trade in that area. For Charles V in particular, however, the Ottoman Empire had become a major, distracting presence in the east as he struggled to extend his empire in the west. All these monarchs had to grapple with new complexities in their seemingly endless struggles with one another, for the scale of warfare was increasing, and the old rules no longer applied.

The Changing Rules of Warfare

As we saw in Chapter 9, the mounted knights of the Middle Ages were being replaced by infantry, and by the sixteenth century, that trend was complete. The primary reason for this change was military technology. By 1500, Europeans had improved on the unreliable early guns of the Hundred Years' War. Now, guns with 50-inch-long barrels gave marksmen a good deal of power and accuracy, and soon the Spanish developed the musket, a 6-foot-long gun that could shoot lead bullets up to 200 yards. Armed with these weapons, soldiers could do a great deal more damage. Indeed, warfare was now dramatically changed, and kings had to pay the price in men and materials for new armies.

The new weapons dictated different military strategies. Now, captains arrayed their troops in a series of long, narrow

Europe, in 1526—Habsburg-Valois Wars **This map illustrates the political division of Europe in 1526 and highlights the Habsburg lands inherited by Charles V. It also shows the Ottoman Empire on Charles's borders.**

lines. The infantrymen carried muskets and were backed by tight formations of pike-wielding foot soldiers. In this new

Growing armies

kind of warfare, sheer numbers often determined a king's success, so monarchs strove to bolster the size of their armies. At the beginning of the century, most armies had fewer than 50,000 men; Charles V's forces boasted a whopping 148,000 (although they were widely dispersed through Charles's extensive lands).

To enlarge their armies, rulers had to resort to creative new ways to fill their ranks. In part, kings relied on mercenaries, hiring soldiers of fortune who offered their services to the highest bidder, but these were never sufficient. Traditionally, kings claimed the right to draft an army from among the able-bodied men of the land. Originally, these draftees were required to fight only on their home soil, but in 1544 Henry VIII sent his conscripts overseas. No one objected, and a

useful precedent was set that helped kings boost their foreign armies. Sometimes men did not wait to be drafted into the growing armies, but instead volunteered. These soldiers joined up for various reasons—some wanted to escape poverty or the hardships of village life; others sought adventure.

Not surprisingly, armies made up of poorly paid mercenaries, conscripts, and volunteers brought new problems to the art of making war. Officers repeatedly complained of soldiers' lack of discipline, and they imposed drilling and strict penalties for disobedience. Military leaders developed other strategies as well to manage their expanding forces. The Spanish evolved a complex military administration, which included the first battlefield hospitals. The Dutch introduced standardized-caliber weapons to help solve the problem of supplying larger numbers of infantrymen. Feeding and outfitting armies were still no easy matter, however. Wives, children, prostitutes, and servants trailed behind the lines

connect to today

War Casualties

This chapter describes how new technology increased the human cost of warfare. Do you think the technology of modern warfare further increased or decreased the human toll of war? What might be the trend in the future?

to take advantage of the regular pay that the armies offered their men. These followers also needed to eat, of course, and at times they plundered the countryside through which the army moved.

Modernized warfare carried a high price. Heavy artillery was especially costly for both offensive and defensive forces. Not only did armies have to spend valuable currency to equip their armies with cannons, but rulers had to rebuild cities into massive fortresses with forts and gun emplacements to guard against opposing artillery. The new warfare also required larger navies, and ships, too, were expensive. Between 1542 and 1550, England spent more than twice its royal revenue on military campaigns. Other European powers also bankrupted themselves on these incessant wars. For example, between 1520 and 1532, Charles V borrowed an astounding 5.4 million gold coins from rich merchants to pay his troops—still, he could not compensate them completely. At his death, Francis I owed bankers one full year's income of all the crown lands.

Winners and Losers

Kings were seldom able to deliver a decisive victory in this seemingly endless warfare, and small victories were soon avenged. Therefore, very few combatants "won" these military contests or profited at all. However, some individuals were able to gain a huge profit. Bankers who lent money to kings recklessly supplying ever-larger armies struck it rich. Guns and ammunition manufacturers, especially in the Netherlands, also profited hugely.

Overall, however, losers vastly outnumbered winners in these wars. As armies ballooned, so did casualties. With the increasing use of bullets and gunpowder, the nature of

PIETER BRUEGHEL THE ELDER, *THE CRIPPLES*, 1568 This painting shows the tragic reality of modern warfare. Many combatants lost their limbs to gunfire and were relegated to a life of poverty.

combat injuries also changed. In the Middle Ages, battlefield surgeons had been skilled at treating sword injuries; in the sixteenth century, surgeons more often had to amputate limbs crushed by artillery shells. As one **Casualties of war** soldier wrote of the new guns: "Would to God that this unhappy weapon had never been invented." To survive, many legless or armless veterans resorted to begging in the towns and villages of Europe.

The wars of this period also contributed to inflation and ruined harvests, both of which tormented even noncombatants. Horrified contemporary witnesses repeatedly described the legions of poor, starving civilians who wandered the landscape in search of food and died along the way. One French writer told of "some thousands of poor people, . . . subdued like skeletons, the majority leaning on crutches and dragging themselves along as best they could to ask for a piece of bread." People weakened by hunger and traveling through the countryside also fell prey to all manner of diseases. In the sixteenth century, outbreaks of plague, typhoid fever, typhus, smallpox, and influenza took a terrible toll.

The Habsburg-Valois Wars

1521–1544

All these costs of making war still did not deter kings from their drive for land and power, and the city-states of Italy—where both Francis I and Charles V had dynastic claims—became the battlefield. Thus began the Habsburg-Valois Wars, named after the ruling houses of Austria and France. These wars were fought sporadically for about twenty-five years.

The wars devastated the Italian city-states, demonstrating that only large states could successfully field large-enough armies for the new warfare. Charles also learned a hazard in using mercenary troops, for in 1527 the emperor was unable **Weary imperialists** to pay them, and his enraged armies stormed Rome in search of booty to cover their pay.

Neither Charles nor Francis could win a decisive victory, so the two men finally negotiated a peace in 1544, and by its terms, Francis agreed to renounce his claim on Italy. Charles, too, wearied by all his problems, and in ill health, troubled by gout, decided to give up his imperial ambitions. He abdicated his various thrones between 1555 and 1556 and split his extensive holdings. He bestowed his Austrian and German lands on his brother Ferdinand I (r. 1558–1564) and the Low Countries, Spain, and Naples on his son Philip II (r. 1556–1598). Weary and disheartened, the ailing Charles V retired to a palace in Spain, where he died two years later. From this point on, these two branches of the Habsburg family went their separate ways.

During the wars, the kings had been willing to ally with unlikely partners. Sometimes Francis sought help from the Turks against Charles, and at times both Catholic kings courted critics of the church—"Lutherans"—to help against the other's Catholic forces. However, the treaty that ended the war attempted to present the Catholic kings as a united front against religious diversity that had flourished in their lands. Charles and Francis agreed to focus their energies on defeating "Muslims and Lutherans" who were threatening the Christian world. The Muslims had been a traditional enemy, but who were these Lutherans who appeared in the sixteenth century and who by 1544 seemed such a threat to the Christian kings?

A TIDE OF RELIGIOUS REFORM

The powerful medieval Christian church had called itself "Catholic," which meant "universal." In the hands of reformers, however, "Catholic" began to mean the traditional church, which even in the Middle Ages had come under criticism. Medieval critics had questioned some of the beliefs and practices of the church—its power, its wealth, and its insistence on obedience to the pope as necessary for spiritual salvation. The last point was central, because from the beginning, Christians had focused on salvation—everything from the best way to worship God to getting into heaven after death. As the sixteenth century opened, criticism began to intensify and many people wondered if their salvation was in good hands.

The Best Path to Salvation?

The church had promised Christians that the path to salvation lay in the hierarchy of the church and its sacramental system, which offered grace to the faithful through the seven **sacraments.** To further confirm this, the Fourth Lateran Council in 1215 (described in Chapter 8) had declared that there was no salvation outside the church. Churchmen also promised that the faithful would be supported by the community of Christians, including the Virgin Mary, all the saints, and the congregations on earth. No Catholic believer, the church claimed, would have to face God alone in the afterlife.

A new popular piety and personal mysticism, along with the spread of Renaissance ideas of individualism, began to raise questions about this path to salvation. Catholicism had emphasized the need for an ordained priest—a "father confessor"—to hear one's confession and offer absolution. This new sensibility of popular piety allowed individuals seeking God to seek Him directly through prayer, breaking the chain of mediators that had marked the Catholic church. Many men and women who called themselves the Brethren of the Common Life tried to create a devout

personal relationship between themselves and Christ, to supplement the complex Catholic theology. This style of popular religion was called the **devotio moderna** (modern devotion), and it influenced many subsequent believers.

One pious follower of the *devotio moderna,* Thomas à Kempis (1380–1471), is reputed to be the author of the best articulation of their ideas, in *The Imitation of Christ* (1425). In this profoundly influential text, Thomas argued that personal piety and ethics were as important as religious dogma. In Thomas's view, individuals could work toward salvation by focusing on their own spiritual growth, and many agreed passionately with Thomas's assertion "Blessed is the soul which hears the Lord speak within it and receives consolation from his mouth." As devoted Christians began to experiment with new forms of a Christian life, intellectuals began to contemplate some of the more complicated aspects of Christian thought.

Desiderius Erasmus: "Prince of Humanists"

As humanism spread to northern Europe, scholars applied the techniques of humanist education to Christian thought. The greatest Christian humanist was Desiderius Erasmus (1466–1536), who became known as the "Prince of the Humanists." Erasmus knew firsthand that some elements of the church needed reform, because he was born in Holland as the illegitimate son of a supposedly celibate priest. He studied at a school that was the center of the Brethren of the Common Life and grew up imbued with the new devotion that called for people to approach God directly in their hearts. Erasmus became a priest and went to study in a traditional university in Paris, which he hated. He dropped out of school, complaining that the university offered "theology as stale as their eggs."

The young priest then went to England, where his intellect was awakened by the humanists in Henry VIII's London. Erasmus became great friends with Thomas More and began a course of study based on a humanist curriculum. His interests remained religious, however, and he turned the humanist emphasis on original texts to biblical studies. He learned Greek so that he could immerse himself in the mental world of the New Testament, and like the Italian humanists, he insisted that language study had to be the starting point for any education: "Our first care must be to learn the three languages, Latin, Greek, and Hebrew, for it is plain that the mystery of all scripture is revealed in them." In this statement, we can see the literary work of the humanists applied to the highest Christian purpose.

Erasmus's greatest contribution to the intellectual life of the West was his critical edition of the New Testament. To approach this, Erasmus rejected the officially accepted version of the Bible—Jerome's (ca. 340–420) Latin translation, called the Vulgate—and returned to the Greek and

Germans Rage Against Papal Exploitation

This document reveals that some in Germany raged against what they saw as exploitation of Germans by a distant pope. It shows that Luther's critique launched in 1517 would find fertile soil.

Critique of Church Wealth, ca. 1480. Author anonymous.

It is as clear as day that by means of smooth and crafty words the clergy have deprived us of our rightful possessions. For they blinded the eyes of our forefathers, and persuaded them to buy the kingdom of heaven with their lands and possessions. But so long as you spend your money on your dear harlots and profligates, instead of upon the children of God, you may be sure that God will reward you according to your merits. For you have angered and overburdened all the people of the empire. The time is coming when your possessions will be seized and divided as if they were the possessions of an enemy. As you have oppressed the people, they will rise up against you so that you will not know where to find a place to stay.

What is the main criticism of the church expressed in this document?

Hebrew texts to create a new rendition. Erasmus even corrected portions of the Vulgate, and his edition became the basis for later translations of the Bible.

The humanist also criticized corruption in the church in many writings. For example, he wrote a satire, *Julius Excluded from Heaven* (1517), in which he showed the famous Renaissance warrior-pope Julius II (see Chapter 10) unable to enter heaven, even though popes had always claimed to hold its keys. His most famous satire, however, was *The Praise of Folly* (1511), in which he used his sharp wit to promote a greater spirituality in religion. In this book, his character, Folly, catalogs vices and in the process makes fun of the author himself, his friends, and the follies of everyday life. His attacks also probed deeply into many of the religious practices of the day, and as readers laughed at his attacks on people who "worshiped" the Virgin Mary over her son and popes who did not live like Jesus, their ideas on worship itself began to change.

Religious satires

Perhaps even more than his disappointment at church corruption, it was his humanist love of education that led him to propose a radically different approach to Christian life. Erasmus argued that Christians should read the Bible directly, rather than relying on priests to interpret it for them: "I would that even the lowliest women read the Gospels and the Pauline Epistles. And I would that they were translated into all languages." A scholar to the core, Erasmus did not advocate separation from the church, but a contemporary of his recognized the long-term impact of the humanist's thought, saying that "Erasmus laid the egg Luther hatched." Revolution in religious thinking had been planted, and the document on this page reveals the anger that served as fertile ground.

Luther's Revolution

Martin Luther (1483–1546), the intelligent son of an upwardly mobile family in Germany, was an improbable revolutionary. His father, a successful mine owner, expected him to further the family fortune by becoming a lawyer, but young Luther's life took a dramatically different turn. During a fierce thunderstorm, Luther was struck to the ground by a bolt of lightning. Frightened, Luther cried out to Saint Anne (the Virgin Mary's mother): "Help me and I will become a monk." He survived the storm and fulfilled his vow (much to his father's initial disapproval). Luther threw himself into his new calling—becoming a monk, priest, and doctor of theology—but he remained plagued with a deep sense of sin and a deep fear of damnation. He even believed he actually saw the devil during the torments of his conscience.

For all Luther's study, prayer, and attempts to live a Christian life, he still did not believe he could ever be worthy of salvation. Even the church's promise of grace in the sacraments and "good works" of the church brought him no comfort. Finally, he found peace in the Bible, especially its statement that the "just shall live by his faith" (Rom. 1:17). Luther interpreted this statement as meaning that people were saved only through God's mercy, not through their own efforts to live as good Christians. Faith alone—not ritual—would save their souls. For Luther, Christ's sacrifice had been complete and for all time, so humans did not have to do anything else for their own salvation. This central point of Luther's belief is called **"justification by faith."**

Inflamed by his newfound belief,

Attack on indulgences

Luther challenged church doctrine over the issue of **indulgences.** Through the Middle Ages, the Catholic Church had developed a complex understanding of how people are forgiven for their sins, including confession, penance, and absolution. As part of this process, churchmen claimed that people had to perform certain "works"—like prayers, fastings, pilgrimages, or similar activities—to receive forgiveness for their sins. If people died before completing full repentance for their transgressions, they could expect to suffer for them in **purgatory** before they could enter heaven, and late-medieval people had come to believe it would be virtually impossible for anyone to do full penance for their sins before death.

Jorg Breu, *The Sale of Indulgences*
ca. 1530

The artists of this engraving intended to show churchmen (called pardoners) on the right watching the pardoner on the left issue indulgences to the faithful lining up in the center. The pardoners are portrayed wearing furs and riding well-appointed mules, both signs of wealth. How would viewers recognize that indulgences were being "sold" here? What evidence is there that the artist was criticizing the practice?

In the Middle Ages, the pope had begun to alleviate some people's fears by offering an "indulgence," a remission of the need to do penance for sins. The pope claimed to control a "treasury of merit"—an infinite supply of good works that had been done by the saints and the Virgin Mary from which he could draw to remit sins. These remissions came in the form of "indulgences," documents that popes gave people in return for certain pious acts. Dating from the fourteenth century, a pious act might be a contribution of money to the church.

In 1517, Pope Leo X had issued a special indulgence to finance the construction of a new St. Peter's Church in Rome that would replace an old, smaller one. Johann Tetzel, a well-known Dominican friar, appeared to sell these indulgences to rich and poor alike in Germany and sent the money to Leo. Tetzel was reputed to have used the crude words "As soon as the coin in the coffer rings, the soul from purgatory springs." Luther, horrified by this apparent traf-

ficking in God's grace, wrote a series of statements decrying the selling of these indulgences and protesting the flow of money from Germany to Rome.

Tradition says that Luther tacked his list of arguments—the Ninety-five Theses—to the door of the church in Wittenberg, but he may well have simply sent it to his bishop. It seems that Luther merely wanted to engage a scholarly debate on the subject, but too many people

Ninety-five Theses

were profoundly interested in this topic. The inflammatory theses were soon translated into German and circulated even more widely than if they had been publicly posted on the church doors—they spread rapidly throughout Germany and beyond by way of the printing press. Their clearly drawn arguments and the passion that lay beneath them appealed to many intellectuals who criticized the church and to Germans who had begun to resent German money going to Italy. With Luther's strong words

"It is foolish to think that papal indulgences . . . can absolve a man," the battle lines were drawn.

Luther's commitment to individual conscience over institutional obedience catalyzed major changes in his life that in turn shaped the emergence of the reformed church. It is somewhat ironic that within a generation, reformers would be enforcing institutional obedience with as much enthusiasm as the Catholics ever had. However, Luther himself pursued the logical consequences of his ideas. In Luther's new understanding, the monastic life made no religious sense; in the presence of God's grace, there was no need for heroic renunciations. Therefore, he left the monastery and married Katherina von Bora, a former nun, and wrote influential works on Christian marriage. He also composed moving hymns that transformed religious services. Furthermore, because he came to his understanding of religion through reading the Bible, he believed that it should be accessible to everyone, so he translated it into German. Indeed, this translation became his most influential legacy. Not only did it make the Bible available to an even wider group of readers; it also, through its popularity, helped shape the form of the developing German language.

Protestant Religious Ideas

Luther articulated a core of beliefs that subsequent religious groups would share, even as they departed from "Lutheranism." Christian churches (except the Roman Catholic and Eastern Orthodox) that share these beliefs today are called **Protestant.** The word derives from the protest of some German princes at the Diet (assembly) of Speier in 1529. Over the objection of the Lutheran princes, that body decided to protect the Catholic Church's right to offer services in Lutheran lands while denying the same privilege to Lutherans in Catholic lands. The name "Protestant" remained long after the issue had been resolved.

For Luther and subsequent Protestant reformers, at the heart of religious belief lay a faith in God's mercy that transcended the need for any good works. The Protestants thus conceived of a "priesthood of all believers," in which women and men were responsible for their own salvation. There was no need for an ordained priesthood to convey grace to believers by performing the sacraments. Church leaders (whom Protestants called ministers, pastors, or preachers) could teach, preach, and guide Christian followers, but they could not help them achieve salvation. Each person stood alone before God throughout his or her life, and on judgment day prayers to saints and to the Virgin Mary were no more helpful than prayers offered by any other Christian. When people's spiritual quests combined with the Renaissance sense of individualism, it changed even the path to God.

With their emphasis on the individual's relationship to God, Protestants rejected many of the elements that had characterized the medieval church. No longer were the faithful to venerate saints or the Virgin Mary, so many claimed the relics of saints and martyrs that filled the churches of Europe were worthless. Protestant faithful would not become pilgrims traveling to the great cathedrals and saints' shrines in search of blessings or miracles. Indeed, the statues of the saints and other icons seemed to many Protestants to promote idolatry, and there was periodic Protestant **iconoclasm,** or destroying of the sacred images in the churches.

Just as Protestants downplayed the importance of the priesthood and the intercession of saints, they restricted the significance and number of the sacraments. In the Middle Ages, Catholics had identified seven sacraments important for salvation (including marriage and the last rites at death). Most (but not all) Protestant reformers accepted only two sacraments—baptism and the Eucharist (the celebration of Christ's Last Supper before his Crucifixion). Furthermore, they rejected **transubstantiation,** which said that the bread and wine offered up at mass were turned into the actual body and blood of Christ—a transformation that only an ordained priest could perform. Although Protestants may have rejected transubstantiation, they held various views on how Christ was present in the Eucharist, but because the bread and wine were not transformed, any believer could celebrate the Last Supper. As other Protestant groups branched off from Luther's initial thinking, they would emphasize some points of this theology over others. However, all of them shared the same basic principles: salvation by faith, not works; the Bible as the sole authority; and a "priesthood" made up of all believers.

These ideas spread rapidly in large part because they offered a simple and elegant answer to the question that had plagued so many: "How do I know I am saved?" Printing presses produced pamphlets and flyers offering these notions to the literate of towns and manors, and popular preachers told peasants in villages about Luther's challenge. Luther's seeds of revolution disseminated widely and found fertile soil.

The Reformed Church Takes Root in Germany

Luther's attack on tradition and hierarchy could not go unnoticed. In 1521, Luther was called to appear before Charles V at the Diet of Worms to defend his views. Though confronted with over a thousand years of tradition, Luther nevertheless adhered to his understanding of scripture, and he reputedly made the famous reply: "To go against conscience is neither right nor safe. Here I stand, I cannot do otherwise." During the Middle Ages, many men and women who had similarly stood by their beliefs had been executed for their stance. The political situation in Germany in the sixteenth century saved Luther from this fate—and turned his personal stance into a religious revolution. Under pres-

Sacraments

Priesthood of all believers

sure from Charles V to recant, Luther sought and received the protection of his prince, the powerful Frederick the Wise of Saxony. The prince offered Luther shelter and protection as the reformer continued his writings.

In addition to reasons of conscience, German princes had other motives for supporting Luther's ideas. The reformer's call to stop sending German money to Rome suited princes who felt the sharp sting of inflation. Princes could also benefit from confiscating wealthy Catholic properties (like churches and monasteries) in the name of religion. Luther's call for a break with Rome also appealed to a growing sense of German nationalism as distinct from the international Christendom represented by the Catholic Church. Some princes may have hoped that any weakening of the pope's authority would also diminish the power of the Holy Roman Emperor Charles V, whose authority derived in part from papal support. A weakened emperor meant more opportunities for the princes to bolster their own power.

Many poor, too, rallied to Luther's banner of religious reform, and this support took a particularly violent form in Germany. Spurred on by fiery preachers, peasants who suffered from hunger, inflation, and skyrocketing manorial dues made Luther's attack on religious abuses part of their revolutionary program. In 1524, German peasants circulated the Twelve Articles, in which they demanded such things as a reduction of manorial dues and services and preservation of their rights to use meadows and woods. These wants dealt directly with the peasants' concerns, but they couched their demands in references to scripture—a direct consequence of Luther's call for people to conduct their lives in accordance with their biblical readings.

Peasants' war

In 1524, a violent peasant war broke out. As the peasants took up arms and stormed manor houses, they called for support from Luther's religious reformers. However, Luther was no John Ball (the religious leader who had led the peasant revolt in England in 1381). He advocated religious reform, not social revolution, for he believed the Bible called for people to obey secular rulers. Appalled by the violence in the countryside, Luther wrote a treatise called "Against the Robbing and Murdering Hordes of Peasants," in which he reprimanded peasants for defying legitimate government. He also urged those in power to "smite, slay and stab" rebellious peasants, but the nobility needed no urging from Luther to protect their privileges. The rebellion was brutally suppressed—more than 100,000 peasants were killed. The princes appreciated Luther's support of their repression and judged the movement perfectly consistent with their political needs. The Protestant Reformation thus found a warm welcome in the courts of many German princes.

By the time Charles V could turn his attention from the wars in Italy in the west and the Turkish threat in the east back to his German lands, the reformed church had taken firm root. At this point, Charles was in no position to uproot Lutheranism, which was supported by many of the great princes of the land. Furthermore, Charles's armies contained many Lutherans—as early as 1527, men among the rioting troops in Rome purportedly were calling for a silk rope to hang the pope. The emperor could not govern any longer without some accommodation.

Charles first tried to demand that his subjects come together under one religion. In 1530, he commanded all Lutherans to return to Catholicism or be arrested, but it was too late. Too many princes were willing to form a military alliance rather than obey. Then Charles tried compromise. In the 1540s, he encouraged talks between Lutherans and Catholics about the possibility of reconciliation, but these failed as well. By the 1550s, Lutheranism had captured about half the population of the empire.

In 1555, Charles's successor, Ferdinand, met with the German princes to negotiate a compromise to settle the religious turmoil. The resulting Peace of Augsburg established the Lutheran Church as a legitimate alternative to Catholicism in Germany. By this treaty, each prince

Peace of Augsburg

defined his principality as either Catholic or Lutheran. This compromise is known by the Latin phrase *cuius regio, eius religio,* which means "who rules determines the religion." Residents of any principality who did not agree with their prince's religious decision were free to move to a more congenial location. The Catholic emperor Ferdinand, the pope, and many churchmen did not like this concession to Lutheranism, which split the unity of the Christian church. However, they had no choice but to accept the compromise forced by the strong German princes.

The Augsburg treaty opened the door for the Reformation to fragment Christian Europe into a complex mix of different Christian sects. In addition, other monarchs and princes besides those in Germany saw the advantage in separating from Rome. Scandinavian kings, for instance, followed the example of German princes in supporting Lutheranism. These conversions left many problems unsolved—what about groups other than Lutherans? What about dissenting voices within either Catholic or Protestant principalities? What was the relationship between the state and religion? While these questions smoldered, the fire of religious reform continued to spread through Europe.

Bringing Reform to the States in Switzerland

While Luther's call for reform was the first to gain a large audience, his was not a solitary voice. Shortly after Luther's challenge, reformers in Switzerland successfully challenged old religious ideas. Switzerland consisted of a loose confederation of states (called cantons) in which many residents were ready for change, and the very independence of the cantons facilitated acceptance of new religious ideas. In addition, many of the young men from the Swiss cantons served as mercenaries in the seemingly insatiable armies of Europe, and service generated a growing disdain for the established order. Just as in Germany, dissatisfaction and growing national spirit combined with a desire for religious reform.

The first leader of the Reformation in Switzerland was Ulrich Zwingli (1484–1531), who lived in the northern canton of Zurich. Zwingli had been strongly influenced by Erasmus's writings, and when he served as a chaplain with Swiss mercenaries, his longing for religious reform became joined with a desire to remove the Swiss confederation from the horrible wars.

Zwingli

In 1519 (a mere two years after Luther's challenge with his Ninety-five Theses), Zwingli became the priest of the main church in Zurich, and from there he began his own attack on traditional church practices. He believed Christians should practice only those things found in scripture, so his church in Zurich rejected such things as the veneration of saints, pilgrimages, purgatory, clerical celibacy, and most of the sacraments. In 1523, the city government in Zurich approved Zwingli's reforms, and Zurich became a Protestant city.

Zwingli and Luther shared many ideas, but would Protestants join together and form one church to oppose Catholicism? One German prince—Philip of Hesse—saw the advantages of consolidation and brought Luther and Zwingli together in 1529 at a meeting in Marburg to try to bring about an alliance. Although the two reformers agreed on virtually all points of doctrine, the meeting fell apart over their respective understanding of the nature of Christ's presence in the celebration of the Eucharist. Zwingli insisted the remembrance was symbolic, whereas Luther insisted that Christ's body was present as well as his spirit. As neither man could compromise with his conscience, there would be no united Protestant church or state. The new reformed churches would go their separate ways.

Just as in Germany, Protestantism came to the Swiss cantons with violence. In 1529, civil wars broke out between Protestant and Catholic cantons, and Zwingli himself died on the battlefield in 1531. The cantons reached a resolution similar to that of the later Peace of Augsburg in Germany—each canton would determine its own religion. However, the fires of reform stirred in more consciences and continued to spread, bringing both more hope and more violence.

Anabaptists: The Radical Reformers

The reforms of Luther and Zwingli appealed to many people but were implemented by princes or urban governments. However, many people saw power and religion as incompatible. New groups took a more radical turn in their efforts to reform the church and to keep it untainted by politics, and these reformers seemed threatening even to Protestants like Lutherans and Swiss reformers. Most members of these sects were referred to by their opponents as Anabaptists, meaning "rebaptizers" (although many of them preferred to be called simply Baptists), because they believed baptism should be reserved for adults, who could make a conscious choice to receive the grace of the sacrament. The radical sects drew heavily from peasants and artisans, especially those suffering from poverty and the relentless warfare of the period.

Confrontation between Anabaptists and the rest of society stemmed mainly from the Anabaptists' views on the relationship between church and state. Many radical reformers advocated a complete separation of these two institutions. They even argued that the "saved" (or the "elect") should not participate in government (including serving in the armies that were vigorously recruiting in the villages).

Church vs. state

While most Anabaptist groups were pacifists, others became revolutionaries fighting for what they believed was a religious cause—the ushering in of a biblically promised age of peace and prosperity during which the "meek shall inherit the earth." Some revolutionaries saw the horrors of war and famine in the sixteenth century as the expected biblical disasters and chose to take up arms to help fight against those who had previously oppressed the poor. In Germany in 1534, a fiery preacher named Melchior established a sect (called the Melchiorites) that gained political control of their city of Münster. They burned all books but the Bible, abolished private property, and introduced polygamy as they settled down to await the expected second coming of Christ. Lutherans and Catholics alike believed this was a threat to society, so they captured the city and massacred the Melchiorites. Thereafter, the radicals were persecuted by Catholics and other Protestants alike.

Radical reformers

Calvinism and the Growing Middle Class

As we have seen, the Swiss cantons with their prosperous middle class had voiced religious longings and aspirations under the guidance of Zwingli. In the mid-sixteenth century, another voice also appealed to many of these well-to-do people in cities throughout Europe. Many people found intellectual and spiritual satisfaction in the teachings of the brilliant French scholar John Calvin (1509–1564). While preparing for a career in law, Calvin had studied many humanist writings, and in about 1533, Calvin

OPINION

Why do you think various socioeconomic groups were drawn to different religious sects, for example, German princes to Lutheranism, peasants to Anabaptism, and middle classes to Calvinism?

read some of Martin Luther's works. He experienced a profound calling to Protestant theology. The new reformer soon experienced pressure from royal authorities who in the reign of Francis I began a periodic suppression of reformers. Calvin had to flee France to avoid persecution and found a safe haven in the Swiss city of Geneva, where he published the first edition of his masterwork, *The Institutes of the Christian Religion* (1536).

What was the nature of Calvin's vision that appealed particularly to the hardworking and often prosperous middle classes? Calvin accepted the basic elements of Protestant belief that Luther had articulated, but he added his own emphasis. Whereas Luther had focused on salvation as the goal of human struggle, Calvin urged people to recognize the majesty, power, and justice of God. Perhaps Calvin's greatest contribution to Reformation thought was to redirect theological speculation from individual salvation to a larger question of humans' place in the universe.

When he turned to the question of salvation, Calvin again emphasized the power of God, shown in **predestination,** the belief that God preordained who would be saved or damned, even before a person was

Predestination

born. Calvin explained that if God were *only* just, everyone would be damned, for all people were sinful. However, God tempered his justice with mercy, reaching down into the flames of damnation and plucking some souls out to share salvation. Calvin called these souls that were predestined to be saved the elect; the rest would experience eternal damnation. Many believers who, like Luther, felt that humans could do nothing to earn their salvation found comfort in the concept of predestination. Although predestination was at the core of Calvin's beliefs, he never stressed it as much as his followers in subsequent generations did.

As Calvinism took hold, Geneva became a vibrant center for Calvinist missionary work. Between 1555 and 1562, Calvin dispersed 100 preachers to the far-flung corners of Europe. Calvin had impres-

Spread of Calvinism

sive organizational abilities, and he laid out directions for organizing congregations that explained how believers could establish underground groups to adopt Calvinism even where civil authorities were hostile. These techniques worked. The Netherlands were particularly receptive to Calvinist thought. In addition, many French cities soon amassed substantial Calvinist minorities, called **Huguenots.** German cities, too, began attracting Calvinist minorities—a problem because the Peace of Augsburg recognized only Lutheranism and Catholicism as acceptable religions. The Scot John Knox (1514–1572) was dazzled by Calvin in Geneva and returned to Scotland, where he established Calvinism as the predominant form of Protestantism. Like Knox, others from the British Isles were drawn to the exciting ideas of the reformers.

Protestant reliance on individual conscience made believers uncomfortable with much of the religious art that had dominated Christian worship in the West. In addi-

DESTROYING IMAGES, 1566 Calvinists believed that the images that graced the churches were idolatry. This illustration from a work published in 1568 by Franz Hogenberg shows people in the Netherlands destroying these images in a riot.

tion, many Protestants believed that religious art smacked of idol worship, drained precious resources better used on the poor, or simply distracted worshipers from focusing on the word of God. These concerns caused believers in many regions to attack religious art. Most of the Reformation leaders disapproved of such violence, but nevertheless, much religious art was destroyed in Protestant countries.

As a second-generation Protestant, Calvin moved the Reformation forward in important ways. In his writings and his life, he worked to establish a positive definition of Protestantism, that is, not simply as "not Catholic." In doing so, he articulated many of the theological principles that would define all Protestant churches. The passion for individualism and religious innovation kept Calvin (and anyone else) from uniting the various protest movements, but his intellect and strong faith made him an able advocate for Protestant thought.

Henry VIII and the English Church

In England in the 1520s, Protestant sympathizers gathered to discuss some of Luther's writings that had been smuggled in. Perhaps even more exciting to the reformers was William Tyndale's English translation of the New Testament, which began to circulate in England in 1526. Protestant sympathies were growing on the island, but they would bear fruit from the actions of an unlikely ally—the king himself.

Henry VIII (r. 1509–1547) was not initially a reformer. In fact, he had written an attack against Martin Luther in 1521 called the *Defense of the Seven Sacraments,* and Pope Leo X awarded him the title Defender of the Faith for his support. (Ironically, Protestant English monarchs still retain this title.) Although many English people wanted religious reform and some felt a strong antipathy toward the pope, it did not seem as if their king would lead them in a break with Rome. But Henry's desperate need for a male heir changed all this.

Remembering the devastating Wars of the Roses (Chapter 9) that had brought his Tudor dynasty to power, Henry believed he needed a male heir to secure the succession. His wife of eighteen years, Catherine of Aragon, had failed to produce one. Henry began to believe that God disapproved of this marriage, for he had married the widow of his brother (a practice normally forbidden) and had received special permission from the pope to do so. Henry also had fallen in love with a beautiful and bright young woman, Anne Boleyn. Anne did not want to become another of the king's mistresses, so she held off his amorous advances, insisting on a promise of marriage; first, Henry needed an annulment from the pope to end his first marriage.

Seeking a male heir

Ordinarily, such royal annulments were easy to obtain because the popes had traditionally acquiesced to royal wishes. However, just as Charles V's absence from Germany in the Italian Habsburg-Valois Wars allowed Lutheranism to take hold, it also facilitated religious reform in England. Henry wanted his divorce in 1527, just as Charles V's troops were sacking Rome and virtually holding Pope Clement VII prisoner. The pope needed the goodwill of Charles to restore order and Henry's queen, Catherine, was Charles V's aunt. The pope dragged his feet in granting Henry his annulment.

In 1533, Anne Boleyn, persuaded that the king would marry her, became pregnant. Now Henry was running out of time for his annulment, for he wanted Anne's child to be born legitimate. Henry's two principal advisors—Thomas Cranmer, archbishop of Canterbury, and Thomas Cromwell—devised a way for Henry to get his annulment. Parliament passed an act making the archbishop of Canterbury the highest ecclesiastical official in England (cutting off the pope's authority). Then Thomas Cranmer ruled that Henry's marriage to Catherine was "null and void," so Henry was free to marry Anne. He did so, and three months later, much to the king's dismay, she gave birth to a girl, the future Queen Elizabeth. (Henry finally had a male heir by his third wife, after Anne was beheaded for adultery, but the king would eventually marry six women in his quest for heirs and personal happiness.)

Henry's annulment

Henry had gotten his annulment, but the force of religious reform he had unleashed continued its momentum. Parliament passed a number of measures designed to control the Catholic clergy and finally passed the Act of Supremacy (1534) that declared the king the supreme

Church of England

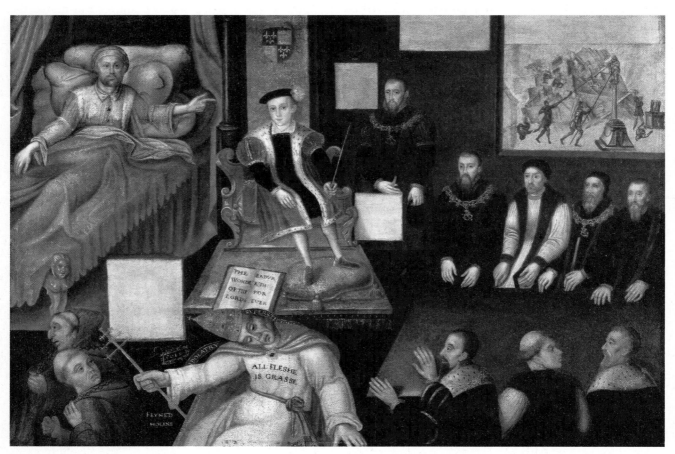

ANONYMOUS, *EDWARD VI AND THE POPE*, 1568–1571 This work commemorates—and tries to ensure—the successful reestablishment of the Church of England by the young King Edward VI, shown at the center while the pope below is depicted crushed by a book of scripture.

head of the Church of England. This break with the papacy established the Church of England as a separate church (which later was also called Protestant), but not everyone in England welcomed this major reform. The most notable dissenter was the humanist Thomas More (1478–1535), whose conscience would not allow him to obey a secular ruler in matters of faith, and he refused to swear an oath acknowledging the king's ecclesiastical supremacy. More was beheaded for his dissent, and this man of high integrity died blessing the king who had been his great friend, saying, "I die the king's good servant, but God's first."

Henry's position toward the reformers vacillated throughout his life. He did not support all the Protestant religious ideas—for example, he reaffirmed transubstantiation, which all the Protestants rejected. In fact, he considered himself a Catholic, although not a "Roman" Catholic. However, the powerful king readily implemented Reformation ideas that enriched his coffers and weakened the power of the Catholic Church. He shared the reformers' rejection of the monastic life and dissolved all the monasteries in England, confiscating their extensive lands and wealth. The king's treasury bulged from the confiscations, and many English religious reformers were satisfied with his new policies. However, the Church of England (also called the Anglican Church) really became Protestant under the reign of Henry's son.

Henry's third wife, Jane Seymour, finally bore him a son, Edward, in 1537. However, the boy was sickly when he took the throne upon Henry's death in 1547. Edward VI (r. 1547–1553) was a bright youth

Edward VI

who was fond of Protestant theology, but he was young. Because of Edward's age, England was in fact ruled by a council of regents who wanted to solidify Protestantism in England.

Archbishop Thomas Cranmer issued a Protestant manual of worship, *The Book of Common Prayer,* and Parliament issued the Act of Uniformity in 1549, making the prayer book's use mandatory for religious service throughout the kingdom. It seemed as if the Church of England was securely established, but the English would suffer more upheavals before religious peace reigned.

The 16-year-old Edward died without an heir, and the kingdom next went to his elder sister, Mary (r. 1553–1558), daughter of Catherine of Aragon, Henry's first wife. A

"Bloody Mary"

staunch Catholic, Mary promptly set about undoing the Protestant reforms and returning England to the protective bosom of Rome. Although many prominent Protestants had fled to the Continent upon Mary's accession, the queen attempted to force remaining Protestants to renounce their beliefs. Bloody Mary ordered some 280 Protestants burned for "religious treason," including Archbishop Cranmer, who had originally granted Henry VIII his divorce. The English public was even more upset by her marriage to Charles V's son Philip II, the Catholic king of Spain. However, the marriage did not produce an heir who could continue her Catholic policies.

ATTRIBUTED TO WILLIAM SEGAN, *PORTRAIT OF ELIZABETH I,* 1585 The shrewd Elizabeth brought a moderate approach to religious reform that allowed England to flourish. Her portraits both advertised her accomplishments and soothed her vanity.

Upon Mary's death, the throne went to her half-sister, Anne Boleyn's daughter, Elizabeth I (r. 1558–1603), whose rule would earn her the affectionate nickname Good Queen Bess. Elizabeth proved a brilliant politician who skillfully positioned herself at the center of a contentious

Elizabeth I

court. She also remained unmarried (the ermine on her left arm in the painting above is the symbol of virginity) and used that condition for her own diplomatic advantage by holding out the possibility of marrying into other European royal houses. Though arrogant and vain, Elizabeth was also a shrewd and frugal ruler who well deserved her people's grateful affection.

In matters of religion, Elizabeth did not worry about the fine points of theology. The young queen was appalled at the violence and destruction caused by the religious controversies, and she felt deeply responsible for maintaining peace in her realm while allowing people to follow their consciences. However, she was insistent on loyalty above all else, and she persecuted Catholics, who she felt had divided loyalties. She wanted to unify England around a Protestant core but also allow her loyal subjects latitude in religious practice and belief. For example, the prayer book that she instituted let people of differing convictions pray together in a national church. This moderate approach was effective: For a while, England basked in a time of peace that fostered an intellectual flowering (see Chapter 10) and an era of international expansion (see Chapter 12).

Even as Elizabeth moved England toward moderation in religion, Scotland clung to the firm Calvinism preached by John Knox. In 1560, a Reformed Parliament gathered in Scotland and made a decisive

Scotland's church break with Catholic France in favor of Protestant England. However, Scotland was to put its own mark on its church, which was established by the Scots Confession of 1560. Knox composed the church's liturgy, the *Book of Common Order*, which demonstrated how the Scottish church departed from the Anglican one. The Scots emphasized individual Christian conscience over ecclesiastical authority, and instead of placing bishops in authority, they established a Presbyterian form of organization that gave authority to pastors and elders of the congregations. The resulting Presbyterian congregations were more independent than the Episcopal congregations of the Anglican Church.

By the end of the seventeenth century, the old medieval notion of a Europe united under the protection of a uniform Christianity had evaporated. The map on page 259 shows the religious diversity that characterized Christian Europe at the end of the sixteenth century. Lutheran and Anglican

Europe divided churches were accepted by princes and rulers. Calvinists formed a solid minority in many areas. Many rulers struggled to grapple with even this degree of diversity. Yet Protestantism, by its very nature, had the potential to yield even more divisions. Once the door had opened for individuals to define their own way to God, there was no limit to the paths that people might create. However, the Catholic Church could not ignore these theological controversies and cries for reform, and in the sixteenth century, Catholicism searched its own conscience.

THE CATHOLIC REFORMATION

Even before Luther circulated his devastating criticism, many leaders in the Catholic Church were working to reform abuses and bring to Catholic worship new insights about textual criticism of Christian humanism. Girolamo Savonarola (1452–1498) in Florence, for example, had urged reform of the Renaissance papacy (see Chapter 10). His was not an isolated voice, though, for even popes in the early sixteenth century called councils and promulgated decrees aimed at reform. This movement of religious reform is called the Catholic Reformation by Catholics and the Counter-Reformation by Protestants, who saw these reforms as a response to the Protestant challenge. However, many of these religious reflections grew out of a continuing Catholic discussion that followed the Great

Schism, the Conciliar movement, and the rule of the politically active Renaissance popes. Popes faced a tough challenge in implementing reforms at that time, because the Habsburg-Valois Wars occupied the attention of the Catholic kings Charles V and Francis I, who in normal times would have backed the papacy. These wars also carried a high financial price for the popes—during the sack of Rome in 1527, for example, imperial troops made off with mounds of gold coins from the papal treasury. To recover their losses, the popes stepped up the sort of fundraising that had so incited Luther. Practical reform had to wait for peace.

The Stirring of Reform in Spain

In the fifteenth century, Spain emerged from its medieval decentralization and became a strong, unified kingdom. In 1469, Isabella (r. 1474–1504) and Ferdinand (r. 1479–1516) married, joining the kingdoms of Leon-Castile and Aragon. They immediately set about reducing the power of the nobility and establishing a centralized power.

Ferdinand and Isabella became known as the "Catholic monarchs," emphasizing their faith and the degree to which they believed they carried the banner of an invigorated Catholicism. As part of their goal of a centralized and religiously homogeneous Spain, they resumed the reconquest of the peninsula that had dominated the history of medieval Spain. The monarchs besieged Granada, the last Muslim stronghold in the south of Spain, and conquered it in 1492.

Ferdinand and Isabella

The religious zeal that grew out of the crusade against Granada continued after the fall of the city. In the same year, all Jews were expelled from Spain. Some 150,000 were given four months to leave. As we will see in Chapter 12, the same crusading zeal would extend across the Atlantic. By 1492, Spain was well placed to take the lead in fostering Catholicism against the forces of Protestantism.

As part of their dynastic aims, Ferdinand and Isabella had arranged marriages for their children to the leading families of Europe. Their daughter Joanna became the wife of the Habsburg archduke, and her son Charles V became heir to both Spain and the Habsburg lands. With such pious grandparents, it is not surprising that Charles V was so vigorous in his support of Catholicism.

The most influential religious figure in Spain during this time was Cardinal Ximénez de Cisneros 1436–1517). He was confessor to the queen, bishop of Toledo, Grand Inquisitor, and regent of Spain after Ferdinand's death. It was Ximénez who brought humanist ideas into Spain.

Ximénez was particularly impressed with Erasmus's emphasis on scholarly study of scripture and the works of the church fathers, and he wanted to strengthen this kind of education in Spain. In 1498, Ximénez received

Cardinal Ximénez

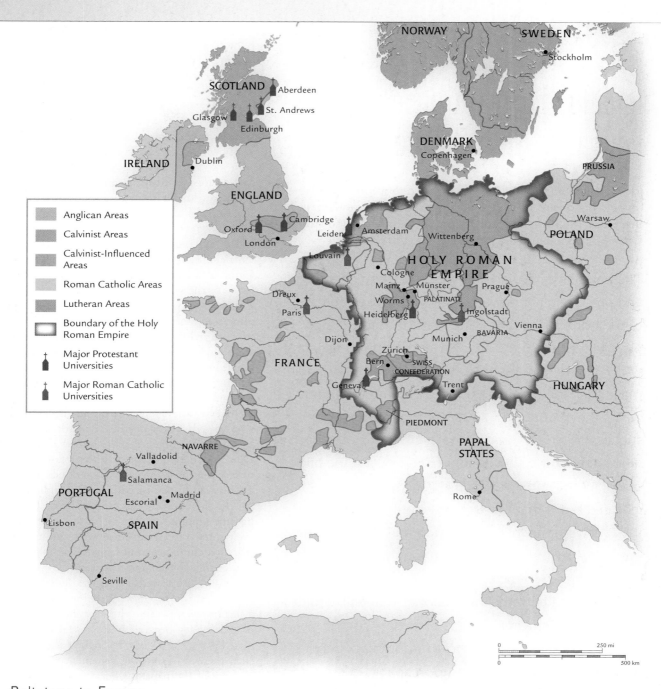

Religions in Europe, ca. 1600 This map shows the distribution of the major centers of Catholics and Protestants in Europe at the end of the sixteenth century. Notice that there were strong Calvinist minorities in some countries.

permission from the Borgia pope Alexander VI to found a new university at Alcalá de Henares that would feature humanist approaches to theological and ecclesiastical studies. The high quality of the scholarship at the school drew notice with the publication of the *Complutensian Polyglot Bible* (1520), an edition of the Bible written in three columns that compared the Hebrew, Greek, and Latin versions. This scholarship represented a high point in humanistic learning and new critical techniques in the study of the Bible.

The Society of Jesus

Throughout its history, the Catholic Church had been reformed by monastic and mendicant orders that infused new life and ideas into the church. This pattern continued in the sixteenth century. Several new orders emerged, but the most influential was the Society of Jesus, whose members were called **Jesuits.**

Ignatius Loyola Argues for Education as a Solution

In August 1554, Ignatius Loyola wrote a letter in which he reveals his desire to stop the growth of Protestantism. In this letter, he advocates education as the best way to stop Catholics from embracing the Protestant theology.

The heretics have made their false theology popular and presented it in a way that is within the capacity of the common people. They preach it to the people and teach it in the schools, and scatter booklets which can be bought and understood by many, and make their influence felt by means of their writings when they cannot do so by their preaching. Their success is largely due to the negligence of those who should have shown some interest; and the bad example and the ignorance of Catholics, . . . Hence it would seem that our Society should make use of the following means to put a stop and apply a remedy to the evils which have come upon the Church through these heretics. . . .

A short catechism [instructional manual] could be taught to children, as the Christian doctrine is now taught, and likewise to the common people who are not too infected or too capable of subtleties. This could also be done with the younger students in the lower classes, where they could learn it by heart. . . .

Another excellent means for helping the Church in this trial would be to multiply the colleges and schools of the Society in many lands, especially where a good attendance could be expected. . . .

What do you think will be the social effects of Loyola's emphasis on education?

The Society of Jesus was founded by Ignatius of Loyola (1491–1556), a soldier in the service of the Spanish monarch. In battle a cannonball shattered Loyola's legs, and he had a long and painful recovery—his legs had to be set and rebroken twice (without anesthesia) because they were healing crookedly. During his recuperation, Loyola read stories of Christian saints and decided to dedicate himself as a soldier of Christ. Loyola trained himself for a spiritual life with the same rigor that marked his military practice. In his quest, he was influenced by Thomas à Kempis's *Imitation of Christ* and wrote his own book that offered a Catholic version of the personal search for God. In the widely read work, *The Spiritual Exercises,* Loyola taught how spiritual discipline could satisfy people's desire to reach up to God while obeying the orders of the Catholic Church. Here was the perfect combination of Catholic orthodoxy and the longings expressed by Protestant reformers.

Jesuits established

In 1540, the pope established the Society of Jesus as a religious order, and the Jesuits, who vowed perfect obedience to the papacy, became the vanguard of reformed Catholicism. These men devoted themselves to education, sharing Cardinal Ximénez's belief that a Christian humanist education would combat the threat of Protestantism. Their schools became among the best in Europe, drawing even some Protestants who were willing to risk their children's conversion to Catholicism in exchange for the fine education.

Jesuits also served as missionaries to bring Catholicism to the New World (see Chapter 12). However, in time the new shock troops of the papacy became controversial in their own right—the vigor with which they pursued their aims and the vehemence of their support of the papacy alienated some Catholics and Protestants alike. But there is no question that in the sixteenth century and beyond, the Jesuits would be a powerful force in the reformed Catholicism.

The Council of Trent

1545–1563

With the conclusion of the Habsburg-Valois Wars, the Catholic monarchs could focus on the divisive religious questions of the day. After the treaty of 1544 that ended the wars, church leaders from all over Europe gathered in northern Italy at Trent, and the council met intermittently from 1545 to 1563. Charles wanted the council to

Reforming corruption

concentrate on reforming abuses, and it confronted this thorny issue honestly, establishing stern measures to clean up clerical corruption, ignorance, and apathy. They even banned the selling of indulgences and the office of indulgence-seller. But the real work of the council took place when it confronted the theological debate that had driven the Protestants from the church. As these leaders clarified their beliefs, it became obvious that there would be no compromise with Protestant Christianity.

The Council of Trent determined that Catholics did *not* stand alone before God. Rather, it claimed, the community of the faithful, both living and dead, could help a

Affirming doctrine

Catholic to salvation. Thus prayers to the saints and to the Virgin Mary *did* matter. The church also affirmed the existence of purgatory and the power of prayer and even indulgences to free souls from their punishment.

These churchmen rejected Protestants by reaffirming their position that Christians needed both faith and good works to go to heaven. For Catholics, the sacraments by their very nature conveyed grace, so the council reaffirmed the existence of all seven rites. In further rejection of Protestant criticism, Catholics retained their idea of transubstantiation, by which priests presided over the transformation of the wine and host into the blood and body of Christ.

While debating and refining their beliefs, the churchmen used principles that had guided previous councils and looked to two authorities—scripture and tradition. Armed with these pillars of Christian thought, they prepared to

Scripture and tradition

answer Luther and the other Protestants, who recognized only their own consciences and the complete authority of the Holy Book. Catholics, the Trent council argued, could draw strength from the body of practices that the faithful had accumulated over the course of a millennium. With its doctrine thus established, the Catholic Church showed a new strength and confidence. Dissenters had gone to other sects, leaving a vigorous corps of dedicated believers to challenge the Protestants head-on.

Catholics on the Offense

Throughout this period, many Catholics expressed their faith with more passion and mystical emotion than they had shown in centuries. Teresa of Avila, Spain (1515–1582), a sixteenth-century mystic who quickly became a saint, exemplified this newfound energy. The daughter of a converted Jew, Teresa entered a convent and experienced a series of visions. Not only a mystic, Teresa was an active reformer, establishing new convents for women as part of her dedication to a reinvigorated Catholicism. Her mystical writing, *Way of Perfection,* ensured her influence, for it

inspired the pope to declare her a Doctor of the Church (which means that her writings were worthy of study). Soon she became the patron saint of Spain, replacing Saint James (Santiago), who had held that honor throughout the Middle Ages. The example of Teresa and other mystics offered the church a strong weapon to show skeptics the deep and passionate faith that came with Catholic worship. However, they also used stronger measures than the writings of gentle mystics.

Reinvigorated, and considering themselves at war with Protestants, the Catholics moved to repress opposition to their views. The Spanish Inquisition took a forceful role in this battle over religious diversity. (This court was separate from the papal inquisition that, as we saw in Chapter 8, had been introduced into Europe in the thirteenth

Spanish Inquisition

century.) Inquisitors now added Lutherans and Calvinists to converted Jews and Muslims in their definition of suspect populations and launched a new round of public trials and executions. In 1542, the Inquisition was reestablished in Rome, as the popes also felt compelled to take extreme measures to protect Catholics themselves from incorrect ideas.

EL GRECO, *BURIAL OF THE COUNT OF ORGAZ,* ca. 1586
Reformed Catholicism disagreed with Protestant views in asserting that the dead can be helped by the prayers of the living and by the intercession of the dead themselves. The famous Spanish painter el Greco illustrated these beliefs in this scene of the burial of a count, who is helped into heaven by the prayers of the living and intercession of the dead.

In addition, the papacy began to publish an Index of Prohibited Books in 1557, which it updated and reissued regularly. (The index was finally abolished in 1966.)

While such measures aimed to control people's beliefs, the church looked to the Spanish king to champion the Catholic cause in the political and military arena. Philip II

| Philip II | (r. 1556–1588), Charles V's heir to the kingdoms of Spain and the Netherlands, had an unparalleled zeal for |

both the Catholic religion and empire. Philip moved his capital from Toledo, a cramped medieval city, to the newly built city of Madrid, chosen because it was the geographic center of the Iberian Peninsula.

Philip faced two dire threats to the Catholic faith: the Turks in the eastern Mediterranean and the Protestants in the north. In 1571, he assembled a league that included a number of Italian city-states and set out to challenge the Turks' supremacy in the Mediterranean. The Venetians, who had a large fleet and were highly motivated by their trading interests in the eastern Mediterranean, were particularly eager to join Philip's navy. Outfitted with 208 galleys—sleek warships rowed by slaves and armed with cannons—Philip's navy confronted the Turks' 230 warships at the Battle of Lepanto, off the coast of Greece.

When the smoke cleared after this spectacular battle, Philip's coalition had scored a decisive victory. The Turks lost two hundred warships, the Europeans only ten. Tens of thousands of men on both sides died in the fighting, and contemporary witnesses described the sea as running red with blood. Nevertheless, the success at Lepanto raised Catholics' spirits throughout the West. The navy had proved that Turkish power in the Mediterranean was not invincible after all. Indeed, some western Catholics began toying with the idea of invading the Ottoman Empire itself. But the Catholic monarchs had other adversaries in mind. Again, the kings of Europe went to war. This time, though, they marched against the Protestants in a series of battles that would drag on for a century and tear apart the soul of Europe.

EUROPE ERUPTS AGAIN: A Century of Religious Warfare

1559–1648

The Reformation had done far more than just establish alternative Christian sects—it raised the possibility that individuals might follow their own consciences in matters of religion. In a society in which the Catholic Church served as the central institution in people's lives, this radical new idea struck at the very foundation of European politics and social realities. From the time the Roman emperor Constantine supported the Catholic Church (see

Chapter 5), people always assumed that there was an identity of belief between rulers and subjects. Political loyalty was considered a religious phenomenon; the Protestant Reformation questioned this assumption.

In fact, the wars of religion that scourged Europe from 1559 to 1648 involved much more than the proper way to worship God. They also centered on the question of what constituted a state—specifically, whether one state could encompass various religious expressions. Like the peasant wars in Germany in 1524, these new hostilities involved religion, but they had significant economic, political, and social dimensions as well.

French Wars of Religion

1562–1598

By the 1550s, Calvinism had gained a good deal of strength in France among the peasants and in the towns of the south and southwest. Although the French Calvinists (Huguenots) remained a minority—only about 7 percent of the population—they were well organized. Local congregations governed by ministers sent representatives to district assemblies that in turn coordinated their efforts with a national assembly and even mustered troops from local churches. This impressive minority even began to recruit members from the nobility—possibly 40 percent of French nobles had become Huguenots. Great noble families took the lead in forwarding their religious (and in turn political) interests—the Guises led the Catholics, and the Bourbons championed the Huguenots. By the mid-sixteenth century, French Protestantism was a force to be reckoned with and the French kings took notice.

Francis I (r. 1515–1547) and his heir, Henry II (r. 1547–1559), were both powerful kings who based their authority in part on a strong Catholic stance. However, this royal power was broken by a freak accident. King Henry was celebrating the wedding of his daughter by fighting in a joust (the war game still much beloved by the nobility), but during the last joust of the day, his opponent's lance shattered, gouging Henry's eye. Henry died of complications of this wound, leaving his widow, the Italian Catherine de' Medici, to rule as regent for her young sons from 1559 to 1589.

Catherine tried to preserve royal control, but her efforts were impeded by the struggle for power between the Guises and the Bourbons, both of whom had family ties to the monarchy and hoped to inherit the throne. Politics here intertwined with religion and the time was ripe for civil war. Fighting broke out in

| Catholics vs. Huguenots |

1562, when the Duke of Guise massacred a Huguenot congregation, and it continued for about thirty-six years (with brief respites). The Huguenot forces, though outnumbered, were too well organized to be defeated. The most infamous point of these wars was the Saint Bartholomew's Day Massacre, which took place on August 23, 1572, just when peace seemed imminent.

A religious compromise seemed to be on the horizon with a marriage between Catherine's daughter and the Bourbon leader of the Huguenots, Henry of Navarre. However, the mutual suspicions and desire for revenge had not subsided—the Guise family persuaded the young king Charles IX (r. 1560–1574) that the Huguenot gathering for the wedding was a plot against the crown. The king then ordered his guard to kill all the Protestant leadership. On the morning of Saint Bartholomew's Day, the soldiers unleashed a massacre against Protestants.

Although the young bridegroom escaped assassination, many others did not. The massacre raged for six days and was particularly brutal. Women and infants were not spared, and even corpses were mutilated as religious fervor introduced a bloodbath. This violence did not end the wars, however. Civil war continued in France until King Henry III (r. 1574–1589) was assassinated, leaving no heir.

The next in line for the throne was Henry of Navarre—the Protestant bridegroom who survived the massacre. Recognizing that the overwhelmingly Catholic population would not accept a reformist king, he converted to Catholicism, reputedly saying, "Paris is worth a mass." Sympathetic to both religions, the new king, Henry IV (r. 1589–1610), issued the Edict of Nantes (1598), which ended the religious wars and introduced religious toleration in France. However, a subsequent king (Louis XIV, discussed in Chapter 13) who believed that a nation was defined by loyalty to one religion would overturn Henry's policy. But for the time being at least, France gained a small respite from the violence of intolerance. The rest of Europe was not so lucky.

Peace in France

A "Council of Blood" in the Netherlands
1566–1609

In addition to Spain, the Catholic king Philip II ruled over the Netherlands, which consisted of seventeen provinces. (Today these provinces are Netherlands, Belgium, and Luxembourg.) Trouble began when Philip began to exert more control over the provinces—he restructured the Catholic Church to weaken the local aristocracy, he insisted on billeting troops locally, and he levied new taxes, all of which offended the Dutch.

In response, riots broke out in 1566, and Dutch Protestants, though still a tiny minority, rebelled against their Spanish, Catholic overlords. In a spasm of violence, they destroyed Catholic Church property, smashing images of saints and desecrating the host. Philip was enraged. Vowing to silence the rebels, he sent the largest

Revolt breaks out

land army ever assembled into the Netherlands to crush the Protestants and bring the province back under his Catholic rule. In 1572, organized revolt broke out and war officially began.

Philip's crackdown ignited a savage forty-year contest in which the Spanish general, the "iron duke of Alba," presided over a slaughter of thousands of Protestants in what he called a "Council of Troubles," but what the Protestants called the "Council of Blood." Calvinist preachers retaliated by giving their congregations complete license to kill the invaders. To protect themselves, the towns of the Netherlands even opened their dikes to flood their country rather than give in to Philip's armies. The Dutch found an able leader in William of Orange, a nobleman known for his wise counsel, who took charge in 1580. William was assassinated four years later, and the murderer was publicly tortured to death as blood continued to flow in the Netherlands.

The defiance of the Dutch cost Philip more than the loss of soldiers and huge amounts of gold to finance the wars. It also diverted his attention northward, away from his victory over the Turks at Lepanto in 1571. Preoccupied by events in the Netherlands, he failed to ride the wave of widespread Christian antipathy toward the Turks and launch a decisive campaign against the enemy in the eastern Mediterranean.

Philip also tried to "save" England from the Protestantism that Henry VIII had introduced. Philip had married Henry's Catholic daughter, Mary (r. 1553–1558), and when she died without an heir, the Spanish king proposed matrimony to her sister, Elizabeth I. But the Protestant Elizabeth refused his attentions and even dared support the Netherlands against him. Philip struck back by hurling the full force of his navy against England, sending a huge fleet across the English Channel in 1588. What happened next stood in stark contrast to Philip's triumph at Lepanto. Instead of scoring an easy victory, the Spanish Armada was wiped out by the well-armed English ships and the sudden onslaught of violent storms in the North Sea (what the English would later call a "Protestant wind").

Armada against England

Philip never succeeded in subduing the Protestants in the Netherlands; the conflict dragged on until the deaths of both Philip and Elizabeth. In 1609, the two sides finally drew up an agreement that gave the northern provinces virtual independence. The final recognition of an independent Netherlands would have to wait until the Peace of Westphalia in 1648. After the final settlement, Protestants in the southern provinces moved north to escape continuing Spanish rule in the south, so the two provinces became divided along religious lines. The northern provinces became the Protestant Dutch Republic, and

Netherlands split

> Although the young bridegroom escaped assassination, many others did not.

Gustavus Adolphus, the Swedish king from 1611 to 1632, brought cannons away from siege work into the field of combat. He brought lighter pieces to accompany his infantry, and ordered gunners to use prefilled bags of powder so that they could load and fire in the middle of a battle. In the decisive battle of 1632, gunpowder smoke blinded the fighters and inflicted enormous casualties on both sides. Gustavus himself died from a gunshot sustained in the battle. From then on, soldiers would face increasingly violent barrages of field artillery as they tried to take contested lands. Today, soldiers use weapons that are more accurate and powerful, but just as potentially lethal. Cannons being employed in Iraq and Afghanistan, such as the new M777 Howitzer, can easily be moved by helicopter, ship, or truck, and require a team of five to man.

the southern (and French-speaking) Spanish Netherlands (which later became Belgium) remained Catholic. But this solution still could not quell the religious tensions tearing at Europe. Instead, the wars shifted east, where they culminated in the bloodiest engagement of them all.

The Thirty Years' War

1618–1648

The Peace of Augsburg had only temporarily answered the question of religious diversity in the Holy Roman Empire. For fifty years after Augsburg, pressure mounted as more and more people followed their consciences and as diverse spiritual beliefs proliferated in the principalities. These tensions reached the boiling point in 1618, when a Catholic prince took over Bohemia (in the modern Czech Republic) and set out to vanquish the substantial Protestant minority in his state. Protestant Bohemian nobles responded by throwing the prince's representatives out the castle window in Prague. The hapless officials landed unhurt in a pile of manure, but the Catholic explanation was that their fall had been broken by angels. The two sides seemed to have irreconcilable points of view.

But the Holy Roman Empire's political structure contained a unique feature that made religious tensions much

War breaks out

harder to resolve than by merely pushing bureaucrats out of windows. The essential problem was that Protestant and Catholic electors (princes who elected the Holy

Roman Emperor) were roughly equal in number. If Bohemia went to a Protestant prince, the balance of power would shift away from the ruling Catholic Habsburgs. Fearing this possibility, the Holy Roman Emperor Ferdinand II (r. 1619–1637) went to war to reclaim Bohemia for Catholicism. His action provoked a civil war that began over the key issue of the authority of the emperor over the princes in Germany but that quickly turned international as Protestants and Catholics across the Holy Roman Empire faced each other in battle.

The first twelve years of the war were marked by the success of Emperor Ferdinand's forces, and it seemed as if the Catholic Habsburgs would be able to roll back the Protestant gains in the German lands. The powerful Catholic Maximilian of Bavaria put at Ferdinand's disposal an army that won a stunning victory over the Bohemians at the Battle of White Mountain in 1620. The Bohemian rebels were killed or exiled, and it seemed as if the war was over. However, the Protestants continued their struggle, but with few gains.

In 1624, the emperor received considerable help when a soldier of fortune came to offer his services to the Catholic cause. Albrecht von Wallenstein, a minor Bohemian nobleman, recognized that the emperor needed a new

Wallenstein

army if he was to succeed, and Wallenstein offered to raise the force if he could billet it and raise its supplies wherever it happened to be stationed. Through these means, Wallenstein introduced a new way of funding wars. Previously, warriors had been paid largely by the losers—that is, through the victors' plunder and sacking of defeated peoples. Wallenstein's innovative requirements served as a kind of war tax levied on all princes and cities who supported the emperor. Now wars would be funded by potential winners as well as losers. This strategy not only funded a large army but also made Wallenstein one of the richest men in the empire. By 1627, Wallenstein's army had begun to conquer the northern region of the empire—the center of Protestant strength. Ferdinand grew so confident that he issued the Edict of Restitution in 1629, ordering all territories lost to Protestants since 1552 to be restored to Catholics.

By 1630, the tide and nature of the war had begun to change. With help from abroad, Protestants made gains, but the war began to shift from a religious struggle to a purely political quest—to weaken the power of the Habsburgs; for example, the Catholic French king was willing to join Protestants in support of this cause. Protestant forces found a worthy champion in the Swedish king Gustavus Adolphus (r. 1611–1632), who was appalled by Ferdinand's treatment of Protestants. At the same time, he feared a Habsburg threat to Swedish lands around the Baltic Sea.

From religion to politics

Gustavus had a clear vision of modern warfare: It would be dominated by gunpowder. He drilled his men incessantly on lining up in squares so that the front line could fire and then move backward to reload while others replaced them. This system, which required ironclad discipline, allowed for sustained firing—an essential tactic for weapons that were still inaccurate.

Arraying his new army, Gustavus fought a decisive battle against Wallenstein at Lutzen in 1632. His armies beat Wallenstein's forces, but in the heat of battle, Gustavus himself was killed by gunshots. The king's death prevented the Swedish forces from following up on the victory. Meanwhile, Wallenstein's loss sealed his fate: The German princes eventually compelled Ferdinand to turn on his enterprising and wealthy general, and the emperor had Wallenstein assassinated a few months later.

Gustavus's successes opened the final phase of the war (from 1632 to 1648), during which the emperor lost all his previous gains. The Protestant princes raised new armies, and by 1635, Ferdinand had to agree to suspend the Edict of Restitution and to grant amnesty to most of the Protestant princes. In return, the Protestants joined the imperial troops in driving the Swedes out of German lands. However, the Catholic French declared open war on Ferdinand in 1635, and for the next thirteen years, French and Swedish troops rampaged through the lands, causing destruction and devastation.

By the 1640s, the war had reached a stalemate. The kings and princes who had started the hostilities had all died, and their successors (as well as civilians) were exhausted. Both sides laid down their arms and took stock of their losses. This war had raged with a violence that astonished even contemporary witnesses used to sixteenth-

Devastation

century battle methods, for armies on both sides had swept through villages and towns and laid to waste everything in their paths. The war had exacted a staggering price: Germany's population had plummeted (although historians do not agree on the figures, some suggest a population loss as high as 30 percent). The economy, too, was damaged. Spain had gone bankrupt and would never recover its standing as a leader on the European stage. France and Sweden emerged somewhat victorious gaining some land at the expense of the exhausted German states.

Peace at Westphalia

The series of agreements that ended the Thirty Years' War are collectively known as the Peace of Westphalia, named for the region of Germany where the agreements were drafted. German princes now had the freedom to choose their own religion, but the religious desires of individuals within the states were still not accepted. However, for the first time, Calvinism was included among the tolerated faiths. The religious landmark of Europe was roughly established along north-south lines. The northwest—England, Holland, Scandinavia, and the northern German states—was Protestant, whereas the south remained Catholic.

The war had marked political overtones at the end, and the treaty accordingly addressed issues of power beyond religious choice. The peace set the political geography of Europe for the next century and established **Political results** a precedent for diplomacy that would shape the way nations resolved political problems in the coming centuries. The map on page 266 outlines the aftermath of the Peace of Westphalia. The representatives at Westphalia conducted all these negotiations with an eye toward "balance of power," a relatively new principle that emerged in fifteenth-century Italy and was now applied to European politics. They believed that they could ensure peace by making all the European powers roughly as strong as their neighbors. This strategy would dominate European diplomacy for centuries.

LIFE AFTER THE REFORMATION

The early modern wars of religion were finally over. Christians with different beliefs would now have to learn to coexist. As the storms of religious rage subsided, Europeans began noticing the dramatic changes in other aspects of everyday life, changes they thought that the Protestant Reformation had provoked.

Legend:
- Ottoman Empire
- Austrian Habsburgs
- Spanish Monarchy
- Swedish Dominions
- Brandenburg-Prussia
- Boundary of the Holy Roman Empire

Europe, 1648 This map shows the political configuration of Europe after the Peace of Westphalia, which ended the Thirty Years' War. Which countries control territories distant from their home center? Which of these remote areas might become centers of conflict in the future? Why?

New Definitions of Courtship and Marriage

When the Protestants excluded marriage as a sacrament, the institution changed in ways they could not have foreseen. After Martin Luther left the monastery and married Katherina, the couple formed a loving partnership and raised five children (along with caring for orphans). Luther explored this relationship in his writings and saw in marriage part of God's plan for humanity. Calvin, too, rejected the church fathers' "too superstitious admiration of celibacy" and extolled the benefits of conjugal partnerships. Although divorce was not easy in any of the Protestant groups, it was possible. With all these changes, the ideal of marriage shifted. Couples began to expect mutual love between man and wife, instead of simply duty that bound extended families together. The Catholic Church also was influenced by the new marital values, and in the late sixteenth century, church manuals began to use the word *love* to refer to conjugal relations.

People still did not marry just for love, however; instead, families continued to arrange suitable matches between young people. Arranged marriages were an essential and logical part of a view that valued family prosperity and continuity more than an individual's happiness. Individual's lives were seen as mere moments in the larger life of the family. Nevertheless, something new was going on in family relations. Although parents still negotiated a suitable match, prospective couples were allowed to consider their compatibility before marriage, and daughters had some say in vetoing disagreeable matches. Courtship customs grew more complex, as men and women evaluated whether they would have a harmonious union.

Courtship

Forging a Link Between Education and Work

The Christian humanists from Erasmus on urged everyone to learn to read. As we saw in the document on page 260 reformed Catholicism under the Jesuits also stressed educa-

Valuing literacy tion as central to a Christian life, and parochial schools and armies of nuns gave young children the rudiments of education. Protestants, too, urged study. As Luther and others emphasized Bible study as part of essential Christian behavior and translated the Bible into vernacular languages, the next logical step was to broaden literacy. Luther encouraged the cities and villages in Saxony to establish publicly funded schools, and many Protestants followed his call. A Bohemian reformer, Jan Amos Comenius (1592–1670), wrote: "All alike, boys and girls, both noble and ignoble, rich and poor, in all cities and towns, villages and hamlets, should be sent to school." This egalitarian notion would take centuries to implement, but it established a new educational goal in the West.

OPINION

What do you think was the most enduring value of the Reformation?

Although education was intended primarily to help people study the Bible and learn to serve as their own spiritual guides, it also had profound implications for the way people viewed work. In response to critics who complained about educating "rustics," the Bohemian educational reformer Comenius answered that universal education would help everyone avoid "that idleness which is so dangerous to flesh and blood."

Valuing work His words hinted at a new philosophy that stressed the value of work.

In the Middle Ages, "those who work" were relegated to the bottom of the social scale. The upper crust consisted of only those who could live off the income of their land and did not need to work to survive. The bourgeoisie—the middle class—that was becoming more and more prosperous since the Renaissance began to change that view and brought a new valuing of work into the consciousness of Western society. The Protestant reformers that appealed to many of the residents of these growing urban areas lent religious support to new ideas about work. In Luther's writings, even women were defined by the work they did. Luther described the ideal wife as follows: "She likes working. . . . She girds her loins and stretches her arms, works with energy in the house."

Calvin, too, believed that men and women were called to work and that work itself was a virtuous activity. Centu-

ries later, the German sociologist Max Weber, in *The Protestant Ethic and the Spirit of Capitalism* (1904), would argue that Calvinists' emphasis on work legitimized and therefore boosted the growth of capitalism in the West. Many Calvinists believed that hard work, efficiency, and frugality all indicated a person predestined to salvation. Not surprisingly, then, Protestants embraced what has come to be called the work ethic with fervor. Historians dispute the details of Weber's thesis, but his argument still offers us an insight into the way religious ideas shaped modern-day views of work in the West. In the Catholic Middle Ages, people had seen work as the curse of Adam laid on the damned; in the Protestant early modern period, work became God's gift to a saved humanity.

Anxiety and Spiritual Insecurity

The striking revolution in thought that the Protestant reformers introduced also prompted some spiritual anxiety and insecurity among Christians. In part, this unease stemmed from the hardship spawned by the relentless warfare of the period. The "community of the faithful" that Catholicism once represented had fragmented, and for

JAN STEEN, *THE SCHOOL MASTER*, ca. 1655 The Reformation stimulated the spread of literacy. The intent was to help everyone to read the Bible. The modern world was born in small village schools—like the one immortalized in this painting—where children struggled under sometimes harsh teachers.

Protestants encouraged to "stand alone before God," the new religious individualism often felt frightening.

The new mind-set began to raise questions about char-itable institutions and their relationship with religious bodies. Where once the universal church had looked after

Charitable institutions the poor and widows and orphans, now separate congregations had to care for their own. The question of who was responsible for whom sometimes became quite murky, and a sense of individual responsibility for one's own plight slowly replaced a collective sense of charity. For example, civic authorities began to consider ways to help the needy, building workhouses for the poor and passing laws prohibiting begging. Such laws could never com-pletely succeed, given the scale of need that we saw in the painting of the cripples in on page 248. Yet, more and more societies tried designing institutional solutions to the problems of poverty.

As communities redivided themselves along religious loyalties, many people's sense of personal anxiety increased. The Catholic Church had also provided community sup-port and at least the hope of miraculous cures for the sick and troubled. Men and women could

Decline of "magic" themselves pray to saints or the Vir-gin Mary for help, and priests could say prayers for members of their congregation in need. The Catholic Church even turned a blind eye to "white" magic, but Protestants rejected saints and any forms of "magic." As village rituals split apart, it became harder to define "com-munity." As changing times and beliefs generated anxieties, some people began looking for scapegoats.

Searching for Scapegoats: The Hunt for Witches

Catholics and Protestants alike shared a long-standing, deeply held belief in charms and potions that could affect people. These might be as benign as healing magical cures and love potions, or as harmful as spells to bring bad weather, illness, or crop failure. Traditionally, Catholic priests offered prayers and countercharms to combat the power of people—often, but not always, called witches—who had the knowledge to cast spells. Protestant preach-ers argued regularly against "superstitious magical prac-tices," but some remained attached to charms and spells, and in England witchcraft accusations usually remained tied to spell-casting.

In the sixteenth century, especially on the Continent, some people began to link a fear of witches to diabolism, or the idea that magical powers came because of a pact with the devil. Martin Luther himself claimed to have confronted the devil several times and constantly remained alert **Fear of the devil** to the presence of this evil being. Church authorities began to stress that witches were in league with the devil and per-formed mysterious ceremonies in his service. To stamp out the devil's assistants, many accused supposed witches, put-ting them on trial and executing them.

People in the sixteenth century were fascinated by the possibility of witchcraft. The best-known work on the subject was the *Malleus Maleficarum* (the "Hammer of Witches"),

timeline

French Wars of Religion 1562–1598

Wars in the Netherlands 1566–1609

Council of Trent 1545–1563

Protestant Reformation 1517–1560

Peak of Witchcraft Trials 1560–1640

| 1515 | 1530 | 1545 | 1560 | 1575 | 1590 |

SALVATOR ROSA, *WITCHES AT THEIR INCANTATIONS* (detail), late seventeenth century Religious insecurity stimulated more witch trials during the early modern period than there had been in the Middle Ages. This painting shows witches engaging in some of their reputed practices, such as performing magic and making pacts with the devil.

which had been written in the late fifteenth century (before the start of the Reformation) for inquisitors to try witches. However, by 1669 it had been reissued in forty editions and had become extraordinarily popular, appealing to Protestants and Catholics alike. In France alone, 345 books about witchcraft were published between 1550 and 1650.

There is no real evidence that any of the convicted "witches" engaged in pacts with the devil. Instead, many people were forced to "confess" under torture. Others may have thought they were confessing to using simple charms only to discover that they were convicted of diabolism.

Catholics and Protestants alike persecuted witches, and the trials in Europe peaked between 1560 and 1640. Although precise numbers elude us, more than 100,000 people were executed for witchcraft, and 200,000 may have endured trials. These trials are probably the most disturbing indicator of the rampant anxiety stirred by the intellectual and social changes of the sixteenth century.

Persecutions

By the eighteenth century, the witchcraft panic had ebbed and the trials gradually ceased, as men and women adjusted to the religious diversity that had split their countries and their communities. However, the ideals of the Protestant Reformation—individualism, a desire for marital harmony, an emphasis on hard work, and a staunch reliance on conscience—left a permanent mark on European society.

SUMMARY

Through the sixteenth century and into the seventeenth, Europe was devastated by warfare among powerful monarchs and religious struggles that split the faithful.

- The Habsburg-Valois Wars brought violent and expensive warfare to Europe as kings tried to expand their territories.

- Some Christians began to question traditional beliefs, and reformers split the Christian unity and established new denominations that offered competing ways to worship.

- The Catholic Church responded to the critique by its own reform and reasserting its ideals at the Council of Trent.

- Europe once again erupted into religious warfare that ended in 1648 with the Thirty Years' War, which devastated Germany.

- The religious ideas of the Reformation affected social and cultural life of everyday people.

This chapter outlined these events on the European continent, but, at the same time, Europeans took the battle between Protestants and Catholics across the seas, as they discovered lands that were new to them thus expanding the West.

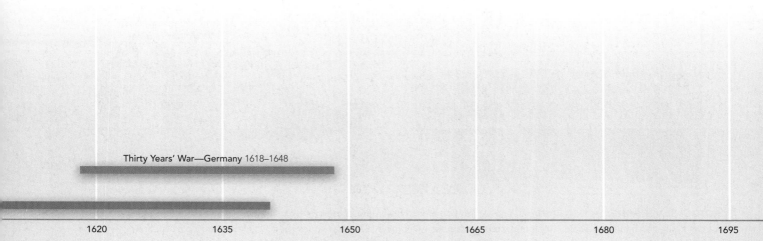

Thirty Years' War—Germany 1618–1648

| 1620 | 1635 | 1650 | 1665 | 1680 | 1695 |

POTOSÍ SILVER MINE, ca. 1584 The European exploration of the New World caused a revolution in economic life as well as exploitation of human beings on a massive scale. This image shows a famous silver mine in Bolivia, worked by more than 13,000 conscripted Amerindians. During the late sixteenth century, the mine supplied huge amounts of silver that contributed to worldwide inflation, and it used mercury to process the ore, which polluted the waterways for a long time.

Faith, Fortune, and Fame

12

European Expansion, 1450–1700

Frightened Sailors "Double the Cape"

In 1498, four Portuguese ships led by Vasco da Gama sailed south from Europe and rounded the southern tip of Africa to reach India in the east. Gaspar Correa accompanied this journey, keeping a careful chronicle that told of the exciting, frightening voyage. In order to sail south with prevailing northwesterly winds, the navigators could not hug the shore but instead had to direct the ships southwest, tacking into the wind and going far away from the sight of land into the unknown sea. For two months, Vasco da Gama tacked out to sea to make sure that when they turned to shore, the ships would "double the cape," skirting the African continent. ▶▶

Correa wrote of the hardships of this venture into the Atlantic: "The fury of the sea [made] the ships seem every moment to be going to pieces. The crews grew sick with fear and hardship, . . . and all clamored for putting back to Portugal. . . . At times they met with such cold rains that the men could not prepare their food. All cried out to God for mercy upon their souls." Vasco da Gama finally ordered the ships about and they sailed southeast again. They circled the southern tip of Africa and with

much celebration they headed northeast toward India.

The ships were to face much more hardship. They pulled into great rivers in Africa looking for food and for people to tell them where they were. They ate unknown fruits—one so toxic it made their gums swell and their teeth loosen. The captain ordered his ill men to rinse their mouths with urine to ease their gums, and the cure worked. Somehow, through all the adversity the crews carried on and finally docked in India at a city

where citizens flocked to the shore, amazed at the Western ships. Correa succinctly and accurately described the confrontation between East and West: "All were much amazed at seeing what they had never before seen." Vasco da Gama's crew was not unique in the fifteenth century; brave sailors sailed east and west from Europe, and the world was transformed as Europeans and indigenous peoples almost everywhere were amazed at their new confrontation. ◄◄

THE WORLD IMAGINED

Western Europeans had long coveted goods from the East, which they generally considered China and India. When they used the name "China," they also meant Japan and the other lands of eastern Asia. When they referred to "India,"

Eastern trade they included southeast Asia and the many islands dotting the Pacific, and although Vasco da Gama reached the mainland of India, he would have been content to land on any of the Pacific islands. More than just a geographic entity, though, the East, in many Europeans' minds, was the source of valuable luxury goods.

Since the Middle Ages, Europe had lusted after the silks, fine carpets, pottery, and precious jewels produced in the East. Europeans were so impressed by these exotic goods that they praised the Chinese as the finest craftsmen in the world. Yet it was the spices from the Orient that riveted Westerners' attention. European diets were bland, and those who depended only on local seasonings—garlic, saffron, and the ever-present salt—found the food tiresome. Recipes of the time and records showing commercial demand reveal that people clamored for cloves, cinnamon, coriander, and pepper in particular—all available only in the East. Throughout the Middle Ages, these products came overland through the Byzantine Empire into western Europe.

But after 1400, intensifying warfare in eastern Europe and Asia made overland travel difficult. (See Chapter 9 for the increased threat posed by the Turks.) Europeans began looking for new trade routes through the eastern Mediterranean to satisfy their appetite for spice. They revived centuries-old memories of journeys to the East by reading accounts like that of the Venetian explorer Marco Polo (1254–1324), who wrote detailed descriptions of his visits to China (see Chapter 9). These works were incorrect in much of their geography, however; for example, Marco Polo

believed that Japan was 1,500 miles east of China. Furthermore, most of these older accounts contained exaggerated descriptions of botanical and biological features of Eastern lands. Nevertheless, no tale of the exotic East seemed too far-fetched to fifteenth-century European imaginations.

During the fifteenth century, western Europeans acquired the *Geography* of Ptolemy (ca. 100–ca. 178). This guide had been translated from Greek, reproduced by the new printing presses, and widely distributed. Now Renaissance explorers had a picture of the world that they **Ptolemy's worldview** could use to venture into the Atlantic, or the "green sea of darkness," as the Arabic commentators called it.

Ptolemy portrayed the world as a globe, divided into the familiar 360 degrees of longitude. The image on page 273, from a 1482 edition of the *Geography,* shows Ptolemy's map of the world. This ancient geographer believed that the world consisted of three continents—Asia, Africa, and Europe—and two oceans—the Indian Ocean and the Western Ocean. The map is surrounded by figures representing the many winds so crucial to a sailing society. In addition to mistaking the number of continents, Ptolemy made two major errors: He underestimated the extent of the oceans, suggesting that land covered three-fourths of the earth's surface, and he miscalculated the earth as being one-sixth smaller than its true size. With only Ptolemy's map to guide them, later explorers understandably expected the journey east to be shorter than it really was. During this age of discovery, however, the theories of Ptolemy dissolved in the face of experience.

THE WORLD DISCOVERED

The explorers expected to capitalize on Europe's desire for Eastern goods and bring back wealth for themselves and their sovereigns. Sixteenth-century rulers were desperate

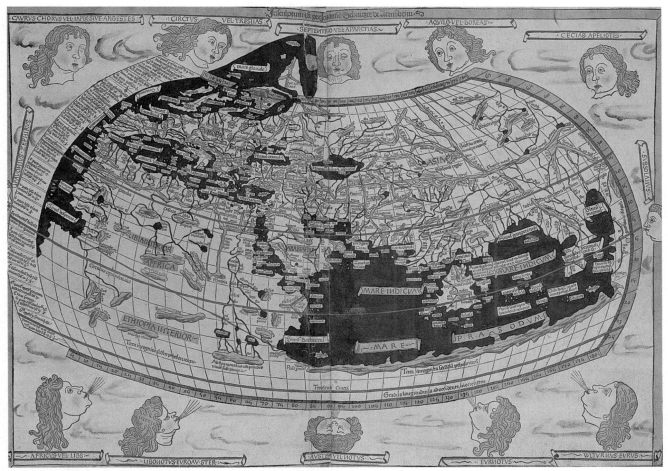

PTOLEMY'S MAP The ancient map shows the world as the explorers expected it to be: largely land, with little sea, and Europe at the center. The four winds in the corners reminded sailors of their source of power.

for money to field their expensive armies, and the conquest of Constantinople by the Turks in 1453 increased the price of the valuable spices as they imposed steep taxes on the goods. This costly trade siphoned precious metals away from an already coin-poor western Europe, and monarchs were willing to reward anyone who hunted for new wealth. Brave, enterprising men eager for fame and fortune took up the challenge.

Fame, Fortune, and Faith: The Drive to Explore

Though the lure of wealth motivated explorers and the sovereigns who funded them, some adventurers had other incentives for embarking on these risky travels. Religion also served as a major impulse for Europeans to seek new worlds. Christians during the fifteenth and sixteenth centuries felt besieged by the Islamic empire of the Ottoman Turks that loomed on Europe's eastern border (see Chapter

11). Some voyages aimed to find allies against the Turks. The Reformation within Europe also stimulated explorations and migrations, as Catholics sought converts to Catholicism overseas and Protestants looked for new lands where they could practice their faith. Faith joined with fame and fortune to drive Europeans across the seas.

New Technologies and Travel

Europeans had a passion for adventure, but they also needed strong navigational tools and skills if they were to survive these hazardous journeys. Fortunately for them, sailors in the Middle Ages had perfected instruments to help them sail out of sight of land. One device, the **quadrant,** aligned with the fixed North Star at night to let navigators determine their latitude. However, this was not useful in the Southern Hemisphere, where the North Star was not visible. Sailors going south had to confront uncharted heavens as well as unmapped lands. During the

Navigation instruments

day, sailors in both Northern and Southern hemispheres could check their calculations with the **astrolabe,** which measured the height of the sun during the day or the altitude of a known star at night.

Finally, mapmakers had gained experience in charting the seas and lands and could graphically document their travels with some accuracy. Earlier skilled seafarers like the Vikings who first discovered North America lacked the cartography skills to allow them to reproduce their long sea voyages with as much certainty as did the sixteenth-century explorers. Navigators felt confident in their charts, and the newly discovered map of Ptolemy, though inaccurate, at least gave them a basic sense of direction.

Sailors lacked only the ships to carry them safely on long ventures. The galleys that had ruled the Mediterranean in the fourteenth century had large, square sails, but their locomotion came primarily from the many slaves who rowed the big ships. These ships were unsuitable for long distances and had little extra space left in their holds to store the provisions necessary for a lengthy sea voyage.

All this changed in the late fifteenth century, when the Portuguese built ships that marked the highest development of a long evolution of Mediterranean sailing ships. In the Middle Ages, shipbuilders had developed a new kind of sail rigging that allowed ships to maneuver near shore in uncertain winds. By the sixteenth century, shipbuilders had improved the mobility of the sails and the rigging of the ropes so that the sails could be moved readily. The image here shows a sixteenth-century watercolor of Portuguese caravels—the small (70 to 80 feet long) ships that conquered the great seas. The large square sails allowed the ships to move in the direction of the wind, or downwind. The real secret to long-distance sailing, however, was the lateen, a triangular, mobile sail at the rear (furled in the image). This device not only let the ship sail faster but also allowed it to sail at an angle to the wind and thus progress upwind—a crucial advantage for traveling into the prevailing westerly winds of the Atlantic. The ships had to be heavy to withstand the storms of the Atlantic, and this weight gave the West an unforeseen advantage: They could support heavy cannons, giving them a military advantage over the lighter ships of the East that sailed the calmer Indian ocean. On these innovative vessels, the Portuguese set out on voyages of discovery that changed the world.

Improved ships

The Portuguese Race for the East

1418–1600

As the chronicler of Vasco da Gama's voyage described in the account at the beginning of this chapter, the Portuguese explorers had an immediate goal in mind: to venture south around Africa to the Indian Ocean and trade directly with natives in India for spices and other luxury items. This route would eliminate the troublesome role of the Ottoman Turks as key players in the eastern Mediter-

ranean trade network. Beginning in 1418, Prince Henry the Navigator (1394–1460) of Portugal sponsored annual expeditions down the west coast of Africa. Bartholomeu Dias continued Henry's work with great success, rounding the southern tip of Africa in 1488. King John II of Portugal (r. 1481–1495), expecting this route to yield the riches of the East, named the tip the Cape of Good Hope. But Dias never reached India. His frightened crew had experienced the storms and hardships that Correa described, but Dias did not maintain the iron control that Vasco da Gama would, and his crew mutinied as he sailed north along the eastern coast of Africa. He was forced to return home.

In 1498, his countryman Vasco da Gama (ca. 1460–1524) set out with four ships to complete Dias's ill-fated voyage to India. He succeeded and returned to Portugal with ships laden with spices worth sixty times the cost of the journey. On his first trip to India, da Gama carried casks of honey, hats, and other trifles to trade for the precious spices. On his second voyage four years later, the explorer brought a new trading item that would transform commerce in the Indian basin: His casks were now filled with gunpowder. Soldiers in India had long known

PORTUGUESE SHIPS, sixteenth century Portuguese caravels, the subject of this informative watercolor, were sturdily designed ships that sailed the great seas. Powered by huge sails, the ships did not need banks of oars, so they could be stocked with water and food for long voyages.

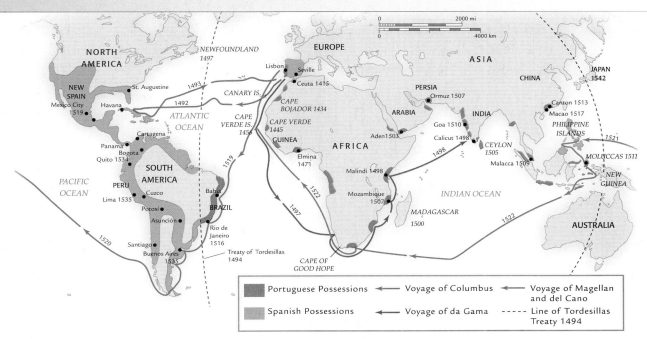

Exploration and Conquest, fifteenth and sixteenth centuries This map shows the routes and dates of the explorations of the fifteenth and sixteenth centuries, as well as the possessions claimed by the Spanish and Portuguese. It includes the Treaty of Tordesillas line, which divided the world between Portugal and Spain.

the recipe for gunpowder, but when they saw its use in da Gama's deadly cannons, a new arms race would begin that would fuel escalating violence in the age of exploration.

Portuguese explorers scored spectacular successes in opening up the trade to the East. As one pleasant surprise, they discovered that India was not simply one location—it included the Moluccas, "spice islands," from which wafted the delightful aroma of cloves as the Portuguese ships approached. As the map above shows, the Portuguese established a string of trading outposts throughout the East. In these small settlements, Europeans lived peacefully near native settlements in a mutually profitable relationship. Portugal's successful entry into the Indian Ocean trade struck a dramatic blow to the economy of the Muslims, who had previously held a monopoly on that trade. At the same time, their neighbors, the Spanish, took a quite different approach. Spain's explorers sailed westward in hopes of reaching the fabulous Orient, believing Ptolemy's claim that the land of plenty lay just over the horizon.

Trading outposts

Spain's Westward Discoveries

1492–1522

Christopher Columbus (1446–1506) perhaps best exemplifies Spain's travel ambitions. The son of an Italian (Genoese) weaver, Columbus traveled to Portugal in 1476 to learn about Portuguese shipbuilding and sailing. During his visit,

he became captivated by the accounts of Marco Polo and the *Geography* of Ptolemy. Inflamed by images of glory and wealth, he asked the Portuguese king to sponsor him on a trip west to Asia. The king rejected him; like many others, he dismissed Columbus as a vague dreamer. Columbus then presented his idea to the Spanish monarchs Ferdinand and Isabella. The queen, impressed with Columbus's proposal, made him an admiral in 1492 and financed his expedition.

Columbus embarked on his journey with three ships, the *Niña,* the *Pinta,* and the *Santa María.* In October, the small fleet landed on an island in the Caribbean Sea. According to the admiral's account, as he stepped ashore, Columbus "claimed all the lands for their Highnesses, by proclamation and with the royal standard displayed." According to Columbus, the many islanders who watched him did not object to his claims, so he accepted this as their tacit agreement—ignoring the language barrier that separated them. Subsequent explorers followed his lead, claiming ownership of already inhabited lands.

Columbus's discoveries

Columbus made four voyages between 1492 and 1502, during which he established settlements on several more Caribbean islands and visited the northern coast of South America and Central America. On his third voyage, he brought women from Spain to ensure the permanence of the settlements. The explorer was not a good administrator, and when Spain sent a judge to look into a revolt in the new lands, Columbus was brought back to Spain in chains. Though he was later released and made a final

Columbus's Discoveries

This contemporary woodcut shows the New World as Columbus wanted to portray it. The king of Spain, on the left, gives Columbus the authority for his voyage, and the navigator's three ships are shown landing on an island to claim it for the king. The island is depicted as a fanciful place, with exotic trees and beautiful, naked natives, showing Europeans a New World that they had expected to find.   Why wouldn't Columbus have portrayed his discovery more realistically, and do modern travel accounts also shade the truth? Why or why not?

way east, they inevitably came into conflict. The Catholic sovereigns of Spain and Portugal appealed to the pope to divide the world into two spheres of influence. In the 1494 Treaty of Tordesillas (shown on the map on page 275), the Spanish received exclusive rights to the lands west of a line drawn 370 leagues (about 1,200 miles) west of the Cape Verde Islands off the west coast of Africa, and the Portuguese received rights to the lands east of the line. This agreement (which was virtually ignored by the other European monarchs) was one of many attempts to apportion the world without regard for the opinions of indigenous residents.

Soon, subsequent travelers convinced Europeans that Columbus was wrong and that a great new landmass had been found. The most influential of these explorers was Amerigo Vespucci (1451–1512), an educated "Renaissance man" who worked for the Medici family of Florence. In 1499, Vespucci set off on a voyage of discovery that took him westward from Spain and across the vast ocean to South America. During his voyage, he took careful navigational measurements and wrote colorful letters to his Medici patron, which were widely circulated. In the introduction to these works, Amerigo's publisher even suggested that Vespucci's name be given to the Mundus Novus (the New World) he had popularized with his maps and vivid tales of a continent across the ocean. The suggestion caught on, and the name "America" became attached to the western landmass that newly captured the European

fourth voyage to the New World, Columbus never received the riches and acclaim he sought. Throughout these years, the Italian adventurer apparently felt sure that he had found Asian islands. He even referred to the natives as Indians because he was certain he was in the general region of India. Columbus never realized that he had discovered a world unknown by virtually all Europeans. Instead, he clung to the image of the world he had imagined. His continued misconceptions encouraged other voyagers, who would soon prove him wrong.

Treaty of Tordesillas

As the Spanish and Portuguese both raced to claim lands on their imagination. See Exploring the Past on page 277 for an example of one of Vespucci's vivid descriptions.

After Vespucci's voyages, people set out purposefully to visit the new continent. For example, the Spanish adventurer Vasco Núñez de Balboa (1475–1517) trekked across the Isthmus of Panama, eventually reaching the Pacific Ocean on the other side.

Circumnavigating the globe

Besides adding to the evidence that a new continent existed, Balboa's discovery intensified the race to the riches of the East. New men with even bigger dreams of wealth joined the rush.

Ferdinand Magellan (ca. 1480–1521) was one of these men. A Portuguese explorer in the service of Spain, Magellan began the first expedition that succeeded in encircling the world. He sailed west from Spain in 1519 with three ships and discovered (and named) the Strait of Magellan at the southern tip of South America. The straits gave him access to the Pacific Ocean (which he also named). He and his crew braved the huge expanses of ocean and withstood mutinies. In 1521, Magellan was killed while interfering in a local war in the Philippines. His navigator, Sevastian Elcano (ca. 1476–1526), finished the journey to Asia and through the Indian Ocean back to Spain. Elcano's voyage took three years and he returned home with only one ship. But that ship was packed with enough spices not only to pay for the cost of the expedition but also to make the crew very rich.

Magellan and Elcano's successful circumnavigation of the globe revealed not that the world was round (they knew that), but its true size. It also demonstrated the impracticality of sailing to the Orient by way of the Pacific. The Spanish would have to search for new sources of wealth—this time in the New World.

The Northern Europeans Join the Race

1497–1650

England, France, and the Netherlands came late to the race for the riches of the New World. Understandably, they were unwilling to accept the terms of the Treaty of Tordesillas. Instead, they began their own explorations. They started by looking for a "northwest passage" to the East that would parallel the southern route around South America. In about 1497, the Genoese captain John Cabot (1450–1498) and his son Sebastian (1476–1557), who both had settled in England, received a letter from the English king Henry VII (r. 1485–1509) authorizing them to take possession for England of any new lands unclaimed by any Christian nation. So empowered, father and son sailed across the North Atlantic to Newfoundland and Maine. They found codfish so plentiful that their ships could not pass through the thick schools of fish. However, the voyage was immediately disappointing because they neither reached Asia nor returned laden with spices.

Exploring the Past

Amerigo Vespucci Describes the New World

In 1499, the naval astronomer Amerigo Vespucci wrote a letter to Lorenzo de' Medici of Florence describing his travels. The letter was particularly influential because of Vespucci's engaging style and sharp observations.

When we arrived at [an island] we saw on the sea-shore a great many people, who stood looking at us with astonishment. We anchored within about a mile of the land, fitted out the boats, and twenty-two men, well armed, made for land. The people, when they saw us landing, and perceived that we were different from themselves—because they have no beard and wear no clothing of any description, being also of a different color, they being brown and we white—began to be afraid of us, and all ran into the woods. With great exertion, by means of signs, we reassured them and negotiated with them. We found that they were of a race called cannibals, the greater part or all of whom live on human flesh.

Your excellency may rest assured of this fact. They do not eat one another, but, navigating with certain barks which they call "canoes," they bring their prey from the neighboring islands or countries. . . .

Still they are a people of gentle disposition and beautiful stature. They go entirely naked, and the arms which they carry are bows and arrows and shields. They are a people of great activity and much courage. They are very excellent marksmen. . . .

How might Vespucci's descriptions of the native peoples influence future interactions between them and the Europeans?

The French also hunted for a northwest passage to the East. In 1534, Jacques Cartier led three voyages that explored the St. Lawrence River in what is today Canada.

Settlements in Canada

He and his crew got as far as Montreal, but the great waterway led only inland, not out to the Pacific Northwest. An early settlement effort in the region of Quebec in 1541 failed, owing to the harsh winter and indigenes' hostility. In about 1600, Samuel de Champlain (ca. 1567–1635) made another try at establishing a settlement in North America. He founded Quebec, signing treaties with the natives to secure the settlement. Canadian settlements remained small in both size and number through the seventeenth century, but their existence ensured the continuous presence of European traders and missionaries in this northern land.

When the much-sought-after northwest passage proved elusive, northern Europeans shifted their journeys of discovery farther south and began to confront the Iberians directly.

Dutch colonies

The Dutch established trading posts in the Spice Islands, and Dutch warships proved their superiority and expelled the Portuguese from the islands that we now know as Indonesia. The Dutch also redesigned their ships to haul more cargo than the small Portuguese caravels that had first mastered the oceans. They then dominated the lucrative spice trade, founding colonies in strategic locations to protect their growing trade empire. As one example, they colonized the tip of South Africa to facilitate their Eastern trade and planted colonies in North America (most famously on Manhattan Island) and in the Caribbean.

The English, for their part, began to install settlements along the North American Atlantic seaboard in the seventeenth century: By 1700, about 250,000 colonists lived along the coast. Many of these people moved there to escape the religious persecution that swept Europe in the seven-

English colonies

teenth century. For this reason, they traveled west with their entire families, with the intent to stay. Their presence irrevocably altered the face of North America.

CONFRONTATION OF CULTURES

When the Europeans arrived in the New World, it was already abundantly populated by peoples who had lived there in resilient societies for millennia. From as early as 35,000 B.C.E., small groups of people walked from Asia northward across a land bridge from Siberia to Alaska. Slowly, over tens of thousands of years, families, clans, and tribes moved southward and settled throughout North, Central, and South America. At first, all these tribes pursued a highly effective hunting-and-gathering existence, with devastating consequences for their future development. As the hunters came through North America, they confronted great herds of large mammals—horses, elephants, camels, and giant ground sloths. Within a few centuries of human arrival, all those large mammals were extinct, probably because of effective hunting. However, this meant that there were no more large animals in North America for domestication—this would represent a fatal disadvantage when the Amerindians confronted Europeans millennia later.

The Original Americans South of the Rio Grande

In about 5500 B.C.E., tribes in central Mexico first developed agriculture, which, as we saw in Chapter 1, allowed large settled populations to become established. These civilizations would become tempting, wealthy targets for European explorers. Agriculture spread north and south from there, but very slowly.

Agriculture

The differing latitudes and varied growing seasons of the large American continents caused agriculture to diffuse more slowly in the Americas than it had in Europe and Asia, where crops spread primarily within similar latitudes. In the Americas, for example, it took about 3,500 years for maize (what we usually call corn) and beans to spread 700 miles from Mexico to the southern farmlands of the modern United States, but spread they did.

With the early use of agriculture in Central America and the western mountains of South America, populations grew large and elaborate empires—the Maya, Aztec, Inca, and others—developed. These civilizations thrived mainly through the cultivation of maize. This highly nutritious, versatile crop originally grew wild in the New World but had been cultivated for so long that it no longer grew without human help. Maize offered high yields with very little effort. Cultivators worked only about fifty days a year to produce an abundant crop that could be eaten even before it was ripe. In these maize-growing societies, men cut and burned brush to clear the land to plant the grain, and women ground the hard kernels into flour to make tortillas, or flat bread.

OPINION

Which areas of the world do you think turned out to be most profitable in the short and long run for the European explorers?

The Incas, a people living in the Andes Mountains of South America, also cultivated a crop indigenous to that region—potatoes. An excellent alternative to maize, which did not grow in the high country, this hardy vegetable grew easily in the adverse conditions and high altitudes of mountain ranges and provided a hearty food supply. Once planted, potatoes required little work to harvest and prepare. Incas living in the mountains dried potatoes for long-term storage.

The small amount of time required to cultivate and harvest maize and potatoes left many days free for other work, and the great Central and South American empires developed a religious and aristocratic culture that demanded human labor for immense building projects. The Maya, Aztecs, and Incas built magnificent cities and roads and imposing pyramids. These constructions seem even more remarkable when we realize that they were built with Stone Age technology and without use of the wheel and (in most places) without the help of powerful, domesticated animals. Among these civilizations, only the Incas had domesticated the llama and alpaca as beasts of burden; throughout the rest of North and South America, people raised only dogs and fowl.

Empire building

The map on page 280 shows the locations of the large South American empires as they existed when the Europeans arrived in the fifteenth century. The illustration shows the narrow Isthmus of Panama, which formed an effective geographic barrier between the two major empires, and which also served to disadvantage the Amerindians in developing increasingly complex societies. For example, the Aztecs in Mexico invented a wheel, but because they lacked draft animals, the wheel remained a children's toy. The Incas had domesticated the llama but had no wheel to convert this animal into an effective beast of burden.

In Mexico, the Aztecs had located their capital at the great city of Tenochtitlán, built on a lake and accessible only by boat or causeway. (Tenochtitlán is the site of present-day Mexico City.) The Aztecs called themselves Meshica, from which we get the word *Mexico*. The Aztecs had conquered all the surrounding local tribes and claimed tribute from the vanquished, including humans sacrificed to the demanding Aztec gods, who people believed claimed human blood to delay an inevitable destruction of Aztec society. The voracious demand for such tribute from the subject peoples catalyzed resentment among them—a force that the new conquerors from Europe would find useful in overpowering the Aztecs.

Aztec Empire

The Original Northern Americans

The spread of maize led to large, settled agricultural communities in North America. In the American Southwest, Pueblo and Navajo peoples adapted to their dry lands by irrigating crops of maize, beans, and squashes. They built permanent adobe buildings, and their populations grew. Farther north and east, Amerindians shaped their environments in different ways. They made extensive use of fire to burn underbrush in forests and, probably more significantly, to burn the great plains and prairies. In doing so, they created a huge pastureland for game, and their populations grew as well. The map on page 280 shows the general patterns of the North American settlements.

The largest settled populations north of the Rio Grande spread along the Mississippi valley with the mound-building cultures. The largest surviving mound, at Cahokia near St. Louis, Illinois, is an astonishing structure, 100 feet high and 1,000 feet long. There were more than a hundred smaller mounds nearby. By 1250 C.E., the settlement surrounding these mounds probably reached between 15,000 and 38,000 inhabitants. These people grew prosperous from long-distance trade along the Missouri and Mississippi rivers, which brought seashells from Florida, copper from the Great Lakes, and other goods from all over the continent. The rise of Cahokia coincided with the spread of maize into the eastern part of the continent, a development that allowed the native populations to grow even more.

Fortunately, we have a visual record of the prosperity that eastern tribes of Amerindians enjoyed before their contact with Europeans, for an artist, John White, accompanied three voyages to the colony of Roanoke. White's detailed watercolors, copied by an engraver in the Netherlands and published in 1590, remain an excellent source of information about the lives and livelihoods of some North American tribes. The village White portrays in the image shown on page 281 is prosperous and orderly and has abundant food available.

AZTEC HUMAN SACRIFICE FROM THE *CODEX MAGLIABECCHIANO,* ca. 1570 Spanish conquerors took advantage of internal warfare among the tribes that generated human sacrifices such as that documented in this Aztec manuscript. The priest at the top removes the heart of the victims.

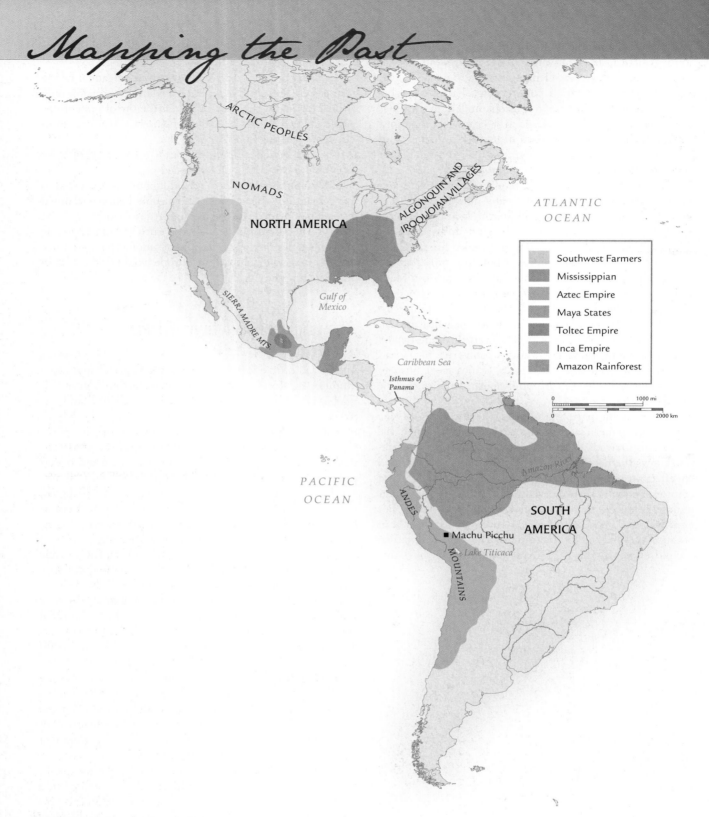

ARCTIC PEOPLES

NOMADS

ALGONQUIN AND
IROQUOIAN VILLAGES

NORTH AMERICA

ATLANTIC
OCEAN

SIERRA MADRE MTS

*Gulf of
Mexico*

Caribbean Sea

*Isthmus of
Panama*

PACIFIC
OCEAN

ANDES

MOUNTAINS

Amazon River

SOUTH
AMERICA

■ Machu Picchu

Lake Titicaca

	Southwest Farmers
	Mississippian
	Aztec Empire
	Maya States
	Toltec Empire
	Inca Empire
	Amazon Rainforest

0   1000 mi
0   2000 km

Indigenous Peoples and Empires in the Americas, ca. 1500   This map shows the locations of the
**Amerindian civilizations in North and South America.   Notice the distances and geographic barriers between
the groups. How did these distances and geographic features contribute to the striking differences among
these populations?**

AMERINDIAN VILLAGE FROM THEODORE DE BRY, *GRANDS ET PETITS VOYAGES*, 1590 This watercolor shows a well-ordered village in North America. Tribes grow tobacco, corn, and pumpkins.

There is much controversy over the size of these indigenous populations in North America, but certainly millions of people prospered in the American North. These flourishing cultures would be drastically affected by the arrival of Europeans.

Early Contacts

Christopher Columbus set the tone for the relationship between the original Americans and Europeans when he claimed land in the New World for the Spanish monarchs and when he treated the people as sources of revenue for the Spanish crown. With few exceptions, subsequent European explorers viewed the native peoples in the same way. Sometimes they traded with them; other times they used them as labor. Still other times, they killed or enslaved the men and women they found living in the new lands.

Explorers of the New World believed they had encountered a major problem: These lands lacked the spices and luxury goods of the East that had brought so much immediate wealth to merchants. These new explorers had to find other forms of riches to bring home. Sometimes they enslaved natives, but this was not particularly lucrative. Instead, they searched for silver and gold to take back to Europe. For the Europeans, all the early contacts involved questions of profit; for the Amerindians, such contacts brought suffering.

Conquest of the Great Empires

1520–1550

While in the Caribbean, the Spanish explorer Hernando Cortés (1485–1547) heard of a fabulously rich society to the west. Their curiosity aroused, he and 600 men sailed across the Gulf of Mexico in search of gold and glory. These Spanish soldiers of fortune were known as **conquistadors.** When Cortés landed on the Yucatán peninsula in southeast Mexico, the people he met there told him of a wealthy civilization in the interior (the Aztecs). As Cortés moved inland, he acquired a gift that proved more valuable to his quest than anything else—the slave woman Malinche.

Cortés's explorations

According to later Spanish sources, Malinche was a princess whose father had died when she was young. The girl's mother gave her to local slave traders when the mother remarried, and the traders included the young woman in their gifts to Cortés. Malinche spoke four Amerindian languages, including the Nahuatl of the Aztecs, and she easily learned Spanish. She converted to Christianity and took the baptismal name of Marina. Malinche was constantly at Cortés's side, interpreting and advising him on matters of policy and customs as he made his way west. The various peoples they encountered on their journey recognized her importance, calling Cortés "Malinche's Captain."

Eventually, Cortés's group marched 250 miles into the interior of Mexico and reached the Aztec capital of Tenochtitlán. There, Cortés and Malinche met with Montezuma II (1502–1520), the Aztec emperor. With the help of Malinche, Cortés garnered the support of nearly 100,000 people from neighboring tribes who were eager to throw off the Aztec yoke. Even with the advantage of gunpowder, armor, horses, and fierce dogs, it took him nearly a year to subdue the empire, and contemporary witnesses captured the violence of the struggle. Bernal Díaz del Castillo described the capture of the last stronghold: "I have read of the destruction of Jerusalem, but I know not if that slaughter was more fearful than this—the earth, the lagoons, and the buttresses were full of corpses and the stench was more than any man could bear." In 1522, Cortés proclaimed the Aztec Empire "New Spain," and he prepared to rule. Although he had fathered

Aztecs conquered

a son with Malinche, he gave her as a bride to one of his soldiers and presented her with expensive estates to thank her for her help.

The Inca Empire fell to another conquistador, Francisco Pizarro (ca. 1475–1541). In 1532, Pizarro landed on the west coast of South America and began to march to Cuzco, the Incan capital. The Inca rulers had just endured

Incas conquered

a five-year civil war over a disputed succession, and the newly victorious ruler, Atahualpa, apparently underestimated the Spanish. Atahualpa came unguarded to meet with Pizarro, and he was promptly captured. He offered a roomful of gold as his ransom, which the Spanish accepted. After collecting the ransom, they killed their hostage. The Incas fought fiercely for a few years after the fall of their leader, but they were unable to overcome the Spanish technical advantages. A new order arose in South America.

How did these small numbers of Europeans manage to conquer the impressive Amerindian empires? They gained a clear advantage from their steel weapons, horses, and

Germs

high organization (including writing, which allowed them to communicate effectively). However, in the long run, their greatest weapon was biological—germs they brought from Europe. When previously isolated populations mingle, it is common for epidemics to break out, but the confrontation between Europeans and Amerindians was particularly devastating because the New World had no history of interaction with domesticated animals. The most devastating acute diseases that Eurasians faced came initially from their animals: measles, tuberculosis, flu, whooping cough, and, perhaps most deadly, smallpox. With thousands of years of exposure to these diseases, Europeans had developed immunities. Amerindians had not. In what turned out to be a biological tragedy that clinched the European conquest, disease and death followed the colonists everywhere they ventured.

North American Contacts

The fortunes of the northern Amerindians in the wake of Europeans' arrival are more difficult to recount because the first contacts between the Europeans and the northern tribes were indirect. Direct contacts in the north did not occur until twenty-five to one hundred years later than the South and Central American contacts. Thus we do not have as many eyewitness accounts for the early period in the north. Yet the effects of the Europeans' arrival were still powerfully felt there, because European germs were able to spread to North America, where they brought diseases to the people and destroyed their societies on a large scale. Thus, when the first accounts of the northern contact were written, the authors described societies that had already been severely disrupted.

One example of the ravages of disease in the north following European contact came in the wake of the Spaniard Hernando de Soto's (ca. 1496/97–1542) landing in Florida in 1539. For four years, de Soto's small force wandered through Florida and Georgia and elsewhere in the South looking for gold. De Soto's band killed many Indians in the course of their travels, but the explorer eventually succumbed to fever and died. Many of de Soto's pigs remained to roam in the woods. As we have seen, domestic animals often served as sources of disease in early modern times, just as they do in the world today, as we are periodically confronted by animal-borne diseases such as swine flu and avian flu. De Soto's pigs similarly brought disease that spread widely through the human population. By the time the next Europeans traveled through the Mississippi valley a century later, the population had fallen steeply, by perhaps as much as 96 percent. Disease had emptied this rich land of its peoples.

Some scholars believe that the rich environmental and animal resources the North American colonists found, from the fertile Great Plains to the innumerable buffalo herds, existed because the native peoples who had tended the land had died off, primarily from imported diseases. The North American world was transformed by the European arrival as surely as was the Southern Hemisphere.

Life and Death Under European Rule
1550–1700

The goal of the newly established European colonial empires was to enrich the home countries. To meet this aim, the colonists exploited natural resources and Amerindian peoples to their fullest. The Spanish crown divided up the lands, placing viceroys in charge of each section. These royal representatives were responsible for delivering to the crown the profits taken from the new lands. The crown claimed one-fifth of all gold and silver mined in the New World, and the treasure ships departed the coasts of the Americas heavily laden.

To get the human labor he needed to search and mine for precious metals, Christopher Columbus proposed enslaving the native peoples. Queen Isabella rejected the plan, for she considered the New World peoples

Enforced labor

her subjects. Instead, the Spanish developed a new structure, called the **encomienda** system, to provide the conquerors with labor. Under this system, the crown would grant an encomienda, which gave conquistadors and their successors the right to the labor of a certain number of Amerindians. Theoretically, in exchange for labor, the Spanish owed the natives protection and an introduction to the Christian faith.

The encomiendas lasted only through the sixteenth century, but this system was replaced by other forms of labor servitude, like the *repartimiento,* which required adult males to devote a certain number of days of labor

Then & Now

"... and a Bottle of Rum"

In the sixteenth century, Europeans were just beginning to drink brandy, distilled from wine, but on the sugar plantations in the Caribbean, slaves discovered that alcohol could be distilled from molasses, the by-product of sugar-making. Seeing the profit available, the owners took over the distillation process and devoted much of their production to making rum, which swept the New and Old Worlds, creating a product for which there was insatiable demand. By 1700, each person in the North American colonies consumed about 4 gallons of rum per year, stimulating the production of sugar and the trade in slaves to produce it. Today, the Caribbean islands remain the major producers of rum, a drink that remains the most popular distilled drink in the United States.

annually to Spanish economic enterprises, such as plantations (called **haciendas**) or mines. Sometimes these contracts stipulated a lifetime of labor (though the subject peoples remained personally free); other times, the Amerindians had to work for the Spanish for a fixed number of years. Life under these contracts proved extremely harsh—with hard labor and a shortage of food—and many laborers died while working for their new overseers.

For the Spanish, the arrangement yielded untold wealth, exemplified by the silver mine in Bolivia—the Potosí—shown in the painting on page 270. From 1580 to 1620, the great age of Spanish imperialism was financed by the silver extracted primarily from the Potosí mine.

The mine was labor intensive, so the mine owners saw the enforced labor of the locals as essential. The Spanish crown gave the owners of the Potosí mine the conscripted labor of 13,300 Amerindians. These workers had to report to the mine on Monday morning and toil underground until Saturday evening. The mine owners did not provide meals; throughout the workweek, the men's wives had to bring them food. Many workers perished under the inhumane conditions.

Not everyone accepted this colonial brutality as a natural consequence of the need for silver. The most severe critic among these was the Dominican friar Bartolomé de Las Casas (1474–1566). In his book *The Tears of the Indians,* Las Casas wrote: "There is nothing more detestable or more cruel, than the tyranny which the Spaniards use toward the Indian." Historians have disagreed about the exact number of lives lost in the Spanish domination of

Amerindian mortality

Central and South America, but all the estimates are shocking. Diseases, overwork, and warfare took a terrible toll on indigenous people everywhere in the New World. When Columbus landed in 1492, for example, the population of the Caribbean Islands was about 6,000,000, and fifty years later, it numbered only a few thousand. The native population of Peru fell from about 1,250,000 in 1570 to just 500,000 in 1620. Mexico fared worse: About 24 million native individuals died between 1519 and 1605. Many fell victim to diseases, overwork, and the abuse that Las Casas had described. Some Europeans abhorred this destruction, but many saw it as merely a source of worry about where to get enough labor to work their mines and the plantations.

In another tragic turn of events, Las Casas proposed a solution that he thought might free the native workers from their burden of labor. He suggested that the king of Spain offer Spanish men and women a license to settle in the New World. In addition to land, each license would give permission for the holder to import a dozen African slaves to the Americas. In his old age, Las Casas recognized the problems with this policy. To his regret, the plan brought a shameful new injustice to the New World: the African slave trade.

The African Slave Trade

By the beginning of the seventeenth century, the new rulers in the Americas were facing alarming labor shortages. The original Americans had died in huge numbers just as

SUGAR PLANTATION, 1667 Sugar was the crop that brought the most wealth to plantation owners. Originally from Egypt, sugar was transplanted wherever it would grow, to satisfy soaring European tastes for sugar and rum. Slaves were brought to work the fields and the processing plants.

colonists stepped up the need for labor in their profitable enterprises. As we saw earlier, mining required countless workers. The sprawling plantations built to exploit demand for new crops also desperately depended on large numbers of ill-paid workers.

Sugar is the overriding example. Although sugarcane grew in Egypt and North Africa, it remained scarce and expensive. Europeans discovered that the cane flourished

Sugar plantations

in the New World and began to cultivate it avidly in hopes of satisfying the intense European craving for its sweet flavor. Sugar also fueled a new vice—the alcoholic beverages (like rum) that it helped make. Throughout the Caribbean and in Brazil, colonists established grand sugar plantations and began using African slaves to work them. On the plantations, workers tended the sugarcane and harvested it with large, sharp knives—a practice that often led to serious injuries. Then the cane had to be crushed to extract its juice.

Sugar and other plantations (for example, cotton in North America) were designed to produce enough of their specified crop to satisfy a world market. Plantation owners took a consuming interest in the success of these endeavors. Indeed, the German naturalist Maria Sibylla Merian (see Past Lives on page 290) wrote that she was ridiculed in the colony of Surinam, in South America, because she

was interested in things other than sugar. This monoculture, or focus on a single crop, forced the plantations to trade with the rest of the world for all their remaining necessities, including labor.

As we saw in Chapter 10, slavery on a small scale began to be reintroduced into Europe during the Renaissance, and the sixteenth-century warfare escalating between Christians and Muslims stimulated even more enslavements in North Africa. For example, in 1627 Muslim pirates from the Mediterranean raided distant Iceland and enslaved nearly 400 descendants of the Vikings. Current studies suggest that between 1580 and 1680, some 850,000 Christian captives were enslaved in Muslim North Africa. Some of these captives who escaped or were ransomed engaged in their own slaving raids against Muslims as a form of revenge.

This growth of slavery between Christians and Muslims likely suggested to Europeans a solution for the labor shortages in the New World. In 1532, the first slave shipments departed from Africa to transport slaves directly across the Atlantic to the plantations of the West

African slaves

Indies and Brazil. Before 1650, only about 7,000 slaves annually crossed the Atlantic, but the figure doubled to about 14,000 between 1650 and 1675. Before the 1680s, the Atlantic slave trade almost exclusively provided slaves for these sugar plantations. During the seventeenth century, blacks brought to North America came from the Caribbean, not directly from Africa—many had European surnames and knew a European language. A significant fraction of these early "servants for life" in North America became free, and some appear in the early records of the colonies (even in the South) as freeholders and voters. By the eighteenth century, the rise in plantations in North America caused slaves to be imported directly from Africa in large numbers (see Chapter 15).

The slave trade generated huge profits, not only for the Europeans, but also for African chiefs who supplied slaves to the traders. Because of long, but periodic, contact with

Impact in Africa

Europe for millennia, Africans had substantial resistance to European diseases, so they survived in larger numbers than the Amerindians had. Slavery had always been part of African warfare, and as early as the seventh century, Muslims profited from slaves brought across the Sahara Desert. However, in the sixteenth century the huge profits created a new scale of trade—chiefs traded slaves to the Europeans in exchange for guns to gain advantage over their traditional rivals. Some tribes (such as the Congo in central Africa) were initially opposed to the trade but became heavily involved to stay competitive with their neighbors.

The political consequences of the trade in Africa varied. In the kingdom of the Congo, the Portuguese quest for slaves weakened the monarchy and led to local warfare and a decentralization of power. In the military kingdom of Dahomey on the west coast of Africa, kings made the slave trade a royal monopoly and profited enormously. When the trade ended, however, the resulting economic depression in Dahomey led to severe political disturbance. Although this discussion shows it is possible to treat the slave trade as one more manifestation of the growing world economy, one cannot ignore the fact that the trade of human beings rendered incalculable costs in human misery.

By 1700, traders were delivering about 30,000 slaves each year, and that number continued to escalate into the late eighteenth century. Packed tightly into the holds of ships and subjected to lack of food, water, and sanitary facilities, as many as 25 percent of these human beings died in transit. Anyone who survived the trip then faced new horrors: starvation and overwork and sometimes harsh physical discipline by their owners.

Some slaves ran away. In Brazil, in particular, many escapees fled into the forest and founded their own communities. The largest of the settlements was Palmares,

Slave rebellions

which the Portuguese attacked in 1692 and destroyed three years later. Although it is impossible to get exact figures, it seems the community consisted of perhaps 10,000 fugitives who had formed a kingdom and designated a king and a council of elders.

Gathering Souls in the New Lands

Early explorers were partially motivated to travel by their desire to spread the Christian faith, and this desire only increased as Europeans found so many "heathens" around the world. Cultures all over the world became exposed to the Christian message. Many missionaries worked to alleviate the misery caused by the conquests, but others traveled from Europe with the zeal of crusaders and with the dogged insensitivity of the conquistadors. Some of them baptized natives in large groups, with no concern for their spiritual inclinations. Columbus and other early explorers, ignorant of native culture, wrote that the indigenous peoples had no religious sensibilities and thus should be easily converted. As a result, subsequent missionaries believed they were offering the benefits of religion to people who had none.

This attitude led to even further ill treatment of native peoples. In 1543, for example, the archbishop of New Spain (Mexico) tried 131 people for heresy, including 13 Aztecs, who he (rightly) believed practiced old forms of piety. In 1555, the Council of Mexico resolved not to ordain anyone of Indian, African, or mixed background— the priesthood was to be reserved for those of European descent. The suspicion extended even to churchmen sympathetic to native peoples. The Spanish crown had banned the writings of Bartolomé de Las Casas that decried Iberian treatment of Amerindians, and the Spanish Inquisition included them on its list of forbidden books.

A significant turning point in the conversion of the indigenous peoples of Mexico came in 1531, when a native convert named Juan Diego claimed to have seen the Virgin Mary. As Diego explained it, Mary had commanded him to build a church in her honor, and when he

Virgin of Guadalupe

needed proof of this command, the Virgin ordered him to gather roses within his cloak and take them to the bishop. Although it was not the season for the flower, Diego claimed to have found them and when he unfolded his cloak in the presence of the bishop, all claimed to see a miraculously formed image of the Virgin Mary left on the cloak. The Virgin of Guadalupe (named for the region near Mexico City where she reportedly appeared) became the patroness of Mexico, and Juan Diego's cloak with the Virgin's image remains in her shrine, where pilgrims gather to see it. For many Mexicans, she lent credence to their belief that Christianity did not belong only to Europeans. Her shrine remains a major pilgrimage site today, and reproductions of the image have been widely circulated. Juan Diego, too, remained a venerated figure, and in 2002, he was declared a saint.

Some missionaries to the Americas proved acutely sensitive to the needs of the new converts and accommodated Christian practice to local religious ways. Las Casas was one such missionary; another was Marie de l'Incarnation

(1599–ca. 1669), a French nun who founded a convent in Quebec to teach native Canadian girls. Marie not only cared for the young women who came to her convent but also learned the Algonquin language and translated some religious writings into that language to make them accessible to the Algonquin-speaking peoples.

Missionaries

Missionaries generally paid more attention to the spiritual salvation of New World natives than to that of the African slaves brought to the Americas. A striking exception to this rule was the Portuguese missionary Pedro Claver (1580–1654), who has now been declared a Catholic saint. Claver settled in Colombia in 1610 and was horrified by the plight of the slaves who worked the plantations. From then on, whenever he signed his name, he added the vow "forever a servant to Africans." He lived up to that vow, converting many Africans to Christianity while caring for their physical needs. He even built and worked in a leper colony, caring for sick, neglected Africans.

Elsewhere across the world, European missionary work took on decidedly different forms than it did in the Americas. In Asia, the missionaries succeeded in their aims only after they acknowledged the validity and strengths of the local cultures. For example, some Jesuit priests in Japan adopted the status of Zen Buddhist priests and strictly observed Japanese etiquette. The Japanese were quite receptive to the missionaries, and by 1580, Jesuits claimed over 100,000 conversions in Japan. The goodwill ended in about 1600, when trade disputes unleashed a Japanese persecution of Christians that was so brutal it virtually stamped out Christianity on the island. The Jesuit Roberto de Nobili in 1605 carried this policy of religious accommodation to its logical extreme in India by dressing in the robes of an Indian holy man, studying Sanskrit, and refusing all contact with fellow Europeans.

The Chinese proved more suspicious of the Westerners, at first denying them entry to their country. Nevertheless, a Jesuit—Matteo Ricci (1552–1610)—approached them with Western gifts (such as a mechanical clock) and gained admission to the court of the Ming emperor Wan-li (r. 1573–1620). While practicing his faith at the Chinese court, Ricci adopted much that was Chinese. He dressed as a Confucian scholar, for example, and preached the Christian message in terms consistent with Chinese ethics. By 1605, 17 missionaries were working in China. Not all the missionaries working in China were as tolerant as Ricci, and many condemned Confucianism as paganism.

As Christianity spread around the world, Christian practice changed as it accommodated the needs of new converts. Mexican Christians, for example, venerated the dark-skinned image of the Virgin of Guadalupe with a vigor unappreciated in Europe. Brazilian and Haitian converts worshiped in the Christian tradition, all the while acknowledging spiritual customs brought from Africa. Chinese Christians continued their practice of venerating ancestors, much to the chagrin of some European priests. In all these cases, the Catholic Church was itself transformed even as it transformed those around it. In time, Protestant worship, too, would be affected—the use of African rhythms in gospel music in modern North American churches offers one vivid example.

Christianity transformed

THE WORLD MARKET AND COMMERCIAL REVOLUTION

Europeans had long traded over extensive distances; after all, it was the spices and silks of the Far East that had first lured them across the Atlantic. During the twelfth and thirteenth centuries, Europeans had enjoyed a growing commerce, creating northern and southern trade routes that brought goods through the Middle East from the farthest reaches of Asia. These centuries introduced a commercial revolution that greatly expanded the opportunities for many in the growing towns of the Middle Ages. However, the disasters of the fourteenth century put the brakes on this growth, and this commercial contraction lasted almost until the middle of the sixteenth century. Now, the navigation of the seas and the exploration of new lands reopened and reshaped this pattern of production and commerce. By the end of the sixteenth century, Europeans were trading in a world market, on a scale larger than they had ever before experienced.

High Prices and Profits: Trading on the World Stage

What exactly stepped up the global demand for luxury goods? In part, the demand was fueled by population growth in the sixteenth and seventeenth centuries. During the sixteenth century, the number of Europeans expanded from about 80 million to 105 million as Europe recovered from the devastation of the Black Death. These increases continued. As the population steadily rose, goods became scarce. Demand intensified and drove prices up. In the sixteenth century, cereal prices escalated about fivefold, and the price of manufactured goods tripled. Contemporary witnesses repeatedly expressed shock at the

Inflation

inflation. As one sixteenth-century Spaniard lamented, "Today a pound of mutton costs as much as a whole sheep used to." People complained, but no one had concrete solutions to the problem.

At mid-century, some Europeans began blaming the influx of precious metals from the New World for their inflation woes. Their frustration was understandable. The Potosí mine alone yielded millions of Spanish coins a year, which poured unchecked into the European economy, moving rapidly from one country to the next. As just one example of the interconnected economy, the massive Spanish ships that transported silver across the Atlantic depended on French canvas for their sails. Silver coins from the New World paid for those sails. Economists can trace Spanish silver from Europe to as far as China, where European merchants snapped up the silks and spices that initially inspired the explorations. Yet the flood of coins into Europe was only part of the picture. In truth, the price revolution stemmed from a combination of the new money, a surge in population growth, and unprecedented appetites for new goods.

The Rise of Commercial Capitalism

Inflation always hurts those with fixed incomes, but high prices also provide incentives for enterprising people to make a profit. The energetic sixteenth-century pursuit of trade stimulated new forms of production and economic concepts that together have been called the commercial revolution, but might more accurately be termed a commercial acceleration, during which trading practices developed in the Middle Ages spread and flourished. During this vital era, a set of business practices (and perceptions) arose that we know as capitalism. The word *capitalism* was actually not used until the nineteenth century. By the mid-seventeenth century, however, some individuals were called **capitalists,** a word indicating how they handled money. Capitalists were people who chose to invest their funds in business activities in order to make more money (capital). For these **entrepreneurs,** the most lucrative business opportunity was the growing world trade. Exploring the Past on page 288 presents a seventeenth-century testimonial on the benefits of this long-distance trade.

Dutch entrepreneurs led the way in implementing capitalist ideas as they engaged in worldwide trade. For example, merchants in Amsterdam built huge warehouses to store goods so that they could control supplies and keep prices **Capitalist ideas** high. Through new strategies like this and through individual initiative, the Netherlands became the leading commercial center in Europe in the sixteenth century.

Capitalist initiative gave rise to fluctuations in demand for goods. We can follow an early example of this economic cycle in the tulip industry. Tulips originally were imported into the Netherlands from Turkey, in the sixteenth century. A Dutch botanist discovered how to grow the many varied colors of this versatile flower. By 1634, buyers not only in the Netherlands but also all over Europe were so enthralled by

JAN VERMEER, *YOUNG WOMAN WITH A WATER PITCHER,* ca. 1664 The global trade brought wealth to new merchant classes. They could then afford beautiful art that celebrated their new acquisitions, such as glass windows, silver pitchers, woven tapestries, and even a world map for the wall.

Thomas Mun Praises Trade

Thomas Mun (1571–1641) was a director in the East India Company, and in 1630 he wrote "Discourse on England's Treasure by Foreign Trade," which was published in 1664. In this excerpt, Mun shows that he shared the mercantilist view that trade could enrich the kingdom.

. . . The ordinary means therefore to increase our wealth and treasure is by Foreign Trade, wherein we must ever observe this rule: to sell more to strangers yearly than we consume of theirs in value. For suppose that when this Kingdom is plentifully served with the Cloth, Lead, Tin, Iron, Fish and other native commodities, we do yearly export the overplus to foreign countries to the value of twenty-two hundred thousand pounds; by which means we are enabled beyond the Seas to buy and bring in foreign wares for our use and Consumptions, to the value of twenty hundred thousand pounds: By this order duly kept in our trading, we may rest assured that the kingdom shall be enriched yearly two hundred thousand pounds, which must be brought to us in so much Treasure; . . .

Let Princes oppress, Lawyers extort, Usurers bite, Prodigals waste, and lastly let Merchants carry out what money they shall have occasion to use in traffique. Yet all these actions can work no other effects in the course of trade than is declared in this discourse. For so much Treasure only will be brought in or carried out of a Commonwealth, as the foreign Trade doth over or under balance in value. . . .

What does Mun consider a favorable balance of trade? How are these views consistent with mercantilist thought, and how do they differ from your understanding of modern economic life?

the exotic and beautiful plants that one rare tulip bulb sold for 1,000 pounds of cheese, four oxen, eight pigs, twelve sheep, a bed, and a suit of clothes. Investors rushed to take advantage of the lucrative tulip market and the supply of the bulbs ballooned. Three years later, however, the increased supply drove down the price, ruining many who had gambled on the rare flower. Novice capitalists learned the hard way about the cruel whims of the market economy.

People with moderate means also yearned to participate in promising financial ventures. To accommodate them, businesses built upon medieval concepts of trading partnerships and developed an innovative entity called the **joint-stock company.** This new economic structure allowed ordinary investors to buy shares in commercial ventures that were run by boards of directors.

Joint-stock companies

With successes in such investments, modest capitalists might generate enough money to set out on their own and gamble on higher-risk opportunities. These joint-stock companies made it easier to raise enough capital for trading ventures around the world. Amsterdam was the site of the first stock exchange, and enterprising people in the colony of New York began trading shares at a tree at the end of Wall Street.

In the seventeenth century, English and Dutch merchants formed exceptionally efficient joint-stock companies that helped them dominate trade in Asia: the English East India Company, founded in 1600, and the Dutch United East India Company, known by its initials VOC (Vereenigde Oost-Indische Compagnie), founded in 1602. Although both companies enjoyed government support, they were privately owned by merchant investors. Their charters granted them remarkable powers—they could buy, sell, and even wage war in the companies' interests. These companies immediately generated huge profits, and both contributed to the early formation of a global network of trade.

Mercantilism: Controlling the Balance of Trade

With so much money at stake, western European governments attempted centralized regulation of their economies—

mercantilism—to profit from the expanded global trade. Mercantilism was based on the assumption that the amount of worldwide wealth was fixed, so countries competed to get a larger piece of the pie. This was essentially economic nationalism, in which governments controlled their economies to increase their acquisition of hard currency. The simple principle "buy low, sell high"

Economic nationalism

led these governments to discourage imports, particularly expensive ones, and encourage exports. In 1586, one Spanish bureaucrat asked King Philip II to forbid the import of candles, glass trinkets, jewelry, cutlery, and other such items, because these sorts of "useless" luxuries drained away precious Spanish gold. Such policies aimed to create a favorable balance of trade and fill bank vaults with gold.

Mercantilist governments passed laws to ensure a favorable trade balance. They imposed tariffs on imports and discouraged manufacturing in their colonies to force

Economic regulations

them to buy exports from the home country. Thus, hard currency would flow from the colonies to enrich royal treasuries in Europe. In fact, mercantilist policy encouraged the founding of new colonies to create new markets to purchase European exports. When other things failed, governments debased their coins to try to maintain a favorable balance.

Some governments even tried to keep wages low so that citizens would have little discretionary income with which to buy expensive imports. All these efforts were meant to enrich the states, not the fortunes of wealthy citizens. Mercantilist policies placed the state before the individual. They achieved their goal, vastly enriching the powerful monarchies of western Europe. Sadly, they also financed the destructive wars that swept over Europe through the mid-seventeenth century. Mercantilist economic policy would continue to shape government policy into the eighteenth century.

OPINION

How did new ideas like joint-stock companies and state banks facilitate the new global trade, and how do they still facilitate trade today?

The Growth of Banking

Neither private capitalism nor mercantilism could have succeeded without innovations in banking practices. Medieval ideas that forbad charging interest and that kept royal treasuries locked in chests in royal bedrooms had become obsolete. In this new age, people needed easier access to

a lot of money, and they refined banking techniques that had been developed in the late Middle Ages in the Italian cities of the Renaissance. Medieval bankers had developed bills of exchange and complex account books to facilitate commerce, but in the late fifteenth century, bankers added checks, bank drafts, and sophisticated double-entry bookkeeping to their skills, all of which made commercial ventures easier than ever.

Through the sixteenth century, private bankers handled most financial transactions. The Fuggers of Germany were the most successful at this profession, taking over a role that the Medicis in Florence had dominated in the fifteenth century. The Fugger family became so

State banks

wealthy that they even lent money to Emperor Charles V. With the emergence of mercantilist ideas about economics serving the state, this kind of practice waned. Instead, government banks developed that controlled profits going to individuals. The Bank of Amsterdam was founded in 1609, followed by the Bank of Sweden in 1657, and the Bank of England in 1694. However, new banking policies could not ensure that even mercantilist governments would grow rich.

The Danger of Overspending: Spain Learns a Lesson

At first, Europeans believed that the wealth flowing into Europe from the New World was the primary payoff from their explorations. Entire countries became rich, and imperial powers grew in previously unheard-of ways. Spain immediately capitalized on the new wealth, its treasure ships offering unlimited prosperity and power to the monarchs. Yet, the vast influx of silver was deceiving, and the Spanish king spent it wastefully on the incessant wars that dominated the sixteenth and early seventeenth centuries.

Consequently, the Spanish crown had to declare bankruptcy several times in the course of the sixteenth and seventeenth centuries. Spain's financial troubles hurt merchants in Germany and Italy, but the real burden fell on the Spanish taxpayers, who were soon saddled with debt. Instead of relieving their debt burdens, the politics of empire only added to them. Domination of the New World passed to the governments of other countries (notably Holland and England) that proved more efficient in fiscal matters.

Ultimately, much of the gold and silver that motivated the expansionist countries did not even end up in Europe. A large percentage of this currency eventually flowed to the East for the purchase of luxury items. As Spain discovered, these precious metals were not enough to keep profligate governments in power.

Maria Sibylla Merian (1647–1717), Naturalist, Artist, and Traveler

MARIA SIBILLA MERIAN
Nat. XII Apr M.DC.XLVII. Obiit XIII. Jan. M.D.CC.XVII.

Maria Sibylla was born in Frankfurt, Germany, the daughter of a well-known engraver and publisher. In her youth, she learned to paint and illustrate books, and also learned to love collecting and studying insects, especially butterflies. In 1665, she married another artist and publisher, and could have lived her life working and drawing in the family business, but the Reformation opened up new opportunities for the talented woman.

In 1685, she was consumed with fervor for religious renewal and left her husband, moving to Amsterdam, where she joined a religious community and a circle of naturalists. In 1699, she and her daughter moved to the Dutch colony of Surinam, on the northern shore of South America, to join a religious colony. Merian lived there for two years, where she observed and illustrated books on the local plants and insects. This work solidified her reputation as a naturalist, and her books remained widely read into the next century. In 1997, the U.S. Postal Service memorialized her by issuing stamps of her drawings.

Merian depended on family ties and religious chaos to forward her dreams of scientific study. What challenges and opportunities do women entering science face today?

Redefining Work Roles

The commercial revolution both enlarged the scale of business and redefined the way people viewed their work. While most people still worked the land, in the cities, which served as the nerve centers of the new economies, people experienced the most remarkable shifts in how they made

Women's work

their living. As the middle class rose to economic power on the dual waves of trade and hard work, the lives of urban women in particular diverged dramatically from earlier times. In the early Middle Ages, women had labored in the stores and workshops of Europe's cities. They dominated trades that they had controlled in the home—textile making and brewing, for example. Women had such a presence in these fields that feminine forms of certain words (ending in *ster*) derived from these jobs—for instance, *webster* (from *weaver*) and *brewster* (from *brewer*)—arose and even became common surnames. Women also owned taverns in such numbers that an instruction manual written for merchants in 1515 assumed that the innkeeper would be a woman and gave instructions on "how to ask the *hostess* how much one has spent."

Still, women's access to the workforce came primarily through their families. Daughters, like most sons, mastered trades in the family workshops, just as Maria Sibylla Merian (in Past Lives) learned printing from her stepfather. Wives worked with their husbands, and widows frequently ran businesses and took their husbands' place in the guilds. During the late Middle Ages, men slowly began to replace women in some of the most lucrative jobs, like cloth making, and just as in banking and commercial enterprises, this late-medieval trend accelerated in the early modern period.

Into the sixteenth century, as work generated more capital and power, it began losing its association with the family and became more linked to the public political arena. Many people (women and men alike) believed that public work and control of money were more appropriately managed by men than women. Late in the sixteenth century, cities accordingly began to issue ordinances restricting women's entry into guilds, which had taken on markedly political overtones. For example, a ruling in France in 1583 limited silk-making apprentices (who had previously been predominantly female) to only two males per master. In another example, a 1508 ordinance in the Netherlands referred to a "brotherhood and sisterhood" of a guild, but the reissued ordinance in 1552 mentioned only a "brotherhood of trimmers." By 1563, when the ordinances were again revised, even widows' rights had been omitted.

Leaving the workforce

Similar examples emerged at local levels throughout Europe. As the commercial revolution spread and urban merchants grew powerful, the old divisions of those who worked and those who did not began to blur. Instead, the growing middle class began to divide the world between those who worked outside the home in the public, political arena and those who worked inside the home. Urban women, relegated increasingly to the domestic sphere, lost much of their visibility in the public arena.

Piracy: Banditry on a World Scale

1550–1700

The expansion of trade into the Atlantic and Pacific brought with it another nettlesome problem: a rise in piracy. Piracy was as old as Mediterranean shipping, when seagoing robbers had preyed mercilessly on the ponderous merchant roundships that moved goods through the inland sea. As the pace of the world economy quickened, pirates moved to take advantage. From about 1550 to about 1700, a "pirate belt" developed that stretched from the West Indies to East Asia. The new entrepreneurial raiding coincided with the weakening of the great Turkish, Spanish, and Chinese empires that we saw in Chapter 11, because these navies could no longer effectively patrol their territorial waters.

Piracy as a way of life actually had a somewhat benign origin—monarchs had often issued licenses for people to steal from other countries in unofficial warfare. Before the seventeenth century, the word *pirate* rarely appeared. Instead, seagoing raiders were called **privateers** or corsairs, terms meaning that they had the authorization of formal commissions from their rulers. Even as late as the eighteenth century, the U.S. Constitution gave Congress the right to issue letters of marque and reprisal,

Early privateers

essentially to hire pirate ships. Privateers earned their profits from captured booty, and in the freewheeling raids that took place on the open seas, it was impossible to distinguish them from pirates acting on their own. The ships that were robbed probably did not draw any distinction between the two.

The difficulties of discerning pirate from privateer may be seen in the case of the famous early English privateers, particularly Francis Drake (ca. 1540–1596). By 1571, Drake had become a major force in the Caribbean, and this champion of the British was considered a ruthless pirate by the Spanish. Drake had numerous bases on land and gained the admiration and support of unconquered Amerindians and Spanish-hating escaped slaves. With the backing and affection of Queen Elizabeth I (r. 1558–1603), Drake and his fellow privateers relentlessly harassed the Spanish ships they found sailing in the Caribbean.

The fortunes of Drake's compatriot Walter Raleigh (ca. 1554–1618) showed how fragile royal support of these independent captains could be. Elizabeth backed Raleigh in his flamboyant enterprises, even knighting her champion. However, her successor, James I (r. 1603–1625) found the privateer less useful. As James began to have political difficulties with English Protestants, he sought an alliance with Spain (as we will see in Chapter 13). As a token of goodwill to Spain, James imprisoned Raleigh in the Tower of London and executed him in 1618.

Pirates included many Africans who had been captured as slaves, because after seizing wealthy slave-trading ships, pirates frequently gave the slaves the choice to continue on their way or join the pirate band. The eighteenth-century trial records of a pirate on the ship *Whydah* indicate that about 30 to 50 of the men on his ship were African and 1 was an Amerindian. The freedom of the pirate life drew many who had few choices elsewhere.

Pirate life

With all its hazards—from fickle royal supporters to war on the high seas—the pirate life could bring amazing riches even for those without a royal patron. Pirate cities sprang up based solely on the illicit trade. For example, Algiers in North Africa became a prosperous Muslim pirate city, and Malta in the Mediterranean was its Christian counterpart. Other pirate cities dotted the Caribbean from the coast of the Yucatán to the islands of the West Indies. These cities served as havens for the violent, reckless sea raiders and their families. They also were places where talented outsiders could rise to positions of considerable power. For example, a poor North African shepherd boy rose through the pirate ranks to become "king" of Algiers in 1569. During the eighteenth century, several women even took command of pirate ships.

Before the seventeenth century, the word *pirate* rarely appeared.

By the mid-eighteenth century, however, governments had begun expanding their navies and set out to suppress the buccaneers. The British admiralty discouraged privateering because it lured sailors away from serving in the navy. The age of informal warfare came to a close and accounts of the bandits' careers retreated to literary works that romanticized their lives. For example, literary pirates made their victims walk the plank; real pirates would not have wasted time on such rituals. If they wanted to kill their captives, they unceremoniously threw them overboard.

> If they wanted to kill their captives, they unceremoniously threw them overboard.

THE WORLD TRANSFORMED

The booming world market that stimulated the movement of goods and the enterprise of pirates also served to spread other aspects of European culture around the world. During the sixteenth century, more than 200,000 Spanish people, 10 percent of them women, migrated to Latin America. In the next century, comparable numbers of English, French, and Dutch settled in North America. These immigrants became a new ruling class that transfused much of European culture into the New World. They built cities featuring the grid pattern that marked Renaissance urban planning and placed their churches in the city centers.

European Culture Spreads

The new immigrants brought their languages and religions, but also unique livestock, tools, plants, and other goods that transformed the lives of native peoples. When European horses escaped (or were stolen), for example, some indigenous peoples took them into their midst. The Plains Indians in the southwest of North America soon made horses central to their way of life. In time, guns, liquor, and many other goods also found their way into the many native cultures.

Plants from Europe, some of them intentionally cultivated, made their mark on the New World as well. For example, Europeans brought wheat **Plants** to make the bread that had long served as their dietary staple. Along with their domesticated plants, they transported their traditional farming methods.

Europeans unwittingly altered the ecology of the New World in many other ways. As we have seen, they brought diseases that ravaged native populations. Less destructive but equally ubiquitous, plants transported to the New World spread with vigor. A sixteenth-century Inca observer (Garcilaso de la Vega) described how quickly the ecology of Peru had been transformed by invasive plants: "Some of them are becoming mischievous, such as the mustard, mint, and camomile, which have spread . . . [and] the first endives and spinach multiplied in such a way that a horse could not force its way through them." Inadvertent transportation of weed seeds also displaced native species. Dandelions are a particularly apt example of a European weed that spread accidentally as people, plants, and animals moved across the sea.

Europeans traveling and trading in Africa and Asia took New World plants to other regions of the world, transforming local consumption habits and economies. Africa, for example, received sweet potatoes and maize in the sixteenth century. In the Congo, the Portuguese introduced maize, although at first the tribes dismissed the vegetable as more suitable for pigs than human beings. In time, these plants became so central to the local culture that people no longer remembered that they were once strange imports. Because the societies of east Asia kept most Europeans at arm's length, they were less influenced by European culture than were the peoples of North and South America, and it would take several more centuries for European trade to exert its full impact in that region.

Finally, the populations themselves mixed as immigrants settled among native societies. Because European men greatly outnumbered women from their home continent, many of them married native and slave women or kept them as concubines. Generations of children born of mixed background, called *mestizos,* preserved aspects of both their parents' cultures. These generations ultimately made the Americas vastly different from Europe in spite of common languages, religions, and political structures.

Population mixing

European Culture Transformed

Europeans were as much transformed by contact with the New World as the original Americans were by their European conquerors. In one of the less savory examples of this exchange, the earliest explorers to the New World probably brought back a virulent form of syphilis. New archaeological excavations have revealed that some form of syphilis existed in Europe from classical times, but this new strain of the sexually transmitted disease ravaged Europe until the twentieth century, when the advent of penicillin offered a cure. The disease never took the kind of toll on Europeans that plagues such as smallpox and measles imposed on native populations. Nevertheless, its presence caused much misery and made some people more cautious about sexual activity.

New foods

New foods changed Europeans' diets and even the landscape. It is difficult to imagine Ireland without the hardy, nutritious potatoes that flourish today in that rocky land, but until the conquest of the Incas, the population of Ireland had to struggle to sustain itself. The tomato—a New World fruit that people first rejected as poisonous—was eventually embraced as an aphrodisiac and became an often-used ingredient in European cuisine. Maize spread more slowly, for Europeans, like the Africans, did not initially view it as a food fit for humans. However, as early as 1500, it began thriving in Spain, from where it soon spread to Italy (near Venice) and eventually to the rest of Europe. Maize had immediate use as animal feed and peasant fare and allowed farming families to sell their more expensive wheat.

In addition to new staples, certain food stimulants from the Americas proved enormously popular in Europe. Chocolate, for example, came to Spain from Aztec Mexico in about 1520 in the form of loaves and tablets that were boiled into a drink. A luxury at first, chocolate had become a common beverage by the eighteenth century. Tea, too, had been a rare treat in the Middle Ages, when some traders brought small amounts from China. Over time, more and more Europeans developed an unquenchable thirst for tea, making the East India Company rich in the process.

New stimulants

Coffee appeared in Europe for the first time in the early seventeenth century and replaced tea and chocolate as the most popular stimulant drink. Coffee seems to have first come from Africa and then spread to the Muslim lands—it was in Mecca by 1511, and Istanbul in 1517. By 1615, coffee had reached Venice, and merchants spread the product rapidly through Europe from there. Physicians praised the drink as medicinal for many ailments, from heart disease to "short breath, colds which attack the lungs, and worms." By the eighteenth century, coffee was so central to European society that even the social life of the West began to be centered at coffee shops.

But it was tobacco that made the biggest impression on European culture. Columbus saw Amerindians smoking it and brought the plant back home as an object of curiosity. Europeans cultivated tobacco at first for medicinal purposes—one sixteenth-century Parisian claimed that it cured all ills—and the plant then spread rapidly all over the world. By the mid-seventeenth century, it had reached as far as China, where virtually the entire population took up the smoking habit. The difficulties of planting tobacco also stimulated settlement expansion. Because the crop rapidly depletes the soil, in an age without chemical fertilizers colonists seeking to profit from the lucrative crop constantly had to annex and cultivate new lands.

Tobacco

The New World's reshaping of European culture unfolded slowly. New products became available gradually, whetting appetites for yet more novelties. The commercial revolution stimulated the movement of goods all over the world, creating more and more demand, which fueled further explorations and commerce. Ironically, the demand for spices, and particularly pepper, that had originally served as the main force behind the voyages of exploration waned by the eighteenth century. Europeans had found other, more intriguing products to satisfy their restless desire for culinary novelties.

connect to today

Global Trade

The movement of people and goods around the world beginning in the fifteenth century transformed the world. In what ways does global trade, or, conversely, embargoes or economic sanctions against trade with certain countries, continue to transform local and global economies today?

A New Worldview

When Europeans first set off across the seas, they had a false, though highly imaginative, view of what they would find. The world proved larger and far more diverse than they had ever imagined, and travelers began to study and write about the new reality. Amerigo Vespucci, the Italian mapmaker and chronicler we met earlier, wrote with awe in 1499 about New World flora: "The trees were

Scientific observations

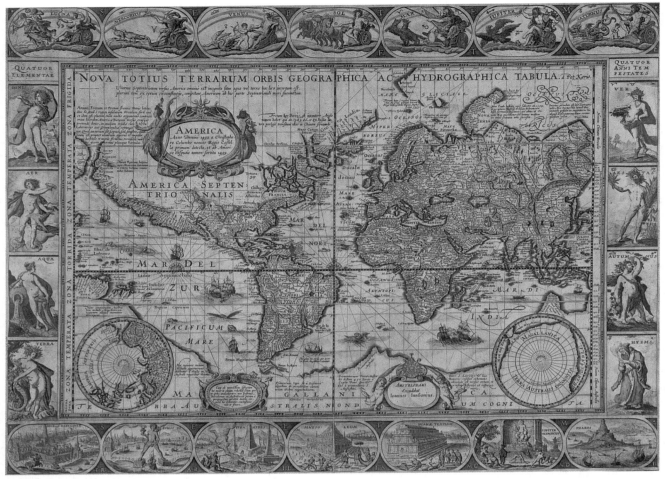

MERCATOR MAP, 1608 The explorers mapped the world and in doing so replaced Ptolemy's vision, shown in the image on page 273. However, the popular Mercator map kept Europe in the center and skewed the perspective of the rest of the world.

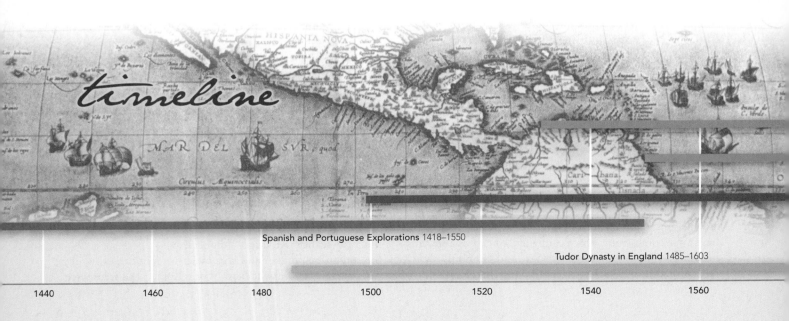

timeline

Spanish and Portuguese Explorations 1418–1550

Tudor Dynasty in England 1485–1603

| 1440 | 1460 | 1480 | 1500 | 1520 | 1540 | 1560 |

so beautiful and so fragrant that we thought we were in a terrestrial paradise. Not one of those trees or its fruit was like those in our part of the globe." Such early descriptions were followed by systematic studies in the seventeenth century. For example, in 1648 a Dutch prince sponsored an expedition that published the *Natural History of Brazil,* followed by many other books by naturalists cataloging the wonders of the Americas.

The new maps created as explorers traveled the global coastlines and great rivers were quite precise. These representations offered a much more realistic picture of the world than Ptolemy's map that guided Columbus. The map in the image on page 294 shows the globe flattened out. This projection method, which let sailors plot straight-line courses, was developed by the Flemish cartographer Gerhard Mercator (1512–1594), who first published it in 1569. Many modern European maps are still based on this technique.

Mercator maps

The **Mercator projection** was a huge step forward in mapmaking, but it still allowed for some measure of geographic illusion. By flattening out the map and placing Europe in the center, mapmakers could not help distorting their graphic representation of the world. Greenland, for example, appears much larger than it is, India becomes smaller, and Asia is divided, thus seeming to have less mass than it really does. Not surprisingly, the Mercator map encouraged the illusion that Europeans occupied the center of the world. This idea shaped Europeans' future mapmaking techniques and their attitudes and actions toward the rest of the globe.

SUMMARY

By the early sixteenth century, Western culture was no longer contained within Europe. Lured by faith, fame, and fortune, Europeans sailed all over the world.

- European explorers used old maps and outdated ideas of the peoples they would find as they tried to discover new routes to the riches of the east.

- The explorers used new ships and traveled around the world, establishing colonies in the new continents of North and South America, and trading posts in Africa and Asia.

- As they traveled, they encountered Amerindians in the New World and wrecked havoc on them by warfare and diseases. Europeans also established the slave trade to fuel Europeans' appetites for new goods.

- The movement of goods stimulated a commercial revolution with the rise of commercial capitalism, mercantilism, and banking. It also stimulated a global age of piracy as bandits tried to interrupt the trade to grow rich.

- The whole world, from Europe and beyond, was transformed as new goods, ideas, and people traveled. A global economy was established.

The resultant blending whetted European appetites for more exploration and conquest, and the new ideas would stimulate more tensions and revolutions in Europe itself.

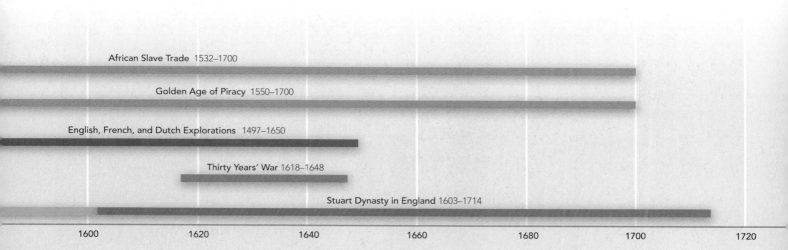

African Slave Trade 1532–1700

Golden Age of Piracy 1550–1700

English, French, and Dutch Explorations 1497–1650

Thirty Years' War 1618–1648

Stuart Dynasty in England 1603–1714

1600 1620 1640 1660 1680 1700 1720

CHARLES LEBRUN,
CHANCELLOR SEGUIER,
ca. 1670   Chancellor Pierre
Seguier (1588–1672) was an
ambitious courtier to the French
king Louis XIV and a member
of France's new nobility that
earned position by service to
the crown, the *noblesse de
robe*. In this painting, Seguier's
office is symbolized by the
formal robes he wears, rather
than by arms. Several well-
dressed pages surround him,
one holding an umbrella over
his head as if he were a minor
monarch. His face conveys a
sense of pleased assurance
with the position he has gained.
Charles Lebrun (1619–1690),
like several other leading artists
of the day, served as painter
to Louis XIV and for eighteen
years created decorations for
the king's Versailles palace.

The Struggle for Survival and Sovereignty

Europe's Social and Political Order, 1600–1715

13

The King's Soldiers Strike Back

"This poor country is a horrible sight," wrote the abbess of a French town in January 1649. "[I]t is stripped of everything. The soldiers take possession of the farms . . . there are no more horses . . . the peasants are reduced to sleeping in the woods . . . and if they only had enough bread to half satisfy their hunger, they would indeed count themselves happy." France had just emerged a victor from the Thirty Years' War (discussed in Chapter 11), only to find itself embroiled in a series of internal revolts. These revolts, like many others erupting throughout Europe, signaled new strains on European society from the bottom to the top of the traditional order. ▶▶

For the vast majority—peasants who worked the fields—pressures came from powers outside their control. The landowning aristocracy required service and obedience; governmental officials demanded ever more taxes and military service; and the impersonal forces that most people attributed to luck, fate, or God brought bad weather, failed harvests, and plagues. Sometimes peasants fled their aristocratic masters or turned violently against isolated governmental officials. However, against the fates and well-armed soldiers, they were powerless.

For those at the top of society, the pressures came from central governments and monarchs. Kings, struggling with the increasingly heavy burdens of war and governance, chipped away at aristocratic independence year after year. They argued that "the royal power is absolute. . . . The prince [king] need render account of his acts to no one." Elites insisted that "our privileges and liberties are our right and due inheritance, no less than our very lands and goods." This contention between monarch and aristocrat sometimes broke out in violence, at other times led to compromises, and often severely strained the elite order.

These two struggles—the first faced by the vast majority on the bottom, the second by the dominant elites on top—colored the West's social and political life during the seventeenth and early eighteenth centuries. This chapter follows these intertwined conflicts in four areas—France, eastern Europe, England, and the Netherlands—where the story took different turns. ◄◄

STRESSES IN TRADITIONAL SOCIETY

"It is necessary that some command and others obey," explained a French judge and legal scholar in 1610. "Sovereign lords address their commands to the great; the great to the middling, the middling to the small, and the small to the people." This description captures the traditional social order that reigned in the West during the seventeenth century. Indeed, people took this order for granted. The structure was based on a hierarchy of ranks, and each rank, from nobility to peasantry, had its set status and occupations. Within each rank were subranks. For example, a hierarchy of titles and offices determined position among the nobility. Artisans divided themselves into masters, journeymen, and apprentices. Within the peasantry, landholders stood above laborers, and all looked down on serfs. Each rank distinguished itself through conventions, dress, duties, and etiquette. Finally, within all these ranks, position went hand in hand with family, itself ranked with men at the top, followed by women, and then children at the bottom.

Together the ranks made up the "body politic," with kings and nobles serving as the head and arms, and artisans and peasants as hands and feet. All worked together to perpetuate life as an organic whole. Everywhere, the church and religious sentiments sanctified this organic social hierarchy. Indeed, the social structure paralleled what Westerners saw as the larger, hierarchic order of the universe—the **Great Chain of Being.** In the Great Chain, everything—from God to the angels, humans, animals, and plants—existed in an ordered, permanent arrangement. During the seventeenth century, new forces tested the smooth running of this traditional society.

Mounting Demands on Rural Life

Facing new demands from many quarters, rural life declined. At the beginning of the century, life for most Europeans typically centered on small, self-sufficient villages that contained a few to a hundred families. A church or manor served as the center of communal activities. Strangers attracted intense scrutiny, and most authorities were local people whom everyone knew. When bad harvests, plagues, or war struck, the villagers received little help from the outside.

The majority of people lived in crowded one-room houses made of timber, thatch, and mud, with one or two narrow windows. At one end of the house stood a stone hearth used for light, cooking, and heat. Wood and peat, which fired the stove, were often in short supply, and the villagers struggled to stay warm during the winters. Grain, in the form of black bread and porridge, made up most meals, though in some areas meat, vegetables, fruits, and dairy products supplemented diets. A few treasured pots, pans, and utensils served all.

The image on page 300 shows a farmyard scene in rural France. Many seventeenth-century Europeans were poorer even than those in this painting. According to one observer in 1696, "They suffer from exposure: winter and summer, three-fourths of them are dressed in nothing but half-rotting tattered linen, and wear throughout the year wooden shoes and no other covering for the foot."

As in past centuries, the family functioned as both a social and an economic unit. Women and men married for practical as well as sentimental reasons. The land, wealth, skills, and position one held counted for much **The family** in a potential marriage partner. Husband, wife, and children lived together, and most marriages, whether happy or not, lasted until death. At various times, relatives, domestics, and laborers might live for a while in the household. Finally, although everyone worked together in the fields, men generally did the heaviest work, while women gardened, raised poultry, and supervised dairy producing.

Fathers, older children, and other relatives might also participate with mothers in raising and socializing young children. Nevertheless, children were not considered at the center of family life, and girls were less valued than boys. Indeed, parents often sent children away to other households to work as apprentices, domestics, or laborers if they could earn more there. Infant mortality ran high; of the five or more children to whom a woman was likely to give birth, only two or three lived beyond 5 years. Parents valued and cared for their children, but in a time of grinding poverty, it is not surprising that parents also viewed children as either assets or liabilities in the struggle for survival; great emotional entanglements with them were risky.

The stresses on these common people are strikingly revealed by the population decreases that occurred during the first half of the seventeenth century. The devastation from the seemingly endless wars took many lives, especially in German lands. The old enemies—poverty, disease, and famine—also roared through these decades. Unusually severe winters—advancing glaciers marked the 1600s as part of the "little ice age"—froze rivers and fields, and wet summers destroyed crops. Suffering, malnutrition, illness, and, too often, death followed. "The staple dish here consists of mice, which the inhabitants hunt, so desperate are they from hunger," reported provincial officials in northern France in 1651. "They devour roots which the animals cannot eat . . . not a day passes but at least 200 people die of famine in the two provinces."

Population changes

OPINION

Which of the factors that caused suffering among the peasants in the seventeenth century do you think were most influential in breaking down traditional society?

Bad times also meant postponed marriages, fewer births, and an increase in the number of deaths among infants and children. Europeans already married late compared to the rest of the world. On average, men waited until their late 20s to wed; women, until their mid-20s. Sometimes so many people died, wandered away in search of food, or fled to the cities that whole villages were abandoned. Conditions improved a bit during the second half of the century, though only enough for the European population to maintain itself and perhaps grow slightly. Life expectancy, which varied by social class and region, was probably less than 30 years (in part because of high infant mortality).

New demands from central governments cut into traditional patterns of rural life. With every new outbreak of war, governmental officials intruded more and more into villages in search of army conscripts. People resisted, and for good reason. Military service took men out of the fields, increasing the burden on the women, children, and elderly who had to shoulder the men's share of the labor. Soldiers embroiled in nearby battles plundered what they could from the villages they passed.

Officials also came with new tax assessments, even though peasants already owed much to those above them. Traditional taxes to the government, tithes to the church, and rents to large landowners used up more than half of the already scant wealth peasants produced.

Peasants avoided collectors and hid what assets they could. In countless incidents, peasants and city dwellers across Europe rose against increasing taxes and attacked the hated collectors. In the 1630s, for example, French peasants rose against tax increases and forced temporary concessions from local officials, only to have those victories reversed by the state. Farther south, in 1647, women demanding more bread led riots that swept through the city of Palermo in Spanish-occupied Italy. Rebels in the city chanted, "Down with taxes!" As in France, government forces eventually reversed early victories and crushed the revolt.

Tax revolts

Other intrusions further eroded the traditional isolation that characterized rural life. Officials and merchants ventured more and more often to the countryside to buy grain for cities, creating food shortages in rural villages. Moreover, as members of the local nobility departed for capital cities and the king's court, new officials appeared and began administering affairs and rendering judgments in courts. For good or ill, villagers found themselves increasingly drawn into the web of national affairs.

Pressures on the Upper Orders

Monarchs faced pressures of their own, especially the demands of war. In the competition for territory and status, kings won by fielding ever-larger armies and mustering the resources needed to support them. During the seventeenth century, armies doubled and redoubled in size, as did the central governments that supported them (see Chapter 11). The costs of making war and supporting government increased accordingly. Governments devoted half or more of their income to the military, and monarchs desperate for money levied more and more taxes just to stay even. The ability to collect taxes could make or break a ruler. More than anything else, a king's unrelenting demands for more taxes sparked widespread resistance to his rule.

Competing centers of power added to the kings' problems. Independent town officials, church leaders, and provincial officials tried to hold on to their authority over local matters. Religious dissidents, for their part, guarded what independence they could. Finally, those who resented the royal tax collectors

Competing centers of power

Louis le Nain, *The Cart*

1641

This painting by Louis le Nain provides a glimpse of everyday life in rural France during the mid-seventeenth century. Here, women and children of varying ages stand on a cart or tend a few animals. One woman sits with her baby on the ground; another has slung a large pot over her back, perhaps in preparation for gathering water. In the background stands a modest house. Considering his portrayal of the figures and details in this painting, what impression of rural life do you think the artist wanted to convey to viewers?

admirers. Their favored supporters, such as France's court preacher and royal tutor Bishop Jacques-Bénigne Bossuet (1627–1704), backed them. Bossuet declared, "The whole state is included in him [the monarch], the will of all the people is enclosed within his own."

Yet the kings used more than words and "yes-men" in this power struggle. Bypassing representative institutions, they sent their royal law courts into the provinces as a way to extend their authority. Sometimes they appointed new local leaders to gain allies. Other times, they attracted aristocrats from the provinces to the royal court, thereby creating a power vacuum that they then filled with their own men. When great nobles resisted being turned into obedient officials, rulers often turned to the lesser nobility or members of the wealthy middle class—men such as Chancellor Seguier, whom we met in the opening of this chapter. Such royal servants received titles or land and were elevated to high office as compensation for their loyalty.

Women also became entwined in these struggles between monarchs and aristocrats. With the royal courts growing in size, many women became important friends and unofficial advisors to kings and influential aristocrats. They used their intelligence, wit, services, and advice to gain privileged positions in royal courts. There they won titles, offices, lands, money, and advantageous marriages for themselves and their families. Mothers encouraged their daughters not to let good marriage opportunities pass by. "It is true that [the proposed groom] is some fifteen years older than you," wrote one aristocratic mother in 1622. "[B]ut . . . you are going to marry a man . . . who has spent his life honorably at court and at the wars and has been granted considerable payments by the king." Royal mistresses also achieved important positions in the king's household. Françoise d'Aubigné (Marquise de Maintenon), mistress (and, secretly, wife) of France's King Louis XIV, influenced court appointments and founded a royal school for the daughters of impoverished nobles in 1686. Some mistresses even persuaded kings to acknowledge their children as "royal bastards" and grant them titles and privileges.

resisted the crown's reach. But the greatest threat to monarchical power came from aristocrats, who tried to retain as much of their social and economic dominance as possible. These nobles often challenged royal policies and decried royal "tyranny" as a violation of divine law. They guarded their traditional rights and local authority, and many of them refused to give up their tax exemptions. Should the crown falter, they stood ready to take back any powers they might have lost.

Monarchs argued with, fought, and schemed against these forms of opposition. They justified their power as a divine right, because they represented God on earth, and surrounded themselves with compliant advisors and

This system of elevated royal authority has been called **royal absolutism** because the kings of the day commanded more loyalty, control, and resources than their predecessors had, and because they justified their right to rule as an absolute. However, no monarch gained true absolute power. Most people understood that even the strongest ruler, divinely ordained, was vaguely subject to tradition and law. As one seventeenth-century French jurist explained, the king's power "seems to place him above the law, . . . [but] his rank obliges him to subordinate his personal interests to the general good of the state." Further, with so many local centers of power, with scores of nobles who persisted in their independent ways, and with too much information to control, no king in this era could hope to dominate everything. Some monarchs even found themselves on losing ends of internal battles for power.

Royal absolutism

> For the peasantry, Henry suggested that prosperity should bring "a chicken in the pot of every peasant for Sunday dinner."

control of some two hundred fortified cities and towns as a guarantee against future oppression. He appealed to the traditional nobility by developing an image as a cultured warrior-king who could be trusted to enforce the law. He catered to rich lawyers, merchants, and landowners by selling new governmental offices, which often came with ennoblement as well as prestige. This growing elite became known as the nobility of the robe because their robes of office, rather than the arms borne by the traditional nobility of the sword, represented their power (see page 296). Many of these nobles gladly paid annual fees for the right to pass their offices on to heirs. For the peasantry, Henry suggested that prosperity should bring "a chicken in the pot of every peasant for Sunday dinner." Not surprisingly, Henry's authority and popularity soared.

With the help of his able, methodical administrator, the Duke of Sully (1560–1641), Henry also launched a comprehensive program of economic reconstruction. Agriculture and commerce benefited from the increased security of life and property brought by better law enforcement; from improved transportation facilitated by the repair of roads, bridges, and harbors; and from the freeing of trade, thanks to lower internal tariff barriers. The monarchy even subsidized and protected new industries that produced luxuries such as glass, porcelain, lace, silk, tapestries, fine leather, and textiles. Sully's efficient collection of taxes and administration of expenditures produced a rare budget surplus.

Henry also dreamed of making France secure from ambitious foreign states and of ensuring his country a supreme position in all of Europe. However, the powerful Spanish and Austrian Habsburgs on France's borders stood in his way. In 1610, he prepared to join his armies for a campaign against his rivals. Yet before he could set out, he was assassinated by a fanatic, and his plans died with him.

ROYAL ABSOLUTISM IN FRANCE

In western Europe, the efforts of French kings to maximize their power exemplified the development of royal absolutism. Building upon the work of predecessors who had enhanced the power of the monarchy, Louis XIV (r. 1643–1715) took personal control of the French monarchy in 1661. By then, France had supplanted Spain as the most powerful nation in Europe. Under Louis' long rule, royal absolutism reached its peak and inspired other monarchs to emulate his style.

Henry IV Secures the Monarchy

French absolutism had its immediate roots in the reign of Henry IV (r. 1589–1610). When Henry IV ascended the French throne in 1589, his country had endured several decades of wars between Protestants and Catholics, combined with conflicts between different political factions. Law and order had broken down, and powerful nobles had reasserted their authority. The finances of the central government lay in disarray, and French prestige abroad had sunk to a low level.

The talented, witty Henry, in his prime at 36, set out to change all this. He defused the religious turmoil by issuing the Edict of Nantes (see Chapter 11), which granted to Huguenots (French Protestants) religious toleration and

Richelieu Elevates Royal Authority

For several years after Henry's death, his Italian wife, Marie de Médicis (1573–1642), ruled as regent for their son, the young Louis XIII (r. 1610–1643). Marie kept opponents at arm's length but made little headway in strengthening the position of the monarchy. Then in 1624, one of her favorite advisors, Cardinal Richelieu (1585–1642), became chief minister and began exercising power from behind the throne. Having come from a minor noble family and possessing a keen intellect, the arrogant and calculating Richelieu handled the young king deftly and controlled others through a skillful blend of patronage and punishment. His twofold policy was to make royal power supreme in France and to maneuver France into a position of dominance in Europe. To Louis XIII, Richelieu promised "to ruin the Huguenot party, to abase the pride of the nobles, to bring back all your subjects to their duty, and to elevate your name among foreign nations to the point where it belongs."

With the royal army at his disposal, Richelieu boldly destroyed the castles of nobles who opposed the king; he disbanded their private armies and executed a number of the most recalcitrant among them. When Huguenot nobles in the southwest rebelled, Richelieu sent in the army and stripped the Huguenots of the special military and political privileges that Henry IV had granted them. Only their religious liberties remained intact. To dilute local centers of political power, the dynamic minister divided France into some thirty administrative districts, placing each under the control of a powerful *intendant*, who was an agent of the crown. He chose these *intendants* from the ranks of the middle class and recently ennobled people and shifted them around frequently, lest they become too sympathetic with their localities. Finally, Richelieu plunged France into the Thirty Years' War in Germany (see Chapter 11). His purpose was to weaken the Habsburgs, chief rivals of the French monarchs for European supremacy.

By the time of his death in 1642, Richelieu had firmly secured royal power in France and elevated France's position in Europe. Nevertheless, the imperious cardinal, having more than doubled taxes to promote his policies, had gained few friends. Far more French subjects rejoiced in his death than mourned his passing.

Mazarin Overcomes the Opposition

Richelieu was succeeded by his protégé, Cardinal Jules Mazarin (1602–1661). Louis XIII's death in 1643, a few months after that of his great minister, left the throne to Louis XIV, a child of 5. Mazarin, who began his career as a gambler and diplomat, played the same role in the early reign of Louis XIV and his regent, Anne of Austria (1601–1666), that Richelieu had played during the reign of Louis XIII.

Early on, Mazarin, Anne, and the child-king faced a series of wide-ranging, uncoordinated revolts that forced them to flee Paris. Known collectively as the **Fronde** (the name of a child's slingshot game, which implied that the participants were childish), these revolts stemmed primarily from French subjects' objections to high taxes and increasing royal power. Between 1648 and 1653, ambitious nobles, footloose soldiers returning from war, urban artisans, and even some peasants fought the monarchy and its supporters in what amounted to a civil war at times. Bad harvests added to the chaos and suffering:

The Fronde

"People massacre each other daily with every sort of cruelty," wrote an observer in 1652. "The soldiers steal from one another when they have denuded everyone else . . . all the armies are equally undisciplined and vie with one another in lawlessness." Nobles conspired and shifted alliances for their own gains, resulting in growing disillusionment with their cause. Gaining support from city dwellers and peasants longing for peace, and shrewdly buying off one noble after another, Mazarin quashed the revolts by 1653. The crown gradually reasserted itself as the basis for order in France.

The Fronde was paralleled by other revolts during the 1640s in Spain, the Italian states, and, much more seriously, England. In each case, the catalysts included new taxes, the demand for more men and supplies for the military, and monarchies' efforts to acquire more power. In the Spanish provinces of Catalonia and Portugal, as well as in the Italian states of Naples and Sicily, rebels murdered tax officials, peasants took up arms, and local nobles joined the fray. Localities demanded and sometimes got concessions, but many of these victories proved short-lived when the crown reasserted its authority. As we will see, matters grew much worse in England. Taken together, these mid-century rebellions served as a warning to monarchs not to push unpopular policies too far—and to the aristocracy not to underestimate the power of the crown.

The Sun King Rises

Upon Mazarin's death in 1661, the 23-year-old Louis XIV finally stepped forward to rule in his own right. "Up to this moment I have been pleased to entrust the government of my affairs to the late Cardinal," he announced. "It is now time that I govern them myself." With his regal bearing and stolid build, young Louis fit the part well. His lack of intellectual brilliance was offset by a sharp memory, a sense of responsibility, and a capacity for tedious work. "One reigns only by dint of hard work," he warned his own son. Haunted by childhood memories of fleeing in terror across the tiled rooftops of Paris during the Fronde revolts, he remained determined to prevent further challenges from rebellious aristocrats. By his mother, Mazarin, and a succession of tutors, Louis had been convinced that he was God's appointed deputy for France. Supporting him was the most famous exponent of royal absolutism, Bishop Bossuet, who argued that the monarchy "is sacred, it is paternal, it is absolute, and it is subject to reason . . . the royal throne is not that of a man but the throne of God Himself." As the document on page 303 indicates, Louis XIV learned these lessons well. In words commonly attributed to Louis, *"L'état, c'est moi"* (I am the state).

However, Louis could not possibly perform all the functions of government personally. The great bulk of the details were handled by a series of councils and bureaus and administered locally by the *intendants*. Distrusting the traditional nobility, Louis instead usually appointed members of modest noble backgrounds to the important offices of his government. Well supervised by the industrious king, the administrative machinery hummed along.

To raise his stature, Louis XIV initiated massive public-works projects that glorified him, his government, and his reign. His greatest architectural project was a new palace. Hating the tumult of Paris, with its streets teeming with commoners, he selected Versailles, 11 miles southwest of the city, as the new seat of government. There, as many as 35,000 workmen toiled for more than forty years to turn marshes and sand into Europe's most splendid palace and grounds.

Versailles

The image on page 304 shows Versailles in 1668. Over the next forty-three years, successive teams of workers added rear gardens and more than doubled the size of the buildings. The exterior of Versailles was designed in long, horizontal, classic lines. The interior boasted a lavish baroque style with richly colored marbles, mosaics, inlaid woods, gilt, silver, silk, velvet, and brocade. Ceiling-to-floor windows and mirrors and crystal chandeliers holding thousands of candles illuminated the salons and halls. In terms of sheer capacity, the palace could house 5,000 people and serve thousands more visitors each day. It faced hundreds of acres of groves, walks, canals, pools, terraces, fountains, statues, flower beds, and clipped shrubs—all laid out in formal geometric patterns symbolizing the triumph of engineering over nature. So dazzling was this hallmark of royal absolutism that other European monarchs soon attempted to copy it.

The Sun King, so named for his chosen symbol, the sun, finally moved to Versailles in 1682. Once established there, he lured the men and women of the nobility away from their local centers of power where they might make trouble and turned them into domesticated court "butterflies." He subjected them to a complex system of etiquette and favoritism that made every aspect of Louis' daily life the center of their concern. Court became a theater where those already in favor, as well as aspiring favorites, had to scheme for gifts, patronage, and position.

Louis XIV Describes Monarchical Rights and Duties

France's Louis XIV embodied the nearly all-powerful king—at least in his glorious appearance and style, if not always in his deeds. In the following excerpt from his writings, he describes his view of kingship to his son.

Homage is due to kings, and they do whatever they like. It certainly must be agreed that, however bad a prince may be, it is always a heinous crime for his subjects to rebel against him. He who gave men kings willed that they should be respected as His lieutenants, and reserved to Himself the right to question their conduct. It is His will that everyone who is born a subject should obey without qualification. This law, as clear as it is universal, was not made only for the sake of princes: it is also for the good of the people themselves. It is therefore the duty of kings to sustain by their own example the religion upon which they rely; and they must realize that, if their subjects see them plunged in vice or violence, they can hardly render to their person the respect due to their office, or recognize in them the living image of Him who is all-holy as well as almighty.

In what ways, according to Louis XIV, should a king take steps to maintain his authority?

PIERRE PATEL THE ELDER, *VIEW OF VERSAILLES,* 1668 A royal procession enters the grounds of Versailles in this aerial view. The new geometrically ordered palace and grounds became a monument to Louis XIV's reign and French royal absolutism.

Winners might secure lucrative rewards, and losers might spend themselves broke trying to stay in the race.

Despite the grandeur of Versailles, this glittering monument to royal absolutism had its critics. In her novel *The Princess of Clèves* (1678), the Countess de Lafayette complained that at Versailles "everybody was busily trying to better their position by pleasing, by helping, or by hindering somebody else." The court reportedly seethed with gossip, scandal, and intrigue. Critics such as Pierre Jurieu, a French Calvinist pastor who fled to Holland, lamented that the king "is the idol to which are sacrificed princes, great men and small, families, provinces, cities, finances and generally everything." Resentful nobles once proudly drawing high status from their lands and lineage came to depend on the approval of and service to the king as the primary route to power. Many hard-toiling, heavily taxed French commoners also grumbled about living in the reflected glory of a pretentious monarch.

Versailles' critics

To enhance the glory of his court, Louis XIV subsidized and attracted to Versailles leading French artists and literary figures. The elegance, the sense of order, and the formalism of royalty all found expression in much of the literature of this **classical style** in French culture. Pierre Corneille (1606–1684), for example, wrote elegant plays modeled on the ancient Greek tragedies. Human beings' conflicts with their own nature and with the workings of fate and the universe furnished the plots. Even more exquisite were the perfectly rhymed and metered couplets of Jean Racine's (1639–1699) dramas. Finally, in his profound comedies, Jean-Baptiste Molière (1622–1673) satirized pompous scholars, social climbers, false priests, and quack physicians. Louis and his court had little to fear from this literature. On the contrary, they appreciated its formal order and laughed along with other audiences at its satire, which was aimed at humankind in general rather than at specific ruling regimes.

Classical literature

While the literature of the seventeenth century amused monarchs, the visual arts of the period positively glorified them. Kings and aristocrats still favored the baroque style of painting and architecture (see Chapter 11). As they saw it, the baroque's swirling forms

Visual arts

and massive, ornamental elegance perfectly reflected their wealth and power. Yet during the second half of the seventeenth century, classicism, with its emphasis on control and restraint, began to gain favor. The appealing paintings of French artists Claude Lorraine (1600–1682) and Nicolas Poussin (1594–1665) helped classicism win official approval in France. Both men spent much time in Italy, studying the Renaissance masters and the Italian landscape. The painting below embodies their style. Compared to the baroque, the classical style shows a logic that echoed the sense of order pervading the Versailles court of the Sun King.

Versailles, the arts, and all other aspects of government cost money. Louis assigned the talented Jean-Baptiste Colbert (1619–1683) to manage his finances. An engine of efficiency, Colbert toiled endlessly, supervising the details of the French economy while also **Colbert** promoting culture by founding the Royal Academy of Sciences in 1666 and subsidizing the arts. In keeping with his bourgeois origins, he chose service to the king as his means of advancement. His family shared in his success, becoming ministers, gaining high offices in the church, marrying well, and securing top positions in the military.

Promoting mercantilistic economic policies (see Chapter 12), Colbert protected industries with high tariffs while subsidizing exports and new industries. To encourage France's growing empire and the commerce it generated, he built a large navy. Finally, Colbert worked to ensure a worldwide reputation for the uniformly high quality of French products. He subjected manufacturing to the most minute regulation and supervision: So many threads of such and such quality and color must go into every inch of this textile and that lace. Although Colbert's restrictive mercantilistic controls in the long run stifled initiative and economic change, French products earned wide acclaim for their quality. By his death in 1683, Colbert had balanced the budget and promoted relative prosperity despite Louis XIV's lavish expenditures.

During the following decades, however, Louis embarked on policies that undermined much of what Colbert had accomplished. The **Revocation of the Edict of Nantes** king's demands for religious conformity and his military ambitions ranked among the most destructive of these policies. Huguenots (French Protestants) paid the highest price for his religious intolerance. In 1685, Louis revoked the Edict of Nantes, which in 1598 had granted tolerance to the Protestant minority. Then he outlawed Protestantism and ordered Protestant churches demolished. The Duke of Saint-Simon lamented that the "ultimate results [of the reversal] were the depopulation of a fourth part of the kingdom and the ruin of our commerce . . . the country was given over to the authorized ravages of dragoons [armed troops], which caused the death of, literally, thousands of innocent people of all ages and both sexes." Although Huguenots were forbidden to emigrate, perhaps as many as 200,000 did, taking their wealth and skills with them to Protestant-friendly areas in Europe and America, "enriching them and causing their cities to flourish at the expense of France," according to Saint-Simon. Up to a million Huguenots who remained in France went underground.

Nor was Louis content to rule in peace as the leader of Europe's most powerful nation. During the last four decades of his 72-year reign, he fought four wars of aggression. The same old reasons prompted him to lead France into battle: more territory, more glory, and more wealth. He set his sights on the Spanish and Austrian Habsburg lands on France's **Wars of aggression** eastern borders and on the Dutch, France's most powerful commercial rivals on the Continent. He put his war minister, the Marquis of Louvois (1639–1691), in charge of organizing France's huge military establishment on the model of a complex business, replete with supply depots and hospitals. While Louvois introduced strict discipline, uniforms, and promotions

CLAUDE LORRAINE, *THE MARRIAGE OF ISAAC AND REBEKAH (THE MILL)*, 1640 This calm, balanced Italian landscape by a leading French artist exemplifies seventeenth-century classicism with its emphasis on control and restraint.

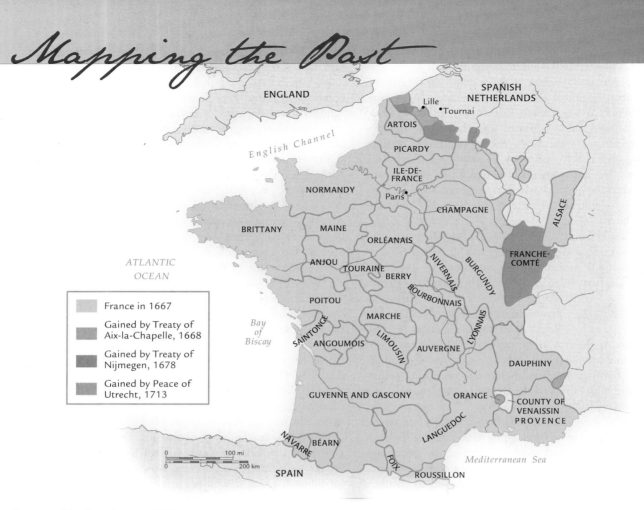

France Under Louis XIV, 1661–1715

This map shows France's provinces and the territorial gains the state made during the reign of Louis XIV. In four wars between 1667 and 1713, France fought against various rivals and coalitions of states to the south, north, and east. **Notice that most of Louis' gains came from Spanish lands and German states on France's eastern border. What might this pattern imply about vulnerable areas of Europe and changing power relationships at the time?**

based on merit, Sébastien de Vauban (1633–1707) designed sturdy fortifications and brilliant siege operations. It was a common saying that whereas a city defended by Vauban was safe, one besieged by Vauban was doomed.

Louis initiated his foreign adventures in the War of Devolution (1667–1668), waged against Spain for French claims in the Spanish Netherlands and Franche-Comté (Burgundy). When victory seemed within reach, the United Provinces, England, and Sweden joined Spain to prevent France from upsetting the balance of power. The Treaty of Aix-la-Chapelle (1668) brought Louis only minor gains (see map above). In 1672, Louis turned against the Dutch, whom he blamed for organizing the alliance against him and who were France's chief trade competitors. The Dutch stopped the invading French only by opening the dikes and flooding the land. Dutch diplomacy brought Spain, Sweden, Brandenburg, and the Holy Roman Empire into an alliance against the French. Louis fought them to a standstill and gained some valuable territories in the Peace of Nijmegen (1679). In the following years, Louis made enemies of the Austrians by refusing to help in their war against the Turks, and he alienated Europe's Protestants by turning against the Huguenots. Fearful that he intended to upset the balance of power and dominate the Continent, much of Europe formed the Grand Alliance against him. The eight-year War of the League of Augsburg (1689–1697) gained France little territory at the cost of much bloodshed and misery. Louis' final struggle, the War of the Spanish Succession, was fought over French claims to the Spanish throne and the partition of Spanish holdings in the Netherlands and Italy. The war lasted eleven years (1702–1713), and the Grand

Alliance defeated French and Spanish forces in a series of battles. Beaten, impoverished, and facing revolts fueled by despair and opposition to taxation, Louis XIV was forced to accept the Peace of Utrecht (1713), which ended Louis' ambitions to create a partnership of Bourbon monarchs in France and Spain—with France the senior partner. The map on page 306 depicts France in 1661, when Louis XIV took control of the monarchy, and the territories he eventually acquired. In the end, he possessed little more than what he had started with some fifty years earlier, and he had even fewer holdings in North America.

Louis XIV died only two years after the Peace of Utrecht. He had long outlived his popularity. One widely circulated letter from an aristocratic critic, Archbishop Fénelon, complained that "for thirty years, your principal ministers have . . . overthrown all the ancient maxims of the state in order to increase your authority beyond all bounds. . . . For the sake of getting and keeping vain conquests abroad, you have destroyed half the real strength of your own state." As the coffin carrying Louis XIV's body was drawn through the streets of Paris, some of his abused subjects cursed his name.

The Sun King had built the French state into the envy of Europe, and his glittering court at Versailles outshone all others. His success relied on knowing how to use the old system, modified by preceding state-builders such as Richelieu, to his advantage. He tamed rather than fought the nobility, who at the same time remained the crown's most important ally and potent competitor. **Assessing Louis XIV** Clearly, strong central governments enjoyed advantages, and none were stronger than France's under Louis XIV. For many monarchs, France under Louis XIV became the model of absolutism. However, his expenditures and wars created unprecedented misery for most commoners saddled with relentlessly rising taxes, more military service, and famines. Recognizing that the continued power of the state required some support of the people, Louis' successors would try to avoid his mistakes and ameliorate the worst threats to the lives of French people.

THE STRUGGLE FOR SOVEREIGNTY IN EASTERN EUROPE

In eastern Europe, people struggled just as fiercely to survive and to define sovereignty as they did in the west. However, the two regions differed sharply, and those differences affected the outcomes of battles over these issues. States east of the Elbe River (see the map on page 308) were less commercially developed than those in west-

ern Europe. Instead of farms worked by legally free and mobile peasants, estate agriculture (large landed estates owned by lords and worked by their serfs) dominated those economies. By the sixteenth century, the nobles who owned these estates had reversed the medieval trends toward greater freedom for the peasantry and the growth of towns. Most people who worked the fields sank into serfdom, bound to the land and owing ever-increasing services to their lords. The middle classes in the towns also declined, failing to gain in numbers and wealth like their counterparts in western Europe. Finally, most central governments at the beginning of the seventeenth century proved weaker than those in western European states, as powerful nobles retained much independence. Despite all this, several monarchs decided to change things in their own favor.

Centralizing the State in Brandenburg-Prussia

In Brandenburg-Prussia, the "Great Elector" Frederick William (r. 1640–1688) inherited a scattered patchwork of poorly managed lands weakened by years of war and population decline. He faced a number of other problems as well. His army was tiny—too weak to keep foreign forces out of his lands or to discipline internal opponents. His nobles, or Junkers, had an independent streak and had found ways to avoid most taxes. Finally, his cities remained uncooperative, asserting their long-established political and economic independence.

Frederick William set out to correct the situation. He believed that the key was to strengthen his standing army. Only then could he gain control of his lands and make Brandenburg-Prussia a desired ally in international affairs. During the 1640s, he more than tripled the size of his army. This new strength and effective diplomacy won him several new territories at the end of the Thirty Years' War (see map on page 308). With energy and skill, he next centralized and administered the governments of his fragmented holdings—while continuing to boost the size of his army. He prevailed over the **Estates**—the representative assemblies of the realm—and acquired the crucial authority to collect taxes. He then used his newly powerful army to enforce tax payments and organize state resources. In a pivotal compromise with landed aristocrats, he allowed them complete control over their serfs in return for support and service in his bureaucracy and army. Through mercantilistic policies, he protected industries, improved communications, and promoted agriculture. Though Frederick William could not afford a lavish court like that of Louis XIV, his policies ratcheted up his power. "Hold fast to the eminence of your superior position . . . [and] rely on your own strength," he advised his

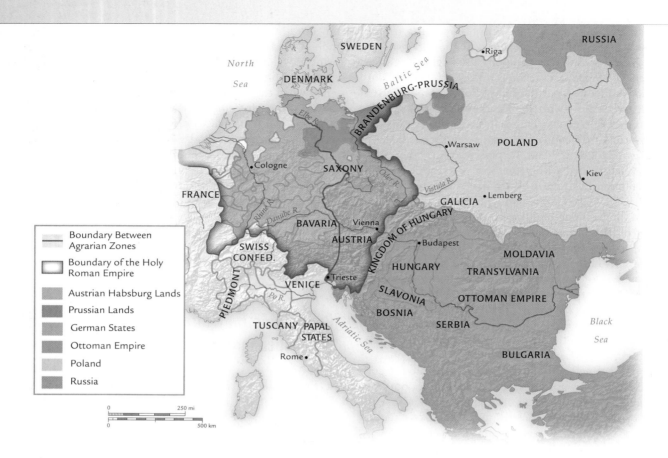

Central and Eastern Europe, 1648 This map shows the border between the western and eastern agrarian zones, running from the mouth of the Elbe River south to Trieste on the Adriatic Sea.

son. At the Great Elector's death in 1688, Brandenburg-Prussia was well on the road to becoming a major player in European politics. He also left a legacy of military values and reliance on armed might that would influence much of Prussia's subsequent history.

In 1701, his son, Frederick I (r. 1688–1713), increased the dynasty's status by acquiring the title of King of Prussia in return for helping the Holy Roman Emperor in a war against France. He used state revenues to turn his Berlin court into a great social and cultural center. By his death in 1713, Brandenburg-Prussia had become a respected force in eastern Europe.

Austria Confronts the Ottomans and Expands Its Control

Austria's Leopold I (r. 1657–1705), facing extreme local, language, and ethnic differences within his diverse lands, could not hope to acquire the same power as that enjoyed by Louis XIV in France or even Frederick William in Prus-

sia. Localities retained considerable autonomy, especially in matters of taxation. The practical Leopold focused on securing his own Habsburg lands, rather than cementing the minimal control he had over the Holy Roman Empire, and allied himself closely with the Catholic Church. He gained the allegiance of the nobles by making them his chief advisors and granting them rights to exploit lands and the peasants on them. Some peasants revolted, but as elsewhere in Europe, they did not pose a serious challenge to authorities. With the help of Poland's king, Jan Sobieski (r. 1674–1696), Leopold also fought the Ottoman Turks, who controlled most of Hungary as part of their large and still-powerful empire.

During the fifteenth and first half of the sixteenth century, the Ottomans had enjoyed great power and relative prosperity. The sultans in Istanbul, wielding secular and religious authority, ran a strong autocratic state that could compete with any European power. Increasingly, they struggled to maintain authority in the face of competition from bandit armies, mutinous army officers, and squabbling elites, but seventeenth-century Ottoman rulers managed to maintain control. In 1683, Ottoman

The Ottomans

armies pushed into Austrian lands and laid siege to the capital, Vienna. Leopold and Sobieski's forces saved the city, however, and then brought most of Hungary under Austrian control (see map on page 310). The loss shocked Ottoman elites, and for good reason. From that point on, the empire ceased to expand, and during the following decades, the Ottomans' sources of wealth dried up. Moreover, the military weaponry and tactics of Ottoman armies and navies lagged behind those of their European foes. Ottoman power and imperial leadership would deteriorate further as weakened rulers struggled against political corruption, provincial revolts, and military insubordination.

After his victory in Vienna, the Austrian king tried to install his own nobility in Hungarian lands and ally himself with powerful Hungarian nobles at the expense of the peasantry. He succeeded only partially, and the still-independent Hungarian nobles remained a thorn in the side of the Austrian monarchy. Facing west, Leopold helped build a coalition that stood against Louis XIV. By the Austrian king's death in 1705, the Habsburg state had become one of the most powerful in Europe.

Russia and Its Tsars Gain Prominence

Even farther east, the Russian monarchy slowly rose to prominence. Already in the sixteenth century, Ivan IV ("the Terrible") (r. 1533–1584) had added both to the authority of the Russian tsars (caesars, or emperors) and to the span of territories over which they ruled. He destroyed the remaining power of the Mongols in southeastern Russia and annexed most of their territory. Next, he began Russia's conquest of Siberia. Within his expanding state, Ivan ruled as a ruthless autocrat, creating his own service gentry to bypass powerful nobles and using torture and terror to silence all he saw as his opponents.

A difficult period known as the Time of Troubles (1584–1613) followed Ivan IV's death. Ivan's feebleminded son Fyodor ruled ineffectively and left no successor upon his death in 1598. Great nobles vied **The Romanovs** for power among themselves and against weak tsars. To end the political chaos, a group of leading nobles in 1613 chose the 17-year-old Michael Romanov (r. 1613–1645) to rule as tsar. He began a dynasty that ruled Russia for over three hundred years.

Despite the political stability Michael and his immediate successors brought, discontent among those below the tsar and the nobility mounted during the century as the authorities increasingly restricted the freedom of the masses. The notorious Law Code of 1649, for example, merged peasants and slaves into a class of serfs and gave the landowning nobility the power to treat them as property. In a spate of uprisings between the late 1640s and early 1670s, the lower classes rebelled against landowners and officials by killing them and looting or burning their estates. The discontent reached a climax in the late 1660s and early 1670s with the revolts of Cossacks (free warriors) in south Russia led by Stenka Razin. A shrewd, seasoned warrior, Razin claimed to "fight only the boyars and the wealthy lords. As for the poor and the plain folk, I shall treat them as brothers." His rebel army marched north, and many towns opened their gates to welcome Razin's forces, now swelling with the addition of discontented peasants and the urban poor. Russian soldiers finally caught, tortured, and executed Razin, and the uprisings tapered off.

By the final decades of the seventeenth century, the Romanov tsars had shored up the government's central administration and extended their authority throughout the country. Lured by visions of wealth from access to Siberian furs, **Russian expansion** Russians had driven eastward into Asia, establishing fortified settlements, bringing indigenous peoples under their control (in the process decimating them with raids and diseases such as smallpox), and planting their flag on the shores of the Pacific. Moreover, through increased trade and travel, Russia's commercial and cultural contacts with the West expanded, bringing new European goods and ideas into the country. The stage was set for a dynamic tsar to propel Russia more fully into European affairs.

This new, energetic emperor came in the person of Peter I ("the Great") (r. 1689–1725). Standing nearly 7 feet tall, Peter seemed born to rule. At the age of 17, he seized the reins of government from his elder sister. He soon concluded **Peter the Great** that the best way to bolster his own political and military power was to copy Western practices. To this end, he traveled to western Europe and learned as much as he could about Western politics, customs, and technology.

Back home, Peter took decisive steps to solidify his authority. In 1698, he crushed a revolt of his bodyguards and silenced critics with a ruthlessness that cowed all potential troublemakers. "Every day was deemed fit and lawful for torturing," wrote an observer. He also made five years of education away from home and state service requirements for the nobility and allowed movement within the ranks only through merit. Peter applied the bureaucratic system of western European monarchs to both central and local government to secure his rule. He also brought Western technicians to Russia in large numbers and protected new industries with mercantilistic policies. Western social customs were introduced to the upper and middle classes of Russian society, such as bringing Russian women out of seclusion to appear in Western dresses at official dinners and social gatherings. In addition, Peter banned the long beards and flowing Oriental robes that Russian men traditionally wore. When the patriarch of the Russian Orthodox Church opposed the tsar's authority and some of his Westernizing policies, Peter took control of the church and confiscated much of

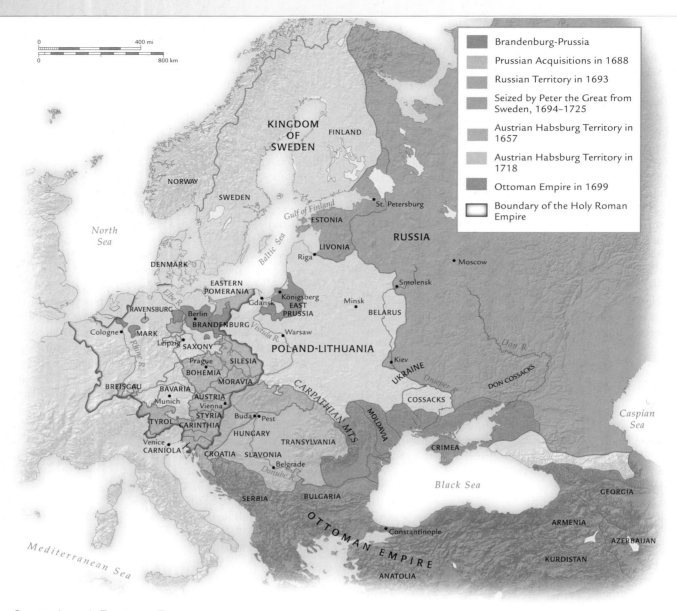

Central and Eastern Europe, 1640–1725 This map shows the changing political landscape in central and eastern Europe during the seventeenth and early eighteenth centuries.

Legend:
- Brandenburg-Prussia
- Prussian Acquisitions in 1688
- Russian Territory in 1693
- Seized by Peter the Great from Sweden, 1694–1725
- Austrian Habsburg Territory in 1657
- Austrian Habsburg Territory in 1718
- Ottoman Empire in 1699
- Boundary of the Holy Roman Empire

its wealth. Henceforth, the Orthodox Church served as a powerful instrument of the Russian government.

All these reforms left the peasantry in even worse straits than before. Peasants made up 97 percent of Russia's population during Peter's reign, and they became tied

Russia's military establishments

down in a system of serfdom bordering on slavery. The taxes they were forced to pay ballooned by a whopping 500 percent, and their feudal obligations and military service increased. Nowhere was peasant life harsher than in Russia, and Peter's efforts to Westernize the nobility only widened the gap between the

educated elites and the enserfed peasantry. "The peasants are perfect slaves, subject to the arbitrary power of their lords," wrote a British envoy to Peter's court. They are usually "transferred with goods and chattels; they can call nothing their own."

To keep Russia in step with the West and support his ambitions for territorial expansion, Peter devoted particular attention to his military establishment. He built a navy and patterned his expanded and modernized conscript army on the model of Prussia. Recruits were drafted for life and even branded with a cross on their left hand to deter desertion. Officials arbitrarily assigned serfs to work in mines and manufacturing establishments to supply the military with equipment and arms.

Peter meant to use his new military might (see image to the right). The tsar waged numerous military campaigns over his long reign, and he designed many of his great reforms to strengthen and modernize his armed forces. In the background of the painting, his troops surge to victory in a mighty battle.

Lacking warm-water access to the West, Peter tried to seize lands bordering the Black Sea that the Ottoman Turks held. Though they had weakened during the seventeenth century, the Ottoman Turks remained a formidable obstacle, and Peter's armies could not dislodge them. Frustrated, Peter turned northwest toward Sweden, which controlled lands bordering the Baltic Sea. Under King Gustavus Adolphus (r. 1611–1632), this Nordic country had become the dominant military power in northeastern Europe in the early seventeenth century (see Chapter 11). At the opening of the eighteenth century, Sweden held large areas east and south of the Baltic in addition to the homeland, and it ranked second only to Russia in size. Much of its success and the power of its monarchs came from the almost constant wars it fought during the seventeenth century. However, it lacked the population and resources to hold its far-flung territories for very long. Though Peter initially lost battle after battle to his brilliant Swedish adversary, Charles XII (r. 1697–1718), his persistence finally paid off. In the Battle of Poltava (1709), the Russians destroyed the Swedish army and managed to wound Charles.

Conflict with Sweden

ANONYMOUS, *THE APOTHEOSIS OF TSAR PETER I THE GREAT* The painter portrayed the Russian tsar as a heroic, all-conquering military figure who is blessed with divine authority. Clad in armor and carrying a sword, Peter asserts his authority over all potential rivals, who offer him their swords.

Through the Treaty of Nystad in 1721, Russia received the Swedish Baltic provinces and some Polish territories (see map on page 310). On the shores of the Baltic Sea, Peter triumphantly built a modern capital, St. Petersburg, that faced west. Reigning from this new court, he emulated the cultured, royal ways of the West to enhance his personal authority. At his death in 1725, Russia had taken its place as a major player on the European stage.

The Victory of the Nobility in Poland

Not all the eastern European states drifted toward monarchical absolutism. In Poland, the competition between the monarchy and the nobility took a different turn—with severe consequences for the nation. In the sixteenth and seventeenth centuries, Poland seemed poised to become a major power. Taking advantage of Russia's Time of Troubles (1584–1613), the Poles had captured Moscow for a few years until the Russians finally drove them out in 1613. In reality, however, the Polish nation, which included Lithuania in a dual kingdom, was far from strong. Sprawling over a large area between Russia and the German states, it had no natural, protective boundaries either to the east or to the west. Ethnic and religious divisions undermined the Polish rulers' hopes for unity, and the economy stumbled. In the late Middle Ages, a sizable overland commerce between the Black and Baltic Seas had flowed across Poland. However, with the shifting of commercial routes and centers to the west in the sixteenth century, Poland's commerce withered. Worse, the Polish nobility, protective of its own power and fearful of an alliance between merchants and the king, deliberately penalized merchants by passing legislation to restrict trade. The great mass of the Polish people remained serfs, bound to the estates of the powerful nobility.

In the face of such forces, only a strong central government could have ensured stability for Poland. Yet this was precisely where Poland proved weakest. For many years, Poland's nobles had been gaining the upper hand, and they closely guarded their power to elect the king. When King Sigismund II died in 1572, ending the long-ruling Jagellon dynasty, the nobles saw to it that no strong king ascended the throne. They monopolized the legislative body (the Diet) and, to safeguard their rights, required a unanimous vote to pass any measure. This system guaranteed political anarchy in which, in the words of a mid-seventeenth-century observer, "there is no order in the state," and "everybody who is stronger thinks to have the right to oppress the weaker."

Over the course of the seventeenth century, revolts by Ukrainian Cossack warriors and wars with Russia, Sweden, and Brandenburg-Prussia resulted in the loss of Polish territories. Rivalries among the Polish nobles worsened the chaos. Moreover, Tatar slave raiders carried off many people. Incursions and internal wars destroyed towns, and the once-thriving Jewish populations were pushed from their homes and often slaughtered. Tens of thousands of Jews were murdered in the pogroms (organized persecutions) that swept through Poland between 1648 and 1658. Protestants also suffered at the hands of the Catholic majority. Not surprisingly, Poland's population declined sharply in these years. By the beginning of the eighteenth century, it lay vulnerable to surrounding powers that boasted stronger central governments.

THE TRIUMPH OF CONSTITUTIONALISM

As the tendency toward absolutism intensified in central Europe, another major struggle began to unfold in a small island nation far to the west. Kings desiring absolute power in England faced a situation significantly different from that in France. In France, the nobility had little history of common action between classes and lost their solitary struggle against absolutism. In England, however, there had been a tradition of joint parliamentary action by nobles and commoners who owned land, and this helped contribute to a different outcome in the struggle for sovereignty. Instead of government residing in the person of an absolute monarch, it rested in written law—constitutions, not kings, would come to rule.

The Nobility Loses Respect

For over one thousand years, the English had taken for granted the idea of separate social classes. Peasants and members of the middle classes showed the high nobility an unmistakable deference, turning out to greet them when they emerged, gazing downward and holding their hats respectfully in their hands. Even upwardly mobile landowners with some wealth (the gentry) knew that they ranked well below the peers (the old nobility). In England, there were only about four hundred noble families, and they jealously guarded their exclusive position. Commentators wrote that "nobility is a precious gift" and accepted this privilege as the natural order of things: "Men naturally favor nobility."

At the beginning of the seventeenth century, several disturbing incidents pointed to ominous cracks in the wall of privilege. One member of the gentry actually jostled and swore at an earl as the two passed in a narrow passageway, and some tenant farmers neglected to turn out, hats in hand, to welcome passing noblemen. Later, a Protestant sect, the Quakers, enacted a religious policy that forbad members to take off their hats to men in authority. Something had changed and nobles no longer seemed so essential or so noble.

What explained this apparent loss of respect for the English upper crust? We can find a partial answer in the shifting role of money. In the early modern world, the old wealth of the nobility had declined relative to the "new money" of merchants and other enterprising individuals. Furthermore, the medieval base of noble power, the military, had also declined. No longer were nobles in charge of defending the realm; mercenary armies made up of commoners now took care of these matters. England had a relatively large sector of independent craftsmen compared to other countries, and noblemen depended more on "free labor"—that is, on wage laborers who could enter into contracts for their labor. These differences led commoners increasingly to feel they could control their own lives rather than defer to their "betters." In addition, education had become the key to upward mobility. More and more, knowledge and service, rather than birth, seemed the measure of a man. But the members of the nobility did not relinquish their traditional place easily. Indeed, critics complained that noblemen were becoming more arrogant than ever in exerting their privileges.

New wealth

As early as the sixteenth century, laws throughout Europe had begun to supplement tradition in keeping the social classes separate, and the situation in England was no different. Governments issued **sumptuary laws** to regulate what kinds of clothing were appropriate for members of each social class. For example, an individual could not wear velvet unless he had an independent income of over 100 pounds a year, and laborers could not wear cloth costing more than 2 shillings a yard. These laws were supposed to preserve social distinction, but the newly rich recognized that the path to gaining social respect lay in part in *looking* noble. Thus, men and women insisted on purchasing luxurious clothing to rival that of the highest classes. Now, it seemed, there was no visual marker of a person's noble status.

Sumptuary laws

The nobles had more success in guarding their property rights than their fashion privileges. In 1671, Parliament passed game laws giving the nobility the exclusive prerogative to hunt on their own lands. The new mandates even allowed them to set lethal trapguns to kill poachers. Not surprisingly, these laws only exacerbated the common people's anger, as the poor continued to poach simply to survive in times of hunger. Still, many members of the nobility tried to hang on to their privilege while others pressed to undo them.

Protestantism Revitalized

A good deal of social criticism also came from Protestants, many of whom believed that the implementation of Reformation ideas in England had not gone far enough. Because many Protestants were involved in the increasingly lucrative commerce, their wealth helped make their concerns more visible. For many, the compromise of Elizabeth I (discussed in Chapter 11) that allowed worshipers of many beliefs to share one Church of England was unacceptable. These critics believed that the Church of England (the Anglican Church) should be "purified"—that is, trimmed of any practice that lacked biblical precedent or smacked of Catholicism. They especially objected to priestly garments and the elaborate rituals of the Anglican Church. Some wanted to eliminate bishops altogether, preferring rule by church elders instead. (This was the practice common in Scotland, where Protestant churches came to be called Presbyterian—"ruled by elders.")

In their zeal, many Protestants became increasingly anti-Catholic, and their political actions were shaped by this prejudice. Other Protestants even wanted to purify daily life, objecting to theater, cockfights, and other seemingly frivolous activities. Although individuals disagreed among themselves on exactly how they wanted the Church of England purified, they all concurred that change was essential. Many members of this loose group of critics, called **Puritans,** became influential members of Parliament.

Puritans in England reconsidered the political relationship between monarchs and their subjects, wondering about competing loyalties between law and conscience, for example. These questions formed the backdrop of a struggle for sovereignty that dominated the seventeenth century. As Puritans gathered to discuss the purification of the church, they could not help but consider the possibility of political action.

James I Invokes the Divine Right of Kings

Because Queen Elizabeth I had died childless, the throne went to her cousin, the king of Scotland, who became King James I of England (r. 1603–1625). As soon as James heard of Elizabeth's death, he rushed to England brimming with great plans. He made promises to many who greeted him on his way south to London, rapidly knighted

ANTHONY VAN DYCK, *JAMES STUART, DUKE OF RICHMOND AND LENNOX,* ca. 1630 The English nobility worked to set themselves apart from lesser folk in their appearance and privileges. Here, James Stuart is shown in the lavish clothing that only the noble could wear, accompanied by the giant dog that accompanied him in the hunt, another privilege reserved for the nobility.

thousands of gentry, and even ordered an accused thief hanged without a trial—assuming incorrectly that as king he had the right to do so. Many of his subjects turned out to see their affable new monarch, but, unfortunately for him, he would not prove as popular, or as politically shrewd, as Good Queen Bess.

The honeymoon of the new monarch and his people faded rather quickly, for unlike his predecessor, he was unable to mollify the varying religious beliefs of his people. He was a Calvinist, yet he favored Anglicanism, and his most enduring heritage was the translation of the Bible he commissioned, the King James Bible, which remains widely admired as both religion and beautiful literature. However, the king managed to offend his subjects who hoped for his support for religious change. At the beginning of his reign, Calvinists approached the king, hoping to eliminate the Anglican episcopal system and bring it in line with the Presbyterian Scottish practice with which the king was familiar. They were sadly disappointed, for James threatened to "harry them out of the land" if they did not conform to Anglicanism.

Religious problems

James also offended his Catholic subjects, banning Jesuits and seminary priests. In 1605, a conspiracy of Catholics planned to blow up Parliament while it was in session. The plot failed and the conspirators were executed. Yet, the "gunpowder plot," as it came to be known, increased the anti-Catholic feelings in the country, which were exacerbated when James planned a political marriage between his son and a Catholic Spanish princess. Although the marriage negotiations fell through, the attempt alienated Calvinists and Anglicans alike.

Thus by 1610, there was much animosity between the king and many of his subjects. James thought the English ungrateful, and they found him arbitrary and arrogant. Unlike Elizabeth before him, James was disinclined to compromise his theoretical notions of divine right monarchy, which offended many Puritans in the House of Commons, as well as many lords who viewed the king as subject to the law of the land.

Divine right

During James's rule, the English colonies in North America grew. In part, the attention to the New World stemmed from James's financial difficulties: The first permanent English colony, named Jamestown after the monarch, was founded in Virginia in 1607. James hoped to generate new income from the Virginia colonies, which in 1619 had imported slaves from Africa to grow tobacco, an increasingly popular crop. Colonial settlement was also forwarded by James's high-handed attitude toward religious dissidents. When the king threatened to harry nonconformists out of the land, some took him literally and emigrated to North America to establish colonies. They avoided Jamestown, which was sympathetic to the Church of England, and instead landed farther north,

Colonies

founding their first colony in Plymouth, Massachusetts, in 1620. The New World was not to be the solution to either James's religious or fiscal problems. He died leaving a shortage of money and an oversupply of ill will among both Parliament and Protestants.

Charles I Alienates Parliament

James's son, Charles I (r. 1625–1649), inherited both his father's rule and his policies. This sober monarch, continuing to invoke the divine right of kings, considered himself answerable only to God, not Parliament. His relationship with his subjects deteriorated rapidly. He approached Parliament in the same way his father had—calling it when he needed money and disbanding it when the members demanded concessions.

Showing a remarkable insensitivity to his Protestant subjects, Charles married a sister of the Catholic king Louis XIII of France. Soon after his wedding, Charles granted concessions to English Catholics, even allowing the queen and her entourage to practice Catholic rituals in the court itself. English Protestants were horrified at what they saw as outrageous behavior by the family of the titular head of the Church of England. Charles responded to critics by persecuting Puritans, whom he viewed as disloyal. More Puritans fled to North America, settling so many colonies in the northeast that the region came to be called New England. Meanwhile, the situation in old England grew more desperate.

Concessions to Catholics

As we saw in Chapter 11, warfare had become extremely expensive, and Charles's costly and fruitless wars with Spain and France had so strained his finances that he even tried to pawn the crown jewels. The king called Parliament several times in the 1620s, only to disband it repeatedly. Things came to a head in 1640, when the Scots, who also objected to the king's high-handed religious policies, invaded the north of England. To raise the army and funds he needed to fight the Scots, Charles called Parliament again. This time, Parliament forced him to agree that he could not disband it without the members' consent. The first crack in Charles's armor of divine right had appeared. The Long Parliament, as it came to be called, continued to meet from 1640 to 1653. Over time, it acquired a measure of power and established protections for the religious freedom of Anglicans and Puritans alike.

Parliament gains power

However, the temporary compromise between the king and Parliament came to an end when troubles in Ireland caused both to agree to send troops. However, their alliance ended there. The question of who would command the army remained. Parliament did not trust the king to suppress his religious sympathies to fight the

Then & Now
Women at War

During the English civil war, some women believed the new revolutionary ideas gave them license to join the army to fight for their freedom. So many women dressed as men to join the battles, King Charles I issued a law forbidding them to "counterfeit their sex" by wearing men's clothing, but he was in no position to enforce such an edict. Today women in Western armies openly serve their country—for example, during Desert Storm in 1991, 41,000 U.S. women served and 15 were killed in battle.

Catholic Irish, and the king did not trust Parliament to share control of any army it raised. In the end, Parliament appointed officers to raise an army, and Charles withdrew from London to raise an army of his own. The Irish no longer seemed the immediate enemy for either side.

"God Made Men and the Devil Made Kings": Civil War

1642–1649

The alignments in the English civil war mirror some divisions in English life. The rural areas were more likely to support the king, and the Puritan strongholds in the cities followed the forces of Parliament. In response to Charles's call for support, noblemen, cavalry officers, and Irish Catholics rallied to his banner. His royalist supporters were called Cavaliers, or horsemen, as a reference to medieval knights who fought for their kings. Back in London, Parliament recruited an army 13,000 strong, drawn from the commoners, merchants, a few noblemen, Scots, and Puritans. All these generalizations, however, are drawn in broad strokes, and frequently the choice to support one side or another derived from private decisions, based sometimes on religion and sometimes on long-standing personal grudges against neighbors.

The strength of the parliamentary forces, called **Roundheads** for their short haircuts, stemmed mainly from their skilled infantry, the support of major sections of the navy, and their religious conviction. Parliament's forces also benefited from the leadership of Oliver Cromwell, a Puritan who not only forwarded the cause of revolutionary change in Parliament but also took charge of the army and forged it into a formidable force called the New Model Army. The royalists had more experience in battles and more skilled generals. The lines were drawn—the royalist forces led by the king fought a civil war against the forces led by Cromwell.

By 1646, Parliament forces had won a series of victories, and Charles surrendered to the Scots, who later turned him over to Parliament in exchange for their back military pay. While the king was moved from prison to prison as royalists conspired to free him, leaders of Parliament confronted new challenges: a series of social upheavals as more and more people were drawn into the turbulent events of the 1640s.

Charles captured

Some previously uninvolved members of society jumped into the fray. After 1646, radicals, both men and women, raised new demands for social justice. Their complaints stemmed mostly from the severe economic problems that had hamstrung England in the 1640s. A series of bad harvests caused food shortages and rising prices, and disabled soldiers returning home discovered they could no longer earn a living. Crime increased as people stole to feed their families, and the social order deteriorated. From these difficult circumstances, groups of radical Protestants arose. Known as **Levellers,** they insisted that social justice become part of Parliament's agenda. A pamphlet sympathetic to their cause claimed that "God made men and the Devil made kings."

Levellers

Levellers were as varied a group as the Puritans, encompassing people with a broad array of agendas. In general, however, they harked back to a tradition of English religious radicals like John Ball (see Chapter 9) and espoused as their goal to level social differences. To that end, they advocated some reforms of Parliament. For example, they believed Parliament should be chosen by the vote of all

A Leveller Condemns the Wealthy

Gerrard Winstanley (1609–1676) was the eloquent founder of the Levellers, and this excerpt from his "True Levellers Standard," 1649, reveals why the elites feared the Leveller agenda.

And that this Civil Property is the Curse, is manifest thus: Those that Buy and Sell Land, and are landlords, have got it either by Oppression, or Murder, or Theft; and all landlords live in the breach of the Seventh and Eighth Commandments, *Thou shalt not steal, nor kill.*

First by their Oppression. They have by their subtle imaginary and covetous wit, got the plain-hearted poor, or younger Brethren to work for them, for small wages, and by their work have got a great increase; for the poor by their labor lifts up Tyrants to rule over them; or else by their covetous wit, they have out-reached the plain-hearted in Buying and Selling, and thereby enriched themselves, but impoverished others. . . .

In what ways are the issues Gerrard Winstanley discusses in this passage still relevant today?

male heads of households, which would represent a dramatic broadening of the vote. Furthermore, they wanted members of Parliament to be paid so that even those with no independent income could serve. Although these ideas may seem natural to us, they posed a major threat to those who believed that only property brought privilege.

The King Laid Low

In the midst of these controversies, the civil war broke out again in 1648 as Charles encouraged his supporters to rise up to free him. Cromwell's forces promptly crushed the uprisings, and some army leaders concluded that they would never come to peaceful terms with the king. With Cromwell's support, they demanded that Charles be tried for treason. The majority of Parliament members refused to take this extreme step, but in December 1648 invading soldiers purged Parliament of the cautious. The remaining members, scornfully called the Rump Parliament by opponents and historians, brought the king to trial.

The Rump Parliament tried Charles as a king, rather than deposing him first and then trying him as a private citizen. In other words, they wanted to find the *king*, not just the man, guilty. This bold act represented a direct clash between two theories of government—one claiming that the king stood above Parliament, the other declaring that he must answer to it. This unprecedented, highly public trial became the first in history to receive full press coverage. Newspapers had initially emerged in England in 1641, on the eve of the civil war; by 1649, six licensed newspapers recorded the testimony in the trial and provided differing opinions on the proceedings.

Charles was accused of claiming to rule by divine right: He who had been "trusted with a limited power to govern . . . had conceived a wicked design to . . . uphold in himself an unlimited and tyrannical power to rule according to his will." Though he genuinely believed in divine right, Charles refused to answer this or any other charge. Instead, he claimed that Parliament had no right to bring charges against him at all. Both sides clearly understood the magnitude of the trial's central question: Who had sovereignty? Charles claimed that God had sovereignty and had delegated it to the king; the Puritans in Parliament claimed that they had sovereignty. There was no room for compromise, and neither side gave way. Charles was found guilty and sentenced to die.

OPINION

Why do you think monarchs' efforts to increase their power in France and England were successful in one case and not in the other?

WEESOP, *EXECUTION OF CHARLES I*, 1649 During the English civil war, King Charles I was put to death. This image documents the shocking event and shows how the audience was both attracted to and repelled by this act.

On January 30, 1649, the condemned king was led to a scaffold erected in front of Whitehall Palace. He bravely addressed the few people near him on the scaffold and repeated his views on sovereignty: "I must tell you that the liberty and freedom [of the people] consists in having a government. . . . It is not for having a share in government. Sir, that is nothing pertaining to them. A subject and a sovereign are clear different things." Charles then laid his head on the block, and the executioner severed it cleanly with one blow. The monarchy had ended, and a new form of government arose to take its place: a republic in which sovereignty rested with representatives of those who owned property. England called its new republic the Commonwealth.

Charles executed

A Puritan Republic Is Born: The Commonwealth

1649–1660

As the Rump Parliament began to rule the republic, chaos erupted throughout the realm. The new commonwealth faced warfare outside its borders and dissension within. Fortunately, Parliament had an able champion in Oliver Cromwell (1599–1658). While Parliament ruled, Cromwell with his army controlled the policies.

Rebellions broke out in Catholic Ireland and Protestant Scotland, and Cromwell led his army to those lands, putting down the revolts so brutally that the Irish still remember his invasion with anger. However, Cromwell was effective and brought Scotland and Ireland tightly

under English rule. Yet Parliament had more to worry about than just these expensive wars.

Within England, Levellers continued to agitate for social reform, and many of their leaders were imprisoned. Then, in 1649, a gathering of women entered the House of Commons bringing a petition asking for "those rights and freedoms of the nation that you promised us." One member of Parliament taunted the women, saying their public stance was "strange," to which a petitioner

Domestic distress

THE ROYAL OAK OF BRITAIN, 1649 Royalists and moderates feared that the civil war would destroy England and its traditions. This cartoon captures these fears as it shows revolutionaries chopping down the oak, symbol of Britain, and bringing down with it religion, the Magna Carta, and other texts hanging from the tree.

responded, "It was strange that you cut off the king's head." These were odd times indeed, and many wondered whether Parliament's victory in the civil war had created more disorder than it had resolved.

Parliament seemed incapable of uniting the various constituents that demanded action after Charles's death. In 1653, when the House of Commons considered a proposal to dismantle Cromwell's large army, the general lost patience.

Lord Protector

He disbanded Parliament altogether, named himself Lord Protector of the Commonwealth of England, Scotland, and Ireland, and established a military dictatorship—the republic remained only as an ideal. Cromwell faced the same problems that had confronted Parliament and the king—foreign wars and religious struggles. A pious Puritan, Cromwell set out to make England the model of a Protestant land, banning horse races, cockfights, and even theater. He ultimately proved as intolerant of Anglicans as they had been of Puritans, and he alienated most of the population with his intrusive policies. The brief experiment with a rule purely by Parliament had failed, and a military dictatorship could not be popular in a land with such a tradition of participatory government.

Who Has the Power to Rule?

Charles's trial and execution, and the disorder that followed, did not resolve the issue of who had the ultimate power in England. In 1651, the English philosopher Thomas Hobbes (1588–1679) wrote a political treatise, *The Leviathan,* that offered an answer to this question in the form of a new theory of government. Perhaps shaken by the chaos of the civil war, Hobbes harbored a pessimistic view of human nature. He claimed that everyone was driven by a quest for power and that given the chance, people would try to exercise their power at the expense of their neighbors—even if it meant taking their property and their lives. In this state of nature where there was no controlling authority, Hobbes described human life as "solitary, poor, nasty, brutish and short." However, he held out a ray of hope: Humans, he explained, recognized their inability to live peacefully, so they created a social contract by which they erected a ruler above them. By this contract,

Thomas Hobbes

subjects willingly surrendered their sovereignty to a ruler who, in turn, agreed to rule over them absolutely.

With this explanation, Hobbes reconciled the Protestant views of sovereignty—in which the people held the right to rule—with absolute monarchy, where the ruler (the king or Lord Protector) possessed sole sovereignty. In the famous frontispiece of *The Leviathan,* shown on page 319, Hobbes visually portrayed the benefits of his system. The ruler is shown at the top wielding the sword and scepter of absolute power. Even more significant, he comprises all the people of the land—he is the body politic. The king derives his power from his subjects, without whom he would not exist. However, with this delegated power, he presides over an orderly and peaceful countryside and village. Church, state, the army, and Parliament are all neatly ordered along the sides of the page.

Hobbes omitted a key point in his thesis: Absolute rule is only as effective as the ruler. Although Cromwell preserved order (albeit while offending many), he failed to develop an institution that could maintain the Puritan republic. When he died in 1658, he named his son Richard his successor. However, the young man could not lead with the same energy and fervor that his father had shown. Under pressure from members of Parliament, Richard resigned, and the right to govern again returned to the people's representatives.

The Monarchy Restored

1660–1688

Sobered by the chaos that had followed Charles's execution, Parliament decided to reinstate the monarchy. It invited Charles II (r. 1660–1685), son of the executed king, to resume the throne. Ships sailed from England to Holland to escort the king home from his place of exile. Charles II came home to a restored monarchy that had all the luxury that his father had enjoyed—and all the problems that had plagued this troubled institution.

Former Cromwell supporters saw the Restoration in a very different light. John Bunyan (1628–1688), for example, who had fought with Cromwell, was imprisoned in 1660 for preaching against the Restoration. His original sentence of three months was extended to twelve years because he refused to stop preaching. After his release in

John Bunyan

---

connect to today

Power Struggle

The Irish still remember Oliver Cromwell's brutal invasion to put down the revolt in Catholic Ireland with anger. This was one of many struggles for power between rulers and groups of their subjects during this time. Why do you think most people in the West today might oppose monarchical rule?

1672, he continued to preach, and he wrote his masterpiece, *Pilgrim's Progress,* in 1678. Probably the most widely read book by an English author, *Pilgrim's Progress* tells of a hero named Christian and his search for salvation through an allegorical world. This tale of hope and confidence in the human power to prevail through times of tribulation was balanced by Bunyan's lesser-known work, *The Life and Death of Mr. Badman* (1680). In this allegory, Bunyan criticized the loose life of Restoration England by describing the journey of a man who goes straight to hell. Bunyan's works strongly suggested that the Restoration had definitely not solved the political struggles of England.

Charles II grappled with the same fiscal problems that had plagued James I and Charles I, but he had to face a Parliament that had proven its strength during the civil

Fiscal problems

wars. The king was bound by law to call Parliament at least every three years, and the members of Parliament had severely curtailed royal power over taxation. Like his predecessors, Charles needed money, and to buttress his revenues without the restrictions Parliament imposed, the

new king tried to exert more control over the colonies in North America. He increased the customs duties permitted by the Navigation Acts (imposed in 1651) and fought a war with the Dutch in 1665. This conflict ended in a treaty that gave the English New York in exchange for Dutch control of Surinam in South America.

Charles's international dealings were hampered by disasters at home. In 1665, England experienced a plague of frightening intensity—70,000 people died in London alone. The following year, a devastating fire broke out in London, engulfing the city and destroying 13,000 dwellings

Plague and fire

and 87 churches, including the venerable St. Paul's Cathedral. After the fire had died out, Charles ordered the city rebuilt and hired the skilled architect Sir Christopher Wren to redesign the main buildings. Wren's masterpiece, the new St. Paul's Cathedral, still marks the London skyline.

In addition to these disasters, the issue of religion again came to the fore. Charles had Catholic sympathies, and to circumvent Parliament, he had several times turned to the Catholic king Louis XIV of France for help and money. The Protestant Parliament, wary of Charles's granting concessions to Catholics, passed the Test Act in 1673. The law required an oath of Protestant loyalties to prevent Catholics from holding public offices, but legislation could not affect the king's conscience, or alleviate Parliament's fears of Catholicism. In 1685, Charles died after converting to Roman Catholicism on his deathbed.

Charles's successor, his brother James II (r. 1685–1688), was not able to avoid direct confrontation with the Protestant Parliament. A Catholic, James demanded in vain that Parliament repeal the Test Act, and he proceeded to place Catholics in high office in violation of Parliament's law. Many English feared that James would adopt Louis XIV's policies against Protestants and even try to institute absolute rule. They may well have been right, but the members of Parliament were not going to wait and see. In 1688, when James's Catholic wife produced a Catholic heir to the throne of England, leading members of Parliament took action.

The Glorious Revolution

To preempt James, parliamentary leaders turned to the king's eldest daughter, Mary, a Protestant and the wife of William of Orange of the Netherlands. William staunchly opposed the policies of the Catholic Louis XIV, so both his politics and his religion suited the English Prot-

William and Mary

estants. William gathered a fleet and an army of 14,000 men and landed in England in November 1688. He marched slowly and peacefully toward London, while most of the English population rallied to his side. Recalling Charles I's fate, James decided to flee to France "for the security of my person." Louis XIV received his Catholic counterpart with kindness.

THOMAS HOBBES, FRONTISPIECE OF HIS WORK *THE LEVIATHAN,* 1651 Thomas Hobbes warned that only an absolute monarchy, shown at the top, would save people from violence, a life he famously called "nasty, brutish, and short."

The Irish Catholics did not welcome the new Protestant king. Indeed, they thought of James II as a Catholic hero, and Irish leaders conspired with James to help him retake his throne while the French king helped fund this enterprise. Early in his reign, William led an army into Ireland and ruthlessly suppressed what he saw as Catholic treason. Abandoning both Ireland and his claim to the throne, James lived out his life in lavish exile in France, leaving the Irish to bear the brunt of William's wrath. The new king reduced Ireland to colonial status and offered new opportunity for English landlords to take possession of Irish Catholic lands. Irish anger toward the English festered and would grow, but William's victory was cheered in England.

> "[N]o person embracing Catholicism or married to a Catholic is eligible to succeed to the throne."

William and Parliament turned to the immediate task of establishing the legitimacy of his kingship. Parliament decided that James's flight from England constituted an abdication of the throne. The sovereignty that, according to Hobbes, the people had surrendered to their king had been returned to Parliament, who now had the right to install a new monarch. Parliament determined to clarify its relationship with the king, and in 1689 it passed a Bill of Rights firmly stating that kings were subject to the laws of the land, thus creating a constitutional monarchy—the triumph of **constitutionalism.** Within the Bill of Rights, William agreed to "deliver this kingdom from popery [Catholicism] and arbitrary power" and to preserve freedom of speech, election, and the rule of law. The bill secured the position of Protestantism in England by ruling that "no person embracing Catholicism or married to a Catholic is eligible to succeed to the throne." Through this bloodless **Glorious Revolution,** Parliament had finally demonstrated that the power to rule rested with the people through their representatives, rather than absolutely with the king. After this, Parliament began to meet annually, which was a practical way to secure its authority.

England's Bill of Rights

Royalism Reconsidered: John Locke

Many English men and women were proud of their bloodless "revolution" that so peacefully changed their monarch, but others were uncertain about the legality of this step. The English philosopher John Locke (1623–1704) wrote an influential political tract—*The Second Treatise of Government* (1690)—to justify "to the world [and] the people of England" the Revolution of 1688 and proclaim the legitimacy of William. Locke did much more—he articulated a new relationship between king and subjects that provided a theoretical framework for constitutional forms of government. Like Hobbes, Locke believed that power originally rested with the people and that citizens themselves established a

monarchy to keep order. However, whereas Hobbes had said that the people turned over their sovereignty completely to the monarch, Locke claimed that they retained it but created a contract of mutual obligations with their ruler. Locke argued that if the king broke the contract, the people had the right to depose him and install a new monarch, just as Parliament had done during the Glorious Revolution.

Locke's political theories were not intended to support full democracies—in his time, the "people" meant only those who owned property. He did not intend for individuals, such as the landless Levellers, to threaten property owners. Nor did he view women as sharing in the popular sovereignty of the privileged social order. Locke's highly influential rhetoric, in which he claimed natural rights of life, liberty, and property, actually applied to relatively few people in 1690. However, in time, his theory would broaden to form the basis for democracy as well as constitutional monarchy.

Parliament soon had the opportunity to exert its king-making authority once again. William and Mary died without an heir, so the crown went to James II's Protestant daughter, Anne. Queen Anne (r. 1701–1714) also died without an heir, whereby the Protestant Stuart dynasty evaporated. Parliament then passed the crown to George I (r. 1714–1727), a great-grandson of James I, who ruled the German principality of Hanover, introducing the Hanoverian dynasty to England. This peaceful transition demonstrated once and for all that the struggle for sovereignty in England was over—Parliament ruled.

Hanover dynasty

The Netherlands Maintain a Republic

The English nobles asserted their rights over the king by exercising their authority through a parliament that ruled over a highly centralized government. This struggle created a strong constitutional monarchy that preserved popular sovereignty while creating a state that would prove highly stable. Another way for people to preserve their sovereignty was to resist a strong central government in order to strengthen local institutions. In the seventeenth century, the Netherlands developed this political structure, which also gave power to the people instead of to absolute rulers. They instituted another form of constitutionalism that structured the government around consent of the propertied.

When the Low Countries split in 1609, the southern Catholic regions remained subject to the absolutist monarch, Philip III of Spain. The map on page 321 shows the division of the Low Countries in 1609. The Spanish Netherlands of the south (now Belgium) formed a buffer between the United Provinces of the north and the divine

The United Provinces

The United Provinces and the Spanish Netherlands,

1609 This map shows the location of the Netherlands in Europe and its division into two separate states. Notice the scale of the map and consider how small the United Provinces were.

right monarchy of France. In the United Provinces, which became largely Calvinist after the wars with Catholic Spain, a Protestant state developed that successfully resisted any attempts at royal absolutism.

The United Provinces—also known as the Dutch Republic—was the only major European power to maintain a republican form of government throughout the seventeenth century. Each province was governed locally by an assembly (called the State) made up of delegates from cities and rural areas. In reality, the States were dominated by an oligarchy of wealthy merchants. The union of the provinces was only a loose confederation, with each province sending deputies to the States General, a national assembly that implemented provincial assembly decisions.

Executive power at the local level was vested in governors (Stadholders) of each province. At the national level, executive power was given to the Council of State, made up of deputies drawn from the provinces.

This remarkable decentralization worked effectively for local issues but had some drawbacks for implementing foreign policy. During the 1650s, Holland—the largest province—began to take an informal lead in directing the state's foreign policy in the first two wars against England. After 1672, William III, a prince of the hereditary house of Orange, became the captain-general of the republic's military forces against France. The House of Orange had

a permanent vote in the States General and served as a unifying point. However, William of Orange exercised more power once he became king of England in 1689 than he ever had in the Netherlands. The 1648 Treaty of Westphalia, which ended the Thirty Years' War (see Chapter 11), formally recognized the Republic of the United Provinces.

What were the special circumstances that led the Netherlands to develop and maintain this strong sense of local sovereignty when other areas of Europe were moving to centralized governments? In **Dutch prosperity** large part, such political independence was facilitated by prosperity. The seventeenth century has been called the golden age of the United Provinces, for this small region was a tremendous European and colonial power. Amsterdam became the commercial and financial center of Europe as ships brought huge quantities of herring from the North Sea, as well as sugar, tobacco, glass, and many other items from around the world, through the bustling port.

In addition to commerce, the Dutch prospered through skilled shipbuilding that was the wonder of Europe. Not only did they design remarkable ships that could sail with fewer crew members than more traditional ships; they also built them quickly and cheaply. They obtained timber, pitch, and rigging from the nearby Baltic regions, and they used the most modern technology for the assembly: mechanical saws, hoists for masts, and the manufacture of interchangeable parts. Contemporary witnesses were amazed to report that given two months' notice, Dutch shipbuilders could turn out a warship every week for the rest of the year. It is no wonder that silver from the New World found its way into the coffers of Dutch builders.

The Dutch also grew rich from their activities as major slave traders in the New World. The population of Amsterdam grew from about 30,000 people in 1570 to 200,000 by 1660, and the growth was testimony to the wealth and opportunities people saw there. Its financial importance was secured in 1609 by the foundation of the Exchange Bank of Amsterdam, the greatest public bank in northern Europe. Europeans were astonished by the prosperity and enterprise of the Dutch.

The Dutch had other elements that contributed to their resistance of absolutism. The Dutch aristocracy was not as wealthy as that of England or France, for example. Their wealth lay more in commerce than in land, so the aristocracy had more in common with the merchants of their land than they did with the landed gentry in England or with the nobility at the court of Versailles. Furthermore, in the United Provinces, the Protestant faith cultivated an ideology of moderation—rather than the aristocratic excess that marked the nobility of other states. That is not to say that the seventeenth-century United Provinces espoused notions of egalitarian democracy—the nobility were as interested in trying to increase their power as those of other countries.

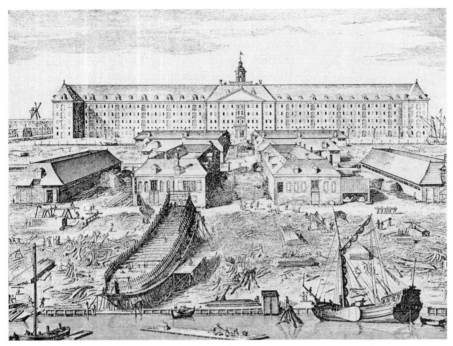

DUTCH SHIPYARD Even small states such as the Netherlands could become rich in the new global marketplace. Dutch shipbuilding was the wonder of Europe, and it was proudly depicted in many images, including this anonymous engraving.

cultural and economic life of the republic. Not only did the United Provinces attract intellectuals, such as René Descartes from France and John Locke from England, but the open-minded assemblies stimulated the spread of ideas through the press. The United Provinces became a leading center for book publishing and transmitted ideas, even revolutionary ones, all over Europe.

The refugees streaming into the Netherlands included some destitute travelers and in some ways burdened the small country. The Dutch, however, generously assisted the needy, who never sank to the same depths of hardship that faced the poor in many other European cities.

The preeminence of the Dutch began to wane by the beginning of the eighteenth century. The economies of England and France had gathered strength both in Europe and abroad and encroached on the commercial empire forged by the Dutch. Yet the two geographically small countries of England and the Netherlands had contributed much to the political development of the West. Both established the sovereignty of the people through constitutionalism—England through Parliament, and the Netherlands through local autonomy. For all their tremendous impact for the future, at the opening of the eighteenth century both nations seemed hardly whispers in a Europe dominated by strong monarchs proclaiming a divine right to rule.

They were just not able to exert much centralized control over the prosperous, Protestant residents that were the wonder of Europe.

Overall, the Dutch exhibited an unusual degree of religious toleration for their time. They even allowed Catholics and Jews to practice their religions, a **Religious toleration** policy that encouraged religious refugees to flock to the Netherlands from all over Europe. These refugees greatly enriched the

timeline

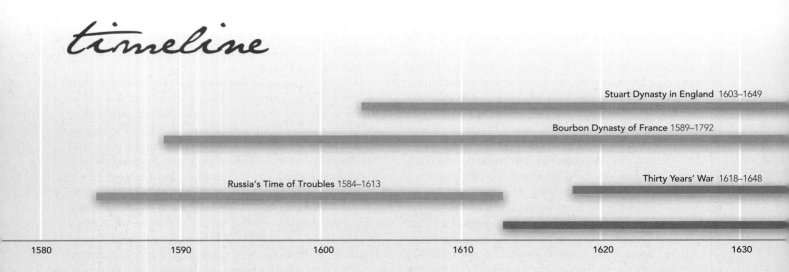

Stuart Dynasty in England 1603–1649

Bourbon Dynasty of France 1589–1792

Thirty Years' War 1618–1648

Russia's Time of Troubles 1584–1613

| 1580 | 1590 | 1600 | 1610 | 1620 | 1630 |

SUMMARY

For upper-crust members of Western societies, the seventeenth century was a period of both comfort and struggle. The comfort came from these elites' continued dominance. From the beginning to the end of the century, they held most of the riches, status, and power. For those below them who toiled in the fields, the period offered struggle without much comfort. In western Europe, demands from expanding central governments for taxes and conscripts only aggravated the hardships wrought by unusually bad harvests and disease. In eastern Europe, landowning nobles added to these problems by burdening peasants under an increasingly heavy yoke of serfdom.

- Population decreases, long wars, and bad harvests as well as competition for territory and status marked some of the growing stress on traditional societies during this period.

- The efforts of French kings such as Louis XIV to maximize their power exemplified the development of royal absolutism in Europe.

- In eastern Europe, states such as Brandenburg-Prussia, Austria, and Russia, monarchs struggled to increase their authority and expand their power.

- Constitutionalism emerged as an alternative to absolutism in England, through a civil war, and in the Republic of the Netherlands.

The structure of this hierarchic society may have loosened enough for some people in western Europe to improve their lot. However, that structure only tightened in eastern Europe. For all of Europe, war, revolt, and even revolution shook societies without breaking the traditional hierarchies. Nevertheless, some traditions started to crumble. Important changes in science and thought were already afoot that would soon transform the intellectual foundations of Western society.

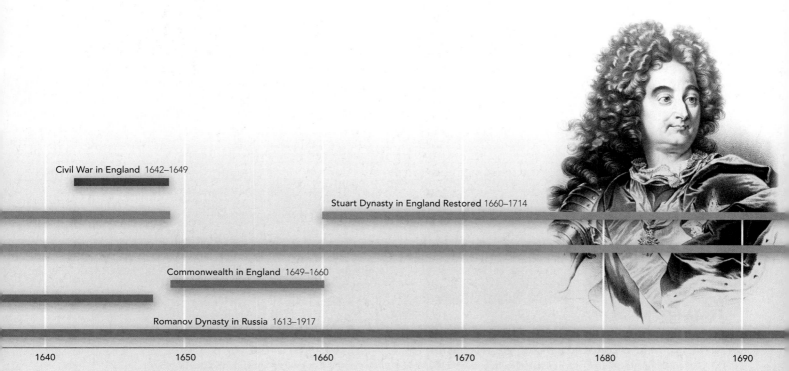

Civil War in England 1642–1649

Stuart Dynasty in England Restored 1660–1714

Commonwealth in England 1649–1660

Romanov Dynasty in Russia 1613–1917

| 1640 | 1650 | 1660 | 1670 | 1680 | 1690 |

ANONYMOUS, *TRIAL OF GALILEO BEFORE THE INQUISITION*

In 1632, Galileo came into conflict with conservative forces in the Catholic Church over his Copernican views. In this painting by an anonymous artist, Galileo sits facing the church officials who will judge him.

A New World of Reason and Reform

The Scientific Revolution and the Enlightenment, 1600–1800

14

Questioning Truth and Authority

On June 22, 1633, the well-known Italian scientist Galileo Galilei (1564–1642) knelt in a Roman convent before the cardinals who served as judges of the Inquisition. The cardinals informed Galileo that he was "vehemently suspected of heresy." They also showed him the customary instruments of torture, though they did not use them. Next, they ordered him to deny "the false opinion that the sun is the center of the universe and immovable, and that the earth is not the center of the same"—views that Galileo had supported in a book he published the previous year. Threatened with being tried and burned as a heretic, Galileo had to denounce his views as heresy. ▶▶

The court and papacy sentenced Galileo to house arrest in Florence for the rest of his life and forbad him to publish on the topic again. Nevertheless, Galileo would not change his mind. The sequence of events leading to Galileo's trial and conviction is a story of its own, but the conflict lay at the core of a major development of the age: the Scientific Revolution.

Until the sixteenth century, most European scholars shared the standard medieval understanding of the physical nature of the earth and the universe. This understanding was based on a long legacy stretching back to the views of the fourth-century B.C.E. Greek philosopher Aristotle. His ideas had been modified in the second century C.E. by Ptolemy of Alexandria and then passed on through Byzantine and Arab scholars to medieval European thinkers. After the thirteenth century, Europeans translated Aristotle's works into Latin and merged his thinking with Christian ideas about the universe.

According to this Christian medieval understanding, the earth rested at the center of an unchanging universe. Around it in ascending order rose the perfect spheres of air, fire, the sun, the planets, and the stars (the firmament), with God (the prime mover) just beyond. Westerners accounted for the succession of day and night by explaining that this finite universe rotated in precise circles around the earth once every twenty-four hours. The heavenly abode of angels consisted of pure matter, and the earthly home of humans was made of changeable, corrupt matter. This universe was clear, finite, and satisfyingly focused on the earthly center of God's concern.

Common sense supported this worldview. A glance at the sky confirmed that the sun and stars indeed circled around the earth each day. Under foot, the earth felt motionless. To careful observers, the motion of planets, whose position often changed, was more perplexing. To explain this mystery, Ptolemy and others had modified their theories, concluding that planets moved in small, individual orbits as they traveled predictably around the earth. People had lived by the wisdom of the ancients and authoritative interpretations of the Bible for centuries. Accordingly, investigation of the physical universe generally consisted of making deductions from these long-accepted guides. But, as with Galileo, changes emerged in scholars' thinking about ideas, the world, and the place of humans in it, as we'll see in this chapter. ◀◀

THE MEDIEVAL VIEW OF THE UNIVERSE, 1559 This woodcut shows the earth at the center of a stable, finite universe. A band with signs of the zodiac suggests the importance of astrology within this Christian understanding.

UNDERMINING THE MEDIEVAL VIEW OF THE UNIVERSE

During the fifteenth and sixteenth centuries, new problems began undermining the traditional view described above. Authorities of all kinds—including Aristotle—came into question during the Renaissance. Some of this questioning stemmed from the Renaissance search for classical writings, which led scholars to discover and read the works of Greek authorities who contradicted Aristotle. **Neoplatonism,** based on the ideas of Plato, stressed the belief that one should search beyond appearances for true knowledge; truth about both nature and God could be found in abstract reasoning and be best expressed by mathematics. Neoplatonic **Hermetic doctrine** provided especially powerful alternatives to Aristotelian thought.

According to Hermetic doctrine, based on writings mistakenly attributed to Hermes Trismegistus (supposedly an ancient Egyptian priest), all matter contained the divine spirit, which humans ought to seek to understand. Among many scholars, this doctrine stimulated intense interest in botany, chemistry, metallurgy, and other studies that promised to help people unlock the secrets of nature. The Hermetic approach also held that mathematical harmonies helped explain the divine spirit and represented a crucial pathway to understanding God's physical world. This approach encouraged scholars to use mathematics and to measure, map, and quantify nature. Moreover, Hermetic doctrine also held that the sun was the most important agency for transmission of the divine spirit and thus rightly

Hermetic doctrine

occupied the center of the universe. Finally, these beliefs fostered the idea of the natural magician who could unleash the powers of nature through alchemy (the study of how to purify and transform metals, such as turning common minerals into gold), astrology (the study of how stars affect people), and magic (see image below). Scholars often saw no distinction between seeking to understand the harmony, oneness, and spiritual aspects of the natural world and what we would call scientific observation and experimentation. Although Hermetic doctrine often proved not useful, all these ideas encouraged investigators to question traditionally accepted knowledge.

In addition to new ideas and beliefs, geographic exploration during the Renaissance also upset traditional assumptions. The discovery of the

Exploration

New World, for example, disproved Ptolemaic geography. Furthermore, overseas voyages stimulated demand for new instruments and precise measurements for navigation. This demand, in turn, encouraged research, especially in astronomy and mathematics.

Finally, the recently invented printing press enabled even out-of-favor scholars to publish their findings, which spread new ideas and discoveries even further. Renaissance rulers supported all these efforts in

The printing press

hopes of gaining prestige as well as practical tools for war, construction, and mining. Church authorities did the same at times, especially backing research in astronomy in the hopes of improving the calendar to date Easter more accurately.

"New philosophy calls all in doubt."

Like the Renaissance, the Reformation unleashed forces that provoked the questioning of long-held views. Most researchers had religious motives for their work, though those motives were not necessarily grounded in tradition. In particular, they yearned for insights into the perfection of God's universe. As we read in Chapter 11, the Reformation shattered confidence in religious authorities. By upsetting hallowed certainties, sixteenth- and seventeenth-century scholars hoped to establish new, even sounder certainties and thereby regain a sense of mastery over nature.

DEVELOPING A MODERN SCIENTIFIC VIEW

Even with these rumblings of change, no sudden breakthrough cleared away the centuries-old understanding of nature. Most scientific work still proceeded slowly, as did scholarly and public acceptance of its findings. Investigators had to demonstrate the effectiveness of their new methods again and again to convince even their colleagues. Indeed, few scholars suggested a wholesale rejection of traditional authorities; most simply chipped away at old notions. By the end of the seventeenth century, however, an entirely new scientific view of reality, initiated by just a handful of scholars, had replaced the traditional view. To understand this startling shift, we need to trace developments in astronomy, physics, and scientific methodology.

Astronomy and Physics: From Copernicus to Newton

During the sixteenth and seventeenth centuries, astronomy and physics attracted the most systematic attention from scholars. Researchers in these fields became particularly dissatisfied with the inability of Aristotelian theory to explain, simply and efficiently, careful observations and mathematical calculations of the stars. The Ptolemaic system for predicting planetary movements seemed overly complex and cumbersome to these scholars. Their findings would dramatically alter Westerners' perceptions of nature and of the earth's place in the universe. As the English poet John Donne complained in 1611, "New philosophy calls all in doubt."

Nicolaus Copernicus (1473–1543), a Polish clergyman with an interest in astronomy, astrology, mathematics, and church law, took the first steps in this intellectual adventure. Like so many other northern European scholars, he

Nicolaus Copernicus

HEINRICH KHUNRATH, *THE LABORATORY AND THE CHAPEL*, 1609 Amid the tools of his trade, an alchemist prays in a small chapel. This seventeenth-century illustration reveals the close connections between spiritual beliefs and alchemy.

crossed the Alps to study in an Italian university. There he became influenced by the rediscovery of Greek scholarship, Neoplatonism, and the Hermetic doctrine. Copernicus sought a simpler mathematical formulation to explain how the universe operated. His search convinced him that the earth was *not* at the center of the universe. Instead, he believed that the sun "sits upon a royal throne" in that location, "ruling his children, the planets which circle around him." Moreover, Copernicus concluded that the earth was not stationary: "What appears to be a motion of the sun is in truth a motion of the earth." According to Copernicus, the earth moved in perfect, "divine" circles around the sun, as did other bodies in the universe. Day passed into night because the earth turned on its axis. This change from an earth-centered (geocentric) to a sun-centered (heliocentric) universe would become known as the **Copernican revolution.**

Copernicus worked on his **heliocentric model** of the universe for almost twenty-five years. However, fearing ridicule and disapproval from the clergy, he waited until 1543—what became the year of his death—to publish it. Few people outside a limited circle of scholars knew of his views, and even fewer accepted them. Nevertheless, Catholic and Protestant authorities who were wedded to the earth-centered system soon recognized the threat to the Christian conception of the universe that these ideas represented. They denounced the Copernican system as illogical, unbiblical, and unsettling to the Christian faith. One Protestant associate of Martin Luther complained that "certain men . . . have concluded that the earth moves. . . . It is want of honesty and decency to assert such notions publicly. . . . It is part of a good mind to accept the truth as revealed by God and to acquiesce in it."

Still, Copernicus's thinking had some supporters. An Italian monk, Giordano Bruno (1548–1600), tested Catholic authorities by openly teaching and extending Copernican thought, arguing that "the universe is entirely infinite because it has neither edge, limit, nor surfaces." Bruno also professed a series of unusual religious notions. Outraged, the Catholic Inquisition burned Bruno at the stake. Nevertheless, Copernicus's views began to influence other scholars who were investigating the physical nature of the universe.

The Danish aristocrat Tycho Brahe (1546–1601) did not share Copernicus's belief in a heliocentric universe, nor did he grasp the sophisticated mathematics of the day. Still,

Tycho Brahe he became the next most important astronomer of the sixteenth century. He persuaded the king of Denmark to build for him the most advanced astronomy laboratory in Europe. There he recorded thousands of unusually accurate, detailed observations about the planets and stars over a period of twenty years—all without a telescope. His discoveries of a new star in 1572 and a comet in 1577 undermined the Aristotelian belief in a sky of fixed, unalterable stars moving in crystalline spheres. Although Brahe mistakenly concluded that some planets revolved around the sun, which itself moved around the earth, other astrono-

mers with better understandings of mathematics would use his observations to draw very different conclusions.

Tycho Brahe's assistant, Johannes Kepler (1571–1630), built on Brahe's observations to support the Copernican heliocentric theory. A German Lutheran from an aristocratic family, Kepler—like other Hermetic scholars—believed in an underlying mathematical harmony **Johannes Kepler** of mystical significance to the physical universe. He sought one harmony that would fit with Brahe's observations. Between 1609 and 1619, he announced his most important findings: the three laws of planetary motion. After determining the first law—which stated that the planets moved in ellipses around the sun—he excitedly wrote, "It was as if I had awakened from a sleep." The second law declared that the planets' velocity varied according to their distance from the sun. The third law concluded that the physical relationship between the moving planets could be expressed mathematically. Kepler thus showed "that the celestial machine . . . is the likeness of [a] clock," further undermining the Aristotelian view and extending the Copernican revolution.

Galileo already believed that the world could be described in purely mathematical terms. "Philosophy," he wrote, "is written in this grand book, the universe, which stands continually open to our gaze. . . . It is writ- **Galileo Galilei** ten in the language of mathematics, and its characters are triangles, circles, and other geometric figures without which it is humanly impossible to understand a single word of it." Galileo also felt that harmonies could be discovered through experimentation and mathematics. By conducting controlled experiments such as rolling balls down inclines, he demonstrated how motion could be described mathematically. He rejected the old view that objects in their natural state were at rest and that all motion needed a purpose. Instead, he formulated the principle of inertia, showing that bodies, once set into motion, will tend to stay in motion. He thus overturned Aristotelian ideas and established rules for experimental physics.

Galileo, hearing about the recent invention of the telescope, then studied the skies through a telescope that he built in 1609 out of a long tube and magnifying lenses. He saw that the moon's surface, instead of being a perfect heavenly body, was rugged (like the earth's), with craters and mountains indicated by lines and shading. The telescope also revealed that Jupiter had moons and that the sun had spots. These observations confirmed the view that other heavenly bodies besides the earth were imperfect and further convinced him of the validity of Copernicus's hypothesis. For years, Galileo had feared the disapproval of the Catholic Church (see Exploring the Past on page 329). Now, however, he was ready to publicly argue that "in discussions of physical problems we ought to begin not from the authority of scriptural passages, but from sense-experiences and necessary demonstrations." Galileo published his findings in 1610.

Six years later, the church attacked his proposition that "the earth is not the center of the world nor immovable, but moves as a whole, and also with a daily motion." This statement, the church said, was "foolish and absurd philosophically, and formally heretical." To back up its claim, the church cited the authority of both the Bible and itself. For the next several years, Galileo kept his thoughts to himself. In 1632, believing that the church might be more open, he decided again to present his views. To avoid challenging the church, he submitted his book to the official church censors and agreed to some changes they demanded. Finally he published his *Dialogue on the Two Chief Systems of the World—* in Italian rather than the less-accessible Latin. This text advocated Copernicanism, portrayed opponents of the Copernican system (such as the Jesuits) as simpletons, and brought Galileo directly into public conflict with conservative forces in the Catholic Church. Because Galileo could show that his book had already been approved by church officials, prosecutors had to use questionable evidence against him. As we saw at the beginning of the chapter, the Roman Inquisition ultimately forced Galileo to renounce his views.

News of Galileo's sensational trial spread throughout Europe, as did fear of publishing other radical views. Soon, however, his book was translated and published elsewhere in Europe, and his views began to win acceptance by other scientists. Even though Galileo admitted that the new science was beyond the grasp of "the shallow minds of the common people," he effectively communicated its ideas to his peers. By the time of his death in 1642, Europe's intellectual elite had begun to embrace the Copernican outlook.

In England, Isaac Newton (1642–1727) picked up the trail blazed by Copernicus, Brahe, Kepler, and Galileo. Late in life, Newton described his

Isaac Newton

career modestly: "I do not know what I may appear to the world; but to myself I seem to have been only like a boy playing on the seashore, and diverting myself in now and then finding a smoother pebble or a prettier shell than ordinary, while the great ocean of truth lay all undiscovered before me." Newton may have held himself in humble regard, but his accomplishments were astonishing.

In 1661, Newton entered Cambridge University, where he studied the ideas of Copernicus and Galileo as well as the advantages of

Kepler and Galileo Exchange Letters About Science

Many leading European scholars of the Scientific Revolution feared publishing their views, which were often unpopular with religious authorities. Such scholars sometimes turned to each other for support, as the following late-sixteenth-century letters between Kepler and Galileo suggest.

Galileo to Kepler: "Like you, I accepted the Copernican position several years ago. I have written up many reasons on the subject, but have not dared until now to bring them into the open. I would dare publish my thoughts if there were many like you; but, since there are not, I shall forbear."

Kepler's Reply: "I could only have wished that you, who have so profound an insight, would choose another way. You advise us to retreat before the general ignorance and not to expose ourselves to the violent attacks of the mob of scholars. But after a tremendous task has been begun in our time, first by Copernicus and then by many very learned mathematicians, and when the assertion that the Earth moves can no longer be considered something new, would it not be much better to pull the wagon to its goal by our joint efforts, now that we have got it under way, and gradually, with powerful voices, to shout down the common herd? Be of good cheer, Galileo, and come out publicly!

In what ways does Kepler's reply suggest that the Scientific Revolution was already a growing movement by the end of the sixteenth century?

scientific investigation. He distinguished himself enough in mathematics to be chosen to stay on as a professor after his graduation. Like most other figures of the Scientific Revolution, Newton was profoundly religious and hoped to harmonize his Christian beliefs with the principles of science. He also believed in alchemy and elements of Hermeticism.

Starting in his early 20s, Newton made some of the most important discoveries in the history of science. He developed calculus and investigated the nature of light; he also formulated and mathematically described three laws of motion: inertia, acceleration, and action/reaction. Yet he is best known for discovering the law of universal attraction, or gravitation. After working on the concept for years, he finally published it in 1687 in his great work *Principia (The Mathematical Principles of Natural Knowledge).* In the book, Newton stated the law with simplicity and precision: "Every particle of matter in the universe attracts every other particle with a force varying inversely as the square of the distance between them and directly proportional to the product of their masses." In his view, this law applied equally to all objects, from the most massive planet to a small apple falling from a tree.

Newton's *Principia*

Newton had managed to synthesize the new findings in astronomy and physics into a systematic explanation of physical laws that applied to the earth as well as the heavens. This Newtonian universe was infinite and had no center. Uniform and mathematically describable, it was held together by explainable forces and was atomic in nature. Essentially, everything in the universe consisted of only one thing: matter in motion.

The Revolution Spreads: Medicine, Anatomy, and Chemistry

Although astronomy and physics led the way in dramatic scientific findings, researchers in other fields made important discoveries as well. Many of these advances also had roots in the sixteenth century. For example, several scholars developed new ideas in the related fields of medicine, anatomy, and chemistry.

In medicine, a flamboyant Swiss alchemist-physician known as Paracelsus (1493–1541) strongly influenced the healing arts. A believer in Hermetic doctrine, Paracelsus openly opposed medical orthodoxy and taught that healers should look for truth not in libraries ("the more learned, the more perverted," he warned) but in the Book of Nature. "I have not been ashamed to learn from tramps, butchers, and barbers," he boasted. As a teacher and wandering practitioner, he treated patients, experimented with chemicals, recorded his observations, and developed new theories. Paracelsus concluded that all matter was composed of salt, sulfur, and mercury—not the traditional earth, water, fire, and air. Rejecting the standard view that

Paracelsus

an imbalance in the humors of the body caused disease, he instead looked to specific chemical imbalances to explain what caused each illness. He also encouraged research and experimentation to find natural remedies for bodily disorders, such as administering mercury or arsenic at astrologically correct moments. Though rejected by most established physicians, Paracelsus's ideas became particularly popular among common practitioners and would later influence the study of chemistry.

Other researchers founded the modern science of anatomy. In the sixteenth century, Andreas Vesalius (1514–1564), a Fleming living in Italy, wrote the first comprehensive textbook on the structure of the human body based on careful observation (see image below). Vesalius himself dissected cadavers, as suggested by the scalpel resting on the table. His dissections of human bodies brought him into conflict with traditional physicians and scholars. Disgusted, he finally gave up his scientific studies and became the personal physician to Emperor Charles V.

Andreas Vesalius

Despite relentless criticism, other scholars continued anatomical research. A line from a poem written for the opening of the Amsterdam Anatomical Theatre in the early seventeenth century reflects the sense that this research needed special justification: "Evil doers who while living have done damage are of benefit after their death." In other

ANDREAS VESALIUS, FROM *ON THE FABRIC OF THE HUMAN BODY,* 1543 Vesalius looks boldly out at the viewer while displaying one of his studies of human anatomy.

words, the body parts of criminals "afford a lesson to you, the Living." The most important of these researchers was William Harvey (1578–1657), an Englishman who, like Vesalius, studied at the University of Padua in Italy. Harvey dissected hundreds of animals, including dogs, pigs, lobsters, shrimp, and snakes. He discovered that the human heart worked like a pump, with valves that allowed blood to circulate through the body: "The movement of the blood occurs constantly in a circular manner and is the result of the beating of the heart." Yet, despite this mechanistic view, he also considered the heart the physical and spiritual center of life—in his words, "the sovereign of everything."

William Harvey

By the seventeenth century, anatomists and others benefited from several newly invented scientific instruments, such as the microscope. Anton van Leeuwenhoek (1632–1723), a Dutchman, became the chief pioneer in the use of this instrument. In observations during the 1670s, he described seeing "little animals or animalcules" in water from a lake. "It was wonderful to see: and I judge that some of these little creatures were above a thousand times smaller than the smallest ones I have ever yet seen, upon the rind of cheese, in wheaten flour, mould and the like." Leeuwenhoek discovered what would later be identified as bacteria in his own saliva: "little eels or worms, lying all huddled up together and wriggling. . . . This was for me, among all the marvels that I have discovered in nature, the most marvellous of all."

Anton van Leeuwenhoek

Around this same time, Robert Boyle (1627–1691), an Irish nobleman particularly interested in medical chemistry, helped lay the foundations for modern chemistry. Drawing inspiration from Paracelsus, Boyle attacked many assumptions inherited from the ancients and began a systematic search for the basic elements of matter. Relying on the experimental method and using new instruments, he argued that all matter was composed of indestructible atoms that behaved in predictable ways. Boyle also discovered a law—which still bears his name—that governs the pressure of gases. His exacting procedures set a standard for the scientific practice of chemistry.

Robert Boyle

The Methodology of Science Emerges

The scientists who challenged traditional views in their fields also used new methods of discovery—of uncovering how things worked and of determining "truth." Indeed, this innovative methodology lay at the heart of the Scientific Revolution. Earlier techniques for ascertaining the truth—by referring to long-trusted authorities and making deductions from their propositions—became unacceptable to the new scientists. They instead emphasized systematic skepticism, experimentation, and reasoning based solely on observed facts and mathematical laws. The two most important philosophers of this methodology were Francis Bacon and René Descartes.

Francis Bacon (1561–1626), an English politician who was once lord chancellor of England under James I, took a passionate interest in the new science. He rejected reliance on ancient authorities and advocated the collection of data without preconceived notions. From such data, he explained, scientific conclusions could be reached through inductive reasoning—drawing general conclusions from particular concrete observations. "Deriv[ing] axioms from . . . particulars, rising by gradual and unbroken ascent, so that it arrives at the most general axioms of all. This is the true way," he proclaimed. In addition, Bacon argued that scientific knowledge would be useful knowledge: "I am laboring to lay the foundation not of any sect or doctrine, but of human utility and power." He believed that science would benefit commerce and industry and improve the human condition by giving people unprecedented power over their environment. As the image below suggests, Bacon became a noted propagandist for the new science as well as a proponent of the **empirical method.**

Francis Bacon

THE NEW SCIENCE The title page of Francis Bacon's book *New Instrument* (1620) asserts optimistically that science is like a voyage of discovery with almost limitless potential.

Despite his brilliance, Bacon did not have a thorough understanding of mathematics and the role it could play in the new science. His contemporary René Descartes (1596–1650) would be the one to excel in this arena. Born in France, Descartes received training in scholastic philosophy and mathematics at one of France's best Jesuit schools and took a degree in law. He entered military service and served during the Thirty Years' War. During his travels, he met a Dutch mathematician and became interested in the new science. An ecstatic experience in 1619 convinced him to commit to a life of the mind. He spent his most productive years as a mathematician, physicist, and metaphysical philosopher in Holland. In 1637, he published his philosophy and scientific methodology in the *Discourse on Method*—in French, not Latin. The book presented an eloquent defense of skepticism and of abstract **deductive reasoning**—deriving conclusions that logically flowed from a premise. "Inquiries should be directed, not to what others have thought, nor to what we ourselves conjecture, but to what we can clearly and perspicuously behold and with certainty deduce; for knowledge is not won in any other way."

Descartes questioned all forms of authority, no matter how venerable—be it Aristotle or even the Bible. He tried to remove systematically all assumptions about knowledge and advocated doubting the senses, which he claimed could be deceptive. Taken to its logical conclusion, his argument left him with one God-given experiential fact—that he was thinking. "I think, therefore I am" became his starting point. From there he followed a rigorous process of deductive reasoning to draw a variety of conclusions, including the existence of God and the physical world. He argued that there were two kinds of reality: mind, or subjective thinking and experiencing; and body, or objective physical matter. According to this philosophy, known as **Cartesian dualism,** the objective physical universe could be understood in terms of extension (matter occupying space) and motion (matter in motion). "Give me extension and motion," vowed Descartes, "and I will create the universe." He considered the body nothing more than "an earthen machine." In his opinion, only the mind was exempt from mechanical laws.

Descartes emphasized the power of the detached, reasoning individual mind to discover truths about nature. Unlike Bacon, he put his faith in mathematical reasoning, not in empirical investigation. By challenging all established authority, by accepting as truth only what could be known by reason, and by assuming a purely mechanical physical universe, Descartes established a philosophy and methodology that became the core of the new science.

René Descartes

OPINION

How did standards for ascertaining the "truth" differ between the new scientific views of the world and the medieval views?

SUPPORTING AND SPREADING SCIENCE

Only a small group of people actually participated in the **Scientific Revolution.** Of these, a handful of women managed to overcome barriers to take part as patrons for scientists or as scientists themselves. Men ignored or discounted their work, and scientific societies usually excluded them. The few women engaged in science, such as the naturalist Maria Sibylla Merian (see Past Lives, page 290) and the Germany astronomer Maria Winkelmann (1647–1717), had to rely on their own resources or work in collaboration with their husbands.

Few scientific scholars—whether male or female—got far without calling on a network of peers and soliciting the support of wealthy patrons. To spread their ideas, these scientists needed to publish their works, interact with like-minded colleagues, and gain the backing of prestigious elites. Fortunately for them, these elites were eager to comply.

Courts and Salons

Governments and wealthy aristocrats served as benefactors and employers of scientists. Kepler, for example, received help from the imperial court, serving in Bohemia as Rudolf II's official mathematician. Galileo became court mathematician to Cosimo de' Medici in Tuscany. Vesalius served as physician to Holy Roman Emperor Charles V, and Harvey as royal physician in England.

Rulers had their own motives—namely, practicality and prestige—for assisting scholars and scientists. Royals especially hoped that scholarship and scientific inquiry would yield discoveries that would enhance the strength and prosperity of the state. For example, they sought experts in building projects, armaments, mapmaking, navigation, and mining. They also tried to burnish their own reputations as powerful, educated people by patronizing scholarship, science, and the arts. In this way, support of science became a supposed hallmark of good government. Enticed by this assistance, learned people gathered at royal courts, which gradually filled rooms with new tools, machines, exotic plants and animals, and books.

Beyond the court, people formed private salons and local academies where those interested in science could meet. In the 1540s, the first academy for scientific study was established, in Naples. Women ran several important salons where scientists discussed their findings along with literature, art, and politics. Some scientists even found benefactors at these meetings.

The Rise of Royal Societies

During the second half of the seventeenth century, central governments stepped up their support of scientific experimentation, publications, and academies. In 1662, for example, Charles II chartered the Royal Society in England; four years later, Louis XIV's finance minister, Jean-Baptiste Colbert, founded the Académie des Sciences in France. These organizations, and others patterned after them, furnished laboratories, granted subsidies, brought scientists together to exchange ideas, published their findings, and honored scientific achievements. This governmental support of science added to the growing prestige of science and the scientific community.

Religion and the New Science

Religious organizations played a mixed role in the spread of the new science. Traditionally, the Catholic Church supported scholarship and learning in general, including, in natural science. Moreover, religious orders staffed most universities, and many key figures of the Scientific Revolution held university positions. Numerous leading scholars also felt a profound sense of spirituality. Copernicus, for example, who dedicated his work to the pope, was a cleric, as were many other natural scientists. Although we may be tempted to assume that the skepticism inherent in the scientific method would lead to atheism, the great scientists attacked neither faith nor established religion. Nor were they dispassionate investigators holding themselves apart from the spiritual nature of their age. They often believed in magic, ghosts, and witchcraft and typically considered alchemy, astrology, and numerology (predicting events from numbers) valuable components of natural science. Galileo, though he later decried his trial as the triumph of "ignorance, impiety, fraud and deceit," remained a believing Catholic. Even Robert Boyle, who like others came to think of the universe as a machine, attributed its origin to God: "God, indeed, gave

motion to matter . . . and established those rules of motion, and that order amongst things . . . which we call the laws of nature." Newton agreed: "This most beautiful system of the sun, planets, and comets, could only proceed from the counsel and dominion of an intelligent and powerful Being. . . . He endures forever, and is everywhere present."

Nevertheless, the new science did challenge certain tenets of faith and the traditional Christian conception of God's place in the ordering of the world. Neither Protestant nor Catholic leaders welcomed Copernican ideas and the implications of the new science. The Catholic Church, itself ordered in a hierarchy that paralleled the old view of the universe, stayed particularly committed to established authorities. Moreover, the church's condemnation of Galileo in 1633 discouraged scientific investigations throughout much of Catholic Europe. Descartes was not alone in deciding not to publish ideas incorporating Copernican assumptions. As he explained in 1634, "It is not my temperament to set sail against the wind. . . . I want to be able to live in peace . . . out of sight." Although the French government would actively promote science, after the mid-seventeenth century most scientific work and publishing took place in Protestant areas—particularly in England and the Netherlands.

The New Worldview

By the end of the seventeenth century, the accumulation of convincing scientific findings and the support for those findings among the educated elites had broken the Aristotelian-medieval worldview and replaced it with the Copernican-Newtonian paradigm. According to the new view, the earth, along with the planets, moved around the sun in an infinite universe of other similar bodies. The natural order consisted of matter in motion, acting according to mathematically expressible laws. Scientific truths came from observing, measuring, experimenting, and making reasoned conclusions through the use of sophisticated mathematics. Religious truths still had their place, and the orderliness of nature reflected God's design. However, science now claimed precedence in explaining the material world.

The Copernican-Newtonian paradigm

→ connect to today←

"yet farther"

At the beginning of the Scientific Revolution, Marco Coronelli, the accomplished Venetian mapmaker and mathematician, opened the world atlas he published with an illustration of a ship, the earth, and scientific instruments and the provocative phrasing "Yet farther," declaring the end of limits to the search for knowledge. In what ways are our present-day assumptions about the physical universe and the workings of nature based on the ideas and discoveries of the Scientific Revolution?

In the sixteenth and early seventeenth centuries, great thinkers such as Copernicus and Galileo had been ridiculed and persecuted for their ideas. By the late seventeenth and early eighteenth centuries, Isaac Newton's fate revealed the acceptance of the new paradigm among educated elites. Famous and popular, Newton became a member of Parliament, served for many years as director of the Royal Mint, and was knighted by Queen Anne.

LAYING THE FOUNDATIONS FOR THE ENLIGHTENMENT

In the course of the eighteenth century, the ideas of the Scientific Revolution spread widely and were applied in stunning new ways. With this broadening, the eighteenth century witnessed the birth of a major cultural movement known as the **Enlightenment.** At the heart of this movement lay the firm conviction—especially among intellectuals—that human reason should determine understanding of the world and the rules of social life. "[H]ave the courage to use your own intelligence," and leave your "self-caused immaturity," exhorted the German philosopher Immanuel Kant (1724–1804). "All that is required for this enlightenment is freedom, and particularly . . . the freedom for man to make public use of his reason in all matters."

The Enlightenment hit its full stride in the middle decades of the eighteenth century, when it particularly influenced literate elites of Europe and North America. Yet, its roots stretched back to the end of the seventeenth century. At that time, the thinking that would characterize the Enlightenment emerged in the writings of people who popularized science, applied a skeptical attitude toward religious standards of truth, and criticized accepted traditions and authorities.

Science Popularized

Unevenly educated and facing challenging findings, members of scientific societies often struggled to understand one another's work. For the nonscientific public, the problem of communicating new, complex ideas was even worse. Late in the seventeenth century, several talented writers, nonscientists themselves but believing that science had established a new standard of truth, began explaining in clear language the meaning of science to the literate public. For example, the French writer Bernard de Fontenelle (1657–1757) enjoyed a long, brilliant career as a popularizer of science. In *Conversations on the Plurality of Worlds* (1686), he presented the Copernican view of the universe in a series of conversations between an aristocratic woman

SCIENCE, EDUCATION, AND ENLIGHTENMENT,
1759 Surrounded by scientific instruments and objects, a teacher instructs three students. This illustration reveals the growing sense during the Enlightenment that an educated person should be familiar with science.

and her lover under starry skies. The English essayist and publisher Joseph Addison (1672–1719), in the March 12, 1711, issue of his newspaper, *The Spectator*, said that he hoped to bring "philosophy out of closets and libraries, schools and colleges, to dwell in clubs and assemblies, at tea-tables and in coffee-houses." He aimed his daily paper not only at men but at women "of a more elevated life and conversation, that move in an exalted sphere of knowledge and virtue, that join all the beauties of the mind to the ornaments of dress, and inspire a kind of awe and respect, as well as love, in their male beholders." Other writers also targeted women. In 1737, for example, *Newtonianism for Women* was published in Naples and was soon translated into English. Writings such as these helped make science fashionable in elite circles.

In the mid-eighteenth century, this popularization of science merged with another foundation of Enlightenment thinking: the belief that every educated man and woman should be familiar with the nature and methods of science.

Teaching science

Soon scientific ideas were being taught to children of the middle and upper classes. For example, the year 1761 saw the publication of *The Newtonian System of Philosophy, Adapted to the Capacities of Young Gentlemen and Ladies*, a book engagingly advertised as the "Philosophy of Tops and Balls." In it, a fictional boy named Tom Telescope gave lectures on science topics to children while also teaching the virtues of good manners and citizenship. The book proved immensely popular, going through many editions in Britain and in other countries.

Many of these books emphasized Newton—and for understandable reasons. Enlightenment thinkers saw this brilliant Englishman as the great synthesizer of the Scientific Revolution, an astute observer who rightly described the universe as ordered, mechanical, material, and set into motion by God. From Newton, they concluded that reason and nature were compatible: Nature functioned logically and discernibly; therefore, what was natural was also reasonable. Many writers of the day agreed with the spirit of a poem written for Newton by the English author Alexander Pope upon the scientist's death in 1727:

Glorifying Newton: reason and nature

> Nature and Nature's Laws lay hid in Night.
> God said, "Let Newton be," and all was Light.

GIOVANNI BATTISTA PITTORI, *ALLEGORICAL MONUMENT TO ISAAC NEWTON*, 1727–1730 This celebratory painting pays homage to Isaac Newton by glorifying the urn that stores his remains and highlighting his scientific discoveries.

In simple terms, Newton had become a European cultural hero, as the painting below suggests.

Enlightenment thinkers also admired the ideas of Newton's compatriot John Locke (1632–1704), who applied scientific thinking to human psychology. This English philosopher did not hold the mind exempt from the mechanical laws of the material universe. In his *Essay Concerning Human Understanding* (1690), Locke pictured the human brain at birth as a blank sheet of paper that sensory perception and reason filled as a person aged. "Our observation, employed either about external sensible objects or about the internal operations of our minds perceived and reflected on by ourselves, is that which supplies our understanding with all the materials of thinking." Locke's empirical psychology rejected the notion that human beings were born with innate ideas or that revelation was a reliable source of truth. What we become, he argued, depends solely on our experiences—on the information received through the senses. Schools and social institutions should therefore play a major role in molding the individual from childhood to adulthood. These ideas, like those of Newton and the Scientific Revolution, also set the stage for the skeptical questioning of received wisdom.

The psychology of John Locke

Skepticism and Religion

Locke's ideas, along with those of Newton and the Scientific Revolution, set the stage for the questioning of established wisdom that came to define the Enlightenment. Among several writers, skepticism—or doubts about religious dogmas—mounted. Pierre Bayle (1647–1706), a French Huguenot forced to flee to the Dutch Republic because of Louis XIV's religious persecutions, became the leading proponent of skepticism in the late seventeenth century. In his *News from the Republic of Letters* (1684), Bayle bitterly attacked the intolerance of the French monarchy and the Catholic Church. In most of Europe, where religious principles shared by ruler and ruled underlay all political systems, nonconformity was a major challenge. Therefore, the book earned him condemnation in Paris and Rome. Eventually, however, Bayle would have the last word. In 1697 he published the *Historical and Critical Dictionary,* which contained a list of religious views and beliefs that Bayle maintained did not stand up to criticism. Bayle cited human reason and common sense as his standard of criticism: "Any particular dogma, whatever it may be, whether it is advanced on the authority of the Scriptures, or whatever else may be its origins, is to be regarded as false if it clashes with the clear and definite conclusions of the natural understanding." Bayle also argued that "morals and religion, far from being inseparable, are completely independent of each other." For Bayle, a person's moral behavior had little to do with any particular religious doctrine or creed. With these stands, Bayle pushed much harder than Galileo in challenging the

Pierre Bayle

Catholic Church and other religious beliefs. He became recognized as an international authority on religious toleration and skeptical criticism of the Bible.

New information and arguments added weight to Bayle's criticism of biblical authority. For example, geological discoveries suggested that life on Earth had actually begun earlier than biblical accounts claimed. Investigators also began casting doubt on reports of miracles and prophecies. David Hume (1711–1776), a first-rate Scottish philosopher and historian, carried the skeptical argument even further. In *An Essay Concerning Human Understanding* (1748), he insisted that nothing—not even the existence of God or our own existence—could be known for sure. Reality consisted only of human perceptions. To Hume, established religions were based on nothing but hope and fear. Reason demanded that people live with skeptical uncertainty rather than dogmatic faith.

David Hume

Broadening Criticism of Authority and Tradition

Travel writing had a long history, and by the eighteenth century many Enlightenment thinkers had read explanations of China's lucid Confucian traditions as well as accounts of customs and beliefs in Islamic, Buddhist, and Hindu lands. Several writers—among them the Baron de Montesquieu (1689–1755), a wealthy judge in a provincial French court, and the French author Voltaire (1694–1778)—used comparisons of place and time to criticize authority and tradition during the early decades of the eighteenth century. Journeying abroad and writing about their experiences gave such people a new perspective on their home societies. Montesquieu and Voltaire, for their part, chastised European customs in general and French institutions in particular for being contrary to reason and good ethics.

Travel writings of Montesquieu and Voltaire

Both presented the traveler as an objective observer. In his best-selling book *Persian Letters* (1721), Montesquieu bitingly satirized the customs, morals, and practices of Europeans from the point of view of two Persian travelers. Through this comparative perspective, Montesquieu painted the French as lacking in both good morals and effective government. Voltaire, in his widely read *Letters Concerning the English Nation* (1733), similarly criticized French politics and Catholic intolerance. In the island nation, "one thinks freely and nobly without being held back by any servile fear." Like many people, Voltaire idealized England because it allowed greater individual freedom, religious differences, and political reform than most other countries, especially France. England was also enviably prosperous and was the home of Newton and Locke, so admired in France. Many French intellectuals wanted for their own country what the English already seemed to have.

Other writers took a new historical perspective to criticize tradition and trumpet rapid change. For them, the tools of science and reason enabled people to surpass their historical predecessors, even the admired Greeks and Romans of antiquity. History became a story of relentless human progress, and people living in the eighteenth century stood on the brink of unprecedented historical achievements. Some people, such as the American scientist and philosopher Benjamin Franklin (1706–1790), embraced the idea of progress with an almost religious fervor: "The rapid Progress of *true* Science now occasions my regretting sometimes that I was born so soon. It is impossible to imagine the Height to which may be carried . . . the Power of Man over Matter, . . . all diseases may by sure means be prevented, . . . and our lives lengthened at pleasure."

History and progress

THE ENLIGHTENMENT IN FULL STRIDE

Building on the foundations of science, skepticism, and criticism, Western intellectuals systematically investigated the ethical, political, social, and economic implications of science after the 1730s. For them, nature—with its laws, order, simplicity, and rationality—served as a guide for human thought and society. "The source of man's unhappiness is his ignorance of Nature," claimed France's influential Baron d'Holbach (1723–1789). The Marquis de Condorcet argued, "The time will therefore come when the sun will shine only on free men who know no other master but their reason" (see document on page 337). These optimistic intellectuals pushed for reform and change, using critical and empirical reasoning to back up their arguments. Specifically, they urged people to shrug off the shackles of tradition and custom and to participate in the accelerating progress of civilization. The spark of reason would soon dispel ignorance and enlighten all human understanding. Indeed, it was this image that lent the Enlightenment its name.

The *Philosophes*

Although Enlightenment ideas bubbled up throughout Europe and North America, France was the true heart of the movement. There Enlightenment thinkers came to be called *philosophes,* the French term for "philosophers." In a sense, the questions these thinkers grappled with were philosophical: How do we discover truth? How should we live our lives? Yet the *philosophes* were not traditional philosophers. Coming from both noble and middle-class origins, they were intellectuals—though often not formally trained by or associated with a university. They tended to extend, apply, or propagandize others' ideas rather than initiate new concepts themselves. They also wrote more plays, satires, histories, novels, encyclopedia entries, and short pamphlets than formal philosophical treatises. Finally, they considered themselves part of a common intellectual culture, an international "republic of letters" held together by literature, correspondence, and private gatherings. In the eyes of leading *philosophes* such as Jean Le Rond d'Alembert (1717–1783), this republic of letters should "establish the laws of philosophy and taste for the rest of the nation."

The witty, versatile François Arouet, who took the pen name Voltaire (1694–1778), best represented the *philosophes*. The son of a Parisian lawyer, Voltaire received a fine classical education from the Jesuits and soon denounced their religious doctrine. He became the idol of French intellectuals while only in his 20s, and the enemy of many others.

Voltaire

He soon ran afoul of state authorities, who imprisoned him in the Bastille for writing verses that criticized the crown. Released, he became embroiled in a dangerous conflict with a prominent nobleman and again landed in the Bastille. By promising to leave the country, he gained his freedom. In England, he encountered the ideas of Newton and Locke and came to admire English parliamentary government and the nation's religious tolerance. As we saw, he popularized Newton's and Locke's ideas and extolled the virtues of English society in his writings.

Slipping back into France, Voltaire hid for a time under the protection of Émilie du Châtelet (1706– 1749),

Émilie du Châtelet

a wealthy woman who became his lover and match. Châtelet had already shown brilliance as a child. By the age of 12, she could speak four languages and had already translated Greek and Latin texts. Her mother worried that she would not find a mate because she "flaunts her mind, and frightens away the suitors her other excesses have not driven off." In 1733, she insisted on joining a group of male intellectuals who met regularly at a Parisian coffeehouse, donning men's clothes after the management refused to admit her because of her gender. Voltaire lived openly with Châtelet and her husband. In the great hall of their country chateau, she hung rods, pipes, and balls from the ceiling for her experiments in physics. She made her reputation by publishing

Condorcet Lauds the Power of Reason

No one lauded the power of reason and the Enlightenment, or had more hope for the future, than the French mathematician and *philosophe* the Marquis de Condorcet (1743–1794). The following is an excerpt from his *Sketch for a Historical Picture on the Progress of the Human Mind*, which he completed in 1794.

Our hopes for the future condition of the human race can be subsumed under three important heads: the abolition of inequality between nations, the progress of equality within each nation, and the true perfection of mankind. Will all nations one day attain that state of civilization which the most enlightened, the freest and the least burdened by prejudices, such as the French and the Anglo-Americans, have attained already? Will the vast gulf that separates these peoples from the slavery of nations under the rule of monarchs, from the barbarism of African tribes, from the ignorance of savages, little by little disappear? . . .

In answering these three questions we shall find in the experience of the past, in the observation of the progress that the sciences and civilization have already made, in the analysis of the progress of the human mind and of the development of its faculties, the strongest reasons for believing that nature has set no limit to the realization of our hopes.

According to Condorcet, what will open the door to such great progress?

a three-volume work on the German mathematician and philosopher Leibnitz and translating Newton's *Principles of Mathematics*. A *philosophe*, accomplished scientist, and leading proponent of Newtonian thought in her own right, Châtelet helped Voltaire gain a better understanding of the sciences and their significance. When she died in childbirth in 1749, the despondent Voltaire accepted an invitation from King Frederick II of Prussia to join his court. However, they soon argued, and Voltaire returned to France.

Having made both a fortune in financial speculations and a rich network of friends and acquaintances, Voltaire was not without resources. He wrote poetry, drama, history, essays, letters, and scientific treatises—ninety volumes in all. The novel *Candide* (1759) became his best-known work. In this dark satire, Voltaire created the epitome of the "ivory-tower" intellectual, ridiculed the pretensions of the nobility and clergy, and skewered the naïveté of optimists who believed that "this is the best of all possible worlds and all things turn out for the best." He aimed his cynical wit especially at the Catholic Church and Christian institutions. His *Philosophical Dictionary* became the most famous, wide-ranging attack on supernatural religion and churches. Voltaire mounted several campaigns for religious toleration, coming to the defense of individuals attacked by prejudice. In his *Treatise on Tolerance* (1763), he attacked the mentality that led to the torture and murder of a Protestant merchant, Jean Calas, on the false charges of murdering his son for threatening to convert to Catholicism. "Christians ought to tolerate one another. I will go even further and say that we ought to look upon all men as our brothers. What! call a Turk, a Jew, a Siamese, my brother? Yes, of course, for are we not all children of the same father, and the creatures of the same God?" Voltaire was celebrated as a national hero and lionized internationally, and his popularity reveals the widespread acceptance of Enlightenment thought throughout the West by the late eighteenth century.

The *Encyclopedia*

No work better summarizes the philosophy of the Enlightenment than the *Encyclopedia*, a collaborative effort by many *philosophes* under the editorship of Denis Diderot (1713–1774) and Jean Le Rond d'Alembert. In the preface, the editors stated their aim: "to overturn the barriers that reason never erected" and "contribute to the certitude and progress of human knowledge." The *Encyclopedia* embodied the notion that reason alone could be used to discover, understand, or clarify almost anything. This massive work explored the complete spectrum of knowledge, offering articles on subjects ranging from music to machinery interpreted through the lens of the *philosophes'* criticism and empiricism. The authors wrote with supreme self-importance: "I can assure you," said d'Alembert in a 1752 letter, "that while writing this work I had posterity before my eyes at every line."

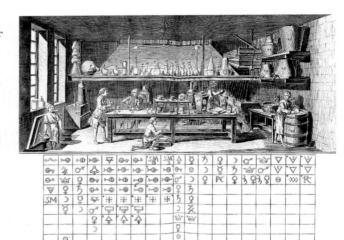

THE *ENCYCLOPEDIA*, 1751 This page from the *Encyclopedia* shows a chemical laboratory and a table with symbols for each chemical substance.

The first volume of the *Encyclopedia* was published in 1751. One of its many illustrations is shown above. Although the study of chemistry and the hundreds of other topics covered in the *Encyclopedia* at first glance may appear innocent enough, they were saturated with the philosophy of the Enlightenment. Church authorities and their governmental allies therefore saw the *Encyclopedia* as a direct threat to the status quo. They censored it, halted its publication, and harassed its editors. Thanks in great part to the persistence of Diderot, who fought the authorities and managed a difficult group of contributing authors, the project was finally completed in 1772.

Battling the Church

Diderot's struggle to publish the *Encyclopedia* was part of a wider conflict between the *philosophes* and the church. Both sides spent much time and effort attacking each other. In countries such as France and Italy, where clerics were strongly entrenched in government, officials censored the writings of the *philosophes* and threatened to imprison or exile them. Governmental censorship was usually more nominal than real. However, Diderot and others trying to publish "offensive" books constantly worried about these threats: "How many times did we awake uncertain if . . . we would be torn from our families, our friends, our fellow citizens." French authors often sent their works to Holland or Switzerland for publication, and private companies then made a business of smuggling the books back into France across Swiss or Dutch borders.

Sometimes the *philosophes'* "crime" was promoting toleration of religious minorities, whether Christian or otherwise. Montesquieu and Voltaire, in France, were among several who attacked discrimination against Jews, for example. These views were particularly controversial because religious tolerance—formal and informal—was not the rule. Most governments maintained a state religion, rooted in law and viewed as the custodian of received views, that discriminated against nonmembers. For example, Denmark barred Catholic priests from entering the country, and the Catholic Inquisition remained active in Spain.

Some *philosophes,* such as the Baron d'Holbach and David Hume, verged on atheism in their attacks on organized religion. "The Christian religion not only was at first

Deism

attended by miracles, but even now cannot be believed by any reasonable person without one," Hume claimed. However, few Enlightenment thinkers pushed matters that far. Most believed in some form of deism—that an impersonal, infinite Divine Being created the universe but did not interfere with the world of human affairs. The prominent author and political philosopher Thomas Paine (1737–1809) stated, "I believe in one God, and no more; and I hope for happiness beyond this life. . . . I do not believe in the creed professed by the Jewish church, by the Roman church, by the Greek church, by the Turkish church, by the Protestant church, nor by any church that I know of. My own mind is my own church." These ideas, like other ideas of the Enlightenment, gained momentum over the course of the eighteenth century. In the long run, the church probably lost more supporters among the upper and middle classes than it gained by so ardently attacking the *philosophes* and their ideas.

Reforming Society

The *philosophes* thought long and hard about reforming society. They wrote and argued about the relationship between the individual and society and reevaluated the

Political thought: Montesquieu and Rousseau

functioning of traditional social institutions. Applying their critical reasoning to fields from government to education, they generated influential ideas for reform.

The most important political thinkers of the Enlightenment—Montesquieu and the Swiss-born writer Jean-Jacques Rousseau (1712–1778)—built on John Locke's work. Locke had pleaded eloquently for the "natural rights"—life, liberty, and property—of human beings. In his *Second Treatise on Civil Government* (1690), Locke had argued that to safeguard these rights, individuals agree to surrender a certain amount of their sovereignty to government. However, the powers of the government, whether it be monarchical or popular, were strictly lim-

OPINION

In what ways did the Enlightenment threaten traditional views and authorities?

ited. No government was allowed to violate the individual's right to life, liberty, and property. If it did, the people who set it up could and should overthrow it—something the English had done in their Glorious Revolution, according to Locke.

An admirer of Locke and the English system of government, the Baron de Montesquieu analyzed political systems from a relativistic perspective. In his widely acclaimed political masterpiece, *The Spirit of the Laws* (1748), Montesquieu argued that political institutions should conform to the climate, customs, beliefs, and economy of a particular country. For instance, limited monarchy is most appropriate for countries of moderate size, like France; and republics for small states, like Venice or ancient Athens. Each form of government had its virtues and vices.

Not only did Montesquieu approve of Locke's doctrine of limited sovereignty, but he specified how it could best be secured—by a separation of powers and a system of checks and balances. The alternative, he warned, was tyranny and an end to liberty: "There would be an end to everything, were the same man or the same body, whether of the nobles or of the people, to exercise those three powers, that of enacting laws, that of executing the public resolutions, and of trying the causes of individuals." This theory, equally applicable to monarchies and to democracies, became Montesquieu's greatest practical contribution to political thought. In North America, framers of the U.S. Constitution incorporated his ideas into their structuring of the United States government, creating separate executive, judicial, and legislative branches of government.

Rousseau offered a more radical political theory than Montesquieu's. In his *Discourse on the Origin of Inequality* (1755), Rousseau argued that people in the "primitive" state of "noble savagery" were free, equal, and relatively happy. Only when some of them began marking off plots of ground, claiming them as their own and thereby founding civil society, did the troubles begin. Private property created inequality and the need for laws and governments to protect people from crime and wars. In *The Social Contract* (1762), Rousseau began by challenging his contemporaries: "Man is born free; and everywhere he is in chains." He then offered a solution to this conflict between individual freedom and social restrictions. In an ideal state, he argued, people entered into a compact with one another, agreeing to surrender their individual liberty, which was driven by self-interest, to the whole society. In return, the individual gained freedom by virtue of being part of the society's "general will," which was driven by the common good. "This means nothing less than that [the individual] will be forced to be free," explained Rousseau. Although Rousseau never made it clear just how the general will operated in practice, he believed that the people themselves—rather than a monarch or a parliamentary body—should make laws. His controversial ideas would powerfully influence the development of democratic theory over the next two centuries. For some people, *The Social Contract* would support participatory democracy, whereas for others, Rousseau's emphasis on conforming to the general will would justify authoritarian political systems.

Then & Now
The Literati

Jean-Jacques Rousseau described himself as a "singular soul, strange, and to say it all, a man of paradoxes." A celebrity both admired and hated in his own time, he wrote more deeply on a wide range of subjects than any of his contemporaries. His *New Heloise* became the most widely read novel of his age, and he is counted among the most important educational theorists in history. Since Rousseau's time, it's become standard for intellectuals to distribute their ideas through their books, magazine articles, and, in recent decades, their appearances on television. But many contemporary intellectuals are still polarizing figures and have achieved similar celebrity status as Rousseau in controversial ways. Author Susan Sontag, for example, starred in one of Andy Warhol's screen-test portraits in 1964, and in 2007 intellectual Cornel West even released a rap album titled *Never Forget: A Journey of Revelations* to share his ideas. It remains to be seen whether or not their body of work will stand the test of time, as has Rousseau's.

Although critical and combative, neither Rousseau, Montesquieu, nor the other *philosophes* were political or social revolutionaries. They did not champion the lower classes, whom they dismissed as ignorant, prone to violence, and, in Voltaire's words, "inaccessible to the progress of reason and over whom fanaticism maintains its atrocious hold." Diderot, of humble parents, admitted that he wrote "only for those with whom I should enjoy conversing . . . the philosophers; so far as I am concerned, there is no one else in the world." Most *philosophes* hoped for painless change from above rather than a revolutionary transfer of power to the still-unenlightened masses. Many shared Voltaire's belief that enlightened absolutism—rule by a well-educated, enlightened monarch—offered the best chance for the enactment of Enlightenment reforms such as religious toleration, rule subject to impartial laws, and freedom of speech (see Chapter 15).

If the functioning of the universe and politics could be described by understandable, rational laws, why should the same not hold true for economic activity? Several Enlightenment thinkers turned their thoughts to this question and attacked mercantilism, the system of regulated national economics that still operated throughout much of Europe. A group of French thinkers known as Physiocrats, led by François Quesnay, personal physician to Louis XV, began to teach that economics had its own set of natural laws. The Physiocrats believed that the most basic of these laws was that of supply and demand, and that these laws operated best under only minimal governmental regulation of private economic activity. This doctrine, which became known as *laissez-faire* (non-

Economic ideas: the Physiocrats and Adam Smith

interference), favored free trade and enterprise. In France, the Physiocrats saw land and agriculture as the main source of national wealth. Other economists would build on their ideas and apply them to different settings.

In 1776, Adam Smith (1723–1790), a Scottish professor of philosophy who associated with the Physiocrats while traveling in France, published *Wealth of Nations*. The book became the bible of laissez-faire economics. By nature, Smith argued, individuals who were allowed to pursue rationally their own economic self-interest would benefit society as well as themselves. Focusing on Britain's economy, Smith emphasized commerce, manufacturing, and labor rather than agriculture as the primary sources of national wealth. Anticipating the industrial age that would first emerge in Britain, he concluded that "the greatest improvement in the productive powers of labor . . . have been the effects of the division of labor." For Smith as well as the Physiocrats, laissez-faire economics held the key to national wealth—whether a nation was built on agriculture or industry.

What Smith and the Physiocrats did for economics, the Italian Cesare Beccaria (1738–1794) did for criminology and penology. Beccaria wrote *On Crimes and Punishments* (1764), an international best-seller, to protest "the cruelty of punishments and the irregularities of criminal procedures, . . . to demolish the accumulated errors of centuries." He argued that criminal laws and punishments, like all other aspects of life, should incorporate reason and natural law. Good laws, he explained, promoted "the greatest happiness divided among the greatest number." Criminal law should strive to deter crime and rehabilitate criminals rather than merely punish wrongdo-

Criminology, penology, and slavery

ers. In Beccaria's view, torture and capital punishment made no sense; indeed, only new penal institutions that mirrored natural law could transform convicted criminals.

Other Enlightenment thinkers used similar arguments to denounce slavery. Abbé Guillaume Raynal (1713–1796), an outspoken and widely read critic of slavery, argued that this institution and many other practices of European and American colonists were irrational and inhumane. In the name of natural rights, he called for a slave rebellion. An article in the authoritative *Encyclopedia* asserted similar views, declaring that all enslaved individuals "have the right to be declared free." These arguments, like the ideas of Beccaria and, in politics, of Montesquieu and Rousseau, would resound again and again through eighteenth-century Western society.

Becoming enlightened required education. Diderot claimed that the *Encyclopedia* was written so "that our children, by becoming more educated, may at the same time become more virtuous and happier." Many Enlightenment thinkers based their ideas on the

Education

psychological ideas of John Locke, which emphasized the power of education to mold the child into the adult. These thinkers often attacked organized religion in particular for controlling education.

Rousseau became the outstanding critic of traditional education. In *Émile*, he argued that teachers should appeal to children's natural interests and goodness rather than impose discipline and punishment. "Hold childhood in reverence," he counseled. "Give nature time to work." He also pushed for less "artificial" schools, maintaining that nature and experience were better guides to independent thinking and practical knowledge—at least for males. "I hate books," he pointed out. "They only teach us to talk about things we know nothing about." By emphasizing practical education, learning by doing, and motivating rather than requiring the child to learn, Rousseau's *Émile* became one of the most influential works on modern education. His ideas on the education of females, however, were not so modern. Like most men of his time (enlightened or not), he believed that girls should be educated to fulfill their traditional domestic roles as wives and mothers.

In theory at least, the Enlightenment emphasis on individualism opened the door to the idea of equality between men and women. Several intellectuals explored this controversial issue. Early in the period, some challenging books on the "woman question" were published by female

The "woman question"

Art Investigation

Léonard Defrance, *At the Shield of Minerva*

1781

In the doorway of an eighteenth-century bookstore in France stand two women, reading books. Just outside are packages of books being delivered from or to Spain, Portugal, Rome, and Naples. In the street, apparently drawn to the bookstore, are people of all classes, from a peasant with his scythe at the left to a cleric in his white robes at the center. The name of the bookstore, "The Shield of Minerva," refers to the Roman goddess of wisdom. In what ways does this painting imply that people of all classes and throughout Europe were being touched by books—and perhaps by Enlightenment ideas?

authors. In one of the best known of these, *A Serious Proposal to the Ladies* (1694), the English writer Mary Astell (1666–1731) argued that women should be educated according to the ideas of the new science—reason and debate—rather than tradition. Later, she explained that men seem to know more than women because "boys have much time and pains, care and cost bestowed on their education, girls have little or none. The former are early initiated in the sciences" and "have all imaginable encouragement" while "the latter are restrained, frowned upon, and beaten." In other writings, she questioned the inequality of men's and women's roles: "If all Men are born Free, how is it that all Women are born Slaves?" Later in the eighteenth century, the British author Mary Wollstonecraft (1759–1797) published *Vindication of the Rights of Women* (1792), in which she analyzed the condition of women and argued forcefully for equal rights for all human beings. Like Astell, Wollstonecraft stressed the need to educate women: "If she be not prepared by education to become the companion of man, she will stop the progress of knowledge and virtue; for truth must be common to all, or it will be inefficacious with respect to its influence on general practice."

Few male writers went that far. Although some men supported better education for women, most held the traditional view that women were weaker than men and best suited for domestic rather than public affairs. According to Immanuel Kant, who spoke so optimistically and eloquently about education and enlightenment, "laborious learning or painful pondering, even if a woman should greatly succeed in it, destroy the merits that are proper to her sex." The editors of the *Encyclopedia* also ignored contributions from women, instead praising those who remained at home. Some of Rousseau's writings were particularly influential among women, primarily because they glorified child rearing, maternalism, and emotional life. Rousseau

never suggested that women were independent beings equal to men. For him, "Woman is made to please and to be subjugated to man."

The Culture and Spread of the Enlightenment

The Enlightenment glittered especially in Paris, and salon meetings became the chief social setting for this intellectual culture. These meetings were hosted by wealthy Parisian patrons, usually women of the aristocracy or upper-middle class. In an environment lush with art, music, and wealth, the *philosophes*, powerful nobles, diplomats, statesmen, artists, and well-educated conversationalists gathered

Salon meetings

regularly to read, listen to, and debate the ideas of the Enlightenment. They also discussed—and sometimes influenced—economic policies, wars, and the king's choice of ministers. The German critic Friedrich Grimm (1723–1807), who published a private newsletter on Parisian life, described the salons of Julie de Lespinasse, who lived openly with the *philosophe* d'Alembert: "Her circle met daily from five o'clock until nine in the evening. There we were sure to find choice men of all orders in the State, the Church, the Court—military men, foreigners, and the most distinguished men of letters. Politics, religion, philosophy, anecdotes, news, nothing was excluded from the conversation." These salon meetings became self-conscious forums for arbitrating and molding public opinion through the open use of reason.

As leaders, patrons, and intellectual contributors to these gatherings, women played a particularly important role in the Enlightenment. Independent, witty, powerful women governed the potentially unruly meetings and discussions

timeline

• Copernicus 1543

• Galileo 1630

• Descartes 1640

• Kepler 1609

Scientific Revolution 1543–1687

1550   1600   1650

by enforcing rules of polite conversation. One of the most famous of these patrons was Madame Marie-Thérèse Geoffrin (1699–1777), a rich middle-class widow who served as a model and mentor for other women leaders of salons.

Smaller meetings in other French and foreign cities, from Berlin to Philadelphia, paralleled the Parisian salon meetings. Moreover, all these meetings went hand in hand with an extensive international correspondence carried out by participants. For some, letter writing, like good conversation in the salons, was an art. People also read and discussed Enlightenment ideas in local academies, Freemason lodges, societies, libraries, and coffeehouses. In addition, most municipalities had clubs where the social and intellectual elites could mingle.

Even bookstores, where people could purchase books or pay small fees to read recent works, became hotbeds of Enlightenment ideas. The image on page 341 shows an eighteenth-century bookstore. In a growing number of bookstores such as this, all sorts of works became increasingly available, from religious tracts and chivalric tales to new novels and Enlightenment literature.

Bookstores

These gatherings and interchanges spread the ideas of the Enlightenment throughout society and enhanced the social respectability of intellectuals. They also helped create a common intellectual culture that crossed class lines and political borders and that contributed to an informed body of public opinion. People who participated in these interchanges came to sense that they could freely express ideas as well as debate political and social issues. By the last quarter of the eighteenth century, Enlightenment ideas could be heard even in the camps of the *philosophes'* traditional opponents—the clergy, governmental officials, and monarchs. As we will see, these ideas pushed some monarchs to enact "enlightened" reforms and encouraged many other people to demand revolutionary change.

SUMMARY

Brimming with new scientific ideas and discoveries, Western civilization relinquished its medieval assumptions and embarked on an innovative journey unique among the cultures of the world.

- During the fifteenth and sixteenth centuries, scholars began questioning the standard medieval understanding of the physical nature of the earth and the universe.

- By the end of the seventeenth century, the Copernican-Newtonian paradigm had replaced the Aristotelian-medieval worldview. Science now claimed precedence in explaining nature and the earth's place in the universe.

- Scientific scholars spread their ideas with the support of courts, salons, and royal societies.

- Enlightenment thinkers carried these daring aspirations further, self-consciously leading a mission of reform and freedom from the shackles of tradition.

- At the heart of the cultural movement known as the Enlightenment was a conviction that human reason and the guide of nature should determine understanding of the world and the rules of social life.

The *philosophes* clearly left a mark on Western culture. As their primary legacy, they widened the gap between religiously influenced doctrines and accepted scholarly thought. Equally significant, they set the intellectual stage for a series of revolutions that would soon sweep America and Europe. Above all, their way of thinking—stressing reason, individualism, and progress—would form the intellectual foundation of modern Western society and further distinguish this civilization from its non-Western counterparts.

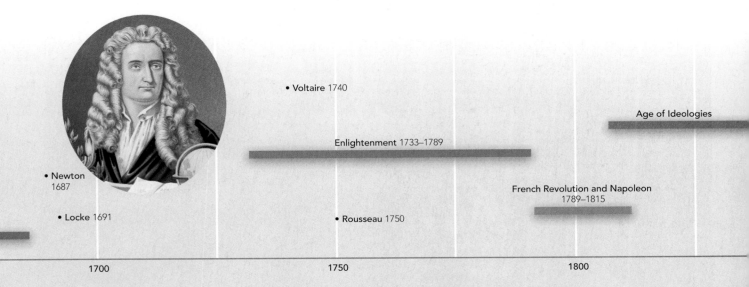

- Newton 1687
- Locke 1691
- Voltaire 1740
- Rousseau 1750

Enlightenment 1733–1789

Age of Ideologies

French Revolution and Napoleon 1789–1815

1700   1750   1800

PHILIP VAN DIJK, *BRISTOL DOCKS AND QUAY,* ca. 1780 This painting shows the British port of Bristol, one of many European port cities that benefited from the lucrative overseas trade that grew during the eighteenth century. On the left, ships arrive and dock on the well-protected canal, where they are loaded and unloaded. On the quay are workers, merchants, and families—some of the many who directly benefited from the activity. Around them are well-kept shops, homes, and buildings that reflect the prosperity of this commercial center and the wealth drawn from Britain's colonial empire.

Competing for
Power
and Wealth

The Old Regime, 1715–1789

15

A King Warns About War

In August 1715, the old and sad Louis XIV fell ill. His legs swelled and turned black as gangrene set in. Remarkably, he had outlived both his son and grandson. On his deathbed, Louis warned his 5-year-old great-grandson, who would succeed him as Louis XV (r. 1715–1774), not to "imitate my love of building nor my liking of war." ▶▶

Neither Louis XV nor many other rulers of the time managed to follow this advice for long. War and building might cost lives and drain royal treasuries, but they made a spectacular show of power in a competitive world. The rulers of Europe clung to their statebuilding ways, straining to secure their central governments and ensure their own position at the top.

During the seventeenth century, this competitiveness had plunged Europe into a series of bloody conflicts—the very battles Louis XIV regretted on his deathbed (see Chapter 13). In western Europe, the violence stopped with the Peace of Utrecht in 1713–1714. Seven years later, the Treaty of Nystad (1721) ended the conflicts in eastern Europe (see map on page 347). For a while, the two treaties held. Monarchs throughout Europe tried to adhere to the principle of a **balance of power** to prevent any one state or alliance from dominating the others. Nevertheless, anyone hoping for an extended period free of war would be sorely disappointed. Up-and-coming states such as Prussia and Britain bristled with ambition and vied with their established competitors for power, prestige, and wealth. Their struggles spread beyond the borders of Europe to overseas colonies on continents from North America to Asia, in this sense turning European wars into global conflicts. As we will see, this competition subjected millions of people to a fresh round of hardship and irrevocably altered the fate and fortunes of nations throughout the West. ◄◄

STATEBUILDING AND RISING AMBITIONS

Within Europe, the fiercest competition took place in eastern Europe. There, Russia and Brandenburg-Prussia were on the rise. Under Peter the Great, Russia had already defeated Sweden, grabbing much of the northeastern Baltic coast in the process. Russia next hoped to take advantage of the sprawling but weak Polish state farther west (see Chapter 13) and to benefit from the decline of the Ottoman Empire, which controlled the Black Sea to Russia's south. Brandenburg-Prussia also saw opportunities in Poland, which divided and bordered its lands. This militaristic state also coveted some of the holdings of the bloated Austro-Hungarian Empire to the south, which in turn intended to hold its own in the power struggle. Someone would have to pay the price for all these ambitions.

Peter the Great had done much to turn Russia toward the West and make it a great power. By the time of his death in 1725, he had modernized Russia's government and military, established Russia as the dominant power in northeastern Europe, and pressured the Russian nobility into the state bureaucracy and army officer corps. In the process, he made many enemies, from the peasants who paid dearly for Peter's accomplishments to all those who had a stake in the very social, cultural, and religious traditions that Peter attacked. His successors would have to face these enemies and shoulder the task of sustaining Russia's expansion to the south and west.

Six mediocre rulers followed Peter—including an infant, a boy of 12, and a mentally unstable tsar. Despite this shaky leadership, Russia held its ground. From 1725 to 1762, its population increased, and the landowning elite grew wealthier than ever. The nobility took back some of the authority it had lost to Peter, diminishing the service it owed to the state; in 1762, nobles freed themselves of all such obligations. Nevertheless, they still staffed the bureaucracy and military officer corps. Moreover, nobles cracked down even more on their serfs, reducing their status to that of mere property. The 1767 Decree on Serfs made the situation crystal clear: "Serfs and peasants . . . owe their landlords proper submission and absolute obedience in all matters."

New leadership in expanding Russia

The decades of weak leadership ended when a dynamic new leader ascended the Russian throne. Catherine the Great (r. 1762–1796) grew up an obscure princess from one of the little German states. For political reasons, her family married her to young Peter III (r. 1762), the tyrannical and intellectually limited grandson of Peter the Great and heir to the Russian crown. He soon rejected her in all ways, and after he became tsar, he quickly lost most of his supporters as well. Catherine had no intention of languishing in obscurity. "I did not care about Peter," she later wrote, "but I did care about the crown." Less than a year after he took the throne, Catherine conspired with a group of aristocratic army officers, who assassinated him and declared Catherine tsarina of Russia.

Catherine the Great

> "I did not care about Peter," she later wrote, "but I did care about the crown."

The new empress used her striking intelligence, charm, and political talent to assert her own power and expand Russian territory and might. Well educated, she thought of herself as attuned to Enlightenment ideas. She often corresponded with French *philosophes* such as Denis Diderot,

French Bourbon Lands	Prussian Lands
Spanish Bourbon Lands	Great Britain
Austrian Habsburg Lands	Boundary of the Holy Roman Empire

Europe, 1721 This map shows Europe after the Treaties of Utrecht (1714) and Nystad (1721). **Identify the lands controlled by Austria. Why might this power's holdings have been vulnerable?**

who spent some time at St. Petersburg as her guest. In 1766, she congratulated Voltaire for triumphing "against the enemies of mankind: superstition, fanaticism, ignorance, quibbling, evil judges, and the power that rests in their hands." Voltaire returned the favor with constant praise for Catherine. She relaxed the traditionally tight constraints on the press in Russia and she confiscated church lands—policies that seemed in line with Enlightenment thinking. Her educational reforms, by which she established new local schools, teachers' colleges, and schools for girls, also suggested a forward-thinking monarch. Most stunningly, Catherine convened a legislative commission, half of whose members were commoners (some even peasants), to reform Russia's legal code. She wrote the *Instruction* (1767) to that commission herself, relying on the works of key Enlightenment figures such as Montesquieu and Beccaria. Her

Instruction called for equality before the law, the abolition of torture, and other liberal reforms.

These programs promised more than they delivered. The commission members squabbled among themselves, and in the end, the effort yielded only minor reforms before it was finally abandoned. Catherine's early talk of easing the burdens on the peasantry also came to little; in return for the support of noble landowners, she allowed them to subjugate the peasants even further. As the document on page 348 suggests, some observers criticized the treatment of Russia's serfs.

In 1768, Catherine provoked a war against the Ottoman Empire. The event seems to have signaled her turn away from enlightened reform and toward power politics. A massive insurrection by Russian serfs in 1773 under the leadership of a Don Cossack, Yemelyan Pugachev (1726–1775),

Landlords and Serfs in Russia

During the eighteenth century, Russian serfs probably fared worse than peasants elsewhere in Europe. Toward the end of the century, Alexander Radischev published a description of Russian serfs and their treatment by noble landowners. For this daring act, the author was imprisoned by Catherine II.

A certain man left the capital, acquired a small village of one or two hundred souls [i.e., serfs], and determined to make his living by agriculture. . . . To this end he thought it the surest method to make his peasants resemble tools that have neither will nor impulse; and to a certain extent he actually made them like the soldiers of the present time who are commanded in a mass, who move to battle in a mass, and who count for nothing when acting singly. To attain this end he took away from his peasants the small allotment of plough land and the hay meadows which noblemen usually give them for their bare maintenance, as a recompense for all the forced labor which they demand from them. In a word, this nobleman forced all his peasants and their wives and children to work every day of the year for him.

In what ways does the landowner described in this excerpt treat his serfs?

further soured her on reform. Pugachev claimed to be Catherine's murdered husband, a "redeemer tsar," and promised his followers land and freedom. Thousands of serfs in southwestern Russia turned against their masters—slaughtering hundreds of landlords and officials—and demanded an end to their plight. Catherine's army managed to put down the rebellion, but only with great difficulty. When some disgruntled followers betrayed Pugachev, the army captured him and tortured him to death.

Catherine proved more successful in her ambitious foreign policy. She defeated the Turks in 1774, extending Russia to the Black Sea and the Balkan Peninsula. She then turned on Poland. At the beginning of the eighteenth century, Poland was the third-largest country in Europe.

The partition of Poland

Yet, as we saw in Chapter 13, it lacked natural boundaries and a strong central government. Weak and without allies, it became a power vacuum that proved all too tempting to its ambitious neighbors. In 1772, Russia, Prussia, and Austria—having plotted Poland's demise among themselves—annexed slices of Polish territory. This aggression at long last stirred the Polish government to action. The Diet passed sweeping reforms, improved the lot of commoners, and gave the central government power to act effectively. These changes came too late. Poland still could not match the combined armies of its enemies, and in 1795, the three aggressors divided the remainder of the hapless nation among themselves. When Catherine died in 1796 after thirty-five years of rule, Russia had grown to an ominous size and had taken its place as a major power in world affairs.

Farther south, military defeats at the hands of the Russians marked the Ottoman Empire's continuing decline. Throughout the eighteenth century, the Ottoman economy suffered from falling population growth and a rising inability to compete commer-

The decline of the Ottoman Empire

cially with Europeans. The English, French, and Venetians took over the trade from the East that used to pass through Ottoman hands. Sultans lost administrative authority to the Muslim clergy. Fearing cultural influences from western Europe, this conservative clergy hindered efforts to introduce European science and even printing presses into Ottoman lands for most of the eighteenth century. Unable to maintain their own armaments industry, moreover, the Ottomans had to rely on European suppliers to outfit the empire's army and navy. At the same time, the Ottomans faced uprisings in their Arabian provinces, where a religious reform movement, **Wahhabism,** challenged the sultans' authority. After mid-century, for good reason, many European elites began calling the Ottoman Empire the "sick man of Europe."

In east-central Europe, the small but rising Brandenburg-Prussia set its sights on the Austrian Empire, a large power struggling to maintain control over its far-flung lands. From 1713 to 1740, the vigorous Frederick William I ruled Prussia. The king was obsessed

Forging a military state in Prussia

with unquestioned absolutism, centralized bureaucratic administration, and, above all, the military. His martial uniforms and preoccupation with Prussian soldiery earned him the label the Sergeant King.

Frederick William's mental image of the perfect military dominated his policies and Prussian society. While he employed his army for road and canal building as well as traditional military service, some 70 percent of the state's budget went to the armed forces, whose size he more than doubled during his reign. Rather than relying on mercenaries, the king required all men to register for military service in local units commanded by German noble officers. The localities, in turn, had to recruit and support these regiments, and soldiers were billeted among the civilian population.

No other state in Europe could boast such a high proportion of men, from peasant to noble, in the military. Nor could any other state point to such a regimented society. In Prussia, the higher ranks of the military and state bureaucracy were reserved for the nobility; the middle classes were clearly prevented from rising to noble status; and the peasantry was a subordinate, overburdened people, often still serfs living in almost slave-like relationships to their landowning masters.

Despite the martial tenor of life in Prussia, the king left a surprisingly progressive legacy. Frederick William I avoided wars, promoted a strong economy, welcomed Protestant and Jewish refugees, and filled the treasury. In 1740, he passed all that he had built, intact, on to his talented son Frederick II (r. 1740–1786), later known as Frederick the Great. The new king soon used this army—the fourth largest in Europe—and the money his father had accumulated to make a bold bid for Austrian lands.

In the same year that Frederick II ascended the throne in Prussia, Maria Theresa (r. 1740–1780) became empress of the Austrian Habsburg dominions. Austria was not a tightly

Austria tries to hold on

controlled, militaristic state like Prussia. Rather, it had already lost most of the indirect control it once held over the central German states as head of the Holy Roman Empire. Austria's own lands contained a complex array of language groups and consisted of some semi-autonomous territories. Austria could barely control Hungary, and its nobility fully dominated its serfs, who paid most taxes directly to their lords rather than to the crown. As a result, Maria Theresa could afford only a relatively small army.

The empress's father had feared that these weaknesses might prove Austria's undoing when he died. More-

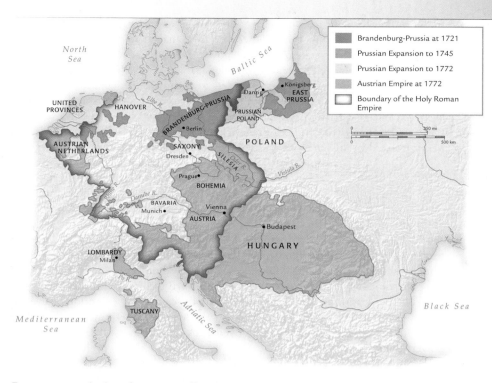

Prussia and the Austrian Empire, 1721–1772 This map shows two growing eighteenth-century powers, Prussia and Austria.

over, there was only weak precedent for a female ruler of Habsburg lands. Therefore, he spent the final twenty years of his life securing agreement among all the European powers (embodied in a document called the Pragmatic Sanction) that his daughter would succeed him without question. In spite of his diligence, when he died in 1740, competitors arose to challenge her authority. As for the principle of balance of power among states implying a desire for peace, Frederick II of Prussia dismissed the idea bluntly: "The fundamental rule of governments is the principle of extending their territories."

As soon as Maria Theresa took the crown, Frederick challenged her authority, a common occurrence when a succession was questionable in any way. Acting on his maxim that "the safety and greater good for the state demands that treaties should

The mid-century land wars

be broken under certain circumstances," the Prussian king marched his troops into Silesia (see map above), the richest of the Habsburg provinces. He also shrewdly forged alliances with other German states against Austria. His aggressive scheming plunged most of the major European states into a series of wars for the mastery of central Europe.

The War of the Austrian Succession dragged on for eight years (1740–1748). Maria Theresa rallied Hungarian arms to her defense and repelled Prussia's allies—Bavarians, Saxons, French, and Spanish. The conflict eventually turned into a military stalemate, which led to a 1748 peace treaty that ended the hostilities. Maria Theresa had managed to preserve the Habsburg state as a major power, but she had been unable to dislodge Frederick from Silesia.

Neither she nor her advisors intended to tolerate this robbery of their fair province by the upstart Prussians—even if it meant starting negotiations for an alliance with their traditional rival, France. Frederick grew fearful of being isolated by his enemies and left vulnerable to invasions. In 1756, when he signed an alliance with Great Britain—Prussia's opponent only a few years earlier—Maria Theresa solidified a new alliance with France. This astounding shift of alliances—the so-called Diplomatic Revolution—suddenly transformed former enemies into friends. Meanwhile, Maria Theresa shored up Austria's internal resources by honing her government's control over taxation, diminishing burdens on the peasantry, and reorganizing the bureaucracy. All this strengthened her position as a ruler who could command strong forces and who enjoyed backing from a powerful ally.

The Diplomatic Revolution

Not one to wait for his enemies to strike first, Frederick reopened hostilities by overrunning Saxony in 1756, initiating the Seven Years' War (1756–1763). However, Frederick soon found himself at bay as France and Austria—now joined by Russia and Sweden, both of which hoped to gain lands at Prussia's expense—closed in on him from all directions. His only backing came from Britain, which saw an opportunity to weaken its longtime opponent, France. After holding off his enemies for six years, the exhausted Prussian king finally seemed near defeat. "I believe all is lost," he confessed in private. Then in 1762 his luck revived. The Russian tsarina Elizabeth, one of his most reviled enemies, died. Her successor, the weak Peter III, happened to admire Frederick and suddenly pulled Russia out of the war. The remaining allies soon lost stomach for the fight. The peace in 1763 left matters much as they had been before the war began, but as we will see (pages 356–357), the fighting in Europe spread to India, the Caribbean, and North America.

Having narrowly escaped destruction, Frederick spent the remaining twenty-three years of his life reconstructing his war-ravaged territories. He encouraged agriculture, subsidized and protected industry, and invited immigrants into his well-governed territories. At no time, though, did he neglect his army or lose his sense of practicality. Indeed, in 1772 he joined Austria and Russia in the first partition of Poland. The map on page 349 shows Prussia's expansion under Frederick, first at the expense of the Austrian Empire when he took Silesia, and then at the expense of Poland as he used the territory to unify the main portions of his country. The map also shows Prussia's chief competitor, Austria, with its farther-flung territories. By the time of his death in 1786, Frederick had raised Prussia to the status of a great power and shared the leadership of central Europe with Austria.

Warfare in the Eighteenth Century

The nature of wars fought by these eighteenth-century nations had evolved and changed from earlier times. Now armies consisted primarily of professional forces whose size and elaborate organization mirrored the centralized, bureaucratic governments they served. Officers were paid as full-time servants of the state in both peace and war. However, the troops they commanded were not all so professional. Conscripts, volunteers, mercenaries, and even criminals made up their rank and file. In this sense, armies served as a depository for men without means and for those seen as threats to the social order. Officers tried to tame these motley groups by stressing harsh discipline and incessant drilling.

Weapons and tactics were also changing. Reliable muskets; bayonets that no longer hindered fire; mobile cannons; and skilled coordination of troops, artillery, and cavalry all made warfare potentially more destructive than ever. Still, generals typically avoided all-out battles, preferring to expend their resources judiciously. "I do not favor pitched battles, especially at the beginning of a war," said Marshall Saxe, a leading French officer and writer on war tactics, in 1732. "I am convinced that a skillful general could make war all his life without being forced into one." Instead of embarking on grand, decisive battles, then, eighteenth-century generals focused on building fortifications, initiating and maintaining sieges, securing supply lines, gaining superior positions, and piling up small advantages. Moreover, most military campaigns lasted only four or five months a year. Meanwhile, life outside the military—commerce, farming, culture, travel, and politics—went on as usual.

Yet, as Frederick the Great recognized, "war is [ultimately] decided only by battles and is not finished except by them." Outright fighting, when it finally occurred, took a heavy toll in human lives. Typically, soldiers arranged themselves in dense rows at least three men deep and fired their muskets, row by row, on command. Each side hurled artillery fire into the opposing troops and sent the cavalry charging in. Casualties mounted, but at the end of the day generals usually pulled their forces back from the battle with enough survivors to fight again.

Maritime battles cost fewer lives than land wars but could be crucial in the overall outcome of war. The largest ships of war in the eighteenth century carried up to one hundred cannons. Often firing at each other at point-blank range, many warships were destroyed or suffered grievous damage in these brutal clashes, and thousands of sailors perished.

A single battle, whether on land or sea, rarely led to a definitive outcome. More likely, the relentless draining away of money and men prompted diplomats to come to the bargaining table and end the war. This hemorrhaging of money and men was not missed by critics of the military, especially Enlightenment thinkers, who denigrated

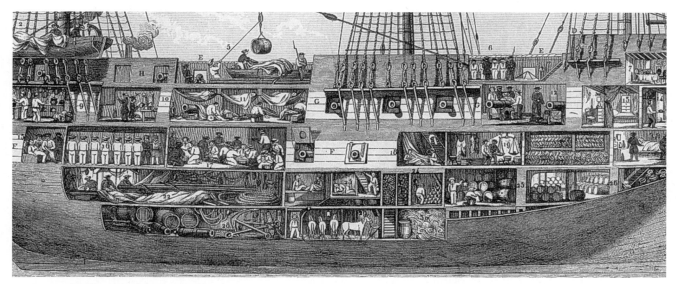

AN EIGHTEENTH-CENTURY FRENCH WARSHIP This view of a French warship shows some of the weapons, men, animals, stores, and equipment carried by this powerful vessel of war.

the old warrior culture as irrational and wasteful. Their criticisms, however, could neither prevent nor end wars in a society in which most people still regarded war as a normal—perhaps necessary—part of life.

Western Europe and the Great Colonial Rivalry

Like eastern Europe, western Europe experienced its own brand of statebuilding and rivalry for power. In this region as well as overseas, France and Britain uneasily shared dominance. Their seventeenth-century rivals, Spain and Holland, were declining. On the Continent, Spain—lacking the finances, manpower, and royal leadership that made it such a power in the late sixteenth and early seventeenth centuries—could no longer threaten France. Holland—damaged by three Anglo-Dutch wars and economic warfare with Britain during the seventeenth century—had gradually lost much of its trade and international position. Overseas, however, Spain and Portugal had managed to hold on to most of their lands. In the Americas, they remained great colonial powers, controlling most of the territory stretching from Mexico to the South American continent. There, they dominated the Amerindians, disrupting their cultures and turning them into laborers on large plantations and in mines, which still produced massive loads of gold and silver for shipment to Europe. Holland also had retained its Pacific colonies, which supported a valuable coffee and spice trade. However, the Dutch had lost some of their empire in Asia and much of their sea power to the British. With Spain and Holland thus occupied, France and Britain became the primary colonial rivals (see map on page 352).

Louis XIV had made France a model of absolutism. However, the French monarchy never again achieved the clout it had enjoyed under his guidance. To be sure, France remained a first-rank power with a large army, a centralized bureaucracy, and a growing economy. Yet, even during the last decades of his reign, Louis XIV's stature diminished. Thoughtful people criticized him for dragging France into what they saw as meaningless foreign conflicts. Louis' expensive wars and unreformed taxation policies also depleted the treasury. As Voltaire reported in 1751, "In the minds of the majority of his subjects, he lost during the last three years of his life all the prestige of the great and memorable things he had accomplished."

> **The French monarchy in decline**

After Louis' death in 1715, French nobles in governmental councils and France's *parlements*—the thirteen judicial courts that had to sign royal decrees before those documents could become law—angled for a restoration of the powers they had lost to the king. The *parlements* claimed to speak for the nation, though in fact they voiced only the interests of the elites. The nobles bargained with the crown, sometimes to the point of open defiance. They faced a stubborn opponent. The young Louis XV, who had ascended the throne at the age of 5, would rule for almost sixty years. Like Louis XIV, he asserted that "sovereign power resides in my person only . . . my courts [*parlements*] derive their existence and their authority from me alone . . . to me alone belongs legislative power without subordination and undivided."

Despite his longevity and support from some able ministers, Louis XV governed far less effectively than his predecessor had. Ignoring administrative matters, he allowed his royal bureaucracy to weaken. As resistance from the *parlements* ate away at the king's authority, France's fiscal pressures from old debts and continued military expenditures

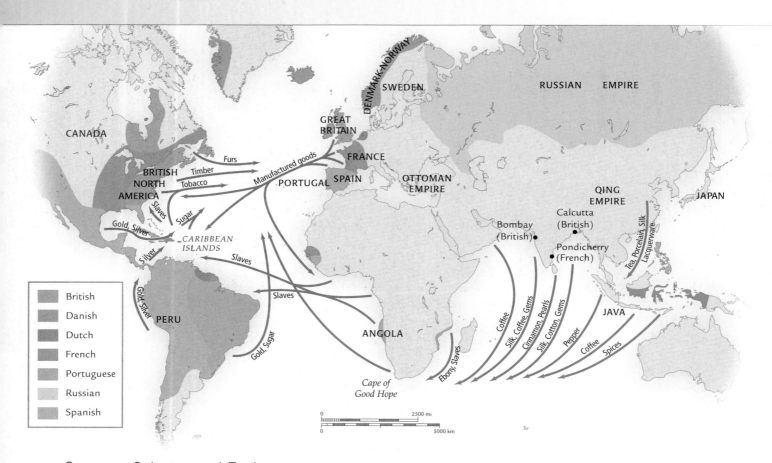

Overseas Colonies and Trade, 1740 This map shows Europe's colonies and overseas trade patterns during the mid-eighteenth century.

grew. The rising tensions centered on the issue of taxes. Specifically, the crown wanted to tap France's wealth by raising taxes, but the nobility sidestepped this move by using the *parlements* to protect their tax exemptions. Moreover, private tax farmers still controlled the collection of taxes, keeping one-third for themselves. Clearly, the monarchy was missing out on large sources of revenue.

Nothing drained money from the treasury more than wars. By avoiding major wars until 1740, the crown achieved relative financial stability. Thereafter the story changed, as France was drawn into a series of costly conflicts with Continental and colonial rivals. Struggling to fund these endeavors and lacking the appropriate financial institutions and taxable resources, France staggered under a relentlessly expanding debt.

In the 1770s, the king and his chancellor finally dissolved the *parlements* and tried to enact an ambitious program of reform. The move came too late. The inept Louis XV had never projected the image of a dynamic, reforming, enlightened monarch. On the contrary, he had a reputation for living lavishly within his opulent court. Underground pamphlets accused him of allowing his mistress and his sexual taste for girls to distract him from attending properly to courtly matters and the demanding business of

managing the state. By the end of his reign, he had earned the dislike and even hatred of his subjects. Louis XV's death in 1774 was met with conspicuous silence, and his tardy reform program evaporated.

Hoping to gain popularity, Louis' successor, Louis XVI (r. 1774–1792), quickly restored the *parlements* and their powers. Again, these aristocratic bodies thwarted new plans for financial reform—even those offered by talented ministers. In France, unlike in most other European powers, the crown and the nobility failed to find a satisfactory way of working together. Again and again, reform efforts faltered, annoying those hoping for change. As frustrations intensified, the crown became increasingly isolated from traditional sources of support within the country.

France needed all the strength it could muster to compete for colonies and stature with Great Britain, where a much different situation had evolved. In 1714, a year before Louis XIV's death, Queen Anne had died. The crown passed to George I (r. 1714–1727), the first of the German Hanoverian line. The British monarchy had already sustained damage from the civil war and revolution of the seventeenth century (see Chapter 13). Though the king remained the chief executive of the state,

Making the British system work

In 1716, the French government supported John Law's private bank with the power to produce its own notes as legal tender and to monopolize overseas commerce. Within just a few years, however, overspeculation in his Mississippi Company—the "Mississippi Bubble"—brought the bank to ruin. At almost the same time, an overseas trading company in Great Britain created its own "South Sea Bubble" and collapsed. Over the next two centuries, various countries would experience other financial bubbles and collapses, such as the real estate bubble that burst in 2008 and created a financial crisis that spread painfully throughout the West. Countries including Iceland, Greece, and the United States were especially hard hit.

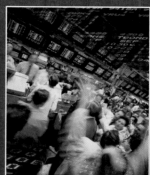

ordained by God and tradition, Parliament now had the upper hand. Divided into the House of Lords (for nobles only) and House of Commons (elected representatives of commoners), Parliament controlled critical functions such as taxation, lawmaking, and the process for bringing grievances to the monarchy. Clearly, king and Parliament had to find a way to work together rather than in opposition.

The answer came in the form of a new institution: the cabinet system. Under this structure, the king chose members of Parliament, usually from the House of Commons, to serve as his ministers. If he hoped to enact policies, he had to select ministers who could command plenty of votes. These men tended to be the leaders of the major groups, or parties, in the House of Commons. By the eighteenth century, two groups dominated the House. Whigs, favoring commercial interests and a strong Parliament, remained staunchly opposed to any return of the Catholic Stuarts to the crown. Whigs also championed popular rights more than the conservative Tories did. Tories usually favored large landowners and a strong monarchy and had stood less firmly against the Stuarts than the Whigs had.

By the middle of the eighteenth century, a pattern had emerged. A group of ministers—themselves led by a prime minister, chosen from Parliament, who could command enough votes in the House of Commons to pass legislation—served the monarch and remained responsible to Parliament. Unlike in France, where most political debate took place outside the government, in Britain, debate occurred within Parliament between the party in power and the "loyal opposition." People thus perceived the nation as being governed by the rule of law rather than the whim of a monarch. This system often moved slowly, but it worked.

Although Britain's government may have been more representative than France's, it was far from democratic. Only some 200,000—most of them the wealthiest males—could vote (see image below). Rich landowners and powerful local elites staffed the government. Not surprisingly, Parliament listened most carefully to representatives of the 400 families whose massive estates included one-fourth of Britain's arable land. British officials did not seek to exempt themselves from taxation, as did most of their counterparts in France, but instead ruled along with the crown by controlling Parliament.

WILLIAM HOGARTH, *CANVASSING FOR VOTES—THE ELECTION*, 1754 This satirical scene of what went on during an election campaign shows an irresponsible candidate and his supporters in front of a tavern bribing people for their votes.

Prosperity formed the foundation of Britain's strong position in these years. The middle class in particular agreed with the popular British author and observer Daniel Defoe that "the greatness of the British nation is not owing to war and conquests . . . it is all owing to trade, to the increase of our commerce at home, and the extending it abroad." Goods poured into Britain from India and North America. The nation transformed itself into an agricultural exporter and a flourishing manufacturing center. By the middle of the eighteenth century, Great Britain had become Europe's leading economic power. It pursued its interest in European affairs through diplomacy, alliances, and the subsidizing of its allies' arms. Its naval dominance alone made it a formidable opponent. After 1740, Britain used both its economic strength and its military might in the great mid-century wars with France that stretched across three continents. To understand this story, we must shift our attention to the West's overseas colonies and the nature of trade among them.

More than anything else, France and Britain fought over colonies. For both countries, foreign trade quadrupled in the eighteenth century, and a large part of that increase derived from transactions with colonies. The two nations also made their greatest profits from trade across the Atlantic. However, their overseas presence differed crucially. The French had only 56,000 colonists living in North America in 1740—a fraction of the British colonial population. Yet French colonists carried out an extensive, highly profitable fur trade. Further, because of their small numbers and trade arrangements, they experienced limited conflict with Amerindians.

Colonies, trade, and war

British colonists, clustered along the eastern seaboard, had a different experience. First, they grew rapidly—from 250,000 in 1700 to 1.7 million in 1760. As they occupied and exploited more and more land, they pushed the Amerindians out. Their expansion, combined with resistance from local tribes, led to savage battles. The fighting, in turn, convinced the colonists that removing or even exterminating the Amerindians was justified. As they became more firmly established, the British colonists bought manufactured goods from Britain in return for tobacco, rice, cotton, and indigo dye, much of which Britain re-exported to the European continent.

These North American colonists participated in the even more lucrative triangle of trade that connected Europe, Africa, and the Americas and that centered on the Caribbean (see map on page 352). The British and French, along with the Dutch and Spanish, held islands there that supported sugar, rum, coffee, and dyestuffs trade produced by slave labor. In particular, the demand for sugar and coffee seemed endless. European craving for these items grew so much that, for many, they became necessities rather than occasional luxuries.

The triangle of trade

At the heart of this thriving colonial commerce was the slave trade (see Chapter 12). Slavery was long common throughout Africa and in other societies. For centuries, Islamic merchants had purchased slaves through well-established African networks and transported them by caravan across the Sahara Desert to the Mediterranean basin or by ship from east African ports across the Indian Ocean to Asia.

The slave trade

In the eighteenth century, the dramatic demand for slaves in the Americas shifted Africa's slave trade westward to the Atlantic coast. Ships from Europe carried manufactured goods (most notably, guns) and gin to western Africa and traded them for slaves—two-thirds of them males, because they best provided heavy labor. Usually captured by African middlemen, slaves languished in pens in towns or forts on the African coast. European trading ships then carried them across the Atlantic in a perilous two-month sea voyage known as the **Middle Passage.**

The image below, an 1846 watercolor, suggests what conditions were like belowdecks on a slave ship. Typically, slaves were packed like cargo into the holds of ships "where the light of day does not penetrate." As many as 700 slaves—naked, branded, and shackled—might be crammed into one ship. A French writer describing these voyages told of a "continuous state of alarm on the part of the white men, who fear a revolt, and . . . a cruel state of uncertainty on the part of the Negroes, who do not know the fate awaiting them." In the document on page 355, Olaudah Equiano, a captured African, describes how this Middle Passage experience soon made him "so sick and low" that he "wished for the last friend, death."

Traders took most of their slaves to the West Indies and Brazil; less than 10 percent went to North American destinations. After unloading their human cargo, the ships filled up with sugar, rum, and other goods—sometimes stopping farther north in the American colonies to take on additional products such as cotton, tobacco, timber, and furs.

A TRANSATLANTIC SLAVE SHIP, 1846 This mid-nineteenth-century watercolor depicts a slave ship where the human cargo is packed tightly belowdecks.

From there, the ships returned to Europe. Merchants then re-exported many of these products to other European nations.

Disease, abuse, and suicide took the lives of many slaves. In addition, African women often suffered the horror of rape by their captors. Those who survived the Middle Passage were then sold for profit and put to work on a plantation or in the mines or households of colonists. Slaves suffered from poor diets, inadequate housing, broken families, and stiff corporal punishment. The uprooting, the trauma of transportation, and the harsh conditions in the colonies stripped much away from these people. Still, slaves often resisted their masters by working slowly, sabotaging equipment, running away, and revolting. Despite their lack of freedom, slaves built hybrid cultural traditions from African, American, and European sources.

Within the slave societies of Brazil, the West Indies, and North America, the notion of race was becoming tied to slavery, adding to earlier notions of racial prejudice. The unprecedented dependence on slavery and the associated development of racism would stain these societies in ways that persist to this day.

The consequences of the slave trade also rippled through sub-Saharan Africa. Traditional trade routes north to the Mediterranean and east to the Indian Ocean disintegrated as more lucrative commerce shifted west to the Atlantic coast of Africa. To supply more human cargo to the Europeans, west African kingdoms raided inland tribes. Bloody internal wars erupted—more deadly than ever thanks to the guns supplied by Europeans to the Africans.

Because many slaves perished in the Americas, and the plantations that depended on them kept expanding, the demand for fresh supplies of slaves increased relentlessly. This rising need perpetuated the triangular commerce among Europe, Africa, and the Americas. European traders took 50,000 to 100,000 slaves across the Atlantic each year during most of the eighteenth century. By the time slave trafficking abated in the mid-nineteenth century, more than 11 million Africans had been ripped from their homes, transported across the Atlantic, and sold into slavery. Another 4 million died resisting seizure or while in transport.

Planters and merchants on both sides of the Atlantic profited from this trade, and European cities serving as slave-trade ports

Olaudah Equiano Describes the Middle Passage

The slave trade between Africa and the Americas involved the horrors of capture and the Middle Passage, a harrowing two-month voyage across the Atlantic. Olaudah Equiano (1745–1797)—a west African who was captured by slave raiders when he was 10 years old—describes the ocean journey. He survived the voyage and twenty-one years of slavery before purchasing his freedom.

I was soon put down under the decks, and there I received such a salutation in my nostrils as I had never experienced in my life; so that with the loathsomeness of the stench and crying together, I became so sick and low that I was not able to eat, nor had I the least desire to taste anything. I now wished for the last friend, death, to relieve me; but soon, to my grief, two of the white men offered me eatables, and on my refusing to eat, one of them held me fast by the hands and laid me across I think the windlass and tied my feet while the other flogged me severely. I had never experienced anything of this kind before, and although not being used to the water I naturally feared that element the first time I saw it, yet nevertheless if I could have gotten over the nettings I would have jumped over the side, but I could not; and besides, the crew used to watch very closely over those of us who were not chained down to the decks, lest we should leap into the water, and I have seen some of these poor African prisoners most severely cut for attempting to do so, and hourly whipped for not eating. This indeed was often the case with myself. . . .

How are captured Africans treated on the slave ship?

flourished, particularly in England. The coastal town of Liverpool, for example, grew from a small town to a major city in the eighteenth century. In 1750, its slave merchants and fleet of almost two hundred ships carried nearly half of Europe's slave trade. Thousands of men from Liverpool worked on both merchant and naval ships, and more than a dozen banks and several insurance companies served slave-trade merchants. The wealth spread outward from Liverpool, helping to finance Britain's burgeoning industry as well as its rising position on the world stage. "Our West-Indies and African Trades are the most nationally beneficial of any we carry on. . . . The Trade to Africa is the branch which renders our American Colonies and Plantations so advantageous to Great Britain," argued one British defender of the slave system in 1746. "The daily bread of the most considerable part of our British Manufacturers are owing primarily to the labor of Negroes." Although the statement may be an exaggeration, slavery generated much commerce and wealth in this eighteenth-century Atlantic economy, whether by direct or indirect means.

As Europeans' commercial activities, profits, and presence increased in the Americas, so did competition and friction, especially between the French and the British. In North America, British colonists along the eastern seaboard pushed inland, beyond the Appalachian Mountains into the Ohio Valley. The French strengthened their holdings by building forts along the Great Lakes and the large rivers of the St. Lawrence and Mississippi valleys. When the War of the Austrian Succession broke out in Europe in 1740, Britain and France soon locked horns on the Continent as well as overseas. Most of the fighting took place in the Americas, however. Wins and losses on each side balanced out, and by the time the conflict ended in 1748, each side had settled for what it had held in the beginning.

Fighting on three continents

The peace would not last long. In 1755, war—sometimes known as the French and Indian War—erupted again, this time initiated by a British offensive against a French stronghold near Pittsburgh in North America. At the same time, the two powers were also competing in India, each trying to take advantage of the declining power of the Mughals (India's Muslim rulers). After 1715, the subcontinent had split apart into bickering, independent kingdoms. India became fertile ground for the British and French, working through their chartered trading companies and backed by their superior weapons of war, to make deals, gain influence, and line up allies among India's opposing princes and political factions. In 1759, British colonialist and soldier Robert Clive (1725–1774), representing Britain's East India Company, explained how a combination of force and bribery could gain the company and England "absolute possession of these rich kingdoms" in India that would provide "an income yearly of upwards of two million sterling." Moreover, he added, Britain would gain advantages over "the several European nations engaged in the commerce here," especially "against

the French." This competition between the British and French for trade and imperial power developed into an undeclared war that, after 1756, coalesced with the hostilities breaking out across Europe (the Seven Years' War), the Caribbean, and North America.

In this widespread war, which involved Asians and Amerindians as well as Europeans, France invested most of its energy and resources in the European arena, whereas Britain focused on the battle overseas. Initially, the French, assisted by the Amerindian allies they had gained, held their own in North America. Then the British, with their superior navy and more extensive population, began capturing French strongholds one by one. The fall of Quebec in 1759 opened all of Canada to British forces. British naval power overwhelmed the French and their Spanish allies in the Caribbean as well. In India, the British also prevailed, crushing the French and subduing several resisting Indian states. During the succeeding decades, as the map on page 357 reveals, the British increasingly took direct control over areas around their bases of power.

The maps on page 358 show the changing fortunes of France and Britain in North America between 1755 and 1763. The Treaty of Paris, which ended the fighting in 1763, gave Britain control of Canada and of France's holdings east of the Mississippi. Britain also received France's West Indian possessions, except for Guadeloupe and Martinique, and most of France's holdings in India. British control over most of India dates from this period. France and several other nations still retained important overseas colonies, but Britain now reigned as the top colonial and commercial power. This "great war for empire" paved the way for the British to establish their worldwide empire in the nineteenth century.

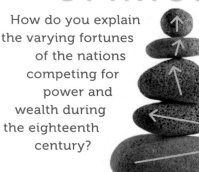

OPINION

How do you explain the varying fortunes of the nations competing for power and wealth during the eighteenth century?

Moving into the Modern World

These global conflicts were just one way the West was shouldering its way into the rest of the world's societies. By the mid-eighteenth century, the West had been sending out explorers, making new commercial contacts, establishing links, and racking up conquests in the non-Western world for almost three centuries. Had this "expansion" of Europe changed the meaning of the West?

During the eighteenth century, the actual "boundaries" of the West did begin to shift. Russia brought under its direct control lands to the east in Siberia. By the second

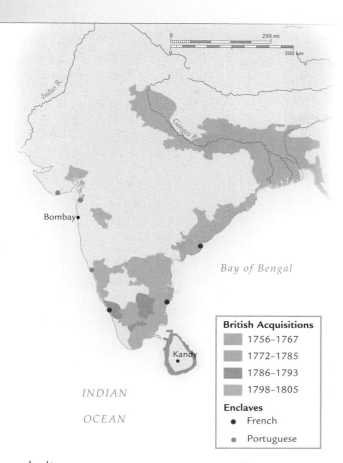

INDIAN

OCEAN

British Acquisitions
- 1756–1767
- 1772–1785
- 1786–1793
- 1798–1805

Enclaves
- ● French
- ● Portuguese

India, 1756–1805 **This map shows British acquisitions in India between 1756 and 1805.**

half of the century, Russians easily outnumbered those regions' indigenous inhabitants. It also pushed its borders south, particularly in the Caspian Sea region. Russia's growing Eurasian empire blurred any line between the West and the non-Western world on the Eurasian landmass. Across the Atlantic, Europeans had colonized parts of the Americas so thoroughly that large sections of the Western Hemisphere were much more than mere outposts. Though thousands of miles away from Europe, they were becoming part of the West itself.

If not in control of other major regions of the world, people from the West were certainly in increasing contact with other cultures and civilizations across the globe. From the broadest perspective, the West shared important similarities with several of these civilizations, such as Japan and China. For example, all of these civilizations had economies based on agriculture and handicrafts; the factories, railroads, and steamships that would mark the industrial era in the West were yet to come. Moreover, several Asian civilizations had enough wealth and military might to put them in the same league as the European nations.

In the mid-eighteenth century, European ships carried goods and people overseas in astounding numbers

and with great regularity. Some sailed to Western ports, others to lands beyond Europeans' control. Demand in the West for goods such as sugar, tea, coffee, and tobacco, along with demand in China for silver, fueled this long-distance commerce. At the same time, burgeoning hunger for slaves forced millions of enslaved Africans across the Atlantic into the Americas. In some areas, Western nations were chipping away at holdings of competitors such as the Ottomans in southeastern Europe and western Asia and the Mughals in southern Asia. In other areas, such as North America beyond the Atlantic colonies and Oceania, Western societies were starting to overwhelm indigenous peoples. But in vast regions of the world, eighteenth-century Europeans gained access only on coastlines. East Asian societies easily kept them at bay, remaining in control of their own affairs. And in Africa, much of the continent remained too difficult for the West to penetrate.

THE TWILIGHT OF MONARCHIES? The Question of Enlightened Absolutism

In both Britain and France, the eighteenth-century monarchies were in decline, but for different reasons. In Britain, the monarchs ruled in partnership with Parliament. However, the kings were undistinguished, and Parliament continued to gain the upper hand. In France, the successors to Louis XIV lacked the interest, talent, and support to make the monarchy dynamic or popular. The twin threats to the crown in these nations—the growing complexity of effective governance, and demands from elites to share power—arose elsewhere as well.

However, in several other nations, monarchs managed to maintain their authority—often by justifying their rule in innovative ways and instituting new policies. In the second half of the eighteenth century, some of these monarchs styled themselves as "enlightened," or attuned to Enlightenment beliefs and willing to initiate reforms for the good of the state and its people. Some historians have distinguished these rulers from their predecessors, calling them "enlightened absolutists" or simply "enlightened." Yet, how valid is this characterization? Several historians claim that these monarchs primarily followed the long tradition of trying to buttress the central government's power and efficiency. Other historians argue that they genuinely initiated reforms in line with Enlightenment thinking.

The most sensational of the self-described enlightened monarchs was Frederick the Great (Frederick II) of Prussia. Even as a boy, Frederick loved music, poetry, and philosophy. After ascending to the throne, he still found time to

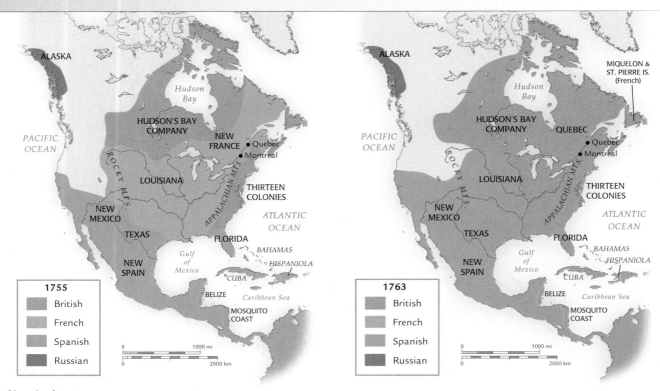

North America, 1755 and 1763 These maps show North America before and after the Seven Years' War.

perform in concerts as an accomplished flutist in his Palace of Sanssouci. There he also hobnobbed with towering cultural figures such as Voltaire, savored books in his library, and carried on a lively correspondence with leading French intellectuals. He knew and spoke the phrases of the Enlightenment. Like several other monarchs, he also wanted to display his awareness of culture and intellectual life to help justify his position as monarch. He described "the good monarch" as one who behaved "as if he were each moment liable to render an account of his administration to his fellow citizens." He claimed to act only in the common interest of the people, declaring himself to be "the first servant of the state" rather than a divinely appointed ruler.

Frederick the Great

At the end of the Seven Years' War (1756–1763), the second of his two wars of aggression, Frederick made some attempts at "enlightened" reforms. For example, he initiated codification of the laws, abolished torture, and ended most capital punishment. Believing that "all religions, if one examines them, are founded on superstitious systems, more or less absurd," he proclaimed religious toleration. Nevertheless, he considered Jews "useless to the state" and taxed them heavily. He advocated public education but spent very little on it compared with what he spent on his army. In his economic policy, Frederick did share the Physiocrats' appreciation of the importance of agriculture and tried to introduce new methods of cultivation (see page 339). Yet he did nothing to free the serfs or lessen their burdens. Neither his wars nor his involvement in the partition of Poland revealed any hint of enlightened principles different from those of the monarchs who preceded him.

No one tried more sincerely to be enlightened than Joseph II of Austria (r. 1780–1790). "Since I have ascended the throne," he said in 1781, "I have made *philosophy* the legislator of my empire." Viewing his rule as a moral and holy calling, Joseph issued thousands of decrees. Unfortunately, he lacked the practical sense of Frederick the Great. He did change laws that had previously limited freedom of the press and religion (including Judaism). He also restricted the death penalty, promoted education, and enacted and tried to enforce equality before the law.

Joseph II

Nevertheless, Joseph still ruled as an autocrat, antagonizing most of the powerful groups in his lands. Even peasants, unable to understand exactly what all the decrees meant, failed to support him. His well-meaning but ill-conceived efforts—to centralize the administration of the widely dispersed Habsburg territories, to replace the numerous languages of his subjects with German, to subordinate the strongly entrenched Roman Catholic Church, and to free the serfs in a society still based on feudalism—all backfired. Opposition and even open revolt swelled in his lands. In 1787, Joseph lamented, "[I] hope that when I am no more, posterity will examine, and judge more equitably . . . all that I have done for my people." His vision would not come to pass. Within a few years of his death in 1790, most of his reforms were abolished and the Habsburg lands reacquired their old, conservative ways.

Certainly these monarchs and others found it easier to manifest their "enlightenment" in style rather than substance. Moreover, they rarely lost sight of traditional goals:

Style, substance, or survival? to increase their own military and economic power. Few attempted to enact fundamental social, political, or economic reforms dictated by Enlightenment thought. Even those who tried, such as Joseph II in Austria, generally failed to overcome opposition to those reforms from tradition-minded people.

Nevertheless, thoughtful observers of the eighteenth century—looking for tendencies and possibilities for reform rather than revolutionary change—believed that several rulers displayed the enlightened spirit of the times. Despite great obstacles to reform within the traditional order, some of these rulers made progress toward fulfilling the *philosophes'* agenda of promoting more religious tolerance, humane social institutions, and rational administration. In the eyes of contemporaries, they earned the label "enlightened."

Finally, from another perspective, **enlightened absolutism** also may have reflected a growing sense that, in the long run, monarchs could no longer *claim* to embody the state. The need for governmental efficiency had grown too much to be entrusted to a poorly qualified individual who happened to be a king or queen. Moreover, governments increasingly had to recognize the emergence of a public sphere within their lands where individuals and groups exchanged information, voiced ideas, and engaged in criticism. Public opinion became a potential tool that monarchs might use to their advantage—or a force they might ignore to their detriment. If the institution of monarchy were to survive, kings and queens had to justify their position in these new, ostensibly enlightened ways.

> "I have made *philosophy* the legislator of my empire."

CHANGES IN COUNTRY AND CITY LIFE

Eighteenth-century European monarchs and officials faced not only the risky politics and wars of their times but also the changes unfolding in their very societies. Especially in western Europe, new economic and social forces began to upset old traditions (see Chapter 13). For some people, these changes created a sense that life was improving and would continue to do so. For others, the changes only deepened their misery. The greatest shifts emerged in the countryside, where the vast majority of the population (some 80 percent) lived and depended on agriculture for their livelihood and very survival.

Historically, toiling in the fields within Europe's traditional subsistence economies produced little more than enough food to survive. During the late seventeenth and eighteenth centuries, new methods of agricultural production that had originated in Holland spread to England and then to other areas of western Europe. These innovative methods allowed fewer people to work the fields and still produce far more food than they needed. The new techniques and the changes flowing from them became so important that they are known as the agricultural revolution.

The Agricultural Revolution

Most early-eighteenth-century farmers used methods that differed only marginally from those employed in previous centuries. They grew the same crops year after year, left one-third to one-half of the land fallow (unplanted) to allow the soil to replenish itself with nutrients for the next planting, and saved only enough fodder to feed small numbers of domestic animals during the winters. Individual families worked small strips of land, and large, uncultivated fields, brushlands, and forests (the commons) were reserved for general use by the community. Traditional community practices usually determined decisions about crops, animals, and land use. Overall, only a small minority of people made their living outside of agriculture, and an even smaller percentage had the good fortune to afford luxuries.

This traditional, agricultural economy had the potential to support a limited measure of population growth. In the eighteenth century, population increases stepped up the demand for food, and hence for hands to clear fields, drain swamps, terrace hillsides, carry water, and till the soil. Most of these efforts were simply an intensification of old methods for increasing agricultural yields, and the growing population consumed most of the extra food they produced. Something had to change if large numbers of Europeans hoped to increase their standard of living and provide enough food for people living in the cities as well as the countryside.

At the heart of the **agricultural revolution** lay two developments: first, the introduction of new crops and the use of new farming techniques that dramatically boosted agricultural yields; and second, the transformation of rural lands farmed for subsistence into large, controlled properties that produced crops for **New crops and techniques** commerce. The primary agricultural advances came first in Holland and Britain, where farmers began experimenting with new crops such as clover, turnips, and legumes, as well as the potato from America. These crops replenished the soil rather than depleting it and therefore could be grown on lands that farmers periodically had to leave fallow. Farmers now used the new crops to feed livestock during the hard winters. More cattle meant more protein-rich dairy products; more horses and oxen eased the workload for humans and provided transportation; and more sheep produced more wool. All this livestock, improving with new crossbreeding practices, yielded more meat, leather, and soap as well as manure with which to fertilize fields. Other new foods, such as nutrient-rich potatoes, also made the land more productive than ever before. Some landowners became renowned for their farming innovations. In England, for example, Charles "Turnip" Townshend (1674–1738) experimented with crop rotation and growing turnips. His compatriot Jethro Tull (1674–1741) advocated the use of a seed drill and manure, which made planting more efficient and productive.

Not all farmers adopted the new agricultural methods. For many, traditional ways were comfortably familiar. Even those who realized how much profit they might make by selling their surpluses in the cities and other distant markets needed money to fund the new farming methods. They also required control over larger tracts of land to introduce the new crops, apply the innovative methods, and specialize in certain products—whether sheep for wool, grain for flour, or cattle for meat and dairy.

By all means, fair and foul, these market-oriented landowners dispossessed individuals of their small plots and communities of their commons to

| Enclosures | enclose land with fences, hedges, and walls as their own. After 1750, Britain's Parliament furthered this trend by authorizing a wave of these **enclosures.** Over the decades, wealthy landowners created large, controlled tracts that yielded products for the market. They reserved only a small part of their land for their own needs or bought their food elsewhere. Through this process, thousands of small, independent landowners,

sharecroppers, and tenant farmers lost their land—and the status and security that had come with it. Rural communities disintegrated, eroding the support and human interactions that had so characterized life in the country.

Manufacturing Spreads in the Countryside: Cottage Industry

The spreading agricultural revolution became one force pushing, forcing, or freeing people to work more in nonagricultural jobs. When families lost their self-sufficient farms, they had to find new sources of income to supplement the meager day-labor wages their landowning employers paid them. Manufacturing seemed to offer a solution. Growing commerce, particularly overseas trade, had heightened demand for manufactured goods—and thus workers to produce them. Traditionally, well-paid urban artisans had done this sort of work. Now, with demand high and rural workers available by the thousands, merchants turned to the countryside to increase production and take advantage of the cheap labor. Moreover, by shifting more production itself to the countryside, merchants avoided urban guild regulations that historically had controlled wages and the quantity and quality of goods.

All these changes stimulated the growth of **cottage industry,** also known as the putting-out system. This system, which had already existed in the sixteenth and seventeenth centuries but to a much smaller degree, worked in a specific way. An entrepreneur provided raw materials (usually for production of textiles such as wool or linen) and sometimes equipment (such as a handloom or a spinning wheel) to peasants. The entrepreneur might be anyone—from a city merchant to a rural landowner—who managed to amass enough money to make an initial investment in raw materials and perhaps equipment. Peasants, who sought employment during times of the year when there was less need for agricultural labor, worked in their homes (hence the term *cottage industry*) to turn these raw materials into finished products. Mainly, they spun wool into yarn and wove the yarn into cloth. Sometimes, enterprising peasants contracted out raw material to other spinners to keep weavers busy, since weavers depended on spinners to provide a steady supply of yarn. Women and children often worked while men were off performing day labor for large landowners. The entrepreneur periodically returned, paid for the peasants' labor by the piece, and distributed the finished products to distant markets. As the image here shows, whole families participated in cottage-industry work. Working in cramped quarters, women and children usually washed, combed,

COTTAGE INDUSTRY, eighteenth century This illustration shows a rural family working together to produce textiles that will be collected for commerce.

and spun the raw material into thread, while men often wove the yarn on looms.

Cottage industry spread rapidly during the eighteenth century, particularly in Great Britain and parts of France and Germany. In addition to textiles, all sorts of goods—from buttons and housewares to knives, nails, and clocks—were produced through this system. The quality of these products varied, and relations between merchants and laborers often broke down over accusations of theft and disputes over wages. Still, more and more people came to depend on the system. For many of these workers, cottage-industry labor changed from a part-time to a full-time occupation.

The primary appeal of the work was its availability. Cottage industry allowed many people to remain in rural areas in a time of shrinking demand for farm workers. It also helped large families keep up and enabled young people to get an earlier start on marriage. On the other hand, the pay rarely rose above starvation wages, and the labor was drudgery.

Wherever it spread, cottage industry extended the money economy and the web of the commercial marketplace. Along with the agricultural revolution, the growth of cottage industry helped set the stage for an even greater economic transformation that would eventually sweep from Britain throughout the West and into the non-Western world: the industrial revolution.

More People, Longer Lives

As these new economic and social forces began to alter traditional ways of life, Europe's population jumped from approximately 110 million in 1700 to 190 million in 1800. The

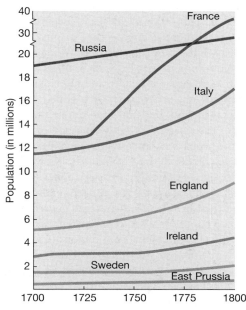

POPULATION GROWTH IN EUROPE, 1700–1800

A GERMAN HOSPITAL, 1746 This illustration from the mid-eighteenth century shows a hospital room and the kinds of activities—from amputations to food deliveries—that commonly took place there.

graph below reveals the population growth throughout most of Europe during the eighteenth century. Relatively large populations help explain the strength of three major powers—England (along with Ireland), France, and Russia (note that much of Russia's increased population came from territorial expansion). Earlier marriages, more and better food, and fewer plagues raised the birthrate and lowered the death rate. Agricultural and commercial prosperity, along with improvements in the transportation of food, reduced the number and severity of famines in many areas. In particular, the widespread cultivation of the potato during the second half of the eighteenth century made this cheap, nutritious food available to millions. A spate of good weather helped to improve harvests. In some areas, new urban sanitation practices—cleaning wells, draining swampy areas, and burying refuse—probably improved health as well.

Population growth

Surprisingly, medical practices rarely contributed to better health. Certainly the medical field saw some advances. Inoculation against smallpox, for example, spread to Europe from the Middle East during the eighteenth century, although it was not used widely until the last decades of the century. Surgeons also made some improvements in the treatment of battlefield injuries. For instance, they learned to treat soldiers for shock before operating, and to clean wounds around the trauma.

Eighteenth-century medicine

Despite these signs of progress, eighteenth-century medicine was still dangerous. The image above provides a glimpse into a German hospital. French hospitals were no better. The French encyclopedist Denis Diderot described the Hôtel-Dieu in Paris, considered one of France's finest hospitals at the time: "Imagine a long series of communicating wards filled with sufferers of every kind of disease who are sometimes packed three, four, five or even six into a bed, the living alongside the dead and dying, the air polluted by this mass of unhealthy bodies, passing the pestilence of their afflictions from one to the other, and the spectacle of suffering and agony on every hand. That is the Hôtel-Dieu."

Deepening Misery for the Poor

The eighteenth-century population explosion exacted an ironic price. Stiffening competition for food drove prices up, while competition for jobs kept wages down. As a result, more and more people fell into poverty. A governmental commission in Austria reported to Empress Maria Theresa that "the peasants live in a condition of real slavery. . . . In their ruinous huts, the parents sleep on straw, the children naked on the wide shelves of earthenware stoves . . . all the charges of the Kingdom are born by the peasants, who are the sole taxpayers." Despite a widespread sense that people were better off than ever and that things would improve, in truth more people meant more misery.

In a desperate attempt to survive, poor people fled to the cities, hoping to find work in trade and manufacturing or as day laborers and domestics. Only some of them managed to find jobs; the rest were left to fend for themselves. A large percentage of urban dwellers missed out on the new wealth and opportunities of the cities. They eked out a living at little more than a subsistence level, and their lot worsened as more and more of them crowded in from the countryside.

Indeed, the surplus of workers; inflation; and disasters such as war, disease, and failed harvests hit the poor in cities and countryside alike. In France, economist Jacques Turgot (1727–1781) described the disastrous harvest of 1769: "The people could exist only by exhausting their resources, by selling at a miserable price their articles of furniture and even their clothes. Many of the inhabitants have been obliged to disperse themselves through other provinces to seek work or to beg, leaving their wives and children to the charity of the parishes." One Spanish official described how "wives and children are without work, and all, piled together in cities or large towns, live at the expense of charity." Even for those who found steady employment, wages simply did not keep pace with escalating prices.

In bad times, food riots and tax revolts broke out in cities and rural areas across Europe. A rise in the price of grain often sparked attacks on merchants, granaries, and convoys of grain slated for armies. People turned on officials as well, blaming them for not keeping grain prices affordable or for allowing food to be shipped out to higher bidders elsewhere. Crime increased and more people slept along the sides of rural roads and city streets. Crowds of mothers pushed into foundling hospitals, desperate to leave children they could not care for. Some foundling hospitals established lotteries to determine which children they could afford to take in.

This deepening of poverty put a huge strain on traditional systems for aiding the poor, such as through the church or private charity. Some people were reduced to begging and to teaching their children this dubious art. Some authorities sympathized; others turned a blind eye. As one French official put it, "Beggary is the apprenticeship of crime; it begins by creating a love of idleness . . . in this state the beggar does not long resist the temptation to steal." A few countries devised legislation, such as the English Poor Laws, that required the impoverished to work on public projects or in workhouses. Officials used these sorts of laws more to control and discipline the poor than to help them. Often the same institution served as a workshop for the unfortunate, a hospital, and a prison. True, the poor had always suffered. Now, however, the population boom pushed their numbers to overwhelming new heights.

Prosperity and the Bourgeoisie

Like the agricultural revolution, urban growth made life worse for some and better for others. Those who gained most during this era were the middle and aristocratic classes, particularly those who seized opportunities in commerce and industry and in the expanding governmental bureaucracies. The urban middle class—in French, the *bourgeoisie*—expanded and found itself in a particularly odd situation. Wealthier than most, the bourgeoisie lived off their investments in trade, manufacturing, or land rather than working with their hands like their fellow commoners. They also found ways to avoid the restrictions of the guild system of production. While those laboring below them envied and resented their success, the bourgeoisie tried to distance themselves from "less respectable" commoners.

Middle-class people also had difficult relationships with those above them—the aristocracy. Successful members of the bourgeoisie resented the privileges enjoyed by the aristocracy, but—even more strongly—they wanted those privileges for themselves. They longed to join the aristocracy, and they were willing to spend money to do it. Money got them titles and offices, large estates, and judicious marriages—the trappings of success that they hoped would earn them acceptance into the ranks of the aristocracy. The aristocrats, for their part, viewed this method of social climbing—and the people who attempted it—with disdain. As they saw it, true nobility derived from birth, not wealth.

Nevertheless, the bourgeoisie persisted and thrived. These merchants, manufacturers, and professionals made money, expanded their businesses, invested in government bonds, and took chances on shaky financial schemes. They valued hard work and the accumulation of money. Moreover, they had the means to purchase a vast variety of luxuries, from coffee and chocolate to wallpaper, cotton clothing, and watch chains—goods produced outside the home, often even outside the country. For them, the market—rather than the household—supplied staples as well as conveniences and luxuries.

Over time, the richest among the bourgeoisie might manage to gain entrance into the aristocracy. Yet even if they could not get into the courts, estates, and homes of the aristocracy, the bourgeoisie developed a public culture of their own. They educated their children at universities and attended public theaters, music halls, and galleries. They filled tea rooms, coffeehouses, literary societies, and clubs and devoured newspapers, journals, and books written especially for them. Over time, they acquired their own sense of identity, as well as an impatience when further opportunities to rise in society were denied them.

THE CULTURE OF THE ELITE: Combining the Old and the New

The culture of the bourgeoisie and the aristocracy reflected the continuance of old trends along with the new developments that characterized the eighteenth century. For example, the courts of Europe still sponsored painters, composers, and musicians. In their private halls, aristocrats savored these artists' paintings, concerts, and operas. The prevailing spirit remained classical, inspired by the Greek and Roman appreciation for formal symmetry, proportion, and reason. On the other hand, artistic styles were changing. Several artists and authors put a new emphasis on emotion and nature in their works, an artistic trend sometimes referred to as the **cult of sensibility.** Audiences for these new cultural forms expanded, and the stream of literature being published for the growing numbers of literate Westerners swelled.

OPINION

Why do you think most of the eighteenth century might be considered one of both growing prosperity and deepening social misery?

The Advent of the Modern Novel

Much of the reading public consisted of members of the middle class, and, not surprisingly, the modern novel reflected middle-class tastes. A compelling story, complex and varied characters, and realistic social situations formed the core of this new literary form. Novels also conveyed current ideas, manners, news, and information in witty and dramatic ways. In several popular novels, the English writer Daniel Defoe (1660–1731) wrote about individuals who planned ahead and used their entrepreneurial skills to meet challenges. The adventures of a character in a Defoe novel might take place at home in England or on exotic islands, as in *Robinson Crusoe* (1719).

Samuel Richardson (1689–1761) and Henry Fielding (1707–1754), also British, used the novel to analyze human personality, emotions, and psychology. In *Pamela, or Virtue Rewarded* (1740), Richardson recounts the story of a servant girl who tries to retain her virtue in the face of her wealthy employer's sexual advances. The book's characters and circumstances powerfully reflected contemporary realities, and the novel inspired a wave of similar works. Many novels appealed particularly to women readers. British writer Fanny Burney (1752–1840) gained fame with the publication of her novel *Evelina or A Young Lady's Entrance into the World* (1778). The book portrays a provincial girl who makes a life for herself in London. Although the story ends with a marriage, it also reveals the social restrictions and dangers facing eighteenth-century women who tried to live an independent life.

During the second half of the century, novels and works of poetry by authors such as Jean-Jacques Rousseau in France and Johann Wolfgang von Goethe (1749–1832) in the German states emphasized emotion, relationships, and social problems. These authors presented the emotions as natural virtues, rejecting the artificiality of formal manners. Their style, which would become known as romanticism, grew in popularity during the last quarter of the century.

Pride and Sentiment in Art and Architecture

Unlike literature, the fine arts still typically reflected the tastes of the dominant aristocracy. Artists vied with one another for commissions to paint the portraits of royals and aristocrats, depicting their proud subjects adorned with plumes, buckles, silks, brocades, and laces. The scenes might include children and dogs and, in the background, lavish estate grounds. The distinctive clothing, haughty poses, and elaborate settings marked subjects as members of the landowning elite.

Many paintings showed intimate scenes of aristocratic private life—meetings, picnics, flirtations, and conversations among the upper classes. In Antoine Watteau's (1684–1721) popular paintings, for example, the context might be classical mythology, but the figures were eighteenth-century aristocrats. Other artists painted well-received, sentimental

Jean-Baptiste Greuze, *The Father's Curse*

ca. 1778

In this dramatic family conflict, the father, on the left, curses his departing son, who is determined to find his own way through life by joining the army. Women and children try in vain to reconcile the two men and to prevent the breakup of the family on such a painful note.   Why might viewers of this family scene be touched and fascinated?

ment buildings and urban residences followed a more neoclassical style, which stressed clarity of line and form modeled on Greek and Roman ideals.

Reaching New Heights in Music

Of all the eighteenth-century arts, music left the most profound legacy. Much of it reflected the tastes of its royal, aristocratic, and ecclesiastical patrons. Composers and musicians, therefore, usually stuck to established forms, and music was typically heard as a pleasing background to conversations, balls, and other social occasions in the bastions of the aristocracy. Increasingly, however, music was played in public concert halls to a larger audience. Opera houses opened everywhere, and composers could now hope to make money from paying audiences as well as from court and aristocratic patronage. Several cities became well-known musical centers, but Vienna topped them all. This Austrian city became the musical heart of Europe, drawing hundreds of musicians who competed for favor there.

The first half of the eighteenth century saw the high point of baroque music, a style that had originated in the seventeenth century and that was still favored in royal courts and aristocratic homes. The greatest practitioners of the baroque style were Johann Sebastian Bach (1685–1750) and George Frideric Handel (1685–1759). Bach was a member of a German family long distinguished by

Baroque music

its musical talent. Noted in his own lifetime chiefly as an organist rather than a composer, he created a vast array of great music for organ, harpsichord, clavichord (forerunner of the piano), orchestra, and chorus. Sadly, much of Bach's work has been lost. Much of his music was religiously inspired, but he also wrote a large amount of secular music. Handel was born in central Germany in the same year and same region as Bach. He studied Italian opera in Germany and Italy and wrote forty-six operas himself. He also became court musician in Hanover. Later, he made

scenes of ordinary people experiencing dramatic moments. The image above, a painting by the French artist Jean-Baptiste Greuze (1725–1805), shows one of these works. William Hogarth's works (see image on page 353) also explored everyday experiences in the lives of ordinary people, but usually from a satirical or moralistic perspective.

Eighteenth-century architecture could not portray sentiments in the same detail as paintings, but buildings in the baroque style still expressed well the gaudy splendor of the eighteenth-century monarchs and their courts. At the same time, architects began deemphasizing size and instead relied on multiple curves and lacy, shell-like ornamentation to convey a sense of pleasing luxury. This style is usually referred to as **rococo.** Some new govern-

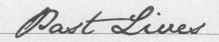
his home in England, as did the elector, who became King George I of England. Handel wrote an enormous quantity of music—both instrumental and vocal—all of it marked by dignity, formal elegance, and harmony.

During the last decades of the century, the restrained baroque style gave way to the more melodic "classical" style, with its striking depth, structure, and emotion. Franz Joseph Haydn (1732–1809) and Wolfgang Amadeus Mozart (1756–1791) led the way. Their most stunning work was the symphony; by the end of their careers, they had created symphonies of rich harmonic complexity and emotional depth within the restrained classical form. During his long career in Vienna, Haydn wrote more than a hundred symphonies in addition to scores of compositions for other forms, particularly chamber music. He became a friend and a source of inspiration for the young Mozart (see Past Lives). Ultimately, Mozart composed more than six hundred works and excelled in all forms, but he became most appreciated for his symphonies, piano concertos, and operas. His music was stunningly clear, melodic, elegant, and graceful. In his hands, the classical style reached its peak.

The classical style

The Grand Tour

The music, art, and literature of the elites were part of a broader, cosmopolitan culture that spilled across national boundaries. This culture manifested itself in elaborate styles of dress, polished manners, and highly structured conversation. French was its international language. The growing popularity of travel and travel literature added to the sense of a common European cultural identity, at least among elites. Indeed, the wealthy often considered the **grand tour** a necessary part of education. Travelers on the tour stopped in main cities to indulge in coffeehouses, storefront window displays, public gardens, theaters, opera houses, and galleries. They might also visit art dealers or public auctions to purchase quality paintings. Family connections offered them accommodations and introduced them to local

Wolfgang Amadeus Mozart (1756–1791)

Musicians quickly recognized the young Wolfgang Amadeus Mozart as a unique genius. Born in 1756, Wolfgang wrote his first compositions when he was just 5 years old. He embarked on the first of many tours throughout Europe as a 6-year-old child prodigy, playing the clavier with his elder sister, Nannerl, also a child prodigy, and his father (see the illustration).

THE MOZARTS

By the time he had reached 14, Mozart had composed several concertos, sonatas, and an opera. Announcements for his performances stressed his virtuosity. For example, for a concert in Italy, the 14-year-old would play "A Symphony of his own composition; a harpsichord concerto which will be handed to him, and which he will play on first sight; a sonata handed him in like manner, which he will provide with variations, and afterwards repeat in another key."

In 1781, after years of traveling, Mozart settled in Vienna. Soon married, he and his wife, Constanze, would have six children. He became a brilliantly successful composer, a virtuoso pianist, and a teacher, eventually attaining appointment as royal chamber composer to Emperor Joseph II of Austria. However, until his death in 1791, he continually borrowed money to support his family.

In what ways was Mozart both an interesting historical figure and a musical genius? Can you think of any contemporary musicians who will be as influential?

society, Enlightenment salons, or potential candidates for marriage. The tour usually continued to historical ruins, which featured revered models of Greek and Roman antiquity that further strengthened the viewers' sense of a common cultural identity.

CULTURE FOR THE LOWER CLASSES

The lower classes were not without cultural outlets that fit their lives and provided a sense of common identity. For peasants, artisans, and the urban poor, culture typically came in the form of shared recreation, songs, tales, and the passing down of wisdom at gatherings and celebrations. Many of these activities also coincided with religious gatherings and celebrations.

Festivals, Popular Literature, and Drink

Villagers worked together and celebrated together—at fairs, harvests, plowings, weddings, and religious holidays. Numerous festivals and public ceremonies had seasonal themes that were of particular importance and interest to people so dependent on agriculture. Other celebratory events related to the Christian calendar and centered on holidays, such as Christmas and Easter. Traditional weddings involved a community procession and festivities as well as a religious ceremony, and they featured music, dancing, feasts, games, and play. In the cities, artisans participated in their own organizations that combined recreational activities with mutual aid and religious celebrations.

Certain forms of literature also became popular among ordinary people. Literacy was growing, thanks to the printing press, the demands of business, and an increase in the number of primary schools. By the end of the eighteenth century, some 40 to 60 percent of the population in England and France could read (more men than women). With the rise in literacy, popular literature also expanded. Stirring religious tracts, almanacs, and tales of chivalric valor—typically, small, cheap booklets—circulated widely. More often, however, the "literature" of ordinary people was passed on orally. At night, people might gather to share folktales and songs that told of traditional wisdom, the hardships of everyday life, the hopes of common people, the dangers of life in the forests or of strangers who could be monsters or princes, and the ways to get along in life.

In the past, elites had fully participated in this popular culture, but during the eighteenth century they increasingly abandoned it to the lower classes. The "respectable" classes now often considered the leisure activities of ordinary people too disorderly and crude. Nevertheless, the middle and upper classes read some of the same popular literature enjoyed by the lower classes. Moreover, everyone—aristocrats and peasants alike—might be found at village festivals, fairs, and sporting events or enjoying jugglers, acrobats, magic lantern shows, and touring troupes of actors. Men of all classes watched and wagered on cockfights and dogfights. Other sports, such as soccer and cricket, gained popularity and drew large, animated crowds.

All the social classes also engaged in drinking—whether wine or brandy in the privacy of a wealthy home, or gin and beer in popular taverns. Especially in England, the ravages of drinking gin seemed to grow to alarming proportions. The problems caused by drinking were so extensive that in 1751 the British government passed a heavy tax on cheap gin to curtail its consumption.

Religious Revivals

Popular culture also merged with deeply felt spiritual beliefs and religious activities. Despite the many secular trends of the period, Christianity still stood at the center of Western culture and life. Churches rather than the state ran the schools and hospitals. The poor, aged, and crippled relied on churches for social services. Church bells announced the time of day everywhere, and religious holidays marked the year.

Within this Western religious culture, popular piety persisted. Indeed, especially among Protestants, a sense grew among ordinary churchgoers that official churches were becoming bureaucratized, complacent, and unresponsive to peoples' spiritual needs. In response, religious **Pietism** revivals spread from community to community and across national borders. In the German and Scandinavian states, **pietism**—which minimized dogma and formal ritual in favor of inner piety, holy living, and the private emotional experience of worshiping—gained strength. Revival movements in Britain and its North American colonies attracted thousands to huge gatherings.

The greatest of these revival movements was Methodism, founded in England by John Wesley (1703–1791). While studying for the Anglican ministry at Oxford, Wesley and a band of fellow students became disillusioned with the spiritual emptiness that had fallen upon the Anglican Church as well as its subservience to the government and the aristocracy. The group's lives became such examples of piety and moderate regularity that their fellow students branded them "Methodists" in derision. Methodism stressed humble faith, abstinence, and hard work. Barred from preaching in the Anglican churches, Wesley rode horseback from one end of England to the other until well into his 80s, preaching the "glad tidings" of salvation in thousands of sermons in streets, fields, and anywhere else he could find even a small audience. He claimed "to lower religion to the level of the lowest people's capacities."

Among Catholics, similar movements—such as Jansenism in France and Italy and Quietism in Spain—spread among elites and others. East European Jews had their own revivalist movement with the founding of the Hasidic sect in the 1740s. Hasidim (meaning "most pious") spread throughout Poland, rejecting formalism, stressing simplicity, and engaging in loud, joyful singing prayers. These religious movements revealed the power with which spiritual matters still influenced people in the West. Nevertheless, like the broader cultural forms of the time, religious revivals left the overall social order intact.

FORESHADOWING UPHEAVAL: The American Revolution

For most of the eighteenth century, neither wars, colonial rivalries, nor changes in country and city life upset the fundamental social and political stability of Western societies. In the last quarter of the eighteenth century, however, new forces erupted that would ultimately transform the West. The first of these disturbances occurred in Britain's thirteen North American colonies. This upheaval shifted the tide of events in North America and foreshadowed a far deeper and broader revolution that would strike at the heart of Europe itself.

Insults, Interests, and Principles: The Seeds of Revolt

By the mid-eighteenth century, more than two million people lived in the colonies. The seaboard cities in particular flourished, benefiting from a thriving commerce with Europe, Africa, and the West Indies. The colonists thought of themselves as British. Furthermore, the thirteen colonies in theory were part of Great Britain, governed in the same way and therefore subject to British trade regulations. In practice, however, the colonists often acted as they pleased, even if that meant quietly ignoring those regulations. They developed their own patterns of local government, manipulated British governors, and worked around British mercantilist policies.

Tensions between the island nation and these prospering colonies arose just after the Seven Years' War ended in 1763. Feeling that they had helped defend the American colonists against the hostile French and Indians, the British expected the colonists to help pay off the huge debt incurred in the fighting. To tighten their control over the colonial empire for which Britain had just fought so long and hard, British officials enacted new commercial regulations and taxes. Perhaps the most irritating of these was the Stamp Act of 1765, which taxed printed documents such as newspapers, pamphlets, and wills.

New commercial
regulations and taxes

The colonists reacted to the new policies with complaints, boycotts, protest meetings, outrage, and sometimes riots. Because colonists were not represented in Britain's Parliament, headlines in newspapers and pamphlets screamed, "No taxation without representation!" In their Stamp Act Congress of 1765, colonists announced that they were "entitled to all the inherent rights and liberties of his [the king's] natural born subjects within the kingdom of Great Britain." Local circumstances and the distance from Britain meant that "the only representatives of these colonies are persons chosen therein by themselves, and that no taxes ever have been, or can be constitutionally imposed on them, but by their respective legislatures." The British compromised, repealing most of the taxes, but many colonists were still not satisfied.

Both sides translated their disagreements into ideological terms. American newspapers, propagandists, and political groups, echoing Enlightenment ideas, argued that violation of their fundamental rights justified a fight for independence. Most people in Britain stood against rebellion and for parliamentary sovereignty as a matter of principle. They argued that they were making only reasonable and minimal demands on the colonies.

In the end, each side felt backed into a corner. The notion of full independence gained appeal among the colonists. American political leaders who were critical of British policies organized the First Continental Congress in 1774, hoping to persuade Parliament to abandon its efforts to directly control colonial affairs. In

→ connect to today ←

Power Struggle

Eighteenth-century kings and queens tried to strengthen their states while gaining status—often through war—in the international arena. How are states in today's world competing politically and economically with one another, both in the West and in the world as a whole?

response, King George III increased British armed forces in America, convinced that "blows must decide whether they are to be subject to the Country or Independent."

A War for Independence

The first blows were exchanged in 1775 between British troops and American militiamen in New England. The Second Continental Congress appointed George Washington (1732–1799) its military commander, setting the course for armed rebellion and independence. On July 4, 1776, that Congress issued the Declaration of Independence, written primarily by Thomas Jefferson (1743–1826) and based on the ideas of John Locke and other Enlightenment thinkers. Citing "self-evident" truths; "inalienable" natural rights such as "Life, Liberty, and the pursuit of Happiness"; and "a long train of abuses" to reduce the people under "absolute Despotism," the Declaration passionately justified rebellion.

Odds favored the stronger British forces, and at first they had the upper hand. Indeed, many British leaders viewed the rebel troops with disdain, one official calling the rebels a "rude rabble without a plan." Nevertheless, despite much internal division, an American victory at Saratoga in 1777 persuaded the French to help the Americans with money, ships, and troops against France's longtime enemy. The Dutch and Spanish eventually declared war on Britain, increasing the stakes for the British. Now British posses-

sions in the West Indies, the Mediterranean, and perhaps even India hung in the balance. In 1781, the victory of the French fleet off Virginia forced a large British army to surrender at Yorktown. This indignity convinced the British that the effort to keep the American colonies was not worth the costs. After two years of negotiations, the combatants drew up the Treaty of Paris in 1783. Britain agreed to recognize American independence and ceded to the United States the lands between the Mississippi River to the west, Canada to the north, and Spanish Florida to the south.

Creating the New Nation

In 1787, a new American constitution established a central government balanced by a separation of powers and strong states' rights. A Bill of Rights was soon enacted, protecting individual liberties and separating church and state. These principles, though lofty, did not apply to everyone. Although the Declaration of Independence had proclaimed that "all men are created equal" as a "self-evident" truth, one-fifth of the people remained slaves, and only property owners and men could vote. Nevertheless, the new nation had instituted—to an unprecedented degree—popular control, personal freedom, and formal toleration.

Some historians deem the American rebellion a war for independence, and others call it a revolution. At the time, people throughout the West—not just in America and Great

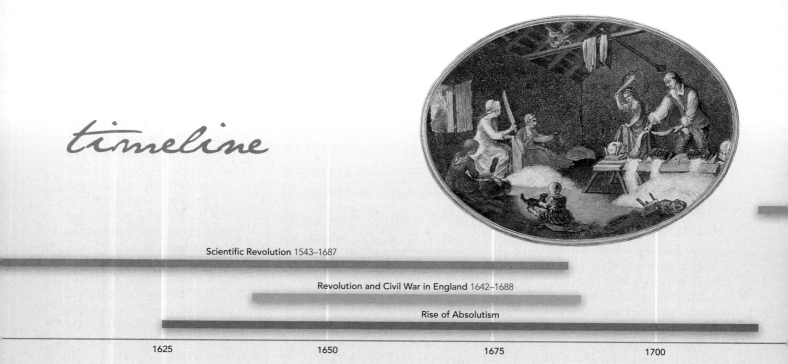

timeline

Scientific Revolution 1543–1687

Revolution and Civil War in England 1642–1688

Rise of Absolutism

1625   1650   1675   1700

Britain—viewed the events as dramatic and significant. A growing body of European readers avidly followed the action in newspaper accounts. Many

War for independence or revolution? of these readers saw the American Revolution as a victory for Enlightenment ideas. They did not realize that the debts incurred by France and the ideas promoted by the American Revolution would soon come back to haunt the French monarchy.

SUMMARY

On the surface, life between 1715 and 1789 seemed to change only incrementally for most Westerners. The vast majority still lived in the countryside and worked the fields. Moreover, society and politics in the so-called Old Regime remained dominated by the aristocracy and, in most places, the monarchy. As in the seventeenth century, cultural forms still reflected elite tastes and the traditional values of commoners below them. Below the surface, however, the West changed in crucial ways during this period.

- European rulers used their growing armies and navies to compete for power and wealth. For example, the political balance of power shifted as Russia and Prussia rose in the east while Britain gained prominence in the west.

Internally, monarchs often struggled for control with the nobility—sometimes their chief allies, sometimes their main competitors.

- Some monarchs enacted reforms and even took on trappings of "enlightened" rulers, whereas others—such as the French kings—failed in these ways.

- Mushrooming commerce, the agricultural revolution, and the spreading of cottage industry altered the ways by which millions of people earned a living, and these changes generated enormous new wealth.

- The music, art, and literature of the elites—especially the modern novel in literature and the baroque and classical styles in art and music—were part of a broader, cosmopolitan culture of old and new trends that spilled across national boundaries.

- The lower classes engaged in cultural outlets, such as festivals, popular literature, and religious revivals, that fit their lives and provided a sense of common identity.

- In Britain's North American colonies, the American Revolution posed a challenge to the status quo that the French would soon take up in a much more fundamental way.

All these developments, combined with the spread of Enlightenment ideas, mark the eighteenth century as a period in which Westerners—knowingly or not—laid foundations for the great transformations to come.

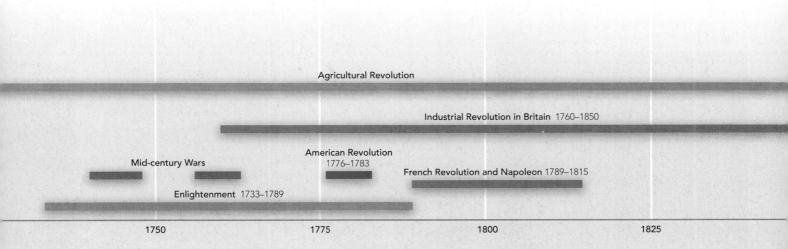

Agricultural Revolution

Industrial Revolution in Britain 1760–1850

Mid-century Wars

American Revolution 1776–1783

French Revolution and Napoleon 1789–1815

Enlightenment 1733–1789

1750　　　　　1775　　　　　1800　　　　　1825

JEAN-PIERRE HOUEL, *THE STORMING OF THE BASTILLE,* ca. 1789   On July 14, 1789, a crowd of Parisians stormed the Bastille, a castle-prison. The painting, one of many illustrating this event, poignantly captures the symbolism of the act. The Bastille, representing the old feudal regime of the past, falls because of corruption within and the heroic power of an outraged people fighting under the revolutionary banner of "Liberty, Equality, Fraternity."

Overturning
the Political
and Social
Order

16

The French Revolution and
Napoleon, 1789–1815

Trouble Brewing in France

France was beginning to stir. On October 17, 1787,
Arthur Young, a British farmer and diarist traveling
through France, described "a great ferment amongst
all ranks of men, who are eager for some change,
without knowing what to look to, or to hope for."
People whom Young talked with in Paris concluded
that "they are on the eve of some great revolution in
the government." ▶▶

Young recognized discontent percolating among the French population, but there was good reason for people everywhere to assume that any crises would pass without a fundamental change in the monarchy or social order. The French monarchy had remained intact for centuries. Both Louis XVI and his predecessor, Louis XV, ruled over the leading nation on the Continent—a country more populous, wealthy, and educated than ever. Although neither king could claim much popularity, Louis XVI could at least bask in the glory of supporting the American revolutionaries in their victory over the British, France's chief competitor.

Then what caused the "great ferment" in France described by our British traveler? Below the surface bubbled growing complaints within France's social orders. Members of the aristocracy and middle classes, many influenced by the ideas of the Enlightenment, wanted more rights and power from the monarchy. Peasants suffered hardships that could, as in the past, create disorder and uprisings. However, the immediate, visible problem came from a conflict over France's finances. ◄◄

THE COLLAPSE OF THE OLD ORDER

When Louis XVI ascended the throne in 1774, he inherited a large—and constantly growing—national debt. Much of that debt had been incurred financing wars and maintaining the military (see Chapter 15). Yet this debt should not have broken a nation as rich as France.

The taxation system

Great Britain and the Netherlands had higher per-capita debts than France, but these countries also boasted taxation systems and banks to support their debts. France lacked an adequate banking system, and most of the national debt was short term and privately held. Moreover, France's taxation system offered little help. The French nobility, clergy, and much of the bourgeoisie controlled the bulk of France's wealth and had long been exempt from most taxes. Nearly all direct taxes fell on the struggling peasantry. There was no consistent set of rules or method for collecting taxes throughout the country, and private tax collectors diverted much revenue from the treasury into their own pockets. Unless something was done, royal bankruptcy loomed ahead.

A succession of ministers tried all kinds of temporary solutions, but to no avail. Costs incurred to support the Americans in their war of independence against England made matters worse. Now interest payments on the debt ate up half of all government expenditures. Bankers began refusing to lend the government money.

Desperate, Louis called an Assembly of Notables in 1787 and pleaded with these selected nobles, clergy, and officials to consent to new taxes and financial reforms. Still they refused, as did the judges (all members of the nobility) in the *parlement*, or law court, of Paris when Louis turned to them. Instead, leading nobles and officials demanded a meeting of an old representative institution, the Estates General. They fully expected to control these proceedings and thereby assert their own interests. With bankruptcy imminent and nowhere else to turn for help, the king gave in. No one knew it at the time, but Louis' decision set the stage for turning France's financial crisis into a political and social movement of epic proportions.

The Underlying Causes of the Revolution

Louis' financial woes were just the most visible part of France's problems. When these tensions combined with the conflicts tugging at the fabric of French society, a dangerous blend resulted. One of the most troubling conflicts stemmed from the relationship between the monarchy and the nobility. For centuries, the French nobility, less than 2 percent of the population, had been the foundation on which the monarchy established its rule. However, the

Revolt of the nobility

nobility was also the monarchy's chief rival for power, and it had grown increasingly assertive during the eighteenth century (see Chapter 15). Through institutions such as the *parlements* that they controlled, nobles resisted ministerial efforts to tax them. More and more, nobles claimed to be protecting their rights as well as France itself from "ministerial despotism." So, when the monarchy turned to this group for financial help, the nobles refused for two reasons. First, they wanted to protect their own financial interests. Second, they used the crisis to assert their independence. Indeed, they argued that they represented the nation. They established a price for their cooperation: a greater share of power. Understandably, France's kings refused to pay that price. Thus, when the Assembly of Notables turned a deaf ear to Louis' pleas in 1787 and instead demanded a meeting of the Estates General, the king faced a financial crisis that was linked to a virtual revolt of his own nobility.

Louis might have thought he could find allies within the middle class in his standoff with the nobility. After all, French and other European kings had occasionally turned to wealthy members of this class for support in the past. Nevertheless, as events would prove in the tumultuous months of 1789, the middle class had changed—it now nursed its own set of grievances. This growing social sec-

Middle-class demands

tor—having almost tripled during the century to some 9 percent of the population—had benefited greatly from France's general prosperity and population boom after 1715. Many talented, wealthy, and ambitious members of the middle class managed to gain the high offices, titles, and privileges enjoyed by the nobility. Others rubbed shoulders and shared ideas with the nobility in salons and did their best to copy the nobles' style of life. Moreover, most had found ways to avoid paying heavy taxes.

However, numerous members of the bourgeoisie—particularly younger administrators, lawyers, journalists, and intellectuals—had encountered frustrating barriers to the offices and prestige enjoyed by the nobility. They also had grown impatient with the monarchy's failure to enact reforms that would benefit them specifically. By 1789, many applauded broad attacks on the privileged orders and the status quo. An example of such an attack was Abbé Emmanuel-Joseph Sieyès' widely circulated pamphlet *What Is the Third Estate?* According to Sieyès, "If the privileged order should be abolished, the nation would be nothing less, but something more." The sorts of reforms that these middle-class critics had in mind were no more palatable to the monarchy than those of the nobility.

People from both the middle class and the nobility had begun expressing ideas and using highly charged political terms that profoundly threatened the monarchy. In the decades before 1789, salon meet-

Enlightenment ideas and language

ings and new publications had spread key ideas of the Enlightenment to an increasingly literate public, particularly the aristocratic and middle-class elite in Paris and other French cities (see Chapter 14). These ideas emphasized the validity of reason and natural rights and questioned long-established institutions. They also undermined notions of the divine rights of kings and traditional ways of life—all while intensifying expectations of rapid reforms. In addition, terms such as *nation, citizen,* and *general will* had increasingly cropped up in the political discourse and reflected a growing sense that politics should include more than the concerns of the monarch and a tiny elite. So, when nobles asserted their own interests against the king, they often used language and ideas that attacked monarchical absolutists as unjustified tyrants and that accused the king's minister of "despotism." Middle-class men and women shared these sentiments and later extended them to demands for legal equality.

Thus, given all the resentments brewing among the nobility and the middle class, Louis and his often unpopular ministers risked much after they exposed themselves to discussions of reform within the Estates General. Three other developments—all beyond the powers of the king, nobility, and middle class—added an underlying sense of disappointment, desperation, and disorder among the French people in these decades.

First, a gap opened between rosy expectations and frightening realities. Before 1770, France had enjoyed a long period of prosperity. This growing wealth engendered a sense of rising expectations—that economically, things would keep getting better and better. After 1770, a series of economic depressions struck, turning

Disappointed expectations

these high expectations into bitter disappointment and frustration. Worse, in 1788 the countryside suffered unusually bad harvests. In May and July of that year, hailstorms wiped out crops throughout France. Drought and then the most severe winter in decades followed. The price of bread soared, and with it came hunger, desperation, and even starvation. Droves of peasants crowded into the cities in search of jobs and help, but the agricultural depression had already spread there and had thrown thousands of artisans and laborers out of work. In the spring of 1789, peasants and urban poor looking for food turned to violence in France's cities and villages. Women led groups demanding grain and lower prices for flour. Desperate people attacked bakeries and stores of grain wherever they could find them. Arthur Young wrote, "the want of bread is terrible: accounts arrive every moment from the provinces of riots and disturbances, and calling in the military, to preserve the peace of the markets." The populace angrily blamed governmental figures and "parasitical agents" of the Old Regime for their plight. Many pamphlets and cartoons portraying the connection between suffering and France's privileged orders circulated throughout France.

The second unsettling development came with the increasing demands for political participation and governmental reform throughout the West in the years before 1789. These movements, arising in various countries, were led by ambitious elites. In Poland, agitation for

Demands for political participation

independence from Russian influence surfaced between 1772 and 1792. Across the Atlantic, what started as a tax revolt in Britain's North American colonies turned into the American Revolution and war for independence that directly involved French aristocrats and common soldiers alike and led to government without a king (see Chapter 15). In the Dutch Republic, demands for reform in the 1780s erupted into open revolt in 1787.

> The populace angrily blamed government figures and "parasitical agents" of the Old Regime for their plight.

FRANCE'S PRIVILEGED ORDERS, ca. 1789 This French cartoon shows an enslaved "common man" as a naked beast of burden carrying the merciless, privileged monarchy, clergy, and aristocracy on his back. Cartoons such as this example not only captured popular opinion but also served as propaganda that helped to fuel the revolution.

In the Austrian Netherlands (Belgium and Luxembourg), elites rose against the reforms initiated by Emperor Joseph II in 1787. Well-informed French elites, keeping abreast of these disturbances, began to surmise that they, too, might successfully challenge the political status quo.

The economic hardship and political uprisings across Europe were damaging enough. A third problem—the French people's disrespect for their own king—made matters worse. For much of the eighteenth century, France had been ruled by the unremarkable, unpopular, and long-lived King Louis XV. Unlike some of his European counterparts, neither he nor his successor, Louis XVI, managed to forge an effective alliance with the nobility or consistently assert their authority over it. Nor did they succeed in enacting reforms or even give the impression of being "enlightened" monarchs. Louis XVI had little particular taste or talent for rule, and his unpopular Austrian wife, Queen Marie Antoinette, increasingly drew fire for her supposed extravagance and indifference to those below her. According to a widely circulated story, she dismissed reports that the poor could not buy bread with the phrase "Let them eat cake!" Though the story was untrue, it reflected the growing anger against the king and queen.

Desperate to stave off the immediate threat of bankruptcy, the relatively weak Louis XVI looked for support.

Unpopular kings

Instead of able allies, he found a jealous nobility, a disgruntled middle class, a bitter and frustrated peasantry, and an urban poor made desperate by hunger.

The Tennis Court Oath

In this ominous atmosphere, Louis XVI summoned the Estates General in 1788. This representative body, which had not met since 1614, was divided into France's three traditional orders, or estates: the first estate, the clergy, owned over 10 percent of France's best land; the second estate, the nobility, owned more than 20 percent of the land; and the third estate, the so-called commoners, included the bourgeoisie, the peasantry, and the urban populace. During the early months of 1789, elections of representatives to the Estates General were held. All men who had reached the age of 25 and who paid taxes could vote. In thousands of meetings to draw up lists of grievances to present to the king, people found their political voices and connected their dissatisfactions with inflating expectations of reform. Hundreds of pamphlets appeared and public debate spread widely. Each of the three estates elected its own representatives. Because the third estate made up more than nine-tenths of the total population, Louis XVI agreed to grant it as many seats as the other two estates combined. However, by tradition, the three estates sat separately, and each group had one vote.

The Estates General

In April 1789, delegates began streaming into Versailles armed only with *cahiers*, or the lists of grievances from all classes of people, that had been called for by the king. Of the 600 representatives of the third estate, not one came from the peasantry. Except for a handful of liberal clergy and nobles elected to the third estate, these delegates—mostly ambitious lawyers, petty officials, administrators, and other professionals—were all members of the bourgeoisie. They fully expected to solve the financial crisis quickly and then move on to addressing the long lists of complaints that they had been accumulating for years. Most bourgeois representatives, like many liberal nobles, wanted to create a constitutional government with a national assembly that would meet regularly to pass taxes and laws.

After religious services and a solemn procession in Paris, the delegates met in Versailles on May 5. Immediately they debated the voting system. The two privileged estates demanded that, according to custom, the three estates meet separately and vote by order—that is, each estate cast one vote. This procedure would place power squarely in the hands of the nobility, which controlled most of the first estate as well as its own order. The third estate demanded that all the orders meet jointly and that delegates vote by head. This method would favor the third estate, for not only did this order boast as many members as the other two combined, but a number of liberal clergy and nobles in the first and second estates sympathized with the reforms called for by the third estate. All sides realized that the outcome of this voting issue would be decisive.

The delegates haggled for six weeks. Louis waffled from one side to the other. Finally, the third estate, backed by some clergy from the first estate, took action and declared itself the National Assembly of France on June 17 and

The National Assembly invited the other two estates to join it in enacting legislation. Three days later, when the third-estate deputies arrived at their meeting hall, they found it locked. Adjourning to a nearby building that served as an indoor tennis court, they took the **Tennis Court Oath,** vowing not to disband until France had a constitution. The painting below dramatizes and glorifies this act of defiance.

On June 23, the king met with the three estates in a royal session. He offered many reforms but also commanded the estates to meet separately and vote by order. Then the king, his ministers, and members of the first two estates regally filed out. The third-estate representatives, however, defiantly remained seated. When the royal master of ceremonies returned to remind them of the king's orders, Count Mirabeau (1749–1791), a liberal nobleman elected by the third estate, jumped to his feet. "Go and tell those who sent you," he shouted, "that we are here by the will of the people and will not leave this place except at the point of the bayonet!" When the startled courtier dutifully repeated these words to his master, Louis XVI, with characteristic weakness, replied, "They mean to stay. Well, damn it, let them stay." A few days later, the king reversed himself and ordered the three estates to meet jointly and vote by head. The third estate had won the first round.

Storming the Bastille

The monarchy might have been able to reassert control had not the new National Assembly received unexpected support from two sources: the Parisian populace and the French peasantry. Both groups had been suffering from the unusually poor economic conditions initiated by bad harvests. Revolutionary events raised expectations in hard times, making these people in the city and countryside particularly volatile. The first important disturbances broke out in Paris, whose population of 600,000 made it one of the largest cities in Europe. In early July, rumors that the king was calling the professional troops of the frontier garrison to Versailles raced through the streets of

SCHOOL OF JACQUES-LOUIS DAVID, *THE TENNIS COURT OATH,* ca. 1792 On June 17, 1789, the third estate took an oath to create a constitution for France. In the center below the presiding officer, from left to right, a white-robed Carthusian monk represents the second estate, a black-robed Catholic curate the first estate, and the brown-clad Protestant minister the third estate. They join, symbolizing the transformation of the meeting into the newly formed National Assembly.

Paris. Alarmed, residents concluded that the king meant to use force against them. Then Louis dismissed his popular finance minister, Jacques Necker (1732–1804). This move seemed to confirm the fears of the third estate, who saw Necker as an ally.

At this critical juncture, the common people of Paris acted on their own. On July 14, riotous crowds of men and women searching for arms marched on the **Bastille,** a gloomy old fortress-prison in a working-class quarter. Few people were actually in the weakly guarded Bastille, but it symbolized the old order. Many died in the confused battle. With the help of mutinous troops, however, the crowd eventually took the Bastille, hacked its governor to death, and paraded around Paris with his head on a pike. "This glorious day must amaze our enemies, and finally usher in for us the triumph of justice and liberty," proclaimed a Paris newspaper.

Uprisings in the country-side echoed events in Paris. That July and August, peasants throughout France revolted against their lords. Burning tax rolls, the peasantry attacked

Peasant revolts

manors, reoccupied enclosed lands, and rejected the traditional rights of noble landowners—dues on land, flour mills, wine presses, and law courts, and the tithes (taxes) landlords charged their tenants. These revolts intensified with the spreading of unfounded rumors that bands of brigands, perhaps assembled by nobles, were on the loose in the countryside. Panicked by this "Great

The "Great Fear"

Fear," many nobles—including one of the king's brothers—fled France and became known as the *émigrés* (exiles).

The End of the Old Order

Now the nobility as well as the monarchy was in retreat. The National Assembly—dominated by the middle-class deputies from the third estate but now including many deputies from the clergy and nobility—tried to pacify the aroused peasantry. On August 4, during a night session of the National Assembly, one nobleman after another stood up and renounced his traditional rights and privileges in an effort to make the best of a bad situation. A leader of the Assembly hailed the "end of feudalism." As the document on page 377 shows, the National Assembly quickly decreed

the end of serfdom, traditional dues owed to landlords, special taxation rights, and privileged access to official posts. The peasantry seemed pacified for the time being.

Success spurred the National Assembly to take further steps. The most important of these actions occurred on August 26, when the Assem-

Declaration of the Rights of Man and Citizen

bly proclaimed the **Declaration of the Rights of Man and Citizen.** Enlightenment ideas and phrases similar to those in the American Declaration of Independence filled this document. "Men are born and remain free and equal in rights," it stated. The natural rights included "liberty, property, security, and resistance to oppression." Sovereignty—supreme authority—rested with the nation as a whole, not the monarchy. Enacted laws should express the "general will"—a term and idea made popular by Jean-Jacques Rousseau (see Chapter 14). The document proclaimed freedom of opinion "even in religion," freedom of the press, and freedom from arbitrary arrest. In 1791, this spirit would lead to the liberation of France's Jews from old legal disabilities.

Some of these rights, such as freedom of the press, applied to women as well as men, but only men gained the full measure of new social and political rights. In the months and years that followed, many women objected to this limitation. Organizing groups and writing petitions and pamphlets, these women demanded to be included. In 1791, Olympe de Gouges (1748–1793), a writer and strong supporter of the Revolution, wrote one of the best-known and more challenging pamphlets, the *Declaration of the Rights of Women.* She argued that women should have the same political and social rights as men: "The only limits on the exercise of the natural rights of woman are perpetual male tyranny; these limits are to be reformed by the laws of nature and reason." Some members of the government, such as the Marquis de Condorcet (1743–1794), voiced similar demands. Despite this rising tide of defiance, Louis refused to sign the August decrees. Instead, he once more assembled troops around Versailles and Paris.

In answer to this new threat of force, on October 5 and 6, a huge crowd of Parisian women, already infuriated by high bread prices and food shortages, marched 11 miles through the rain to Versailles, where they surrounded

March to Versailles

→ connect
to
today ←

Vive la Revolution!

The compelling banner of "Liberty, Equality, Fraternity" proved so potent that the French Revolution's impact spread far beyond the borders of France. It soon spawned wars that engulfed most of Europe for more than two decades. How do the causes of the French Revolution compare to those of uprisings and revolutions today?

---

the palace. With the help of members of the recently formed National Guard—units of armed civilians under Lafayette—they forced the king and his family to accompany them back to Paris, bringing him closer to the people and away from the protected isolation of Versailles and the king's aristocratic advisors. As the carriage bearing the royal family rolled toward the capital, where the royal family would be virtually imprisoned in the Tuileries Palace, the surrounding crowd of women and men shouted jubilantly, "We have the baker [the king], the baker's wife, and the little cook boy! Now we shall have bread!" Although this image of women taking political action into their own hands made them heroines of the Revolution in some eyes, others would nervously look back on the women's behavior as something inappropriate and even frightening. Most men were not ready to accept such a change in women's traditional roles.

A few days later, the National Assembly moved its sessions to Paris. The third estate, building on the anger and hunger of the peasantry and the urban poor, had triumphed. The old order had disintegrated.

THE CONSTITUTIONAL MONARCHY: Establishing a New Order

Flushed with success, the National Assembly now turned to the task of transforming French institutions. Guiding principles were represented by the revolutionary banner

Liberty, Equality, Fraternity

"Liberty, Equality, Fraternity." At that time, the idea of liberty meant freedom from arbitrary authority and freedom of speech, press, conscience, assembly, and profession. Equality meant equal treatment under the law and equality of economic opportunity—at least for men. Fraternity meant comradeship as citizens of the nation. During the next two years, the Assembly passed a series of sweeping reforms that altered almost all aspects of life in France.

The central government, now based on national sovereignty, was transformed into what amounted to a constitutional monarchy. The National Assembly served as its

Constitutional monarchy

legislature, and the king (still an important symbol of authority for many) remained its chief executive officer. Because only taxpaying males could vote and win election to office, the bourgeoisie firmly held the reins of power. For the time being, the governance of France was decentralized. To undermine old loyalties and the power of the provincial nobility, the National Assembly created eighty-three newly named departments, each almost equal in size and administered

New Laws End the Feudal System in France

Cracking under the pressures of the summer of 1789, nobles in the National Assembly moved on August 4 and 5 to abolish their own feudal rights and privileges. The following excerpts describe some of the laws passed to end the feudal system.

ARTICLE I. The National Assembly hereby completely abolishes the feudal system. It decrees that, among the existing rights and dues, . . . all those originating in or representing real or personal serfdom or personal servitude, shall be abolished without indemnification.

IV. All manorial courts are hereby suppressed without indemnification. . . .

VII. The sale of judicial and municipal offices shall be suppressed forthwith. Justice shall be dispensed *gratis*.

IX. Pecuniary privileges, personal or real, in the payment of taxes are abolished forever. Taxes shall be collected from all the citizens, and from all property, in the same manner and in the same form. . . .

XI. All citizens, without distinction of birth, are eligible to any office or dignity, whether ecclesiastical, civil or military; and no profession shall imply any derogation.

What conclusions about the grievances underlying the French Revolution might this document support?

THE MARCH TO VERSAILLES In this spirited scene from the times, determined Parisian women, carrying weapons and hauling a cannon, march to Versailles to confront the king with their demands and to force the royal family back to Paris.

by locally elected assemblies and officials. Similarly, the National Assembly took France's judicial system out of the hands of the nobility and clergy. It created new civil and criminal courts, with elected judges. France's complex, unequal system of taxation was also swept away, replaced by uniform taxes on land and the profits of trade and industry.

The new government linked reform of the Catholic Church with the financial problems it faced. Repudiating France's debt was out of the question because part of it was owed to members of the bourgeoisie. To pay for its expenditures, the National Assembly issued what amounted to paper money called *assignats*. To back up the *assignats*, pay off the debt, and at the same time bring the church under governmental control, government officials confiscated and sold church property.

This seizure of property constituted a major step toward the nationalization of the church. Next the Assembly dissolved all convents and monasteries and prohibited the taking of religious vows. People would elect the clergy, including non–Roman Catholics, and the state would pay their salaries. These measures were incorporated in the **Civil Constitution of the Clergy,** to which all members of the clergy were required to take an oath of allegiance in order to perform their functions and draw their salaries. This last step proved too much for many religious officials, for it threatened the very independence of the clergy. Pope Pius VI called the oath of allegiance "the poisoned fountainhead and source of all errors." Approximately half the clergy of France, including nearly all the bishops, refused to take the oath. This defection of the nonjuring clergy created a long-lasting division among France's Catholic population. Many people, especially rural women, fought against this disturbance of their religious life, vowing to defend their faith "with the last drop" of blood. The Revolution would lose the support of many French citizens who felt loyal to the old church and their local priests.

Civil Constitution of the Clergy

The King Discredited

Louis XVI must have bitterly resented these changes, for they diluted his power and put Paris under the control of his former subjects. Nonetheless, he managed to make things even worse for himself. On June 20, 1791, the royal family, in disguise, escaped from Paris and headed by coach to France's northeastern frontier, where Louis hoped to find supporters and perhaps reverse the tide of events. Unfortunately for him and his family, a postmaster recognized them just before they could reach safety. Officials arrested the royal family in Varennes and returned them to Paris. To save face, the government concocted a thin story about the royal family being kidnapped, but in many eyes the king and queen had now become traitors.

Flight of the royal family

In October 1791, the National Assembly gave way to the Legislative Assembly, with all new representatives elected under the new rules. In only two years, and with relatively little bloodshed, France had been made over. A written constitution ruled supreme over the diminished monarchy. The church lost its independence from the state. The nobility forfeited its special rights and privileges. Men gained individual rights and liberties and legal equality. Though excluded by the reformers, women would nevertheless continue to voice demands for political and social rights and play important roles as the Revolution evolved. France now boasted a more democratic electoral system than England or the United States. Events had already gone well beyond anything our British traveler, Arthur Young, might have imagined two years earlier.

Reactions Outside France

Outside France, writers and reformers in Europe and the United States hailed the French Revolution or the principles underlying it. In elegant salons, elites spiritedly discussed these dramatic events, and in newspapers and pamphlets, writers dissected and debated their meaning. Supporters established societies in Britain and in states along France's eastern borders. Some activists, such as the American writer Tom Paine, traveled to Paris to participate directly. In Britain, Charles Fox, a leader of the Whigs, called the Revolution "much the greatest event that ever happened, and much the best." Others argued against the French Revolution. The most famous attack was launched by Edmund Burke in his *Reflections on the Revolution in France* (1790). This British statesman argued that France moved too quickly in the name of abstract notions of natural rights and justice. As a result, revolutionaries replaced a despotic monarchy with anarchy. In his view, societies should evolve slowly, drawing reforms from the long historical experience of a national culture. Good government came from good habits. Reforms worked well when based on a nation's best traditions.

Most governments opposed the Revolution when they realized the threat it posed to their own security. If a revolution could rise in France, end aristocratic privileges, and undermine the monarchy, the same might happen elsewhere. Officials welcomed and listened to the aristocratic émigrés who fled France. They suppressed pro-revolutionary groups within their borders. Within a few years, most states joined coalitions to fight against the revolutionary armies.

OPINION

What do you think Louis XVI could have done to keep as much power as possible?

TO THE RADICAL REPUBLIC AND BACK

The new government, launched with such optimism in October 1791, lasted less than a year. Up to that point, the bourgeoisie and the peasants had been the primary beneficiaries of the Revolution. The bourgeoisie had gained political control over the country and social mobility. The peasantry had won freedom from feudal obligations. To the many peasant landowners who owned their land before the Revolution were now added others who had seized the lands of émigré nobles or had purchased confiscated church lands (though many of these lands went to middle-class buyers).

However, other groups remained quite dissatisfied. The royal family and much of the aristocracy and high clergy yearned for the restoration of their traditional positions. On the other hand, many Parisians urged a more radical approach to the Revolution. These shopkeepers, artisans, bakers, innkeepers, and workers had won little beyond theoretical rights and legal equality. Those who owned no property still could not vote, yet they had supplied much of the physical force and anger that had saved the third estate and made the reforms possible. Increasingly, these men and women formed organizations, held meetings, and intently discussed the numerous pamphlets, petitions, and newspapers printed daily in Paris. Some of these clubs became egalitarian meeting places for women and men; others, such as the Society of Revolutionary Republican Women, insisted that women should participate more fully in the Revolution. Many of the most politically active came to be known as the **sans-culottes**

Sans-culottes

because they wore long pants instead of the fashionable knee breeches of the elites. A pamphlet described a *sans-culotte* as "a man who has no mansions, no lackeys to wait on him, and who lives quite simply. . . . He is useful, because he knows how to plough a field, handle a forge, a saw, or a file, how to cover a roof or how to make shoes and to shed his blood to the last drop to save the Republic." Typically the *sans-culottes* carried pikes and addressed people as "Citizen" or "Citizeness." Eventually they and their supporters gained control over the municipal government of Paris—the Commune.

Leadership for this urban populace fell into the hands of radical members of the bourgeoisie, who allied themselves with the *sans-culottes* and favored overthrow of the monarchy and extension of the Revolution. Well organized and ably led, these radicals came together in numerous clubs that formed to debate and plan political matters. The **Jacobin** Club, which had hundreds of affiliated clubs outside of Paris, became the most important of these political organizations. Its membership included more than 200 deputies, and over time, militant radicals gained strength within the organization.

The Jacobin Club

War and the Breakdown of Order

Events—particularly the rumors of war that had begun circulating throughout France—soon played into the hands of the Parisian radicals. The monarchs of Austria and Prussia, fearing the spread of revolutionary ideas to their own lands and urged on by French émigrés, began to make threatening moves and to issue meddlesome warnings to the French revolutionaries. In France, many groups welcomed the prospect of war, though for different reasons. The royal family and its supporters believed a French victory would enhance the prestige and power of the throne; even a French defeat could help by restoring the Old Regime and royal power. Radicals, who wanted to turn France into a republic, believed that war would expose the inefficiency and disloyalty of the king and topple the monarchy.

The war that broke out in April 1792 became the first of a series of conflicts that would span twenty-three years and ultimately embroil most of the Western world. At first, inflation, food shortages, and breakdowns of order hampered France's war effort. The French armies suffered from lack of experienced leadership; nearly all the high-ranking officers were members of the nobility and had either fled or been deposed. The Austrian and Prussian armies badly defeated the French and advanced toward Paris. Panic broke out in the city. "Everywhere you hear the cry that the king is betraying us, the generals are betraying us, that nobody is to be trusted . . . that Paris will be taken," exclaimed an observer. When the Prussian commander, the Duke of Brunswick, announced that he would deliver the royal family "from their captivity," French radicals

The Jacobins' Revolutionary Politics

In the years following 1789, the Jacobin Club of Paris became the most influential political club in the city and, with many affiliated clubs outside of Paris, the most important in France. The Jacobins pushed politics in an increasingly more radical direction. The following document, which they circulated on September 12, 1792, reveals some of the club's evolving goals and tactics.

The people of Paris have felt the necessity of preserving an imposing attitude and of exercising a strict surveillance over the Minions and agents of the traitor, Louis the Last. Be apprehensive, brothers and friends, lest new intrigues shall follow the baffled intrigues. The head, the cause and the pretext of the machinations still lives! Despotism moves in the darkness; let us be ready to engage in a combat to the death with it, under whatever form it presents itself. . . .

These orders are in substance:

The purgatorial examination of the National Convention, in order to reject from its midst the suspected members who may have escaped the sagacity of the primary assemblies;

The revocability of the deputies to the National Convention who have attacked or who attack by any motions the rights of the sovereign;

The sanction, or the popular revision of all the constitutional decrees of the National Convention;

The entire abolition of royalty and the penalty of death against those who may propose to reestablish it;

The form of a republican government.

What tensions within France does this document expose?

rightly accused Louis XVI and Marie Antoinette of being in treasonable communication with the enemy. On August 10, local leaders in Paris organized a huge Parisian crowd of men and women, who then attacked the king's palace. The royal family fled for their lives to the Legislative Assembly. The invading crowd wrecked the interior of the palace and slaughtered hundreds of the king's guards. The Legislative Assembly suspended and imprisoned the hapless Louis XVI. Under pressure from the people of Paris, it called elections—this time with almost all men enjoying the right to vote—for a National Convention to draw up a new, more radical constitution.

Meanwhile, one of the Jacobin leaders, Georges-Jacques Danton (1759–1794), used his great skills as an orator and organizer to gather recruits for the army and rush them to the front. As the **Panic and massacres** recruits prepared to leave Paris to meet the invading Prussians, rumors—spurred by the propaganda of radical journalists like Jean-Paul Marat (1743–1793)—spread that reactionary clergy and nobles planned to murder their wives and children. Frightened and enraged people began murdering members of the nonjuring clergy (who would not swear allegiance to the new order) and nobles being held in the prisons of Paris. During the first three weeks of September 1792, more than a thousand fell victim to these massacres.

In the elections for the National Convention, held amid this hysteria, republicans—favoring elimination of the monarchy altogether and the creation of a French republic— **National Convention** won a sweeping victory. Most of the conservative elements fearfully stayed away from the polls. This Convention ruled France for the next three years, taking the Revolution down a new, more radical road.

Radical Republicans Struggle for Power

The struggle for political dominance among the different Jacobin factions intensified after the election. The Girondins, so called because many of their leaders came from the vicinity of Bordeaux in the department of the Gironde, had once been the most powerful and radical faction of the Legislative Assembly. Because they had sat on the speaker's left, they had come to be known as "the Left." In the new National Convention, the Girondins found themselves on the Right as the more conservative faction. Now the Left consisted mostly of members of the Jacobin political club from Paris. These Jacobins came to be called "the Mountain" because they occupied the highest seats in the convention hall.

Girondins and Jacobins

On September 22, 1792, the National Convention declared France a republic. The government then disposed of the king, who had squandered most of his support since his flight to Varennes in 1791. The Convention tried Louis and found him guilty of treasonable communication with the enemy. An extended debate ensued over whether to execute the king, with most of the Girondins opposed and the Mountain in favor. On January 21, 1793, the Convention voted by a narrow margin to execute Louis.

The Republic

The image on this page depicts the scene of Louis' execution. On the platform, Louis addressed the crowd for the last time: "I die innocent." An eyewitness described how the executioners "dragged him under the axe of the guillotine, which with one stroke severed his head from his body." The revolutionary government adopted the newly invented guillotine as its instrument of choice because it considered the device more efficient and therefore humane than other methods of execution, such as hanging and the ax. In the painting an executioner holds up the head of the king for the troops and crowd to view. An observer reported that a few seconds later, "cries of 'Vive la Républic' [long live the Republic] were heard . . . and in less than ten minutes this cry, a thousand times repeated, became the universal shout of the multitude, and every hat was in the air." Although other executions would not have the same significance or draw the same crowds, this scene would be repeated thousands of times over the next two years. Beheadings not only served as affirmations of revolutionary justice but also provided entertainment—people often rented chairs and purchased food, drinks, and souvenirs, including miniature guillotines. Those who could not attend might purchase widely sold prints such as the one pictured.

Execution of the king

Ten months later the queen, Marie Antoinette, followed Louis XVI to the guillotine. These executions sent a shudder of horror through the royal courts of Europe, as did the new French army recruits' surprising success against the Austrian and Prussian coalition. The hastily assembled revolutionary armies, swelling with numbers and enthusiasm, had checked the advancing Austrian and Prussian armies at Valmy in September 1792. France now went on the offensive. Alarmed, Britain, the Dutch Netherlands, Spain, Portugal, Sardinia, and Naples joined Austria and Prussia in a great coalition against France.

Internal and external enemies

EXECUTION OF LOUIS XVI, ca. 1794 In this depiction, an executioner holds up the head of Louis XVI, who has just been guillotined before a crowd of troops and other onlookers in central Paris.

This new external threat was compounded by internal threats to the revolutionary government. The peasants of the Vendée region in western France, stirred up by the nonjuring clergy and others, rebelled against the republican government. "We want our king, our priests and the Old Regime," cried the rebels. The uprising spread until some sixty of the eighty-three departments suffered revolts. Lyons, France's second-largest city, rose against the government in May. Toulon, the chief French naval base on the Mediterranean, invited in the British fleet to help in the fight against France's radical government. All-too-real enemies outside and within France's borders surged forward to fight against the Revolution.

The Terror

Faced with a seemingly inevitable demise of their cause and threatened by radical demands from the *sans-culottes*, the leaders of the Mountain decided to take drastic action. For support they turned to the Paris Commune, as the city government was called, which radicals and the *sans-culottes* controlled. The *sans-culottes* wanted to carry the Revolution even further, toward more direct democracy and governmental controls over the price of bread. Although the Mountain's leaders did not fully agree with the *sans-culottes*, they were willing to work with them to gain supremacy.

The National Convention, now dominated by the Mountain and surrounded by a threatening Parisian crowd of women and men urged on by *sans-culotte* leaders, voted the expulsion and arrest of their chief competitors, the Girondin leaders, on June 2, 1793. To pacify the *sans-culottes*, the National Convention also agreed to enact the Law of the Maximum to control the price of bread, flour, and other essentials. Finally, the Convention drafted a democratic constitution

Committee of Public Safety

based on universal male suffrage that promised rights to education and even subsistence (a job or poor relief). However, the Convention soon suspended the constitution and formed the 12-member **Committee of Public Safety** to guide the country. The committee had two main tasks: to secure the Republic against its enemies—both internal and external—and to carry out a radical republican program. With the vast authority granted by the Convention, it enjoyed dictatorial powers. The committee came under the ideological leadership of the gifted and feared Maximilien Robespierre (1758–1794). A lawyer from the provinces when elected to the Estates General in 1789, he quickly rose to head the Jacobin Club in Paris. This stern, determined idealist was influenced by Rousseau and was bent on the creation of a virtuous republic. In pursuit of this dream, Robespierre and his fellow committee members struggled both to appease and to control the unpredictable, threatening *sans-culottes*.

To protect the Republic from its internal enemies and to satisfy demands from the *sans-culottes* for immediate action, the Committee of Public Safety instituted a Reign of Terror. "We must annihilate the

Reign of Terror enemies of the Republic at home and abroad, or else we shall perish," Robespierre warned. He justified the Terror by arguing that in this time of revolution, "the first maxim of our politics ought to be to lead the people by means of reason and the enemies of the people by terror." Accordingly, agents of the committee searched out and summarily tried anyone suspected of being counterrevolutionaries. Even those who had once supported the Revolution—such as the Girondins, whose views had fallen out of favor—were arrested and executed. Though many people became victims of arbitrary justice, officials used the Terror most often where real threats arose—regions in revolt and vulnerable areas near France's borders. During this violent phase of the Revolution, probably between 200,000 and 400,000 victims of the Terror went to prison. Some 25,000 to 50,000 died in jail or at the hands of executioners.

To secure the Republic against external enemies, the government ordered a *levée en masse*, or general call-up of all men, women, and children to serve the nation. As able-bodied young men were rapidly

Levée en masse trained and rushed to the front, the army swelled to 850,000 men—a number that far exceeded the forces of France's opponents. Everyone else was supposed to contribute to the war effort by collecting or manufacturing supplies for the troops and by bolstering spirits. Women stitched clothing and served as nurses, children made bandages, and old men delivered stirring, patriotic speeches. This united activity for defense of the country produced an intense national patriotism.

One soldier wrote home from the front to explain his feelings: "When *la patrie* calls us to her defense, we ought to fly there. . . . Our life, our wealth, and our talents do not belong to us. It is to the nation, *la patrie*, that all that belongs." With the officer corps now open to talent and the massive mobilization of men, materials, and spirit, the citizen armies turned back coalition forces by the end of 1793. By the summer of the following year, they had carried the war beyond France's borders.

The Republic of Virtue

While fighting this war, Robespierre and the Committee of Public Safety carried out their radical republican program. They attempted to reform institutions and infuse all aspects of French life with revolutionary politics. They intended to create a Republic of Virtue based on Rousseauian ideas of reason and natural law.

Attacking the Catholic Church

First, they targeted those institutions that, in their view, represented the worst of the Old Regime. Many officials saw the Catholic Church in this negative light and sold church buildings, turned them into warehouses, or rededicated them as "temples of reason." Angry radicals disfigured religious statues, even sending some wooden figures of saints to the guillotine and melting down church treasures. The most enthusiastic radicals searched out nonjuring clergy for prosecution and pressured even the clergy who had sworn to uphold the Revolution to leave their vocations. Some radical leaders hoped that the new festivals established to celebrate the Revolution would provide a sufficient substitute for Christian rituals. Other revolutionaries tried to create new beliefs, such as the Cult of Reason, to replace Christianity. Robespierre tried in vain to institute his own deistic Cult of the Supreme Being.

The National Convention also enacted legislation that took the rules governing family life and education away from the church and placed them in state hands. Marriage became a civil rather than a religiously ordained act. New rules for

Family life and education divorce allowed thousands of couples to end marriages they would have been bound to under church rules. Births were registered at city halls rather than local churches. Women could sue for equal inheritance for the first time. Education became a responsibility of the state. New legislation mandated free primary schooling for all girls and boys and state-run secondary schooling, though in fact the government had neither the funds nor enough trained teachers to support such a system.

> Women stitched clothing and served as nurses, children made bandages, and old men delivered stirring, patriotic speeches.

Then & Now

Terrorist Activities

Between 1793 and 1794, France experienced the most radical phase of the Revolution, known as the Reign of Terror. During this period, France was essentially ruled by the Committee of Public Safety, led by Maximilien Robespierre. In a 1794 speech, Robespierre argued that "if the basis of popular government in time of peace is virtue, the basis of popular government in time of revolution is both virtue and terror: virtue without which terror is murderous, terror without which virtue is powerless." In recent years, particularly since 9/11, we have again been made aware of the weapons of terror and the ways their use have been justified by different groups. We also have seen how controversial antiterrorism measures are justified, such as the Patriot Act, which was signed into law by President George W. Bush in 2001 and reduces restrictions on authorized agencies' abilities to search individuals' records—including phone, email, and financial—if they are suspected of containing information about terrorist activities.

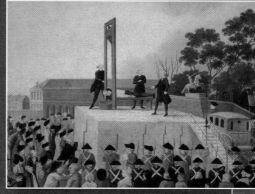

Women—especially those living in the cities—welcomed the new marriage, divorce, inheritance, and education laws, for they increased women's rights. However, the Jacobins had no desire to free women from their traditional role in the private sphere. Rather, they rejected women's participation in politics and outlawed female associations such as the Society of Revolutionary Republican Women. Jacobins declared that women's primary duties lay in nurturing children. They concluded that women had no proper role as active citizens and that women's political groups only disrupted the republican order. As one member of the government explained, "It is horrible, it is contrary to all laws of nature for a woman to want to make herself a man."

The new government went far beyond simply rooting out opponents of the Revolution and attacking institutions tied to the Old Regime. It also tried to create support for

Revolutionary symbols

the Republic by infusing the objects and activities of everyday life with revolutionary symbols. The figure of Liberty replaced royal symbols on everything from coins and statues to plates and posters. Patriotic groups planted liberty trees throughout France. Women adopted the flowing robes and hairstyles of ancient Greece that reflected rejection of the traditional social order. People sported revolutionary ribbons on their hats. Songs such as the "Marseillaise," rallying the "children of the nation . . . against . . . the

bloody standard of tyranny!" rang out among crowds and troops. Plays and paintings that supported the Revolution were encouraged. Officials promoted festivals that featured revolutionary symbols, mass loyalty oaths, and patriotic celebrations. Titles of all kinds were discarded and replaced with the terms "citizen" and "citizeness."

In the name of reason and revolutionary principles, the government revamped the calendar, making the months equal in length and naming them after the seasons. Weeks were made ten days long, with one day of rest. (This change eliminated Sunday, a day of traditional Christian importance.) September 22, 1792—the date of the declaration of the Republic—became the first day of Year I. The new metric system of weights and measures, based on units of 10, was introduced and eventually would spread beyond France's borders to countries throughout the world.

The Revolution Spreads Outside of France

Since 1792, France had fended off various coalitions of European powers. After initial defeats, France's citizen armies had gone on the offensive. During the struggles that ensued, France incorporated lands on its northern and eastern borders, claiming that these additions conformed to France's "natural boundaries" of the Rhine and the Alps. By 1799, more victories on the battlefield enabled France to set up "sister" republics in Holland, Switzerland, and Italy. To these areas, the French brought their own Enlightenment—inspired revolutionary principles and legislation. However, the gains carried a tremendous price tag: Hundreds of thousands died in the fighting, and the constant warfare disrupted trade and created shortages of essential goods.

Sister republics

The Revolution also powerfully influenced opinion outside France. Initially, many groups in nearby countries supported the Revolution and its principles. However, part of that support rested on seeing France, a powerful rival, weakened. As people began to understand the seriousness of the attacks on monarchy and aristocracy and the threat to their own political independence, support waned. Still, many intellectuals and liberal political groups continued to uphold the ideals of the Revolution, at least until 1793, when the Revolution took a more radical turn.

Outside opinion

The Revolution helped promote other developments farther away. In Poland, patriots tried to use inspiration from France to assert independence from Russia. Despite some initial successes, however, their efforts failed. In Ireland, the revolutionary doctrines of liberty, equality, and natural rights touched many, encouraging them to rise against their British lords and make Ireland a republic. Irish patriots even anticipated a French invasion to help their own rebellion, although the invasion never took place.

Uprisings

In the Caribbean, slaves in France's lucrative colony of St. Domingue (Haiti) took heart from revolutionary principles and revolted. The 1791 slave uprising struck fear in the hearts of white settlers. Reports from French settlers, such as the wealthy Madame de Rouvray, described how the slaves "slaughtered and torched much of the countryside hereabouts" and warned, "how can we stay in a country where slaves have raised their hands against their masters?" After much maneuvering and the abolishing of slavery by the National Convention in February 1794, the rebel leader Toussaint L'Ouverture and his black generals gained control of St. Domingue. The determined group would go on to successfully oppose English, Spanish, and French armies, turning the island into the independent republic of Haiti in 1804.

Resistance to the Republic Rises

Despite the Reign of Terror and efforts to establish a Republic of Virtue, violent resistance to the Republic persisted and in some cases grew. Its leadership consisted primarily of local aristocrats and notables, officials who had fallen out of favor with the Jacobins, Girondin sym-

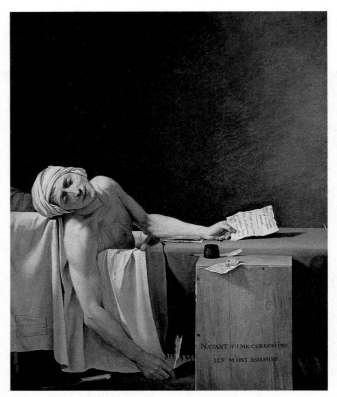

JACQUES-LOUIS DAVID, *THE DEATH OF MARAT*, 1793 In this scene vividly capturing the French revolutionary conflict and resistance, radical journalist and deputy Jean-Paul Marat lies mortally wounded by an assassin while in a bath. On the side of his writing stand are the words "Not having been able to corrupt me, they assassinated me."

pathizers, and members of the nonjuring clergy who had gone underground. They gathered additional support from remaining royalists, conservative peasants who had already gained most of what they wanted, opponents of military conscription, and the many citizens who remained loyal to Catholicism and their nonjuring priests. Of the many armed revolts that broke out across France, the most important occurred in the Vendée, a region in western France. In what amounted to a regional civil war that raged for most of 1793 and dragged on for years thereafter, both sides committed atrocities and thousands lost their lives before republican soldiers gained the upper hand. The image above reveals another form of resistance and the symbols of conflict during the radical phase of the Revolution.

Meanwhile, discontent with Robespierre and his policies increased. With the defeat of the invading coalition armies and the suppression of internal rebellion, most people no longer saw any need for the Terror—yet the Terror only intensified. When the influential Danton counseled moderation, Robespierre sent him and his most prominent followers to the guillotine. No one, not even the members of the National Convention, felt safe. Finally, on July 27, 1794 (9 Thermidor on the Revolutionary calendar, and thus referred to as the **Thermidorian Reaction**),

Thermidorian Reaction

the Convention overthrew Robespierre. In an ironic ending, the Jacobin leader died by the guillotine: the same device to which he had sent so many others to their deaths.

Reaction: The "White" Terror and the Directory

With the leader of the Terror now dead, the propertied bourgeoisie quickly gained control of the government. Eliminating the "Red" Terror of the Committee of Public Safety, they replaced it with the "White" Terror of reaction. They executed the former terrorists and imprisoned many supporters of Robespierre, including the painter, Jacques-Louis David. Armed bands of bourgeois hirelings roved around beating and killing Jacobins. Restrictive measures of Robespierre's regime were repealed, and many individuals, weary of the Republic's code of discipline and restraint, reveled in an outburst of licentious living. Middle- and upper-class women wore revealing clothing; mistresses appeared publicly, even in the political arena. On the other hand, women of the poor in the small towns and countryside often turned back to the Catholic Church. They hoped that a return to God would end the turmoil of the revolutionary years.

A new constitution in 1795 reflected conservative reaction. The right to vote for members of the legislative bodies was limited to the wealthier property owners. Executive functions were placed in the hands of five directors—the **Directory.**

Men of reasonable competence staffed the Directory (1795–1799), but they failed to restore tranquillity. War dragged on, governmental finances unraveled further, and brigands terrorized the countryside and the cities. The five directors tried to balance threats from the royalists on the Right and the Jacobins on the Left. They turned against the *sans-culottes* by removing price controls and had to be saved by governmental forces when the *sans-culottes* stormed the Convention in May 1795. Five months later, the government barely put down a royalist uprising, thanks to a quick-acting artillery officer named Napoleon Bonaparte. The directors finally resorted to purges to control the legislature and increasingly relied on the army for support. All in all, the situation was ripe for the arrival of a strongman who could bring both order at home and peace abroad.

NAPOLEON BONAPARTE

Within France, the Revolution provided unprecedented opportunities for ambitious soldiers of talent. Most prerevolutionary army officers had come from the nobility and had fled the country or lost their commands as the Revolution gathered momentum. This leadership drain, as well as the need to expand the army, created a huge demand for skilled officers. Napoleon Bonaparte, a talented artillery officer, stepped in to take full advantage of these opportunities.

Napoleon's Rise to Power

Born into a poor but well-known family on Corsica in 1769, just a few months after the Mediterranean island was transferred from the Republic of Genoa to France, Napoleon was hardworking, assertive, independent, and even arrogant as a youth. These qualities would stay with him for the rest of his life. The young Napoleon attended French military school (where he proved particularly strong in mathematics) and received his commission as second lieutenant when he was just 16. When the Revolution broke out in 1789, Napoleon was already familiar with Enlightenment ideas and resented the aristocratic pretensions of those around him. He quickly sided with the revolutionaries. In 1793, he attracted attention during the recapture of Toulon. Two years later, when he happened to be in Paris, the National Convention called on him to quell a threatening Parisian crowd. Using artillery—his legendary "whiff of grape-shot"—Napoleon quickly dispersed the crowd and became the hero of the Convention. He fell in love with and married the politically well-connected Josephine de Beauharnais (1763–1814), a 32-year-old widow eager to provide security for her children.

Napoleon then used his growing prominence to secure command of the French army still fighting in northern Italy. Calling his forces "soldiers of liberty" and announcing to the people of Italy that "the French army comes to break your chains," he skillfully galvanized the lethargic French forces into defeating the Austrians and Sardinians. Along with loads of Italian art, Napoleon sent home glowing reports of his exploits. In 1797, he personally negotiated the favorable Treaty of Campo Formio with Austria, which recognized French expansion and the creation of the Cisalpine Republic in northern Italy (see map on page 386). Over the next two years, French armies moved south, helping to set up more French-controlled republics throughout the Italian peninsula. Napoleon's successes in Italy established his reputation as a brilliant military leader and able statesman.

Turning toward the British, Napoleon and the Directory concluded that an expedition to Egypt would deal a telling blow to British commerce with its colonies in Asia. Egypt could also serve as the foundation for a new French colony. Moreover, a conquest there might enhance **Expedition to Egypt** Napoleon's image as a daring, heroic conqueror. Yet, despite some spectacular battlefield successes, the expedition failed; Admiral Nelson (1758–1805), who became one of Britain's most admired naval commanders, destroyed the French fleet at the Battle of the Nile on August 1, 1798. The French land campaign in Egypt and Syria persisted for a while, but it was doomed by a lack of supplies and reinforcements.

France and Its Sister Republics

This map shows the expansion of France and the creation of its sister republics between 1792 and 1798. Notice the dates of annexation and of the creation of sister republics. Who do you think was most threatened by these developments? Why?

Napoleon avoided personal disaster by slipping back to France with a few chosen followers, cleverly controlling the reports from Egypt and emphasizing the expedition's scientific explorations and exotic discoveries (he sent 165 scholars to Egypt in hopes that they might help him control the country) as well as its few victories.

Meanwhile, matters took a bad turn for France's government, the Directory. The expedition to Egypt prompted Great Britain, Austria, and Russia to join in a new coalition. These allies inflicted defeats on French armies and threatened to invade France itself. Eyeing this foreign threat, as well as bankruptcy, insubordinate army commanders, and disruptions in the countryside, rival factions within France vied for power. One conservative faction, led by a member of the Directory, Abbé Sieyès, concluded that a coup d'état would gain them needed control over the gov-

Coup d'état

ernment. This situation provided Napoleon with another opportunity to advance his career. Sieyès and others conspired with him to overthrow the Directory on November 9, 1799 (18 Brumaire). The conspirators expected that the 30-year-old military hero would make a popular figurehead representing authority, and they would actually govern the country. As events would prove, they were very mistaken.

Napoleon Consolidates Control

Napoleon quickly outmaneuvered his partners. He had a new "short and obscure" constitution drawn up and accepted by members of the old legislature. In a national **plebiscite** where people could vote to accept or reject

First consul

the new constitution, the French overwhelmingly approved it (though the government falsified the results to give it a more lopsided victory). As one observer explained, people "believed quite sincerely that Bonaparte . . . would save us from the perils of anarchy." Napoleon named himself "first consul" and assumed the powers necessary to rule—all with the ready support of the Senate. The remaining two consuls, as well as voters and the handpicked legislative bodies they thought they were electing, had only minimal powers. Next, Napoleon placed each of France's eighty-three departments under the control of a powerful agent of the central government—the *prefect*. Thus, at both the local and the national levels, Napoleon ended meaningful democracy in France.

With the touch of a skilled authoritarian politician, Napoleon proceeded to gather support. He welcomed former Old Regime officials as well as moderate Jacobins into his service. By approving the end of serfdom and feudal privileges as well as all transfers of property that had occurred during the Revolution, he won favor with the peasantry. He gained the backing of the middle class by affirming the property rights and formal equality before the law that adult males had secured during the Revolution. He welcomed back to France all but the most reactionary émigrés, most of whom had come from France's old aristocracy. The educated elite admired Napoleon for patronizing science and inviting leading scientists to join him in his government. To deter opposition, he created a secret police force, suppressed independent political organizations, and censored newspapers and artistic works. Finally, for those who displayed the highest loyalty and the most spectacular achievements (particularly in the military), he created the prestigious Legion of Honor.

Keenly aware of the political and social importance of religion—once calling religion "excellent stuff for keeping the common people quiet"—Napoleon made peace with

The Concordat

the pope and ended the ten-year struggle between the French revolutionary governments and the Roman Catholic church. Their Concordat (formal agreement) of 1801 declared the Catholic religion the religion of the majority of the French people but ensured freedom for Protestants. Later, Napoleon granted new rights to Jews, as well. Under his rule, the clergy was paid by the state and required to take an oath of allegiance to the state. Confiscated Catholic Church property was not returned.

Reforming France

Napoleon followed up this pattern of blending compromise and authoritarian control with a remaking of France's legal, financial, and educational systems. The Civil Code of 1804 (the **Napoleonic Code**), for example, generally affirmed the

Napoleonic Code

Enlightenment-inspired legal reforms that the early French revolutionaries had sought. Progressives throughout Europe and even overseas would embrace this law code. For

men, the code guaranteed legal equality, careers open to talent, and paternal authority over women, children, and property. In particular, it catered to middle-class employers by forbidding strikes and trade unions. At the same time, the code rejected many of the rights and liberties gained in 1789 as well as the more radical measures enacted after 1792. For women, the code represented a clear defeat. Rather than granting them legal or political equality, it gave power over property and the family to men and left married women legally and economically dependent on their husbands. The code also severely restricted the right to divorce, particularly for women. These measures reflected Napoleon's belief that women belonged in the home and that their concerns should center on domestic life.

To stabilize France financially, Napoleon established the Bank of France to handle governmental funds and issue money. To promote economic health, he involved the state in a huge program of public works, supported certain industries, and established price controls. To restructure educational institutions, he created a long-lasting system of secondary schools tied to the University of France and infused it with patriotic trappings. Napoleon also actively supported scientific research and rewarded surgeons, chemists, mathematicians, and other scientists with governmental posts and honors.

Finance and education

Creating the Empire

Napoleon's rise to power hinged on his ability to remove external military threats as well as internal disruptions. This he managed by crossing the Alps in 1800 with a French army to crush the Austrian forces in northern Italy and knock Austria out of the coalition of powers opposing France. Next, he made peace with Russia and persuaded Great Britain to sign the Peace of Amiens in 1802.

In the first five years of his rule, Napoleon scored spectacular successes. Law and order reigned at home, and he secured peace abroad. Public morale was high. Napoleon's vision of a centralized, paternalistic state that would make France the model of a modern nation through reason, authority, and science seemed almost real.

However, two problems lurked beneath this promising exterior. First, Napoleon had an insatiable craving for public recognition and legitimacy. He satisfied this need at least partially with a bold move in 1804. That year, with the approval of the Senate and the French people

Emperor Napoleon

in a lopsided plebiscite, Napoleon formally established France as an empire—and then crowned himself emperor. As Jacques-Louis David's painting on page 388 reveals, Napoleon controlled all aspects of the coronation.

The new emperor then elevated members of his family to princely status and granted new titles and honors to his wealthy supporters who had proved themselves, usually as

JACQUES-LOUIS DAVID, *NAPOLEON'S CORONATION*
Napoleon stands in front of Pope Pius VII preparing to place a crown on his kneeling wife, Josephine, to make her his empress. He has already boldly crowned himself emperor with a laurel wreath that alludes back to Roman emperors and Charlemagne, crowned emperor by the pope in the year 800.

officers on the battlefield. Later, he divorced Empress Josephine, whose relationship with Napoleon became more formal than intimate, and who failed to produce a male heir. He married Princess Marie-Louise of Austria, giving him a stronger image as legitimate royalty.

In addition to his hunger for formal recognition, Napoleon had a second problem. He had risen to prominence and power through his military conquests. "I am an upstart soldier," he admitted. "My domination will not survive the day when I cease to be strong, and therefore feared." These martial ties would push Napoleon to seek still greater conquests on the battlefield. "Conquest has made me what I am; only conquest can maintain me." Yet even when battle after battle brought him victory, war also came at great cost and risk.

Need for conquests

War and Conquest

The interests of Great Britain and Napoleon clashed too often for their peace to last long. By the end of 1803, the two countries were again at war, and by 1805, the ambitious Napoleon had to battle a new coalition of European powers. That year, he marched to the English Channel with a huge army and seemed poised to invade England. Before him stretched 24 miles of water and British sea power. To overcome those barriers, Napoleon amassed a combined French and Spanish fleet and plotted his next move. Alert for any opportunity, he suddenly turned his army eastward, surrounded an exposed Austrian army, and on October 20, forced it to surrender. The next day, however, England's Admiral Nelson sighted the combined French and Spanish fleets off Cape Trafalgar on the southwest point of Spain and annihilated them. Although Nelson perished early in the battle, his navy's victory saved Great Britain from the menace of an invasion and limited Napoleon's conquests to the European continent.

Battle of Trafalgar

On land, Napoleon fared much better—in fact, he seemed invincible. His success stemmed in part from his independent units that could move quickly and then join in a mass attack. Equally important, he possessed an unusually talented officer corps and enjoyed the loyalty of a large number of nationalistic citizen—soldiers. The strategy of sending a mass of spirited soldiers in a column of attack aimed at dividing opposing forces served Napoleon well. Fighting alongside his troops, he cleverly used these military strengths to crush the combined forces of Austria and Russia at Austerlitz in December 1805. Prussia made the mistake of declaring war on France after it was too late to join the Austrians and Russians. As the French troops moved east through villages and cities, people reported how "the dreadful cry was heard in the streets, 'the French are coming!'" Napoleon virtually obliterated the Prussian forces. When the Russian troops began massing again, Napoleon moved eastward and decisively defeated them in the great Battle of Friedland (1807). Although the resulting Treaties of Tilsit (July 1807) were technically between equals, they actually left Russia only a junior partner to France. France commanded the greater resources, and Napoleon expected to have his way on the European continent.

Military strengths

Despite all these triumphs, Napoleon still could not find a way to get his troops across the Channel to attack England directly. He finally hit on an alternative plan—the **Continental System**—that he hoped would destroy his rival's commercial economy by preventing the importation of British goods into continental Europe. To implement the plan, he ordered a continent-wide blockade against British ships, confiscated all British goods, and set French privateers upon British merchant ships. Britain responded with new regulations that amounted to its own blockade on shipping to continental ports. Now the naval war between France and Britain affected even neutral states, including the United States.

The Continental System

By 1810, Napoleon had redrawn the map of Europe (see map on page 389) and the political balance of power. He

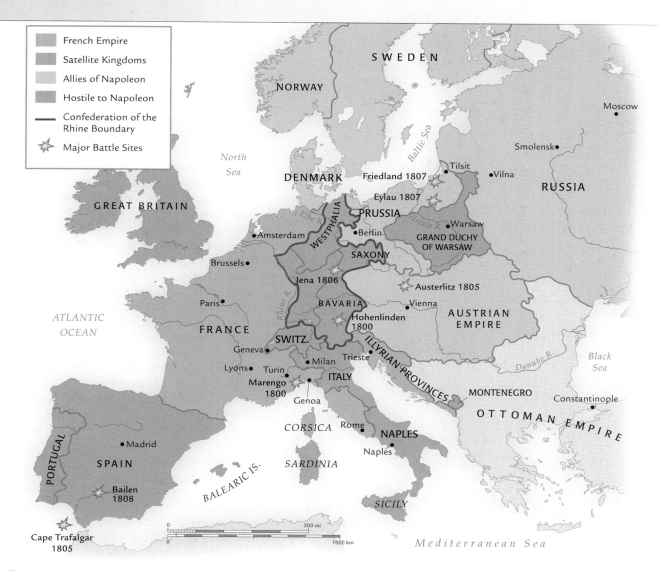

Europe, 1810 **This map shows Europe at the height of Napoleon's empire.**

had dismembered Prussia and abolished the Holy Roman Empire. Now most German states were unified into the Confederation of the Rhine. Holland and the Italian peninsula had come under French control. Spain was a dependent state, and Austria, Russia, and a diminished Prussia had become reluctant allies of France. Only Great Britain and still-defiant parts of Spain and Portugal remained active opponents.

The new European order

In those areas annexed to France, Napoleon ruled directly and imposed all of France's laws and institutions. In dependent states, he installed French-controlled governments to rule with the help of local elites. He usually made members of his family monarchs in these areas—his brother Louis, king of Holland, his brother Jérôme, king of Westphalia, and his brother Joseph, king of Spain. In these areas, he also introduced some of France's "enlightened"

institutions and policies. These usually included constitutional government, equality before the law, careers open to talent, the Napoleonic Code, civil rights to Jews and other religious minorities, and the creation of similar public works improvements—schools, roads, bridges—that Napoleon supported in France. Wherever Napoleon conquered, except Russia, he abolished serfdom. At the same time, the reforms included tax increases and conscription quotas to help finance and provide soldiers for Napoleon's armies.

The Impact Overseas

Naturally, Napoleon's policies exerted their greatest impact in Europe, but other areas—particularly in the Western Hemisphere and the British Empire—also felt the effects of his rule and expansion. In the Caribbean, Napoleon failed to

Remaining Colonial Possessions

- Spanish Possessions
- Former Borders of Spanish Viceroyalties
- LA PLATA Former Names of Spanish Viceroyalties
- British Possessions
- French Possessions
- Dutch Possessions

Date of independence from colonial power / Date of separation from other states
1821/1823

Latin America After Independence **This map shows that within a twelve-year period, Spain and Portugal lost most of their possessions in the Americas.**

won its independence. Elsewhere, Simón Bolívar (1783–1830), known as The Liberator, led the fight for independence against Spanish forces.

As the map on this page shows, by 1822 almost all of Spain's colonies, as well as Portugal's huge colony of Brazil, had gained their independence. Nevertheless, Bolívar's and others' hopes for unity within Spain's old colonies soon faded as various South American regions began dividing into separate states. Most of these new states would adopt the Napoleonic Code as their basis of civil law, and oppressive white minorities would rule them for many years.

Napoleon's dominance over the European continent inspired England to step up its overseas expansion and tighten control over its own colonies and areas of influence. Sea power enabled it to capture and take over French and Dutch colonies in Africa, Asia, and America. In addition, England began trading more briskly with South America. However, one of England's strategies—its counterblockade of Napoleonic Europe—had a major, unintended drawback. By enforcing the blockade, England ended up embroiled in the War of 1812 with the United States. That war, in turn, spread farther north when the United States attempted to invade Britain's loyal colonies in Canada.

England's overseas expansion

In Egypt, Napoleon's invasion failed, but in its wake local elites rebelled against Ottoman overlords. In 1805, the Egyptian general Muhammad Ali was victorious, and he set himself up as effective ruler of Egypt for the next three decades. Using European models, he strengthened and modernized Egypt's army, which eventually became the most powerful force in the Islamic world.

In the decades that followed, states from Asia to the Americas that reformed their own governments and laws would look to the Napoleonic Code and adopt parts of it. In this way, some of the ideals of the Enlightenment and the French Revolution would be translated through the Napoleonic Code to many areas around the globe.

Adopting the Napoleonic Code

put down the black population's struggle for independence and freedom in St. Domingue (Haiti). He also cut his losses in North America and sold Louisiana to the United States.

The Napoleonic Wars had dramatic consequences in the colonies of Spain and Portugal in the Americas. Discontent with colonial rule had been mounting during the eighteenth century. In particular, the colonists resented the economic and political restrictions imposed by the mother country. As the native-born Creoles began to outnumber the Spanish and Portuguese-born settlers, the ties of loyalty to home countries weakened. The successful revolt of the English colonies to the north and the birth of the United States also impressed colonial liberals and intellectuals. Spanish colonists' attachment to Spain faltered further when Napoleon overthrew the Spanish king and placed his own brother, Joseph Bonaparte, on the throne. By 1810, many colonists were in open revolt.

Revolt in Latin America

Over the next ten years, Spain struggled to regain its colonies. In 1814, Argentina drove off a Spanish army and

Decline and Fall

Napoleon had an even more ambitious vision—to rule Europe as the head of a single imperial administration. Before he could make his vision real, new problems plagued him. Even at the height of his power, Napoleon and his empire suffered from dangerous weaknesses. Between 1808 and 1812, three crucial vulnerabilities—

flawed policies, resistance to his rule, and overextension of his military reach—would intensify and erode Napoleon's power.

The Continental System that Napoleon devised to cripple England economically was not working well enough. With control of the sea, Great Britain applied an effective counterblockade against the Napoleon-dominated Continent. Port cities and industries relying on external commerce suffered. Smuggling further weakened the system.

Flawed policies

In some areas, such as Holland and Russia, the restrictions of the system became a constant source of irritation and resentment against the French. In the long run, the Continental System stiffened opposition to Napoleon on the Continent and failed to weaken England. Again and again, that island nation would finance Napoleon's enemies.

People across Europe had other reasons besides the Continental System to resist Napoleon's rule. In the wake of France's conquering armies, a new national spirit developed among many subject peoples. In Spain, for example, Napoleon had no sooner placed his brother Joseph on the Spanish throne than his unwilling subjects rose up against him. The painting on this page by the influential

Growing resistance

Spanish artist Francisco de Goya depicts the popular resistance in Spain to the Napoleonic occupation and the reprisals that resulted.

The Madrid rebellion and reprisals by Napoleon's soldiers inspired other Spanish uprisings and organized resistance against French troops in the years to come. Larger French armies, even when led by Napoleon himself, managed only limited success against the hit-and-run guerrilla tactics used by the Spanish. England took advantage of the situation by sending supplies and troops to Spain under the Duke of Wellington (1769–1852), the British commander who would plague Napoleon's forces to the end. Spain became a running abscess that drained Napoleon's military strength.

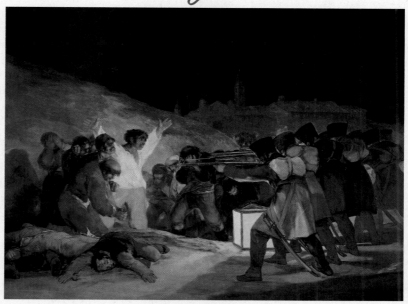

Francisco de Goya, *The Executions of the Third of May*

1808

In this night scene, a firing squad of anonymous French soldiers brutally executes citizens in retaliation for riots against French troops in Madrid. The magnitude of the French atrocity is emphasized by the central figure, who resembles a crucified Christ about to be shot. Monks and commoners, selected at random for execution, surround the man at the center, and the bodies of those already executed lie scattered on the bloody earth around him. In the background, shrouded under a black sky, stands the monastery. What message might Goya have been trying to convey to Spanish viewers by means of this painting?

In Prussia, similar national sentiments encouraged the government—partly in secret—to modernize its army and civil institutions in preparation for liberation from France. In Austria, the government again declared war on Napoleon in a premature effort to free itself from subservience to the French emperor. In Holland, opposition to

Napoleon's policies ran so strong that in 1810 he had to annex the country to France to bring it under control. All this resistance drained French forces and raised the specter of open revolt at the least opportunity.

Napoleon himself created that opportunity by overextending his imperial reach. Successes on the battlefield added to his growing dreams of creating an empire ruled from Paris that would encompass all of Europe. Russia, already chafing against the commercial restrictions of the Continental System and harboring its own ambitions for expansion in eastern Europe, stood as the main barrier to Napoleon's dreams. In 1812, these conflicting ambitions soured the alliance between Russia and France. Against the advice of his closest associates, Napoleon decided to invade Russia. Amassing an immense army of more than 600,000, he plunged into the vastness of Russia. Half of his troops, however, were unenthusiastic conscripts from dependent states. The Russian army retreated into the interior of their huge country, following a scorched-earth policy and luring Napoleon ever farther from his base of supplies. "We believed that once in Russia, we need do nothing but forage—which, however, proved to be an illusion. . . . All the villages were already stripped before we could enter," wrote Jakob Walter, a German conscript in Napoleon's army. One of Napoleon's aides explained the deepening problem: "We were in the heart of inhabited Russia and yet we were like a vessel without a compass in the midst of a vast ocean, knowing

Overextension

Invasion of Russia

nothing of what was happening around us." At Borodino, the Russians turned and made a stand. In one of the bloodiest battles of the nineteenth century—taking a toll of more than 80,000 casualties—the two armies fought until the Russians withdrew.

The French army may have won the battle, but it failed to destroy Russia's forces. In September, Napoleon's Grand Army, weakened by battlefield losses and even more so by hunger, fatigue, and disease, finally entered Moscow. Tsar Alexander I, however, refused to capitulate. The future looked even worse for the French when a fire destroyed much of Moscow, leaving the invaders without enough shelter or supplies to ride out the notorious Russian winter. "Here in the white country we'll all have to die of hunger," wrote Johann Wärncke, a German soldier in Napoleon's army. Napoleon began his retreat, but too late. The winter caught his forces overburdened with loot. Tens of thousands of them froze, starved, or succumbed to disease. Russian Cossacks, riding out of the blizzards, cut down or captured thousands more. Many of Napoleon's men surrendered to Russian forces. Of the

OPINION

Do you think Napoleon's accomplishments were worth the costs?

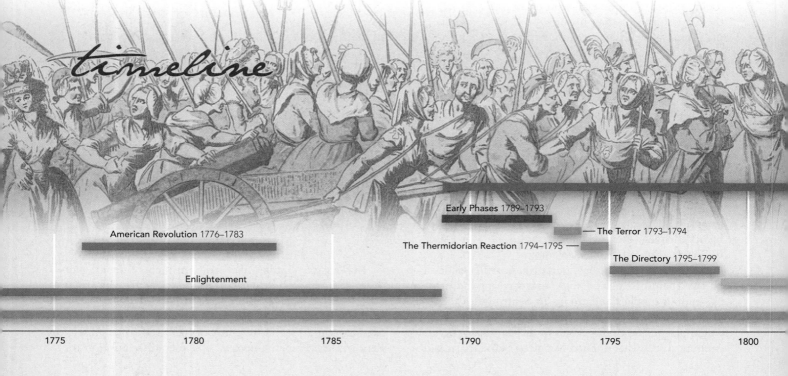

timeline

American Revolution 1776–1783

Enlightenment

Early Phases 1789–1793

The Thermidorian Reaction 1794–1795 ——

—— The Terror 1793–1794

The Directory 1795–1799

1775   1780   1785   1790   1795   1800

original 600,000 who marched into Russia, fewer than 100,000 struggled home.

Napoleon himself was able to dash back to France. Behind him, one nation after another, aided by British money, joined the Russians in a war of liberation. Back home, Napoleon raised new conscripts for his army and again rushed them eastward. At Leipzig in central Germany, in October 1813, allied armies at last decisively defeated Napoleon. The next year, the allies entered Paris and exiled Napoleon to the island of Elba, off the coast of Italy.

Defeat at Leipzig

Napoleon still had some fight left in him. While the allies squabbled over the peace settlement and discontent weakened France's new government under Louis XVIII, Napoleon escaped back to France. "Soldiers! In exile I heard your voice," he announced. "Now I have landed [in France]." He quickly raised yet another army from the remains of his old, still loyal supporters. However, he was finally defeated in June 1815 by British and Prussian forces at Waterloo in Belgium. This time his captors imprisoned him on the bleak island of St. Helena in the South Atlantic. "Posterity will do me justice," he wrote while in exile. "The truth will be known; and the good I have done will be compared with the faults I have committed." Six years later, Napoleon died, probably of stomach cancer.

Waterloo

SUMMARY

In 1789, the French Revolution brought the French monarchy to its knees. During the following years, revolutionaries eliminated the monarchy, overturned France's social system, and transformed the nation's institutions. Wars eventually propelled to power Napoleon Bonaparte, who in turn almost conquered the European continent and, in the process, spread the ideals of the French Revolution. The course of history in the West shifted permanently.

- Conflicts over France's finances sparked events that led to the Revolution. Below the surface, members of the aristocracy and middle classes, drawing on Enlightenment ideas, demanded more rights and power from the monarchy. The anger and hunger of the peasantry and the urban poor fueled the upheaval that brought down the old order.

- Guided by the revolutionary banner "Liberty, Equality, Fraternity" and basing the central government on national sovereignty, the National Assembly transformed French institutions.

- In 1792, the Revolution entered a new, more radical phase. A republic replaced the constitutional monarchy, the nation went to war with much of Europe, and the Terror spread throughout France. Two years later, a conservative reaction ended the Revolution's most radical stage and brought the Directory to power.

- In 1799, a coup d'état brought Napoleon to power. He consolidated his control, reformed French institutions, and used his military might to create a new empire. Growing resistance and overextension eventually led to his fall and the end of France's European empire.

In 1815, a king again ruled France. Many aristocrats and royalists hoped to turn back the clock to the days before 1789, when they enjoyed unchallenged power and prestige. However, too much had changed. The Revolution had destroyed a French monarchy based on the divine right of kings. French aristocrats might still boast impressive titles, but the revolutionaries and Napoleon had secured legal equality for French men, if not women. Members of the middle class, though no longer enjoying the control they had exercised during the revolutionary years, would not relinquish the opportunities for position and prestige they had gained. The peasantry would never again be burdened by the traditional dues and services they once owed to lords.

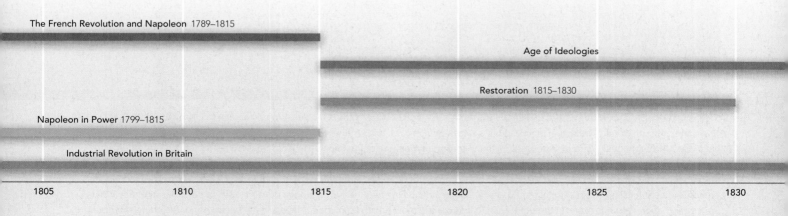

The French Revolution and Napoleon 1789–1815

Age of Ideologies

Restoration 1815–1830

Napoleon in Power 1799–1815

Industrial Revolution in Britain

1805   1810   1815   1820   1825   1830

J. M. W. TURNER, *DUDLEY, WORCESTERSHIRE,* 1832   In his 1832 watercolor of Dudley, Worcestershire, a city of about 23,000 in 1831 in the heart of Britain's industrial Black Country, British painter J. M. W. Turner shows the transformation of old towns and traditional landscapes wrought by the industrial revolution. In the foreground on one of the canals that crisscrossed this region, barges laden with cargo—typically coal for fuel, iron ore for smelting, and lime for flux, all plentiful in the region and used in the production of iron—dock for unloading and wait to receive goods from factories along the banks. The vessel at the right carries hoops of sheet iron destined for one of Dudley's finishing shops. The numerous mills' chimneys and coal-fired hearths produce dense clouds of polluting smoke that dim the city and encrust it with soot. On the right, a white and orange glow bursts from iron furnaces. In the background, the church steeples and battlements of a ruined castle rise into the moonlit sky, indicating how the old town has had to adapt to the new realities of modern industry, where work never seems to stop.

Factories, Cities, and Families in the

Industrial Age

17

The Industrial Revolution, 1780–1850

A Merchant Family Rises, a Railroad Worker Falls

In this new era, Britain led the way. There a middle-class couple such as Richard and Elizabeth Cadbury might expect to work hard and see the Birmingham cloth and dry goods store they opened in 1794 support them and their several children. Thirty-five years later their sons, Benjamin and John, had become wealthy retailers and manufacturers. ▶▶

Others did not consider the industrial age such a boon. One railroad worker told of a day when two thousand of his coworkers lost their jobs: "They were all starving, the heap of them, or next door to it." This worker had recently injured his leg at work and was laid up for one month, living "all that time on charity; on what the chaps would come and give me. When I could get about again, the work was all stopped, and I couldn't get none to do.... I went to a lodginghouse in the Borough, and I sold all my things—shovel and grafting-tool and all, to have a meal of food. When all my things was gone, I didn't know where to go.... Now I'm dead beat, though I'm only twenty-eight next August."

Stories about successful merchants like the Cadburys and less-fortunate laborers like this railroad worker give us a glimpse at the two faces of Britain's industrial revolution. Year by year, the work and home lives of these people and others changed only gradually. However, between the 1780s and 1850s—little more than a single lifetime—astonishing developments transformed economic and social life in Britain. The scene pictured on page 397 captures some of what that transformation meant to people. ◄◄

THE INDUSTRIAL REVOLUTION BEGINS

In the mid-eighteenth century, most British people had lived in the countryside. Women and men who laboriously spun fibers into thread and yarn and then wove it into cloth with the aid of only simple tools and hand-looms barely noticed the few new machines that could quickly spin American cotton into thread and weave it into cloth by the thousands of yards. To transport their goods to markets, these people, like their predecessors from centuries back, relied on coaches drawn by horses over rutted dirt roads, and on wooden ships pushed by currents and winds across the seas. Steam engines, already present for several decades, were inefficient and rare outside of coal mines.

By 1850, things had changed dramatically. Over half of Britain's population, which had more than doubled during the period, now lived in cities. Cotton factories churned out hundreds of millions of yards of cloth that were sold throughout the world every year and were driving those who still made cloth the old way out of business. New mines, machines, and production techniques made vast quantities of iron cheap to produce, easy to work, and available everywhere. Railroads carried people and merchandise to their destinations quickly, inexpensively, and reliably. Recent generations of efficient coal-burning steam engines powered these factories, foundries, and railroads. Waves of inventions and innovations built on earlier break-throughs cheapened production while improving quality. Although marked by periodic crises and downturns, a self-sustaining process of economic growth and technological change had been achieved and would continue through the decades after 1850.

What created this phenomenon—which French observers in the 1820s termed an industrial revolution—and why did it happen first in the West and particularly in Britain?

A Booming Commercial Economy in the West

Why the industrial revolution emerged first in the West rather than in other civilizations such as China or India is difficult to say. Before 1500, Europeans enjoyed no fundamental advantages in how they produced goods over their Asian counterparts; in some areas, such as iron and steel production, they even lagged behind. Many qualities, such as intellectual traditions and politics, differentiated Eastern civilizations from the West and may help explain the early appearance of the industrial revolution in the West. However, the rise of commerce during the sixteenth, seventeenth, and eighteenth centuries distinguished the West economically. Civilizations elsewhere usually participated in this growing commerce only reluctantly. China, for example, may have produced luxury goods dearly desired by Westerners, but, except for gold and silver, the Chinese wanted little in trade from the West. Moreover, the occupation of merchant had a low social status in China, further discouraging any potential bloom of commerce in that part of the world. In the West, however, the growth of commerce encouraged people to produce more agricultural and manufactured goods and sell them for a profit in the marketplace. Merchants and entrepreneurs became devoted to buying low and selling high, thereby amassing more and more wealth. The growth of commerce helped create the potential markets, producers, entrepreneurs, and capitalists that would fuel the industrial revolution in the West.

The Western and non-Western worlds

Britain's Unique Set of Advantages

Commerce also helps explain why Britain industrialized first. During the sixteenth and seventeenth centuries, commercial activity in England intensified along with English sea power and overseas holdings. In the eighteenth century,

WILLIAM WYLD, *VIEW OF MANCHESTER*, 1851 In this hazy vista, smokestacks in Manchester, England, stand in sharp contrast to the surrounding unspoiled rural landscape. Between 1780 and 1851, Manchester grew from a small country town to become one of England's leading industrial centers.

Britain became Europe's leading commercial and colonial power (see Chapter 15). Britain's economy efficiently turned out goods for export, and the island **Commercial vigor** nation enjoyed considerable access to expanding markets—both internal, from its rapidly growing and relatively wealthy population, and external, from its colonies and established commercial connections.

Commercial vigor, however, is not enough to answer the question of why Britain led the industrial revolution. Other areas of Europe enjoyed advantages that would be important for industrialization. For example, during the first half of the eighteenth century, Holland's agriculture and financial institutions were second to none. France was the wealthiest nation in the West. Britain, however, boasted a unique combination of advantages that, when added to its commercial leadership, laid a solid foundation for the birth of the industrial revolution.

Water transportation—far cheaper and quicker than overland shipping—played a crucial role in moving the coal, iron, cloth, and machines pumped out by Britain's new factories and mines. Already **Transportation** crisscrossed with countless navigable rivers, Britain enhanced its natural internal transportation system even more by building an extensive network of canals after 1760.

Certain raw materials—especially coal, iron, and cotton—also had an essential part in the island's industrialization. Britain's American colonies harvested large quantities of cotton. Not only did the British countryside contain plentiful depos- **Raw materials** its of coal, but they were often conveniently located near iron deposits where foundry workers used the two materials in the newer processes of smelting to make iron products.

An expanding population and a particularly large and mobile force of both skilled and unskilled workers gave Britain another advantage. Already less tied to villages than others in many parts of the Continent, this class of rural labor- **Labor** ers grew as waves of enclosures in the eighteenth century made many small farmers landless (see Chapter 15). These men and women could fill the rising demand for cheap industrial labor in the cities.

Britain had the capital to invest in industry for several reasons. First, its growing agricultural and commercial prosperity made it one of the wealthiest countries— per capita—in Europe. Second, it gained an unusual ability to amass **Capital** and mobilize that wealth into capital for potential investment, thanks to the development of a national banking system. Third, unlike most of its continental competitors, Britain was long free of internal tariff barriers, had a uniform and stable monetary system, and—since the Glorious Revolution of 1688 (see Chapter 13)—had a government that sympathized with business interests. All this encouraged wealthy individuals and families to risk money on commerce and industry. Therefore, inventors, innovators, and those who saw an opportunity could more easily find the means to start an industrial enterprise in Britain than elsewhere in Europe.

Finally, and according to some analysts, most important, entrepreneurship—at the heart of industrialization—was more socially acceptable in England than elsewhere. "In England commerce is not looked down upon as being derogatory, as it is in France and Germany," concluded an eighteenth-century Swiss observer. Members of England's aristocratic families—especially younger sons left without inherited lands—often sought careers in commerce and manufacturing. Social barriers between them and the business-minded middle class were lower than elsewhere. More than in most European nations, British merchants and **entrepreneurs** occupied a strong, respected place in society. On the other hand, in France, for example, most elites looked on commerce and industry as a means—often regrettable—to gain money to purchase office, estates, and aristocratic status; as soon as possible, French aristocrats usually left commerce or distanced themselves from their businesses.

In short, Britain had the most potential both to nurture and to take advantage of Europe's first industrial stirrings. Yet, what was it that finally transformed this potential into reality? Oddly, the crucial development came with advances in agriculture.

A Revolution in Agriculture

The agricultural revolution, with its new crops, methods of rotating crops, breeding of animals, and enclosures of open fields, spread in Britain during the late seventeenth and eighteenth centuries (see Chapter 15). Production increased, as did profits for the large landowners who shipped their crops to markets near and far. Declining food prices enabled more British families to purchase manufactured goods such as shoes, knives, and cloth. As the agricultural revolution picked up speed, fewer and fewer people produced more and more food. The new, large-scale farmers grew crops and livestock to feed the growing number of people working in factories, digging in the mines, and building their lives in the cities. Moreover, these well-to-do, enterprising landowners could use their profits to invest in the many business and commercial opportunities becoming available.

By 1850, the majority of Britain's population no longer raised food or lived in the countryside. Most lived and worked in cities and factory towns. Whether people were better off in these urban centers is a question we will turn to later. For now, the stage was set for Britain's industrial revolution.

NEW MARKETS, MACHINES, AND POWER

As wealth increased and people moved away from subsistence farming toward the burgeoning urban centers, the demand for manufactured goods reached unheard-of levels. Inventors and entrepreneurs rushed to fill this demand, dreaming up new machines and designing novel manufacturing methods. The machines, gaining complexity almost every year, seemed like mechanical wonders. The methods of production transformed the workplace. Coal and steam provided all the power necessary to make these machines and production methods work. Manufactured goods poured forth, available to all with the money to purchase them.

The Rising Demand for Goods

The old methods of production—slow, unreliable, and costly—could not satisfy the rising clamor for manufactured goods (see pages 359–361). In fact, the population growth in Britain and Europe alone created an ever-expanding pool of potential customers for low-cost clothing, nails, pottery, knives, and so forth. Eager overseas buyers, particularly in the colonies, offered raw materials in return for Britain's manufactured goods. At home, Britain's own successful farmers and merchants added to the demand.

Between the middle decades of the eighteenth century and 1850, inventors and entrepreneurs introduced new machines and methods that began to satisfy these hungry markets. Most inventors were practical men who embodied the widespread British **Inventors and entrepreneurs** interest in devices, gadgets, and machines of all kinds and had more talent as curious tinkerers than as scientific thinkers. Industrial entrepreneurs were also practical. Sometimes inventors themselves, they more often used the new devices and processes invented by others. Entrepreneurs purchased machines, employed workers, ran factories and mines, and found the necessary capital and markets.

Some entrepreneurs were landowning aristocrats; others rose from rags to riches. Many were Protestant dissenters, such as Calvinists and Quakers, who had been discriminated against by the dominant Anglican Church. Denied careers in government, they jumped at the opportunities presented by commerce and industry. Most, however, came from the middle classes. They took advantage of journals that promoted new techniques and ideas, divided and redivided the processes of production, and trained a workforce unaccustomed to working with machines in factory conditions. Buying raw materials from both local and distant suppliers, they promoted their products to the public. Through their resourcefulness and sometimes outright greed, they pursued profits. Navigating a risky competitive environment, they often reinvested their profits in their shops and factories, buying new machines and boosting production. The story of how they took advantage of new markets in the early decades of the industrial revolution is a narrative of new developments in cotton, iron, and steam.

Cotton Leads the Way

Changes in cotton production came first and with dramatic results. Before 1750, most thread and yarn was spun by women and woven into cloth by men who worked in rural cottages or small urban shops. Using only simple spinning wheels and handlooms, these laborers produced thread, yarn, and cloth of uneven quality. How much they produced was limited by many things—the supply of fiber, farmwork that took them away from their spinning and weaving, the wages paid by the entrepreneurs who organized much of this work, and, above all, the tools and methods they used.

In 1733, John Kay (1704–1764) invented a device called the flying shuttle, which doubled the speed at which cloth could be woven on a loom. The shuttle, in turn, intensified the demand for thread. In the 1760s, **Weaving and spinning** James Hargreaves (d. 1778) invented the spinning jenny, which revolutionized thread production. By 1812, one spinner could produce as much cotton thread as 200 spinners had in 1760. Other inventions, such as Richard Arkwright's (1732–1792) water frame and Edmund Cartwright's (1743–1823) power loom, allowed weavers to turn cotton into cloth in tremendous quantities. Two American developments added to the acceleration in textile production: Eli Whitney's (1765–1825) cotton gin (1793), which efficiently removed seeds from raw cotton; and the expanding slave plantation system in the South. Indeed, British manufacturers' growing demand for cotton became an important force perpetuating slavery in the cotton-growing areas of the United States.

By 1850, British cotton manufacturers had boosted cloth production from less than 40 million yards per year during the 1780s to more than 2,000 million yards per year. Cotton had become hugely popular and, alone, accounted for some 40 percent of British exports.

Iron: New Processes Transform Production

Machines for the new cotton industry were just one source of a growing demand for iron. Armies needed guns and cannons; civilians needed nails and pans. Until the eighteenth century, British iron makers were limited by the island nation's dwindling forests, for they knew how to smelt iron ore only with charcoal, which came from wood. Even during the days of plentiful charcoal, ironworkers had only their own and their animals' muscle power with which to work the iron into usable forms. Most of this iron production came out of small family firms or homes of artisans.

In 1708, Abraham Darby discovered an efficient way to smelt iron with coal in a blast furnace. This innovation would make the iron industry a key driver of the industrial revolution. By the end of the century, other new processes enabled iron makers to double production **Smelting with coal** again and again. As suggested by the image below, foundry workers began using steam engines to operate smelting furnaces, drive forge hammers to shape the iron, and roll the iron into sheets. New ironworks such as these, with their tall, smoke-belching furnaces, were joining cotton factories as symbols of the industrial revolution.

The Steam Engine and the Factory System

Both the cotton and the iron industries created ever-higher demands for power. At the beginning of the eighteenth century, people had to rely on muscle, wind, and water to supply the energy to do their work. Early mills used water-power, which meant that their owners had to build them near waterfalls. A drought in the summer or a cold snap in the winter could threaten to dry up or freeze this essential power source.

PHILIP JAMES DE LOUTHERBOURG, *THE COALBROOKDALE IRONWORKS AT NIGHT*, 1801 Flames and smoke light up the night at Coalbrookdale, one of England's iron-producing centers.

FRANÇOIS BONHOMME, *WORKSHOP WITH MECHANICAL SIEVES,* 1859 This interior view of a French zinc factory reveals the processing of raw materials, rows of machines, and division of labor that characterize the factory system. Men, women, and children work together in this hot, noisy building; the men have the more authoritative and skilled jobs (a foreman sits in the rear to the left) while the women and children sort and split chunks of ore.

The steam engine, first used in the early eighteenth century to pump water out of deepening coal mines, provided a solution and would become the industrial revolution's most important technological advance. Portable and easily controlled, the earliest models were nevertheless not yet efficient enough for widespread application. Over the course of the eighteenth century, inventors such as Thomas Newcomen (1663–1729) and James Watt (1736–1819) improved the power and efficiency of these engines. Watt, a skilled craftsman backed by the daring entrepreneur Matthew Boulton (1728–1809), worked for years on the engine, making several design changes and eventually converting the reciprocal motion of the piston into a rotary motion. Now steam engines could be used not only to pump coal mines but also to drive the other new machines of the day, such as powering bellows for iron forges, mills for grains, and looms for textiles. The steam engine came to symbolize the new industrial age.

Reliable power from steam engines also made it possible for entrepreneurs to locate factories away from waterpower sites and build even larger cotton, iron, and other factories. In huge buildings, entrepreneurs hoped to guard their industrial secrets and mold a new labor force. Hundreds of workers, who produced goods in a repetitive series of steps and specialized tasks, tended rows of machines. The **factory system** had emerged. "The principle of the factory system . . . is to substitute mechanical science for hand skill, and the partition of a process into its essential constituents, for the division or graduation of labor," explained Andrew Ure, a professor of applied science, in 1835 (see Exploring the Past on page 401). As we will see, factories generated unprecedented wealth for their owners and investors but brought new hardships for the people who toiled in them. The image above reveals the nature of the factory system.

Coal: Fueling the Revolution

As the industrial revolution hit its stride, the demand for coal also intensified. Steam engines devoured coal as fuel. Iron makers required more and more coal to run their furnaces. Britain's doubling population needed coal to heat their homes.

People poured huge amounts of money and labor into digging mines, extracting the coal, and developing the roads, canals, and rails necessary to transport the mineral to waiting customers. Not only did coal fuel the industrial revolution; mining and manufacturing became so entwined that it was hard for people to think of one without the other.

Railroads: Carrying Industrialization Across the Land

The advent of the railroad age brought everything together. In the eighteenth century, horses had pulled carts along rails radiating out from mines, hauled barges along the growing network of canals, and pulled carriages along roads. Only wind in the sails of ships could move heavy cargoes and passengers across the seas.

During the 1820s, as steam engines began to power ships, the British inventor George Stephenson (1781–1848) developed the practical modern railroad. In 1830 his new train, the Rocket, initiated the Liverpool-to-Manchester railway line. The Rocket's speed (16 miles per hour) and reliability excited the imaginations of everyone. People eagerly invested in railway companies, rode the new lines out of curiosity, and traveled by rail to vacation spots.

The railway carried heavy freight with unprecedented ease and speed. By 1850, trains were chugging over 2,000 miles of track in Britain, reaching astonishing speeds of up to 50 miles an hour. Steaming across bridges and through tunnels to the railway stations dotting the land, the new locomotives embodied the power and the promise that seemed to characterize the industrial age. Optimistic observers such as the British politician Edward Stanley argued that "of all the promoters of civilization, the Railway System of communication will be amongst the foremost in its effects, for it cannot fail to produce many and mighty changes in manufactures, in commerce, in trade, and in science." The image on page 402 captures the drama and excitement of the railroad age.

The railroad seemed to pull together all the trends that emerged during the industrial revolution. It ignited demand for an array of related products—coal-thirsty steam engines to power the trains, iron to build the

Andrew Ure Defends Industrial Capitalism

From the beginning, industrialization had its critics and defenders. Andrew Ure, a British doctor, was one of the most effective public advocates of industrial capitalism. In the following excerpt from his 1835 book, *The Philosophy of Manufacturers*, Ure focuses on the factory system.

The principle of the factory system ... is, to substitute mechanical science for hand skill, and the partition of a process into its essential constituents, for the division or graduation of labour among artisans. On the handicraft plan, labour more or less skilled, was usually the most expensive element of production—*Materiam superabat opus*; but on the automatic plan, skilled labour gets progressively superseded, and will, eventually, be replaced by mere overlookers of machines.

By the infirmity of human nature it happens that the more skilful the workman, the more self willed and intractable he is apt to become, and, of course, the less fit a component of a mechanical system, in which, by occasional irregularities, he may do great damage to the whole. The grand object therefore of the modern manufacturer is through the union of capital and science, to reduce the task of his workpeople to the exercise of vigilance and dexterity,—faculties, when concentred to one process, speedily brought to perfection in the young. ...

What is the essence of the factory system?

William Powell Frith, *The Railway Station*

1862

The Great Continental Express is about to depart from Paddington Station in London. At the center is a middle-class family. The mother kisses her son, who is holding a cricket bat and is being sent away to school with his brother. Farther right, a wedding party bids adieu to a bride and groom. Behind them, a boy sells newspapers to departing passengers, and a soldier in a red uniform kisses his plump baby good-bye. On the far left, working-class people hurry toward the third-class cars. Above the bustling platform and trains, the wrought-iron-ribbed ceiling and numerous hanging lamps mark the train station as one of London's appealing industrial wonders.   In what ways does this painting celebrate the connection between railroads and modern urban life?

1870) described in *Dombey and Son* (1846), a new rail line meant that "houses were knocked down; streets broken through and stopped; deep pits and trenches dug in the ground; enormous heaps of earth and clay thrown up . . . everywhere carcasses of ragged tenements, and fragments of unfinished walls and arches, and piles of scaffolding, and wilderness of bricks, . . . mounds of ashes blocked up rights of way." All this "wholly changed the law and custom of the neighborhood," before the railroad "trailed smoothly away, upon its mighty course of civilization and improvement."

Finally, like the other new industries, the railroads could be a risky investment opportunity. Some owners and investors grew fabulously wealthy; others suffered devastating financial losses. Just as the cotton and iron industries continued to face competition from older methods such as the putting-out system (cottage industry), handicrafts, small family firms, and agriculture, the railroads had to fight to steal business from the roads and canal systems that were expanding across Britain at the same time. Those who had thrown their lot in with the railroads need not have worried too long about the wisdom of their investment, however. Like the cotton and iron factories, the railways were the wave of the future, and they rolled inexorably across the British landscape.

Britain's Triumph: The Crystal Palace Exhibition

In 1851, that shining future was put on display for all the world to admire. That year, London hosted the first international industrial fair at the glass and iron Crystal Palace. At this dazzling exhibit, millions of visitors came to gaze reverently at the British miracle.

The image on page 403 shows the interior of the Crystal Palace—its arching glass roof like a cathedral, its steel framing a testament to modern engineering. To many in

rails and cars, cloth and leather to make furnishings, and bricks and glass to erect the new stations. Like the cotton factories, iron foundries, and coal mines, the railroad industry created new jobs while destroying old ones. In addition, it left its own permanent mark on the land and neighborhoods it affected. As Charles Dickens (1812–

Effects of the railroad

THE CRYSTAL PALACE EXHIBITION Under a majestic glass and iron roof, visitors from around the world viewed commercial and industrial displays. This 1851 international fair marked Britain's new industrial might.

1851, the Crystal Palace was at once an architectural masterpiece and a jewel of mass production that could not help but appeal to popular taste. In addition to admiring the building itself, visitors could view displays from various nations.

The awe-inspiring palace confirmed economic realities. Britain produced more than half the world's cotton cloth and iron, and, despite periodic downturns, the nation enjoyed sustained economic growth. Britain had become the world's first industrialized nation.

INDUSTRIALIZATION SPREADS TO THE CONTINENT

It was not until after 1830 that industrialization spread with much force outside Britain (see the graphs on page 404). Before then, people from France, the German states, and elsewhere were interested in Britain's economic wonders. Some traveled to Britain to copy machines, and others enticed British technicians and capital to their own countries. A few modern industrial shops and machines sprang

up on the Continent, but overall, agriculture and tradition still dominated economic life there.

After 1830, industrialization spread to certain regions, especially Belgium, northeastern France, the northern German states, and northwestern Italy (see the graphs).

These areas had plenty of urban **Governmental aid** laborers, deposits of iron and coal, and developed transportation facilities. Envious of British wealth, pressured by British competition, and recognizing the military potential of cheap iron and rail transportation, continental governments took a more active role in supporting industrialization than British rulers had. They enacted tariffs to protect their manufacturers from British goods, and they subsidized new industries. Railroads, partially financed by governments and foreign capital, led rather than followed the advent of other industries, widening markets and creating demand for coal and iron. These countries could not yet hope to catch up to Britain. At mid-century, a German official complained that Germany would never "be able to reach the level of production of coal and iron currently attained in England." But soon Germany and other nations would manage to industrialize more selectively and quickly, thanks to the groundwork that Britain had laid.

As the map on page 405 indicates, by 1850 large industrial centers had arisen in Belgium, France, and those areas of northern Germany bounded by the 1834 Zollverein (a customs union that eliminated tariffs between independent German states). Other regions, particularly around Milan in northern Italy and in the northeastern United States, had also begun to industrialize.

Most of southern, central, and eastern Europe, however, remained virtually untouched by industrial development. Lacking well-placed resources, efficient transportation, mobile workforces, commercialized agriculture, and capital for investment, these regions retained their traditional and rural character. The vast majority of people in these areas **Remaining traditional** remained in the countryside tied to **economies** subsistence farms or, especially in the east, large agricultural estates. Small villages rather than booming cities were the rule. Wealthy urban elites might purchase manufactured goods from industrial regions to the west, but their own countries could not produce them in the same way. Governments and perhaps a few ambitious and wealthy individuals sometimes imported the latest

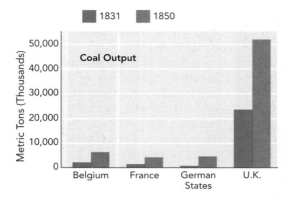

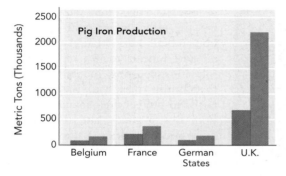

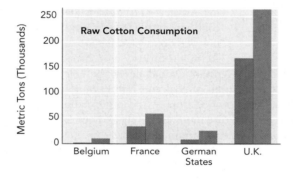

INDUSTRIAL PRODUCTION IN EUROPE, 1831–1850

BALANCING THE BENEFITS AND BURDENS OF INDUSTRIALIZATION

How did industrialization affect everyday life for Europeans? To answer this complex question, we might first explore the impact of the new machines, factories, and railroads on people's work conditions, home lives, and social relationships. It is also important to ask who received the lion's share of the new wealth.

Foreign observers marveled at Britain's wealth; indeed, to this day many of us associate machines, factories, and railroads with prosperity. Statistics seem to confirm this impression: Britain's national product increased more than threefold between 1780 and 1850. The population in Europe also surged during the same period and absorbed some of the new wealth. Probably thanks to better food supplies (especially cultivation of the potato), earlier marriages, and declining mortality rates, Europe's population ballooned from fewer than 175 million in 1780 to 266 million in 1850. During this same period, Britain's population more than doubled.

New wealth

These startling numbers suggest a sense of economic well-being on the part of Europeans, but they also frightened some contemporaries. In his influential *Essay on the Principle of Population* (1798), British economist Thomas Malthus (1766–1834) warned that population growth would inevitably outstrip food supplies. A few years later, another well-known economist, David Ricardo (1772–1823), argued that overpopulation would restrict wages to no more than subsistence levels.

Population growth

Nevertheless, industrialization generated new wealth so rapidly that personal income rose faster than population growth in these years. Between 1800 and 1850, per-capita income skyrocketed by a whopping 75 percent in Britain. As other countries—such as Belgium, Germany, and France—industrialized, they too enjoyed similar gains. But who exactly was receiving these new riches?

The Middle Class

The middle classes (bourgeoisie), still a minority of the population even in Britain, prospered. The newest, most dynamic group within the middle classes was the industrial entrepreneurs—the factory and mine owners. They gained the most, some amassing enormous fortunes. Many bankers, smaller factory owners, professionals, merchants, and shopkeepers enjoyed more modest gains, as did those who

machines and built a few railroad lines, but these signs of industrialization primarily had symbolic or military value. Relying on old methods of production, merchants in these lands had trouble selling their manufactured goods in international markets. Nations, such as Spain and Russia, that once exported cloth saw their sales dry up in the face of British textiles.

There were a few exceptions in these traditional economies. For example, Austria's Bohemian lands developed a spinning industry, and a few factories sprang up around St. Petersburg and Moscow in Russia. Even so, British technicians and industrialists were often needed to support these limited efforts. On the whole, all these countries would have to wait before experiencing both the benefits and the burdens of the industrial revolution.

The Industrial Revolution in Europe, 1850

This map illustrates the spread of industrialization in Europe by 1850. **How does the extent of industrialization in England compare to that in the nations of continental Europe?**

earned interest and profits from investing their savings in industrial and commercial ventures. All investments, however, did not pay off. Some loans were not repaid. People took financial risks, and some lost their bets. Firms failed all the time, and periodic economic downturns spawned a string of losses and bankruptcies.

Still, over the long haul, the middle class as a whole benefited the most from industrialization. As their wealth and numbers grew, so did their prestige, political power, and cultural influence. The Scottish philosopher and scholar James Mill (1773–1836) claimed that the "heads that invent . . . the hands that execute, the enterprise that projects, and the capital by which these projects are carried into operation" all came from the middle class. Marked by their modest, sober clothing, the middle class gradually displaced the once-glittering aristocracy who were still tied by tradition to the land. This process unfolded slowly, and some aristocrats and landowners managed to adjust quite well to the change.

The Working Classes

The picture is far less clear for the working classes—those who labored in the factories, tended the machines, and toiled in the mines. For people who shifted from the agricultural life or jobs as artisans to work as factory laborers, industrialization may have hurt more than it helped, especially in its earlier decades. These people worked six days a week, twelve to sixteen hours a day, earning only subsistence-level wages. William Harter, a British silk manufacturer, justified the long hours to a parliamentary commission: Reducing the hours of labor "would instantly much reduce the value of my mill and machines . . . every machine is valuable in proportion to the quantity of work which it will turn off in a given time." In textile factories, whole families typically labored together. Women's earnings were between one-third and two-thirds of men's, and children's wages were a mere fraction of that. As a result, factory owners employed women and children whenever possible to save money, and they even contracted with orphanages to provide cheap child laborers.

The image below shows the interior of a cotton factory. One governmental investigation of child labor described how children "were rendered pale, weak and unhealthy" from "labouring for hours like little slaves." Employers, anxious to keep their machines running and wages low, replied that "it was absolutely necessary that the children should be employed within the mills from six o'clock in the morning till seven in the evening, summer and winter."

Factory labor

After the 1820s, factory workers' wages started to climb. By the 1840s or 1850s, they were earning more than their agricultural counterparts. This change did not make them rich, however, for most of them had to spend some two-thirds of their income on food alone. In 1842, Flora Tristan reported that most workers in English factories "lack clothing, bed, furniture, fuel, wholesome food—even potatoes!" and that their bodies were "thin and frail, their limbs feeble, their complexions pale, their eyes dead."

THE WHITE SLAVES OF ENGLAND.

CHILD LABOR, 1853 New factories typically employed women and children. As this woodcut of a cotton factory interior suggests, supervisors sometimes used harsh methods of discipline.

Money was only one variable in the quality-of-life equation. Industrial workers faced job insecurity, physical dangers, and painful changes unique to their way of life. The worst insecurity centered on employment itself. Even in good times, some firms failed. During economic downturns and crises, such as the "Great Hunger" of the 1840s, wages plummeted below subsistence levels, and many workers lost their jobs. For these industrial laborers there was no unemployment insurance to turn to, and no foraging, cottage industry, or gardening that people living in the countryside could resort to in hard times.

Insecurity

The work itself carried a high risk of severe physical injury. Factory owners made no provisions for safety. In cotton factories, children regularly climbed under and on top of the equipment to free jammed machines, collect cotton, and tie broken threads; many young workers suffered terrible injuries to their hands and even lost fingers. Long hours and exposure to chemicals, dust, smoke, and industrial residue all led to ill health. Indeed, industrial populations had a far shorter life expectancy and higher incidence of disease and deformity than rural populations. In the 1840s, the military turned down 90 percent of volunteers from some urban areas for health reasons—double the rate of rejection for rural volunteers.

Risks of injury

Besides job insecurity, injury, and ill health, the new industrial age brought lifestyle changes that are harder to evaluate. Industrial workers experienced a new rhythm of labor that no longer bore any resemblance to the natural rhythms of daylight and seasonal changes. Now, workers toiled unrelentingly to keep pace with the machines and schedules of the factory owner. Employers and their stewards maintained workplace discipline with fines, curses, and whippings. Children who could not keep up were beaten at times; some were even chained to their machines. There were no slack days, like the traditional Monday of preindustrial times. Wages took the form of cash, which workers had to save and apportion carefully over the week for food and housing despite the temptations of alcohol and other leisure activities. At the end of the long workday, laborers trudged home to poor housing clustered around noisy mills or mine entrances or to cheap, overcrowded rooms and cellars of industrial cities.

Lifestyle changes

People growing up on farms and in small villages at least had traditions they could rely on. But this traditional life also had its own harsh side. Poverty was no stranger to

OPINION

Do you think the burdens and consequences of industrialization during the decades before mid-century outweighed their benefits?

the countryside, nor was child labor, cold, uncertainty, and squalor in windowless hovels. One contemporary, Frederick Eden, argued that the difficulties experienced by small farmers and villagers were only "temporary" and a small price to pay for "the greater good which may be expected from the improvement." However we evaluate all this, life in the city did give the working class something no one could have foreseen: a new sense of class consciousness, an awareness of their own unique burdens and hardships that emboldened them into action and alarmed the onlooking middle classes.

Developing Working-Class Consciousness

Because industrial workers lived in the same areas, labored in the same oppressive buildings, grappled with similar problems, socialized and commiserated together, and joined the same trade or civic organizations, they began to see themselves as a separate class. This sense of solidarity came partly from a tradition among artisans and craftsmen of membership in guilds. Although guilds were made illegal after 1791 and were opposed by middle-class people committed to gaining control over the workplace, other workers' organizations such as fraternal societies, trade organizations, and mutual aid societies persisted. These groups laid the foundation for the emergence of trade unions, made legal (though severely restricted) in England in 1824 and elsewhere after 1850. By mid-century, labor leaders had formed the beginnings of national unions, such as the Grand National Consolidated Trades Union in Britain in 1834, the National Trades Union in the United States in 1834, and the General Workers' Brotherhood in Germany in 1848.

Workers' organizations

Sometimes, workers turned to violence against what they saw as threats from industrialization by destroying the new machines. After 1811, English hand weavers, losing their work to the new power looms, went on rampages, smashing the machines to pieces or campaigning to get rid of them. Glove makers destroyed the new stocking frames that threatened their jobs. These forms of protest came to be known as **Luddism** in honor of a legendary (and perhaps fictitious) leader, Ned Ludd. The British Parliament quickly named industrial sabotage a capital offense and heavily suppressed the violence. Nevertheless, sporadic episodes of violence continued to erupt for several years, not only in Britain but elsewhere as the industrial revolution spread. In the 1830s, silk workers in Lyons, France, rose up against attempts to lower their pay. In 1836, Spanish workers burned a textile factory in Barcelona. During the 1840s, several governments had to call out troops against strikers.

Luddism

Most of these efforts brought few concrete results in the period before 1850. In addition to the power wielded by wealthier classes and governments, many internally divisive forces chipped away at the fledgling working-class solidarity. Labor leaders, for example, who usually came from the more skilled trades—the cabinetmakers, printers, tailors, masons, and blacksmiths—tended to look down on unskilled industrial workers. Most women were not invited to join worker organizations, though they forged some of their own trade associations. Other loyalties based on religion, region, trade, or even neighborhood undermined worker unity. Sometimes the only connection holding laborers together was a sense of shared problems, the belief that workers had a right to a just wage, and the impression that their employers were exploiters rather than economic partners.

Despite the forces dividing workers, their sense of themselves as a separate, unique class strengthened over time. Increasingly, members of the middle class began to see them as dangerous and even savage. As we will see in following chapters, with the sharpening of working-class consciousness, the power of the traditional artisan groups and the peasantry would decline—quickly in the decades after 1850, especially in highly industrialized places such as Britain, Belgium, and parts of Germany. The process would unfold more gradually in moderately industrialized places, such as France, and slowly in most of southern and eastern Europe.

For good or ill, industrialization was transforming everyday life across Europe. The economic and human balance shifted from the countryside to the city. Now the dramatic social transformations took place in the growing urban centers where, as one young worker described London in the 1820s, "a wilderness of human beings" lived.

LIFE IN THE GROWING CITIES

The unprecedented growth of cities from 1780 to 1850 stemmed from a combination of forces. Population was increasing in both urban and rural areas. Enclosures of land by market-oriented landowners that dispossessed individuals of their small farms and communities of their commons further uprooted rural families. These pressures pushed people from the land. At the same time, the cities, with their promise of jobs and the lure of beer halls and theaters, attracted people in droves. Industrial towns sprang up where none had existed before. Towns ballooned into cities, and already large cities grew even more imposing. Some of the most spectacular urban growth happened in industrial cities, such as Manchester, which expanded from 25,000 in 1772 to 367,000 in 1850; and Birmingham, Leeds, and Saint-Étienne in France,

Urban growth

A Middle-Class Reformer Describes Workers' Housing

The following is a description of housing in Nantes, France, during the 1830s.

If you want to know how he [the poorer worker] lives, go—for example—to the Rue des Fumiers which is almost entirely inhabited by this class of worker. Pass through one of the drain-like openings, below street-level, that lead to these filthy dwellings, but remember to stoop as you enter. One must have gone down into these alleys where the atmosphere is as damp and cold as a cellar; one must have known what it is like to feel one's foot slip on the polluted ground and to fear a stumble into the filth: to realise the painful impression that one receives on entering the homes of these unfortunate workers. Below street-level on each side of the passage there is a large gloomy cold room. Foul water oozes out of the walls. Air reaches the room through a sort of semi-circular window which is two feet high at its greatest elevation. Go in—if the fetid smell that assails you does not make you recoil. . . . You will see two or three rickety beds fitted to one side because the cords that bind them to the worm-eaten legs have themselves decayed. . . . No wardrobes are needed in these homes. Often a weaver's loom and a spinning wheel complete the furniture. There is no fire in the winter. No sunlight penetrates [by day], while at night a tallow candle is lit. Here men work for fourteen hours [a day].

What most bothers the author about workers' housing?

which more than tripled in size. Other already substantial cities, such as London and Paris, became increasingly crowded and sprouted new suburbs.

Most cities flourished through industrial activity, such as mining and manufacturing. Other areas scarcely touched by industrialization, such as Naples, St. Petersburg, and Vienna, also grew dramatically through the expansion of governmental bureaucracies and traditional commerce.

The Promise and Pitfalls of Work in the Cities

Industry, however, had the strongest pull. It inevitably attracted new commerce and gave rise to a broad range of consumer and service needs. Women flocked to the textile factories, but even more women living in the cities worked as domestics. Many young women came for what jobs they could find, perhaps hoping to send home part of their pay and still save enough to start a new life. The building trades drew growing numbers of men, who sometimes left their wives and children in the countryside to survive on a patch of land and dwindling cottage-industry employment. Many men periodically returned to the countryside, particularly in winter, when construction slowed, or during planting and harvest times.

Living with Urban Growth

Industrialization and urbanization also altered the landscape that people traveled through to reach the cities. Forests shrank as people cut down more and more trees for construction of cities, mines, factories, and railroads. The same mines and railroads cut scars into the land, and the cities and factories ate up rural landscapes. Rivers once fit for fish or drinking became polluted with industrial and human wastes.

Approaching the cities, travelers saw smoke in the air from the dirty coal fires used to heat buildings and from the engines of industry. In the city, and particularly in the poor working-class areas, the air smelled foul, for there were no

Environmental changes

modern sewers, sorely inadequate toilet facilities, and not enough clean water. Garbage and animal waste collected in the streets until heavy rains washed them away. In Manchester, only two-thirds of the houses had toilets, and many of those flushed into inadequate cesspools. Human and animal waste mixed in rivers that people used for drinking water. Charles Dickens's description of the fictionalized Coketown in his novel *Hard Times* (1854) would have struck a familiar chord for nineteenth-century travelers to Britain's industrial cities: "It was a town of machinery and tall chimneys, out of which interminable serpents of smoke trailed themselves for ever and ever. . . . It had a black canal in it, and a river that ran purple with ill-smelling dye, and vast piles of buildings full of windows where there was a rattling and a trembling all day long, and where the piston of the steam-engine worked monotonously up and down."

Overwhelmed by these surroundings, newcomers to the cities tended to settle in areas where they knew someone else. Whole neighborhoods grew up populated by people who had come from the same rural region. This tendency led to a sense of segregation and separate identities within the cities, as people familiar with one another clustered together.

Few neighborhoods were planned. Indeed, the expansion of most cities became increasingly uncontrolled. The rampant growth created far more problems for the working **Different neighborhoods** class than for anyone else. The middle classes, for example, most likely lived in lower-floor apartments in the more desirable sections of town and had the benefit of some running water. They also could afford to employ servants. It was in the working-class sections and poverty-stricken areas that the social ills and squalor of the age reached their worst levels. As the manufacturer and socialist Friedrich Engels (1820–1895) described, "The houses are packed from cellar to attic and they are as dirty inside as outside." In the Irish quarter of London, as many as 38 people crowded into small buildings down narrow alleys where the walls were crumbling, and "piles of refuse and ashes lie all over the place and the slops thrown out into the street collect in pools which emit a foul stench." In the bad quarters lived "the poorest of the poor. Here the worst-paid workers rub shoulders with thieves, rogues and prostitutes." Exploring the Past on page 408 describes conditions where poor workers lived. The image here, a mid-nineteenth-century woodcut, also portrays the squalor and crowding of a London slum.

Worrying About Urban Society: Rising Crime

One of those social concerns centered on patterns of criminal behavior. People in the upper classes complained about crime and the social disorder it implied. Had cities become

GUSTAVE DORÉ, *A LONDON SLUM*, mid-nineteenth century Dark, crowded urban areas such as the district shown in this woodcut were home to innumerable poor workers and other impoverished individuals.

hotbeds of crime, as some middle-class observers claimed, or were these critics simply overly worried about their own safety and well-being?

Crime certainly plagued people in the West long before the industrial revolution. In rural areas, along highways, and in the preindustrial cities of Europe, crimes ranging from pickpocketing to murder occurred all too frequently. Professional thieves had reportedly run rampant in Germany, England, and France in past centuries.

In the early stages of industrialization, theft and robbery in particular did rise in the cities. Crowds provided prime opportunities for pickpockets. In urban taverns and dance halls, men sometimes fell into violent brawling, sometimes over women. In these establishments, alcohol flowed freely and almost certainly played a role in outbreaks of fighting. The widening gaps between rich and poor and the desperation of living in hard times also made tempers short. Finally, the anonymity of life in the city and the tempting array of luxury items to steal made crime harder to resist.

Whether justified by the realities of more crime or not, the specter of urban crime and fear of disorder prompted new efforts to improve law enforcement. In 1829, under

Crime and law enforcement

the leadership of Robert Peel, Parliament passed a law establishing the first modern police force in London. Peel's new police, called "Bobbies" in his honor, emphasized regular patrols by uniformed officers as a way to deter crime and present a visual image of security. Both the middle and the working classes accepted the Bobbies, in part because the police were not allowed to be engaged for political purposes such as domestic espionage, and in part because people saw them as the first line of defense against all disorder. By the early 1830s, there were some 3,000 uniformed officers in the force.

The frightening consequences of rapid urbanization were becoming all too apparent. Year by year, the cities grew more densely packed and seemingly more dangerous. In bad times, they teemed with desperate people hoping to find jobs; in good times, they drew even more people eager to take advantage of the available work and other opportunities. Contemporaries associated the cities with overcrowding, filth, crime, moral degeneracy, and an unruly working class. "They [the working class] live precisely like brutes . . . they eat, drink, breed, work and die," complained a middle-class British observer in 1850. "The richer and more intelligent classes are obliged to guard them with police." Perhaps most disturbing, however, were the disease and death that haunted urban centers.

OPINION

In what ways do you think moving from the countryside to the city changed people's lives during this period?

PUBLIC HEALTH AND MEDICINE IN THE INDUSTRIAL AGE

People had good reason to fear for their health and safety in the growing cities, especially in the poorer sections of town. On average, city dwellers fell ill more often and died at a far earlier age than their rural counterparts. Within the cities, the poor lived half as long as the rich.

Industrialization itself was dangerous. The new machines maimed factory workers, and cave-ins, floods, and explosions killed miners. Various diseases stemmed directly from mining and manufacturing. Coal miners became ill and died from black-lung disease. Cotton workers developed brown-lung disease. In textile factories, women suffered particularly high mortality rates. Metalworkers, especially grinders, developed lung diseases from inhaling shavings. Poisonings from mercury, lead, and phosphorus used in industrial processes also increased.

The Danger of Disease

The greatest danger came from infectious diseases. They were the great causes of sickness and death before the nineteenth century, and the rapid growth of crowded cities that lacked sanitation facilities made matters worse. People living in working-class quarters and urban slums were most vulnerable. Tuberculosis and diphtheria thrived in the most heavily populated areas and killed millions during the nineteenth century.

Worse, plagues periodically swept through cities. Cholera epidemics struck Europe several times, causing great panic as people in city after city awaited the arrival of the illness (see map on page 411). Suggested remedies included taking several measures to restore warmth to the body, giving laudanum (opium dissolved in alcohol), and seeking medical aid. In 1831 alone, cholera killed some 100,000 in France and 50,000 in England.

People disagreed about the causes of diseases. Some observers blamed illnesses on physical weakness and immorality of individuals. In these critics' view, disease was rooted in inferior genetic background, overindulgence,

Causes of disease

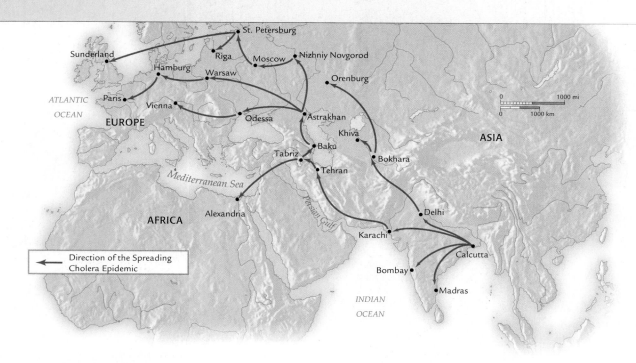

The Spread of a Cholera Epidemic
This map shows the spread of the cholera epidemic that originally broke out in eastern India in 1817.

degenerate lifestyle, poor hygiene, and irresponsibility. Only self-help could solve the problem, they argued.

Other commentators and some doctors theorized that disease spread through contagion—that people caught diseases from one another. This theory had more to do with magic, belief in the devil, or a desire to keep the ill out of sight than any notion of modern germ theory. It seemed to explain sexually transmitted diseases like syphilis but could not answer the question of why some people contracted various diseases while others did not. In these commentators' minds, quarantine offered the best solution to fighting contagious diseases.

Most doctors eventually concluded that disease stemmed less from personal contact than from environmental forces. They believed in miasma, the centuries-old notion that people caught diseases by breathing fumes given off by human waste, rotting vegetables, decaying flesh, marshes, or stagnant ponds. They also blamed poor diets for weakening resistance to these sources of disease. In a widely respected 1840 study, the French physician Louis Villermé attributed the prevalence of disease in the working-class slums of Lille to the cellars and crowded rooms where "the air is never renewed," where "everywhere are piles of garbage, of ashes, of debris from vegetables picked up from the streets, of rotten straw," where "one is exhausted in these hovels by a stale, nauseating, . . . odor of filth, odor of garbage." This helped him and others explain why people living in barracks, workhouses, and the worst parts of cities more often fell ill and died.

Seeking Medical Care

None of these theories about disease aided individuals seeking medical care. Doctors may have been well-meaning, but in 1850, anyone visiting a doctor was more likely to be hurt than helped. Most people consulted physicians reluctantly and had little trust in the power of treatments or medicine. To our twentieth-century sensibilities, medicine in the early 1800s can indeed seem quite alarming. To alleviate a fever, for example, doctors often turned to traditional cures such as initiating bloodletting by opening a vein or applying leeches to the skin, or they recommended laxatives to purge the bad humors and fluids from the body. Physicians routinely prescribed pills that at best did nothing and more likely contained toxic substances such as mercury. Frequently, the addictive drug laudanum was suggested for the treatment of pain, sleeping problems, difficulties with children, and a variety of other complaints. Such treatments more often led to fluid depletion, poisoning, and addiction than any improvement of the patient's condition.

Doctors

More benignly, doctors might recommend fresh-air cures or taking the waters at health spas. Many of the wealthy traveled to coastal resorts and centers in Caldas da Rainha in Portugal, Bath in England, and Baden-Baden in Germany for these health cures. They may have gained some temporary relief from conditions such as arthritis,

CAROLINE NAUDET, *JOURNEY OF A DYING MAN TO THE OTHER WORLD*, 1820 In this grim scene, a wealthy doctor in black robes leads a procession that includes a dying man, a clergyman pointing up, a surgeon with a fluttering bat over his head, a sinister-looking apothecary carrying an enema device, and an undertaker. A harsh commentary on patients' fate under the care of early-nineteenth-century doctors, the work captures popular attitudes toward physicians.

but they more likely enjoyed the lively social events and casinos that also attracted them to these spas.

The image above, an 1820 print by the French artist Caroline Naudet (1775–1839), reveals popular attitudes toward physicians. Many sufferers looked for treatments opposed by

Alternative medicine

ordinary doctors to cure their ailments. Homeopathy, which emphasized the use of herbal drugs and natural remedies, gained in popularity during the period. Other options—from vegetable laxatives, claimed to be effective for all ills, to faith healers—saw wide use. These alternatives at least gave sufferers a sense of controlling their own health.

As for surgery, people turned to this option only as a last resort. Surgical methods became safer in the first half

Surgery

of the nineteenth century, but anesthesia and antiseptics still lay in the future. Those who managed to survive the pain of an operation faced a likelihood of dying from an infection afterward.

Promising Developments for Public Health

Despite all the dangers, the period had a few bright spots for the future of public health. Improvements in diet probably held the most promise. Many nutritious foods had become more available than ever, especially potatoes, which were an affordable, rich source of vitamin C and minerals; dairy products, which helped newborns survive infancy and childhood; and meat, which contained high-grade proteins. Inexpensive cotton underwear, thanks to the new cotton mills, kept people warmer and cleaner than before. The smallpox vaccine, developed during the eighteenth century and made into a safe form in 1796 by Edward Jenner in England, would virtually erase a disease that had once afflicted almost 80 percent of Europeans and killed millions. The discovery of anesthetics—nitrous oxide and, after 1846, ether and chloroform—began to make surgical trauma bearable.

Other developments showed some potential as well. Following the lead of a small group of influential French physicians, European doctors applied scientific methods to medicine and made great strides in pathology and physiology. Hospitals proliferated and increasingly became places to observe the sick and gather

New developments in medicine

information. New laboratories allowed doctors to conduct more experiments. Professional organizations and educational institutions for doctors and nurses formed, and governments, particularly in France, began taking some responsibility for medical education and licensing.

Many doctors no longer relied solely on a patient's description of the problem. Physical examinations became common—feeling the pulse, sounding the chest, taking the blood pressure, looking down the throat. Some doctors used the new stethoscope, which became a crucial tool for diagnosing bronchitis, pneumonia, and pulmonary tuberculosis (commonly called consumption). Among the upper classes, the family physician was even gaining some favor as a respected social contact and confidant.

In England, Edwin Chadwick (1800–1890) initiated a campaign to improve public health. In his 1842 report for a parliamentary commission, *The Sanitary Condition of the Laboring Population of Britain*, he emphasized that the accumulation of human and animal waste near people's dwellings was a crucial cause of disease. He proposed a system of underground tunnels that would allow constantly running water to carry waste out of the city.

Nevertheless, the gains from these promising new developments would not come until the second half of the nineteenth century. In Britain, one of every three people still died of contagious diseases in the decades surrounding 1850. Health, therefore, remained a great public and private concern. It was not the only concern that crossed the lines between public and private life, however. The day-to-day events in everybody's lives, whether in illness or health, unfolded within a crucial setting: the family. In this period of industrialization and urbanization, the family as an institution and the roles within it began to shift in the face of enormous economic and social pressures.

FAMILY IDEALS AND REALITIES

The ways that people come together into families and the roles they play in their families usually evolve slowly, if at all. During this period, however, the middle class redefined accepted notions of the family, and working-class families struggled under the new pressures beleaguering them. In subtle but important ways, family ideals and realities were changing.

Middle-Class Ideals: Affection, Children, and Privacy

With their numbers, wealth, and status in urban societies rising, the middle class not only developed its own ideas about what the proper family should be but also propagated those ideas as the norm for everyone else. The result

> People were supposed to marry because of affection, love, and emotional compatibility.

was an evolution of, rather than a break from, old notions about the family. Compared with families of earlier times, the ideal middle-class family emphasized emotional bonds, attention to children, and privacy.

People were supposed to marry because of affection, love, and emotional compatibility. Social rank and wealth remained important, but these values exerted less influence than they had in the past. Love could bridge social and economic gaps. Indeed, one of the great themes in the flood of new novels that appeared during the nineteenth century centered on this very conflict: the tension between love and money in **Marriage** marriage. In stories that ended happily, love won out—though most characters in these plots never were relegated to a life of poverty as a consequence of their choice.

The new middle-class family was smaller and more child centered than before. Europeans were choosing to limit the size of their families, and by mid-century this preference led to declining rates of population growth. Women gave birth to fewer children—two or three rather than the five or six of an earlier era—and more infants than ever survived the first, riskiest years of life. Unlike workers and **Family size** peasants, middle-class parents did not have to view their children as economic assets—as hands to work the fields, help with the crafts, or labor in the factories. Wealthier urban parents could afford to raise perhaps just two or three children as fulfilling products of a good home. More than ever, children came to be seen as innocent, impressionable, vulnerable persons who should be separated from the corrupting influences of adult society. Mothers **Children** and fathers began investing more time, effort, and other resources in child rearing. Boys, especially, needed training and education designed to ensure their success as adults in the changing urban world. To arm them with these essentials, parents extended the time period of childhood and economic dependence. All this required planning and intensified emotional ties between parents and children. Parents increasingly centered their attention and family activities on children.

More than ever, mothers and fathers idealized their home as a private "haven in a heartless world," separate from and above the world of paid work. The home represented the reward for competing on the job—a protected, glorified place **The home** for a satisfying personal life. There husband and wife could enjoy the delights of material possessions and, hopefully, the rewarding intimacy of family life. As indicated by the growing number of popular books by authors such as Jane Austen (1775–1817), Mary Ann

Evans (1819–1880) (writing under the pen name George Eliot), and Charlotte Brontë (1816–1855), home was a setting of many appealing, moralizing dramas where the virtues of prudence, love, sacrifice, self-reliance, and persistence could usually overcome all obstacles.

Separate Spheres: Changing Roles for Middle-Class Women and Men

With the rise of industrialization and urban life, the roles of middle-class husbands and wives grew more and more separate. In the seventeenth and eighteenth centuries, most middle-class families had worked together as one economic unit—sharing the responsibilities of running a shop or business and living near their place of work in back rooms, upstairs, or next door. During the nineteenth century, the tasks assigned to men and women, and the private world of home and the public place of paid work, became increasingly distinct. As the locus of work shifted from the home to the factory, store, or office, women lost their traditional employments that contributed to the family economy. Paid employees working outside the home now occupied the role previously played by women who had run thriving family businesses. The new economic growth also allowed middle-class families to afford the homes, servants, and leisure previously reserved for the elite. Eventually, the ability of middle-class women to devote more time to their homes and families without having to do paid work, and to hire servants to lighten domestic burdens, became symbols of social success. The home became women's sphere, and within the home, child rearing began requiring far more maternal attention than ever. As the task of raising children and socializing them with the values and training needed for success expanded, so did the responsibilities of motherhood. Becoming "rational mothers," fully able to meet the new demands of child rearing, turned into a revered duty.

The man was supposed to be the respected economic provider who operated primarily in his sphere: the competitive world of work outside the home. He was expected to behave in an authoritative, competent, and controlled manner. These qualities reflected the legal and economic realities of the time. Under British **The man's sphere** common law and the Napoleonic Code on the Continent, for example, a man had legal authority over his wife and children. He also had control over his wife's personal property as well as over any money earned by her. Furthermore, only men could vote. Most positions in the middle-class world of work were reserved for men. Those jobs usually required specialized skills in planning and information managing—abilities that came primarily from formal schooling. Young men were more likely than women to receive a for-

mal education in areas of study such as accounting or law. Through apprenticeships and clerkships in commerce, industry, or finance, men also found many opportunities to equip themselves for success in the growing industrial-urban economy.

Women faced a very different set of cultural expectations. A host of marriage manuals, medical tracts, advice books, and religious dictates reminded women that their place was within the domestic sphere. A woman should provide emotional support for her husband and cultivate a virtuous home environment to counteract the amoral, competitive marketplace. She should care for the children, make sure the house was **The woman's domestic sphere** clean and the meals served, supervise domestic servants (a requirement for any middle-class home), and manage other domestic tasks, from sewing to administering household accounts.

In some ways, a middle-class woman's domestic sphere extended outside the home. She might manage the family's social life, for example, or lead in religious matters. If she had the time and means, she might also participate in philanthropic activities, social movements such as temperance or the abolition of slavery, and certain cultural events—but only as long as these activities added to her image as virtuous, dutiful, maternal, supportive, and sensitive. These activities put women in a position of power as representatives of the family in religious, social, and cultural matters and often gave them the last word on such matters within the family.

Involvement in politics was out of the question for most women. A few middle-class women joined movements to gain political and legal rights, but their efforts did not lead to real reforms during this period. Nor did paid work fit the domestic image. Although a woman might serve without wages as a clerk or secretary in her husband's store or office, paid work outside the home was considered inappropriate and generally not available to married women. Even for unmarried women, only occupations directly connected to the domestic role, such as governess, elementary school teacher, lady's companion, or seller of women's clothing, were deemed acceptable. There were exceptions, especially in cultural fields such as painting and writing, but most people raised a skeptical, disapproving eyebrow at women who had such careers.

At home, a wife was expected to be the counterpart to her controlled, strong husband. "In every thing . . . that women attempt, they should show their consciousness of dependence" on men, explained Elizabeth Poole Sandford in her widely read book, *Woman in Her Social and Domestic Character* (1842). Law hindered most married women from acquiring economic independence and generally placed them, as well as children, under the formal power and protection of men. Women were supposed to be emotional and even frail, and therefore capable of only domestic tasks. The training of young women reinforced these qualities.

Instead of a secondary schooling or professional education, women's formal training focused on religion, music, and perhaps languages. Any other skills a young woman might need, she picked up at home.

Educators and scientists generally agreed that women were ill suited for occupations outside the home and that they lacked the emotional control, mental acuity, and assertiveness of men. Doctors usually held the same views, and even believed that menstruation incapacitated women and that women had no interest in sex. Clothing, too, emphasized this vision of women's proper role. Middle-class husbands wore prudent and practical clothing for the world of work—trousers and jackets in modest black or gray. Their wives endured tight corsets and full decorative skirts more suited for display than action.

In short, the middle-class ideal was a small, private family bonded by love and authority. In such a family, the wife and husband willingly fulfilled the expected roles of their separate spheres. Families measured their success in achieving this ideal by the luxury items they bought, collected, and self-consciously displayed; by the accomplishments of their children; by how well their lives matched the uplifting dramas that the novels and paintings of the day depicted; and by their participation in appropriate social, religious, and philanthropic activities.

connect to today

Industrialization

During the industrial revolution, life for everyone was rapidly changing. In bad times, unemployment and business failures made urban life particularly harsh. In prosperous times, filth and disease still marked these cities. In what countries today do you see people struggling with the prospect of industrialization?

of an older child or neglectful "babyfarmers," women who took in far too many children. Many mothers resorted to drugging their children with laudanum to keep them out of harm's way while the adults were at work.

Middle-class critics demanded reforms that would limit women's ability to work away from home, although working-class women objected that they had no better alternatives.

As one group of women factory workers from Manchester pointed out, "Hand loom has been almost totally superseded by power loom weaving, and no inconsiderable number of females, who must depend on their own exertions, . . . have been forced . . . into the manufactories, from their total inability to earn a livelihood at home." During recessions, women's plight worsened. Employers laid off the more highly paid men first, leaving women with the overwhelming burden of managing both a paid job and all the domestic tasks at home.

Working-class and peasant families were being pulled apart in other ways as well. Adolescent boys left home to seek work in the mines or cities. Daughters, too, sought jobs as factory laborers or as domestics in middle- or upper-class homes. In the cities, women were all the more vulnerable during economic downturns when low-paying jobs disappeared.

Working-Class Realities

The middle class assumed that its vision of the proper family served as the standard for all. However, this vision did not fit the urban and industrial realities facing the far more numerous working classes.

Industrialization pulled many working-class women away from their homes and into factory jobs. Employers preferred to hire women because they worked for lower salaries and seemed more pliable than men. In the early decades, young children often accompanied their mothers, providing even cheaper labor and falling victim to the harsh, disciplined factory environment. During the 1830s and 1840s, public outcry against child labor (led by middle-class reformers, not the working class) prompted women to leave their younger children at home in the care

Women workers

Prostitution

Hard times left unmarried and married women alike in particularly desperate straits. To survive, some women turned to prostitution, which grew along with Europe's mushrooming cities. In 1850, there were probably some 30,000 prostitutes in Paris and 50,000 in London. Unemployment and the dangers of solitude were probably the main forces driving women to prostitution. Many prostitutes had come from outside the cities and had no family to help them. Others were out-of-work domestics, seamstresses in need of income during a slow season, daughters of unemployed workers, or women abandoned after being impregnated by masters or lovers. Low wages also led to prostitution; a woman earned as much money in one night prostituting herself as she could acquire in an entire week of work at the factory.

Many of these women worked as prostitutes for relatively short periods, and only part-time. While the work helped

Then & Now
Office Hours

In 1844, a Berlin factory posted rules for workers. The normal workday began "at all seasons at 6 A.M. precisely," and ended, "after the usual break of half an hour for breakfast, an hour for dinner and half an hour for tea," at 7 P.M. Workers arriving 2 minutes late would "lose half an hour's wages." Those who were more than 2 minutes late could not start work "until the next break." Though different in harshness and details, labor laws and restrictions on workers' workdays still exist throughout the West. For example, workers in Italy can expect to work no more than 8 hours a day or 40 hours a week. While German workers also have an 8-hour workday, collective agreements in many cases have reduced their workweek to 35 to 38.5 hours.

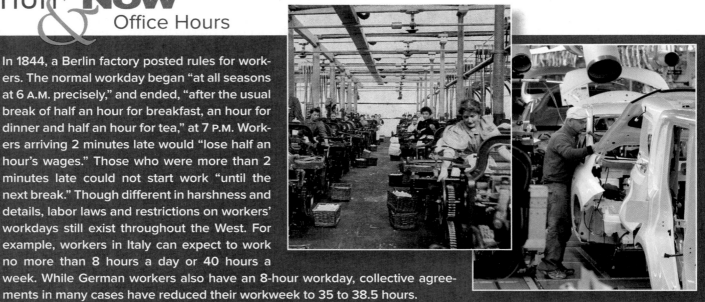

them financially, it also exposed them to venereal disease, which ran rampant during this period. Finally, in some people's minds, prostitution linked working-class women to images of urban crime and immorality. To middle-class moralists, prostitutes embodied unrestrained sexuality and therefore were the ultimate outcasts. However, despite its dangers, prostitution would persist as a sign of the difficulties that many working families faced in Europe's growing cities.

timeline

Industrial Revolution in Great Britain 1760–1850

French Revolution and Napoleon
1789–1815

The "Old Regime"

| 1750 | 1760 | 1770 | 1780 | 1790 | 1800 |

Stress and Survival in the Working Classes

The new tensions swirling through working-class family life had severe consequences for some. Peasant, artisan, and working-class families had worked together as economic units for longer than the middle class had, and industrialization and urbanization corroded this unity. The stresses proved so great that some families broke apart, leaving a growing number of women to work and manage households on their own.

However, the picture was not all bleak. As a rule, the family survived, providing a haven for workers and a home for children. Like peasants' and artisans' families, many working-class families clung to the old putting-out system or the newer piecework system, in which entrepreneurs distributed jobs, such as tailoring or decorating, to workers at their homes. Unions, better wages, and new social policies would ease the burdens on workers in the decades after 1850. In the end, most families adjusted and found ways to meet the many challenges of the industrial age.

SUMMARY

Industrialization meant unprecedented, sustained economic growth, and it soon became a measure of whether people considered a society "modern" or "traditional." Carrying in its wake fundamental changes in literally all aspects of life, industrialization altered the ways people worked, what they could buy, how they lived their lives, and where they stood on the social ladder. Its railroads, dams, bridges, factories, and mines transformed the land, the rivers, and the air.

- The growth of commerce helped create the potential markets, producers, entrepreneurs, and capitalists that would fuel the industrial revolution in the West. Britain, Europe's leading commercial and colonial power, used its unique set of advantages to industrialize first.

- In Britain, growing demand for manufactured goods encouraged inventors and entrepreneurs to create new machines and manufacturing methods. Coal and steam provided the power while factories transformed the workplace.

- After 1830, industrialization spread to the Continent, especially Belgium, northeastern France, the northern German states, and northwestern Italy.

- The middle classes, especially factory and mine owners, bankers, professionals, and shopkeepers, benefited most from industrialization. The picture, at least in the short run, is far less clear for those who labored in the factories, tended the machines, and toiled in the mines.

- Despite a host of social problems, the cities had a vibrancy and an image of opportunity that continued to attract people. While some people lost ties to traditional communities and beliefs when they migrated to the cities, others gained, whether by hard work, luck, or the advantages of birth.

- Both industrialization and life in the growing cities brought increased exposure to health risks, especially infectious diseases. While some developments in public health and medicine were promising, doctors still lacked the means and understandings to help most individuals seeking medical care.

- Middle-class families responded to their improving positions by developing a compelling new set of ideals about how men and women should behave.

Nations that industrialized left others behind in the competition for wealth. That wealth was all too easily translated into power, leaving traditional agrarian societies in the West vulnerable to their industrialized neighbors. The new riches pumped out by the machines of industry also propelled the West into an even stronger position to dominate unindustrialized, non-Western societies throughout the world.

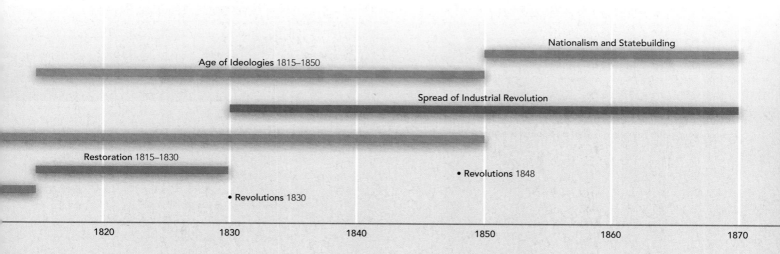

HENRI-FÉLIX EMMANUEL PHILIPPOTEAUX, *REVOLUTIONARY TRIUMPH IN PARIS*

This vibrant painting shows the poet and liberal leader Alphonse de Lamartine triumphantly saluting a Parisian crowd in 1848.

Coping
with
Change

Ideology, Politics, and Revolution,
1815–1850

18

A Gathering of Victors

In the autumn of 1814, the leaders of the powers who had finally vanquished Napoleon gathered to redraw territorial boundaries and fashion a lasting peace. The conference also attracted representatives of every state in Europe, hundreds of dispossessed princes, agents of every interest, and adventurers. Nearly everyone who thought he or she was somebody of importance in high circles attended. ▶▶

The representatives reveled in the glittering gatherings and entertainments. In addition to the public conferences, many private meetings took place—though just how private remains uncertain, for Austrian spies regularly opened letters and searched wastebaskets. Elsewhere, in newspapers from St. Petersburg, Rome, and Paris to London and even Boston, people closely followed the daily events in the beautiful Austrian capital. Something immensely important and exciting seemed to be unfolding there. ◄◄

THE CONGRESS OF VIENNA

The four major victors over Napoleon—Great Britain, Prussia, Russia, and Austria—set peace terms with France around the time of Napoleon's overthrow in April, and these four dominated the congress. The elegant, arrogant Metternich led the Austrian delegation and became the most influential figure of the congress. Jean-Baptiste Isabey's formal portrait of the principal figures at the Congress of Vienna (see image on page 421) gives a sense of the seriousness of this event and the ideals that the victors represented.

The victors

As guiding principles in the negotiations, the conferees decided on legitimacy and stability. By *legitimacy* they meant that territories should once more be placed under the control of the old ruling houses of the traditional order. By *stability* they meant establishing and maintaining a balance of power within Europe, with particular focus on restraining France. The main powers agreed that the settlement should apply to all of Europe.

Legitimacy and stability

Yet the conferees proved lenient in their settlement toward France. Thanks to the victors' desire to turn France into an ally rather than a resentful enemy, France, the original force behind all the turmoil, escaped the proceedings with only light penalties. Having already restored the French throne to the Bourbons, the powers merely reduced France roughly to its 1789 boundaries. Because of Napoleon's 100-day return, they also required France to pay an indemnity of 700 million francs, return stolen art treasures, and submit to occupation by allied forces until the indemnity was paid.

To confine France within its frontiers and discourage future French aggression, the powers established strong buffer states along France's borders. As the map on page 422 shows, Prussia received a sizable block of territory along the Rhine; the Austrian Netherlands (Belgium) and the Dutch Netherlands were unified; Piedmont-Sardinia in northern Italy was enlarged; and the old monarchy was restored in Spain.

Territorial arrangements

Trading among themselves, the four main powers took new territories. Great Britain gained several strategic islands and colonies, all of which boosted its sea power and overseas dominance. Prussia added some areas in central Europe. Russia acquired control over a reduced, nominally independent Poland, thereby edging farther into the heart of central Europe. Russia also took Finland from Sweden, which in turn got Norway at the expense of Napoleon's ally Denmark. Austria gained Lombardy and Venetia in northern Italy as well as the permanent presidency over the weak German Confederation—the thirty-nine German states that remained after Napoleon's destruction of the Holy Roman Empire.

Although they displayed little concern for the wishes of the peoples being placed under the control of one power or the other, the conferees did produce a settlement that contributed to a century of freedom from Europe-wide war. Moreover, thanks to the persistent efforts of the British, the powers agreed in principle to abolish the slave trade. They also achieved—at least temporarily—their conservative goals of promoting legitimacy and stability that meant so much to them.

The Concert of Europe: Securing the Vienna Settlement

Metternich and his colleagues, pleased with their handiwork, set up the political machinery for perpetuating the Vienna settlement. Conveniently at hand was the Holy Alliance, conceived by Russia's tsar Alexander I to establish and safeguard the principles of Christianity.

The Holy Alliance

Russia, Austria, and Prussia—the three bastions of conservatism—formed the nucleus of this alliance. Though Metternich and professional diplomats put little faith in it, the Holy Alliance did symbolize a commitment to preserving the Vienna settlement. Perhaps more important, it suggested a possible willingness to intervene in other countries in support of its conservative principles.

The Quadruple Alliance, also known as the **Concert of Europe,** proved a much more earthly agency for perpetuating the Vienna settlement. Austria, Russia, Prussia, and Great Britain created this military alliance

The Concert of Europe

in November 1815 to guarantee the Vienna settlement. The powers agreed to hold periodic meetings to discuss

JEAN-BAPTISTE ISABEY, *THE CONGRESS OF VIENNA,* 1815 Isabey's painting shows the main diplomats and officials who negotiated the peace settlement after the Napoleonic Wars. Their clothing marks them as members of the aristocracy, though they lack the more elegant outfits and wigs of the eighteenth century. Above the men, as if approving of what they are doing, hangs a symbol of the restoration of the Old Regime: a portrait of a king draped in regal robes.

common problems. In 1818, France completed its payment of indemnities and joined the Alliance.

Soon this conservative partnership showed its strength. In 1821, it authorized an Austrian army to put down an insurrection in Naples against King Ferdinand I. The Neapolitan liberal rebels, no match for the Austrian troops, were soon defeated and their leaders executed, imprisoned, or exiled. In 1822 the Alliance, despite Britain's withdrawal, authorized France to intervene against a liberal revolt in Spain. A French army streamed across the Pyrenees and easily crushed the rebellion. That same year, the conservative powers supported Alexander's proposal to send a Russian fleet to help put down the revolt of Spain's Latin American colonies (see Chapter 16).

The great strength of the Alliance, however, remained bound within the European continent. Across the Atlantic Ocean, President Monroe of the United States announced what would come to be called the Monroe Doctrine: The United States would regard any interference on the part of European powers in the affairs of the Western Hemisphere as an "unfriendly act." British support of the doctrine—

stemming from Britain's own economic interests in Latin America—killed any further thought of Holy Alliance intervention in the Western Hemisphere, for Great Britain enjoyed unchallenged dominance of the seas.

IDEOLOGIES: How the World Should Be

The principles underlying the settlement at Vienna and the international cooperation to enforce it reflected the deep conservatism of Metternich and many others during these years. Their conservatism was more than just a whim or political mood. Under the impact of the French Revolution and the industrial revolution, the centuries-old aristocratic order and agriculturally based society had started to crumble. Intellectuals in particular tried to grasp these changes by exploring ideologies, or sets of beliefs about the world

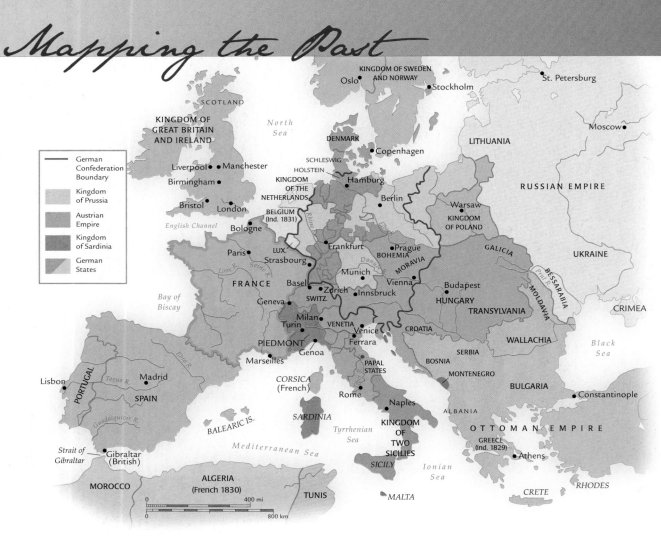

Mapping the Past

Europe, 1815 This map shows Europe after the Congress of Vienna in 1815. **Locate the enlarged states—the Netherlands, Prussia, and Piedmont-Sardinia. Why did the Congress of Vienna strengthen these states?**

and how it should be. These ideologies exerted immense power. People wrote, marched, fought, and died for them. Indeed, they fueled many of the struggles that would erupt in the years to come and ultimately would shape our very definition of the modern world.

Conservatism: Restoring the Traditional Order

The changes initiated during the French Revolution and supported by Enlightenment ideas threatened and even terrified conservatives. They wanted desperately to preserve the traditional way of life. **Conservatism** provided the ideas to refute Enlightenment and revolutionary principles and all those who stood behind them. At the heart of conservatism lay a belief in order and hierarchy. The social and political order, conservatives believed, should be based on a hierarchy of authoritative institutions whose legitimacy rested on

God and tradition. As conservatives saw it, the revolutionary notion of equality was wrong: The elite were equipped to rule; the rest were not. The most formidable enemy was the bourgeoisie, "this intermediary class" ready to "abandon itself with a blind fury and animosity . . . to all the means which seem proper to assuage its thirst for power," according to Metternich. Conservatives also warned that the idea of individualism promoted by the Enlightenment and favored by the rising middle class would fragment society and lead to anarchy. In the mind of a conservative, all change was suspect. If change did come, it should take the form of slow evolution of social and political institutions.

In 1790, the influential Anglo-Irish writer and statesman Edmund Burke (1729–1797), horrified with the outbreak of the French Revolution, outlined some of the principles of conservatism (see page 378). He argued that the revolutionaries' radical reforms based on abstract reason and notions of equality unraveled hard-won victories against savagery: "[I]t is with infinite caution that any

Burke

man ought to venture upon pulling down an edifice which has answered . . . for ages the common purposes of society." The monarchy and nobility should be preserved because they, like the church, were established links to an organic past and the best hopes for preserving the order necessary for societies to thrive.

The French writers Joseph de Maistre (1753–1821) and Louis de Bonald (1754–1840) represented a later generation of conservative thinkers who proved more rigid and ultra-royalist than Burke. As the docu-

De Maistre and de Bonald

ment here suggests, they attacked everything about the French Revolution and Enlightenment as contrary to religion, order, and civilization. De Maistre called the French Revolution an "insurrection against God." Both writers argued that authority rightly rests in the monarchy and the church, both of which derive that authority from God. "When monarchy and Christianity are both attacked, society returns to savagery," declared de Bonald. These conservatives felt that deep down, humans were more wicked than good, more irrational than rational. Only the time-tested traditions and institutions could hold the bad impulses of humans in check. All means, including fear and violence, should be used to roll back the changes from the French revolutionary and Napoleonic periods and return to societies dominated by monarchs, aristocrats, and clergy.

Not surprisingly, people from these same three groups found conservatism most appealing. Conservatism also attracted many who believed in a Christian view of society,

Appeal of conservatism

particularly members of the established churches rather than religious minorities. Some even saw the revolutionary and Napoleonic periods as divine retribution for the presumption and evil that had long marred human beings. In the international field, conservatism was epitomized by Metternich's policies, the Holy Alliance, and the Concert of Europe. In domestic policies, this conservatism was characterized by the restoration of power to the traditional monarchs and aristocrats, the renewed influence of Christianity, and the suppression of liberal and nationalistic movements.

However, conservatives faced formidable opponents, even during the early years after the fall of Napoleon. The French Revolution had turned the ideas of liberalism into a powerful, persistent force. The clash between conservatism and liberalism had just begun and would endure into the twentieth century.

Liberalism: Individual Freedom and Political Reform

In contrast to conservatism, **liberalism** drew on the promises of the French Revolution and the Enlightenment. Conservatives sought to maintain traditional society; liberals fought to change it. Liberals wanted a society that

A Conservative Theorist Attacks Political Reform

Many conservatives resented the reforms sparked by the French Revolution. The extremely conservative theorist Joseph de Maistre was no exception. Here, de Maistre attacks written constitutions and the reform of political institutions.

Every thing brings us back to the general rule—*man cannot create a constitution; and no legitimate constitution can be written.* The collection of fundamental laws, which must essentially constitute a civil or religious society, never has been written, and never will be, *a priori.* It is only when society finds itself already constituted, without being able to say how, that it is possible to make known, or explain, in writing, certain special articles; but in almost every case these declarations or explanations are the effect of very great evils, and always cost the people more than they are worth.

. . . Not only does it not belong to man to create institutions, but it does not appear that his power, *unassisted,* extends even to change for the better institutions already established. . . . *Nothing* [says the philosopher, Origen] . . . *can be changed for the better among men, without God.* . . .

On what basis does de Maistre object to written constitutions?

promoted individual freedom, or liberty. However, many laws, customs, and conditions of the traditional order stood in their way. Liberals therefore opposed the dominance of politics and society by monarchs, aristocrats, and clergy, and governments' arbitrary interference with individual liberty. To the extent that these elements of the traditional order remained in place, liberals demanded reform and fought resisting conservatives.

From the Enlightenment and the theories of John Locke, liberals adopted ideas about natural laws, natural rights, toleration, and the application of reason to human affairs (see Chapter 14). From political thinkers such as Montesquieu, they took the idea that governmental powers should be separated and restricted by checks and balances. From the French and American revolutions, they drew on the principles of freedom, equality before the law, popular sovereignty, and the sanctity of property.

Sources of liberalism

Liberalism reflected the aspirations of the middle class, which was gaining wealth but lacked political and social power in the traditional order. Not surprisingly, then, liberals advocated government limited by written constitutions, the elimination of political and social privileges, and extension of voting rights to men of some property and education (most liberals stopped short of suggesting universal male suffrage or extension of the vote to women). In addition, liberals desired representative institutions where none existed and an extension of the right to participate in representative institutions that remained the preserve of the aristocratic and wealthy elite. They demanded that governments guarantee the sanctity of property and individual rights, such as freedom of the press, speech, assembly, and religion.

Certain economic policies also had great importance to liberals and reflected the stake that the middle class had in commerce and industry. The Scottish economist Adam Smith (1723–1790) formulated the ideas that guided economic liberalism (see page 340). In *The Wealth of Nations* (1776), Smith argued that economics, like the physical world, had its own natural laws. The most basic economic law was of supply and demand, he explained. When left to operate alone, economic laws, like an "invisible hand," would keep the economy in balance and, in the long run, create the most wealth. According to Smith, self-interest—even greed—was the engine that motivated people to work hard and produce wealth: "It is not from the benevolence of the butcher, the brewer, or the baker that we expect our dinner, but from their regard to their own interest." Governments should therefore follow a policy of laissez-faire (hands-off), limiting their involvement in the economy to little more than maintaining law and order so that an unfettered marketplace could flourish.

Smith

Other liberal economic thinkers extended Smith's ideas. The British economist Thomas Malthus (1766–1834) cast gloom on hopes for progress among workers. He argued that population would always increase more than food supplies, resulting in poverty and death by "the whole train of common disease, and epidemics, wars, plague and famine." Malthus concluded that workers themselves were "the cause of their own poverty," because they lacked the moral discipline to avoid sexual activity. The politically influential Englishman David Ricardo (1772–1823) refined Malthus's arguments into the "iron law of wages," explaining that wages would always sink to subsistence levels or below because higher salaries just caused workers to multiply, thereby glutting the labor market and lowering wages. He emphasized that the economy was controlled by objective laws. The lessons for these "classical" liberals (to distinguish them from modern American liberals, who usually favor government programs to regulate certain economic and social affairs) were clear: no intervention in economic matters by government, no tariffs or unions that artificially raise prices or wages, and no restrictions on individual enterprise.

Malthus and Ricardo

Over time, liberalism evolved and developed several variations. The English philosopher Jeremy Bentham (1748–1832) and his followers advocated a kind of liberalism that became particularly influential in Britain. Known as utilitarianism, it held that all activities and policies should be judged by the standard of usefulness. "Nature has placed mankind under the governance of two sovereign masters, *pain* and *pleasure*," explained Bentham. What was useful, the utilitarians decreed, was what created more pleasure than pain; the best laws and policies were therefore those that promoted "the greatest good for the greatest number" of people. Bentham's utilitarians fought for more governmental intervention in economic and social affairs than other liberals. For example, they supported reforms to protect women and children workers in factories and to improve urban sanitation. Democracy was implicit in utilitarianism, for the best way for the greatest number to maximize their own happiness was for each person to vote. Nevertheless, most liberals during this period actually opposed democracy. They feared the supposedly unruly "masses" and hoped to keep government in the hands of the propertied and well educated. They would not start to embrace democratic reforms until the middle of the nineteenth century. At that time, some of them, such as John Stuart Mill (1806–1873) (see Past Lives on page 425), would also begin arguing for major social programs to protect workers and even the right to vote for women.

Bentham

Mill

As we saw earlier, liberalism appealed especially to the rising middle classes, who were prospering from commerce and industry and wanted political power along with their growing wealth and confidence. Liberals had faith that history was on their side, that liberalism, like progress, was inevitable and that the forces they opposed were of the past. That optimism gave them strength to fight against the conservative forces of tradition and rally to protect their gains.

John Stuart Mill (1806–1873) & Harriet Taylor (1807–1858)

John Stuart Mill and Harriet Taylor were one of the most famous and extraordinary couples of the nineteenth century. They met in 1830 when Harriet was already married and with two children. They became "intimate and confidential friends." Mill was a constant visitor to the Taylor household and a frequent companion to Harriet in London. Although their relationship created a scandal in London society, John Taylor, unwilling to see his wife unhappy, acquiesced in it.

In 1843, Mill published *A System of Logic*, the first of several major works that marked him as one of the leading thinkers of the nineteenth century. In 1851, Harriet published anonymously *The Enfranchisement of Women*, which argued for universal suffrage and more equal companionship between men and women. Mill would go on to publish *On Liberty* (1859), his most famous political work, in which he argued for freedom of thought and warned against the tyranny of the majority. In 1869, he published *The Subjection of Women*, which made him one of the leading feminists of the century. It is fundamentally wrong, he said, for society to "ordain that to be born a girl instead of a boy, any more than to be born black instead of white, or a commoner instead of a nobleman, shall decide the person's position through all life."

Mill was happy to describe most of his works as jointly produced by himself and Harriet. But

JOHN STUART MILL AND HARRIET TAYLOR

Mill may have been too generous in his praise of her role. Just how much she contributed has long been a matter of heated debate. In 1849, two discreet years after John Taylor's death, Mill and Harriet Taylor married. They were proud that their relationship was based on rationality, intellectual companionship, affection, and intimacy, but not sex. They imagined their marriage as a utopian union of equals. It lasted until 1858, when Harriet died.

Harriet Taylor and John Stuart Mill embodied many nineteenth-century trends. Liberalism, romanticism, and socialism all played a role in their lives. In addition, what brought them together was the middle-class ideal—affection, companionship, the shared life at home. In other ways, however, they did not reflect the times at all. Their views on marriage and relations between men and women, and the intensity of their intellectual collaboration, alarmed many of their contemporaries. Only in the decades to come would these unusual views gain more favor.

In his life, writings, and politics, why is Mill considered a leading feminist of the nineteenth century?

Nationalism: A Common Identity and National Liberation

Like the liberals, nationalists harbored a spirit of optimism. They, too, were aroused by the French Revolution, for it promoted the idea that sovereignty rested not in a monarch or a church but in the people, and that they, banded together, constituted the nation. **Nationalism** promised to unify nations, liberate subject peoples from foreign rule, create a sense of fraternity among members of a national community, and lead that community to a common destiny. At its core was a feeling of cultural identity among distinct groups of people who shared a common language and traditions and who belonged in a nation-state of their own.

France became an early source of nationalist sentiments. There a sense of membership in the state became especially important when the Revolution transformed the kingdom into a nation. Popular sovereignty, wider political participation, and the abolition of old provincial boundary lines gave the French a feeling of solidarity among themselves and with the national government. Universal conscription into the revolutionary armies added to feelings of fraternity in a righteous cause and helped make those armies strong. Powerful new symbols, such as the tricolor flag, stood for national unity and willingness to sacrifice for the sake of the nation.

The French Revolution

Nationalism also moved people who did not yet share a state. In the German-speaking areas, for example, scholars and intellectuals developed a cultural basis for nationalism. Writers such as Johann Gottfried von Herder (1744–1803) fostered a sense of common national identity arising from German folk culture and oral traditions. Georg Wilhelm Friedrich Hegel (1770–1831) provided philosophical and historical bases for German nationalism and the importance of the national state. Romantics such as Ernst Moritz Arndt (1769–1860) urged Prussians, Austrians, Bavarians, and others with common roots to "be Germans, be one, will to be one by love and loyalty, and no devil will vanquish you." Groups and secret societies such as Young Germany—usually composed of students, intellectuals, and members of the middle class—promoted a sense of national identity and unity.

Cultural nationalism

In Italy, Poland, and elsewhere, nationalists formed similar organizations and intellectuals created interest in national languages and folk culture. Scholars resurrected and developed languages from previous eras and elevated myths to national histories. Schoolteachers taught these languages and histories to their students and thereby spread a sense of ethnic unity. Nationalists used this growing interest in language and history to proclaim their nation's special mission—for example, of the Czechs to become leaders of the Slavs, or the Italians to lead Europe again as it had during Roman times.

Nationalism promised a new sense of community as the old order with its traditional allegiances declined. It offered a sense of strength and unity that appealed to many peoples: to those threatened with foreign domination, such as the Spaniards and Italians under the French during the Napoleonic era; to those dissatisfied with the dominance of one ethnic group, such as Czechs, Magyars, or Serbs under the Germans within the Habsburg Empire; and to those feeling suppressed by what they considered foreign domination, such as the Greeks under the Ottomans, the Poles under the Russians, and the Italians under the Austrians.

Sense of community

From such sources, it was a short step to calls for national liberation and political unification. Nationalism soon acquired attributes of a religion and became a powerful political force. For example, the Italian nationalist Giuseppe Mazzini (1805–1872), who founded the revolutionary Young Italy movement in 1831, called Italy "the purpose, the soul, the consolation of our thoughts, the country chosen of God and oppressed by men." Some nationalist leaders, such as Mazzini, began demanding loyalty and solidarity from members of their organizations.

National liberation and unification

Before 1848, most nationalists supported liberal causes, for liberals also struggled for national rights. Both liberals and nationalists typically believed that sovereignty should rest with the people, united by common loyalties and language. They also had faith that change would bring political, social, and economic progress. Campaigns by liberals to promote agricultural improvement and industrial development often merged into German, Italian, and Hungarian calls for national unity.

Later, nationalists would ally themselves with conservatives, for both believed in the value of historical traditions and in an organic society over the rights of the individual. Nationalism would also become more entwined with notions of national superiority and special national missions that so often appealed to conservatives. All nationalists, however, insisted that each nation of people, unified into a self-governing state, should be the primary focus of political loyalty and that the political boundaries of the state should be the same as ethnic boundaries of the people. The widespread political and emotional appeal of nationalism made it an increasingly powerful ideology over the course of the century.

Romanticism: Freedom, Instinct, and Spontaneity

The origins of nationalism in literature and history also made it attractive to believers in **romanticism.** This ideology became the dominant spirit in literature and art during the first half of the nineteenth century. Its significance stretched beyond culture, however. Romanticism reflected a new recognition that human beings were complex, emotional, and only sometimes rational creatures. In a civilization that was growing ever more scientific, materialistic, industrial, and urban, romanticism became a counterweight for the human experience. It stood against eighteenth-century classicism and the Enlightenment and the ideals of reason and order that so characterized those eras. Instead, romanticism emphasized individual freedom and spontaneity.

The origins of romanticism can be traced back to Jean-Jacques Rousseau, the acclaimed writer and philosopher we met in Chapter 14. Though a central figure of the Enlightenment, Rousseau had stressed feeling, instinct, emotions, and love of nature. He described walking away from the city into the fields and woods, stretching himself out on the ground, digging his fingers and toes into the dirt, kissing the earth, and weeping for joy. In several of his most widely read writings, he seemed to idealize love, childhood, and "the noble savage."

Rousseau

Other strands of romanticism came from the German "Storm and Stress" (Sturm und Drang) literature of the late eighteenth century. German writers gave much weight to inner feelings fully experienced and expressed by sensitive individuals. Johann Wolfgang von Goethe provided a model of the emotional individual searching for love and self-understanding in his novel *The Sorrows of the Young Werther* (1774). Like Rousseau, Goethe had many interests. He delved into philosophy, science, and public affairs as well as literature. His masterpiece, the philosophical drama *Faust*, featured a medieval scholar who, dissatisfied with the fruits of knowledge, sells his soul to the devil in return for earthly pleasure and wisdom. In Goethe's medieval interests, his emotional spontaneity, and his love of nature and of individual personality, this renowned writer exemplified the heart of romanticism.

"Storm and Stress" literature

All these qualities explored by Rousseau and Goethe came to characterize the work of succeeding romantic writers and artists. Many romantics expressed a new interest in the Middle Ages. They revived the popularity of medieval tales, Gothic architecture, the Knights of the Round Table, and heroic figures, thereby turning the medieval era from the Dark Ages into the Age of Faith.

Reviving the Middle Ages

This fascination with the Middle Ages reflected romanticism's passionate concern with the drama of history. Written by scholars such as Thomas Babington Macaulay (1800–1859) in Great Britain, history was literary and exciting, featuring heroic individuals, great accomplishments, and national struggles. These same themes were explored by the Prussian philosopher Hegel. In Hegel's view, history was a great spiritual drama of heroic individuals that would lead to a new sense of national identity and freedom.

History

Romanticism also stressed the emotion of Christianity and the mystical presence of God in nature. According to romantic theologians, the important part of religion was the feeling of dependence on an infinite God rather than religious dogma or institutions. In his widely read book *The Genius of Christianity*, the French writer François Auguste-René de Chateaubriand (1768–1848) described in lush words how "every thing in a Gothic church reminds you of the labyrinths of a forest; every thing excites a feeling of religious awe, of mystery, and of the Divinity." In part, religious revivals during the late eighteenth and early nineteenth centuries, with their stress on piety and emotional outpourings, reflected these spiritual qualities of romanticism.

Christianity

The connections among the love of nature, the spiritual presence of God, and the power of emotions were most striking in the romantic literature, art, and music of the period. In the literary realm, the English poets William Wordsworth (1770–1850) and Samuel Taylor Coleridge (1772–1834) became closely associated with the beautiful lake country of northwest England—Wordsworth by birth and Coleridge by adoption. Together the two men traveled to Germany, where they fell under the influence of German romanticists. They collaborated on *Lyrical Ballads* (1798), which included Wordsworth's "Lines Composed a Few Miles Above Tintern Abbey" and Coleridge's "Rime of the Ancient Mariner." Both writers glorified nature and sensed a brooding, mystical presence of the divine. Wordsworth saw in nature a higher wisdom than what scholars might offer:

Literature

> One impulse from a vernal wood
> May teach you more of man,
> Of moral evil and of good
> Than all the sages can.

Wordsworth's and Coleridge's ardent appreciation of nature, their introspective concern for the individual, and their preoccupation with the spiritual rather than the material made them leaders among Britain's many romantic poets.

In France, Germaine de Staël (1766–1817) led the romantic movement in literature. Although she admired the passionate Rousseau, she attacked most Enlightenment thinkers for not being free enough. She turned to writing in order to grapple with her own emotional experiences with several lovers and to argue for living the passionate life. Often writing about female heroes and genius in works such as *Corinne*, de Staël also looked to history for a vision of another, better world. She and other romantics created an image of the ideal romantic heroine who followed her emotions rather than tradition or reason— a model that some tried to follow in life. Also in France, George Sand (Amandine Dupin Dudevant) (1804–1876) became an extraordinarily creative writer and an unconventional woman. Abandoning her tyrannical husband for an independent life in Paris, Sand became an intellectual leader whose private life included several love affairs with

Karl Friedrich Schinkel, *Medieval Town on a River*

1815

In this romantic painting, the artist depicts an imaginary medieval town. A stunning Gothic cathedral, its spires stretching toward the heavens above and basking in the sun's blessings, dominates the people below as well as the scene itself. The finely built town in the background appears well ordered, as do the town's humble citizens, working calmly and enjoying the fruits of this civilization. What impression of medieval life do you think the artist intended to convey to viewers? How might this scene contrast with a realistic urban scene of the nineteenth century or today?

key elements of romanticism: glorification of nature, religious mysticism, adoration of an idealized medieval era, and expression of emotion. The romantic love of magnificent landscapes can be found in the painting on page 429.

Music

In music, a number of romantic composers followed in the footsteps of Ludwig van Beethoven (1770–1827). The music of this famed German composer overflowed the bounds of classic forms, becoming freer, more individualistic, and more emotional than anything that had come before. Beethoven composed his *Pastoral Symphony* as a musical link to nature. "How happy I am," he wrote in 1810, "to be able to stroll in the woods, among the trees, bushes, wild flowers and rocks. No one can love the country as much as I do." The lyrics to one of his choral works explain his feelings about music:

> *When the magic of sound holds sway*
> *and works bring inspiration,*
> *glorious things must appear,*
> *darkness and turmoil become light.*

One critic explained that romantic music should "paint to the eyes of the soul the splendors of nature, the delights of contemplation, the character of nations, the tumult of their passions, and the languor of their sufferings."

Through much of romanticism, strands from all the ideologies combined and recombined in a variety of ways. Nationalism, for example, played a prominent role in some romantics' lives. In the 1820s, England's romantic poet Lord Byron (1788–1824) fought for Greek national independence against the

Connections to nationalism

well-known people. At her own convenience, she dressed as a man or a woman. Like several other women writers, she also took a male pseudonym to add legitimacy to her writings. Several of her novels explored romantic love and featured strong, intensely emotional heroines.

Leading romantic painters also stressed emotional images. The image above, an oil painting by the German artist Karl Friedrich Schinkel, shows an idealized image of a medieval town at twilight. The painting contains the

Art

Turks. Some of Frederic Chopin's (1810–1849) dramatic music self-consciously evoked nationalistic sentiments for his native Poland, which was still under Russian rule. The Italian Giuseppe Verdi (1813–1901) and the German Richard Wagner (1813–1883), who developed the opera into a fully integrated art form of music, theater, ballet, and special effects, were among many other composers whose works brought together romantic and openly nationalistic themes.

JOHN MARTIN, *THE BARD*, 1817 This vision of a poet immersed in nature in a dramatic medieval landscape exemplifies the romantic impulse in art.

Liberals, too, found comfort in various aspects of romanticism, which helps explain the movement's wide appeal. By breaking sharply with past forms, romanticism attracted liberal and revolutionary spirits. Indeed, many romantic writers and artists sided with liberal causes. Germaine de Staël, for example, in her own life as well as in her novels, histories, and political tracts, fostered romanticism and liberalism in France. Few liberal romantics, however, were more popular than the French writer Victor Hugo (1802–1885), who idealized the masses of underprivileged humanity and preached redemption and purification through suffering.

Connections to liberalism

At the same time, certain dimensions of romanticism appealed to conservatives as well—especially the return to the past, the emphasis on Christianity, and the stand against the rationalism of the Enlightenment. Sir Walter Scott (1771–1832), who in novel and verse glorified the Middle Ages and his native Scotland, was a conservative. So was the French writer François Auguste-René de Chateaubriand, who advocated a return to mystic Catholicism and dreamed of noble Indians in tropical America.

Connections to conservatism

Romanticism found expression in many cultural forms—in the new English gardens that imitated nature rather than confining it to geometric forms, in the image of the artist as a nonconforming genius, in the glorification of walks down wooded lanes, in the popularity of the Grimm fairy tales that evoked images of medieval life, and in the sentimentalization of love in life and literature. In its qualities, its popularity, and its persistence, romanticism proved to be more than a casual change of taste or a mood. It reflected the revolutionary social, political, and intellectual developments of the era.

Early Socialism: Ending Competition and Inequities

Romantics questioned the existing system from cultural and emotional perspectives. **Socialists** questioned it from social and economic perspectives. As socialists saw it, the common people—the workers—were missing out on the astounding power and wealth generated by the industrial revolution. Socialists called for a reordering of society so as to end the competition and class divisions that caused inequalities and suffering. Such calls made the socialists enemies of both the conservative and liberal camps.

During the early decades of the nineteenth century, a few intellectuals—some of whom came to be called Utopian Socialists—contended that society should be based on cooperation rather than competitive individualism and that property should be owned communally. One of the first of these early socialists was the French nobleman Henri de Saint-Simon (1760–1825). During the French Revolution, Saint-Simon abandoned his noble title. Turning to land speculation, he made and lost a fortune. He and his followers believed that society should be reorganized on the basis of a "religion of humanity," that all people should work, and that the inheritance of private property should be abolished. In Saint-Simon's ideal world, women would be elevated from their inferior social positions. Superior artists, scientists, engineers, and businesspeople would be rewarded according to the formula "from each according to his capacity, to each according to his deserts." Saint-Simon's influential followers became convinced that the best scientists and managers could use their expertise to plan and run prosperous societies for the benefit of everyone.

Utopian Socialists

Saint-Simon

Charles Fourier (1772–1837) was also an early Utopian Socialist who, like Saint-Simon, gathered a following. A Frenchman who had been a traveling salesman, he advocated doing away with economic competition, which he saw as the very source of evil. In his utopian society, agriculture and industry would be carried on by voluntary cooperatives whose members would pool their resources and live in communal apartment houses (*phalansteries*). Housework and child care would be a shared

Fourier

responsibility of the community. Women, like men, would have the right to work and to control their own money. Fourier also considered traditional marriage too restrictive sexually. Work and pleasure would merge as people did as they pleased while still carrying out the tasks their society required to survive. People would be paid according to the labor, capital, and talent that each contributed.

In fact, the communities that Fourier's followers established in the United States and Europe rarely lasted for long. Fourier's ideas, however, inspired many people looking for a more joyful, communal alternative to the competitive industrial societies spreading in the West.

Robert Owen (1771–1858) had different ideas. Born in Wales, Owen quickly made an industrial fortune in Manchester and bought large cotton mills **Owen** in New Lanark, Scotland. Early in the nineteenth century, he set out to make New Lanark a model community. He raised wages, shortened work hours, improved working conditions, abolished child labor, provided educational and recreational facilities for employees, and established sickness and old-age insurance. Productivity in his mills soared, and profits rose. Owen spent years drawing up plans for model socialist communities, which he envisioned as being located in rural settings and as mostly self-sufficient. The plans called for community members to raise children together and for women to share in governing. Like Fourier, Owen advocated loosening the bounds of marriage to create greater sexual freedom for women and men. Several such communities were established in America, most notably New Harmony, Indiana. However, all soon succumbed to internal disagreements and economic difficulties. The efforts cost Owen most of his fortune. He retained his fame, especially within the labor movement and among those establishing modest workers' cooperatives. However, he died in 1858 without having created a lasting alternative to the harsh industrial capitalism he deplored.

In the 1830s, several Frenchwomen began linking socialist demands with calls for the emancipation of women. The most famous of these women was Flora Tristan (1801–1844), who was influenced by **Tristan** Fourier's ideas. French law discriminated against women in many ways, including automatically awarding custody of children to fathers after a marital separation. When Tristan's abusive husband was awarded their children, she fought back. Eventually she turned this dispute into a campaign to end discrimination against women within marriage, in the law, and on the job. She traveled throughout Europe and Latin America, speaking passionately for unions and the creation of centers for the care and education of workers. In her *Worker's Union* (1843), she argued that equality between

women and men could free the whole working class and transform civilization.

These and other early socialists recognized both the significance of the industrial revolution and its possibilities. They attacked the unbridled pursuit of profits in an unregulated, industrial economy. Only a well-organized society, they explained, could eliminate the misery of industrial capitalism and promote happiness. Most early socialists also attacked middle-class restrictions on women, emphasized the importance of sensual pleasure, and questioned traditional Christianity. The wave of socialist thought that these leaders unleashed became profoundly influential by the middle decades of the nineteenth century. As it evolved, it took on a more revolutionary quality, and it bore the distinctive stamp of one of the most authoritative thinkers of the nineteenth century: Karl Marx.

"Scientific Socialism": Karl Marx and *The Communist Manifesto*

"A specter is haunting Europe—the specter of Communism," announced Karl Marx (1818–1883) in 1848. "Let the ruling classes tremble at a Communist revolution." Born into a German middle-class family, his father was a Jewish lawyer who had converted to Christianity. A brilliant student, Marx attained his doctorate in philosophy and history, but he was denied an academic position because of his radical views. After embarking on a career in journalism, he was exiled from Germany for his attacks on censorship and his economic views; later, France exiled him because of his revolutionary socialist ideas. He spent the last thirty-four years of his life in London researching, writing, and trying to build organizations to put his ideas into action. Marx collaborated with his friend Friedrich Engels (1820–1895), son of a wealthy German manufacturer, in writing the seminal work ***The Communist Manifesto*** (1848). This treatise, along with the later *Das Kapital*, contained the fundamentals of what Marx called "scientific socialism."

Marx argued that economic interest, more than anything else, drove human behavior. He also thought that the dominant characteristic of each historical epoch was its prevailing **Economic interest** system of economic production— how people made a living. In his view, politics, religion, and culture were all shaped mainly by economic and social realities.

Marx also described how human societies in each historical era became divided into the "haves" and the "have-nots." The haves owned the means of economic produc-

> "A specter is haunting Europe—the specter of Communism[.]"

tion—in nineteenth-century Britain, for example, the industrial capitalists who owned the machines and factories.

Class struggle They also controlled the state and the ideas that dominated their societies. The have-nots were the exploited laborers—for example, Britain's industrial working class. Each side consisted of classes of people with opposing interests. As Marx wrote, "[T]he history of all hitherto existing society is the history of class struggle." At a certain point, economic and social change would bring these class struggles to a revolutionary crisis. The French Revolution, he explained, was an example of one of those conflicts coming to a violent head, as the bourgeoisie (the middle-class capitalists) overcame the aristocracy (the feudal landlords.)

Marx focused much of his analysis on his own industrial society of the nineteenth century. In this society, he explained, the bourgeoisie (capitalists) exploited workers by paying them only subsistence wages **Industrial capitalism** rather than compensating them for the true value created by their work. "These labourers, who must sell themselves piecemeal, are a commodity, like every other article of commerce," Marx lamented. At the same time, Marx saw capitalists as locked in a competitive struggle with one another. This contest forced them continually to introduce new, costly machines and build larger factories: "Constant revolutionizing of production, uninterrupted disturbance of all social conditions, ever-lasting uncertainty and agitation distinguish the bourgeois epoch from all earlier ones." Soon, Marx warned, greater and greater quantities of goods would be produced by a system running out of control. Eventually, the relentless competition and the periodic economic crises that plague industrial societies would thin the ranks of the bourgeoisie. At the same time, the working class would grow stronger as its numbers and consciousness increased. Inevitably, the workers—with "nothing to lose but their chains" and with "a world to win"—would revolt, seize the factories, destroy the capitalist system, abolish private property, and establish a classless socialist society.

Marx only hinted at the general nature of this new socialist society. His writings suggest that the elimination of capitalism would end the division of **Socialist society** society into classes of haves (capitalists) and have-nots (workers). The state itself would eventually wither away, for its only purpose was to protect the interests of the haves against the have-nots. Freed from exploitation and the pressures of capitalist competition, all people would lead more varied, cooperative, creative lives—in this sense, free and truly human.

Marx's socialism gained immense appeal. Because he based much of his analysis on evidence and logic, it attracted intellectuals and students. Because his socialism reflected the social and emotional turmoil being produced **Appeal of socialism** by the industrial revolution, especially the suffering of the working poor, it spoke convincingly to workers and their leaders. During the second half of the nineteenth century, Marx's socialism would become a major force in the West.

RESTORATION AND REPRESSION

Socialism as well as the other ideologies reflected the political and social realities of their era, particularly the efforts of people to understand and cope with changes that either threatened them or offered promise. In the three decades following 1815, however, socialism played only a limited part in the great struggles for policies and power. During these years, it was the forces representing conservatism, liberalism, and nationalism that instead took center stage.

The struggles for influence and power among believers of these ideologies took place in pamphlets and newspapers, in courts and parliaments, in universities and police barracks, and in streets and fields throughout Europe. In the first years after the defeat of Napoleon, conservatism held sway in international and diplomatic affairs. The Vienna agreements and the cooperative arrangements to repress the threat of revolution in Europe epitomized this ideology. Conservatism also prevailed in domestic politics across most of Europe.

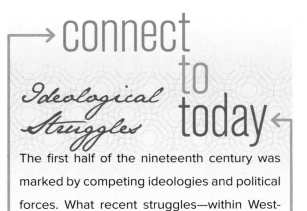

→ connect to today ←

Ideological Struggles

The first half of the nineteenth century was marked by competing ideologies and political forces. What recent struggles—within Western countries or elsewhere in the world—might be comparable to these?

The Return of the Bourbons in France

When the victorious armies of the coalition powers entered France and deposed Napoleon in the spring of 1814, they brought "in their baggage" the members of the Bourbon royal family who **Louis XVIII** had fled the Revolution. In their wake trooped the émigré nobility. The brother of the guillotined Louis XVI was placed on the throne as Louis XVIII (r. 1814–1824). (The son of Louis XVI, who had died in prison without having ruled, was considered Louis XVII.)

The "restored" king ruled with an odd mixture of conservatism and moderation. He issued a charter that retained Napoleon's administrative and legal system as well as civil and religious liberties. He also placed lawmaking in the hands of a two-chamber legislature. However, only a small, wealthy elite could vote, and the king kept most of the power.

Nevertheless, Louis XVIII used his authority with moderation, thinking that a mild leadership style would help ensure his hold on the crown and tranquillity in France. Most of the returned émigrés, however, had little appreciation for his relaxed rule—they were more conservative and angry than he was and wanted action. Led by the king's younger brother, the comte d'Artois, these ultraroyalists controlled the legislature. Through the rest of Louis XVIII's reign, they agitated for a return of their privileges and indemnification for their lost lands.

After Louis XVIII's death in 1824, d'Artois was crowned King Charles X (r. 1824–1830); he followed more conservative policies that favored the old aristocracy and the Catholic Church. He offered money to indemnify those who had lost land in the Revolution and gave the church greater control over education. Those policies provoked growing opposition to his rule. When elections increased the size of the opposition, he dissolved the Chamber of Deputies. In the face of still-increasing opposition, he abolished freedom of the press and drastically restricted the right to vote.

Charles X

Reaction and Repression in the German States

The German states in 1815 consisted of thirty-seven little states and two large ones—Prussia and Austria. All belonged to the German Confederation, which lacked an army, a treasury, and even a flag. Austria and Prussia politically dominated the German lands. Both states were firmly conservative, if not reactionary.

In multilingual Austria, the Habsburg emperor and Metternich, the conservative diplomat we met at the beginning of the chapter, held sway. The Austrian leaders had good reason to fear liberalism and nationalism like the plague, for the empire included many ethnic groups—including Hungarians, Czechs, Serbs, and Italians—with their own languages and customs. In the wake

Metternich

of the French Revolution, they began to stir with national consciousness. Metternich used all means—police, spies, censorship, and travel restrictions—to ensure the status quo. The only possible threats to conservative control came from within some of the small states in the weak German Confederation, and Austria enjoyed permanent presidency over that organization.

When students and professors formed organizations and staged festivals that supported liberal and nationalistic principles, conservative officials became alarmed. "We want a constitution for the people that fits in with the spirit of the times and with people's own level of enlightenment," explained one student. "[A]bove all, we want Germany to be considered *one* land and the people *one* people."

The murder of a conservative dramatist by a member of a student organization, Karl Sand, gave Metternich his opportunity to strike. After Sand's trial and public execution, Metternich called the princes of the leading German states to Carlsbad and had them draw up a set of harsh decrees outlawing the organizations. He also issued an ominous warning: "The duty of especial watchfulness in this matter should be impressed upon the special agents of the government." The Carlsbad Decrees established strict censorship and supervision of classrooms and libraries. Spies and police terrorized liberal students and professors. Although Sand became a political martyr in the eyes of many young nationalists, the crackdown worked: The small liberal and nationalistic movements evaporated.

Carlsbad Decrees

In Prussia, the conservative, militaristic Hohenzollern kings reigned. Behind them stood the equally conservative landed aristocracy, the Junkers. The Junkers served as officers in the Prussian army and filled the key posts in the civil service and administration. They had no sympathy for any reforms that seemed even faintly liberal or nationalistic, and they reversed many of the changes of the Napoleonic era. However, to better connect its separated territories, Prussia began making commercial treaties with its smaller German neighbors, providing for the free flow of trade among them. By 1834, nearly all the states of the German Confederation except Austria had joined the Prussian-sponsored **Zollverein** (customs union), which would prove of great importance in the march toward national unity.

Prussia

Restoration in Italy

Austria dominated Italy even more completely than Germany. Metternich described Italy as only a "geographical expression." Austria annexed the northern states of Lombardy and Venetia outright. Most other states were ruled by Austrian princes or under Austria's protection and guidance. Piedmont-Sardinia in the northwest was free from Austrian control, but its ruling House of Savoy was no less conservative than Metternich.

In 1815, the deposed aristocracy and clericals trooped back to the Italian states intent on regaining their old positions. They and their Austrian masters soon sent nearly all the Italian intelligentsia to prison or exile. When revolts in Naples, Sicily, and Piedmont flared up in 1820, the forces of order quickly used overwhelming force to put them down.

The Papal States in central Italy were no exception in this period of restoration. Pope Pius VII revived the Inquisition, reconstituted the *Index* of prohibited books, annulled Napoleonic laws of religious toleration, and even did away with French innovations such as street lighting. His successor, Pius VIII, followed equally conservative ideas. In 1829, he condemned almost everything even faintly liberal, including secular education and civil marriage.

Conservatism in Russia

Russia remained a vast agricultural nation with a feudal social structure and a tiny urban bourgeoisie. The Orthodox Christian Church, dominated by an upper clergy drawn from the aristocracy, served as an arm of the government. After fighting against the French, suffering a ravaging invasion in 1812, and playing a major role in Napoleon's defeat, Russia commanded considerable respect and power in Europe. Russia's tsar was the unstable Alexander I—at first a man open to reform, such as granting the Poles a constitution and proclaiming religious toleration, and later more of a reactionary mystic who resumed religious repression. He fell under the influence of Metternich in international affairs and his own aristocratic magnates at home. At his death in 1825, Russia remained a champion of autocracy and conservatism.

His successor, Nicholas I (r. 1825–1855), was an austere autocrat whose military career wedded him to the concepts of discipline and authority. When he assumed the throne in December 1825, a group of his young liberal military officers—hoping to write a constitution and free the serfs—revolted. Nicholas immediately crushed these "Decembrists"

and bitterly turned against any hints of liberalism. He followed a policy of demanding submission of everyone to the autocracy and to the Orthodox Church. Although the Decembrists would later gain a reputation as liberal political martyrs, Russia's government now stood as a bastion of conservatism and would remain so for many decades.

Holding the Line in Great Britain

Although Great Britain had for years been a home of representative government, conservatives dominated its government in 1815. Property qualifications so severely restricted the suffrage that only about 5 percent of adult males could vote. The distribution of seats in Parliament was so distorted that a relatively small number of families dominated the House of Commons. Furthermore, the emerging industrial cities of the north were scarcely represented at all. The conservative landed aristocracy and the Tory Party, which had seen the country through the Napoleonic Wars, had a firm grip on power.

Things became even more restricted when an economic depression left thousands of returning veterans jobless. Luddite riots (see page 407) and the specter of revolutionary activity prompted the government to take strong measures against the restless workers. The climax came in 1819 when troops charged on a crowd that had assembled in St. Peter's Fields, outside Manchester, to listen to reform speeches. A number were killed and hundreds injured in this Peterloo Massacre.

Peterloo Massacre

GEORGE CRUIKSHANK, *THE PETERLOO MASSACRE*, 1819 Cruikshank's print shows Britain's conservative forces violently breaking up a rally for liberal and radical reform.

The image on page 433 shows the troops of the conservative British government breaking up this rally for liberal and radical political reform.

The government treated the Irish no less harshly. The Irish had long been ruled and exploited as a conquered people. In the 1801 Act of Union, Britain formally absorbed **Ireland** into the United Kingdom. In this predominantly Catholic land, the Protestant minority controlled most of the land and political power. The Catholic peasantry suffered from such acute poverty that the threat of famine was not uncommon. Irish nationalists organized to agitate for the right to send elected Catholic representatives to Parliament. In 1829, fearing a civil war in Ireland, the conservative British government reluctantly passed the Catholic Emancipation Act, which allowed Roman Catholics to become members of Parliament.

A WAVE OF REVOLUTION AND REFORM

Despite conservative efforts to maintain order and halt change during the years after 1815, liberal and nationalistic causes simmered just under the surface. The demands for greater political participation and recognition of national identity strengthened and spread. Moreover, Europeans could no longer ignore the changes stemming from early industrialization and urbanization. In some cases, revolts and revolutions broke out. In other cases, people clamored for and gained major reforms.

The Greek War for Independence

A hint of the problems to come occurred during the 1820s, when Greeks mounted a national liberation movement against their Ottoman Turk overlords. The Ottoman Empire still sprawled over vast territories, from the north African coast and southwest Asia to southeastern Europe, but it had been weakened by internal dissension and external threats. By 1815, revolts had enabled Serbia to gain virtual independence, and in Egypt, Muhammad Ali ruled with only nominal subordination to the Ottomans. The Greek revolt began in 1821, which resulted in the death of many defenseless Turks. After the Turks met Greek insurrections with force and atrocities, romantic and liberal idealists formed an international movement to support Greek independence. Britain's well-known romantic poet Lord Byron was one of several who traveled to Greece to contribute to the cause. He brought money and enlisted in a regiment but lost his life to malaria at Missolonghi.

EUGÈNE DELACROIX, *GREECE EXPIRING ON THE RUINS OF MISSOLONGHI*, 1827 The canvas captures Greece's struggle for independence. A woman symbolizing Greek liberty kneels in the ruins of a Greek city in a plea for help against Turkish overlords. It is already too late for the martyred freedom fighter whose arm is thrust forward toward the viewer. Behind the woman, a Turkish soldier strikes a victorious pose.

The image above, by the romantic French artist Eugène Delacroix (1798–1863), captures Greece's struggle for independence.

In the end, intervention by Great Britain, France, and Russia finally secured Greek independence. Although Europeans thought of Greece sympathetically as Christian and as the birthplace of European civilization, these countries' motives had more to do with their own greedy hopes of gains at the expense of the Turks than with genuine support for the Greek revolutionaries. They achieved their objective, but this dramatic chapter in Greek history still revealed the strength of nationalistic movements and the power of liberal and romantic ideals to fuel these movements.

Liberal Triumphs in Western Europe

In 1830, a new series of revolutions tested and sometimes overwhelmed established governments. In France, a struggle arose for liberal reforms against the reactionary King Charles X. Since ascending the throne in 1824, Charles had tried to reverse the moderate policies of his predecessor, Louis XVIII, and return France to the days before the French Revolution. He aligned himself with the most extreme ultraroyalists and the Catholic Church, angering the wealthy bourgeoisie and even the peasantry with his reactionary policies. Support for his regime weakened and he lost control over the Chamber of Deputies, the most representative of France's two-chamber legislature. His efforts to dissolve the Chamber, censor the press, and narrow the electoral laws only stiffened liberal opposition. In July 1830, things came to a head. Liberals in Paris joined with workers outraged by rising food prices. Workers took to the streets of Paris and set up barriers against the king's unenthusiastic troops. Uprisings—fueled by hunger, suspicions of hoarding, and resentment against taxes—spread throughout France. After three days of haphazard fighting, the insurgents gained the upper hand. Charles X, the last Bourbon king of France, fled to Great Britain.

The July Revolution in France

While many in France had hoped for a republic to replace the Bourbon monarchy, more conservative liberals took control and created a constitutional "bourgeois monarchy" under Charles X's cousin, Louis-Philippe (r. 1830–1848). Recognizing that a new, more liberal era had dawned in France, Louis-Philippe assumed the role of "citizen king," casting aside the clothes and ornaments of royalty and dressing in the style of his Parisian upper-middle-class supporters. He reduced property qualifications for voting, thereby doubling the electorate (though still only the property-owning elite could vote).

The year 1830 also brought revolutionary trouble in the Belgian provinces of the kingdom of the Netherlands. The union forced on Belgium (predominantly Catholic) and the Netherlands (mainly Calvinist) at Vienna had never been a happy one. Although numerically a minority, the Dutch staffed most of the country's political institutions. As one Belgian nationalist put it in 1830, "By what right do two million Dutchmen command four million Belgians?" Desires for national liberation combined with tensions over high food prices to fuel a revolt in August 1830. When the half-hearted efforts of the Dutch government failed to suppress the revolt, Austria and Russia threatened to intervene. Britain and France resisted the intervention and secured Belgian independence. Belgium soon adopted a liberal constitution.

Revolution in Belgium

By that time, liberal reformers had also scored successes in Switzerland, making that country the first to grant universal male suffrage. In 1834, a new constitution introduced at least the form of liberal institutions to Spain as well.

Switzerland and Spain

Testing Authority in Eastern and Southern Europe

As the map on page 436 shows, revolutionaries also tested regimes in eastern and southern Europe. In November 1830, a Polish nationalistic movement led by students and army cadets tried to end Russian rule. They managed to establish a provisional government in Warsaw, but conflict within different social groups and among reformers weakened that government. Russian troops soon defeated the revolutionaries. Nicholas sent thousands of Poles to Siberia in chains and began a harsh program of Russification to crush any hint of Polish independence.

Poland

In Italy, nationalists began gathering in secret societies called *Carbonari*. (The word means "charcoal burners," suggesting an image of common people meeting around charcoal fires.) The Carbonari had long plotted for political freedom and national unification. In 1831, liberal and nationalist revolutions broke out in central Italy, but Austrian forces promptly suppressed them. The movement again went underground but was kept alive under the leadership of the romantic nationalist Giuseppe Mazzini.

Italy

Liberal Demands in Great Britain

In Britain, conservatives had to contend not only with demands for liberal reforms but also with pressures rising from early industrialization and urbanization. Despite the Peterloo Massacre and the restrictive Six Acts, Britain had already shown signs of political flexibility in response to public opinion in the 1820s. By 1822, it had deserted the conservative Concert of Europe. The government repealed laws preventing laborers from organizing unions and removed civil restrictions against nonconforming Protestants and Catholics. Yet these measures, however encouraging to liberals, did not get at the fundamental issue that had raised reform demands for decades: broadening popular participation in the government.

Now the industrial middle class, gaining in wealth and number, added weight to radicals' demands to extend the right to vote and relocate political strength from the countryside to the underrepresented industrial cities. However, the conservative Tories, who controlled Parliament, remained unwilling or unable to effect electoral reform. In 1830, elections brought the more liberal Whigs to power. These Whigs believed that moderate reform rather than reactionary intransigence was the best way to preserve elite institutions from revolutionary change.

Reform Bill of 1832

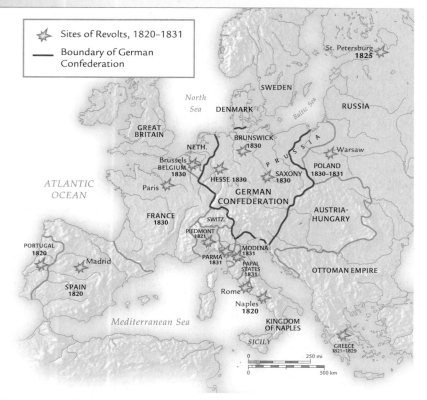

European Revolts, 1820–1831 This map shows the locations of revolts in Europe between 1820 and 1831.

Map legend:
- Sites of Revolts, 1820–1831
- Boundary of German Confederation

Worried that the July Revolution in France might spread to Britain, and facing increasing public demonstrations for reform as well as violent acts of protest, the Whigs decided to bend rather than break. They introduced the Reform Bill of 1832, which answered some of the demands. Speaking in favor of the bill, the English historian and politician Thomas Babington Macaulay warned that "now, while the crash of the proudest throne of the Continent [France] is still resounding in our ears . . . now, while the heart of England is still sound," the Reform Bill must be passed. After considerable effort, the Whigs finally enacted the new law.

The Reform Bill did not grant the universal manhood suffrage called for by radicals, but it lowered property qualifications so that most upper-middle-class men (still a small minority) could vote. More important, the bill redistributed electoral districts, taking power away from the "rotten boroughs" (no-longer-important towns and rural areas) and giving it to the underrepresented cities where commercial and industrial elites dominated. The political struggle to pass the bill enabled the House of Commons to gain power over the House of Lords, which had opposed the law. The long era of dominance by the conservative landed aristocracy was ending. More liberal property owners, including the commercial and industrial bourgeoisie, rose to power. From that point on, Britain's leading politi-

cal groups realigned themselves into the modern Conservative and Liberal parties.

Britain's government soon turned to other reforms. Britain had for several decades led in the antislavery movement, abolishing its own slave trade in 1807 and pushing the Congress of Vienna to declare against the trade in 1815. Europeans, however, often violated principled declarations against slavery and shipped hundreds of thousands more African slaves to the Americas—especially to the Caribbean and Brazil. In 1833, Parliament bowed to humanitarian radicals and Protestant reformers and abolished slavery in Britain's colonies. Fifteen years later, France would follow suit by abolishing slavery in its colonies, and in 1888, Brazil joined the list, ending slavery in the Americas.

Antislavery

Britain's Parliament and reformers also tried to cope with growing pressures exerted by the industrial revolution. Several new laws aimed to ease some of the disturbing harshness of industrial employment. Between 1833 and 1847, Parliament forbad the employment of women and children in underground mines, prohibited the employment of children under 9 in textile mills, and limited children 9 or older and women to ten hours a day in those factories. Other legislation also reflected the British economy's shift from agriculture to industry. In the name of free trade and lower bread prices, liberals mounted a major attack on the Corn Laws, which imposed tariffs on grain imports. An anti–Corn Law movement spread throughout the country, accusing the aristocratic landowners who benefited from the Corn Laws of being enemies of the middle and working classes. Victory for the movement came in 1846 with the repeal of the Corn Laws. The repeal reduced the price of bread, but it also opened up the possibility that employers—knowing that workers could afford the cheaper bread—would slash wages.

Economic and social reforms

Corn Laws

These liberal principles and reforms, however, only added to the suffering of millions facing the horrible potato famine in Ireland. This mostly rural and impoverished population relied on the potato for food. In 1845, a new, unknown fungus attacked potato plants, ruining the crop. Famine spread as the crops failed year after year. Despite some charitable assistance, Britain's liberal government concluded that the state should not meddle in the economy. More than a million died in Ireland and another

Irish famine

million fled overseas while Britain's liberals—often sympathetic and believing that the free market would alleviate the distress—held fast to their principles and did little.

Nor were liberal reforms enough for the hard-pressed urban workers. They were bitterly aware that they had been bypassed by the Reform Bill of 1832: "The Reform Act has

Chartism

effected a transfer of power from one domineering faction to another, and left the people as helpless as before," explained one of their leaders. They also complained that Britain's unprecedented national prosperity had not benefited workers: "With all these elements of national prosperity, and with every disposition and capacity to take advantage of them, we find ourselves overwhelmed with public and private suffering." In 1838, working-class leaders took action and drew up The People's Charter. The document called for several democratic reforms, including universal male suffrage, election by secret ballot, and the removal of property qualifications for office. "We perform the duties of freemen; we must have the privileges of freemen," announced the charter.

The so-called **Chartists** presented their demands twice to Parliament, which summarily rejected them. Nevertheless, the movement persisted within the working class for years. Women aided the cause by raising money and passing petitions for signatures. They also, unsuccessfully, demanded that the charter include provisions for female suffrage. Finally, in April 1848, the Chartists planned a huge demonstration in London to back up their petition. The frightened government and middle classes prepared to use force to control the gathering, as they had several times against strikes and workers' protests. However, when the reforms were refused once more, only a few mild protests arose, and the Chartist movement sputtered out. Nevertheless, Britain's political parties were becoming aware of the growing influence of the working classes and began considering ways to win their favor.

In Britain, then, reforms designed to meet demands for broader representation and manage the social consequences of industrialization and urbanization were under way by the 1840s. Under pressure, Britain's government bent enough to satisfy much of the middle class. The discontented working classes were not yet powerful enough to force their views on the resisting government. Liberalism, the strongest ideology challenging Britain's traditional order, remained a force for reform rather than revolution.

On the Continent, however, nations followed a different path. Throughout western Europe, liberal and nationalistic movements gained stunning successes in these same years. In eastern and southern Europe, these two ideologies also rose and served notice, but, with the exception of

> "While half of the population of Paris dies of starvation, the other half eats for two."

Greece, the conservative forces of order beat them down. In 1848, however, the complicated interplay among all these movements finally reached a volatile turning point.

THE DAM BURSTS

On New Year's Day, 1848, one could look back to 1830 and conclude that the forces that had opened the gates to a wave of revolutions and reforms had since been held under control. In February 1848, everything would change.

Trouble had already been brewing across Europe. In 1846 and 1847, poor harvests had driven up food prices and even brought famine. These disasters, along with financial crises, undermined markets for manufactured goods, created business failures, and left thousands of workers jobless. Governments tried to maintain order, but the growing resentments of liberals, nationalists, and now socialists, who blamed governments for failing to enact overdue reforms, made things even more difficult.

Antigovernment groups had also begun taking on a disturbing complexity and variety. Some protesters wanted only to widen political participation and institute accepted liberal reforms; others demanded full democracy. Several ethnic groups desired national autonomy; workers wanted jobs and rights. Together, the potential opposition to established governments not only loomed large but also cut across class and ideological lines. Intense, shared opposition to the status quo masked any differences these groups might have had. As the pressure of their frustration mounted, the economic crisis threatened to unlock the floodgates.

The "Glory Days"

The dam broke first in France. Louis-Philippe's constitutional monarchy had allied moderate conservatives and moderate liberals into a regime of wealthy property owners. Presenting itself as the bearer of national patriotism and political

France

caution, the government managed to quiet both conservative and radical opponents during the 1830s. However, beneath the surface of this apparently stable regime, discontent grew. The king and his chief minister during the 1840s—the moderately liberal historian François Guizot (1787–1874)—opposed any further extension of the suffrage. Workers, who had not shared in the relative prosperity of the period, clamored for the right

ANTON ZIEGLER, *THE BARRICADE IN MICHAELER SQUARE ON THE NIGHT OF MAY 26TH,* 1848 Men and women of various classes in Vienna guard a revolutionary barricade made of paving stones, timbers, and carts. Behind the barricade, a community of people stands ready to help one another politely in the common effort (notice the man aiding a woman across a wooden footbridge). The atmosphere has an almost festive quality.

ers, the government tried to prohibit the event. Opposition erupted in the Parisian streets. King Louis-Philippe tried to quiet people by dismissing his unpopular prime minister, François Guizot. Long in office, Guizot's response to those not rich enough to have the right to vote was "Get rich, then you can vote." The king's effort at appeasement failed. A shot fired during a brawl between a crowd and troops guarding government houses unnerved the troops, who fired a murderous volley into the mob and set off a full-scale insurrection. Barricades against governmental troops flew up all over Paris, and when the king's citizen militia, the National Guard, began taking the rebels' side, Louis-Philippe followed Guizot into exile.

The romantic poet Alphonse de Lamartine (1790–1869) and a group of bourgeois liberals proclaimed the Second Republic and hastily set up a provisional government. The new ruling body was republican in sentiment, but, tellingly, it had only one prominent radical member: the socialist writer Louis Blanc (1811–1882). The provisional government immediately called for the election by universal male suffrage of an assembly to draw up a new constitution. Yet that government turned down demands for political and economic rights by the new woman's newspaper, *The Voice of Women*, and by women's political clubs. Under pressure from the Paris populace, the provisional government did admit workers to the National Guard, thereby giving them access to arms.

The government, in response to popular demand for the right to work, also set up national workshops. The workshops—an idea once proposed by Louis Blanc—however, were a parody of Blanc's socialist **National workshops** vision. Blanc lamented that they were deliberately planned so as to ensure failure. In this ill-designed undertaking, laborers were assigned to hastily arranged projects. When more laborers enrolled than could be used, the surplus workers were paid almost as much as the employed ones to remain idle. To make matters worse, tens of thousands of job-hungry laborers rushed to Paris to join the workshops. The resulting demoralization of labor and the cost to the tax-payers frightened peasant and bourgeois property owners alike. Elections held in April 1848 swept conservative republicans and monarchists back into office.

to vote and the right to organize unions but got neither. The poor harvests and financial crises in 1846 and 1847 heightened frustration with the regime. In Paris, more than 40 percent of the workforce was without a job. One Parisian radical complained, "While half of the population of Paris dies of starvation, the other half eats for two."

The parliamentary opposition and bourgeois reformers began holding banquets to rally support for widening the right to vote. When a banquet to be held in Paris on February 22 in honor of George Washington's birthday (the United States served as a symbol of democracy in this period) promised to attract thousands of sympathetic work-

As the map on page 441 reveals, the February explosion in Paris set central Europe aflame with revolt. One core of the revolutions settled in Vienna, the seat of the Habsburg government. After news of the Paris events arrived in Vienna, Austrian students, middle-class reformers, and workers charged into the streets, clamoring for an end to Metternich's

Then & Now

Student Revolutionaries

On a late February morning in 1848, Carl Schurz heard from a friend that the French had just "driven away" their king and "proclaimed the republic." With his fellow students, Schurz rushed into the street and to a spontaneous rally in the market-square. The revolution had begun in the German states. In recent decades, college students have also played important roles in revolutions in the West and elsewhere—from Berkeley and Paris in 1968 to Eastern Europe in 1989. During the disputed election victory of Iranian president Mahmoud Ahmadinejad in 2009, students at Iranian universities took to the streets, demanding their votes be accounted for. More than 100 students at Shiraz University alone were arrested in the wake of the protests.

---

system. There, as elsewhere in the streets of Europe's cities, women joined men in the effort, building the barricades,

Austria

taking care of the wounded, supplying the fighters with meals, and sometimes taking part in battles against armed forces. The painting on page 438 captures the flavor of this revolutionary activity. As the uprising gained momentum, Metternich fled for his life. The Habsburg emperor, Ferdinand I, hastily abolished the country's most repressive laws, ended serfdom, and promised constitutional reform.

In Hungary, the Magyars, under the leadership of the eloquent Louis Kossuth (1802–1894), rose and demanded

Hungary

national autonomy from Austria. The Czechs followed suit in Bohemia and called for a Pan-Slavic congress to meet at Prague. In Austria's Italian provinces of Lombardy and Venetia, the rebellious populace drove the Austrian forces into defensive fortresses and declared their independence. By June 1848, it appeared that the Habsburg Empire was splintering along ethnic lines and that its German core would commit to liberal reforms.

When the Hohenzollern ruler of Prussia, Frederick William IV (r. 1840–1861), heard of

OPINION

What issues and actions did the several revolutions and movements for reform that developed between 1820 and 1848 have in common?

events in Austria, he granted some reforms and promised a liberal constitution. Nevertheless, as the document on page 440 suggests, the news from Paris and Vienna sent middle-class liberals and artisans demonstrating in the streets of Berlin, the capital of Prussia. Frederick William sent in the troops, but their brutality stiffened support for

Prussia

the revolutionary cause. A few days later, he withdrew his troops and promised more reforms and support for German national unity. Hohenzollern Prussia, like Habsburg Austria, appeared on the road to liberal government.

In several other German states, rulers quickly gave in to revolutionary demands. Then a self-appointed group of liberal leaders made a bold move: They called for a popularly elected

Frankfurt Assembly

assembly representing all German states to meet at Frankfurt to construct a liberal German nation. "[A]t last the great opportunity had arrived for giving to the German people the liberty which was their birthright and to the German fatherland its unity and greatness," explained a participant. Three crucial questions confronted the Frankfurt Assembly: (1) whether German-speaking portions of the multilingual Habsburg Empire and other states should be included in the projected

German Liberals and Nationalists Rally for Reform

The February 1848 revolution ending Louis-Philippe's regime and establishing a republic in France inspired many others throughout Europe who thirsted for reform. In Germany, liberals and nationalists rallied in hopes of uniting the German states and initiating liberal reforms. In the following selection, the journalist Carl Schurz (1829–1906) describes the feelings he shared with others.

.... Now had arrived in Germany the day for the establishment of "German Unity," and the founding of a great, powerful national German Empire. In the first line the convocation of a national parliament. Then the demands for civil rights and liberties, free speech, free press, the right of free assembly, equality before the law, a freely elected representation of the people with legislative power, responsibility of ministers, self-government of the communes, the right of the people to carry arms, the formation of a civic guard with elective officers, and so on—in short, that which was called a "constitutional form of government on a broad democratic basis." Republican ideas were at first only sparingly expressed. But the word democracy was soon on all tongues, and many, too, thought it a matter of course that if the princes should try to withhold from the people the rights and liberties demanded, force would take the place of mere petition. ... Like many of my friends, I was dominated by the feeling that at last the great opportunity had arrived for giving to the German people the liberty which was their birthright and to the German fatherland its unity and greatness. ...

What reforms does Schurz long for?

German nation, (2) what should be done with non-German ethnic groups living within German states, and (3) who should head the new nation. After almost a year of debate, the assembly decided on a smaller Germany and offered the crown to the king of Prussia.

Meanwhile, in Italy several states established new constitutions. The movement for national unification kept alive by the idealist Giuseppe Mazzini found additional strength. He backed up his ideas with action: "Insurrection—by means of guerrilla bands—is the true method of warfare for all nations desirous of emancipating themselves from a foreign yoke," he explained. Just one year after the first revolt broke out in France, popular demonstrations brought down the papal government and forced Pius IX to flee Rome. Mazzini soon gained a foothold as head of the newly formed Republic of Rome.

Italy

The Return to Order

For the revolutionaries of 1848, a new, victorious age seemed to have dawned. Within a few months, the old governments almost everywhere had been swept from power or seriously weakened. The upheavals were so widespread that at one point Tsar Nicholas I of Russia exclaimed to Britain's Queen Victoria, "What remains standing in Europe? Great Britain and Russia." Unfortunately for the revolutionaries, however, the forces of order showed resiliency and even new strength when events took more radical turns.

In France, divisions rose among those once unified against the monarchy. The more conservative peasantry and landowners in the countryside stepped back from the radical reforms demanded by Parisian artisans, shop owners, and intellectuals. The gap also widened between the middle class, which felt that reforms had gone far enough or even too far, and workers, who agitated for more social programs. These divisions reached a boiling point when the Constitutional Assembly, which had been elected in the late spring of 1848, abolished the national workshops. Officials told the workers to join the army or go look for work in the provinces. The desperate men and women of the Paris working class resorted to arms and

June Days in France

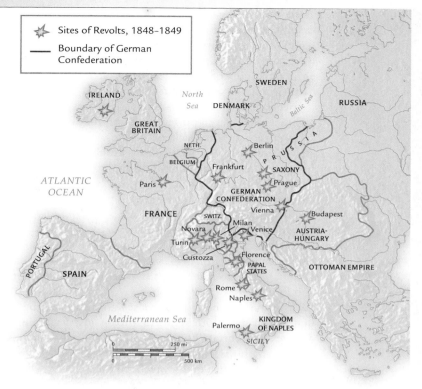

Sites of Revolts, 1848–1849
Boundary of German Confederation

European Revolts, 1848–1849 This map shows the locations of the 1848–1849 revolutions.

barricades. For four days, war raged in the streets of Paris between the working class, armed with National Guard rifles, and the regular army. The French liberal writer and politician Alexis de Tocqueville (1805–1859), an observer of the events, described the "June Days" as "the revolt of one whole section of the population against another. Women took part in it as well as men . . . and when at last the time had come to surrender, the women were the last to yield."

The image on page 442 depicts the fate of the revolutionary workers of Paris during the June Days of 1848. When the last barricade had fallen during the bloody June Days, some 1,500, mostly workingmen, had perished. Several hundred were sent overseas to French colonial prisons. Louis Blanc fled to Great Britain. The events widened the cleavage between radical urban Paris and conservative rural France—a cleavage that would long complicate France's public life. As a final insult to the revolutionaries, the December presidential elections swept Louis-Napoleon Bonaparte (1808–1873), nephew of Napoleon Bonaparte, to victory. Promising something for everyone and projecting an image of order and authority, Louis-Napoleon held

office for three years and then destroyed the republic in 1851 by taking power for himself in a coup d'état.

In Austria, the revolutionaries' inexperience and the rivalries among various ethnic groups gave the Habsburgs the upper hand. Playing one group against another and using their still-formidable military force, the Austrian **Austria and Hungary** rulers beat down the liberal and national revolts one after the other. In Hungary, they had the help of the reactionary Nicholas I of Russia, whose army overwhelmed the Magyar rebels. In Italy, Austrian might (and in Rome, French arms) eventually prevailed.

In Prussia, Frederick William IV fell under the influence of his militaristic and reactionary Junker advisors. Heartened **Prussia** by the news from Vienna that the Habsburgs had regained their position, he spurned the German crown offered him by the Frankfurt Assembly, contemptuously calling it "a crown from the gutter." His rejection of the crown blasted the Frankfurt Assembly's hopes for a united, liberal Germany. He accused liberals in the Frankfurt Assembly of "fighting the battle of godlessness, perjury, and robbery, and kindling a war against monarchy," and his Prussian troops drove the point home by ousting the few remaining liberals determined to keep the assembly alive.

What Happened?

By 1850, the conservative forces of order had regained control. What happened? How could so many victories by liberals, nationalists, workers, and students be turned into defeats so quickly?

There are several explanations. First, the alliances among middle-class liberals, radicals, socialists, artisans, and workers was one of convenience (based on their shared opposition to the status quo) rather than genuine fellowship. After revolutionary forces gained power, the interests of the various groups proved too divergent for the alliances to endure. These divisions emerged most clearly in France, where the frightened

OPINION

In what ways did the ideas and actions of liberals, nationalists, and socialists challenge conservatives between 1815 and 1850?

JEAN-LOUIS-ERNEST MEISSONIER, *MEMORY OF CIVIL WAR (THE BARRICADE)*, 1849 Revolutionary workers lie mortally wounded in the streets of Paris after the forces of order crushed the uprising in June 1848.

"were inspired by the hatred of royalty," while the socialists "were inspired . . . by the progress of humanity. The republic and equality was the aim of the one; social renovation and fraternity the aim of the other. They had nothing in common but impatience . . . and hope."

Internal divisions

Second, liberal and nationalistic forces worked best together when out of power; in power, they often stood at cross-purposes. This lack of harmony between liberals and nationalists was particularly pronounced in central Europe, where the nationalist aspirations of German, Polish, Magyar, Croatian, Serbian, and other groups conflicted with efforts to form new governments with liberal institutions. For example, liberals in the Frankfurt Assembly who sought to unify Germany turned against other nationalities who rose up against German rule in Austria and Prussia.

Holding power: liberalism vs. nationalism

Third, the strength of conservatism should not be underestimated. With industrialization just beginning to emerge in central Europe, the middle and working classes—both discontented with the conservative status quo—were still weak. Revolutionary leaders were inexperienced as well. In Germany, for example, the journalist Carl Schurz explained the failure of the Frankfurt parliament: "That parliament was laboring under an overabundance of learning and virtue and under a want of . . . political experience."

Conservatism

Finally, once the shock of initial defeat at the hands of revolutionaries had faded, the seasoned leaders of the forces of order marshaled their resources, drew on their own armies and those of allies, and overcame the divided revolutionary forces. After they reestablished control, conservative leaders tore up most of the reforms and impris-

middle class and conservative peasantry broke with the Parisian working classes. Alphonse de Lamartine, a poet and leading politician at the time, explained how the revolutionaries were divided into two groups: the republicans

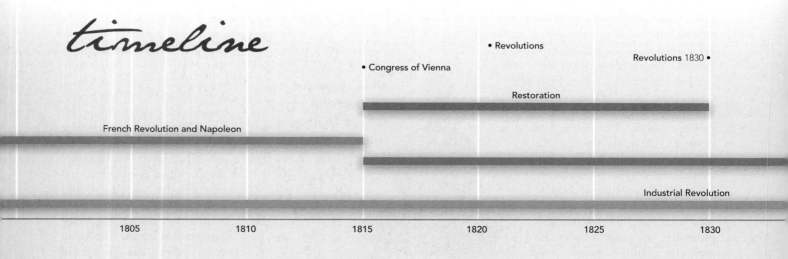

timeline

• Revolutions

Revolutions 1830 •

• Congress of Vienna

Restoration

French Revolution and Napoleon

Industrial Revolution

| 1805 | 1810 | 1815 | 1820 | 1825 | 1830 |

oned, executed, or exiled revolutionaries. In December 1848, Pope Pius IX summarized the views of angry conservatives: "We . . . declare null and of no effect, and altogether illegal, every act" of reform during 1848. In fact, a few liberal reforms, such as the abolition of serfdom in Austria and Hungary and the limited constitutions in Piedmont and Prussia, would survive, but the great changes and power that for a few months seemed within the grasp of revolutionaries were gone.

Force

SUMMARY

In 1815, the conservative forces of order tried to secure their own survival by repressing all those heartened by the principles and reforms of the French Revolution and the Enlightenment.

- At the Congress of Vienna, the victors tailored the settlement to meet their conservative goals of promoting legitimacy and stability.

- Powerful ideologies such as conservatism, liberalism, socialism, and nationalism fueled many of the struggles that would erupt during the nineteenth century and ultimately would shape our definition of the modern world.

- In the first years after the defeat of Napoleon, conservatism prevailed in domestic and international politics.

- In the early 1820s, a cycle of revolution and reform timidly emerged. In 1830, revolutionary forces posed a broader challenge, gaining some important victories in western Europe.

- The cycle returned in full force in 1848, as revolutions broke out through Europe and scored victory after victory. Those victories proved short-lived. By 1850, conservatives were back in power.

The overall failure of 1848 did not necessarily ensure a permanent victory for conservatism. As industrialization and urbanization spread year by year, traditional life and the old order it represented kept crumbling. Moreover, participants and observers had witnessed the power of ideologies, as well as economic and social realities, to galvanize people into political action. However, the reestablished governments had learned important lessons from 1848, too, and would try to secure their positions with new vigor.

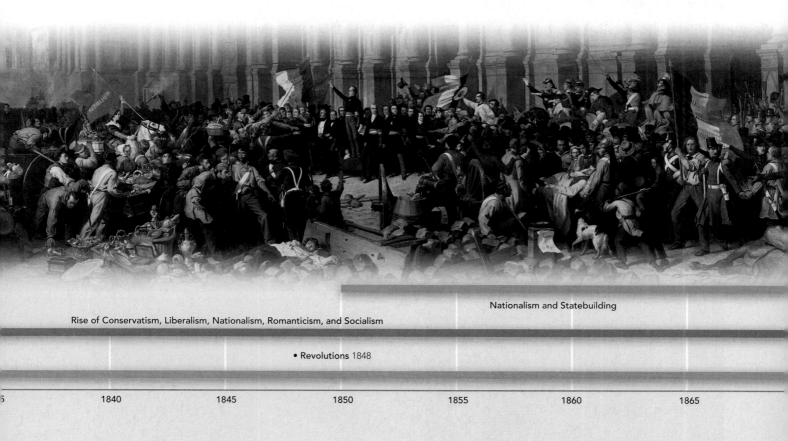

Rise of Conservatism, Liberalism, Nationalism, Romanticism, and Socialism

Nationalism and Statebuilding

• Revolutions 1848

ADOLPH MENZEL, *THE DEPARTURE OF WILLIAM I FOR THE ARMY ON JULY 31, 1870,* 1871 This 1871 painting by German artist Adolph Menzel suggests that the inhabitants of Prussia's capital, Berlin, greeted a statebuilding war against France with an outburst of Prussian patriotism and broader German nationalism.

Nationalism and Statebuilding

Unifying Nations, 1850–1870

19

Building Unified Nation-States

"Every German heart hoped for it," wrote the Baroness Spitzemberg in Berlin in 1871. "United into one Reich, the greatest, the most powerful, the most feared in Europe; great by reason of its physical power, greater still by reason of its education and the intelligence which permeates it!" So the baroness expressed her longing for national unification, a passion felt by many others in the West. ▶▶

In the two decades after 1850, no political force was stronger than nationalism. It pushed people toward national unity in Italy and Germany and threatened to tear the Habsburg and Ottoman Empires apart. In the United States, the principle of national unity helped spark a brutal civil war. In France and elsewhere, rulers enacted major reforms designed to bolster national unity and their authority as leaders of a nation of citizens. All these efforts were intended to build strong, unified nation-states led by central governments that could enjoy the support of their citizens.

Unlike in 1848, however, the nationalist political figures were neither revolutionaries nor idealists. As one advocate of Italian unification observed, "To defeat cannons and soldiers, cannons and soldiers are needed." From positions of established power, this new generation of leaders molded nationalism to fit harsh political realities. They focused their eyes on practical policies, not ideals. As we'll read in this chapter, they gambled, compromised, manipulated, and fought to achieve their goals. Few struggled more persistently and cleverly than Count Camillo di Cavour. ◄◄

THE DRIVE FOR ITALIAN UNIFICATION

Count Camillo di Cavour (1810–1861) was born into a well-to-do, noble family living in Piedmont-Sardinia, a small but relatively powerful independent state in northern Italy that also included the island of Sardinia. As a young man, he gambled, played the stock market, experimented with agricultural techniques, and succeeded in business—a pattern of taking calculated risks he would later try to follow in politics. By the 1840s, he had become committed to Italian unification. Shortly before the revolution of 1848, he founded the newspaper *Il Risorgimento (The Resurgence)*, which passionately argued for a unified Italy. In 1850, Piedmont-Sardinia's King Victor Emmanuel II (r. 1849–1878) made Cavour his minister of commerce and agriculture and, two years later, prime minister.

Cavour

Cavour's goals were clear. First, he wanted to modernize Piedmont economically and thereby win strength and respect for his homeland. Second, he sought to make Piedmont the central engine of the drive for national unification. Third, he advocated forming a new Italian state as a constitutional monarchy under Piedmont's king rather than a democratic republic or a confederation under the pope. To achieve all these ends, Cavour lowered tariffs, built railroads, and balanced Piedmont's budget. He supported the nationalistic Italian National Society and its Feminine Committee, which worked toward national unification with Piedmont at the helm. Finally, he employed diplomacy and Piedmont's relatively small army to gain

Cavour's leadership

international support for the struggle against the primary obstacle to unification—Austria.

When the Crimean War broke out between Russia and the Ottoman Empire in 1854, Cavour saw an opportunity. He brought Piedmont in on the side of Great Britain and France, countries that had joined the Ottoman Turks against Russia. Cavour hoped to gain the friendship and support of France and Britain and thereby elevate Piedmont-Sardinia's status among the European powers. "I believe that the principal condition for the improvement of Italy's fate," he explained to the Parliament of Piedmont in 1855, "is to lift up her reputation once more . . . to prove that Italy's sons can fight valiantly on battlefields where glory is to be won." Victory in the east, he claimed, "will help the future state of Italy more than all that has been done by those people who hoped to regenerate her by rhetorical speeches and writings."

His risky plan may have paid off. At the Paris Peace Conference in 1856, which ended the war, he pleaded Piedmont's case against Austria so skillfully that he captured the attention of the international community. Two years later, Cavour and France's Emperor Napoleon III met at a French resort to discuss ways to move against Austria, a competitor of France on the Continent and the chief barrier to Cavour's hopes for Italian unity. The two decided to provoke Austria into a war against Piedmont and thereby bring France into the fray. "Together we began to . . . search for those grounds for war which were so difficult to find," explained Cavour in a note to his king. Then "we discovered what we had been trying so hard to find," a way to manipulate Austria into a war that "would not alarm the other continental powers." After Austria declared war, France would help Piedmont drive the Austrians out of Lombardy and Venetia, and these two states would then be annexed to Piedmont-Sardinia. In return, Piedmont would cede

> The opposing troops had little heart for their own cause.

the two small, French-speaking provinces of Savoy and Nice to France and allow a kingdom of Central Italy to be created for Napoleon III's cousin.

In 1859, after Cavour mobilized the Piedmontese army and refused an Austrian demand to reverse the act, the unsuspecting Austrians declared war on Piedmont. French armies, using new railroad lines, poured across the Alps to fight alongside the Piedmontese. In the bloody battles of Magenta and Solferino, the French and Piedmontese ousted the Austrians from Lombardy. But to the dismay of Cavour, Napoleon III suddenly made a separate peace at Villafranca with Austria that gave Piedmont Lombardy and left Venetia in Austrian hands. Cavour's side now had momentum, however. Nationalists in other Italian states, inspired by Piedmont's success, rose to the cause of national unity. By early 1860, most of northern and central Italy had joined Piedmont voluntarily.

War with Austria

At this pivotal point in the action, the rawboned nationalist Giuseppe Garibaldi (1807–1882) made a daring exploit. Garibaldi had long struggled to create a unified and republican Italy—organizing people, conducting campaigns of guerrilla warfare, and leading insurrections. Often in exile, he had become a well-known figure in Europe and the Americas. In May 1860, accompanied by a thousand civilian warriors dressed in red shirts, he sailed for Sicily in southern Italy, where many peasants had already launched a revolt. "It is the duty of every Italian to succor them [the Sicilians in revolt] with words, money, arms, and above all, in person," he announced (see Exploring the Past). Garibaldi's goal was nothing less than the conquest of the Kingdom of Naples, the largest and most populous of the Italian states, and then Rome itself. Cavour officially condemned the seemingly foolhardy expedition but secretly assisted it.

Garibaldi

As the painting on page 448 suggests, Garibaldi's exploits read like an adventure novel. In rapid succession, Garibaldi conquered Sicily, crossed the Strait of Messina, and triumphantly entered Naples (see map on page 449). The opposing troops had little heart for their own cause. Many, along with civilian women and men by the thousands, joined Garibaldi after his first victories. Made

Garibaldi Appeals to Italians for Support

The campaign that resulted in the unification of Italy required not just idealism but also a realistic outlook and daring action. With his political manipulations, Cavour provided the realism. With his invasion of Sicily in 1860, Giuseppe Garibaldi provided the daring action.

The brave man finds an arm everywhere. Listen not to the voice of cowards, but arm, and let us fight for our brethren, who will fight for us tomorrow.

A band of those who fought with me the country's battles marches with me to the fight. Good and generous, they will fight for their country to the last drop of their blood, nor ask for other reward than a clear conscience.

"Italy and Victor Emmanuel!" they cried, on passing the Ticino. "Italy and Victor Emmanuel!" shall re-echo in the blazing caves of Mongibello.

At this cry, thundering from the great rock of Italy to the Tarpeian, the rotten Throne of tyranny shall crumble, and, as one man, the brave descendants of Vespro shall rise.

To Arms! Let me put an end, once and for all, to the miseries of so many centuries. Prove to the world that it is no lie that Roman generations inhabited this land.

In what ways does this proclamation echo the appeal of nationalism?

Garibaldi Landing in Sicily

This illustration shows Garibaldi heroically landing at the island of Sicily to fight for Italian unification. In the background, his band of volunteer soldiers (the "Red Shirts") pours from three ships and marches in rough formation. Carrying a sword and flag representing Italian unity, Garibaldi is welcomed by admiring children, women, men, and a priest.   In what ways does this depiction glorify Garibaldi's exploits and the unification movement?

charter. The king, along with a parliamentary government elected by limited suffrage, would rule. The red, white, and green Piedmontese flag now flew over all of Italy, from the Alps to Sicily, except in Venetia and Rome. These two provinces (with the exception of the Vatican palace) joined the Italian state in 1866 and 1870, respectively.

Sadly, Cavour did not live to enjoy the fruits of his labors. Less than three months after the birth of his beloved Italian nation, he died. Paunchy, with ill-fitting glasses, he had never cut an impressive figure. Nor had he made a particularly powerful orator. "I cannot make a speech," he once said, "but I can make Italy."

GERMANY "BY BLOOD AND IRON"

Like Italy, Germany as we understand it did not exist in 1850, except in the hearts of nationalists. Most of the many German states belonged to the loose Germanic Confederation, but this organization, under the dominance of Austria, did not function as a **Prussian leadership**

ever bolder by his conquests, the confident Garibaldi advanced north toward Rome.

Not wanting to lose control of the rapidly changing situation and fearing that an attack on Rome by Garibaldi might lead France and Austria to come to the aid of the pope, Cavour sent troops southward in September 1860, gained control over the Papal States, and then skirted the area around Rome. King Victor Emmanuel, marching at the head of his army, met Garibaldi's forces south of Rome. Garibaldi yielded to Victor Emmanuel and his Piedmontese troops. Two years later, Garibaldi, hoping to annex Rome as the capital of Italy, fomented an unsuccessful uprising. The gallant patriot soon retired to his farm on the rocky island of Caprera.

Kingdom of Italy The Kingdom of Italy was formally declared in March 1861, with Victor Emmanuel II as monarch and the Piedmontese Constitution of 1848 as the national

unified nation. Would someone like Piedmont's Count Cavour rise to overcome the obstacles to German unification? By 1860, no one of this caliber had yet stepped forward.

The best hope for German unity rested with Prussia, which had achieved a position of strength thanks to its economic expansion and leadership over the Zollverein, a German customs union that fostered industrialization in Prussia and the Rhineland (see page 432). By 1853, every German state except Austria had joined the Zollverein. However, Prussia was torn by the political struggle between liberals in the legislature and the conservative aristocracy. The two sides fought over plans to strengthen Prussia's military. When Prussia's new king, William I, and his military advisors proposed to double the size of the army, the liberals, who distrusted Prussian militarism and hoped to gain a stronger role for the legislature in the Prussian government, defeated the measure. Faced with a deadlock between these uncompromising forces and convinced that his royal authority was being threatened, William I called on Otto von Bismarck (1815–1898).

"I was born and raised as an aristocrat," Bismarck once explained. He would remain loyal to Prussia's landowning aristocracy his whole life. As a young man, Bismarck showed little promise of future greatness. While attending university, he spent more time gambling than studying. A religious conversion in 1846 and marriage seemed to give him more of a sense of purpose. He entered politics in 1847 and came to believe that only an alliance of conservatism and nationalism could preserve the aristocracy and strengthen Prussia. His enemies were the liberals, who had failed in 1848, and Austria, Prussia's chief competitor and supposed senior partner within the German states.

Bismarck

Bismarck assumed the office of prime minister of Prussia in 1862. With the backing of the king, the aristocracy, and the army, he promptly defied the liberals in the legislature, violated the constitution, and ordered taxes collected for military reform. "Necessity alone is authoritative," he argued. He would pursue a policy of realism—**Realpolitik**—to achieve his goals. "Not by speeches and majority resolutions," Bismarck rumbled, "are the great questions of the time decided—that was the mistake of 1848 and 1849—but by blood and iron." As the prime minister argued, Germans looked to Prussia for leadership not because of its liberalism but because of its power.

Like Cavour in Italy, Bismarck sought out political opportunities, created them when they failed to materialize, and did not hesitate to take calculated risks, including war. In 1864, Denmark provided his first opportunity when it tried to incorporate Schleswig and Holstein, two small provinces lying between Prussia and Denmark. The provinces' legal status had been disputed for decades. Posing as a defender of German nationalism, Prussia promptly declared war on Denmark, pulling Austria—anxious to retain leadership of the German Confederation—in as Prussia's reluctant ally. In the complicated settlement—Schleswig and Holstein were to be ruled jointly by Prussia and Austria—Bismarck shrewdly planted the seeds for a future conflict with Austria.

Wars for unification

Bismarck soon used this unworkable arrangement to stir up trouble with Austria. He obtained the support of

The Unification of Italy **This map shows the unification of Italy in the years after 1859.**

Italy by promising Austria's province of Venetia as a prize. He gained Russia's sympathy by supporting its intervention against rebellious subjects in Poland. He neutralized Napoleon III by personal persuasion and deception. Finally, he manipulated domestic politics to achieve his ends. In 1866, Bismarck took a risk by using threats and maneuvers to provoke Austria into declaring war on Prussia. Austria was twice the size of Prussia, with double the population, and had long dominated central Europe. Nevertheless, Prussia's modern and mobile armies managed to overwhelm the surprised Austrian forces in just seven weeks. Austria suffered four times as many casualties as Prussia, in great part because of the fast-firing needle-guns used by Prussian troops and the army's use of railroads to move forces quickly to battlefields. Bismarck boldly expelled Austria from the German Confederation and even annexed several German states that had sided with Austria. Nevertheless, hoping for Austrian support in the future,

Austro-Prussian War

Then & Now
National Pride

Bismarck described himself as driven throughout his career toward one goal: "to unify Germany, taking any path, and employing any means." Not only did he use three wars to that end, he was willing to adopt almost any legal and domestic policies to promote national unification under Prussia. Nationalism and the call to patriotism have proven to be a potent political force throughout the West since Bismarck's time. In today's world, political parties and leaders in many countries often stand with patriotic symbols and sound the call for "national unity" and sacrifice for "the nation." What sorts of policies might politicians and movements justify in the name of nationalism and patriotism?

Bismarck refused the desires of Prussia's king and army leaders to annex Austrian territories.

Prussia now controlled the newly created North German Confederation. Despite some democratic forms, such as a legislative body (the Reichstag) elected by universal male suffrage, the government was fundamentally an **autocracy.** The legislature had no control over the chancellor—appointed by and responsible only to the king or his cabinet—and little control over the budget or armed forces. However, some of the southern German states, with larger Catholic populations than Prussia had, still lay outside Bismarck's grasp (see map on page 451). He wisely recognized that these remaining, reluctant states might join the fold if German nationalism could be rallied against a common, foreign threat. France, Bismarck decided, might just fit the bill.

Franco-Prussian War

Bismarck's opportunity to confront France came in 1870 when the Spanish crown was offered to a Hohenzollern prince—a relative of Prussia's William I. When Bismarck persuaded the reluctant prince to accept the Spanish offer, the French immediately took alarm at the prospect of being surrounded by Hohenzollerns. The French exerted heavy pressure on Prussia, and both the prince and King William yielded. However, the unsatisfied French ministers demanded more. After a meeting at Ems between the French ambassador and the Prussian king, the chancellor saw an opportunity to provoke the French into war. Cleverly editing the Ems telegraph dispatch so as to make it appear that the French ambassador and the Prussian king had insulted each other, he published it to the world. The French government was offended and walked into Bismarck's trap. Buoyed by public demands for action, France declared war.

The chancellor had taken his greatest risk, for France seemed to possess enough military might and economic resources to humble Prussia. As France's confident prime minister stated, "We go to war with a light heart." Again, however, the able Prussian troops quickly scored resound-

ANTON VON WERNER, *PROCLAMATION OF THE GERMAN EMPIRE*, 1885 Prussian officers hail William, who stands at the left. But the center of the painting belongs to Bismarck, dressed in white. He alone holds the document proclaiming the new empire that he, more than anyone else, had built. The dramatic scene is set in France's Versailles palace, emphasizing that Prussia had achieved German unity by defeating France in war.

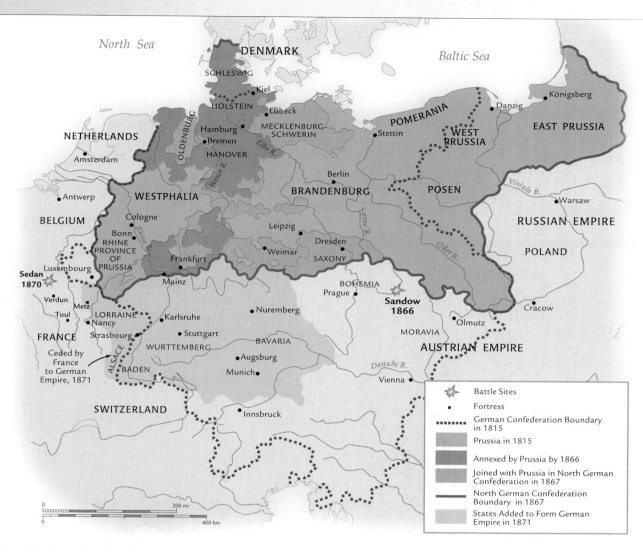

Map labels:

North Sea · Baltic Sea · DENMARK · SCHLESWIG · Kiel · HOLSTEIN · Lübeck · Danzig · Königsberg · NETHERLANDS · OLDENBURG · Hamburg · MECKLENBURG-SCHWERIN · POMERANIA · WEST PRUSSIA · EAST PRUSSIA · Bremen · Stettin · Amsterdam · HANOVER · Elbe R. · Weser R. · Berlin · BRANDENBURG · POSEN · Vistula R. · Antwerp · WESTPHALIA · Spree R. · RUSSIAN EMPIRE · Warsaw · BELGIUM · Cologne · Leipzig · Oder R. · POLAND · Bonn · RHINE PROVINCE OF PRUSSIA · Rhine R. · Weimar · Dresden · SAXONY · Frankfurt · Sedan 1870 · Luxembourg · Mainz · BOHEMIA · Prague · Sandow 1866 · Verdun · Metz · Karlsruhe · Nuremberg · Cracow · Toul · LORRAINE · Nancy · Olmutz · FRANCE · Strasbourg · WURTTEMBERG · BAVARIA · MORAVIA · AUSTRIAN EMPIRE · Ceded by France to German Empire, 1871 · ALSACE · BADEN · Stuttgart · Augsburg · Danube R. · Munich · Vienna · SWITZERLAND · Innsbruck

Legend:

- ☆ Battle Sites
- ▪ Fortress
- ····· German Confederation Boundary in 1815
- Prussia in 1815
- Annexed by Prussia by 1866
- Joined with Prussia in North German Confederation in 1867
- ── North German Confederation Boundary in 1867
- States Added to Form German Empire in 1871

0   200 mi
0   400 km

The Unification of Germany This map shows the steps taken to achieve German unification in 1871.

ing successes. One French army was surrounded at the fortress city of Metz. The Prussians encircled another French army at Sedan, forcing it to surrender. Napoleon III himself was one of the captives. When this news reached Paris, the liberals overthrew the government of the Second Empire and declared the Third French Republic. Paris held out for a few more months, surrounded by the Germans, but finally surrendered in January 1871.

On January 18, 1871, Bismarck called the heads of all the German states to Versailles in France. Gathering in the Hall of Mirrors, the dignitaries proclaimed Prussia's King Wil-

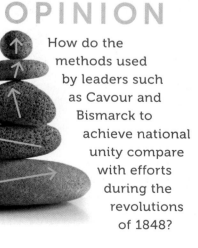

OPINION

How do the methods used by leaders such as Cavour and Bismarck to achieve national unity compare with efforts during the revolutions of 1848?

liam I emperor of the new German Empire; he would rule until 1888. The painting on page 450 celebrates that moment.

The constitution that Bismarck had drafted for the North German Confederation became the constitution for the new German Empire. Its twenty-five states retained control over many domestic matters, but Prussia dominated the union. Known as the Second Reich (Germans honored the old Holy Roman Empire as the First Reich), the powerful nation included a large and rapidly growing population, a vibrant industrial economy, and a feared military. Bismarck, of course, remained chancellor and lived to rule over his creation for the next nineteen years. In Germany, as in Italy, a clever, realistic political leader had employed diplomacy and war to transform the unruly forces of nationalism into German unification.

THE FIGHT FOR NATIONAL UNITY IN NORTH AMERICA

The struggle for unification flared up in other parts of the West besides Italy and Germany. Between 1800 and 1861, the United States' political institutions had evolved along democratic and nationalistic lines. **The United States** Almost all white men had gained the right to vote. A modern, broad-based political party system had formed and wrestled political power from the elite circles of the old colonial well-to-do. The nation had expanded westward to the Pacific Ocean, conquering the Amerindians and displacing them to reservations. When Mexico stood in the way of expansion, it also lost its lands to the United States armed forces. Commercial interests led the United States across the Pacific to Japan. Finally, American culture began to free itself from strictly European influence. Citizens proudly thought of themselves and their institutions as having a distinct flavor within Western civilization.

However, as the nineteenth century progressed, the nation labored under growing regional differences. The North was an expanding, urban, industrial society based on free labor. The top image here, a **North-South divisions** lithograph of the Stillman, Allen & Co. Novelty Iron Works of New York City, illustrates one of the many manufacturing facilities growing up in the North's cities in the middle decades of the nineteenth century. The South remained agricultural, dependent on plantation crops such as cotton, and based on slave labor. The bottom image here, a painting of a Southern plantation, portrays this rural society with its large population of slaves. The North enjoyed a growing population and generally favored federal over state power. The South, worried that its influence over national policies was slipping away, emphasized states' rights over federal power. In the decades before 1861, these two regions, with their increasingly different societies and interests, clashed politically on several occasions.

It was the issue of slavery, though, that gave these clashes a dangerous emotional intensity and tied together **Slavery** the other problems dividing the North and the South. By the early 1800s, the northern states had eliminated slavery. However, the institution persisted in the South, where agriculture, and especially cotton plantations, reigned supreme. There, slaveholders viewed slaves as the very basis of their wealth, power, and status. Meanwhile, in the free-labor North, antislavery sentiment grew. "[T]his government cannot endure permanently half slave and half free," declared Abraham Lincoln (1809–1865) in 1858, just two years before the nation elected him president.

In 1861, all these regional differences, fueled by the question of whether to abolish slavery, ignited a bloody war between the North, led by Lincoln, and the South, under Jefferson Davis (1808–1889). The **The Civil War** conflict raged for four years until the North finally defeated the Southern armies. Ultimately the war took more than 600,000 lives, making it the bloodiest conflict in the Western world since the end of the Napoleonic Wars. Lincoln had achieved his primary goal: to reestablish national unity and affirm the power of the national government. In the aftermath, slavery was abolished in the United States.

A NORTHERN FACTORY The smokestacks and busy harbor activity in this print illustrate the U.S. North's industrial might, which played a crucial role in the Civil War.

CHARLES GIROUX, *A SOUTHERN PLANTATION*, ca. 1850s The economic strength and social structure of the U.S. South were represented by cotton plantations such as the one immortalized in this painting.

Farther north, a different struggle for national independence and unity had been unfolding in Canada. William Lyon Mackenzie (1795–1861), a nationalist politician,

Canada

called for Canadians to "put down the villains [the British] who oppress and enslave our country" and gain "freedom from British tribute." Britain responded to a rebellion in 1837 by granting Canada some control over its own domestic affairs. Nevertheless, the Canadian territories were not yet joined into a single nation, and Canadians feared the growing power of the United States. Demands for union and complete nationhood increased. Finally, in 1867, the British North American Act united Canada into a single nation with its own constitution.

DIVIDED AUTHORITY IN THE AUSTRIAN AND OTTOMAN EMPIRES

Nationalism pulled Austria's multiethnic empire apart rather than bringing it together (see map on page 454).

Austria

Czechs, Serbs, Romanians, Magyars (Hungarians), and other ethnic groups wanted to form their own, independent nations rather than rally behind Austria, which was predominantly German.

Austria's emperor, Francis Joseph (r. 1848–1916), was no reformer or politician in the mold of Bismarck, Cavour, or Lincoln. Under pressure from liberals and nationalists, he agreed in 1860 to a moderate decentralization of the empire and the creation of a parliament. After Austria's defeat by Prussia in 1866, the dominant German minority in Austria compromised with the assertive Magyars rather than fight them over issues of nationality. Their agreement, the Compromise of 1867, set up the **Dual Monarchy** of Austria-Hungary. Each country had its own separate parliament, but the two were united under a common ruler, the head of the House of Habsburg. This arrangement was

Austria-Hungary, 1867

essentially an alliance between the Germans of Austria and the Magyars of Hungary against other competing ethnic groups. The empire therefore divided authority in an effort to control even more threatening movements for

national independence. This arrangement did not please other national groups, especially the Czechs, who would persistently demand equality with the Hungarians.

Like the Austrians, Ottoman rulers also had to struggle with the divisive forces of nationalism. In 1850, at least nominally, the Ottoman Empire was still extensive. From its base in Anatolia, it maintained varying degrees

The Ottoman Empire

of control over much of southeastern Europe, as well as over provinces stretching from North Africa to the Persian Gulf. However, the empire was already in decline. Its North African provinces—Egypt, Libya, Tunisia, and Algeria—were virtually autonomous. Egyptian rulers in particular tried to modernize the army, bureaucracy, and economy using western European models; Muhammad Ali (r. 1805–1848) at one point had become strong enough to threaten Ottoman control in Syria and Anatolia. To the north, powerful, ambitious neighbors—especially the Russians, who attacked the Turks in 1853 and again in 1877—maneuvered to take advantage of the Ottomans' weaknesses: lack of economic development, declining finances, internal dissension, and difficulties instituting reforms. But the greatest threats to the empire's integrity came from its restless Balkan provinces in southeastern Europe. In this area, nationalism rose, producing the same sorts of movements for independence that had weakened the Austrian Empire.

By 1830, the Ottoman Empire had already lost Serbia and Greece to independence movements (see map on page 455). Nationalism had fueled an unsuccessful revolt by the Romanians in 1848 as well. In 1856, the Romanians gained international support as part of the set-

Balkan nationalism

tlement of the Crimean War. Over the next twenty years, they pressed the Ottomans for their freedom, finally winning full independence in 1878.

Nationalist movements also cropped up among the Bulgars. Encouraged by Serbia and Russia, the Bulgars revolted in 1876. Each side in the conflict committed atrocities, but those committed by the Turks especially shocked Europeans. That year, Bosnia and Herzegovina also rose against the Turks. Serbia and Russia then joined forces against the Ottoman Empire. By 1878, international agreements, most notably the Treaty of Berlin, had secured the independence of Bulgaria and placed Bosnia and Herzegovina under Austro-Hungarian rule. Movements for national independence, with the aid of powers eager to take advantage of the empire's declining strength, had ended Turkish control throughout most of the Balkans. However,

OPINION

In what ways was nationalism divisive in the Austrian and Ottoman Empires?

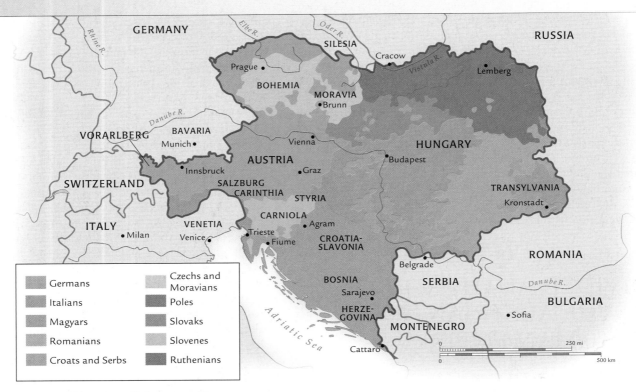

Language Groups of Austria-Hungary
This map shows the concentrations of language groups in Austria-Hungary at the end of the nineteenth century.

these developments also left a jumble of dissatisfied groups and nationalities—a few who had their own states, some who longed for political independence, and others who did not like being annexed by Austria-Hungary.

USING NATIONALISM IN FRANCE AND RUSSIA

The power of nationalism to motivate people to join revolutionary organizations, form new political allegiances, follow powerful politicians, and go to war in the name of national unity made itself clear in Italy and Germany. Under different conditions, nationalism weakened and dismembered long-established multinational states such as the Austrian and Ottoman empires.

Nationalism also pushed governments in well-established states to reach out to citizens for support. These governments tried to justify and sustain their authority by performing public services, and they bolstered their power by promoting the idea of national greatness. They paid more attention to everyday life so as to maintain social peace and cultivate loyalty to the nation—and especially

to its leaders. These efforts to channel nationalism into statebuilding are especially well illustrated by the paths that France and Russia took after 1850.

Napoleon III and the Second Empire

In France, Louis-Napoleon Bonaparte, nephew of Napoleon Bonaparte, promised reform while creating a regime based on authoritarian nationalism. Louis-Napoleon was originally elected president of France's Second Republic in 1848. He benefited from his illustrious name, his appeal to property owners longing for order, and his well-publicized promises to link democracy from below with reforming leadership from above. When the National Assembly refused to change the constitution so that he could run for a second term, he organized a coup d'état and seized power on December 2, 1851. Resistance was limited, although hundreds were killed and thousands were arrested and deported. He quickly granted universal male suffrage, and during the following year, he held two plebiscites in which more than 90 percent of the voters supported him, establishing the Second Empire and making him hereditary emperor—Napoleon III. "I believe," he confidently wrote, "that there are certain men who are born to serve as the

Napoleon III

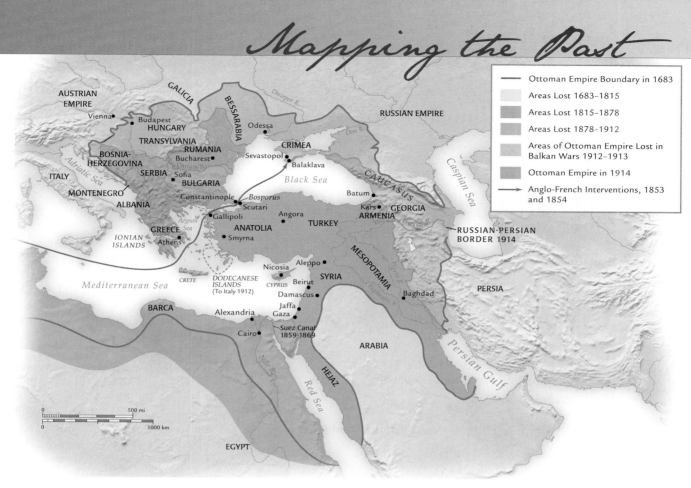

The Decline of the Ottoman Empire, 1683–1914   This map shows the loss of territory from the Ottoman Empire between 1683 and 1914.   Why did the growth of nationalism become such a threat to the Ottoman Empire?

means for the march of the human race. . . . I consider myself to be one of these."

Building on his uncle's legend, Napoleon III tried to convince citizens that he would lead the nation to new heights in domestic as well as foreign affairs. Napoleon III kept the elected legislature firmly under his thumb by minimizing its authority over his ministers and manipulating the electoral machinery. When it served his purposes, he encouraged industrialization and economic growth by promoting railroad construction, public works, and financial institutions—policies that appealed to the middle and working classes. His prefect of Paris, Georges Haussmann (1809–1891), rebuilt Paris into an envied model of a modern, wealthy, powerful capital (see Chapter 20). To project a progressive image, Napoleon also directed the building of hospitals, nurseries, and homes for the aged. To gain support from workers, he kept bread prices low, instituted a system of voluntary social insurance, encouraged cooperatives, and partially legalized labor unions.

The French emperor's foreign adventures gained him prestige at first but lost him everything in the end. He

brought France into the Crimean War and played the glorious host to the peace conference that ended that conflict. In addition, he tried to increase French influence on the Italian peninsula by joining Piedmont in a war against Austria, but he underestimated the strength of Italian nationalism; that nation unified without becoming beholden to France. In 1862, his armies marched into Mexico City and set up a Habsburg prince, Maximilian, as puppet emperor for France. A few years later, problems at home and a threatening army from the United States forced Napoleon to withdraw his troops, leaving the doomed Maximilian to the mercy of Mexican forces.

Meanwhile, declining prosperity further weakened Napoleon's position within France. Trying to allay the mounting discontent of liberals and workers, he made one concession after another. By 1870, the liberal parliament had begun gaining the upper hand. That year, **Fall of Napoleon III** the ailing and discouraged Napoleon III blundered into a war with Prussia. Defeated and captured, he and his government fell.

Florence Nightingale (1820–1910)

FLORENCE NIGHTINGALE IN THE MILITARY HOSPITAL AT SCUTARI.

J. A. BENWELL, *FLORENCE NIGHTINGALE IN THE MILITARY HOSPITAL*, 1856

In October 1854, a British journalist in Constantinople reported the successes enjoyed by the British army in the Crimean War. He also described in dramatic detail the horrendous condition of the army's medical facilities where the wounded and sick languished and died.

One of the many readers outraged by the report was Florence Nightingale.

Using her family's wealth and political connections, she obtained from the British government a commission to lead a team of 38 nurses to Turkey.

She described conditions at Scutari: "We have no room for corpses in the wards. . . . Not a sponge, nor a rag of linen, not anything have I left. . . . These poor fellows have not had a clean shirt nor been washed for two months before they came here. . . . I hope in a few days we shall establish a little cleanliness." She advocated fresh air, sunshine, hygiene, and diet. The image above shows Nightingale organizing care for the patients. Within six months and despite opposition, incompetence, and corruption within the British army, she transformed the medical facility.

How does Nightingale's experience reveal the different ways in which war can alter people's lives? How do you think it compares to those experiencing war today?

Alexander II and Russia

Napoleon III had stood for order, reform from above, and national grandeur. Until he faltered, the French gave up their liberal sentiments for those ends. In Russia, Tsar Alexander II made similar appeals in an effort to overcome that country's troubles.

By 1850, Russia had earned a reputation as the most conservative of European powers. Its government remained autocratic under the tsar, its feudalistic society still bound serfs to the land and their lords, and its large army enjoyed an aura of near invincibility. After the Crimean War, it became clear that things would have to change.

Russia's autocracy

In 1853, war broke out between Russia and the Ottoman Turks. Although the causes for this outbreak of hostilities were complex, Russia hoped to snatch territory from the weakening Ottoman Empire. In addition, Russia sought to gain shipping access to the world from the Black Sea through the Turkish Straits and gain influence in the Near East. Early the next year, after the Russian navy sank the Ottoman fleet in a single devastating battle, France, Britain, and Piedmont-Sardinia, driven by their own ambitions rather than principles, joined the Ottoman Turks and poured their military forces into the Black Sea. They laid siege to Russia's naval base Sebastopol, on the Crimean peninsula.

Crimean War

The war dragged on until 1856, and both sides fought with gross incompetence. The flavor of this war, and in particular one suicidal charge by the British light cavalry, would be immortalized in a poem by Alfred, Lord Tennyson:

> *"Forward, the Light Brigade!"*
> *Was there a man dismay'd?*
> *Not tho' the soldier knew*
> *Some one had blunder'd:*
> *Their's not to make reply,*
> *Their's not to reason why,*
> *Their's but to do and die:*
> *Into the valley of Death*
> *Rode the six hundred*

Thanks to new telegraph lines and expanded press coverage, the public in the West could follow the conflict closely. People learned almost immediately, in graphic detail, about the horrific loss of life both on the Crimean battlefield and in the pitifully inadequate medical facilities (see Past Lives on page 456). More than 250,000 soldiers died, most of them from disease caused by poor sanitation, starvation, and lack of medical assistance. In the end, no one could claim much of a victory, but Russia, whose massive military no longer looked so formidable, was humbled.

Even before the Crimean disaster, peasant revolts and workers' protests had plagued Russia. In all of Europe, only Russia still allowed serfdom, which left millions tied to the land. Russia's serfs deeply resented the labor and dues they owed for the right to farm lands, and protests and insurrections broke out with alarming frequency. Between 1825 and 1855, more than five hundred serf rebellions occurred in Russia. Food shortages struck all too often, yet most aristocrats took little responsibility for the suffering of their serfs. Many within the privileged class feared rebellion. The peasants' low standard of living is revealed in the image on page 459, a photograph of peasants in a Russian village during the second half of the nineteenth century.

Not surprisingly, serfs conscripted into Russia's armies showed a distinct lack of enthusiasm. Their sullenness finally helped make Russia's leaders see that their country was being left behind by the other powers. The country simply lacked the social support, armaments, and railroads (it took Russia months instead of weeks to move troops and supplies to the Crimean front) to win a modern war. Moreover, because serfs were bound to the land, Russia lacked a large mobile labor force to support industrialization and thereby keep up with nations to the west.

The new tsar, Alexander II (r. 1855–1881), was a complex, well-educated individual who recognized Russia's problems from the moment he took office. He was determined to introduce reforms to strengthen and modernize Russia and prop up his own rule. Like Napoleon III's policies, Alexander's **"Great Reforms"** came from above but proved much more far-reaching and dramatic. In 1861, Alexander freed Russia's 22 million serfs and, a few years later, 25 million state-owned peasants. "It is better to abolish

Alexander II's "Great Reforms"

A Serf Reacts to the Russian Emancipation Proclamation

In 1861, Tsar Alexander II issued a dramatic proclamation emancipating Russia's serfs. Many people anticipated great changes stemming from this proclamation. The following excerpt depicts the reaction of Aleksandr Nikitenko, a former serf.

5 March. A great day. The emancipation manifesto! I received a copy around noon. I cannot express my joy at reading this precious act which scarcely has its equal in the thousand-year history of the Russian people. I read it aloud to my wife, my children and a friend of ours in my study, under Alexander II's portrait, as we gazed at it with deep reverence and gratitude. I tried to explain to my ten-year-old son as simply as possible the essence of the manifesto and bid him to keep inscribed in his heart forever the date of March 5 and the name of Alexander II, the Liberator.

I couldn't stay at home. I had to wander about the streets and mingle, so to say, with my regenerated fellow citizens. Announcements from the governor-general were posted at all crossways, and knots of people were gathered around them. One would read while the others listened. I encountered happy, but calm faces everywhere. Here and there people were reading the proclamation aloud, and, as I walked, I continually caught phrases like "decree on liberty," "freedom." . . .

How might members of Russia's aristocracy have reacted to this proclamation?

serfdom from above than to wait until the serfs begin to liberate themselves from below," he told a group of his nobles. This bold move, occurring at almost the same time that millions of slaves were emancipated in the United States, put an end to a notorious form of human bondage and transferred land to the freed peasantry. The document on page 457 reveals one serf's reactions to the decree that abolished serfdom. However, emancipation did not make the peasants fully independent and self-sufficient. In general, they received the poorest land, owed payments for their land and freedom, and were tied by collective ownership to their village commune, the *mir,* whose elected officials assigned parcels of land and determined what could be planted.

Other reforms made the judicial system more independent, created local political assemblies (*zemstva*) with elected officials, encouraged primary and secondary education by opening thousands of new schools, and reduced military service. However, expectations for further reform rose too fast for Alexander and came to haunt him. His efforts to relax control over Poland and grant amnesty to thousands of Poland's political prisoners seemed only to provoke a major Polish revolution in 1863, leading Alexander to repress the divisive nationalistic uprisings there and elsewhere within Russia's empire. To counter budding nationalism among minorities, he tried to force them to adopt the Russian language and culture. The universities

→ connect to today ←

Patriots

In the decades between 1850 and 1870, people in regions ranging from the Americas in the west to the Ottoman Empire in the east rallied, fought, and died in the name of national unity. What do you think are nationalism's benefits today? What is an example of its drawbacks?

he reopened became centers of intellectual discontent. Nor did his emancipation of the serfs end peasant rebellions.

Alexander intended to transform Russia into a modern authoritarian state that could command the allegiance of its citizens and wield power through a reformed, supported military. At best, he succeeded only partially. Certainly some of his reforms created important, long-lasting changes, but he did not turn his nation into a modern, national monarchy. Alexander himself, though called the "tsar liberator," was never popular. After an assassination attempt in 1866, he became more close-minded and increasingly turned Russia into a police state. Unrest still simmered among Russia's different nationalities. In addition, dissatisfaction among the peasantry and growing dissent among Russia's intellectuals, middle classes, and workers spelled trouble for the years ahead.

SUMMARY

By the 1870s, the most successful political leaders had learned new lessons about the power of nationalistic sentiment. Nationalism was a mighty force more easily used than opposed. It could fuel successful movements for national

timeline

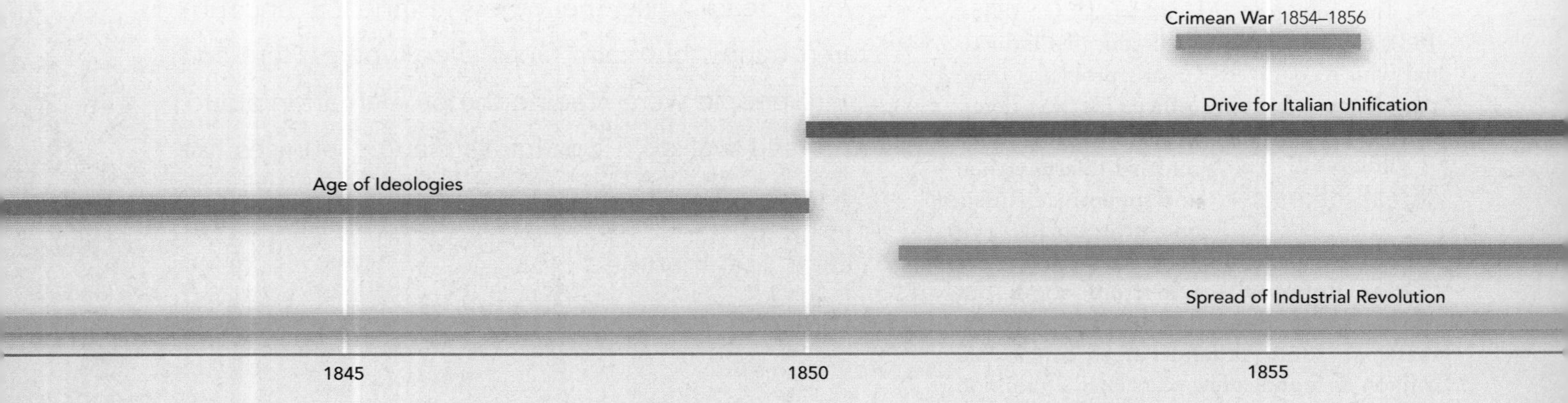

Crimean War 1854–1856

Drive for Italian Unification

Age of Ideologies

Spread of Industrial Revolution

| 1845 | 1850 | 1855 |

PEASANTS IN A RUSSIAN VILLAGE The mud streets, rude housing, and worn clothing in evidence in this photo from the second half of the nineteenth century suggest the low living standard of Russia's peasants.

- The drive for Italian unification was led by Count Cavour of Piedmont-Sardinia and Giuseppe Garibaldi, who succeeded in creating the Kingdom of Italy in 1861. Many lost their lives in the effort, and the new nation was still relatively poor and plagued with regional differences.

- Prussia's Otto von Bismarck took advantage of wars and opportunities to create the new German Empire in 1871. From that point on, German nationalism remained linked with military prowess rather than liberal ideals.

- In North America, the United States reestablished national unity after a costly civil war that would mar American society for generations and cost President Lincoln his life. With difficulty, Canada managed to become united into a single nation with its own constitution.

- Nationalism weakened the multiethnic Austrian and Ottoman Empires, threatening to dismember each of them.

In France and Russia, central governments tried to justify and sustain their authority by reaching out to citizens and promoting the idea of national greatness. They recognized that reforms initiated from above could foster needed national unity and win them greater power. Increasingly, the cry "for the good of the nation" served as the only rationale for such leaders' policies and whims. As the era unfolded, even war could be presented to an unwary public as an act of national will and politics.

unification, disintegrate multinational empires, enhance existing unity in already established nations, and strengthen central governments.

- In the two decades after 1850, shrewd political realists led successful nationalist struggles to build unified nation-states. These leaders relied on power politics, war, and diplomacy to achieve their aims.

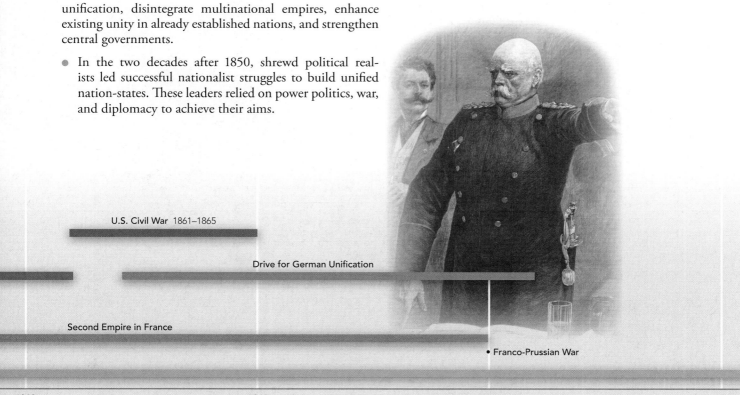

U.S. Civil War 1861–1865

Drive for German Unification

Second Empire in France

• Franco-Prussian War

| 1860 | 1865 | 1870 | 1875 |

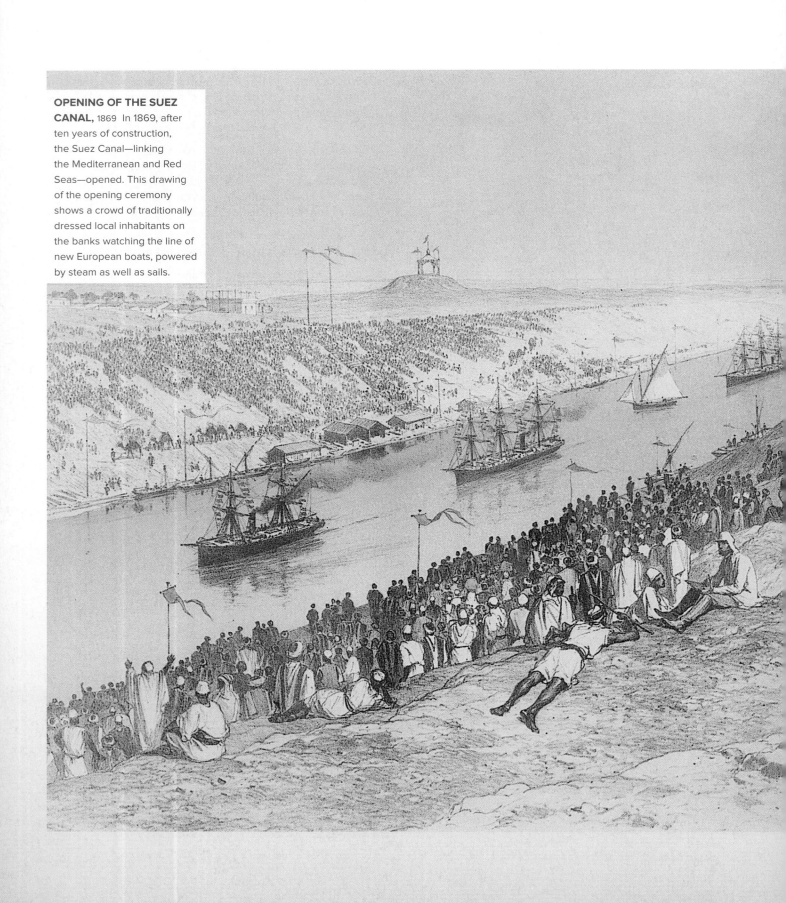

OPENING OF THE SUEZ CANAL, 1869 In 1869, after ten years of construction, the Suez Canal—linking the Mediterranean and Red Seas—opened. This drawing of the opening ceremony shows a crowd of traditionally dressed local inhabitants on the banks watching the line of new European boats, powered by steam as well as sails.

Mass Politics and Imperial Domination

Democracy and the
New Imperialism,
1870–1914

20

A Place in the Sun

"We have conquered for ourselves a place in the sun," announced Germany's Kaiser William II (r. 1888–1919) in 1901. Addressing an audience from Hamburg's business community, he boasted that "it will now be my task to see to it that this place in the sun shall remain our undisputed possession, in order that the sun's rays may fall fruitfully upon our activity and trade in foreign parts, that our industry and agriculture may develop within the state." William was referring to Germany's territories, gained in the scramble for overseas conquests that had been going on over the previous two decades. His audience and many others in the industrialized Western world expected to gain wealth from this recent imperial expansion. ▶▶

He also may have been reminding his listeners that the German
nation had been unified in the 1860s
through war and conquest (see
Chapter 19). Indeed, underlying his
words was an appeal to pride in the
growing power of this new nation.
Like other political leaders in the
West, William had learned to use

nationalism to gain support from listeners and readers.

Politicians such as William could
no longer ignore public opinion, for
democracy was on the rise. Between
1870 and 1914, demands for democracy, or political participation by common people, spread as more and
more people struggled to gain access

to politics. Now the new politics of
nationalism combined with industrialism to multiply the power of the West
and push it outward into Africa and
Asia in a great imperial expansion.
The West was rising to a new level of
world dominance. ◀◀

DEMANDS FOR DEMOCRACY

In 1896, the Russian statesman Konstantin Pobedonostsev
(1827–1907) published what would become a widely read
attack on democracy. "What is this freedom by which so
many minds are agitated, which inspires so many insen-
sate actions, so many wild speeches . . . ?" His answer was
democracy, "the right to participate in the government of
the State." He complained that "the new Democracy now
aspires to universal suffrage—a fatal error, and one of the
more remarkable in the history of mankind."

However, between 1870 and 1914, it became increasingly clear to those who had long enjoyed political power
in the West that, sooner or later, the beliefs of the masses
would count in politics. Since the French Revolution in
1789, a widening pool of Europeans had tasted political power, a trend that ruling elites feared. Some politicians, such as Pobedonostsev, tried to turn their backs on
democracy. Others tried to tame it, and still others flourished with it.

During the 1870s and 1880s, three developments
became entwined with demands for democracy. First,
many governments established national systems of free
and compulsory public education at
the primary-school level. With this
policy, they hoped to create more
patriotic citizens. They also wanted to provide citizens
with the skills and discipline needed by modernizing
economies and military establishments. Moreover, they
wanted their voting electorate to be educated. To liberals
especially, access to the schoolhouse and democracy went
hand in hand.

Second, educated, voting citizens could read newspapers, and popular journalism responded to the call. Before
1850, newspapers were few, small, expensive, and written
for a limited readership. By the end
of the century, a new kind of newspaper had popped up everywhere—

Public education

Popular journalism

one that was cheap, sensational, and wildly popular. In the
United States, publishers such as Joseph Pulitzer (1847–
1911) and William Randolph Hearst (1863–1951) built
influential newspapers featuring screaming headlines, flag-
waving patriotism, an easy style, sensational news, and
attention-getting columns. Other newspapers throughout
Europe, especially in the capital cities, followed the same
pattern. They catered to the newly educated public's hunger
for news and, in turn, powerfully molded public opinion.

Third, politicians realized they had to appeal to the
new voters. They devised innovative campaign strategies,
such as crisscrossing the country by railroad and delivering
stirring campaign speeches to cheer-
ing crowds in large halls and outdoor forums. They listened to newly
formed interest groups—whether business organizations,
reformers, or labor unions. These interest groups held rallies on their own, to gather support and gain influence
through newspaper coverage of their meetings. Finally,
politicians began creating all sorts of state institutions,
from census bureaus to social security administrations, to
satisfy the demands of their politically aroused societies
and persuade new voters to support them. All these
changes vastly reshaped parliamentary politics.

Political campaigns

Such developments put pressure on politicians to adjust
the way they conducted themselves, for democratic reform
meant more than widening the right to vote and bringing
new faces into government. To succeed in the new world
of mass politics, politicians had to learn to monitor—and
navigate—the shifting tides of public opinion. More and
more, rising to and staying in political office meant pleasing interest groups, journalists, educated readers, and
newly enfranchised voters.

Liberal Democracy in Western Europe

Would European societies ease toward a liberal democratic
consensus? Many people hoped so, particularly in western
Europe, where Great Britain and France had experimented
with democratic reforms, but in different ways.

Great Britain started the second half of the nineteenth century in a strong, stable position. It had avoided the revolutionary turmoil that swept over the European continent between 1848 and 1850, largely because the British adapted just enough to contain the pressures for radical change (see Chapter 18). Liberalism—stressing little governmental involvement in economic and social affairs, low taxes, and free trade—seemed to work well in Britain, and the island nation boasted the most modern economy in the world.

For most of the 1850s and 1860s, liberals controlled the British government. But they were more willing to call

Reform bills of 1867 and 1884

on national pride, sympathize with movements for national liberation abroad, and parade British naval might than to accommodate those who demanded entry into the political system. It was the Conservative Party, under Benjamin Disraeli (1804–1881), that finally decided to bend and take the credit for democratic reform before the Liberals themselves could grab it. The Conservatives passed a new measure—the Reform Bill of 1867—which doubled the electorate and gave the vote to the lower-middle class for the first time. In addition, they gathered support from the working class by passing laws that limited working hours, established sanitary codes, created housing standards, and aided labor unions. In 1884, the Liberal Party, under William Gladstone (1809–1898), countered by pushing through another reform bill that gave two-thirds of adult males the vote. To sweeten the deal even further, the Liberals opened the army and civil service to talent and made primary education available to all.

Having both jumped on the reform bandwagon, British Conservatives and Liberals now had to compete for power in new ways. For the first time, politicians such as Gladstone used the railways to campaign throughout the nation, speaking before crowds of thousands. A growing corps of journalists followed the campaigns, shaping public opinion by reporting speeches and scandals daily in cheap newspapers with mass circulation. New interest groups, mostly from the middle class, bent the ears of politicians who wanted their support in return. Britain was moving toward democracy, but in ways that worried traditional politicians used to deciding things among their "own kind."

France's path toward democracy took more violent turns than Britain's. A birthplace of democracy, France nevertheless started the 1870s on a turbulent note. The

France's Third Republic

Franco-Prussian War of 1870 spelled the end of Napoleon III's Second Empire and the emergence of the Third French Republic (see Chapter 19). The first elections, held in February 1871 after Napoleon III's fall and the surrender of Paris, resulted in a victory for the monarchists, who hoped to limit democracy and open the door for the restoration of a monarchy. Still

THE PARIS COMMUNE, ca. 1871 This altered photo portrays executions during the Paris Commune period. It was used by government troops as propaganda against Communards.

the city of Paris refused to submit to the domination of conservative, rural France. It demanded home rule and set up its own city government, or commune.

The **Paris Commune** would gain a reputation as a democracy out of control or as an experiment in Marxist socialism. In reality, the Commune stood for decentralizing power in France, self-governance, support of working-class organizations, and greater equality for women. Its roots lay in the city's resistance to the Germans between

The Paris Commune

September 1870 and January 1871. During those horrific months, Parisians had braved starvation and isolation in the face of the German siege. Most of the rich fled the city. The lower classes not only resented this exodus but also took over positions of power that the wealthy had abandoned. The February 1871 elections ended the German siege, but not the division between Paris and the rest of the nation. Parisians felt betrayed by France's new conservative government when it concluded the peace with Germany. When government troops tried to disarm them, they rebelled and fighting erupted. The government troops withdrew, and again Paris was put under siege, this time by French troops. Two months later, the government troops attacked, killing some 25,000 Parisians, arresting thousands more, and deporting more than 5,000 to distant penal colonies. Both sides in the Paris conflict committed bitter reprisals (see image above).

The fall of the Paris Commune ended the immediate threat to the integrity of France, but not the political and social uncertainties that still lurked below the surface. A period of restless political struggle followed. At first, monarchists almost regained power, but they failed to agree on which of three possible royal houses (the Bourbon, the Orleanist, or the Bonaparte) they should rally around. By the end of the 1870s, liberals, elected by universal male suffrage, controlled the French Republic.

Meanwhile, several forces reoriented politics toward the wider voting public. First, public schooling spread throughout France. Republican teachers replaced Catholic teachers, bringing in a common secular curriculum and promoting patriotism and republican virtues. Second, military service became compulsory and helped turn young, rural men into

Spread of democratic institutions

French citizens with new political awareness. Third, a popular national press took root in Paris and attracted readers throughout the nation. These papers reported all the political scandals, especially the sensational and far-reaching **Dreyfus affair** (see page 468), and soon readers in the provinces began avidly following national politics. In France, as in Britain, democratic institutions were spreading throughout the nation and redefining the nature of politics.

For and Against Democracy in Central and Eastern Europe

In contrast to the western European governments, national leaders in central and eastern Europe were more autocratic. Monarchs and their ministers in these regions had the last word in political decision making. Like nations in western Europe, those in central and eastern Europe struggled with pressure to institute democratic reforms. In some cases, these nations took reluctant steps toward democracy; in others, they declined to change. In addition, the tensions between autocratic and democratic forces in central and eastern Europe became particularly entwined with aggressive nationalism. The cases of Germany, Austria, and Russia provide apt examples of the various ways in which this struggle manifested itself.

In Germany, the constitution stipulated universal suffrage, but real power rested with the king and his ministers. Bismarck, who dominated as Germany's chancellor

Germany under Bismarck

between 1870 and 1890, supported universal male suffrage from the beginning only because "in a country with monarchical traditions and loyal sentiments" such as Germany, "universal suffrage would lead to . . . eliminating the influence of the liberal bourgeois classes." Bismarck believed that most workers and peasants would vote for his conservative policies.

In a twelve-year crusade against the Socialists, who attacked the autocratic nature of Germany's government and were gaining popularity in elections, Bismarck outlawed the Social Democratic Party's publications, organizations, and meetings and set the German police force on them. When his repressive tactics did little to diminish Socialist votes, Bismarck tried to undercut the party's appeal to the working class by removing "the causes for

socialism." Borrowing some of the Socialists' programs, between 1883 and 1889 he established a comprehensive system of social insurance that provided accident, sickness, and old-age benefits.

Ironically, in fighting against the Social Democrats, the conservative Bismarck made Germany a leader in enacting progressive social policies. Nevertheless, Bismarck's campaign against the Social Democratic Party would fail. The Socialists had built a solid following and continued to gain public support. In 1890, two years after the death of Kaiser William I, the new monarch, Kaiser William II, dismissed the aging chancellor. William II, eager to rule himself, "dropped the pilot" of the German ship of state and ended an era in German history.

In Austria, liberalism spread during the 1870s along with the rise of the bourgeoisie in that country. Liberals supported the constitutional monarchy, parliamentary government, and restricted suffrage. They also believed that it was possible to hold a multinational empire together. In the 1880s, nationalistic demands from

Nationalistic discontent in Austria

different language groups began to overwhelm liberals and play into the hands of conservatives. Parliamentary sessions in Austria frequently degenerated into shouting matches, in which representatives from different language groups hurled inkstands at one another. This nationalistic discontent proved even more intense in Hungary than in Austria. Moreover, the partnership between Austria and Hungary threatened to disintegrate altogether (see page 453). The introduction of universal male suffrage in 1907 only made the empire more difficult to govern. More often than not, the emperor and his advisors bypassed parliament and ruled by decree.

In Russia, Alexander II's "Great Reforms" did little to open the doors to democracy beyond the local level (see pages 456–457). Indeed, they may have sparked more dissatisfaction than celebration. For serfs, liberals, and intellectuals, the reforms did not go far enough. A group of sons and daughters of the

Radical action in Russia

aristocracy and middle classes decided to take action. In a well-intentioned but ill-fated movement, they traveled to rural areas in an effort to uplift the lives of country dwellers. They received a rude welcome in several ways: Rural people resented what they saw as condescending attention from inexperienced urban intellectuals, and the tsar's police promptly repressed them.

Some of the young idealists fled; others remained and turned to terrorism. One group, The People's Will, defined terrorism as "the destruction of the most harmful persons in the Government, the protection of the party from spies, and the punishment of official lawlessness and violence." Vera Zasulich became an early heroine in this movement

> Some of the young idealists fled; others remained and turned to terrorism.

when she attempted to assassinate the St. Petersburg chief of police in 1878. Her action initiated a series of violent eruptions and assassinations, in which terrorists killed numerous bureaucrats and police officials, and the government brutally suppressed the rebels. The cycle of terrorism and repression turned Alexander II to a more conservative course, and he halted all further reforms. In 1881, members of The People's Will retaliated by murdering Alexander II with a bomb.

The new tsar, Alexander III (r. 1881–1894), blamed his father's death on softness and set out to erase every trace of liberalism and democracy in Russia. His secret police

Reaction under Alexander III

arrested thousands of suspects, and the tsar himself initiated a sweeping program of Russianization. Authorities forced minority groups to use the Russian language and persecuted followers of non-Orthodox religions, especially Jews. Russia, much more so than Austria, would not yet bend to the democratic winds blowing from the west.

INSIDERS AND OUTSIDERS: Politics of the Extremes

During the late nineteenth century, those democratic winds in the West spread beyond what had been the mainstream of politics. New groups and causes emerged to challenge the established center of liberal and conservative politics. These new groups gained strength and complicated the trend toward democracy. To the political left of liberals stood the unions, socialists, and anarchists. To the political right of conservatives were anti-Semites and ultranationalists. Still outside, without the vote, were women, who increasingly demanded a voice in national politics.

These groups and causes appealed to large numbers of people, particularly those who had previously been left out of politics. They became so prominent that established political leaders could not ignore them. With the political spectrum widening, it seemed less and less likely that Europe's nations would find some consensus or social peace.

The Spread of Unions

Until the 1880s, labor unions were limited chiefly to skilled workers, organized by crafts, who proved moderate in their aims and methods. In the 1880s, unionization spread rapidly to unskilled workers. These new union members adopted more radical methods and turned toward socialist programs. Seeking more than mutual aid, they demanded a say in working conditions and wages. They went on strike and flexed their political muscle through the vote. As a

Strikes

man who employed thousands of dockers in Marseilles, France, explained, "The days of the employer's arbitrary power are past, unfortunately. . . . For long we could hope to subdue these trade unions that rose against our authority. . . . That too is finished, over." The image below captures some of the ideals of the new unions.

As the end of the century approached, organized labor became a formidable force. Labor unions in Great Britain formed the National Trades Union Congress and became identified with the new Labour Party. In Germany, unions, especially among the unskilled workers, grew dramatically and coalesced into a national Marxist organization. In France, various unions banded together into the giant General Confederation of Labor, with a radical political program. In the United States, the abundance of cheap immigrant labor and the determined resistance by industrial capitalists hindered the emergence of unions. In 1886, however, Samuel Gompers founded the American Federation of Labor—the first successful national labor organization in America. By 1914, unions had become sufficiently large and organized to make them a major power, both in the workplace and at the polls.

PAUL LOUIS DELANCE, *STRIKE*, 1908 Under red flags symbolizing their cause, striking French union members stream out of distant factories. The strikers are supported by humble people upon whom a few rays of blessing sunshine fall.

Socialism Gains Strength

Like the labor unions, socialism also became a major force within the working class and in politics during the late nineteenth century. Most socialists looked to the ideas of Karl

The First International Marx for inspiration (see Chapter 18). Marx had argued that modern industrial society was splitting into two opposing classes: the capitalists, or owners of the means of production, and the workers. Capitalism, he explained, was bound to be replaced by a socialist system through revolution by the working class. Marx helped union organizers to form the International Working Men's Association (the First International) in 1864. The organization fell apart in the 1870s, but in 1889, socialists formed the Second International. These organizations helped socialists unify and spread their cause. A sense of shared struggle and beliefs inspired them to form unions, create political parties, and fight powerful employers and strong politicians.

Yet, the strength of socialism varied in each country. In Britain, established politicians excluded the working classes or socialist thinkers from politics until the 1880s.

The Fabians Then a group of well-known intellectuals formed the **Fabian Society,** which advocated the adoption of socialist policies through politics rather than revolution. Beatrice Webb (1858–1943), one of the founders of the Fabians, explained that she became a socialist because of "the physical misery and moral debasement following in the tracks of the rack-renting landlord and capitalist profit maker in the swarming populations of the great centres of nineteenth century commerce and industry." Webb could see no way out of "the recurrent periods of inflation and depression—meaning for the vast majority of the nation, alternate spells of overwork and unemployment."

During the 1890s, both unions and socialists in Britain developed enough political muscle to form the Labour Party and elect members to Parliament. By 1906, Labour had pressured the Liberals, led by David Lloyd George (1863–1945),

Britain's Labour Party to adopt new policies providing accident, sickness, old-age, and unemployment insurance for workers. As Labour members of Parliament argued, these old men and women were "the veterans of industry, people of almost endless toil, who have fought for and won the industrial and commercial supremacy of Great Britain. Is their lot and end to be the everlasting slur of pauperism?" To pay for the new policies, the Liberals shifted the "heaviest burden to the broadest backs." A steeply graduated income tax and high taxes on inheritances landed on the rich. When Conservatives in the House of Lords resisted, the Liberal and Labour parties passed a bill that stripped the House of Lords of most of its former power.

In France, socialism gained strength during the 1890s. During the following decade, socialist parties helped push France's republican government to enact a limited program of unemployment, old-age, accident, and sickness insurance for workers.

France and Jaurès By this time, the different wings of the French socialists had joined to form the United Socialist Party under the leadership of scholar-orator Jean Jaurès. By 1914, the United Socialist Party numbered 1.5 million voters and had 110 seats in the Chamber of Deputies.

Socialism enjoyed its greatest success in Germany. In 1890, Germany's main socialist party, the Social Democrats, won the vote of 20 percent of the electorate. Officially the party adhered to the idea that revolution was historically inevitable. A party leader, August Bebel,

German Social Democrats expressed the optimism of this view: "Every night I go to sleep with the thought that the last hour of bourgeois society strikes soon." In practice, however, the party usually followed the ideas of the "revisionist" socialist Eduard Bernstein (1850–1932). This German writer and politician urged socialists to cooperate with the capitalist classes to obtain immediate benefits for labor and advocated a gradual approach to socialism. By 1914, the Social Democrats polled some 4.5 million votes, making it the largest political party in Germany.

Even in conservative Austria, socialists gained strength in industrial areas for the same reasons they did elsewhere in the West. The plight of workers was their top priority. Anna Maier, who started a life of work in a tobacco factory when she was 13, captured this concern when she explained that "young girls were often abused or even beaten" on the job. One day Maier read a copy of the *Women Workers'* newspaper smuggled into the factory by one of the older women. Eventually, she managed to join the Social Democratic Party. After she had taken part in demonstrations, her factory manager took her "off a good job" and put her "in a poorer one," but as she later reported, "nothing stopped me." When the tobacco workers union formed in 1899, she joined them and became "a class-conscious fighter." Maier's story was repeated by many other workers throughout the West in the decades before 1914.

> All too easily, this spreading strain of nationalism strengthened racist and anti-Semitic thought.

Anarchism: Freedom from All Authority

While sometimes associated with socialists, **anarchists** made more radical demands. Drawing on the ideas of leaders such as the Russian activist Mikhail Bakunin

(1814–1876) and Russian theoretician Pyotr Kropotkin (1842–1921), they stressed the elimination of any form of authority that impinged on human freedom. "So long as there exist States, there will be no humanity," Bakunin argued. "The masses of the people will be de facto slaves even in the most democratic republics." Anarchists believed that human beings, once freed from the corrupting institutions that oppressed them, would naturally cooperate with one another.

Anarchism became particularly influential in Spain, Italy, and France, where it appealed to trade unionists, artisans, agricultural laborers, and shopkeepers suffering from unemployment and declining wages. Its supporters favored direct action through unions and cooperatives rather than parliamentary politics. After the turn of the century, many anarchists hoped the grand solution to their problems would come with a "general strike," as described by the popular French writer Georges Sorel (1847–1922). Such a strike, they believed, would force the capitalist system to grind to a sudden halt. A small wing of the anarchist movement went beyond hoping for a general strike and turned to violence. Among its victims were President Sadi Carot of France in 1894, King Umberto I of Italy in 1900, and President William McKinley of the United States in 1901.

Anti-Semitism and Ultranationalism

Usually at the opposite end of the political spectrum from socialism and anarchism, **anti-Semitism** often appealed to conservative nationalists. Followers of Judaism had long suffered from anti-Semitism—hostility toward or hatred of Jews. Since the Middle Ages, Jews had been accused of murdering Christ, segregated into special quarters known as ghettos, and persecuted. However, between 1789 and the 1870s, the spreading ideals of the Enlightenment and the French Revolution had enabled Jews to gain new rights and a degree of legal equality, though rarely full acceptance. At least in western and central Europe, this progress led many Jews to believe that finally they could join their nation-states as full citizens.

During the last decades of the nineteenth century, however, nationalism took on militant and authoritarian tones. All too easily, this spreading strain of nationalism strengthened racist and anti-Semitic thought. Comte de Gobineau (1816–1882), a Frenchman, and Houston Stewart Chamberlain (1855–1927), an Englishman who became a German citizen, wrote widely read tracts arguing that race determined much of history. The two men helped formulate the Aryan myth, which held that Germans belonged to a special race and therefore possessed superior qualities: "[T]he Germanic races belong to the most highly gifted group, the group usually termed Aryan. . . . Physically and mentally the Aryans are pre-eminent among all people; for that reason they are by right . . . the lords of the world." Chamberlain's ideas veered off into anti-Semitism, as did the thinking of other well-known racist writers. Their pseudoscientific thought—which labeled Jews as a separate, inferior race—became increasingly popular.

During the same period, anti-Semitic politics gained force, especially among artisans, small shopkeepers, rural workers, and others who felt threatened by liberalism and capitalism and saw Jews as being linked to both. These people scornfully called Jews outsiders and capitalists and blamed them for their own economic ills and fears. Ultranationalist politicians used anti-Semitism to rally crowds, shift the blame for failed policies away from themselves, and win votes.

Right-wing newspapers such as *La Libre Parole* popularized scandals as well as anti-Semitic stories that coalesced

SAMUEL HIRSZENBERG, *THE BLACK BANNER*, 1905 Horrified and grief-stricken Jewish people, bearing their dead, flee anti-Semitic attacks (pogroms) in Russia-dominated Poland. The sky echoes the ominous dangers still facing these people.

most dramatically in the Dreyfus affair. People throughout France followed every development of "the affair" day after day and year after year. In 1894, a

The Dreyfus affair

group of bigoted army officers falsely accused and convicted a Jewish captain, Alfred Dreyfus, of treason and sent him to solitary imprisonment on Devil's Island in South America. Three years later, evidence of Dreyfus's innocence appeared. Nevertheless, high-ranking officers refused to reopen the case. Newspaper articles, sensational trials, accusations, and huge public demonstrations divided the nation between the political Left and Right. Republicans, socialists, and intellectuals, inspired by the famous French writer Émile Zola, who attacked the judgment of the military and judiciary in the case, rallied for Dreyfus. Nationalist, conservative, monarchist, and anti-Semitic forces supported the army. In 1899, a second court-martial again convicted Dreyfus, despite evidence of another officer's guilt in the affair. The president of the Republic pardoned Dreyfus, but it took seven more years to get Dreyfus fully acquitted.

The Dreyfus affair marked not only the battle over anti-Semitism but the evolution of French politics as well. The victory for Dreyfus became a victory for republicanism and anticlericalism. Electoral victories made republicans strong enough to separate church and state in 1905 and initiate a program of social legislation. Socialists, who had joined republicans in the Dreyfus case, gained greater legitimacy and popularity. The political power of monarchists and the Catholic Church had been dealt a debilitating blow.

For Jews, persecution was worse in central and eastern Europe. These regions had the highest Jewish population and the most aggressive strain of nationalism. Nationalis-

Central and eastern Europe

tic anti-Semitic organizations, such as the Pan-German Association and the Christian Social Workers' Party, emerged in Germany. Anti-Semitic journals warned of the dangers to "the native-born Christian population" as Jews gained access to the press, to state offices, and to professions such as teaching and law. One anti-Semitic deputy in Germany's parliament explained in an 1895 speech that "every Jew who at this moment had not done anything bad may nevertheless under the proper conditions do precisely that, because his racial qualities drive him to do it."

In Austria, the Christian Socialist Party and the German National Party took a decidedly anti-Semitic stand. By the 1890s, a new breed of politics based on symbols, charisma, nationalism, racism, anticapitalism, and anti-Semitism had arisen. The election of Karl Lueger in 1897 as mayor of Vienna symbolized this political trend; Lueger campaigned on an anti-Semitic platform and triumphed even in this bastion of Austrian liberalism.

Some of the most violent anti-Semitic acts occurred in Russia. Tsars Alexander III and Nicholas II (r. 1894–1917) sanctioned the persecution of Jews and required them to live in designated areas. Officials labeled Jews as outsid-

ers and excluded them from mainstream society. Whenever anyone wanted to assign blame for their problems, they could point to the Jews. This hostility culminated in a series of pogroms, or organized mass attacks on Jews, led by anti-Semitic groups and government officials (see image on page 467). Between 1870 and 1914, these persecutions helped push more than 2 million eastern European Jews out of their homes and to the west, particularly to the United States.

Concerns about persecutions in eastern Europe as well as the weakening of Jewish identity through assimilation in western Europe gave rise to **Zionism**, a Jewish nationalist movement to create an independent state for Jews in Palestine—the ancient homeland of the Jews. The

Zionism and Herzl

Hungarian writer Theodor Herzl (1860–1904) became the leading figure in the Zionist movement. In 1896, he published an influential pamphlet, *The Jewish State: An Attempt at a Modern Solution of the Jewish Question,* urging formation of an international movement to make Palestine a Jewish homeland. He envisioned the homeland transformed into a socialist community of hardworking cooperatives. The following year he led the new World Zionist Organization to prominence. He gained a large following in eastern Europe, found financial support from several sources, and won cautious political support from British governmental officials. "It might be many years before the founding of the State is under way," Herzl warned. "In the meantime, Jews will be ridiculed, offended, abused, whipped, plundered, and slain in a thousand different localities." After Herzl's death in 1904, other leaders advanced his aims and secured more support—including the financial aid of donors such as the French banker Baron de Rothschild, and the cooperation of Arthur Balfour (1848–1930), Britain's prime minister. By 1914, some 85,000 Jews had emigrated to Palestine, primarily from eastern Europe.

Still Outsiders: Women, Feminism, and the Right to Vote

By 1914, most of the political groups that had been outside the mainstream of politics had gained a political voice. In the majority of Western countries, universal male suffrage had become the rule by 1914. However, women still remained on the political sidelines, hampered by an ideology that left them unequal economically, trapped in their own "separate sphere" by laws that declared them legally inferior, and excluded by political institutions that deprived them of the vote. Few men in any of the political parties, movements, or unions offered their support for women's suffrage.

During the last decades of the nineteenth century, many women finally turned to political activism. Numerous women—whether as individuals or as activist group members—were already calling themselves "feminist."

Political activism

Groups of feminists organized several movements to promote women's issues, demand legal equality of the sexes, and advocate social and political change. In 1878, representatives of these groups from twelve nations came together in Paris at the International Congress of the Rights of Women and initiated a period of increased activism and international cooperation. Although feminists were still a minority among women, their strength grew dramatically. In Britain and the United States, women with middle-class and aristocratic backgrounds fought especially hard for the right to vote. They argued that without the vote, women would continue to suffer from a range of inequalities. "The idea that the possession of political rights will destroy 'womanliness,' absurd as it may seem to us, is very deeply rooted in the minds of men," British writer Frances Power Cobbe (1822–1904) pointed out in 1884. Men, Cobbe explained, "really prize what women now are in the home and in society so highly that they cannot bear to risk losing it by any serious change in their condition." A few years later, Elizabeth Cady Stanton (1815–1902) expressed the views of many Americans in the women's suffrage movement: "If we are to consider [a woman] as a citizen, as a member of a great nation, she must have the same rights as all other members."

Another group of feminists tried to gain equality through social reform—focusing on the needs of the working class and often voicing socialist sympathies. Led by women such as Louise Michel (1830–1905) in France and Clara Zetkin (1857–1933) in Germany, they argued that only when workers as a whole gained freedom from economic and social oppression would women achieve justice. In 1885, Michel looked forward to a transforming revolution that would introduce a new era "when men and women will move through life together as good companions, and they will no more argue about which sex is superior than races will argue about which race is foremost in the world." Ten years later, Zetkin explained that proletarian women could attain "salvation only through the fight for the emancipation of labor."

The strongest women's suffrage movements arose in Great Britain. The movement was exemplified by organizations such as the National Union of Women's Suffrage Societies, led by Millicent Fawcett (1847–1929), and the more radical Women's Social and Political Union, led by Emmeline Pankhurst (1858–1928) and her two daughters.

Suffrage movements

OPINION

What do you think were the most significant problems that resulted from the large number of people who were incorporated into politics between 1870 and 1914?

The leaders of these movements had reached a crucial conclusion: Being polite was not going to win them the right to vote. They worked as other political groups did, forming organizations, presenting petitions, pressuring politicians, forging alliances, holding demonstrations, publishing newspapers, and marching for the franchise. They continued despite scorn from men, ridicule by newspapers, rejection by politicians, cold shoulders from labor unions and socialists, and force by the police. "We have presented larger petitions than were ever presented for any other reform, we have succeeded in holding greater public meetings than men have ever had for any reform . . . we have faced hostile mobs at street corners . . . we have been ridiculed, we have had contempt poured upon us . . . we know that we need the protection of the vote even more than men have needed it."

In 1908, a rally for female suffrage drew some 250,000 women to Hyde Park in London. After 1910, feminism in Britain took a more public and violent turn as women resorted to window smashing, arson, assaults, bombing of railway stations, and chaining themselves to the gates of Parliament. Police arrested them, judges imprisoned them, and, when they went on hunger strikes, authorities force-fed them.

Still the British government as well as most other Western authorities refused to give in to the feminists' demands. Finland granted women the right to vote in 1906—the first victory for the women's suffrage movement—but other victories would take years. Women would not gain the vote until after 1918 in Britain, Germany, and the United States; until the 1940s in France; and until the 1970s in Switzerland.

EMIGRATION: Overseas and Across Continents

By 1914, most Western societies had taken great, often reluctant, steps toward democracy. A swirl of forces—the growing pressures of nationalism, the spread of industry and commerce, and the competition for military might—fueled those steps and molded the politics that resulted. Some of those same forces also pushed a new wave of Europeans and their governments across the globe.

Eugène Laermans, *The Emigrants*

1896

This triptych (three-paneled painting) by Eugène Laermans shows stages in the process of emigration that many Europeans experienced. In the right-hand panel *(The Exordium)*, a parish priest addresses the crowd of departing villagers for the last time. For the priest, the news seems bad; this departure of his flock may mark the decline and possibly death of his village. In the background lies the village under dark clouds. The central panel *(The Exodus)* shows a seemingly endless line of humble men, women, and children carrying their meager belongings and dragging their pets. They march along the road and, for the last time, look back at their homeland and village in the distance. In the left-hand panel *(The Exile)*, they crowd into the port. The darkening clouds to the west warn of a difficult voyage across the Atlantic and their unknown fate in new lands. In what ways might this painting be considered a realistic rather than an idealistic depiction of emigration across the Atlantic?

the same: Imperial powers raced to carve up Africa and establish control in Asia. With their new presence, wealth, and power, Europeans dominated the world as never before.

Leaving Europe

Ever since the first sixteenth-century settlements, Europe had sent a sizable trickle of emigrants to the Americas. The trickle became a flowing stream in the mid-nineteenth century. Great numbers of British, Irish, and then German immigrants landed in the United States during the 1840s, 1850s, and 1860s. After 1870, the stream swelled to a rushing torrent, as peoples from southern and eastern Europe joined the flow. Between 1870 and 1914, some 30 million Europeans left their homelands and emigrated, mostly to the Americas and Australia.

What explains this immense movement? As suggested in the images above by Belgian artist Eugène Laermans (1864–1940), many of the vast numbers of peasants and workers who emigrated overseas left Europe reluctantly. They felt pushed by the difficulties of their lives on the land and in the villages more than pulled by the apparent opportunities in foreign lands. In several parts of Europe, such as Scandinavia, the British Isles, and southern Italy, the land could no longer support the expanding population. Moreover, the shift to commercial agriculture throughout Europe had left a flood of small farmers landless or unable to compete. Natural catastrophes also played a part. A deadly potato famine in Ireland in the late 1840s forced

After the mid-nineteenth century, a great migration of people from Europe gained momentum. Europeans streamed overseas and across continents, hoping to start new and better lives. As they fanned across the globe, they brought money and great quantities of manufactured goods to nonindustrialized areas. Their governments did

many Irish to flee their homeland to escape starvation. These hardships impelled people—even in relatively rich western European countries such as Laermans's Belgium—to head for more promising shores. Many emigrated to the Americas, especially between 1880 and 1892.

Causes for the migration

Many opportunities, both real and imagined, also beckoned from across the oceans. Visions of free or cheap land, already taken away from native peoples, attracted Europeans to the Americas, Australia, and New Zealand. People heard news of plentiful jobs in America's growing cities. Steamships and railroads made the trip faster and cheaper than ever, though not pleasant for the crowds who traveled in ships' bottom compartments with baggage and supplies.

Unfortunately for these hopeful travelers, reality often proved far less appealing than their dreams. New arrivals usually got only the most remote or poorest lands and the lowest-paying jobs. Lonely or adrift in their new world, they sent letters and money back home, maintaining ties to old communities for a while or asking others to join them. Millions gave up the search for a better life or found reason to turn back; about one-third of those emigrating overseas from Europe eventually returned home.

THE NEW IMPERIALISM: The Race for Africa and Asia

In the 1880s, this mass migration of individuals was paralleled by an expansion of Western power into non-Western parts of the world. European nations raced to gain control over Africa and Asia especially. They subdued local opposition and reshaped the existing societies to fit their own purposes. They brought Western culture and institutions to Africa and Asia whether those peoples wanted them or not. By 1914, imperial powers had seized most of Africa and much of Asia, taking direct or indirect control over almost half a billion people.

Imperialism was not new. Since the fifteenth century, Europeans had been extending their influence over the globe. Increasingly during the eighteenth and nineteenth centuries, Western nations developed and mobilized the ships, weapons, and finances that gave them advantages over other civilizations. Spurred on by competitive rivalries

Kaiser William II Links Nationalism and Imperialism

For many people, the distance between the increasingly assertive nationalism of the late nineteenth century and the new imperialism of the period was short. The following speech at Hamburg in 1901, delivered by Kaiser William II of Germany, exemplifies this view.

In spite of the fact that we have no such fleet as we should have, we have conquered for ourselves a place in the sun. It will now be my task to see to it that this place in the sun shall remain our undisputed possession, in order that the sun's rays may fall fruitfully upon our activity and trade in foreign parts, that our industry and agriculture may develop within the state and our sailing sports upon the water, for our future lies upon the water. The more Germans go out upon the waters, whether it be in the races of regattas, whether it be in journeys across the ocean, or in the service of the battleflag, so much the better will it be for us. For when the German has once learned to direct his glance upon what is distant and great, the pettiness which surrounds him in daily life on all sides will disappear. . . .

As head of the empire I therefore rejoice over every citizen, whether from Hamburg, Bremen, or Lübeck, who goes forth with this large outlook and seeks new points where we can drive in the nail on which to hang our armour.

How does William II connect nationalism and imperialism?

Exploring the Past

Economics and Imperialism in Africa

With new conquests made in the scramble for Africa, many people expected commerce to accelerate and new markets for manufactured goods to emerge. This attitude shows up in Lord Lugard's account of his experiences in colonial service.

The "Scramble for Africa" by the nations of Europe—an incident without parallel in the history of the world—was due to the growing commercial rivalry, which brought home to civilised nations the vital necessity of securing the only remaining fields for industrial enterprise and expansion. It is well, then, to realise that it is for our *advantage*—and not alone at the dictates of duty—that we have undertaken responsibilities in East Africa. It is in order to foster the growth of the trade of this country, and to find an outlet for our manufactures and our surplus energy, that our far-seeing statesmen and our commercial men advocate colonial expansion. . . .

There are some who say we have no *right* in Africa at all, that "it belongs to the natives." I hold that our right is the necessity that is upon us to provide for our ever-growing population—either by opening new fields for emigration, or by providing work and employment which the development of over-sea extension entails—and to stimulate trade by finding new markets, since we know what misery trade depression brings at home.

How does Lugard respond to arguments against imperialism?

among themselves for power and wealth, European states used these advantages to impose their will again and again in Asia and Africa. But the burst of expansion between about 1880 and 1914 was so rapid and extensive that historians call it the **new imperialism.**

Money and Glory

There were many forces driving this wave of imperialism. For one thing, as the document on page 471 indicates, people thought they could make money from it. "It is in order to foster the growth of the trade of this country, and to find an outlet for our manufacturers and our surplus energy, that our far-seeing statesmen and our commercial men advocate colonial expansion," concluded a British colonial administrator. Industrial nations hungered for new markets, cheap raw materials, and juicy investment opportunities. Western manufacturers, merchants, financiers, shippers, investors, adventurers, and settlers thought they would find all these things in Africa and Asia, and European workers believed that the guaranteed markets would keep them employed. Political leaders, egged on by other pressures as well, usually agreed.

Economic causes

Yet the race for riches often proved more difficult than people expected. Many colonies cost European governments far more to acquire and maintain than riches received. The colonizing process got complicated politically as well. Imperial powers took some colonies not because they saw them as money-makers but because they wanted to protect the borders of other, more lucrative colonies. In many such buffer colonies, loans were never paid off, mines never yielded enough minerals to cover their expenses, and markets proved not worth the cost of building railroads to reach them. But in the beginning, people hoped for great profits or at least security for money-making ventures in distant lands. Competition and the optimistic taking on of risks were at the heart of capitalism, and this led many Westerners and their nations into Africa and Asia.

Politics of imperialism

A different, probably more powerful competition—the drive for international prestige—also drove governments, cheered on by millions of their citizens, to snap up

Nationalism and imperialism

colonies. The renewed burst of imperialism came at precisely the time when nationalism was on the rise in Europe. As the document on page 472 suggests, nationalistic sentiment easily translated into a new struggle for imperial conquest—for remote islands, barren deserts, and impenetrable jungles as well as for more lucrative prizes. Governments used such conquests to display their muscle, especially when such a display was lacking at home. France's expansion, for example, helped French citizens feel compensated for losses suffered in the Franco-Prussian War. Italian conquests overseas promised to make up for Italy's failure to acquire first-rate power status on the Continent. Gaining colonies became a measure of status, proof of a nation's political and economic prowess. To be left behind in the imperial race marked a nation as second class. "[A]ll great nations in the fullness of their strength have desired to set their mark upon barbarian lands, and those who fail to participate in this great rivalry will play a pitiable role in the time to come," the nationalist German historian Heinrich von Treitschke announced. People in the West avidly followed the race for colonies. Newspapers reporting on incidents and conquests in Asia and Africa framed these developments as adventures and patriotic causes. Thrilling stories about action overseas sold countless papers. In books and classrooms, people could see their national colors spreading across oceans and continents.

This competition for economic gain and international prestige gained a life of its own, a momentum that became hard to curb. When one nation moved into a new area, others followed, for fear of being left with nothing. To protect established colonies, imperial powers seized adjoining territories. To ensure supply lines to distant colonies, nations grabbed up islands, ports, and bases. To form alliances and collect bargaining chips for when disputes arose, imperial powers made colonial claims.

Finally, people found ways to justify imperialism. Westerners saw themselves as bringing "blessings" of their civilization to "backward" peoples. The British writer Rudyard Kipling (1865–1936) expressed the belief of many Western-

Justification

ers when he wrote of the "white man's burden" to civilize the "lesser breeds" of the earth. Missionaries took to heart the injunction to "Go ye into all the world and preach the gospel to every creature" (see image above).

Some people put imperialism in a less rosy context. These observers described colonial competition and conquest as part of an unavoidable, Darwinian struggle for survival of the fittest. In such a struggle, the white "race" would surely prevail, they believed. France's prime minister even claimed that "the superior races have rights over the inferior races," a view supported by many.

A EUROPEAN VISION OF IMPERIALISM This pro-imperialism publication depicts a member of a Catholic order teaching Ugandan girls how to improve their lives. The implied promise is that the West will bring its technology, faith, and civilization to a new generation of thankful Africans.

There were people who opposed imperialism. Intellectuals, reform clubs, and politicians such as Jean Jaurès called it an unjustifiably cruel and costly exploitation. However, such voices did not carry enough weight. Powerful economic interests and politicians had found imperial expansion irresistible, and

Opposition to imperialism

most citizens were all too willing to support the adventure. Moreover, imperial conquest became so easy it seemed foolish not to take advantage of it.

The Tools of Conquest

Before 1850, it was either too difficult or not worth the effort for Westerners to penetrate into Africa's interior or extensively expand colonial holdings in Asia. After 1850, science and technology gave the industrialized nations the tools they needed to conquer and control nonindustrialized lands.

Steam-powered iron ships conveyed messages, materials, and people across oceans quickly and cheaply. Smaller steamboats took travelers up rivers. Railroads carried them across vast stretches of land. The Suez Canal cut thousands of miles off journeys to Asia, and the Panama Canal promised much the same

Transportation facilities

(see the drawing on page 460). In 1800, mail took as long as one year to get from London to India. In 1880, a telegram took just hours.

Innovations in weaponry also gave the West new clout. Europeans had long possessed more firepower than non-

Force

Western peoples. The new breech-loading rifles and machine guns multiplied that advantage. Local societies resisted, but with the destructive power of these new weapons, European soldiers numbering only a few hundred annihilated local forces in the thousands. Winston Churchill, Britain's future prime minister and an observer of the 1898 Battle of Omdurman in the Sudan, described the effects of the machine gun on natives: "It was not a battle but an execution. . . . The bodies were . . . spread evenly over acres and acres." In that particular battle, 11,000 Muslim tribesmen died, whereas only 28 British soldiers lost their lives. Many other battles, large and small, took place in the series of open and guerrilla wars over the years. Imperial powers usually prevailed, but conquest and control came with much bloodshed and brutality. As the British novelist Joseph Conrad wrote in his 1902 classic, *Heart of Darkness,* "The conquest of the earth, which mostly means the taking it away from those who have a different complexion or slightly flatter noses than ourselves, is not a pretty thing when you look into it much."

Disease, more than distance or resistance, had also kept Europeans out of most of Africa. But by 1830, the French had discovered the power of quinine to protect their soldiers from deadly malaria long enough to take

Medicine

Algeria in North Africa. After 1850, explorers, missionaries, traders, soldiers, and officials came into sub-Saharan Africa armed with the new medicine.

Various Europeans used these tools of conquest at different times. Sometimes missionaries and explorers entered

OPINION

What do you think was the most significant result of the great expansion of European peoples and powers across the globe between 1880 and 1914?

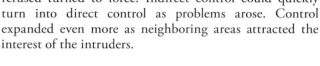

"The soldiers drive the people into the bush. If they will not go they are shot down, and their left hands cut off and taken as trophies."

new lands first; at other times, traders or even military officers made decisions on

Patterns of conquest

their own to move in. Once there, they called on home governments to provide support, enforce contracts, and protect private interests. Newspapers reported "atrocities" committed against the unwelcome intruders and stirred up European cries for revenge and protection of national honor. Western governments that had requested the cooperation of local political leaders and had been refused turned to force. Indirect control could quickly turn into direct control as problems arose. Control expanded even more as neighboring areas attracted the interest of the intruders.

The Scramble for Africa

Imperial control spread most dramatically in Africa. In the early nineteenth century, Africa was the seat of several vital civilizations. In the north were the long-established Islamic societies. In sub-Saharan Africa—particularly in the western and central Sudan, where the Sahara Desert gave way to grasslands and trade flourished—a rich array of societies and states had developed over the centuries. In most kingdoms of the Sudan and western Africa, Islam had become a major cultural influence. Trade and contact with Europeans affected Africa, but except for coastal and certain other limited areas, such as South Africa, most of Africa remained free from European control.

By the middle decades of the nineteenth century, however, the French had conquered and annexed Algeria in North Africa and had pushed their way up the Senegal River in the west. The Brit-

North Africa

ish had taken the Cape Colony in South Africa from the Dutch during the Napoleonic Wars, and the Dutch settlers had moved northward into the interior (see map on page 475). In the late 1870s, two developments initiated an international scramble to carve up Africa.

The first occurred in Egypt. This North African state had long interested France and Britain as a market

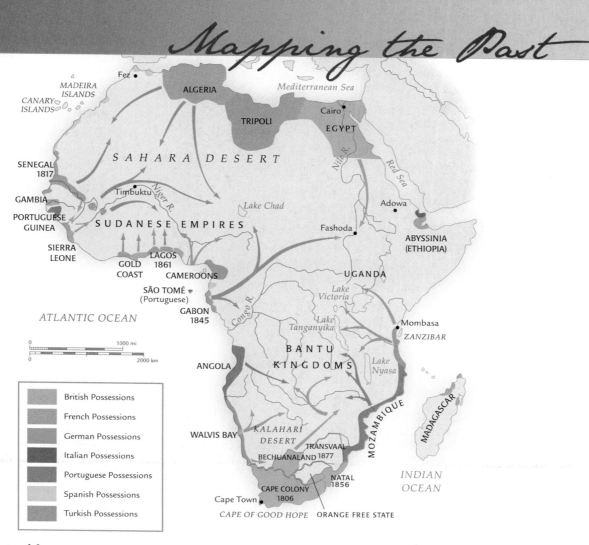

Imperialism in Africa, ca. 1885

Comparing this map, which shows European holdings in Africa in 1885, with the map on page 476, which shows European holdings in 1914, reveals the results of the Europeans' grab for African lands. Notice the dates of acquisition by the European powers. What do these dates reveal about the timing of the scramble for African lands?

for European goods and investments and as a bridge to Asia. European bankers financed the construction of port facilities, railroads, and telegraph lines in Egypt, granting high-interest loans to Egypt's government. In 1869 the Suez Canal, built by a French company, opened and became the vital link from the Mediterranean Sea through Egypt to the Red Sea and the Indian Ocean. The British desired control over the canal so as to secure their lucrative position in India. In 1875, Great Britain took advantage of the Egyptian government's financial distress and purchased the Egyptian ruler's, or khedive's, controlling portion of the canal stock. Four years later, France and Britain seized Egypt's treasury to secure their investments. When nationalist groups in Egypt revolted, British troops occupied Egypt. Formally, the khedive remained

in office, but after 1882, Britain held most of the real power. By then, 3,000 ships a year passed through the Suez Canal.

The British reshaped Egypt's economy so that it produced cotton, silk, and wheat for export in return for manufactured goods. They also disrupted local work life by hiring Egyptian laborers for their own projects—whether as railroad builders or servants. Worse, they insulted unfavored groups—such as Muslims and Arabs—by paying them less than favored groups.

The French reluctantly acquiesced to British control in Egypt in return for Britain's support of French ambitions in northwestern Africa. In the following years, Britain expanded south to secure Egypt and east to maintain its position in India and China. For similar reasons, France

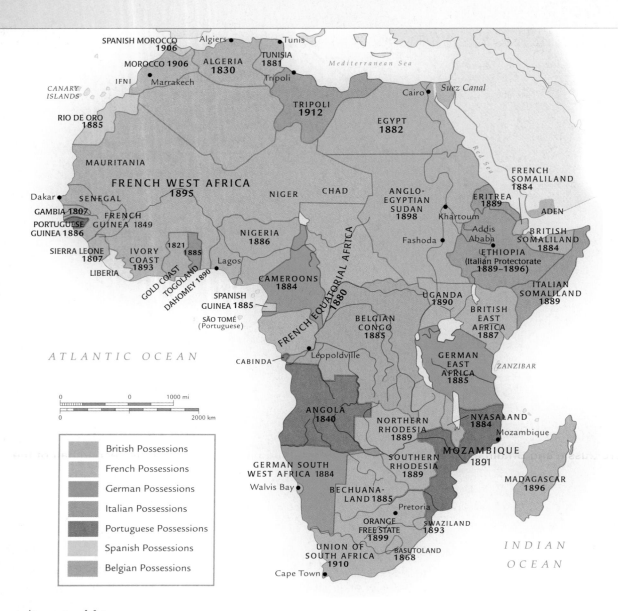

Imperialism in Africa, 1914

expanded from its stake in Algeria to Tunisia, Morocco, and most of northwestern Africa.

At the same time, King Leopold II of Belgium (r. 1865–1909), set out to get "a slice of this magnificent African cake." Hungry for ivory, rubber, hardwoods, palm oil, and glory, he initiated a new competition for acquisitions in sub-Saharan Africa by devouring the Congo. He had claimed that his purpose was "to open to civilization" central Africa, "to pierce the darkness which envelopes whole populations." In fact, his troops killed and mutilated thousands of local peoples in the process of conquest. An American missionary described the brutality with which Leopold's officials forced people into the forest to collect rubber: "The soldiers drive the people into the bush. If they will not go they are shot down, and their left hands cut off and taken as trophies."

Worried about missing out on the land grab, the other European powers voiced their own claims. The French centered their efforts in western Africa, the Germans in eastern Africa, and the British up and down the center, "from Cairo to Capetown." The Berlin Conference of 1885 formalized this scramble for Africa, setting ground rules for territorial acquisition on that continent.

Sub-Saharan Africa

By 1914, most of the huge continent had been carved up by the various European powers (see the map above). The main exception was Ethiopia. There, Emperor Menelik II (r. 1889–1913) cleverly played one European power off another. In the process, he manipulated the Europeans into supplying his country with modern arms, which he then used to defeat the invading Italians in 1896.

The Middle East and Central Asia, 1850–1914

This map shows the Middle East and parts of Central Asia where Russia and Britain expanded their areas of control and influence during the second half of the nineteenth century.

For the Europeans, the costliest struggles occurred among themselves. The imperial powers averted most conflicts by diplomacy. In South Africa, however, even the most skilled diplomacy failed to keep the peace. British settlers began to move into the South African Cape Colony early in the nineteenth century. The Dutch Boers (Afrikaners), who had settled there in the seventeenth century and resented Britain's abolition of slavery, trekked northward far into the interior, slaughtering the resisting Zulus in their way. Eventually, the British recognized the independence of the two Boer states, Transvaal and the Orange Free State.

However, when rich gold mines were discovered in Transvaal in the 1880s, British immigrants flooded in. The British entrepreneur and empire builder Cecil Rhodes (1853–1902), backed by powerful interest groups concerned about the growing German presence in southwestern Africa, decided to brush aside the two little Boer republics. But what the British thought would be an easy victory took three years (1899–1902) of military effort and involved severe casualties and enormous costs. Backed by 300,000 troops from India and the homeland, Britain finally won the brutal contest and in the end treated the defeated Boers leniently. The British took them into partnership in the Union of South Africa, and the Boer hero General Louis Botha (1862–

Boer War

1919) was elected the Union's first prime minister. Botha's government announced that it would "permit no equality between colored people and the white inhabitants," a policy that South Africa would hold on to for the next eighty years.

Europeans usually ruled directly over African societies so they could create the economic conditions they wanted. Colonial administrators trained cooperative tribes as their clerks, soldiers, and favored workers. These preferences often sparked bitter tribal jealousies and rivalries. Throughout Africa, Europeans made it clear by their words and actions that they considered themselves, their civilization, and their "race" superior to the Africans. Their dominance established, Europeans prided themselves on bringing Christianity and civilization to the "dark" continent. They had scant appreciation for the qualities of African societies and dismissed the Africans as inferior peoples useful only for manual labor. Often they treated them little better than slaves. They also established new political boundaries that ignored the long-standing social, cultural, and political realities of local peoples. Some officials even worked to "submerge" Africans from different societies "into a single colored working class," a policy that prevented Africans from maintaining kinship and community ties. Those Africans who resisted might be decimated in armed battle or

Dominance, conflict, and consequences

Then & Now
Drug Trafficking

Between 1839 and 1842, the British used war to force the Chinese to legalize the lucrative opium trade. Over the following decades, the British continued to import opium into China. Isabella Bird Bishop, a British traveler in China during the 1890s, reported that "opium houses are as common as gin shops in our London slums." In today's world, we are well aware of the many continuing problems associated with use and trade of addictive drugs. In Mexico, for example, a powerful drug cartel has existed for decades. In recent years, fighting between cartels has increased as they compete for control of the lucrative U.S. trafficking routes.

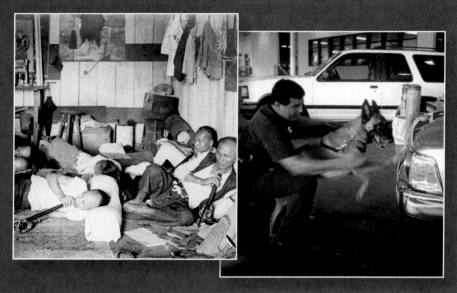

dispossessed and forced onto reservations. Yet resentment and desperation led many Africans to rebel against their conquerors, despite the hopelessness of their situation. A warrior in South Africa explained the reasons for one of these rebellions: "Our King gone, we had submitted to the white people and they ill-treated us until we became desperate and tried to make an end of it all. We knew that we had very little chance because their weapons were so much superior to ours. But we meant to fight to the last, feeling that even if we could not beat them we might at least kill a few of them and so have some sort of revenge."

Establishing Control in Asia

In Asia, Western powers usually got what they wanted by ruling through local elites. In these large, well-organized societies, where the potential for effective resistance remained great, Westerners' tampering with the established power structure was risky.

India was as linguistically and regionally diverse as Europe. Nevertheless, by the nineteenth century, the British had brought together a variety of states, territories, and

The Middle East and India

tribal groups to create an Indian state under British control. The Indian subcontinent became Britain's richest imperial prize. Nearly twenty times larger than Great Britain and more than seven times as populous, India bought and sold more goods than any other British colony. Britain directed much of its imperial

policy toward preserving this lucrative colony. Part of the reason Britain annexed new colonies in Africa and widened its sphere of influence in the Middle East was to protect India from other European states. One of these was Russia, which was expanding its control in areas near India (see map on page 477). Competition for power and influence in these lands brought Russia and Britain to the brink of war in 1881 and again in 1884–1887.

Until 1858, the British East India Company, a private-stock company, governed much of India. However, the great Sepoy Mutiny of 1857, the first large-scale uprising of Indians against British rule, almost drove the British out of India. This prompted the British government to take direct control. Instead of meddling with the structure of Indian society, the British used India's elites to support their rule. They employed a half-million Indians to administer the huge country and built railroads, canals, ports, schools, and medical facilities. In one sense, India benefited in that population increased rapidly. On the other hand, living standards for most fell as population increases outstripped economic growth. The British paid low wages and labeled Indians as inferior—at best, in the words of the British historian and politician Thomas Macaulay, "a great people sunk in the lowest depth of slavery and superstition." Through use of tariffs, they forced India to collapse its own cotton industry and accept British imports of cotton cloth instead. They restructured India's economy to specialize in products the British wanted, such as jute, raw cotton, opium, tea, and wheat. As one Indian nationalist explained, "*Pax Britannica* [Britain's peace] has been established in this country in order that a foreign government may exploit the country."

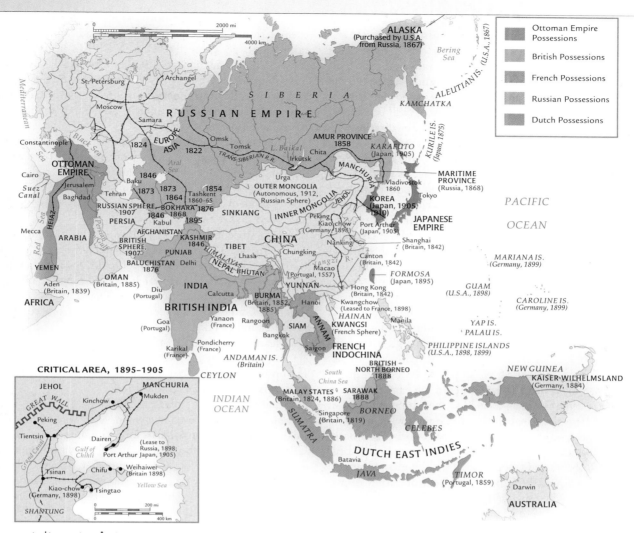

CRITICAL AREA, 1895–1905

Imperialism in Asia, 1840–1914 This map shows the expansion of imperialism in Asia by the Western powers and Japan.

Britain permanently altered this ancient civilization by creating a national unity, whether the Indians desired it or not. Moreover, British men and women in India imported their own cultural standards, lived separately from the "inferior" native societies, and expected the Indians they dealt with—from elites to servants—to adjust to British ways. For example, in her book *The Complete Indian Housekeeper and Cook* (1898), British author Flora Annie Steel boasted that "to show what absolute children Indian servants are," she has "for years adopted castor oil as an ultimatum," adding that this is "considered a great joke, and exposes the offender to much ridicule from his fellow-servants."

The British showed no inclination to grant India self-government. As a result, nationalism—already a potent force in Europe—rose in Asia. Indian dissatisfaction with British rule mounted steadily. In 1885, the nationalist Indian elite formed the Indian National Congress, which would launch a long struggle for Indian independence.

France followed the same pattern as Britain in its southeast Asia colonies. By the 1860s, open resistance to the intruding French had become hopeless. As one of Vietnam's leading statesmen explained in 1867, "The French have come, with their powerful weapons of war . . . no one can resist them. They go where they want, the strongest ramparts fall before them." During the 1880s and early 1890s, France took what would become Vietnam, Cambodia, and Laos and grouped them into the Union of Indochina under French control. As in India, medicine, sanitation, canals, roads, and other projects financed by the French led to population growth in Indochina. French rule also spawned economic dependence and resentment against the European assumption of superiority. A southeast Asian elite arose that, as in India, would struggle to expel Western rule.

Southeast Asia

China, with its highly structured society, strong central government, and large armed forces, had long kept

Westerners at arm's length. Although the Chinese admitted some European traders and Christian missionaries in the sixteenth and seventeenth centuries, they closed their doors rather tightly thereafter. At the beginning of the eighteenth century, China ranked among the world's most prosperous and powerful societies. The Chinese still considered their huge, populous country the center of civilization surrounded by lesser civilizations. As late as 1793, China's emperor could easily dismiss a proposed trade agreement with Britain: "Our Celestial Empire possesses all things in abundance. We have no need of barbarian products."

China

However, during the nineteenth century, population explosion, famine, rebellions, and poor leadership under the declining Qing (Ch'ing) dynasty weakened the ancient civilization. The country became a power vacuum that proved all too tempting to the Western powers. Armed with their guns and goods, Westerners streamed into China.

First, the British forced themselves on the Chinese. During the 1830s, Britain began trading Indian opium in China for tea, silver, silk, and other products. Soon opium became one of Britain's most important commodities. Chinese officials tried to stop the economic drain, addiction, and criminal activities stemming from the opium trade by making the drug illegal. As the Chinese official in charge exclaimed to the British, "You do not wish opium to harm your own country, but you choose to bring that harm to other countries such as China. Why?" In response, Britain sent gunboats and troops armed with modern weapons. They easily defeated the Chinese in a series of clashes known as the Opium Wars. By the terms of the Treaty of Nanking (1842), which ended the conflict, the Chinese ceded Hong Kong to the British, opened several tariff-free ports to foreign trade, exempted foreigners from Chinese law, and paid Britain a large indemnity.

Opium Wars

At mid-century, disaster struck. China suffered a devastating civil war—the Taiping Rebellion (1850–1864). Subsequent rebellions extended the internal conflict another ten years. In the end, these wars took perhaps fifty million lives, and the famines that followed cost the lives of millions more. All this strife weakened the Qing dynasty and revealed the government's inability to control a nation threatened by external enemies and internal upheaval.

Taiping Rebellion

In the years that followed, China fought a series of wars against foreigners. It lost them all, and each defeat chipped away at its sovereignty and racked up yet more indemnities. The Western powers grabbed up spheres of influence and

semi-independent treaty ports where all foreigners were exempt from Chinese jurisdiction. In addition, they built railroads to penetrate farther into China's heartland. As shown on the map on page 479, they also took lands on the huge country's periphery. By all these means, the French and British added to their possessions in south Asia, Russia gained territory in the north, and Japan snapped up Korea and Taiwan in the east.

The United States joined in the frenzy, grabbing the Philippine Islands after a war with Spain in 1898 and a long struggle against Filipino nationalist forces that cost the lives of perhaps 200,000 Filipinos. President William McKinley explained that the United States had the duty "to educate the Filipinos and uplift and Christianize them." To protect its commercial interests in Asia, the United States called for an "Open Door" policy that would avoid further territorial annexations by the imperial powers. Rivalry among the great powers themselves, as much as Chinese resistance, saved China from complete loss of its independence.

The Philippines

Meanwhile, Chinese nationalism rose in response to foreign aggression. In 1899–1900, the Boxer Rebellion, a serious uprising against Western influences, erupted. Furious at those who had betrayed Chinese religion and customs, the Boxers, a secret organization that believed in the spiritual power of the martial arts, killed thousands of Chinese Christians and a number of foreigners—all with the encouragement of China's dowager empress. Combined forces from the imperial powers brutally suppressed this nationalist movement and forced China to pay large indemnities (see image below).

Boxer Rebellion

JOHN CLYMER, *THE BOXER REBELLION,* 1900 This dramatic painting shows U.S. marines firing on the Boxers, who in 1899 staged a rebellion against foreign influence in China.

Even propped up by imperial powers, the corrupt Chinese central government could not last. In 1911, reformers led by Sun Yat-sen (1866–1925), a Western-educated doctor, launched a revolution aimed at freeing China from foreign exploitation and modernizing its society. Rebellions swept most of China and pushed the corrupt, inept, disintegrating dynasty to its final collapse. Sun proclaimed a republic, but power soon dispersed among imperial generals, who became warlords. China's struggles to cope with the encroaching world and its internal problems were far from over.

Japan, even more than China, had long refused direct contact with the West. At the beginning of the nineteenth century, the island nation remained in great part a feudal society ruled by the shogun—a strong military governor—and his military chieftains. The Japanese emperor had only limited powers. Though long influenced by Chinese culture, Japan also had a sharply defined sense of identity: "[O]ur country is the source and fountainhead of all other countries, and in all matters it excels all the others," explained one Japanese writer.

Japan

In 1853, however, the Japanese witnessed an imposing sight: a squadron of well-armed, steam-powered American ships under Admiral Matthew Perry (1794–1858) sailing uninvited into Edo (Tokyo) Bay. Perry's instructions from the American government stressed the United States' desire to "establish commercial intercourse with a country whose large population and reputed wealth hold out great temptations to mercantile enterprise." If friendly negotiations should fail, the instructions continued, Perry should "change his tone" and threaten force. Perry took the charge to heart: "The World has assigned this duty to us," he asserted.

Japan's efforts to resist Perry's encroachment proved futile. Soon the well-armed Western ships intimidated the Tokugawa government into signing unequal treaties with the United States. Japan also inked agreements with Britain, Russia, France, and the Netherlands that opened the country to trade and foreign presences.

Fifteen years after Perry's arrival, the 250-year-old Tokugawa shogunate collapsed in a revolution led by powerful aristocrats who ushered into power the boy emperor Meiji (Enlightened Rule). Weakened by decades of population growth, declining agricultural productivity, popular revolts, and failed efforts at reform, the shogunate gave way. According to Count Ito, a leader of the **Meiji Restoration,** members of the new government "set themselves to the task of introducing Western civilization into Japan." These leaders quickly dismantled the country's traditional military and social order. Using French, German, British, and American ways, they created a new conscript army, introduced universal education, established a written constitution, and began industrializing the economy. In 1889, Ito declared success: "If we . . . compare the present state of affairs with that which existed some twenty years ago, we shall not exaggerate if we say that the country has undergone a complete metamorphosis." Within a few decades, Japan had transformed itself on its own terms. Once a feudal society with a preindustrial economy, it was now a modern industrialized nation.

The Meiji Restoration

The industrialized nation soon began flexing its new muscle in Asia. Japan viewed China no longer as a source of culture to be respected but as a weakened land open to conquest and exploitation. In 1894, the Japanese invaded China, forcing it to pay a large indemnity and give up Korea and Taiwan. In 1904, after Russia angered Japan by increasing its presence in China's northern province of Manchuria, the Japanese attacked the tsar's troops. To the world's surprise, Japan defeated the inept Russian forces both on land and at sea and became the dominant power in Manchuria. Industrialized, militaristic, and imperialistic, Japan had taken its place alongside other world powers by 1914.

Russo-Japanese War

→ connect to today ←

Colonial Expansion

Between 1870 and 1914, Western powers expanded their power into many parts of the globe, and the political, economic, and cultural consequences of this imperial expansion were great for both Western and non-Western peoples. What legacies and consequences of imperialism might still be influencing world affairs today?

The Legacy of Imperialism

With its technology, its industrial capitalism, and above all its aggressive nationalism, the West had subjected most of Africa and Asia to its domination between 1870 and 1914. In Australia and New Zealand, European powers had already established large settler colonies. As in North America, contact and clashes with the incoming settlers proved disastrous for the indigenous populations. In the Pacific, the pattern of imperial conquest that the West had established in Africa and Asia held true. Western adventurers, missionaries, traders, gunboats, troops, and businesses came, took over, and destroyed the world that native peoples had long known. Worse, the Westerners carried diseases that decimated Pacific populations.

Certainly, life in non-Western lands had not been idyllic before the intrusion of the West. As one Ndebele warrior in South Africa put it, "Even in our own time there were troubles, there was much fighting and many innocent people were killed." Many from the West in these lands may have been well meaning, and they may have brought elements of Western civilization that were of some benefit to people in the non-Western world. In 1900 Lord Curzon, the celebrated British viceroy of India, wrote about the consequences of British rule over India: "I do not see how any Englishmen, contrasting India as it now is with what it was . . . can fail to see that we came and have stayed . . . in obedience to . . . the decree of Providence, . . . for the lasting benefit of millions of the human race." In India, British rule probably prevented internal wars and promoted order. In Africa, Europeans did abolish slavery. Imperial powers built ports, railway lines, hospitals, schools, and sanitation facilities. Colonized peoples also learned about Western politics, economics, and education, eventually making use of them to assert their own liberation from imperial powers.

Yet, rather than striving to understand and appreciate non-Western societies, most people in the West viewed them from a condescending, arrogant, or downright racist perspective. The colonized peoples had to endure being treated as menials and subordinates by men and women whose only necessary qualification was being Western. The insults to local peoples' self-respect and their relentless humiliation fueled resistance to Western control.

Western powers not only forcibly drew non-Western lands into a world economy but also exploited the natural and human resources of the conquered lands and profoundly undermined the cultural, social, and religious traditions of the African and Asian peoples. In addition, they distorted non-Western economies to serve the demands of their own commerce. They imposed what one observer called "the European system of monotonous, uninterrupted labour," in which industries such as mining and railroad building subjected native laborers to inhumane and dangerous working conditions. Forced to migrate to find jobs in the alien economy, local workers left behind shattered families and communities. Political structures that had long functioned effectively in these lands broke down in just a few years.

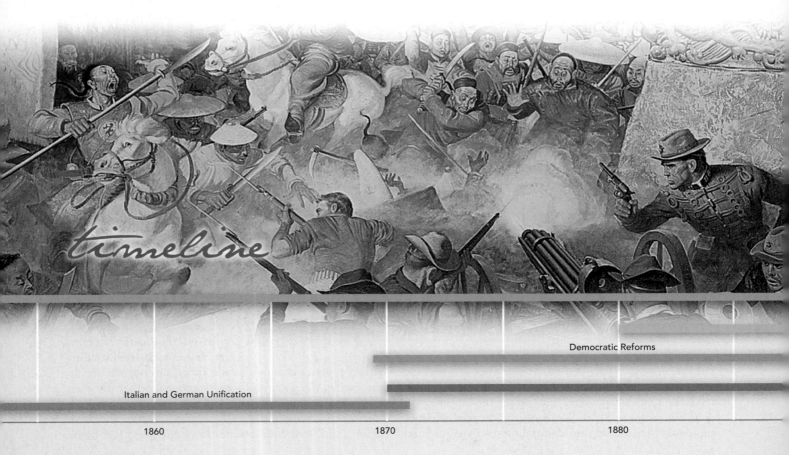

timeline

Democratic Reforms

Italian and German Unification

1860   1870   1880

By 1914, tens of thousands of colonial administrators, soldiers, and settlers relied directly on imperialism for their careers, status, and livelihood. They, along with Western tourists, enjoyed a sense of privilege and superiority over Africans and Asians. Many also enjoyed, though less often discussed, sexual contact with their colonized peoples. Indeed, most Westerners had come to view imperialism as normal and harmless. In their home countries, some people in the West visited the proliferating zoos with "exotic" animals, studied anthropology, viewed new works of art, and read literature that reflected interaction with non-Western lands. But few Westerners recognized how destructive it could be—not only to colonial peoples but also to themselves. In Asia, for example, Russia's expansion south brought it to the borders of British India and nearly ignited a war with that nation. Farther east, Russia pushed to the Sea of Japan and Manchuria; the action sparked hostilities with Japan. More than once, Britain, France, and Germany narrowly avoided war in Africa. Imperialism extended the already intense economic and political competition among the European states, heightening the potential for major conflict among these powers.

SUMMARY

In the years 1870–1914, Europe grew more powerful, democratic, nationalistic, and imperialistic.

- More and more Westerners gained access to the political process. Nationalism opened these doors for them, as did the movement toward democracy. Many political leaders recognized nationalism and democracy as forces that they could use to their advantage. Others simply adjusted to them. Those who resisted did so at their own peril.

- New groups emerged to challenge the established center of liberal and conservative politics. To the political left of liberals stood the unions, socialists, and anarchists. To the political right of conservatives were anti-Semites and ultranationalists. Still without the vote were women, who increasingly demanded a voice in national politics.

- Europeans were moving, not only to their own cities but out of Europe by the millions.

- Industrialization and the promise of wealth in new places combined with nationalism and mass politics to push the imperial West throughout the world as never before. As a result, Western power—economic, political, military, and imperial—expanded in an environment of intense international competition.

In the years just before 1914, the strain of this competition on Western societies grew obvious. Labor unrest, the movement for women's suffrage, politics of the extremes, civil violence, diplomatic crises, military threats, and a growing sense of uncertainty all pointed to trouble in the making. Yet this was a complex era. During the same period, the civilization that produced such uncertainty also created new engines of wealth, transformed its cities, and supported an explosion of creative thought and culture.

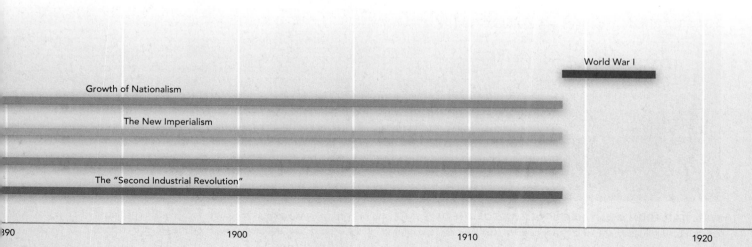

Growth of Nationalism

The New Imperialism

The "Second Industrial Revolution"

World War I

1890　　　　1900　　　　1910　　　　1920

WILLIAM P. FRITH, *MANY HAPPY RETURNS OF THE DAY,* 1856 In this painting, a family gathers for a birthday. The rich clothing, carpeting, paintings on the wall, heavy curtains, solid bricks showing through the window, and attentive servant on the left all mark this as an urban middle-class home.

Modern Life
and the Culture of
Progress

Western Society, 1850–1914

21

Urban Sprawl

In 1864, an observer described Milan in northern Italy as vibrant "without being feverish like Paris or London." Though Milan had become one of the great cultural centers in the newly unified Italian state, workers still lived along narrow, winding streets in the heart of this city. Everyone knew each other and spoke the local Milanese dialect. Citizens "huddled around the cathedral, like a family warming itself at the hearth." ▶▶

This quaint image would not last long. Over the next thirty years, wide avenues and expensive "great white houses, all straight," replaced Milan's narrow streets and old dwellings. Each year thousands of immigrants—mostly peasants and artisans—streamed into the city looking for jobs and all kinds of other opportunities. In just one decade, the city's population grew by almost a third. By the 1890s, the center of Milan teemed with people from the city's outlying quarters and suburbs who traveled there to work, shop, or amuse themselves. They spoke the common Italian language and shoved "on and off the trams . . . day and night." More people purchased goods in the huge new department store near the cathedral than prayed in that Gothic church. Nearby, in the newly built Gallery, musicians, singers, businesspeople, shoppers, and diners congregated in the shops and cafés under a magnificent glass roof. Milan—like Paris, London, and other great cities in the West—had become a center of industry, growth, and culture—a thriving embodiment of modern life.

In the decades after 1850, industrialization pulled masses of Westerners to new jobs in cities like Milan. Urban growth began to overwhelm the West's centuries-old land-based society. In cities, the continuing spread of liberal ideas and the optimism of wealthy urban leaders created a culture of progress. Dominated by science, which seemed to promise so much, and by competitive values that served the up-and-coming middle class so well, this urban culture altered the ways people thought about the world and their place in it. Those who recognized these engines of change saw their civilization being pushed to modernity. In 1850, however, few understood what modernity meant or even how difficult the ride there could be. ◄◄

THE SECOND INDUSTRIAL REVOLUTION

"Steam and electricity have conquered time and space to a greater extent during the last sixty years than all the preceding six hundred years," gushed a special issue of *The Illustrated London News* in 1897. Yet in 1850, most people knew little about the industrial revolution. Outside Britain and a few limited areas in the West, more people still lived in the countryside than in the cities, and more worked at home or in home workshops than in factories. Most had never set foot in a railway car. Even in the cities, people probably made their living much as their parents had—as helpers in shops, domestics, artisans, merchants, and day laborers.

By 1914, this scenario had changed so drastically that even Britain had been left behind. Between 1850 and 1870, the coal mines, iron foundries, textile factories, steam engines, and railroads that had made Britain an industrial giant spread broadly into western and central Europe and North America. After 1870, new inventions, manufacturing processes, and methods for getting products to market and selling them rendered the earlier milestones of industrialization out-of-date. Science, technology, and industry marched hand in hand. Large-scale factories dwarfed the textile mills and iron foundries of the early industrial era, and huge department stores displayed endless goods to entice consumers. For the first time in history, people began to expect continuing economic growth. According to some historians, these developments created a "second industrial revolution."

Steel Leads the Way

Steel led the way in this new wave of industrialization. The Bessemer processes for removing impurities from molten iron speeded up and cheapened steel production, transforming it from an expensive luxury product into a strong, affordable improvement over iron. The image here, an 1880 photograph of the Krupp Steelworks, reveals the new technology and massive factories that produced steel and enabled countries such as Germany to become industrial leaders. Out of this steel, manufacturers made efficient tools and machines to fabricate metal, textile, leather, and wood products.

THE KRUPP STEELWORKS, 1880 This photograph of a German steel factory shows the powerful new machines that helped make Germany an industrial leader. On the left are the huge converters that turned iron into steel.

With advances in chemistry, textile manufacturers could now use inexpensive synthetic dyes to color their cloth, and paper manufacturers could process wood pulp more efficiently than ever. By 1914, new chemical-based fabrics and processes had spawned a host of infant industries. Germany's chemical laboratories and their development of industrial uses for chemicals helped propel that nation ahead of Great Britain as an industrial leader.

Chemicals

Electricity and petroleum became practical sources of power, thanks to the invention of the electrical dynamo, the steam turbine, and the internal combustion engine. By the end of the century, electric lamps glowed in city streets, large stores, and wealthy neighborhoods throughout Europe. Electricity powered factories and workshops and was the magic behind the refrigerators and vacuum cleaners that would start to appear in middle-class homes.

Electricity and petroleum

New Transportation and Communication Networks

Getting around, moving things, and communicating became dramatically easier as well. Before 1850, few people had seen more of the world than they could view on foot or by cart or horseback. By 1914, millions traveled enormous distances each year. Even in China, Turkey, and Brazil, trains chugged along, hauling people for astonishing stretches. This was the greatest era of railroad building in history, and with the railroads came hundreds of bridges and long tunnels. At the same time, huge steamships with steel hulls, turbine engines, and screw propellers replaced sailing ships. The opening of the Suez Canal (between the Mediterranean Sea and the Indian Ocean) in 1869 and the Panama Canal (between the Atlantic and Pacific Oceans) in 1914 cut thousands of miles off long sea voyages and brought the Western and non-Western worlds into closer contact.

Railroad building

However, the future lay with yet another revolutionary invention: the internal combustion engine. In 1887 the German inventor Gottlieb Daimler (1834–1900) attached his little combustion engine to a wagon—and the automobile was born. Two decades later in the United States, former bicycle mechanic Henry Ford (1863–1947) introduced the assembly line to the automobile industry. By 1914, cars, taxis, and trucks jammed city streets in Europe and America and created new demand for oil, rubber, and concrete.

Internal combustion engine

Just as these new means of transportation linked millions of people physically, the telegraph and telephone connected them in a giant communication network. In 1844, Samuel Morse sent a message by wire 40 miles from Baltimore to Washington. In 1866, ships laid telegraph cable across the Atlantic, enabling news to travel from London to New York as quickly as it had moved from one side of London to the other. Ten years later, Alexander Graham Bell (1847–1922), an American born in Scotland, invented the telephone.

Telegraph and telephone

The Birth of Big Business

These telephone companies, railroads, shipping lines, steel mills, chemical plants, and new factories became too large for all but a very few individuals to finance. Capitalists now raised money by organizing corporations and selling shares of stock—partial ownership—to investors. Governments helped out by passing laws that limited stockholders' risk to only the money they invested. Luck helped, too, for the discovery of gold in California and Australia in the 1850s and 1860s, and in Alaska and South Africa later in the century, increased the supply of money. This was big business, and it was controlled by large banks and wealthy executives. These executives functioned much as heads of state, conferring with boards of directors and lesser executives. Under them were layers of managers who specialized in areas such as sales, finance, and production and who hired, fired, and supervised employees.

In this new world of business, the big and strong often destroyed the small and weak. Corporations combined into gigantic, monopolistic trusts (called "cartels" in Germany) that commanded markets, prices, and wages. Rockefeller's Standard Oil trust in the United States and the I. G. Farben chemical cartel in Germany are examples of the spectacular business successes of the age. By 1914, big business controlled a large share of industrial production in the West. In Japan, too, which adapted quickly to Western industrialization, five giant corporations dominated three-quarters of that nation's industry.

Monopolies

The Lure of Shopping

With all the new technology, manufacturers habitually churned out more products than they could sell. So, merchants found new ways to create customer demand. Grandiose department stores, such as the Bon Marché in Paris and Bocconi's in Milan, rose up in major cities across the West. The stores displayed a dazzling array of enticing goods—ready-made clothes, furniture, rugs, umbrellas, stationery, toilet paper—a cornucopia of foreign and domestic

Department stores

temptations. Prices were fixed and aimed at the middle classes, but even members of the working class might afford some items. Posters announced "sales" to draw more people to their stores' massive glass and iron emporiums. Glossy catalogues mailed to potential customers in other cities and the countryside encouraged people to order the practical goods and the luxuries of modern urban life for delivery by the new national postal services.

Winners and Losers in the Race for Wealth

In this intense economic struggle, some people flourished, others fell behind, and many worried about their future. Cycles of prosperity and recession made economic life precarious. New economic powers such as Germany and the United States rose to challenge and sometimes surpass mighty Great Britain, which failed to invest sufficiently in new processes and marketing techniques. Industrialization spread unevenly east to Russia—St. Petersburg alone would sprout more than nine hundred factories by 1914. Areas in southern and eastern Europe that held on to old ways of making a living fell further behind, although even in these poorer regions industrialization gained some footholds. Overseas, Australia and Canada began to industrialize, and Japan—with its new machines, factories, and railroads—became a major industrial power.

| Western and non-Western worlds |

However, most of Latin America, Africa, and mainland Asia scarcely entered the industrial race before 1914. Although Latin American nations boasted some railway lines and substantial foreign trade, they lacked the machinery and manufacturing that marked industrial economies. A similar pattern held in mainland Asia and most of Africa, which produced cash crops and raw materials to trade to the industrialized West for manufactured goods but were unable to develop industrial economies.

Did this second industrial revolution make life better overall for Westerners? As we saw with our discussion of the first industrial revolution in Chapter 17, this question is difficult to answer. Statistically, the answer is yes. It certainly paid to be living in the industrializing nations of the West. In these thriving regions, most people benefited from the new wealth—even those living outside the cities. Food prices came down, and larger farms, chem-

| New wealth |

ical fertilizers, and threshing machines boosted harvests and lowered costs. Agricultural producers in North America, Argentina, and Australia sent inexpensive grains and meat in new, refrigerated ships. Prices for manufactured products also dropped as the new machines and processes made production more efficient. With declining prices came a rise in real wages for workers, which almost doubled in Britain between 1850 and 1914. Meat, dairy products, sugar, tea, and coffee were no longer luxuries. People snapped up previously out-of-reach manufactured goods. With care and luck, they even saved a bit of money for hard times.

Those hard times visited some more than others, and here the old pattern held true. The middle classes benefited more than the working classes, skilled workers more than unskilled, and owners of large farms more than agricultural laborers. Nor did the new wealth end

| Hard times |

misery for those at the bottom of the socioeconomic ladder. Many people remained mired in poverty. Among workers, few could expect to retire without sinking into dependence or impoverishment, let alone ease into the dream of a comfortable cottage with a small garden. The gaps between rich and poor were all too apparent. The upper 20 percent of the population generally received more of a nation's income than the remaining 80 percent. Every day the urban poor could see but not afford the fine apartments, carriages, and clothes of the wealthy.

OPINION

Why do you think industrialization so quickly doomed traditional society in the West?

THE NEW URBAN LANDSCAPE

City life became the new norm for masses of people in the West. Many rural villages declined or died, slowly in some areas, quickly in others. People from outside the local community moved in, bought the land, and hired migrant laborers to work it. Residents flocked to the cities, and those who had established themselves there stayed. An observer in 1899 reflected the experience of millions: "[T]he most remarkable social phenomenon of the present century is the concentration of population in cities." Europe's population ballooned from 270 million in 1850 to 450 million in 1914, and well over half of western Europeans lived in cities. In Britain, only 8 percent of the workforce remained in the countryside. London, Europe's greatest urban center, grew from 2.5 million in 1850 to more than 4.5 million in 1914.

Rebuilding Cities

As these numbers multiplied everywhere, even the physical foundations of cities changed. Urban centers grew out, up, and belowground. Milan, the thriving Italian center described at the beginning of this chapter, was not the only city to rebuild. Governments, entrepreneurs, and speculators tore apart centuries-old housing and winding streets in Paris, Vienna, Brussels, Stockholm, Barcelona, Cologne, and Mexico City. In place of these older features, they constructed broad, tree-lined avenues, parks, fashionable apartment houses, department stores, fancy cafés, government buildings, museums, hospitals, opera houses, schools, and libraries. New neighborhoods, open spaces, transportation systems, and underground water and sewer systems transformed the face and substance of city life.

Paris led the way in this wave of reconstruction. In the French capital, Emperor Napoleon III and his technocratic administrator, Baron Haussmann, initiated the most ambitious plans for demolishing some of the oldest and poorest neighborhoods. According to Napoleon, Haussmann, and their advisors, these reconstruction efforts offered several important benefits. Doctors and reformers argued that filth from overcrowding caused the diseases that often swept through Paris. Wide streets and open spaces, they explained, would let in much-needed fresh air. But those wide streets also gave governments a political advantage: They deterred people from again throwing up revolutionary barricades to fight the forces of order, as they had in 1848, and afforded troops ready access to working-class areas. Finally, reconstruction projects generated untold wealth for investors, speculators, influence brokers, schemers, architects, engineers, and workers from all over France.

As in Milan, the new construction drove the poor out of the center of Paris to the east end or into working-class suburbs. Wealthier Parisians felt little sympathy. After all, they reasoned, the capital city represented the nation in the eyes of citizens and visitors alike. As Haussmann explained, "The splendor of this city reflects on the whole country." The power, wealth, beauty, and modernity of Paris must not be marred by images of poverty and misfortune.

Sewers and Subways

Below Europe's city streets, less glamorous but no less important projects hummed along. In 1850, most houses in Europe's major cities did not have running water. Sewage in cities such as Berlin still ran in open gutters, creating an atmosphere of filth and tremendous stench. During the following decades, these standards began to change. First in London and then elsewhere, engineers and workers built water and sewer systems. Doctors, reformers, and planners led the drive to bring in freshwater in aqueducts or pipes from sources upstream and to create hundreds of miles of underground sewers to carry waste downstream. These measures made urban life healthier and more comfortable than before.

More than water and waste moved below the city, however. In 1863, London's underground railway opened. Over the next fifty years, Paris and New York built subways of their own. Along with carriages, trams, and railroads, the efficient, predictable subways enabled people to shop and work in places farther from home than ever. People moved their residences out of crowded urban centers to city fringes and suburbs—whether upscale neighborhoods for the middle class or less expensive areas for workers.

CITY PEOPLE

Who were these people filling the cities of the West? How did they make their way in life, so far away from the land and surrounded by industrial advances and new wealth? Part of the answer is revealed in the image shown on page 490, a mid-century engraving of a typical Parisian apartment house. At this time, the city's various social classes still lived in close proximity but in different conditions.

On Top of It All: The Urban Elite

At the top of the urban social order was a small, elite class of wealthy aristocrats and the richest of the bourgeoisie—the millionaire factory owners, merchants, and bankers. Amounting to less than 1 percent of the population, these people socialized together, turned to each other for help, and intermarried. Through strategic matchmaking, new wealth from the daughter or son of an American captain of industry or banker might enable an aristocratic family to maintain its position. More often, however, aristocrats kept their positions by making shrewd investments, serving governments, holding on to top spots in the military and diplomatic corps, and wisely managing their lands and businesses. They, along with members entering their ranks, had prestige but not the formal privileges that their eighteenth-century predecessors had enjoyed.

Those who had been born into aristocratic families clung to what was left of the old lifestyle. Those aspiring to the aristocratic life used their money to copy that lifestyle. These newly rich bought estate houses in the country and opulent townhouses along the best avenues and parks, attended fancy balls, took hunting trips to Africa, and supported large staffs of servants. They also kept up with the latest fashions and made grand gestures toward cultural and philanthropic activities. However, a few rules of the aristocratic game had changed. Obvious arrogance was frowned upon, as this elite made an effort to comply with middle-class morality. At the very least, they strove to appear responsible, domestic, and religious. Of course, their children got the best of everything. In every way, these elites were truly the upper crust, on top and intent on staying there.

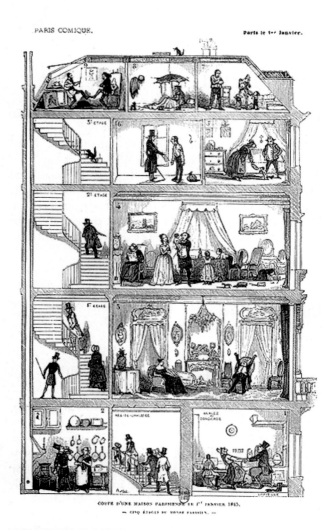

THE URBAN CLASSES, mid-nineteenth century In a typical Parisian apartment house, the wealthy bourgeoisie lived on the second floor in luxurious comfort; above them lived families of lesser means, with the lower classes and aspiring artists living on the bottom and upper floors in increasing poverty.

Pride and Success: The "Solid" Middle Class

Well below this upper crust, the "solid" bourgeoisie held the better jobs, lived in the finer apartments, dined at fashionable restaurants, and commanded at least one good servant. These were the families of small factory owners, merchants, managers, doctors, druggists, local bankers, lawyers, professors, and architects who earned and spent more money than most.

Worried about competitors from below, many middle-class men established "professional" associations designed to keep standards up and rivals down. Nor did they open their professions to women. Wives and daughters, they intoned, "best" not work for pay. Beliefs that women and men belonged in "separate spheres"—women at home, men in the public world of work—persisted. "Of all those acquirements, which more particularly belong to the feminine character," explained Isabella Mary Mayson Beeton in her best-selling advice book for women, "there are none which take a higher rank . . . than such as enter into a knowledge of household duties; for on these are perpetually dependent the happiness, comfort, and well-being of a family."

Women and work

Some women managed to swim against the current, however. They engaged in philanthropic activities—in support of the poor and uneducated, or against alcohol and prostitution. British philanthropist Angela Burdette-Coutts (1814–1906), for example, gave away a fortune to schools and housing for the poor. In France, many wealthy women followed the example of Empress Eugénie (consort of Napoleon III), who supported societies that provided assistance to new mothers. In the United States, educated middle-class women staffed hundreds of settlement houses in urban centers that helped immigrants adjust to the customs and language of their new country as well as middle-class values. Only a few women managed to carve out careers in business, teaching, writing, or painting. Exclusion from universities kept most ambitious upper-middle-class women from pursuing lucrative professions, though schools such as Queens College in Britain and the Female Medical College of Pennsylvania promised some professional opportunities to women.

If not arrogant, this bourgeoisie was proud. Who else better represented their civilization? As they saw it, success flowed from character, ability, and effort; in a world open to talent, rewards came from achievement. These people praised discipline, control, and respectability, while attacking public drunkenness, emotional outbursts, and—especially in **Victorian** Britain—open displays of sexual affection. In addition, they respected Christian morality and marital fidelity. Cleanliness went hand in

Values

hand with purity and modernity, as did running water for regular baths and several changes of clothes. Certainly, they argued, all good people should live up to these standards, at least in appearance.

Hardworking and Hopeful: The Lower Middle Class

Those just below the solid bourgeoisie probably tried as hard as any group to succeed in modern society. These lower-middle-class people performed skilled services as tellers in banks, sorters in mailrooms, and salespeople in department stores. Reading, writing, and mathematical skills (and for more and more, the new typewriter) enabled thousands to become schoolteachers, postal workers, and clerks in places from government agencies and insurance firms to accounting offices and train stations. Some of these lower-paying "white-collar jobs" became open to educated women, particularly if they were unmarried.

Lower-middle-class people made their living in settings that sometimes resembled factories. The image below shows a French telephone exchange. As shown here, even when jobs opened for middle-class women, they were often separate from men's work and of lower status. With the height-ening tempo of industrialization,

Social mobility these lower-middle-class occupations multiplied. People might move up the economic ladder, and better-off workers could hope to see their educated children rising into this class. In turn, a few children from lower-middle ranks might move into the also-expanding solid middle class. Although moving

FRENCH TELEPHONE EXCHANGE, late nineteenth century In this large telephone office all the employees are middle-class women, with the exception of male supervisors and a boy who delivers messages.

up remained more the exception than the rule, the possibilities were far greater than before 1850. By 1914, the middle classes overall had grown from between 3 and 10 percent of the population to more than 20 percent in much of the West.

The "Other Half": The Working Classes

Unlike the elites and the middle classes, the working classes lived on crowded side streets, the poorer east side of cities such as London or Paris, or the edge of town where land and rents were cheaper. Though better off than before 1850, they still faced the threat of job loss, which could send them into poverty in an instant (see images on page 492).

Even employed workers struggled to make ends meet. A new demand for certain skilled work helped some. Those who could read directions; could build or repair machines; or were printers, plumbers, or cabinetmakers earned respectable wages. They might also join unions and demand reforms. Other skilled workers lost out, for factory owners fit laborers to jobs that had become nothing more than mindless, repetitive tasks. Automaker Henry Ford expressed the views of many industrial managers toward this kind of labor: "I could not possibly do the same thing day in and day out, but . . . to the majority of minds, repetition holds no terrors. . . . The average worker, I am sorry to say, . . . wants a job in which he does not have to think." Whether former artisans with obsolete skills or migrants from the country-side, these workers earned paltry wages and worked at an exhausting pace. They and their children tended to remain low-paid industrial laborers for the rest of their lives.

Despite legislation restricting women from certain jobs, many labored outside and inside the home. Jeanne Bouvier, a Frenchwoman born in 1865, worked as millions of other working-class women did. When she was 11 years old, she took her first job in a silk factory near Lyons. Three years later, she moved to Paris, where she worked as a domestic and then in the hatmaking industry. Later, she worked a twelve-hour day as a seamstress and did piecework on her own.

In addition to their jobs in factories and small shops, many women took in work at home finishing clothes, polishing items for sale, wrapping chocolates, or decorating toys. Some of the new machines of industry even added to the demand for this older piecework. For example, Singer's sewing machine, invented in the 1850s, enabled entrepreneurs to hire women for low wages to work at home or in small "sweatshops." Such women proved especially appealing to these employers because they were easy to fire and posed little threat of forming a union or going on strike.

Still more women worked in traditional urban jobs. Domestic servants could count on meals and housing

Léon Frédéric, *The Stages of a Worker's Life*

1895–1897

Belgian artist Léon Frédéric (1856–1940), for a time Belgium's most famous painter, tried to encompass all stages of a worker's life in this large triptych. In the central panel, children, parents, and young couples dominate the foreground while in the background a funeral coach approaches. The left panel depicts the man's work world, where men of all ages engage in manual labor or observe it. The right panel shows the women's world, all mothering and nurturing. What impression of working-class life do you think the painter intended to convey to viewers?

revolt, commit crimes, or create disorder, and sympathy for the harshness of working-class life. Most middle-class people agreed with the popular writer Samuel Smiles that the working classes suffered from their own faults rather than injustices in the social system: "no laws . . . can make the idle industrious, the thriftless provident, or the drunken sober. Such reforms can only be effected by means of individual action, economy, and self-denial."

However, other members of the middle class—especially younger, college-educated people who were also connected to religious causes—joined organizations to ease the plight of the urban poor. With high optimism and idealism, they established clinics, settlement houses, and maternal-wellness societies. Thousands of middle- and upper-class women visited the poor; ran schools; and inspected asylums, workhouses, and prisons. One Spanish charity worker wrote a guide for visitors to the poor: "In viewing their faults, vices, and crimes, we must ask ourselves this question: Would the poor be what they are, if we were what we ought to be?" Some of these workers spread birth-control information; others touted the benefits of religion. Women's groups in particular distributed prayer books to the poor or sold Bibles to raise money to aid the needy—a reflection of the still-close link between the churches and

and perhaps even some savings from their salaries. On the other hand, they suffered from the whims of their employers and the threat of sexual abuse. Women in laundries labored at drudgery for low wages, although some of them enjoyed the sense of comradeship that came with the job at times. The growth of cities may have increased the work available to these women, but the machinery of the industrial revolution did not yet ease job conditions for them.

What to Do About "Them"

Members of the middle classes looked upon their working-class counterparts with a mixture of fear and sympathy: fear that these were dangerous people who might rise in

charitable work. Still others tried to help the poor through political activism, joining socialist organizations such as the Fabian Society in London, which decried the capitalist system as unjust and inefficient.

Building Character Through Athletics

For turn-of-the-century Europeans who had the time and money, city life could be fun. New forms of recreation and sports not only offered entertaining diversions but also built character values important for industry and war. Soccer, rugby, and cricket, once games only for schoolchildren, became extremely popular, competitive team sports for adults. In 1901, more than 100,000 attended a championship game of soccer in Britain. The emphasis on teamwork, competition, and discipline in the sports world reflected the qualities of industrial work and military service so prized during the era. Other new sports, such as bicycle and auto racing, stressed the speed and power of machines; by no coincidence, industrial firms sponsored some of these contests. Even the growth of scouting and, in Germany, the "wandering youth" clubs revealed the belief that good character required physical vigor and outdoor living. Accordingly, the modern Olympic games—stressing competition and nationalism—were established during this period, with the first games held in Athens in 1896.

Women's sports were less professional and less competitive than men's. Even scouting for girls was designed to instill homemaking values. But women did take to bicycles, despite warnings from the old guard that the loose clothing necessary for bicycling was unfeminine, that the activity would damage enthusiasts' ability to have children, and that women might inappropriately experience sexual pleasure from riding.

The New Tourist

Increasingly, people vacationed away from the cities. More and more, people left town. Those who had the means might imitate the eighteenth-century aristocratic habit of visiting the great cities, museums, and monuments of Europe. Others traveled to resorts on the Mediterranean coast, the Alps, or the shores of the Baltic Sea. By 1890, some 100,000 people visited the resort town of Vichy in central France to "take the waters" (cure their ills), relax, and socialize. Tourism became so popular that special books appeared, and professionally organized tours formed to guide people on their travels.

Workers usually lacked the time or money for such luxuries. Some managed short trips on trains that left cities every day for the coast, perhaps to Dieppe in France or Brighton in England, where piers and amusement parks beckoned. Most, however, stayed in the cities. There, some

went to café concerts to see singers, comedians, jugglers, and acrobats. Others attended theaters featuring fast dancing or enjoyed boxing matches, vaudeville shows, and (after the turn of the century) movies.

PRIVATE LIFE: Together and Alone at Home

As the tempo of life in factories, stores, government offices, and streets increased, private life grew more precious. The individualism trumpeted by the liberal bourgeoisie accentuated the longing to withdraw from the public arena into the family, the home, and the self. The personal—one's body, sexuality, and internal life—became a subject of intense fascination. The home—the realm of the family protected by walls and locked doors—was the center of private life.

Family: The Promise of Happiness

People believed in the family. Like a religion, the family promised happiness in a difficult world, a meaning that would extend beyond death, and a sacred place free from intrusion by the outside world. As much as their means permitted, people celebrated the family through daily gatherings at meals and special occasions such as weddings, vacations, and birthdays (see the painting on page 484). For individuals, these occasions marked points in their own life cycles. At more private moments, the family home served as a place where individuals shared emotions, or perhaps confessed silently to themselves or in a diary in the solitude of a bedroom.

More than ever, people recorded moments of private life in letters, diaries, and photographs. Families exchanged

→ connect
to
today ←

A Civilization's Value

"In order to estimate the value of a civilization," explained a high Chinese official educated in European universities in the early twentieth century, "the question we must finally ask is not what great cities . . . it has built . . . what clever and useful implements . . . it has made . . . what institutions, what arts and sciences it has invested: the question is what type of humanity, what kind of men and women it has been able to produce." In what ways do you think we struggle with this question today as societies in the West and the world continue to modernize?

Beeton's Guide for Women

Mrs. Beeton's Book of Household Management became the most popular "guidebook" for the proper middle-class woman in Victorian England. In the following selection, Isabella Beeton describes the overall role of the "mistress of a house" and the correct treatment of servants.

1. As with the Commander of an Army, or the leader of any enterprise, so is it with the mistress of a house. Her spirit will be seen through the whole establishment; and just in proportion as she performs her duties intelligently and thoroughly, so will her domestics follow in her path. Of all those acquirements, which more particularly belong to the feminine character, there are none which take a higher rank, in our estimation, than such as enter into a knowledge of household duties; for on these are perpetually dependent the happiness, comfort, and well-being of a family.

***

19. The Treatment of Servants is of the highest possible moment, as well to the mistress as to the domestics themselves. On the head of the house the latter will naturally fix their attention, and if they perceive that the mistress's conduct is regulated by high and correct principles, they will not fail to respect her. If, also, a benevolent desire is shown to promote their comfort, at the same time that a steady performance of their duty is exacted, then their respect will not be unmingled with affection, and they will be still more solicitous to continue to deserve her favour.

What attitudes toward women does this selection reflect?

---

thousands of letters over a lifetime that told of children, deaths, visits, and health. Such correspondence held the family together when travel and migration to different cities threatened to pull it apart. Diaries of the day reveal much self-concern and introspection. One Frenchwoman explained, "When I am alone, I have plenty to do in following the movement of my ideas **Recording private life** and impressions, in exploring myself, in examining my dispositions and my various ways of being, in drawing the best out of myself, in registering the ideas that come to me by chance or that are suggested to me by my reading." People took photographs to capture family occasions—from baptisms to Sunday meals and partings—especially after the invention of the small Kodak camera in the 1880s. They carefully enshrined these photographs in frames and collected them in well-organized albums.

A Home of One's Own

The dream of family life and privacy required having a home of one's own—a private kingdom apart from city and society. But home had another purpose as well: It announced the material success of the bourgeoisie and the pleasures of private life (see image on page 495).

Servants shared middle-class homes but remained on the fringes of the family's private life. Relegated to their own small quarters in the attic or basement, servants had little free- **Servants** dom to move about the house at their leisure or take part in their employers' lives. Indeed, with the era's emphasis on both individualism and privacy, employers increasingly saw servants as potential intruders into private life. The bedroom and bathroom became off-limits, and people complained about how hard it was to find "good," affordable servants. By the turn of the century, many middle-class families managed with just a single female domestic, or none at all.

For the typical middle-class man, home was a retreat from public life, to be savored at the end of the workday or on weekends. For the middle-class woman, it was much more. Society glorified her domestic role more than ever. No longer would she be praised for

MIHALY MUNKACSY, *PARIS INTERIOR*, 1877 Middle-class apartments in large cities typically bulged with possessions.

doing "productive" work such as managing a husband's shop. Instead, she orchestrated every aspect of the family's home life, managing the meals, chores, visits, and guests.

Women's roles Her highest duty, however, was to bear and raise children. No longer was reproduction regarded as simply a natural function: It had become a complex, demanding activity. Most likely, a middle-class woman had fewer children than her mother, but she was expected to lavish greater attention on them. Her children would probably remain at home through adolescence, though many families sent their offspring to boarding schools. To help women meet all these expectations, books, magazines, pamphlets, and advice columns offered tips on how to attract a man and marry well; manage a household; sharpen "home economics" skills; and cultivate an appropriate social life that included teas, afternoon visits, and dinner parties.

At the same time, disturbing crosscurrents started to undermine this picture of the home and women's role in it. As the document on page 494 indicates, prominent people circulated new ideas about the restrictions imposed on women. Many women demanded more independent lives, even choosing to live outside the confines of the middle-class home. The British reformer Florence Nightingale (1820–1910) complained of "the petty grinding tyranny of a good English family," refused to marry, and helped found the modern profession of nursing. A few occupants outside the home were gradually opened to middle-class women, and some women entered universities and professions. Growing numbers of "new women" lived in women's clubs or apartments, dressed more practically, and did more "daring" things such as traveling alone and entering the public space as activists.

> The loss of a job might well doom a family to homelessness.

Poor Housing

Workers could not afford to draw such sharp lines between public and private life. Their homes, typically only one or two rooms in deteriorating buildings, rarely fulfilled all their needs. Often they relocated from one residence to another, carrying what they could. In some cases, they moved so as to search for something slightly better; in others, they sought to avoid a landlord demanding back rent.

The loss of a job might well doom a family to homelessness. With little hope of saving enough to pay for decent housing, workers tended to spend their extra money on clothes to "cut a good figure" and thereby present a well-groomed image in their public lives. For them, the city streets held far more promise than the buildings in which they lived. While the bourgeoisie retreated into homes or private clubs, workers used the public buildings, streets, and spaces of the city for their social and even private lives.

Working-class women enjoyed neither the space, furnishings, nor servants that graced the typical middle-class home. They usually worked at a factory or did poorly paid piece-work at home, where they could **Working-class women** care for their children. If their children seemed more unruly and independent than those of the middle classes, moralists condemned these mothers for failing to create a proper home life. Such critics ignored the fact that working-class women lacked the money needed to cultivate the "ideal" family life. Worse, this disapproval helped employers justify paying these women less than men and treating them poorly.

Intimacy and Morality

Private life for working-class families was burdened by tensions involving basic survival. Middle-class families experienced tensions, too, but of a different sort. Founded on love, companionship, and intimacy, the middle-class family could become a pressure cooker of conflicting feelings and desires, of guilt and shame, of misunderstood communication and resentment. Family members often fought over money, but the confining expectations of intimacy could be worse. "Do not admit anyone else into our private life, into our thoughts," counseled a French man to his prospective wife in 1873. People understood such warnings. The home was a center of secrecy. More often than not, at the heart of that secrecy was sex.

For Britain's middle classes in particular, this era witnessed the height of Victorian sexual morality. Sex was supposed to be little discussed and limited to the marriage bed, enclosed in a separate "master" bedroom with locked doors. Sexual problems "shouldn't arise," but if they did, "enlightened" sufferers might turn to their doctor—the expert on sex, hygiene, and morality all rolled into one. Mixing moralisms with an image of scientific authority, most doctors confirmed the standard views of other commentators: Healthy and prudent sexuality could take place only within the marriage. Affairs risked scandal (especially for the woman) and illegitimacy. Sex with prostitutes was unhygienic and somehow dangerous to the race. Doctors vaguely connected prostitution, syphilis, tuberculosis, and alcoholism as physical and social "scourges," all resulting from "venereal excesses." Most often, they blamed women for being prostitutes, for forcing their husbands to visit prostitutes, or for having inappropriate sexual appetites.

Victorian morality

Masturbation also caught the attention of doctors, priests, and parents. Physicians warned men that masturbation would drain their strength. They condemned masturbation by females even more strongly. To prevent youths from "abusing themselves," they prescribed orthopedic devices, special bandages, and belts.

As for homosexuality, people viewed it in an even worse light. Doctors labeled it a sickness or psychological disorder. Newspapers added to the public condemnation of homosexuality by reporting "scandalous" affairs among public figures and "uncovering" homosexual subcultures. The trial and imprisonment for gross indecency of the famed British author Oscar Wilde (1854–1900) in 1895 promoted a new awareness of homosexuality while revealing how far officials and the public would go to denounce it.

Sexual Realities

Despite these idealized, restrictive notions about proper sexual conduct, reality was quite different. Somehow people, especially the middle classes, discussed sex enough to limit births. While many used the old methods—abstinence and withdrawal—new information and methods also became available. Men began using condoms, and women douched or used diaphragms and sponges soaked in disinfectants. Many resorted to abortion as a method of birth control, particularly in cases of illegitimacy.

Birth control

These methods seem to have worked. The birthrate declined in these years. In France, for example, it dropped from 33 per 1,000 in 1800 to 19 per 1,000 in 1910. Many people chose to limit births for economic reasons. As people moved from farms to the cities, they no longer needed so many children to help with the work. In the cities, the increasing costs of raising children deterred couples from having large families. Yet successful birth control among the middle classes caused concern, for many worried that the "best" of society were not reproducing themselves as quickly as the "poor" and "uncompetitive." Commentators argued that "good" families needed more children. Nationalists complained that competing states or "alien peoples" would overwhelm their nation or "race" if "the fittest" did not increase their fertility.

Certainly actual sexual behavior failed to live up to the standards of Victorian moralists. The "best" people had affairs, and illegitimacy remained high. Deadly sexually transmitted diseases rose and spread widely among all classes. In addition, prostitution thrived in many urban areas. Tens of thousands of prostitutes in the largest cities displayed themselves on streets and in city parks and in windows and doorways. Some worked in bars or elegant brothels for a more select clientele. Working-class women who lost jobs, domestic servants dismissed because of pregnancy, or young women on their own might turn to prostitution to survive. Men of all classes patronized prostitutes. Governments tried to control prostitution, requiring medical exams of prostitutes and limiting its practice to certain districts. Worse than these inconveniences were the risks of this life. Prostitutes were often subjected to violence, the most famous example of which was the serial killings committed by Jack the Ripper in London in the late 1880s.

By the end of the century, new attitudes, or perhaps the weight of reality, had broken down some of the more restrictive notions of Victorian sexual propriety. More people accepted and expected mutual sexual enjoyment within marriage, and people became educated about the physical facts of sexual contact. Books, pamphlets, and talks about sex enabled women and men to read about the subject and sometimes even discuss it openly. Doctors, psychologists, and intellectuals began to study sex and see that it played a major role in individuals' sense of identity.

New attitudes

Psychic Stress and Alcoholism

Growing concern with sex and private life in this period reflected a broader preoccupation with psychological well-being. Anxieties and emotional disorders seemed all too common. Women especially suffered from fits, paralysis, convulsions, numbness, headaches, oversensitivity to light, digestive disorders, and fatigue. Doctors listened, prescribed pills, and suggested expensive cures such as surgery and health-spa retreats. They sometimes blamed the complexities of city life or the noise and speed of modern life for these disturbing health problems. Other commentators suggested different causes. Within the confines of middle-class life, perhaps people worried too much about being judged by others. Or maybe the rapid changes of the era led to insecurity. Whatever the causes,

SCIENCE IN AN AGE OF OPTIMISM

EDGAR DEGAS, *ABSINTHE*, 1876–1877 This painting of a woman drinking a strong alcoholic beverage in a Paris café suggests links between drinking and stress.

the evidence of psychic stress was growing in diaries, in the rise of psychoanalysis, in the new descriptions of proliferating "mental illnesses," in the spread of psychiatric clinics, and in the mounting number of chronic patients in insane asylums.

Was widespread alcoholism a sign of psychic stress? The image above, an 1876 painting by Edgar Degas (1834–1917) of a woman drinking absinthe (a strong alcoholic beverage) in a Parisian café, seems to indicate a link between drinking and stress. Drinkers now seemed more depressed than jovial, and drunkenness appeared to be everywhere—in the streets, at work, in bars, and, increasingly, behind closed doors. New temperance movements attacked the "scourge" of alcohol, and with legitimate reason. In France, the average person consumed more than 60 gallons of wine a year, not including brandy, beer, and the more addictive absinthe shown in this painting. Even drugs such as opium, morphine, heroin, cocaine, and hashish gained footholds, especially among artists. Fear of drug-induced suicides led France to ban such drugs in 1908.

By no coincidence, the practice of **psychoanalysis** emerged during this period (see page 504). Various other movements also focused on psychic stress. One of the best known and popular of these was Christian Science, founded in America by Mary Baker Eddy (1821–1910). Having suffered interminable ailments and nervous disorders as a youth, Eddy turned to a spiritual approach to healing in her adult years. As she explained in her bestselling book *Science and Health* (1875), "mind healing" could dispel sickness and pain. Whatever the causes and supposed cures, stress and emotional pain seemed too widespread to ignore, and many observers connected them to the pressures of modern life.

Despite these concerns about the pressures of modern life, most observers embraced the new age enthusiastically. "I see no limit to the extent to which intelligence and will, guided by sound principles of investigation, and organized in common effort, may modify the conditions of existence, for a period longer than that now covered by history," announced British biologist T. H. Huxley (1825–1895) in 1893. "And much may be done to change the nature of man himself," he added.

The eighteenth-century optimism about science spread during the second half of the nineteenth century. Many people—especially members of the rising middle classes—felt certain that their generation would find solutions to the problems that had plagued human beings from the beginning. Scientists confirmed this optimism by making discoveries that answered fundamental questions and that could be translated into practical products, such as industrial goods and medicines. Intellectuals proffered new ways to explain the world and human beings' place in it. Writers and artists found answers to similar questions by looking hard at the lives of people in their changing world. These scientists, intellectuals, and artists thrived in big cities such as London, Paris, Berlin, Milan, and Vienna. In these cultural hubs, some taught in universities or conducted experiments in laboratories. Others might debate in learned societies, do research in libraries, or paint in studios. Still others chatted in cafés or simply wrote in back rooms. Their work generated provocative ideas and added to the sense that life could be understood more fully than ever before.

Science, Evolution, and Religion

The best news came from science. After 1850, word of scientific advances spread from elite circles to the broader public. Stunning discoveries emerged and directly affected people's lives. However, certain conclusions that appealed to some provoked outrage in others.

No one became a greater hero, or villain, than Charles Darwin (1809–1882). Born into a distinguished British family, Darwin studied medicine and theology. Yet these disciplines failed to challenge him. Instead, the world of plants and animals became his consuming passion. His answer to a single question—how have all living species come to be as they are today?—caused an intense controversy that still continues in some circles.

Darwin

In 1831, Darwin, despite frail health, began a voyage around the world as a ship's naturalist on the *Beagle*. He

For the most part, it was only during the nineteenth century that universities began offering the study of natural science. These schools advanced scientific knowledge in two main ways: They promoted scientific research and helped train future teachers, physicians, and other professionals, who in turn would spread scientific thinking and the fruits of science throughout society. Today, most universities still aim to advance science in these same ways. What are some of the other main goals of today's colleges and universities?

observed and collected fossils and specimens in different environments. He made his most important finds in South America and the Galápagos Islands off the coast of that continent. Gradually he developed his theory of evolution, which, for him, answered his question. In *On the Origin of Species by Natural Selection* (1859), he described the slow evolution of present plant and animal species from earlier, simpler forms through a process of natural selection. Survival, he explained, came from struggle. In the competition for survival, those that possessed the most useful characteristics in a given environment—for example, the horse with the longer legs—survived to produce the most offspring. Through this process, they transmitted their successful qualities to future generations.

These ideas were not completely new. By the mid-nineteenth century, many intellectuals had accepted the concept of a slow and gradual development of the earth's crust and its inhabitants. Liberalism included ideas about the competitive struggle among human beings for food and survival, something that Thomas Malthus had written about at the beginning of the century (see Chapter 17). In addition, Enlightenment thinkers had already popularized the notion of "progress." Many in the mid-nineteenth century already embraced the sense that the present had evolved in progressive stages from a lower past. But no one had ever before supplied an all-encompassing explanation, supported by convincing evidence, for the origin of plants and animals.

What about human beings? Most people believed that humans remained a species apart from all others. At first Darwin avoided the delicate question. In his 1871 work, *The Descent of Man*, he finally took the bold step of arguing that humans evolved from more primitive species by the same process as plants and animals. "Man still bears in his bodily frame the indelible stamp of his lowly origin," he proclaimed. No longer could people "believe that man is the work of a separate act of creation."

Though many people already believed in evolution, Darwin's claims became front-page news. Few ideas have provoked such widespread controversy. To some people, his ideas made sense. Much of the scientific world, for example, quickly accepted Darwin's theory of evolution. Dominant social groups everywhere also derived comfort from it. The rising bourgeoisie, for instance, seized upon evolution as a way to explain and justify its own success. Scientists, including Darwin, also found confirmation for their views that women were inferior to men and destined to play a dependent domestic role in the male-dominated family.

Controversy

As the document on page 499 suggests, philosophers and scholars also expanded Darwin's thesis and applied it to all human behavior, a doctrine known as **Social Darwinism.** British philosopher Herbert Spencer (1820–1903) built a whole system of influential ideas around the concept of evolution; he and other Social Darwinists extended Darwin's theory far beyond its scientific foundations by making it the key to truth and progress. Spencer even saw the notion of survival of the fittest as justification for the harsh competitiveness of human society: "Under the natural order of things society is constantly excreting its unhealthy, imbecile, slow, vacillating, faithless members," he explained. Helping such people "encourages the multiplication of the reckless and incompetent . . . and discourages the multiplication of the competent and provident." Other Social Darwinists, such as British criminologist Francis Galton (1822–1911), suggested that the human race could be improved through selective breeding, or eugenics.

Social Darwinists

Darwin's ideas threatened many people wedded to traditional Christian beliefs. He tried to reassure his alarmed readers: "I see no good reason why the views given in this volume should shock the religious feelings of anyone." Though many Christians accepted some of Darwin's ideas, his views offended numerous others. Spe-

Darwinism and religion cifically, the notion of a long and mechanistic evolution of all present species, including human beings, from simpler forms seemed to contradict the account of divine creation given in the Bible: "If the Darwinian theory is true," complained one theologian, "Genesis is a lie, the whole framework of the book of life falls to pieces, and the revelation of God to man, as we Christians know it, is a delusion and a snare." Evolution, Darwin's critics cried, left God out of the world and diminished the uniqueness of human beings in it.

Some of Darwin's opponents suppressed his books and the teaching of evolution in schools. The Catholic Church angrily rejected Darwin's theory along with many other ideas of the time. In 1864, Pope Pius IX (1846–1878) issued a *Syllabus of Errors* attacking the idea of evolution and secular education. He also railed against religious toleration, free speech, and much else: It is "an error to believe that the Roman Pontiff can and ought to reconcile himself to, and agree with, progress, liberalism, and modern civilization." In 1870, the First Vatican Council bolstered the pope's authority by declaring that, under certain circumstances, the pope's statements on issues of morality and faith should be considered divinely sanctioned truths.

Darwin's allies rushed to his defense. T. H. Huxley, a biologist, surgeon in the British navy, and president of a leading scientific society, popularized Darwin's work in dozens of vigorous and lucid books and pamphlets. Heaping withering scorn on opponents, Huxley called himself "Darwin's bull-dog." Alfred Russel Wallace (1823–1913), a British naturalist, claimed that Darwin "is the Newton of natural history" who "established a firm foundation for all future study of nature."

Over time, many of Darwin's critics moderated their hostility to Darwin's findings. Toward the end of the century the Catholic Church, under Pope Leo XIII (1878–1903), even began taking the position that natural science was not the province of the church, that evolution could be taught as a hypothesis, and that parts of the Bible should be taken figuratively.

Walter Bagehot on Natural Selection and Human History

Social Darwinism and related doctrines spread, especially among liberals, during the second half of the nineteenth century. The Englishman Walter Bagehot (1826–1877) won notice for presenting views shared by his liberal, middle-class contemporaries.

The strongest nation has always been conquering the weaker; sometimes even subduing it, but always prevailing over it. Every intellectual gain, so to speak, that a nation possessed was in the earliest times made use of—was invested and taken out—in war; all else perished. Each nation tried constantly to be the stronger, and so made or copied the best weapons, by conscious and unconscious imitation each nation formed a type of character suitable to war and conquest. Conquest improved mankind by the intermixture of strengths; the armed truce, which was then called peace, improved them by the competition of training and the consequent creation of new power. Since the long-headed men first drove the short-headed men out of the best land in Europe, all European history has been the history of the superposition of the more military races over the less military—of the efforts, sometimes successful, sometimes unsuccessful, of each race to get more military; and so the art of war has constantly improved. . . .

In what ways might someone use Bagehot's argument to justify war or imperialism?

Mysteries of the Material and Human World

Research multiplied in many fields besides natural science. Scientists focused especially on the nature of matter. Discovery after discovery in chemistry and physics led them

Physics and chemistry to conclude that all matter was composed of atoms, that each atom was in turn made up of smaller particles that moved in circles like a miniature solar system, and that each chemical element of matter had a specific atomic weight. In 1870, the Russian chemist Dmitri Mendeleev (1834–1907) compiled a new chart showing the atomic weight of all the known elements and indicating by gaps the other elements that remained to be discovered. Chemists and physicists proved him right. Year after year, researchers discovered new elements that fit into the periodic table. In the 1870s, James Clerk Maxwell (1831–1879) analyzed the relationship between light, magnetism, and electricity. His ideas led to a greater sense of physical unity in the universe and practical developments such as the development of the electronics industry.

The successes of Darwin and of chemists, physicists, and others in the natural sciences encouraged scholars to apply the same scientific techniques and principles to psy-

Psychology chology, or the study of human behavior. One of the first to bring this discipline into the laboratory was Wilhelm Wundt (1832–1920). In his laboratory at Leipzig, Wundt and his enthusiastic students tested human reactions and carried out carefully controlled and measured experiments on cats and dogs, assuming that the findings would also apply to human beings.

The Russian scientist Ivan Pavlov (1849–1936), pursuing Wundt's line of inquiry, discovered the conditioned reflex. Pavlov showed meat to a hungry dog until the dog's mouth watered. Then Pavlov rang a bell while showing the meat. Eventually, the dog's mouth would water when only the bell was rung. The implication was that many of our human responses are purely mechanical reflexes prompted by stimuli of which we are often unaware.

The field of sociology also acquired status as a social science. Auguste Comte (1798–1857) named the new discipline. He argued that humankind was entering a stage of history in which truths would be discovered by the scientific gathering of factual data. Humans and society,

Sociology he said, are as susceptible to scientific investigation as minerals, plants, and the lower animals are. He believed that his philosophy, which he called **positivism,** would reveal the laws of human relations and allow social scientists to engineer harmonious societies. Comte's followers, eager and numerous during the

second half of the nineteenth century, placed great faith in statistics and amassed copious statistical data on numerous social problems. Like Comte, most of them believed that sure social knowledge would enable people to remake society for the better.

Historians such as the German Leopold von Ranke (1795–1886) strove to turn history into a social science. Ranke rejected history based on tradition or legend. He also attacked the notion that history could come in the form of a purposeful story about the progress of humanity, the working out of God's will, or other such **History** themes. He argued that historical accounts should be based on an exhaustive accumulation and analysis of documentary evidence. Conclusions could be drawn only from facts, he insisted. In this way, Ranke believed, history would become coldly scientific and morally neutral. His attitude and methodology spread widely, particularly in Germany and the United States.

These scholars believed that individual and social behavior could best be studied by careful, objective observation, experimentation, and analysis. Like scientists, they considered themselves professionals with specialties rather than amateurs. They also formed societies and published their findings in their own journals. Part of what drove them was their faith that these findings would point the way to improving the quality of human life, and they conveyed that faith to a wider public. In this sense, these scholars and scientists shared and promoted the optimism of the period.

Germs, Cures, and Health Care

No field of science promised more new understanding and dramatic applications than medicine. At mid-century, medicine entered a golden age. The most important discovery came not from a doctor but from a chemist. Louis Pasteur (1822–1895), the son of a French **Pasteur and germ theory** tanner, became interested in what happened to wine and beer during the fermentation process. In the 1860s, he discovered the airborne microorganisms responsible for fermentation and showed that bacteria caused milk to sour. He demonstrated that heating milk—"pasteurizing" it—destroyed the bacteria that caused diseases. His long years of work eventually enabled him to identify disease-producing organisms in humans and create vaccines to prevent diseases such as rabies. Here, finally, was the explanation for how people caught infectious diseases: germ theory.

Many doctors and scientists, still wedded to old ideas and practices, dismissed Pasteur's findings. The German scientist Robert Koch (1843–1910) confirmed the French

For most diseases, however, cures lay in the future.

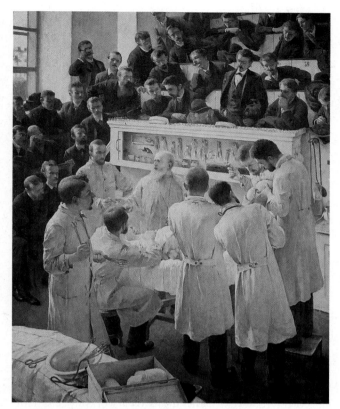

ALBERT SELIGMANN, *OPERATION BY GERMAN SURGEON THEODOR BILLROTH*, 1890 This painting of a Viennese operating room reveals a growing confidence in modern science but the persistence of old patterns in medical practice, including the absence of surgical masks and gloves, the use of unsterilized instruments, and males' dominance of the profession.

chemist's conclusions, convincing doctors that bacteria indeed caused diseases. In the early 1880s, Koch discovered the bacteria responsible for two of the most deadly diseases of the time: tuberculosis and cholera. His students used the same research methods to find microbes that caused a list of other diseases from pneumonia and meningitis to syphilis.

Modern doctors of the late nineteenth century now understood that specific microorganisms (germs) caused specific infectious diseases. In addition to this realization, new tools increased physicians' stature as scientists and improved their ability to diagnose ailments. The thermometer, for example, allowed them to measure body temperature, and the stethoscope let them hear what was going on inside the body. The microscope permitted examination of tissue samples, the X-ray (1896) revealed the body's internal structures, and the electrocardiograph (1901) recorded the workings of the heart.

The most advanced doctors realized that although they may have known more about illnesses and the inner workings of the body, they still could do little to cure diseases.

Remedies Aspirin (1899) reduced fever, inflammation, and minor pain; morphine controlled more serious pain; and

barbiturates might induce sleep—but none of these constituted a medical cure. The first great exception was an antitoxin against diphtheria developed in Robert Koch's Berlin laboratory in 1891. For most diseases, however, cures lay in the future. The best that doctors could do was to stop prescribing poisonous pills and dangerous procedures such as bloodletting and purges.

Within medicine, the field of surgery saw especially remarkable progress. During the 1860s and 1870s, the British surgeon Joseph Lister (1827–1912) developed procedures that included the use of antiseptics during operations. These procedures dramatically lowered the **Surgery** risk of infection from the operation itself. Over the following decades, surgeons applied Lister's methods with great success. No longer did they operate in dirty, bloodsplattered back rooms, wearing black coats or street clothes. Increasingly, they washed their hands, worked in relatively sterile environments, and wore white surgical gowns, face masks, and rubber gloves to lessen the risks of infection (see image to the left).

Medical advances also made a huge difference in the field of nursing. In hospitals, emergencies, and war, nurses often had the most direct contact with sufferers and the wounded. During the Crimean War (1853–1856), Florence Nightingale **Nursing** transformed nursing into a modern profession. Her reforms stressed cleanliness, fresh air, and discipline and helped make nursing an attractive path to independence and service. A few years later, the philanthropist Dorothea Dix (1802–1887) led similar reform efforts in the United States during the Civil War, and in Switzerland a banker established the International Red Cross, creating new demand for professional nurses.

By the turn of the century, much in medicine had gained the authority of science and was "professionalized." Better nursing gave the wounded a fighting chance at survival. Doctors who understood diseases and surgeons who performed operations safely now helped more than hurt their patients. Even so, many doctors insisted on practicing traditional medicine, and most remained too expensive for working-class families to afford except when they were in dire need. Many working-class women were forced to prescribe their own curative regime or find some inexpensive "cure."

CULTURE: Accepting the Modern World

Faith in science and technology reflected a growing sense that people could observe the facts of everyday life carefully, understand them, and use that understanding to control the world more successfully than ever before. Writers and artists also closely observed contemporary life in their books and paintings. During the second half of the nineteenth century, their focus included the methods of science and the realities of urban life. The romanticism of early-nineteenth-century culture—which had idealized love, religion, and the exotic—gave way to a gritty sense of realism (see Chapter 18). Realists felt free to look modern life full in the face and both praise its successes and criticize its failings.

Realism and Naturalism: The Details of Social Life

The age witnessed the rise of realistic and naturalistic literature, which explored the social dislocation brought about by the industrial revolution, commercial values, and city life. Eugène de Vogüé (1848–1910), a nineteenth-century French writer, explained that a realist "observes

Literature

life as it is in its wholeness and complexity with the least possible prejudice on the part of the artist. It takes men under ordinary conditions, shows characters in the course of their everyday existence." Authors, often focusing on the unpleasant, sordid side of human nature and society, examined how environment and heredity together shaped people's lives. With scientific thoroughness, these writers examined people's public and private lives, their individual and social failings, and the hypocrisy of their religious and moral values.

The French novelist Gustave Flaubert (1821–1880), for example, deftly captured the full flavor of **realism.** His *Madame Bovary* (1857) related the illicit sex life of the wife of a small-town French physician in such full and unblushing detail that it scandalized a public not yet accustomed to such unrestrained revelations. *Madame Bovary* became a model for other novelists. Few writers, however, were as popular as Charles Dickens (1812–1870). As we saw in Chapter 17, Dickens's novels presented realistic descriptions of the middle and lower classes in Britain's urban, industrial society. For example, in *The Old Curiosity Shop*, he refused to shy away from the realities of nighttime in impoverished sections of cities, "when bands of unemployed labourers paraded in the roads . . . when carts came rumbling by, filled with rude coffins . . . or when orphans cried, and distracted women shrieked and followed in their wake, . . . when some called for bread, and some for drink to drown their cares."

Mary Ann Evans (1819–1880), writing under the pen name George Eliot, also wrote popular novels examining the realities of British social life. In *Middlemarch*, for instance, she linked psychological conflict to the determining social realities surrounding her characters. The

Norwegian playwright Henrik Ibsen (1828–1906) presented another perspective on such realities. Ibsen ridiculed bourgeois society in his popular dramas. In *A Doll's House,* probably his best-known play, the heroine, Nora, rebels against her expected role in the "doll's house" that her stodgy, hypocritical, middle-class husband, Helmer, has created for her:

> NORA: What do you consider my holiest duties?
> HELMER: Need I tell you that? Your duties to your husband and children.
> NORA: I have other duties equally sacred.
> HELMER: Impossible! What do you mean!
> NORA: My duties toward myself.
> HELMER: Before all else you are a wife and a mother.
> NORA: That I no longer believe. Before all else I believe I am a human being just as much as you are.

The French writer Émile Zola (1840–1902) explained that the naturalist novel, having evolved from the realistic novel, "substitutes for the study of the abstract man . . . the study of the natural man, governed by physical and chemical laws, and modified by the influences of his surroundings; it is in one word the literature of our scientific age." He wrote in almost clinical detail about the social problems spawned by industrialism. In one series of novels, he portrayed several generations of a working-class family battered by the forces of heredity and the environment. They struggle to survive, fighting poverty, strikes, alcoholism, and conflict among themselves.

Russia produced some especially talented writers who created stunning realistic literature. An example is Leo Tolstoy (1828–1910) and his masterpiece *War and Peace* (1865–1869). This sweeping novel about Russia during the Napoleonic Wars features scores of characters who battle impersonal social forces and the overwhelming details of

GUSTAVE COURBET, *THE STONE BREAKERS,* 1849 In this realistic painting, an old worker breaks up stones, probably for use in building a road. His young assistant carries the stones away in a basket. Their tattered clothing and averted faces make them seem anonymous and therefore representative of many other workers. The scene, like the men's lives, is harsh.

everyday life. Even the strongest individuals in the story become ensnared in forces beyond their control. In other writings that reflected the social realities of his own times, Tolstoy attacked capitalism and materialism: "Money is a new form of slavery, and distinguishable from the old simply by the fact that it is impersonal."

Fyodor Dostoyevski (1821–1881), another legendary Russian author, focused more on psychological and moral realities in his novels. His characters—such as the anguished student Raskolnikov in *Crime and Punishment* (1866), who murders an old woman—struggle with moral conflicts in an age marked by spiritual bankruptcy. Like other realistic writers, Dostoyevski shone a spotlight on the harshness of modern life, particularly its power to overwhelm individuals.

Innovative painters turned to realistic depictions of life on their canvases. The French artist Gustave Courbet (1819–1877), who believed that an

Art

artist should "never permit sentiment to overthrow logic," led the attack on romantic art by painting sober scenes of urban life and rural labor. In *The Stone Breakers*, shown on page 502, Courbet portrays rural laborers as a passerby might see them. He claimed he "saw these people every day on my walk." Courbet and other realistic artists depicted everyday life on large canvases and thereby earned the wrath of those artists and critics who believed that only paintings of historical, mythological, religious, or exotic scenes should be considered great art.

Impressionism: Celebrating Modern Life

Like the realists and naturalists, impressionist painters embraced modern life—but in a different way. Specifically, they applied a new understanding of color, light, and optics to their work. Their paintings—with their informal quality and emphasis on angles—suggested randomness of reality. Such artists ventured outside their studios to paint scenes. They especially sought to convey the impression of a view that the eye actually sees at first glance—the impression created by light reflected off a surface at a single moment—rather than what the knowing brain interprets from visual cues, hence the name **impressionism** for this school of painting. The French artist Claude Monet (1840–1926) described the way he painted: "Try to forget what objects you have before you—a tree, a house, a field, or whatever. Merely think, here is a little square of blue,

CLAUDE MONET, *THE DOCKS OF ARGENTEUIL*, 1872 In this scene near Monet's home just outside of Paris, middle-class women carrying parasols stroll along the Seine. Sailboats on the river suggest pleasure; a bridge in the distance implies that the city is not far away.

here an oblong of pink, here a streak of yellow, and paint it just as it looks to you . . . until it gives your own naive impression of the scene before you."

Monet's *The Docks of Argenteuil* shown above, is an example of many paintings of the suburban countryside—the places to which the urban bourgeoisie might travel on Sundays or vacations. The bourgeoisie purchasers of Monet's paintings would recognize this sort of place,

Monet

where civilization and countryside meet under a broad sky. Impressionists also painted psychologically subtle portraits, bedroom and dance-hall interiors, urban parks, and city streets.

FROM OPTIMISM TO UNCERTAINTY

The impressionists' delight in the beauty and charm of modern life fit well with the continuing belief in reason, individual rights, and progress that marked the decades after 1850. Economic growth, improving conditions in the cities, and new conquests by science buoyed a broad sense of moderate optimism about the world. However, from the 1880s on, signs of a disturbing new undercurrent rose to the surface of Western culture. Some of the West's best intellectuals, writers, and artists injected themes of pessimism and painful introspection into their work. They emphasized how strongly irrational forces guided human behavior. Though still a minority, these thinkers and critics undermined rather than overwhelmed the prevailing certainty and optimism of the period. They added to the growing social and political tensions of the turn-of-the-century decades described in Chapter 20.

Everything Is Relative

In part, this disillusionment stemmed from the growing feeling of uncertainty creeping into elite scientific circles—the sense that the more people learned, the less solid and reliable the material world became. The work of Albert

Einstein

Einstein (1879–1955) exposed this uncertainty in physics. A German who later fled to America, Einstein assailed time-honored concepts about the stability of matter and the nature of the physical universe. In 1905, while still earning a living as a patent clerk in Switzerland, he proposed what would become the seminal theory of relativity. According to this theory, time, space, and motion are relative to one another as well as to the observer—they are not the absolutes scientists had believed in for so long.

Building on the work of the German physicist Max Planck (1858–1947), who had shown that heated bodies emit energy in irregular packets (quanta) rather than a steady stream, Einstein also derived a groundbreaking formula, $E = mc^2$ (E = energy; m = mass; c = speed of light). This formula blurred the distinction between mass and energy and described the immense energy contained within each atom. The atomic energy in a lump of coal, for example, was revealed to be some three billion times as great as the energy obtained by burning the coal. This unsettling notion later contributed to the development of the atomic bomb. By showing that matter could be transformed into energy, Einstein again challenged Newtonian physics. More conservative scientists, wedded to time-honored Newtonian physics, dismissed his theories. Eventually, however, Einstein's views gained support, further undermining scientists' assumptions about the physical nature of the universe.

Sex, Conflict, and the Unconscious

Ideas about the human mind—the internal, mental universe—also took a disturbing turn in these years. Sigmund

Freud and psychoanalysis

Freud (1856–1939), the Viennese neurologist, concluded that nervous disorders stemmed from psychological causes, not physiological sources

as most doctors had believed. Basing his ideas on the words, experiences, and dreams of troubled patients, he founded psychoanalysis, which he described as "the scientific method by which the unconscious can be studied."

Freud argued that much of human behavior was irrational, unconscious, and instinctual. Conflict, he claimed, was a basic condition of life, particularly when it occurred between people's innate biological drives (such as sex or aggression) and their social selves. According to Freud, these conflicts developed on a mostly unconscious level and in stages during childhood. At war within all people are what Freud called the id, the superego, and the ego. The id is the source of our basic desires, the most important and disturbing of these being sexual. The superego imposes socially acceptable standards of behavior on the individual. The ego tries to find ways to satisfy both the demands of the id and the restraints of the superego. Typically, the mind responds to this conflict by repressing the id's desires from consciousness. However, the unconscious psychic struggle continues, creating a mental life of great tension.

Freud added fuel to his already controversial ideas by emphasizing the importance of sexual conflicts originating in childhood. He argued that children inevitably come into conflict with their parents, competing with the same-sex parent for the love of the opposite-sex parent. At an unconscious level, he claimed, this competition for the parent of the opposite sex strongly shapes the development of an individual's personality.

> "[T]he price of progress in civilization is paid in forfeiting happiness."

Freud believed that much psychic pain and many emotional disorders stemmed from the suppressed and frustrated drives of early life—frustrations that then festered outside of people's awareness. He concluded that the correct therapy for such disorders was to make the sufferer conscious of the facts and circumstances of his or her original frustration. Hence, he encouraged patients to talk about their dreams, for by interpreting dreams the unconscious could be revealed.

Freud's controversial explanation of human behavior had several disturbing implications: Neither adults nor children are innocent beings after all; too few people lead happy lives; sex and aggression play powerful roles in children and adults alike; people cannot escape from internal conflict and frustration. Although he hoped that reason and understanding would ease humanity's psychological plight, Freud was far from an optimist. He eventually concluded that "the price of progress in civilization is paid in forfeiting happiness."

Fear of Social Disintegration

The French scholar Émile Durkheim (1858–1917), a founder of modern sociology, offered a different sort of warning about trends in modern society. Though a strong believer in science, Durkheim argued that industrial society—especially with its competitive individualism and lack

Durkheim of collective values—was weakening the ties that connected people with one another. As people became more concerned with their own freedom and advancement, he believed, the restraints and the spiritual beliefs that held traditional societies together would break down. This trend toward social disintegration, Durkheim warned, disoriented individuals, made them feel cut off from others, and left them without a sense of purpose. As a result, more and more people were experiencing despair, which in turn led to rising suicide rates. Like Freud, Durkheim believed that advancing civilization left psychic pain in its wake.

Disenchantment Sets In

Perhaps the deepest sense of disenchantment with the optimistic, bourgeois, urban society of the nineteenth century emerged in philosophy. Friedrich Nietzsche (1844–1890), a brilliant German philosopher, is one example. Reason could not solve human problems, Nietzsche concluded.

Nietzsche Instead, he believed in "will," which in his view enabled people to survive and the strongest among them to achieve power. Great leaders, he argued, rose through strength, intelligence, and above all, "the will to power." Nietzsche further claimed that if a superior society were to emerge, it would have to come about through the efforts of gifted individuals who would rise to positions of leadership because of their superior strength, will, and intelligence. Anything that contributes to power is good, he explained—be it strength of will, boldness, cunning, or intelligence. Likewise, whatever leads to weakness is bad—be it gentleness, modesty, generosity, or compassion.

In Nietzsche's view, Christianity stood in the way of a better human society. "Christianity has taken the side of everything weak, base, ill-constituted; it has made an ideal out of opposition to the preservative instincts of strong life," he announced. "God is dead; we have killed him." For Nietzsche, the idea of the death of God was liberating: Now humans could cast off all conventions. Nietzsche also decried democracy for amounting to rule by the supposedly mediocre "masses . . . or the populace, or the herd, or whatever name you care to give them." He went on to attack many other accepted tenets of nineteenth-century civilization, such as liberalism, rationalism, and science. Although Nietzsche was not a nationalist or racist himself, others would later use his ideas to support militant nationalism and racism.

Art Turns Inward

Many talented artists also turned away from the mainstream of nineteenth-century civilization. Their work grew more pessimistic and critical of middle-class life. The slogan "Art for art's sake" reflected the trend of

Expressionism

various artistic movements, such as **expressionism** and symbolism. They self-consciously attacked social and artistic taboos in ways that mystified much of the public. Their often introspective works proved understandable mainly to themselves and a small artistic elite. The Russian abstract expressionist painter Wassily Kandinsky (1866–1944) spoke for many of his fellow artists when he explained that his work was not intended to represent how things looked. "Look at the picture as a graphic representation of a mood and not as a representation of objects," he suggested.

Many artists focused on peripheral members of a society that seemed to be disintegrating, painting prostitutes, solitary drinkers, blind beggars, and circus performers. Moreover, threatening symbols of science, machinery, and speed began to crop up on canvases. Photography had already displaced traditional representation art. The French poet Guillaume Apollinaire (1880–1918) explained that modern painters "avoid any representation of natural scenes . . . since

JAMES ENSOR, *CHRIST'S TRIUMPHANT ENTRY INTO BRUSSELS*, 1888 Ensor shows a parade and a mob of people whose faces are in coarse caricatures or masks that reflect pretense and false smiles. Behind their masks lurk isolation and anxiety. Banners cynically proclaim "Long Live Socialism," "Political Spectacles Always Succeed," and "Long Live Jesus."

everything is sacrificed by the artist to truth." Now avant-garde painters created distorted, subjective, and abstract images. We can see evidence of these trends in expressionist paintings such as those by the Belgian artist James Ensor (1860–1949) (see image on page 505).

EDVARD MUNCH, *THE SCREAM*, 1893 A wide-eyed figure standing on a bridge lets out a terrified shriek. The distorted land, water, and sky echo the cry. In this painting, themes of death, anxiety, loneliness, and fear coalesce.

Like Ensor, the Norwegian artist Edvard Munch (1863–1944) expressed a deep current of horror in middle-class life, but in a deeper, more personal way. In *The Scream* (shown here), themes of death, anxiety, loneliness, and fear coalesce. Munch once exclaimed, "How much of my art I owe to suffering!" Many other artists painted similarly anguished scenes, emphasizing social anxieties, urban loneliness, violence, horror, and a turning inward toward the unconscious. Their paintings penetrated through surface-level appearances into a deeper, disturbing psychic reality.

OPINION

In what ways do you think "modern life and the culture of progress" is an apt description of Western culture during this period?

In music, expressionism also challenged artistic conventions and public tastes. The Russian composer Igor Stravinsky (1882–1971) led this movement in his music for the ballet *The Rite of Spring*. The premiere of the ballet on May 29, 1913, in Paris has been called the most notorious event of the twentieth century. Upon hearing the music—with its offbeat rhythm and unrestrained, dissonant sounds—the audience rose in outrage. Fights broke out, and many listeners stormed from the theater after complaining loudly. Yet among certain elites, Stravinsky became the leading composer of the day.

Music

Like science and philosophy, art and music were slipping away from the grasp of ordinary people. The new understandings of modern life that had seemed so promising a few decades earlier now appeared shadowed by doubt and even foreboding.

timeline

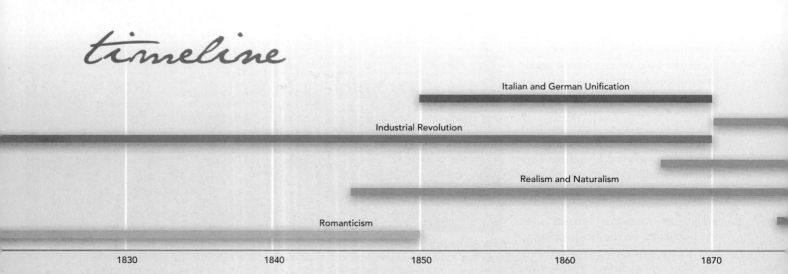

Italian and German Unification

Industrial Revolution

Realism and Naturalism

Romanticism

| 1830 | 1840 | 1850 | 1860 | 1870 |

SUMMARY

By 1914, industrialization, urban growth, and the culture of progress had pulled much of the West into new territory. Life in large parts of Europe and North America had undergone a huge transformation. Someone who had lived during the late eighteenth century would have found virtually everything about the turn-of-the-century West strange or even shocking.

- After 1870, a "second industrial revolution" marked by new inventions, manufacturing processes, and methods for getting products to market and selling them spread in the West.

- Life in great urban centers, many of them rebuilt, became the new norm for masses of people in the West.

- People of all classes filled the cities. The middle classes fared particularly well while the working classes struggled to make ends meet.

- For many in the cities—particularly the middle classes—private life, centered around the family, home, and self, became more highly valued than in the past.

- Optimism about the promises of science to unravel the mysteries of the material and human world spread widely.

- Writers and artists tended to accept the modern, closely observing contemporary life in their books and paintings.

- From the 1880s on, some of the West's best intellectuals, writers, and artists introduced themes of pessimism and painful introspection into their work.

People have called the years 1850–1914 the Age of Progress. The reasons are clear. Income for most people rose at least a little, and for some quite considerably, while the machines of industry pumped out endless new products that promised to ease the burdens of everyday life. Science promised even more. Many of the cultural forms of the period gazed directly at the modern world and embraced it. In the 1920s, the French would look back to the two decades surrounding the turn of the century as La Belle Époque—the beautiful era.

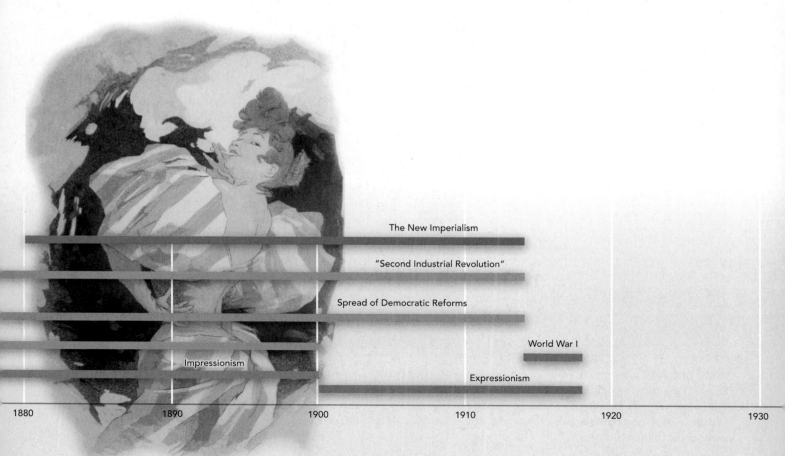

The New Imperialism

"Second Industrial Revolution"

Spread of Democratic Reforms

World War I

Impressionism

Expressionism

1880   1890   1900   1910   1920   1930

OTTO DIX, _WAR_, 1929–1932 The German expressionist painter Otto Dix (1891–1969) fought in the trenches of World War I and was wounded several times. In this triptych he depicts the destructiveness of war. In the panel on the left, soldiers march toward the bleak battlefront. Their fate is depicted in the following panels: the gore and destruction of the front lines, trenches that serve as coffins for the numberless dead, and the endless haunting nightmares of those who somehow survive. This painting all too accurately captured the reality of the period as experienced by millions of people.

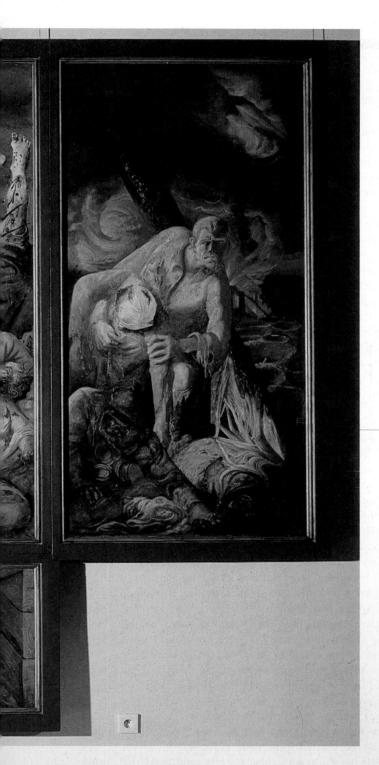

Descending into the Twentieth Century

22

World War and Revolution,
1914–1920

Assassination in Sarajevo

On June 28, 1914, 19-year-old Gavrilo Princip, gun in hand, waited along a parade route in Sarajevo, the capital of the Austro-Hungarian province of Bosnia. Princip was a member of a Bosnian nationalist organization that had been trained by the Black Hand, a Serbian terrorist group. He was not alone. That day, Archduke Ferdinand, the heir to the Austro-Hungarian throne, was visiting Sarajevo. Princip, waiting with several conspirators, planned to kill the archduke to promote Slavic liberation from Austro-Hungarian control. ▶▶

As Ferdinand's open car passed by, Princip's co-conspirators lost their nerve and did not shoot. Then Ferdinand's driver took a wrong turn. Realizing his mistake, he stopped the car and, by chance, backed up to where Princip stood. Princip fired, killing Ferdinand and his wife, Sophie. ◄◄

ON THE PATH TO TOTAL WAR

In the years leading up to the killing of Archduke Ferdinand, several political leaders had been assassinated without great risk of war. Yet in just four weeks, this incident would lead Austria-Hungary, a second-rate power, to declare war on Serbia, a third-rate power in the southeast corner of Europe—the Balkans. Within one more week, most of Europe was engulfed by war. The Great War ended the era that had begun 125 years earlier with the French and industrial revolutions. It spawned a new round of revolution, destroyed several empires, and altered politics and society for the rest of the twentieth century. The consequences of this war even spread into the non-Western world, drawing in troops from Asia and Africa and changing how people around the globe viewed the West.

How could this incident in Sarajevo, far from the heart of Europe and not directly involving any of Europe's major powers, result in an all-out war that would end an era and transform Western society?

Rivalries and Alliances

Part of the answer to this question lies in the national, economic, and imperial rivalry percolating in Europe at the time. Militant nationalism, intensifying since the mid-nineteenth century, encouraged countries to view one another as dangerous rivals in the struggle for power and prestige. Politicians used this nationalism to glaze over domestic problems and win public support. The growth of industrial capitalism created an environment of competitive economic struggle as nations tried to promote their industries and gain markets. The outburst of imperialism in the decades before 1914 pitted these rivals against one another in a race to acquire colonies and expand their arenas of influence around the world.

These rivalries fueled international affairs and pressured European states to form a system of alliances among themselves. The German statesman Otto von Bismarck initiated the alliances in the 1870s. Concerned about being encircled by enemies, he allied Germany with Austria-Hungary and Russia to avoid any possibility

of a two-front war—to the east against Russia and to the west against France. After forcing Bismarck's retirement, the new German kaiser—hoping to extend German influence over areas of concern to Russia—allowed the reinsurance treaty with Russia to lapse. **The alliance system** This opened the door to major shifts in international relations. New alliances formed as European states tried to protect themselves and pursue their ambitions. Italy, looking for support against France in the competition for colonies, joined Germany and Austria-Hungary in 1882 to form the Triple Alliance. Russia, hoping to expand into southeastern Europe and gain access to the Mediterranean at the expense of the declining Ottoman Empire, came into conflict with Austro-Hungarian and German ambitions in the Balkans. By 1894, Russia had joined in a new alliance with France, which eagerly sought an ally in case of a clash with Germany. In 1904, Britain, threatened by the rise of Germany as a new naval, industrial, and imperial power, joined its old rival France in an alliance called the Entente Cordiale. In 1905 and again in 1911, German challenges to French sovereignty over Morocco in North Africa created international crises that drew France and Britain closer together.

By 1914, Europe had divided itself into two powerful alliance systems: the Triple Entente, comprising France, Russia, and Great Britain; and the Triple Alliance, made up of Germany, Austria-Hungary, and Italy. On the one hand, these alliances may have encouraged Europeans to believe that they could avert major wars. Between 1870 and 1914, a balance of power did generally prevail. Statesmen solved most conflicts diplomatically, and military scuffles remained brief and local. On the other hand, the alliance system gave smaller powers an opportunity to influence the decisions of larger powers; everyone feared that losing an ally—even a relatively weak supporter making decisions in its own interests—would upset the balance of power and make strong nations vulnerable.

Meanwhile, military might played a large part in politics in this world driven by competition and a struggle for international stature. Germany built a new navy; Britain kept ahead and in 1906 launched the *Dreadnought*, the first of a new class of battleships armed entirely **Military buildup** with big guns; and most powers reinforced their armies. Between 1870 and 1914, France and Germany more than doubled the size of their standing armies by requiring citizens to serve for set periods of time. Politicians justified

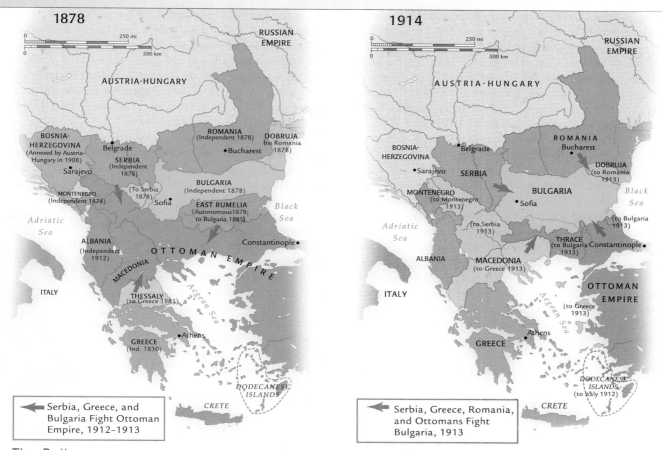

The Balkans, 1878 and 1914 **The map on the left shows the Balkans in 1878 and highlights fighting and territorial changes to 1913. The map on the right shows the same region in 1914, after new warfare had resulted in further territorial changes.**

huge expenditures for the military buildup with nationalistic slogans and claims that military spending promoted industry, jobs, and trade. Military staffs made plans emphasizing quick offensive thrusts and drew up timetables for mobilizing their forces in case of war. Most people assumed that any war that broke out would be short, like the Franco-Prussian War of 1870 (see pages 450–451), and that their own nation would win it. This armaments race and military planning only heightened the suspicion and fear brewing between nations. It also made national leaders feel ever more dependent on their allies for support in case of war.

Crises in the Balkans

These rivalries and hardening alliances became enmeshed in a series of crises that exploded in the Balkans (see maps above). Why the Balkans? This was Europe's most unstable area—a land of strong nationalistic aspirations felt by several peoples who had been long dominated by the declining Austro-Hungarian and Ottoman empires. As the Ottoman Empire disintegrated during the late nineteenth and early twentieth centuries, various Balkan peoples, such as the Romanians, Bulgarians, and Serbs, had established independent nations. Peoples still under Ottoman or Austro-Hungarian rule agitated for their own independence or sought support from their linguistic kin—especially the Serbs—in these new Balkan states. The Ottoman Turks had long struggled to maintain what power they still retained in the area. Their efforts to modernize economically, reform the government, and maintain unity in the face of demands for a constitution failed to reverse the empire's decline. In 1908, a coup overthrew the sultan and brought the nationalistic Young Turks to power, but their efforts to make Turkish the official language in Balkan areas and to increase Turkish control made the region more volatile. The Austro-Hungarians feared dismemberment of their multinational empire by these nationalistic sentiments. They hoped to expand into the Balkans and thereby weaken any movements for independence among their own ethnic minorities. These hopes brought Austria-Hungary into conflict with Russia, which had long hungered for influence and expansion in the Balkans and wanted to secure a port into the Mediterranean. Russia had fought two limited wars in pursuit of these aims during the second half of the nineteenth century. It also envisioned itself as the honorable, fraternal protector of Slavic peoples in the Balkans.

The first Balkan crisis erupted in 1908, when Austria-Hungary suddenly annexed two provinces, Bosnia and Herzegovina, which were home to Serbs, Croats, and others. Serbia had wanted to annex these territories, peopled by its own linguistic kin. Serbia appealed to Russia, and Russia threatened Austria-Hungary, whereupon Germany joined its ally and forced Russia to back down. The second Balkan crisis occurred in 1912–1913. The various Balkan states defeated Turkey in a war and then fought among themselves over the spoils. Victorious Serbia longed for more territory. Austria-Hungary thwarted the small country's expansion to the Adriatic Sea and threatened to annihilate Serbia. Again Serbia appealed to Russia, and again German pressure forced Russia to back down.

The assassination of Archduke Ferdinand on June 28, 1914, precipitated the third Balkan crisis. The government of Austria-Hungary, certain of Serbian involvement in the assassination, decided to crush Serbia and establish its own dominance in the Balkans once and for all. But this plan would require the backing of Germany, for Russia might come to the support of its Serbian allies and defend its own interests in the Balkans. At a fateful conference in Berlin eight days after the Sarajevo shooting, the German government encouraged Austria-Hungary's scheme with a "blank check" of full support. Emboldened by Germany's backing and advice to act quickly, Austria-Hungary presented Serbia with an ultimatum that Serbia could not hope to meet. The Austrians may not have wanted a Europe-wide war, but they felt they needed a war with Serbia. Upon hearing of Austria's demands on Serbia, Russia's foreign minister told Austria's ambassador, "You are setting fire to Europe." On July 28, even after Serbia had yielded on all but one of the ultimatum's terms (which would have allowed Austria to investigate Serbian involvement in the assassination plot), Austria-Hungary declared war.

Germany's blank check

To back Serbia against Austria-Hungary, Russia ordered its clumsy military establishment to mobilize. However, Russian military planning, which assumed a war against both Austria and Germany, did not allow for only partial mobilization against Austria. Russia's order of full mobilization on July 29 was almost the same as a declaration of war—especially to German military leaders.

Mobilization

Germany's main war plan assumed a two-front war against Russia and France, requiring the German army to knock France out of the fighting before Russia could bring the weight of its slow-moving forces against Germany.

Therefore, Germany mobilized and sent ultimatums to Russia, demanding demobilization, and to France, requiring a declaration of neutrality. When Russia failed to reply and France gave an unsatisfactory response, Germany declared war on Russia on August 1 and on France two days later. On August 4, when German troops violated Belgian neutrality on their way to attack France, Great Britain declared war on Germany.

Thus the great powers of Europe were sucked into a general war they did not want by the very alliances they had formed to protect themselves and feared to violate. The growing tensions in European societies—violent domestic politics, strikes, threats from the political Left and Right, and themes of uncertainty and disintegration expressed in the arts—all worsened matters. These tensions made many Europeans, including many intellectuals and well-known observers, welcome war as a quick, all-encompassing relief. Facing these perils and tensions, Europe's stunningly inept political and military leaders made decisions based more on blind optimism and fear of humiliation than on reason and concern for their nation's well-being. At the time, few Europeans guessed how long the brutality would last.

THE FRONT LINES

Off to Battle

Almost everywhere in Europe, people greeted the declarations of war with outbursts of nationalistic joy. As the Austrian writer Stefan Zweig (1881–1942), a volunteer himself, recalled, "There were parades in the street, flags, ribbons, and music burst forth everywhere, young recruits were marching triumphantly, their faces lighting up at the cheering." Young men volunteered in droves, "honestly afraid that they might miss this most wonderful and exciting experience of their lives; that is why they hurried and thronged to the colors, and that is why they shouted and sang in the trains that carried them to the slaughter."

Celebrating war

Here, suddenly, was a way to end domestic divisions and renew one's sense of purpose in the world. Political opponents set their differences aside and came together to support the war effort. As the document here reveals, even socialists, long opposed to war and nationalistic calls, joined in the effort to promote national defense. Most feminists also suspended their political demands and offered ardent support for the military cause. The troops, people assumed, would surely be home by Christmas. Indeed, the British government promised that life would go on as usual with no shortages and no new regulations. Each combatant expected to win.

Nations initially on the sidelines soon enlisted with one side or the other (see the map on page 514). Hoping to gain territory in a victorious fight, Turkey and Bulgaria joined Germany and Austria-Hungary to become the **Central Powers.** Italy, long a member of the Triple Alliance with Germany and Austria-Hungary, had declared its neutrality at the beginning of the war, claiming that Austria had violated the alliance by launching a war of aggression on Serbia. Italy shifted its loyalty to France and Britain after receiving better promises of victory spoils. This side, eventually joined by many other nations from the Americas and the non-Western world, became known as the **Allies.** The Allies had the advantage of sheer numbers, but the Central Powers were led by Germany's better-equipped, well-trained army and could more easily move troops and coordinate military strategies.

The Central Powers versus the Allies

The Schlieffen Plan

Anticipating a confrontation with both Russia and France, the German high command resorted to a military strategy known as the **Schlieffen Plan.** This plan called for a holding action against the slow-moving Russians while the main German forces thrust through neutral Belgium to knock out France. Then the Germans could concentrate on destroying Russia. Great Britain, her allies hobbled, would sue for peace, the Germans expected.

Day after day, the Schlieffen Plan worked. Four weeks after the outbreak of hostilities, German forces arrived just outside Paris ahead of schedule. Some surprises, however, lay in store for them. Stubborn Belgian

Exploring the Past

A Russian Socialist Supports the War Effort

At the beginning of World War I, even socialist parties—which had long argued that they would not support a nationalistic war entered into by a government dominated by capitalists—supported the effort. The following letter from V. Bourtzeff, a Russian socialist, appeared in the London *Times* about six weeks after the outbreak of the war in 1914.

The representatives of all political parties and of all nationalities in Russia are now at one with the Government, and this war with Germany and Austria, both guided by the Kaiser, has already become a national war for Russia.

Even we, the adherents of the parties of the Extreme Left, and hitherto ardent anti-militarists and pacifists, even we believe in the necessity of *this* war. *This* war is a war to protect justice and civilization. It will, we hope, be a decisive factor in our united *war against war,* and we hope that after it, it will at last be possible to consider seriously the question of disarmament and universal peace. There can be no doubt that victory, and decisive victory at that (personally I await this in the immediate future), will be on the side of the Allied nations—England, France, Belgium, Serbia, and Russia.

To Russia this war will bring regeneration. . . .

What might this document suggest about the political advantages of going to war?

World War I
This map shows the two alliances and the major fronts in World War I. **What does this map reveal about the surrounded position of the Central Powers and the importance of Turkey during the war?**

resistance had held up the Germans long enough for the French to redeploy their forces to the north and for the British to send their small army across the Channel. Germans suffered unanticipated casualties and transportation problems. At a critical moment, the German command detached 100,000 of their best troops under Generals Hindenburg (1847–1934) and Ludendorff (1865–1937) and sent them east to fight the Russians, who had invaded Germany with unexpected speed. Nearing Paris, the German First Army detoured from its planned route in order to concentrate its force on the French capital. This move opened a gap in the Germans' eastern flank and exposed its western flank. At this juncture, the desperate French armies seized the opportunity and turned on the Germans. Parisian taxicabs rushed army reserves to the front in the effort to save Paris. Units of Britain's army arrived to enter the fray at a crucial moment. In the bloody seven-day Battle of the Marne, the Allies at last halted the Germans, drove them back several miles, and shattered German

hopes that the Schlieffen Plan would succeed. As the map on page 515 indicates, both sides extended their lines more than 400 miles from the Swiss border to the North Sea and dug in for the winter. Germany was now stuck with what it had tried so hard to avoid—a war on two fronts.

Slaughter and Stalemate on the Western Front

The defensive lines proved superior to offensive thrusts. To the surprise of almost everyone, the armies on the western front fought a war of attrition from their networks of trenches protected by barbed wire, mines,

Trench warfare

and machine guns. The trenches became filled with mud, rats, human bodies, lice, waste, poison gas, and the stench

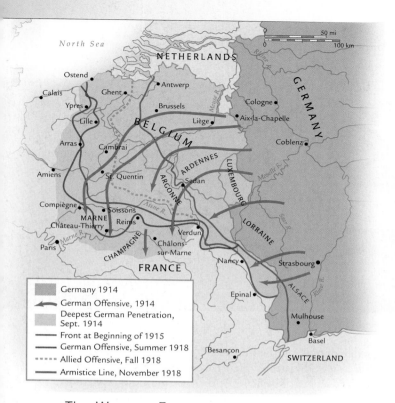

The young British poet and soldier Wilfred Owen related how the brutal reality of the war wiped out old images of its glory. Owen warned that anyone who saw the suffering

> *. . . would not tell with such high zest*
> *To children ardent for some desperate glory,*
> *The old Lie: Dulce et decorum est*
> *Pro patria mori. ("It is sweet and proper*
> *to die for one's country.")*

Military leaders failed to realize that machine guns, modern artillery, mass mobilization, and trenches had utterly changed the nature of warfare. Acting on old assumptions and oblivious to these new military realities, generals ordered offensives again and again. Each time the charges moved lines only yards, if at all, and each time the human costs were staggering. "We lie under the network of arching shells and live in a suspense of uncertainty," wrote German war veteran Erich Maria Remarque (1898–1970) in his novel *All Quiet on the Western Front*. "Over us Chance hovers." The wartime life expectancy of a front-line officer such as Wilfred Owen was only two months. After a year and a half of this mutual slaughter, nothing had changed.

The Western Front This map shows the western front at various stages of World War I.

of death. But they also served as homes and protection for troops under fire, as shown in the image here. Between the trenches, mortar and massive artillery bombardments created a barren, pockmarked landscape of mud and death that few soldiers could cross and still hope to live. The British introduced tanks in 1916 but did not manage to use them effectively to cross trenches until the last year of the war.

Despite the defensive advantages of **trench warfare,** military commanders remained wedded to notions of an offensive breakthrough. Again and again, they sent troops scrambling out of their trenches, over the top and into no-man's-land, where enemy machine-gun fire mowed them down by the thousands. Fritze Franke, a German soldier, described his experience of trench warfare in a November 1914 letter: "Every foot of ground contested, every hundred yards another trench; and everywhere bodies—rows of them! All the trees shot to pieces; the whole ground churned up a yard deep by the heaviest shells; dead animals; houses and churches . . . utterly destroyed. . . . And every troop that advances in support must pass through a mile of this chaos, through this gigantic burial ground and the reek of corpses." Fololiyani Longwe, an African serving in the British army on the western front, described how soldiers stood "buried in a hole with only your head and hands outside, holding a gun" for days with "no food, no water," and "only death smelling all over the place."

TRENCH WARFARE Rows of men in gas masks wait in trenches protected by barbed wire in this war of attrition on the western front.

Trench warfare created a demand for an armored, self-propelled weapon that could bridge trenches, maneuver across the cratered battlefields of the western front, and enable the infantry to break through enemy lines to victory. The British and French led efforts to develop this weapon: the tank. Today tanks remain a critical component of ground operations, although they have become much more sophisticated to meet the challenges of modern warfare. The Challenger 2, the current tank employed by British armies, is equipped with nuclear, biological, and chemical protection systems.

In 1916, the Germans tried for a draining victory by attacking the French fortress at Verdun (see map on page 514). Their plan was, in the words of the German commander, to "bleed to death" the French by forcing them to sustain massive casualties defending this historic strongpoint. During the ensuing nine-month battle, the Germans sometimes fired as many as a million shells in one day. The French managed to hold off the Germans, but 700,000 men on both sides lost their lives in the effort. "You found the dead embedded in the walls of the trenches, heads, legs, and half-bodies, just as they had been shovelled out of the way by the picks and shovels of the working party," recalled one French soldier.

Great battles of 1916

That same year the British attempted a breakthrough in the Battle of the Somme in northeastern France (see map on page 514). They suffered 60,000 casualties, with more than 20,000 killed in just the first day. "As far as you could see there were all these bodies lying there—literally thousands of them. . . . It didn't seem possible," wrote a British soldier. By fall, Britain had endured 400,000 casualties; France, 200,000; and Germany, 500,000, in this one battle. It ended in a stalemate. "Here chivalry disappeared for always," wrote the German Ernst Jünger. In the Passchendaele offensive (see map), the British again tried to break through the German "crust," losing some 400,000 soldiers in the effort. Like other great battles in the west, Passchendaele scarcely moved the front lines at all.

Neither the politicians nor the generals found the will to call a halt to the slaughter. Anything short of complete victory, they feared, would mean that all the deaths and casualties were in vain. The troops were not so stubborn. Sometimes they agreed to avoid battles. They even occasionally fraternized across the trenches, sang together, and allowed each other to eat meals in peace or collect the bodies of fellow soldiers in no-man's-land. They also were capable of making their outrage known to their superiors. After a new, disastrous offensive ordered by France's commander General Nivelle in April 1917, mutinies broke out in almost half the French divisions on the front. Thousands of soldiers were court-martialed and more than 500 sentenced to death, although most executions were never carried out. New commanders and troops tacitly agreed to stop these hopeless offensive onslaughts.

The photograph on page 517 illustrates how all means, old and new, were used to fight this war. Armies would use poison gas, flamethrowers, and tanks for the first time. Even dogs—75,000 of them—were employed to search for wounded men on the battlefronts.

Weapons of war

On the seas, both sides in the war hoped for decisive victories. The British navy set up a blockade of Germany, and the Germans responded with the submarine. Germany and Britain never met in a conclusive naval showdown, however. In the Battle of Jutland, the only major naval battle of the war, the British fleet prevented the German fleet from breaking the blockade—but suffered serious losses as a result. Most of the massive struggle took place on the ground. After three years of fighting, neither side could break through on the western front. By then, the French alone had sustained more than 3.5 million casualties. Yet the war dragged on.

Victory and Defeat on the Eastern and Southern Fronts

As the map on page 514 indicates, the war proved far more mobile and offensive on the eastern front than in the west. In eastern Europe, the terrain did not favor trench warfare, and in any case the Russians lacked the resources to sustain such a defensive effort. Initially, Russia, with its huge but inadequately supplied army, pushed into German and Austro-Hungarian lands. At the end of August 1914, however, the reinforced German armies, bolstered by their superior technology and leadership, trapped the Russians at Tannenberg and administered a crushing defeat. The Russian commander, General Samsonov, committed suicide on the spot. Farther south, the Russians defeated an Austro-Hungarian army at Lemberg only to bring in a German army that delivered a series of hammer blows to the Russians. The Germans drove deep into Russia and inflicted immense casualties, making Generals Hindenburg and Ludendorff heroes. In the Balkans, German, Austrian, and Bulgarian forces had eliminated Serbia from the war by the end of 1915. That same year, a disastrous Anglo-French effort to help the hard-pressed Russians by landing at Gallipoli and breaking through Turkish defenses at the nearby Dardanelles was beaten back by the Turks with heavy losses to the Allies (see map on page 514).

In 1916, Russia made one more great effort against the Austro-Hungarian forces in the south. Under General Aleksei Brusilov, Russian armies almost forced the Austro-Hungarians to withdraw from the war. The Austro-Hungarians resorted to recruiting men over the age of 50 into the army and, in the end, kept going only with German support. But the Russians could not sustain the effort. Lack of effective leadership, insufficient supplies, and desertions plagued Russia's armies. "Half of them have no rifles," Tsar Nicholas admitted, "the troops are losing masses and there is nobody to collect them on the battlefields." Germany's renewed push in 1917 resulted in massive Russian losses. These losses, along with internal strife that toppled the tsar, his government, and the succeeding provisional government (see pages 526–528), knocked Russia out of the war in December 1917. Nevertheless, for more than two years, the Russian effort had drawn German troops east, weakening the German forces in the west.

Russia's military collapse

Meanwhile, in northeastern Italy, Austrian and German troops won some costly battles, but the Italian forces limited the Central Powers' advances. Farther south and east, Allied forces attacked the Ottoman Empire. In 1915, after an Anglo-French fleet failed to open the Dardanelles strait so that Russia could receive supplies in her Black Sea ports, a 400,000-man force of British, French, Australian, New Zealand, and other troops landed at Gallipoli. The invaders suffered terrible defeats at the hands of the Turkish defenders and were forced to evacuate. Even more crippling, malaria, cholera, dysentery, and other diseases spread among the troops fighting in the Middle East. Eventually, the British, most notably the charismatic officer and writer T. E. Lawrence (1888–1935), stirred up Arab resentment into a desert revolt against the

Southern fronts

OLD AND NEW MEANS OF WARFARE In World War I, all means, from the traditional cavalry horses to the new airplanes, were used on the battlefront, as this period photograph documents.

Ottoman Turks in Palestine and Mesopotamia. Together, British and Arab forces gradually gained the upper hand against the Ottoman Turks.

The War Spreads Across the Globe

The war itself soon spread outside of Europe and the Mediterranean basin, in great part thanks to the West's colonies and imperial interests throughout the world. In the South Atlantic, British and German naval forces clashed off the Falkland Islands. In Africa, minor battles erupted around Germany's colonies. In East Asia, Japan joined the war on the Allied side and promptly seized German holdings in the Pacific and China. When Russia seemed on the verge of falling apart, Japan also sent soldiers into the tsar's far eastern provinces. Britain and France drew troops from Canada, Africa, Asia, and Australia to fight on several fronts. More than 1 million Indian soldiers served under the British, particularly in the Middle East campaigns, and hundreds of thousands of African soldiers from French colonies served in Europe. The Western nations also called on workers from these lands, including a 200,000-man labor battalion from China, to work in France and elsewhere in the war effort.

However, non-Western peoples often resisted the European powers' efforts to gain their support. Nomadic tribes fled Russia's central Asian provinces rather than serve in the tsar's army. In French West Africa, local tribes revolted when the French tried to mobilize labor brigades. Moreover, non-Westerners did not automatically favor the Allied cause. Most of those who followed the conflict in Asia viewed World War I as a European civil war. In addition, they were likely to favor Germany over France and Britain, two nations that had a tradition of Asian conquest. Indeed, for the most part, the first world war remained a European affair. Raging on year after year, the conflict shattered the lives of soldiers and civilians alike.

WAR ON THE HOME FRONT

No Western society could come through such a protracted war unscathed. As the toll on lives and supplies climbed, whole societies had to mobilize to support the military effort. In this sense, World War I became the first **total war,** blurring the traditional distinctions between combatants and civilians and between battle lines and the home front. The first world war transformed whole economies, societies, and governments, as well as the lives of soldiers.

Total war

Mobilizing Resources

After the first few months of hostilities, armies began to run out of ammunition, supplies, and troops. The French alone were firing more than 100,000 artillery shells a day—far more than their armaments factories could supply. Entire economies were reorganized to churn out huge quantities of bullets, guns, and machines in just days and weeks rather than the usual months and years. The war effort required untold quantities of other materials as well—everything from food and uniforms to trucks and coffins. Overall, the war demanded unprecedented industrial capability and organizational agility to produce and move supplies for the armed forces.

To varying degrees, the governments of the major powers took control of their economies. Government agencies, rather than the free marketplace, determined production, consumption, wages, and prices. In Germany, the War Raw Materials Board located, rationed, and distributed raw materials. To meet the need for products that Germany could no longer import, such as rubber, the board helped develop synthetic substitutes. In Britain, the Ministry of Munitions, led by David Lloyd George, supervised the armaments industry. The ministry's bureaucracy of 65,000 clerks controlled prices, supplies, and production of war materials.

Governments take control

This tightly controlled mobilization of resources also included people. Not only were men drafted into the armed services, but women and men on the home fronts were often required to work in accord with priorities determined by the government. Labor unions were brought into partnership with business and government. In addition, governments suspended laws limiting the length of the workday and controlling workplace conditions. People were thus forced to work longer hours under dangerous circumstances.

Demand for troops on the front lines and labor on the home front altered traditional social and national boundaries. Although the war did not eliminate class conflict, social distinctions blurred as people from all walks of society joined the war effort and worked or fought side by side. Conventional national distinctions were sometimes violated: For a while, the hardpressed Germans forced thousands of Belgians to move and work in German factories. The war effort could even include children: Some German teachers organized their students to go through garbage and collect anything that might be useful. Perhaps most striking, officials challenged traditional gender roles by calling women into the labor force.

WOMEN WAR WORKERS This interior view of a British armaments plant reveals how mass production, supported by women workers, created the huge quantity of materials needed for the war effort.

New Gender Roles

Gender roles changed radically under the pressures of all-out war. At first, many women were left on their own financially as their husbands marched off to battle. Later, when economies began straining with the war effort, women got new jobs previously reserved for men. The image on page 518 shows women working in a large British armaments plant, producing the huge quantity of shells needed on the battle lines. Such women participated in all aspects of the munitions industries. They became army clerks and streetcar conductors and drove taxis and ran farms. Some served as firefighters at home and as nurses at the front. Others gained entry into white-collar jobs in banks, commercial businesses, and urban offices. In Great Britain, the number of women working outside the home had increased twentyfold to some five million by 1918. In Russia, women made up over 40 percent of the labor force. Similar patterns held in other European countries.

These shifting labor patterns created new tensions over women's roles as men began fearing they would lose their jobs to women permanently. "Workmen have to be handled with the utmost tenderness and caution lest they should actually imagine . . . that women could do their work equally well," wrote a female British munitions factory worker in 1916. Women themselves often had conflicted feelings about their new role. Many gained a new sense of independence from earning a paycheck. Some displayed their newfound freedom by living alone, going out socially on their own, wearing shorter dresses, cutting (bobbing) their hair, and smoking cigarettes. By no coincidence, several nations would grant women the right to vote at the war's end.

Maintaining the Effort

As the war persisted, governments became more involved in manufacturing consent and less tolerant of dissent. Propaganda specialists tried

Propaganda

to inspire support for the war and hatred for the enemy. The more the propaganda succeeded in its aims, the harder it became for governments to compromise or withdraw from the conflict. Officials deliberately manipulated information and censored private letters to shape

Let Us Never Forget

Numerous propaganda posters were produced on all sides of the war. This image from a French magazine depicts Germans as having committed atrocities during their march through Belgium and northern France. Here an innocent, horror-stricken, assaulted woman kneels on a blood-soaked crib and cradles the body of her murdered child. The empty wine bottles and helmet scattered on the ground around her leave no doubt that immoral German soldiers have committed these acts.   In what ways has the artist used visual clues to prompt the viewer to read this picture as a dramatic series of events that have just occurred?

public opinion about the war. In particular, they tried to create the impression that their own country was completely virtuous and that it was the other nations that were committing crimes against humanity. To combat war weariness, governments painted the enemy as evil incarnate and whipped up people's sense of outrage. There was no way, political leaders declared, that "good" people could ever make peace with such diabolical opponents.

Governments also tried to promote dissent among their opponents and turn neutral countries into allies. Germany supported the Irish in their 1916 Easter Rebellion in Dublin for Irish independence, which British forces brutally crushed. Germany also aided the Bolsheviks against Russia's government. The British promoted rebellion among the Arabs against the Turks and used propaganda to help bring the Americans in on their side.

Victories or defeats on the front lines reflected the abilities of civilian societies to mobilize effectively for the war effort—materially, politically, and psychologically. Those nations less able to develop and sustain this vast homefront effort—such as the Austro-Hungarian and Russian empires—faltered first. They lacked the solid industrial base and organizational strength of Germany, France, and Great Britain. Over time, however, even the strongest nations weakened under the strains of total war. Food shortages spawned malnutrition, disease, and high infant mortality, especially in Germany, which acutely felt the impact of Britain's naval blockade. Governments tried to pay for the war by printing more money, thereby creating an inflation of prices.

By 1917, hunger and war weariness were igniting strikes and domestic disorders throughout Europe. Beleaguered governments suspended civil liberties, ignored democratic procedures, and ruled by **Rising dissent** emergency police powers. In France, Georges Clemenceau (1841–1929) became a virtual dictator after November 1917. He sent troops against strikers and arrested those agitating for peace. "I wage war," he declared. "I wage nothing but war!" In Austria, political unity unraveled as different nationalities clamored for independence. In Germany, some socialist and Catholic legislators came out for peace, and Generals Hindenburg and Ludendorff assumed control over the German war effort. By the end of 1917, Russia's whole war effort had collapsed. Clearly, World War I would be won or lost on the home front as well as on the battle lines.

TO THE BITTER END

Early in 1917, the German high command grew desperate to bring the draining war to a victorious conclusion. The generals decided to launch an unrestricted submarine campaign against enemy and neutral shipping alike. Germany's leaders knew this policy could bring the United States into the war. Up to that point, the United States had remained neutral but had become increasingly invested in the Allied cause through trade and loans. The sense that Germany and its partners were the aggressors, along with the 1915 sinking of the passenger liner *Lusitania* during a German submarine blockade of Britain, had also nudged American public opinion toward support of the Allies. Now Germany's high command gambled that they could defeat Britain and France before the Americans could send enough supplies and troops to Europe to make a difference. Indeed, Ludendorff and Hindenburg promised victory within only six months.

At about the same time, British intelligence turned over to the United States an alarming note that it claimed to have intercepted. In that document, called the Zimmermann note, Germany offered to grant U.S. territory to Mexico—the very territory lost by Mexico in the 1848 Mexican-American War—if **The U.S. enters the war** Mexico agreed to attack the United States. When German submarines began sinking American cargo ships, U.S. entry into the conflict was ensured. On April 6, 1917, the United States declared war on Germany. President Woodrow Wilson promised to "make the world safe for democracy."

The Germans had good reason to think that they might prevail. At the beginning of 1918, the United States' contribution to the war was still relatively small. In addition, the Italians had suffered a disastrous blow at the Battle of Caporetto, almost putting them out of the war. Romania had been defeated, and Russia had withdrawn from the war. Now Germany could at last focus its efforts on a one-front war. In the Atlantic, its U-boats (submarines) were sinking one-fourth of all ships taking supplies to Britain—350 ships went down in one month alone.

On the other hand, Germany's allies—the Austro-Hungarian and Ottoman Empires—were teetering, and Germany was suffering from lack of materials and food, thanks to Britain's naval blockade. The British had also discovered a way to foil the U-boats by using heavily escorted convoys armed with depth charges. Now the race was between Germany and the United States. Germany transferred troops from the Russian front in an effort to overwhelm Great Britain and France before waves of American troops could arrive, while the United States struggled to raise, train, and transport sufficient forces to France to stem the German tide.

In March 1918, General Ludendorff launched, on the western front, the first of a series of massive German blows designed to end the war. The British and French were driven back with heavy losses. Desperate, they finally agreed to a unified **Final battles** command under France's General Ferdinand Foch (1851–1929). By mid-June, after the fourth of the great drives, the Allied lines were so badly battered that when the climactic fifth drive began along the Marne River in mid-July, Ludendorff wired the kaiser: "If the attack succeeds, the war will be over and we will have won it." When Foch heard the opening German barrage, he wired his government: "If the present German attack succeeds, the war is over and we have lost it." The Allies stopped the Germans by a narrow margin. Foch, now receiving a swelling stream of fresh American soldiers—more than 250,000 soldiers a month—immediately ordered a counterattack. British tanks helped break through German lines. The balance shifted. Suddenly, the Germans were in retreat. German strength and morale waned rapidly. That spring and summer, Germans suffered more than 2 million casualties.

At the end of October, Germany's Bulgarian and Turkish allies surrendered. On November 3, Austria-Hungary, its ethnic minorities in revolt, also surrendered; a week later, the last Austro-Hungarian emperor abdicated. The next day, mutiny broke out in the German navy and spread to workers in German cities. Popular uprisings brought down the kaiser's government, and on November 9 he fled the country. On November 11, the new German Republic government accepted an armistice.

For many, however, even the last days of the war were too long. In Britain, Wilfred Owen's mother, like so many others, received news of her son's death (he was machine-gunned in a final attack) just as church bells began ringing for victory. Those last days would also leave a haunting legacy in Germany. German commanders manipulated reports from the front so that most of Germany's population remained unaware of the extent of their country's military collapse. The new civilian government of republicans and socialists in Germany would later be blamed by many Germans for the surrender. This development would in turn set the stage for future charges that Germany had not really lost the war but had been stabbed in the back by the very political forces that would rule Germany during the 1920s.

connect to today

Causes of Wars

By itself, the events on June 1914 would not have led nations to commit to such a costly endeavor as World War I. But people turned the event into a spark that ignited a deadly fire they could not put out. What insights from studying World War I might we use to analyze the potential causes of wars in today's world and to anticipate how a war, once started, unfolds?

ASSESSING THE LOSSES

The war had shattered much of Europe. Some 10 million soldiers and perhaps another 7–10 million civilians had perished from the war and its hardships. Russia lost almost 2 million soldiers, as did Germany. Serbia lost some 15–20 percent of its population. All across northern France and Belgium, war cemeteries spread, many with unmarked graves, others with elaborate monuments to the fallen such as those shown on page 522. Europe lost the cream of a generation of its future leaders. Colonial troops from Asia and Africa also suffered. The image on page 523, showing a Senegalese soldier learning to use artificial limbs with the help of a Red Cross nurse, indicates the price many such veterans paid for their service.

For those left behind, the hardships persisted. Many survivors would have to spend the rest of their lives in veterans' hospitals. In many places, mutilated people, widows, and spinsters seemed the rule rather than the exception. Many survivors would remain obsessed with the experience of this war, like the British poet Siegfried Sassoon, who wrote, "The rank stench of those bodies haunts me still, And I remember things I'd best forget" (see Exploring the Past on page 524). In addition to all the death and misery, the fighting brought incalculable financial and material losses. The war laid to waste a tenth of the richest region of France and devastated the most developed part of Russia. It also saddled European nations with heavy debts, especially to a new international creditor—the United States. Finally, it was difficult not to merge the losses from the war with the tens of millions of deaths caused by the 1918 flu pandemic. That flu, which spread rapidly around the globe, was not *caused* by World War I, but the close quarters of troops and the mass movements of people spurred by the war probably added to the suffering and the staggering death toll.

THE PEACE SETTLEMENT

No peace settlement could make up for the losses of World War I. Nevertheless, delegates who gathered at Versailles near Paris in January 1919 and the people they represented expected a resolution that could somehow justify those losses. Other burdens weighed on the delegates as well. The end of fighting did not stop wartime hatred and suffering. Starvation threatened central and eastern

Käthe Kollwitz (1867–1945)

By the eve of World War I, Käthe Kollwitz's prints, drawings, and posters had made her one of Germany's leading artists. "[M]y art has purpose," she said. "I want to be effective in this time when people are so helpless and in need of aid."

In early August 1914, just after World War I broke out, the Kollwitz family heard German soldiers singing as they marched in the streets. Käthe wept in horror. During those same days, her youngest son, Peter, only 18 years old, volunteered for the army. On August 27, 1914, she wrote, "Where do all the women who have watched so carefully over the lives of their beloved ones get the heroism to send them to face the cannon? I am afraid that this soaring of the spirit will be followed by the blackest despair and dejection." A month later, she wrote, "It seems so stupid that the boys must go to war … how can they possibly take part in such madness?" Three weeks later, on October 22, 1914, Peter was killed in the war.

This loss of her son haunted Käthe for the rest of her life. In letters and diaries, she expressed endless grief for her fallen boy. She expanded her sorrow to embrace grieving mothers in all countries. Reflecting on the causes of the war, she described how Peter and others she knew had "subordinated their lives to the idea of patriotism. The English, Russian and French young men have done the same. The conse-quence has been this terrible killing and the impoverishment of Europe."

After her son's death, Käthe began a long struggle to create monumental sculptures in memory of Peter and other sons killed in the war. It would take her ten years to start work on the final forms for these sculptures and another eight years before the figures were completed in stone. A photograph of the two sculptures is shown here.

How does Kollwitz's life reflect the impact of World War I on European society? How does war today impact society?

KÄTHE KOLLWITZ, *THE MOURNING FATHER AND MOTHER*

Europe. In addition, a growing fear of revolutionary communism haunted the delegates, who primarily represented the forces of order and wealth in their nations. Already in power in Russia, communists had a real chance of triumphing in Germany and in the newly independent states of eastern Europe.

Versailles: A Victors' Peace

Although all thirty-two of the victorious Allies participated in the peace conference, the leaders of France, Great Britain, the United States, and Italy made the major decisions. Representatives of colonized peoples, ethnic and religious groups, women's organizations, and various national groups went to Versailles hoping for a hearing but received none. The vanquished Germany and Austria-Hungary were excluded from the talks, as was Russia, which had dropped out of the war a year earlier.

Premier Georges Clemenceau, the aged Tiger of France, headed the French delegation. As host of the conference and leader of the nation that had done the most to defeat Germany, Clemenceau expected to dominate the decision making. The eloquent and fiery Prime Minister David Lloyd George led the British delegation. He also intended to dominate the conference. Premier Vittorio Orlando (1860–1952), head of the Italian delegation, wanted all the territory that the Allies had promised in the first place to draw Italy into the war. The idealistic President Woodrow Wilson (1856–1924), expecting approval of his Fourteen Points as the basis for peace, led the American delegation. The United States had attained much prestige during the war and was the first non-European country in centuries to influence the fate of European nations.

A fundamental and bitter clash immediately developed between France's Premier Georges Clemenceau, who wanted a "hard" peace that would render Germany harmless, and U.S. President Woodrow Wilson (1856–1924),

Wilson's Fourteen Points

who wanted a "just" peace free of vindictiveness that would leave Germany resentful or ripe for takeover by extreme political forces. In his Fourteen Points, Wilson called for the self-determination of peoples, armaments reduction, and a "general association of nations" to guarantee the safety of "great and small states alike." British Prime Minister David Lloyd George often sided with Wilson but, like Clemenceau, wanted a victory worthy of the sacrifices made during the war.

It took six months of hard work and wrangling to draw up the peace terms. Although the Treaty of Versailles reflected many of Wilson's ideals, it was more of a victors' peace reflecting France's desire for security and an eager-

CASUALTY FROM THE COLONIES A nurse helps one of the many soldiers from Europe's colonies who became casualties of the war.

ness to punish Germany. In what came to be known as the **war guilt clause,** the agreement forced Germany and its allies to accept full responsibility for the war. Germany lost all its overseas colonies and concessions; several victorious nations gained control over these territories in Africa and the Pacific. France regained Alsace and Lorraine, lost in the Franco-Prussian War of 1870. In addition, the victors would occupy German territory on the west bank of the Rhine for the next fifteen years. The Polish-speaking areas of eastern Germany were ceded to the resurrected Polish state, and a "Polish corridor" was cut through German territory to give Poland an outlet at Danzig to the Baltic Sea. Germany's armed forces were limited to 100,000 soldiers and saddled with severe armament limitations. Finally, Germany was held liable for reparations that in 1921 were set at $33 billion.

Redrawing the Map of Europe

As the map on page 525 reveals, the treaties dealt the harshest blow to Germany's allies because the territorial rearrangements were usually based on the principle of unifying national language groups. Austria-Hungary was cut down from a polyglot empire of 50 million—second in area only to Russia among the nations of Europe—to an Austria of 6.5 million German-speaking Austrians and a Hungary of 8 million Magyars. Many in Austria wanted

In the Trenches and Beyond

Some of the most poignant accounts of experiences on the front lines come from poets who have served in the military. Unlike many poets, Siegfried Sassoon (1886–1967) survived World War I. But the experience would haunt him for the rest of his life. The following is from "Does it Matter?"

Does it Matter?

Does it matter?—losing your legs? . . .

For people will always be kind,

And you need not show that you mind

When the others come in after hunting

To gobble their muffins and eggs.

Does it matter?—losing your sight? . . .

There's such splendid work for the blind;

And people will always be kind,

As you sit on the terrace remembering

And turning your face to the light.

Do they matter?—those dreams from the
   pit? . . .

You can drink and forget and be glad,

And people won't say that you're mad;

For they'll know you've fought for your
   country

And no one will worry a bit.

What do you think Sassoon means by "Does it Matter?"

---

their new country to merge with Germany, but the settlement specifically forbad this arrangement. The Czechs and Slovaks were joined into the new state of Czechoslovakia, which included sizable German and other minorities. Serbs, Croats, Slovenes, Bosnians, and others populated the new state of Yugoslavia. The Ottoman Empire was dismembered, and parts of its Anatolian homeland were occupied by British, French, Italian, and Greek forces. Perhaps unavoidably, all these new national boundaries created many internal ethnic divisions and pockets of discontent that would breed future conflicts.

Woodrow Wilson had placed his chief hopes for peace in an association of countries—the **League of Nations**—that he expected would guarantee borders and peaceably settle the tensions and conflicts that were certain to arise in the future. The League was incorporated into

The League of Nations

the treaty with Germany but had no military forces at its command. Its only weapons were economic sanctions and moral condemnations. Though perhaps well intentioned, the League was doomed almost from the beginning. The exclusion of Germany and the Soviet Union from the association weakened its potential effectiveness. In addition, the self-righteous President Wilson—reluctant to compromise with political opponents back in the United States and physically weakening—failed to persuade the isolationist American Senate to ratify the peace accords and join the League. What little faith Great Britain and France had in Wilson's ideas quickly disappeared.

Legacy of the Peace Treaty

The peace settlement negotiated in Paris satisfied no one and left a legacy of deep resentments. France's Clemenceau considered the terms too lenient. Moreover, both Great Britain and the United States refused French pleas to join France in a defensive alliance. Not surprisingly, the French felt betrayed and abandoned. The Germans, for their part, considered the terms outrageous. Many Germans refused to believe that their armies had lost the war. The Germans also resented not being allowed to participate in the talks. Their representatives were presented with a humiliating settlement that they signed only after the Allies threatened to invade. Italy's leader, Orlando, walked out of the conference to protest broken Allied promises of more territorial gains.

Nationalists in Turkey, led by their wartime hero of Gallipoli, Mustafa Kemal (1881–1938), refused to accept the Treaty of Sèvres, which had been negotiated by the Allies and the sultan's tottering regime in 1920. That treaty allowed foreign powers to occupy eastern and southern Anatolia. Mustafa Kemal's national army drove out the occupying troops, toppled the sultan's regime, and

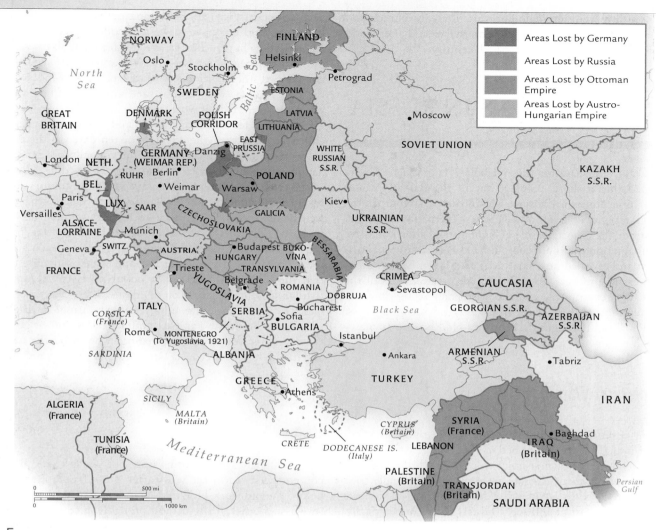

Europe, 1923 **This map shows Europe after the settlement that ended World War I.**

established the Republic of Turkey—an act affirmed by the Allies in the Treaty of Lausanne (1923).

In areas of North Africa and the Middle East, Arabs were outraged by decisions of the Allied powers. Arab nationalists had been promised independence by the British and French during the war. Now mandates from the League of Nations authorized the French to exercise administrative control over Lebanon and Syria, and the British over Mesopotamia and Palestine. According to the League of Nations, these peoples were "not yet able to stand by themselves" and their "tutelage . . . should be entrusted to the advanced nations." Making matters worse, Britain had promised Jewish nationalists a homeland in Palestine.

China refused to sign because the Treaty of Versailles gave the Japanese rights in the Chinese mainland, and Japan left offended because the conference refused to

declare formally the equality of all races. Russia, which had suffered huge losses, had not even been invited to the conference, and the U.S. government failed to ratify the treaty.

John Maynard Keynes (1883–1946), an influential British economist who attended the talks, perhaps best summed up the flaws in the Paris agreement in his book *The Economic Consequences of the Peace* (1919). "[T]he treaty," Keynes warned, "includes no provisions for the economic rehabilitation of Europe—nothing to make the defeated Central Empires into good neighbors, nothing to stabilize the new States of Europe, nothing to reclaim Russia."

World War I had unleashed passions and destruction of such magnitudes that possibly no settlement could have sufficed. Nowhere in the West did those passions rage stronger than in Russia, defeated by Germany in 1917 and still reeling from internal upheavals. There, revolution and civil war were forging a new union that would alter world affairs for the rest of the twentieth century.

REVOLUTIONS IN RUSSIA

In 1914, the Russian tsar Nicholas II and his advisors hoped that a short, painless war in the Balkans would overcome domestic divisions within Russia, strengthen the tsar's regime, and improve Russia's international stature. Instead, the "short, painless" fight turned into a massive conflagration that only compounded Russia's internal discord and revealed how far Russia had fallen behind other powers to the west. In addition, the greatest fears of the tsar, his government, and the aristocracy whose interests he represented came true: World War I devastated Russia militarily and brought the centuries-old Romanov dynasty crashing down.

The First Warnings

1905

Long-simmering discontent made Russia ripe for violent upheaval. This discontent had its roots in the Russian government's historical resistance to change. Throughout the nineteenth century, Russia's government had usually tried to ignore rather than adapt to the liberalizing movements that swept most of Europe. The tsar ruled autocratically, relying on the nobility, the church, the army, and the bureaucracy without allowing a hint of political participation to the vast majority of Russian society. Industrialization, initiated in the 1880s and surging in the 1890s—encouraged by the aggressive policies of Sergei Witte (1849–1915), the finance minister, and an infusion of foreign capital into Russia—stimulated the growth of the middle and working classes in cities such as Moscow and St. Petersburg. These people chafed against Russia's traditional society and archaic government. Frustrated Russian intellectuals turned to revolutionary doctrines and even terrorism in an effort to promote rapid change. Others hoped for more moderate liberal reforms. Still the tsarist government, particularly under Nicholas II (1894–1917), refused to bend.

A turning point came with the embarrassing defeat of the tsar's army and navy by Japan in the 1904–1905 Russo-Japanese War. The various liberal and radical groups took advantage of the government's weakness and clamored for reform. The mounting pressures for change finally exploded early in 1905. On Sunday, January 22, thousands of workers gathered in front of the tsar's palace in St. Petersburg to protest economic hardships. "We have

become beggars; we have been oppressed; we are burdened by toil beyond our powers; we are scoffed at; we are not recognized as human beings; we are treated as slaves who must suffer their bitter fate and who must keep silence," complained the petitioners. Marchers sang "God save the tsar," but the tsar's troops fired on them, killing and wounding hundreds of women, men, and children.

Demands for reform increased, and in October, a general strike paralyzed the country for ten days. In the cities, workers organized themselves into councils, or **soviets.** Sailors mutinied on the battleship *Potemkin,* as did soldiers in the army. At the same time, peasants in the countryside revolted and attacked wealthy landowners. Several officials were assassinated. With much of its army pinned down thousands of miles away in the Russo-Japanese War, the tsar's government wavered. Surrounded by dissension and revolt, Nicholas II yielded at last and issued a manifesto that promised civil liberties, a popularly elected Duma (parliament), and legalization of unions. These concessions had little lasting meaning, however. The return of the Russian troops from the Far East and a fresh round of governmental repression had restored order by 1907. The tsar and his advisors reduced the Duma to a nondemocratically elected body.

The Fall of the Tsar

The few halfhearted reforms were not enough, and discontent persisted in the years after 1905. In the months before the outbreak of World War I, strikes proliferated in Russia's cities. This turmoil probably encouraged the tsar to bring Russia into the war, for he immediately banned strikes and suspended the Duma, whose members still agitated for liberal reforms. As we saw earlier, Russia soon suffered staggering losses at the hands of the German armies. Its leadership, transportation facilities, supplies, and armaments simply could not withstand the demands of total war. Moreover, many non-Russian subjects living within the empire became more interested in establishing their own independent states than supporting the war effort.

In August 1915, a desperate Nicholas made a fatal mistake: He left the capital to take personal command of the army. As a result of Nicholas's actions, the Russian people blamed the tsar for their country's military losses. Equally problematic, the inept, unpopular government in the capital now fell under the sway of Nicholas's wife, Alexandra. When the tsarina came under the influence of Grigori Efimovich Rasputin (ca. 1871–1916), a corrupt Siberian mystic who claimed to have the power to heal the tsar's hemophiliac son, things took a more bizarre turn. Even the tsar's aristocratic supporters, a group of whom finally murdered Rasputin late in 1916, demanded fundamental change.

In early March 1917, the dam broke. The strains of war drove hungry working-women to initiate strikes and demonstrations. With industrialization, Petrograd (St. Petersburg), Moscow, and other Russian cities had grown rapidly. Women, who made up more than half of the labor force in Petrograd, had to work long hours for low wages and then stand in long bread lines to buy food for their families. Rising prices and shrinking supplies, especially during the winters, translated into hunger and starvation.

The March revolution

DEMONSTRATIONS IN PETROGRAD, 1917 Marches such as this one in March 1917 by Petrograd women led to the revolution that overthrew Russia's tsar and his government.

Women rightly blamed the government for Russia's continuing involvement in the war and for the food shortages. On March 8, in recognition of International Women's Day, they made their voices heard. That day, 10,000 women marched into Petrograd, shouting, "Down with war and high prices! Down with starvation! Bread for workers!" The protesters also demanded an end to the rule of Nicholas II. Thousands of sympathizers, both women and men, joined the demonstrations in the wintry days of March 1917. Yet police and troops were reluctant to fire on the crowds, especially because so many of them were women. Many troops actually joined the demonstrators. The French ambassador to Russia reported watching "a disorderly mob carrying a red flag" marching toward an oncoming regiment of troops. But instead of restoring order, "the army was fraternizing with the revolt." Too many people had lost their respect for the rigid, poorly led autocracy. As Russia's minister of foreign affairs put it, "The Emperor is blind!" Many of his colleagues agreed. On March 12, the Duma organized a provisional government, and three days later Nicholas II abdicated. Railroad workers took him and his family into custody.

The Provisional Government

Most members of the provisional government hoped that Russia would move toward constitutional parliamentary democracy. Led by moderate liberals Pavel Milyukov (1859–1943) and Prince Georgi Lvov (1861–1925), these politicians represented the upper classes. The provisional government enacted into law civil liberties, religious freedom, equality before the law, union rights, and other liberal reforms. They also promised more fundamental social reforms and a constitution.

However, in addition to its inexperience, its rival factions, and the intensifying pressures for change, the provisional government labored under three key burdens. First,

it had to share power with the soviets—the political organizations of workers, soldiers, and radical intellectuals—particularly the strong Petrograd soviet. The soviets favored socialist self-rule and stood against the upper classes represented by the provisional government. Second, the government chose to continue Russia's draining involvement in World War I. The links between these first two burdens came to light with the Petrograd soviet's issuance of Order Number 1 on March 14. This significant mandate declared that military officers would be democratically elected by soldiers and that military decisions would be democratically made. Order Number 1 further unraveled authority and discipline within Russia's armed forces. Third, neither the provisional government nor the soviets could control the peasantry, which made up some 80 percent of the population. Peasants refused to wait for the land-redistribution legislation that the government had promised. They seized land and hoarded food for themselves, worsening hunger in the cities as prices rose and supplies became more scarce. The peasantry's defiance also attracted soldiers, who deserted the front to make land claims of their own.

The soviets

The provisional government failed to satisfy many. The peasants wanted still more land, and workers demanded more bread. Russia could no longer support the unpopular war effort, yet the government could not find a way to withdraw gracefully from it. Again and again the provisional government tried to rally the Russian troops to victory. In desperation, it even created the Women's Battalion of Death in an effort to shame male soldiers into greater effort. More than 80 percent of these women became casualties. The desertions continued.

In May, the liberal heads of the provisional government resigned and the moderate socialist Alexander Kerensky (1881–1970) became the leading figure in the government. Kerensky, however, faced new political divisions, for by this time many radical intellectuals had returned to Russia from the west, where they had fled from the tsar's repression, or rose from Russia's social ranks. They tried to push ideas and events in one direction or the other. Those who proved most influential came from a group of Marxist revolutionaries, the Social Democrats—in particular their minority faction, the Bolsheviks. This faction was led by Vladimir Ilich Ulyanov (1870–1924), known by his revolutionary name, Lenin.

Kerensky leads

The Rise of the Bolsheviks

Marxism had become influential among some Russian intellectuals, revolutionaries, and groups critical of Russia's tsarist autocracy toward the end of the nineteenth century. In 1898, Russian Marxists had formed the Social Democratic Party, whose principal leaders were Georgi Plekhanov (1857–1918) and his disciple Lenin. Repression by the tsar's government forced the Social Democrats into exile. At a London conference in 1903, the radical Bolshevik wing under Lenin split from the more moderate Mensheviks.

Until 1917, Lenin's **Bolsheviks** remained only a minor party within Russia. Its leaders were hunted down by the state police and shot, imprisoned, or exiled. For seventeen years, Lenin remained in exile in Switzerland, keeping his party alive from a distance and plotting the eventual overthrow of the tsar's government. During that time, he developed theoretical and tactical principles that the Bolsheviks would later use. Three of these principles set forth the most crucial guidelines and, for the most part, set Lenin's Bolsheviks apart from other Marxist organizations. First, the party should be an elite, highly trained, and constantly purged (cleaned of disloyal ideas and people) group of dedicated Marxist revolutionaries capable of instructing and leading the masses. This elite would not be seduced by short-term gains. Second, contrary to what Marx had argued, the socialist revolution need not include only the industrial working class. In Russia, it could be a dual revolution of workers and poor, land-hungry peasants—all part of an even broader socialist revolution that would sweep through other European countries. Third, the party

Lenin's principles

should firmly oppose participation in the war, which Lenin considered a product of imperialist rivalries and a continuing civil war among capitalists.

In April 1917, the German government secretly transported Lenin from his place of exile in Switzerland to a Baltic port, from which he made his way to Russia, in an effort to worsen the chaos in Russia and remove Russia from the war. The Germans had good reason to consider Lenin a threat to stability in Russia. John Reed, a sympathetic American journalist and observer, described Lenin as "a strange popular leader—a leader purely by virtue of intellect; colorless, humorless, uncompromising and detached; without picturesque idiosyncrasies—but with the power of explaining profound ideas in simple terms, of analyzing a concrete situation." Back in Russia, Lenin refused to cooperate with the provisional government. Instead, he unleashed a barrage of compelling slogans, such as "Peace to the Army," "Land to the Peasants," "Ownership of the Factories to the Workers," and "All Power to the Soviets." He argued that the time was ripe for a socialist revolution against capitalism. To achieve this revolution, he urged his followers to gain control over the soviets, particularly the powerful Petrograd soviet.

When Kerensky failed to extract Russia from the war, Bolshevik influence grew, especially among the Petrograd workers and soldiers. In July 1917, a massive popular demonstration against the provisional government erupted in that city. Most members of the Bolshevik Party supported the demonstration, though in the end the leadership did not. In these bloody July Days, the provisional government put down the demonstrators with force. The Kerensky government arrested many Bolsheviks and impelled others, including Lenin, to flee to Finland.

Yet Kerensky soon suffered a fresh round of failures in the war as well as the threat of an impending coup d'état by General Lavr Kornilov (1870–1918). To avert disaster, in September the desperate Kerensky released the Bolsheviks and relied on the soviets to defend the capital against Kornilov. Kornilov's plans failed when most of his soldiers refused to follow his orders to attack Petrograd.

By October, many leading figures from larger socialist parties had become discredited through their association with the provi-

"Peace to the Army"

Russia's July Days

OPINION

Why do you think historians find it easier to understand why a revolution toppled the tsar than why the Bolsheviks came to power several months later in a second revolution?

Communism and Civil War

LENIN PROCLAIMING SOVIET POWER This propagandistic painting by Vladimir Serov shows Lenin, backed by Stalin, announcing the Bolshevik victory in 1917.

sional government. This turn of events helped the Bolsheviks, under the leadership of Lenin and the brilliant Leon Trotsky (1879–1940), finally gain control over the Petrograd and Moscow soviets. Bolshevik women created a network to call for demonstrations, organize women in factories, and do paramilitary work. Lenin judged the time right for his next move.

On November 6, he and Trotsky launched a well-organized seizure of power. His Red Guards (workers' militia units) took over crucial control centers and arranged for the transfer of power to the soviets and Lenin. Within just hours, the deed was complete. Kerensky, unable to reorganize his forces, fled. Although some of the fighting was violent, the success of the Bolshevik revolution stemmed mostly from the revolutionaries' organizational talents, a lack of effective resistance by the provisional government, and Trotsky's success in portraying the uprising as *defense* of the soviets rather than a Bolshevik *offensive*. On November 7, the Bolshevik majority enthusiastically elected Lenin the head of the new government.

The November revolution

The Bolsheviks, who now called themselves Communists, immediately moved to fulfill their promises and consolidate their power. In place of the old tsarist hierarchy, they set up a pyramid of people's soviets, or councils. These councils were elected by universal suffrage but were actually dominated by relatively few Communist Party members. When national elections failed to return a Communist majority to the Constituent Assembly, Lenin had armed sailors disperse that elected body. Capitalism was abolished outright. A barter system of exchange replaced money, the value of the ruble having been destroyed by inflation and devaluation. Committees of workers responsible to party commissars took over management of industry and commerce. The government nationalized the land and turned over its management to local peasant committees, who then distributed it to individual peasants to be worked by their own labor. All crop surpluses were to be given to the state. Finally, the state expropriated church lands and enacted laws to establish the legal equality of the sexes—the first Western government to do so.

To buy time and free the new regime for the enormous task of refashioning Russian society, Lenin immediately opened peace negotiations with Germany. The Germans, realizing Russia's helplessness, demanded the harshest of terms. Lenin attempted to stall them, but in March 1918, when the Germans threatened to attack Petrograd and Moscow, he signed the Treaty of Brest-Litovsk. Russia lost Finland, Estonia, Latvia, Lithuania, the Ukraine, Bessarabia, the Polish provinces, and some of the Trans-Caucasian territory. Lenin had paid a high price for peace. These lands contained one-third of Russia's European population, three-fourths of its iron, and nine-tenths of its coal. In addition, Germany compelled Russia to pay a heavy indemnity. Lenin gambled that a socialist revolution in Germany would reverse some of these losses and provide the support that the fledgling socialist system desperately needed to survive in Russia.

Nevertheless, these hard peace terms were not the worst of Lenin's woes. A bitter civil war broke out in Russia following the peace with Germany (see map on page 530). The Russian aristocracy, including most of the higher army officers, launched a series of uncoordinated attacks against the Bolshevik regime. These "White" forces were aided by various other groups disaffected by the revolution. They also had the support of French, British, Greek, Polish, Japanese, Czech, and U.S. troops that were in Russia for various reasons, but in great part to oppose the anti-capitalist Bolshevik government. For decades afterward, the Communists would remember how the outside world had turned against them during this vulnerable time.

Creating an emergency policy of "war communism," the Bolshevik government mobilized Russia's economy and society for the civil-war effort. Urban workers and troops

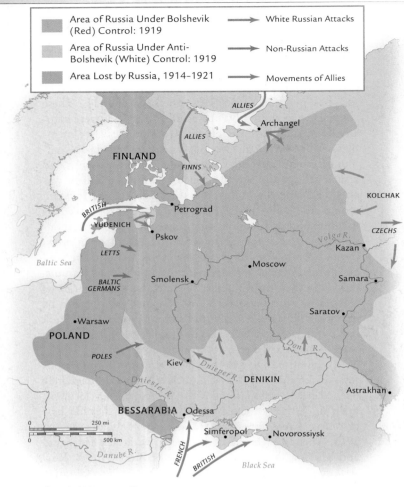

Civil War in Russia, 1919 This map shows Russia during the civil war.

Map legend:
- Area of Russia Under Bolshevik (Red) Control: 1919
- Area of Russia Under Anti-Bolshevik (White) Control: 1919
- Area Lost by Russia, 1914–1921
- → White Russian Attacks
- → Non-Russian Attacks
- → Movements of Allies

Map labels: ALLIES, Archangel, FINLAND, FINNS, KOLCHAK, BRITISH, YUDENICH, Petrograd, CZECHS, Pskov, LETTS, Volga R., Kazan, Baltic Sea, BALTIC GERMANS, Smolensk, Moscow, Samara, Saratov, Warsaw, POLAND, POLES, Kiev, Dnieper R., Don R., DENIKIN, Astrakhan, Dniester R., BESSARABIA, Odessa, Simferopol, Novorossiysk, FRENCH, BRITISH, Danube R., Black Sea

Scale: 0 – 250 mi; 0 – 500 km

swept through the countryside and confiscated grain from the peasantry to feed the cities and the army. The Bolsheviks sharply suppressed any internal opposition. A secret police force—the Cheka—unleashed the Red Terror to hunt down "class enemies" and ensure internal conformity to the Bolshevik regime. To avoid the possibility of White forces freeing the imprisoned Nicholas II and his family, the Bolshevik government ordered them executed. However, the Red armies faced numerous obstacles in their all-out effort to defeat the Whites. When peasants realized that the government intended to seize their surpluses, for example, they resisted or refused to raise more crops than they needed for themselves. Moreover, the government had to contend with violent ethnic hatreds that further divided the country. Only with the greatest difficulty did the Red armies, well organized by Trotsky, finally defeat the Whites. In doing so, the Bolsheviks regained the Ukraine.

By 1920, World War I and the Russian civil war had ended. In addition to the two million Russian soldiers who died in the world war, some four to six million had lost their lives in the civil conflict. The once-powerful nation lay defeated, impoverished, and exhausted. Starvation hung like a specter over millions. The fighting was over, but Russia and other Western nations now faced the challenge of rebuilding social stability in an environment of continuing political and economic turmoil.

timeline

The Alliance System

Rising Nationalism and Militarism

The "New" Imperialism

The "Second Industrial Revolution"

| 1910 | 1911 | 1912 | 1913 | 1914 | 1915 | 1916 |

SUMMARY

British historian Arnold Toynbee said that in the years before 1914, his generation expected that "life throughout the World would become more rational, more humane, and more democratic . . . that the progress of science and technology would make mankind richer . . . that all this would happen peacefully." World War I shattered that vision.

- Militant nationalism, an environment of competitive economic and imperial struggle, an armaments race, and a system of alliances set the stage for the outbreak of World War I.

- On the western front, armies fought from trenches in a war of attrition. On the eastern and southern fronts, the war proved far more mobile and offensive. The war soon spread outside of Europe and the Mediterranean basin.

- Whole societies mobilized to support the military effort, blurring the traditional distinctions between combatants and civilians and between battle lines and the home front.

- Eventually, the flow of forces from the United States and the exhaustion of Germany and its allies brought the fighting to an end on November 11, 1918.

- Along with millions of human lives, the war destroyed or weakened European empires.

- The peace treaties "to make the world safe" and "to end all wars" left a legacy of disappointment and resentment.

- Military losses and revolution ended the Russian Empire, replacing it with the Soviet Union and communist rulers who were transforming that society and would alter the political landscape throughout the world in the next decades.

- The calamities of those years were not limited to the war itself. In Turkey, the nationalistic government responded to Armenian demands for independence with actions that amounted to modern mass genocide costing over a million lives.

In 1918 an influenza epidemic hit, killing some 50 to 100 million people worldwide. In central and eastern Europe, postwar starvation threatened millions despite relief efforts by the United States and the International Red Cross. In the next two decades, all these losses, sufferings, disappointments, and resentments would draw Europe and the world once again into a maelstrom of violence.

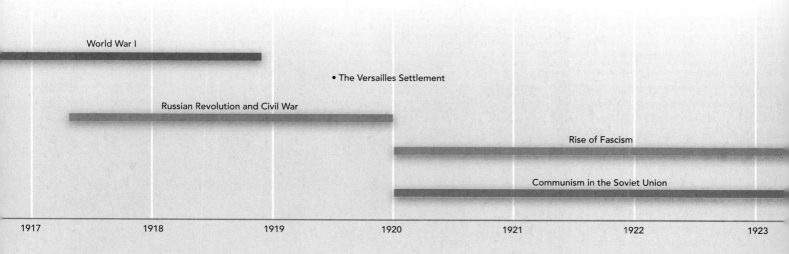

World War I

• The Versailles Settlement

Russian Revolution and Civil War

Rise of Fascism

Communism in the Soviet Union

| 1917 | 1918 | 1919 | 1920 | 1921 | 1922 | 1923 |

GIACOMO BALLA, MUSSOLINI'S MARCH ON ROME, 1922 Italian futurist painter Giacomo Balla (1871–1958) shows Benito Mussolini, in the center wearing a respectable coat and tie, joining leaders of his Italian Fascist Party for the 1922 March on Rome. As suggested by their outfits and assertive bearing, many in this march of some 25,000 are members of Mussolini's Black Shirts—a paramilitary group formed just after the end of World War I. During these uncertain postwar years, many paramilitary groups in places such as Italy, Germany, and Eastern Europe marched and fought for power.

Darkening Decades

Recovery, Dictators,
and Depression, 1920–1939

23

What's to Come

Liberation, Loss, and Reality

In a haunting preview of troubles lurking over the era, Erich Maria Remarque, a German author and war veteran, described his life in Berlin during the early 1920s. "Prices have been soaring everywhere" and "poverty is greater than it was during the war." One afternoon he heard that demonstrations had been called for. In the streets, ominous rumors circulated that "troops have been concentrated at the barracks." Groups of strikers began marching through the streets. ▶▶

A disturbance broke out, people were yelling, and on corners speakers harangued small crowds. "Then suddenly everywhere is silence." A procession of maimed and wounded war veterans in the "faded uniforms of the front-line trenches" moved slowly toward him. Men with one arm carried white placards: "Where is the Fatherland's gratitude? The War Cripples are starving."

For Remarque and millions of others living in the post–World War I West, reality soon undermined the sense of liberation that the end of the war had brought. Families tried to care for their wounded sons, fathers, and brothers, and to endure the loss of those who had perished in battle. Many veterans came home angry. They had been promised moral purification during the war

and compensation for their service after. Now they sensed that, in some ways, civilians did not fully appreciate their sacrifices. Too often, their old jobs had disappeared. For some, their wives or lovers had deserted them or developed a new, disturbing sense of independence. Many veterans, returning to homelands whose economies lay in ruins, struggled just to get enough food. ◄◄

TRYING TO RECOVER FROM THE GREAT WAR

1919–1929

Indeed, economic uncertainty had settled like a pall over most of Europe. In the decades after the war, nations struggled to retool their economies from wartime needs back to ordinary requirements and to reestablish international trade.

Across Europe, recessions followed short periods of relative prosperity all too quickly. Among the Western powers, only the United States emerged from the war richer than ever. In Asia, Japan also emerged from the war stronger and richer—a new competitor looking to expand in East Asia and gain recognition as a great power. Europeans now looked to their governments for relief and leadership.

The Victors Hold On

Solutions to Europe's economic problems depended greatly on the politics of the postwar era. However, within the democracies, no one seemed to step forward with innovative ideas for change. Some people hoped that the addition of women to the voting roles in these countries (with the notable exception of France, Italy, and Sweden) would improve politics. In fact, however, women's suffrage seemed to change politics little, if at all. Most women voted as men did, and relatively few women gained political office.

International relations showed the same lack of innovation as domestic politics. Although the dominant military power on the Continent, France still feared a resentful Germany and defensively held on to what it had salvaged in the Versailles treaty following the war. The nation fiercely resisted any efforts by colonized people to move toward independence in its overseas holdings. Various conservative parties generally held power, and domestic policies changed little from the prewar period. The conserva-

Defensive France

tives concentrated on rebuilding France and trumpeting anti-German nationalism.

Great Britain might have worked with its ally France to find solutions to postwar problems, but each nation usually acted alone or in opposition to the other. Various political parties—Conservatives, Laborites, and

Britain and its empire

Liberals—alternated in power in Britain. Sometimes they formed coalitions with each other, but none came forth with fresh solutions to the economic and diplomatic problems plaguing the British. Instead, Britain pulled away from extensive involvement in European affairs and tried to solve the Irish problem and to hold on to its restless colonies in Asia and Africa.

In the decades before World War I, British governments had attempted in vain to enact home rule for Ireland to quell growing demands for Irish independence. Leaders such as Constance Markievicz (1868–1926), a founder of republican and women's organizations, called on the Irish to "fix your mind on the ideal of Ireland free, with her women enjoying the full rights of citizenship in their own nation," warning that "our national freedom cannot, and must not, be left to evolution." In 1914, Parliament had finally passed the Irish Home Rule Bill, but it postponed the bill's implementation until after the war. In 1916, impatient Irish nationalists in Dublin rose up against the British but were crushed (see page 520). Executed leaders quickly became national martyrs, and the extremist organization Sinn Fein (Ourselves Alone) gained leadership in the nationalist cause. Its military wing became the Irish Republican Army. When the Sinn Fein Party declared Irish independence in 1919, fighting broke out between the IRA and the British army. With the British cast in the role of oppressors, the bloodshed persisted for two years. In December 1921, a treaty created the Irish Free State, although the six predominantly Protestant counties of Ulster (Northern Ireland) remained tied to Great Britain. Even then, a civil war broke out between pro-treaty and antitreaty forces. This legacy of violence would haunt the British and Irish again and again.

The British also faced nationalist problems elsewhere in the world. In West Africa, nationalistic leaders pressured the British to establish representative institutions; the British agreed to new constitutions in Nigeria in 1923 and the Gold Coast in 1925. In North Africa, opposition to foreign rule forced the British to grant independence to Egypt in 1923. In the Middle East, Britain faced uprisings in Iraq and conflicts in Palestine, where Zionist immigrants bumped up against native Arabs. In Asia, nationalist parties developed into powerful political forces. Perhaps the strongest movement for national liberation emerged in India. Many Indians, hoping they would be rewarded with self-government, had fought for Britain in World War I, and the Indian economy had grown with India's support of Britain's war effort. Indian leaders, such as Mohandas Gandhi (1869–1948) and Jawaharlal Nehru (1889–1964), who had been Westernized by education and experience while employed by British rulers, led the drive for independence. Gandhi used the tactic of civil disobedience—publicly and nonviolently breaking the law—to promote widespread sympathy for his cause. Even Britain's leaders, reacting to these pressures, began talking about granting self-rule to India.

The United States, for its part, could have taken a leadership role in international affairs. However, it refused to ratify the Versailles treaty, join the League of Nations, or involve itself extensively in tensions overseas. Europe's troubles came to center more and more on events in Germany, an unstable nation that would soon become enmeshed in a round of political and international turmoil.

The U.S. turns inward

"France and Germany Ban War Forever"

emburg (1870–1919) and Karl Liebknecht (1871–1919) led an uprising of radical Marxists (Spartacists). The government responded with repression, using the Free Corps—right-wing paramilitary groups made up mostly of veterans—to murder the two leaders and put down the communist threat. Nevertheless, communists continued to stir discord for several more years. In 1920, the German government faced a new threat, this time from right-wing nationalists under Wolfgang Kapp (1858–1922). A general strike by workers in support of the government paralyzed the economy and ended Kapp's effort to take over Berlin.

Then economic and international crises added to Weimar's political woes. In January 1923, after the German government defaulted on the huge war reparations bill, French and Belgian troops responded by occupying the Ruhr Valley, Germany's richest industrial area. The Germans struck back with passive resistance—opposing the occupiers in every way but with violence. Enraged, the French tried to create a secession movement from Germany in the Rhineland. Although the occupying forces failed to collect any reparations, the occupation paralyzed Germany's economy, and wild inflation swept the country. At the crest of the inflation wave, four trillion German marks were worth only one dollar. People literally took wheelbarrows full of money to go shopping. Within days, the inflation wiped out countless Germans' life savings.

Wild inflation

Continuing Crises in Germany

Germany emerged from World War I defeated and angry. However, it had the potential to regain its strength quickly. More populous than France, Germany still had an intact industrial infrastructure. It also occupied an advantageous position in the postwar rearrangement of the European map. On its eastern borders lay weak nations newly created at the end of World War I. Farther east, Russia was isolated and preoccupied with shoring up its struggling new communist society.

Soon after the war, the Germans set up the **Weimar Republic** (named after the city where its constitution was drawn up) as a model liberal democracy. Moderate Social Democrats led the republic, but they had inherited the taint of defeat from the outcome of the war. Moreover, many officials in the bureaucracy, judiciary, and army were the same people who had occupied these positions before 1918. They were not particularly dedicated to the new republic. Nationalists and right-wing parties looked on the new parliamentary system with contempt.

The Weimar Republic

Challengers within Germany arose almost as soon as the Social Democrats came to power. From the Left, Rosa Lux-

Conciliation and a Glimpse of Prosperity

Germany's international and economic picture looked bleak in 1923. But near the end of that year, a series of events unfolded that held out hope for international cooperation and a return to prosperity, not only for Germany but also for other nations in the West. In August, Gustav Stresemann (1878–1929) rose to leadership in the German government and offered to reconcile the country's differences with France. Having lost more money and international standing than it had gained from its occupation of the Ruhr, France reversed its policy and agreed to cooperate with Stresemann. An international commission headed by Charles Dawes (1865–1951) of the United States drew up a plan for the occupying forces' withdrawal from Germany. The commission also arranged for international loans to Germany and set up a system by which Germany would pay lower reparations in installments. In 1925, Germany signed the Treaty of Locarno with France, Great Britain, Italy, and Belgium—an agreement that guaranteed Germany's existing frontiers with France and Belgium. Optimistic headlines in the *New York Times* declared, "France and Germany Ban War Forever." In 1926, the

The Dawes plan

League of Nations admitted Germany and elected Strese-mann its president. With international relations apparently normalized, France retreated, hoping that alliances with smaller eastern European states and the **Maginot Line**—a string of defensive fortresses on the French/German border it began building in the late 1920s—would contain the economically revived Germany.

Most of the remaining Western economies also perked up after 1924. In several countries, automobile manufactur-

Uneasy prosperity ing, aviation, synthetics, and electronics took off. Vacuum cleaners, washing machines, refrigerators, and electric irons—now often purchased on installment plans—became the norm in middle-class homes. New production techniques spread, especially among big-business employers who began using the principles and methods of "scientific management" promoted by the American efficiency engineer Frederick W. Taylor (1856–1915). After conducting time and motion studies, Taylor and other industrial psychologists recommended a sharper division of labor and detailed control over every aspect of work in order to boost worker productivity. Taylor especially emphasized the division between thinking by managers and physical labor by workers: "We do not want any initiative [from workers]," he wrote. "All we want of them is to obey the orders we give them, do what we say and do it quick." These techniques may have made production more efficient, but for laborers, work became more mindless, dull, and repetitive than ever.

Outside of manufacturing, many people found jobs in the fast-growing service and housing sectors. Women in particular took positions as salesclerks, social workers, nurses, telephone operators, manicurists, hairdressers, and processors of convenience foods such as pudding mixes and dried cereals. Housing projects with indoor plumbing, electricity, and central heating sprang up throughout Europe—many of them boasted common-use day-care centers, laundries, and gardens. With all these developments, the West seemed to be back on the path of material progress that characterized the decades before World War I.

At the same time, several industries declined, unable to keep up with the new products, enhanced technology, and stiffer competition. Britain, especially, clung to its old expertise in metals and textiles and failed to invest in the rising new technologies. Its coal industry sank dramatically, sparking massive strikes that in 1926 turned into a general strike by miners and other industrial workers. The economies of nations outside of Europe—particularly in the United States, Canada, Australia, and Japan—benefited at Britain's and Europe's expense.

The Roaring Twenties?

The popular culture of the 1920s reflected these complex political and economic changes of the postwar era. This uneasy, worrisome time has been called the Jazz Age and the Roaring Twenties. Both terms convey the exuberance of the period's popular culture. They also hint at the superficial nature of the gaiety. This glittering culture had an edgy, frenetic quality that suggested a people haunted by a profound insecurity.

In the image on page 537, a depiction of a cabaret scene, the German expressionist painter Otto Dix captures these contradictions of life during the 1920s. Berlin in particular became famous for cabarets such as this. The painting echoes a description of Berlin in that era by a leading German journalist, Hans Sahl: "It was a time of great misery, with legless war veterans riding the sidewalks on rolling planks, in a nation that seemed to consist of nothing but beggars, whores, invalids, and fat-necked speculators."

While millions of people read the proliferating practical books, popular fiction, and newspapers, no new forces of popular culture shaped and reflected national attitudes more than the radio and movies. In France, the first radio broadcast station opened in 1920. It transmitted **The radio and movies** poor-quality sound to a limited audience, but by 1939, the number of radios in France had reached almost five million. The movie industry also flourished, particularly in Germany, Russia, France, and the United States. More than 100 million people saw a film each week.

Filmmaking itself became an art form, a visual record of social attitudes, and an account of people's ambitions and dreams. Films were thoughtfully and cleverly edited to promote drama and show scenes from different perspectives. Increasingly, creating movies involved specialized roles, such as producer, director, and editor. Marketed actors became envied celebrities, and millions followed the lives and careers of these movie stars. Many filmmakers projected their nations' self-images in stunning, creative ways—perhaps none more so than the legendary Russian Sergei Eisenstein (1898–1948). His epic films about the 1905 and 1917 revolutions in Russia represented the Soviet view of events in those "heroic" years.

Other films revealed deep-seated concerns about modern society. The image on page 538, for example, shows an eerie, futuristic scene from the German director Fritz Lang's (1890–1976) film *Metropolis* (1925). This image emphasizes the overwhelming power of urban architecture and technology and demonstrates cinema's potential to serve as an artistic medium. It seems to complement visually lines from "The Waste Land" (1922), a work by one of the period's leading poets, T. S. Eliot (1888–1965):

Unreal City,
Under the brown god of a winter dawn,
A crowd flowed over London Bridge, so many . . .
And each man fixed his eyes before his feet.

On another level, this scene also hints at other harbingers of modernity: the advent of skyscrapers, already rising in New York City, and the daring flights being made in small planes. Just two years after this film was made, the solo flight across the Atlantic of the American pilot

Charles Lindbergh (1902–1974) won acclaim on both sides of the ocean. Americans and Europeans alike saw embodied in Lindbergh and New York the promise of something young, exciting, and dynamic that just might push the West forward into a bright future.

Indeed, throughout the West, cities such as Berlin, Paris, and New York became even more dazzling cultural centers than before. Office buildings and skyscrapers shot up, some of them displaying striking

The Bauhaus school

new trends in architecture. The most influential architect was the German Walter Gropius (1883–1969), who in 1919 founded the **Bauhaus** school of art in Germany. This school created new standards for modern architecture and for the design of ordinary objects, from chairs and lamps to dishes. Emphasizing clean, functional lines, this international style of architecture symbolized acceptance of the modern, industrial world. These buildings unabashedly displayed their efficient structure, prefabricated materials, and steel and glass features. Many architects would follow this new style over the next half-century in creating office buildings, workers' housing, and private homes.

In addition to trends in entertainment and the arts, the phrase "Roaring Twenties" implied new attitudes toward sex. Especially in leading cities, clothing fashions, often popularized in movies, exhibited these changing attitudes. Women's clothing, featuring thinner fabrics, shorter skirts, and tight-fitting styling, became more revealing. Along with fashion, women's hairstyles grew progressively shorter as well. Women discarded confining corsets that had long been in fashion and

New attitudes toward sex

even donned trousers for sporting activities. Bathing suits, too, became increasingly skimpy. The "flapper," whom we see in the painting below, was now the new symbol of the ideal, free, sexually liberated woman.

The new focus on body image and sexual appeal intensified concerns about hygiene. People began regularly using toothbrushes, deodorants, and cosmetics. In addition, they bathed more often than before and shaved more closely. Tanned, thin women and muscular men became the new standards of health and sexual attractiveness.

As sex became more openly discussed and encouraged, governments also searched for ways to revive declining birthrates and thereby replace the lives lost during the war. In France, for example, the government made distributing birth-control information illegal and abortion punishable by death. The French proclaimed a new holiday, Mother's Day, an innovation that other Western countries soon copied. Many governments provided maternity benefits, and increasingly, births took place in hospitals under the control of specialized nurses and doctors. Separate rooms for testing, labor, delivery, and recovery made the process of giving birth almost factory-like. Doctors, nurses, and

OTTO DIX, *GROSSTADT (BIG TOWN)*, 1927–1928 These scenes from just outside (left) and inside (right) a Berlin cabaret show the contradictions of postwar life as impoverished, crippled veterans on the street look in on revelers frolicking on the dance floor. The painting suggests artificial celebration and underlying misery more than joy.

MOVIES AND MODERN LIFE This scene from Fritz Lang's film *Metropolis* (1925) shows a plane flying through the canyons of a modern city. It suggests the power of the cinema to convey images and ideas about modern life.

social workers told women the "best" way to care for their children, and child-rearing courses for girls became compulsory in some countries.

The Anxious Twenties

Of all the forms of culture that gained currency during these years, high culture most powerfully reflected the stressful undercurrents of the postwar period. Many writers, intellectuals, and artists emphasized the uncertainty of the era and explored the widespread feelings of insecurity that people harbored.

Several philosophers, reacting to the horrors of the Great War, attacked nineteenth-century optimism and rationalism. These thinkers expanded on the ideas set

| Sense of decay and crisis |

forth earlier by Friedrich Nietzsche in Germany and Henri Bergson in France (see page 505). The most widely read of the post–World War I philosophers was a German, Oswald Spengler (1880–1936). In his book *The Decline of the West* (1918), Spengler argued that all civilizations were like biological organisms, each with its own life cycle. Western civilization, he claimed, had passed its high point, and World War I signaled the beginning of its end.

Sigmund Freud's ideas (see Chapter 21) about the irrational, unconscious, and instinctual aspects of human thought and behavior—which had first emerged just before World War I—gained more acceptance during the 1920s. The unconscious and irrational played particularly

prominent roles in the most acclaimed literature of the postwar era. The Irish writer James Joyce (1882–1941), German author Franz Kafka (1883–1924), and French writer Marcel Proust (1871–1922) created disquieting, introspective works of literature that elevated personal psychological experience over reason. In *Ulysses* (1922), Joyce in particular mastered the stream of consciousness technique, which displayed to the reader the rambling thoughts, free associations, and erotic fantasies going on in the mind of a character. At first, critics and the public dismissed the novel as "morbid," "nonsense," and "foul." Eventually, however, this book about a single day in the lives of a group of Dubliners, which also served as a commentary on the human condition, was hailed as one of the century's greatest works of literature. In her novel *Mrs. Dalloway* (1925), British author Virginia Woolf used similar techniques to describe one day in the inner life of a woman, including fragmented conversations, partial remembrances, and fantasies.

Novels and memoirs of the Great War also proliferated during these years. As in *All Quiet on the Western Front* by the German author Erich Maria Remarque, these works emphasized themes of brutality and suffering, disillusionment with civilian life, and a sense that the war had spawned a generation of lost souls. At the same time, Remarque's and others' books revealed a longing for the sense of purpose and comradeship that so often arises during a war effort but subsides in times of peace.

Similar themes marked artistic styles of the day. The **Dada** movement stressed the absence of purpose in life. Surrealist painters explored dreams and the world of the subconscious. Other painters, such as Käthe Kollwitz (see the Chapter 22 Past Lives) and Otto Dix (see image on page 537), created moving images of suffering, destruction, and social despair.

In the 1920s, then, Western democratic societies struggled mightily both to come to terms with the consequences of the war and to move on to better days. In the early postwar years, the difficulties seemed overwhelming. Even with the revival of healthier economies and easing of international tensions after 1923, underlying doubt and insecurity persisted and made themselves plain in the period's cultural expression.

TURNING AWAY FROM DEMOCRACY: Dictatorships and Fascism

1919–1929

The sense of unease and the difficult realities clearly burdened politics in the Western democracies, but things were far worse on the political front elsewhere in Europe.

Among the states of east-central and southern Europe, the strain of the postwar years became too much for the fragile democratic systems budding there.

Authoritarianism in East-Central Europe

In 1919, Admiral Miklos Horthy (1868–1957), the reactionary former commander of the Austro-Hungarian navy, led forces, aided by anticommunist Allies and ambitious Romanians, that overthrew the newly formed regime led by the communist Béla Kun (1885–1937) in Hungary. Horthy's rule, like other right-wing authoritarian regimes that followed in Poland (1926) and Yugoslavia (1929), amounted to a dictatorship backed by the nation's military and conservative forces—the bureaucracy, high church, and wealthy elites. Why did these east-central European nations, most of which emerged from the dissolution of the Austro-Hungarian Empire during World War I with new democratic regimes, turn away from parliamentary democracy?

Part of the answer may be that the newly created nations in this area faced enormous economic problems. Although the old Austro-Hungarian Empire had suffered from ethnic and political divisions, it had functioned as an economic whole—its industrial areas trading with its agricultural regions. Now split up, the individual nations were mostly agricultural and too unproductive to create prosperity. Only Czechoslovakia, whose parliamentary system would survive the longest, boasted an advanced industrial economy.

Struggling with these problems, the new democratic regimes seemed divided and ineffective. Many conservative groups feared the kind of change represented by liberal democracy, socialism, and communism. Such changes promised to dilute conservatives' power, diminish their economic base, and undermine their beliefs in the traditional social order. This lack of experience with democracy and the strength of these conservative groups made these nations vulnerable to authoritarian men like Horthy, who promised order and advocated nationalism backed by armed force. One by one, the democratic governments fell to authoritarian takeovers. As in Horthy's regime, the new rulers sometimes used "White Terror" to silence opponents and often repressed Jews and other minority groups.

To the south, Turkey became a republic in 1923 under the leadership of the nationalist Mustafa Kemal and displayed some of the same authoritarian characteristics. Kemal soon became known as Atatürk (Father of the Turks). Theoretically, the nation was a constitutional democracy based on universal male suffrage, but in fact, Atatürk acted as an authoritarian ruler. He secularized Turkey completely, separating the state, legal system, courts, and schools from the Muslim religious establishment. In 1934, women gained the right to vote. Many of Atatürk's reforms, including the importation of the Roman alphabet and Western clothing, were based on European models. Yet, although Kemal was a modernizer, his regime became a one-party dictatorship that promoted Atatürk—a military man who was willing to use brutality to get his way—as the all-important nationalistic hero.

This rise of authoritarian governments during the 1920s spread to the West. The most dramatic and ominous move came in Italy. There, the charismatic Benito Mussolini (1883–1945) took power, bringing with him a new governance system and ideology: **fascism.**

The Rise of Fascism in Italy

At its core, fascism in practice meant dictatorship by a charismatic leader. However, it was more than that. It included a set of antidemocratic, anti-individualistic, and anticommunist ideas or attitudes. Fascist doctrine hailed the people while denouncing the principles of the French Revolution. Fascist leaders such as Alfredo Rocco (1875–1935) **Fascist doctrine** viewed the state as a living organism and rejected liberal democratic forms of government, complaining that the liberal state "is dissolving into a mass of small particles, parties, associations, groups and syndicates that are binding it in chains." The fascist call was to nationalism and military prowess. In Italy, people angry and dismayed by events following World War I heard this call and followed it.

Italy had emerged from World War I a battered, disappointed victor. Its armies, on the verge of collapse, had nevertheless managed to hold on and ultimately contributed to the final Allied victory. However, the Treaty of Versailles denied Italy **Turmoil in Italy** some of the territories on the Adriatic coast that the Allies had promised in return for Italy's contribution to the war effort. Many Italians felt that at Versailles, their nation lost its rightful status as a great power. All this left Italian nationalists bitter and convinced many more Italians that the war had not been worth the price Italy had paid.

Near chaos within this troubled nation multiplied these disappointments. Italy's already weak economy staggered under a huge national debt. Its inflated currency, together with a shortage of consumer goods, made prices skyrocket. Hundreds of thousands of veterans could find no jobs. In the summer of 1919, disorder spread. Farmworkers threatened property owners by joining unions called red leagues. Veterans and poor families began seizing idle lands. Banditry in the south grew out of control, and

> The fascist call was to nationalism and military prowess.

strikes plagued the cities. During the winter of 1920–1921, workers seized control of several hundred factories. Socialists and communists gained strength within industrial and rural unions.

Italy's newly elected government, plagued by political divisions, seemed powerless in the face of these pressures. Frightened landlords and factory owners, along with thousands of veterans and a middle class ravaged by inflation and insecurity, longed for vigorous leadership and a strong, dependable government. The vigorous leader who stepped forward was Benito Mussolini. The strong government was his fascist dictatorship.

Mussolini was born into a family of socialist artisans; he received enough education to become a teacher and then a radical journalist. At the outbreak of World War I,

Mussolini takes power

he used the socialist paper he edited to advocate antimilitarism and to demand that Italy remain neutral during the war. A year later, he changed his mind, now convinced that "only blood makes the wheels of history turn." He broke from his socialist allies, started a new newspaper, and joined the army. After the war, he organized mostly unemployed veterans into the National Fascist Party—the term *fascist* alluding to Roman prowess, unity, and justice. His Fascist Party soon attracted enough support to bring down Italy's parliamentary government.

Why did Mussolini's political movement hold such appeal? The answer to this question is complex. Fascism

The appeal of fascism

attracted veterans hoping for a sense of renewal after the disappointments of the war and the immediate postwar years and appealed to young men who felt they had missed out on the war experience and therefore responded to the call of wounded national pride. "When

I returned from the war—just like so many others—I hated politics and politicians, who . . . had betrayed the hopes of soldiers, reducing Italy to a shameful peace," explained Italo Balbo, a future associate of Mussolini. These men became the members and muscle of the new party. Factory owners, merchants, and landowners also embraced fascism when Mussolini vowed to save Italy from communism. These groups provided Mussolini with money when he organized squads of black-shirted Fascisti to terrorize radical workers and their liberal supporters. Finally, those who blamed the parliamentary government for Italy's postwar woes warmed to fascist promises to act decisively and create unity through nationalistic policies. Fascism seemed to offer a third way—a path above socialism and conventional parliamentary democracy—to security and success for Italy.

In 1922, building on this support, squads of black-shirted Fascists marched on Rome under Mussolini's vow that "either we are allowed to govern or we will seize power." The indecisive Italian king Victor Emmanuel III (r. 1900–1946) buckled under the pressure and appointed Mussolini prime minister. With great speed, the Fascist leader acquired extraordinary powers.

Between 1924 and 1926, Mussolini turned his office into a dictatorship. Under his rule, only the Fascist Party could engage in organized political activity. Il Duce (the leader) sent his secret police everywhere. "Everything within the State," he demanded, and "Nothing outside the State." Musso-

The Fascist system

lini next struck a deal with the powerful Catholic Church and signed the Lateran Treaty of 1929. In return for money and the right to teach religion in the public schools, the papacy finally recognized the existence of the Italian state. The agreement ended the sixty years of division between the church and the state since unification.

To guide Italy's economy toward self-sufficiency and industrialization while carefully protecting private property and profits, the Fascists worked closely with business leaders. They organized the different industries and trades into confederations, or corporations. Each corporation included a syndicate of workers and one of employers, each in turn headed by a Fascist official. The Fascists also abolished all independent labor unions, strikes, and lockouts. Instead, compulsory arbitration under the party's direction now settled issues of wages and working conditions and disputes between labor and management. The complicated economic and political machinery that Mussolini put in motion for these purposes became known as the corporate state, or corporatism.

Although the state would gain a controlling hand in several major industries, Mussolini's corporate state mainly enlarged the bureaucracy and hamstrung workers' unions. A few well-publicized achievements, such as new railroads, highways, building projects, and educational reforms, hid more fundamental deficiencies. His ambitious agricultural

MUSSOLINI AND HIS BLACK SHIRTS Mussolini and his Black Shirt followers, in paramilitary uniform, raise their arms in a military salute. The scene has been self-consciously set up to present an image of strong leadership and military prowess, and it suggests the appearance of ritual and participation in a mighty movement.

policies generally failed to improve per capita output. People of property fared well, but workers, especially women, suffered declining income. Even though women flocked to hear him, Mussolini cut their wages by decree and banned them from several professions. Those who did not heed his call to take up their maternal duties were pushed toward low-paying jobs. Nevertheless, growing numbers of Italian women still managed to enter universities and find positions in the world of paid work.

By 1929, Mussolini stood unchallenged. Using films, radio addresses, biographies, newspapers, and schools, he amassed a huge following of supporters who repeated his reassuring phrase "Mussolini is always right." Some artists and intellectuals supported at least his image of dynamic leadership. Mussolini also won a reputation among groups throughout Europe, South America, and the United States as someone who could "make the trains run on time," gain peace with the Catholic Church, and stand up to communist threats.

In reality, Mussolini—like many twentieth-century politicians—was more of an actor able to manipulate appearances than an effective ruler who could solve domestic or international problems. Many people immune to his charm saw him as merely a strutting, boasting carnival performer. Mussolini's vision of historical destiny—to create a Second Roman Empire and turn the Mediterranean into an Italian lake—perhaps most revealed a disturbing lack of touch with reality. Even with Il Duce in control, Italy was no major power.

To the east, the situation was entirely different. Russia had been a major power and might well rise again. Now transformed into a communist state and reformed into the Soviet Union by the Bolsheviks, its radical left-wing policies represented an even more frightening threat to capitalist democracies than the extreme right-wing politics of Italian Fascism.

TRANSFORMING THE SOVIET UNION

1920–1939

In 1920, Russia's bloody civil war had finally ended. The suffering, however, dragged on. Industrial production sank to only 13 percent of pre–World War I levels. A famine struck, taking four to seven million lives. Countless thousands of veterans and city dwellers roamed the countryside in search of food, shelter, and employment. "Green Armies" of peasants revolted against forced requisitions of their crops and restrictions against selling products at market prices. Workers struck against declining wages and lack of control over the factories. Sailors at the Kronstadt naval base mutinied, demanding political liberty. Many

Communist Party and union members called for more democracy. How could Lenin's still vulnerable Communist government survive?

Lenin's Compromise: The NEP

Lenin retreated. In 1921 he launched the **New Economic Policy (NEP),** a "temporary" compromise with capitalism. This policy allowed peasants to manage their own land and sell their own crops. In addition, small-scale industries could operate under private ownership, and money and credit were restored. Although the state still supervised the economy, the NEP provided enough capitalist incentive to pull the Russian economy out of chaos.

Lenin's retreat did not extend to politics, however. Russia remained a "dictatorship of the proletariat," symbolized on Russia's flag by the red of socialism, the hammer of industrial workers, and the sickle of peasants. Lenin and the Communist Party elite maintained a tight grip on power and brutally suppressed any opposition. Local soviets submitted to the central government in Moscow, dominated by its 16-person Politburo and, above all, the secretariat of the Communist Party. The formal creation of the Union of Soviet Socialist Republics (USSR, or Soviet Union) in 1922 paid only lip service to desires for autonomy in "republics" such as the Ukraine, Armenia, and Georgia. Russia, home to four-fifths of the USSR's total population, dominated the Union.

Soviet society in the 1920s reflected its revolutionary origins as well as the temporary compromise with capitalism. The Communists had eliminated the old aristocracy, church, and traditional class distinctions. But party, military, and cultural elites enjoyed higher standards of living, better housing, and more educational opportunities than anyone else. Some peasants who took advantage of NEP opportunities also became relatively wealthy, as did their urban counterparts running small businesses.

Moreover, women enjoyed unprecedented legal equality. In addition to the right to vote, they received the right to equal pay, education, and professional opportunities. The government set up programs and agencies such as the Women's Bureau to promote equality, day care, housing, medical care, and information on birth control and divorce. Alexandra Kollontai (1872–1952), head of the Women's Bureau, urged collectivization of child rearing and a new family form: "The narrow and exclusive affection of the mother for her own children must expand until it embraces all the children of the great proletarian family. In place of the indissoluble marriage based on the servitude of woman, we shall see rise in the free union [of two people] . . . equal in their rights and in their obligations."

These new policies all showed promise, but in fact the burdens on Soviet women probably increased. Programs to help them lacked the resources to make a real difference. Greater access to jobs rarely translated into higher-level positions. Women were still expected to retain their traditional burdens at home, their "second shift."

Although the NEP was a retreat from strict Communist policies, Lenin's regime still envisioned itself as leading the world into modernity. The government turned churches and great mansions into museums and meeting halls. Cultural activities promoted proletarian pride, the benefits of technology, and the glories of the future. Avantgarde artists created utopian visions by connecting images of mass production and social justice.

The NEP may have encouraged the outside world to end its isolation of Russia. Between 1922 and 1924, all Western nations recognized the Soviet Union except the United States, which remained aloof until 1933. Indeed, to many socialists throughout the West, the Soviet Union stood as a source of hope and inspiration.

The Struggle to Succeed Lenin

Lenin would not live to witness the results of the NEP. After a series of paralytic strokes, he died in 1924. Three of his chief associates—Leon Trotsky (1879–1940), Nikolai Bukharin (1888–1938), and Joseph Stalin (1879–1953)—jockeyed to succeed him. Most observers assumed that the brilliant but arrogant Trotsky, who had led the Red Army during the civil war, would win. He argued that the Soviet Union must promote revolutions elsewhere in the West to survive and that the Soviet economy should be tightly controlled and massively industrialized from above. By contrast, the popular Bukharin, who had been appointed by Lenin to lead the NEP, argued for socialism by slow, careful steps. The shrewd political manipulator Stalin claimed a middle-of-the-road position between these two but believed that Russia must survive alone—"socialism in one country." His opponents vastly underestimated him.

Stalin (a pseudonym meaning "man of steel") was born in Georgia the son of poverty-stricken ex-serfs. His mother managed to get him into an Orthodox seminary school, where he received a formal education. Expelled from the seminary because of his

Joseph Stalin

Marxist views, he joined revolutionary groups. Repeatedly arrested, he kept managing to escape. In 1917, he took advantage of the revolutionary turmoil and hastened to Petrograd from his exile in Siberia. A poor speaker and writer, he used daring and organizational talents to rise in the party. He played a prominent role in Russia's civil war and became executive secretary of the Communist Party. In this key position, he made himself master of the all-important party machinery and pursued his drive for power.

Toward the end of his life, Lenin warned that "Stalin is too rude" to lead. Nevertheless, after Lenin's death, Stalin cleverly played on the Soviet people's love of Lenin by posing as his heir and leading a movement to deify him. He also brought into the party new people, who thereby owed him a debt. Playing his rivals against each other, he used his control over the Central Committee of the Communist Party to edge the overconfident Trotsky and his supporters on the Left out of powerful positions and, in 1927, expel them from the party. The next year, he turned against Bukharin and the Right. Party members who had doubts about Stalin accepted the need for party loyalty. By the end of 1928, Stalin had maneuvered himself into a position of dominance over the Communist Party and of dictatorship over the Soviet Union. Now he set out to transform the nation.

Stalin's Five-Year Plans

By 1928, Soviet industry had probably attained little more than 1913 levels of production. Stalin and his party leadership wanted much more. That year, he ended the NEP and launched the First **Five-Year Plan.** The fundamental goal of the plan could not have been more ambitious: "We do

THE FIVE-YEAR PLAN IN FOUR YEARS, 1930s This propaganda poster portrays Stalin as leading efforts to industrialize the Soviet Union rapidly. He faces the old "enemies" of the Communist Party: capitalism and religion.

not want to be beaten. . . . Old Russia . . . was ceaselessly beaten for her backwardness. . . . We are fifty or a hundred years behind the advanced countries. We must make good this lag in ten years . . . or they crush us." The plan called for the rapid, massive industrialization of the nation. Goals included more than doubling industrial production, increasing the generation of electric power almost fivefold, and building 1,500 new factories within five years. To achieve the goals, the State Planning Commission, or Gosplan, would strictly regulate all aspects of production, including targeting crucial industries such as steel, regimenting the industrial labor force, and hiring foreign engineers to help build the new factories. The 1930s Soviet propaganda poster shown on page 542, *The Five-Year Plan in Four Years,* portrays the idea that Stalin will lead Soviet industrial development against the threatening reactionary forces of capitalism and religion. As if preparing for another war, Stalin ordered the USSR's entire society to mobilize for industrialization.

> ## "We do not want to be beaten."

To help accomplish the Five-Year Plan's goals (which included doubling agricultural production), the state took

Collectivization

agriculture out of the control of individual peasants by consolidating their lands into huge collective farms that used modern machines. Elected managers and party officials ran the farms. Individuals could own tools, keep small gardens for fruits and vegetables, and raise pigs and chickens for private use or sale. By determining prices and distribution of crops, the state expected to use agricultural "surpluses" to pay for industrialization—to buy the equipment to build factories, transportation facilities, and power plants. **Collectivization,** it was believed, would also push peasants to become industrial workers in the cities.

The process of collectivization proved ruinous. Hundreds of thousands of peasants, especially wealthier landowners derisively called *kulaks,* powerfully resisted the new policies. In protest, they even destroyed their own crops and livestock— some 50 percent of horses and cattle between 1929 and 1933. Officials terrorized such resisters into submission. "The expropriation of the kulaks is an integral part of the formation . . . of the collective farms," announced Stalin. The kulaks should be "eliminated as a class." Hundreds of thousands of peasants were killed and far more were exiled to Siberia, never to return. This violent battle of wills was accompanied by plummeting agricultural production and government pressure to increase agricultural exports at all costs to finance

industrialization. The results were disastrous: Between 1930 and 1933, famine struck, taking the lives of four to six million people. An observer reported that in Ukrainian villages, peasants resorted to eating "dogs, horses, rotten potatoes, the bark of trees, grass—anything they could find . . . and no matter what they did, they went on dying, dying, dying." The effort to collectivize agriculture and the deadly hunger tore apart rural families, communities, and established ways of life. Nevertheless, Stalin finally got his way: More than half the land was collectivized within the first year, and over 90 percent after ten years. As one Communist Party worker put it, "It took a famine to show them who is master here. It has cost millions of lives, but the collective farm system is here to stay."

To industrialize the Soviet Union, planners had to start almost from ground level and build up. They concentrated on producer goods such as engines and tractors rather than consumer goods such as shoes and clothes. Gradually, steel mills, dams,

Mobilizing for industrialization

power plants, foundries, mines, refineries, chemical factories, and railroads appeared all over the Soviet Union. Technocrats and officials faced pressure to produce targeted results. The government fostered a sense of emergency to inspire people, especially the young, to work hard. Presenting the effort as a great adventure, officials pointed out that those who most contributed to the industrialization drive could achieve a status similar to that of

PROMISES OF SOVIET SOCIETY, 1930s This poster shows an idealized scene of Soviet industrial and social accomplishments and announces, "People's Dreams Have Come True!"

Stalin Collectivizes Agriculture

As part of his campaign to collectivize agriculture, Stalin used massive coercion against the Russian kulaks (relatively rich independent peasants). Widespread destruction and death resulted. In the following excerpt, Lev Kopelev recounts his own participation in this collectivization drive.

We were raised as the fanatical [believers] of a new creed, the only true *religion* of scientific socialism. The party became our church militant, bequeathing to all mankind eternal salvation, eternal peace and the bliss of an earthly paradise. It victoriously surmounted all other churches, schisms and heresies. The works of Marx, Engels and Lenin were accepted as holy writ, and Stalin was the infallible high priest.

. . . Stalin was the most perspicacious, the most wise (at that time they hadn't yet started calling him "great" and "brilliant"). He said: "The struggle for grain is the struggle for socialism." And we believed him unconditionally. And later we believed that unconditional collectivization was unavoidable if we were to overcome the capriciousness and uncertainty of the market and the backwardness of individual farming, to guarantee a steady supply of grain, milk and meat to the cities. . . .

How does Kopelev justify his participation in the drive?

the heroes of the 1917 revolution. The government moved "shock brigades" of enthusiastic, efficient workers from factory to factory to stimulate production, while the press celebrated new "Heroes of Labor" who exceeded production targets. Officials encouraged women to work both on the collective farms and in factories; by 1940, women made up almost half the labor force.

All elements of Soviet society were mobilized to support the effort to make the USSR an industrial power. Schools, adult education classes, newspapers, union meetings, and youth associations became saturated with official doctrines of Soviet communism, efficiency, and class pride. "We must make every school child aware of . . . how the great people of our epoch—Lenin, Stalin, and their companions in arms—organized the workers in the struggle for a new and happy life," explained a Soviet text on teaching methods. Officials, minor bureaucrats, and members of the secret police ranged everywhere and monitored progress. Within families—the "school for socialism"—mothers were urged to raise their children to fit into communist society. Earlier policies supporting women's choices were reversed. The state made abortion illegal and promoted traditional marriage and relationships. In this more repressive era, homosexuality became a crime.

The state also tightened controls over cultural productions, ending the experimentation of the 1920s. The Central Committee of the Communist Party told publishing houses that "books must be an instrument for the mobilization of the workers for the tasks of industrialization and collectivization." A government ministry took control over filmmaking to make sure movies promoted revolutionary enthusiasm and favorable views of the communist state. Socialist realism became the required orthodoxy in art. In this style, approved murals, art, and literature portrayed realistic images of people carrying out the dreams of a communist society. The poster on page 543 is an example of this effort to make art relevant and compelling to the working masses.

At the end of 1932, Stalin announced that all goals of the First Five-Year Plan had been accomplished several months ahead of time. He recited a list of accomplishments in iron, steel, tractors, automobiles, machine tools, chemicals, and aircraft production. "Our country has been converted from an agrarian into an industrial country," he proclaimed. These gains, however, came at a high price. For the hard-pressed workers, consumer goods beyond the necessities remained scarce. Clearly, some Soviet citizens—namely, party members—benefited more than others. One refugee cynically compared life before and after the Bolshevik Revolution: "In Tsarist times there were the rich and the poor; under Soviet power there were the party members and the non-party members." Similar Second and Third Five-Year Plans would follow, this time with more emphasis on consumer goods and armaments. The terrifying Great Purges would also follow.

Blood and Terror: The Great Purges

In 1934, Leonid Nikolayev assassinated Sergei Kirov (1888–1934), a high Soviet official. Stalin used the murder as an excuse to eliminate potential rivals. The incident introduced a long period of party purges, marked by terror, house arrests, bizarre show-trials, torture, imprisonments, and executions—all approved by Stalin.

Historians still debate Stalin's motives for the **Great Purges.** Stalin and party officials blamed difficulties during the five-year plans on many—engineers, technocrats, army officers, older party members, regional nationalists, foreign conspirators, saboteurs—and purged the accused. Lower-level officials probably contributed to the waves of purges by trying to rise at the expense of higher-level officials. Stalin himself was extremely suspicious. He saw enemies everywhere. Certainly he worried about threats from within the party. He eradicated all potential opposition—real or imagined, and even on foreign soil. In 1940, Soviet agents assassinated Trotsky in Mexico.

By the time the Great Purges ended in 1939, authorities had killed some one million people. Another seven million died or languished in forced-labor camps; still more had been sent into exile. The terror spread throughout Soviet society, for everyone knew of someone accused and arrested. Almost all the original Bolshevik leaders and the Red Army's top officer corps were gone. New, younger figures beholden to Stalin now staffed the government, the Communist Party, and the military.

In the end, Stalin got most of what he wanted. By 1939, the Soviet Union had a fully planned economy, with the state determining production, prices, and distribution. Although officials announced successes whether they occurred or not, the USSR had in fact become the third-greatest industrial power in the world. More than 90 percent of peasants lived on collective, mechanized farms. Millions more had moved to the cities, where new housing, schools, libraries, and hospitals had sprung up. For the first time, most of the population could read. Within the Soviet Union, no one dared oppose Stalin, and now he

had the armaments to face a new challenge already rising in the west. But the cost had been tremendous. Between 15 and 20 million people (some scholars argue that the figure might be much higher) had died from starvation, execution, or the harsh conditions in forced-labor camps, and far more had suffered as a result of Stalin's policies.

THE GREAT DEPRESSION
1929–1939

The forces to the west creating that challenge to the USSR had begun to coalesce and gather momentum, and the Soviets were not the only ones threatened by them. As we saw earlier, authoritarianism and fascism—fierce opponents of communism—had already started to rise in the 1920s. In 1929, a new crisis struck the Western democracies: the **Great Depression.** Reeling from years of hard times and pulling much of the world with them, Western societies began edging toward a new darkness that would more than rival the horrors of World War I.

Crash!

In October 1929, the New York stock market crashed. In one month, stocks lost almost two-thirds of their value. The financial crisis quickly spread from the United States, the world's leading industrial nation and creditor, to Europe, where nations depended heavily on American loans and trade. The crash ended the relative prosperity since 1924 and provoked an unprecedented global depression. Within two years, thousands of banks and businesses throughout the West failed. Spending, production, employment, and income all dropped sharply. Plant closings, farm foreclosures, and joblessness haunted the Western nations. People's confidence in the economy died, and too often with it went their faith in themselves.

A complex series of events had led to the disaster. The postwar economic order was built on a fragile foundation of international credit, reparations payments, and foreign trade. Much of Europe remained dependent on the United States for credit. Germany in particular relied on American loans to support its reparation payments.

Causes of the economic collapse

In 1928, American investors began pulling their money out of Germany and demanding repayment of loans to invest in the unregulated, soaring U.S. stock market. Credit dried up in Germany and in east-central European nations tied to the German economy. The 1929 crash sent people running to banks to withdraw funds, further undermining credit. Soon the West's entire economic house of cards collapsed.

Then & Now
Government Interference

No nation was hit harder by the Great Depression than Germany. By 1932, it had more than six million unemployed workers and countless people wandering homeless along its streets and roads. As a result, most people stopped believing that the government should interfere as little as possible in the face of economic threats. Since then, when recessions occur most Western governments have quickly stepped in to stabilize the situation. For example, during the economic downturn in the United States in 2008, President Bush intervened to bail out the financial institutions. When President Obama succeeded him in office the following year, he continued to try to manage the economic crisis by reducing taxes and increasing spending.

The collapse took much of the globe with it. Over the years, non-Western lands had become important suppliers of raw materials—such as rice, cotton, cocoa, rubber, oil, copper, and tin—for Western industry and urban populations. With their economies more and more dependent on international trade, these regions were now tied to the economic fate of the West. Ties to the West particularly marked industrialized Japan's economy. The lure of increasing trade with the United States during the 1920s had persuaded Japan to halt its imperial expansion in Asia. The Great Depression—which quickly slashed exports to the United States in half and left three million people unemployed—brought an end to Japan's prosperity and revived its imperial ambitions. Japan's leaders looked to make East Asian markets their own, by conquest if necessary.

Effects in non-Western lands

In the Teeth of the Depression

By 1932, Europe's economies had shrunk to one-half their 1929 size. Unemployment in the West rose to a shocking 22 percent, leaving 30 million people out of work. Along with their jobs, people lost their savings, their farms, and their homes. One British woman echoed the feelings of many: "These last few years since I've been out of the mills . . . I've got no spirit for anything." Masses of people sank into poverty, and malnutrition and diseases spread. Families suffered from new tensions as men lost their traditional role as breadwinners. "When he was out of work," lamented a woman from Liverpool, "we were always having rows over the children."

In eastern and central Europe, hard-pressed farmers and unemployed workers looked for scapegoats. They blamed Jews, whom they saw as controlling the banks, bureaucracy, jobs, and policies responsible for the depression. People also pointed their fingers at socialists, communists, big business, and even modernity. Ethnic groups and major powers turned on one another, and throughout the West, popular protests by desperate, angry people spread.

Searching for Solutions

At first, governments met the depression the old way: by balancing the budget and increasing tariffs on imported goods. However, these policies just made matters worse by dampening spending and hindering trade. A moratorium on reparations and war debts in August 1931 came too late to do much good. Imperial powers such as Britain and France turned to their colonial holdings for secure trade and profits, only to meet rising demands for independence in India, Iraq, Vietnam, Algeria, and elsewhere. The British economist John Maynard Keynes (1883–1946) argued for new policies—more government expenditures financed by budget deficits to stimulate consumer spending and raise employment—but few listened to his still little-known ideas.

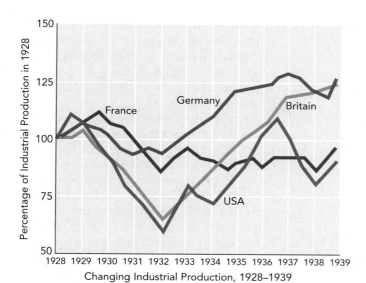

Changing Industrial Production, 1928–1939

INDUSTRIAL PRODUCTION, 1928–1939

After 1932, new regimes in the United States, Britain, and Germany adopted policies to increase government spending and provide some relief. Similar policies had already enabled Scandinavian democracies to weather the depression with relative ease. However, even with these measures, most Western democracies recovered slowly and not fully until the late 1930s, thanks to spending for rearmament. The graph above indicates that France and the United States in particular had difficulty raising industrial production to figures approaching pre-1929 levels. By then, these democracies faced new threats that made even the anxious 1920s look like "roaring" good times. The most ominous menace came from Germany.

OPINION

In what ways do you think the Great Depression was much more than an economic downturn?

NAZISM IN GERMANY

In 1928, Germany's fascist party, the Nazis (National Socialists), won less than 3 percent of the vote in national elections. Five years later, the party and its leader, Adolf Hitler, gained power and ended German democracy—all through legal means. How did this happen?

The Young Adolf Hitler

The story of Nazism's rise begins with the life of Adolf Hitler (1889–1945). Hitler was born to a middle-aged Austrian customs official and his much younger wife. When his father died in 1905, Hitler quit school and traveled to Vienna, where he hoped to become an artist or architect. Denied admission to the art academy, he lived on his orphan's pension, selling postcards and hanging wallpaper. He compulsively followed daily routines and would do so for the rest of his life. He also picked up nationalistic, anti-Semitic, and racist ideas circulating in Vienna that he embraced with deadly seriousness.

When World War I broke out, Hitler "thanked heaven out of an overflowing heart." For this ardent German nationalist, here was a righteous crusade to end a life of drifting. He served as a courier in the German army and was decorated three times. War's end found him in a hospital recovering from a poison gas attack. He revered World War I as "the greatest of all experiences." As for Germany's defeat at the end of the conflict, he blamed Jews and Marxists, who he felt sure had "stabbed Germany in the back."

The Birth of Nazism in Germany's Postwar Years

Hitler spotted opportunities in Germany's turbulent postwar years. Several right-wing groups had formed that offered extreme solutions to Germany's problems and that threatened the newly formed parliamentary government of the Weimar Republic. In 1919, while working in Munich as an informer for the army, Hitler joined one of those groups—the German Workers' Party. A year later, he rose to leadership in the party and renamed it the National Socialist German Workers' Party, or the **Nazi Party** (despite the party's name, it was neither socialist in the traditional sense nor well supported by urban workers). Hitler also organized a paramilitary wing—the SA "stormtroopers"—to back the party. Copying Mussolini's techniques, the SA troopers wore brown shirts and carried pagan symbols (the swastika). They marched through the streets, sang patriotic songs, and beat up communists, socialists, and anyone else they considered their opponents.

Nothing yet marked this small group as destined for success. Nevertheless, in 1923 Hitler and the popular war hero General Ludendorff made an ambitious grab for power. From a beer hall in Munich, the Nazis marched on the local government. Republican troops easily put down this "Beer Hall Putsch," and Hitler, after a highly publicized trial, spent nearly a year in jail. While in prison, he wrote *Mein Kampf (My Struggle),* a work that set forth the core of his Nazi doctrine.

Goebbels's Nazi Propaganda Pamphlet

Propaganda was strongly emphasized by the Nazis as a method of acquiring and maintaining power. Joseph Goebbels (1897–1945), an early leader in the Nazi Party, was made chief of propaganda in 1929. The following is an excerpt from a 1930 pamphlet, written by Goebbels, describing why the Nazis are against Jews.

WHY DO WE OPPOSE THE JEWS?

We are the ENEMIES OF THE JEWS, because we are fighters for the freedom of the German people. THE JEW IS THE CAUSE AND THE BENEFICIARY OF OUR MISERY. He has used the social difficulties of the broad masses of our people to deepen the unholy split between Right and Left among our people. He has made two halves of Germany. He is the real cause for our loss of the Great War.

The Jew has no interest in the solution of Germany's fateful problems. He CANNOT have any. FOR HE LIVES ON THE FACT THAT THERE HAS BEEN NO SOLUTION. If we would make the German people a unified community and give them freedom before the world, then the Jew can have no place among us. He has the best trumps in his hands when a people lives in inner and outer slavery. THE JEW IS RESPONSIBLE FOR OUR MISERY AND HE LIVES ON IT. . . .

WE ARE ENEMIES OF THE JEWS BECAUSE WE BELONG TO THE GERMAN PEOPLE. THE JEW IS OUR GREATEST MISFORTUNE.

In what ways might this excerpt be a convincing piece of propaganda?

Nazism, like other brands of fascism, assaulted the liberal, democratic tradition in the West. According to Nazi doctrine, the political order should be dominated by a single party headed by a dictatorial leader (Hitler) who appealed to the masses. In addition, the doctrine reflected the sense among many Germans of being haunted by defeat in World War I and "humiliated" by the settlement that followed, and it fostered the belief that Germany therefore should rearm and redress the "injustices" of the Versailles treaty. At the center of Hitler's beliefs lurked biological racism and anti-Semitism. He glorified the mythical German "Aryan race" as superior and destined to conquer all other peoples in the struggle for racial supremacy. He also condemned the Jews as corrupt, landless parasites who created Marxist communism, caused Germany's humiliating defeat in World War I, and propagated liberalism. Underlying this element of the Nazi doctrine was a sense that everything in politics and in life was a constant struggle between peoples. Perils and enemies—whether from Jews, Poles, Bolsheviks, or others—lurked everywhere, plotting Germany's destruction. These fears seemed to justify ambitions to conquer the Slavic people to the east, to gain living space *(Lebensraum)*, and to follow policies to rid Germany of all opponents.

> **Nazi doctrine**

The Growth of the Nazi Party

Hitler exited jail in 1924 determined to acquire power from within, legally. Between 1925 and 1929, the Nazi Party grew in numbers somewhat but still remained a small splinter group. Then in October 1929, Germany's foreign minister, Gustav Stresemann, whose effective leadership for five years held center parties of the Weimar Republic together, died. That same month, the New York stock market crashed. Soon the Great Depression had Germany in its grip. It spelled the end of American loans and ignited unemployment and panic. Internal divisions immobilized parliamentary government, and the political extremes on both the Left and Right rapidly gained strength.

In 1930, the aged president Paul Hindenburg, Germany's military commander during

World War I and no friend to democracy, authorized rule by decree over Germany's unstable parliament. In elections held that year, the Nazis won a startling 18.3 percent of the vote—up from 2.6 percent in 1928. Hindenburg turned to conservative politicians to lead the republic, but they failed to govern effectively. The moderates, socialists, and communists, for their part, could not unify into a strong political force. In 1932, the Nazi Party became the largest political organization in Germany, winning an astonishing 37.3 percent of the vote. In elections for the office of president, Hitler gained 13.5 million votes against Hindenburg's 19 million.

The Appeal of Nazism

Nazism offered certainty to confused, frightened people; a sense of emotional belonging and unity in a time of crisis and anxiety; and action in a time of political immobility and conflict. Hitler and the doctrine of Nazism captured the imaginations of many Germans, especially young people and displaced veterans eager to achieve some measure of social stature in the new elite. Indeed, Hitler presented Nazism as "the organized will of the youth." For some, this included the appeal of being part of a street gang. He also appealed to the millions of Germans—the lower-middle class in particular—who had been traumatized by the Great Depression.

Much of Hitler's appeal stemmed from the alluring promises he made—promises that offered comfort and reassurance to a people in desperate need. He claimed that he would get rid of the despised war reparations, economic hardship, incompetent leadership, threats from the Left, and parliamentary government. In addition, he vowed to restore national unity and order in Germany and revive both the German people's shattered pride and their military might. The document on page 548 suggests how Hitler and the Nazi Party used nationalism and anti-Semitism to gain support.

To wealthy industrial leaders and landowners who feared the growing strength of unions, socialists, and communists, Hitler and his party held less of a personal attraction. Instead, Nazism represented the lesser of two distasteful options in the minds of these groups. Many such people who voted for the Nazis did so as a way to vote *against* the Weimar Republic, the terms of the Versailles treaty, and the communist path, rather than *for* the Nazi ideology. Indeed,

most of these Germans probably would have preferred to elect more traditional conservatives, but none of the existing candidates passed muster.

Whatever the appeal, those drawn to Hitler and the Nazis either ignored the party's strident nationalism, racism, and anti-Semitic fervor or embraced those sentiments. After all, such calls had been heard throughout central and eastern Europe for decades. However, many Germans failed to detect the especially virulent quality of the Nazis' version of these feelings. Even experienced politicians never saw the danger in the situation. In fact, some conservative leaders, such as Franz von Papen, supported Hitler under the assumption that they could control him. As they would discover, they were greatly mistaken.

Hitler Takes Power

In January 1933, President Hindenburg offered Hitler the chancellorship, and the Nazi leader accepted. Jubilant stormtroopers marched through Berlin's streets, holding their blazing torches high. In his new position, Hitler immediately called for another round of parliamentary elections. Now in official control of the state police and the agencies of information, the Nazis used propaganda and terror to confuse and frighten voters. As Hitler explained it, "Terror at the place of employment, in the factory, in the meeting hall, and on the occasion of mass demonstrations will always be successful."

Five days before the elections, Hitler discredited the communists by accusing them of burning the Reichstag building. He used the fire to justify the suspension of civil liberties and the arrest of many communists. On election day, the Nazis gained 44 percent of the vote; with their nationalist allies, they now had enough for a majority. The Reichstag quickly passed an enabling act granting Hitler the power to make laws on his own for four years. He soon outlawed all other political parties, and when Hindenburg died in 1934, Hitler became the sole leader of the German government. That same year, Hitler ordered Heinrich Himmler (1900–1945) and a handpicked private armed force, the elite **SS,** to "blood purge" his own paramilitary organization, the SA. Hitler saw the leader of the SA, Ernst Röhm (1887–1934) as a rival with plans to establish control over the army. That Night of the Long

→ connect to today ←

Rise of Regimes

Many Europeans, especially in Italy, Germany, and east-central Europe, turned to right-wing leaders who attacked parliamentary government and raised the compelling banner of militant nationalism. What circumstances in the present day might facilitate the rise of regimes like the dictatorships or fascist governments of the 1920s and 1930s?

ADOLF HITLER AT BUCKEBERG, 1934 Carefully organized mass rallies such as this one from the mid-1930s helped create a sense of belonging among the German people and increased Hitler's power.

it is worthwhile to live and die for such German womanhood." Officials launched campaigns to honor and reward pregnant women, prevent birth control, and improve racial stock. The government provided subsidies for large, racially German families. Women who gave birth to more than four children received the bronze Honor Cross of the German Mother; more than six warranted a silver medal, and more than eight, the coveted gold. In 1937, the Nazi Art Council of the Reich demanded that painters cease depicting families with only two children. A new program in 1938 went so far as to encourage SS soldiers to breed children with "racially fit" women outside of marriage.

Nazi youth organizations such as the Hitler Youth and the League of German Girls expanded rapidly, absorbing the majority of teenage boys and girls by the late 1930s. Boys were molded into Nazi supporters with military values and sometimes encouraged to spy on their teachers and parents. "I don't want an intellectual education" for boys, Hitler said. "They must learn in the face of the most difficult trials to conquer the fear of death for my sake." Girls were trained to become housewives and mothers, which the Nazis saw as the perfect complement to the loyal, fearless German soldier.

Nazi youth organizations

Knives eliminated potential opponents to Hitler within the party and the powerful SA as a rival to the reviving German army. Now the army swore allegiance to Hitler. The Nazi leader's dictatorship was complete.

Life in Nazi Germany

His power consolidated, Hitler proceeded to turn Germany into a police state. The government abolished freedom of speech, press, and assembly. An elaborate and all-powerful secret police, the Gestapo, uncovered and destroyed opposition. Nazi officials took over top positions in the government and pressured churches to conform to the new order. Professional organizations of doctors, teachers, lawyers, and engineers were transformed into Nazi associations. Officials even pushed people into joining Nazi leisure-time organizations.

The Nazis set out to bring family and private life under their control. As one step, the German Women's Bureau established guidelines for "proper" womanhood. Women, the bureau proclaimed, belonged at home, where they could fulfill their primary duties as homemakers, as subordinates to their husbands, and as producers of children. According to Guida Diehl, the leader of a pro-Nazi women's organization, "A woman's honor rests on the province specifically entrusted to her . . . love, marriage, family, motherhood. . . . The German man wants to know . . . that

Family and private life

Hitler inspired and manipulated people with his stirring, inflammatory speeches, rallies, parades, and symbols. His organizers choreographed mass meetings such as the one at Buckeberg in 1934, shown in the photograph above, to whip up excitement and a sense of belonging among the populace. At such rallies, Hitler made a carefully staged, dramatic entrance and delivered a long, emotionally charged speech. "It is the belief in our people that has made us small men great, that has made us poor men rich, that has made brave and courageous men out of us wavering, spiritless, timid fold," he proclaimed at the Nuremberg rally in 1936. Listeners described feeling "eternally bound to this man." The ministry of propaganda, under Joseph Goebbels (1897–1945), reinforced the psychological power of the rallies by controlling

Promoting Nazism and Hitler

OPINION

What do you think were the main factors that led to the rise and acquisition of power by Hitler?

information and spreading Nazi ideology through the press, radio, films, textbooks, pamphlets, and posters. For example, the ministry commissioned Leni Riefenstahl (1902–2003) to create the documentary film *Triumph of the Will* (1935), which portrayed the Nazis and their leaders as awe inspiring and gloriously on the march. Goebbels also painted an image of Hitler as the people's heroic leader, the one who could even be trusted to limit any excesses by over-zealous extremists within the Nazi Party itself.

In addition to promoting enthusiasm for their leader and ideology, the Nazis attacked "decadent" modern art and the popular culture of the Jazz Age. Only those whose works conformed to Nazi tastes—usually sentimental, pro-Nazi subject matter—could exhibit, publish, or perform. Officials promoted the burning of liberal books, sometimes even those of Germany's greatest literary figures of the eighteenth and nineteenth centuries, such as Goethe and Schiller. The Nazi minister of culture told university professors, "From now on it will *not* be your job to determine whether something is true but whether it is in the spirit of the [Nazi] revolution." Although some intellectuals and artists supported these policies, many opposed them and left Germany.

Both to solidify their power and to carry out their racist ideas, the Nazis targeted many groups for repression. For example, they sent communists, socialists, resisting Catholics, Jehovah's Witnesses, and the Roma (Gypsies) to concentration camps. Mixed-race children, criminals, prostitutes, alcoholics—all considered genetically inferior or "community aliens"—became candidates for sterilization. Homosexuality warranted at least incarceration or castration. A frightening glimpse of the future for all these groups came in 1939 when the Nazis created euthanasia programs designed to eliminate the mentally ill, handicapped, aged, and incurably ill.

No group, however, was more systematically repressed than the Jews. According to Joseph Goebbels, Jews had "corrupted our race, fouled our morals, undermined our customs, and broken our power." He blamed them as "the cause and the beneficiary of our misery." In 1933, the government excluded Jews from higher education and pub-

Nazi repression and persecution

FELIX NUSSBAUM, *SELF-PORTRAIT WITH JEWISH IDENTITY CARD,* 1943

The man in this painting grimly regards the viewer. In one hand, Nussbaum holds up his identity card, which in red letters states that he is Jewish. The yellow Star of David on his coat also identifies him as Jewish to the public. The walls of a prison yard tower ominously above him. Although this painting dates to 1943, the Nazis subjected Jews in Germany, such as Nussbaum, to increasingly harsh repression during most of the 1930s. What do the yellow Star of David and the identity card indicate about the evolving Nazi policy toward Jews in Germany?

lic employment. By 1935, most Jewish professionals in Germany had lost their jobs. That year the **Nuremberg Laws** took citizenship away from Jews and forbade marriage or sexual relations between Jews and non-Jews. In 1938, an episode of unrestrained violence revealed the mounting intensity of the Nazis' anti-Semitism. Incited by Goebbels, who blamed Jews for the assassination of a German diplomat in Paris, Nazi stormtroopers vandalized Jewish residences, synagogues, and places of business, smashing windows and plundering shops during the night of November 9–10. The troops then attacked Jews themselves, killing dozens and imprisoning tens of thousands in concentration camps. After this attack—known as **Kristallnacht,** or Crystal Night, for its images of shattered glass—the Nazi government increasingly restricted Jews' movements, eliminated their jobs, and confiscated their assets. By 1939, over half of Germany's Jews had emigrated, even though they had to leave their possessions behind, pay hefty emigration fees, and face rejection in other countries. Soon, though, it became too late to escape Germany. The painting on page 551 depicts the repression closing in on the Jews.

What did ordinary Germans think of this repression and persecution? Historians still debate this question. Although many people seemed to share Hitler's attitudes, at least to a degree, most people outside the persecuted groups may not have understood Hitler's extreme, ultimate purpose. Certainly some knew and many should have known. A few Germans objected. However, open resistance was dangerous. For those who disagreed with Hitler, it was much easier and safer to retreat into private life and apathy. Moreover, they, and many other Germans, found reason to overlook Hitler's repressive measures and support him in his efforts to revive their prostrate nation.

Rebuilding and Rearming the New Germany

Governmental expenditures fueled economic recovery, but Hitler's main goal was rearmament. Superhighways, hospitals, sports stadiums, and apartment houses sprang up all over Germany; so did rearmament plants that created jobs for millions. To make Germany self-sufficient in case of another war, the Nazis supported the development of synthetics for the manufacture of such items as rubber and petroleum that Germany would otherwise have to import. The planned conquest to the east, Hitler hoped, would provide needed raw materials and eventually pay for Germany's governmental expenditures.

For the most part, the Nazis left business organizations and the capitalist economy alone. However, big business, forced to bow to the will of governmental policy, did lose some freedom. The real assault was on independent labor unions, which the government abolished and replaced with the Nazi Labor Front.

All these efforts worked. Germany regained the economic and military strength to make it a great power. By 1935, Hitler had taken Germany out of the League of Nations and the Geneva Disarmament Conference. Unwilling to back the letter of the Versailles treaty with force, the Allies offered only muted opposition to Hitler's renunciation of the Versailles disarmament provisions. The next year, Hitler initiated a secret Four-Year Plan to prepare Germany for war. By 1939, the Nazis had increased armaments expenditures thirtyfold. Hitler felt ready to flex his newly developed muscles. His aggressive ambitions, combined with disturbing events outside Germany, were pushing the world toward war.

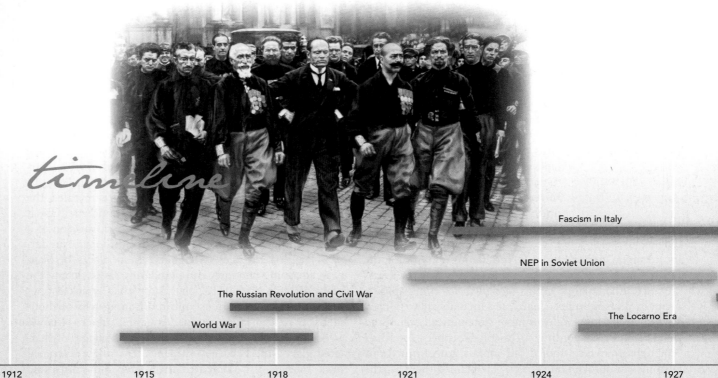

timeline

Fascism in Italy

NEP in Soviet Union

The Russian Revolution and Civil War

The Locarno Era

World War I

1912   1915   1918   1921   1924   1927

SUMMARY

During the 1920s, the West struggled to recover from the terrible World War I years. But any optimism generated by the end of the war was tempered by problems such as inflation and unemployment as well as the growth of authoritarian regimes. The Great Depression dealt an even more crushing blow to post–World War I hopes.

- Among the Western powers, economic uncertainty and political timidity marked the years after World War I. However, most Western economies perked up after 1924.

- In east-central and southern Europe, postwar strains overwhelmed fragile democratic systems. Several authoritarian regimes arose during the 1920s, most ominously in Italy with the rise of fascism.

- Under Lenin and especially Stalin, the Communists transformed the Soviet Union. By 1939, the Soviet Union had a fully planned economy.

- The 1929 stock market crash marked the beginning of the Great Depression, a widespread economic collapse with massive social and political consequences.

- In 1933 the Nazis, under Adolf Hitler, came to power in Germany, rearming the military and turning the country into a totalitarian state.

By the end of the 1930s, capitalist democracies had weakened, the authoritarian nations had become ominously belligerent, and the communist Soviet Union under Joseph Stalin had collectivized agriculture and built up its industrial base through the Five-Year Plans. But no country seemed to grow stronger, and for many in a more frightening way, than Germany under Adolf Hitler and the Nazis. The decade would not end before a return to the horrors that so many had hoped were behind them when that terrible storm lifted in 1918.

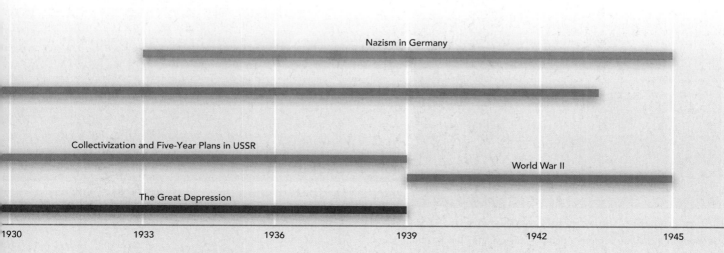

Nazism in Germany

Collectivization and Five-Year Plans in USSR

World War II

The Great Depression

| 1930 | 1933 | 1936 | 1939 | 1942 | 1945 |

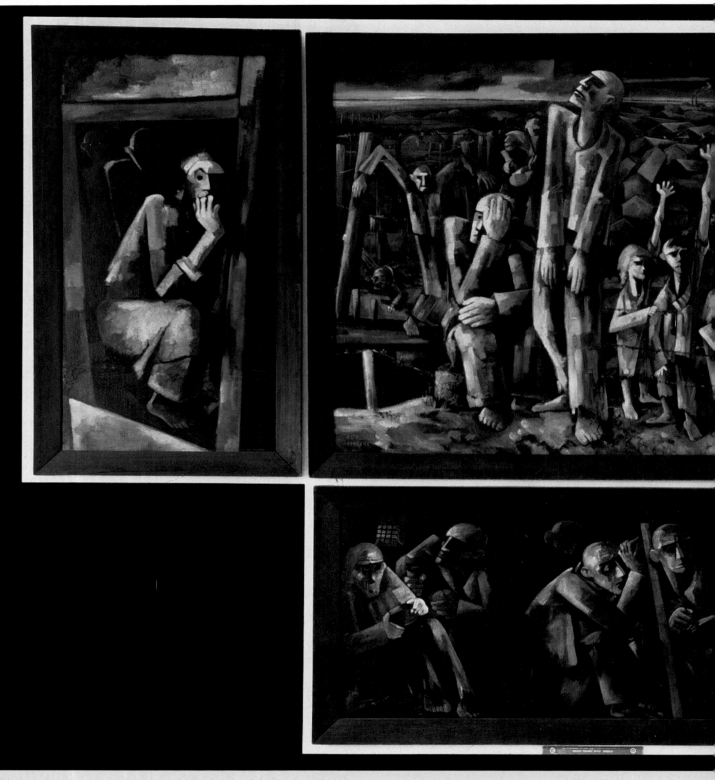

HORST STREMPEL, *NIGHT OVER GERMANY*, 1945 This 1945 painting by German artist Horst Strempel (1904–1975) depicts the fate of Germany in World War II. More broadly, it conveys the human suffering brought on by that horrendous conflict.

Into the Fire
Again

World War II, 1939–1945

24

Hopes Crashed into Ruins

In September 1938, British prime minister Neville Chamberlain flew home from a conference with leaders of France, Germany, and Italy. At the airport north of London, he announced to cheering crowds that an agreement at that meeting, known as the Munich Conference, had achieved "peace for our time." British newspapers proclaimed him a hero. ►►

Less than a year later, Chamberlain delivered another speech on the same topic. But this time, he made a painful admission to Britain's House of Commons. "This is a sad day for all of us, and to none is it sadder than to me," he confessed. "Everything that I have worked for, everything that I have hoped for . . . has crashed into ruins." The events that had devastated Chamberlain had just taken place in eastern Europe. On September 1, 1939, Germany had invaded Poland. ◄◄

THE ROAD TO WAR

1931–1939

What happened in the West and the world that led to that day? As we saw in Chapter 23, in the tense years of the 1920s and 1930s a new wave of authoritarian governments had washed across eastern and southern Europe; by 1938, only Czechoslovakia remained a parliamentary democracy. Many of these regimes included elements of fascism, but most were simple dictatorships by royal or military figures. Fascist movements, such as the Cross of Fire organization in France and the "Rex" Party in Belgium, also sprouted up in western Europe.

The democratic nations turned inward as they grappled with the depression and political divisions within their own borders. After 1934, communists in those nations sought to form alliances with socialists and moderates against the growing strength of fascism. The **Popular Front** in France is an example of such a partnership. The Front governed from 1936 to 1938. It was unable to pull the nation out of the depression, however, and ultimately fell from power. Its defeat left France more politically divided and discouraged than ever.

International Affairs Break Down

For France and the other democracies, international affairs soon slipped out of control. Rearmament spread, aggression became the order of the day, and neither the democratic powers nor the League of Nations responded forcefully to stop it.

In 1931, Japan initiated the new pattern. Many in Japan had long viewed China as their immediate rival—an enemy with the potential to stand in the way of their ambitions for economic and political dominance in east Asia. On the orders of young officers, the Japanese army invaded Manchuria in northern China and began a drive for conquest. Crowds in Japan cheered the news of the Manchurian campaign, and a heightened sense of nationalistic militarism gradually pervaded Japanese political life. The

Japan on the march

League of Nations condemned Japan but took no action. By 1937, China had managed to shake off the most onerous Western controls over the country but still bore the scars of decades of a sporadic, bloody civil war. China's dominant Nationalist Party, under Jiang Jieshi (Chiang Kai-shek) (1887–1975), had expended much of its strength opposing the growing Chinese Communist Party, led by Mao Zedong (1893–1976). In the early 1930s, Jiang had almost vanquished the Communists, but Mao and the core of his movement held on.

In 1937, Japanese troops invaded China proper. Less than six months later, the Japanese Imperial Army captured Nanking, capital city of China's Nationalist government. Over the following six weeks, Japanese army officers gave their troops free rein of the city. An American reporter in Nanking described the Japanese victory as "accompanied by the mass killing of the defenders, who were piled up among the sandbags, forming a mound six feet high." Victory did not end the slaughter: "Thousands of prisoners were executed by the Japanese . . . the killing of civilians was widespread . . . Nanking's streets were littered with dead." In what probably amounted to a deliberate policy, the Japanese carried out mass killings and executions of up to 300,000 Chinese soldiers and civilians and raped thousands of women.

Appalled, the rival Chinese Communists and Nationalists finally forged an alliance against the Japanese, and the Soviet Union provided military assistance to China against its powerful rival in the east. Nevertheless, city after city in China fell to Japanese bombs and invading armies. With its expanding industrial economy hungry for new markets, Japan was determined to create "a new order in East Asia," under its domination. To secure its position, it moved to form an alliance with two other aggressive, authoritarian states: Italy and Germany.

In 1935, Mussolini ordered his troops to invade Ethiopia in East Africa, hoping to win popularity at home despite the unemployment and failing social policies there. Ethiopia appealed to the League of Nations for protection. The League condemned Il Duce's actions, but the democratic powers did not follow up with enough action to stop him. Indeed, these responses to his aggression only pushed Mussolini toward Hitler, and in 1936 the two leaders agreed

Italy invades Ethiopia

to a friendship alliance—the Rome-Berlin **Axis.** In 1939, that alliance solidified into the military Pact of Steel. To show unity with Hitler, Mussolini promptly adopted anti-Semitic racial laws for Italy. To further his own military ambitions, he invaded Albania.

Civil War in Spain

In 1936, civil war broke out in Spain. Five years earlier, Spain had become a democratic republic for the first time. But when the Popular Front, made up of radicals, socialists, and communists, won election in 1936, a group of generals led by the conservative Francisco Franco (1892–1975) launched an armed rebellion against the new government. Franco's nationalist rebels enjoyed the support of the fascist Falange Party, the army, the church, and most of the wealthy elites; nevertheless, they could not easily overturn the popular Loyalists—the supporters of the Popular Front government.

The Spanish civil war soon became an international battlefield. Hitler and Mussolini, spotting an opportunity to advance the cause of fascism, gain an ally, and test their new weapons, sent arms and troops to aid Franco. At one point in 1937, Germans manning new airplanes on behalf of Franco's nationalists attacked the small Spanish town of Guernica, raining death on the civilian population there. The slaughter became the subject matter of one of the most haunting paintings of the twentieth century, *Guernica* (1937; see above), by the Spanish artist Pablo Picasso (1881–1973).

The Loyalists appealed to the other Western democracies for aid, but no help came. These nations hoped to maintain good relations with Italy and Germany and thus committed to a policy of neutrality, even though the fascist powers only pretended to agree. Unofficial Loyalist support came from some 40,000 idealistic volunteers, such as the Garibaldi Brigade and the Lincoln Brigade, who traveled to Spain from abroad and fought as individuals in the Loyalist cause. Otherwise, only the Soviet Union (until 1938) and Mexico provided assistance. The Loyalists also suffered from internal divisions between competing communists, anarchists, and liberals. In 1939, after three years of slaughter and atrocities on both sides, Franco's

Pablo Picasso, *Guernica*

1937

This 25-foot-long mural in black and white captures the worst features of this war—terror, brutality, disjointedness, lack of direction, and despair. On the left, a woman shrieks while holding a dead child. In the center, a warrior and horse lie shattered into fragments as the wounded sorrowfully look on. On the right, a woman plummets from a burning building. The image expresses both a wailing lament and a warning: Modern war not only kills indiscriminately but also targets civilians in order to terrorize all into submission. In what ways might details of this painting serve as a warning today?

rebels finally beat down the last of the Loyalist resistance (see map on page 558). The authoritarian Franco ruled Spain until his death in 1975.

Trying to Cope with Germany

In March 1936, Hitler gambled by ordering his armed forces into the Rhineland, that part of Germany on the west bank of the Rhine River that the Treaty of Versailles had deemed a demilitarized zone (see map on page 559). France fretted and fumed but, lacking Britain's support, did nothing. Hitler's bold gamble paid off. With a new confidence, he turned to the three countries that bordered Germany to the east: Austria, Czechoslovakia, and Poland.

In 1938, the Nazis incorporated Austria without opposition, annexing the 6.5 million Austrians to the German Reich (empire) (see map on page 559). Hitler then claimed

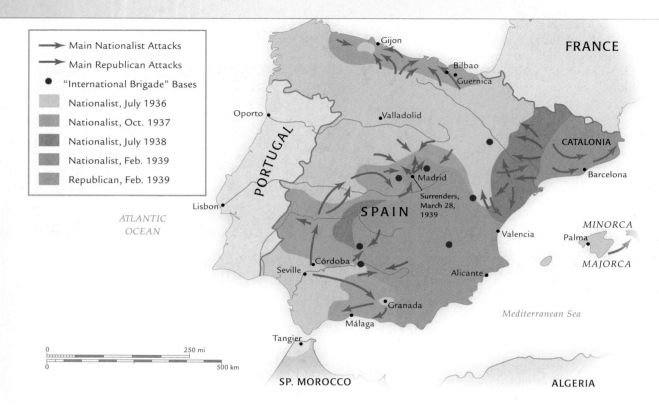

The Spanish Civil War, 1936–1939 This map shows the evolution of the Spanish Civil War between 1936 and 1939.

a portion of Czechoslovakia—the Sudetenland—that included 3.5 million German-speaking people. The Czechs, however, surprised him by rushing to their defenses. For months, Hitler churned out a barrage of propaganda that painted the German-speaking Czechs as a persecuted minority. He threatened and roused his people to readiness for war, finally vowing to march if the Sudetenland was not surrendered to him.

A difficult question now arose for the rest of Europe as it watched Hitler's actions: What should be done? For complex reasons, no one opposed Hitler with force. For one thing, World War I had made many Europeans reluctant to risk general war again. In addition, disagreement swirled over the justice of Hitler's demands. Some people agreed with Germany that the Versailles treaty was too harsh and sympathized with those who wanted to appease Germany's injured feelings. Many other people saw Hitler as sometimes reasonable and as a force that at least might be used to stop the spread of communism. British prime minister Neville Chamberlain (1869–1940), aware of Britain's lack of armed forces and public support to halt Hitler, tried for a compromise with the German ruler.

On September 29, 1938, the leaders of Germany, Italy, France, and Britain met in Munich to resolve the Sudetenland question. In the end, the two democratic powers chose **appeasement**—giving in to Hitler's demands in hopes of satisfying him. Hitler grabbed the piece of Czechoslovakia

that he wanted. British and French leaders, underestimating Hitler's territorial ambitions and determination to go to war, felt pleased with the agreement. Their nations still suffered from the Great Depression and could not endure another conflict, they told themselves. Moreover, many Europeans—particularly the British and French—considered a renewal of horrors akin to those of the Great War of 1914–1918 unacceptable. However, the Czechoslovak and Soviet governments expressed outrage; they hadn't been invited to attend the conference. The agreement would force the Czechs to capitulate. For Stalin, the deal confirmed the continuing unwillingness of the Western democracies to unite with the Soviet Union against the growing fascist threat.

> **Appeasement at Munich**

Back in Britain, Chamberlain announced that the **Munich Conference** agreement had "saved Czechoslovakia from destruction and Europe from Armageddon." Across Europe, crowds cheered, celebrating what they saw as the preservation of peace. But a few months later, Hitler showed his true colors: Without warning, he sent forces to overrun the remainder of the Czechoslovakian Republic (see map on page 559).

When Hitler next threatened Poland, Great Britain got tough and promised to come to Poland's aid. They turned to the Soviets for help, but it was too late. Isolated or excluded for too long from international affairs and disillu-

Legend:
International Boundaries, 1936
Germany in 1933
Remilitarized in 1936
Annexed in 1938
Satellite States, March 1939
Conquered by Germany in September 1939
Annexed by Soviet Union in September 1939

German Expansion, 1936–1939 **This map shows German expansion between 1936 and September 1939, as well as the territory annexed by the Soviet Union thanks to the Nazi-Soviet nonaggression pact of August 1939.**

sioned by France's and Britain's weak response to German aggression, Stalin stunned the world by signing a nonaggression pact with Hitler on August 23, 1939. In return for the Soviet Union's neutrality while Germany carved up Poland, Hitler gave Stalin a free hand to reannex territories in eastern Europe—including eastern Poland—that Russia had lost during World War I (see map above). By making this cynical pact with his greatest ideological enemy, Nazi Germany, Stalin may have gambled that the Soviet Union could stay on the sidelines, growing in strength, while the fascist and democratic capitalists destroyed one another.

At dawn on September 1, the Germans launched an all-out attack on Poland by land, sea, and air. Hitler remained convinced that France and Britain would not go to war over Poland. He was wrong. Two days later, Great

Nazi-Soviet nonaggression pact

Britain and France declared war on Germany. In a poem titled "SEPTEMBER 1, 1939," poet W. H. Auden (1907–1973) moaned that

The unmentionable odor of death
Offends the September night

World War II had begun.

AXIS VICTORIES

1939–1942

Perhaps the war initiated in 1914 never quite ended, and the 1920s were just a pause in three decades of fighting and crises after 1914. Maybe if the depression had not struck,

Hitler and the Nazis would not have come to power, the democracies would have continued to grow, and war could have been averted. Tragically, the war that did break out in September 1939 would blaze six long years and encompass the globe as never before.

Triumph of the German Blitzkrieg

The German **blitzkrieg**—a "lightning war" of highly coordinated air strikes and rapid deployment of tanks and motorized columns—overwhelmed Polish forces. But that did not end matters within Poland: German occupiers and Germans already living within Poland soon began destroying the Polish people, actions that would form a pattern to be repeated and magnified in the years to come. The French and British mobilized their armies along the German border, and the British fleet blockaded Germany by sea—all to no avail.

For the next six months, in what became known as the "phony war," almost no military action took place. France and Great Britain seemed paralyzed. Meanwhile, the Soviet Union took advantage of its agreement with Hitler and reannexed territories in Poland and eastern Europe—including Estonia, Latvia, and Lithuania—that Russia had lost in World War I. When Finland refused to yield strategic territories, the Soviets attacked. The Finns put up a determined resistance, and it took several months for the Soviet army finally to defeat these stubborn soldiers.

In April 1940, the Germans suddenly overran both Denmark and Norway. German planes fended off Britain's fleet, inflicting heavy losses. The next month, German armies assaulted Luxembourg, the Netherlands, Belgium, and France. Tiny Luxembourg offered no resistance, while the Dutch fought heroically but fell after six days. To support the beleaguered Belgians, the British army and a large part of the French army moved into Belgium. The French trusted that their fortresses—the Maginot Line— would hold along the German border. However, the line proved useless against the highly mobile German tanks. The Germans skirted the fortresses to the north through the Ardennes Forest. German general Erwin Rommel recalled the break-

The Battle of France

through: "The tanks now rolled in a long column through the line of fortifications. . . . Our artillery was dropping heavy harassing fire on villages and the road far ahead. . . . Engines roared, tank tracks clanked and clattered . . . civilians and French troops, their faces distorted with terror, lay huddled in the ditches." And then, he noted, "the flat countryside lay spread out around us under the cold light of the moon. We were through the Maginot Line."

The German blitzkrieg drove quickly to the English Channel, cutting off Allied armies in Belgium and then trapping them at Dunkirk, a seaport in northern France. A flotilla of military and civilian ships, including fishing boats and pleasure craft, rescued 330,000 British and French troops off the beach at Dunkirk.

The Battle of France ended after only five weeks. Although almost equal in numbers to the Germans, the French seemed demoralized from the beginning of the war. According to one French journalist, they felt abandoned by the British, "who were ready to fight to the last French soldier." On June 16, 1940, the aged, right-wing Marshal Philippe Pétain became premier of France and quickly surrendered to Hitler. With the surrender, Germany took the northern half of France and the entire Atlantic coast. The new authoritarian French regime would govern the remaining unoccupied portion of France from the city of Vichy. French general Charles de Gaulle escaped to Great

LAURA KNIGHT, *THE BATTLE OF BRITAIN,* 1943 Women and men pull in balloons used to hinder flights by German bombers during the Battle of Britain. In the background are buildings destroyed by bombing, but numerous smokestacks in the distance indicate that Britain's ability to fight survives.

Britain and declared himself leader of the Free French government in exile.

France's collapse left Great Britain to face Germany alone. The audacious and eloquent Winston Churchill (1874–1965), who had replaced Neville Chamberlain as prime minister, warned his people of the serious struggle to come: "This is no war of chieftains or of princes, of dynasties or national ambition; it is a war of peoples and of causes." The Germans, determined to gain control of the English Channel and prepare for an invasion of Britain, unleashed massive air attacks against Britain in July 1940. As the Battle of Britain erupted, Churchill rallied his country, offering his "blood, toil, tears, and sweat" and vowing "we shall never surrender."

The Battle of Britain

For almost two months that fall, the Germans bombed London every night. A British civilian described some of the ordeal: "Bombs fell by day as well as by night. We became accustomed to the sudden drone of an airplane in the middle of the morning, the screech of a bomb, the dull crash of its explosion and the smell of cordite that filled the air a moment later." The image on page 560 reveals some of the effort involved in the Battle of Britain. In cellars and subway stations, the British people holed up while their planes and antiaircraft guns, now aided by radar, fought off the Germans. Boosted by the high morale of the people, the increased output of aircraft factories, and Churchill's leadership, the island nation miraculously held. By November, the British had prevailed.

> "This is no war of chieftains or of princes, of dynasties or national ambition; it is a war of peoples and of causes."

War in North Africa and the Balkans

Even though Italy was not yet ready to take on another major war, Mussolini did not want to miss out on the spoils of an easy victory. He, too, invaded France as it fell to the Germans. Then in September 1940, his armies in Africa moved east from Libya into Egypt. A few weeks later, they attacked Greece from Albania.

However, Mussolini's forces met disaster at every turn. Mobile British forces routed Italian armies in North Africa, and British planes crippled the Italian fleet in southern Italy. The Greeks also contributed to the rout, driving the Italians back into Albania.

In response, Germany's forces streamed into the Balkans and North Africa. Hitler had several goals in mind for this move. He coveted the Balkans for their rich supplies of raw materials, especially the Romanian oil fields. He also hoped to save the Italian forces in North Africa and take the Suez Canal, Britain's lifeline to its empire.

Hungary and Romania yielded to Hitler's threats and joined the Axis alliance in November 1940; Bulgaria did the same in March 1941. Yugoslavia and Greece refused, and they were overrun by German forces within a few weeks. Germany's Afrika Korps drove the British back into Egypt. Pro-German movements broke out in Iraq, Iran, and French Syria. At this point, however, Hitler hurled his main forces against the Soviet Union, giving the British a breathing spell to recoup their strength in North Africa and the eastern Mediterranean.

Operation Barbarossa: Germany Invades the Soviet Union

The eventual conquest of the Soviet Union had always been uppermost in Hitler's thoughts, despite his deceptive pact with the USSR. Even before that 1939 deal, Hitler had revealed his true intentions to a group of associates: "Everything I do is directed against Russia. If the West is too stupid and blind to understand that, I shall be forced to reach an agreement with the Russians and strike at the West. Once [the West] is defeated, [I shall] turn my concentrated forces against the Soviet Union." Conquest of the Soviet Union would bring Germany "living space" as well as vast industrial and agricultural resources. It would also eliminate any threat from Nazism's great ideological enemy. And it would afford Germany access to millions of Jews—Hitler's "blood enemy"—living in the Soviet Union. Still, the Nazi leader had hoped to subdue the British before turning to the Soviets. Failing that, he decided to invade the Soviet Union anyway.

In June 1941, the Germans launched Operation Barbarossa, sending more than three million soldiers, 3,700 tanks, and 2,500 planes against the USSR. Hitler expected to crush Soviet resistance in six weeks, well before the notorious Russian winter set in. "You only have to kick in the door, and the whole rotten structure will come crashing down," he claimed. But he also warned his generals, "The war against Russia will be . . . one of ideologies and racial differences and will have to be conducted with unprecedented, unmerciful and unrelenting harshness."

Stalin had long suspected that Hitler would someday turn against him, yet he believed that a German invasion was impossible before spring 1942, when Britain would be too crippled to constitute much of a diversion to German forces. Moreover, recent evidence suggests that Stalin himself may have planned to turn the tables on Hitler and launch his own full-scale preemptive attack on German forces in eastern Europe. In the days before the June invasion by Germany, Stalin refused to believe numerous reports from many sources that Hitler's forces were about to attack. He even ignored warnings from some of his top generals.

On the morning of June 22, the Germans launched their assault. Caught off guard, Stalin delayed his response. For a few days, he disappeared from the public eye. Finally, he urged the Soviet people to rally to "the Great Patriotic War." Not everyone rose to the challenge. Indeed, the Ukrainians and some other Soviet groups initially greeted the Germans as liberators. The German forces quickly shattered Soviet armies. On July 3, the chief of Germany's General Staff wrote in his journal, "The Russian Campaign has been won in the space of two weeks." In just the first twenty days of the campaign, 600,000 Soviet soldiers lost their lives.

Even in the face of such destruction, most Soviet peoples put up a determined resistance. The weather worked against the enemy. The September mud season slowed German troops and tanks, and the unusually harsh winter that followed caught the invaders unprepared. Nevertheless, the German war machine crunched forward. By December 1, it had come within sight of Moscow and had nearly surrounded Leningrad (see map on page 563). A confident Hitler announced the imminent, permanent destruction of the USSR.

Once again, the weather intervened. The winter tightened its grip, subjecting the lightly clothed and weakly supplied Nazis to frigid temperatures. Moreover, Japan's decision not to go to war against the USSR saved the Soviets from a disastrous two-front struggle. Stalin could now move troops from the Far East to the West. The combination of punishing weather and Russian counterattacks forced the Germans to halt and in some places even retreat—but only temporarily. By then, German forces had slaughtered more than three million Soviet soldiers and captured another three million. But the Soviet forces were not yet broken.

Japan Attacks

Farther east, events were brewing that would add yet another dimension to the war. Specifically, Western imperial presence in Asia and the Pacific had frustrated Japan's dreams of expansion. The resource-poor island nation depended on foreign raw materials and markets to fuel its industrial economy. During the 1930s, the Great Depression had weakened Japan's democratic regime and made the army a more potent political as well as military force. As military men gained control of the government, Japan's foreign policy shifted to expansionism. By 1939, Japan had conquered the populous coastal areas of China

and pushed Chinese forces well into the interior. When the war in Europe weakened European colonial powers—which controlled much of Southeast Asia, with its wealth of essential resources such as oil, tin, and rubber—Japan joined the Rome-Berlin Axis. It quickly occupied French Indochina and threatened the Dutch East Indies. The United States responded with a total economic embargo on all exports to Japan, threatening Japan's oil supplies in particular.

Hoping that the war in Europe would induce the United States to cede dominance to the Japanese in Southeast Asia, Japan struck. On December 7, 1941, Japanese air forces surprised the American fleet anchored in Pearl Harbor, Hawaii, crippling the U.S. naval and air forces. President Franklin D. Roosevelt (1882–1945) called it "a day that will live in infamy." The United States immediately declared war on Japan, and within days Germany and Italy declared war on the United States. Several Latin American nations joined the United States in the Grand Alliance against the Axis.

The U.S. enters the war

The long-isolationist United States had an army with limited capabilities. In addition, it had sent huge quantities of arms, equipment, and food across the Atlantic in its role as "the arsenal of democracy." Roosevelt agreed with Churchill to make the war in Europe the United States' first priority, and Americans started mobilizing their country's vast resources for the fight.

Meanwhile, the Japanese conquered a vast area in Southeast Asia and the Pacific (see map on page 564), creating The Greater East Asia Co-Prosperity Sphere. Japan claimed to be liberating Asia from the imperial West, but it dominated the new territories through nationalist leaders ready to collaborate with Japan's occupation forces and treated the conquered peoples as inferior subjects. Scoring victory after victory, the Japanese and Germans seemed to be winning the war.

"[A] day that will live in infamy."

BEHIND THE LINES: The Struggle and the Horror

By 1942, Hitler ruled most of continental Europe from the English Channel to the outskirts of Moscow (see map on page 563). In administering his lands, he pursued two primary goals. First, he hunted for ways to keep Germany supplied with war materials and maintain the standard of living for Germans without having to call

Hitler's "New Order"

Legend:
- Hitler's Greater Germany
- Allied with Germany
- Occupied by Germany and Its Allies
- Grand Alliance
- Neutral Nations
- ✦ Major Battle Sites

World War II in Europe This map shows Hitler's empire at its height in 1942, the front lines in the following years as the Allies closed in on Germany in 1945, and the major battles of the war. **What does this map indicate about the military problems confronting Hitler after 1942?**

on them to make unpopular sacrifices. Second, he sought to fulfill his racist agenda. To these ends, he implemented his "New Order," a program of economic exploitation and racial imperialism in the lands that he now controlled. He used conquered peoples according to their ranking in his racial hierarchy. Those most directly related to the Nazi conception of the Aryan race, such as Scandinavians, Anglo-Saxons, and Dutch, were treated well and might be absorbed into the Nazi empire as partners with the Germans. He considered the Latin races, such as the French, inferior but tolerable as supportive cogs in the New Order. Slavs ranked toward the bottom of Hitler's hierarchy; they were to be isolated, shoved aside, treated like slaves, or killed.

The Holocaust

Lowest on Hitler's racial scale were the Jews, and they fared the worst in Hitler's scheme. Nazis herded Jews into ghettos in German, Polish, and Russian cities. For a while, the Nazis envisioned forced emigration of Jews, perhaps to the island of Madagascar off the east coast of Africa, to solve the "Jewish problem." In 1941, such ideas ended and Hitler initiated a policy of genocide, formally adopted in a January 1942 meeting, which came to be known as the **Holocaust.** Mobile SS squads under Reinhard Heydrich (1904–1942) and Heinrich Himmler began the wholesale killing of Jews, along with Slavic prisoners of war, in Poland and Russia.

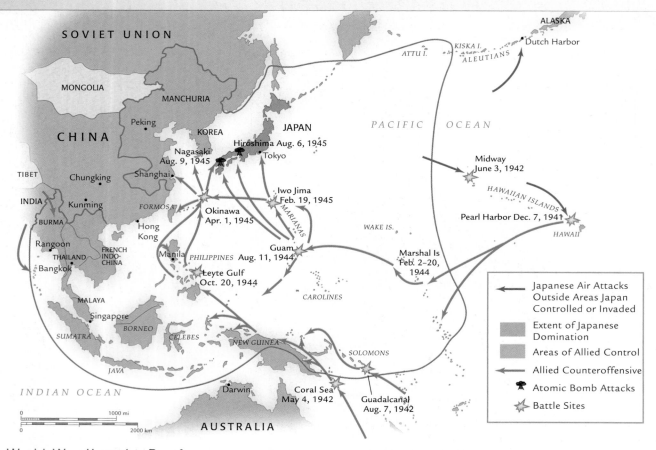

World War II in the Pacific

This map shows Japan's empire at its height in 1942 and traces the course of the Allied counteroffensive that led to Japan's defeat in 1945.

Firing squads shot victims en masse. Dissatisfied with the pace of the killings, the Germans began using mobile vans that murdered people by gas. Finally, when that method still did not seem efficient enough, the Nazis used large gas chambers that killed thousands at a time. Heydrich, the Plenipotentiary for the Preparation of the Final Solution of the European Jewish Question, promised that this campaign—"a historic moment in the struggle against Jewry"—would be carried out "effectively but silently." Heydrich charged Adolf Eichmann (1906–1962) with managing this task.

The Nazis built six huge death camps in what had been Poland.

Death camps From gathering points all over Europe, unknowing victims were crowded into cattle cars, where they soon became dehydrated, disoriented, and terrorized; many died in transit. Upon their arrival, officials divided families, segregated people by sex, and made the first

OPINION

In what ways was the Holocaust a consequence of Nazism and the war?

"selection." "Inside the camp, one's first view was fixed on a mountain of children's shoes," recalled a woman survivor. "To tell the truth I did not understand what that meant." Those who could not work as the Nazis wanted—therefore more women, children, and elderly—were sent to the "showers"—the Nazis' euphemism for the gas chambers. Officials especially targeted pregnant women to prevent the birth of more Jews. They sent the rest, now physically and mentally terrorized, to the work camps.

The scale and depravity of this programmed inhumanity, torture, and death were unprecedented; thus the victims simply could not grasp what was happening until it was too late. Some Jews rebelled—in the Warsaw ghetto and the Treblinka camp, for example. They and others who fought back may have made important moral statements, but they stood no real chance against the Nazis. The masses of Jews trapped in ghettos or camps, their strength sapped by hunger and illness, had little choice. For many, the only way to maintain a shred of dignity against the degradation and death was silence. The Nazis had trapped these victims in a merciless, thoroughly organized system from which few escaped.

Struggling to survive in the camps, many people tried to help one another, though the desperate conditions at times also brought out the worst in people. In this surreal world, the Germans applied assembly-line methods to the destruction of millions of human beings. A French doctor described the killing process at the Auschwitz-Birkenau camp: Once prisoners were herded and forced into the gas chambers, "the massive oak double doors are shut. For two endless minutes one can hear banging on the walls and screams which are no longer human. . . . Five minutes later the doors are opened. The corpses, squashed together and distorted, fall out like a waterfall" (see Exploring the Past on page 566). In a particularly brutal twist, the Nazis forced Jewish prisoners to carry out much of the dirty work of killing. Nazi guards subjected their captives to torture and abuse, and German doctors conducted gruesome experiments on camp prisoners.

In the end, almost all prisoners slaved in the camps on starvation rations until they died or were sent to the gas chambers when no longer useful to their captors. In Auschwitz alone, the largest of these camps, the Nazis murdered more than 12,000 people a day and more than one million Jews by the end of the war. Although Jews were the Nazis' main target, many people from non-Jewish groups—communists, gypsies, Jehovah's Witnesses, Soviet prisoners of war, Slavs, homosexuals—suffered the same fate. Moreover, the elite Nazis had other ominous plans—including an eventual genocidal "resettlement" to Siberia of more than 30 million people, mainly Slavs—if the Nazis should win the war in the East. Rudolf Höss, commander of the Auschwitz camp, would describe the order for mass kill-ings as "something extraordinary, something monstrous. However the reasoning behind the order of this mass annihilation seemed correct to me . . . I wasted no thoughts about it." Ultimately these genocidal efforts took priority over even the war effort and continued right up until the last days of the war (see image below).

Who knew about the brutal realities of the camps during the war? The Nazis had gone to great lengths to cover up the process of killing, swearing everyone involved to secrecy and presenting more benign concentration camps outside Poland for international inspection. As reports of what really was happening filtered out, many people expressed disbelief. Atrocities on such a mass scale seemed impossible. But it had taken thousands of officials, bureaucrats, soldiers, police, and SS guards to carry out the murders. At least these thousands knew. Indeed, many concentration- and death-camp officials followed orders with enthusiasm, competing for approval from their superiors. Several large German companies, including the industrial giant I. G. Farben, benefited from contracts with the camps. Most German civilians may have been apathetic or may have chosen not to think about what was going on in the east, but information—from witnesses, from individuals indirectly involved, and by word of mouth—about the camps and massive killings was widespread. While perhaps not fully comprehended, the Final Solution had become an open secret in Germany by the end of 1942. Authorities on the outside who might have tried to help did nothing. At some point, British and American commanders probably knew. While the full extent of the Holocaust may not have been clear, from almost the beginning Allied leaders had received information about the Nazi killing programs from various sources. After 1942, some Western newspapers published reports about mass murders and the death camps, though how much was widely understood or accepted before 1944 is unclear. Eventually, Jewish leaders pleaded to Allied governments to bomb the gas chambers and the railway lines leading to the death camps. But Allied officials claimed that other military targets were more important for the overall war effort.

NAZI ATROCITIES, 1945 This grim photo taken in the Landsberg concentration camp is one of many that testify to Nazi atrocities.

Collaboration and Resistance

Collaborating governments often copied or cooperated with the Nazis. In some countries, such as Croatia, officials willingly rounded up Jews and carried out the killing themselves. The anti-Semitic government of Vichy France under Pétain transported thousands of Jews to Nazi death camps. In almost all conquered lands, the Nazis managed to find individuals who would collaborate with them.

However, many others resisted. The Danes saved most of the Jews living in their lands. In Italy, officials often ignored Nazi

The Nazi Death Camps

The "final solution" took the form of death camps where Nazis could kill on a larger scale. Testimonies from witnesses paint vivid pictures of the horrors that occurred daily in these camps. The account below is from Abraham Bomba, who in 1942 was transported with his family from a Polish ghetto to the Treblinka death camp, where his job was to cut women's hair before they were gassed.

Filling the Treblinka Gas Chambers

The gas chamber . . . was all concrete. There was no window. [It] had two doors . . . [and] the people went in to the gas chamber from the one side . . . [and] they pushed in as many as they could. It was not allowed to have the people standing up with their hands down because there was not enough room, but when the people raised their hand[s] . . . there was more room. . . . And on top of that they throw in kids, 2, 3, 4 years old. . . . The whole thing took . . . between five and seven minutes. The door opened up . . . from the other side. People working in Treblinka number two took out the corpses. Some of them dead and some of them still alive. They dragged them to the ditches . . . big ditches, and they covered them. That was the beginning of Treblinka.

What might be the significance of these actions, which occurred on such a large scale?

directives, despite Mussolini's alliance with Hitler. Numerous stories, such as the experience of the young Anne Frank hiding in the Netherlands, record individual heroism and tragedy. Resistance organizations rose in almost every occupied territory, particularly in France, Yugoslavia, and the Soviet Union. At great risk, men and women alike established underground networks, provided intelligence to the Allied forces, conducted guerrilla actions, aided escaping prisoners, sabotaged German military installations, and engaged Nazi forces that might have been used on the war fronts. Communists, such as those in Yugoslavia under the command of Josip Broz, often formed the core of the most determined resistance movements. Tito's organization became one of the most effective resistance forces in Europe.

But the price of fighting back was high. The Germans infiltrated resistance groups and brutally crushed any hints of threats. Collective retribution for attacks against German leaders deterred many. In one case, the Nazis massacred 7,000 people in one town in retaliation for the killing of 10 Germans by Yugoslav partisans. In some places, such as Ukraine, Greece, and Yugoslavia, resistance groups with different political agendas fought among themselves, eroding their ability to oppose the Nazis.

Mobilizing the Home Fronts

Even more than in World War I, whole societies mobilized for the war effort in the 1940s. Governments controlled production and rationed goods. As labor shortages arose, women again assumed jobs normally reserved for men. Political leaders acquired unusual powers and discouraged dissent. Even outside the Nazi empire, some groups of citizens fell victim to the suspicion that the war engendered. In the United States, for example, government agents removed Japanese Americans living on the West Coast from their homes and businesses and placed them in camps. Propaganda on all sides painted distorted, racist pictures of the enemy and whipped up civilian support of the troops.

Britain, taking the brunt of German aggression early on, mobilized thoroughly. The government drafted men between the ages of 18 and 50 and women between 20 and 30 into military or civilian war service. Women accounted for most of the increase in Britain's labor force. The government also enlisted scientists to help break the German code and work on an atomic bomb.

The Soviet Union tried everything to brace itself against the Germans. Hundreds of thousands of Russian women served in the Soviet armed forces; millions took jobs, replacing men sent to the front. In October 1941, the Soviets managed an astounding feat: They dismantled more than five hundred factories in Moscow and elsewhere and reassembled them in the east, away from the encroaching German troops. By 1942, Soviet factories were producing far more tanks, guns, and combat airplanes than their German counterparts.

In World War II, the major combatants recognized that victory hinged on the ability to increase industrial production. With so many men serving in the armed forces, nations called on women to work in jobs traditionally reserved for men. In the United States, many factory workforces were transformed. In recent decades throughout the West, women have moved into jobs once considered reserved for men. Today, many scholarships and grants have been created to encourage more women to enter fields that were traditionally reserved for men, including math, science, engineering, and technology.

The United States, less threatened geographically by the war, mobilized unevenly; still, it boosted its wartime production by 400 percent in two years and sent large quantities of supplies to its British and Soviet allies. Germany was also slower to mobilize its citizens. In the early years, Hitler instead relied on quick victories and spoils from conquered lands to fulfill his nation's needs. Millions of conscripted foreigners and prisoners of war served as Germany's laborers. Only after 1942 did Hitler turn to full mobilization, multiplying Germany's production over the following two years despite concentrated Allied bombing.

TURNING THE TIDE OF WAR

1942–1945

The now-global war was fought in three major theaters: the Soviet Union, the Mediterranean and western Europe, and the Pacific. The turning points in all theaters came between June and August 1942. The largest, bloodiest battles occurred in the Soviet Union and were fought by some nine million soldiers. The Germans had already conquered most of that nation's lands west of the Volga River, leaving nearly half of the Soviet people under German rule.

The Eastern Front and the Battle of Stalingrad

The Germans, refreshed and reequipped, resumed their offensive against the Soviet Union in June 1942, this time in the southern sector of the USSR. In July, one German soldier expressed confidence that "the Russian troops are com-pletely broken," and "the Führer knows where the Russians' weak point is." The soldier recorded in his diary that he fully expected German forces to "take Stalingrad and then the war will inevitably soon be over." In early August, as German forces pushed forward, he and others anticipated the rewards of victory: "What great spaces the Soviets occupy, what rich fields there are to be had here after the war's over." By mid-August, they had reached the outskirts of Stalingrad on the Volga River. However, this soldier noted that the "doomed" Russian divisions "are continuing to resist bitterly."

The Battle of Stalingrad became the greatest of the war and raged for seven months. "Not a step backward," ordered Stalin. He spared no resource, including the many women who served on the front lines as combat soldiers, tankers, and snipers. Indeed, some airforce regiments were made up entirely of women. The most revered pilot, Lily Litvak, shot down twelve German planes.

As the Russian winter again approached, Hitler ordered his army not to retreat. That decision took a huge toll on the German army. By the end of October, the German soldier's diary entries revealed a change in his optimistic attitude: "Who would have thought three months ago that instead of the joys of victory we would have to endure such sacrifice and torture, the end of which is nowhere in sight." The Germans mounted their final assault on November 11 and penetrated to the Volga. But a stalemate ensued, dragging on until November 19, when the Russians launched their long-planned encircling offensive. Though the Russian winter loomed, Hitler ordered his forces to stand firm. That decision took a huge toll on the German army. In December, the same German soldier complained, "Everybody is racked with hunger. Frozen potatoes are the best meal." Just before his death, he wrote, "The soldiers look like corpses or lunatics, looking for something to put in their mouths. They no longer take cover from Russian shells; they haven't the strength to walk, run away and hide."

In January 1943, the Russians finally surrounded the remainder of the 300,000-man German army, now reduced by casualties to 80,000. German Sixth Army commander General Friedrich Paulus sent a note to the German high command: "Further defense senseless. Collapse inevitable. Army requests immediate permission to surrender in order to save lives of remaining troops." Hitler replied: "Surrender is forbidden. Sixth Army will hold their positions to the last man." A few days later, the German Sixth Army surrendered.

The Soviets lost one million soldiers in the bitter struggle over Stalingrad. And Germany never recovered from the massive loss of men and material, and morale suffered during the epic seven-month battle. Over the next two and a half years, Soviet forces slowly beat back the invaders (see map on page 563).

The Southern Fronts

In North Africa the German general Rommel's (1891–1944) tough Afrika Korps fought to within 65 miles of the Egyptian coastal city of Alexandria. But in August 1942, at the Battle of El Alamein, the British forces, bolstered by supplies from the United States, held. Over the following months, British and newly arriving American forces managed to push the Germans back, and in May 1943, the cornered Afrika Korps surrendered.

The Mediterranean

The war-weary Stalin now urged Britain and America to open up a major western front in France to take the pressure off his forces. Instead, in an effort to protect British interests in the Mediterranean without risking a battle against major German forces, the Allies attacked Italy. First, they moved from the island of Sicily up into the southern Italian mainland. In July 1943, the Italian government arrested Mussolini, and two months later Italy surrendered. However, strong German forces still held most of the country. German commandos rescued Mussolini and set him up as

THE BATTLE OF STALINGRAD, 1942 In this staged photograph that exemplifies the use of propaganda during the war, Russian soldiers pose in ways suggesting the difficulty of this deadly battle.

the head of a puppet government in the north. The Allies' progress slowed through the Italian mountains, and the rest of the Italian campaign became a long and costly effort.

Meanwhile, Allied planes rained bombs on German targets. These dangerous missions took a heavy toll on both sides. In 1943, for example, only one-third of British crews flying planes across the channel would survive their first tour of duty. In late July of that same year, systematic bombing raids by British and American air forces set off a devastating firestorm in the German city of Hamburg. A survivor described what happened: The sky became "absolutely hellish" in minutes. "No noise made by humans—no outcry—could be heard. It was like the end of the world." The firestorm killed 40,000 people.

The Western Front

On June 6, 1944 (**D-Day**), American, British, and Canadian forces under General Dwight Eisenhower (1890–1969) finally swept across the English Channel to make a run at German forces holding France. Hitler, overextended in Russia and the Mediterranean, had to defend a 3,000-mile coastline in the west. Forced to gamble on where the Allies would invade, he bet on Calais, where the English Channel was narrowest. Instead, the invasion—supported by an armada of more than 6,000 vessels and 12,000 aircraft—came on the Normandy beaches. Hitler's "Atlantic Wall" of defenders took a huge toll on the invaders. In many cases, lead companies suffered 90 percent casualties; boats and tanks were often destroyed before their troops could even fire a shot. One American soldier reported that within the first ten minutes, "every officer and sergeant of the leading company had been killed or wounded. . . . It had become a struggle for survival and rescue."

Despite these losses, the Allies established a northwestern European front. Two months later, they opened a new front in southern France. Aided by French forces and resistance fighters, the Allies pushed the Germans out of most of France before year's end. Meanwhile, Allied bombs pulverized German cities and crippled Germany's transportation network.

Under the steady onslaught, Germany began running out of oil and soldiers. Early in 1945, American and British forces at last succeeded in crossing the Rhine into Germany. By that time, the Russians had swept through most of eastern and southeastern Europe. Along the **Germany defeated** 1,500 miles between Stalingrad and Berlin lay the wreckage of Hitler's once-mighty war machine. The painting on page 569 by Canadian artist Charles Fraser Comfort reveals the fate of so many combatants toward the end of World War II. It echoes scenes from World War I, suggesting ways in which the two wars were tragically related.

Still, Hitler would not give up. Even in the case of Berlin, he refused to evacuate civilians from the cities, despite

CHARLES FRASER COMFORT, *DEAD GERMAN ON THE HITLER LINE*, ca. 1944 This painting of a single German soldier's remains stands for the loss of millions during this tragic, devastating war.

the deaths and hardships that would result, so that his troops would feel compelled to fight even more desperately—a tactic Stalin had already used. On April 20, 1945, Berlin civilians heard the approaching Soviet troops. "Our fate is rolling in from the east," reported one woman in her diary. "What was yesterday a distant rumble has now become a constant roar. We breathe the din; our ears are deafened to all but the heaviest guns."

Germany finally surrendered on May 8, and the war in Europe ended. In what one survivor described as "the carcass of Berlin," Hitler, his wife, Eva Braun, and several other top Nazis committed suicide. In Italy, Italian partisans had already shot Mussolini and his mistress.

The War in the Pacific

In the Pacific, the turning point of the war came in the late spring of 1942 (see map on page 564). American and Australian troops stopped the Japanese army in New Guinea, and the Americans turned back Japanese naval forces in the Battle of the Coral Sea, northeast of Australia. Soon, American ships, aided by intelligence from intercepted cipher transmissions, positioned themselves off Midway Island to ambush the incoming Japanese. At first, the Japanese fared well, destroying two-thirds of the American planes. Then, aided by luck, dive-bombers from American aircraft carriers spotted four Japanese carriers with their planes being refueled and rearmed. The encounter proved a disaster for the Japanese. In just five minutes, the course of the Pacific war was reversed. Three Japanese carriers went down, followed later by the fourth. The Japanese lost the advantage permanently. The U.S. arms industry was already on its way to outproducing the Japanese and creating an overwhelmingly strong fleet. The Battle of

Battle of Midway

Midway condemned the Japanese to fight defensively for the rest of the war.

In August 1942, the Americans attacked Guadalcanal in the Solomon Islands northeast of Australia. Capitalizing on their growing naval superiority and having broken the Japanese code, the Americans conducted an island-hopping campaign toward Japan. One American Marine described the "brutal, primitive hatred" that developed between the Japanese and American soldiers in this costly campaign, which "resulted in savage, ferocious fighting with no holds barred." As the battles raged on Pacific islands, "the fierce struggle for survival . . . eroded the veneer of civilization and made savages of us all."

In October 1944, the Japanese fleet made a final, desperate effort near the Philippines, but American forces annihilated it in the Battle of Leyte Gulf. However, as the United States and its allies closed in on the Japanese home islands, the most brutal land battles of the war lay ahead: Iwo Jima and Okinawa. During these battles, Japanese soldiers often fought to the death or took their own lives rather than surrender. During the battle of Okinawa, Japanese pilots volunteered to fly almost 2,000 **kamikaze** missions in which they dive-bombed their planes into Allied ships (see Exploring the Past on page 570). The Allies lost dozens of ships and thousands of soldiers to these desperate tactics.

Isolated, exposed, and subjected to ceaseless air and sea attacks, Japan was doomed. In February 1945, the United States began massive bombing raids on Japan's home islands, igniting huge firestorms that destroyed vast sections of Japan's cities and killed hundreds of thousands of people. After Germany surrendered in May 1945, American and British troops rushed to the Far East. In mid-July, American and British scientists finished developing and testing the atomic bomb, a new, powerful weapon the two countries had been working on for several years. To avoid the heavy casualties that a direct assault on the Japanese home islands would cause, the United States decided to use the bomb to shock Japan into surrender—a decision that has sparked controversy ever since.

The atomic bomb

While some Japanese political leaders recognized the hopelessness of continuing the war and pressed the government to pursue a peace settlement, Japan's military leaders promised a bloody fight to the finish. The fighting on Okinawa had convinced many American soldiers that the enemy would not give up. As one survivor of that battle put it, "Japan would have to be invaded with the same gruesome prospects." At the same time, many of the scientists who had developed the weapon opposed using it. So did General Dwight Eisenhower: "First, the Japanese were ready to surrender and it wasn't necessary to hit them with that awful thing. Second, I hated to see our country be the first to use such a weapon."

On August 6, 1945, a U.S. plane dropped an atomic bomb that destroyed the Japanese city of Hiroshima and some 80,000 of its inhabitants; tens of thousands more died later from the effects of radiation. One survivor, Yamaoka

"We Shall Plunge into Enemy Ships"

During the last year of the war in the Pacific, the Japanese responded to widespread losses by resorting to suicide attacks on U.S. ships. The Kamikaze Special Attack Corps carried out these attacks. The following is an excerpt from a letter written by Heiichi Okabe, a member of that corps, on February 22, 1945.

I am actually a member at last of the Kamikaze Special Attack Corps. My life will be rounded out in the next thirty days. My chance will come! Death and I are waiting. The training and practice have been rigorous, but it is worthwhile if we can die beautifully and for a cause. . . .

The sortie has been scheduled for the next ten days. I am a human being and hope to be neither saint nor scoundrel, hero nor fool—just a human being. . . .

We shall serve the nation gladly in its present painful struggle. We shall plunge into enemy ships cherishing the conviction that Japan has been and will be a place where only lovely homes, brave women, and beautiful friendships are allowed to exist.

What is the duty today? It is to fight.
What is the duty tomorrow? It is to win.
What is the daily duty? It is to die.

We die in battle without complaint. I wonder if others, like scientists, who pursue the war effort on their own fronts, would die as we do without complaint.

Do you agree with his statement that he is "just a human being" and neither a hero nor a fool? Explain.

Michiko, described the horror: "There were people, barely breathing, trying to push their intestines back in. People with their legs wrenched off. Without heads. Or with faces burned and swollen out of shape. The scene I saw was a living hell." Three days later, a second atomic bomb demolished the industrial city of Nagasaki, killing an additional 50,000. On August 8, the Soviet Union declared war on Japan and sent troops into Manchuria. The Japanese surrendered on August 15, 1945.

PEACE AND THE LEGACY OF WAR

In 1945, Europe lay prostrate as some 50 million refugees drifted across the land and countless people faced starvation and homelessness. Memories of **Europe in shambles** lost loved ones and homes, the horrors of the concentration camps, the hardships of occupation, and the echoes of mass bombings would haunt people for the rest of their lives.

Outrage, fear, and violence continued to stalk Europe. Many resistance fighters and Soviet troops executed surrendering Nazi soldiers on the spot. Angry officials and ordinary people hunted down and punished collaborators after only summary trials. To shame women they suspected of sleeping with German soldiers, irate citizens shaved off women's hair and marched them through the streets. The Soviets, Poles, and Czechoslovakians pushed 13 million ethnic Germans out of homes in Eastern Europe toward the west. One eyewitness described how "families with children, packages, hand wheelbarrows, horse-drawn wagons, and bicycles were making their way, and were being assaulted" as they fled along the roads to Germany. Stalin's officials sent thousands of returning Soviet prisoners to forced-labor camps or to the executioner for being "contaminated" by dangerous, anti-Soviet ideas. Jews who had managed to survive often found their homes destroyed, and they still suffered from flagrant anti-Semitism.

With agricultural and nonmilitary industrial production at a fraction of their prewar levels, Western Europe looked to the United States for loans, relief, defense, and leadership. Eastern Europe, in even worse shambles, was falling under the dominance of the Soviet Union. Political leaders and diplomats involved in the peace settlement hoped this time to avoid the "mistakes" made at the close of World War I. The main challenge facing them was to find a way to deal with defeated nations without spawning new conflicts.

The Settlement

The leaders of Great Britain, the United States, and the Soviet Union shaped postwar Europe in two wartime conferences, at Tehran in December 1943 and Yalta in February 1945, and one postwar conference at Potsdam in July 1945. They agreed to accept only unconditional surrender by Germany and Japan and to require complete restructuring of the aggressors' governments. Germany, which had proved so powerful in two world wars, would be disarmed and divided. The Soviet Union, having suffered so much from Germany's massive invasion, demanded and received pledges of territories on its western border as well as reparations from Germany. To further weaken Germany and recognize the impact of the war, Poland's border with Germany was pushed westward. Finally, a **United Nations** organization was founded in 1945 by fifty-one nations to promote international peace and cooperation.

Discord over Eastern Europe On other matters, however, discord among the wartime allies created a more ominous view of the future. The most crucial disagreements came over the fate of the Eastern European countries. Stalin argued that because the Soviet Union had endured invasions through these countries in both world wars, he needed them to serve as a buffer zone of states loyal to the USSR. The United States and Great Britain demanded complete independence and democracy for these countries. Concessions on both sides at the Yalta Conference in February 1945 left Eastern Europe vaguely democratic but "friendly" to the Soviet Union. This arrangement quickly proved unworkable. Two nations—Poland and Bulgaria—were already under communist control, and pro-Soviet "coalition governments" quickly formed in other Eastern European states.

At the final conference, at Potsdam in July 1945 (the war ended without a formal peace treaty), Stalin had the upper hand. President Roosevelt had died. Although the American president, Harry Truman, firmly demanded free elections in all of Eastern Europe, he had been in office only

THE UNITED NATIONS, 1947 This period poster by Henri Eveleigh celebrates the founding of the United Nations and conveys the hopes of its founders for peace and international cooperation.

three months. Churchill might have been able to exert more pressure on Stalin, but the newly elected Clement Attlee replaced him during the conference. Stalin, insisting that the Soviet Union must obtain complete security against Germany and any potential Eastern European allies, refused to budge on the issue: "A freely elected government in any of these East European countries would be anti-Soviet," he admitted, "and that we cannot allow."

U.S. leaders had trouble swallowing the reality behind Stalin's words. In fact, Eastern Europe was already behind Soviet lines and occupied by Soviet troops by war's end, just as Western Europe remained behind Anglo-American lines and within the United States' and Britain's sphere of influence. "Everyone imposes his own system as far as his armies can reach," observed Stalin privately. "It cannot be otherwise."

The Legacy of War

Human beings have waged war on each other since the beginnings of civilization. But World War II, especially when viewed in connection with its twentieth-century predecessor, World War I, shook the West and the world as nothing before.

One crucial difference stemmed from technology. Bloody battles, massacres, torture, and cruelty were not new to the twentieth century. But for the first time, combatants had developed weapons to translate these acts into tens of millions of deaths on and off the battlefields. The use of chemicals, machines, and organizations to inflict a wide range of horrors on so many people so quickly was also unprecedented.

Certainly, World War I set a well-remembered precedent for the decision makers of the Second World War. The 1914–1918 conflict had become a relentless mutual slaughter with single battles costing hundreds of thousands of lives and total deaths surpassing 20 million. Those years of war also carried in their wake genocidal actions by the Turks against the Armenians and Allied blockades for months after the end of the war that inflicted widespread starvation on defeated nations.

The two decades after World War I brought to power regimes in Russia, Germany, and Japan that hinted at what a second world conflict might wreak on humanity. In Russia,

connect to today

Civilian Casualties

During World War II inhumanity—from indiscriminate bombing to programmed genocide—gained the upper hand in the West, Asia, and the Pacific. In what ways do we see problems in maintaining a meaningful distinction between civilians and combatants in today's wars?

transformed into the Soviet Union, Stalin inflicted a terror-famine on Ukraine, which cost millions of lives, and established the system of slave-labor camps (the Gulag) that also killed and imprisoned millions more. In Germany, the rise of the Nazis to power under Adolf Hitler in 1933 soon led to concentration camps, anti-Semitic terror, and policies of euthanasia. In Japan, the initiation of war against China in 1937 resulted in what is generally called the Rape of Nanking.

The outbreak of war in Europe in 1939 led to even worse acts and consequences. Violence raged across oceans and continents. The death toll alone was staggering. More than 60 million people—some scholars argue that the actual figure might be much higher—were killed during World War II.

Even more ominous, far more civilians than soldiers died, owing in part to the tactics and weapons of modern war. The drive to inflict massive damage led to indiscriminate carpet and fire bombings. These raids not only made little distinction between military and civilian targets but

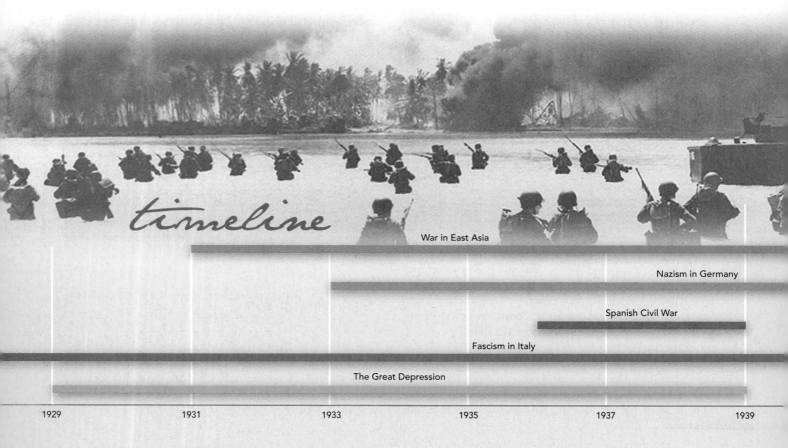

timeline

War in East Asia

Nazism in Germany

Spanish Civil War

Fascism in Italy

The Great Depression

| 1929 | 1931 | 1933 | 1935 | 1937 | 1939 |

literally flattened German and Japanese cities such as Dresden and Tokyo. The search for revolutionary superweapons also bore frightening fruit. The atomic bomb—the weapon that finally ended the war in the Pacific—made it all too clear that human beings now had the ability to inflict unimaginable destruction with a single blow.

Meanwhile, the 11 to 12 million deaths resulting from the Nazis' genocidal program revealed a new capacity for bureaucratized and industrialized killing. Only a relatively few individuals survived the death camps to "tell the story, to bear witness." They and the rest of humanity have had to find ways to live with the realization, in the words of the Auschwitz survivor Primo Levi, "that such a crime should exist," and that it had been "introduced irrevocably into the world of things that exist."

More broadly, terror—of combatants and civilians alike—became a standard tactic during World War II. Officially sanctioned mass rape—in particular by advancing Russian forces in retaliation against the Germans and by Japanese soldiers against the Chinese—made the experience of war all the more vicious. Rape took tragic forms. For example, some 300,000 women, most of them from Korea, were forced to serve the Japanese military as "comfort women."

After World War II, it was clear that humans had acquired the capacity to annihilate peoples and civilizations. This realization called into question some of the very developments that had most characterized the West over the previous two centuries: science (used to destroy lives), industrialization (which made the war machines possible), nationalism (which mutated into militarism), ideological beliefs (which justified everything from sacrifice to terror and genocide), and humanism (which seemed irrelevant in the face of blatant inhumanity). In the European heart of the West, many people prayed that a conflict on the scale of World War II would never strike again. But even as they hoped, tensions between two countries that had once lain at the peripheries of the West—the Soviet Union and the United States—suggested that peace might prove short-lived.

SUMMARY

World War II devastated much of Europe and left scars across the globe from North Africa and the Middle East to East Asia and the Pacific. The first battles erupted in Asia when the Japanese, eager to expand their empire, invaded China. Then Nazi Germany and Fascist Italy struck in Europe.

- The legacy of World War I, the breakdown of international affairs, and the rise of Nazi Germany under Adolf Hitler led to the outbreak of World War II in Europe in 1939.

- Between 1939 and 1942, German and Japanese forces scored victory after victory and seemed to be winning the war.

- Behind the battle lines, Hitler and the Nazis carried out the genocidal Holocaust. To support the war effort, nations mobilized their home fronts.

- In 1942, the tide of war changed as the Allies gained the upper hand in the long struggle against Axis forces.

- Peace was finally achieved in 1945, but the cost had been great and the legacy of twentieth-century wars was ominous.

- The war took a staggering toll. The Nazis not only waged war against the Allies, millions of European Jews, and other "undesirable" groups but also conducted nothing less than a campaign to destroy eastern European nations.

At war's end, tens of millions of Europeans had been uprooted and were homeless. Western and non-Western societies, weary and bloodied, now faced an overwhelming task: to recover from the devastation of the war and regain some sense of order. Moreover, a shadow of a sobering new realization had been cast: Through modern warfare and new technology, human beings now had the power to obliterate the entire world.

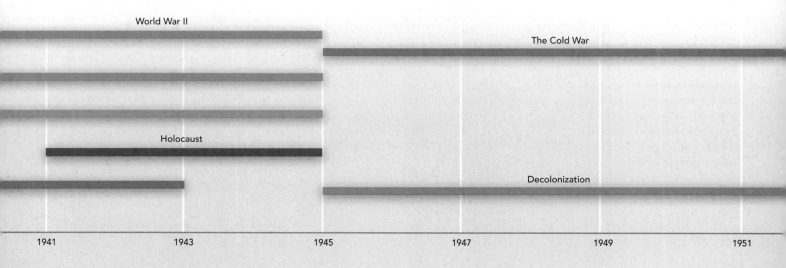

World War II

The Cold War

Holocaust

Decolonization

1941   1943   1945   1947   1949   1951

DON EDDY, *NEW SHOES FOR H,* 1974 In this 1974 painting, Don Eddy uses the artistic style known as photo-realism to depict a shoe-store display in New York City. Reflected in the store window are cars, buses, a department store sign (S. Klein), office and apartment buildings, and a pedestrian in blue jeans—all in all, a typically vibrant street scene in a leading Western city of the era.

Superpower
Struggles
Global and
Transformations

The Cold War, 1945–1980s

25

"Another World"

In 1974, a retired Frenchwoman, Françoise Giroud, contrasted her early life as a stenographer in the 1930s with the lives of young women of the 1970s. "[T]here is simply no comparison. . . . A month of paid vacation, . . . organized travel, . . . paperback books, . . . blue jeans and the T-shirts, instant mashed potatoes, the transistor, . . . the boyfriend who has a [used car], . . . and the Pill! It's not a better world; it's another world altogether." This new world that Giroud described boasted unheard-of material well-being, international peace throughout most of the West, innovative day-to-day conveniences, and striking new medical knowledge. The painting in the chapter opener is an apt illustration of this new age. ▶▶

The image reveals a wealthy, commercial society awash in consumer goods. In effect, the painting offers a view of reality from different perspectives, paralleling the efforts that many Westerners made to understand their rapidly changing world.

Yet these decades also had their dark side. Nations around the world labored to recover from the devastation of World War II. As they did so, a new menace emerged—growing tensions between the United States and the Soviet Union that for decades would overshadow international relations and everyday life. At the same time, colonial peoples took advantage of Europe's weakness and changing attitudes toward imperialism and demanded their independence in ways the West could not ignore. New nations and international organizations soon emerged throughout the world, and global interactions grew so complex that the traditional lines between Western and non-Western societies blurred more than ever.

As Giroud said, "It's not a better world; it's another world altogether." ◂◂

ORIGINS OF THE COLD WAR

"At the present moment in world history nearly every nation must choose between alternative ways of life," announced U.S. President Harry Truman on March 12, 1947. Ominously, he added, "The choice is too often not a free one," referring to what he termed the "coercion and intimidation" used to force "totalitarian regimes" on the peoples of several countries. Eight months later, his secretary of state, George Marshall, pointed to the heart of the problem: "The present line of division in Europe is roughly the line upon which the Anglo-American armies coming from the west met those of the Soviet Union coming from the east. . . . Developments in the European countries to the east of that line bear the unmistakable imprint of an alien hand." According to Truman and Marshall, the "alien hand" over Eastern Europe belonged to the Soviet Union, only two years earlier an ally of the United States in World War II.

The conflict over the fate of Eastern Europe drove a sharp wedge between the World War II allies. Long-standing antagonisms and new differences soon combined to break down further any cooperation between the Western democracies and the Soviet Union. Ever since the communists had come to power in 1917, they and the capitalist democracies had viewed each other as opponents (see Chapter 23). As ideologies, communism and capitalism had always been in direct opposition. As practiced in the Soviet Union under Lenin and Stalin, the political system of communism took a dictatorial form, in sharp contrast to the democracies of Great Britain and the United States. Hitler's invasion of the Soviet Union in World War II and the United States' entry into the war only temporarily united Great Britain, the United States, and the Soviet Union. The three powers joined as allies more in opposition to Nazi Germany than in agreement over principles or goals. Not surprisingly, when negotiations over war aims and settlement terms took place, the history of hostility, distrust, and fear between the capitalist and communist powers caused problems. After the war, when the threat of Nazi Germany no longer held the Allies together, tensions worsened.

In 1945, the U.S. cut off all aid to the USSR. The rhetoric of discord between the powers increased. The next year, Winston Churchill, speaking at a small college in Missouri, warned the world of an **Iron Curtain** descending from the Baltic to the Adriatic Seas, dividing Europe between communist East and capitalist West.

Churchill's warning proved apt. Within the next few years, Soviet-backed communist parties in Eastern Europe pushed their opponents aside and rose to power; only communist Yugoslavia and Albania would manage to follow independent courses. In Western Europe, despite the presence of popular communist parties, American-backed anticommunist politicians controlled the governments. In Greece, the two sides clashed as the British and the Americans supported the repressive anticommunist monarchy in an armed conflict against the Greek communists. The **Cold War** had begun.

The Heart of the Cold War

At the heart of the Cold War lay a troubled Germany. As the map on page 577 indicates, the peace settlement had divided the aggressor nation into four occupation zones: American, Soviet, British, and French. The city of Berlin, in the Russian zone, was also divided into the same four sectors. Sharp disagreements soon surfaced among the occupiers. The Soviets alarmed their allies by grabbing valuable resources from Germany, including entire factories, and transporting them to the Soviet Union as reparations for war losses rather than waiting for cash payments. The Soviets also hoped to keep their old enemy Germany economically weak and fully divided. The United States and Britain, on the other hand, set out to restore and integrate economically the western sectors of Germany, seeing those regions as essential allies in the growing split with the USSR.

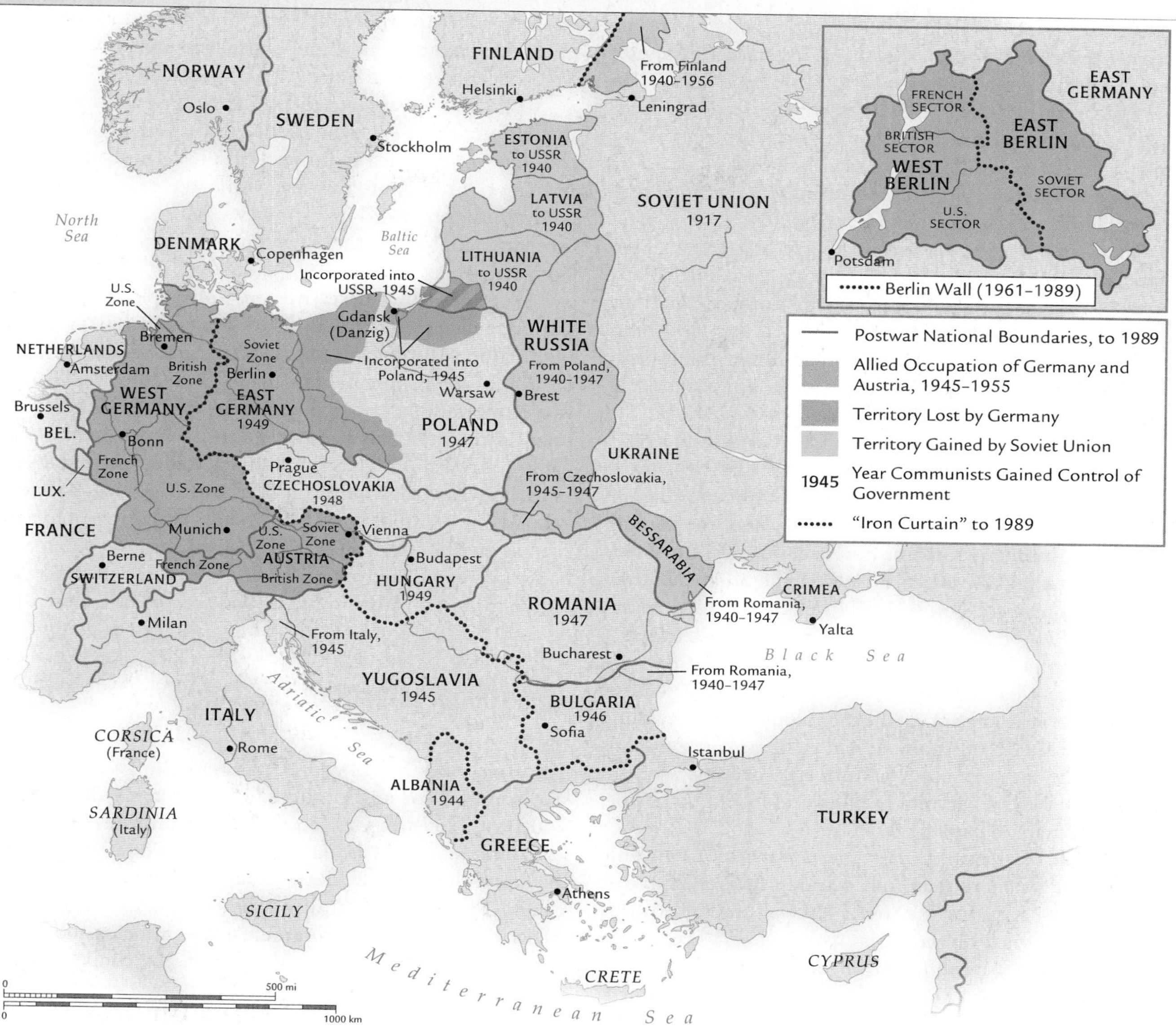
NORWAY
Oslo
SWEDEN
Stockholm
FINLAND
Helsinki
From Finland 1940–1956
Leningrad
ESTONIA to USSR 1940
LATVIA to USSR 1940
LITHUANIA to USSR 1940
SOVIET UNION 1917
North Sea
Baltic Sea
DENMARK
Copenhagen
Incorporated into USSR, 1945
U.S. Zone
Bremen
NETHERLANDS
Amsterdam
British Zone
Soviet Zone
Berlin
Gdansk (Danzig)
Incorporated into Poland, 1945
WHITE RUSSIA
From Poland, 1940–1947
Brest
Warsaw
WEST GERMANY
EAST GERMANY 1949
Brussels
BEL.
Bonn
POLAND 1947
French Zone
LUX.
Prague
CZECHOSLOVAKIA 1948
U.S. Zone
UKRAINE
From Czechoslovakia, 1945–1947
FRANCE
Munich
U.S. Zone
Soviet Zone
Vienna
AUSTRIA
Berne
French Zone
British Zone
SWITZERLAND
Budapest
HUNGARY 1949
BESSARABIA
CRIMEA
From Romania, 1940–1947
Yalta
Milan
ROMANIA 1947
From Italy, 1945
Bucharest
Black Sea
From Romania, 1940–1947
YUGOSLAVIA 1945
Adriatic Sea
BULGARIA 1946
Sofia
ITALY
CORSICA (France)
Rome
Istanbul
ALBANIA 1944
SARDINIA (Italy)
TURKEY
GREECE
Athens
SICILY
CYPRUS
CRETE
Mediterranean Sea
0 500 mi
0 1000 km
EAST GERMANY
FRENCH SECTOR
BRITISH SECTOR
EAST BERLIN
WEST BERLIN
SOVIET SECTOR
U.S. SECTOR
Potsdam
Berlin Wall (1961–1989)
Postwar National Boundaries, to 1989
Allied Occupation of Germany and Austria, 1945–1955
Territory Lost by Germany
Territory Gained by Soviet Union
1945 Year Communists Gained Control of Government
"Iron Curtain" to 1989

Europe After World War II This map shows Europe after World War II and the dates that communists gained control of governments in Eastern Europe.

The Berlin blockade and the division of Germany

Matters came to a head in 1948 when the United States and Britain tried to spur economic recovery by introducing a new currency in the western zones of Germany despite Soviet opposition. Stalin countered by blockading the three western zones of Berlin. From June 1948 to May 1949, the Soviets stopped all land traffic across their zone from the West to Berlin. In response, the Western powers mounted a daring and continuous airlift that carried supplies to the city. If "Berlin falls," warned the American military commander General Lucius Clay, "western Germany will be next . . . if we withdraw, our position in Europe is threatened. . . . Communism will run rampant." The **Berlin airlift** eventually prompted the Soviet Union to back down.

In September 1949, the Western allies followed through on their plan to merge the three western zones of Germany and to create an independent West German state—the German Federal Republic. One month later, the Soviet Union established the German Democratic Republic in its eastern zone, completing the division of Germany into the capitalist West and communist East.

The Cold War spreads

Meanwhile, the Cold War chill was already spreading across the rest of Europe. In 1947, U.S. president Harry Truman (1884–1972) initiated the Truman Doctrine, a policy that offered military and economic aid to countries threatened by a communist takeover. "The peoples of a number of countries of the world have recently had totalitarian regimes forced upon them against their will," he warned. "[I]t must be the policy of the United States to support free peoples who are resisting attempted subjugation by armed minorities or by outside pressures." His immediate concern was the civil war in Greece, where local communists aided by neighboring Yugoslavia were making gains against the royalist government. His larger goal was to create a military ring of "**containment**" around the Soviet Union and its satellite states.

That same year, Truman's secretary of state, George Marshall (1880–1959), launched the **Marshall Plan,** a package of massive economic aid to European nations designed both to strengthen them and to tie them to American influence. The Soviet Union forbad Eastern European governments to accept the aid and soon established the Council for Mutual Economic Assistance (COMECON), a Soviet version of the Marshall Plan for Eastern Europe.

In 1949, the United States organized the **North Atlantic Treaty Organization (NATO),** a military alliance among the United States, Canada, and most of the nations of Western Europe against the Soviet Union. Within a few years, Greece and Turkey had joined the alliance. After West Germany signed on in 1955, the Soviet Union countered NATO by creating its own military alliance in Eastern Europe, the Warsaw Pact. Now thousands of troops in each alliance—backed by the presence and might of the two superpowers—faced each other along a line dividing Eastern and Western Europe. It had taken only a few years for each side in the Cold War to forge economic, political, and military ties among its allies and form two hostile camps (see map on page 579).

The Cold War would color international relations and everyday life for more than four decades. Andrei Zhdanov (1896–1948), a powerful Soviet official, described the official Soviet view of the Cold War in 1947: U.S. goals were "domination in all countries marked out for American expansion" and "the creation in peacetime of numerous [military] bases . . . for aggressive purposes against the USSR." John Foster Dulles (1888–1959), President Dwight Eisenhower's secretary of state, presented the U.S. view in 1953: "Soviet communism . . . is the gravest threat that has ever faced . . . Western civilization, or indeed, any civilization . . . dominated by a spiritual faith." Compromise between such extreme, hostile views seemed impossible.

Terror lurked just below the surface of the Cold War. By 1949, both superpowers had the atomic bomb; by 1953, the hydrogen bomb. Each country supported growing military budgets and stockpiled huge caches of weapons, including intercontinental ballistic missiles (ICBMs) that could carry nuclear warheads. The danger rippled outward as other nations—Britain, France, India, China, Israel, and Pakistan—also developed nuclear weapons. In fact, the Cold War was fought in all ways except open military conflict between the United States and the Soviet Union. Networks of spies fanned out over the globe. Political struggles anywhere, even purely internal matters, became arenas for

Cold War weapons

defining a victory or defeat in the Cold War. The competition expanded to include nonpolitical activities as well, such as space exploration and the Olympic Games.

Cold War posturing and imagery also saturated the media (see image on page 580). From the United States, the Voice of America radio station spread anticommunist messages throughout Europe, while the station's Soviet counterpart presented its own views. Most European governments controlled the news on their radio and television programs.

All this led to a pervasive sense of suspicion and fear. Novels, movies, and television shows featuring spies and international intrigue proliferated. In the United States, for example, Senator Joseph McCarthy (1908–1957) led a massive name-calling campaign between 1950 and 1954 "to uncover" communists and communist sympathizers; these "fellow travelers," McCarthy claimed, had infiltrated every aspect of American life, from the armed services to Hollywood movie studios. Atomic bomb drills in American schools and bomb shelters in city basements and suburban backyards completed the picture of a Western democratic nation menaced by communism and the Soviet Union.

The Global Impact of the Cold War

The Cold War quickly spread around the globe as each side searched for allies and victories wherever they could find them. No area escaped from the worldwide competition, but events in Asia and Latin America especially reveal the far-reaching impact of the Cold War. In both areas, the United States forged anticommunist alliances while the Soviet Union supported communist governments and revolutionary movements. More than once, the contest fueled crises and armed conflict in these areas.

Japan had emerged from World War II defeated on sea and land, the shocked victim of history's first two atomic bombs used for military purposes. Because the United States by far had played the major role in the defeat of Japan, it refused to share the occupation and governing of the Japanese islands with its former allies. The U.S. quickly promoted political democratization and used financial aid to help Japan rebuild and conform to U.S. policies. In this way, Japan, like West Germany, would become a link in the Cold War containment "chain" that the U.S. was forging around the Soviet Union. The strategy paid off handsomely. During the 1950s and 1960s, Japan became a firm ally and used its modern industries and skilled labor to make an astounding economic recovery that surpassed even that of West Germany.

China, just across the Sea of Japan, moved in a different direction. The civil war between Mao Zedong's zealous Communist forces and Jiang Jieshi's conservative Nationalist forces was suspended during World War II. Mao's forces

The Cold War in Asia

Europe During the Cold War

This map shows how the Cold War had divided Europe by the 1950s. **What connections between military and economic cooperation are revealed by this map?**

waged a more incessant guerrilla warfare against the Japanese than the Nationalists did and thereby gained a growing following among the Chinese people. After the surrender of Japan in 1945, the bitter, internal struggle for control of China began anew. The United States supported the Nationalists, while ever-increasing numbers of Chinese supported the Communists. In 1949, the victorious Communists swept over the entire Chinese mainland. Jiang's Nationalists fled to the nearby island of Taiwan, where they came under the protection of the U.S. Navy. Mao promptly proclaimed the People's Republic of China and joined in an alliance with the Soviet Union. With Soviet aid, he began the daunting task of industrializing and communizing China.

Less than a year later, the Cold War merged with simmering internal forces in nearby Korea to produce a major conflict that embroiled both the new Chinese communist regime and the United States. At the end of World War II, in accordance with the Yalta agreements, Soviet troops occupied Korea north of the thirty-eighth parallel, while American forces controlled the south. The Soviets and Americans had withdrawn by 1949, leaving North and South Korea as armed client states rather than a united Korean nation. The new governments of the North and South, each ruled by dictators, talked loudly of conquering each other.

The Korean War

In 1950, the Soviet-backed North Korean communists—with the approval of both Stalin and Mao—suddenly invaded U.S.-backed South Korea. The determined, well-armed North Korean communists easily defeated the South Koreans. Supported by the UN, the U.S. quickly intervened. The American and UN forces soon overcame the North Koreans, but as their troops approached the Korean-Chinese border and threatened to bomb North Korean sanctuaries in China, the Chinese entered the fray. They pushed the U.S. and UN forces back to the thirty-eighth parallel, where a stalemate developed. By the time of the armistice in 1953, the war had cost some 1.5 million casualties on each side and had left much of Korea in ruins.

These experiences with Korea and China prompted the United States to involve itself in nearby Vietnam, Laos, and Cambodia. The U.S. feared that the fall of one nation in that region to communism would, as with a row of dominoes, lead to the fall of other adjacent nations.

PEACE MUST BE SAVED, 1948 In this 1948 poster created for the French Communist Party, atomic bombs hover over the prostrate victim, spreading death (the crosses in the background) and destruction (the burning buildings). The poster warns France against any alliance with Germany, which the communists claimed would amount to preparation for war against the Soviet Union.

"Vietnam represents the cornerstone of the Free World in Southeast Asia, the keystone to the arch, the finger in the dike," warned Senator John F. Kennedy in 1956. "Burma, Thailand, India, Japan, the Philippines, and obviously Laos and Cambodia are among those whose security would be threatened if the red tide of Communism overflowed into Vietnam."

Accordingly, the U.S. helped the French fight against Vietnamese nationalists. Vietnam had been a French colony before World War II and, under the leadership of Ho Chi Minh (1890–1969) and his Vietnamese Communist Party, had fought for its independence from France in the years after World War II. After suffering a series of defeats, France finally agreed to withdraw in 1954. The 1954 Geneva Accords provisionally gave Ho Chi Minh's Communists control of the nation north of the seventeenth latitude and provided for elections throughout the whole country in 1956. The U.S. refused to sign the accords, and Ngo Dihn Diem (1901–1963), who took power in the south where the remnants of the old French-supported Associated State of Vietnam had fled, refused to hold the elections. The nation was divided between the North, ruled by the victorious Ho Chi Minh, and the South, under an authoritarian, anticommunist government that tried to maintain the aristocratic society of a vanishing era (see map on page 581).

The unpopular regime in the South relied for its survival on the economic and political support of the United States and its allies. Military aid and armed forces soon followed, as the United States sought to increase its influence not only in South Vietnam but also in Laos and Cambodia, which had gained freedom from the French. During the mid-1960s, the U.S. sent more than 500,000 troops to Vietnam. American planes dropped more explosives there than had been used by all combatants during World War II, pummeling the tiny nation. Still, the opposing North Vietnamese—helped by material aid from the Soviet Union and China—proved skilled and tenacious fighters, and the war dragged on.

The cost, futility, and unpopularity of the Vietnam War put increasing pressure on U.S. leaders to end American involvement in the conflict (see image on page 582). In 1973, after long negotiations, the U.S. and Vietnamese forces finally signed peace agreements, and the United States withdrew its forces. The civil war in Vietnam, however, persisted for another two years before the Communists swept to victory—not only in Vietnam but also in neighboring Laos and Cambodia.

The Cold War tide shifted in Asia several times. China, which had backed the Vietnam Communists, had continued in its own direction. During the 1950s, China was engaged in trying to meet overly ambitious goals in industry and agriculture. To that end, it communized its society even more completely than had ever been attempted in the Soviet Union. In a plan

The Vietnam War

China's Great Leap Forward

called the Great Leap Forward, China's huge and burgeoning population was set to building irrigation dams and ditches, steel mills, factories, railroads, schools, and hospitals at a frenetic pace. In 1959, an alternating cycle of droughts and flooding struck, producing one of the deadliest famines in history; some 20 million Chinese may have died of starvation and malnutrition over the next three years. Overzealous local party officials provoked resentment and resistance among the already harried populace, and for years the Communist Party hierarchy was wracked by a power struggle between moderates

Mao's Cultural Revolution

and radicals. In 1966, Mao tried to reignite the revolutionary spirit by launching the Great Proletarian Cultural Revolution. He empowered youthful zealots to cleanse China of those who did not enthusiastically support him. Over several years, millions of people suffered humiliation or death.

At the same time, relations between China and the Soviet Union began to cool. As early as

The Chinese-Soviet split

1956, China started criticizing the USSR, which that year under Nikita Khrushchev (1894–1971) began backing away from Stalin's harshest policies. Mao denounced Moscow for softening toward the capitalistic, imperialist West and for abandoning strict Marxist-Leninist principles. In 1960, the Soviet Union began to withhold promised economic and technological aid to China. When China exploded its first nuclear device in 1964, the two communist nations moved further apart, and by 1968, they were embroiled in border disputes.

With the Soviet Union a common enemy, China and the United States tentatively looked to each other for support. During the 1970s, China normalized relations with the U.S., replaced Taiwan in the UN, and, after the death of Mao in 1976, initiated policies emphasizing economic decentralization and free-market activities. The statue of Mao shown on page 583 symbolizes the new, assertive strength of communist China.

The Cold War soon took another turn in central Asia, where the Soviet Union became entangled in its own version of the Vietnam War. In 1979, Soviet troops intervened

Soviets in Afghanistan

to support a communist coup in Afghanistan, a nation on the USSR's southern border that the Soviets considered within their own sphere of influence. They promptly became locked in a ten-year war against tenacious guerrilla forces backed by the U.S. Central Intelligence Agency. In

Vietnam and Southeast Asia This map shows Vietnam and its neighbors during the 1950s, 1960s, and 1970s, when war wracked the area.

1989 the Soviets finally withdrew, leaving Afghanistan in shambles and wracked by internal violence.

Even the Latin American countries, far from the conflicts in Asia and long considered "friends" by the United States, got pulled into the Cold War. At the end of World War II, the governments of independent Latin American states were republics in name. In reality, however, most of them were right-wing dictatorships, representing the interests of the well-to-do bourgeoisie, the landowning classes, and the professional military. The Roman Catholic Church, which had been a powerful conservative force in this region during the nineteenth

The Cold War in Latin America

Wolf Vostell, *Miss America*

1968

In this 1968 collage, German artist Wolf Vostell conveys impressions of the war in Vietnam. A female figure suggesting a fashion model or contestant from a Miss America pageant struts provocatively, but parts of her body are blotted with red. Below, photographic images of disturbing events during the war intrude. Much of the coloring suggests not only blood but also the American flag. Should this collage be viewed primarily as a thoughtful, realistic depiction of the war or as a piece of propaganda?

the Soviet Union. The United States, on the other hand, supported the conservative governments.

Over the next four decades, the U.S. intervened in or invaded several Latin American nations to shore up conservative forces in its global struggle against communism. The Soviets, for their part, supported sympathetic revolutionary movements and regimes. Of all the Latin American countries, Cuba became the most volatile staging ground for the intensifying feud between the superpowers. In 1959, Marxist rebel leader Fidel Castro ousted the American-supported dictatorship in Cuba and launched a sweeping program of social and economic reforms. The new program included the seizure of property owned by citizens and corporations of the United States. The U.S. government promptly terminated aid to the island nation, and Castro turned to the Soviets for help. These developments threatened the Americans in two crucial ways. First, a revolutionary, left-wing regime backed heavily by the Soviet Union had suddenly gained a beachhead in Latin America—a mere 90 miles from the U.S. mainland. Second, the Americans worried that Castro's success would embolden other opposition and revolutionary movements— also typically led by Marxists— throughout Latin America. Such uprisings would lead to more Cold War victories for the communists. Three years after the Cuban revolution, the U.S. government sponsored the Bay of Pigs invasion, an ill-fated attempt by Cuban refugees to topple the Castro regime.

Tensions soon reached a new high in the Caribbean. On October 12, 1962, a U.S. spy plane discovered Soviet missiles being installed in Cuba. Privately, President Kennedy admitted: "What difference does it

Crisis in Cuba

century, had grown more liberal during the twentieth century. Sometimes it even exerted its influence in social and economic reform movements. In the years following World War II, the poor in Latin America became increasingly restless. Many of them turned to communism, encouraged by

make? They've got enough to blow us up now anyway. . . . This is a political struggle as much as military." Although the U.S. had missiles on Russia's border in Turkey, the Americans decided that Soviet missiles in Cuba were intolerable. With the USSR's ships steaming toward the Caribbean,

EAST AND WEST: Two Paths to Recovery in Europe

MAO AND COMMUNIST CHINA, 1970 A statue of Mao towers over a 1970 victory parade in China, suggesting the growing strength and political will of that nation.

the U.S. Navy under orders to intercept them to prevent the arrival of more missiles in Cuba, and American forces mobilizing, people around the world braced themselves for a possible nuclear war. On October 27, the U.S. Joint Chiefs of Staff urged an all-out attack on Cuba if the Soviets did not immediately remove the missile bases. Two days later, USSR leader Nikita Khrushchev backed down, and an agreement ended the crisis.

Détente

The two superpowers would not again come so close to war with each other. Indeed, at times Cold War tensions relaxed as each side backed away from the sort of conflict that promised to devastate each nation and much of the world. Nuclear test-ban treaties in the 1960s and strategic arms limitation talks in the 1970s eased fears of confrontation. The Helsinki agreement in 1975, confirming Europe's political frontiers and recognizing certain human rights, seemed to solidify a period of **détente**—growing cooperation between Cold War adversaries. But détente went only so far. The 1980s witnessed a return to combative rhetoric and policies with the Soviet invasion of Afghanistan and the tougher anticommunist policies of the Reagan administration in the United States. By the middle of that decade, few people saw any end to the Cold War.

OPINION

What do you think was the most important result of Cold War tension on international affairs in the Western and non-Western worlds?

Under the long shadow of the Cold War, Europeans again tried to return to normal life after World War II. Beyond the astounding number of deaths and widespread destruction, whole cities—such as Berlin, in the heart of Europe—had been devastated. "Nothing is left in Berlin," wrote a reporter for the *New York Herald Tribune* in 1945. "There are no homes, no shops, no transportation, no government buildings. . . . Berlin can now be regarded only as a geographical location heaped with mountainous mounds of debris." Realists declared that economic recovery alone might take twenty-five years. Others wondered whether European society would ever recover.

European nations followed two main paths toward recovery that reflected Cold War differences and the politics underlying those differences. In the Soviet Union and Eastern Europe, communist governments promised clear planning and an unquestionable sense of direction under firm party direction. In Western Europe, the capitalist democracies relied on an alliance of the free market and governmental controls to transform their societies from the wartime devastation. Each path would have its successes and problems.

Tight Control in the Soviet Union and Eastern Europe

Nowhere was the damage and upheaval from World War II worse than in the Soviet Union and Eastern Europe. Soviet citizens longed for an end to wartime deprivations and Stalin's strict controls. Eastern Europeans living along the USSR's border wondered uneasily what to expect as their governments and economies came under the rule of communist parties controlled by Moscow.

Stalin refused to relax his grip over the Soviet Union. He asserted dictatorial control, crushing the merest hint of political dissent and purging those whom he perceived as potential threats. Prisons and forced-labor camps overflowed with his victims. Nor did his economic policies—tight planning and extreme sacrifice for heavy industrialization—change. To help rebuild what the war had destroyed in the Soviet Union, Stalin drained off economic resources from the Eastern European states.

Those countries under Soviet dominance—the "satellite" states—were required to cooperate with the Soviet Union. Single-party "people's democracies" in Poland, East Germany, Czechoslovakia, Hungary, Romania, Yugoslavia, and Albania initiated Soviet-style economic planning, nationalization, collectivization of agriculture, and industrialization. Officials allowed little contact with Western Europe.

Nevertheless, Eastern Europe refused to become a mere appendage to the Soviet Union. These nations harbored strong desires for national autonomy and they often resented Soviet restrictions. Within these states, discontent also rose over the persistent shortage of consumer goods, low wages, and poor working conditions. The Soviets and their followers often had difficulty maintaining control as resistance flared into open rebellions.

Yugoslavia snapped first. The Soviet Union had a weak foothold there because the Yugoslav resistance had liberated the nation from Nazi control almost on its own. In 1948, Yugoslavia's strong and popular dictator, Tito, stood up to Stalin's threats and headed his nation on an independent course. Tito's decentralized form of communism stressed more local control and worker participation in management than the Soviet model.

The death of Stalin and new opportunities

In 1953, Joseph Stalin, the man who had led the USSR for a quarter-century, died. In the Soviet Union, millions mourned Stalin as the leader who had saved them from Nazism. However, some Eastern Europeans saw his death as an opportunity to step up their demands for greater independence. Workers in East Berlin initiated protests against governmental efforts to increase workloads without raising wages. Crowds soon gathered in the streets, demanding political reform and a loosening of ties to the USSR. Police and Soviet tanks promptly crushed these uprisings.

In Moscow, potential successors to Stalin jockeyed for power. They quickly agreed to eliminate the dreaded head of the secret police, Lavrenti Beria (1899–1953), and restricted that organization's terrorist activities. After two years of collective leadership, Nikita Khrushchev, the son of a miner, moved up from the party bureaucracy to emerge as Stalin's successor. In a 1956 unpublished speech to startled communist leaders, Khrushchev denounced the "cult of personality" fostered by Stalin. He also accused Stalin of using "the most cruel repression, violating all norms of revolutionary legality . . . mass arrests and deportations of many thousands of people, executions without trial." Khrushchev slightly loosened government control of Soviet cultural life; authors such as Boris Pasternak (1890–1960) even managed to publish works that implied some criticism of the Soviet regime. New policies also stressed the production of consumer goods, increased

housing, and better health care. Workers throughout the USSR gained more freedom to move from one job to another.

Eastern Europeans hoped that this de-Stalinization would spell a relaxation of Soviet control over their nations. In Poland, worker strikes against wage cuts expanded into demands for political change in 1956, and the Soviets threatened to intervene. Nevertheless, Poland's Communist Party elected the moderate Wladyslaw Gomulka (1905–1982) instead of the Soviet candidate. Gomulka refused to cave in to Soviet demands but promised military loyalty. A compromise left Poland within the Soviet sphere of control while enjoying some new levels of economic and cultural independence—including increased toleration of the Roman Catholic Church.

Protests and uprisings in Eastern Europe

Next, Hungarians issued a challenging demand for independence. When Hungary's communist leaders called on troops to put down protesters in the streets, the troops refused to fire and instead switched sides. A new government under the reforming communist Imre Nagy (1896–1958) initiated major economic and political reforms that included the introduction of a multi-party system. Nagy even proposed to withdraw Hungary from the Warsaw Pact—Moscow's military alliance with its Eastern European satellites. The Hungarians had crossed the line. The Soviets sent in tanks and troops, slaughtering thousands and forcing hundreds of thousands to flee to the West. Nagy was hanged, and the lesson was made crystal clear: Cooperate with Moscow or pay the highest penalty.

In 1961, relations between East and West hit a new low. Under orders from Khrushchev, the East German government erected a 100-mile, heavily armed wall in Berlin to keep its citizens from fleeing to the West. Berlin had served as an escape route for 2.6 million people, especially professionals and the well educated who sought a higher standard of living in Western Europe. The wall graphically marked the division of Germany and symbolized the hostility between Western and Eastern Europe.

The Berlin Wall

In 1964, competitors within the Communist Party's Central Committee suddenly ousted Khrushchev, who had been weakened by foreign policy embarrassments such as the Cuban missile crisis, and installed the more conservative Leonid Brezhnev (1906–1982). The new Soviet leader took a firm line in dealing with Soviet satellites in Eastern

connect to today

Another World Altogether?

As Françoise Giroud said at the beginning of the chapter, the 1970s were "not a better world; it's another world altogether." In what ways do you think this statement could also be accurate when comparing the Cold War era to today?

THE BERLIN WALL Workers, soldiers, and onlookers gather on both sides as the wall dividing East and West Berlin is repaired. East German soldiers, such as those on the left side of the photograph, guard the wall against East Germans trying to escape. To the right, West Germans look on.

Europe. Most of these states posed no problem for him. East Germany, for example, closely followed the Soviet line while developing its industrial capacity, and it became the richest nation in Eastern Europe. Hungary remained tranquil, orienting its economy toward consumer goods, loosening state control, and introducing limited capitalistic practices at the local level.

Other satellite states caused conflict—none more than Czechoslovakia. In 1968, reformers gained control of the Czechoslovak Communist Party and replaced the coun-

The Prague Spring

try's Stalinist leader with Alexander Dubcek (1921–1992), who believed that communism could be made compatible with internal party democracy and personal freedom. In this **Prague Spring** uprising, the Dubcek government initiated economic decentralization, greater national independence, democratic reforms, and elimination of censorship— "socialism with a human face." The reforms gained enthusiastic support within Czechoslovakia, especially among optimistic students and intellectuals thirsting for free speech.

Like Hungary in 1956, Dubcek's reforms went too far for the USSR's comfort. Especially fearful that the Prague Spring could inspire similar movements throughout Eastern Europe, the Soviets sent in Warsaw Pact troops to reverse Dubcek's policies and halt Czechoslovakia's steps toward independence. The Czechs reacted with passive resistance; they could do little more. The Soviets removed Dubcek and his liberal supporters from power, and Brezhnev established his "Doctrine": Soviet intervention is justi-

fied in order to ensure the survival of socialism in another state. The conservative Brezhnev would make sure that Eastern Europe, like the Soviet Union itself, would not stray too far from the tightly controlled communist path followed since the early post–World War II years.

Parliamentary Politics and Prosperity in the Western Democracies

Western European nations proceeded on a strikingly different course to recovery, dictated by both Cold War considerations and the internal histories of those societies. In 1945, most Western European nations quickly returned to prewar democratic forms of government, and political parties leaning toward the center of the political spectrum soon gained control. In some countries, one political party dominated for long stretches of time—the Christian Democrats reigned in West Germany for two decades, for example, and in Italy for four decades following World War II. In other countries, major parties alternated in power, as the Labor and Conservative parties did in Britain. Some governments lasted only months, as happened in France, though the same group of well-known politicians usually rotated into the high offices of new governments and worked with a stable bureaucracy that carried out policy.

Initially, communist parties also gained strength after the war, especially in France and Italy. In France, elections in 1945 resulted in a sweeping victory for parties of the Left, including the communists, as well as the retirement of the conservative general Charles de Gaulle, who had set up a government in Paris in 1944. In Italy, the communists also emerged from World War II strong. For decades, the Italian Communists would command 25 to 35 percent of the vote and win local elections. But after 1947, when the Cold War heated up, these communist parties in France, Italy, and elsewhere were systematically excluded from participation in national governments.

In the struggle to repair their broken economies, European nations benefited greatly from U.S. aid. Having emerged from the war the world's preeminent economic power, the United States pumped almost $13 billion of Marshall Plan aid into

U.S. aid and economic recovery

Western Europe between 1947 and 1952. More than a sense of humanity motivated the Americans. The economic aid also served U.S. Cold War interests by supporting anticommunist forces. The aid came with strings attached: international cooperation and freer trade by the recipients. By demanding these conditions, the U.S.—

> Initially, communist parties also gained strength after the war, especially in France and Italy.

Exploring the Past

A Warning About the United States

By the mid-1960s, many Europeans sensed that the United States, although friendly, had grown overbearing in some ways. This sense was particularly strong in France, as evidenced by the following selection from Jean-Jacques Servan-Schreiber's *The American Challenge*, first published in 1967.

Europeans can regain control over their destiny in this confrontation with the American challenge only by taking stock of themselves and, as we will now try to describe, by hard work and patience. . . .

To build a powerful and independent Europe means strengthening the economic and political bonds of the Common Market. No single nation is strong enough to support efficient production in all areas of advanced technology, for the national framework is too narrow and cannot provide adequate markets for such products. Also, the growing diversification of these products demands a specialization that makes any attempt at national self-sufficiency virtually impossible. . . .

Our back is to the wall. We cannot have both economic self-sufficiency and economic growth. Either we build a common European industrial policy, or American industry will continue taking over the Common Market.

What does this excerpt suggest about Europeans' perceptions of the United States during the 1960s?

now producing more than half the world's industrial goods—gained unprecedented access to large European markets.

Europeans helped themselves as well. Drawing on lessons from the Great Depression, World War II, and the British economist John Maynard Keynes, governments adopted policies to dampen recessions by deficit spending (priming the pump) and to counter inflation by tightening expenditures and interest rates. Several European states, from France to Norway, went even further by engaging in economic planning. This typically included nationalizing certain industries. In France, for example, major banking and insurance companies, coal mines, and gas and electrical utilities came under government control. In such countries, technocrats—bureaucrats with technological or scientific expertise—made economic decisions that were once the province of business owners or parliaments. Other nations avoided such extensive planning. West Germany, for example, broke up prewar corporate cartels instead and pressured labor and management to cooperate for industrial peace.

At the same time, most European nations created social programs to protect citizens from severe hardship and to promote social peace. These **welfare state** programs had roots in the late nineteenth century, when governments had begun taking responsibility for the inequities of capitalism. Concerned about declining population growth, Europeans also wanted to encourage women to have more children. In the years after World War II, many governments followed Sweden's early lead and initiated programs providing health-care benefits and family allowances as well as prenatal care, maternity benefits, child care, and nursery schooling.

The welfare state

Nowhere was the welfare state more dramatically introduced than in Britain. Having shared the toil and suffering of World War II under the effective governmental direction of the economy, British citizens believed that everyone should get a piece of the prosperity that they expected would follow the war. In 1945, they elected a Labor government under Clement Attlee (1883–1967). The new government soon nationalized about 20 percent of Britain's economy and initiated what some called "cradle-tograve" social-welfare policies. All British citizens could now look to governmental support during times of need—whether those times involved raising children, suffering job loss or an accident, paying for adequate housing, or ensuring adequate resources for retirement. Above all, Britain's National Health Service guaranteed free medical care to all.

Scandinavian countries continued to lead, going the furthest in ensuring a decent standard of living for everyone in both good times and bad. By contrast, the Americans swam against the tide. Prosperous, with its high-spending military in close alliance with big business, the United States strenuously resisted programs smacking of socialism. Not until the 1960s did it pursue moderate social reform, such as new educational programs, low-income housing projects, and limited governmental support of medical services.

Of course, all social programs came at a price. Taxes rose, particularly for the middle and upper classes, and government bureaucracies ballooned. Moreover, critics questioned the quality of the services provided, particularly medical care. Yet once established, most social programs served enough people and gained sufficient political backing to become permanent fixtures.

The nations of Western Europe recognized that cooperation offered the best hope for competing economically in a world of superpowers. Encouraged by the Marshall Plan, these countries moved toward economic integration.

Beginning European economic integration

In 1950, France and West Germany created the French-German Coal and Steel Authority to remove tariff barriers and manage coal and steel resources regionally. Jean Monnet (1888–1979), the architect of this organization, held high hopes: "If only the French could lose their fear of German industrial domination, then the greatest obstacle to a united Europe would be removed. . . . It could, in fact, become the germ of European unity." In 1952, the organization expanded into the European Coal and Steel Community with the addition of Italy, Belgium, Luxembourg, and the Netherlands. Five years later, these same six nations signed the Treaty of Rome establishing the **European Economic Community** (the EEC, also referred to as the Common Market). The treaty proposed to eliminate tariff barriers, cut restrictions on the flow of labor and capital, and integrate the economies of the member nations.

The Common Market ended tariff and immigration barriers ahead of schedule, and its member nations enjoyed increased trade, productivity, and industrial production. In 1967, the organization combined with other cooperative bodies to form the European Community (EC) to work toward even greater economic and political integration. As Exploring the Past on page 586 indicates, optimistic supporters hoped that the European Community would make Western Europe an independent regional power that might economically and even politically challenge its superpower ally, the United States, as well as the opposing Soviet bloc in Eastern Europe.

Assessing the Paths Taken

Throughout Europe, early fears about how long reconstruction would take proved unfounded (see the table below). The Soviet and East European economies expanded after the war, though not as rapidly as Eastern Europeans expected or hoped. The Soviets applied advanced science, technology, and engineering to establish a strong industrial base, support a huge military, and build large urban projects. Some Eastern European nations, such as East Germany and Czechoslovakia, also developed extensive industrial bases and even outperformed the Soviets.

The Eastern-bloc nations

Although communism stood for the end to class differences, some citizens within each nation were, in the words of British author George Orwell, "more equal" than others. Certainly the Communist Party elite and professionals enjoyed better services and a higher standard of living than everyone else. But all citizens gained access to education, free medical care, and job security under communism. Subsidies made their usually overcrowded housing inexpensive, and unemployment and abject poverty virtually disappeared.

Women participated fully in economic life in these nations, often outnumbering men in the labor force. Moreover, a majority of doctors and teachers were women. Far more women engaged in manual labor such as logging and heavy construction work than their counterparts did in the West. They also received family allowances, maternity benefits, and child-care support. Outside the higher levels of government, Soviet women gained widespread

COUNTRY	1938	1953	1963	1980
Britain	181	258	330	441
France	74	98	194	362
Germany	214	224	416	747
West Germany		180	330	590
East Germany		44	86	157
Italy	46	71	150	319
Poland	19	31	66	169
Sweden	21	28	48	83
Soviet Union	152	328	760	1630

EUROPEAN INDUSTRIAL PRODUCTION, 1938–1980 Figures are a percentage of British industrial output in 1900.

political representation in parliamentary bodies, especially in local government. Nevertheless, women's pay lagged behind men's and women usually remained responsible for traditional domestic duties.

But even with all these improvements, Eastern-bloc nations could not keep up with their citizens' growing desires for a higher standard of living and more independence. Eastern Europeans had relatively few choices in consumer goods, food, and housing. In satellite nations, longing for autonomy from the Soviet Union persisted. Within each nation, Soviet-backed regimes—for the most part dictatorships—labored under questions about their political legitimacy. For many people, a sense of isolation from the West and a stifling of free expression within their own societies dampened cultural life in those nations.

In the capitalist democracies of Western Europe, government spending and welfare-state programs, as well as

Western Europe

U.S. aid, fueled a strong revival (see table on page 587). Europeans used this money, their growing store of new technology, and their skilled workforce to rebuild factories and transportation networks into models of efficiency. Falling tariff barriers and a population enlarged by increased birthrates created new demand for consumer goods. Food and clothing prices declined, jobs abounded, and wages rose. By 1955, the standard of living for even those in the bottom half of society rose. In just a decade, Western Europe had recovered fully from the economic devastation of the war.

During the 1960s, some Western European nations achieved unimagined levels of prosperity. West Germany, Switzerland, and Sweden became the wealthiest nations in Europe. People in northern Italy spoke of their own "economic miracle." On the other hand, areas farther south still wedded to more traditional agricultural economies lagged behind, and once-mighty Britain—reeling from the loss of overseas trade and investments, and hampered by the antiquated state of most of its mines and factories—suffered a relative decline.

Overall, however, Western Europe took on the look and substance of wealth. Industries such as electronics, automobiles, plastics, petroleum, prefabricated housing, and airlines flourished. Newly restored city centers attracted hordes of shoppers, suburban commuters, tourists, and pedestrians. The number of cars on Europe's streets jumped tenfold from fewer than 5 million in 1945 to over 50 million by 1970. Stores overflowed with a cornucopia of foods and clothing. Electronic gadgets—from electric can openers to hand-held audiotape players—cropped up everywhere. The proliferation of restaurants, theaters, travel, and hotels reflected the affluence and the widespread standard of a forty-hour workweek and four weeks of paid vacation each year.

The good economic news outweighed almost everything else in Western Europe, and nothing helped its politicians more, for economic growth became the key measure of political success. Moreover, as observers and visitors looked at the paths to recovery taken in Eastern and Western Europe, the West's stunning prosperity clearly contrasted with the slower growth in the East. However, Western Europe also had problems that reflected its decline from the heights of power and certainty. Not only had these nations forfeited leadership to the United States, but they lost their colonial empires as well.

THE TWILIGHT OF COLONIALISM

Even before World War II, national liberation movements around the globe had gathered momentum. When Germany defeated imperial nations such as France and the Netherlands, and Japan conquered Western holdings in Asia and the Pacific, Europe's control over its colonial territories weakened. The United Status further undermined the imperial powers by pushing them to dismantle their empires at war's end. At the same time, the Soviet Union continued to spread its decades-old denunciation of Western imperialism throughout the world. In the United Nations, sentiment grew toward the view that colonial "subjugation, domination and exploitation constitutes a denial of fundamental human rights." In the colonies, people seethed with anger against the Europeans. "Leave this Europe where they are never done talking of Man, yet murder men everywhere they find them," wrote the French West Indian philosopher Frantz Fanon (1925–1961) in his widely read book *The Wretched of the Earth.* "For centuries they have stifled almost the whole of humanity. . . . Look at them today swaying between atomic and spiritual disintegration." The last emperor of Vietnam, Bao Dai, warned his French overlords about "this desire for independence which is in everyone's heart and which no human force can any longer restrain."

Despite the intensity of these sentiments, many European settlers felt they had lived in the colonies too long to cede control to the local populations. Several political leaders in Europe agreed with Winston Churchill's sentiments: "I did not become the king's first minister in order to preside over the liquidation of the British Empire." The French

OPINION

What were the strengths and weaknesses of the two paths to recovery followed by Western and Eastern Europe during this period?

announced that "the attainment of 'self-government' in the colonies, even in the distant future, must be excluded." The struggle to end colonialism was on.

Revolts in Southern Asia

At the end of World War II, national liberation revolts threatened the huge British, Dutch, and French empires in southern Asia. Of the Western imperial powers, only the United States escaped direct embroilment in this revolt, by granting independence to the Philippines in 1946.

In India, the world's second most populous country, Mohandas K. Gandhi (1869–1948) led the independence movement. Educated in Great Britain, this astute middle-

India

class Hindu used passive resistance and civil disobedience rather than direct violence to pressure British officials to grant Indian independence. In 1947, Britain's Labor government finally freed India, partitioned into the separate states of India and Pakistan because of growing political divisions between Hindus and Muslims. Great Britain also relinquished Ceylon (Sri Lanka), Burma (Myanmar), and Malaya.

Independence, however, did not end problems in this troubled region. Religious and national strife soon broke out between Hindu India and Muslim Pakistan. Gandhi tried to quell the hostilities, but a fanatical Hindu nationalist assassinated him in 1948. Open war between the two states erupted in 1949 over possession of the disputed state of Kashmir. The United Nations managed to stop the shooting but failed to resolve the dispute, which would simmer for decades. This conflict, as well as border clashes with China, persuaded India to accept military aid from both the United States and the Soviet Union. India and Pakistan also faced the huge tasks of unifying their populations—divided by languages, caste, and class—and helping their millions of poverty-stricken and illiterate citizens.

In the rich and populous Dutch East Indies, nationalist leaders had established underground organizations during the wartime Japanese occupation. These leaders now stepped

Indonesia

in and declared independence when the invaders left. The Dutch resisted fiercely for four years before yielding control. In 1949, they finally recognized the Republic of Indonesia as an independent nation.

A similar but more painful pattern emerged in France's Asian empire after the Japanese left Indochina in 1945. As we have seen (page 580), the popular Indochinese national-

Vietnam

ists, led by Soviet-educated communist Ho Chi Minh (1890–1969), proclaimed the independent Democratic Republic of Vietnam. Heavy fighting between the French imperialists and communist nationalists ensued. In 1954, France finally admitted defeat, pulling out of Vietnam and freeing the neighboring countries of Laos and Cambodia.

Conflict in the Middle East

In the Middle East, Britain had been the dominant imperial power since World War I. However, under pressure from nationalists who had agitated for full independence since the first decades of the twentieth century, the British relaxed their control in the years before World War II. At the end of the war, British influence remained strong in several states, but only Cyprus, Palestine, and the Suez Canal were still official British possessions. Moreover, Britain was making a pronounced bid for Arab friendship and, to that end, helped to form the League of Arab States in 1945. Yet, the admission of tens of thousands of Jews into Palestine under the Balfour Declaration of 1917—a British promise to create a "national home" for Jews in Palestine—made Palestine a new trouble spot.

Palestine was the ancient home of the Jews—a people with a long history of being displaced by others. In the seventh century, the Islamic Arabs conquered Palestine and lived there until the twentieth

century. In the late nineteenth century, a new movement—Zionism—

Palestine

emerged to restore Palestine as the national home for the Jews (see pages 467–468). During the anti-Semitic persecutions of the Hitler era, Jewish refugees poured into Palestine and bought land, enraging the dispossessed Arabs. The British were caught between their obligations to the Arab nationalists in Palestine and the Jewish settlers eager to reclaim Palestine as their homeland.

In 1948, the beleaguered British finally turned Palestine over to the United Nations. The Jews immediately proclaimed the State of Israel and accepted the boundary lines that the United Nations drew up dividing Palestine between the Jews and the Arabs. However, the League

Israel founded

of Arab States protested this arrangement, and fighting broke out between the two sides. Although outnumbered, the well-organized Jewish forces held on. After a year, the United Nations brokered a truce. During the conflict, Israel had gained some territory and had expelled more than a half-million Palestinian Arabs. Most of these refugees, not welcomed by neighboring Arab states, settled in rough camps just outside Israel's new borders. The vigorous new nation, with financial help from abroad and a social-democratic government at home, began building modern cities and a strong economy. The Arab nations, however, refused to recognize Israel, and Palestine nationalists, without a country of their own, continued to conduct border raids on the fledgling nation. Conflicts stemming from the birth of the Israeli state would drag on for decades (see map on page 590).

These conflicts only compounded the broader anti-Western sentiment percolating in the region, especially in nearby Egypt, where Britain still controlled the Suez Canal. In 1952, a

Egypt

military coup in Egypt brought the dynamic nationalist leader Gamel Abdul Nasser (1918–1970)

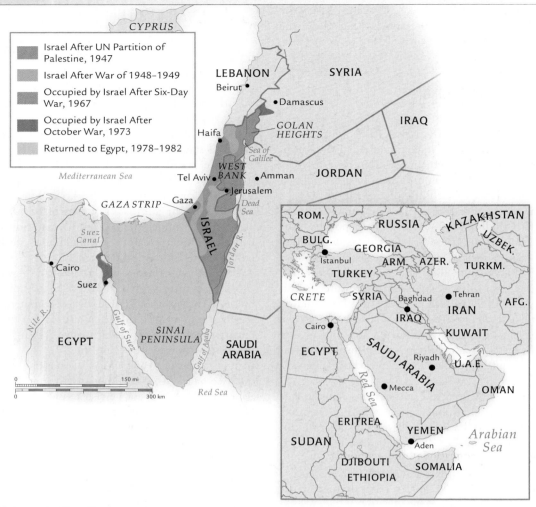

The Arab-Israeli Conflict, 1947–1982 This map shows some of the results of the various Arab-Israeli conflicts between 1947 and 1982.

Map legend:
- Israel After UN Partition of Palestine, 1947
- Israel After War of 1948–1949
- Occupied by Israel After Six-Day War, 1967
- Occupied by Israel After October War, 1973
- Returned to Egypt, 1978–1982

to power. Although Nasser kept much political power for himself, he promised parliamentary institutions, drew up a constitution guaranteeing individual rights, and distributed land to the poorer peasantry. In 1956, when the United States refused to support his plans to develop the Egyptian economy, he seized the Suez Canal. As he saw it, control of the canal would not only enrich Egypt but also symbolize Egypt's independence and Arab nationalism.

Nasser's bold action provoked a military attack by Israel, Britain, and France. Cold War rivalries quickly came into play when the Soviet Union threatened to intervene on the side of Egypt. At this point, the United States pressured the three invading powers to retreat. Though defeated militarily, Nasser ended up a national hero and the leader of the Arab world for standing up to Israel and the Western powers. Moreover, Britain lost the canal and soon its last holdings in the Middle East, and the Soviets gained influence in the region.

When war broke out again in 1967 and 1973—between Egypt (with its Arab allies) and Israel—the Soviet Union and the United States rushed billions more dollars of arms and advisors to their respective allies. The area had become another crucible of superpower competition that would continue to generate anti-Western resentment.

Liberating Africa

As in Asia and the Middle East, movements for national liberation stirred in Africa, where France and Britain held the most territory. France faced its greatest challenge in North Africa, where the largely Islamic population seethed with nationalistic unrest. In the face of this growing force, France granted indepen-

The French in North Africa

dence to Morocco and Tunisia in 1956 but drew the line at Algeria. The imperial power had held Algeria for over a century and considered it part of France rather than just a colony. In addition, more than a million French settlers lived there. They feared loss of property and reprisals from the eight million Islamic Algerians in the case of France's withdrawal. Complicating matters, the French military was determined to hold Algeria so as to repair the damage that France's reputation had sustained in Vietnam. At the same time, Arab nationalists living in Algeria believed that, with enough resolve, they just might oust the colonialist regime.

A long, bloody stalemate resulted. As one French soldier noted, "There's this staggering fact: The entire Arab population is joining the resistance against us." When the French government eventually showed a willingness to compromise, disgruntled colonial army officers threatened to overthrow the government in Paris. In 1958, as France's government teetered on the verge of collapse, retired general Charles de Gaulle was recalled to power. The World War II hero alone had the stature and legitimacy to negotiate with the forces of Arab nationalism. He granted Algeria independence in 1962 and freed almost all the other remaining French colonies.

Britain experienced similar challenges to its authority in its African colonies. The Labor government tried to prepare for the gradual freeing of British territories by

Britain dismantles its empire

sharing power with Africans in the civil service and bolstering funds for educational and economic development. The experience with Nasser in Egypt and a rebellion in Kenya from 1951 to 1956 finally persuaded the British to hasten their departure from Africa. By 1965, Britain had formally dismantled its African empire.

Yet even with most imperialists gone, trouble still brewed on the African continent. Sizable white minorities

Rhodesia and South Africa

living in Rhodesia and South Africa clung desperately to their power over black majorities. In Rhodesia, despite persistent guerrilla attacks by angry members of the black majority, the exclusively white regime held on until 1980. In long-independent South Africa, the prosperous white minority held fast to its power over the nonwhite majority. The white minority harshly suppressed the increasingly restless black majority and enforced **apartheid** (racial segregation). This policy earned the all-white South African government decades of heated protests from nonwhites and condemnation throughout the world. Only in the 1990s would the white government under F. W. de Klerk at last allow the popular African National Congress, headed by the venerated Nelson Mandela, to assume leadership. By then, all European powers had pulled out of Africa. As the map on page 592 shows, their departure ended Europe's domination of Africa and Asia.

Decolonization did not end Western influence in the non-Western world or bring peace and prosperity to the previously subject peoples. Newly independent nations were often left with illogical borders drawn arbi-

The legacy of colonialism

trarily by nineteenth-century European imperialists, depleted economies, and internal political divisions that drew in Cold War agents from both sides to exploit the chaos. Especially in Africa, ethnic conflict sometimes flared up into bloody civil wars, such as in Nigeria, where the Ibos in the eastern region attempted to secede and set up the independent Republic of Biafra. Because the newly freed countries—especially in Africa—were generally left without internally generated political institutions, instability, bloodshed, and rule by military strongmen often resulted. In southern and southeastern Asia, religious and political differences broke out into wars in the years after liberation. Growing but impoverished populations lived under the threat of hunger and, in bad weather, starvation. Droughts, for example, in the huge sub-Saharan region of northern Africa during the 1970s, 1980s, and 1990s, brought famine and death to tens of thousands. Most former colonies remained "Third World" nations—relatively poor, supplying raw materials to industrialized nations and dependent on the wealthier countries' goods and aid. Interaction between Western and non-Western peoples had transformed life on both sides, and resentments nurtured by years of colonial suppression still lingered in many non-Western nations.

A SENSE OF RELATIVITY IN THOUGHT AND CULTURE

Decolonization forced Western Europeans to reevaluate themselves and their civilization. So did the rise of the United States and the Soviet Union as superpowers and the ensuing Cold War that quickly cast its shadow over the West and the world. In these decades of such accelerating change, thoughtful people struggled to understand and define their lives and the culture in which they lived. The idea of universal truths that had prevailed in earlier times gave way to a growing sense that truth was relative—to the individual, to time, and to place. Increasingly, intellectuals, scholars, and writers argued that values were defined by the cultures in which they arose, judgments stemmed from individual perceptions, and conclusions hinged on the evidence selected. In these subtle senses, the postwar decades stressed shifting meanings rather than certainties.

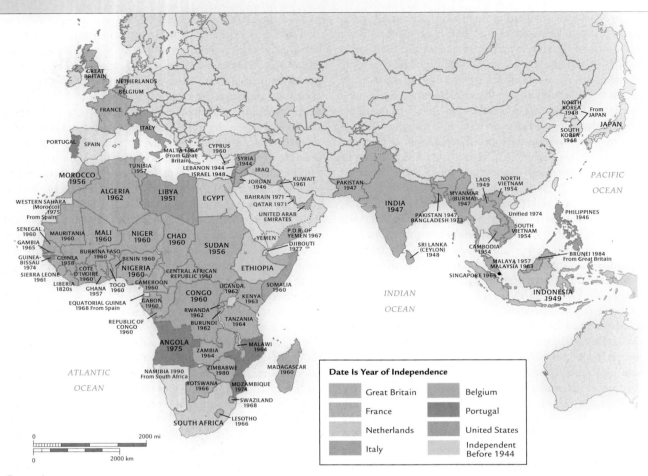

Decolonization This map shows the colonial empires held by Western powers before World War II and the dates when the former colonies gained their independence.

Existentialism: Responsibility and Despair

During the 1940s and 1950s, the philosophy of existentialism captured much attention in the West. Originating in an era marked by war, depression, mass death, and the decline

Sartre and Camus

of traditional standards of morality and religious beliefs, **existentialism** offered a stark interpretation of reality. France's Jean-Paul Sartre (1905–1980) became the most influential proponent of this body of thought. In novels, plays, and philosophical works, Sartre argued that there is no meaning to existence, no universal right or wrong. As he saw it, individuals are born and simply exist. They must make their own decisions, define their own purpose and values, and take responsibility for their actions. "Man cannot escape from the sense of complete and profound responsibility . . . one ought always to ask oneself what would happen if everyone did as one is doing." In the end, according to

Sartre, one simply dies without there being any philosophical meaning to death. The French writer Albert Camus (1913–1960) also popularized existentialism, in novels and plays such as *The Stranger* (1942) and *The Plague* (1947). He stressed the plight of the responsible individual seeking understanding and identity in an amoral, purposeless world.

The sense of despair that existentialist assumptions often engendered came forth graphically in the Theater of the Absurd, which dispensed with linear plots, definable action, and conventional sets and costumes. Samuel Beckett's (1906–1989) plays are good examples of

Theater of the Absurd

this genre. In *Waiting for Godot* (1952), two tramps wait for someone who never arrives. There is no purpose in what they do, for people in this culture no longer shared a sense of meaning. In Beckett's *Endgame* (1958), one character adrift in a world out of control describes his situation: "All life long the same questions, the same answers." In this absurd life, all responsibility rested with individuals, who had to make their own choices and decide how best to use their time on Earth.

A Culture of Contrasts and Criticism

The uncertainty and relativity implied by existentialism emerged not only in theater but also in other cultural forms. Writers, artists, and critics often disagreed with one another and with popular taste. In **Cinema** cinema, a stream of what critics dismissed as undistinguished movies nevertheless poured forth year after year. Yet cinema was perhaps the most original art form produced during the twentieth century. In the late 1940s and 1950s, several thoughtful movies, such as *The Bicycle Thief* by Italian filmmaker Vittorio de Sica, stressed the realistic struggles of ordinary people. During the 1960s and 1970s, the works of filmmakers such as Ingmar Bergman in Sweden, Federico Fellini and Liliana Cavani in Italy, Jean-Luc Godard in France, and Stanley Kramer in the United States exemplified the potential of cinema as a sophisticated, creative, artistic medium. These films contrasted sharply with the flashy artificiality of innumerable Hollywood movies—although many Hollywood motion pictures did feature stunning re-creations of the past, finely honed acting, and a creative mix of lighting, sound, and special effects.

Many educators and commentators hoped that television would become a worthy cultural and educational medium as well. By the 1960s, people spent on average fifteen to thirty hours per week watching television. To be sure, numerous situation comedies, adventure shows, dramas, and game shows celebrated the joys, anguish, and pains of everyday life—as well as violence, romance, and fantasy. Yet most television critics were disappointed. Like radio and newspapers, television crossed lines between serious news, politics, and entertainment alike. TV had an especially powerful impact on politics. Politicians sought or purchased TV exposure, shortened and simplified their messages, and cultivated an image created with the help of media and advertising professionals.

In the more traditional cultural fields, a similar pattern of conflict over new works emerged. Some of the most critically acclaimed works seemed inaccessible to ordinary people. In art, abstract expressionistic paintings, such as those created by the American artist Jackson Pollock (1912–1956), who dripped paint onto canvases, drew attention but not crowds. The painting below is one of Pollock's best-known works. Pollock explained why he avoided realistic representations of recognizable objects: "The modern artist is living in a mechanical age and we have a mechanical means of representing objects in nature such as the camera and photograph. The modern artist . . . is working and expressing an inner world . . . expressing his feelings rather than illustrating." **Art**

Pop art, with its images of everyday objects such as hamburgers in advertisements, also gained attention but bewildered audiences. The image on page 594, by the American artist Andy Warhol (1928–1987), looks like nothing more than rows of soup cans. From another perspective, however, viewers might interpret it as an image of striking, colorful unity that reproaches our commercial, prepackaged society with its standardized tastes.

Such paintings sometimes drew popular ridicule. One American newsmagazine, *Time*, called Jackson Pollock "Jack the Dripper." On one level, this popular rejection of bold new artistic forms was nothing new. Indeed, artistic styles that were once unpopular and considered avant-garde or elite—such as nineteenth-century postimpressionism and the twentieth-century paintings of Pablo Picasso—now attracted admiring crowds.

A related, but more puzzling, pattern emerged in literature and music. For example, the "new novel," which consciously avoided clear plots and well-defined characters, gained critical acclaim but attracted little popular attention. **Literature and music** Yet other, hard-to-categorize novels that critics praised just as heartily—for example, works by German author Günter Grass, French author Marguerite Duras, and British author Doris Lessing—won wide popularity. In music, the dissonant, atonal music of Arnold Schoenberg (1874–1951) garnered few fans compared with the hugely popular rock and roll, whereas jazz—a creation of African-American culture that emphasized sophisticated improvisation and rhythm—enjoyed a large following.

Perhaps cultural products and tastes, like the civilization they reflected, were changing too fast for most people. To be sure, many Westerners worried about the speed of and the forces behind cultural changes. In Europe especially, people talked about maintaining their own cultural tastes and identities in the face of "Americanization." **Americanization** They complained about the Hollywood movies, blue jeans, Coca-Cola, hamburgers, and fast food that poured from the United States into Europe. They also bemoaned the drain of intellectuals and artists moving to

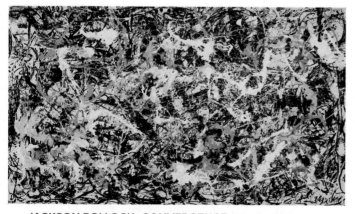

JACKSON POLLOCK, *CONVERGENCE*, 1952 Paintings such as this work by American artist Jackson Pollock avoided realistic representations and seemed inaccessible to ordinary people.

ANDY WARHOL, *ONE HUNDRED CANS,* 1962 Pop art painters such as Warhol created images filled with everyday objects that were not usually thought of as objects of art.

the United States. However, they could do little about the rapid spread of ideas, tastes, talent, and culture across political boundaries. Western Europeans found themselves losing the control they once had, and even the relative stability and prosperity gained in the 1950s and 1960s came under attack.

PROTESTS, PROBLEMS, AND NEW POLITICS: The 1960s to the 1980s

As the two postwar decades came to a close, the course of history in the West shifted. Events in the 1970s and 1980s unfolded in a context similar to that of the earlier decades: Cold War competition led by the United States and the USSR. Each side represented different political and economic systems that divided Europe and much of the world. Each side also marched to the beat of economic growth—more rapid in the capitalist West than the com-

munist East. However, within this same context, economic and political trouble was afoot. During the late 1960s and early 1970s, the road to social peace grew bumpy.

A Flurry of Social Protests and Movements

During these years, the gap between the ideals and realities of democracy, equality, and prosperity became more obvious and irritating than before. In some cases, unprecedented access to education fueled a growing awareness of this gap, while in others prosperity itself gave people the confidence to demand change. Often the well-publicized efforts of one group to force change inspired similar efforts by others. Protest movements frequently began in the United States and attracted close attention throughout the West. These dissatisfied groups voiced their demands with an assertiveness that shook several Western societies and even threatened governments.

The first of the great social movements began in the United States during the 1950s. There, African Americans initiated the civil rights movement, which inspired several other protest and liberation efforts in the West. The civil rights movement stemmed from America's long failure to integrate its large black popula- **The civil rights movement** tion. African-American veterans returning from World War II felt particularly frustrated with the discrimination they again faced at home.

In 1954, the Supreme Court took a major step in the fight against discrimination by outlawing racial segregation in public schools. "Separate educational facilities are inherently unequal," the Court concluded. A year later, a quiet act by a courageous individual set a series of additional changes in motion. A black civil rights activist, Rosa Parks, took a seat in the white-only section of a bus in Montgomery, Alabama. A yearlong boycott of segregated public transportation by African Americans in Montgomery followed, the first of many mass actions throughout the United States in the 1950s and 1960s.

White resistance to the black struggle for equality flared up in the American South, and more than once the federal government had to send troops and marshals there to overcome white resistance. White opposition also mounted in the large industrial cities of the North. Many whites fled to the suburbs to avoid integration. In 1964 and 1965, Congress passed a series of civil rights acts that guaranteed voting rights for all and broadly outlawed racial discrimination. Still, the turmoil continued. Racially charged riots broke out in major cities. The violence reached a climax in 1968 following the murder of Martin Luther King, Jr. (1929–1968), the prominent African-American leader.

In the face of growing opposition and divisions within its own ranks, the civil rights movement lost steam in the

1970s, but not before inspiring other groups, such as Spanish-speaking Americans, Native Americans, young people, and women. The protests by youths became especially threatening. Like the civil rights movement, these protests began in the United States. Soon, however, they spread throughout the West.

College students, whose numbers in the West more than tripled during the 1950s and 1960s, created movements of their own. The sheer mass of this first postwar generation of students and the emergence of a separate youth culture helped give these young people an acute sense of their own power. The civil rights movement and growing opposition to the Vietnam War provided causes and experiences for many. In 1964, students at the University of California at Berkeley attacked the restrictive values, social inequities, and competitive impersonality of the university and the traditional society it represented. Students also decried racism, poverty, and the growing American participation in the Vietnam War. Sometimes the protests turned into riots when authorities used force. Similar demonstrations soon boiled up across the United States.

Student movements

In 1968, the unrest spread to the campuses and streets of capitals from Tokyo and Mexico City to London, Amsterdam, Milan, and Berlin. Even in Eastern Europe—especially in Czechoslovakia—youthful protesters added to dissident movements demanding social change and political democratization. "We are intensely aware, in a way perhaps not possible for the older generation, that humanity stands on the edge of a new era," declared students at the University of British Columbia in Canada. Exploring the Past reveals the views of some of the radical student groups. The most dramatic confrontations took place in Paris—the Days of May uprisings. Fed up with the rigid, overcrowded university system and fearing that many would miss out on France's new prosperity after graduation, Parisian students rampaged through the streets of the French capital. Charles de Gaulle, president of France since 1958, met the demonstrators with police repression. The students then gained the support of sympathetic workers, who in turn demanded higher wages and an end to police brutality. This alliance between students and workers paralyzed France and even threatened to overturn the government. But the danger was short-lived. Agreements to raise wages appeased workers

An Oxford Student Explains Revolutionary Attitudes

Between the mid-1960s and early 1970s, university students throughout the West organized radical attacks on the status quo. The following selection by Tariq Ali, a student at Oxford and a leading revolutionary socialist, demonstrates the more extreme attitudes among these activists.

What is absolutely clear is that the revolutionary movement is in a period of upswing throughout the world. The war in Vietnam, the events of May 1968 in France and the invasion of Czechoslovakia symbolize this upswing. Vietnam is at the moment the battlefront against imperialism. France showed the extreme vulnerability of monopoly capitalism and the strength of the working class. Czechoslovakia has initiated the struggle for political revolutions in Eastern Europe and the Soviet Union itself. . . .

Those of us who form the hard core of today's new revolutionaries . . . are puzzled by the tendency among many Left factions in the developed countries to devote as much time and energy to attacking each other as to attacking capitalism. The new revolutionaries fight against sectarian tendencies. And what is most important of all, we are not to be bought off by the State. WE mean business.

What developments of the 1960s does Ali's analysis reflect?

and siphoned them off from the movement, and the government once more regained control. However, the protests provoked major reforms in higher education and probably played a role in de Gaulle's resignation a year later.

Like the civil rights movement, student activism waned in the 1970s. As universities adopted reforms that met many of the protesters' demands and the war in Vietnam came to an end, the sparks of protest faded. Among women, however, an international feminist movement was still gaining momentum.

Although feminism had a lengthy history in the West, the traditionally defined domestic role of women still had

The women's liberation movement

not changed much, even as late as the 1950s. In most Western nations, the dominant message from pulpits, welfare offices, doctors, and governmental officials was the same: Women should stay at home and serve as the anchor of the family, defining their social identity through their husband and focusing on raising children. But that age-old message increasingly came under attack as women gained access to higher education, experience in various protest and liberation movements, and greater awareness of the social restrictions on their lives.

One key to this increasing awareness came from new books. In 1949, the French writer Simone de Beauvoir (1908–1986) published *The Second Sex*, the century's most pivotal analysis of the condition of women. In this powerful book, de Beauvoir uncovered the myths that had relegated women to second-class status relative to men. "There is an absolute human type, the masculine. . . . He is the Subject, . . . she is the Other." De Beauvoir argued that women remained in cultural and economic dependence to men and therefore did not live as free human beings. The passive role assigned to women, she explained, forced them to live according to standards set up by men. De Beauvoir recommended a difficult but rewarding role for women: a life of work, self-definition, and independence.

The Second Sex became the fundamental text for feminist movements in the 1960s. Other writers, such as the American Betty Friedan, popularized de Beauvoir's ideas and added to them. In her widely read book *The Feminine Mystique* (1963), Friedan urged women to escape the confines of home, go back to school, move into new careers, and become more independent.

These ideas struck a chord, especially among many middle-class women. Increasing life expectancy and fewer children meant that more of these women than ever were living longer and devoting less of their lives to raising a family. They now had the time and resources to seek fulfillment outside the home—if they could find a way to break down traditional barriers. As more women enrolled in universities and pursued careers, discrimination against them

on the job because of their gender only heightened their sense of injustice and outrage.

Starting in the late 1960s, women in several Western nations founded organizations, conducted marches, held rallies, started journals, opened feminist bookstores, and pressured officials to recognize their needs. In 1969, an English women's group described the essence of the women's liberation movement: "We are economically oppressed: In jobs we do full work for half pay, in the home we do unpaid work full time. We are commercially exploited by advertisements, television and the press; legally we often have only the status of children. We are brought up to feel inadequate, educated to narrower horizons than men. This is our specific oppression as women. It is as women that we are, therefore, organizing."

Such efforts inspired a barrage of specific demands, including full citizenship in the political arena, equitable wages, and access to new careers. Despite opposition from conservative and religious groups, women pushed controversial issues such as day care, maternal leave, legalized abortion, and liberalized divorce into the spotlight of public discourse. They also protested stereotypical portrayals of femininity and widespread assumptions—among women and men alike—that raised the barriers facing them. Finally, they persuaded universities to introduce women's studies programs and prompted scholars in numerous academic disciplines to include feminist perspectives in their books.

By the early 1980s, the sharp edge of women's movements had dulled, but many long-term victories were already theirs. Women had gained greater control over fertility and sexuality from governments, churches, and male-dominated medical establishments. Moreover, lesbians demanded and received some recognition of their rights. As French author Monique Wittig noted in 1979, without feminism, lesbian culture and society "would still be as secret as they have always been." More women than ever flocked to universities, began careers in law, medicine, education, government, and business, and won political office. "Every girl now thinks in terms of a job. This is progress," said one Swedish vocational counselor. "They don't intend to be housewives for some future husband."

> Indeed, the very forces that had brought prosperity for some threw others out of work.

Stagnant Growth and Rising Inflation

While the protest movements inspired optimism among their proponents and anger among conservative opponents, disturbing economic developments spawned worry and doubt. A new phenomenon that became known as "stagflation"—stagnant economic growth paired with rising inflation—spread in the West. The main culprit was oil and its central role in providing cheap energy for the Western economy. During the 1950s and 1960s, Western interests had kept oil prices low by expanding production and discouraging oil-producing countries in the Middle East, Africa, and South America from presenting a united front to raise prices. The low prices encouraged many users of coal to switch to oil and helped control inflation.

In 1973, a war broke out in the Middle East between Israel and its Arab opponents. Middle Eastern oil-producing states, now organized into the Arab-dominated **Organization of Petroleum Exporting Countries (OPEC),** began

The oil crisis

to punish the West for supporting Israel in this conflict. As they limited production and increased prices, the cost of oil rose sixfold between 1973 and 1975. Prices again surged in 1979, spurring global inflation that particularly distressed the poorer nations of Asia and Africa and sent Western nations into a downward spiral of debt. Western economies, also facing disruptions in the international monetary system and growing competition from Japan, fell into recession.

In Europe and the United States, expectations of perpetual economic growth and limitless natural resources gave way to doubt. Indeed, the very forces that had brought prosperity for some threw others out of work. For example, the increased automation of industrial plants, the substitution of oil for coal, and the growing use of computers often eliminated more jobs than they created. The "green revolution" in agriculture boosted productivity but also forced people off the land and into the urban labor market. Equally alarming, large transnational corporations cut jobs as they moved their plants to regions offering cheap labor.

All these forces worsened unemployment, which by the early 1980s hit a whopping 10 percent and higher in many Western nations. In Britain—once an economic giant—

Growing unemployment

unemployment stayed at more than 12 percent year after year through the 1980s. Unions weakened, unable to protect workers in this perilous economic climate. The gap between rich and poor widened, and for many people—especially lower-wage earners—the economic good times seemed over. Least able to protect themselves were immigrant workers.

As is common during periods of economic uncertainty, wealthier nations turned against "outsiders." During the prosperity of the 1950s and 1960s, Western Europeans had opened their doors to desperate immigrants from southern

Turning against immigrants

Europe, Turkey, North Africa, and former colonies lured north by the promise of work. Immigrants filled the jobs that British, French, German, and Swiss workers passed over—the hardest, lowest-paid work in factories and fields, undesirable night shifts, street cleaning, and garbage collecting. Immigrant women were particularly vulnerable to exploitation in these jobs and in positions as domestics. Immigrant workers also labored

under obligations to send money back home. Many, having heard myths about "lands of plenty," assumed that someday they would return home rich.

In fact, officials often denied them social services and discouraged them from settling permanently. West Germany refused to grant citizenship to even those "immigrants" born in Germany. In the 1970s and 1980s, many governments, fearing worsening unemployment in their own countries, slammed the door shut against immigrants. The millions of foreign-born residents or "outsiders" who managed to arrive in the West increasingly suffered racial and anti-immigrant attacks.

The New Political Landscape

Reacting to social movements and uneasy about their economic fate during the 1970s and 1980s, voters throughout the West turned to political parties that they had once ignored or even disdained. Socialists, who accommodated these voters by toning down their radical message,

Turning to the Left

gained the most from this new development. In 1969, the Social Democrats in West Germany won control for the first time in almost fifty years. During the 1970s, under Willy Brandt (1913–1992) and Helmut Schmidt, they eased Cold War tensions by pursuing a policy of increased diplomatic and economic relations with Eastern Europe and the Soviet Union. By the late 1970s and early 1980s, Spain, Portugal, and Greece had also elected new Socialist governments that endured and led these nations into the European Common Market. In 1981, socialists under the leadership of François Mitterrand (1916–1996) came into power in France. They nationalized industries, shortened working hours, and enacted progressive social programs. However, persisting inflation and high unemployment soon led them to reverse some of these policies.

Communist parties in Western Europe also tried to adapt to voters' demands so as to garner popularity. In Italy, Spain, and France, the communists turned to "Euro-communism," supporting more moderate policies and vowing to cooperate with other leftist parties. They even gave up the Soviet model and its call to worldwide revolution and promised to work within Western democratic institutions and economic systems that blended free enterprise and state planning. For a while during the late 1970s and early 1980s, communists gained strength in Italy and played roles in governments in Spain and France.

Britain turned the other way. In 1979, voters handed a sweeping victory to the Conservatives and their right-wing leader, Margaret Thatcher, Britain's first female prime minister. Thatcher initiated policies to diminish state control over the economy, crush union power, and cut

Turning to the Right

spending for Britain's welfare state. Some state-owned and subsidized industries were "privatized"—sold to private enterprise. Thatcher also cut taxes on the wealthy, hoping to encourage investment and a "trickling down" of wealth to the rest of British society. Bitter strikes and urban riots by workers and the unemployed decrying her hard-line policies did not dissuade her.

Across the Atlantic, Thatcher found an ideological ally in Ronald Reagan, elected president of the United States in 1980. Reagan pursued similarly conservative policies, reversing some of the liberal social policies of the 1960s, moving against unions, privatizing governmental services, cutting taxes, increasing military spending, and reviving Cold War posturing against the Soviet Union. Thatcher's and Reagan's partially successful efforts in the 1980s to limit governmental spending on social programs marked the beginning of a gentle but broad turn toward conservative politics in the West.

Despite the changes, some groups still felt left out of politics. They demanded attention, even at the price of violence. In the 1970s and 1980s, political terrorism spread

Terrorism

across the West, conducted by groups such as the Red Brigades in Italy, the Red Army Faction in West Germany, and the Palestine Liberation Organization (PLO). Many of these groups had radical political goals. Others, such as the militant Basque separatists in Spain and the Kurdish rebels in Turkey, demanded national liberation. All desperately wanted recognition and had concluded that only assassinations, abductions, and bombings would achieve their aims.

No area in Europe suffered more from terrorism than Northern Ireland. There the Roman Catholic minority struggled fiercely to gain equality with the Protestant majority. Many Roman Catholics demanded total separation from Britain and union with Ireland. The Provisional Wing of the Irish Republican Army (IRA) conducted a long campaign of terror to this end. As the Protestants fought fiercely to maintain their supremacy, violence begot even more violence.

Governments responded to terrorists, sometimes with violence and occasionally by making deals. Security measures increased, as did the presence of armed police, and occasionally governments were able to penetrate the urban anonymity of modern society to capture terrorists. For the most part, however, terrorism remained an exceptional means of protest that never gained enough support to threaten governments.

POSTINDUSTRIAL SOCIETY

The political fluctuations of the 1970s and 1980s reflected more than just economic ups and downs or politicians' efforts to garner popular support. Underlying many changes during this period was a fundamental development: The industrial societies of the West had begun transforming themselves into **postindustrial societies.** This term refers to a culmination of economic and social changes occurring in the West over several decades. Traditional manufacturing industries declined in importance as more competitive plants employing cheap labor opened outside of Europe and North America. In place of manufacturing, demand for financial, health, educational, informational, and consumer services mushroomed—all services at which the West excelled. Well-educated and handsomely paid professionals, managers, and financiers rose to prominent positions in corporations and government, joining or replacing property owners and entrepreneurs as key economic figures. The bulk of the middle class—most of them well educated and with white-collar jobs—also grew in number and wealth. Industrial workers saw their jobs disappearing while demand for service employees expanded. Yet many of these service employees, who seemed white collar or middle class in their appearance or lifestyle, made the same income or even less than blue-collar workers. Traditional class lines were blurring.

Changing Fortunes in the Postindustrial Society

Some people gained more than others in this mobile society. The gap between rich and poor may have narrowed between the 1940s and 1960s, but that gap remained formidable and even increased in the 1970s and 1980s. Only the growing numbers of married women entering the paid workforce maintained or improved most families' standard of living after the early 1970s. Nor did overall prosperity solve problems of economic discrimination. Women generally received only two-thirds to three-fourths of men's salaries for the same work. Minority and immigrant groups still occupied the most poorly paid jobs. In many Western cities, a core of impoverished slum dwellers remained. Often without regular jobs and marked by their race or ethnic origin, they suffered the worst problems of urban life.

For most people in postindustrial societies, however, material life improved. Housing mushroomed, in France alone increasing to a half-million new units per year during the 1970s. New apartments had distinct rooms—bedroom, kitchen, living room, bathroom—and were not just for the middle class. Most homes boasted running water, indoor toilets, a bath or shower, and heating as well as an array of appliances. In the 1980s, one Italian woman reflected in amazement how her children "have grown up in a world in which washing machine, refrigerator, vacuum cleaner, and television set are taken for granted."

Daily patterns of life also changed as more and more people lived and worked in different parts of the cities and their expanding suburbs. People commuted on crowded trains or by car through traffic jams. The neighborhood cafés or pubs where people used to gather after work steadily lost customers, as did local, small stores where shoppers knew the merchants and each other. In their place, restaurants, supermarkets, and shopping malls sprang up, adding to the sense of urban anonymity.

The Baby Boom and the Booming Cities

Underlying the development of this postindustrial society were shifting populations that fueled economic growth and transformed patterns of life. Skyrocketing birthrates that had started during the war years led to the so-called **baby boom** soon after. An increase in life expectancy and the influx of immigrants added to the population growth. Europe's population, for example, increased from 264 million during the war to 320 million in the early 1970s. But the baby boom and the rapid jump in population did not last long. In the 1960s, birthrates began to decline as people returned to the long-term pattern of choosing to have fewer children. In the 1970s, these rates fell to less than half the pre–World War II figures in some areas.

Fewer of those populations lived on farms anymore. By 1955, less than a quarter of the population worked in agriculture. Over the next thirty years, that figure would fall to below 10 percent almost everywhere. Thanks to mechanization, fertilizers, pesticides, new seeds, and larger farms, dwindling numbers of farmers produced more than enough for everyone else, as well as surpluses for export. Rural economies could no longer offer employment to more than a small minority of the population. Once the heart of Western civilization, rural areas became places that city people traveled through and nostalgically imagined. Small country towns dominated by church steeples tried to stay viable by attracting tourists, people wanting second homes, or small industries looking to relocate. With the spread of highways, telephones, televisions, and computers, rural life retained only a hint of the isolation that formerly distinguished it from city life.

As they had for decades, people left rural areas and small towns in droves and headed for the cities. These migrations spread well beyond national borders. Wealthy northern European cities absorbed waves of newcomers from southern Italy, Greece, Turkey, and Africa, just as cities in North America took in Latin Americans and Asians. These immigration trends added to the traditional urban problems of congestion, overburdened transportation systems, pollution, and crime. Large parts of great cities deteriorated while the surrounding suburbs, with their own industrial plants, corporate offices, apartment complexes, and housing projects, expanded.

The Shifting Foundations of Family and Private Life

Along with this movement of people and transformation of cities, the very foundations of family and private life within postindustrial society began to shift. After the baby boom years of the 1940s and 1950s, families became smaller as people, aided by more widely available birth-control devices, chose to limit births. Families also became less stable, as married people used changing attitudes and laws concerning divorce to break apart more often. Many people decided to put off or avoid marriage altogether. Increasing numbers of single parents and same-sex partners now headed households.

The old family structure, in which the man wielded authority, weakened and began to be replaced by a sense of the family as a democratic partnership of equals. Married women streamed out of their roles as housekeepers, child rearers, and supporters of their "breadwinning" husbands. They now took paying jobs outside the home not only for the income but also for the equality and independence that paid employment offered. Especially within the middle classes, work outside the home became a sign of emancipation for women. With these changes, some homes became zones of domestic cooperation; others witnessed new battles between couples over household chores and child rearing. Overall, however, the burdens of housework and child care still rested primarily with women.

The process of raising children also changed. Children spent more years than ever in school to acquire the skills needed to excel in the competitive postindustrial society, a shift that made them financially dependent on their parents into their late teens and even early twenties. With

FAMILY WATCHING TELEVISION, 1950s In mid-century, television viewing widely became the focal point of family gatherings and foreshadowed a continuing decline in family interactions.

nursery schools becoming standard, children now started school at age three rather than age six. More than ever, the socialization, training, and career choices of youths were taking place outside the home.

Within the home, an individual's private life became no longer secondary to family life. The photograph on page 599 presents the image of the small family together watching television. But this image may also depict a decline of family interaction. Larger apartments and houses let family members spend more time than ever in separate rooms, coming together only for meals or TV watching. Much of home life became private, with individuals spending most time apart and alone rather than joining other family members.

Growing concern for private satisfactions

This growing concern for private satisfactions, which fit so well with the competitive economic individualism of postindustrial society, also played a role in the frequent separation of families. More often than ever, the ties holding marriages together began breaking apart. With love as the primary motive for marriage, the declining intensity of love that often occurs with time seemed enough to warrant divorce. As the sexual satisfaction of both partners became a core purpose of marriage, trouble in this domain also became a volatile source of discord and divorce.

Legal changes and statistics reflected these new realities. The grounds for divorce eased in most places to the point where mutual consent was enough. By the 1980s, between 25 and 50 percent of those who married would eventually get divorced. The old image of the breadwinning father, the homemaking wife, and the dependent children bonded together in a life-long relationship remained true for only a minority of the population.

The "Sexual Revolution" and the Youth Culture

Within or outside marriage, people gained new degrees of sexual freedom. Innovative methods of contraception, particularly the birth-control pill and the intrauterine device (and abortion, especially in Eastern Europe), achieved widespread acceptance in the 1960s and further separated sexual pleasure from reproduction. Manuals, sex education in schools, and the portrayal of sex in movies, books, magazines, and marketing materials became far more explicit than ever, reflecting the changing attitudes toward sex. Many conservative and religious groups strongly opposed these developments and the increase in premarital sex, though they were losing this battle by the 1970s. They also lost ground to gays, lesbians, and others who demanded respect and freedom.

Young men and women coming of age in the late 1950s and the 1960s, an era sometimes called the sexual revolution, led these widespread changes in sexual values.

Their clothing—flowered shirts and beads for men, blue jeans and miniskirts for women—and long hairstyles symbolized their new sexual freedom as well as the wider challenge of their youth culture to the older generation.

Young people's taste in music and movies also announced a break between generations. In the United States, Elvis Presley led the explosion in rock and roll's popularity in the late 1950s. With his suggestive dancing, slicked-back hair, and devoted following of young, screaming fans, Presley embodied eroticism and sexual abandon. The Beatles and other popular rock groups had a similar impact. Social dancing evolved from a carefully choreographed, chaste ritual to a no-holds-barred celebration of the body and sexuality. In popular movies, brooding, sullen young actors such as James Dean and Marlon Brando portrayed rebellious youths and became icons of the expanding youth culture.

BREAKTHROUGHS IN SCIENCE

The postindustrial society and the changing patterns of urban life that characterized it owed much to the many scientific breakthroughs of the period following World War II. More than ever, science became linked to economics and the needs of large institutions—from governments and industrial corporations to universities. These links were particularly strong in "big science." Before World War II, most scientific research was carried out by individuals or small groups of scientists in a university setting. The applica-

The rise of big science

BIG SCIENCE, 1969 This photo of Americans on the moon serves to illustrate the combined power of large universities, big business, and governmental backing to carry out major scientific and technological projects.

Then & Now
Computer Technology

The Z3 was the world's first electromechanical computer. Developed by Konrad Zuse in 1941, the project was funded by the German government and originally employed by their military. The machine weighed a staggering 2,200 pounds. Today, technology is widely available to populations across the West in much lighter and more portable forms. The Apple iPad, for example, weighs less than 2 pounds.

tion of their discoveries by engineers and technicians came later. After the war, funds for scientific research poured in from government and big business, forming what some called the military-industrial-university complex. With the influx of money and interest, the number of scientists jumped fivefold between 1945 and 1985, and the fields they entered divided into more and more subspecialties. Organized teams of scientists, technicians, and managers worked in large research laboratories, using expensive equipment and aiming for specific goals. The results were stunning.

From the Universe Above to the Universe Within

Cold War competition especially fueled the massive effort to put satellites and humans into space. By the 1960s, satellites spun around the earth, providing a steady stream of military surveillance, weather observations, communications, and scientific information. The "space race" between the United States and the Soviet Union climaxed with a televised walk on the moon's surface in 1969 (see photograph on page 600). While taking his first step, the American astronaut Neil Armstrong spoke his now-famous words: "That's one small step for man, one giant leap for mankind."

Government money funded other scientific and technological efforts as well. Teams of physicists used powerful particle accelerators to explore the subatomic world. From innovations in radar systems during World War II came microwave technology, which became central to the television and long-distance telephone industries. Work on the atomic bomb led to nuclear power plants.

Similar efforts by teams of scientists and individuals led to fundamental discoveries in fields such as genetics. In 1953, the structure of DNA, the material in chromosomes that contains hereditary information, was discovered. This implied that the characteristics of all living things, including humans, could be controlled, and it opened the controversial possibility of tampering with this molecule to create new forms of life. Research into gene splitting and genetic engineering would turn this possibility into reality.

The Information Revolution

Much of the new scientific work depended on computers, which became the core of the "**information revolution.**" The computer first emerged in the 1940s as a tool for storing and manipulating information. Encouraged by business and government during the 1950s and 1960s, its scientific and economic impact widened. With miniaturization during the 1970s and 1980s, computers the size of a notebook could outpower their room-size predecessors. These new "personal computers" cropped up on desktops and in briefcases everywhere. Now most people involved in science, scholarship, and business relied on computers, and the new devices became the core of a booming, worldwide industry.

Transforming Medicine

In the decades after World War II, medicine also entered new territory—itself becoming a big business with strong links to science and economics. Long gone were the days of visits by horse-and-buggy doctors. Now most physicians saw patients in offices, clinics, and especially hospitals, which employed medical personnel working in coordinated teams with complex machines. The era of the family doctor also faded. Now patients consulted more prestigious specialists. Finally, doctors gained a new degree of power to battle medical problems. Whereas in earlier centuries physicians may have done more harm than good with their treatments, now medicine became a major lifesaver in the Western and non-Western world.

The keys to these changes were antibiotic drugs and vaccines. In the 1930s, researchers discovered that sulfa drugs could cure infectious diseases. Penicillin and other antibiotics soon followed. By the 1940s, once-fatal illnesses such as meningitis and pneumonia could be cured by antibiotic drugs. Tuberculosis, a disease so deadly that it was called the "white plague," was almost eliminated by a vaccine and antibiotics. In 1977, smallpox was literally eradicated throughout the globe. The spotlight on medicine shifted from traditional infectious diseases to cancer, heart disease, arthritis, and AIDS.

New surgical techniques also offered more hope than in previous centuries. Antibiotics let surgeons perform lung and other operations that had been too risky before because of the danger of infection. In the 1960s, open heart surgery and heart bypass operations became almost routine. Then organ replacement—first of kidneys and then even hearts— became possible. Surgery became more a process of continuous repair and replacement than cutting and removing.

Expensive new machines for diagnosis and treatment complemented all the new medical techniques. Ultrasound machines, CT scanners (which combined X rays with computer analysis), and MRI devices that used radio waves gave doctors a window into the body without having to open it up. Dialysis machines and pacemakers offered new hope to kidney and heart patients.

For those suffering from mental illnesses, effective medications emerged in the 1950s. Doctors prescribed a growing list of these psychotropic drugs for people with schizophrenic and manic-depressive conditions. Though the success of these drugs was far from complete, they contributed to the closing of many mental hospitals and asylums.

By the 1980s, medicine had become dominated by large hospitals, groups of doctors, insurance companies, and governmental agencies. Health "consumers" expected more and more from medicine—including cures for most ailments and what many saw as a right to live to retirement and a robust old age. Nations devoted more resources than ever to medicine—often more than 10 percent of the national income. Britain's minister of health once complained, "There is virtually no limit to the amount of health care an individual is capable of absorbing."

In several senses, then, the evolution of medicine since World War II reflected broader qualities of the era. Science, especially big science, enabled doctors to expand and even revolutionize the field. Medicine also relied on the overall prosperity and governmental support of those decades, which enabled people to demand, and the health-care industry to provide, so many services. The very growth of this service industry as well as the high status and income enjoyed by its leading practitioners echoed the development of the postindustrial society, with its stress on services and technical expertise. Finally, like much else, Western medicine spilled across borders and into the non-Western world—though also in ways that highlighted the disparities of wealth between the Western and non-Western worlds and the conflicts that often arose when those different cultures met.

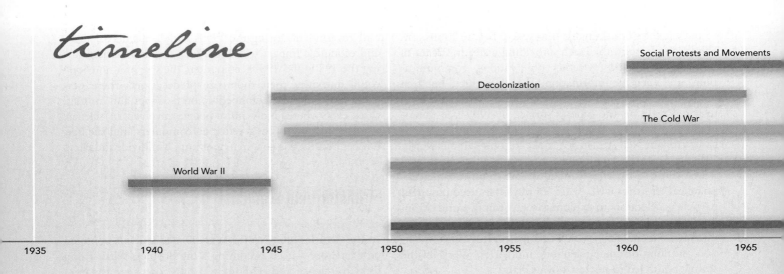

timeline

Social Protests and Movements

Decolonization

The Cold War

World War II

1935   1940   1945   1950   1955   1960   1965

SUMMARY

The decades between 1945 and 1989 witnessed a quickening pace of change as more people than ever were drawn into the swirl of politics, economic development, and urban life.

- The Cold War conflict between the United States and the Soviet Union, drawing on deep differences in their political and economic systems, quickly spread across Europe and the rest of the world.

- In the Soviet Union and Eastern Europe, communist governments firmly directed their countries' economic and social life, while in Western Europe, capitalist democracies relied on a combination of the free market and government controls to transform their societies.

- During the two decades following World War II, most of the colonial empires held by Western powers disintegrated and former colonies gained their independence.

- In a period of accelerating change, the ideal of universal truths gave way to a growing sense that truth was relative—to the individual, to time, and to place.

- The 1960s and early 1970s witnessed a flurry of social protests and movements. New economic and social problems as well as shifting political realities marked the late 1970s and the 1980s.

- Postindustrial society, marked by a long-term decline of traditional manufacturing industries and the rise of service industries, spread throughout the West.

- Increasingly, major scientific efforts and breakthroughs relied on the economics and the needs of large institutions—from governments and industrial corporations to universities.

As the final decade of the twentieth century approached, the West as a whole remained powerful and was often envied abroad. At the same time, it had become clear that the Western powers could no longer act without taking into account the concerns, power, and problems of the non-Western world. Soon, stunning developments in Eastern Europe would mark 1989 as the dawn of a new historical era.

Fall of Communism

Toward European Unification

Economic Reforms in China

Communism in China

| 1970 | 1975 | 1980 | 1985 | 1990 | 1995 |

CHINA, 2008 On a late afternoon in November 2004, workers bicycle home from the large steel mill in Baotou, China. The mill supports this rapidly expanding one-industry town, located just west of China's capital city, Beijing, and, along with similar cities, testifies to China's growing role as a leading industrial nation. The carbon-rich smoke pouring into the air and creating pollution that will spread east to Beijing and beyond also reveals the accelerating environmental problems—above all, global warming—facing China and the world in the twenty-first century.

Into the Twenty-First Century

The Present in Perspective

26

Opening a New Era

"The 20th century is now over." The historian John Lukacs made this announcement in a 1991 issue of the *New York Times*. By "20th century," Lukacs meant the 75-year era that began in 1914 and ended in 1989. The year 1914 marked the outbreak of World War I, which for most historians represented the beginning of the twentieth century. That conflict and World War II dominated the period. "The Russian Revolution, the atom bomb, the end of the colonial empires, the establishment of the Communist states, the emergence of the two superpowers, the division of Europe and of Germany—all of these were the consequences of the two world wars, in the shadow of which we were living, until now," wrote Lukacs. The year 1989 saw the nations of Eastern Europe break from their Soviet ties and from communism. ▶▶

In just two more years, the Soviet Union itself would fall apart.

Other developments, also with roots in the past, added to the sense that the world had just lived through the closing of one historical era and the opening of another. The movement toward economic integration in Western Europe, the growing strength of the newly unified Germany, and the changing position of the United States altered international relations. Beyond the West, the Pacific Rim—particularly East Asia—gained enormous economic clout. In the Islamic world, stretching from North Africa through the Middle East to Indonesia, mounting pressures posed a variety of threats to stability in those regions and beyond. From a global perspective, three regional power centers had emerged—Europe, North America, and East Asia. Almost everywhere, people, problems, cultures, and histories spilled across national borders, challenging those living in the Western and non-Western worlds to broaden their understanding of the world and their place in it. ◂◂

THE COLLAPSE OF COMMUNISM

Of all these developments, the collapse of communism in the Soviet Union and Eastern Europe arguably had the most dramatic and far-reaching global impact. In a

THE BERLIN WALL, November 1989 Demonstrators celebrate the fall of the Berlin Wall, which served as a barrier between Eastern and Western Europe. "In the Name of the People," written in English, credits popular will for tearing down the wall and announces the importance of the event to a watching world.

startling public announcement early in November 1989, East Germany's communist leader succumbed to months of growing pressure and ordered the Berlin Wall, the most powerful symbol of the Cold War, torn down. This photograph shows Germans from East and West climbing over the Berlin Wall near the Brandenburg Gate. A reporter described the scene: "Nearby, before the Brandenburg Gate . . . people climbed up onto the rim of the wall during the night of November 9 . . . taking pickaxes to it." Then the cranes and bulldozers came. "People stared unbelieving, as East German cranes lifted away the slabs of concrete." As the wall crumbled, another observer described the Berlin border crossings: "The streets were packed with people streaming past the East German border guards. . . . Cars from East Berlin slowed to a crawl alongside the crowds of West Berliners waiting just over the white stripe painted on the asphalt, cheering every car . . . handing cans of beer to the drivers." In those first heady days, millions of East Germans crossed the border, some to stay, others to return again and again "loaded down with full plastic shopping bags." The mayor of West Berlin declared, "This [is] the greatest historical event since the French Revolution."

Everywhere in Eastern Europe, communist governments were collapsing. The Soviet bloc, which had seemed so impenetrable, quickly dissolved. Soon the Soviet Union itself would break apart.

Undermining Communism in the Soviet Union

What explains this massive historical reversal? The story begins in the Soviet Union, where communist power was most firmly entrenched. During the two or three decades following World War II, the Soviet Union, like other communist nations, enjoyed economic growth and relative prosperity (see Chapter 25). The USSR boasted impressive factories and elaborate technical projects such as dams, railway systems, military hardware, and manned rockets. Rapid industrialization, which pulled peasants and women into the urban workforce by the millions, boosted productivity.

However, during the 1970s and 1980s, central planning and collectivization—the hallmarks of the Soviet economic system—failed to match new consumer demands. Keeping up with the rapidly changing, technologically

Problems with central planning

sophisticated economy of the 1970s and 1980s required flexibility, a willingness to experiment with new production methods, and local decision making—all of which the Soviet economic system lacked. Instead, economic decisions came from high officials more sensitive to political pressures than to economic realities. Central planners, pursuing out-of-date strategies or unaware of changes in grassroots needs, often ordered factories to produce goods that did not meet consumers' demands. Local plant managers, struggling to get needed materials and labor, suffered long delays while distant officials made decisions. Workers, their jobs guaranteed, had little incentive to work hard or even show up consistently. Similar problems plagued agriculture, where collectivization discouraged effective decision making and hard work. As the rate of economic growth declined, embarrassed Soviet planners had to import grain again and again from the capitalist West. Government leaders worried that the Soviet economy would never catch up with formidable capitalist competitors such as the United States, Germany, and Japan.

Worse, everyday dissatisfactions spread. Soviet workers had money but not the selection or quality of goods that they wanted and that they knew were available to

Spreading dissatisfaction

people in the West. Instead, they regularly stood in lines for as long as two hours a day just to buy basic supplies. Even urban professionals, managers, and technicians, although relatively wealthy and well educated, experienced similar frustrations. Far too obviously, only a small corps of Communist Party officials and privileged elites enjoyed access to the most desirable goods and services in this supposedly egalitarian society, fueling resentment. For everyone else, the only alternative was the thriving, but expensive and illegal, black market. Faith in the communist system, even among members of the Communist Party, began to evaporate. "I'm not a good Party member because I don't believe in Communism . . . nor do a lot of Party members," admitted one 40-year-old Communist in 1990. "Joining the Party was for me entirely a calculated way of furthering my career."

Three pivotal developments during the late 1970s and 1980s exacerbated the problems undermining the Soviet brand of communism. First, the spread of modern com-

Growth of dissent

munications broke down the old Stalinist policy of enforced isolation from the rest of the world and fueled the growing dissident movement. By watching television, people saw for themselves the material wealth enjoyed by Western nations. They also perceived the swirling cultural and intellectual currents that officials tried to stifle within the Soviet Union. Yet photocopiers and computers spread information easily, making censorship difficult. Privately published manuscripts criticizing Soviet life circulated among the educated elite. The dissident movement grew, led by the Nobel Prize–winning physicist Andrey Sakharov (1921–1989) and others. Dissidents demanded more democracy, greater civil liberties, and some independence for nationalities within the Soviet Union. Although such demands earned Sakharov and others exile, the dissident movement persisted. Moreover, among many people not yet ready to join the dissident movement, the increasingly obvious contradictions between the official party line and the harsh realities of Soviet life engendered cynicism and apathy.

Second, military and wartime expenditures increasingly burdened the Soviet economy. In the 1980s, the United States under President Ronald Reagan vigorously pursued the Cold War arms race, forcing the

Military burdens

Soviets—with their fundamentally weaker economy—to struggle to keep up. At the same time, the 1979 Soviet invasion of Afghanistan turned into a costly military quagmire. The widely condemned conflict wore on for years, straining the USSR's economy and diminishing the Soviet leadership's popularity.

Third, the quality of the Soviet leadership declined in the 1970s and 1980s. Leonid Brezhnev weakened noticeably and repeatedly fell ill in the seven years before his death in 1982. Most of his colleagues were long estab-

Declining leadership

lished in their offices. Brezhnev's immediate successors, Yuri Andropov (1982–1984) and Konstantin Chernenko (1984–1985), each died shortly after assuming office. These older men were reluctant to alter the USSR's course or to make way for a younger generation of reformers. But in 1985, a new leader—Mikhail Gorbachev—was appointed head of the Soviet Union. Just 54 years old, he had very different ideas about how the Soviet Union should operate.

Gorbachev Launches Reforms

Born into a peasant family, Mikhail Gorbachev (1931–) studied law as a youth at the University of Moscow. He moved rapidly up through the Communist Party ranks, eventually taking responsibility for agricultural policy. Charming and astute, he became a capable manipulator of people and events. Britain's prime minister, Margaret Thatcher, recognized him as a man "with whom we can do business." Gorbachev also had bold plans to lead the Soviet Union in new directions. Soon after assuming power in 1985, he replaced a third of the old party leadership with new supporters. By then, he shared the views of reformers who recognized the fundamental economic problems plaguing the Soviet Union. In his willingness to grapple with problems, Gorbachev echoed Khrushchev's attack on

Stalinism some thirty years earlier. Nevertheless, he had no intention of loosening the party's hold on power.

Gorbachev embarked on a three-pronged policy: **perestroika** (restructuring), **glasnost** (openness to discussion),

Perestroika

and disarmament. All three were intended to bring the Soviet economy up to the standard of Western capitalist societies. No one—not even Gorbachev—imagined the consequences that would flow from these daring reforms.

Perestroika involved a thorough restructuring of the Soviet economy. The program's goals included decentralizing planning, allowing market forces rather than officials to set prices, and putting control of land and agricultural practices into the hands of families and cooperatives rather than large state farms. In short, *perestroika* would create a mixed economy featuring a blend of socialist planning and a capitalist, free market. Gorbachev knew that the transformation would take time and cause short-term pain, including further shortages of consumer goods, inflation, and unemployment. To gather the political backing and the financial resources he needed to carry out the program, he initiated *glasnost* and an arms-reduction plan.

Glasnost curtailed censorship, encouraged freer discussion of everything from culture to politics, and opened the doors to the partial democratization of the Communist

Glasnost

Party and the Soviet political system. Officials freed dissidents such as Andrey Sakharov. Some governmental proceedings were made visible to the public and even televised. In the spring of 1989, the government held the first open elections since 1917, which resulted in the defeat of numerous communist dignitaries. Gorbachev hoped that *glasnost* would elevate his prestige internationally, win him foreign political and financial support, and inspire intellectuals and workers at home to accept his bold restructuring of the Soviet economy.

His arms-reduction plan served the same ends. In meetings with U.S. presidents almost every year between

Arms reduction

1985 and 1991, Gorbachev pushed for more and more reductions in both countries' military stockpiles. These meetings bore fruit: Both the USSR and the United States agreed to limit nuclear weapons and conventional forces not only on their own soil but also in Europe. At the same time, Gorbachev tried to extract Soviet forces from the war in Afghanistan. The effort took four years, but in 1989 the last Soviet troops finally came home. These feats burnished Gorbachev's reputation at home and abroad and promised to ease the USSR's heavy burden of military expenditures.

> "A spectre is haunting eastern Europe: the spectre of what in the West is called 'dissent.'"

However, implementing *perestroika* proved more difficult than Gorbachev and his supporters expected. Entrenched officials resisted the changes, as did many Soviet individuals whose jobs and incomes were threatened by economic restructuring. Gorbachev's promises also raised the Soviet people's expectations to impossible heights. Some reformers even criticized him for moving too slowly.

To complicate matters, ethnic groups and republics within the Soviet Union began agitating for national autonomy and the freedom to express their own cultural beliefs. Peoples from central Asia and Armenia to the Baltic republics had long harbored resentments against the Soviet state. Most of these republics had been forced to

Demands for autonomy

join the Soviet Union during the devastating civil wars of 1917–1921. When Gorbachev weakened the monopoly power of the Communist Party, he undermined the principal institution holding the multinational Soviet Union together. Emboldened by Gorbachev's promised leniency in Eastern Europe, the republics took action. The greatest threat came from elites in Latvia, Lithuania, and Estonia on the Baltic coast, who led demands for political autonomy. As tensions mounted, events in Eastern Europe took a dramatic turn, overshadowing developments in the Soviet Union.

Revolutions in Eastern Europe

Ever since coming under the USSR's control, many people living in the communist nations of Eastern Europe had yearned to reclaim their national autonomy. Moreover, economic and cultural problems similar to those undermining communism in the Soviet Union plagued these societies and their governments. Though dissent did not always result in public protests, strikes, or demonstrations, it still simmered. In 1978, the Czechoslovakian playwright Václav Havel mocked the words of the *Communist Manifesto:* "A spectre is haunting eastern Europe: the spectre of what in the West is called 'dissent.'" Underground publications demanding honesty and civil rights circulated through intellectual and artistic circles in Poland, Hungary, and Czechoslovakia.

Two developments in the late 1980s strained the communist regimes trying to maintain control over these satellite states. First, economic difficulties mounted as Eastern European governments labored to keep prices artificially low. To make matters worse, foreign loans from the West to Eastern European nations such as Poland became

Economic problems

more expensive and began drying up. When those governments finally tried to increase prices without raising wages, public opposition mushroomed. Second, Gorbachev revoked the long-standing Brezhnev Doctrine. In 1989, he made his intentions clear: "Any interference in domestic affairs and any attempts to restrict the sovereignty of states, both friends and allies or any others, are inadmissible." Gorbachev had decided to let events in Eastern Europe unfold without Soviet intervention. For reformers and dissenters, this policy was a green light to action.

Revoking the Brezhnev Doctrine

Poland led the way in the rush for liberation. This nation already had a history of protest movements that made it a weak link in the Soviet chain. In 1980, shipyard workers in Gdansk struck against rising consumer-goods prices. The strikers organized a noncommunist union, Solidarity, under the leadership of Lech Walesa. Support for Solidarity spread throughout the nation, forcing the government to recognize the new organization and accede to some of its demands. When the union pushed for more, resistance from Moscow and conservative elements in the Polish government stiffened. In late 1981, General Wojciech Jaruzelski, the new leader of the Polish Communist Party, declared martial law, arrested Walesa, and outlawed Solidarity.

Poland leads

However, the union survived these reversals. Early in 1989, with the Polish economy in crisis, negotiations began between Jaruzelski and Solidarity, still led by Walesa. The Polish Catholic Church, which had maintained a position in the nation and indeed enhanced its own prestige with the visit of Pope John Paul II in 1979, helped mediate discussions. The talks resulted in the legalization of Solidarity and, in June, new elections. Solidarity's stunning victory at the polls prompted Jaruzelski to ask the union to form a new government. A few months later, the communist leader stepped down, and the Communist Party gave up power in Poland without a fight.

Hungary soon followed suit. This satellite state already had a mixed economy, with almost one-third of its wealth coming from a private sector of small enterprises, crafts, and family agriculture. Reformers within the Hungarian Communist Party gained some power in 1988 and removed the old leader, János Kádár, from office. In the summer and fall of 1989, Hungary held elections, established a multiparty political system, and initiated economic reforms to open the country to private enterprise. The image above, a poster published by the Hungarian Democratic Forum, captures the sense of ushering out a bygone era.

Hungary

Next came Czechoslovakia. In the fall of 1989, student demonstrators took to the streets demanding academic freedom and human rights. When police responded with clubs and tear gas, the demonstrators turned against them and other authorities. Workers and employers alike joined the

ISTVAN OROSZ, *COMRADES, IT'S OVER*, 1989 This poster published by the Hungarian Democratic Forum announces the fall of communism in Hungary and elsewhere in Eastern Europe.

students in the streets of Prague and in the great St. Wenceslas Square in the city center. In November, the call went out for a general strike. Within a few days, the hard-line Communist government resigned. Václav Havel, the playwright and dissident leader who had been imprisoned for his views, and Alexander Dubcek, who had tried to liberalize Czechoslovakia in 1968, quickly rose to power. As in Poland and Hungary, the fall of the communist regime in Czechoslovakia was bloodless—a "velvet revolution."

The "velvet revolution" in Czechoslovakia

In East Germany, the wealthiest and most powerful of the Eastern European states, even people who did well under communism wanted to head west by the thousands. An American woman residing in East Germany described the growing dissatisfaction. "Too many . . . things were wrong. . . . Too much was missing from the shops. . . . There were no spare parts to fix home appliances or cars.

East Germany

Assembly lines were halted for want of supplies from auxiliary plants. It was the same on building sites, and the workers stood idle and furious. What good was this kind of socialism? Why did everything work so smoothly in the Germany next door?" When Hungary opened its borders with Austria in September 1989, tens of thousands of East Germans used that escape route to stream into the West. "They had been watching it longingly on West German television all their young lives. They knew from the commercials exactly how they would furnish their homes and make them shine."

In October 1989, antigovernment demonstrations spread throughout East Germany. People brandished signs proclaiming "We are the people." Long-suppressed criticism of the state's feared "security" forces surfaced. The hard-line communist leader was ousted from office. In November 1989, his communist successor bowed to the inevitable and ordered the Berlin Wall torn down. Joyful demonstrators celebrated for days. Soon, communists lost power, and within a year East and West Germany had reunified.

The rest of Eastern Europe also quickly followed. In Bulgaria, an internal coup deposed the Stalinist ruler. In Romania, the relatively independent but dictatorial communist leader Nicolae Ceaușescu ordered troops to fire on demonstrators, setting off a bloody revolution. His overthrow cost many lives and ended with the execution of Ceaușescu and his wife. The following year, Albania's independent but highly Stalinist regime also collapsed.

The freeing of Eastern Europe took less than a year. One after another, these nations cut the ties binding them to the USSR, enacted democratic reforms, and introduced capitalism into their economies (see map above). The repercussions of these events echoed throughout the Soviet Union, quickly pushing developments beyond the control of Gorbachev and his supporters.

Eastern Europe, 1989 **This map shows the upheavals that toppled the communist regimes in Eastern Europe.**

The Soviet Union Disintegrates

The Soviet leader had managed only halting steps in his effort to restructure the Soviet economy—*perestroika*. High officials announced plans to move the economy away from central planning and then delayed the plans in the face of determined opposition by hard-liners. These officials also worried about the difficulties—including unemployment, inflation, and dislocation—that the transition would cause. Gorbachev watered down his reforms to the satisfaction of no one. The waffling and controversy only worsened the frustrations of hard-liners and reformers alike. Reformers who wanted Gorbachev to move faster grew disgusted with the moderate pace of change, while the old communist guard became increasingly alienated. As the economy began to spin out of control, the Soviet leader's popularity dwindled.

Problems with reform

Gorbachev tried pushing through promising political reforms as part of his *glasnost* policy, but, as with *perestroika*, each step taken to enact reforms opened the door further for new expressions of dissatisfaction. In 1990, he persuaded the Communist Party's Central Committee to eliminate the party's constitutional monopoly on political power. He created a new, strong presidency—an office separate from the Communist Party hierarchy. Equally daring, he called for new elections.

All these changes democratized Soviet politics and undermined the power of the Communist Party—in the process exposing the corruption of the old Soviet regime. Party members resigned in droves. These policies also facilitated the rise of Gorbachev's chief rival, Boris Yeltsin (1931–2007), the newly elected president of the Russian Republic. A charismatic, liberal reformer, Yeltsin publicly resigned from the Communist Party in July 1990. In another bold move, he declared the Russian Republic an independent state.

At the same time, movements for independence gained momentum within several ethnic groups and nationalities throughout the USSR. The Soviet Union contained more than a hundred ethnic groups, as well as some 50 million Muslims in central Asia. Many of these groups considered themselves separate nations and the Soviet Union as a collection of nations rather than a single whole. The republics of Estonia, Lithuania, and Latvia led in pressing Moscow for independence. In 1991, the Ukraine joined the Russian Republic in declaring itself independent. Ethnic conflict and nationalistic demands spread in the Soviet republics of Armenia, Azerbaijan, Moldova, Georgia, and elsewhere. Though Gorbachev resisted these demands and tried to quell the ethnic conflicts, the situation had gone beyond anyone's control. In the spring of 1991, he proposed a compromise: the Treaty of Union, in which all the Soviet republics would be independent but held together as a confederation.

Independence movements

In August 1991, with the Treaty of Union about to take effect, communist hard-liners from inside the government and the KGB tried to oust Gorbachev. Within three days, the hard-liners' ineptitude and the opposition marshaled by Russian president Yeltsin doomed the coup to failure. Indeed, Gorbachev's authority was slipping away to Yeltsin even at this moment. In late 1991, after the two leaders stripped the Communist Party of much of its power, Gorbachev resigned.

Hard-liners' coup

The End of the Cold War

By 1991, the Soviet Union had lost control over the states of Eastern Europe and was itself disintegrating—the Cold War was over. In the following selection, historian John Lewis Gaddis analyzes the causes of the Cold War's end.

What no one understood, at the beginning of 1989, was that the Soviet Union, its empire, its ideology—and therefore the Cold War itself—was a sandpile ready to slide. All it took to make that happen were a few more grains of sand. The people who dropped them were not in charge of superpowers or movements or religions: they were ordinary people with simple priorities who saw, seized, and sometimes stumbled into opportunities. In doing so, they caused a collapse no one could stop. Their "leaders" had little choice but to follow.

One particular leader, however, did so in a distinctive way. He ensured that the great 1989 revolution was the first one ever in which almost no blood was shed. There were no guillotines, no heads on pikes, no officially sanctioned mass murders. People did die, but in remarkably small numbers for the size and significance of what was happening. In both its ends *and* its means, then, this revolution became a triumph of hope. It did so chiefly because Mikhail Gorbachev chose not to act, but rather to be acted upon.

What role did Gorbachev play in the upheavals of 1989?

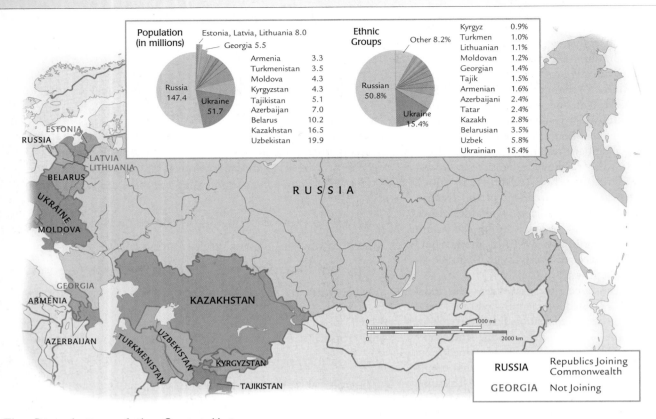

Population (in millions)	
Estonia, Latvia, Lithuania	8.0
Georgia	5.5
Russia	147.4
Ukraine	51.7
Armenia	3.3
Turkmenistan	3.5
Moldova	4.3
Kyrgyzstan	4.3
Tajikistan	5.1
Azerbaijan	7.0
Belarus	10.2
Kazakhstan	16.5
Uzbekistan	19.9

Ethnic Groups	
Other	8.2%
Russian	50.8%
Ukraine	15.4%
Kyrgyz	0.9%
Turkmen	1.0%
Lithuanian	1.1%
Moldovan	1.2%
Georgian	1.4%
Tajik	1.5%
Armenian	1.6%
Azerbaijani	2.4%
Tatar	2.4%
Kazakh	2.8%
Belarusian	3.5%
Uzbek	5.8%
Ukrainian	15.4%

RUSSIA	Republics Joining Commonwealth
GEORGIA	Not Joining

The Dissolution of the Soviet Union, 1991 This map shows the division of territory resulting from the disintegration of the former Soviet Union.

In the end, no one, including the once-dominant Russians, wanted to save the old Soviet Union. Gorbachev had unleashed the forces of revolution, and he—along with the USSR itself—became revolution's victim. The long Cold War was over (see Exploring the Past on page 611). In 1999, Gorbachev would look back and explain, "Communism—as the inventors of the theory imagined it—never existed anywhere. . . . What did exist was Stalinist socialism. That system had exhausted itself and was doomed to disappear." The map above shows what became of the former Soviet Union. Most of the republics within the old structure joined the new Commonwealth of Independent States, a loose confederation. A few republics, such as the Baltic states, broke away altogether.

Life After the Collapse of Communism

After the celebrations in the former communist bloc ended, people awoke to new, dismaying realities. In his 1990 inaugural address, Václav Havel had issued a warning that applied just as much to other nations in Eastern Europe as it did to Czechoslovakia: "Our country is not flourish-ing. . . . Entire branches of industry are producing goods which are of no interest to anyone, while we are lacking the things we need. A state which calls itself a workers' state humiliates and exploits workers. Our obsolete economy is wasting the little energy we have available. . . . We have polluted our soil, our rivers and forests." Leaders in Eastern Europe and the former USSR faced a crucial problem: how to institute capitalism and liberal democracy in nations with little experience of either.

The economic transition proceeded quickly in Poland and Hungary, but more moderately in Bulgaria, Romania, and Albania. Almost everywhere, however, it brought pain. When governments closed the doors of inefficient state industries or sold them, many workers lost their jobs. The removal of price controls also provoked instant inflation that especially hurt those living on fixed incomes. Some people took advantage of new opportunities that came with the transition; for example, former communist officials in particular benefited from lucrative insider deals. Several cities—such as Prague in the Czech Republic, with its domes, spires, cobblestone alleys, pubs, cafés, and secondhand bookstores—also fared well with heightened tourism. But too many people had let them-

Eastern Europe

selves expect more than the eradication of communism could deliver. In the face of widespread bitterness, governments struggled to gain stability and institute unpopular but apparently necessary economic policies such as closing state industries and allowing prices to rise.

In the former Soviet Union, people were unaccustomed to democratic politics, managers were unfamiliar with the market economy, and many officials resisted reform. The economy stumbled badly. Year after year, **The former Soviet Union** Russia's economic output decreased, as did its population. Removing price controls and privatizing industry had eliminated lines in front of stores and created economic opportunities for some. However, prices skyrocketed beyond the reach of average consumers, the Russian currency lost its value, and some 30 percent of the population struggled to subsist on approximately $1 per day.

The collapse of communism proved particularly stressful for Russian men. From Communist Party officials and generals to physicists and professors, men who had once enjoyed status, security, and relative wealth lost these benefits in the turmoil of the postcommunist era. Life expectancy for Russian men plummeted to fifty-eight years, a decline that was "the steepest and most severe ever documented anywhere in the world" according to one researcher. Alcoholism more than tripled in the years after the collapse. For women, the story was different. Although many women suffered from unemployment when state industries folded, perhaps their losses were not so great and were eased by new opportunities. In any case, they seemed to manage the transition better than men, maintaining a life expectancy of seventy-three years. Indeed, a growing elite of women entered managerial positions and earned increasing salaries.

Boris Yeltsin retained a precarious hold on power as president of Russia and, despite illnesses, was reelected in 1996. But the Russian people **Yeltsin's problems** resisted his inconsistent efforts at reform. In the parliament, with its tangled array of different political parties, fragmentation ruled. Moreover, "reformed" communists retained positions of power, as they did in Eastern European states such as Serbia, Bulgaria, and Lithuania. With control disintegrating, lawlessness—from street crime to organized crime—rapidly spread. By 1998, the fumbling Yeltsin had lost his popularity and much of his power as the Russian economy verged on collapse.

When he resigned on the last day of 1999, turning power over to Vladimir Putin, many Russians yearned for the power, order, and stability that communism had brought. While rich oligarchic figures and organized crime still sapped Russia's wealth, Putin, supported by an increasingly loyal bureaucracy and some genuine popularity, provided some functional stability and considerable respect within and outside Russia. He effectively supported Russia's evolving market economy and legal system. Although he moved against the independent media and undermined political opposition, he provided a welcome relief from Yeltsin, whose uneven and unpopular reign witnessed the collapse of basic industries and social services along with the growth of crime and widespread corruption.

In 2008, Putin gave up the presidency to his protégé, Dmitry Medvedev (1965–), and moved to the post of prime minister. By then, political stability and increasing wealth from oil and gas had propelled Russia's economy forward. While no longer a superpower, the country—described by Putin as a "managed democracy"—increasingly acted like a regional power ready to assert itself in disputes with neighbors.

Nationalism Unleashed

Despite its drawbacks, communism had provided many people with a sense of unity and security. Its fall opened a void that nationalistic sentiments rose to fill. As had often been the case in nineteenth- and twentieth-century history, nationalism provoked heated conflict along with a feeling of belonging. Ethnic and cultural struggles raged in several republics of the former Soviet Union. In Azerbaijan, the Azerbaijanis and Armenians clashed. The most violent outburst came in secessionist Chechnya, where Russians fought an unpopular war with Chechnyans demanding their independence. The indecisive two-year conflict cost some 80,000 deaths and 250,000 wounded, although the Chechnyans gained many of their goals. In 1999, another draining war broke out between Chechnyans and Russians.

In Eastern Europe also, nationalistic, ethnic, and religious rivalries opened old wounds and created new divisions. The maps on page 614 reveal some of these problems. In 1993, the Slovak minority in Czechoslovakia, pushed by ambitious Slovak politicians, voted for independence. Czechoslovakia reluctantly agreed to divide itself into the Czech Republic and Slovakia. In Romania, ethnic friction between the Romanian majority and the Hungarian minority flared up.

The bloodiest conflicts broke out in Yugoslavia, where chaotic civil wars marked the disintegration of that country. The six republics that constituted Yugoslavia had been held together under communist rule since World War II (see bottom map **Civil wars in Yugoslavia** on page 614). With the death of Tito in 1980 and the fall of communism in the rest of Eastern Europe in 1989, Yugoslavia began to crack. In 1991, Slovenians, angered by the refusal of the dominant Serbian communists to liberalize economic and political policies, detached themselves from Yugoslavia. Peoples in Croatia, Bosnia-Herzegovina, and Macedonia

Disintegration of Czechoslovakia and Yugoslavia,

1991–2007 **These maps respectively show the division of Czechoslovakia into the Czech Republic and Slovakia and the disintegration of Yugoslavia.**

the mostly Muslim Bosnians and other peoples who lived as minorities in these areas.

The war for a Greater Serbia raged with appalling brutality. The worst fighting took place in Bosnia-Herzegovina. On this bloody battlefield, the Serbs initiated a policy of **ethnic cleansing,** driving Muslim Bosnians from their homes; placing them in concentration camps; and raping, murdering, and starving them. In 1992, a Serb guard at one concentration camp proudly explained, "We won't waste our bullets on them. . . . They have no roof. There is sun and rain, cold nights, and beatings two times a day. We give them no food and no water. They will starve like animals." A survivor reported seeing "corpses piled one on top of another. . . . The bodies eventually were gathered with a forklift . . . this happened almost every day." The photograph on page 615 shows some of the hastily created graves in Bosnia-Herzegovina's capital city, Sarajevo.

The Bosnians, supported by aid from the Islamic world, fought back desperately for more than four years. Only a Western embargo and NATO intervention brought an uneasy end to the violence and peace accords in 1996. The conflict had killed 250,000 people, displaced three million, and left 800,000 antipersonnel mines embedded in the land. Moreover, peace still depended on the continued presence of international troops. In 1997, a NATO commander in Bosnia warned that "if we withdraw our forces, there will be slaughter in the streets" and predicted that complete recovery would take decades.

Just two years later, brutality like that unleashed in Bosnia rose in nearby Kosovo—another region within Yugoslavia. Serbians, led by President Slobodan Milosevic, met rising demands for independence from the Albanian majority in Kosovo with overwhelming military force. Renewing the practice of ethnic cleansing, Serbian troops slaughtered thousands of Kosovar Albanians and forced hundreds of thousands to flee to neighboring states.

After diplomacy failed, NATO unleashed its military resources for the first time in its fifty-year history. Member air forces, led by the United States, opened a three-month bombing campaign on Serbian forces and on Serbia itself. Milosevic finally agreed to terms and withdrew his forces. Protected by NATO troops, the Kosovar Albanians streamed back to their badly damaged land, bringing with them few hopes for ethnic cooperation in the region. In 2000, Vojislav Kostunica defeated Milosevic in Yugoslavia's presidential election, and soon Milosevic found himself standing trial for war crimes before an international tribunal in The Hague, Netherlands.

followed suit. War soon erupted between the religiously Orthodox Serbs, attempting to expand the territory they controlled, and their longtime Catholic Croatian rivals to the northwest. Trapped between the two antagonists were

REPERCUSSIONS AND REALIGNMENTS IN THE WEST

CIVIL WAR IN BOSNIA-HERZEGOVINA The dead and the suffering from the civil war in Bosnia-Herzegovina mingle in a cemetery in January 1993.

Repercussions from the collapse of communism spread around the world. As communism lost its credibility, nations still committed to the Soviet model, such as Cuba and North Korea, were left isolated. Capitalism gained renewed respect and even inspired awe in both the Western and non-Western worlds. For many, the collapse of communism in Eastern Europe and the USSR signified the final triumph of capitalism. With the end of the Cold War, the contours of domestic and international politics began to shift.

The United States Unchallenged and Germany Rising

With the former Soviet forces in decline and the Warsaw Pact dissolved, the United States and Germany rose in stature. The United States emerged as the world's only military superpower. It flexed its military muscle in 1991 by leading a United Nations–authorized coalition that repelled Iraq's invasion of tiny, neighboring Kuwait. In the short war, the U.S.-dominated coalition easily defeated Saddam Hussein's forces. In 2001 and 2003, it again demonstrated its military might, in Afghanistan and Iraq. The U.S. also contributed to international peacekeeping efforts by sending forces to troubled areas such as Somalia, Haiti, Bosnia, and Kosovo. Despite years of large budget deficits and apparent decline, the U.S. economy rebounded in the mid-1990s to a position of leadership that inspired envy the world over.

Germany's influence and potential also rose. In 1990, German unification confirmed Germany as a European and world economic leader—in exports, in balance of trade, and in gross domestic product. Emerging victorious from the first national elections, the former West German chancellor Helmut Kohl and his conservative Christian Democrats vowed to bring eastern Germany's economy up to the high standard enjoyed in the West. The costs of the transition mushroomed far beyond expectations; as state industries collapsed in the East, unemployment and the cost of welfare benefits shot

> "We won't waste our bullets on them. . . . They have no roof. There is sun and rain, cold nights, and beatings two times a day. We give them no food and no water. They will starve like animals."

up. Nevertheless, the reunified state still ranked as the top economic power in Europe. Clearly, Germany stood poised to exert new influence in Eastern Europe and the European Community.

Politics Shift to the Right

In the United States, Germany, and elsewhere in the West, politics shifted to the Right. The reasons behind this change were complex, but economic forces played a major role. Despite the continued overall prosperity enjoyed in the West, many nations suffered from high unemployment and declining growth rates during the 1980s and 1990s. In part, the free flow of trade and capital had created a new international labor market that operated outside the control of national governments and labor unions, resulting in the loss of many business opportunities and manufacturing jobs in the West. As global economic competition stiffened and nations struggled to stay in the game, many people blamed costly social programs—often supported by the political Left—for their nation's economic problems. The changes wrought by the postindustrial society, especially the shift from manufacturing to services, also weakened labor unions—the Left's traditional source of support. The previous sense that government was obligated to provide for rich and poor alike—a belief that had fueled the post–World War II welfare state—

faded along with memories of those older times. Government regulation of economic affairs and the cost of social programs came under question everywhere.

Conservatives began scoring record successes at the polls. Citing the apparent triumph of capitalism, they attacked expensive programs and sometimes fanned the flames of anti-immigrant sentiments, playing on the popular perception that foreign-born newcomers took jobs. France's right-wing National Front, led by Jean-Marie LePen, attained particular prominence by blaming immigrants from North Africa and elsewhere for France's economic problems. The traditional communist parties in Western Europe declined, and socialist parties, whether in power or not, moderated their policies to shore up their popularity. In Austria, Italy, Germany, and Spain, conservative and right-wing politicians gained popularity. Even when traditional parties of the Left regained power, as they did in many countries during the late 1990s, their platforms were more muted and conservative than in the past. No other nation ventured as far down the conservative path as Great Britain and the United States. In Great Britain, the Conservatives led by Margaret Thatcher and her successor dominated throughout most of the 1980s and 1990s, cutting taxes, attacking social programs, and selling state-owned industries to private investors. When the Labor Party finally came to power in Great Britain in 1997, it pursued only mild changes. In the United States, Republicans rolled back liberal programs and Democrats scrambled to adopt more conservative platforms. The sharply conservative administration of George W. Bush came to power in 2001. Mostly in the name of economic development and the war against terrorism, it aggressively pursued many policies initiated by the Reagan administration in the 1980s, including loosening environmental protections, reducing social programs, lowering taxes in ways that favored the wealthy and corporations, increasing military spending, and cutting into the protection of civil liberties.

By the mid-1990s, this conservatism had merged with a broader questioning of traditional politics in the West. As anxieties over economic problems intensified and as scandals rocked governments, people voted for unknowns or stopped voting altogether. Especially in France, Italy, and Austria, candidates who voiced disenchantment with the standard politics of the Left and Right attracted popular support.

In 2008, elections swept Barack Obama into office as president of the United States. Backed by national and international popularity, as well as a more liberal admin-

Questioning traditional politics

istration, Obama promised to reverse some of his predecessor's conservative policies. Whether this new focus represents a broader political change in the West remains to be seen. All these shifts in domestic politics gained much attention. However, events beyond state borders would soon overshadow these internal concerns throughout the West.

Toward European Integration

The end of the Cold War may have left the United States the world's sole superpower, but it also strengthened the movement toward unity that had been unfolding in Europe since the 1950s.

In 1992, the 12 members of the European Community (EC) eliminated all major internal barriers to trade, the flow of capital, and the movement of people. That same year, the EC joined with the seven-member European Free Trade Association to form the European Economic Area, creating the world's largest trading bloc and paving the way for several new countries to seek full membership (see map on page 617). Between 1999 and 2004, a number of Eastern European nations, such as Poland, the Czech Republic, Hungary, Lithuania, and Slovakia joined NATO and were accepted for membership in the European Union. Also in 1992, France and Germany formed a joint army corps, the European Corps, open to other participants in the European Union. With the Maastricht Treaty of 1992 (which changed the name of the EC to the European Union), most members of the **European Union (EU)** agreed to establish a common currency (the **Euro**) controlled by a central European bank by 1999. The plan required great economic discipline, above all controlling the large yearly budget deficits most nations ran. By 2002, people in most countries of the European Union carried Euros in their pockets, wallets, and purses.

The potential of the European Union seemed tremendous. In 2011, the twenty-seven member nations had more than 491 million inhabitants and a combined gross national product greater than that of the United States. Perhaps in response to the growing power of the European Union, the United States joined with Mexico and Canada in 1994 to create a new free-trade zone—the **North American Free Trade Agreement (NAFTA).** Not everyone embraced the idea of such alliances. Many Europeans opposed further integration, clinging to national preferences and warning against the dangers of giving up sovereignty to an international body of bureaucrats. To be sure, the European nations had great difficulty

OPINION

What consequences flowed from the collapse of communism outside Eastern Europe and the Soviet Union?

joining forces to put down the crisis in Bosnia, but their joint action as part of a NATO force to quell the violence in Kosovo in 1999 led to a vow by the leaders of fifteen European countries to make the European Union a military power for the first time. The Union adopted plans to build its own military of up to 60,000 troops. Moreover, by that same year, the European Union had opened its arms to possible membership for Turkey as well as virtually all of central and eastern Europe. Despite many reservations, most Europeans seemed willing to cooperate. The statement by a German woman early in 2002 reflected the sense of many: "I feel German, but also European."

In 2005, French and Dutch voters rejected a newly drafted constitution designed to strengthen the European Union. This outcome signaled the voters' broad ambivalence about taking further steps toward European integration and, in particular, their concerns about welcoming the populous, Muslim, and relatively poor Turkey into the Union—as well as their worries about a potential influx of immigrants and migrant workers. However, in 2009, member states finally ratified the Lisbon Treaty designed to streamline European Union institutions.

THE WORLD AND THE WEST FROM A GLOBAL PERSPECTIVE

The European Union, 2011 **This map shows the European Union in 2011 and identifies nations that have applied for membership.**

As they took further steps toward unity, Europeans had more in mind than competing with the United States. They also knew that they had to meet the changes sweeping through much of the Western and non-Western worlds. Since the end of colonialism, European nations could no longer rely on colonies as controllable markets. By the 1990s, all nations faced a global economy marked by the presence of multinational enterprises beyond the command of individual states. Waves of huge corporate buyouts and mergers increased this concentration of economic power. By 2000, small handfuls of these corporations controlled more than half the global market in oil, automobiles, electronics, multimedia, and personal computers. Westerners also confronted new competitors, from Latin

Globalization

America to East Asia, who wielded growing economic and political clout. In addition, various international agencies and organizations, such as the International Monetary Fund, the World Bank, and the World Trade Organization, wielded great economic clout over financial aid and international commerce that affected governments, corporations, and ordinary people throughout the world. Finally, the pace of global economic integration and change had quickened, complicating international business for everyone. Certain technological advances, above all the development of the computer, the Internet, and genetic engineering, had the potential of creating the equivalent of a third industrial revolution.

By 2000, the mushrooming use of computers and the Internet in business and commerce had already transformed many economies. Increasingly, goods could be designed in one country, financed internationally, produced overseas, sold world-wide, and serviced through phones and the Internet from numerous locations. All these changes tended to blend local and national markets into global markets and called into question the very issue of national identity. Even in the poorest nations, signs of this **globalization** proliferated. As just one example, workers in new manufacturing plants owned by multinational corporations wore the same brand-name athletic shoes and drank the same beverages as their Western counterparts. Moreover, thanks to films, television, radio, computers, cellular phones, fax machines, satellites, and travel, ideas and images flowed across international borders as easily as money, goods, and services, further blurring the distinctions between cultures.

East Asia and the Rise of the Pacific Rim

The greatest challenge to the West's economic dominance came from East Asia. Since the 1960s, Japan had grown into a major economic power. Year after year, this island nation enjoyed the world's largest favorable balance of trade. By the 1980s, it boasted the world's second-largest gross domestic product. A giant in automobile production and electronics, Japan replaced the United States as the world's topmost creditor nation. Although reversals brought Japan's economic momentum to a virtual standstill during the 1990s, and even a decline during the 2001 and 2002 world economic slowdown, the nation still led the world in per capita gross domestic product.

In the 1990s, other regions on the periphery of the Pacific Ocean attracted wealthy investors with their political stability, cheap and disciplined labor force, and openness to capitalism. Multinational corporations opened offices and made investments throughout this so-called Pacific Rim. Hong Kong, Taiwan, South Korea, Malaysia, Indonesia, and Singapore all boomed, drawing manufacturing jobs away from Europe and the United States in industries such as electronics, textiles, plastics, metals, computers, automobiles, and leather goods. Visitors found thriving cities such as Kuala Lumpur in Malaysia—with the world's two tallest buildings marking its skyline and its high-rise apartment houses serviced by climate-controlled malls—"unrecognizable to anyone who knew it 30 years ago." On the outskirts of such glittering urban centers, satellite communities and industrial parks rose where jungles used to thrive. Similar developments transformed other great cities of East Asia, from Singapore and Bangkok to Jakarta and Hong Kong.

Yet no country experienced a more stunning economic transformation than China. In 1978, the successors to Mao, led by Deng Xiaoping (1904–1997), had initiated the Four

Most Muslim leaders and clerics rejected violence and terrorism.

Modernizations program to foster rapid economic development and greater productivity. The program departed dramatically from Mao's economic policies by decentralizing decision making and introducing a market-oriented economy into the countryside and, later, into some urban areas. By the mid-1980s, these policies had opened China to tourism and foreign investment, stimulated new economic growth, and created greater economic freedom within China. Agreements with Japan and the United States rapidly expanded trade as well. For the first time, Chinese farmers produced a surplus of food for export. In certain areas of the country, particularly the New Economic Zones in the southeast, capitalistic investments and manufacturing practices spurred high rates of growth. By the first decade of the twenty-first century, China had become the world's most important manufacturing nation and a major player in international finance.

The economic transformation of China

Nevertheless, China made these economic reforms without corresponding political reforms. Whether that practice could continue was called into question in 1989, when students and intellectuals demanding political reform organized massive demonstrations in Beijing. After a brief standoff, the government, supported by China's rural population and most of the army, violently crushed the demonstrations and jailed the leaders. In the years that followed, as China's leadership aged and pressures for political reform persisted, analysts watched carefully for change within the great Asian country. By the first decade of the twenty-first century, China stood as a rapidly growing economic power with tremendous political potential on the international stage.

The Challenge of Islam

Other areas of the world presented different challenges to the West. In particular, several Islamic nations in North Africa and the Middle East developed a new assertiveness and a willingness to make their dissatisfaction with Western ways known. They had long resented the former Western imperial powers' condescension toward them. The West's support of Israel only irritated an already raw nerve.

The emergence of combative leaders in states such as Libya, Syria, Iran, and Iraq—some of whom advocated Islamic or Pan-Arab unity against Israel and Western influence—stepped up tensions further. Moreover, in nations from Algeria and Turkey to Afghanistan and Pakistan, Islamic fundamentalists had gained strength. Western secular notions such as individualism, capitalism, materialism, commercialism, gender equality, and sexual freedom were flooding across airwaves and borders into the Islamic world.

These notions seemed to insult and threaten fundamentalists' traditional and religious beliefs. Condemning Westernization and the secularization of life in their countries, they demanded a return to traditional symbols of their conservative views, such as the veil that they required women to wear in public. Iran's fundamentalist leader Ayatollah Ruholla Khomeini (1900–1989), who had come to power as the leader of a revolution in 1979, epitomized rejection of the West. "With the Qur'an in one hand and a gun in the other, defend your dignity and honor" against the "oppressive powers" of the West, he told his nation in 1980. He especially castigated the United States, labeling it the "great Satan" because it had supported Israel and had intervened several times in the region. Finally, many Middle Eastern Islamic states possessed the crude-oil reserves on which the West and Asia depended, and they used the precious resource to command international respect and attention. The potential of Middle Eastern states to pull Western nations into armed conflict was made all too clear in 1990 when Iraq invaded oil-rich Kuwait, prompting a UN-backed military response, in 2003 with the U.S.-led invasion of Iraq, and with the persisting violence in Afghanistan that threatened to spread into neighboring Pakistan.

International Terrorism and War

On the morning of September 11, 2001, coordinated teams of terrorists hijacked four American airliners. They slammed two of the planes into Manhattan's famed World Trade Center (Twin Towers) office buildings and a third into the Pentagon, headquarters of the U.S. Department of Defense in Washington D.C. Passengers apparently brought down the fourth plane before it could reach its target. Nearly 3,000 people lost their lives in the attacks, most of them perishing when the Twin Towers collapsed later that morning. Blame soon fell on the shoulders of a well-financed international terrorist group, **al-Qaeda,** which professed a radical version of Islamic fundamentalism, under the leadership of Osama bin Laden.

The forces behind this tragedy and the responses to it were complex, and historians can make only tentative analyses at this point. However, analysts point to the intensifying anger toward the West among radical Islamic fundamentalists as one major underlying force for the attack. Islamic fundamentalists had long lamented what they saw as the West's corruption of regimes within the Islamic world. Authoritarian governments that fundamentalists viewed as too secular and too connected to the West ruled most Islamic states. Fundamentalism found growing support among people who were outraged by this supposed perversion of Islamic law and who were enraged at the reality of masses of people living far below the wealthy elites in these countries.

Most Muslim leaders and clerics rejected violence and terrorism. But against the overwhelming military, politi-

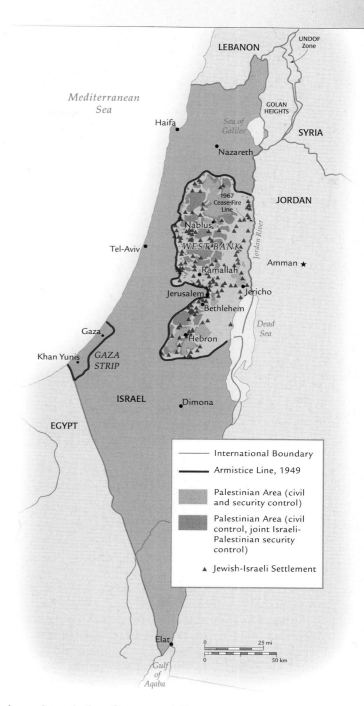

Israel and the Occupied Territories, 2011 **This map shows Israel, the occupied territories of the West Bank, and the Gaza Strip. It also identifies areas of varying Palestinian and Israeli control, as well as Jewish-Israeli settlements.**

cal, and economic forces that Western nations and non-fundamentalist Islamic states could marshal, terrorism seemed a legitimate and even religiously justified way to assert some fundamentalists' point of view. For a group such as al-Qaeda, terrorism might catalyze widespread

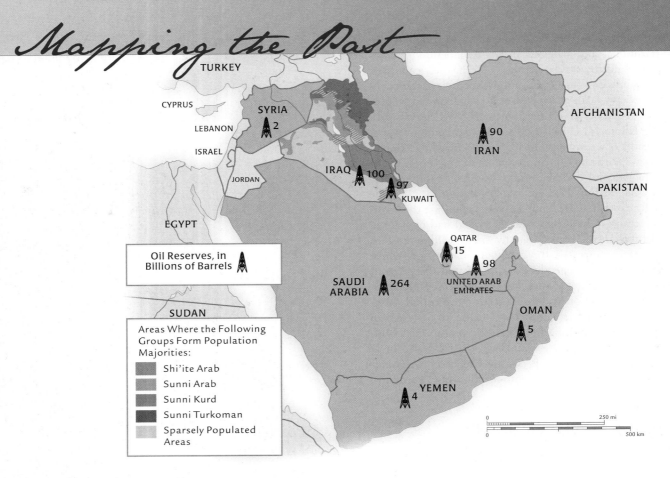

Mapping the Past

The Middle East and Iraq, 2003 This map shows the Middle East, estimated oil reserves in several nations, and ethno-religious groups in Iraq at the beginning of the U.S.-led invasion in 2003. In what ways might the war in Iraq change this region?

fundamentalist revolts that would bring down "corrupt" governments in the Islamic world.

A second force came in the form of the festering Israeli-Palestinian conflict. This struggle deepened Islamic funda-

Israeli-Palestinian conflict

mentalists' rage toward the West—in particular the United States. In various ways, Israel and the Arab world had been at odds since the mid-twentieth century (see Chapter 25). Moreover, Israel had long been perceived as a Western outpost in the Middle East. The close relationship between Israel and the United States encouraged that perception, and many held the United States partly responsible for the sufferings of Palestinians. For example, al-Qaeda's Osama bin Laden railed against "the crusader-Jewish alliance, led by the United States and Israel."

Fueled by these forces and religious enthusiasm, terrorist organizations grew in the 1980s and 1990s and adopted bolder tactics aimed at both military and civilian targets. Some of these groups gained strength and reach through financial support by wealthy patrons. The growing avail-

ability of modern communications and military technology also enhanced their power.

During the first years of the new century, tensions grew. After efforts to forge a U.S.-sponsored settlement of the Israeli-Palestinian dispute collapsed in 2000, a new, more deadly round of violence erupted between Israelis and Palestinians (see map on page 619). Day after day, pictures, reports, and stories of the conflict focusing on Palestinian deaths at the hands of the Israelis spread across the Islamic world. In Israel, suicidal terrorists bombed shopping centers, restaurants, and buses. Within Palestinian areas, the death tolls from missiles, planes, and guns fired by the well-armed and trained Israeli forces rose dramatically. By 2004, much of the violence had subsided, and in 2005 Israel unilaterally withdrew from the Gaza Strip. However, in 2006 an election gave the militant Islamic organization Hamas—considered a terrorist group by many in the West—governing power in Palestine, raising tensions again. That same year, a war broke out in Lebanon between Israel and Hezbollah, a radical Islamic organization apparently backed by Iran and Syria. In 2008, Israel, citing a growing number of rocket attacks on its territory, invaded the Gaza Strip, now controlled by Hamas.

The devastating attacks of September 11, 2001, against the United States were intended to strike at symbols of U.S. "imperial" power. The United States answered the attacks by declaring war against terrorism. President George W. Bush vowed to pursue terrorists wherever they lurked in the world and punish those who harbored them. Drawing on the sympathy and support of many nations, the U.S. military launched a massive aerial assault on al-Qaeda strongholds in Afghanistan, as well as on the Taliban, the radical fundamentalist regime that ruled the mountainous nation (see map on page 620).

Afghanistan had a history of strife. During the 1980s, the Afghani people had endured a long, bloody war against

War in Afghanistan

Soviet invaders. The impoverished, war-torn country again suffered from the turmoil following the Soviet withdrawal in the late 1980s. In the mid-1990s, the Taliban seized power in most of Afghanistan, and there al-Qaeda found a home.

In 2001 and 2002, the U.S. military, using anti-Taliban Afghan forces for much of the campaign on the ground, crushed most of the al-Qaeda and Taliban forces harbored within Afghanistan. However, President George W. Bush declared the war on terrorism far from over, pointing to the possibility that other terrorists and regimes might acquire and wield weapons of mass destruction. He warned that other states might also feel the force of U.S. military power in the future.

In March 2003, the United States took another step in the name of its war on terror. The U.S. military, backed by British forces and the token support of other nations, attacked Iraq. During the months leading up to the war,

War in Iraq

the Bush administration, building on fears stemming from the September 11, 2001, terrorist attacks, cited the development and existence of terrifying weapons of mass destruction (chemical, biological, and nuclear) in Iraq that threatened the United States and the whole international community. Administration officials also claimed that Iraqi leader Saddam Hussein's dictatorial regime had links with international terrorist organizations such as al-Qaeda. The United States, officials said, had a duty to rid the world of Iraq's violent, brutal regime. Under these justifications for invading Iraq lay a vision within the Bush administration of aggressively and, if necessary, single-handedly reforming oil-rich Iraq. Other authoritarian regimes in the strategic Middle East, administration officials hoped, would then transform themselves into democracies or at least reform. These new regimes would become friends of the United States and its allies as well as stable sources of oil (see map on page 620).

Within weeks, U.S. and British air and ground forces overwhelmed Iraqi defenders and toppled Saddam Hussein and the Baathist Party, which had ruled Iraq with an iron fist for more than twenty years. Although President Bush declared victory in June 2003, achieving peace, stability, or international acclaim in the months that followed proved daunting. The United States, backed by Great Britain, refused to cede authority over the stabilization and rebuilding of Iraq to the United Nations. Many potential allies who had opposed the war in the first place—including France, Germany, Russia, India, Turkey, and most Arab states—refused to lend a hand under those conditions. The cost and responsibility for the process fell squarely on the shoulders of the United States and Great Britain, though other allies provided some support. Within Iraq, guerrilla and suicide attacks steadily raised the death toll into the thousands each month. Looting and sabotage further undermined efforts to establish security and promote recovery. Some of these problems are suggested by the image below. The photograph shows a United States Marine sitting in a schoolroom below a damaged mural of the country he and his fellow soldiers are occupying and trying to pacify. He is part of a military operation in western Iraq, which in 2005 was still a stronghold of insurgent activities. In the following two years, violent insurgent attacks increased. By 2007, Iraq seemed on the verge of civil war.

THE OCCUPATION OF IRAQ A United States Marine rests below a map of Iraq in an Iraqi schoolroom.

Then & Now
Terrorist Activities

Terrorism is not new. During the French Revolution, the term was used to describe the systematic state of terror inflicted against the population. Terrorist organizations grew alarmingly in the 1980s and 1990s and adopted bolder tactics aimed at both military and civilian targets. On September 11, 2001, terrorists struck targets in the United States, killing thousands of people. Today, more than ten years later, we are starting to gain some historical perspective on what has come to be known as 9/11. Several important developments—including wars, changes in international affairs, and altered domestic policies—flowed from 9/11 and reactions to it.

Moreover, U.S. ambitions to usher in a new, democratic government met with mounting discord among factions within Iraq. Historic rivalries between majority Arabs and minority Kurds in the north, and between the majority Shi'ites and minority Sunnis in the center and south, stymied efforts to create a new, effective government (see map on page 620). Finally, despite the eventual capture of Saddam Hussein in December 2003 and extensive searches, U.S. investigators could find no weapons of mass destruction or links to the sort of international terrorist organizations that carried out the September 11, 2001, plot.

Only time will enable us to make firm judgments about the U.S. actions in Iraq and the policies underlying them. However, these actions and policies may prove to have greater historical significance than the toppling of Saddam Hussein's regime. First, the Bush administration set what many critics worldwide considered dangerous precedent by initiating a **preemptive war,** based on the *assertion* that Iraq had imminent plans to attack the United States, or, even worse, a "preventive war," based on the *possibility* that Iraq might attack sometime in the distant future. In these relatively nonthreatening circumstances, such a war violated long-established rules of international relations and dashed ambitions of those hoping to strengthen international barriers to the outbreak of wars.

Preemptive war, unilateralism, and the occupation

Second, the Bush administration not only failed to win important UN and international support for the war but also appeared to punish those who disagreed with its foreign policies—including longtime major allies such as France and Germany. Indeed, the United States seemed to discard the principles of internationalism that had informed global diplomacy since the end of World War II. In place of those principles, it appeared to favor a kind of **unilateralism** in which the world's only superpower pursued its own interests regardless of its allies' views and interests. The administration's abandonment of the Kyoto Protocol, which sought to limit global-warming emissions; its plans to develop an antiballistic missile shield and a new class of nuclear weapons; its desertion of international efforts to strengthen rules against biological weapons, land mines, and small arms; and its attacks on the International Criminal Court all added to the impression that the United States had decided to go it alone.

Third, the way the U.S. government justified its invasion of Iraq and what many in the world saw as the destructive mishandling of the occupation that followed diminished the sympathy and support for the United States that had been offered after the September 11 attacks. Moreover, the bloodshed and political turmoil that reigned in Iraq year after year during the presence of U.S.-led coalition forces served to increase the regional influence of Iran, still ruled by a fundamentalist regime that now embarked on a policy to develop its own atomic resources. These developments, along with veiled threats by the U.S. government to launch strikes against Iran, cast a darkening shadow over the Middle East.

Starting in 2008, some of the violence within Iraq abated. The new president of the United States, Barack Obama, riding a wave of national and international popularity, signaled changes in U.S. policy in Iraq and committed to the withdrawal of U.S. forces by 2011. But already, with U.S. troops and money diverted to Iraq since 2003, violence and instability were worsening in neighboring Afghanistan, where Taliban and al-Qaeda forces had gained new life and threatened the weak central government that relied heavily on financial and military aid from the West.

Terrorism and the war in Afghanistan also had implications for neighboring Pakistan. This pre-

Crisis over Kashmir

dominantly Muslim nation had long-simmering problems with India, a primarily Hindu country, over Kashmir. These two nations' struggle for control over Kashmir (see map here) had sparked armed conflict several times over previous decades. The growing threat of terrorism made the area even more volatile. In 2002, the two sides again seemed on the verge of war. This time, however, both Pakistan and India had demonstrated to each other and the world their ability to use nuclear weapons. In 2008 a terrorist organization, apparently based in Pakistan, launched a deadly suicidal attack on one of India's major cities, Mumbai, an event that again threatened peace in the region. By the next year, the ability of Pakistan's central government to exercise control over the nation was in question, especially in its northern and western lands, where openly aggressive Taliban and pro-Taliban forces had found sanctuary and were gaining strength.

Afghanistan, Kashmir, and South-Central Asia, 2002
This map shows Afghanistan, Kashmir, and the surrounding areas in 2002.

Upheavals in North Africa and the Middle East

Turbulence in the region was not simply about terrorism. In 2009, people swirled through the streets of Tehran, Iran, in massive protests against the government and its handling of elections. While the regime was seriously threatened, it eventually cracked down brutally against the protesters. In January 2011, growing demonstrations against the long-standing dictatorial regime in Tunisia led to that government's fall. That upheaval soon spread to other countries in the region. In February, massive demonstrations broke out in Egypt. Within weeks, President Mubarak, who had held office for decades, was forced out along with several of his supporters.

By March 2011, demonstrations had rocked the authoritarian regimes in Bahrain and Yemen, while in Libya a revolution against Muammar Qaddafi, who had ruled the country for more than forty years, resulted in an armed conflict, splitting the country apart and leading to the partial

intervention of Western powers under the authorization of the United Nations and the Arab League. Other nations in the region, from Morocco and Algeria to Iraq and Syria, felt the challenge of unrest and upheavals within their borders.

While each case was different and reflected its own history, there were some commonalities in these upheavals, often referred to as the "Arab Spring."

The "Arab Spring"

First, most were directed at authoritarian regimes without any democratic component or with only "sham" democratic institutions. Second, most protesters were young women and men, many of them educated but unable to find good jobs. Third, a sense of humiliation and suffering from powerlessness often fueled passions underlying the upheavals. Finally, modern communications—from televised news reports to cell phones, emails, Facebook, and Twitter—played important roles in organizing demonstrations and keeping people abreast of events.

In various ways that drew the attention and involvement of the West, much of the region from the southern shores of the Mediterranean to India suffered from instability, threats of conflict, and outbreaks of violence. The roots of these problems reach far back into the twentieth century and are entwined with the legacy of the West's imperialism, periodic wars within the region, the world's growing reliance on the area's oil deposits, and complex sectarian politics within Islamic states. But to many people around the world, it seemed clear that the conflicts, poverty, and political tensions of this strategically crucial region had greater global significance than ever before. The images of peace and security that many people had envisioned after the fall of communism gave way to a new sense of vulnerability in a world that seemed to be slipping out of control.

Across Borders: Cultural Conflict and Convergence

All these developments—in the Middle East, North Africa, and East Asia—revealed the West's inextricable ties with the non-Western world. They also posed new challenges to the dominance that the West had enjoyed for so long. Perhaps most important, they illustrated a problem that spread

Resistance to globalization

well beyond any one region: the chafing of local cultures against global and even national influences. On one level, globalization meant the invasion of Western culture into centuries-old but vulnerable non-Western cultural legacies. On another level, nationalism and religious fundamentalism revealed a deep resistance to globalization. The struggles of minorities to retain their own sense of identity in the face of demands for national and religious conformity within their own nations reflected a parallel resistance to outside meddling. In one terrifying variation of this pattern, in the central African state of Rwanda, ethnic Hutu extremists slaughtered more than 500,000 ethnic Tutsi during the mid-1990s; fighting and civil war plagued the area for years. Another variation of this violence occurred in the western Sudan region of Darfur, where political disputes between Arabs and non-Arab rebels arose. Between 2004 and 2006, government-backed Arab militias carried out a systematic campaign that killed 300,000 non-Arab farmers and displaced two million people. In 2011, people in southern Sudan voted to form their own state, raising hopes that violence in the region will diminish. In the West and elsewhere, these multilayered resentments and struggles formed a complex backdrop for other emerging developments.

While ethnic conflict and nationalism intensified in several parts of the globe, cultural differences among Western nations and between Western

Immigration

and non-Western peoples also softened with an increase in international contacts. People migrated in droves to the West and other wealthy areas of the world, such as the oil-rich Middle East, and crossed countless borders in the search for work.

The new immigration opened doors for many people, but it also had its dark side. The opening of frontiers within Europe during the 1990s and the desperation of millions throughout the world made the movement of people difficult to control. Illegal immigration skyrocketed to more than 10 million people a year globally. For example, immigrants from Iran, Turkey, Iraq, Pakistan, Bangladesh, Albania, and elsewhere risked dangerous boat passages and expulsion to reach places such as Italy's long, exposed southern coast. "We lived like animals. . . . If we had not brought some biscuits and water, we would have starved," said a Kurdish immigrant in 1997. Some of the thousands who crossed North American borders each year—legally and illegally—told similar stories.

Germany in particular drew people from Turkey, Yugoslavia, Italy, Eastern Europe, and Russia and attracted asylum-seekers from many other parts of the world. In 1997, almost 9 percent of Germany's population were immigrants, many of whom remained unassimilated and yet alienated from their lands of origin. One Turkish woman who worked in her father's pizzeria in Berlin described the situation: "People like me are foreigners in Turkey. . . . There you are not a real Turk, and here you are not a complete German. We are somewhere in between." Her father agreed: "Even if I had a German passport, I would still feel like a foreigner and be regarded as a foreigner."

By 2010, some 20 million Muslims lived in Western Europe, many of whom were frustrated by bleak job prospects, outraged by discrimination, and yearning for a sense of respect. A French youth of Algerian descent living in one of the rough housing projects just outside of Paris explained: "You wake up every morning looking for work. But why? There isn't any." Like millions of other Arab and African immigrants and their French-born children and grandchildren, he had not been well integrated into French society. In 2005 and 2006, groups of young immigrants displayed their frustration in riots.

During these same decades, a common popular culture, especially among the youth in American, European, and non-Western cities, spread with increasing speed across all borders. The worldwide popularity of Hollywood movies, Disney products, soccer, Nintendo computer games,

Popular culture

hamburgers, pizza, shopping malls, noodle soup, Nike shoes, Benetton clothes, TV series, and rock and roll all reflected this standardization of cultural tastes. The spread of English as the world's second language and the beaming of television shows across borders by satellite facilitated the convergence of cultures. No medium offered more potential for this crossing of cultural lines in the future than the Internet. Instantaneous electronic communication and access to burgeoning informational, commercial, and scientific resources on the World Wide Web seemed to have dissolved time and space as well as national borders, spawning what some observers called the "global village."

Other cultural changes also set off the 1990s as unique. In the arts, what was once seen as modern in 1914 or even as late as mid-century—the glass skyscrapers and the abstract paintings of Mondrian and Pollock, for example—now seemed old and were taken for granted. Artistic and intellectual movements adopted the "postmodern" label. In the arts, followers of **post-modernism** became less concerned with austere principles. Architects, for example, rejected the pure forms and plain glass walls of the modern style in favor of buildings with elaborate shapes and ornamentation. Intellectuals and critics sympathetic to postmodernism attacked all ideologies—from liberalism to Marxism—and even the intellectual foundations of most academic disciplines as outmoded, oppressive distortions of the truth. Skeptical that objective truth was possible, they claimed that science itself was infected by the dominant values and beliefs of the culture that produced it.

Postmodernism

OPINION

In spite of all of the forces dividing the global community, what forces do you see pulling the world together?

corporations and financial institutions. Trying to stem the losses, governments from the United States to Europe and China intervened massively in their economies.

Oil presented another long-term problem that spilled across borders in recent decades. Economic development in the West and elsewhere heightened demand for energy derived from oil and natural gas. Most Western nations consume far more oil than they produce, and nations with rising economies such as China and India want the oil-fueled wealth enjoyed in the West. In a competitive international arena, they vie for supplies from major producers such as Saudi Arabia, Iran, Iraq, Russia, Venezuela, and Nigeria. Webs of politics, arms, money, and influence surround this growing international need for oil. More insidiously, the divisions between rich and poor presented pressing across-borders dilemmas. The relatively affluent West, with its multinational corporations, could no longer ignore nations scourged by crushing debts, pressing economic needs, and unmet demands. The evolving global economic landscape added to the uncertainty. Despite the rise of East Asia and India, the gap between the affluent, industrialized nations of the northern latitudes and the poorer, developing nations of the south widened. Incomes in most nations in sub-Saharan Africa and Latin America actually declined from 1960s levels. In 2005, more than two billion people in the world subsisted on the equivalent of less than $1 per day.

Growing international economic ties

As world population in 2010 approached seven billion—more than double that at the end of World War II—the poorer southern half of the globe carried the heaviest burden of population growth. The table below shows population changes for major areas of the world since 1900 and estimates population figures for the mid-twenty-first century.

Beyond Borders: Uncertainty and Opportunity in a Shrinking World

The spreading webs of communications and the goods and services radiating out from the West promised satisfactions galore for anyone who wanted to—and could afford to—participate. However, recessions during the 1980s and after 2000 reminded Westerners and non-Westerners alike that economic growth could not be taken for granted. Despite the West's overall prosperity, inflation and declining personal incomes for the bottom half of society spawned social discontent in these decades. In most of Europe, unemployment continued to hover above 10 percent and reached as high as 20 percent during the 1990s. Unions everywhere lost membership and clout, leaving more workers than ever without protection in a shifting, competitive marketplace.

In addition, with international economic ties proliferating, problems in one area of the world quickly made themselves felt in other regions. For example, the financial crisis and economic turmoil that struck Asia in 1998 spread rapidly, creating huge losses for investors and trading partners throughout the world. In 2008, another financial crisis, this time much more serious and combined with a collapse of real estate values, struck the United States. Repercussions quickly spread to Europe and around the globe, leading to what some economists have called the worst financial crisis, economic crisis, and recession since the Great Depression of the 1930s. Tens of millions of people lost their jobs. Stock markets plunged, and bankruptcies felled large

MAJOR AREA	1900	1950	2000	2050
	POPULATION (IN MILLIONS)			
Asia	947	1402	3672	5428
Africa	133	221	794	2000
Europe	408	547	727	603
Latin America	74	167	579	806
North America	82	172	389	438
Oceania	6	13	31	47
World (total)	1650	2522	6192	9322

POPULATION CHANGES ACROSS THE TWENTIETH AND TWENTY-FIRST CENTURIES

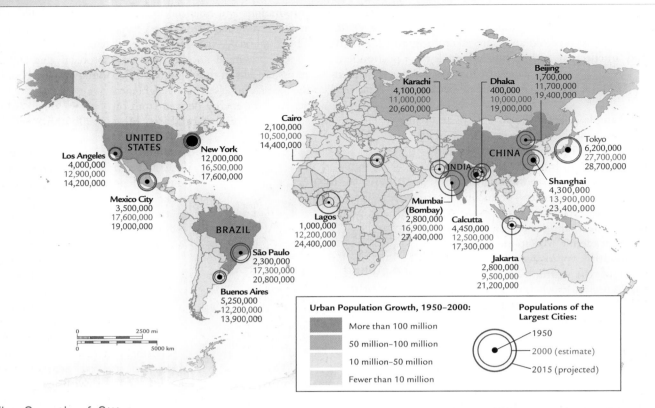

Karachi
4,100,000
11,000,000
20,600,000

Dhaka
400,000
10,000,000
19,000,000

Beijing
1,700,000
11,700,000
19,400,000

Cairo
2,100,000
10,500,000
14,400,000

Tokyo
6,200,000
27,700,000
28,700,000

UNITED STATES

CHINA

New York
12,000,000
16,500,000
17,600,000

Los Angeles
4,000,000
12,900,000
14,200,000

INDIA

Shanghai
4,300,000
13,900,000
23,400,000

Mexico City
3,500,000
17,600,000
19,000,000

Mumbai
(Bombay)
2,800,000
16,900,000
27,400,000

Calcutta
4,450,000
12,500,000
17,300,000

Lagos
1,000,000
12,200,000
24,400,000

BRAZIL

São Paulo
2,300,000
17,300,000
20,800,000

Jakarta
2,800,000
9,500,000
21,200,000

Buenos Aires
5,250,000
12,200,000
13,900,000

0   2500 mi
0   5000 km

Urban Population Growth, 1950–2000:

- More than 100 million
- 50 million–100 million
- 10 million–50 million
- Fewer than 10 million

Populations of the Largest Cities:

- 1950
- 2000 (estimate)
- 2015 (projected)

The Growth of Cities
This map shows those areas with the largest urban populations and the growth of population in the world's largest cities.

Europe, with declining birthrates, will experience a drop in population, while Asia and Africa will gain the most. Many Western nations—particularly the United States—have relied on immigration to bolster population figures.

The distinction between Europe and the rest of the world in population trends is also reflected in the process of urbanization (see map above). Although the wealthy areas of the West once experienced the most rapid urban growth, other parts of the world gained the lead during the second half of the twentieth century. Moreover, in 1950, six out of the ten largest cities were in Europe and the U.S.; by 2000, most of the world's largest cities were in the non-Western world, a trend that has continued into the second decade of the century.

Economic growth, population increases, and urbanization created alarming environmental problems in recent

GLOBAL WARMING, 1941–2004 Two photographs of Muir Glacier, Alaska, in 1941 (left) and 2004 (right) reveal the signs of global warming.

decades. The earth's air, water, and seas became more and more polluted, while acid rain, caused by smoke and fumes, damaged more than one-third of Germany's remaining forests. Great rivers such as the Rhine and the Danube became like sewers, and waters such as the Mediterranean and Black seas were fouled by runoff from industrial sites and cities. Even the monuments of ancient Greece and Rome were rapidly deteriorating and crumbling from the onslaught of fumes and vibrations of city life. In Eastern Europe and the Soviet Union, environmental problems had been virtually ignored for decades. The collapse of communism in those areas revealed staggering environmental degradation. In many Western countries, the growing importance of Green parties pushed environmental concerns into the political spotlight.

Environmental costs

Environmental problems extended well beyond the West. Thirteen of the fifteen cities with the worst air pollution in the world were in Asia. Of the estimated 2.7 million people worldwide who died each year from illnesses caused by air pollution, the majority were Asians. Each year, Asia lost 1 percent of its forests. As humanity consumed more and more resources and disrupted the globe's natural balance, thousands of plant and animal species became extinct each year. Humanity's need for more and more energy also led many nations to rely increasingly on nuclear power. The 1986 accident at the Chernobyl plant in the Soviet Union shed new light on the potential dangers of nuclear power—the accident released two hundred times the radiation of the two bombs dropped in World War II.

In March 2011 a gigantic earthquake just off Japan's northwestern coast unleashed a massive tsunami that not only caused great damage and loss of life, but also disabled a large nuclear power facility. As a result, authorities lost control over radioactive materials at the plant and large amounts of dangerous radiation were released into the environment. Once again, the feasibility of nuclear power becoming cheap and safe enough to substitute for coal and petroleum plants, which produce great quantities of carbon waste, was called into question.

Many observers believe that **global warming** has become our most threatening environmental problem. Most scientists agree that in recent decades the Earth's atmosphere

The Copenhagen Accord on Climate Change

While many scientists have long warned about the dangers of global warming, only in recent years has the international community recognized the gravity of the problem. Building on earlier conferences, the United Nations organized a major conference on climate change in Copenhagen, Denmark, late in 2009. The following is an excerpt from the resulting Copenhagen Accord.

We underline that climate change is one of the greatest challenges of our time. We emphasise our strong political will to urgently combat climate change in accordance with the principle of common but differentiated responsibilities and respective capabilities. To achieve the ultimate objective of the Convention to stabilize greenhouse gas concentration in the atmosphere at a level that would prevent dangerous anthropogenic interference with the climate system, we shall, recognizing the scientific view that the increase in global temperature should be below 2 degrees Celsius, on the basis of equity and in the context of sustainable development, enhance our long-term cooperative action to combat climate change. We recognize the critical impacts of climate change and the potential impacts of response measures on countries particularly vulnerable to its adverse effects and stress the need to establish a comprehensive adaptation programme including international support. . . .

Why might some countries be unwilling to accept legally binding actions to stem global warming?

has heated up at an alarming rate, in great part thanks to the heat-trapping so-called greenhouse gases, such as carbon dioxide, that have been created through the combustion of coal and petroleum products. Factories, power plants, urban growth, and gas-guzzling motor vehicles in the West and in rapidly developing nations such as China and India add to those greenhouse gases every day.

Global warming

According to most scientists, the warming process is probably irreversible and, unless slowed by policies that crucial nations seem unwilling to adopt, could produce dramatic climate changes, resulting in the melting of ice sheets and glaciers, coastal flooding, widening droughts, worsening hurricanes, and rapid extinction of plant and animal species by the end of this century. The images on page 626 show one example of the many glaciers that have been melting throughout the world. Some experts feel that such dramatic environmental developments will diminish or destroy our ability to sustain Earth's population. Climate-induced food shortages, mass migrations, and possible pandemics could destabilize entire regions of the world. Global warming is "the single biggest challenge facing the planet, the equal in every way to the nuclear threat that transfixed us during the past half-century and a threat we haven't even begun to deal with," warned one distinguished scientist.

People have turned to science and government to solve these environmental problems, but thus far the results have been mixed at best. On the one hand, scientists and governmental officials finally recognized the severity of these problems and have begun to address them by committing more funds to research and coming to agreements on new regulations to minimize the damage (see Exploring the Past on page 627). On the other hand, anxieties about the environment have often conflicted with a stronger desire of many people for continued economic growth. Businesses and governments, reflecting this desire, have often proved reluctant to commit to expensive environmental-protection programs.

Like the environment, health issues have also received an ambivalent response. In the last few decades of the twentieth century, many officials and commentators recognized that an aging population, particularly in the West, presented a growing health problem that would strain medical facilities and budgets, but they were unsure

AIDS

JENNIFER BARTLETT, *SPIRAL: AN ORDINARY EVENING IN NEW HAVEN*, 1989 A firestorm sweeps away everything in its path. In a world that still had unimaginably destructive weapons of war at its fingertips, this scene may well have offered a visual warning to the West and the rest of the world as the twenty-first century began.

what to do. With certain health problems—the worldwide AIDS (acquired immune deficiency syndrome) epidemic is just one example—recognition of the dangers came too late. Even then, many efforts to address such crises proved halfhearted. Again, AIDS is an apt example. Between 1978 and 2006, 26 million people died from this disease. AIDS became the most deadly epidemic in recent global history, yet many people initially denied its existence or criticized those who had contracted it (see image to the right). After several years, some help began to arrive, but not nearly enough. In 2011, some 34 million people in the world were living with AIDS or HIV, the virus that causes AIDS. In some sub-Saharan countries of Africa, some one in four adults were infected.

In the face of frightening diseases, environmental degradation, economic uncertainty, and devastating weaponry, many people looked to the new century with cynicism or dread. Some found it all too easy to imagine even the violent destruction of all life on Earth, as the painting on page 628 suggests.

Perhaps in response to these anxieties, the last two decades of the twentieth century saw a renewal of religious commitment among many people. In the United States and Europe, evangelical Christianity—with its emphasis on personal salvation and spiritual experience—became the fastest-growing religious movement.

Movements of religious revival

In Russia, an outpouring of religious sentiment within the Orthodox Church followed the collapse of communism. Islamic fundamentalism, calling for a return to traditional ways and a rejection of alien ideologies, intensified in lands from West Africa to East Asia. All of these movements reflected a hunger for a sense of meaning and a clarity of values by which to live in an uncertain time.

Yet, despite these anxieties, there were also reasons to look to the coming century with hope and optimism. After all, the West had surmounted major obstacles. It had enjoyed more than sixty years of relative peace and had

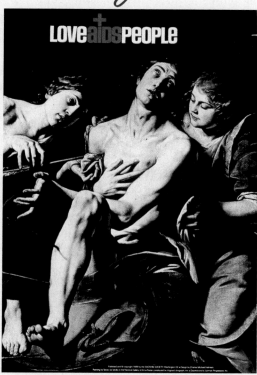

Charles Michael Helmken, *Loveaidspeople*
1989

In this poignant image, a modern-day AIDS victim, portrayed as the Christian martyr Saint Sebastian, has been wounded by the "arrows" of officials and social attitudes that condemn him as morally dirty and sinful. As he looks up desperately for help, two figures lovingly aid him. The poster makes an urgent plea for assistance. How, as a viewer, do you interpret the details and colors in this poster?

managed to avert the dreaded clash of superpowers during the Cold War. In Eastern Europe, most nations had gained their long-sought independence with a minimum of violence. In some areas, seemingly hopeless problems showed signs of being

Accomplishments and optimism

solved. For example, in Northern Ireland, Protestants and Catholics created a power-sharing government, ending a decades-long bitter conflict.

For many people around the world, the standard of living had risen to unprecedented levels. In Asia, for example, increasing prosperity had lifted some 400 million people out of abject poverty. Between 1999 and 2008, the global economy doubled. Although social equality still remained only an ideal, the Western promise of continually improving well-being for everyone seemed to hold firm. The increasing human life span and rising numbers of elderly—in part thanks to the global increase in food production and better access to health care—attested to that well-being. Moreover, many women gained access to opportunities once available only to men: By the late 1990s, roughly equal numbers of women and men in the West received higher education and pursued paying careers. Women's presence in professional life and in politics continued to grow. True, traditionalists worried about the destruction of the family as an institution, citing the growing prevalence of two-career parents, a rise in cohabitation and single motherhood, and accelerating divorce rates. Nevertheless, family structures persisted, although many of them took new forms, such as "an emotionally bound partnership."

Continuing scientific discoveries suggested that the West and the rest of the world could look forward to dramatic developments in the future. Perhaps most stunning was the prospect of changes stemming from the decoding of the human genome—determining the chemical sequence of the DNA in every cell of the human body. In 2001, this costly, long-term project carried out by hundreds of scientists in six countries was completed. With this "blueprint" of human life, scientists hoped to revolutionize medicine and gain new insights into human nature.

Overall, the West has gained a much needed appreciation of its place in the world, and human beings around the globe have new tools to understand themselves within a widening universe. Technology, trade, and instant communications provide growing opportunities for cooperation across national boundaries. As the second decade of the twenty-first century opens, life offers more options to more people than ever.

connect to today

Twenty-First-Century Challenges

There have been major political, environmental, and social developments since 1989. Which do you think will prove the most serious in the years to come?

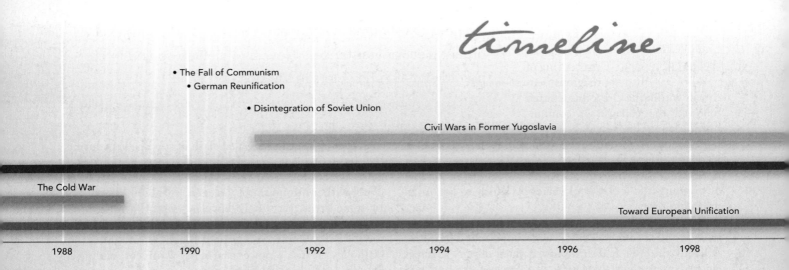

timeline

• The Fall of Communism
• German Reunification

• Disintegration of Soviet Union

Civil Wars in Former Yugoslavia

The Cold War

Toward European Unification

| 1988 | 1990 | 1992 | 1994 | 1996 | 1998 |

SUMMARY

In 1989, history in the West abruptly shifted course. The communist regimes in Eastern Europe fell, severing these nations' ties to the Soviet Union and sparking unprecedented political and economic reforms. Two years later, the Soviet Union itself disintegrated. The Cold War ended and along with it a sharply defined historical era stretching back to 1914.

- Fundamental economic problems, widespread calls for national independence, and new policies initiated by Mikhail Gorbachev led to the fall of Europe's communist governments.

- The end of the Cold War renewed the commitment to democracy and capitalism in the West, accelerated the existing movement toward unification in Europe, and left the United States standing as the sole military superpower in the world.

- Globalization—marked by the movement of goods, information, people, problems, and cultures across traditional borders—has become a dominant development in today's world.

Our time may mark the beginning of a new global society. The human desire for limitless economic growth seems relentless, but also leaves its mark on the environment in ways that spread concern across national boundaries. Western civilization, so long centered on the western tip of the Eurasian continent, now seems to be one of many lights shining on this shrinking globe. Great challenges face all of humanity. Whether and how the West—and the world—will embrace these challenges remains to be seen.

Growing Importance of Computers and "The Information Revolution"

2002   2004   2006   2008   2010   2012

Glossary

Note to users: Terms that are foreign or difficult to pronounce are transcribed in parentheses directly after the term itself. The transcriptions are based on the rules of English spelling; that is, they are similar to the transcriptions employed in the *Webster* dictionaries. Each word's most heavily stressed syllable is marked by an acute accent.

A

Absolute monarch (máh-nark) A seventeenth- or eighteenth-century European monarch claiming complete political authority.

Absolutism (áb-suh-loo-tism) (Royal) A government in which all power is vested in the ruler.

Abstract expressionism (ex-présh-un-ism) A twentieth-century painting style infusing nonrepresentational art with strong personal feelings.

Acropolis (uh-króp-uh-liss) The hill at the center of Athens on which the magnificent temples—including the Parthenon—that made the architecture of ancient Athens famous are built.

Act of Union Formal unification of England and Scotland in 1707.

Afrikaners Afrikaans-speaking South Africans of Dutch and other European ancestry.

Age of Reason The eighteenth-century Enlightenment; sometimes includes seventeenth-century science and philosophy.

Agora In ancient Greece, the marketplace or place of public assembly.

Agricultural revolution Neolithic discovery of agriculture; agricultural transformations that began in eighteenth-century western Europe.

Ahriman In Zoroastrianism, the evil god of darkness.

Ahura Mazda In Zoroastrianism, the beneficial god of light.

Akkadian (uh-káy-dee-un) A Semitic language of a region of ancient Mesopotamia.

Albigensians (al-buh-jén-see-unz) A medieval French heretical sect that believed in two gods—an evil and a good principle—that was destroyed in a crusade in the thirteenth century; also called Cathars.

Alchemy (ál-kuh-mee) The medieval study and practice of chemistry, primarily concerned with changing metals into gold and finding a universal remedy for diseases. It was much practiced from the thirteenth to the seventeenth century.

Allies (ál-eyes) The two alliances against Germany and its partners in World War I and World War II.

Al-Qaeda A global terrorist network headed by Osama bin Laden.

Anarchists (ánn-ar-kissts) Those advocating or promoting anarchy, or an absence of government. In the late nineteenth and early twentieth centuries, anarchism arose as an ideology and movement against all governmental authority and private property.

Ancien régime (áwn-syáwn ráy-zhéem) The traditional political and social order in Europe before the French Revolution.

Antigonids (ann-tíg-un-idz) Hellenistic dynasty that ruled in Macedonia from about 300 B.C.E. to about 150 B.C.E.

Anti-Semitism (ann-tye-sém-i-tism) Prejudice against Jews.

Apartheid "Separation" in the Afrikaans language. A policy to rigidly segregate people by color in South Africa, 1948–1989.

Appeasement Attempting to satisfy potential aggressors in order to avoid war.

Aramaic (air-uh-máy-ik) A northwest Semitic language that spread throughout the region. It was the language that Jesus spoke.

Archon (áhr-kahn) A chief magistrate in ancient Athens.

Areopagus (air-ee-áh-pa-gus) A prestigious governing council of ancient Athens.

Arête (ah-ray-táy) Greek term for the valued virtues of manliness, courage, and excellence.

Arianism (áir-ee-un-ism) A fourth-century Christian heresy that taught that Jesus was not of the same substance as God the father, and thus had been created.

Assemblies, Roman Institutions in the Roman Republic that functioned as the legislative branch of government.

Assignats (ah-seen-yáh) Paper money issued in the National Assembly during the French Revolution.

Astrolabe (áss-tro-leyb) Medieval instrument used to determine the altitudes of celestial bodies.

Augury (áh-gur-ee) The art or practice of foretelling events though signs or omens.

Autocracy (au-tóc-ra-cee) Government under the rule of an authoritarian ruler.

Autocrat (áuto-crat) An authoritarian ruler.

Axis World War II alliance whose main members were Germany, Italy, and Japan.

B

Baby boom The increase in births following World War II.

Babylonian Captivity Period during the fourteenth century in which seven popes chose to reside in Avignon instead of Rome. Critics called this period the "Babylonian Captivity" of the papacy.

Bailiffs Medieval French salaried officials hired by the king to collect taxes and represent his interests.

Balance of power Distribution of power among states, or the policy of creating alliances to control powerful states.

Balkans States in the Balkan Peninsula, including Albania, Bulgaria, Greece, Romania, and Yugoslavia.

Baroque (ba-róak) An artistic style of the sixteenth and seventeenth centuries stressing rich ornamentation and dynamic movement; in music, a style marked by strict forms and elaborate ornamentation.

Bastard feudalism (feúd-a-lism) Late medieval corruption of the feudal system replacing feudal loyalty with cash payments.

Bastille (bas-téel) The royal prison symbolizing the Old Regime that was destroyed in the French Revolution.

Bauhaus (bóugh-house) An influential school of art emphasizing clean, functional lines founded in Germany by the architect Walter Gropius just after World War I.

Bedouin (béd-oh-in) An Arab of any of the nomadic tribes of the deserts of North Africa, Arabia, and Syria.

Berlin airlift The airborne military operation organized to supply Berlin's Western-occupied sectors during the Soviet Union's 1948 Berlin blockage.

Berlin Wall The wall erected in 1961 to divide East and West Berlin.

Bessemer (béss-uh-mer) **process** A method for removing impurities from molten iron.

Black Death Name given the epidemic that swept Europe beginning in 1348. Most historians agree that the main disease was bubonic plague, but the Black Death may have incorporated many other diseases.

Blackshirts Mussolini's black-uniformed Fascist paramilitary forces in the 1920s and 1930s.

Blitzkrieg (blíts-kreeg) "Lightning war," a rapid air and land military assault used by the Germans in World War II.

Boers (boars) Dutch settlers in south Africa.

Bolshevik (bówl-shuh-vick) "Majority faction," the Leninist wing of the Russian Marxist Party; after 1917, the Communist Party.

Bourgeoisie (boor-zhwa-zée) The middle class.

Boxers A nineteenth-century Chinese secret society that believed in the spiritual power of the martial arts and fought against Chinese Christians and foreigners in China.

Boyar A Russian noble.

Brezhnev (bréhzh-nyeff) **Doctrine** Policy that justified Soviet intervention in order to ensure the survival of socialism in another state, initiated by USSR leader Brezhnev in 1968.

Brownshirts Hitler's brown-uniformed paramilitary force in the 1920s and 1930s.

Burschenschaften (bóor-shen-sháhf-ten) Liberal nationalist German student unions during the early nineteenth century.

C

Cabinet system Government by a prime minister and heads of governmental bureaus developed by Britain during the eighteenth century.

Caesaropapism (see-zer-oh-pápe-ism) The practice of having the same person rule both the state and the church.

Cahiers (kye-yéah) Lists of public grievances sent to the French Estates General in 1789.

Caliph (káy-liff) A title meaning "successor to the Prophet" given to Muslim rulers who combined political authority with religious power.

Capitalists Those promoting an economic system characterized by freedom of the market with private and corporate ownership of the means of production and distribution that are operated for profit.

Capitularies (ka-pít-chew-làir-eez) Royal laws issued by Charlemagne and the Carolingians.

Caravel (care-uh-véll) A small, light sailing ship of the kind used by the Spanish and Portuguese in the fifteenth and sixteenth centuries.

Carbonari (car-bun-áh-ree) A secret society of revolutionaries in nineteenth-century Italy.

Cartel (car-téll) An alliance of corporations designed to control the marketplace.

Cartesian (car-tée-zhen) **dualism** A philosophy developed by René Descartes in the seventeenth century that defines two kinds of reality: the mind, or subjective thinking, and the body, or objective physical matter.

Catacombs Underground burial places. The term originally referred to the early Christian burial locations in Rome and elsewhere.

Cathars (cáth-arz) A medieval French dualist heretical sect; also called Albigensians.

Central Powers World War I alliance, primarily of Germany, Austria, and the Ottoman Empire.

Centuriate (sen-chúr-ee-ate) **Assembly** An aristocratic ruling body in ancient Rome that made the laws.

Chancellor A high-ranking official—in Germany, the prime minister.

Chartists English reformers of the 1830s and 1840s who demanded political and social rights for the lower classes.

Checks and balances A balanced division of governmental power among different institutions.

Chivalry (shív-el-ree) Code of performance and ethics for medieval knights. It can also refer to the demonstration of knightly virtues.

Christian humanists During the fifteenth and sixteenth centuries, experts in Greek, Latin, and Hebrew who studied the Bible and other Christian writings in order to understand the correct meaning of early Christian texts.

Civil Constitution of the Clergy New rules nationalizing and governing the clergy enacted during the French Revolution.

Civic humanists Those practicing a branch of humanism that promoted the value of responsible citizenship in which people work to improve their city-states.

Classical style A seventeenth- and eighteenth-century cultural style emphasizing restraint and balance, and following models from ancient Greece and Rome.

Cold War The global struggle between alliances headed by the United States and the Soviet Union during the second half of the twentieth century.

Collectivization The Soviet policy of taking agricultural lands and decisions away from individual owners and placing them in the hands of elected managers and party officials.

Comecon (cómm-ee-con) The economic organization of communist eastern European states during the Cold War.

Committee of Public Safety Ruling committee of twelve leaders during the French Revolutionary period of the Terror.

Common law Laws that arise from customary use rather than from legislation.

Common market The European Economic Community, a union of Western European nations initiated in 1957 to promote common economic policies.

Commonwealth of Independent States A loose confederation of several former republics of the disintegrated Soviet Union founded in 1991.

Commune (cómm-yune) A medieval or early modern town; a semi-independent city government or socialistic community in the nineteenth and twentieth centuries.

Communist Manifesto A short, popular treatise written by Karl Marx and Friedrich Engels in 1848 that contained the fundamentals of their "scientific socialism."

Complutensian Polyglot (comm-plue-tén-see-an pólly-glàht) **Bible** An edition of the Bible written in 1520 that had three columns that compared the Hebrew, Greek, and Latin versions.

Compurgation (comm-pur-gáy-shun) A Germanic legal oath taken by twelve men testifying to the character of the accused.

Concert of Europe The alliance of powers after 1815 created to maintain the status quo and coordinate international relations.

Conciliar (conn-síll-ee-ar) **movement** The belief that the Catholic Church should be led by councils of cardinals rather than popes.

Concordat (conn-córe-dat) A formal agreement, especially between the pope and a government, for the regulation of church affairs.

Condottieri (conn-duh-tyáy-ree) From the fourteenth to the sixteenth century, captains of bands of mercenary soldiers, influential in Renaissance Italy.

Congress of Vienna The peace conference held between 1814 and 1815 in Vienna after the defeat of Napoleon.

Conquistadors (conn-kéy-stah-doors) Spanish adventurers in the sixteenth century who went to South and Central America to conquer indigenous peoples and claim their lands.

Conservatism An ideology stressing order and traditional values.

Constitutionalism The idea that political authority rests in written law, not in the person of an absolute monarch.

Constitutional monarchy Government in which the monarch's powers are limited by a set of fundamental laws.

Consuls (cónn-suls) The appointed chief executive officers of the Roman Republic.

Containment The Cold War strategy of the United States to limit the expansion and influence of the Soviet Union.

Continental System Napoleon's policy of preventing trade between continental Europe and Great Britain.

Contra posto (cón-tra páh-sto) A stance of the human body in which one leg bears weight, while the other is relaxed. Also known as counterpoise, it was popular in Renaissance sculpture.

Copernican (co-pér-nick-an) **revolution** The change from an earth-centered to a sun-centered universe initiated by Copernicus in the sixteenth century.

Corinthian order One of three architectural systems developed by the Greeks to decorate their buildings. The Corinthian order is marked by the capitals of columns decorated with acanthus leaves.

Corn Laws British laws that imposed tariffs on grain imports.

Corporate state Mussolini's economic and political machinery to manage the Italian economy and settle issues between labor and management.

Corsair A swift pirate ship.

Cossacks The "free warriors" of southern Russia, noted as cavalrymen.

Cottage industry Handicraft manufacturing usually organized by merchants and performed by rural people in their cottages.

Coup d'état (coo-day-táh) A sudden taking of power that violates constitutional forms by a group of persons in authority.

Creoles (crée-ohlz) People of European descent born in the West Indies or Spanish America, often of mixed ancestry.

Crusades From the late eleventh century through the thirteenth century, Europeans sent a number of military operations to take the Holy Land (Jerusalem and its surrounding territory) from the Muslims. These military ventures in the name of Christendom are collectively called the Crusades.

Cult of sensibility The eighteenth-century emphasis on emotion and nature forwarded by several European artists and authors.

Cuneiform (cue-née-uh-form) A writing system using wedge-shaped characters developed in ancient Mesopotamia.

Curia Regis (kóo-ree-uh régg-ees) A medieval king's advisory body made up of his major vassals.

Cynicism (sín-uh-sism) A Hellenistic philosophy that locates the search for virtue in an utter indifference to worldly needs.

Cyrillic (suh-ríll-ik) **alphabet** An old Slavic alphabet presently used in modified form for Russian and other languages.

D

Dada (dáh-dah) An early twentieth-century artistic movement that attacked traditional cultural styles and stressed the absence of purpose in life.

Dauphin (dough-fán) Heir to the French throne. The title was used from 1349 to 1830.

D-Day The day of the Allied invasion of Normandy in World War II—June 6, 1944.

Decembrists (dee-sém-brists) Russian army officers who briefly rebelled against Tsar Nicholas I in December 1925.

Declaration of the Rights of Man and Citizen France's revolutionary 1789 declaration of rights stressing liberty, equality, and fraternity.

Decolonization The loss of colonies by imperial powers during the years following World War II.

Deductive reasoning Deriving conclusions that logically flow from a premise, reasoning from basic or known truths.

Deism (dée-iz-um) Belief in a God who created the universe and its natural laws but does not intervene further; gained popularity during the Enlightenment.

Demotic A form of ancient Egyptian writing used for ordinary life. A simplified form of hieratic script.

Détente (day-táhnt) The period of relative cooperation between Cold War adversaries during the 1960s and 1970s.

Devotio moderno (day-vóh-tee-oh moh-dáir-noh) A medieval religious movement that emphasized internal spirituality over ritual practices.

Diaspora The dispersion of the Jews after the Babylonian conquest in the sixth century B.C.E. The term comes from the Greek word meaning "to scatter."

Diet The general legislative assembly of certain countries, such as Poland.

Directory The relatively conservative government during the last years of the French Revolution before Napoleon gained power.

Division of labor The division of work in the modern process of industrial production into separate tasks.

Doge (dóhj) The chief magistrate of the Republic of Venice during the Middle Ages and Renaissance.

Domesday (dóomz-day) **Book** A record of all the property and holdings in England, commissioned by William the Conqueror in 1066 so that he could determine the extent of his lands and wealth.

Doric order One of three architectural systems developed by the Greeks to decorate their buildings. The Doric order may be recognized by its columns, which include a wide shaft with a plain capital on the top.

Drachma (dróck-mah) Hellenistic coin containing either 4.3 grams (Alexander's) or 3.5 grams (Egypt's) of silver.

Dreyfus (drý-fuss) **affair** The political upheaval in France accompanying the unjust 1894 conviction of Jewish army officer Alfred Dreyfus as a German spy that marked the importance of anti-Semitism in France.

Dual Monarchy The Austro-Hungarian Empire; the Habsburg monarchy after the 1867 reform that granted Hungary equality with Austria.

Il Duce (ill dóoch-ay) "The Leader," Mussolini's title as head of the Italian Fascist Party.

Duma Russia's legislative assembly in the years prior to 1917.

E

Ecclesia (ek-cláy-zee-uh) The popular assembly in ancient Athens made up of all male citizens over 18.

Edict of Nantes (náwnt) Edict issued by French king Henry IV in 1598 granting rights to Protestants, later revoked by Louis XIV.

Émigrés (em-ee-gráy) People, mostly aristocrats, who fled France during the French Revolution.

Emir (em-éar) A Muslim ruler, prince, or military commander.

Empirical method The use of observation and experiments based on sensory evidence to come to ideas or conclusions about nature.

Ems (Em's) **Dispatch** Telegram from Prussia's head of state to the French government, edited by Bismarck to look like an insult, that helped cause the Franco-Prussian War.

Enclosure Combining separate parcels of farmland and enclosing them with fences and walls to create large farms or pastures that produced for commerce.

encomienda (en-koh-mee-én-da) A form of economic and social organization established in sixteenth-century Spanish settlements in South and Central America. The encomienda system consisted of a royal grant that allowed Spanish settlers to compel indigenous peoples to work for them. In return, Spanish overseers were to look after their workers' welfare and encourage their conversion to Christianity. In reality, it was a brutal system of enforced labor.

Enlightened absolutism (áb-suh-loo-tism) Rule by a strong, "enlightened" ruler applying Enlightenment ideas to government.

Enlightenment An eighteenth-century cultural movement based on the ideas of the Scientific Revolution and that supported the notion that human reason should determine understanding of the world and the rules of social life.

Entente Cordiale (on-táhnt core-dee-áhl) The series of understandings, or agreements, between France and Britain that led to their alliance in World War I.

Entrepreneur (on-truh-pren-óor) A person who organizes and operates business ventures, especially in commerce and industry.

Epic (épp-ik) A long narrative poem celebrating episodes of a people's heroic tradition.

Epicureanism (epp-uh-cúre-ee-an-ism) A Hellenistic philosophy that held that the goal of life should be to live a life of pleasure regulated by moderation.

Equestrians (ee-quést-ree-ans) A social class in ancient Rome who had enough money to begin to challenge the power of the patricians.

Essenes (Ess-éenz) Members of a Jewish sect of ascetics from the second century B.C.E. to the second century C.E.

Estates Representative assemblies, typically made up of either the clergy, the nobility, the commoners, or all three meeting separately.

Estates General The legislature of France from the Middle Ages to 1789. Each of the three Estates—clergy, nobility, and bourgeoisie—sent representatives.

Ethnic cleansing The policy of brutally driving an ethnic group from their homes and from a certain territory, particularly prominent during the civil wars in the Balkans during the 1990s.

Eugenics (you-génn-iks) The study of hereditary improvement.

Euro (yóu-roe) The common currency of many European states, established in 1999.

Eurocommunism The policy of Western European Communist parties of supporting moderate policies and cooperating with other Leftist parties during the 1970s and 1980s.

European Economic Community The EEC, or Common Market, founded in 1957 to eliminate tariff barriers and begin to integrate the economies of western European nations.

European Union (EU) The community of European nations that continued to take steps toward the full economic union of much of Europe during the late twentieth century.

Evolution Darwin's theory of biological development through adaptation.

Existentialism (ekk-siss-ténn-sha-lism) A twentieth-century philosophy asserting that individuals are responsible for their own values and meanings in an indifferent universe.

Expressionism A late-nineteenth- and early-twentieth-century artistic style that emphasized the objective expression of inner experience through the use of conventional characters and symbols.

F

Fabian (fáy-bee-an) **Society** A late-nineteenth-century group of British intellectuals that advocated the adoption of socialist policies through politics rather than revolution.

Factory system Many workers producing goods in a repetitive series of steps and specialized tasks using powerful machines.

Falange (fa-láhn-hey) A Spanish fascist party that supported Francisco Franco during the Spanish civil war.

Fascism (fáh-shism) A philosophy or system of government that advocates a dictatorship of the extreme right together with an ideology of belligerent nationalism.

Fealty (fée-al-tee) In the feudal system, a promise made by vassals and lords to do no harm to each other.

Federates In the late Roman Empire, treaties established with many Gothic tribes allowed these tribes to settle within the Empire. The tribes then became "federates," or allies of Rome.

Fibula (pl. fibulae) An ornamented clasp or brooch, favored by the ancient Germanic tribes to hold their great cloaks closed.

Fief (feef) In the feudal system, the portion—usually land—given by lords to vassals to provide for their maintenance in return for their service.

Five-Year Plan The rapid, massive industrialization of the nation under the direction of the state initiated in the Soviet Union in the late 1920s.

Forum The central public place in ancient Rome which served as a meeting place, marketplace, law court, and political arena.

Fourteen Points U.S. President Wilson's plan to settle World War I and guarantee the peace.

Frankfurt Assembly Convention of liberals and nationalists from several German states that met in 1848 to try to form a unified government for Germany.

Free companies Mercenary soldiers in the Middle Ages and Renaissance who would fight for whoever paid them. They were called "free" to distinguish them from warriors who were bound by feudal ties to a lord.

Free Corps (core) Post–World War I German right-wing paramilitary groups made up mostly of veterans.

Free trade International trade of goods without tariffs, or customs duties.

Fresco A technique of painting on the plaster surface of a wall or ceiling while it is still damp so that the colors become fused with the plaster as it dries, making the image part of the building's surface.

Fronde (frawnd) Mid-seventeenth-century upheavals in France that threatened the royal government.

Fundamentalists Those who believe in an extremely conservative interpretation of a religion.

G

Galley A large medieval ship propelled by sails and oars.

General will Rousseau's notion that rules governing society should be based on the best conscience of the people.

Gentry People of "good birth" and superior social position.

Geocentric Earth-centered.

Gerousia (gay-róo-see-uh) Ruling body in ancient Sparta made up of male citizens over age 60.

Gestapo (guh-stóp-po) Nazi secret police in Hitler's Germany.

Girondins (zhee-roan-dán) Moderate political faction among leaders of the French Revolution.

Glasnost (gláz-nost) Soviet leader Gorbachev's policy of political and cultural openness in the 1980s.

Globalization Twentieth-century tendency for cultural and historical development to become increasingly worldwide in scope.

Global warming The heating of the earth's atmosphere in recent decades, caused in part by the buildup of carbon dioxide and other "greenhouse gases" produced by burning fossil fuels.

Glorious Revolution In 1688, English Parliament offered the crown of England to the Protestant William of Orange and his wife Mary, replacing James II. This change in rule was accomplished peacefully and clarified the precedent that England was a constitutional monarchy with power resting in Parliament.

Gosplan The Soviet State Planning Commission, charged with achieving ambitious economic goals.

Gothic (góth-ik) A style of architecture, usually associated with churches, that originated in France and flourished from the twelfth to the sixteenth century. Gothic architecture is identified by pointed arches, ribbed vaults, stained-glass windows, and flying buttresses.

Grand tour An educational travel taken by the wealthy to certain cities and sites, particularly during the seventeenth and eighteenth centuries.

Great Chain of Being A traditional Western-Christian vision of the hierarchic order of the universe.

Great Depression The global economic depression of the 1930s.

Great fear Panic caused by rumors that bands of brigands were on the loose in the French countryside during the summer of 1789.

Great Purges The long period of Communist Party purges in the Soviet Union during the 1930s, marked by terror, house arrests, show-trials, torture, imprisonments, and executions.

Great Reforms Reforms instituted by Russia's tsar Alexander II in 1861 that included freeing Russia's serfs.

Great Schism (skíz-um) Period in the late Middle Ages from 1378 to 1417 when there were two (and at times three) rival popes.

Greek fire A Byzantine naval weapon made of combustible oil that was launched with a catapult or pumped through tubes to set fire to enemy ships.

Guild An association of persons of the same trade united for the furtherance of some purpose.

Guillotine (ghée-oh-teen) A device for executing the condemned used during the French Revolution.

H

Hacienda (ha-see-én-da) Large landed estates in Spanish America that replaced encomiendas as the dominant economic and social structure.

Haj (hodge) The Muslim annual pilgrimage to Mecca, Medina, and other holy sites.

Hasidim (hah-see-déem) Sect of Jewish mystics founded in Poland in the eighteenth century in opposition to the formalistic Judaism and ritual laxity of the period.

Heliocentric (hee-lee-oh-sén-trick) Pertaining to the theory that the sun is the center of the universe.

Hellenes (Héll-eenz) The name ancient Greeks assigned to themselves, based on their belief that they were descended from a mythical King Hellen.

Hellenistic Of or related to the period between the fourth century B.C.E. and the first century B.C.E.

Helot (héll-ots) A serf in ancient Sparta.

Heresy A religious belief that is considered wrong by orthodox church leaders.

Hermetic doctrine Notion popular in the sixteenth and seventeenth centuries that all matter contains the divine spirit.

Hieratic (high-rát-ick) A form of ancient Egyptian writing consisting of abridged forms of hieroglyphics, used by the priests in keeping records.

Hieroglyph (high-roe-gliff) A picture or symbol used in the ancient Egyptian writing system—means "sacred writing."

Hijra (hídge-rah) (also *Hegira*) Muhammad's flight from Mecca to Medina in 622 B.C.E.

Holocaust (hóll-o-cost) The extermination of some six million Jews by the Nazis during World War II.

Holy Alliance Alliance of Russia, Austria, and Prussia to safeguard the principles of Christianity and maintain the international status quo after the Napoleonic Wars.

Homeopathy (home-ee-áh-pa-thee) Medical treatment emphasizing the use of herbal drugs and natural remedies.

Hoplites (hóp-lights) Ancient Greek infantrymen equipped with large round shields and long thrusting spears.

Hubris Excessive pride, which for the ancient Greeks brought punishment from the gods.

Huguenots (húgh-guh-nots) French Protestants of the sixteenth, seventeenth, and eighteenth centuries.

Humanists Students of an intellectual movement based on a deep study of classical culture and an emphasis on the humanities (literature, history, and philosophy) as a means for self-improvement.

Hundred Years' War A series of wars between England and France from 1337 to 1453. France won and England lost its lands in France, thus centralizing and solidifying French power.

I

Icon (éye-con) A sacred image of Jesus, Mary, or the saints that early Christians believed contained religious power.

Iconoclasm (eye-cónn-o-claz-um) A term literally meaning "icon breaking" that refers to an eighth-century religious controversy in Byzantium that argued that people should not venerate icons.

Ideogram (eye-dée-o-gram) A hieroglyph symbol expressing an abstract idea associated with the object it portrays.

Ideograph A written symbol that represents an idea instead of expressing the sound of a word.

Ideology (eye-dee-áh-lo-gee) A set of beliefs about the world and how it should be, often formalized into a political, social, or cultural theory.

Imam Muslim spiritual leader, believed by Shi'ites to be a spiritual descendant of Muhammad who should also be a temporal leader.

Imperialism The policy of extending a nation's authority by territorial acquisition or by the establishment of economic and political control over other nations or peoples.

Impressionism A nineteenth-century school of painting originating in France that emphasized capturing on canvas light as the eye sees it.

Indo-European Belonging to or constituting a family of languages that includes the Germanic, Celtic, Italic, Baltic, Slavic, Greek, Armenian, Iranian, and Indic groups.

Inductive reasoning Drawing general conclusions from particular concrete observations.

Indulgence A certificate issued by the papacy that gave people atonement for their sins and reduced their time in purgatory. Usually indulgences were issued for performing a pious act, but during the Reformation, critics accused the popes of selling indulgences to raise money.

Industrial revolution The rapid emergence of modern industrial production during the late eighteenth and nineteenth centuries.

Information revolution A rapid increase in the ability to store and manipulate information accompanying the development of computers during the second half of the twentieth century.

Inquisition A religious court established in the thirteenth century designed to root out heresy by questioning and torture.

Intendant (ann-tawn-dáunt) A French official sent by the royal government to assert the will of the monarch.

Internationalism The principle of cooperation among nations for their common good.

Ionia (eye-ówn-ee-uh) Ancient district in what is now Turkey that comprised the central portion of the west coast of Asia Minor, together with the adjacent islands.

Ionic order One of three architectural systems developed by the Greeks to decorate their buildings. The Ionic order may be recognized by its columns, which are taller and thinner than the Doric columns and capped with scroll-shaped capitals.

Iron Curtain The dividing line between Eastern and Western Europe during the Cold War.

Islamic fundamentalism A movement within Islam calling for a return to traditional ways and a rejection of alien ideologies that gained strength during the second half of the twentieth century.

J

Jacobins (jáck-o-bins) A radical political organization or club during the French Revolution.

Jacquerie (zhak-rée) The name given to the peasant revolt in France during the fourteenth century.

Jansenism A religious movement among French Catholics stressing the emotional experience of religious belief.

Jesuits (jéh-zu-its) Members of the Catholic religious order the Society of Jesus, founded by Ignatius Loyola in 1534.

Jihad (jée-hod) Islamic holy war in which believers feel they have the authority to fight to defend the faith.

Joint-stock company A business firm that is owned by stockholders who may sell or transfer their shares individually.

Journeyman A worker in a craft who has served his or her apprenticeship.

Joust A medieval contest in which two mounted knights combat with lances.

Junkers (yóong-kers) Prussian aristocracy.

Justification by faith The belief that faith alone—not good works—is needed for salvation. This belief lies at the heart of Protestantism.

K

Kamikaze (kah-mih-káh-zee) Usually refers to suicidal attacks on Allied ships by Japanese pilots during World War II.

Kore (kóh-ray) (pl. *korai*) Greek word for maiden that refers to an ancient Greek statue of a standing female, usually clothed.

Kouros (kóo-ross) (pl. *kouroi*) Greek word for a young man that refers to an ancient Greek statue of a standing nude young man.

Kristallnacht (kriss-táhl-nahkt) The "night of the broken glass"—a Nazi attack on German Jewish homes and businesses in 1938.

Kulak (kóo-lock) A relatively wealthy Russian peasant labeled by Stalin during the period of collectivization as a "class enemy."

Kulturkampf (kool-tóur-kahmpf) Bismarck's fight against the Catholic Church in Germany during the 1870s.

L

Laissez-faire (léss-say-fair) "Hands-off." An economic doctrine opposing governmental regulation of most economic affairs.

Laudanum (láud-a-numb) Opium dissolved in alcohol, used as a medicine in the eighteenth and nineteenth centuries.

League of Nations A post–World War I association of countries to deal with international tensions and conflicts.

Lebensraum (láy-benz-rowm) "Living space." Hitler's policy of expanding his empire to the east to gain more land for Germans.

Legume (lég-yoom) A pod, such as that of a pea or bean, used as food.

Levée en masse (le-váy awn máhss) General call-up of all men, women, and children to serve the nation during the French Revolution.

Levellers Revolutionaries who tried to "level" the social hierarchy during the English civil war.

Liberalism A nineteenth- and twentieth-century ideology supporting individualism, political freedom, constitutional government, and (in the nineteenth century) laissez-faire economic policies.

Liege (léezh) **lord** In the feudal system, a lord who has many vassals, but owes allegiance to no one.

Linear perspective An artistic technique used to represent three-dimensional space convincingly on a flat surface.

Lollards Followers of the English church reformer John Wycliffe who were found heretical.

Long March An arduous Chinese communist retreat from south China to north China in 1934 and 1935.

Luddism The smashing of machines that took jobs away from workers in the first half of the nineteenth century.

M

Ma'at (máh-aht) An Egyptian spiritual precept that conveyed the idea of truth and justice, or, as the Egyptians put it, right order and harmony.

Maccabean (mack-uh-bée-en) **Revolt** Successful Jewish revolt led by Judas Maccabeus in the mid-second century B.C.E. against Hellenistic Seleucid rulers.

Madrigal Musical composition set to a short poem usually about love, written for several voices. Common in Renaissance music.

Magi (máyj-eye) Ancient Persian astrologers or "wise men."

Maginot (máh-zhin-oh) **Line** A string of defensive fortresses on the French/German border that France began building in the late 1920s.

Magna Carta The Great Charter that English barons forced King John of England to sign in 1215 that guaranteed certain rights to the English people. Seen as one of the bases for constitutional law.

Marshall Plan A package of massive economic aid to European nations offered in 1947 to strengthen them and tie them to American influence.

Marxism A variety of socialism propounded by Karl Marx stressing economic determinism and class struggle—"scientific socialism."

Megalith An archaeological term for a stone of great size used in ancient monuments.

Meiji (máy-jee) **Restoration** The reorganizing of Japanese society along modern Western lines; initiated in 1868.

Mendicant orders Members of a religious order, such as the Dominicans or Franciscans, who wandered from city to city begging for alms rather than residing in a monastery.

Mercantilism (mírr-kan-till-ism) Early modern governmental economic policies seeking to control and develop the national economy and bring wealth into the national treasury.

Mercator (mer-káy-ter) **projection** A method of making maps in which the earth's surface is shown as a rectangle with Europe at the center, causing distortion toward the poles.

Mesolithic Of or pertaining to the period of human culture from about 15,000 years ago to about 7000 B.C.E. characterized by complex stone tools and greater social organization. "Middle Stone Age."

Methodism A Protestant sect founded in the eighteenth century that emphasized piety and emotional worship.

Metics (métt-iks) Foreign residents of Athens.

Miasma (my-ázz-ma) Fumes from waste and marshes blamed for carrying diseases during the eighteenth and the first half of the nineteenth centuries.

Middle Passage The long sea voyage between the African coast and the Americas endured by newly captured slaves.

Minoan (mínn-oh-an) A civilization that lived on the island of Crete from 2800 to 1450 B.C.E.

Mir (mere) Russian village commune.

Missi dominici (mée-see do-min-ée-kee) Royal officials under Charlemagne who traveled around the country to enforce the king's laws.

Mithraism (míth-ra-ism) A Hellenistic mystery religion that appealed to soldiers and involved the worship of the god Mithra.

Mughals (móe-gulls) Islamic rulers of much of India in the sixteenth, seventeenth, and eighteenth centuries.

Munich Conference The 1938 conference where Britain and France attempted to appease Hitler by allowing him to dismantle Czechoslovakia.

Myceaean (my-sen-ée-an) A civilization on the Greek peninsula that reached its high point between 1400 and 1200 B.C.E.

Mystery religions Ancient religions that encouraged believers to cultivate a deep connection with their deity. Initiates swore not to reveal the insights they had gained during rites and ceremonies; the shroud of secrecy resulted in the name "mystery" religions.

N

Napoleonic (na-po-lee-ón-ik) **Code** The legal code introduced in France by Napoleon Bonaparte.

Nationalism A nineteenth- and twentieth-century ideology stressing the importance of national identity and the nation-state.

Natural law Understandable, rational laws of nature that apply to the physical and human world.

Nazi Party Hitler's German National Socialist Party.

Neolithic (nee-oh-líth-ik) Of or denoting a period of human culture beginning around 7000 B.C.E. in the Middle East and later elsewhere, characterized by the invention of farming and the making of technically advanced stone implements. "New Stone Age."

Neoplatonism (nee-oh-pláy-ton-ism) Views based on the ideas of Plato that one should search beyond appearances for true knowledge; stressed abstract reasoning.

New Economic Policy (NEP) Lenin's compromise economic and social policy for the USSR during the 1920s.

New imperialism The second wave of Western imperialism, particularly between 1880 and 1914.

Night of August 4 Surrender of most privileges by the French aristocracy at a meeting held on August 1, 1789.

Nominalism (nóm-in-al-ism) A popular late-medieval philosophy based on the doctrine that the universal, or general, has no objective existence or validity, being merely a name expressing the qualities of various objects resembling one another in certain respects. Also called New Nominalism.

North American Free Trade Agreement (NAFTA) The 1994 agreement between the United States, Mexico, and Canada to create a free trade zone.

North Atlantic Treaty Organization (NATO) A military alliance against the Soviet Union initiated in 1949.

Nuremberg Laws Hitler's anti-Jewish laws of 1935.

O

Ockham's razor A principle that states that between alternative explanations for the same phenomenon, the simplest is always to be preferred.

October Revolution The 1917 Bolshevik revolt and seizure of power in Russia.

Old Regime (re-zhéem) European society before the French Revolution.

Oligarchy (áh-luh-gar-kee) Rule by a small group or by a particular social class—often wealthy middle classes, as in ancient Greek or medieval European cities.

Operation Barbarossa (bar-bar-óh-ssa) The German invasion of the USSR during World War II.

Optimates (ahp-tuh-máht-ays) The nobility of the Roman Empire. Also refers to the political party that supported the nobility. Contrast with the *populares*.

Ordeal An ancient form of trial in which the accused was exposed to physical dangers that were presumed to be harmless if the accused was innocent. Ordeals might include grasping hot pokers, trial by battle, immersion in water, and other similar challenges.

Organization of Petroleum Exporting Countries (OPEC) An Arab-dominated organization of Middle Eastern oil-producing states that became effective during and after the 1970s.

Ostracism (áhs-tra-sism) A political technique of ancient Greece by which people believed to be threats to the city-state were chosen, by popular vote, for exile.

P

Paleolithic (pay-lee-oh-líth-ik) Of or pertaining to the period of human culture beginning with the earliest chipped stone tools, about 750,000 years ago, until the beginning of the Mesolithic, about 15,000 years ago. "Old Stone Age."

Pantheon (pán-thee-on) A great temple in Rome built in 27 B.C.E. and dedicated to all the gods. In 609 C.E., it was rededicated as a Christian church called Santa Maria Rotunda.

Paris Commune The revolutionary government of the city of Paris, first in the 1790s and then in 1871.

Parlement (parl-máwn) A French court of law during the Old Regime.

Parliament Britain's legislature, including the House of Commons and House of Lords.

Parthenon (párth-uh-non) A famous Doric temple of Athena on the Acropolis in ancient Athens.

Patricians The ancient Roman aristocracy who populated the Senate and were particularly powerful during the Republic.

Pax Romana ("pocks" or "packs" row-máhn-ah) Literally, "Roman Peace." Two hundred years of relative, internal peace within the Roman Empire beginning with the rule of Caesar Augustus.

Peace of Paris The 1919 peace settlement after World War I.

Peers Members of the House of Lords in England.

Perestroika (pair-ess-trói-ka) Gorbachev's policy of "restructuring" the Soviet economy during the 1980s.

Petrine (pée-tryn) **doctrine** The belief that the popes, bishops of Rome, should lead the church because they are the successors of Peter, who many claim was the first bishop of Rome.

Phalanstery (fa-láns-ter-ee) The model commune envisioned by the French utopian socialist Fourier.

Phalanx (fáy-langks) An ancient Greek formation of foot soldiers carrying overlapping shields and long spears.

Pharaoh The title of the rulers of ancient Egypt. Also refers to the household and administration of the rulers.

Pharisees (fáir-uh-sees) Members of an ancient Jewish sect that rigidly observed purity laws, including dietary rules. They also believed in the resurrection of the just and the existence of angels.

Philosophes (fee-low-zóffs) Leading French intellectuals of the Enlightenment.

Phonogram A character or symbol used to represent a speech sound used in ancient writing.

Physiocrats (fízz-ee-oh-crats) Eighteenth-century French economic thinkers who stressed the importance of agriculture and favored free trade.

Pictogram A picture representing an idea used in ancient writing.

Pietism (píe-uh-tism) An eighteenth-century Protestant movement stressing an emotional commitment to religion.

Plebeians (pleb-ée-ans) The members of the urban lower classes in ancient Rome.

Plebiscite (pléb-uh-sight) A direct vote that allows the people to either accept or reject a proposed measure.

Pogrom (puh-grúhm; also: póe-grom) An organized persecution or massacre of Jews, especially in eastern Europe.

Polis (póe-liss) (pl. *poleis* [póe-lease]) An ancient Greek city-state.

Poor Laws Eighteenth- and nineteenth-century British laws enacted to deal with the poor.

Populares (pop-you-lahr-ays) In Roman history, the political party of the common people. Also refers to the people themselves. Contrast with the *optimates*.

Popular Front The political partnership of parties of the Left, particularly in France and Spain, during the 1930s.

Positivism A mid-nineteenth-century theory of sociology holding that scientific investigation could discover useful fundamental truths about humans and their societies.

Postindustrial societies Late-twentieth-century societies that moved from manufacturing to services led by professionals, managers, and financiers.

Postmodernism A late-twentieth-century approach to the arts stressing relativism and multiple interpretations.

Praetorian guard Personal bodyguard of the Roman emperors.

Pragmatic Sanction The international agreement secured by the Habsburg emperor in the 1730s to ensure that his daughter would succeed him without question.

Prague Spring The brief period of democratic reforms and cultural freedom in Czechoslovakia during 1968.

Predestination Doctrine claiming that since God is all-knowing and all-powerful, he must know in advance who is saved or damned. Therefore, the salvation of any individual is predetermined. This doctrine is emphasized by Calvinists.

Preemptive war War initiated by one side on the justification that another side was on the verge of attack.

Prefect Powerful agents of the central government stationed in France's departments.

Preventive war War initiated by one side on the justification that another side might attack sometime in the future.

Principate (prínce-a-pate) The governmental system of the Roman Empire founded by Octavian (also known as Caesar Augustus).

Privateer An armed private vessel commissioned by a government to attack enemy ships.

Protestant Of or pertaining to any branch of the Christian church excluding Roman Catholicism and Eastern Orthodox.

Psychoanalysis Pioneered by Sigmund Freud, a method of investigating human psychological development and treating emotional disorders.

Ptolemaic (ptah-luh-máy-ik) **system** The traditional medieval earth-centered universe and system of planetary movements.

Ptolemies (ptáh-luh-meez) Hellenistic dynasty that ruled in Egypt from about 300 B.C.E. to about 30 B.C.E.

Purgatory In Roman Catholic theology, a state or place in which those who have died in the grace of God expiate their sins by suffering before they can enter heaven.

Purge Expelling or executing political party members suspected of inefficiency or opposition to party policy.

Puritans In the sixteenth and seventeenth centuries, those who wanted to reform the Church of England by removing all elaborate ceremonies and forms. Many Puritans faced persecution and were forced to flee to the American colonies.

Q

Quadrant An instrument for taking altitude of heavenly bodies.

Quadrivium (quad-rív-ee-um) The medieval school curriculum that studied arithmetic, music, geometry, and astronomy after completion of the trivium.

Quadruple (quad-róo-pull) **Alliance** Alliance of Austria, Prussia, Russia, and France in the years after the Napoleonic Wars to maintain the status quo.

Quietism (quíet-ism) A movement among seventeenth-century Spanish Catholics that emphasized the emotional experience of religious belief.

Qur'an (also Koran) The Muslim holy book recorded in the early seventh century by the prophet Muhammad.

R

Racism Belief that racial differences are important and that some races are superior to others.

Raison d'état (ráy-zawn day-táh) "Reason of state." An eighteenth- and nineteenth-century principle justifying arbitrary or aggressive international behavior.

Rationalism The belief that, through reason, humans can understand the world and solve problems.

Realism A medieval Platonist philosophy that believed that the individual objects we perceive are not real, but merely reflections of universal ideas existing in the mind of God. In the nineteenth century, this referred to a cultural style rejecting romanticism and attempting to examine society as it is.

Realpolitik (ray-áhl-po-lee-teek) The pragmatic politics of power; often a self-interested foreign policy associated with Bismarck.

Redshirts Garibaldi's troops used in the unification of Italy.

Reform Bill of 1832 English electoral reform extending the vote to the middle classes of the new industrial cities.

Reichstag (ríkes-tahg) German legislative assembly.

Reign of Terror The violent period of the French Revolution between 1792 and 1794.

Relativity Einstein's theory that all aspects of the physical universe must be defined in relative terms.

Relics In the Roman Catholic and Greek Orthodox churches, valued remnants of saints or other religious figures. Relics usually are parts of bodies but may also include objects that had touched sacred bodies or that were associated with Jesus or Mary, such as remnants of the True Cross.

Renaissance Literally, "rebirth." The term was coined in Italy in the early fourteenth century to refer to the rebirth of the appreciation of classical (Greek and Roman) literature and values. It also refers to the culture that was born in Italy during that century that ultimately spread throughout Europe.

Resistance movements Underground opposition to occupation forces, especially to German troops in conquered European countries during World War II.

Restoration The conservative regimes in power after the defeat of Napoleon in 1815 that hoped to hold back the forces of change or even turn back the clock to prerevolutionary days.

Risorgimento (ree-sor-jee-mén-toe) A nineteenth-century Italian unification movement.

Rococo (roe-coe-cóe) A style of art developed from the baroque that originated in France during the eighteenth century that emphasized elaborate designs to produce a delicate effect.

Romanesque (Roman-ésk) A style of architecture usually associated with churches built in the eleventh and twelfth centuries and that was inspired by Roman architectural features. Romanesque buildings were massive, with round arches, barrel vaulted ceilings, and dark interiors.

Romanticism A cultural ideology during the first half of the nineteenth century stressing feeling over reason.

Rosetta Stone A tablet of black basalt found in 1799 at Rosetta, Egypt, that contains parallel inscriptions in Greek, ancient Egyptian demotic script, and hieroglyphic characters. The stone provided the key to deciphering ancient Egyptian writing.

Rostra The speaker's platform in the Forum of ancient Rome.

Roundheads Members or supporters of the Parliamentary or Puritan party in England during the English civil war (1642).

Royal absolutism The seventeenth- and eighteenth-century system of elevated royal authority.

S

Sacraments In Christianity, rites that were to bring the individual grace or closeness to God. In Roman Catholicism and Greek Orthodoxy there are seven sacraments: baptism, confirmation, the Eucharist, penance, extreme unction, holy orders, and matrimony. Protestants in general acknowledge only two sacraments: baptism and the Lord's Supper.

Sadducees (sád-juh-sees) Members of an ancient Jewish sect that emphasized worship at the Temple in Jerusalem. They rejected new ideas such as resurrection, insisting on only those ideas that could be found in the Torah.

Saga A medieval Scandinavian story of battles, customs, and legends, narrated in prose and generally telling the traditional history of an important Norse family.

Salon (suh-láhn) Seventeenth- and eighteenth-century social and cultural gatherings of members of the upper and middle classes.

Sans-culottes (sawn-key-lóht) Working-class people of Paris during the French Revolution.

Sarcophagus (sar-kóff-a-gus) A stone coffin.

Satellite states Eastern European states under the control of the Soviet Union during the Cold War.

Satrap (sát-trap) An ancient Persian governor in charge of provinces called "satrapies."

Schlieffen (shléaf-en) **Plan** German military strategy in World War I that called for a holding action against Russia while German forces moved through Belgium to knock out France.

Scholasticism The dominant medieval philosophical and theological movement that applied logic from Aristotle to help understand God's plan. It also refers to the desire to join faith with reason.

Scientific Revolution The new sixteenth- and seventeenth-century methods of investigation and discoveries about nature based on observation and reason rather than tradition and authority.

Scutage (skyóot-ij) Medieval payment in lieu of military service.

Second Reich (rike) German regime founded in 1871 and lasting until the end of World War I.

Seleucids (se-lóo-sids) Hellenistic dynasty that ruled in Asia from about 300 B.C.E. to about 64 B.C.E.

Semitic (sem-ít-ik) Of or pertaining to any of a group of Caucasoid peoples, chiefly Jews and Arabs, of the eastern Mediterranean area.

Senate, Roman The deliberative body and influential governing council of Rome during the Republic and Empire. Composed of ex-magistrates with lifetime membership, the Senate did not legislate, but conducted foreign policy and warfare and authorized public expenditures.

Sepoy (sée-poy) **Mutiny** The 1857 uprising of Indians against British rule.

Septuagint (sep-tu-eh-jint) A Greek translation of the Hebrew scriptures (the Old Testament), so named because it was said to be the work of 72 Palestinian Jews in the third century B.C.E., who completed the work in seventy days.

Serfs Medieval peasants who were personally free, but bound to the land. They owed labor obligations as well as fees.

Shi'ite (shée-ite) **Muslims** Those who accepted only the descendants of 'Ali, Muhammad's son-in-law, as the true rulers. It was not the majority party in Islam but did prevail in some of the Muslim countries.

Shire An English county.

Sinn Fein (shín féign) "Ourselves Alone." An extremist twentieth-century Irish nationalist organization.

Skepticism (skép-ti-cism) The systematic doubting of accepted authorities—especially religious authorities.

Social Darwinism The effort to apply Darwin's biological ideas to social ideas stressing competition and "survival of the fittest."

Socialists Those promoting or practicing the nineteenth- and twentieth-century ideology of socialism, stressing cooperation, community, and public ownership of the means of production.

Socratic method The method of arriving at truth by questioning and disputation.

Solidarity A Polish noncommunist union that became the core of resistance to the communist regime during the 1980s.

Sophists (sóff-ists) Fifth-century B.C.E. Greek philosophers who were condemned for using tricky logic to prove that all things are relative and success alone is important.

Sovereignty (sóv-rin-tee) The source of authority exercised by a state; complete independence and self-government.

Soviet A workers' council during the 1905 and 1917 Russian revolutions and part of the structure of government in the Soviet Union.

SS The Schutzstaffel, Hitler's elite party troops of the 1930s and 1940s.

Stadholder (stáhd-holder) A governor of provinces in the Dutch United Provinces.

Statutory law Laws established by a king or legislative body. Contrast with common law.

Stoicism (stów-i-cism) A Hellenistic philosophy that advocated detachment from the material world and an indifference to pain.

Strategoi (stra-táy-goy) Generals in ancient Athens who eventually took a great deal of political power.

Struggle of the Orders The political strife between patrician and plebeian Romans beginning in the fifth century B.C.E. The plebeians gradually won political rights as a result of the struggle.

Sturm und drang (shtúrm unt dráhng) "Storm and stress." A literary movement in late eighteenth-century Germany.

Sumptuary (súmp-chew-air-ee) **laws** Laws restricting or regulating extravagance (for example, in food or dress), often used to maintain separation of social classes.

Sunna (sóon-a) A collection of sayings and traditions of the prophet Muhammad that delineates the customs adhered to by Muslims.

Supply and demand Adam Smith's liberal economic doctrine that demand for goods and services will stimulate production (supply) in a free-market system.

Surrealism (sur-rée-a-lism) A twentieth-century literary and artistic style stressing images from the unconscious mind.

Symphony A long sonata for orchestra.

Syncretism (sín-cre-tism) The attempt or tendency to combine or reconcile differing beliefs, as in philosophy or religion.

Syndicalism (sín-di-cal-ism) A late-nineteenth-century anarchist ideology envisioning labor unions as the center of a free and just society.

T

Taliban The strict, fundamentalist Islamic regime that ruled most of Afghanistan from 1996 to 2001.

Tennis Court Oath Oath taken by members of the French Estates General not to dissolve until they had created a constitution for France.

Tetradrachma (tet-ra-drák-ma) Hellenistic coin worth four drachmas.

Tetrarchy (tét-rar-key) The governmental system of the Roman Empire founded by Diocletian that divided the empire into four administrative units.

Theocracy (thee-áh-kruh-see) Government by priests claiming to rule by divine authority.

Theme A division for the purpose of provincial administration in the Byzantine Empire.

Thermidorian (ther-mi-dór-ee-an) **Reaction** The overthrow of Robespierre and the radicals in July 1794, during the French Revolution.

Third Estate Commoners, or all people except the nobility and clergy, in early modern European society.

Third French Republic The republican government established in 1871 and lasting until Germany's defeat of France in 1940.

Torah (tór-uh) The first five books of the Jewish sacred scriptures, comprising Genesis, Exodus, Leviticus, Numbers, and Deuteronomy.

Tories A conservative British political party during the eighteenth and nineteenth centuries.

Totalitarianism A twentieth-century form of authoritarian government using force, technology, and bureaucracy to effect rule by a single party and controlling most aspects of the lives of the population.

Total war A form of warfare in which all the forces and segments of society are mobilized for a long, all-out struggle.

Transubstantiation (trán-sub-stan-chee-áy-shun) In the Roman Catholic and Greek Orthodox churches, the belief that the bread and wine of the Eucharist were transformed into the actual body and blood of Christ.

Trench warfare An almost stagnant form of defensive warfare fought from trenches.

Triangular trade Trade pattern between European nations and their colonies by which European manufactured goods were traded for raw materials (such as agricultural products) from the Americas or slaves from Africa.

Tribune An official of ancient Rome chosen by the common people to protect their rights.

Triple Alliance Alliance of Germany, Austria-Hungary, and Italy in the years before World War I.

Triumvirate (try-úm-vir-ate) A group of three men sharing civil authority, as in ancient Rome.

Trivium (trív-ee-um) The basic medieval curriculum that studied grammar, rhetoric, and logic; after completion, students could proceed to the quadrivium.

Troubadour (tróo-buh-door) Poets from the late twelfth and early thirteenth centuries who wrote love poems, meant to be sung to music, that reflected the new sensibility of courtly love, which claimed that lovers were ennobled.

Truman Doctrine U.S. policy initiated in 1947 that offered military and economic aid to countries threatened by a communist takeover with the intention of creating a military ring of containment around the Soviet Union and its satellite states.

Tsar The emperor of Russia.

Twelve Tables According to ancient Roman tradition, popular pressure in the fifth century B.C.E. led to the writing down of traditional laws to put an end to patrician monopoly of the laws. The resulting compilation—the Twelve Tables—was seen as the starting point for the tradition of Roman law.

U

Ultra-royalism The nineteenth-century belief in rule by a monarch and that everything about the French Revolution and Enlightenment was contrary to religion, order, and civilization.

Unconscious According to Freud, that part of the mind of which we are not aware; home of basic drives.

Unilateralism Actions or policies taken by one nation in its own interests regardless of the views and interests of its allies.

United Nations (UN) An international organization founded in 1945 to promote peace and cooperation.

Universal A metaphysical entity that does not change, but that describes particular things on earth—for example, "justice" or "beauty." Explained by the ancient Greeks and examined by subsequent philosophers. (Also called "forms" or "ideas.")

Utilitarianism (you-till-a-táre-ee-an-ism) A nineteenth-century liberal philosophy that evaluated institutions on the basis of social usefulness to achieve "the greatest happiness of the greatest number."

Utopian (you-tópe-ee-an) **socialism** A form of early nineteenth-century socialism urging cooperation and communes rather than competition and individualism.

V

Vassal In the feudal system, a noble who binds himself to his lord in return for maintenance.

Versailles (ver-sígh) **treaty** Peace treaty between the Allies and Germany following World War I.

Victorian Referring to the period of Queen Victoria's reign in Britain, 1837–1901.

Vulgate (vúll-gate) A version of the Latin Bible, primarily translated from Hebrew and Greek by Jerome.

W

Wahhabism (wuh-háh-biz-uhm) An Islamic reform movement founded in the eighteenth century that stressed a strict, literal interpretation of the Qur'an.

War guilt clause Article 231 of the Treaty of Versailles that places all blame on Germany for causing World War I.

Warsaw Pact A military alliance in Eastern Europe controlled by the Soviet Union and initiated in 1955.

Waterloo Site in Belgium of a decisive defeat of Napoleon in 1815.

Weimar (wy'e-mar) **Republic** The liberal German government established at the end of World War I and destroyed by Hitler in the 1930s.

Welfare state Governmental programs to protect citizens from severe economic hardships and to provide basic social needs.

Wergeld (véhr-gelt) In Germanic law, the relative price of individuals that established the fee for compensation in case of injury.

Whigs A British political party during the eighteenth and nineteenth centuries.

Witan The ancient Anglo-Saxon men who participated in the Witenagemot.

Witenagemot (wí-ten-uh-guh-mote) Ancient Anglo-Saxon assembly of nobles.

Z

Zealots (zéll-ets) An ancient Jewish sect arising in Palestine in about 6 C.E. that militantly opposed Roman rule and desired to establish an independent Jewish state. The sect was wiped out when the Romans destroyed Jerusalem in 70 C.E.

Zemstva (zémst-fah) Municipal councils established in Russia in the second half of the nineteenth century.

Ziggurat (zíg-gur-raht) A pyramid-shaped Mesopotamian temple.

Zionism A late-nineteenth- and twentieth-century Jewish nationalist movement to create an independent state for Jews in Palestine.

Zollverein (tsóll-ver-rhine) Nineteenth-century German customs union headed by Prussia.

Zoroastrianism (zorro-áss-tree-an-ism) An ancient Persian religion that had a belief in two gods: a god of light named Ahura Mazda and an evil god named Ahriman.

Credits

PHOTO

Chapter 1

Page xxxii: Rites before the tomb. Page from the Book of the Dead of Hunefer. Thebes, Egypt, 19th Dynasty, ca. 1300 BCE. Papyrus, 45.7 x 83.4 cm. Inv.: EA 9901, sheet 5. Location: British Museum, London, Great Britain. © The Trustees of The British Museum/Art Resource, NY; p. 2: Marijan Murat/dpa/Corbis; p. 3: PhotoDisc/Getty Images; p. 6: World Religions Photo Library/The Bridgeman Art Library; p. 8: Ashmolean Museum, Oxford, UK/Bridgeman Art Library; p. 12: Corbis; p. 13R: © Fancy Photography/Veer; p. 13L: The Palma Collection/Getty Images; p. 14: Private Collection/ The Bridgeman Art Library; p. 15: Aegyptisches Museum, Staatliche Museen zu Berlin, Germany/ Erich Lessing/Art Resource, NY; p. 16: M. Busing/ Bildarchiv Preussischer Kulturbesitz/Art Resource; p. 24: PhotoDisc/Getty Images.

Chapter 2

Page 26: PRISMA ARCHIVO/Alamy; p. 30: Archaeological Museum, Heraklion, Crete, Greece/Erich Lessing/Art Resource, NY; p. 32L: National Archaeological Museum, Piraeus, Greece/Nimatallah/Art Resource, NY; p. 32R: Acropolis Museum, Athens, Greece/Nimatallah/ Art Resource, NY; p. 34: Archives Charmet/The Bridgeman Art Library; p. 36: Attributed to The Bryn Mawr Painter. Red-figure Plate with Woman Playing Kottabos, 480 BC. Terracotta; actual: 2.5 x 21.8 cm (1 x 8 9/16 in.). Harvard Art Museums, Arthur M. Sackler Museum, Bequest of David M. Robinson, 1960.350. Photo: Michael Nedzweski © President and Fellows of Harvard College; p. 39: National Archaeological Museum, Athens, Greece/Erich Lessing/Art Resource, NY; p. 41R: USDOD; p. 41L: The Art Archive/National Archaeological Museum Athens/Dagli Orti; p. 43: Acropolis Museum, Athens, Greece/Nimatallah/Art Resource, NY; p. 48: Digital Vision/Getty Images.

Chapter 3

Page 50: Archaeological Museum, Istanbul, Turkey/ Erich Lessing/Art Resource, NY; p. 54L: The Art Archive/Musée Archéologique Naples/Alfredo Dagli Orti; p. 54R: Dynamic Graphics Group/ PunchStock; p. 59: The British Museum, London, England/Art Resource, NY; p. 60a: Hermitage, St. Petersburg, Russia/Bridgeman Art Library; p. 60b: © The Trustees of the British Museum/ Art Resource, NY; p. 62: Bibliotheque Nationale, Paris, France/Bridgeman-Giraudon/Art Resource, NY; p. 64: Bildarchiv Preussischer Kulturbesitz/Art Resource; p. 65: Vanni/Art Resource; p. 69: Museo di Villa Albani, Rome, Italy/Alinari/Art Resource, NY; p. 70: © s. Stoltzfuss/Iconotec.

Chapter 4

Page 72: Museo Archeologico Prenestino, Palestrina, Italy/The Bridgeman Art Library;

p. 75: The Louvre Museum, Paris, France/ Erich Lessing/Art Resource, NY; p. 80: Galleria Nazionale d'Arte Antica (Pal. Barberini-Corsini), Rome,Italy/Alinari/Art Resource, NY; p. 81R: Tom A. Peter/Christian Science Monitor/Getty Images; p. 81L: Scala/Art Resource, NY; p. 82L: Mansell Collection/Alinari/Art Resource, NY; p. 82R: Scala/Art Resource, NY; p. 83: Museo Pio Clementino/Vatican Museums, Vatican State/ Scala/Art Resource, NY; p. 86: © Mary Evans Picture Library/The Image Works; p. 88: Scala/Art Resource, NY; p. 92: © iStockphoto.com/Ammit; p. 93: The British Museum.

Chapter 5

Page 94: Scala/Art Resource, NY; p. 98: Braccio Nuovo/Vatican Museums, Vatican State/Scala/ Art Resource, NY; p. 103: R. Balsley; p. 104L: Scala/Art Resource, NY; p. 104R: Royalty-free/ Corbis; p. 105: Scala/Art Resource NY; p. 106TL: Corbis; p. 106TR: Corbis; p. 106B: Deutsches Archäologisches Institut, Rome, Italy; p. 108: Alinari/Art Resource, NY; p. 114L: David H. Wells/Corbis; p. 118: Museo Pio Cristiano, Vatican Museums, Vatican State/Scala/Art Resource, NY; p. 119: Mausoleum of Galla Placidia, Ravenna, Italy/Scala/Art Resource, NY; p. 121: © Image Source.

Chapter 6

Page 122: Scala/Art Resource; p. 125B: Heribert Proepper/AP Images; p. 125TL: Photodisc/Getty Images; p. 125TR: © Imagestate Media (John Foxx)/Imagestate; p. 129: The Board of Trinity College, Dublin, Ireland/Bridgeman Art Library; p. 130: Bibliotheque nationale de France/Art Resource, NY; p. 132: Bayerische Staatsbibliothek, Muenchen, Germany, Clm 4452, fol.152v; p. 134: John A. Rizzo/Getty Images; p. 136T: S. Vitale, Ravenna, Italy/Scala/Art Resource, NY; p. 136B: S. Vitale, Ravenna, Italy/Scala/ Art Resource, NY; p. 138: Prado, Madrid, Spain/ The Bridgeman Art Library; p. 141: Pergamon Museum, Berlin, Germany/The Bridgeman Art Library; p. 145: Real Monasterio del Escorial Spain/Granger Collection/Art Archive; p. 146: © iStockphoto.com/Xavier de Tarade.

Chapter 7

Page 148: Viking Ship Museum, Bygdoy, Norway/ Werner Forman/Art Resource, NY; p. 154: British Library, London, UK/© British Library Board. All Rights Reserved/The Bridgeman Art Library; p. 155T: The Louvre Museum, Paris, France/Erich Lessing/Art Resource, NY; p. 157: S. Giovanni in Laterano, Rome, Italy/Alinari/Art Resource, NY; p. 159: Private Collection/ The Bridgeman Art Library; p. 162: Viking Ship Museum, Oslo, Norway/Giraudon/The Bridgeman Art Library; p. 166: Vassal pledging fealty and receiving a fief from his Lord (fol. 6v. of the Heidelberg MS. Cod., Pal. Germ.164). Ruprecht-Karls Universitaatsbibliothek Heidelberg; p. 168TL:

HIP/Art Resource, NY; p. 168TR: Tom Grill/ Corbis; p. 168B: Viking Ship Museum, Bygdoy, Norway/Werner Forman/Art Resource, NY.

Chapter 8

Page 170: Detail from the Bayeux Tapestry, before 1082 (wool embroidery on linen)/Musee de la Tapisserie, Bayeux, France/The Bridgeman Art Library; p. 173: Sts. *Oswald and Aidan and the beggars who will share their dinner.* Master of the Berthold Sacramentary (13th CE). The Weingarten Missal. Germany, Weingarten Abbey, c. 1200–1232. M.710, f.101v. The Pierpont Morgan Library, New York, N.Y./Art Resource, NY; p. 174R: Kim Steele/Getty Images; p. 174L: Andrew Ward/Life File/Getty Images; p. 177: Snark/Art Resource, NY; p. 178L: Ste. Madeleine, Vézelay, France/Scala/Art Resource, NY; p. 178R: Amiens Cathedral, France/Scala/Art Resource, NY; p. 179: Sainte Chapelle, Paris, France/Bridgeman-Giraudon/Art Resource, NY; p. 180: Photo: Joerg P. Anders.Bildarchiv Preussischer Kulturbesitz/Art Resource, NY; p. 181: TTL Images/Alamy Images; p. 182: University Library Heidelberg/Gianni Dagli Orti/The Art Archive; p. 190: Bildarchiv Preussischer Kulturbesitz/Art Resource, NY; p. 196: Detail from the Bayeux Tapestry, before 1082 (wool embroidery on linen)/Musee de la Tapisserie, Bayeux, France/The Bridgeman Art Library; p. 197: British Library/HIP/Art Resource, NY.

Chapter 9

Page 198: *Danse Macabre* (oil on canvas) (detail of 197686), Notke, Bernt (c.1440–1509)/ St Nicholas' Church, Art Museum of Estonia, Tallinn, Estonia/The Bridgeman Art Library; p. 202T: *Les Belles Heures de Jean, Duc de Berry* by Pol, Jean and Herman de Limbourg (active ca. 1400–1416). Folio 74v: Procession of Flagellants. Tempera and gold leaf on parchment. Accession #54.1.1. The Metropolitan Museum of Art, The Cloisters Collection, 1954. (54.1.1) Photograp. © 1987 The Metropolitan Museum of Art/Art Resource; p. 202B: British Library, London, UK/ Bridgeman Art Library; p. 207B: Erich Lessing/ Art Resource, NY; p. 207TL: © ullstein bild/ The Granger Collection; p. 207TR: Purestock/ Superstock; p. 210: Duomo, Florence, Italy/Scala/ Art Resource, NY; p. 211: Photo: R.G. Ojeda. Musée Condé, Chantilly, France/Réunion des Musées Nationaux/Art Resource, NY; p. 213: Bibliotheque nationale de France; p. 216: Erich Lessing/Art Resource, NY.

Chapter 10

Page 218: Accademia, Venice, Italy/Erich Lessing/Art Resource, NY; p. 221: The Sistine Chapel, Vatican Palace, Vatican State/Scala/ Art Resource, NY; p. 229: Pinacoteca, Vatican Museums, Vatican State/Scala/Art Resource, NY; p. 231: Gabinetto dei Disegni e delle Stampe, Uffizi, Florence, Italy/Scala/Art Resource, NY; p. 233: Camera degli Sposi, Palazzo Ducale,

Mantua, Italy/Scala/Art Resource, NY; p. 234T: Reproduced by kind permission of the Ministero per i Beni e le Attivita Culturali, Italy/Biblioteca Nazionale Centrale di Firenze; p. 235L: Duomo, Florence, Italy/Scala/Art Resource, NY; p. 235R: Corbis; p. 236: Stanza della Segnatura, Stanze di Raffaello, Vatican Palace, Vatican State/Scala/Art Resource, NY; p. 238: Bettmann/Corbis; p. 241B: The Granger Collection; p. 241TR: © Contographer/Corbis; p. 241TL: C. Bowman/Getty Images; p. 242: Accademia, Venice, Italy/Erich Lessing/Art Resource, NY.

Chapter 11

Page 244: Musée des Beaux Arts Lausanne/Gianni Dagli Orti/The Art Archive; p. 248: The Louvre Museum, Paris, France/Scala/Art Resource, NY; p. 251: Bildarchiv Preussischer Kulturbesitz; p. 255: The Granger Collection, NY; p. 256: National Portrait Gallery, London, UK/The Bridgeman Art Library; p. 257: Courtesy of The Marquess of Salisbury, Hatfield House/Fotomas Index/Topfoto/The Image Works; p. 261: S. Tome, Toledo, Spain/Bridgeman-Giraudon/Art Resource, NY; p. 264L: Erich Lessing/Art Resource, NY; p. 264R: © Mary Evans/Castle Howard/The Image Works; p. 267: Giraudon/The Bridgeman Art Library International; p. 268: Bildarchiv Preussischer Kulturbesitz; p. 269: National Gallery, London/Art Resource, NY.

Chapter 12

Page 270: Library of the Hispanic Society of America, New York; p. 273: Royal Geographical Society, London, UK/Bridgeman Art Library; p. 274: The Pierpont Morgan Library/Art Resource, NY; p. 276: Private Collection/The Bridgeman Art Library; p. 279: Biblioteca Nazionale, Firenze/Fotomas/Bridgeman Art Library; p. 281: The Granger Collection; p. 283L: © iStockphoto.com/FabioFilzi; p. 283R: © OSWALDO RIVAS/Reuters/Corbis; p. 284: SSPL/Science Museum/Art Resource, NY; p. 287: *Young Woman with a Water Pitcher*. Ca. 1662. Oil on canvas, 18 x 16 in. (45.7 x 40.6 cm). Vermeer (van Delft), Jan (1632–1675). The Metropolitan Museum of Art, Marquand Collection, Gift of Henry G. Marquand, 1889. (89.15.21). Photograp. © 1993 The Metropolitan Museum of Art/Art Resource, NY; p. 290: Typ 732.18.567, Department of Printing and Graphic Arts, Houghton Library, Harvard College Library; p. 294T: Royal Geographical Society, London, UK/Bridgeman Art Library; p. 294B: Fototeca Storica Nazionale/Getty Images.

Chapter 13

Page 296: The Louvre Museum, Paris, France/Scala/Art Resource, NY; p. 300: Erich Lessing/Art Resource, NY; p. 304: Réunion des Musées Nationaux/Art Resource, NY; p. 305: © National Gallery, London/Art Resource, NY; p. 311: Russian Historical Museum Moscow/Alfredo Dagli Orti/The Art Archive; p. 313: Dyck, Anthony van (1599–1641) *James Stuart (1612–1655), Duke of Richmond and Lennox*. ca. 1634–35. Oil on canvas, 85 x 50 1/4 in.

The Metropolitan Museum of Art, Marquand Collection, Gift of Henry G. Marquand, 1889. (89.15.16). Photograp. © 1998 The Metropolitan Museum of Art/Art Resource, NY; p. 315R: © HIP/Art Resource; p. 315L: © Lalage Snow/Corbis; p. 317T: The Granger Collection; p. 317B: British Library, London, UK/ Bridgeman Art Library; p. 319: British Library/HIP/Art Resource, NY; p. 322: The Granger Collection, New York; p. 322: © Pixtal/age Fotostock.

Chapter 14

Page 324: Erich Lessing/Art Resource, NY; p. 327: Charles Walker/Topfoto/The Image Works; p. 330: Snark/Art Resource, NY; p. 331: Image Select/Art Resource, NY; p. 334: Houghton Library, Harvard University; p. 335: Fitzwilliam Museum, University of Cambridge/Bridgeman Art Library; p. 338: Private Collection/The Stapleton Collection/The Bridgeman Art Library; p. 340L: © The Granger Collection, New York; p. 340R: Richard Alan Hannon/Getty Images; p. 341: Musee des Beaux-Arts, Dijon, France/Erich Lessing/Art Resource, NY; p. 342L: © Pixtal/age Fotostock; p. 342R: Library of Congress Prints and Photographs Division [LC-USZ62-47604]; p. 343: © Pixtal/age Fotostock.

Chapter 15

Page 344: Bristol City Museum and Art Gallery, UK/Bridgeman Art Library; p. 351: Mary Evans Picture Library; p. 353B: Harper Collins Publishers/The Art Archive; p. 353TL: Sandra Baker/Getty Images; p. 353TR: © Digital Vision Ltd./Getty Images; p. 354: National Maritime Museum, Greenwich, London, UK/The Art Archive; p. 360: The Granger Collection; p. 361: Germanisches Nationalmuseum, Nuremberg; p. 364: Réunion des Musées Nationaux/Art Resource, NY; p. 365: Réunion des Musées Nationaux/Art Resource, NY; p. 368: The Granger Collection.

Chapter 16

Page 370: Musee Carnavalet/Roger-Viollet/The Image Works/Bridgeman-Giraudon/Art Resource, NY; p. 374: Bettmann/Corbis; p. 375: Réunion des Musées Nationaux/Art Resource, NY; p. 378: Réunion des Musées Nationaux/Art Resource, NY; p. 381: Erich Lessing/Art Resource, NY; p. 383L: Scala/Art Resource; p. 383R: © Sean Adair/Reuters/Corbis; p. 384: Erich Lessing/Art Resource, NY; p. 388: Erich Lessing/Art Resource, NY; p. 391: Erich Lessing/Art Resource, NY; p. 392: Réunion des Musées Nationaux/Art Resource, NY.

Chapter 17

Page 394: Lady Lever Art Gallery, National Museums Liverpool/Bridgeman Art Library; p. 397: The Royal Collection © 2011, Her Majesty Queen Elizabeth II; p. 399: Science Museum, London, UK/Bridgeman Art Library; p. 400: Conseratoire National des Arts et Métiers - CNAM, Paris/Photo: P. Faligot, Seventh Square; p. 402: New Walk Museum, Leicester City Museum Service, UK/Bridgeman Art Library; p. 403: Guildhall Library, Corporation

of London, UK/Bridgeman Art Library; p. 406: General Research Division/Print Collection/Science, Industry & Business Library. New York Public Library/Art Resource; p. 409: The New York Public Library/Art Resource, NY; p. 412: Naudet, Caroline. *Voyage Et Conduite D'Un Moribund Pour L'autre Monde*. 1988-102-116. Philadelphia Museum of Art: The William H. Helfand Collection, 1988; p. 416TL: © Balean/TopFoto/The Image Works; p. 416TR: KAZUHIRO NOGI/AFP/Getty Images; p. 416: Library of Congress Prints and Photographs Division [LOC-USZC4-2860].

Chapter 18

Page 418: Musée du Petit Palais, Paris, France/Bridgeman-Giraudon/Art Resource, NY; p. 421: AKG Images, London; p. 425: London Stereoscopic Company/Getty Images; p. 428: Bildarchiv Preussischer Kulturbesitz/Art Resource, NY; p. 429: Yale Center for British Art, Paul Mellon Collection, USA/Bridgeman Art Library; p. 433: The Granger Collection; p. 434: Musée des Beaux-Arts, Bordeaux, France/Bridgeman-Giraudon/Art Resource, NY; p. 438: Erich Lessing/Art Resource, NY; p. 439L: bpk, Berlin/Art Resource; p. 439R: © SERGEY DOLZHENKO/epa/Corbis; p. 442: The Louvre Museum, Paris, France/Bridgeman-Giraudon/Art Resource, NY; p. 443: Musée du Petit Palais, Paris, France/Bridgeman-Giraudon/Art Resource, NY.

Chapter 19

Page 444: Bildarchiv Preussischer Kulturbesitz/Art Resource, NY; p. 448: Culver Pictures, Inc.; p. 450B: Bildarchiv Preussischer Kulturbesitz/Art Resource, NY; p. 450TR: Ingram Publishing; p. 450TL: © JULIEN WARNAND/epa/Corbis; p. 452T: Image copyright © The Metropolitan Museum of Art/Art Resource, NY; p. 452B: *Cotton Plantation*, 1850s (oil on canvas), Giroux, Charles (fl.1850–80)/Museum of Fine Arts, Boston, Massachusetts, USA/Gift of Martha C. Karolik for the M. and M. Karolik Collection of American Paintings, 1815–65; p. 456: National Army Museum, London/The Bridgeman Art Library; p. 459T: The Granger Collection; p. 459B: Ingram Publishing.

Chapter 20

Page 460: Bildarchiv Preussischer Kulturbesitz/Art Resource, NY; p. 463: Eugene Appert/Hulton/Getty Images; p. 465: Musée d'Orsay, Paris, France/Erich Lessing/Art Resource, NY; p. 467: Hirszenberg, Samuel (1865–1908). *The Black Banner (Czarny Sztandar)*, 1905. Oil on canvas, 30 x 81". Gift of the Estate of Rose Mintz. The Jewish Museum, New York, NY, USA. Photo by Richard Goodbody, Inc./Art Resource, NY; p. 470: Eugène Laermans, *Les émigrants*, 1896. (3 panels) Right panel: L'exorde; Central panel: L'exode; Left panel: L'exil. Koninklijk Museum voor Schone Kunsten, Anver. Royal Museum of Fine Arts, Antwerp. Image courtesy of Reproductiefonds Vlaamse Musea NV/Lukas Art in Flanders; p. 473: Mary Evans Picture Library; p. 478L: Library of Congress Prints and

Photographs Division [LC-USZ62-103376]; p. 478R: David R. Frazier Photography; p. 480: Marine Corp. Historical Society; p. 482: Marine Corp. Historical Society.

Chapter 21

Page 484: Harrogate Museums and Art Gallery, North Yorkshire, UK/Bridgeman Art Library; p. 486: ullstein bild/The Granger Collection; p. 490: Archives Charmet/The Bridgeman Art Library; p. 491: Archives Charmet/The Bridgeman Art Library; p. 492: Frederic, Leon (1856–1940) © ARS, NY. *The Ages of the Worker*, triptych. Oil on canvas, 1895–97. Musee d'Orsay, Paris, France Musée d'Orsay/Reunion des Musées Nationaux/Art Resource, NY; p. 495: Magyar Nemzeti Gallery Budapest/Gianni Dagli Orti/The Art Archive; p. 497: Musée d'Orsay, Paris, France/Réunion des Musées Nationaux/Erich Lessing/Art Resource, NY; p. 498L: © Bettmann/Corbis; p. 498R: David Buffington/Getty Images; p. 501: Allgemeines Krankenhaus (General Hospital), Vienna, Austria/Erich Lessing/Art Resource, NY; p. 502: Bildarchiv Preussischer Kulturbesitz/Art Resource, NY; p. 503: Musée d'Orsay, Paris, France/Réunion des Musées Nationaux/Erich Lessing/Art Resource, NY; p. 505: *Christ's Triumphant Entry into Brussels*, 1888 (oil on canvas), Ensor, James (1860–1949)/J. Paul Getty Museum, Los Angeles, USA. © ARS, NY. © DACS/Lauros/Giraudon/© 2010. ARS, NY/SABAM, Brussels/The Bridgeman Art Library; p. 506: Munch, Edvard (1863–1944) *The Scream*. 1893 (Tempera and pastels on cardboard, 91 x 73.5 cm.) © Copyright ARS, NY. National Gallery, Oslo, Norway. Erich Lessing/Art Resource, NY; p. 507: Getty Images.

Chapter 22

Page 508: Dix, Otto (1891–1969) *The War*. Triptych, oil on wood, 1929–32. © 2010. ARS, NY./VG Bild-Kunst, Bonn. Staatliche Kunstsammlungen, Dresden, Germany. Erich Lessing/Art Resource, NY; p. 515: Roger Viollet/Getty Images; p. 516L: Mary Evans/Robert Hunt Collection/The Image Works; p. 516R: Purestock/Superstock; p. 517: Imperial War Museum, London; p. 518: Imperial War Museum, London; p. 519: Mary Evans Picture Library; p. 522: *Memorial depicting the artist and her husband mourning their dead son*, Peter Kollwitz, dedicated in 1931 (stone), Kollwitz, Käthe Schmidt (1867–1945)/Vladslo German Military Cemetery, Vladslo, Ypres, Belgium © 2010. ARS, NY./VG Bild-Kunst, Bonn. © DACS/© Paul Maeyaert/© 2010. ARS, NY./VG Bild-Kunst, Bonn/The Bridgeman Art Library; p. 523: Bettmann/Corbis; p. 527: Sovfoto; p. 529: © DACS/Archives Charmet/The Bridgeman Art Library; p. 530: Library of Congress Prints and Photographs Division [LOC-USZ62-52290].

Chapter 23

Page 532: DEA/M. E. SMITH/De Agostini/Getty Images; p. 537: Dix, Otto (1891–1969) © 2012. ARS, NY./VG Bild-Kunst, *Bonn. Grosstadt - Big town*, tryptick, left wing. 1927/28, wood, distemper 181 x 101 cm. Inv. 0-1890. Kunstmuseum, Stuttgart, Germany. Erich Lessing/Art Resource, NY; p. 537: Dix, Otto (1891–1969) © 2010. ARS, NY./VG Bild-Kunst, *Bonn. Grosstadt - Big town*, tryptick, left wing. 1927/28, wood, distemper 181 x 101 cm. Inv. 0-1890. Kunstmuseum, Stuttgart, Germany. Erich Lessing/Art Resource, NY; p. 538: UFA/The Kobal Collection; p. 540: AP Images; p. 542: Fotomas/Bridgeman Art Library; p. 543: RUSU 2225, Poster Collection, Hoover Institution Archives; p. 546L: Archive Photos/Getty Images; p. 546R: Mario Tama/Getty Images; p. 550: Heinrich Hoffmann/Timepix/Time Life Pictures/Getty Images; p. 551: Nussbaum, Felix (1904–1944) *Self-portrait with Jewish Identity Card*. 1943. Oil on canvas, 56 x 49 cm. © 2010. ARS, NY./VG Bild-Kunst, Bonn. Bildarchiv Preussischer Kulturbesitz/Art Resource, NY; p. 552: DEA/M. E. SMITH/De Agostini/Getty Images.

Chapter 24

Page 554: Strempel, Horst (1904–1975) © 2010. ARS, NY./VG Bild-Kunst, *Bonn. Night Over Germany*. 1945. Oil on canvas. Inv. A III 257. Photo: Joerg P. Anders. National galerie, Staatliche Museen, Berlin, Germany. Bildarchiv Preussischer Kulturbesitz/Art Resource, NY; p. 557: Picasso, Pablo (1881–1973) *Guernica*. 1937. © ARS, NY. Oil on canvas, 350 x 782 cm. Museo Nacional Centro de Arte Reina Sofia, Madrid, Spain. John Bigelow Taylor/Art Resource, NY; p. 560: Imperial War Museum, London. IWM ART LD 2750; p. 565: AP Images; p. 567L: MPI/Archive Photos/Getty Images; p. 567R: Corbis; p. 568: Archive Photos/Hulton Archive/Getty Images; p. 569: Charles Comfort Fraser, *Dead German on the Hitler Line*, c. 1944 (w/c on paper). Canadian War Museum, Ottawa, Canada/Bridgeman Art Library; p. 571: Archives Charmet/The Bridgeman Art Library; p. 572: Corbis/Royalty Free.

Chapter 25

Page 574: Don Eddy (American, b. 1944). *New Shoes for H*, 1973–74. Acrylic on canvas; 111.7 x 121.9 cm. © The Cleveland Museum of Art, Purchased with a grant from the National Endowment for the Arts and matched by gifts from members of The Cleveland Society for Contemporary Art, 1974.53.; p. 580: © DACS/Roger Perrin/The Bridgeman Art Library; p. 582: Museum Ludwig/Rheinisches Bildarchiv; p. 583: Goksin Sipahiouglu/Sip. Press; p. 585: Bettmann/Corbis; p. 593: Pollock, Jackson (1912–1956) © ARS, NY. *Convergence*. 1952. Oil on canvas, framed: 95 1/4 x 157 1/8 x 2 7/8" (241.935 x 399.0975 x 7.3025); support: 93 1/2 x 155" (237.49 x 393.7 cm.). Gift of Seymour H. Knox, Jr., 1956. Albright-Knox Art Gallery, Buffalo, New York. Albright-Knox Art Gallery/Art Resource, NY; p. 594: © 2003 Andy Warhol Foundation for the Visual Arts/ARS, NY/TM Licensed by Campbell's Soup Co. All rights reserved. Albright-Knox Art Gallery, Buffalo, New York, Gift of Seymour H. Knox, Jr., 1963/Art Resource, NY; p. 599: Lambert Studios/Hulton Archive/Archive Photos/Getty Images; p. 600: NASA; p. 601L: AKG Images/ullstein bild; p. 601R: David Planchet/McGraw-Hill Companies; p. 603: © StockTrek/Photodisc/Getty Images.

Chapter 26

Page 604: China Photos/Getty Images; p. 606: © Régis Bossu/Corbis Sygma; p. 609: Musee d'Histoire Contemporaine, BCIC, Universite de Paris, France; p. 615: Antoine Gyori/Sygma/Corbis; p. 621: Jehad Nga/Corbis; p. 622L: Réunion des Musées Nationaux/Art Resource, NY; p. 622R: Courtesy of Bri Rodriguez/FEMA; p. 626R: Bruce F. Molnia/USGS; p. 626L: William O. Field; p. 628: Jennifer Bartlett. *Spiral: An Ordinary Evening in New Haven*, 1989. Painting: oil on canvas, tables: painted wood and steel, cones: break formed hot rolled welded steel painting: 108" x 192", tables: 30" x 32" x 35", 39" x 41" x 35" cones: 20" x 30" x 21", © J. Bartlett. Private Collection, Greenwich, CT. Courtesy of the Paula Cooper Gallery, NY; p. 629: Courtesy of the National Library of Medicine; p. 631: Heath Korvola/Getty Images.

TEXT CREDITS

Chapter 11

From VAN VOORST. Readings in Christianity, 1e. © 1997 Wadsworth, a part of Cengage Learning, Inc. Reproduced by permission. www.cengage.com/permissions.

Chapter 14

Jean Antoine Nicholas Caritat Marquis de Condorcet, Sketch for a Historical Picture on the Progress of the Human Mind, tr. June Barraclough, Weidenfeld and Nicolson (Orion Books), 1955, pp. 236–237, 244.

Chapter 17

Sidney Pollard and Colin Holmes, Documents of European Economic History, Source: vol. 1, St. Martin's Press, 1968. Reproduced with permission of Palgrave Macmillan.

Chapter 22

"Does It Matter", from COLLECTED POEMS OF SIEGFRIED SASSOON by Siegfried Sassoon, copyright 1918, 1920 by E.P. Dutton. Copyright 1936, 1946, 1947, 1948 by Siegfried Sassoon. Used by permission of Viking Penguin, a division of Penguin group (USA) Inc. Copyright Siegfried Sassoon by kind permission of the Estate of George Sassoon.

Chapter 24

Reproduced by permission of The United States Holocaust Memorial Museum.

Diego, Juan, 285
Diehl, Guida, 550
Diet of Speier, 252
Diet of Worms, 252
dietary laws, 18–20, 113–114
Dijk, Philip van: *Bristol Dock and Quay, ca. 1780, 344*
dikes, 174, 263, 306
dinars, 144
Diocletian, *108,* 108–110, 116
Diocletian's Division of the Empire, 304 C.E., 109*f*
Diogenes, 68, *69*
Diogenes, Ramonos, 190
Dionysius Exiguus, 131, 152
Dionysus, 33, 69
diphtheria, 410, 501
diplomacy, 229–230, 239, 477
　　Byzantine, 137–138
Diplomatic Revolution, 350
Directory, 385–386
disarmament, 513, 552, 608
diseases. *See also specific diseases*
　　of European expansion, 282–283
　　of imperialism, 474
　　in Industrial Revolution, 410–411
　　infectious, 410, 500–501, 602
　　sexually transmitted, 237, 293, 411, 416, 496
Disraeli, Benjamin, 463
dissections, 70, 178, 238, *238,* 330–331
dissent, growth of, 520, 583–585, 608
divination, 33, 75, 80
Divine Light Wisdom, 145
divine right of kings, 300, 302, 313–314, 316, 321–322
divorce, 9, 266, 387, 599
Dix, Dorothea, 501
Dix, Otto, 536, 538
　　Grosstadt (Big Tech), 537
　　War, 508
DNA
　　evidence, 75, 201
　　structure of, 601, 630
Dnieper River, 161
doctorate degrees, 178
doge, 227
Dome of the Rock, ca. 691, *122,* 141, 145
domes, 147, 235
Domesday Book, 184
domestic animals, 3–4, 6
domesticated plants, 3–4
Dominic de Guzmán, 195
Dominican order, 195–196
Dominici, Giovanni, 232
Domitian, 100
Donation of Pepin, 131
Donne, John, 327
Doré, Gustave: *A London Slum, 409*
Dorian Greeks, 31
Doric order, 43, *43*
Dostoyevski, Fyodor: *Crime and Punishment,* 503
Douai, 203
double-entry bookkeeping, 289
douches, 104, 496
dowry, 232
drachma, 60
Drake, Francis, 291
Dreadnought battleships, 510
dream interpretation, 504
Dresden, 573
Dreyfus, Alfred, 468
Dreyfus affair, 464, 468
Drinking Game, ca. fifth century B.C.E., 36
drones, *207*
drug cartels, 478
Dual Monarchy, 453
Dubcek, Alexander, 585, 609
Dubois, François: *St. Bartholomew's Day Massacre,*
　　ca. 1576, 244
Il Duce, 540–541, 556
due process of law, 185
Dulles, John Foster, 578

Duma (parliament of Russia), 526–527
Dunkirk, 560
Dura Europus, 58
Duras, Marguerite, 593
Dürer, Albrecht: *Portrait of Katharina,* 1520, *231*
Durkheim, Émile, 504–505
Dutch East Indies, 562, 589
Dutch Republic, 263, 321, 335, 373
Dutch Shipyard, 322
Dutch United East India Company, 288
dynamo, electrical, 487
dynasties, clash of,1515–1555, 246–249
dysentery, 517

E

earls, 153
early marriages, 361, 404
early socialism, 425, 429–430
earthquakes, 627
East
　　empires of, in late Middle Ages, 212–217
　　meets West, in Hellenistic Age, 60–66
　　Portugal's race for the east, 1418–1600, 274–275
　　West and, in Cold War, 583–588
East Germany
　　Berlin Wall in, 584–585, *585,* 606, *606*
　　fall of communism in, 610
　　Soviet Union's domination of, 576–577
East India Company, 288, 293, 356, 478
Easter, date of, 131, 133, 327
Easter Rebellion, 1916, of Ireland, 520
Eastern Europe
　　1640–1725, 310*f*
　　1648, 308*f*
　　1989, 610*f*
　　in Cold War, 583–585
　　economic transition in, 612–613
　　fall of communism in, 606–615
　　revolutions in, 608–610
　　struggle for sovereignty in, 307–312
Eastern Universalism, 212–214
Eastern-bloc nations, 571, 587, 606
Ebro River, 83
EC. *See* European Community
Ecclesia, 37–38
eclipses, solar, 33
ecology, of Americas, 292
economic cycles, 287, 625–627
economic disparity
　　in Cold War era, 598, 602
　　in Europe, eighteenth century, 362
　　in Europe, nineteenth century, 430–431
　　in Hellenistic Age, 63–64
　　in Industrial Revolution, 410
　　in present, 630
　　in Renaissance, 230
　　in Roman Empire, 103
　　in Rome (republic), 86–87
　　in Western society, 1850–1914, 488
economic interest, 430–431
economic nationalism, 289
economic regulations, 289
economics, and imperialism, 472
ecumenical council, 118
Eddy, Don: *New Shoes for H, 574*
Eddy, Mary Baker: *Science and Health,* 497
Eden, Frederick, 407
Edessa, 193
Edict of Milan, 116
Edict of Nantes, 263, 301, 305
Edict of Restitution, 265
Edmund Ironside, 162
Edo Bay, 481
education
　　Charlemagne and, 157–158
　　in early Middle Ages, 151–154, 157–158
　　in Enlightenment, 341
　　in French Revolution, 382–383
　　in Hellenistic Age, 67
　　in high Middle Ages, 177–178, 187

　　in Protestant Reformation, 249–250, 258–260, 267
　　public, 462, 463–464
　　in Renaissance, 222–223
　　in Rome (republic), 85
　　science and, 334–335
　　sex education, 600
Edward I, 185, 187
Edward III, 206–207, 209
Edward the Confessor, 184
Edward V, 209
Edward VI, *256,* 257
EEC. *See* European Economic Community
efficiency, 536
ego, 504
Egypt
　　afterlife in, 1, 12
　　Alexander the Great's conquest of, 54
　　art in, 12, 14–16
　　Bonaparte in, 385–386, 390
　　ca. 3100–1000 B.C.E., 10–16
　　command economy of, 60
　　family life in Old Kingdom, 11
　　First Intermediate period, 13
　　fresco from, ca. 1295–1186 B.C.E., *14*
　　Great Britain in control of, 474–475, 535, 590
　　Hebrews in, 15, 17–18
　　Hyksos invasion of, 14
　　Mesopotamia and, ca. 2000 B.C.E., 5*f*
　　Middle Kingdom, 13–14
　　New Kingdom, 1, 14–16
　　obituaries of, 11
　　Old Kingdom, 10–11
　　Ptolemaic dynasty of, 57–58, 66
　　railroads in, 475
　　religion in, 10, 15–16
　　Second Intermediate period of, 14
　　Suez Canal and, 460, *460,* 474, 475, 487, 561, 590
　　trade in Old Kingdom of, 10–11, 13–14
　　in World War II, 561
Eichmann, Adolf, 564
An Eighteenth-Century French Warship, 351
Einstein, Albert, 504
Eisenhower, Dwight, 568, 569, 578
Eisenstein, Sergei, 536
El Alamein, Battle of, 568
El Greco: *Burial of the Count of Orgaz, 261*
Elagabalus, 107
Elba, 393
Elbe River, 174, 307
Eleanor of Aquitaine, 184
electrical dynamo, 487
electricity, 486–487, 500, 536
electrocardiograph, 501
elephants, in warfare, 61, 83
Eliot, George, 414, 502
Eliot, T. S: "The Waste Land," 536
Elizabeth, tsarina, 350
Elizabeth I, 223, 241, 256–258, 291, 313
Elizabeth of York, 209
emails, 383, 623
embalming, 1, 12
emigration, 469–471
emirs, 146
emotional life, in classical Greece, 36
empires. *See also* imperialism; *specific empires*
　　in Central America, 278–282
　　in early Middle Ages, 154–158, 164
　　in East in late Middle Ages, 212–217
　　growth of, 1200–500 B.C.E., 20–25
　　indigenous peoples and empires in the Americas,
　　　ca. 1500, 280*f*
empirical method, 331–332, 338
enclosures, 360
encomienda system, 282
Encyclopedia, 1751, 338, *338,* 341, 342
Engels, Friedrich, 409, 544
　　The Communist Manifesto, 430–431, 608
engineering, 3, 75, 102, 172, 601
England. *See* Britain; Great Britain
English Channel, 155, 388, 560, 561

James I, 291, 313–314, 331
James II, 319–320
James the Elder, Saint, 186
Jamestown, 314
janissaries, 215
Jansenism, 367
Japan
  1942, 564f
  in Cold War containment chain, 578
  earthquake in, 627
  economic power of, 487, 546
  Industrial Revolution in, 481, 488
  invasion of China, 556
  invasion of Manchuria, 556
  Japanese ultranationalism, 562
  Kamikaze Special Attack Corps, 569, 570
  Meiji Restoration, 481
  missionaries in, 286
  Pearl Harbor attach by, 562
  in Rome-Berlin Axis, 557
  Russo-Japanese War, 481, 526
  Tokugawa shogunate, 481
  trade and, 272
  in World War I, 517, 525
  in World War II, 556, 562, 569–572
Japanese Americans, in United States, 566
Jarrow, 151, 153, 154
Jaruzelski, Wojciech, 609
Jaurès, Jean, 466, 473
javelins, 14, 53
jazz, 593
Jazz Age, 536, 551
Jefferson, Thomas, 368
Jehovah's Witnesses, 551, 565
Jenner, Edward, 412
Jericho, 4
Jerome, 249
Jerusalem, 145
  in Crusades, 190, 192–193
  destruction of, 114–115
  pilgrimages to, 116, 190
  Second Temple of, 20, 66, 112, 114
  Western Wall, ca. 19 B.C.E., 114, *114*
Jesuits, 259–260, 267, 286, 314
Jesus Ben Sirach: *Ecclesiasticus*, 66
Jesus of Nazareth, 13, 96, 112–113, 122, *132*, 140
  Christ as the Good Shepherd, ca. 450 C.E., *119*
  Christ as the Good Shepherd, second century C.E., *118*
  Jesus movement, in Christianity, 113–114
  nature of Christ, 118, 138–139
  second coming of Christ, 254
jewelry, of Vikings, 160, 162, *162*
Jews. *See also* Hebrews; Judaism
  accused of bringing the plague, 201
  in Alexandria, 65–66
  anti-Semitism, 466–468, 547–548, 551, 557, 590
  Babylonian captivity of, 19–20, 22, 24
  in Crusades, 193
  dispersion of, 114
  expelled from Germany, 230
  expelled from Spain, 230, 258
  in France, 376, 387, 389
  genocide of, 561, 563–565, 573
  Hasidic, 367
  Hellenized, 65–66
  Islam and, 143–144
  Kristallnacht, 551
  in Nazi Germany, 561, 563–565, 573
  origin of, as southern Israelites, 18
  persecution by Visigoths, 131
  pogroms (massacres) against, 312, 467
  in Poland, 312, 367
  in Prussia, 358
  in Renaissance, 230
  in Roman Empire, 112–115
  in Russia, 468
  Spanish Inquisition and, 261
  urban, in high Middle Ages, 175
Jezebel, 18
Jiang Jieshi (Chiang Kai-shek), 556, 578–579
jihad, 143, 146, 192–193

Joan of Arc, 208–209
John (of England), 185, 187
John II (of Portugal), 274
John of Monte Corvino, 214
John of Toul, 16
John Paul II, Pope, 609
John the Baptist, 113
John XII, Pope, 188
joint-stock companies, 288
Joseph II of Austria, 358–359, 365, 374
Josephus, 66, 67, 115
journalism, popular, 462
journeymen, 175
jousts, 183, *185*
Joyce, James: *Ulysses*, 538
Judah, kingdom of, 18–20, 20f
Judaism
  afterlife in, 112
  of Diaspora, 19–20, 114
  in exile, 19–20
  four faces of, 112–113
  Hasidic, 367
  in Hellenistic Age, 65–66
  law codes of, 112
Judas Maccabeus, 66, 67, 112
Judea, 65–66, 112–114
Julia, 91
Julia Maesa, 107
Julian calendar, 92
Julius Caesar, 112
  Commentaries, 88–89
  military success of, 91, 95–96
  political career of, 91–93
  writings of, 88–89
Julius II, Pope, 229, 236, 250
July Days, of Russian Revolution, 528
July Revolution, 435, 436
June Days of 1848, in France, 440–441
Jünger, Ernst, 516
Junkers, 307, 432, 441
Juno, 80
Jupiter, 80, 88
Jurieu, Pierre, 304
justice, 8
justification by faith, 251
Justinian, 131, 136
  conquests of, 134–135, 137f
  Corpus Iuris Civilis (*Body of Civil Law*), 135, 178
Jutes, 128
Jutland, Battle of, 516

K

Ka'bah, 140, 142
Kádár, János, 609
Kadesh, Battle of, (1299 B.C.E.), 16
Kafka, Franz, 538
kamikaze missions, 569, 570
Kamikaze Special Attack Corps, 569, 570
Kandinsky, Wassily, 505
Kant, Immanuel, 334, 342
Kapp, Wolfgang, 535
Kashmir, 589, 623, 623f
Kay, John, 399
Kemal, Mustafa, 524, 539
Kennedy, John F., 580, 582
Kenya, 591
Kepler, Johannes, 328–329, 332
Kerensky, Alexander, 528–529
Keynes, John Maynard, 546, 586
  The Economic Consequences of the Peace, 525
KGB, 611
Khadijah, 140, 141
Khanate of the Golden Horde, 216
khedive, 475
Khomeini, Ayatollah Ruholla, 619
Khrushchev, Nikita, 581, 583, 584–585, 607
Khufu, 12
Khunrath, Heinrich: *The Laboratory and the Chapel*, 1609, 327
Kiev, 161, 213

Kievan Rus, 139
King, Martin Luther, Jr., 594
King James Bible, 314
King Oswald with his Bishop Aidan, ca. 1200, 173, *173*
kinship groups, 52, 124, 166, 477
Kipling, Rudyard, 473
Kirov, Sergei, 545
Knight, Laura: *The Battle of Britain*, 1943, *560*
Knights of Saint John, 216
Knights Templars, 193
Knossos, 28–29
  fresco from, ca. 1500 B.C.E., *30*
Knox, John, 255
  Book of Common Order, 258
Koch, Robert, 500–501
Kodak cameras, 494
Kohl, Helmut, 615
Kollontai, Alexandra, 541
Kollwitz, Käthe, 522, 538
  The Mourning Father and Mother, *522*
Komnene, Anna: *The Alexiad*, 191–192
Komnenian dynasty, 190–193
Konigshofen, Jacob von, 201
Kopelev, Lev, 544
kore, 32
Korea, 213, 223, 480
Korean War, 579
Kornilov, Lavr, 528
Kosovo, 614–615, 617
Kossuth, Louis, 439
Kostunica, Vojislav, 615
kouros, 32
Kramer, Stanley, 593
Kristallnacht, 551
Kronstadt naval base, 541
Kropotkin, Pyotr, 467
The Krupp Steelworks, 1880, 486, *486*
Kublai Khan, 213–214
kulaks, 543–544
Kun, Béla, 539
Kurds, 598, 622, 624
Kuwait, 615, 619
Kyoto Protocol, 174, 622

L

labor unions, 417, 437, 462, 465–466, 625
  strikes of, 407, 465
Labour Party, 465–466, 534, 585, 586, 616
labyrinths, 29–30
laconic, 38
Laermans, Eugène: *The Emigrants*, 470, *470*
Lafayette, Countess de: *The Princess of Clèves*, 304
laissez-faire economics, 340, 424
Lamartine, Alphonse de, *418*, 438, 442
Lancaster family, 209
land mines, 622
land redistribution, 527
Landucci, Luca, 226
Lang, Fritz: *Metropolis*, 536, *538*
Laocoön, *65*
Laos, 589
Las Casas, Bartolomé de: *The Tears of the Indians*, 283, 285
Lateran Council, Fourth, 190, 249
Lateran Treaty, 540
latifundia, 110
Latin America, 390f, 562, 581–582, 625
Latin language, 75, 88–89, 102, 138, 210
Latin League, 78
latitude, 71, 273, 278
Latvia, 529, 560, 608, 611
laudanum, 410–411, 415
Law, John, 353
law codes
  of Byzantine Empire, 134–135
  canon law, 190
  Code of Hammurabi, 8–9
  common law, of Great Britain, 153, 414
  of early Middle Ages, 150–151
  equality under, 373, 387